D0984683

BIOGRAPHICAL
DICTIONARY OF
EVANGELICALS

BIOGRAPHICAL
DICTIONARY OF
EVANGELICALS

Editor:
Timothy Larsen, PhD, FRHistS
Associate Professor of Theology, Wheaton College, IL, USA

Consulting editors:
D. W. Bebbington, Ph.D.
Professor of History, University of Stirling

Mark A. Noll, PhD
McManis Professor of Christian Thought, Wheaton College, IL, USA

Organizing editor:
Steve Carter
Reference Books Editor, Inter-Varsity Press, Leicester

Inter-Varsity Press, Leicester, England
InterVarsity Press, Downers Grove, Illinois, USA

INTER-VARSITY PRESS
38 De Montfort Street, Leicester LE1 7GP, England
Email: ivp@uccf.org.uk
Website: www.ivpbooks.com

INTERVARSITY PRESS
PO Box 1400, Downers Grove, Illinois 60515, USA
Email: mail@ivpress.com
Website: www.ivpress.com

First published 2003

British Library Cataloguing in Publication Data
A catalogue record for this book is available from the British Library.

UK ISBN 0-85111-987-5

Library of Congress Cataloging-in-Publication
Data has been requested.

US ISBN 0-8308-2925-3

Set in 9.25/10.5 Sabon

Typeset in Great Britain by CRB Associates, Reepham, Norfolk
Printed in Great Britain by Creative Print & Design (Wales), Ebbw Vale

Inter-Varsity Press is the publishing division of the Universities and Colleges Christian Fellowship (formerly the Inter-Varsity Fellowship), a student movement linking Christian Unions in universities and colleges throughout Great Britain, and a member movement of the International Fellowship of Evangelical Students. For more information about local and national activities write to UCCF, 38 De Montfort Street, Leicester LE1 7GP, email us at email@uccf.org.uk, or visit the UCCF website at www.uccf.org.uk.

InterVarsity Press® is the book-publishing division of InterVarsity Christian Fellowship/USA®, a student movement active on campus at hundreds of universities, colleges and schools of nursing in the United States of America, and a member movement of the International Fellowship of Evangelical Students. For information about local and regional activities, write to Public Relations Dept., InterVarsity Christian Fellowship USA, 6400 Schroeder Road, PO Box 7895, Madison, WI 53707-7895.

CONTENTS

ABBREVIATIONS AND CROSS-REFERENCES

c.	about, approximately	n.d.	no date
ch(s).	chapter(s)	no.	number
ed(s).	editor(s)	n.s.	new series
edn	edition	NT	New Testament
e.g.	for example	OT	Old Testament
ET	English translation	p(p).	page(s)
et al.	and others	repr.	reprinted
etc.	and so on	sic	thus
f., ff.	and the following	tr.	translated, translation
idem	the same author	vol(s).	volume(s)
i.e.	that is to say		

An asterisk before a name indicates that the person is the subject of an article.

ABOUT THE EDITORS

Timothy Larsen is Associate Professor of Theology at Wheaton College, IL, USA. A Fellow of the Royal Historical Society, he earned his PhD from the University of Stirling, Scotland. He was previously Lecturer in Church History and then Principal at Covenant College, Coventry, England, and then Professor of Church History at Tyndale Seminary, Toronto. He has published two monographs, *Friends of Religious Equality: Nonconformist Politics in Mid-Victorian England* (Boydell, 1999) and *Christabel Pankhurst: Fundamentalism and Feminism in Coalition* (Boydell, 2002). In addition to co-editing two collections of scholarly articles and contributing chapters to several books, research articles of his have also been published in numerous learned journals and annuals, including *Church History*, the *Scottish Journal of Theology*, *Fides et Historia*, the *Journal of Victorian Culture*, the *Bulletin of the John Rylands University Library of Manchester*, *Studies in Church History* and the *Journal of Ecclesiastical History*.

David Bebbington is Professor of History at the University of Stirling, Scotland. His doctorate is from Cambridge, where he was Research Fellow of Fitzwilliam College before moving to Stirling. He has also taught at the University of Alabama, Birmingham, at Regent College, Vancouver, at Notre Dame University, Indiana, and at the University of Pretoria, South Africa. He is the author of *Patterns in History* (IVP, 1979), *The Nonconformist Conscience* (Allen & Unwin, 1982), *Evangelicalism in Modern Britain* (Unwin Hyman, 1989), *William Ewart Gladstone: Faith and Politics in Modern*

Britain (Eerdmans, 1993) and *Holiness in Nineteenth-Century England* (Paternoster, 2000). He has also edited *The Baptists in Scotland* (Baptist Union of Scotland, 1988) and *The Gospel in the World: International Baptist Studies* (Paternoster, 2002), and has co-edited with Mark Noll and George Rawlyk *Evangelicalism: Comparative Studies of Popular Protestantism in North America, the British Isles and Beyond, 1700–1990* (Oxford, 1994) and with Roger Swift *Gladstone Centenary Essays* (Liverpool, 2000).

Mark A. Noll is McManis Professor of Christian Thought in the history department at Wheaton College, IL, USA. He has taught at Wheaton for a quarter of a century, with periods as a visiting professor at Westminster Seminary, Regent College and the Harvard Divinity School. His books include *America's God, from Jonathan Edwards to Abraham Lincoln* (Oxford, 2002), *The Old Religion in a New World: The History of North American Christianity* (Eerdmans, 2002), *Turning Points: Decisive Moments in the History of Christianity* (2nd edn, Baker, 2000), *American Evangelical Christianity: An Introduction* (Blackwell, 2001) and others. With David Bebbington and George Rawlyk he edited *Evangelicalism: Comparative Studies of Popular Protestantism in North America, the British Isles, and Beyond, 1700–1990* (Oxford, 1994), and with David Livingstone and Darryl Hart, *Evangelicals and Science in Historical Perspective* (Oxford, 1999). His other books, essays and reviews address subjects in North American and evangelical history.

LIST OF CONTRIBUTORS

To the best of the editors' knowledge, this information was correct at the time of publication.

Amos, Scott (PhD University of St Andrews) was formerly Instructor in History, Lynchburg College, VA, USA.

Aponte, Edwin D. (PhD Temple University) is Assistant Professor of Christianity and Culture, Perkins School of Theology, Southern Methodist University, TX, USA.

Armstrong, John H. (DMin Luther Rice Seminary) is President of Reformation and Revival Ministries, Carol Stream, IL, USA.

Atherstone, Andrew C. (DPhil University of Oxford) is Curate of Christ Church, Abingdon.

Bademan, R. Bryan (MA Wheaton College) is a PhD student, University of Notre Dame, IN, USA.

Barker, William S. (PhD Vanderbilt University) is Professor of Church History Emeritus, Westminster Theological Seminary, PA, USA.

Barnes, Peter (ThD Australian College of Theology) is a Presbyterian minister and Lecturer in Church History, Presbyterian Theological Centre, NSW, Australia.

Belcher, Richard P. (ThD Concordia Theological Seminary) is Director, Pastoral Ministries Department, Columbia International University, SC, USA.

Berends, Kurt (DPhil University of Oxford), is Co-ordinator of the Christian Scholars Program and Assistant Professor of History, University of Notre Dame, IN, USA.

Berk, Stephen (PhD University of Iowa) is Professor of History, California State University, CA, USA.

Binfield, Clyde (PhD University of Cambridge) is Professor Associate in History, University of Sheffield.

Birtwistle, Graham M. (PhD Free University of Amsterdam) is Lecturer in Modern Art History, Free University of Amsterdam, Netherlands.

Blumhofer, Edith L. (PhD Harvard University) is Professor of History and Director of the Institute for the Study of American Evangelicals, Wheaton College, IL, USA.

Bolt, John (PhD University of St Michael's College, Toronto) is Professor of Systematic Theology, Calvin Theological Seminary, MI, USA.

Bonk, Jonathan J. (PhD University of Aberdeen) is the Executive Director of the Overseas Ministries Study Center, New Haven, CT, USA, and editor of the *International Bulletin of Missionary Research*.

Boobbyer, Philip C. (PhD University of London) is Senior Lecturer in Modern European History, University of Kent.

Brackney, William H. (PhD Temple University) is Professor, Department of Religion and Director of Program in Baptist Studies, Baylor University, TX, USA.

Bratt, James D. (PhD Yale University) is Professor of History and Director of the Calvin Center for Christian Scholarship, Calvin College, MI, USA.

Brereton, Virginia Lieson (PhD Columbia University) is a lecturer in English, Tufts University, MA, USA.

Briggs, John H. Y. (MA University of Cambridge) is a Professor Emeritus, University of Birmingham, and Senior Research Fellow and Director of the Baptist History and Heritage Centre, University of Oxford, and was formerly Pro-Vice Chancellor, University of Birmingham.

Bundy, David (Licentiate Université Catholique de Louvain) is Associate Provost for Library Services and Associate Professor of History, Fuller Theological Seminary, CA, USA.

Bush, Harold K., Jr (PhD Indiana University) is Associate Professor of English, Saint Louis University, MO, USA.

Cadle, Penelope J. (BA Trinity College, Indiana) is a PhD student, University of Wales.

Caldwell, Robert W., III (MDiv Trinity Evangelical Divinity School) is a PhD student, Trinity Evangelical Divinity School, IL, USA.

Cantor, Geoffrey (PhD University of London) is Professor of the History of Science, University of Leeds.

Carter, Craig A. (PhD University of St Michael's College, Toronto) is Vice-President, Academic Dean and Associate Professor of Religious Studies, Tyndale College, ON, Canada.

Chatfield, Graeme R. (PhD University of Bristol) is Lecturer in Church History, Morling College, NSW, Australia.

Christie, Nancy (PhD University of Sydney) is an independent scholar, Hamilton, ON, Canada.

Clements, Keith (PhD University of Bristol) is General Secretary, Conference of European Churches, Geneva, Switzerland.

Coffey, John (PhD University of Cambridge) is Reader in History, University of Leicester.

Coolman, Boyd Taylor (PhD University of Notre Dame) is a member of the Adjunct Faculty, Duke Divinity School, NC, USA.

Coolman, Holly Taylor (MDiv Princeton Theological Seminary) is a PhD student, Duke University, NC, USA.

Cooper, Tisha L. (MA Wheaton College) is Assistant Chaplain and a Religious Studies teacher, Kingham Hill School, Oxfordshire.

Cornick, David (PhD King's College, London) is General Secretary of the United Reformed Church and a Fellow of Robinson College, Cambridge.

Currie, David A. (PhD St Andrews University) is an instructor in Church History, Gordon-Conwell Theological Seminary, MA, USA.

Davies, D. Eryl (PhD University of Wales) is Principal, the Evangelical Theological College of Wales, Bridgend.

D'Elia, John A. (ThM Fuller Theological Seminary) is Director of Development, Fuller Theological Seminary, CA, USA, and a PhD student, University of Stirling.

De Gruchy, Stephen M. (DTh University of the Western Cape), is Director of Theology and Development Programme School of Theology, University of Natal, South Africa.

De Jong, James A. (ThD Free University of Amsterdam) is President Emeritus and Professor of Church History, Calvin Theological Seminary, MI, USA.

Dickey, Brian (PhD ANU Canberra) is Associate Professor of History, Flinders University, SA, Australia.

Dickson, Neil (PhD University of Stirling), is Assistant Principal Teacher of English, Kilmarnock Academy.

Dieter, Melvin E. (PhD Temple University) is Professor Emeritus of Church History and Historical Theology, Asbury Theological Seminary, KY, USA.

DiPuccio, William (PhD Marquette University) is Director, Institute for Classic Christian Studies, OH, USA.

Dorries, David W. (PhD University of Aberdeen) is Associate Professor of Church History and Theological Librarian, Oral Roberts University, OK, USA.

Dorsett, Lyle W. (PhD University of Missouri, Columbia) is Professor of Evangelism and Spiritual Formation, Wheaton College, IL, USA.

Dotterweich, Martin H. (PhD University of Edinburgh) is Assistant Professor of History, Crichton College, TN, USA.

Dowling, Maurice J. (PhD University of Belfast) is a teacher of Church History and Historical Theology, Irish Baptist College, Belfast.

Duriez, Colin (BA University of Ulster) is a freelance writer, editor and lecturer, and a former commissioning editor, Inter-Varsity Press, Leicester.

Eddison, John (MA University of Cambridge) was formerly on the staff of Scripture Union.

Ely, Richard (PhD University of Tasmania) is Honorary Research Associate in the School of History and Classics, University of Tasmania, Australia, and Senior Fellow in the History Department, University of Melbourne, Victoria, Australia.

Enns, James C. (MA University of Calgary) is an instructor in history and philosophy, Prairie Bible College, AB, Canada.

Eskridge, Larry (MA University of Maryland) is Associate Director, Institute for the Study of American Evangelicals, Wheaton College, IL, USA, and a PhD student, University of Stirling.

Faris, Tommy L. (MDiv Northern Baptist Theological Seminary) is a PhD student in Religion, Columbia University, NY, USA.

Ferguson, Sinclair B. (PhD University of Aberdeen) is Minister of St George's Tron Parish Church, Glasgow.

Finlayson, Sandy (MLS University of Toronto, MTS Tyndale Seminary, Toronto) is Director of Library Services and Associate Professor of Theological Bibliography, Westminster Theological Seminary, PA, USA.

Forsaith, Peter, is on the staff of the Wesley Centre, Oxford, and a PhD student, Oxford Brookes University.

Frame, John M. (MPhil, Yale University) is Professor of Systematic Theology and Philosophy, Reformed Theological Seminary, Orlando, FL, USA.

Francis, Keith A. (PhD University of London) is Associate Professor of History, Pacific Union College, CA, USA.

Friesen, Paul H. (PhD University of St Michael's College) is University Chaplain and a lecturer, King's College, NS, Canada, and a lecturer, Atlantic School of Theology, NS, Canada.

Gasque, Ward (PhD University of Manchester) is President, Center for Innovation in Theological Education, Seattle, WA, USA.

George, Timothy (ThD Harvard University) is Dean, Beeson Divinity School, Samford University, AL, USA and an executive editor of *Christianity Today*.

Gloege, Timothy E. W. (MA Wheaton College) is a graduate student in history, University of Notre Dame, IN, USA.

Goertz, Donald A. (MCS, MDiv Regent College, MA University of St Michael's College) is a teacher of Church History and Christian Spirituality, Tyndale Seminary, ON, Canada and a PhD student, University of St Michael's College, ON, Canada.

Goff, Philip (PhD University of North Carolina) is Director, Center for the Study of Religion and American Culture, Indiana University – Purdue University Indianapolis, IN, USA.

Goodhew, David (DPhil University of Oxford) is Vicar, St Oswald's, Fulford, York.

Goodwin, Daniel C. (PhD Queen's University) is Assistant Professor of History, Atlantic Baptist University, NB, Canada.

Gordon, Grant (DMin Princeton University) is an Intentional Interim Pastor near Toronto, ON, Canada.

Gouldbourne, Ruth M. B. (PhD University of London) is Tutor in History, Bristol Baptist College.

Graham, Stephen R. (PhD The University of Chicago) is Dean of Faculty and Academic Life, North Park Theological Seminary, IL, USA.

Grass, Timothy G. (PhD University of London) is an associate lecturer at Spurgeon's College, London.

Greenman, Jeffrey P. (PhD University of Virginia) is Academic Dean and Professor of Christian Ethics, Tyndale Seminary, ON, Canada.

Grenz, Stanley J. (DrTheol University of Munich) is Distinguished Professor of Theology, Baylor University and Truett Theological Seminary, TX, USA.

Gundlach, Bradley J. (PhD University of Rochester) is Assistant Professor of History, Trinity International University, IL, USA.

Hambrick-Stowe, Charles E. (PhD Boston University) is Director of the Doctor of Ministry Program, Pittsburgh Theological Seminary, PA, USA.

Hamm, Thomas D. (PhD University of Indiana) is Archivist and Professor of History, Earlham College, IN, USA.

Hankins, Barry (PhD Kansas State University) is Associate Professor of History and Church-State Studies, Baylor University, TX, USA.

Hargreaves, John A. (PhD University of Huddersfield) is a Methodist Local Preacher, Halifax Circuit.

Harrell, Jr, David E. (PhD Vanderbilt University) is Breeden Eminent Scholar in Humanities, Auburn University, AL, USA.

Harris, Maureen (PhD University of Durham) is a retired lecturer in English living near Bishop Auckland.

Haykin, Michael A. G. (ThD University of Toronto) is Professor of Historical Theology and Reformed Spirituality, Toronto Baptist Seminary, ON, Canada, and Adjunct Professor of Church History, Southern Baptist Theological Seminary, KY, USA.

Heath, Gordon L. (MDiv Acadia Divinity College) is a PhD student, University of Toronto, Canada, and Assistant Professor of History, Tyndale College, ON, Canada.

Hedges, Daniel J. (DMin McCormick Theological Seminary), is Professor of Practical Theology at the School of Theology and Missions, Oral Roberts University, OK, USA.

Heitzenrater, Richard P. (PhD Duke University) is William Kellon Quick Professor of Church History and Wesley Studies, Duke University, NC, USA.

Hensley, Jeffrey (PhD Yale University) is Assistant Professor, Virginia Theological Seminary, VA, USA.

Hilliard, David L. (PhD Australian National University) is Reader in History, Flinders University, SA, Australia.

Hindmarsh, D. B. (DPhil University of Oxford) is James M. Houston Associate Professor of Spiritual Theology, Regent College, BC, Canada.

Holmes, Finlay (MLitt University of Dublin) was formerly Professor of Church History, Union Theological College, Belfast.

Hopkins, Mark T. E. (DPhil University of Oxford) is a lecturer, Theological College of Northern Nigeria, Nigeria.

Husbands, Mark (MRel Wycliffe College, University of Toronto) is Assistant Professor of Theology, Wheaton College, IL, USA, and a PhD student, University of St Michael's College, ON, Canada.

Hutchinson, Mark (PhD University of NSW) is Dean of Graduate Studies and head of the History of Society Program, Southern Cross College, NSW, Australia.

Jauhiainen, Peter D. (PhD University of Iowa) is an Assistant Professor of Religion and Humanities, Kirkwood Community College, IA, USA.

Jeffrey, David L. (PhD Princeton University) is a Fellow of the Royal Society of Canada and Distinguished Professor of Literature and Humanities, Baylor University, TX, USA.

Johnson, Stuart B. (MA Macquarie University) is an Adjunct-Lecturer, Macquarie Christian Studies Institute, Macquarie University, NSW, Australia, and a PhD student, University of New South Wales, NSW, Australia.

Johnson, Wayne J. (PhD University of Keele) is Senior Lecturer, York St John College.

Jones, Helen M. (MA Universities of Cambridge and London) is a PhD student at King's College, London.

Jones, Margaret P. (MPhil University of Cambridge) is a Methodist minister and Senior Methodist tutor, North Thames Ministerial Training Course.

Kemeny, P. C. (PhD Princeton Seminary) is an Assistant Professor of Religion and Humanities, Grove City College, PA, USA.

Kidd, Thomas S. (PhD University of Notre Dame) is Assistant Professor of History, Baylor University, TX, USA.

Lam, Wing-hung (PhD Princeton University) is Research Professor in Church History and Chinese Studies, Tyndale College and Seminary, ON, Canada.

Lambert, Frank (PhD Northwestern University) is Professor of History at Purdue University, IN, USA.

Lane, Anthony N. S. (BD University of Oxford) is Professor of Historical Theology and Director of Research, London Bible College.

Larsen, David K. (PhD University of Chicago) is Head of Access Services, University of Chicago Library, IL, USA.

Larsen, Timothy (PhD University of Stirling) is Associate Professor of Theology, Wheaton College, IL, USA.

Leonard, Bill J. (PhD Boston University) is Dean and Professor of Church History, Wake Forest University Divinity School, NC, USA.

Letham, Robert W. A. (PhD University of Aberdeen) is Senior Minister at Emmanuel Orthodox Presbyterian Church, Wilmington, DE, USA.

Lewis, Donald M. (DPhil University of Oxford) is Professor of Church History and Dean of Faculty, Regent College, BC, Canada.

Lim, Paul C.-H. (PhD University of Cambridge) is Assistant Professor of Historical and Systematic Theology, Gordon-Conwell Theological Seminary, MA, USA.

Lineham, Peter (DPhil University of Sussex) is Associate Professor of History, School of Social and Cultural Studies, Massey University's Auckland campus and Chair of the Academic Advisory Committee, Bible College of New Zealand and Tyndale Graduate School of Theology, New Zealand.

Long, Kathryn Teresa (PhD Duke University) is Associate Professor of History, Wheaton College, IL, USA.

Maas, David E. (PhD University of Wisconsin) is Professor of History, Wheaton College, IL, USA.

McCasland, David (MA Wheaton College) is a full-time writer living in Colorado Springs, CO, USA.

McGee, Gary B. (PhD Saint Louis University) is Professor of Church History and Pentecostal Studies, Assemblies of God Theological Seminary, MO, USA.

McGonigle, Herbert (PhD University of Keele) is Principal and Senior Lecturer in Historical Theology and Wesley Studies, Nazarene Theological College, Manchester.

McKinley, Edward H. (PhD University of Wisconsin) is Professor of History, Asbury College, KY, USA.

MacLeod, A. Donald (AM Harvard University, MDiv Westminster Theological Seminary) is Minister of St Andrew's Presbyterian Church, Trenton, ON, and Lecturer in Church History, Tyndale Seminary, ON, Canada.

Macquiban, Timothy S. A. (PhD University of Birmingham) is Principal of Sarum College, Salisbury.

Manley, Ken R. (DPhil University of Oxford) was formerly Principal of Whitley College, The University of Melbourne, Victoria, Australia.

Maple, Grant S. (PhD University of New England) is Director of the Anglican Education Commission, Diocese of Sydney, NSW, Australia.

Mason, Alistair F. (PhD University of Leeds), was formerly Senior Lecturer in Christian Studies, Department of Theology and Religious Studies, University of Leeds.

Mathers, Helen (PhD University of Sheffield) is Centenary History Research Fellow, University of Sheffield.

Matthew, David (BA University of Bristol) is a Christian writer, itinerant teacher and member of the eldership team, Five Towns Christian Fellowship, Castleford.

Maxwell, Ian D. (PhD University of Edinburgh) is minister of Kirk o'Field Parish Church, Edinburgh.

Meyer, Dietrich (DrTheol University of Hamburg) was formerly Archivdirektor of the Evangelical Church of the Rhineland, Germany.

Miedema, Gary R. (PhD Queen's University, Canada) is Assistant Professor of History, Tyndale College, ON, Canada.

Mitchell, Christopher W. (PhD University of St Andrews) is Director of the Marion E. Wade Center, Wheaton College, IL, USA.

Mobley, Kendal P. (STM Boston University School of Theology) is a Baptist clergyman in Tiverton, RI, USA.

Morgan, D. Densil (DPhil University of Oxford) is Reader in Theology and Religious Studies, University of Wales.

Muirhead, Andrew T. N. (MLitt University of Stirling) is a librarian working for Stirling Council.

Munden, Alan F. (PhD University of Durham) is Rector of Weddington and Caldecote, Nuneaton.

Murray, Derek B. (PhD University of St Andrews) is Lecturer in Baptist History, Scottish Baptist College, Paisley, and was formerly Chaplain of St Columba's Hospice, Edinburgh.

Nation, Mark T. (PhD Fuller Theological Seminary) is Associate Professor of Theology, Eastern Mennonite Seminary, VA, USA, and was formerly the Programme Director of the London Mennonite Centre.

Noll, Mark A. (PhD Vanderbilt University) is McManis Professor of Christian Thought, Wheaton College, IL, USA.

Nordlof, John (PhD Delaware University) is Assistant Professor of English, Regis College, MA, USA.

Olbricht, Tom (PhD University of Iowa) is Distinguished Professor Emeritus of Religion, Pepperdine University, CA, USA.

Oldstone-Moore, Christopher (PhD University of Chicago) is Instructor of History, Wright State University, OH, USA.

Owen, David Rhys (MTh Rhodes University) is an ordained Methodist minister and Chaplain and Head of Religious Studies, Taunton School.

Packer, J. I. (DPhil University of Oxford) is Board of Governors Professor of Theology, Regent College, BC, Canada.

Paproth, Darrell (PhD Deakin University) is lecturer in church history and church and culture in Australia, Bible College of Victoria, Victoria, Australia.

Pearse, Meic (DPhil University of Oxford) is Lecturer in Church History and BA Course Leader, London Bible College, and Adjunct Professor of Church History, Evangelical Theological Seminary, Croatia.

Peterson, Kurt (PhD University of Notre Dame) is Assistant Professor of History, North Park University, IL, USA.

Pierard, R. V. (PhD University of Iowa) is Professor of History, Emeritus, Indiana State University, IN, USA, and Scholar in Residence and Adjunct Professor, Gordon College, MA, USA.

Piggin, Stuart (PhD University of London) is Master of Robert Menzies College, Macquarie University, NSW, Australia.

Pointer, Richard W. (PhD Johns Hopkins University) is Professor of History, Westmont College, CA, USA.

Pooley, Roger F. (PhD University of Cambridge) is Lecturer, School of English and Philosophy, University of Keele.

Pratt, Andrew (MA University of Durham) is a PhD student, Liverpool Hope University College.

Randall, Ian (PhD University of Wales) is Lecturer in Church History and Spirituality, Spurgeon's College, London.

Raser, Harold E. (PhD The Pennsylvania State University) is Professor of the History of Christianity, Nazarene Theological Seminary, MO, USA.

Reid, Darrel (PhD Queen's University, Ontario) is President, Focus on the Family Canada, Langley, BC, Canada.

Rennie, Ian S. (PhD University of Toronto) is a retired minister of the Presbyterian Church in Canada and was formerly Professor of Church History, Regent College, BC, Canada, and Vice-President, Academic Dean and Professor of Church History, Tyndale Seminary, ON, Canada.

Roberts, Michael B. (MA University of Oxford), is Vicar of Cockerham, Glasson and Winmarleigh, Lancaster, and Honorary Research Associate, University of Lancaster.

Robertson, David A. (MA University of Edinburgh) is the minister of St Peter's Free Church of Scotland, Dundee, and a PhD student, University of Edinburgh.

Robins, Roger G. (PhD Duke University) is Archivist of the David J. du Plessis Center for Christian Spirituality, Fuller Theological Seminary, CA, USA.

Roney, John B. (PhD University of Toronto) is Professor of History, Sacred Heart University, Fairfield, CT, USA.

Rosin, Robert L. (PhD Stanford University) is Professor and Chairman of the Department of Historical Theology, Concordia Theological Seminary, MO, USA.

Rowdon, Harold H. (PhD University of London) was formerly Senior Lecturer in Church History, London Bible College.

Roxborogh, John (PhD University of Aberdeen) is Co-ordinator of Lay and Recognized Ministry Training, Presbyterian School of Ministry, Knox College, New Zealand.

Roxburgh, Kenneth B. E. (PhD University of Edinburgh), is Chair, Department of Religion, Samford University, AL, USA.

Ryken, Philip Graham (DPhil University of Oxford) is senior minister of Tenth Presbyterian Church, Philadelphia, PA, USA.

Schmalzbauer, John A. (PhD Princeton University) is Assistant Professor of Sociology and E. B. Williams Fellow, College of the Holy Cross, MA, USA.

Scorgie, Glen G. (PhD St Andrews University) is Professor of Theology, Bethel Seminary, CA, USA.

Scotland, Nigel (PhD University of Aberdeen) is Field Chair, School of Theology and Religious Studies, University of Gloucestershire.

Shaw, Ian J. (PhD University of Manchester) is Lecturer in Church History, International Christian College, Glasgow.

Shelley, Bruce L. (PhD University of Iowa) is Senior Professor of Church History, Denver Seminary, CO, USA.

Shepherd, Victor A. (ThD University of Toronto) is Professor of Historical Theology and Chair of Wesley Studies, Tyndale Seminary, ON, Canada.

Shuff, Roger N. (BD University of Wales), is a Baptist minister and a PhD student, Spurgeon's College, London.

Sider-Rose, Michael J. (PhD University of Pittsburgh) teaches on the Chicago Semester, Trinity Christian College, IL, USA.

Sivasundaram, Sujit (PhD University of Cambridge) is Research Fellow in History, Gonville and Caius College, Cambridge.

Smith, Karen E. (DPhil University of Oxford) is tutor in Church History, South Wales Baptist College and Department of Religious and Theological Studies, University of Wales.

Smith, Mark (DPhil University of Oxford) is Lecturer in Modern Church History, King's College, London.

Solberg, Winton U. (PhD University of Pittsburgh) is Professor Emeritus of History, University of Illinois, IL, USA.

Spencer, Stephen R. (PhD Michigan State University) is Blanchard Professor of Theology, Wheaton College, IL, USA.

Stackhouse, John G., Jr (PhD University of Chicago), is Sangwoo Youtong Chee Professor of Theology and Culture at Regent College, BC, Canada.

Stanley, Brian (PhD University of Cambridge) is Director of the Henry Martyn Centre, Cambridge, and a Fellow of St Edmund's College, University of Cambridge.

Starr, J. Barton (PhD Florida State University) is Associate Vice-President and Academic Dean (Humanities and Social Sciences) and Chair Professor of History, Lingnan University, Hong Kong.

Steinacher, C. Mark (ThD Wycliffe College, University of Toronto) is a member of the adjunct faculties of McMaster Divinity College, ON, Canada, and Tyndale Seminary, ON, Canada.

Sutton, William R. (PhD University of Illinois) is Teaching Associate at University Laboratory High School, University of Illinois, IL, USA.

Sweeney, Douglas A. (PhD Vanderbilt University) is Associate Professor of Church History and the History of Christian Thought, Trinity Evangelical Divinity School, IL, USA.

Thimell, Daniel P. (PhD University of Aberdeen) is Associate Professor of Theological and Historical Studies and Chair of the Department of Theology and Missions, Oral Roberts University, OK, USA.

Thomas, Arthur D., Jr (PhD Union Theological Seminary) is Professor of Christian Spirituality, The Ecumenical Institute of Theology, St Mary's Seminary, MD, and University and Adjunct in Spirituality, Wesley Theological Seminary, DC, USA.

Thomas, Joseph L. (MTh Fuller Theological Seminary) is a PhD student, Trinity Evangelical Divinity School, IL, USA.

Thompson, David M. (PhD, BD University of Cambridge) is Senior Lecturer in Church History, University of Cambridge.

Thompson, T. Jack (PhD University of Edinburgh) is Senior Lecturer in the History of World Christianity, New College, University of Edinburgh.

Torbett, David (PhD Union Theological Seminary) is visiting professor at Mount Union College, OH, USA.

Treloar, Geoffrey R. (PhD University of Sydney) is Dean, and Director of the School of Christian Studies, Robert Menzies College, Macquarie University, NSW, Australia.

Trollinger, William Vance, Jr (PhD University of Wisconsin) is Associate Professor of History, University of Dayton, OH, USA.

Trueman, Carl R. (PhD University of Aberdeen) is Associate Professor of Church History and Historical Theology, Westminster Theological Seminary, PA, USA.

Tudur, Geraint (DPhil University of Oxford) is Lecturer in Church History, Department of Theology and Religious Studies, University of Wales, and Director of the Centre for the Advanced Study of Religion in Wales.

Tyson, John R. (PhD Drew University) is Professor of Theology at Houghton College, NY, USA.

Unruh, Heidi (MA Eastern Baptist Theological Seminary) is affiliated with Eastern University, PA, USA, as Associate Director of the Congregations, Communities and Leadership Development Project.

Van Die, Margaret (PhD University of Western Ontario) is an Associate Professor of History at Queen's University and Queen's Theological College, ON, Canada.

Vedder, Chris (MA University of Manchester) teaches in the UK and Eastern Europe.

Vickery, Jon (MDiv Tyndale Seminary), is a ThD student, Wycliffe College, University of Toronto, ON, Canada.

Wainwright, Geoffrey (DrTheol University of Geneva, DD University of Cambridge) holds the Cushman Chair of Christian Theology at Duke University, NC, USA.

Wallace, Peter J. (MDiv Westminster Theological Seminary) is a PhD student, University of Notre Dame, IN, USA.

Ward, W. R. (DPhil University of Oxford, DrTheol h.c. University of Basel) is Emeritus Professor of Modern History, University of Durham.

Wellings, Martin (DPhil University of Oxford) is a minister in the Oxford Circuit of the Methodist Church and British Section Secretary of the World Methodist Historical Society.

Wenger, Robert E. (PhD University of Nebraska-Lincoln) is Dean of School of Arts and Sciences and Professor of History, Philadelphia Biblical University, PA, USA.

Westerkamp, Marilyn J. (PhD University of Pennsylvania) is Professor of History, University of California, Santa Cruz, CA, USA.

Wigger, John H. (PhD University of Notre Dame) is Associate Professor of History, University of Missouri, MO, USA.

Wilson, David B. (PhD Johns Hopkins University) is Professor of History, Mechanical Engineering and Philosophy, Iowa State University, IA, USA.

Wilson, Linda (PhD Cheltenham and Gloucester College) is a distance learning tutor, the Open Theological College.

Wright, David F. (DD University of Edinburgh) is Professor of Patristic and Reformed Christianity, University of Edinburgh.

Yarnell, Malcolm (DPhil University of Oxford) is Academic Dean and Associate Professor of Historical Theology, Midwestern Baptist Theological Seminary, MO, USA.

Yates, Timothy E. (ThD University of Uppsala) is Canon Emeritus of Derby Cathedral.

INTRODUCTION

Attempting to define the complex reality of modern evangelicalism is always a challenge in books such as this one. In proposing such a definition I have drawn on the studies of two leading scholars of evangelicalism with whom I have been privileged to work on this project and to whom I refer jokingly as my 'patron saints' (though always behind their backs, since this is really not a very evangelical designation!). In tackling the thorny questions of definition, I have sought to blend the complementary approaches that they have adopted in earlier published works.

David Bebbington, in his landmark study *Evangelicalism in Modern Britain*, proposed a remarkably useful definition that has become the standard one. The Bebbington quadrilateral identifies four crucial characteristics of evangelicals (conversionism, activism, biblicism and crucicentrism) and has been adopted for this study. Nevertheless, the approach taken by Mark Noll in his seminal work, *Between Faith and Criticism*, has also served as a guide. Noll uses a thoroughgoing descriptive approach, arguing that the evangelical community is a readily identifiable network and that therefore those who can be seen to be a part of that network are the proper subjects of studies in evangelicalism. Noll's approach also informed this study. This influence means that the book has been biased towards figures who have had a substantial impact in the wider evangelical movement (that is, across denominational lines) and away from those whose influence was contained within denominational, ethnic, theological or regional subcultures.

Chronologically, a birth year of 1935 was chosen as the *terminus ad quem* (although a mistake over dates led to the inclusion of one person born in 1936!). The subjects were not limited to people who had died, as so many of the leading evangelicals who shaped the movement from the 1940s onwards have been blessed with long life. On the other hand, turning the work into a 'who's who' of the current evangelical scene was also to be avoided. Those born in 1935 or earlier have now passed the standard retirement age of 65 and therefore some perspective can be gained when assessing their achievements and reputations. Bebbington regards the 1730s as the decade that launched the evangelical movement, and his judgment is accepted here. Nevertheless, the inclusion of a 'prehistory' of evangelical forbears was thought to be useful – those by whose work evangelicals have often been shaped and with whose examples they have identified. The earliest figure who has been included is John Wyclif. Thus my rule of thumb for the chronological scope of the volume has always been 'from John Wyclif to John Wimber' (and, I suppose one might add, 'via John Wesley'). The Reformers and Puritans are the most obvious examples of individuals included because of their influence on the evangelical community, even though they were not 'evangelicals' in a technical sense.

Geographically, the scope is the English-speaking world, understood in its traditional sense as the UK, the USA, Canada, Australia, New Zealand and South Africa. A few figures from non-English speaking countries have also been included if their ministries or reputations made a significant impact upon English-speaking evangelicals. Occupationally, the focus has been, naturally enough, upon the kind of work that those who gain a wide reputation amongst evangelicals are apt to do. Most subjects are ministers, theologians, evangelists, preachers, writers or missionaries, although a variety of other professions leaven the whole, as the reputations of various subjects in the evangelical community appeared to warrant.

In general, my goal has been to include those figures that would be of interest to scholars, ministers, ordinands, students and others interested in the history of evangelicalism.

I have tried to resist the temptation to decide what people *ought* to want to know and then to shape the project accordingly. Thus I have not attempted to 'balance' the list in terms of denominational identity or gender. Instead I am trusting that the attention paid by the wider evangelical network to some people rather than others will reflect well or badly on it and not on me as a historian and compiler.

The bibliographies at the end of the entries are designed to point readers towards a few of the most useful secondary sources that address the subjects at greater length (and primary sources too, if autobiographical). Contributors were asked to confine themselves to these rather than listing all the sources they had consulted.

It has been a pleasure to work with Steve Carter, Reference Books Editor at IVP, whose knowledge, competency, efficiency, fair-minded good sense and natural congeniality made this project a smoother one for the editor than it might have been. Special thanks are due to David Goodhew, Mark Hutchinson, Peter Lineham, Ian Rennie and Brian Stanley, who cheerfully acted as unpaid experts in order to fill lacunae in my knowledge when the list of entries was being composed. Nevertheless, since hard choices had to be made, all their well-reasoned wish-lists were cut, so they cannot be blamed for the final results. I am grateful also to Susan Rebis for her skilful and meticulous copy-editing of the volume.

The greatest hidden determinant of the scope of such a project, of course, is the amount of space available in a single-volume work, a ruthless factor that resists all special pleading. George Marsden, in his classic study of Fuller Seminary, *Reforming Fundamentalism*, tells of a heated controversy on the doctrine of Scripture amongst the seminary's faculty. Daniel Fuller argued that inerrancy was an untenable position because of various difficulties in the text that he could itemize. E. J. Carnell, on the other hand, began his impassioned defence of the verbal inspiration of the Scriptures with the words, 'My list of discrepancies is longer than yours, Dan Fuller.' Although I do not intend to argue that my final list of subjects is inerrant, I can, I believe, truthfully reply to those who might question it that my list of subjects who ought to have been included but were not is longer than theirs. If those who use this work find in it most of the standard figures whom they have heard named in historical surveys or in the evangelical community, and perhaps stumble upon some other interesting figures along the way, then I will consider my task to have been successfully completed.

Timothy Larsen

■ **ABERHART, William** (1878–1943), Canadian preacher and politician, was born on 30 December 1878, on a farm near Kippen, Huron County, Ontario, the fourth of eight children. Raised in a Presbyterian environment, Aberhart would always consider himself a Calvinist, but he was also greatly influenced by the revivalists who regularly itinerated in the area.

After graduating from Hamilton Normal College in 1899, Aberhart began to teach in Brantford, Ontario. By 1905 he had been appointed a principal. Having taken several correspondence courses, he graduated in 1911 from Queen's University with a BA.

Early in Aberhart's teaching career, his study of science and biblical criticism led to a major crisis of faith. It was resolved by his discovery of the teachings of Cyrus *Scofield, which provided him with a hermeneutical framework. Brantford was also a stronghold of both fundamentalism and the Plymouth Brethren movement in Ontario. Aberhart quickly modified Scofield's teaching, adopting a radical futurist version of ultradispensational premillennialism.

In 1910 Aberhart moved to Calgary, Alberta, where he took a position as a school principal. An excellent administrator and educator, he was appointed principal of a new model high school, Crescent Heights, in 1915. He would serve there with distinction until elected as provincial premier.

In Calgary Aberhart also quickly established himself as a popular Bible teacher and preacher. Finding a home church was not so easy. Having initially attended Grace Presbyterian Church, he moved in 1912 to the large Wesleyan Methodist Church and finally, in 1915, to Westbourne Baptist Church, which was without a pastor. He remained there until 1929. Ironically, although he was neither a Baptist nor ordained, he exercised complete control over the congregation. His Thursday evening class, the 'Prophetic Bible Conference', grew rapidly, increasing his reputation in the city.

Aberhart saw himself as an evangelist, not a prophetic preacher. Prophecy, he believed, was the servant of evangelism, so it should normally take place in the context of the proclamation of Christ's death on the cross. It was the cross that served as the fulcrum of history. But Aberhart's call to conversion combined evangelism and prophecy; conversion was presented as the way to escape the terrors of the AntiChrist. Interestingly, Aberhart's evangelistic techniques were later directly transferred to his work of political recruitment. The message changed, but the means of eliciting commitment did not.

In all areas of life, Aberhart liked absolute answers. Scripture, he believed, provided such answers if one had the proper key to unlock it. Various biblical texts presented serious problems for his hermeneutic. This hermeneutic, especially the literal interpretation of prophecy, required a text which was literally true, just waiting to be decoded. Aberhart found his text in the King James Version, which he believed to be inerrant. Since the Textus Receptus had, he believed, been miraculously preserved by God in the Swiss Alps, every syllable and all the punctuation of the King James Version was inspired.

In the early 1920s Aberhart moved increasingly toward the sectarian fringe. His lectures, and his magazine, *The Prophetic Voice*, begun in 1924, popularized his views. In 1920 he came under the influence of the 'Jesus Only' Pentecostal movement. As a result, he adopted their baptismal formula and a charismatic understanding of the Spirit, although without accepting the doctrine of initial evidences, and introduced to his church the office of 'Apostle'. He believed that the Spirit was received through the laying on of hands by the Apostle, Aberhart himself. This office gave him unprecedented power in Westbourne. Aberhart also abandoned his Reformed view of sanctification.

Central to Aberhart's interpretation of history was his belief in race names. The Bible spoke of peoples, and by studying these, Aberhart believed, one could understand their status in the present dispensation. No matter where they lived, they always remained a part of their race. Aberhart argued that inter-racial marriages were evil, and that the children of such marriages were 'Daughters of Babylon'; in consequence of these remarks, he has been charged with anti-Semitism. He did attack Zionism as futile, believing that the Jews' return to Palestine was not for this dispensation. But after the rise of Nazism, he took a strong stand against anti-Semitism. The system of race names was the basic conviction of

British Israelism, another movement that influenced him.

Aberhart's dispensationalism gave him a very pessimistic view of humanity. It was also the means by which he tried to identify the primary sources of evil in the world. He believed that capitalism, which was symbolized by Babylon in the book of Revelation, was the worst of these. Aberhart's social critiques were devastating.

Although Aberhart did not believe that any biblical prophecies were related to the present dispensation, he did believe in cause and effect. Many current events had 'presignificance'; they would lead to the tribulation.

Aberhart had a great ability to identify and meet the needs of his society. In the 1920s there was a shortage of clergy, especially among the small rural churches. So in 1925 Aberhart founded the Calgary Bible Institute to train lay people in his fundamentalist faith. Courses were also available by correspondence. Ernest Manning, later premier of Alberta, was in the first Bible Institute class.

That same autumn Aberhart began broadcasting the services of the Prophetic Bible Conference on CFCN Calgary, the most powerful radio station in western Canada. Soon he was also broadcasting the morning and evening services of Westbourne Baptist. Probably his most successful religious venture was his Radio Sunday School, for children from the ages of five to sixteen, which he founded in 1926. Pupils' achievements were recognized on the air. Eventually over 9,000 children were enrolled. Aberhart became immensely popular, and in 1926 he had to build a large centre for his growing operation.

In 1925 Aberhart supported T. T. *Shields in his dispute with the Ontario Baptists. Then, when charges of modernism were levelled against the Baptist college in Brandon, Aberhart took Westbourne out of the Baptist Union of Western Canada, probably in 1926. This secession left him free from all external oversight, but exacerbated tensions within his congregation. Westbourne, rebelling against his absolute control, split in 1929; 65% of the members left. They went back to their old building and aligned themselves with Shields' Regular Baptists. Aberhart then formed the Bible Institute Baptist Church, firmly under his own control as Apostle.

The Great Depression brought dramatic changes to Alberta, which was badly affected by the economic collapse. Aberhart, still principal of a high school with over 1,000 students, saw the impact of the slump on their lives. In 1932 he discovered Social Credit, an economic theory developed by Clifford Douglas. Douglas placed the blame for the economic crisis on banks and financiers, accusing them of taking away from the people the purchasing power that was needed to balance production and consumption. The result was poverty in the midst of plenty. Aberhart was attracted by what seemed to be a definite solution to the problems of the Depression. He began to include economic theory in his radio broadcasts. He drew liberally from the ideas contained in the *Communist Manifesto* especially state control of credit and production, public ownership of property, heavy taxation of non-sympathizers and aliens and abolition of inherited wealth. All these ideas were combined with the social critiques of the biblical prophets. If the Bible was true, Aberhart maintained, then so was his version of Social Credit.

Unable to persuade the existing parties to adopt his ideas, Aberhart founded the Social Credit Party. The next election campaign was vicious. When the Bible Institutes, led by Prairie Bible Institute, charged Aberhart with betraying the gospel by entering politics, he accused them of being like the priest and Levite in the parable of the good Samaritan. His attacks almost destroyed them.

The 1935 election brought Aberhart to power at the head of a coalition representing all the province's religious groups. Aberhart drew people from all denominations into his party; only 11% of its members came from fundamentalist groups. At the Bible Institute Baptist Church, however, the pastor was not allowed even to have fellowship with other Christian groups. Aberhart was able to turn the widespread dissatisfaction in the province to his advantage. As premier, he was prevented by the constitution from implementing his most controversial ideas. Some of his supporters were dissatisfied, but Aberhart was able to take a number of constructive measures. He reorganized the educational system, including the University of Alberta. He also fixed wages and prices, improved working conditions, raised pensions, improved health care, strove to lower interest rates and established a provincial bank. Against those who accused him of changing his theology, he argued that what the people needed was not more Bible teaching, but more application.

As premier, Aberhart exerted rigid control over his government and saw his party as a vehicle for his personal ideas. A populist politician, he was an excellent organizer and dynamic speaker, able to capture and hold people's attention by the sheer power of his personality.

William Aberhart died on 23 May 1943 in Vancouver.

Bibliography
D. R. Elliott and I. Miller, *Bible Bill: A Biography of William Aberhart* (Edmonton: Reidmore Books, 1987); D. A. Goertz, 'The Development of a Bible Belt: The Socio-Religious Interaction in Alberta Between 1925 and 1938' (MCS thesis, Regent College, 1980).

D. A. GOERTZ

■ **AINSWORTH, Henry** (c. 1570–1622), Separatist, was born in Swanton Morley in Norfolk. He studied at St John's and Gonville and Caius Colleges in Cambridge. A mild mannered man, he gained a reputation for his scholarly, moving exposition of Scripture. He became a part of the Separatist Church that had been organized in 1592 under the leadership of Francis Johnson, John Greenwood and others.

After the death of Henry *Barrow and John Greenwood in 1593, the congregation moved from London and settled in Amsterdam. Ainsworth became a teacher of the congregation in 1596, though his authority was disputed; it was claimed that he was a 'reformed apostate', that is, that he had attended a parish church, albeit for a service conducted by a Puritan minister. In spite of this claim, Ainsworth remained in office, and in the same year he led the congregation in its publication of *A True Confession* (1596), which highlighted some key doctrinal issues that would later prove to be somewhat contentious. They included the nature of the ordinances, the authority of the ministry and the importance of discipline within the church.

A True Confession was a defence against those who had falsely called the church 'Brownists' and an attempt to clear themselves from 'unchristian slanders of heresie, schisme, pryde, obstinacie, disloyaltie, sedicion, etc' (*A True Confession* in W. L. Lumpkin, *Baptist Confessions of Faith* [Valley Forge: Judson Press, revised edition 1969, p. 82]). The confession expressed a sincere belief in congregational church government, but at the same time it strongly emphasized the authority of the ministry: 'for the keeping of this Church in holy and orderly communion, as Christ hath placed some speciall (sic) men over the Church, who by their office are to govern, oversee, visit, watch, etc ...' (Lumpkin, p. 90).

According to the *Confession*, leaders appointed by the congregation were not to force it to go against conscience, but they were recognized as having authority to lead and to administer the ordinances. Its organization, particularly in relation to leadership and discipline, continued to trouble the congregation. For several years the ordinances of baptism and the Lord's Supper were not celebrated because the church had no pastor and no-one was deemed competent to administer them.

In 1597 Francis Johnson joined the congregation as pastor. Initially he and Ainsworth seemed to agree over the organization of the church, but by 1610 they were divided over Johnson's desire to elevate the presbytery above the congregation. At first Ainsworth agreed that Christ had ordained a presbytery or eldership to which the church members should submit. Later, perhaps after reading the argument of John *Smyth, he changed his mind. Denying that ministers should have authority over the members, on 16 December 1610 he and some of the members seceded from the congregation led by Johnson.

Ainsworth and his party were then embroiled in a lawsuit as they sought to gain the right of ownership of the meeting house. This dispute sharpened the debate over the authority of leadership within the church. Ainsworth argued that although authority was given to the ministers by the church, and at times members were to submit to their authority, in congregational polity the church never fully surrendered all authority to them, because the congregational meeting, under the Lordship of Christ, had final authority.

Ainsworth wrote a number of works that helped to explain congregational ecclesiology. In 1607 he published a book entitled *The Communion of Saincts* (sic), in which he outlined a view of the church based on the idea of covenant relationship with God and one another. In this devotional work, he claimed that the covenant, which was agreed by the congregation, stood on two pillars: to keep faith in God by Jesus Christ and to observe his laws in love (*Communion of Saincts*, 1615 edn, p. 340). His belief in congregational polity was made still clearer when he wrote that all saints have 'a right and interest in the covenant of God ... each one according to his place, calling and measure of grace, given him from Christ the head' (p. 375).

Ainsworth's writings, particularly *The Communion of Saincts*, which was reprinted several times (1615, 1618, 1628 and twice in 1640), proved to be very influential in expounding the Separatists' belief that the covenanted church or gathered community was the scriptural model for the church. This congregational doctrine of the church was rooted in the Separatist tradition and, as disseminated in the writings of Ainsworth and others, continued to flourish among Dissenters in succeeding generations.

Bibliography

H. Ainsworth, *The Communion of Saincts* (Amsterdam: 1607); H. Ainsworth, *Counterpoyson* (Amsterdam?: 1608); H. Ainsworth, *A Defence of the Holy Scriptures* (Amsterdam: 1609); B. R. White, *The English Separatist Tradition, from the Marian Martyrs to the Pilgrim Fathers* (Oxford: Oxford Theological Monographs, 1971); M. R. Watts, *The Dissenters* (Oxford: Clarendon Press, 1978).

K. E. SMITH

■ **ALEXANDER, Archibald** (1772–1851), Old School Presbyterian pastor and Princeton theologian, was born in Rockbridge County, Virginia, to a Scots-Irish family. His father, William, served as a Presbyterian ruling elder, and Archibald was converted during the 1789 revival through the preaching of his teacher and pastor, William Graham. After studying theology with Graham at Liberty Hall Academy (later Washington and Lee University), he was licensed to preach by the Presbytery of Lexington at the age of nineteen.

Alexander acquired from Graham a predilection for the theology of Francis Turretin (1623–1687), a commitment to Scottish common-sense realism and a fascination with the developing field of psychology. Having grown up in Jeffersonian Virginia and being an heir to the Great Awakening, he insisted upon the need for a rational defence against deism and displayed a lifelong concern for the experience of saving faith, blending rational faith with heartfelt piety.

On 7 June 1794 Hanover Presbytery ordained him as pastor of two small churches in the Virginia piedmont. From 1797 to 1806 he served as president of Hampden-Sydney College, continuing to pastor various churches in the area. In 1801 he was sent to the General Assembly in Philadelphia, where he was commissioned to represent the Assembly to the General Association of Connecticut in the establishment of the famous Plan of Union, an arrangement Alexander would later work to end.

During his presidency at Hampden-Sydney, Alexander trained several young men for the ministry and urged the creation of a theological seminary. In addition he helped establish *The Virginia Religious Magazine* (1804–1807) to foster experimental religion and encourage foreign and domestic missions. He resigned the college presidency in 1806 because of increasing student misbehaviour and accepted a call to the Third Presbyterian Church of Philadelphia, of which he was pastor from 1806 to 1812.

In Philadelphia Alexander deepened his friendship with Ashbel Green, and his national reputation was confirmed by his election as moderator of the 1807 General Assembly. In his sermon to the 1808 Assembly he urged the creation of regional seminaries in order to train ministers throughout the church. During his Philadelphia years Alexander helped to establish the First African Presbyterian Church of Philadelphia (1809) and the Philadelphia Bible Society (1808). Later, while at Princeton, he assisted in the formation of the American

Colonization Society (1816), writing a history of the movement in 1846.

In 1812 the General Assembly called Alexander as Professor of Didactic and Polemical Theology at the Theological Seminary at Princeton, where he spent thirty-nine years inculcating orthodox Reformed theology and revival-oriented piety through the philosophy of common-sense realism. Less exegetically oriented than his student, colleague and successor Charles *Hodge, Alexander's approach to theology and piety is demonstrated in his writings, such as *A Brief Outline of the Evidences of the Christian Religion* (1825; expanded and revised in 1836 as *Evidences of the Authenticity, Inspiration, and Canonical Authority of the Holy Scriptures*), *Thoughts on Religious Experience* (1841), *Biographical Sketches of the Founder and Principal Alumni of the Log College* (1845) and *Outlines of Moral Science* (1852), as well as in numerous articles in the seminary's journal, the *Biblical Repertory and Princeton Review* (1825–1871).

Alexander argued that 'God has so constituted our minds that we cannot avoid believing in certain truths as soon as they are presented to the mind.' Convinced that there were certain intuitive truths or fundamental principles that must be universally accepted by all reasonable persons, such as the existence of the external world, cause and effect, the soul and God, Alexander attempted to utilize these truths to undergird the rationality of the Christian faith. Hence he argued that apologetic proofs for the existence of God were a necessary starting point for Christian theology, though he acknowledged that no-one could be converted apart from the direct work of the Holy Spirit.

Alexander believed that proper religious experience would flow from a theology that embraced the whole of biblical teaching. He insisted that defective theology invariably produced defective experience, as evidenced, he claimed, in the revivalism of Charles *Finney.

During the debates over the New Haven theology, congregational polity and voluntary associations that characterized the 1830s, Alexander attempted to maintain a moderate position. He agreed with the Old School but desired to maintain the unity of the church. Finally, in 1837 he became convinced that unity was no longer possible and approved the abrogation of the Plan of Union which he had helped create.

In 1802 Alexander married Janetta Waddell, daughter of the blind Virginia Presbyterian minister, Dr James Waddell. Six sons and a daughter survived them, including two sons, James Waddell Alexander and Joseph Addison Alexander, who taught at Princeton Seminary.

Bibliography

J. W. Alexander, *The Life of Archibald Alexander* (New York: Scribner's, 1854); A. W. Hoffecker, *Piety and the Princeton Theologians* (Grand Rapids: Baker Book House, 1981); L. A. Loetscher, *Facing the Enlightenment and Pietism: Archibald Alexander and the Founding of Princeton Theological Seminary* (Westport: Greenwood, 1983).

P. J. WALLACE

■ **ALLEINE, Joseph** (1634–1668), Puritan divine, had a profound influence on the piety of later evangelicalism through his famous book, *An Alarme to Unconverted Sinners*.

Alleine was converted in 1645 as a result of the death of his much older brother Edward, a clergyman, who was then twenty-six years of age. Subsequently, he was educated at Exeter College, Oxford, and from April 1649 at Lincoln College. On 3 November 1651 he was appointed a scholar of Corpus Christi. Then, on 6 July 1653, he took his BD. He became a tutor and chaplain (in preference to being elected a fellow).

The 1650s at Oxford were dominated by the towering figure of the Puritan vice-chancellor, John *Owen, a man of broad intellectual interests. This period thus witnessed the maturing of new trajectories of learning, such as oriental languages, and the rise of new scientific approaches to the world that were to bear fruit in coming years in the work of the Royal Society. It would seem that Alleine was fully immersed in this culture, being an intimate friend of numerous founding members of the Royal Society. Out of this context he produced a work (now lost) entitled *Theologia Philosophica*, which represented an attempt to harmonize revelation and philosophical thought, and which won great praise from Richard *Baxter. In producing such a work, Alleine was typical of the generation of English Reformed thinkers who had come to maturity in the middle years of the seventeenth century and who had started to appropriate the latest philosophical and scientific developments for the cause of orthodoxy.

In 1654 Alleine was ordained in Taunton and ministered there until he was ejected in 1662. He continued to preach despite the strictures of the Clarendon Code, working as an evangelist, at one time with the grandfather of John and Charles *Wesley. For his pains, he endured repeated imprisonment and finally, worn out by the demands of work and constant persecution, he died on 17 November 1668.

Alleine's most famous work, *An Alarme to Unconverted Sinners*, was first published in 1671, selling 20,000 copies. A second printing, entitled *A Sure Guide to Heaven*, was published in 1675, this time selling 50,000 copies. The work has been reprinted many times. In it, Alleine expounds the strongly conversionist and experimental piety that typified much Puritan theology, whilst presupposing a fundamentally Reformed Orthodox soteriology. As such, it is typical of the tradition of Reformed pastoral theology, found among the English Puritans and the writers of the Dutch *Nadere Reformatie*, that combined elements of both pietism and Reformed Orthodoxy. This is also evident in the posthumously published work of casuistry, *Divers practical cases of conscience satisfactorily resolved* (1672). Nevertheless, the reader of Alleine's *Alarme* should bear in mind that he was a man who socialized with members of the Royal Society and wrote a major work of philosophical theology; thus, the conversionist pietism of the *Alarme* gives only a partial picture of a man who was undoubtedly sophisticated and subtle regarding matters of the intellect.

C. R. TRUEMAN

■ **ALLEN, Richard** (1760–1831), African American minister, was a founder and the first bishop of the African Methodist Episcopal (AME) Church, the first African American denomination in the United States. His authority extended far beyond the AME Church. Allen became an influential figure in the general development of Protestantism in the United States and in the formation of African American Christianity, as well as in the abolitionist movement during the antebellum period.

Born a slave in Philadelphia, Pennsylvania on 14 February 1760, Allen and his family were owned by the lawyer Benjamin Chew, who later sold them to Stokley Sturgis, a farmer who lived near Dover, Delaware, south of Philadelphia. Allen was converted to Christianity in 1777 under Methodist influence while in Delaware. In the immediate aftermath of his conversion Allen urged his acquaintances to convert, but later experienced a period of doubt. The uncertainty of this time was ended by what Allen described as a filling of his soul, which left him with an abundant confidence in his faith. A sister and a brother also became Christians, and Allen himself became a Methodist lay preacher. Although Allen's master was not a Christian, Sturgis allowed him to join the Methodist society and be a member of a class for several years.

When white neighbours criticized Sturgis for allowing slaves to attend Methodist meetings and suggested that their work was suffering as a result, Allen and his brother decided that they would work harder and prove that Christianity did not reduce productivity. Sturgis became convinced that Christianity was a positive influence and agreed, at Allen's request, to host a Methodist meeting in his own home. Sturgis was himself converted, became persuaded that slavery was wrong and allowed Allen to purchase his and his brother's freedom. Allen was permitted to hire himself to others and earned the purchase prices within five years.

To support himself in his freedom and ministry as a lay preacher, Allen worked as a woodcutter, a bricklayer and driving a wagon team. He thus established a practice of self-supported ministry that would continue in his later life. Allen continued his preaching ministry to both blacks and whites in Delaware, Maryland, Pennsylvania, New Jersey and New York. While he was working in one preaching circuit, he came to the attention of prominent leaders in early American Methodism, including Francis *Asbury and Richard Whatcoat.

After the Methodist Episcopal Church was formally established at the Christmas conference of 1784, Allen travelled around the Baltimore circuit with Whatcoat in early 1785. In that same year Asbury asked Allen to accompany him on a ministry tour of the South. Allen felt compelled to decline Asbury's request, partly because of the segregation that would be imposed in the churches there.

In 1786 Allen was invited to assist in the ministry at St George's Methodist Episcopal Church in Philadelphia. African Americans throughout the city heard his open-air preaching and attended prayer meetings. Black membership at St George's grew significantly during Allen's ministry. Allen and other blacks advocated the establishment of a separate African congregation in the interests of more effective ministry, but their suggestion was scorned and rejected by the congregational leadership. Partly as a response to this rejection, Allen, Absalom Jones and a number of blacks from St George's Church founded the Free African Society in 1787. This society initially acted as a burial society to provide help for widows and orphans and later became a benevolence and mutual support organization.

A pivotal and decisive event in the history of American Christianity occurred because of the discrimination experienced by African Americans at St George's Church. The increase in the number of blacks at St George's became a matter of concern for some whites in the congregation, who instituted a policy of segregated seating. In 1787 (some scholars say 1792) Allen, Jones and other blacks left St George's after Jones and William White were pulled from their knees and out of a section of the church building reserved for whites. Those African Americans who left St George's in protest founded a new congregation, the African Church of Philadelphia. Because of the persecution and discrimination they had experienced at the hands of the Methodists the congregation became affiliated to the Protestant Episcopal Church.

Despite his appalling experience at St George's, Allen remained committed to Methodist principles, believing that Methodist Christianity was the kind best suited to African Americans. He declined the invitation to be the preacher of the African church on the grounds of his commitment to Methodism. Allen bought an old blacksmith's shop

and moved it to a piece of land in Philadelphia that he had purchased as the first site for a Methodist meeting house for blacks. On 9 April 1794 Bethel Church was founded there with the Methodist bishop Francis Asbury participating in the dedication. The ministry and membership of Bethel Church grew in the ensuing years under Allen's leadership. As other African Methodist congregations were established the church became known as Mother Bethel. Allen continued his work of promoting the welfare of the black community in Philadelphia and was ordained by Asbury in 1799 as a deacon.

Once Bethel Church was established, Allen had to contend with renewed efforts by white Methodists and the leadership at St George's to bring Bethel Church under their jurisdiction. Allen and Bethel Church refused to sign over the building and its property to the Methodist Conference as they were instructed. Through a combination of trickery and bad advice the transfer occurred anyway, but Bethel Church subsequently recovered the title. The leadership of St George's took Bethel Church to the civil court to obtain legal authority over the black congregation, and the case eventually reached the Pennsylvania Supreme Court. Finally, on 1 January 1816, St George's lost their case, and the separate identity of Bethel AME Church was confirmed.

Later that year representatives from several black congregations, many of whom also had experienced discrimination, met to form the African Methodist Episcopal Church and officially established an independent self-governing church. Allen was elected and consecrated as the first bishop of the AME Church on 11 April 1816 but continued to serve as pastor of Bethel Church. The new denomination grew significantly in the ensuing years.

During Allen's episcopacy the AME Church sent missionaries to Haiti, Canada and Africa and was active in the abolitionist movement, as well as opposing the mission of the American Colonization Society. For example, Bethel Church hosted a major convention of African Americans in 1817, which protested against the deportation of blacks as a response to the problem of slavery and the issues raised by the presence of people of African descent in the United States. Mother

Bethel also became a stopping-place for escaped slaves travelling on the Underground Railroad to freedom. In 1830 the American Society of Free Persons of Color for Improving Their Condition in the United States met at Bethel Church under the leadership of black ministers striving for the abolition of slavery and discrimination.

Throughout his ministry Allen was committed to the principle of an independent African American church as part of his larger goals of holiness and the elevation of African peoples, especially in the light of the continuing existence of slavery in the United States. His family shared his vision. In 1800 Allen married his second wife, Sarah Bass Allen, a prominent leader in the AME Church. Together they had six children, Richard Jr, James, John, Peter, Sarah and Ann. Allen died on 26 March 1831 in Philadelphia.

Bibliography

R. Allen, *The Life Experience and Gospel Labors of the Rt. Rev. Richard Allen* (Philadelphia: Martin & Boston, 1833); C. V. R. George, *Segregated Sabbaths: Richard Allen and the Emergence of Independent Black Churches, 1760–1840* (New York: Oxford University Press, 1973); H. D. Gregg, *History of the African Methodist Episcopal Church* (Nashville: AME Sunday School Union, 1980).

E. D. APONTE

■ **ALLINE, Henry** (1748–1784), New Light revivalist, hymnist and anti-Calvinist theologian, was born in New Port, Rhode Island, the second son of New England Congregational parents, William Alline and Rebecca Clark. When Alline was twelve years old his formal education ended as his family joined a northward migration of New England Yankees and settled along the Minas Basin of Nova Scotia, on the lands that had been vacated by the French-speaking population in 1755.

Like many early North American settlers, Alline's family had limited access to regular worship and preaching, which left him free to pursue his spiritual journey with little ecclesiastical influence. Having been 'moved upon by the spirit of God' at a young age, Alline read theology and became concerned with controversial points of doctrine such as predestination, ecclesiology, hell and the sacraments. Although caught in what he later called the 'frolicking and carnal mirth' of his youth, Alline privately endured periodic episodes of spiritual angst and morbid introspection from adolescence until 26 March 1776 when he finally received assurance of eternal salvation. He declared, 'My whole soul, that was a few minutes ago groaning under mountains of death ... crying to an unknown God for help, was now filled with immortal love, soaring on the wings of faith, freed from the chains of death and darkness.' This classic New Light New Birth profoundly changed the course of Henry Alline's life.

Shortly after his conversion Alline experienced an inescapable 'call to preach the gospel' but faced a number of obstacles. First, there was the problem of education. New England Congregational ministers were usually not considered candidates for ordination unless they possessed a college education from Harvard or Yale. Secondly, coming from a family with ageing parents who could not spare him from the farm, let alone fund a college education, made the possibility of obeying the 'divine call' even less likely. So bound to religious convention was Alline that he waited a full year after experiencing conversion and a sense of call to ministry before he 'came out and spoke by way of exhortation' on 18 April 1776. The day was one appointed for fasting and prayer for the deteriorating relationship between Britain and the American colonies.

Alline's earliest preaching efforts brought visitors from nearby townships to hear him as he grew in confidence and boldness. In July 1776 he preached outside the confines of his own township, in the adjacent township of Newport. His goal was to help others be 'wrapped up in God' and experience the ecstasy of conversion as he had. Indeed, his conversion became the model for all others in the New Light movement in Nova Scotia. By September of the same year Alline had enough followers who had experienced the New Birth to establish formal churches in Falmouth and Newport. During these months Alline continued his trade as a tanner and agricultural labourer while he preached. However, when his preaching began to resonate further afield, in Horton (present-day

Wolfville), Alline abandoned 'labour with my hands' and began an itinerant career that would continue until his death.

From 1777 to 1783 Alline preached for an increasingly broadening circuit that included the Sackville-Amherst townships and communities around the Minas Basin, down the Annapolis Valley, up the St John River and along the south shore of Nova Scotia from Yarmouth to Liverpool. In this area he established eight churches in total. The communities most open to his ministry were, not surprisingly, those that shared his own cultural background: transplanted Yankees who were trying to eke out an existence on the periphery of British North America. Also, many in his congregations had witnessed the First Great Awakening in New England under the preaching of Jonathan *Edwards and George *Whitefield, and they clearly identified the revivalistic ethos of Alline as being in the same tradition. By the mid-1770s New Englanders accounted for more than half of Nova Scotia's population.

Some scholars have understood the Great Awakening among Nova Scotians as led by Alline as a retreat from the 'grim realities of their outward environment' to the ecstasy of religious enthusiasm. Others have interpreted the response of Nova Scotia's Yankees as a means of fashioning a Nova Scotian identity separate from New England, as a 'People Highly Favoured of God'. More recent research has studied the inner dynamics of New Light piety as it gave meaning and purpose to living the Christian faith.

Alline was a profoundly effective preacher who, according to one scholar, 'instinctively knew how to link words together to create literary images which drilled into the human mind, first transforming doubt into agony, and then agony into intense spiritual relief'. His earthy use of language was also employed in his more than 500 published hymns and songs that made him the most productive North American hymn-writer of his day. Combining sermons, songs and an anti-formalism that despised religious hierarchy, religious rituals and organization, Alline triggered the most extensive religious 'awakening' in the history of Canada. Some historians have argued that in spite of significant opposition from clerics such as Jonathan Scott (the Calvinistic Congregational preacher from

Chebogue who called him the 'Ravager of Churches'), his critics could not deny his success. In 1777 two Presbyterian clergymen challenged Alline's right to preach since he was not formally ordained, to which he replied that his 'authority' was from God. Alline was later ordained, somewhat reluctantly, in the spring of 1779 by members from three of his churches.

If Alline's ambivalence to ecclesiastical tradition challenged the Congregational establishment in Nova Scotia, his sometimes heterodox theology, found in his two books *Two Mites on Some of the Most Important and much disputed Points of Divinity* (1781) and *The Anti-Traditionalist* (1783), was met with suspicion and condemnation from a number of quarters. Influenced by Jacob Boehme's theology mediated through William Law's works, Alline held to such beliefs as Adam's pre-creation existence, Adam's nature as both male and female, the spiritual presence of all persons in Adam at the fall and the spiritual, not physical resurrection of Christ. Jonathan Scott declared Alline's theology to be 'erroneous and horrible', while John *Wesley considered it as 'gold and dross shuffled together'. While Alline's theological works were not particularly original and may be the least impressive of his accomplishments due in part to his lack of formal education, they were republished in New England in 1797 and 1804 by the Freewill Baptist sect. Benjamin Randall, their leader, was attracted to Alline's anti-Calvinist stance and his emphasis on the role played by the freedom of the will in the New Birth. While some of Alline's more peculiar theological ideas were initially embraced by the Freewill Baptists, they were discarded in the nineteenth century.

In late 1783 Henry Alline set out to preach in New England even though he knew that because he was dying of consumption he would probably not return to Nova Scotia. He died in New Hampshire at the home of the Revd David McClure, the Calvinistic minister of the Northampton Congregational Church on 2 February 1784. It is ironic that Alline's funeral took place within the 'Calvinistic Puritan establishment of New England' against which the New Light preacher had chafed for most of his ministry.

Alline's legacy in the Maritimes was not

that of the theologian so much as that of the itinerant evangelist and revivalist who shaped the contours of regional religious culture and whose hymns are still sung by a few congregations today. It is ironic that even though he rejected ecclesiastical authority and considered baptism as a 'non-essential', the two major Maritime Baptist groups that emerged in the nineteenth century grew significantly from the churches and tradition he forged in the eighteenth. The Regular Baptists (Calvinistic) and the Free Christian Baptists (Arminian) perpetuated Alline's emphasis on the ecstatic New Birth experience and revival as they became formal groupings in the nineteenth century. By 1861 these two groups of Baptists together represented the largest Protestant grouping in New Brunswick and the second largest in Nova Scotia, and in 1905 to 1906 united to form one denomination, though much of the Allinite tradition had been jettisoned by that time.

Bibliography

D. G. Bell, 'Henry Alline and Maritime Religion' (Canadian Historical Association Historical Booklet 51, 1993); G. A. Rawlyk (ed.), *Henry Alline: Selected Writings* (New York: Paulist Press, 1987).

D. GOODWIN

■ **AMES, William** (1576–1633), Puritan theologian, was a leading English Puritan of the generation after William *Perkins, whose theology was to have a significant impact not only in England but also in Holland and North America.

Ames was born in 1576 in Ipswich, Suffolk, and when orphaned at an early age, he was adopted by an uncle, Robert Snelling, who lived in Oxford. He matriculated at Christ's College, Cambridge, where he came under the influence of the leading Puritan theologian, William Perkins, who became not only his tutor but also his close friend.

Ames received his AB degree in 1607 and then accepted an invitation to a college fellowship. In 1609 he was even in the running for the college mastership, but his outspoken objections to clerical vestments and other aspects of Anglican ceremonial undermined his application, and he was

passed over. Subsequent to this rejection, he resigned his college position.

At this point, he received a call to become pastor of a congregation in Colchester. Unfortunately, the increasingly anti-Puritan policies of the government were to prevent him from accepting this invitation. His translation into Latin of William Bradshaw's polemical tract, *English Puritanism*, had earned him the attention of the authorities, and the bishop of London blocked the call. Harassed by the authorities, Ames decided to leave England and fled to Holland in 1610. Here he met the English Separatist John *Robinson at Leiden, whom he managed to persuade to adopt a less radical position on church polity.

For some years Ames supported himself through pastoral work on behalf of the English Merchant Adventurers in the Netherlands. He was successor to John Burgess as chaplain to the British in the Hague in 1611 and married Burgess's daughter, who died childless shortly thereafter. Diplomatic pressure from England led to his dismissal in 1618, but in 1619 the Synod of South Holland recommended him for a professorial chair at the University of Franeker, a post that he assumed in 1622. His colleagues on the faculty included the vigorously orthodox but somewhat dissipated theologian, Johannes Maccovius (1588–1644), and Sibrandus Lubbertus (1557–1625). It was while on the faculty at Franeker that Ames wrote his influential theological works, *Bellarmine Disarmed* (1628); *The Marrow of Theology* (1622); and *Conscience with the Power and Cases Thereof* (1632), all of which enjoyed influence well beyond the borders of the Netherlands.

Ames's life in Holland was thereafter closely linked with the continuing controversy between the Reformed Orthodox and the Remonstrants. This debate had originally focused on the appointment of Jacob *Arminius to a chair at the University of Leiden (1603), had reached a climax at the Synod of Dordt (1618–1619), where Ames had been a paid consultant to the president, and had continued to divide theologians. At issue were a number of questions relating to the nature of God's grace, free will, the ordering of the covenants and the atonement of Christ. Ames himself clashed at various times with a number of Remonstrant theologians, including Jan Uitenbogaert (1557–1644) and Simon Episcopius (1583–1643).

In the late 1620s Ames began to consider the possibility of a move to the New World, largely as a result of letters written by Puritans there who urged him to join them. In December 1630 he wrote to John *Winthrop to the effect that he would indeed come out to join them, but his plans never came to fruition. Instead, he accepted a call in 1632 to pastor an Independent congregation in Rotterdam. There Ames was the victim of the cold and damp caused by a serious flood in October 1633, contracting a fever and dying within a few days.

Ames's theology represents the blend of Reformed Orthodox theology and concern for practical, experiential piety that is so typical of the greatest Puritan divines. His most famous work, Medulla Theologica (ET The Marrrow of Theology), began as a series of lectures for the sons of wealthy Leiden merchants, and it covers a wide range of theological topics in an orderly and methodical way. English Puritans did not on the whole produce the kind of all-embracing systematic doctrinal syntheses of continental counterparts such as Voetius and Turretin, but to see this omission as a sign of an unsystematic or undogmatic temper would be wrong, as the Medulla of Ames shows.

The work is interesting for a number of reasons. First, Ames shows the familiarity with the broad Western tradition of theology, from the patristic era through the Middle Ages up to the present, that is typical of Puritan and Reformed divines. Indeed, in his careful delineation of topics and concern for precise definition when dealing, for example, with the nature of divine willing, he makes extensive use of terminology developed in the Middle Ages. Like other Puritans and Reformed Orthodox, Ames is catholic in the true sense of the word, in that he quarries the whole of church tradition for arguments and terms that are useful in explicating the Bible's teaching in a coherent manner.

One good example of the way in which Ames self-consciously locates his Medulla within the ongoing Western tradition is seen in his definition of theology as a practical science. Here he echoes the position of the medieval scholastic Duns Scotus, and

indicates his awareness of the medieval debate about whether theology was a practical or a speculative science. His own answer stands in contrast to the majority of the Reformed tradition, which regarded theology as a mixed science, embodying both practical and speculative elements. The difference in definition is not massively significant in terms of content, as Ames then divides his work into two main sections, dealing with faith and observance, doctrine and practice respectively. Nevertheless, the existence of the discussion in a work such as Ames's Medulla is a clear sign that Puritan theology, as it established itself in the university context, was happy to adopt much of the historic terminology and concerns of that context. In addition, Ames' definition reflects his distaste for metaphysical speculation and his emphasis upon the intimate connection between doctrinal belief and practical piety. In this, he exemplifies the kind of practical theology that was so typical of the Dutch Nadere Reformatie ('Second Reformation').

Secondly, the work shows clear signs of the influence of the writings of Peter Ramus (1515–1572). Often regarded as an anti-Aristotelian thinker, Ramus's approach to philosophy is, rather, a modification of certain elements in Aristotelian logic. He is most famous for his technique of bifurcation (something he emphasized but that did not originate with him), whereby topics are divided into two subtopics to facilitate clear analysis and discussion. Despite certain scholarly claims to the contrary, his influence on Ames and other Puritans seems to be primarily formal. Ames's predilection for bifurcation helps him to give a graphic representation of the interrelationship of his topics, but it does not exert significant influence on the content of his theology.

Thirdly, the work offers a significant exposition of the concept of the covenant of grace, with particular reference to the covenant dispensations before Christ (chapter 38) and after Christ until the end of the world (chapter 39). In this exposition Ames made a significant contribution to Reformed theology which impacted not only upon the theology of subsequent English Puritans, for whom the Medulla was a respected and significant authority, but also upon Dutch Reformed thinking. One of Ames' pupils,

Johannes Cocceius (1603–1669), was to become one of the most significant formulators of covenant theology.

Ames' concern for the inseparability of doctrine and practice along with his development of federal themes, as manifested in both the *Marrow* and his casuistical treatise, meant that his work was to prove a decisive influence on the shape of the theology of later English Puritanism, the New England divines and the Nadere Reformatie. Like Perkins, he was a crucial figure in the development of Reformed theology in the early seventeenth century.

Bibliography
K. L. Sprunger, *The Learned Doctor William Ames* (Urbana: 1972); M. Nethenus, H. Visscher and K. Reuter, *William Ames*, trans. D. Horton (Cambridge, Massachusetts: 1965); E. Dekker, 'An Ecumenical Debate between Reformation and Counter-Reformation? Bellarmine and Ames on *liberum arbitrium*', in W. J. van Asselt and E. Dekker (eds.), *Reformation and Scholasticism: An Ecumenical Enterprise* (Grand Rapids: 2001).

C. R. TRUEMAN

■ **ANDERSON, Sir James Norman Dalrymple** (1908–1994), legal scholar, was born on 29 September 1908 in Aldeburgh, Suffolk, England. After working as a missionary in Egypt and then rising to the rank of colonel in the British Intelligence Corps, Anderson entered academia. He rapidly became an authority in legal studies, while retaining an involvement in church activities that culminated in his becoming chair of the House of Laity within the Church of England's new General Synod from 1970 to 1979. A gifted speaker and writer, he played a prominent role as an apologist for Christianity.

Norman Anderson (as he was known) was educated at St Lawrence's College, Ramsgate, and Trinity College, Cambridge, where he read law (BA 1930, LLB 1931, MA 1934). Raised within a Christian family, his path to faith was gradual rather than turning on a specific experience of conversion. At Cambridge he became heavily involved in the Cambridge Inter-Collegiate Christian Union

(CICCU), eventually becoming its president. Anderson became firmly convinced of the truth of a conservative evangelical view of Christianity, without subscribing to the view of sanctification advocated by the Keswick Convention, then popular among CICCU members and British conservative evangelicals in general.

Drawn to work among Muslims but feeling he lacked the gifts to be a pioneer missionary, Anderson went to Cairo through the Egypt General Mission in 1932. There he learnt Arabic and began to utilize his capacity as an apologist for Christianity. In 1933 he married Patricia Hope; they had three children. When the Second World War began Anderson joined the British army and, because of his linguistic ability, was assigned to the Intelligence Corps, where he rose to the rank of colonel. Returning to England at the war's end, Anderson became warden of Tyndale House, a research library for biblical studies, recently founded by the Inter-Varsity Fellowship. In an austere national climate Anderson helped to nurture the fledgling organization and experienced a period of personal spiritual renewal.

In 1947 he was appointed Lecturer in Islamic Law at London University's School of Oriental and African Studies. From there he wrote a definitive study of Islamic law in Africa and travelled widely; he became professor in 1954. In 1959 Anderson was made Director of the Institute of Advanced Legal Studies in London, where he played a pivotal role in British and international legal studies, influencing governments and churches. Thus, for instance, Anderson had significant input into a legal code for Kenyan Muslims. In 1965 he was called to the Bar at Gray's Inn and became Dean of the Faculty of Law of London University. In 1974 he was made a Queen's Counsel and knighted. His academic career concluded in 1976 when he oversaw the opening of the Institute's new headquarters in London. He received an honorary DD from St Andrew's in 1974 and an honorary LittD from Wheaton College in 1980.

Anderson remained heavily involved in church matters. Had it not been for family health problems, he might have returned to missionary work. He immersed himself in the work of a number of evangelical bodies, including the Inter-Varsity Fellowship (later the Universities and Colleges Christian Fellowship) and the Egypt General Mission (later the Middle East General Mission, then Middle East Christian Outreach). From the mid-1960s Anderson became increasingly involved in the government of the Church of England. A member of its Church Assembly from 1965, he became the first chair of the House of Laity in the new General Synod in 1970 and then a member of the Anglican Consultative Council. He played a significant role in the National Evangelical Anglican Congress at Keele in 1967, encouraging Anglican evangelicals to engage more with the wider society and with the wider church. In 1975 he was re-elected chair of the House of Laity, retiring in 1979. His ecclesiastical and legal experience were invaluable in negotiations with the then prime minister, Harold Wilson, over significant reform of the Crown Appointments Commission (the body that appoints Anglican bishops), reform that effectively loosened the ties between church and state.

Anderson was a frequent speaker and writer in the field of Christian apologetics. He wrote both to defend core Christian beliefs, such as the resurrection and the incarnation, and to deal with current dilemmas, such as the relation of Christianity to other faiths and contemporary ethical concerns. Anderson was happy to face opposition by debating with radical theologians such as Don Cupitt and by defending the historicity of the resurrection at Harvard University.

Anderson's faith was all the more impressive given that his family life was marked by a series of tragedies, as a result of which his three children predeceased him. Anderson himself died on 2 December 1994. In the course of a long life Norman Anderson played many roles: missionary, soldier, scholar and church leader. Most prominent as an academic and as a leading Anglican layman, he was constant in his reasoned attachment to conservative evangelical Christianity, which he did much to commend by his words and actions.

Bibliography

J. N. D. Anderson, *An Adopted Son: The Story of My Life* (Leicester: IVP, 1985).

D. J. GOODHEW

■ **ANDREW, Brother** (1928–), pioneer and missionary to the suffering church worldwide, founder of Open Doors International, was born on 11 May 1928 and grew up in a Protestant family in the northwest of Holland. Around the time when Winston Churchill delivered his 'Sinews of Peace' speech, in which he affirmed that an iron curtain had descended across the continent of Europe, Andrew volunteered for military service against communist insurgents in the Dutch colony of Indonesia. Invalided home in 1949, he began reading the Bible and was converted in 1950. By 1953 he was training for mission at WEC College, Glasgow. He married the former Corry Van Dam in 1958; they have five children.

As the Cold War developed, Andrew began his controversial ministry to Central and Eastern Europe. He sought an enduring, spiritual solution to the problem of communism, perhaps as an alternative to relatively ineffective military and political action. In 1955 Andrew made his first trip behind the Iron Curtain, to a communist youth festival in Poland. Touring other Iron Curtain countries, he discreetly distributed Christian literature and began to formulate an overall strategic plan for his ministry. These guiding principles included a commitment to cooperating with local pastors and other indigenous leaders, particularly by providing assistance in response to their priorities. By late 1955 Andrew had founded 'Open Doors', an international and non-denominational missionary organization; it began its work well before secular agencies such as Amnesty International (1961) were created. In 1960 he adopted the pseudonym 'Brother Andrew' to preserve his anonymity for security reasons; as the major powers began to trade spies on Berlin's Glienecke Bridge, Andrew continued to conduct his clandestine Bible-smuggling into Warsaw Pact countries.

Andrew's biography, *God's Smuggler*, was published in 1965 and has sold over ten million copies in more than thirty languages. After the publication of *God's Smuggler*, Andrew was no longer able to obtain visas for Eastern Europe and Russia, so he began travelling extensively in other countries where the church was persecuted. Opposition, however, was not restricted to communist-led governments; Andrew's work did not receive universal acclamation among evangelicals either. Some objected to his decision to circumvent customs regulations. Faced with mounting criticism from within the Christian community, in 1974 Andrew issued a theological justification for his activities, *The Ethics of Smuggling*. The core of this book's argument was Acts 5:19, in which the apostles chose to defy an order issued by a legitimate government because it contradicted God's commands. This argument has addressed the concerns of many Christians, but there is evidence of lingering suspicion over the legitimacy of Andrew's activities. Andrew described his 1985 book, *Is Life So Dear?*, as 'an amplification of ideas' from *The Ethics of Smuggling*. Throughout his Christian life, he has been an agent for change, and has helped to redefine the boundaries of the modern missionary movement in areas of limited access.

In the meantime, Open Doors has achieved substantial results in Africa, Asia, China, Latin America and the Middle East. Beginning in the early 1980s, Andrew's attention turned to largescale delivery of Bibles to countries where they were in limited supply: one million Bibles to China (Project Pearl: 1981); five million pieces of Christian literature for young people in Latin America (Project Crossfire: 1985); one million New Testaments to Russia (1988); one million Children's Bibles throughout the former Soviet Union (Project Samuel: 1991–1992); the first 20,000 copies of a simplified Chinese script Study Bible, developed in conjunction with New Life Literature and the Bible League (1992); 50,000 Bibles in standard Albanian (1993); a printing of the Chinese Children's Bible Storybook (1994); the Latin American Agape Study Bible (1996); one million Bibles and one million other items of Christian reading material to China (1999). A striking vignette brings into focus the profound changes that have occurred since Brother Andrew began his ministry. The Albanian Bibles were formally presented to the president of Albania. At one time, Albania was the country that most fiercely prosecuted anyone caught smuggling a Bible.

Open Doors began formal relief work in 1998, its first project being to fly food and supplies to Christians in remote areas of southern Sudan. Another facet of their work has been the instigation of major prayer campaigns, for example, the Seven Year Prayer Campaign for the Soviet Union, from 1984 to 1990 (which concluded when the Iron Curtain came down).

Another significant initiative was the 'Ten Years of Prayer for the Church in the Muslim World' (1990–2000). For quite some time, Andrew observed, the Muslim world had been growing by means of Islamist revival, while the Christian church in the region had been declining. Andrew's call for prayer reflected his conviction that many Muslims, especially in the Middle East, have not actually rejected Jesus because they have never had the opportunity to hear a clear presentation about his life, death and resurrection. Andrew's private meetings with Muslim leaders in various countries have resulted in new ministry opportunities. One such leader gave him an open invitation to lecture in an Islamic university on what real Christianity is. Andrew is among the few Western leaders to go regularly to Muslim groups as an ambassador for Christ. However, the constant danger faced by Christians in the Muslim world, particularly by the national workers, is a grave cause for concern. Open Doors campaigns for Christian prisoners and delivers Bibles, often secretly, throughout the Muslim world.

Andrew's worldwide work has received public recognition in recent years. In 1994 he was knighted by Queen Beatrix of the Netherlands. The World Evangelical Fellowship conferred their Religious Liberty Award on him in 1997, acknowledging not only his own efforts to provide Bibles and Christian literature, but also his advocacy on behalf of the persecuted church. The thrust of his current work is the continuing need to speak to Muslim governments on behalf of Christians being persecuted by Islamic fundamentalists.

The ministry of Brother Andrew and Open Doors may be summarized as: first, to strengthen the body of Christ living under restriction or persecution by providing Bibles, materials, training and other aid, and encouraging it to become involved in world evangelism; secondly, to train and encourage Christians in threatened or unstable areas to prepare for persecution and suffering, so that they will be able to maintain their Christian witness; thirdly, to educate, motivate and mobilize the church in the free world increasingly to identify with and assist the suffering church. Open Doors currently has over 300 full-time workers in more than twenty countries, as well as thousands of volunteers. Its *Open Doors* magazine reaches more than 200,000. Brother Andrew has written ten inspirational books.

Bibliography

Brother Andrew with J. and E. Sherrill, *God's Smuggler* (New York: New American Library, 1965; London: Hodder & Stoughton, 1968); Brother Andrew with V. Becker, *For the Love of My Brothers* (Minneapolis: Bethany House Publishing, 1998).

C. M. STEINACHER
C. VEDDER

■ **ANGAS, George Fife** (1789–1879), Baptist businessman and Australian colonist, was born on 1 May 1789 into a Baptist merchant family of Newcastle upon Tyne, England, and apprenticed to his father's coach-building firm. His religious views were shaped at an early age and did not significantly change for the remainder of his life. At the age of twenty he was baptized and received into membership of New Court Baptist Church in Newcastle. In 1812 he married Rosetta French, who died in 1867. They had three sons and four daughters.

As a young man Angas became active in many evangelical and philanthropic societies. His family's business interests in Central America, importing mahogany for carriage building, led him to campaign for the liberation of those Indians in the British settlement in Belize (British Honduras) who were illegally used as slaves by British merchants. At his expense, in 1822 the Baptist Missionary Society sent its first missionary to the region. In 1816 Angas played a leading part in establishing the interdenominational Newcastle Sunday School Union, and in 1820 he was a founder of the Bethel Seamen's Union, which was later absorbed into the British and Foreign Sailors' Society.

In 1824, as his business interests expanded into shipping and banking, Angas moved to London. From 1834 to 1839 he divided his time between London and his main residence at Dawlish, Devonshire. In the early 1830s he was attracted by the prospect of planting a new British colony based on the principle of religious equality, where Nonconformists could live without the legal and social disadvantages they still encountered in England. William Penn, the founder of Pennsylvania, was one of his heroes. Angas thus became involved in the plans to found a colony in South Australia, and in 1834 he was appointed to the board of the Colonization Commissioners. To rescue the faltering scheme, in 1835 he founded the South Australian Company which bought large tracts of unsold land at a reduced price. After the beginning of settlement in South Australia in 1836 Angas closely followed developments in the new colony and was an enthusiastic promoter. To encourage 'pious Dissenters' to emigrate there he addressed meetings, wrote newspaper articles, distributed pamphlets and helped to recruit ministers. His hope was that South Australia would become 'the headquarters for the diffusion of Christianity in the Southern hemisphere'. The largest religious group he induced to settle in the colony, in 1838, was a band of several hundred 'Old Lutherans' who, having refused to accept the state-imposed union church, were seeking to leave Prussia. Angas lent money from his own capital for their passage to South Australia and the purchase of land where they would settle as tenants on arrival. He expected to (and did) make a large profit, but he also wanted to assist fellow Christians who had been suffering persecution for the sake of conscience.

In 1851 Angas emigrated to South Australia and made his principal residence at Lindsay Park, near the country town of Angaston. He was soon prominent in many areas of the colony's political, business and religious life. From 1851 to 1866 he was a member of the Legislative Council. However, he was too inflexible in his views to be successful in politics. He neither sought nor attained popularity, and his dictatorial manner often caused offence. He regretted the democratic and levelling trends he saw emerging in the colony.

Angas was described by his biographer as 'a Puritan of the Puritans'. His personal life was disciplined and austere: he rose early, wasted nothing and delegated as little as possible. Convinced that God had allowed him to accumulate wealth in order to further the gospel, he was a generous, often unpublicized, supporter of evangelical clergy and societies, churches, schools and charitable institutions. He preferred to give relatively modest sums to small causes rather than large benefactions to benefit the wider community; his gifts often had conditions attached.

Angas was deeply hostile to Roman Catholicism because he thought it was both in error doctrinally and opposed to religious liberty. He was affronted by the marriage of his artist son George French Angas to an Irish Roman Catholic. During the 1860s, supported by his private secretary Henry Hussey, he financed the distribution of tracts and other literature to warn Protestant colonists of the 'true character of Popery'. This sectarian crusade was out of tune with the growing mood of religious tolerance.

During his lifetime Angas's fortunes fluctuated, but when he died at Lindsay Park on 15 May 1879 he was one of the richest men in South Australia. He was respected for his firm and consistent principles, his shrewdness in business and his part in founding the colony, but he was a hard man to like.

Bibliography
E. Hodder, *George Fife Angas: Father and Founder of South Australia* (London: Hodder & Stoughton, 1891); D. Pike, *Paradise of Dissent: South Australia, 1829–1857* (Melbourne: Melbourne University Press, [2]1967).
D. L. HILLIARD

■ **ARMINIUS, Jacobus** (c. 1559–1609), Dutch Remonstrant Reformer, was born Jacob Harmenszoon in Oudewater near Utrecht. His middle-class family was devastated when his father, a maker of kitchen utensils, died during Arminius's infancy and his mother, together with all his siblings, were killed during his adolescence in the Spanish massacre of Oudewater in 1575. Thereafter, family friends raised him. Like most classically trained humanist scholars of his era, he eventually Latinized his name, recalling the first-century Germanic leader Arminius, noted for his resistance to the Romans.

In 1574 he began his studies at Leiden, centre of a tradition reaching back into the pre-Reformation ferment of the north Netherlands in the fourteenth and fifteenth centuries. The atmosphere included a biblically informed piety, a sacramentarianism in which medieval sacraments were viewed as largely superstitious, and a humanist perspective that identified corruptions in the church. It would be anachronistic to speak of this movement as (proto-)Lutheran or Zwinglian, as these titles entail a doctrinal specificity that was not operative in the Leiden tradition. Studies followed at Geneva, Basel and Geneva again, culminating, after years of leadership in city, church and university, in a doctorate from Leiden in 1603.

Leiden accommodated the older Reform as well as the precise Calvinism that Reformed refugees had brought with them. The ensuing conflict was less concerned with predestination (although the issue was never far from the surface) than with the relationship of the Calvinist consistory (an ecclesiastical court in Reformed churchmanship) and the city (which reflected the less doctrinally exact, humanist-informed piety indigenous to the Low Countries). The consistory, for instance, in the rigorous spirit of Calvinism opposed the observance of Christian festivals (e.g. Christmas) that happened not to fall on Sundays.

Financed by Amsterdam merchants, Arminius began studying under *Beza at Geneva on New Year's Day 1582. Beza, *Calvin's sixty-two-year-old successor, was venerated in Reformed circles everywhere. By rearranging Calvin's emphases, Beza largely retained the major tenets of Calvin's theology while significantly altering its spirit. Calvin, for instance, had spoken of the grandeur of God and the majesty of God but not of the 'sovereignty' of God; Beza thrust into the centre of his thought a sovereignty that was to appear to Remonstrants indistinguishable from the arbitrary assertion of naked power.

Having graduated from Geneva, Arminius studied next at Basel, and then at Geneva once more. A trip to Italy in 1587 led to his being accused of compromising himself with Roman Catholic potentates and also of having 'lost his [Calvinist] faith' through exposure to Jesuits.

Upon returning to Amsterdam, he was

ordained pastor to the 'Old Church', the focal point of church life in the city. In 1590 he married Lijsbet Reael, an aristocrat who thereafter ensured that he moved among the most influential merchants and leaders of the city. Like all the magisterial Reformers before him, Arminius would remain a pastor for virtually all of his working life, spending fifteen years in the Amsterdam pulpit and six in the Leiden pulpit. (It is interesting to note his conviction that exercising the pastoral office, rather than theological wrangling, facilitates the holiness of the minister.) From 1603 until his death in 1609 he was professor of theology in Leiden, where he was also elected rector (president) of the university, even though a minority of the theologians opposed him. In Leiden he brought together the key themes of his writing on earlier controversies, and in 1608 published his most mature work, *Declaration of Sentiments*.

While the notions pertaining to his name are commonly thought to include the rejection of all things Calvinist, Arminius's appreciation of Calvin's *Commentaries* is noteworthy. They occupy, he said, second place only to Scripture: 'I recommend that the *Commentaries* of Calvin be read ... For I affirm that in the interpretation of the Scriptures Calvin is incomparable, and that his *Commentaries* are more to be valued than anything that is handed to us in the writings of the Fathers ... so much so that I concede to him a certain spirit of prophecy in which he stands distinguished above others, above most, indeed, above all.'

Arminius's preaching on Romans became the occasion of a theological controversy that he was never to escape. His first opponents were humanists who denied original sin. Uncompromisingly he replied to them, 'I believe that our salvation rests on Christ alone and that we obtain faith for the forgiveness of sins and the renewing of life only through the grace of the Holy Spirit.' Opposition arose next from the Calvinists, who differed from him on his insistence that Romans 7 describes the pre-Christian. Immediately he was accused of Pelagianism, Socinianism (Unitarianism) and noncompliance with the Belgic Confession and the Heidelberg Catechism. Not trusting the Calvinist clergy of the church courts, he defended himself on charges of doctrinal deviation only in the presence of civic officials whom he recognized as his assessors. They acquitted him.

In his detailed exposition of Romans 9, another major area of protracted controversy, Arminius insisted: that the question his opponents said that the doctrine of predestination answered, namely, 'Why do some individuals believe and others do not when all alike are dead *coram Deo*?', is neither asked nor answered in the chapter; that the chapter does not discuss individuals but rather classes of people, those who affirm righteousness by faith in the Righteous One and those who seek to merit God's recognition; that to speak of the predestination of individuals before they have been created, and therefore to speak of the reprobation of individuals before they could have sinned, is to render God monstrous; that to postulate both a hidden and a revealed will of God is to deny the New Testament's declaration that in Jesus Christ (whom everyone admits to be the revelation of God's will) 'the whole fullness of deity dwells bodily' (Col. 2:9 RSV); that God's command and God's promise are co-extensive (it is not the case that God commands all to repent and believe but visits only some with the mercy that quickens both repentance and faith; God does not predestine who will or will not believe, but rather God predestines to salvation in Christ all who believe in Christ); that the position of Beza and his supporters can mean only that God is deemed to be the author of sin (Cardinal Bellarmine agreed with Arminius, adding that the high Calvinist position rendered God the only sinner), thus denying human culpability and implying that God's judgment is pointless.

Arminius's chief writing during his pastorate in Amsterdam, *Examination of Perkins' Pamphlet*, has often been judged his single best contribution to theological discussion. William *Perkins (1558–1602), the major spokesperson for English high Calvinism, maintained as a strong supralapsarian that creation and the fall are (merely) the means whereby the decree of election or reprobation is implemented. Arminius's arguments in the *Examination* are those found throughout his works, but their exposition is more detailed and more nuanced here than anywhere else. Most pointedly, Arminius insists that grace is the love of God meeting humankind as sinful. Grace is not a synonym for 'decree' or 'will' or 'sovereignty'; grace is God's love addressing humans in their depravity rather than 'affecting' them as creatures without reference to their sin.

Perkins maintained that Christ died only for the elect, the parameters of the atonement being identical with the parameters of faith. Arminius argued that Christ had died (and thereby gained salvation) for all, but that only some are saved; i.e. the cross is sufficient for all but effectual only in believers.

Consonant with his understanding of the free will, Arminius eschewed the notion of the Christian life as the 'state' of grace (and therefore static), preferring to understand it as dynamic: graced concurrence acknowledges and appropriates greater grace in an upward spiral that also involves the believer advancing in godliness through greater immersion in grace. Whereas Perkins had denounced this position as Pelagian, Arminius maintained that Pelagianism predicated the will's response to grace entirely or partially on nature, whereas the will's response to grace is wrought by grace without being compelled by grace. A concomitant of his position is that believers can 'make shipwreck' of faith. Yet they need not fear doing so, paradoxically, in that the gift of grace (and therefore of faith) includes a gift of filial fear that prevents believers from becoming presumptuous and cavalier and renders them spiritually vigilant. In this way they are 'kept' by the power of God.

Those who esteem Arminius frequently do so on account of his views concerning predestination, but he must not be thought to be a one-issue thinker. Unlike the first and second generation magisterial Reformers, Arminius was a scholastic evincing immense affinities with the scholastic 'family', whether Catholic and predestinarian (e.g. Banez and Baius), Catholic and non-predestinarian (e.g. Suarez and Molina), Protestant and predestinarian (e.g. Junius and Gomarus) or Protestant and non-predestinarian (e.g. his successors, Episcopius and Limborch). Although the non-predestinarian, biblical humanism of the older north Netherlands is found in Arminius, it does not typify him. Rather he is indebted to late medieval and Renaissance Aristotelianism.

Like all scholastics, Arminius has a metaphysical concern foreign to the earlier Reformers, and unlike the latter, he is indebted to Thomas Aquinas. In fact Aquinas is the most frequently quoted thinker in Arminius's works, and the only scholastic whom he names as an influence. Certainly not a Jesuit, Arminius none the less preferred the Jesuit reading of Aquinas to the Dominican reading with its Augustinian character. Arminius was not a crypto-Catholic, but he stands squarely in a tradition indebted to Thomistic metaphysics and Aristotelian logic. Most Protestants are unaware that these elements characterize the theologies of the seventeenth century.

Whereas the Reformed schools differed markedly on the issue of supra- or infralapsarianism, Arminius differed from *both* with respect to his understanding of God's will and foreknowledge. Here he owed much to Molina's *scientia media*; God foreknows future contingencies without thereby determining them. Molina furnished him with a matrix that included God's foreknowledge, the efficacy of grace, and a freedom of the will that is genuine rather than merely apparent. In short, Arminius adopted the Jesuit-Thomistic tradition of *scientia media*, in which divine determination was denied, yet the infinitude of the divine intellect and the scope of human freedom was preserved.

Arminius's life unfolded amidst relentless conflict. Denied external tranquillity, he was never distracted from the practical, non-speculative understanding of theology he absorbed from his reading of the medieval Duns Scotus, and credibly stated that his sole ambition was 'to inquire in the Holy Scriptures for divine truth ... for the purpose of winning some souls for Christ'.

Bibliography

C. Bangs, *Arminius: A Study in the Dutch Reformation* (Grand Rapids: Zondervan, 1985); R. A. Muller, *God, Creation and Providence in the Thought of Jacob Arminius* (Grand Rapids: Baker, 1991).

V. SHEPHERD

■ **ARTHUR, Sir George** (1784–1854), colonial administrator and penal reformer, was born in Plymouth, England, on 21 June

1784, and died in England on 19 September 1854.

Born into a Church of England merchant family prominent in Plymouth, Arthur may have attended Plymouth Grammar School. He saw service in the Napoleonic Wars and in 1812 reached the rank of major. '[P]romotion', he remarked in 1814, 'had been my ideal.' This declaration was made in the setting of a personal religious crisis: he had become convinced that he was a sinner and of the 'truth and power' of the gospel. In retrospect, Arthur's conversion redefined rather than restricted his career ambitions, giving them a religious dimension. Arthur also gained powerful religious connections, becoming part of the evangelical network Sydney Smith jokingly called the 'Clapham sect'. Arthur corresponded regularly with such leading evangelicals as William *Wilberforce, James *Stephen Jr, Zachary *Macaulay and Fowell *Buxton.

While Arthur's family background was Anglican, it was not evangelical: indeed his family feared he had become a 'Methodist'. He had not, although his churchmanship was not exclusivist. He saw churchmen whose 'manners, habits and pursuits' disinclined them from the 'condescension' involved in being 'the very servant of slaves' as generally less effective than Moravians and Methodists in ministering to the moral and religious needs of native peoples. In Van Diemen's Land (from 1856 called Tasmania) he sometimes attended worship in the Presbyterian church, and he employed Wesleyans as catechists to convicts: they rendered 'the most essential service to morals, if not to religion'.

In 1814 Arthur married Elizabeth Usher. In the same year he purchased a commission as major in a Jamaican black regiment. In 1815 he was promoted to lieutenant-colonel and in 1816 appointed Superintendent of the colony of British Honduras. In his Jamaican years, if not earlier, he came to see slavery as morally and religiously repellent. In 1816 he told the British Colonial Secretary, Lord Bathurst, that he was 'a perfect Wilberforce as to slavery'. Evangelically active in Honduras, he hoped to make the colony the base for spreading Christianity in the region, but efforts to recruit the new king of the Mosquito Shore in that venture failed.

From 1834 to 1836 Arthur was Lieutenant-Governor of Van Diemen's Land, a penal colony. Here he implemented, with Colonial Office approval, a unique 'system' of convict administration, through which he hoped to make the entire island a kind of out-of-doors panopticon.

As an administrator Arthur was efficiency-minded, autocratic and usually remote. He was also worldly-wise in the sense that when he left Van Diemen's Land he had become wealthy through shrewd local investment. Like most Clapham 'saints' he believed in the subordination of ecclesiastical to secular power. He treated colonial chaplains and senior churchmen as subordinates in religious as well as temporal matters; in effect he was the colony's pastor-in-chief as well as its commander-in-chief. His hand held, ultimately, the sword of mercy as well as that of justice.

Arthur's 'system' depended on careful invigilation and classification. The motor was choice. On arrival in the colony two pathways lay open to the convict: one upwards, the other down. If the convict chose to conduct himself or herself badly, this would be carefully recorded and the convict set on a downward path. This led first to chain gangs, then to so-called places of 'secondary punishment', such as Port Arthur, and finally to the gallows. For female convicts, the Female Factory in Hobart was the equivalent place of secondary punishment. Progress on the upward path was recorded with equal care. This led through four stages: assignment to a free settler, a ticket of leave, a conditional pardon and finally full freedom. Often, when a boatload of convicts arrived at Hobart, Arthur came on board to explain how the system would work.

Arthur claimed that his system addressed 'two orders of crime': 'the one predisposing and internal, consisting of the evil passions of a man – the other exciting and external, consisting of all those things which may be objects of desire or ambition'.

External causes of crime in Britain required external remedies, for instance transportation. This removed British criminals 'from a part of the empire in which the inducements to commit crime surpass their power of resistance, to another part [Van Diemen's Land] ... in which these are more nearly balanced'. Arthur once expressed this principle by likening transportation to moving weak plants from an exposed to a sheltered part of a garden.

The system was to be the shelter under which, for most convicts, 'the silent yet most efficient principle of self interest' would find expression in outwardly honest behaviour. Furthermore, the *de facto* gaolers, the masters to whom well-behaved convicts were assigned, could be expected to recognize that the reformed convict was the better worker and so see advantage in assisting the process of reform. 'Bentham's notion that gaolers should possess a personal interest in the reform of convicts', Arthur remarked, 'is beautifully realised' in Van Diemen's Land. Operating with almost a Lockean or *tabula rasa* concept of the human mind, Arthur hoped to address the 'external' causes of crime. 'We are in great measure', he wrote, 'the creatures of education.'

What of predisposing 'evil passions', Arthur's 'internal' cause of crime? Ministers of religion were key agents 'by which the *reformation of expediency* may be elevated *into the reformation of principle*' (Arthur's emphasis). Chaplains were to foster in convicts what Arthur called 'mind', discomforting feelings of degradation. Thus 'minded' (shamed), the convict was to be encouraged to cultivate the 'inward (moral and religious) regulator'. Conjoining Arthur's belief in original sin (that 'the heart of every man is desperately wicked') and his Lockean/Benthamite concept of the malleability of human nature, creates logical difficulty. However, the conjunction has a context, being common among the meliorist Calvinists of Clapham.

Arthur's punishment-redemption machine proved impressively effective in fostering at least outward reform and respectability, but it did not long survive his departure from the colony. Assignment to free settlers was the crucial lever in setting newly arrived convicts on the redemptive track. However, the British government, faced with growing free-settler complaints that assignment 'tainted' colonial society and British complaints that the very success of assignment was stripping transportation of its power to intimidate would-be British criminals, scrapped assignment in the late 1830s.

Towards Tasmanian Aborigines, Arthur was anxiously benevolent, but he lacked effective power to prevent murderous by-products of settler expansion. He employed G. A. Robinson in 1831 to persuade the few remaining aborigines to move to Flinders Island. Arthur hoped to save them from settler aggression and convert them from hunter-gathering to farming and Christianity. He did not save them from illness and demoralization. Later, he expressed deep distress at the 'necessity' (he still saw it as that) of 'driving a simple but warlike, and as it now appears, noble-minded race, from their native hunting grounds'. 'Disguise it as we may,' he reflected, 'we are the intruders.'

'The saint of Hobart Town' (as some enemies called him) defied and defies easy interpretation. His recall in 1836 closed an episode of singular penal and evangelical originality. Arthur himself, writing on the voyage home, saw in his governorship cause for remorse: 'What I now most desire is to give glory to God, and what I most highly lament is that I have hitherto been such an unprofitable servant to him.'

Arthur remained a trusted career governor and a firm evangelical, although less provocatively so. From 1837 to 1841 he was Lieutenant-Governor of Upper Canada. In 1841 he became a baronet. From 1842 to 1846 he was governor of the Presidency of Bombay. He died in 1854, wealthy and laden with secular honours (e.g. an honorary DCL from Oxford in 1848 and a lieutenant-generalship in 1853). He was survived by five sons and seven daughters.

Bibliography

A. G. L. Shaw, *Sir George Arthur, Bart, 1784–1854* (Melbourne: Melbourne University Press, 1980).

R. ELY

■ **ARTHUR, William** (1819–1901), Wesleyan Methodist minister and author, was born in Ireland on 3 February 1819, the son of James and Margaret Arthur. There is some dispute about his exact place of birth, but his early years were spent in Kells, County Antrim. When Arthur was twelve the family moved to Westport, County Mayo. Given the family's straitened circumstances, it is likely that Arthur's education was largely informal. He worked briefly in the corn business, before and after joining the Wesleyan Methodists at the age of fifteen. In 1837 he was accepted as a candidate for the Wesleyan ministry and, although under the discipline of the Irish Conference, he was sent to train at the Theological Institution at Hoxton. While training he volunteered for missionary service and left for India in April 1839. He spent less than two years in the subcontinent, mostly at Gubbi in the Mysore district, being forced by deteriorating health to return home in 1841. Arthur continued to work under the auspices of the Wesleyan Methodist Missionary Society (WMMS) as an effective advocate for missions, and the combination of his first-hand experience and powerful platform oratory with the pathos of his broken health made him for eight to ten years 'the most popular speaker in England'. His first book, A Mission to the Mysore, published in 1847, drew on articles which had previously appeared in the Wesleyan Methodist Magazine.

From 1846 to 1849 Arthur was stationed in France. On his return he defended Jabez *Bunting during the gathering reform agitation, and he criticized the reformers' policy of putting pressure on the Conference by 'stopping the supplies' to the WMMS. He worked briefly in two London circuits, but the breakdown of his voice in 1851 brought his itinerant circuit ministry to an end. During his convalescence he wrote The Successful Merchant (1852), a biography of the Bristol Wesleyan and self-made businessman Samuel Budgett. The Successful Merchant reflected a concern in evangelical circles to offer practical advice to Christians engaged in commerce. Budgett's sons James and Arthur were among the cofounders of The London Quarterly Review (1853), to which Arthur was a regular contributor. He joined the WMMS secretariat in 1851, returning to Ireland in 1868 as the first president of Methodist College, Belfast. From 1871 until his retirement in 1888 he was honorary secretary of the WMMS. Arthur was elected president of the Wesleyan Conference in 1866. Bouts of ill health periodically curtailed his preaching and teaching activities, and on a number of important occasions his speeches were read in Conference or

committee by T. B. Stephenson. Neither persistent throat problems nor poor eyesight, however, prevented him from playing a prominent part in connexional affairs, and he made effective use of his London base in Clapham, the considerable financial means inherited through his wife and his network of influential friends. Arthur helped to initiate the creation of the Metropolitan Chapel Building Fund. He differed sharply with his friend J. H. Rigg over connexional education policy in the early 1870s (Arthur opposed the maintenance of a denominational system of education) and warmly advocated the admission of lay representatives to the Conference (1876). A staunch opponent of ultramontanism, Arthur rallied Nonconformist opposition to Gladstone's proposal to give state funding to the Roman Catholic university in Ireland in the early 1870s, and he wrote a widely circulated pamphlet on Home Rule, Shall the Loyal be Deserted and the Disloyal Set Over Them? (1886). Arthur was a secretary of the Evangelical Alliance for many years and a speaker at the first Methodist Oecumenical Conference , which met in London in 1881.

Arthur's literary output included a dozen books and many pamphlets, besides lectures, articles and reviews. He wrote on missions, defending British colonialism as a providential opportunity for the extension of Christianity. He commented on contemporary political issues, on Roman Catholicism and on philosophy, challenging the views of Comte, Mill, Fitzjames Stephen, Frederic Harrison and Herbert Spencer, and giving as the Fernley Lecture of 1883 a discourse entitled On the Difference Between the Physical and the Moral Law. His most enduring work was The Tongue of Fire (1856), a study of the impact of the Holy Spirit on the life of the church. More biblical exposition and exhortation than systematic pneumatology, The Tongue of Fire influenced the holiness movements on both sides of the Atlantic.

In June 1850 Arthur married Elizabeth Ellis Ogle, and they had four daughters. Elizabeth Arthur died in 1888 after three years of illness, and Arthur retired to Cannes, where he died on 9 March 1901.

Bibliography

T. B. Stephenson, William Arthur: A Brief Biography (London: C. H. Kelly, 1907);

N. W. Taggart, *William Arthur: First Among Methodists* (London: Epworth Press, 1993).

M. WELLINGS

■ **ASBURY, Francis** (1745–1816), Methodist preacher and bishop, was the single person most responsible for shaping American Methodism, the largest popular religious movement in America between the Revolution and the Civil War. Under Asbury's leadership, American Methodism grew at an unprecedented pace, rising from a few thousand members to more than 200,000. Asbury was born on 20 August 1745 in a cottage in the parish of Handsworth, Staffordshire, about four miles outside Birmingham. His parents were Joseph and Elizabeth Asbury (née Rogers). Joseph was a farm labourer and gardener, employed by two wealthy families in the parish. While Francis was still quite young the family moved to a cottage on Newton Road, near West Bromwich. In all likelihood they rented the cottage, which at the time was attached to a brewery and is still standing. Despite limited resources, Joseph Asbury was determined that his son would receive a good education. Accordingly, he sent Francis to the only school in the area at Snail's Green, about a mile from the family home. But the schoolmaster's severity filled Asbury 'with such horrible dread, that with me anything was preferable to going to school'. At about the age of thirteen Asbury left school and soon entered an apprenticeship to a local metalworker. As a metalworker's apprentice and the son of a gardener, Asbury understood the lives of working people, and this later enabled him to establish a close bond with American Methodists, the vast majority of whom came from the lower and middle ranks of society. The bond was particularly strong between Asbury and American Methodist preachers, almost all of whom came from artisan and farming backgrounds, and almost none of whom attended college or came from families of more than moderate wealth. The formal education of most was limited to a few years of common school. They accepted Asbury so thoroughly because he was one of them. He felt at home in their small cottages and they knew it. These were the kinds of relationships that cannot be easily feigned, and that formed the foundation of Asbury's authority over American Methodism.

The death of Asbury's sister Sarah in May 1749 at the age of six was a severe blow to Elizabeth Asbury. According to Asbury, his mother sank 'into a deep distress at the loss of a darling child, from which she was not relieved for many years'. Perhaps events surrounding his sister's death and his mother's subsequent depression were part of the reason why Asbury never married. The tragedy of Sarah's death drove Elizabeth to search for a deeper spiritual meaning in life. Elizabeth soon gained a reputation for seeking out almost anyone in the area with evangelical inclinations, including local Methodists. Asbury's religious convictions seem to have grown along with his mother's. As his spiritual curiosity grew, Elizabeth directed him to a Methodist meeting at Wednesbury, where he heard John *Fletcher, the vicar of Madeley parish and one of John *Wesley's closest partners among the Anglican clergy, and Benjamin Ingham, a former member of the Wesleys' group at Oxford, the so-called 'Holy Club'. Asbury was impressed by the zeal of the preachers and their listeners, and after an intense search for the assurance of salvation, he experienced conversion at about the age of fifteen. In its basic outline, Asbury's conversion was classically evangelical. It would have been thoroughly recognizable to all early Methodists, who had themselves passed through a similar set of experiences. Had their hearts burned when they first heard zealous prayer and passionate, extemporaneous preaching? So had his. Had they struggled under the weight of their sins? So had he. Had they found forgiveness and assurance in Christ? So had he. This common set of experiences provided a crucial bond between Asbury and other early Methodists, both in England and America.

Asbury soon joined a class meeting and a band, and at about the age of seventeen he began to exhort and then preach in public. At twenty-one he took the place of the travelling preacher assigned to the Staffordshire circuit. In August 1767 he was admitted on trial (a probationary period for new itinerant preachers) and assigned to the Bedfordshire circuit. In August 1768 Asbury was admitted into full connection and assigned to the Colchester circuit, followed by the Bedfordshire circuit in 1769 and the Wiltshire circuit in 1770. At the Bristol annual conference in August 1771 he answered Wesley's call for volunteers to go to America.

When Asbury arrived in America in October 1771 there were fewer than 400 Methodists in the colonies. Asbury soon discovered that Joseph Pilmore and Richard Boardman, Wesley's only official missionaries in America before his arrival, had largely confined their ministries to Philadelphia and New York City, rather than following Wesley's principle of itinerancy. Pilmore and Boardman had little contact with Methodists in the South, and they apparently had not enforced the requirement that members attend a class meeting. Asbury's example, however, led Pilmore and Boardman to itinerate more widely, with Pilmore journeying as far south as Georgia in 1773. Establishing Methodist discipline in New York City and Philadelphia would prove a more difficult task and would take Asbury and others several years to accomplish.

In the spring of 1773 John Wesley sent Thomas Rankin and George Shadford to enforce the Methodist system of probationary membership and closed class meetings and love feasts. This led Pilmore and Boardman to return to England in January 1774. In September 1773 Asbury travelled south to Maryland, where he was struck with what in all probability was malaria. The disease dogged him into the spring of 1774, yet he continued to travel and preach widely. In 1775 and 1776 Methodism in southern Virginia experienced a large-scale revival, making the upper South the centre of American Methodism. These revivals were noted for their enthusiasm, which Asbury defended against the objections of Rankin and others.

With the outbreak of the American Revolution all the British preachers sent by Wesley returned home, save Asbury. As the war intensified in the middle states and the South, so did the suspicion of Methodists as loyalist sympathizers. In early 1778 Asbury took up residence at the home of Judge Thomas White in Delaware, unable to travel far because of anti-Methodist sentiment. For much of the next two years Asbury remained in Delaware. By 1779 Methodist preachers in the South had begun ordaining themselves to administer the sacraments. They did this because

obtaining the sacraments through the Anglican Church had become impossible in many places. The ordinations were a clear break from Wesleyan practices, and one to which Asbury and the northern preachers strenuously objected. In May 1780 Asbury, Freeborn *Garrettson and William Watters attended the annual conference at Manakintown, Virginia, to attempt a reconciliation. At first the Southern preachers flatly rejected their offer, but the next morning they abruptly changed their minds, voting to suspend the ordinations for one year and to recognize Asbury's authority over the movement both North and South. This was the first time that many of the Southern preachers had seen Asbury, and their change of heart is an indication of his ability to persuade and inspire confidence in others. Rather than returning north following the agreement, Asbury immediately set out on an extended tour of Virginia and North Carolina that would carry him into the autumn of 1780. This tour cemented Asbury's authority in the South, effectively ending the sacramental crisis.

The 1780s were a decade of unprecedented expansion for American Methodism, with membership rising from 8,500 in 1780 to 57,600 in 1790. Much of this increase was the result of a series of dramatic revivals in the South. By March 1781 Asbury estimated that he had travelled nearly 4,000 miles over the preceding eleven months. He now began a pattern he would follow for most of the rest of his career of spending the winter in the movement's southern reaches and the summer farther north. Beginning in the early 1780s, Asbury and other northern Methodists attempted to enact strict rules against Methodists owning slaves. These efforts culminated in 1784 with the passage of rules requiring all Methodists gradually to liberate their slaves. But within six months outcry and resistance from Southerners forced the suspension of the 1784 rules. Asbury would be haunted by the question of Southern Methodists holding slaves for the rest of his life. In 1784 John Wesley ordained Thomas *Coke as superintendent over American Methodism and sent him to America to ordain Asbury as co-superintendent (or bishop). Coke ordained Asbury at the so-called Christmas conference of 1784, at which the independent Methodist Episcopal Church was organized.

One of the hallmarks of episcopal authority in early American Methodism was the bishop's power to appoint preachers to their circuits without appeal. Since Coke spent relatively little time in America, for all practical purposes Asbury alone exercised this authority until relatively late in his career. At the 1792 General Conference James O'Kelly attempted to limit this authority by proposing that the conference be given the right to overrule the bishop. Although it initially enjoyed widespread support, O'Kelly's motion was eventually lost, at least in part because a majority of the preachers came to believe that he intended to use the provision to usurp authority over the southern Virginia circuits. O'Kelly and a band of dissidents soon left to form the Republican Methodist Church. Owing in part to the O'Kelly schism and to unrest over the church's anti-slavery rules, membership declined considerably in the Southern states of Delaware, Maryland, Virginia and Georgia during the 1790s. But these losses were offset by gains in the North, particularly in Pennsylvania, New York and parts of New England.

Between 1800 and 1810 Methodist membership in America increased from 63,700 to more than 171,700. Asbury continued to travel widely, limited only by his declining health after 1794. In 1811 alone he rode 6,000 miles, presided over eight annual conferences, preached 200 sermons and stationed 700 preachers. During his career in America, Asbury rode more than 250,000 miles on horseback and crossed the Allegheny mountains some sixty times. One biographer estimates that he stayed in 10,000 households and preached 17,000 sermons. Over a thousand children were named after him. Despite the church's phenomenal success, Asbury's lifestyle changed little during his forty-five years in America, and his salary never exceeded that of an ordinary travelling preacher. Like George *Whitefield and John Wesley before him, Asbury never fell prey to greed, womanizing or the temptation of a life of leisure. Indeed he had no private life outside his friendships with Methodist preachers and others whom he visited periodically in his travels. He rarely owned more than could be carried on horseback. By the 1810s Asbury's

renown had spread throughout much of the nation, owing in part to his evident piety and remarkable stamina. Yet in many ways he had outlived his time. He always wore knee buckles and gaiters, never approving of the new-style pantaloons, though nearly all his preachers wore them by the 1810s. While Methodists throughout the nation grew more prosperous, Asbury clung steadily to the old ways. He 'observed the most rigid economy in every thing that related to spending money', recalled the itinerant preacher Jacob Young. His clothes were plain and inexpensive, as were his horses, saddles and saddlebags. He preferred to travel on horseback because it was simpler and cheaper, but if he was forced to use a carriage it was always 'of the plainest and cheapest kind'.

For many of his later years Asbury was troubled by asthma and rheumatism, particularly in his feet. By 1812 Asbury's travelling companion, Henry Boehm, had to carry him 'in my arms' from the two-wheeled sulky in which he now travelled to each church or home, where the bishop would sit to preach. In 1814 Asbury suffered a severe three-month bout of pleurisy, from which he never fully recovered. The illness left him so thin that his bones 'appeared in da[n]ger of cutting through the skin'. Yet he continued to travel, crossing the Allegheny mountains four more times, visiting New England and making two trips to South Carolina and Georgia. Fittingly, Asbury died while on the road in Spotsylvania County, Virginia, on 31 March 1816, on his way to the General Conference in Baltimore.

Asbury embodies early American Methodism's greatest successes and its most wrenching failures. His success as a leader was a combination of several factors. Asbury was a consensus builder and tireless grassroots organizer. He maintained extensive face-to-face relationships with a wide range of people across the nation. Early in his career Asbury identified excessive 'levity', or the love of talking too much, as his besetting sin. He considered this a drain on his piety, but it also allowed him to build many deep and lasting relationships and to feel closely the pulse of the church and the nation. Ordinary people welcomed Asbury into their homes and conversed freely with him about their hopes, fears and aspirations. Asbury also embraced many elements of American popular culture, willingly coopting them into the Methodist system. Though fairly staid in his own religious practices, he defended the enthusiasm of Southern Methodists, white and African American, when Rankin, Pilmore and others attempted to quell the noisy worship they encountered in the South. He encouraged his preachers to use popular modes of speech and styles of singing, and eagerly promoted camp meetings when they burst on to the scene in the early 1800s. But coopting popular culture inevitably required compromise. Asbury initially succeeded at instilling a commitment to voluntary poverty among Methodist preachers, but by the end of his career he saw this position substantially eroded. The issue of slavery also demonstrated the limits of Methodism's appeal. After the failed attempts to combat slavery in the 1780s, Asbury became increasingly willing to divide his personal convictions from his public pronouncements for the sake of popular appeal among whites.

During his forty-five years in America Asbury kept a journal and wrote thousands of letters. He published extracts of his journal from August 1771 to April 1773 in the *Arminian Magazine* (Philadelphia) in 1789 and 1790. Two other portions of the journal were published in 1792 and 1802. An edited version of the entire journal was first published in three volumes in 1821, with a second edition in 1852. The manuscript journal was destroyed in a fire in 1836.

Bibliography

E. T. Clark, J. M. Potts, and J. S. Payton (eds.), *The Journal and Letters of Francis Asbury*, 3 vols. (London: Epworth; Nashville: Abingdon Press, 1958); E. S. Tipple, *Francis Asbury: The Prophet of the Long Road* (New York: Methodist Book Concern, 1916); L. C. Rudolph, *Francis Asbury* (Nashville: Abingdon Press, 1966).

J. H. WIGGER

■ **BACKUS, Isaac** (1724–1806), American Baptist clergyman, one of the outstanding advocates of the principle of the separation of church and state, was born on 9 January 1724 in Norwich, Connecticut, the son of Samuel Backus and Elizabeth Tracy. Backus's parents were farmers, and he received a rudimentary primary education and worked as a labourer on the family farm in his early life. The death of his father in 1740 led to a close relationship with his mother, from whom Isaac derived many of his religious convictions. Norwich was dramatically affected in 1741 when the revivalist James Davenport arrived and led many to a deeper Christian commitment. The widow Backus and her son Isaac were soon numbered among the New Lights. In 1745 they joined others in the community in forming a Separate Church at Bean Hill. The following year Isaac sensed a call to the ministry, and in the next two years he joined preaching tours in Connecticut, Rhode Island and Massachusetts. At length he visited Middleborough, Massachusetts, and was invited to become pastor of a new congregation being formed in a new parish, Titicut. Despite his lack of education and experience, he was selected in February 1748 to be the minister of the 'Church of Christ in the Joining Borders of Bridgewater and Middleborough' (Titicut) and was ordained in April. The congregation was New Light or Separate Congregationalist; it stressed the New Birth and progressive revelation and was supported by the voluntary contributions of its membership. Local authorities refused to recognize the church or Backus's ministry. When the tax-collector attempted to collect dues from the congregation in support of the recognized Congregational Church, Backus took the lead in creating a petition for exemption from paying religious taxes. He and his mother were threatened with imprisonment for not paying their taxes.

During the years from 1749 to 1756 Backus wrestled with several issues. The first was the drive to unite the Separates in favour of a defence of exemption from paying religious taxes; the second was his own identity among the Separates; and the third was his becoming a Baptist. Much influenced by the English Baptist theologian John *Gill, Backus adopted an antipaedobaptist position and was himself baptized in 1751. Between 1753 and 1755, as the leader of the antipaedobaptist Separates, Backus experimented with open communion, at times in bitter debate with members of his congregation about the acceptability of members who favoured infant baptism. Unable to achieve exemption from the religious tax as Separates and divided from the rest of the Middleborough church over communion, Backus and his loyal antipaedobaptist following adopted closed communion and antipaedobaptist articles of faith. The new congregation called itself the 'Baptist Church of Christ in Middleborough, Bridgewater, and Raynham'. Backus served this congregation, to be known as 'Middleborough First Baptist Church', for the rest of his life.

As a Baptist minister in revolutionary America, Isaac Backus identified with important causes and leaders. Within his own denomination he rose to regional and then national prominence. At the time of his commencing the Baptist phase of his ministry in Titicut there were scarcely eighteen Baptist congregations in all of New England. Half a century later, at the end of Backus's ministry, there were over 300 Baptist churches in the region. More than any other figure, Isaac Backus led the transition from New Light to Baptist and rallied the various Baptist factions into a unified movement. In 1767 he was a founder of the Warren Baptist Association, the leading coalition of Baptists in New England. He travelled widely among the churches and had had several works published by 1790. When the Baptists founded the College of Rhode Island in 1764, Backus was appointed to the board of trustees, and he remained one of its staunchest advocates. In 1789 the Warren Association commissioned him to itinerate in the southern states, and he spent five months in Virginia and North Carolina, travelling over 1,250 miles and preaching 117 sermons. In 1777 he published the first volume of his *Church History of New England*, one of the earliest historical accounts of Baptists in the United States. The second and third volumes of this seminal work were completed in 1784 and 1796 respectively. His travels and historical work placed him among the most quoted leaders of the denomination.

Backus's advocacy of religious liberty, and in particular the separation of church and state, made a permanent contribution to political ideology and American evangelical thought. He began with the principle that religious liberty required the unrestrained exercise of religious principles. Influenced by John Locke and Adam Smith, Backus opposed all forms of encroachment by the state into the inalienable right of every person to act in all religious affairs according to the full persuasion of his or her own mind. He followed Locke's logic of natural rights and claimed that freedom of conscience should be added to the rights to life, liberty and property. Moreover, governments had no right to interfere with voluntary religious expression or belief, or to enforce their judgments with the sword. As an evangelical Backus held that piety, religion and morality were essential for maintaining the civil order, and he fully anticipated a time when true saints would be in a majority. The Revolution was as much spiritual as political, he thought, allowing America to declare its spiritual independence and move as a nation towards the gospel.

In 1774 the Warren Baptist Association deputed Backus to represent them at the First Continental Congress in Philadelphia on the issue of the free exercise of conscience. Backus and James Manning presented a memorial to the Massachusetts delegation, which included John Adams and Samuel Adams, both of whom rejected the Baptist case. Undaunted, however, Backus returned to Massachusetts to answer the criticism that Baptists were enemies of the Patriot cause and that taxation for religious purposes should be abolished. In 1779 he again forcefully advocated his positions in widely distributed tracts and in a draft of instructions to the Massachusetts General Assembly on the writing of a state constitution.

As a respected figure among the Baptist community Backus also wrote thirty-eight tracts on a variety of topics, including the Shaker movement, Universalism, the Freewill Baptists, Sandemanians and hyper-Calvinism. He was particularly antagonistic towards the Shakers, against whom he wrote as early as the 1750s. In the 1770s he charged them with being morally disreputable and with propagating their schemes with strange powers, signs and lying wonders. The issue of the interpretation of Calvinism occupied a central place in Backus's thinking over several decades. On the one hand, as a moderate Calvinist, he disagreed with the Unitarians, Universalists and Freewill Baptists over their emphasis on human achievement and diminishing of God's sovereignty. On the other hand, he also inveighed against hyper-Calvinism, 'consistent Calvinism' and the New Divinity over their doctrine of extreme predestination, which seemed to him to be a form of fatalism. He felt that the new writers did not faithfully represent Jonathan *Edwards, for whom he had a great admiration.

Among historians of the Baptists in the United States, Backus ranks very high. His three-volume historical account of the rise of New England religious traditions was primarily an attempt to compensate for the absence of Baptists from early accounts of the Puritan history of New England. He thus began his story with the founding of John Robinson's congregation (1602–1608) in England. He introduced the almost forgotten figure of Roger *Williams into his account of the 1630s and cast him in a major role, both as a champion of religious liberty and as a forerunner of the Baptists. Backus thus created a myth around Williams that lasted for a century in Baptist historiography. Backus's account of the years from the 1640s focused on the Baptists as the guardians of religious liberty and the true inheritors of the Great Awakening. He proved his worth as an historian of New England, compiling useful statistical data and detailing the interactions between the sects in that region. His treatment of Baptists and others in the South is less reliable, and it has been suggested that he used uncritically the unpublished materials of Morgan Edwards, the Philadelphia Baptist itinerant and historian.

Isaac Backus died of the effects of multiple strokes on 20 November 1806 at his home in Middleborough. He was married in 1749 to Susanna Mason of Rehoboth, and they had nine children. Throughout his life Backus was a robust, muscular person, accustomed to hard labour. In 1797 he sat for a portrait at the request of John *Rippon for use in the English periodical the *Baptist Annual Register*, from which other likenesses are derived.

Backus was a symbol of the pilgrimage to Baptist principles in eighteenth-century America. The survival of his diary and correspondence make him one of the best-documented personalities among his peers. Religious historians compare Backus favourably with Francis *Asbury and George *Whitefield as one of the great itinerants: from 1747 to 1806

he made over 900 journeys covering 67,000 miles, preaching over 9,800 sermons or an average of four per week for over sixty years.

Bibliography

W. G. McLoughlin (ed.), *Diary of Isaac Backus*, 3 vols. (Providence: Brown University Press, 1979); *Isaac Backus and the American Pietistic Tradition* (Boston: Little, Brown, 1967); T. B. Maston, *Isaac Backus: Pioneer of Religious Liberty* (Rochester: American Baptist Historical Society, 1962).

W. H. BRACKNEY

■ **BARCLAY, Oliver Rainsford** (1919–), mission worker, was born on 22 February 1919 in Kobe, Japan. Barclay spent his working life with the Inter-Varsity Fellowship (IVF; renamed the Universities and Colleges Christian Fellowship [UCCF] in 1974), acting as general secretary between 1964 and 1980. Little known outside evangelical circles, he is none the less a significant figure in the history of twentieth-century British Christianity.

Barclay owed his Japanese birthplace to his missionary parents, but he was British and was educated at Gresham's School in Norfolk and Trinity College, Cambridge. He went to Trinity in 1938, leaving in 1945 after completing a PhD in Zoology. Brought up an Anglican, Barclay had a Quaker grandfather, whose influence led both Barclay and his father to become pacifists. He was a conscientious objector in the Second World War, although he grew less convinced of the pacifist viewpoint in later life. Barclay came to faith as a schoolboy in Norfolk, but was decisively influenced by the Cambridge Inter-Collegiate Christian Union (CICCU), in which he became a leading member. CICCU (and IVF, of which it was part) saw themselves as holding to Christian orthodoxy, in contrast to the then much larger and theologically broader Student Christian Movement (SCM). Barclay's theology was largely formed by CICCU, T. C. *Hammond's writings and the preaching and speaking of Dr Martyn *Lloyd-Jones. Hammond's and Lloyd-Jones' conservative Calvinism formed the theological backbone of IVF from the late 1930s. Barclay has retained a conservative evangelical faith throughout his life, but in 1976 he abandoned his Anglicanism and began worshipping at a free evangelical church. He was twice married: first to Dorothy, by whom he had one daughter and three sons; then, following her death from cancer, to Daisy.

In 1945 he began a two-year appointment as graduates' secretary for IVF. He then held various posts within the organization, becoming its general secretary in 1964. He retired in 1980, but remained active in its affairs and as an author. Barclay succeeded the long-serving Douglas *Johnson, who had been crucial to the establishment of IVF as a force within British universities. Barclay followed a similar path to Johnson, combining a staunchly conservative theology with great tactical and strategic vision and a deep pastoral concern. He contributed greatly to the rise of IVF in the post-war period and especially through the 1960s and 1970s, when many other Christian groups in universities were in sharp decline. Placing a strong emphasis on the intellectual underpinnings of faith, he was wary of the charismatic movement. However, Barclay was sensitive to cultural shifts, and under his leadership Christian Unions adapted their worship and shed some evangelical taboos in response to the surrounding culture. While Barclay was general secretary, IVF/UCCF established itself in the new universities of the 1960s and expanded into other sectors of higher education. IVF/UCCF has had an increasing influence on Christianity in Britain because of its growth, the greater proportion of the population going to university, and because many churches look to graduates for their leadership. IVF/UCCF has also been a key player in the establishment of conservative evangelicalism as a major force in universities across the world through the International Fellowship of Evangelical Students.

In his writings Barclay was concerned to show how a conservative view of Christianity was intellectually credible; his books included *Reasons for Faith* (1974) and *Developing a Christian Mind* (1984). Encouraged by Douglas Johnson, Barclay did much to promote a network of groups through which evangelical students could develop a distinctively Christian approach to their professions after they had graduated. Barclay was amongst those evangelical leaders who began to emphasize more strongly the social

implications of the gospel in the early 1970s. Concerned lest his views be seen as those of IVF, he published his work on these subjects under the pseudonym of A. N. Triton (*Whose World,* 1970). More recently, Barclay has written on historic and contemporary evangelicalism, stressing the need to retain a strong grasp of doctrine, lest Christianity be swallowed up by its surrounding culture. Barclay's most widely-read work was *Guidance: Some Biblical Principles* (1956). He was also in demand as a speaker.

At the same time as Barclay was president of CICCU, John A. T. Robinson, later an Anglican bishop, was president of the Cambridge branch of the more liberal SCM. Their subsequent theological trajectories say much about the shifting currents in Christianity within universities and in Britain generally. Robinson's controversial *Honest to God* embodied the swing towards liberalism in the 1960s, but SCM withered away in the 1960s and 1970s. Barclay, a layman who is little known outside evangelical circles, helped to promote the vitality of IVF/UCCF in this period. Barclay's combination of conservative theology, cultural flexibility and emphasis on the intellect has deeply marked both student Christianity and English evangelicalism in the second half of the twentieth century.

Bibliography

G. Fielder, *Lord of the Years: Sixty Years of Student Witness. The Story of the Inter-Varsity Fellowship, Universities and Colleges Christian Fellowship, 1928–88* (Leicester: IVP, 1988); O. R. Barclay, *Evangelicalism in Britain, 1935–95* (Leicester: IVP, 1997).

D. J. GOODHEW

■ **BARKER, Frederic** (1808–1882), second Anglican bishop of Sydney, Australia, was born at Baslow, Derbyshire, on 17 March 1808, the fifth son of the Revd John Barker (1762–1824) and his wife Jane (1768–1838). His grandfather served as the Duke of Devonshire's chaplain in Ireland and Dean of Raphoe. His father was for thirty years vicar of Baslow.

Barker was educated at Grantham School and Jesus College, Cambridge (BA 1831, MA 1839, DD 1854), where he came under the influence of Charles *Simeon's evangelical circle. He shared their Calvinist theology, love for the Prayer Book, Bible study and extemporary prayer, and their rejection of Roman Catholic dogma.

He was made deacon on 10 April 1831 and was ordained priest by Bishop J. B. *Sumner of Chester on 10 April 1832. Barker's appointment as perpetual curate of Upton (1832–1837) was interrupted by service as missioner to Ireland in late 1834. This was a test of his stamina and evangelical fervour as he travelled 800 miles and preached fifty-two sermons in a month. He returned to England to take up the incumbency of St Mary's, Edge Hill, Liverpool, on 23 January 1835.

Barker was strongly influenced by Sumner's church extension programme. The Church Building Society, St Aidan's College, Birkenhead, the Diocesan Board of Education and the training college for teachers provided models for similar bodies in Sydney. He adopted Sumner's expectations that clergy would be resident, improve their pastoral standards, visit the sick, read and expound the Scriptures, create Sunday schools, give lectures and encourage lay assistance in pastoral work. Between 1835 and 1854 St Mary's developed from a new church on the rural fringe into a vibrant suburban parish with one daughter church and another in the planning stage. It had a day school and a Sunday school, each with 350 pupils, and supported a number of missionary societies.

On 15 October 1840 Barker married Jane Sophia, elder daughter of John and Janet Harden of Ambleside. Jane had a charming and hospitable manner, a lively wit, a sharp intellect, a frankness of speech and artistic qualities. She proved to be a worthy companion and support during their childless marriage. Her death at Randwick on 9 March 1876 was a heavy blow for Barker.

Recurrent health problems led Barker in April 1854 to accept the lighter duties of the rural Baslow parish following the death of his older brother. Three months later when offered the bishopric of Sydney he accepted it in a spirit of missionary service. He was consecrated in Lambeth parish church on St Andrew's Day 1854 and sailed for Sydney on 28 February 1855, after a three-month recruitment drive for clergy and funds.

Nothing had prepared the Barkers for the culture shock they met when they stepped ashore in Sydney on 25 May 1855. Evangelical Archdeacon William Cowper's warm welcome contrasted with the cool reception from Sydney's predominantly High Church clergy. The blatant materialism and the lifeless outward observance of Christianity appalled the Barkers. Frederic believed that the efficient discharge of his duties, his positive leadership and courteous treatment of clergy would win over the disaffected.

During August 1855 Barker conducted his first episcopal visitation. He saw the need for enhanced pastoral oversight for the unwieldy diocese that covered two-thirds of New South Wales and part of Queensland. His first step was to secure an endowment for the new see of Goulburn (1863). Bathurst followed in 1870 and North Queensland in 1877. Evangelical bishops were installed in each. Further diocesan reforms in 1867 included the establishment of deaneries of four or five parishes to overcome the isolation many younger clergy experienced as they moved straight from theological training into parishes. Rural deans were given the responsibility of mentoring these men as well as overseeing their pastoral performance and property matters.

To supplement the diminishing number of clerical recruits from England and Ireland, Moore Theological College was established in 1856. By 1882 it had trained 30% of Sydney clergy as well as another ninety-nine ordinands for other Australian dioceses. To fund new churches and to supplement clerical stipends, Barker established a Church Society. Its inspiration came from the Chester Church Building Society, the Church Pastoral Aid Society and the Newcastle Church Society. It played a vital role after the phasing out of state aid in 1862.

Barker encouraged lay pastoral visitation, parish ministries for young people, the British and Foreign Bible Society and the Sydney City Mission. He was only moderately successful in finding suitable clergy to staff working-class parishes. The removal of pew rents from many parishes opened them to a wider social spectrum.

He and his clergy gave outstanding leadership to flood and drought-affected communities. Work among indigenous Australians lacked continuity and direction, while that among the Chinese came to a halt as they dispersed from the goldfields in the mid-1860s.

His comprehensive achievements in education included the establishment in 1856 of the position of inspector to improve the quality of education in diocesan schools, which numbered 107 by 1861. A Church of England Training School for teachers was founded in 1857. To Barker's regret, the constitution of St Paul's College in the University of Sydney gave him a titular rather than an active role. He secured amendments to the 1866 Public Schools Act that gave clergy right of entry into public schools for denominational religious instruction. In 1879 he fought to retain church schools as a focus for evangelism and instruction in Christian living. However, he lacked the support of many of his clergy and laity, who formed a Protestant–secularist alliance to promote government schools. Barker won increased right of entry for religious instruction under the 1880 Public Instruction Act. Without public funding, his church school programme withered. Offsetting this was a dramatic increase in Sunday school enrolments. Barker also established a Lay Readers' Institute in 1875 and planned a training institute for deaconesses.

In constitutional matters Barker was hesitant because of the unclear relationship of the colonial church to the state. It took him until 1866 to negotiate a suitable form of synodical government that gave an equal role to laity and clergy. It was a conservative solution that favoured the autonomy of the diocesan bishop and meant that provincial and general synods were chiefly consultative bodies. The Sydney synod worked to make clerical appointments more democratic, to set minimum standards for clergy stipends and housing and to establish clergy widows' and orphans' superannuation funds. Barker refused to let synod become the platform for those with political causes, such as temperance, because of the way they confused middle-class values with the gospel message of salvation. He considered evangelism to be the most effective means of social reform.

While in England attending the 1878 Lambeth Conference, he married Mary Jane Woods (1848–1910), elder daughter of Edward and Mary Woods, before returning to Sydney. Barker's failing health caused him to leave for England again in 1881 to convalesce. He died at San Remo, Italy, on 6 April 1882 and was buried next to his father and brother in Baslow churchyard. His passing was widely mourned because his contemporaries considered him a judicious administrator and a warm and gentle pastor.

Bibliography
W. M. Cowper, *Episcopate of the Right Reverend Frederic Barker ... A Memoir* (London: Hatchards, 1888); S. Judd and K. Cable, *Sydney Anglicans* (Sydney: AIO, 1987); G. S. Maple, 'Evangelical Anglicanism – Dominant, Defensive or in Decline? A Study of ... the Episcopate of Frederic Barker 1855–1882' (MA thesis, Macquarie University, 1992).

G. S. MAPLE

■ **BARNARDO, Thomas** (1845–1905), humanitarian, was born in Dublin on 4 July 1845, the son of a German businessman and a Quaker mother. Barnardo was raised in the Church of England, the church of his father, but was influenced by the evangelical faith of his mother. At the age of sixteen, amidst the Irish evangelical revival of the 1860s, Barnardo converted, against the explicit objections of his father, to the Plymouth Brethren, a premillennial sect. Although first apprenticed to a wine merchant by his father, Thomas Barnardo chose to become a medical student at the London Hospital in Whitechapel at the age of twenty-two, in the hope of joining the China Inland Mission. He was not accepted for overseas missionary work, in part because of his overbearing personality. However, as a result of his teaching at an evangelical Ragged School in Stepney, he redirected his missionary efforts towards the rescuing of slum children. In 1867 he opened the East End Juvenile Mission, which established prayer meetings, industrial training and penny savings banks for children, though it also addressed the needs of the adult poor by offering sewing classes and mothers' meetings for impoverished widows. In addition, during the 1870s Barnardo engaged in a popular crusade of temperance preaching that resulted in the establishment of the People's Church, which housed more than 3,200 people at a time, and a series of coffee houses that were intended to attract working-class men away from the pub.

Barnardo's forays into child rescue work were, in many ways, a direct extension of his evangelical faith. He sought to provide evidence for Christianity by rescuing child waifs and strays and exhorting them to convert. Not only was Barnardo at the forefront of a wider evangelical movement that linked social reform to evangelicalism, but in focusing upon children he was also among the first to stress their importance to the perpetuation and growth of evangelicalism. Believing that children were born in sin rather than innocence, Barnardo placed great emphasis on childhood conversion. He held that the rebuilding of the British citizenry must occur not through reform of the social environment, as some philanthropists argued, but primarily through a process of Christian rebirth within each individual. Although Barnardo saw Christian conversion as the best means for integrating poor and orphaned children into society, he stressed obedience, duty, thrift and a strong work ethic as the outward signs of this Christian rebirth.

The focus of Barnardo's vast child-rescue network was, therefore, Christian conversion, and as a result of his missionary zeal, he not only opened his doors to evangelicals like himself, but also sought out in particular Anglican and Roman Catholic children, whom he wished to convert to his brand of evangelicalism. This policy brought him into increasing conflict with both the clerical leadership and the laity of those denominations. In addition, Barnardo's charismatic personality, his organizational skills and missionary zeal made him into one of the most successful fundraisers within the increasingly competitive world of London evangelical charity. By the 1870s he had established a chain of juvenile homes for boys and a number of coffee houses, which were also popular preaching venues. In 1873, after his marriage to Syrie Louise Elmslie, Barnardo established girls' homes intended to rescue girl prostitutes from the streets of London. Moreover, following the lead of Annie MacPherson, he also established a programme of child emigration to Canada, Australia and South Africa, as a solution to the problem of high unemployment in London.

By the mid-1870s Barnardo dominated the evangelical charitable network in London, and as a result came into direct conflict with other evangelical ministers who were with difficulty carving out their own missionary empires. In 1876 George Reynolds, an obscure Baptist minister, and Fred Charrington, a purity crusader, began a public attack upon Barnardo, charging him with immoral behaviour when he was boarding with a widow, and claiming that he had misappropriated funds, cruelly treated his juvenile charges and doctored photographs of ragged children for the purposes of soliciting funds for his rescue work. Although this challenge was largely the result of struggles between various evangelical groups, it erupted into a major legal scandal once the powerful Charity Organization Society (COS) became involved.

Because of his emphasis on saving souls for God, Barnardo opened his boys' and girls' homes to destitute orphans and children of widows who were trying to avoid the workhouse test, a policy that brought him into increasing conflict with the COS. The COS blamed the upsurge in pauperism and the decline in the work ethic among the working-classes upon the proliferation of charities. Barnardo, however, remained a vociferous critic of the workhouse, arguing that the state had a responsibility to train and educate the poor, especially orphaned children, and that a respectable citizenry could be fashioned only through the creation of family settings or 'homes' where the tenets of Christianity were inculcated. His private conduct as well as his public work was excoriated in the newspapers, and in 1877 the essentially internecine evangelical dispute went to arbitration. Eventually Barnardo won his court case, but the revelations concerning his overbearing leadership and his personal control of finances forced him to place his juvenile homes in the hands of trustees. The public allegations and the lengthy court case also caused Barnardo to remain in debt for several years. In the long run the case, although it was brought by disgruntled evangelical missionaries, severely damaged the reputation of the evangelical charitable network in London at a time when the Anglican and Roman Catholic churches were making new inroads in the slums of the East End by establishing their own societies for waifs and strays.

The financial constraints that the public scandal henceforth placed upon Barnardo forced him to find new and less expensive avenues for child rescue, as his previous system of homes was found to be too expensive. As a result, the 1880s saw a tremendous expansion in his overseas work. Barnardo's juvenile emigration schemes, especially those in Canada, where homes were established in Toronto, Peterborough and Winnipeg, and an Industrial Farm founded in Manitoba to provide agricultural training for boys, expanded apace in this decade. Never one to back down from a fight, Barnardo went on further to promote the rights of children against those of parents. Still smarting from the accusations brought in the court case that he had flouted the rights of parents, especially those concerning the religious education of their children, Barnardo campaigned to restrict the legal rights of those parents whom he and the courts deemed to be 'irresponsible'. In 1889 the Poor Law Adoption Act took the first step in challenging the rights of working-class parents, and in 1891 the Custody of Children Act was passed, which severely restricted parental control over both abandoned and mistreated children. Although this law in large part fulfilled Barnardo's aim of subordinating parental rights to child welfare, significantly it preserved the rights of parents to determine the religion of their children, a principle which had been at the centre of Barnardo's controversies with working-class parents.

Barnardo's career was not only important in transforming the very idea of childhood; he was also instrumental in the assertion of children's rights. His evangelical insistence upon early childhood conversion helped not only to reinvigorate older networks of evangelical philanthropy, but also to focus reform interests around the question of child welfare. The longstanding influence of Barnardo's view of charity well into the twentieth century illustrates the strength of the voluntaristic and non-secular roots of modern welfare initiatives. Barnardo died on 14 September 1905, of heart disease.

The British children's homes continued their work for many years; the last one closed in 1984. The local government policy of fostering children within the empire was discontinued in the 1950s. Although a 'spiritual' (though not explicitly Christian) emphasis continues to animate the Barnardo organization, it now focuses on adoptions, the regulation of day-care for children, and the development of government social policy.

Bibliography
J. W. Bready, *Doctor Barnardo: Physician, Pioneer, Prophet: Child-like Yesterday and Today* (London: Allen & Unwin, 1931); A. E. Williams, *Barnardo of Stepney: The Father of Nobody's Children* (London: Allen & Unwin, 1966); J. H. Batt, *Dr Barnardo: The Foster Father of Nobody's Children* (London: S. W. Partridge, 1904).

N. CHRISTIE

■ **BARNHOUSE, Donald Grey** (1895–1960), fundamentalist minister, was a leader among American Presbyterian evangelicals. Born in Watsonville, California, on 28 March 1895, Barnhouse was raised in the Methodist Church. His father, Theodore Barnhouse, was a carpenter and private contractor. His mother, Jennie Carmichael Barnhouse, was a strong-willed individual, who had a strong influence on his religious life. As a fifteen-year-old, Barnhouse attended a Christian Endeavor convention and received the 'assurance' of life eternal. He then sensed a call to Christian ministry. In 1912 he entered the Bible Institute of Los Angeles (BIOLA) and came under the influence of Reuben Archer *Torrey, an early colleague of Dwight L. *Moody and a prominent evangelist. Torrey's dispensational approach to the second coming of Christ shaped Barnhouse's own eschatology. He then attended the University of Chicago, but he found its liberal atmosphere unacceptable and transferred to Princeton Theological Seminary in 1915. He left the school two years later without a degree, but having established a reputation as a polemicist who never hesitated to challenge professors with whom he disagreed. On leaving Princeton, Barnhouse enlisted in the Army Signal Corps and achieved the rank of First Lieutenant. Following the war, he worked for the Belgian Gospel Mission from 1919 to 1921 and helped to organize the *Ecole Biblique de Belgique*. He then spent two years in France as pastor of two Reformed churches in the Alpine region.

Barnhouse married missionary Ruth Tiffany in 1922; the couple produced four children. (Ruth Tiffany Barnhouse died of cancer in 1944.) They returned to the United States in 1925, where Barnhouse studied at the University of Pennsylvania and served as pastor of Grace Presbyterian Church. In 1927 he became pastor of Philadelphia's Tenth Presbyterian Church, a position he held until his death. His education continued, and in 1927 he received the Master of Theology degree from Eastern Baptist Theological Seminary. In 1933 Dallas Theological Seminary conferred the honorary degree of Doctor of Divinity upon him. In 1952 he received the Doctor of Theology degree from Aix-en-Provence, a seminary founded by a small group of French Reformed Churches.

As a pastor Barnhouse soon became known for his expository preaching, a practice of intense analysis of and reflection on biblical texts. For example, he spent over three years preaching only from the book of Romans. He generally eschewed topical preaching, preferring to link a specific verse with 'the whole Bible'. He replaced the standard Sunday evening service with an early vesper service, which was broadcast on local and, ultimately, national radio, and which enabled him to take Sunday night preaching engagements elsewhere. In 1949 his radio programme became the 'Bible Study Hour' broadcast on more than one hundred stations by the National Broadcasting Company (NBC). The number of stations broadcasting the programme had risen to 455 by the time of his death in 1960. Barnhouse's radio success increased his popularity at Bible conferences and other events around the country.

In 1931 Barnhouse established an evangelical magazine, *Revelation*, which published his sermons, Bible studies, commentaries and devotions along with those of other evangelical preachers. In 1950 he gathered a largely new editorial staff and became editor of another magazine, *Eternity*. He became widely known as a Bible class teacher and travelled extensively conducting classes. These activities kept him away from Tenth Presbyterian Church. His continual absences from the pulpit were generally accepted by the congregation, although not without controversy; some members left because of them. Nonetheless, Barnhouse continued to extend his own work and ultimately created a staff numbering over fifty individuals, who helped to coordinate his schedules, activities and the work of the church. In 1955 he reported that for more than thirty years he had preached, on average, six nights each week, a total of more than 12,000 sermons.

Theologically, Barnhouse was a dispensational fundamentalist within the Reformed tradition. He emphasized divine sovereignty and election, did not permit 'invitations' or altar calls at Tenth Presbyterian Church. He asserted that the church was called not to 'Christianize' society but to evangelize it, and opposed the Social Gospel movement. He agreed that social action should be taken, but only as a result of personal faith. Although he affirmed the eternal punishment of the damned, he did not believe that it necessarily involved actual hell-fire. As a fundamentalist, he insisted on three foundational doctrines: the incarnation of Christ as the second person of the Trinity; Christ's death and resurrection as essential for the salvation of human beings; and the infallible inspiration of the Bible as the inerrant Word of God.

Concerning the 'end times', Barnhouse was a dispensationalist who ultimately developed his own detailed expectations regarding Christ's return, based particularly on texts in Jeremiah, Daniel, Ezekiel and Revelation. These included the following. First, Jews would retake the Holy Land and would control the region from Egypt to the Black Sea. Secondly, European nations would form an alliance with a leader who would be recognized as the Antichrist. A great tribulation would occur after the true church was raptured from the world, leaving an organized religion which would unite with the antichrist to control the world. Thirdly, Russia, as leader of the remaining nations, would lead an attack against the United States of Europe in the Palestinian region of Armageddon, an event that would trigger the return of Jesus Christ. Christ would defeat all earthly armies and bind the devil for eternity. Unlike many traditional dispensationalists, however, Barnhouse did not believe that the church of his day was false and that true believers should separate themselves from it. Thus, he would not align himself with fundamentalist separatists such as C. I. *Scofield, J. Gresham *Machen and Carl *McIntire.

Barnhouse's outspoken criticism of liberalism and his unbending conservatism created controversy among Presbyterians in the Philadelphia region. In 1929 seventeen pastors in the Philadelphia presbytery accused Barnhouse of creating divisions and mistrust among the churches. Ultimately, a judicial committee was appointed from the synod of Pennsylvania, and he was found guilty of bearing false witness and violating ordination vows. The presbytery that urged him to 'put away from you the evil of your doings' gave him a simple 'admonition'. This controversy estranged him from many Presbyterian colleagues on the left, while his refusal to leave the Presbyterian Church in the USA led to his isolation from many fundamentalists.

Barnhouse's social views were shaped by his conservative theology. He believed that married women were to maintain the home, submit to their husbands and nurture their children in faith. The Barnhouses educated their children at home and refused to allow them to have contact with other children, even those from church families, since they could not be sure that the families followed the same principles in raising their children. Barnhouse rejected divorce and remarriage under any circumstances, yet three of his four children were divorced. In the light of their experiences he moderated his view of divorce, claiming that it was 'not the unpardonable sin'. Throughout his ministry he also opposed racism, communism and Roman Catholicism.

Towards the end of his ministry, however, Barnhouse moderated his personal response to those with whom he had long disagreed. In 1953 he announced a New Year's resolution that marked a change in his previously conservative attitudes, although he continued to maintain conservative theology. He acknowledged that his earlier zeal for correct doctrine had led him to treat people badly and hurt them deeply. He also began to urge greater cooperation between Christians and even praised the World Council of Churches, a target of fundamentalist criticism, for its many fine activities. His ecumenical endeavours extended to Seventh Day Adventists and Pentecostals, groups often shunned by liberals and conservatives alike. However, he did not

compromise his long-held doctrinal positions, and throughout the 1950s he frequently criticized Unitarians, Universalists, Christian Scientists and Jehovah's Witnesses, who could in his view make no claim to be part of the true church of Christ. He also questioned the Christianity of contemporaries such as ethicist Reinhold Niebuhr, Quaker Elton Trueblood, and missionary-theologian Albert Schweitzer.

Barnhouse was a tireless preacher, a fearless polemicist, and an individual who, while never renouncing his conservative convictions, was certainly willing to rethink them, often at the cost of friendships within his own fundamentalist constituency.

Bibliography

C. A. Russell, 'Donald Grey Barnhouse: Fundamentalist Who Changed', *Journal of Presbyterian History* 59 (1981); *Dictionary of Christianity in America* (Downers Grove: InterVarsity, 1990); D. G. Barnhouse, 'Can a Sane Man Believe in Hell?', *Eternity* 11 (June 1960); A. C. Guelzo, 'Barnhouse', in J. M. Boice (ed.), *Making God's Word Plain* (Philadelphia: Tenth Presbyterian Church, 1979).

B. J. LEONARD

■ **BARROW, Henry** (c. 1550–1593), English Separatist, was born at Shipdam in Norfolk and educated at Clare Hall, Cambridge. In 1576 he entered Gray's Inn and seemed destined for a career in law. Precisely when and how he became a strict Puritan and later a Separatist is not known. However, by 1586 he and John Greenwood, another important Separatist leader from Norfolk, were in fellowship with a London congregation. On 19 November 1587, on the orders of Archbishop Whitgift, he was arrested while visiting Greenwood in prison. He was accused of not attending church, of being disobedient to the Queen and of teaching that the Church of England was not the true church. While in prison, Barrow continued to write treatises and became one of the leading proponents of Separatism.

Although Barrow was called a 'Brownist', he engaged in controversy with Robert *Browne, the erstwhile Separatist, and tried to argue that he owed no theological debt to Browne or to his writings. However, like

Browne and other Congregationalists, he argued that congregational government was the scriptural model for the church. He stressed that the covenant relationship was at the heart of a true understanding of the church and, like Browne, seems to have believed that it was conditional, in that the believer was expected to be obedient to God and to his will as revealed in Scripture. His opponents accused him of denying that salvation was according to God's mercy, but he argued that to the contrary, the grace of God at work in the elect would lead to an active obedience to the covenant. Hence he was not claiming that an individual could keep the covenant unaided, but that by God's grace one might be obedient to God.

Barrow and Greenwood believed that the Church of England was in a state of total apostasy because: members of parish churches could not testify to an experience of conversion; the ministry of the church was not based on an apostolic pattern of presbyters and deacons appointed by the congregation; the worship was directed by a book other than Scripture; and the government of the church was not shared by all its members. Barrow and his followers argued that reform of the church was badly needed and, for Barrow, to reform the church was 'to reduce all things and actions to the true and ancient and primitive pattern of God's word' (L. H. Carlson [ed.], The Writings of Henry Barrow, 1590–1591, pp. 354f.).

Barrow insisted that the Congregationalists' ecclesiology was the right one, but he did not totally abandon the idea of having appointed officers within the church. He and Greenwood argued that officers were a part of the scriptural pattern for the church; officers should be appointed by the congregation and should share in making decisions and administering the ordinances. Indeed, in Barrow's congregation in London it seems that the ordinances were not celebrated until Francis Johnson was appointed as pastor about 1592. Officers were also to help with the discipline of the congregation, which Barrow believed to be vital to the life of a covenant community. But members were to submit to the discipline of the whole fellowship of believers, and leaders were not to act apart from the shared decision of the congregation.

Although Barrow stressed the voluntarist principle, he did insist that it was the duty of the government to compel people 'to the hearing of the word'. And it was the duty of government to reform both church and nation. However, he insisted that the prince could not 'compel any to be a member of the Church, or the Church to receive any without assurance by the public profession of their own faith, or to retain any longer, than they continue and walk orderly in the faith' (Writings, 1590–1591, p. 40).

Barrow's contribution to the Separatist movement was his ability to write and effectively disseminate its ideas. In his writing he argued forcefully that the church was best expressed through a congregational form of church government. He sought to base his arguments on Scripture, although they reflected his own experience within a covenant community as well.

Barrow was arrested on a charge of publishing seditious writings and, with Greenwood, was hanged at Tyburn in April 1593.

Bibliography
B. R. White, The English Separatist Tradition, from the Marian Martyrs to the Pilgrim Fathers (Oxford Theological Monographs, 1971); L. H. Carlson (ed.), The Writings of Henry Barrow, 1587–1590 (London: 1962); L. H. Carlson (ed.), The Writings of Henry Barrow, 1590–1591 (London: 1966); L. H. Carlson (ed.), The Writings of John Greenwood and Henry Barrow, 1591–1593 (London: 1970).

K. E. SMITH

■ **BAVINCK, Herman** (1854–1921), Dutch Reformed theologian, was largely responsible with Abraham *Kuyper for the revival of orthodox Calvinism in the late nineteenth century. Bavinck is not as well-known in the English-speaking world as Kuyper, but his four-volume Reformed Dogmatics remains the standard reference work for classic Dutch Reformed theology more than a hundred years after its initial publication in the 1890s. Its continuing relevance is evidenced by the fact that all four volumes are being translated into English and from English into other languages, including Korean.

Bavinck was born on 13 December 1854 in Hoogeveen, province of Drenthe, where his father, Jan Bavinck, was an influential minister in the Secession Dutch Christian Reformed Church, which had been formed in 1834 in protest against state control of the national Dutch Reformed Church. Initially persecuted for their faith and refusal to cease meeting 'unofficially' for worship, the secessionists remained at the margins of nineteenth-century Dutch life and were apprehensive about culture and society shaped by modernity.

Though the Bavinck home shared the Pietism of this community, it was more cosmopolitan than that of most secessionists. Jan Bavinck was a self-taught learned man who, only a few months before Herman's birth, had declined his church's request to teach at the newly established Kampen Theological School. Herman's mother, the stronger of the two parents, had grown up in the National Dutch Reformed Church and counterbalanced the Bavincks' tendency towards Pietist withdrawal.

To the end of his life Bavinck prized the piety of the church in which he was raised and made it his own. Yet his own thought was more catholic. A gifted student, he chose, after one year of study for the ministry, not to stay at the church's seminary in Kampen but to pursue a more 'scientific' training at the State University of Leiden; he 'desired to become acquainted with the modern theology first hand'. This decision was supported by his mother but opposed by his father. Bavinck obtained a doctorate in theology from Leiden with a dissertation on the ethics of Ulrich *Zwingli. In later reflection on his Leiden years Bavinck judged that the experience had enriched him intellectually and refined his theology, but that it had also impoverished him spiritually.

For the rest of his life Bavinck wrestled with these two formative influences. As one of his contemporaries said, Bavinck was a man between two worlds, at the same time 'a Secession preacher and representative of modern culture'. In a revealing assessment of the liberal social-gospel theology of Albrecht Ritschl, Bavinck contrasts the goals that inspire Pietism and Ritschl's liberalism respectively. The former, he says, sees salvation in Christ as 'primarily a means to separate man from sin and the world, to prepare him for heavenly blessedness'. In contrast,

'Ritschl posits the very opposite relationship: the purpose of salvation is precisely to enable a person … to exercise his earthly vocation and fulfill his moral purpose in this world.' Bavinck's evaluation of these goals is revealing: 'Personally, I do not yet see any way of combining the two points of view, but I do know that there is much that is excellent in both, and that both contain undeniable truth.'

Upon completing his theological studies, Bavinck honoured the piety of his childhood church and home by becoming the minister of the Christian Reformed Church in Franeker, Friesland. Bavinck served this church faithfully from 1880 to 1883, declining two invitations from prestigious institutions in Amsterdam, one to be minister of its Christian Reformed Church and the other to teach theology at Abraham Kuyper's new Free University of Amsterdam, which had opened in 1880. He indicated to the university that although he honoured the ideal of independent Reformed higher education, his love for his own church and his concern about the quality of theological education at its school in Kampen made acceptance of the invitation impossible.

Recognizing his undeniable intellectual gifts, the synod of the Christian Reformed Church appointed Bavinck to teach theology at its Kampen school in 1883; he taught there with distinction from 1883 to 1902. He was the first teacher at Kampen to possess a doctorate, and he raised the level of Kampen's theological education considerably. Bavinck collated his teaching in the first edition of his major work, the four-volume *Reformed Dogmatics*, published between 1892 and 1901. He also developed a close relationship with Abraham Kuyper, whose Neo-Calvinism enabled him to synthesize his experiential piety with his world-affirming appreciation for modern culture and learning. The *Reformed Dogmatics* are characterized by this integration; Bavinck links piety to the difficult issues and questions facing the modern person, such as those relating to creation and evolution.

Already as a student Bavinck had been drawn to Kuyper and his effort to revive classic Dutch Reformed thought in church and nation alike. The theological tool that Bavinck utilized in this endeavour was the trinitarian and profoundly Irenaean claim that grace restores nature. His favourite and oft-repeated definition of Christianity was some version of the following: 'The essence of the Christian religion consists in this, that the creation of the Father, devastated by sin, is restored in the death of the Son of God, and re-created by the Holy Spirit into a kingdom of God.' In an important address on common grace he summarized his understanding of grace: 'Christianity does not introduce a single substantial foreign element into the creation. It creates no new cosmos but rather makes the cosmos new. It restores what was corrupted by sin. It atones the guilty and cures what is sick; the wounded it heals.'

After declining repeated invitations, Bavinck finally accepted an appointment to teach theology at the Free University in 1902. After revising and expanding the *Reformed Dogmatics*, he turned his attention away from theology to culture and society, including politics, education and pedagogy, psychology and philosophy. He continued to venture beyond the boundaries of orthodox Reformed thought while maintaining his commitment to it.

In 1912 Bavinck engaged in a conversation with modernist clergy about 'Modernism and Orthodoxy', the title of his 1911 rectoral address at the Free University of Amsterdam. Here Bavinck expressed in familiar terms his wonder at the new modern world and the remarkable changes taking place in it. Although uncertain about the future, he was also hopeful, declaring 'God is busy doing great things in our times.' He did not, however, hide his Pietist sympathies. 'I am and always hope to remain a child of the Secession,' he said, adding that much of his theological training at Leiden had been 'stones for bread'. He concluded that to accept the modernist credo was to reduce the great realities of the Christian faith (creation, fall, atonement, regeneration) to 'clanging cymbals, symbols'. But, he added, 'They remain realities and if I gave them up I would be lost. So I reminded myself that [the liberal critique of Scripture] cannot be true. The biblical realities are so much more real than the conundrums of Scripture and nature. I am thus not bound by mere tradition but by what is in the deepest part of my soul, my very life, the salvation of my soul.'

This thoroughly modern man of deep faith and piety died on 29 July 1921.

Bibliography
Our Reasonable Faith, trans. by Henry Zylstra (Grand Rapids, 1956); *The Certainty of Faith*, trans. Harry der Nederlanden (Jordan Station, Ont.: Paideia, 1980); *The Last Things: Hope for this World and the Next*, ed. by John Bolt, trans. by John Vriend (Grand Rapids, 1996); *In the Beginning: Foundations of Creation Theology*, ed. by John Bolt, trans. by John Vriend (Grand Rapids, 1999).

J. BOLT

■ **BAXTER, Richard** (1615–1691), Puritan pastor, evangelist, theologian and leader, was known throughout England for his landmark ministry in Kidderminster over fourteen years (1641–1660, with five years away as a Parliamentary army chaplain, 1642–1647) and for his massive literary output, 135 books in just over forty years, which earned him the nickname 'scribbling Dick'. An alert observer with a tenacious memory for all he saw and read, his posthumous memoirs (*Reliquiae Baxterianae*, 1696) remain a main source for much seventeenth-century history. Baxter was essentially a cross-bench conservative for whom the Puritan idealism he absorbed in his youth was always the point of reference. He was a theocratic monarchist who thought *Cromwell was spoiled by power and the Commonwealth and Protectorate were a mistake, so he welcomed the Restoration as the right move. The first clergyman to decline the terms of ministry in the national church imposed by the 1662 Act of Uniformity (curtain-raiser to the persecuting Clarendon Code), he wrote untiringly on behalf of the more than 1,700 who, like him, accepted ejection but hoped for a future comprehension that would restore national church ministry to them, or if not that, then some form of toleration that would allow them to preach and pastor lawfully. (Toleration did not come until 1689, following the Revolution.) In an era of upheaval and bitter strife, both political and religious, Baxter sought unity in theological, ecclesiastical, socio-political and personal terms, identifying himself after 1662 as a mere Christian, a mere catholic, a mere Nonconformist and a reconciler seeking church peace. He also supported John Dury's quest for pan-European Protestant reunion and is properly seen as an ecumenical pioneer.

Often called a Presbyterian, Baxter never was one, but as a paedobaptist who approved England's parochial system and multitudinous congregations he could not favour any form of separatism nor countenance the covenantal church-gathering of Congregationalists and Baptists. His ideal polity was an episcopal system shorn of prelatical autocracy and made synodical, according to a plan devised by Archbishop Ussher, whereby each chief pastor would be viewed as bishop of his congregation and diocesans would chair clerical gatherings as first among equals. Much as he valued extempore prayer, Baxter did not object to a fixed liturgy as such, and could have served in the restored Church of England had not the terms of the Act of Uniformity effectively required all clergy to renounce all thought of further reformation at any point.

The most prolific English theological writer of all time, Baxter gave the world four classics: The Saints' Everlasting Rest (1650), an electrifying exploration of how the hope of heaven should shape life on earth; The Reformed Pastor (1656), a plea to ministers to teach, evangelize, catechize from house to house and maintain and model full Christian vitality – 'the best manual of the clergyman's duty in the language' according to Broad Church bishop H. Hensley Henson (1925); A Call to the Unconverted (1657), in Baxter's phrase a 'wakening persuasive' that became a fountain-head of evangelistic literature; and A Christian Directory (1673), the fullest compendium of Puritan lore on Christian life and conduct that was ever produced. Baxter's learned doctrinal folios Catholick Theology (1675), a tour de force squaring current Reformed, Lutheran, Arminian and Roman Catholic systems with each other, and the Latin Methodus Theologiae (1681), an attempt to break into the world of international Protestant scholarship with an analytical compendium of Ramist type, only trichotomizing rather than dichtomizing, were stillborn. So too, it seems, were his brilliant apologetic treatises Reasons of the Christian Religion (1667) and More Reasons for the Christian Religion (1672), which deserved a better fate; and his polemics against papal imperialism, his pleas for comprehension and his apologias for Nonconformity were tracts for the times that have now only historical interest. It is as a practical, devotional writer on regenerate living that Baxter lives today.

The son of a small landowner, and thus a gentleman in the seventeenth-century sense, Baxter came to faith in his teens through reading William *Perkins, Richard Sibbes and other Puritan pundits. After a brilliant school career he was sent to London to become a courtier rather than to the university to become a scholar, but he hated it. He came home to Shropshire, began to suffer from the sicknesses that would be with him all his life, sought ordination in order to do the most good possible before he died and was made deacon by the Bishop of Worcester in 1638. A year as a preaching schoolmaster and another as a pastoral assistant led to his call to Kidderminster, a weaving town of some 2,000 adult inhabitants, which he transformed. He filled the parish church with over half the population twice a Sunday, saw hundreds of conversions, established family devotions in most homes, nurtured his young people, trained layfolk as witnesses and prayer warriors and, with the help of an assistant, gave every family two separate hours of catechizing each year, using the Westminster Shorter Catechism as the text. He insisted that as minister he must have full freedom and authority to discipline his flock as well as teach them, and he would accept at the Lord's Table only the six hundred or so who were willing to be rebuked by him if he saw the need. In this he was implementing the ideal of parish discipline that the first Puritans formulated before he was born.

From his weekly fellowship with neighbouring clergy emerged in 1653, within the Cromwellian religious climate and practice, the Worcestershire Association, a ministerial fraternity covenanted for discipline and, after 1656, for family catechizing on the Kidderminster model. Similar associations sprang up in other counties, and by 1660 Baxter was England's best-known clergyman.

Having in that year declined the entangling offer of the bishopric of Hereford, and having failed at the 1661 Savoy Conference, where he was the Puritan leader, to get Puritan objections taken seriously in the revision of the 1604 Prayer Book, and having been barred that same year from all future ministry in Worcestershire, Baxter realized that his days as a pastor were over. So in 1662 he married (very happily, as his 1681 memoir of his just-deceased wife shows) and lived from then on near or in London, writing furiously and preaching periodically, sometimes risking fines and imprisonment by so doing. Twice he was imprisoned as a contumacious Nonconformist, once for a week and once for nearly two years. Having viewed himself as at death's door for more than fifty years (and with justice, be it said), he died at seventy-six, and a huge procession came out for his funeral.

Baxter was a mainstream exponent of Puritan Calvinism, as in the standards of Dort and Westminster, except on justification by faith. Viewing justification as a kingdom blessing, and conceiving God's kingdom as analogous to a seventeeth-century European monarchy, Baxter explained Christ's death as an act of universal reparation for sin in virtue of which God has made a new law offering amnesty to breakers of the old law who now repent and receive Christ as their Saviour and Lord, whom henceforth they seek to obey. God's justifying of them extends beyond initial pardon to continued and final acceptance of them in virtue of their obedience to his new law. Baxter developed this scheme, which he thought was scriptural, to counter antinomianism. His peers called it neonomianism, a version of justification by works, and critiqued it as obscuring Christ's solidarity with believers and the true significance of his righteousness imputed to them.

Bibliography
N. H. Keeble (ed.), *The Autobiography of Richard Baxter* (London: J. M. Dent, 1974); N. H. Keeble and G. F. Nuttall, *Calendar of the Correspondence of Richard Baxter*, 2 vols. (Oxford: Clarendon Press, 1991); G. F. Nuttall, *Richard Baxter* (London: Nelson, 1965).

J. I. PACKER

■ **BEECHER, Lyman** (1775–1863), American Congregational and Presbyterian clergyman and president of Lane Theological Seminary, was one of the most famous preachers of his day.

Beecher held two major concerns throughout his career. First, he was dedicated to 'the revival spirit' (Cross, *Autobiography*, p. 45). Beecher sought to persuade sinners to commit themselves to Christ, and he evaluated his success as a preacher by the number of souls he converted. The second of Beecher's concerns was moral reform. He believed that a revival of the Christian church should lead to the moral revitalization of the nation. He encouraged Christians to band together in voluntary societies in order to eradicate what he considered social evils.

Beecher was born on 12 October 1775 in New Haven, Connecticut, the son of a blacksmith, David Beecher, and his third wife, Esther Lyman Beecher. His mother died days after his birth. Beecher was raised by an uncle and aunt, Lot and Catharine Benton, on a farm in Guilford, Connecticut. He entered Yale at the age of eighteen, at which time President Timothy *Dwight was encouraging a revival of religion among students. Beecher was converted under Dwight's exhortations in 1796. Upon graduating in 1797, Beecher prepared for a career in ministry, studying theology under Dwight for one year. He briefly supplied Congregational pulpits in Connecticut before he was called to minister to the East Hampton Presbyterian Church on Long Island, New York, in 1799, the same year that he married his first wife, Roxana Foote.

Two sermons, published during Beecher's tenure at East Hampton, brought him his earliest notoriety. His *Remedy for Dueling* (1806), delivered after Aaron Burr fatally wounded Alexander Hamilton in a duel, was an early call to social reform. *The Government of God Desirable* (1807) is an example of Beecher's revival-oriented preaching.

In 1810, after a salary dispute with the congregation at East Hampton, Beecher accepted a call to the Congregational Church of Litchfield, Connecticut. From this pulpit, Beecher advocated a number of causes. He helped to form the Domestic Missionary Society and the American Bible Society and other voluntary associations. He spoke out against intemperance, at first encouraging abstention only from 'ardent spirits' and later from all forms of alcohol. His *Six Sermons on Intemperance* (1825) went through several editions and was translated into several languages.

One cause Beecher later regretted advocating was the continued state support of the Congregational Church in Connecticut. Beecher later called disestablishment, which occurred in 1817, 'The best thing that ever happened in the state of Connecticut. It cut churches loose from dependence on state support. It threw them wholly on their own resources and on God' (Cross, *Autobiography*, pp. 252–253).

In the early nineteenth century, Unitarianism made significant advances among Boston Congregationalists. Beecher opposed Unitarianism in *The Bible a Code of Laws* (1817) and in *The Faith Once Delivered to the Saints* (1823). Also during Beecher's tenure at Litchfield, Roxana Beecher died of consumption in 1816. Beecher married Harriet Porter the following year.

In 1826 Beecher left Litchfield to pastor the Hanover Street Church in Boston. A phalanx of orthodox Congregational ministers had recently organized the thirty-seven-member congregation as a beach-head against Unitarianism. Under Beecher's leadership the church rapidly gained hundreds of members, giving birth to other new churches. After the church building was destroyed by fire in 1830, the congregation rebuilt on Bowdoin Street.

In Boston Beecher continued to engage in public controversy, not only against Unitarianism, but also against contemporary secular reform movements. Beecher called on Christians to correct social injustices and to show charity to the poor in order to quell the complaints and stem the tide of what he considered atheistic socialism. He later rewrote and published these sermons under the title *Lectures on Political Atheism* (1852).

At times, Beecher's zeal manifested itself as intolerance. In January 1831 he delivered a series of lectures in which he described Roman Catholics, who were then emigrating to Boston from Ireland in great numbers, as 'a danger ... to Republican liberty' because of 'the allegiance which they owe to a foreign sovereign', the Pope (Harding, *A Certain Magnificence*, p. 297).

Beecher developed an interest in the mission of the Protestant Church in the American West. In 1832 he moved to Cincinnati,

Ohio, to become president of Lane Theological Seminary and pastor of the Second Presbyterian Church. In *A Plea for the West* (1835) Beecher exhorted easterners to support Protestant institutions like Lane, which would Christianize the west and counter the success of Roman Catholic missions on the American frontier.

As president of Lane, Beecher became embroiled in a conflict over American slavery. Many Lane students, including Theodore Dwight Weld, were abolitionists. They advocated the immediate, rather than the gradual, emancipation of slaves and opposed the work of the American Colonization Society, which sought to move freed slaves to a colony in Africa. The Lane trustees, anxious about antagonizing the white citizens of Cincinnati, forbade discussion of slavery among students and restricted students' charitable work among Cincinnati's African American population. Beecher considered slavery an evil, but he did not share Weld's commitment to immediate emancipation or his opposition to colonization. Nor did he understand Weld's and his compatriots' need to associate freely and openly with local African Americans. While Beecher opposed the rules issued by the trustees, he also tried to persuade Weld to make compromises that would allay their anxieties. The 'Lane rebels' refused to compromise and transferred *en masse* to Oberlin College in 1834.

Beecher's years in Cincinnati also brought theological conflict. As a revivalist, Beecher, like his friend, Yale professor Nathaniel *Taylor, addressed his listeners as free agents, exhorting them to submit voluntarily to the benevolent 'government of God'. Many conservative Presbyterians found Beecher's emphasis on free will incompatible with the traditional Reformed doctrines of predestination and original sin. His opponents brought Beecher to trial before the Presbyterian adjudicatory. Beecher was exonerated of heresy by the Synod of Cincinnati in 1835. He defended his orthodoxy in his *Views on Theology* (1836). The debate surrounding Beecher was one of the causes of the division of the Presbyterian Church in the United States into Old School and New School factions from 1837 to 1869. The same year that Beecher was tried for heresy, Harriet

Porter Beecher died. Beecher married Mrs Lydia Jackson of Boston the following year.

Beecher resigned as pastor of the Second Presbyterian Church in 1843. In 1846 Beecher visited England to preach at the World Convention of Evangelical Protestant Churches and the World Temperance Convention. He retired from the presidency of Lane in 1850. Beecher moved to Boston in 1851, where he collected and published some of his writings in his three-volume *Works* (1852–1853). In 1856 Beecher moved to Brooklyn, New York, to live near his son, Henry Ward Beecher, who was by this time a famous preacher himself. There Beecher died on 10 January 1863. His autobiography, published posthumously, consisted of his personal reminiscences (which he dictated to his son, Charles), letters, excerpts from his other writings and contributions from his children. In the years after his death, Beecher's memory was all but overshadowed by the fame of his talented children, including Henry Ward Beecher and Harriet Beecher *Stowe, the author of *Uncle Tom's Cabin*.

Bibliography

B. M. Cross (ed.), *The Autobiography of Lyman Beecher*, 2 vols. (Cambridge, Massachusetts: Harvard University Press, 1961); V. Harding, *A Certain Magnificence: Lyman Beecher and the Transformation of American Protestantism, 1775–1863* (Brooklyn, New York: Carlson, 1991).

D. TORBETT

■ **BELLAMY, Joseph** (1719–1790), Congregational minister, theological educator and leading New Divinity theologian, was born in Cheshire, Connecticut to a family of little means, professional status or social standing. Little is known of his early life save that he graduated from Yale College in 1735 at the age of sixteen and for the next year, through a theological apprenticeship, studied for the ministry under Jonathan *Edwards in Northampton. He was licensed to preach at eighteen and ordained at twenty-one, and he subsequently served as minister in Bethlehem for over fifty years from 1739 to the time of his death. Thus he began his ministry in the midst of evangelical revival (i.e. during the First Great Awakening of 1740) and ended it

in the midst of political upheaval and uncertainty (i.e. during the early years of the new Republic following the American Revolution). Considered one of the most gifted preachers of his day, Bellamy was thought by some to be equal in expository and rhetorical ability to George *Whitefield. His writings were also influential, especially his defence of the moral perfections of God and their relationship to the moral government of the world in *True Religion Delineated* (Boston, 1750) and his controversial *The Wisdom of God in the Permission of Sin, Vindicated* (Boston, 1769), in which he argued that God permitted sin as a necessary means of bringing about the greatest good such that the universe is 'more holy and happy than if sin and misery had never entered'. Bellamy married Frances Sherman, with whom he had eight children. He died in 1790 after an incapacitating stroke.

One of the most significant aspects of Bellamy's influence on the development of eighteenth- and early nineteenth-century American Christianity was his role as theological educator. Prior to the establishment of theological seminaries in America, apprenticeships were the common mode of theological education beyond undergraduate study. On the model of his own study with Edwards, Bellamy established a theological boarding school in his home in Bethlehem for the education of aspiring ministers. Between 1750 and 1780, his 'School of the Prophets', as it was called, combined the study of speculative divinity with practical piety and thus provided theological training for more than sixty ministers, who were eventually appointed to influential pastorates throughout Connecticut and southern New England. His students included the famous New Haven minister Jonathan Edwards, Jr, the son of his mentor, and even the infamous Aaron Burr, who later became a sceptic.

But perhaps Bellamy's greatest contribution to American religious history was his attempt, along with Samuel *Hopkins, Nathaniel Emmons and other 'New Divinity' thinkers of the 1760s and 1770s, to refashion Edwards' Calvinism into, in the words of Mark Valeri, 'a popular moral idiom' (*Law and Providence*, p. 55); this would contribute 'creatively to the single most brilliant and most continuous indigenous theological tradition that America has produced' (S. Ahlstrom, *A Religious History of the American People* [1972], p. 405). Bellamy and the New Divinity theologians went beyond Edwards by specifying the relation between providence and moral law and muted the more evangelical themes of Edwards' theology, namely the transcendence of God, the soul's union with Christ, and the inner experience of grace. These changes of emphasis in (and arguably revisions of) Edwards' theology represented accommodations to the norms of the Revolution: fairness in government and personal responsibility in citizens, which were both seen as necessary for human happiness and individual rights.

Although Bellamy clearly sought to be faithful to the experiential Calvinism that he had inherited from Edwards, he and other New Divinity theologians nevertheless opened the way for further modifications in Edwards' system during the early nineteenth century, as the Reformed tradition in America appropriated more of the voluntary, democratic spirit of the Enlightenment. Thus in attempting to defend Reformed orthodoxy from the challenges of Enlightenment rationalism and deism, Bellamy arguably adopted many of the presuppositions of his opponents and thereby inadvertently hastened the downfall of Reformed orthodoxy in New England during the nineteenth century.

Bibliography

G. Anderson, 'Joseph Bellamy (1719–1790): The Man and His Work' (PhD thesis, Boston University, 1971); *The Works of Dr. Joseph Bellamy* (New York: Garland Publishing, 1987); J. Conforti, 'Joseph Bellamy and the New Divinity Movement', *The New England Historical and Geneological Register*, 87 (1983), pp. 126–138; B. Kuklick, *Churchmen and Philosophers: From Jonathan Edwards to John Dewey* (New Haven: Yale University Press, 1985); M. Valeri, *Law and Providence in Joseph Bellamy's New England: The Origins of the New Divinity in Revolutionary America* (New York: Oxford University Press, 1994).

J. HENSLEY

■ **BENNETT, Dennis** (1917–1991), pioneer of the charismatic movement in American Protestantism, made national headlines in 1960 when he claimed to his Episcopalian congregation that he had received the spiritual experience of speaking in tongues. Moving to another parish, Bennett found himself becoming the chief spokesperson for a growing number of Protestants who were no longer willing to hide experiences that they identified as the gifts, signs and wonders of the Holy Spirit. These adherents, who were found in every Protestant denomination, formed the nucleus of the rapidly expanding charismatic movement.

Bennett was born in England on 28 October 1917 and emigrated to the United States in 1927. After earning an undergraduate degree at San Jose State University, he began theological training and graduated with a Master's degree at the University of Chicago. Ordained as a Congregational minister in 1949, Bennett served as a pastor in San Diego, California, during 1949–1950. He joined the Episcopal Church in 1951, and moved to Lancaster, California. Bennett was ordained a deacon in February 1952 and an Episcopalian priest in October 1952. He became rector of St Mark's in Van Nuys, California, in 1953.

While at St Mark's, Bennett and his wife Elberta came under the influence of certain people who claimed to have received the baptism of the Holy Spirit, evidenced by their speaking in unknown tongues. Having had the same experience, the Bennetts found fresh vitality in their Christian lives. They were motivated to share their experience with others in their congregation, and a sizeable number of members claimed to be baptized in the Spirit. As the news spread, an opposition group was formed of members embarrassed by such 'enthusiasms', who sought to suppress their expression within the church.

On 3 April 1960, in the early Sunday service, Bennett felt compelled to announce publicly to his congregation that he had spoken in tongues and had encouraged others to seek this experience. Opposition was so vocal that he made the decision to resign as rector in the eleven o'clock service that day. Strange tongues among Episcopalians proved to be newsworthy. Bennett became a national figure almost overnight as *Newsweek*, *Time* and other major news publications carried his story. Yet his future as a minister was momentarily in jeopardy.

Bennett's supervising bishop looked upon his case sympathetically. He was willing to protect Bennett's ministerial status within the Episcopalian Church, without forcing him to retract his testimony. He assigned Bennett to a new appointment as rector of a small, struggling parish near Seattle, Washington. St Luke's Episcopal Church was a congregation in desperate straits, on the brink of financial collapse. The congregation welcomed the 'notorious' Dennis Bennett as their new rector, knowing that he would be bringing with him his message of Spirit baptism. Bennett's first service at St Luke's was on 15 July 1960.

Dennis Bennett and St Luke's proved to be an ideal match. The congregation offered him acceptance and support and did not resist his vision of spiritual renewal. The majority of the church embraced the distinctive charismatic experience, and in turn ministered to the many seekers who made their way to St Luke's. Bennett had unexpectedly touched a central nerve in the Christian conscience of America; thousands of Protestants found the courage to declare openly that they had received Spirit baptism. Bennett emerged as the national spokesperson, and St Luke's the centre of attention and activity of a new movement. The charismatic movement, also known as the renewal movement, gained adherents not only from Episcopalianism, but from every Protestant denomination. St Luke's, now given a challenging new role as the centre of charismatic renewal, experienced a dramatic reversal of fortunes. Within twelve years of Bennett's arrival, it had become one of the most prosperous and dynamic Episcopal churches in the northwest.

Bennett soon found himself in demand as a speaker. Groups from both within and outside Episcopalianism wanted to hear his story. As early as 1961 he sensed a call to travel and share his message. Entering into a new era of growth and hope, St Luke's was willing to share the services of their pastor as a part of their mission of outreach. Yet in the midst of exciting ministry that was helping to promote an emerging Protestant renewal movement, tragedy struck the Bennett household. Bennett's faithful companion, Elberta,

succumbed to cancer in 1963. She left behind three children as well as her husband.

Bennett poured himself into ministry, travelling extensively throughout the United States and abroad. In 1966 he married Rita Reed, who joined him at St Luke's. Rita's previous ministry experience was well suited to Bennett's role as a speaker. Their communication styles complemented each other, and they increasingly ministered together, both as speakers and as writers. In 1968 they formed the Christian Renewal Association, and after Bennett's retirement from the rectorship of St Luke's in 1981 they devoted themselves to it full time for the next ten years, conducting conferences and seminars and writing books and articles as the charismatic movement continued to thrive.

Bennett's most compelling book proved to be *Nine O'clock in the Morning*. Rita collaborated with him in the writing of *The Holy Spirit and You* (1971), an immensely popular book. She has also written her own books. Their ministry together ended on 1 November 1991, when Bennett died. Rita maintains the ministry of Christian Renewal Association, serving as president. She has defined the organization's mission: 'to bring emotional, spiritual and physical wholeness to those in need'. Her two most recent books, *You Can Be Emotionally Free* and *To Heaven and Back*, have been major bestsellers.

Bibliography

D. Bennett, *Nine O'Clock in the Morning* (Plainfield: Logos International, 1970); D. and R. Bennett, *The Holy Spirit and You* (Plainfield: Logos International, 1971); D. and R. Bennett, *Trinity of Man* (Plainfield: Logos International, 1979).

D. W. DORRIES

■ **BERKHOF, Louis** (1873–1957), Reformed theologian, was born in Emmen, the Netherlands, in 1873 to parents who were members of the Christelijke Gereformeerde (the body which had broken with the state-supported Reformed Church in the Netherlands and was related to the Christian Reformed Church in America). In 1882 he emigrated with his parents to Grand Rapids, Michigan, where he lived most of the rest of his life. Some time in 1893 he publicly professed his faith in Christ in the Alpine Avenue Christian Reformed Church.

Also in 1893, Berkhof began studies at the Theological School of the Christian Reformed Church (later Calvin College and Calvin Theological Seminary). After graduation in 1900, he was ordained in the Christian Reformed Church and became pastor of the church in Allendale, Michigan. Two years later, he entered Princeton Theological Seminary and, after earning his BD in 1904, returned to Grand Rapids as pastor of Oakdale Park Church. While at Oakdale Park, he also took some courses, primarily in philosophy, by correspondence through the University of Chicago.

In 1906 Berkhof began a thirty-eight-year teaching career at Calvin Theological Seminary. Appointed first as Professor of Exegetical Theology, Berkhof taught all biblical courses from 1906 to 1914. In 1914, when the department was divided into Old Testament and New Testament, he moved to an exclusive focus on the latter.

In the early part of his career Berkhof came to play an important part in two notable controversies. In 1917 H. Bultema, a Christian Reformed minister, published *Maranatha: A Study Concerning Unfulfilled Prophecy*, in which he argued for literal interpretation of biblical prophecy and defended dispensational premillennialism. Berkhof responded with admiration for the respect for Scripture that Bultema and others displayed, but he went on to argue that such an interpretation neither understood prophecy rightly nor did justice to the evidence of Scripture itself. Berkhof's view was eventually upheld by a decision of a church synod.

Then, in 1919, Berkhof was involved in initiating events that led to a new controversy. Along with three of his colleagues Berkhof wrote a letter questioning the teachings of fellow professor R. Janssen, charging that, by his acquiesence to modern criticism, Janssen had set himself at odds with principles of scriptural authority and infallibility. Following up on these accusations, a church synod deposed Janssen from his teaching position. The Janssenist controversy represents the issues that came to concern Berkhof most. The second half of his career was marked by consistent efforts to oppose reliance on

autonomous human reason and other tendencies of Modernism which Berkhof saw coming to hold sway.

From 1926 Berkhof continued his teaching career at Calvin as Professor of Dogmatic [systematic] Theology. He also served as Calvin's first president from 1931 until his retirement in 1944. When Berkhof died on 18 May 1957, he was still writing regularly on church doctrine for publications of the Christian Reformed Church.

In 1924 the language of instruction at Calvin Seminary was changed from Dutch to English, both languages in which Berkhof was thoroughly fluent. This transition, and the ease with which Berkhof made it, could perhaps be considered symbolic of his entire career. Berkhof was an outstandingly articulate voice among many who, deeply committed to their heritage of Dutch Reformed faith, sought, in the cultural and religious context of America, to make known the riches it contained. This transmission of the Reformed tradition to new generations is certainly his greatest accomplishment. He is not known for creative or innovative work; his goal was rather to preserve and hand on a classic Calvinistic formulation of theology in the tradition of A. *Kuyper, G. Vos, C. *Hodge and, especially, H. *Bavinck, whose work he closely followed. His work bears the mark of essential Reformed doctrines: the sovereignty of God and the need for an obedient response from humanity, with the Bible serving as the infallible guide for faith. To this task of exposition he brought an unusual gift for careful analysis and clear presentation. He is the single most influential theologian within the Christian Reformed Church, having trained virtually all its ministers over a period of nearly forty years.

In the early part of his career, Berkhof wrote on cultural issues, calling the church to remember not only its responsibility in spiritual matters, but also its rightful role in social reform. Later, however, he showed greater concern for the way in which social concerns were displacing theological ones. A man of faith as well as a scholar, Berkhof has been described as 'a fusion of simple piety, a high theology, and an unswerving devotion to the Reformed faith'.

Berkhof was a highly prolific author. Indeed, a full bibliography of his writings runs over fifty pages. His *Systematic Theology* is his most significant work. First published in 1932 as a collection of class lectures under the title *Reformed Dogmatics*, it was later revised, expanded and published under its new title in 1938. It has been widely used in theological seminaries and Bible institutes in North America, and has earned Berkhof international recognition as a Reformed theologian. To his *Systematic Theology*, Berkhof added an *Introductory Volume to Systematic Theology* in 1932 and, in 1937, *The History of Christian Doctrine*, which traced the development of Christian doctrine from the patrisitic to the modern period. His other significant works include *New Testament Introduction* (1915), *The Assurance of Faith* (1928), *Introductory Volume to Reformed Dogmatics* (1933), *The Vicarious Atonement through Christ* (1937), *Recent Trends in Theology* (1944), *Riches of Divine Grace* (a collection of sermons, 1948), *Principles of Biblical Interpretation* (1950), *The Kingdom of God* (1951), *Aspects of Liberalism* (1951) and *The Second Coming of Christ* (1953).

Bibliography
D. F. Wells (ed.), *Reformed Theology in America* (Grand Rapids: Baker Book House, 1997).

H. TAYLOR COOLMAN

■ **BERKOUWER, Gerrit Cornelis** (1903–1996), Dutch Reformed theologian, was one of the most influential voices in twentieth-century evangelical theology, due to his irenic temperament and openness to new currents in the life of the church and contemporary society. As his major works were quickly translated into English, his influence was felt in both Europe and North America.

Berkouwer was born in Amsterdam on 8 June 1903 to devout Dutch Reformed parents. After completing his secondary school education, he attended Abraham *Kuyper's Free University of Amsterdam, beginning his theological studies in 1922. Kuyper, the major force behind Dutch Neo-Calvinism, died in 1920, and his colleague, the great theologian Herman *Bavinck, died only a year later. With these two giants gone, a struggle ensued for the soul of the Reformed Churches. Younger theologians and clergy

pleaded, on the basis of Bavinck's irenicism and openness, for a new engagement with modern culture, particularly on questions of science and creation. The decade following Kuyper and Bavinck's death was one of considerable turmoil as the church wrestled with these issues at its synodical gatherings. The polemical and contentious character of the decade of Berkouwer's maturing as a theologian may have contributed to his lifelong passion for mediating in conflicts between people and theological ideas.

Also in 1922 Karl Barth published the influential second edition of his *Römerbrief*. Along with Roman Catholic theology, Barth's theology would become Berkouwer's conversation partner in his own theological pilgrimage. Though Berkouwer shared with Barth a profound distaste for the traditional, scholastic Roman Catholic notion of *analogia entis* and its derivative, natural theology, he was initially critical of Barth. But his affinity for key Barthian themes is reflected in the title of his definitive work on Barth, *The Triumph of Grace in the Theology of Karl Barth* (1954; ET 1956). For Berkouwer as for Barth, the mystery of God is never accessible to us by our own reaching into heaven through philosophy but always and only through God's merciful revelation to us in Christ as it is appropriated in faith.

After completing his dissertation on 'Faith and Revelation in the Newer German Theology' in 1932, Berkouwer became involved in pastoral work and also published several monographs, mainly on the themes of Scripture and revelation (e.g. *The Problem of Scripture Criticism*, 1938). He was appointed to the Faculty of Theology at the Free University in 1945. Berkouwer's pastoral work profoundly affected the method and content of his later dogmatic writings.

Berkouwer explicitly sets aside the philosophical, scholastic method in favour of a biblical, pastoral one. Though he did not include a theological prolegomena in the eighteen volumes of his *magnum opus*, *Dogmatic Studies*, his theological method can be discerned inductively. Berkouwer's approach to doctrine can be described as 'biblical-inductive'; he claims to have learned it from *Calvin. Like Calvin, Berkouwer is opposed to all speculation about God's essence, 'which we ought more to adore than meticulously to search out' (Calvin, *Inst.* 1.5.9). His biblical motto is 1 Corinthians 4:6, 'Do not go beyond what is written.' Berkouwer's emphasis on biblical rather than systematic theology is motivated in large part by his negative attitude to the Dutch Reformed theological tradition he inherited. He judges it to be scholastic, abstract and (very importantly) of little use for preaching and pastoral care.

Theology, in Berkouwer's view, must be restricted to truth directly appropriated from Scripture as it is received in faith. This conviction issues in the method called correlation. The first three volumes of Berkouwer's *Dogmatic Studies* (1949) were entitled *Faith and Justification* (ET 1954), *Faith and Sanctification* (ET 1952) and *Faith and Perseverance* (ET 1973). For Berkouwer the truth of a Christian doctrine is inseparable from its being appropriated in faith by the believer. True doctrine must be believed, and it must be preachable.

This emphasis on the existential character of doctrinal truth was influential in the Dutch Reformed Church. The Gereformeerde Kerken in Nederland adopted a relational view of scriptural truth in its controversial 1979 report *God met Ons* ('God with Us'). It is here, in Berkouwer's lifelong effort to move beyond the traditional, formal understanding of Scripture's authority ('It is true because God said so') to a more material one, focusing on the content of Scripture as God's saving revelation in Christ, that we find his most important substantive contribution to evangelical theology. In the English-speaking world this approach was utilized by Jack B. Rogers (a student of Berkouwer) and Donald K. McKim in their influential *The Authority and Interpretation of the Bible* (1979) and played a significant role in the debates over inerrancy among American evangelicals in the 1980s.

Berkouwer's approach to theology can also be stated in terms of the relation between subject and object. Berkouwer, from the beginning, consciously sought to overcome what he judged to be the false polarity between an objective theological approach (based on the formal authority of Scripture) and a subjective one (based on faith experience). Drawing on the opening chapters of Calvin's *Institutes* (which discuss the relation between knowledge of God and self-knowledge), Berkouwer sought to overcome the subject–object dichotomy by focusing on the relation between God and humanity, revelation and faith. This correlative method, Berkouwer believed, would result in a theology that was biblical, preachable and believable.

The implications of this approach can be seen in Berkouwer's reinterpretation of Reformed doctrine in his *Divine Election* (1955; ET 1960). Judging the traditional, scholastic Reformed system to be an abstract and static decretal theology, Berkouwer's study of Romans 9 – 11 led him to a revisionist reading of the apostle Paul. For Berkouwer, the key phrase for understanding Paul's doctrine of election is in Romans 9:11–12: 'God's purpose of election ... *by his call*'. Divine election is realized through preaching. God's electing work belongs to his mission of mercy to save. Election reveals the sovereign, merciful heart of God. Election should not generate speculation about the numbers of elect and reprobate but a doxology to the sovereign God (Rom. 11:33–36). The truth of the doctrine of election can be grasped only by a believing theologian in faith.

Responses to Berkouwer's 'new' way of doing theology have been mixed. Many of his doctoral students have gone on to significant teaching posts in Reformed and evangelical institutions and continued in the anti-scholastic trajectory he helped to initiate. But critics are not sure whether Berkouwer's efforts to transcend key scholastic distinctions clarify difficult theological issues or obscure them by eliminating useful categories. In particular, Berkouwer's rejection of the biblical realist notion of truth in favour of an existential view is seen by many as problematic. Recent scholarship has also defended Protestant scholastic theology against the charge that it is unbiblical, unprofitable, impersonal and abstract. It has argued that Reformed scholastic theologians such as Gijsbertus Voetius and Wilhelm à Brakel were as concerned about piety as they were about orthodox doctrine and that their theology reflects this dual concern.

Bibliography
L. B. Smedes, 'G. C. Berkouwer', in P. E.

Hughes (ed.), *Creative Minds in Contemporary Theology* (Grand Rapids: Eerdmans, 1966), pp. 93–98.

J. BOLT

■ **BEZA, Theodore** (1519–1605), French Reformed theologian, successor to *Calvin at Geneva, was born at Vezelay in Burgundy to a family of the lesser nobility. Beza learned Greek and Latin from Melchior Wolmar, who was sympathetic to the Reformation and also taught Calvin. From 1534 he studied law in Orleans; he received a licentiateship in 1539 and moved to Paris to practise. However, his interests were more literary, and he started to write poetry. He had an affinity for the classics but was also attracted to the teachings of the Reformation. In 1548 he published a book of poems, which later he revised and reissued, since the first edition contained a number of items he regretted having included.

Against the strong wishes of his family for him to be ordained, Beza privately married Claudine Desnoz. Following a grave illness in 1548 he renounced Catholicism, becoming a Protestant. He went to Geneva, making his marriage to Claudine public. In his absence, he was condemned by the Parlement of Paris and burned in effigy in 1550.

At the instigation of Pierre Viret, Beza was appointed Professor of Greek in the academy at Lausanne, staying there until 1558. During this time be became rector. He taught and wrote extensively. He defended Calvin in the Bolsec controversy on predestination, which generated his first theological work, *Tabula praedestinationis* (ET *The sum of all Christianity*) (1555). More rigorously logical than Calvin's work, it traced the order of the causes of salvation and damnation in a table, with double predestination as the source of all that followed. Beza also defended Calvin after the execution of Servetus. In 1556 he published an annotated edition of the Greek New Testament. In 1558 he issued his *Annotations on the New Testament*, followed by the Geneva Bible (in 1560) and his *Confession de la foi chrétienne* (*Confession of the Christian faith*).

On Calvin's invitation, Beza moved to Geneva in 1558 as Professor of Greek. Rector from 1559 to 1563, he eventually taught theology in the Genevan academy from 1559 to 1599. There he began to complete Clement Marot's translation of the Psalms into French. He represented the French Protestants at the Colloquies of Poissy in 1561 and Saint-Germain in 1562. He continued to give support to the Huguenots and their leader Gaspard de Coligny during the wars of religion in France (1564–1572), attending the Synod of La Rochelle in 1571.

On Calvin's death in 1564, the main burden of responsibility in Geneva fell on Beza. Besides being the head of the academy and teaching there, he was moderator of the company of pastors until 1580, and the main pastor until shortly before his death. He strongly influenced the Genevan magistrates, helping to preserve a delicate balance of power between church and civil authorities, so avoiding Erastian control of the church. He was also a major spokesman of Reformed Protestantism as a whole. He published the first edition of his *Life of Calvin* in 1564.

Beza had a wide range of interests. His textual scholarship was seen at its best in his 1565 Greek text of the New Testament, which included the Vulgate and his own translation. It was the best Greek text available at the time. Beza used the Codex Bezae and Codex Claromontanus. Continuing his active concern for the Huguenots after the St Bartholomew's Day massacre (1572), he wrote *Du droit des magistrats sur leurs subjects* (*The right of magistrates over their subjects*) in 1574, arguing for the right of lesser magistrates to revolt. Since all political authority comes from God through election by the people, the people may revolt against tyrants under the leadership of their elected magistrates, not simply those of royal blood as some had suggested hitherto. This work was an important contribution to political theory. Beza's other publications included *Quaestionum et responsionum Christianorum libellus* (*Book of Christian questions and answers*) (1570/1576) and a history of the Reformed movement in France (1580). In 1586 he was a chief figure at the Colloquy of Montbéliard, disputing with the Lutheran Jakob Andreae in an attempt to resolve the increasingly acrimonious divisions between the two traditions on the Lord's Supper. Here his belief in limited (definite or effective) atonement was made clear, but in the debate he was more moderate and irenical than Andreae. The colloquy failed in its aim, and the division remained a serious problem for Protestantism. Despite this failure, Beza continued to seek reconciliation with the Lutherans.

Beza consolidated the theology of Geneva in the generation or so after the death of Calvin. A vigorous defender of double predestination, he consolidated and strengthened the movement and prepared the way for the development of Reformed scholasticism. A clear supralapsarian, he made a sharp distinction between the decree of election and its execution, which affected the rest of his theology, including his view of the church and sacraments. He was faithful to Calvin's doctrine of the sacraments.

Beza's influence was felt throughout Europe through personal contact, his writings, his correspondence, and those he taught. He wrote dozens of theological works, which had a profound impact, partly because of his literary gifts. His influence was evident in England, where many of his works were available in the late sixteenth and early seventeenth centuries. His chart of the order of causes of salvation and damnation was adopted and adapted by the leading Puritan William *Perkins, who opposed *Arminius, another of Beza's students. Beza's 1565 New Testament, the best text available at the time, was dedicated to Queen Elizabeth. He requested Elizabeth to come to the aid of Huguenot refugees when Geneva was unable fully to cope with the consequences of drought and famine. The Geneva Bible was the preferred choice of many English Puritans. Beza sent his Codex Bezae, one of the earliest extant texts of the New Testament, to Cambridge University in 1581. His New Testament textual work was important in the development of textual criticism, eventually influencing the Authorized Version of 1611. His works were published in English, French and Latin, having a powerful impact in the second half of the sixteenth century. His completion of Marot's translation of the Psalms was important in the development of Reformed psalmody.

Interpretation of Beza has been varied. Heinrich Heppe in the nineteenth century, and Hans-Emil Weber, Walter Kickel, Brian Armstrong and R. T. Kendall in the twenti-

eth, all argued that he replaced Calvin's biblical and dynamic theology by a logical system based on Aristotelian philosophy and ecclesiastical authority. Richard A. Muller, Jill Raitt and others have revised this assessment. Despite obvious differences, underlying continuities run deeper. Calvin also used Aristotelian logic and ecclesiastical authorities. Beza's Reformed contemporaries, Calvin included, saw him as a colleague, not a competitor. His particular theological foci were set within a commitment to the Reformed faith, while his humanist, biblical and textual interests belie the idea of a radical departure from his predecessor's theology.

Bibliography

P.-F. Geisendorf, *Theodore de Bèze* (Geneva: Alexandre Jullien, 1967); W. Kickel, *Vernunft und offenbarung bei Theodor Beza: zum problem des verhaltnisses von theologie, philosophie und staat* (Neukirchen-Vluyn: Neukirchener Verlag des Erziehungsvereins, 1967); R. Letham, 'Theodore Beza: a reassessment', *SJT* 40 (1987), pp. 25–40; J. Raitt, *The Colloquy of Montbéliard* (New York: Oxford University Press, 1992).

R. W. A. LETHAM

■ **BICKERSTETH, Edward** (1786–1850), Anglican clergyman and missionary apologist, was born in Kirkby Lonsdale, Westmoreland, on 19 March 1786, the fourth son of Henry and Elizabeth Bickersteth. He was educated at the local grammar school and in 1801 joined his brother in London. At first he was employed as a clerk in the Post Office, then as an articled clerk in a solicitor's office. He was hard working and his employer commended his diligence.

From 1804 he took his religion seriously, kept a spiritual journal and became active in good works. By 1807 he had been converted. In April 1811 Bickersteth moved to Surrey Street, Norwich, and entered into partnership as a solicitor with Thomas Bignold, and in the following month he married Bignold's sister, Sarah. Throughout their marriage their home was simple and pious. They had a family of six children (two others were stillborn), and for a time two nieces also lived with them. Their only son, Edward Henry, became a well-known hymn-writer and was Bishop of

Exeter from 1885 to 1900. Their eldest daughter, Elizabeth Sarah, married the Revd T. R. *Birks, who was Bickersteth's curate and after his death his biographer. Subsequent generations of the Bickersteth family became church leaders and missionaries.

Besides working as a solicitor, Bickersteth spent much of his time reading theology and involved in Christian activity in Norwich. It was hard going, and he reported that 'All are alive to worldly things here, while religion meets either with opposition or a most cold and heartless reception.' But in September 1813 he helped to establish the Norfolk and Norwich Church Missionary Association. He became the lay secretary, and his brother-in-law and partner became the treasurer. Bickersteth discussed his future with the Revd Josiah Pratt, the secretary of the Church Missionary Society (CMS). Pratt encouraged Bickersteth to work for the Society and to seek ordination. Although he had no degree or title for orders, Bickersteth was accepted for ordination by the Bishop of Norwich, who ordained him deacon on 10 December 1815; he was ordained priest by the Bishop of Gloucester on 21 December. In January 1816 he sailed to West Africa and inspected the small CMS mission in Sierra Leone, and his findings were published as an appendix to the sixteenth annual report of the Society. While he was there he admitted six African boys to communion, one of whom returned with him to England. In August 1816 Bickersteth and his family moved into the headquarters of CMS at 14 Salisbury Square, London. Between 1816 and 1830 he was a clerical secretary of the Society and responsible for the organization and visitation of local associations. He spent much of his time away from London and spoke on behalf of the Society throughout the United Kingdom, speaking on the theme of mission in upwards of 900 churches. The growth and development of CMS during this period was due mainly to Bickersteth's activity. He was also responsible for the training of the Society's missionaries, first at Salisbury Square, then from 1820 at a larger house in Barnsbury Park, Islington. He was also the afternoon preacher at Wheler Chapel, Spitalfields, and for twelve months the minister of the chapel. During this period of his ministry the congregation increased and people were converted.

In 1830 Bickersteth succeeded William Dealtry as the Rector of Watton, a small rural parish of about 800 people, five miles from Hertford. For the next twenty years he continued to speak as a deputation speaker for CMS and for many other evangelical societies. He was an able and effective preacher and often spoke at the annual 'May' meetings in Exeter Hall, London. He preached the annual sermon for CMS in 1832 and one of the five jubilee sermons in 1848. Of the four-day jubilee celebration he said, 'It was really heaven upon earth.' He supported both the British and Foreign Bible Society (and opposed the involvement of Unitarians) and the Trinitarian Bible Society. He was generous in his outlook towards other denominations and deplored the divisions within Protestantism; he believed that its differences were in externals, not in matters of faith. 'I dislike any party feeling,' he said and made clear his view that 'The Church of England is not the whole Church of Christ in England.' He was involved with the foundation and leadership of the Evangelical Alliance, which promoted both evangelical unity and opposition to Roman Catholicism. Bickersteth was a staunch Protestant who opposed the teaching of the Oxford Movement in England and supported the minority Anglican Church in Ireland. He was against the government grant given to support the training of Roman Catholic priests at Maynooth College and was involved with the formation of the Society for Irish Church Missions.

Throughout his life Bickersteth was an avid reader; he had a library of nearly 11,000 books. His literary output was considerable, and after his death a cheap edition of his works was published in sixteen volumes. Much of his writing was popular and pious, and he produced thousands of tracts. From 1832 Bickersteth edited the *Christian Family Library* and compiled the *Christian Psalmody* (1833, enlarged 1841). This book, which included eight of his own hymns, has been described as having 'had a most powerful and lasting influence upon the hymnody of the Church of England'. It became the basis for his poet-son's widely used *Hymnal Companion to the Book of Common Prayer* (1870, revised 1876). Edward Bickersteth's other publications were polemical, or concerned with the interpretation and fulfilment of biblical prophecy. Like his friend Lord Shaftesbury, he became a convinced pre-millennialist. 'My conviction increases', he said, 'that Christ's coming is at hand.' This belief strengthened his support for the evangelization of the Jews and the establishment of an Anglican bishopric in Jerusalem. He was an early supporter of the London Society for Promoting Christianity amongst the Jews, frequently spoke at its annual meetings and in 1834 preached the annual sermon. From 1836 he edited *The Testimony of the Reformers*, and four years later was involved with the formation of the Parker Society, which republished the works of the English Reformers.

In 1841 he suffered a mild stroke, and five years later was seriously injured after being thrown from his carriage. After his recovery his literary and deputation work continued unabated. He suffered another stroke in 1850 and died at his home at Watton on 28 February 1850.

Bibliography

T. R. Birks, *Memoir of the Rev. Edward Bickersteth*, 2 vols. (London: Seeleys, 1852); M. Hennell, *Sons of the Prophets* (London: SPCK, 1979), pp. 29–49; F. K. Aglionby, *The Life of Edward Henry Bickersteth* (London: Longmans, 1907).

A. F. MUNDEN

■ **BINGHAM, Rowland V.** (1872–1942), Canadian missionary statesman and evangelical entrepreneur, was born in East Grinstead in the county of Sussex, amid the beautiful countryside of south-eastern England. He grew up in Headcorn in Kent, where his father had relocated his modest construction business. His father's premature passing and deathbed call to his children to seek salvation added a note of solemnity to the spirit of the boy. He became a pupil teacher at the age of thirteen, and within a short period of time was converted through the joyful testimony of a group of young Salvation Army cadets. Discipled in the Army in its early years, he was never to lose its emphasis on the primacy of evangelistic outreach in Christian ministry. At the age of sixteen he left for Canada, becoming a Salvation Army officer in Toronto, which would be his home base

throughout the rest of his life. After a couple of years he found the Army too restrictive, becoming involved, as a result, with the nascent Christian and Missionary Alliance.

Bingham was introduced to the Alliance as assistant to John Salmon, an Englishman who was engaged in planting the first congregation of the new denomination in Toronto. Salmon had a peripatetic ministerial career, moving from the Methodists to the Congregationalists, then to the Baptists and finally to the Alliance, but these peregrinations evidenced not so much instability of character as an unremitting hunger for God's best. It was Salmon who taught Bingham that an essential element of Christian spirituality involved believing the promises that God had made in the Bible, seeking to act upon them, and thus inevitably being involved in spiritual warfare with satanic and demonic forces. Through this teaching another indispensable element was added to Bingham's life and ministry. Although he highly esteemed the Alliance for its missionary vision, he did not throw in his lot with them, believing rather that he should strike out on his own in missionary endeavour.

In the 1890s Toronto was sometimes called the 'missionary capital of the world', because in its Christian population there existed a large measure of missionary interest and enthusiasm. In this setting Bingham readily found two willing associates and naively assumed that financial support would follow. In 1893, while still only twenty years of age, he travelled to Nigeria with his colleagues, determined to penetrate the northern part of the country with its great Islamic centres, its areas of animistic strength and its malarial climate. By late 1894 his two friends were dead, and he had returned home with malaria; yet like his model William *Carey, he determined to persevere. He took some medical training in a hospital in Cleveland, studied at the Alliance Bible School in New York, engaged in pastoral work and married Helen Blair, from an Ontario family, who shared his missionary commitment. During this time he sought to organize a missionary society with a board of directors, raise funds and secure recruits. In 1900 Bingham returned to Nigeria with two new recruits, where almost immediately upon arrival he contracted malaria again and was invalided home, with his two associates following on the next boat. These sufferings did not overwhelm Bingham but served to make him a remarkably mature young leader.

Back in Canada, while still in his twenties, Bingham began to display many of the characteristics of strong leadership. He was a man of vision, expressed in the title of the missionary organization which he founded, the Sudan Interior Mission (SIM). This title referred not to one country in north-eastern Africa but to the whole sub-Saharan area, sometimes called the Sahel, for which northern Nigeria was the most accessible sector and could be the doorway. As with most people of vision, Bingham had a magnetism which attracted some very capable people, particularly in the pioneer days. Among these were A. W. Banfield, who became a famous linguist; Andrew Stirrett, who gave up his thriving pharmaceutical business, turned his financial portfolio over to the Mission and became a medical doctor; Guy Playfair, a promising young Manitoba athlete; the irrepressible 'Tommy' Titcombe, who with almost no official qualifications entered the most dangerous places with phenomenal success; and Dr Thomas Lambie, who entered southern Ethiopia with Bingham in 1927. Bingham also had great administrative abilities, which enabled him to develop strong home bases in many Western countries and at the same time, through his constant international travels, to maintain necessary standards on the mission fields. A man of boundless faith and seemingly limitless energy, Bingham also had the capacity to go on learning; after a number of years of concentration on evangelism, he was persuaded of the need for education and set about organizing an inspiring array of institutions.

The motto of Carey, 'Attempt great things for God and expect great things from God', was ever before Bingham, and he saw SIM grow into one of the largest interdenominational 'faith' missions. After his death it actually became the largest of such missions, making it one of the greatest Christian missionary agencies. Although the SIM had difficulties with indigenization, as did most missionary societies, it gradually grew in understanding and worked its way through them, producing effective African denominations and congregations, including the Evangelical Church of West Africa, centred in Nigeria, and a dynamic Ethiopian church with several million members and adherents. In the latter part of the twentieth century the Mission became known as SIM-International, linking itself in a global structure with a mission in Latin America.

Among Bingham's other ventures was the founding, in Toronto in 1904, of the monthly magazine *The Evangelical Christian*, which contained a broad range of missionary articles, devotional material and Christian news. For six decades it was the major interdenominational Christian magazine in Canada. He established the Evangelical Publishers bookshop, with its large premises in the heart of Toronto on the major financial artery of Bay Street, and Canadian Keswick, a summer Christian conference centre with its own buildings situated in the beautiful Muskoka country of rocks, lakes and fir trees. Early in the Second World War Bingham established the Soldiers' and Airmen's Christian Association, patterned on British models of which he knew. Its friendly urban centres, situated as near as possible to Canada's major military installations, provided a healthy atmosphere, a place of encouragement and a locus of evangelism. In 1928, when speaking at the Cambridge Inter-Collegiate Christian Union and being impressed with what the Inter-Varsity Fellowship was accomplishing throughout the British universities, Bingham urged the students to send someone on a similar mission to Canada. When he arrived home he wrote an article in *The Evangelical Christian* describing what was taking place in the British universities and urging Canadian Christian students to engage in the same work. Howard Guinness arrived as representative of the British student movement that autumn and established Inter-Varsity in Canada.

Bibliography

J. H. Hunter, *A Flame of Fire: The Life and Work of R. V. Bingham* (Toronto: Sudan Interior Mission, 1961); B. A. McKenzie, 'Fundamentalism, Christian Unity, and Premillennialism in the Thought of Rowland Victor Bingham (1872–1942): A Study of Anti-Modernism in Canada' (PhD thesis, University of Toronto, 1985); L. Reynolds, *Footprints: The Beginnings of the Christian* and Missionary Alliance in Canada (Toronto: Christian and Missionary Alliance, 1982).

I. S. RENNIE

■ **BIRKS, Thomas Rawson** (1810–1883), Anglican clergyman, was born on 28 September 1810 in Staveley, Derbyshire, the son of Thomas and Sarah Birks. His father was a farmer, and the family were Congregationalists. Birks was educated at nearby Chesterfield, then at the Nonconformist Mill Hill School, Middlesex. He entered Trinity School, Cambridge, where he obtained numerous prizes, and as a student taught in the Jesus Lane Sunday School. In 1834 he graduated BA (MA in 1837) and became a member of the Church of England and a fellow of Trinity College. He was ordained deacon in 1837 and priest in 1841.

Between 1837 and 1844 Birks was the curate of Edward *Bickersteth at Watton, Hertfordshire. While in the small country parish he continued his theological studies, during which he adopted premillennialist views; in due course he wrote over fifteen works on prophecy. On leaving Watton, Birks published ten parting sermons. The following year he married the rector's eldest daughter, Elizabeth ('Bessie') Sarah Bickersteth (d. 1856), and they had a family of eight children, two of whom died in infancy. Two years after Bickersteth's death Birks published his father-in-law's biography (1852).

From 1844 Birks was the rector of the small rural parish of Kelshall, Hertfordshire. (Between 1914 and 1923 his son, Edward Bickersteth Birks, was the incumbent of the same parish.) For the next twenty-two years Birks continued to write, publishing about fifty works. They included editions of William Paley's *Evidences of Christianity* (1848) and *Horae Paulinae* (1850), and his own *Horae Apostolicae and Horae Evangelicae* (1852). In 1853 Birks published two lectures, *Modern Rationalism* and *The Inspiration of the Scriptures*, in which he rejected dogmatic inerrancy and declared, 'The Bible ... is the Word of the living God.' He became involved in some of the contentious theological issues of the day. He responded to *Essays and Reviews* in *The Bible and Modern Thought* (1861), and he replied to Bishop Colenso's arithmetical work of biblical criticism on the Pentateuch in *The Exodus of Israel: Its Difficulties Examined, and Its Faith Confirmed* (1863). Birks's convictions about prophecy led him to stress the importance of studying the Old Testament and to claim, 'Our faith as Christians, our message as preachers, must begin with Genesis and not with St Matthew.' Like his father-in-law, Birks supported the principle of evangelical unity, and from 1850 he was the honorary secretary of the Evangelical Alliance. Twenty years later his views on hell proved unacceptable to the EA, and he resigned his office, but not his membership. Birks was also in demand as a preacher and speaker. In 1852 he preached the annual sermon for the London Society for Promoting Christianity Amongst the Jews, and he delivered a number of lectures to the annual premillennial gathering held at St George's, Bloomsbury, London. His link with the rector, H. M. Villiers, continued, and when Villiers became the Bishop of Durham (on his translation from Carlisle), Birks became his examining chaplain. Unfortunately, Villiers died a year after his appointment. In 1861 Birks preached the annual sermon for the Church Pastoral Aid Society. In it he condemned a gospel which made 'religion wholly a private affair for the conscience and the closet, instead of proclaiming the authority of the true King over every faculty of the human mind ... over nations and kingdoms' and the whole earth. Birks supported the main evangelical societies. He was deeply critical of Roman Catholicism and published a number of works on Protestantism, and he was a vice-president of the militant Church Association. He was critical too of what he called the 'gross fallacy' of the Revised Code, in which payment by results became the practice in those day schools to which a government grant was paid. The national protests delayed the legislation, and Birks published three works against the code.

In 1866 Birks succeeded Charles Clayton as the vicar of Holy Trinity, Cambridge, and married a widow, Georgina Agnes Douglas, at Christ Church, Clifton, Bristol. In 1867 and 1868 he was a theological examiner at the University of Cambridge, a member of the board of theological studies and a frequent preacher before the university. In 1871 Birks became a canon of Ely Cathedral, and in the following year was the conservative successor of F. D. Maurice as the Knightbridge Professor of Casuistry, Moral Theology and Moral Philosophy at Cambridge. He published his inaugural lecture as *The Present Importance of Moral Science* (1872) and also several of his lectures on moral science. Meanwhile, he continued his biblical studies and in 1871 published a *Commentary of the Book of Isaiah*. In the 1870s he was involved in a number of evangelical initiatives in Cambridge. In 1875 a meeting took place at Holy Trinity vicarage at which plans were made to establish an evangelical theological college in Cambridge (opened six years later as Ridley Hall). Birks was at Holy Trinity when the Cambridge Inter-Collegiate Christian Union began in 1877, and two years later he became a member of the Cambridge University Prayer Union. He and his wife were known for their hospitality to undergraduates, and he continued the tradition of his predecessors by delivering Bible studies to students. Alongside his academic works he wrote about a hundred hymns. He suffered a mild stroke in 1875, and after a second stroke in 1877 he resigned from Holy Trinity.

The historian of the Church Missionary Society, Eugene Stock, described Birks as 'one of the most learned and thoughtful of Evangelical leaders', and his brother-in-law, Bishop E. H. Bickersteth, said, 'I shall always esteem him as one of the most original and clear-sighted thinkers of the Church of England.' Birks was debilitated by a third stroke in 1880 and died in Cambridge on 19 July 1883.

Bibliography
F. W. B. Bullock, *The History of Ridley Hall Cambridge* (Cambridge: Council of Ridley Hall, 1941); I. Randall and D. Hilborn, *One Body in Christ: The History and Significance of the Evangelical Alliance* (Carlisle: Paternoster Press, 2001).

A. F. MUNDEN

■ **BLAIKLOCK, Edward Musgrave** (1903–1983), classicist, was born on 6 July 1903, the son of an artisan, in Birmingham, England. Edward (Ted) Blaiklock emigrated with his family to Auckland, New Zealand, in 1909. The family purchased a small farm at Titirangi, in a dramatically beautiful setting on the fringes of the small city. As a schoolboy Ted became a keen naturalist as well as a lover of books, to which his family, who were committed to self-improvement, gave him ready access. At the age of thirteen he won a Junior National Scholarship and a place in the academically oriented Auckland Grammar School. In 1920 the family experienced a financial crisis precipitated by the post-war depression, and their farm had to be sold; Blaiklock became a pupil teacher instead of going to university.

Blaiklock was converted in May 1921 through the preaching of J. W. *Kemp, the new pastor of the Auckland Baptist Tabernacle, who had ministerial experience in prominent Scottish and American churches. He trained as a teacher and engaged in part-time study at university. He married Kathleen Mitchell on 13 November 1928; they had two sons, David and John. Blaiklock began to work as a primary school teacher, but then visited Europe for a year before accepting an appointment to teach Latin and French at Mount Albert Grammar School. Meanwhile, he studied Latin and French and acquired two MA degrees under A. C. Paterson and the famous Ronald Syme, and developed a deep interest in classical history and archaeology.

Blaiklock was appointed a lecturer at Auckland University College in 1927, declining an overseas scholarship. He was grieved not to be appointed as Professor of Classics in 1933, although in 1939 he was placed in charge of the Greek course, following complaints about the deficiencies of the professor, Charles Cooper. At last, honoured with a DLitt. for his thesis on Euripides, he was appointed professor late in 1947. He became a great figure in Auckland as the symbol of protest against modern life, particularly in battles within the faculty of arts. No administrator, he was essentially a teacher and scholar and was old-fashioned in his approach to learning. In the 1960s he created a sub-department of biblical history and literature. He retired in 1968. In New Zealand he was best known as 'Grammacticus', the classicist who romanticized about the New Zealand landscape in a weekly newspaper column.

Blaiklock's faith matured in the face of sarcasm and cynicism from colleagues. As he wrote in *Between the Morning and the*

Afternoon, 'It was difficult for a young man who had felt the warm appeal of Kemp's uncomplicated faith, to go back on Monday to a world which appeared less and less Christian and to an academic society which took it for granted that religion was a spent, irrelevant force' (p. 19). In his spare time he lectured in New Testament Greek at the Bible Training Institute founded by Kemp, and was thus drawn into New Testament studies, though not of a literary kind. He associated himself with the infant Inter-Varsity Fellowship and its little Evangelical Union.

In later life Blaiklock's role was that of a scholarly symbol of evangelicalism, part of the increasingly global evangelical scholarly community. His works were published by respected evangelical publishers in Britain and the United States, and he was a member of the Tyndale Fellowship and the author of the commentary on the book of Acts in the Inter-Varsity Press Tyndale New Testament Commentary series. Yet he was fundamentally a classicist, and in his scholarly writing on biblical subjects he showed little interest in or awareness of the issues that increasingly preoccupied biblical scholars. These he did not understand. He was a wordsmith and a preacher, and his evocation of personalities and places made him best known in later years as a preacher and a writer of semi-serious biblical material (such as Scripture Union bible reading aids), though this relegation pained him. Yet no-one could equal his moving, evocative prose at the Keswick Conventions or at mainstream church functions where he was the one evangelical Baptist deemed respectable enough to preach. Among the New Zealand conservative Christian public he was adulated, and he served as president of Scripture Union, the Inter-Varsity Fellowship and the Bible Training Institute, although he was not a good committee person, being too emphatic and not a good listener.

His symbolic role in New Zealand reached its zenith at the time of the Geering dispute in 1968, when he was asked by a publisher to write a response to the liberal theological stance of the Old Testament scholar and Presbyterian college principal, Lloyd Geering. In his book, *Layman's Answer*, he showed little interest in Geering's specific views, which he treated as simply a version of liberal German Protestant thought. It was in his account of the physical resurrection and its historic attestation that he revealed his passion and his priority.

In his later years Blaiklock was increasingly isolated within the rather populist conservative evangelical world, leading tours of Greece for the Evangelical Travel Association and criticizing the charismatic movement, with which he had no sympathy. The death of his wife grieved him deeply, and his moving tribute to her, which recalls C. S. Lewis's *A Grief Observed*, reflects the pain and personal travail of a noble but fragile man unfitted for contemporary life. He died in Auckland on 26 October 1983.

Bibliography
E. M. Blaiklock, *Between the Morning and the Afternoon: The Story of a Pupil Teacher* (Palmerston North: Dunmore Press, 1980); E. M. Blaiklock, *Between the Foothills and the Ridge, A Tale of Two Climbers* (Palmerston North: Dunmore Press, 1981); E. M. Blaiklock, *Between the Valley and the Sea: A West Auckland Boyhood* (Palmerston North: Dunmore Press, 1979); E. M. Blaiklock, *Ten Pounds an Acre* (Wellington: Reed, 1965); T. Shaw, *E. M. Blaiklock: A Christian Scholar* (London: Hodder & Stoughton, 1986).

P. J. LINEHAM

■ **BLANCHARD, Jonathan** (1811–1892), social reformer, educator and college president, was born near the Green Mountains in Rockingham, Vermont. In his early days Jonathan enjoyed dancing, cards and alcohol. He wrote in his autobiography, 'I hated liquor, though I loved its taste; for I saw that it ruined men.' At the age of sixteen he accepted Christ and gave up his former practices, graduating in 1832 from Middlebury College, Vermont. For the next two years he taught at Plattsburg Academy. It was while teaching there that he struggled with a question that would dominate the rest of his life: 'What is a perfect state of society? The question thrilled me, and I have since thought and written more on that one theme than any other. I could see that from my childhood I had been seeking a perfect state of society by resisting social evils.'

In order to prepare to fight social evils,

Blanchard in 1834 entered Andover Theological Seminary in Massachusetts. Here, however, he caused trouble when he organized an anti-slavery society, and so he dropped out and spent from 1834 to 1835 as an abolitionist spokesman in Pennsylvania working for Garrison's American Anti-Slavery Society. Then in the autumn of 1837 he resumed his theological studies at Lane Seminary in Cincinnati, Ohio. Although he attended two seminaries, he never graduated from either school. In the autumn of 1838 he married Mary Avery Bent, and within a month was ordained a Presbyterian minister, accepting the call to the Sixth Presbyterian Church in Cincinnati.

After Blanchard became a pastor it was his custom for years to read some portion of Scripture each day in Hebrew, Greek, Latin and French. In the eight years of his pastorate in Cincinnati the church grew by 500 members, and Blanchard helped establish a Presbyterian newspaper, the *Cincinnati Observer*. In addition, 'I rode 800 miles at my own expense to start the paper now called the *Herald and Presbyter*, in which I printed lectures on Sabbath reform and public morals; and by appointment of Presbytery, I preached as an evangelist; and received members to twenty churches in southern Indiana and Ohio.'

Because Jonathan and Mary were ultra-abolitionists who advocated the immediate freedom of slaves, from 1838 their home in Cincinnati was a stop on the Underground Railroad for slaves escaping from Kentucky over the Ohio River. Blanchard became increasingly famous as an abolitionist spokesman. In 1842 he preached and printed a *Sermon on Slave-holding* by appointment of the Synod of Cincinnati, and in 1843 he was the American vice-president at the World's Anti-Slavery Convention in London. On his return he lectured in the Cincinnati College on the wrongs of Ireland. Then in October 1845 Blanchard engaged in a famous debate, lasting sixteen hours over four days, with another Presbyterian pastor, Nathan Rice, on the subject 'Is slave holding in itself sinful, and the relation between master and slave necessarily a sinful relation?' The complete text of this debate was published in 1845 under the title *A Debate on Slavery*. After reading it, the trustees at Knox College in Galesburg, Illinois, who were looking for a new president, invited Blanchard to accept the post.

Now Blanchard started a career as an educator of future pastors. He was president at Knox for thirteen years and then in 1860 began a twenty-two year presidency at Wheaton College in Wheaton, Illinois. Although he is often called the 'founder' of Wheaton College, in reality the school had been founded seven years earlier by Wesleyan Methodists. While serving as president of the two colleges Blanchard frequently preached sermons, in college chapel and as a Congregational pastor in both Galesburg and Wheaton, promoting his reform ideas. In 1868 he founded a newspaper, the *Christian Cynosure*, using his position as editor to promote reform.

Blanchard's reform perspective was best reflected in 1884 when he ran for president of the United States as candidate of the American Party, the political party of the National Christian Association. He identified the author of civil government as God, urged sabbath observance, stressed civil equality, proposed arbitration between nations to secure permanent peace, promoted the use of the Bible in state schools, supported gold alone as a currency, urged protection of all loyal citizens and justice to Indians, and advocated women's suffrage. He also urged abolition of the electoral college and prohibition of alcohol, strongly condemned secret societies (especially the Freemasons, who he thought had caused the Civil War) and opposed monopolies.

Critics of Blanchard misinterpreted him as a 'bigot' who was against modernity. In reality, Blanchard was an evangelical social reformer who never equivocated in his quest for a 'perfect society'.

Bibliography
J. Blanchard, *Sermons and Addresses* (Chicago: National Christian Association, 1892); C. S. Kilby, *Minority of One: The Biography of Jonathan Blanchard* (Grand Rapids: Eerdmans, 1959); R. S. Taylor, 'Seeking the Kingdom: A Study in the Career of Jonathan Blanchard, 1811–1892' (PhD thesis, Northern Illinois University, 1977).

D. E. MAAS

■ **BLOESCH, Donald** (1928–), American theologian, has proved to be an exceedingly productive and creative evangelical systematician. Born on 3 May 1928 in Bremen, Indiana, he is the descendant of Swiss missionaries sent to German-speaking immigrants in the USA and the son of a minister of the Evangelical Synod of North America (a denomination that in 1934 merged with the Reformed Church in the United States [German] and subsequently joined with the Congregational Christian churches to form the United Church of Christ). The legacy of Reformed and Lutheran Pietist traditions has had a lasting impact upon Bloesch.

Bloesch came to a personal and living faith in the gospel as a young man in high school. At this early stage, one of his most formative experiences was his confirmation in the Evangelical and Reformed Church, a two-year process involving considerable catechetical and biblical study. Following high school, he enrolled in Elmhurst College, a denominational school that boasts both H. Richard and Reinhold Niebuhr among its alumni. In 1950, rather than following what was then an established practice of proceeding from Elmhurst to Eden Seminary, Bloesch decided to accept a full scholarship at the Chicago Theological Seminary. As a result of this decision, Bloesch encountered a form of liberal theology that resembled the process philosophy of Alfred North Whitehead. Reading Kierkegaard, Brunner, Barth, Bultmann and Tillich drew Bloesch's attention to a theological world beyond the dominant modernist (rationalist) approach to theological method and discourse within the academy. American evangelical theology did not influence him substantially at this time; he believed that it shared too deeply the rationalist principles of argument that had been so deleterious to modern liberal theology.

After graduating from the Chicago Theological Seminary (1953), Bloesch was ordained into the ministry of the United Church of Christ and soon afterwards began doctoral studies in theology at the University of Chicago. Studying under such luminaries as Charles Hartshorne, Daniel Jenkins, Wilhelm Pauck and Daniel Day Williams, he encountered a self-consciously mature form of liberal theology. In 1956 he successfully defended his dissertation on 'Reinhold Niebuhr's Re-Evaluation of the Apologetic Task'.

During this period Bloesch's spiritual development was influenced by his maternal grandmother, whose piety and concern for her grandson's spiritual wellbeing were considerable. Bloesch's involvement with Inter-Varsity Christian Fellowship at the University of Chicago provided him with genuine and moving Christian fellowship. In addition, his exposure to the religious life of British Anglo-Catholic monasticism, which he encountered during his postdoctoral work at Oxford University (1956–1957), left a deep impression upon him. The expression of genuine devotion that he discovered in the monks' shared life of worship and prayer not only encouraged him to hope for the spiritual renewal of mainstream churches, but is also largely responsible for his ongoing interest in Christian spirituality, evident in both his early works, *Centers of Christian Renewal* (1964), *The Crisis of Piety* (1968) and *Christian Spirituality East and West* (1968), and his subsequent research projects on *Spirituality Old and New*, *The Doctrine of the Saints*, *The Christian Meaning of Love in Light of the Cross* and *The Paradox of Holiness*.

But systematic theology rather than Christian spirituality has been the primary focus of Bloesch's teaching and research. In his two-volume work *Essentials of Evangelical Theology* (1978, 1979), he urged evangelicals to move beyond parochial debates in order to rediscover resources latent within classical Christian doctrine. The principal sources for Bloesch's own *resourcement* (rediscovery of tradition) have included Tertullian, Augustine, Anselm, *Luther, *Calvin, P. T. *Forsyth, Barth and T. F. *Torrance. Since around 1990 Bloesch has focused upon the task of writing a largescale systematic theology under the title *Christian Foundations*. Within just eight years, he has published five of the proposed seven volumes. This project has secured for him a reputation as one of the pre-eminent North American evangelical theologians of his generation, which rests largely upon his extensive use of Anselm's theological axiom, 'faith seeking understanding'. He has affirmed not only an infinite qualitative distinction between God and humanity, but more importantly, God's reconciliation of humanity in Christ. He seeks to articulate a theology of revelation in which God is not understood as an all-powerful, distant and unchanging deity, but rather as the incarnate Lord, the one true God, who has graciously entered the world 'for us and for our salvation'.

Bloesch might have provided a more nuanced account of the epistemic basis of reason (alongside his 'qualified fideism' and rejection of Protestant scholasticism) and a more thorough treatment of the ontological connection between the divine Word and holy Scripture, but he clearly expresses 'Reformed and evangelical catholicity' in which the unbounded love of the Father, in and through the Son, is made effectively present by the ongoing work of the Holy Spirit. Donald Bloesch is a theologian in the service of the gospel.

Bibliography
D. J. Adams (ed.), *From East to West: Essays in Honor of Donald G. Bloesch* (Lanham: University of America Press, 1997); E. M. Colyer (ed.), *Evangelical Theology in Transition: Theologians in Dialogue with Donald Bloesch* (Downers Grove: InterVarsity Press, 1999).

M. HUSBANDS

■ **BODDY, Alexander** (1854–1930), early pioneer in the British Pentecostal movement, was born on 15 November 1854, the son of James Boddy, rector of St Thomas Church, Cheetham, Manchester, and later of Elwick Hall, County Durham. He was educated at Manchester Grammar School and went on to study law. He was admitted by Sir George Jessel, Master of the Rolls, to be a solicitor of the Supreme Court of Judicature in December 1876. His time at the Keswick Convention that year proved to be a moment of spiritual crisis, which led him to refuse a legal partnership. Though successful in the law, he felt called to the ministry. With help from family and friends he was able to enter Durham University where he graduated LTh. He was ordained deacon in 1880 and priest in 1881. He was successively curate of Elwick Hall (1880), Castle Eden (1880–1881), Low Fell, Gateshead (1881–1884) and St Helen's, Bishop Auckland (1884). In the same year he moved to All Saints, Monkwearmouth,

Sunderland, first as curate (1884–1886) and then as vicar (1886–1922).

Monkwearmouth was to be the scene of his significant influence on the modern British Pentecostal movement. Boddy was a convinced evangelical much influenced by Keswick holiness teaching. In his early days he was also an enthusiastic traveller and visited (among other places) Russia, North Africa, Lapland and North America. On hearing a report that there was an outpouring of the Holy Spirit in Norway, Boddy went in March 1907 to witness it for himself. As a result he persuaded Thomas Ball Barratt (1862–1940), an English Methodist minister working in Oslo, to come to Sunderland. Barratt arrived on 31 August 1907 and stayed until 2 December. During his visit, Boddy's wife Mary and his two daughters Mary and Jane all had a profound experience which they identified as baptism in the Holy Spirit. Alexander had to wait until 2 December for his Pentecostal experience.

From this time All Saints Church, Monkwearmouth, became the first centre of the modern Pentecostal movement in Britain. Boddy provided both a focus and leadership for the many Christian leaders and church workers who came to the Whitsuntide convention meetings which he organized. Among their number was the Bradford plumber Smith *Wigglesworth (1859–1947), who received 'baptism in the Spirit' when Mrs Boddy laid hands on him. Others were Pastor G. Polman of Amsterdam and Stanley Frodsham and George and Stephen *Jeffreys from Britain. During the period from September 1907 to April 1908 about 500 seekers were 'baptized in the Holy Spirit'. Through the generosity of these people the debt on the church hall was finally paid, and a commemorative stone in the front wall reads, 'When the fire of the Lord fell it burned up the debt.' Until the outbreak of the First World War, Boddy continued to organize an important series of annual Pentecostal conventions, which were attended by Christian leaders of all denominations. Some of the historic denominational churches turned against missionary clergy who had received a Pentecostal experience. In order to support them, The Pentecostal Missionary Alliance was formed in 1909 with Boddy chairing the inaugural meeting. He also travelled to a number of places, including Hamburg, Oslo and the USA, and spread his message with the publication of his magazine entitled *Confidence*, which continued from 1908 until 1926, his pamphlet *Pentecost for England* and a series of *Roker Tracts*.

Boddy was also a devoted and much-loved parish priest whose strong leadership and clear teaching were greatly appreciated by his congregations. His dedicated pastoral labours during the Durham miners' strike of 1892 and his efforts in raising £500 for the relief of the iron workers in his parish were long remembered. Boddy was greatly assisted in his ministry by his wife Mary, with whom he had a long and happy marriage. Due to her failing health, he left Monkwearmouth in 1922 for the rural parish of Pittington. Boddy was a gifted and lucid teacher and was the acknowledged leader of early Pentecostalism in Britain. His influence has been somewhat underestimated by historians of Pentecostalism.

Bibliography

Anon., 'Rev Alexander Boddy, F.R.G.S.', *YMCA Flashes* vol. 2.8 (April 1895); E. Blumhofer, 'Alexander Boddy and the Rise of Pentecostalism in Britain', *Pneuma* 8 (spring, 1986), pp. 31–40; D. Gee, *Wind and Flame* (London: Assemblies of God Publishing House, 1967); W. Hollenweger, *The Pentecostals* (London: SCM Press, 1972); P. Lavin, *Alexander Boddy: Pastor and Prophet* (Wearside Historic Churches Group, 1986).

N. A. D. SCOTLAND

■ **BÖHLER, Peter** (1712–1775), Moravian bishop, was born on 31 December 1712 at Frankfurt-on-Main, Germany, the son of John Conrad Böhler, a brewer. After schooling in the city, he entered the University of Jena in 1731, where he attended the lectures of Spangenberg and *Zinzendorf, leading members of the United Brethren (Moravians) who had settled in Saxony in 1722. Through them he became familiar with the works of *Spener and German Pietism. He experienced instantaneous conversion and decided to begin ministry with the Moravians. He became academic tutor to a son of Count Zinzendorf, who then sent him to Savannah,

having ordained him with Bishop Nitschmann, as pastor of the infant church in the new colony of Georgia in America, where German Protestants were allowed to settle.

The year 1738 was pivotal in the history of the Methodist movement in Britain. Rupp claims for Böhler the role of 'Evangelist in his [John *Wesley's] Pilgrim's Progress' (*Religion in England*, p. 356). He brought from Germany a form of Pietism which, through exposure to the works of *Luther and an emphasis on justification by faith, cross-fertilized the high church Anglicanism of the Wesleys to create a distinct Methodist theology and praxis, at the vanguard of the Evangelical Revival. The Wesleys had already encountered Moravians on their journey to Georgia across the Atlantic in *The Simmonds* in 1735. When they returned two years later in some disarray, Böhler, passing through England on his way to Georgia, met them in London and Oxford. He offered spiritual direction and guidance to their tormented souls. He urged John Wesley to purge away 'that philosophy' (of proving faith by works) by preaching 'faith until you have it; and then, because you have it, you will preach faith'. He ministered to Charles *Wesley in his dangerous illness. He convinced them both of the need for instantaneous conversion with examples from Scripture and the testimony of fellow Moravians, who introduced them to the works of Luther and the necessity of personal faith in Jesus Christ, conversion and assurance. The subsequent conversion of Charles and John in May 1738 (21 and 24 May respectively: the 'Aldersgate Experience') owed much to the intervention and guidance of Böhler, of whom John later wrote, 'O what a work hath God begun since his coming to England!' Böhler was also responsible for the growth of groups, in both Oxford and London, that met for Bible study and the sharing of testimony, resembling the segregated Moravian bands in which discipline was exercised. He may have been the inspiration for Charles's memorable verse 'O for a thousand tongues to sing my great Jehovah's praise', a claim challenged by supporters of *Whitefield.

Before Böhler left for Georgia in 1738, he met at Fetter Lane, London, with a group organized by James Hutton, forming a society with rules devised by himself and modified by

John Wesley. This became the first English congregation of Moravians, from which followers of Wesley separated to form the Foundery Society in 1740 after disagreements surfaced. The love feast of 1 January was the high point of Moravian and Methodist co-operation, at the start of a year remarkable for revival that saw the development of Moravian and Methodist groups in Bedford, Bristol, Cambridge, Oxford, Reading and Yorkshire.

In the meantime, Böhler served in Georgia, building a school for black children on land given by Whitefield, and visiting congregations in Philadelphia and New York. He was recalled to Europe and arrived in Bristol at the beginning of 1741, resuming his ministry among growing congregations in London and West Yorkshire. He married an English-woman, Elizabeth Hobson, and had four surviving children born between 1743 and 1751. Bereft of Böhler's irenical influence and friendship with the Wesleys, the Moravians and Methodists had experienced a growing rift over issues surrounding Molther's doctrine of stillness, to which Böhler was never committed, and mutual suspicions over the religious enthusiasm of the Methodists and their emphasis on perfect love and its fruits. Böhler and Spangenberg engaged in talks with John Wesley but there was no reconciliation over the issue of Christian perfection. Böhler regretted the breach to the end of his life. Wesley too regarded his relationship with the Brethren as close, loving them 'beyond any body of men upon earth except the Methodists'.

Later that year Böhler returned to America, attending the Synod of Pennsylvania and visiting the settlements at Nazareth and Beth-lehem. In 1742 he was chosen as moderator by the Synod. On a visit to New York, he was arrested for his ministerial activities. In his defence, he claimed that the Archbishop of Canterbury had declared the Moravians to be 'an apostolical, episcopal Orthodox Church'. Expelled from the city, he returned to Beth-lehem where he continued his ministry until the arrival of Spangenberg released him to return to Europe in 1743.

At the Synod of Marienborn his wife Elizabeth was appointed a deaconess, and Böhler was sent to Lindheim as Dean of the University for the Brethren. In 1748 he was consecrated bishop by Zinzendorf, de Witte-ville and Nitschmann. As an able administrator as well as preacher and pastor, he was involved in talks with the Church of England as a sister church. On his third visit to America in 1753 (exchanging with Spangen-berg) he spent much energy in resolving difficulties in the communities, resulting in a period of depression from which he recovered. A new community at Bethabara in North Carolina was established, and he served the major congregation in New York until 1755. He returned to Germany that year but resumed duties in America the following year, staying until 1764.

By then he was an elder statesman of the Brethren, acting as director and principal member of the Elders' Conference. His last visit to London was in 1775 when he preached in the Fetter Lane Chapel. He died on 27 April aged sixty-three after a stroke.

Bibliography

J. P. Lockwood, *Memorial of the Life of Peter Böhler* (London: Wesleyan Conference Office, 1868); C. Podmore, *The Moravian Church in England 1728–1760* (Oxford: Clarendon Press, 1998); G. Rupp, *Religion in England 1688–1791* (Oxford: Clarendon Press, 1986); C. W. Towlson, *Moravian and Methodist* (London: Epworth Press, 1957).

T. S. A. MACQUIBAN

■ **BONAR, Horatius** (1808–1889), Scottish Presbyterian minister and hymn-writer, was born into a ministerial family, his great-great-grandfather being John Bonar, inducted as minister at Torphichen, near Edinburgh, in 1693. Bonar's two brothers, Andrew Alex-ander and John James, were also ministers in Scotland in the nineteenth century.

Bonar was educated at Edinburgh High School and then at the University of Edinburgh, where he met Robert Murray *McCheyne and came under the influence of Thomas *Chalmers. Chalmers possessed a powerful mind, an evangelical spirituality and a social awareness that affected a whole generation of Scottish Presbyterian ministers.

Bonar was then licensed to preach and became assistant to the Revd John Lewis, minister of St James's in Leith. During his work in Leith, Bonar began to write songs for the children in the parish, an indication of his concern to communicate the good news of the gospel to as many people as possible. He was ordained minister of the North Parish in Kelso on 30 November 1837 but left the established church at the Disruption in May 1843, remaining in Kelso as a minister of the Free Church of Scotland. In 1866 he moved back to Edinburgh to minister at Chalmers Memorial Chapel, and he stayed there until his death in 1887.

Throughout his ministry he was a tireless evangelist. His experience, along with his close friends William C. Burns and Robert Murray McCheyne, of the important spiritual movements which affected many places in Scotland in the 1830s and 1840s encouraged him in the work of evangelism. He regarded the Scottish Borders as a mission field ripe for evangelization, and in every village and even in individual farmhouses he held meetings to preach the gospel with great earnestness and authority. His labours were successful, as his accounts to his fellow ministers show: 'During this season there were all the marks of a work of God which we see in the account given of the preaching of the gospel by the apostles. The multitude was divided, families were divided; the people of God were knit together, they were filled with zeal and joy and heavenly-mindedness; they continued steadfast, and increased in doctrine and fellowship, being daily in church and in prayer-meetings; and numbers were constantly turning to the Lord.' He had a strong conviction that the outpouring of the Holy Spirit in revival was the only hope for the church, and in 1845 he edited John Gillies' Historical Collections to encourage an expectation of this hope within the minds and hearts of Scottish Christians. Despite opposition from contemporary ministers within the Free Church of Scotland such as John Kennedy of Dingwall, Bonar helped to organize D. L. *Moody's evangelistic meetings in Edinburgh in 1887.

Bonar was also an author of practical theology. God's Way of Peace and God's Way of Holiness were the most popular of his practical works. He served as the editor for The Quarterly Journal of Prophecy from 1848 to 1873 and for the Christian Treasury from 1859 to 1879.

In 1843, along with over 450 ministers of the Church of Scotland, Bonar left the established church to form the Free Church of Scotland, in which he exercised a significant ministry as a preacher and author, serving as moderator of the Free Church General Assembly in 1883. His wider ministry was recognized by the University of Aberdeen, which conferred upon him an honorary DD in 1853.

Prior to 1872 the singing of hymns within the Free Church of Scotland was not allowed. Bonar realized that the influence of the Psalter was declining among young people, and he began to write hymns, using the popular tunes of the day. He wrote more than 600 hymns, characterized by an evangelical simplicity and devotional warmth that became widely loved in different parts of the world. His collection of hymns, Hymns of Faith and Love, sold 140,000 copies during his lifetime. Many are still in use in the worship of churches in the twenty-first century, and among the most popular are 'I heard the voice of Jesus say', 'Fill Thou, my life, O Lord my God' and 'Here, O my Lord, I see Thee face to face', the last being used particularly as a communion hymn.

Bonar, along with many of his contemporaries, was influenced by the new interest in premillennialism as shaped by the thought of Edward Irving. He abandoned postmillennial theology, regarded as the evangelical orthodoxy of the early nineteenth century, and held that the physical, visible, imminent return of Christ should be the expectation of God's people. His first sermon in Kelso and his last sermon in Edinburgh both contained the text 'Behold I come quickly!'

Bonar maintained a Calvinistic theology throughout his life and was concerned at the lack of understanding which many Christians demonstrated with respect to the Christian faith. While ministering at Kelso, he began to write short tracts on the Christian faith and, in all, he completed thirty-six titles which he used in his evangelization and pastoral work. His first book, The Night of Weeping, was published in 1845, and a year later he wrote Truth and Error as a forceful warning against the superficiality appearing in religious life at that time. Another book, Man: His Religion and His World (1851), expressed his concern about the dangerous trend of diluting the gospel in an attempt to make it 'pleasant' and 'easier' to accept. He was well aware of the pitfalls of shallow and superficial evangelism, declaring, 'We think if we can but get men converted, it does not much matter how. Our whole anxiety is, not how shall we secure the glory of Jehovah, but how shall we multiply conversions?' To the end of his life he continued to sound warnings against contemporary tendencies that threatened the Christian church. Significantly, one of the last books he wrote, *Our Ministry, How It Touches the Questions of the Age* (1883), contained this perceptive observation: 'Man is now thinking out a Bible for himself; framing a religion in harmony with the development of liberal thought; constructing a worship on the principles of taste and culture; shaping a God to suit the expanding aspirations of the age.'

In 1843 he married Jane Lundie, and for forty years they shared joy and sorrow. Five of his children died in their early years. Towards the end of their lives, one of their daughters was left a widow with five small children and she returned to live with her parents. The gracious spirit of Horatius and his wife could be clearly seen from a letter to a friend in which he wrote, 'God took five children from life some years ago, and He has given me other five to bring up for Him in my old age.'

Bonar's health began to decline in 1887, but only when approaching the age of eighty did he preach in his church for the last time, dying on 31 May 1889.

Bibliography

B. R. Oliphant, 'Horatius Bonar' (PhD thesis, Edinburgh, 1951); *Memoirs of Dr Horatius Bonar, by Relatives and Public Men* (Edinburgh, 1909).

K. B. E. ROXBURGH

■ **BOOTH, William** (1829–1912) and **Catherine** (1829–1890), co-founders of the Salvation Army, are still venerated in their own movement, but they deserve to be better known outside it. The works of those who eclipsed the Booths in fame in their own day and in history have mostly passed away. The Salvation Army, the largest Protestant charity in the world and still an effective agency for evangelism among the marginalized in many parts of the world, survives as their legacy and their memorial.

William Booth was born on 10 April 1829, the second child and only son of Samuel Booth and his second wife Mary Moss, in Sneinton, then a village very near Nottingham, England. For several years William's father, a small-scale building contractor, could afford to send William to a local grammar school. In 1842 Samuel Booth was ruined financially. William, aged thirteen, was withdrawn from school and sent to learn a trade as a pawnbroker's apprentice. Although a conscientious and faithful employee, Booth despised the trade he was learning and found his only comfort in the fervent Christianity of a local chapel. Converted on 1 February 1847, William soon joined a group of young Methodist men who preached outdoors in the slums of Nottingham. At the expiry of his apprenticeship in 1849, Booth moved to London, where he lodged for a time with a married sister.

He hoped by this move to find another kind of work, but he was soon forced back into his old trade as a pawnbroker's assistant. His great love by now, however, was in lay preaching, for which he soon discovered that he had gifts of empathy and expression. His zeal commended him to Edward Rabbits, a wealthy boot and shoe manufacturer who attended the same chapel. In April 1852 Rabbits agreed to pay William's expenses for three months so that he could devote himself entirely to evangelism. At a small dinner organized by Rabbits to celebrate this, Booth met Catherine Mumford, his future wife.

Catherine Mumford was born on 17 January 1829 at Ashbourne, Derbyshire, the only daughter of five children (of whom she and one brother survived infancy) born to John and Sarah Mumford. John was a Methodist preacher and temperance worker; Sarah was exceptionally devout, zealous and protective. Catherine, a delicate child, was raised in an atmosphere of prayers, devotional literature and unremitting piety. Highly intelligent, alert and sensitive on the one hand, forthright and courageous on the other, Catherine as a young woman was intense in her convictions but always open to what she regarded as the leading of the Spirit, which saved her from narrow zealotry. Married to William Booth on 17 June 1855, Catherine came to exercise a profound influence upon her husband and the work they created together.

For several years the Booths served in pastorates in four denominations in various parts of Britain. The last of these was the Methodist New Connexion. Although subject to wide fluctuations of mood in his private life, William was steady in his faith. He undertook a small amount of supervised theological study in Wesleyan literature that strengthened his commitment to a simple and direct theology of personal salvation. He became a respected and popular preacher in his denominational home, but he increasingly felt restricted by rules that limited his evangelistic trips away from his own pulpit. The family was never poor. For most of their married life they enjoyed a comfortable middle-class existence, almost always having at least one domestic servant, although for years they lived in rented homes and moved often. The first of the Booths' eight children was born March 1856, but it was not until the seventh was born, in Hackney, London, in December 1865, that the family had a permanent home.

During these years, while William honed his skills as an evangelistic speaker, Catherine, alongside her growing domestic responsibilities, devoted herself to a range of theological and devotional literature. She came particularly to value the writings of the American Phoebe *Palmer, from whom she adopted the idea of 'holiness' as an instantaneous work of grace. Catherine was a lifelong advocate of the kind treatment of domestic animals, an important cause in an age when almost all commercial and passenger vehicles were horsedrawn. She was also an early advocate of the right of women to preach the gospel. The fact that she substituted for her husband in the pulpit in Gateshead was widely known, but Catherine's reputation was truly made in 1862 with the publication of her pamphlet on 'female ministry'.

In 1861 the Booths withdrew from the Methodist New Connexion to become independent itinerant evangelists, free from denominational control. There followed several years of wandering evangelism in which William became established as an effective revival speaker. He had a strong and colourful personality; he was gifted with compelling imagery; and he was fired with an all-consuming passion to rescue the lost, whom he saw and graphically described as faced with the immediate choice between the fires of hell and eternal happiness.

William Booth was also that rare figure among great leaders, the person who recognizes in another a superior mind and heart to which he willingly defers. By 1865 Catherine had become so well-established as a writer and speaker in her own right that she was the family's prime support. She was conducting a series of meetings of her own for six weeks in Rotherhithe, London, when William was invited by a different group of urban missionaries to conduct a revival service in a different part of town, on an abandoned Quaker burial ground on Mile End Waste, in the slums of east London.

The first of these meetings was held on 2 July 1865. This was a turning-point for the Booths. William's passion for lost souls was genuine and lifelong. His experience as a pawnbroker had given him sincere compassion for the helpless poor, the children, elderly and unemployed for whom Victorian society made just such provision as they could beg or steal for themselves. Booth was not a social revolutionary, but he was deeply moved by the plight of those who could not rise by their own efforts to the level of bare subsistence. Speaking to the east London crowds who flocked to hear him convinced Booth that he had a particular calling from God to evangelize the urban poor. Catherine, already a success in her own London meetings, accepted this decision gladly, and the couple established their own permanent missionary organization in London.

The new organization, which went through several name changes, was known for a time as the East London Christian Mission; in September 1869 it became the Christian Mission. During these years William and Catherine worked together to strengthen and focus the ministry of the mission in ways that proved highly effective and were adopted permanently. Mission preaching emphasized evangelism for the lost and holiness as an instant second word of grace for those who were already saved. Heavily influenced by Catherine's strong views on the dangers of drink, William agreed that the new movement should require all permanent members to abstain totally from alcohol. Because they believed that Christ commanded charity for the poor and because they could plainly see that hungry, homeless people could not concentrate properly on eternal things, the Booths started small-scale welfare programmes such as soup kitchens. The Christian Mission opened stations around London and beyond. By 1878 there were fifty-seven of these. The Mission published its own magazine, *The Christian Mission Magazine.*

During these years the organization of the Christian Mission developed as well, along lines that suggested themselves to William and Catherine Booth and their closest associates, including Bramwell, their oldest son, and George Scott Railton, an educated and exceptionally single-minded man, who served as Booth's private secretary. These leaders came to realize that William's powerful personality, which had become only more self-assured and autocratic with the passage of time and which deferred only to Catherine and then only in private, did not lend itself to the system of government by committee which was then in use in the mission. At the same time, the leaders of the mission believed that there was an additional and irresistible theological argument for giving William Booth centralized control. The Christian Mission was engaged in active spiritual warfare with Satan and his devils, and Booth was their battlefield commander. Mission workers thought in terms of a 'holy war', in which military imagery seemed natural.

Seen in this light, the selection of a new name for the organization had a history, although it appeared at the time as the result of a momentary whim. In preparing text for the September 1878 issue of the mission magazine, William and Bramwell Booth and Railton worked together. The latter hit upon the phrase 'volunteer army' to describe the mission. Bramwell, dissatisfied with this, said he was no volunteer, but a 'regular'. After a moment's pause, William reached over to write that the Christian Mission was a 'Salvation Army'.

The speed and thoroughness with which the Mission adopted military forms after its change of name shows how well the change suited the spirit of the organization. But even the most cheerful estimate of the Mission's prospects could not have foreseen the dramatic results of the change. Not only did it suit Booth's commanding style (he was now the 'General' in name as well as in fact) and the militant theology of the missionaries; the Salvation Army's new style also had enormous appeal among the very elements in society whom the Booths hoped to reach with the gospel. Flags, uniforms and the use of brass bands marching in the streets and playing gospel songs and popular tunes 'converted' with Christian words all drew powerfully upon the popular taste of the age. Army officials appeared in a striking array of new uniforms and ranks, drawn freely from the British Army and the Empire. Prayers became 'volleys', money contributions were 'cartridges' and the birth of a child to a converted couple was heralded as 're-inforcements'. The official magazine became *The Salvationist* in 1879, and in 1880 *The War Cry.* At the end of the first five years of its existence, the Army had nine times as many stations as the Christian Mission in its last, best year.

The Salvation Army did not strike every observer as a great and welcome work of God. Many were irritated by it, and some found it intolerable. Representatives of established denominations and many intellectuals looked down upon the Army as irresponsible, uncouth and a menace to good order.

Brewers and tavern keepers who cared little about good taste regarded the Army's effective temperance campaign as a mortal threat. Rough men were encouraged to ridicule or, if that failed, to attack Army meetings. Civic authorities resented the Army for being the occasion of public disruptions, which they tried in vain to prevent by refusing to protect Salvationists or by actually harassing them. At the same time, they looked upon those who sold alcohol as an important element in the commercial life of the community.

Opposition, of course, only stimulated Salvationist zeal and was in any case neither widespread nor prolonged. Much public opinion favoured the Army from the start, and the best-known critics were won over or shamed into silence. The Church of England eventually offered to adopt the Army as an official branch of the established church. The Roman Catholic Church sympathized with the Army from the start, recognizing in the new movement a common concern for the urban poor and a willingness to make Christianity colourful and appealing to sight and hearing, regretting only the extreme form of Protestantism which the Army represented.

The Salvation Army continued and expanded the practical charity of the Christian Mission, but the majority of its energy during the first years was focused on direct evangelism. By the end of the 1880s the Army's parades and street-corner meetings were familiar parts of urban life in the English-speaking world, including North America, Australia, the West Indies, Africa and India, and in Europe. In 1890 William Booth published his mature thinking on the role of social welfare in the Army's redemptive scheme, an event which deliberately drew public attention to the Army's welfare programmes. Eventually these welfare programmes became closely identified with the Army in the mind of the public, upon whose financial support they depended.

The book *In Darkest England and the Way Out* appeared late in 1890. Written with the assistance of W. T. Stead, a sympathetic London editor, it explained what Booth called the 'Cab-Horse Charter'. Booth accused the people of England of caring more about draught horses than about people. When a cab horse fell to the ground, bystanders did not stop to ask whose fault it was, but worked together to lift the horse up and help it back to work. So long as it lived, the horse was guaranteed three things which humans often did without: shelter, food and work. To remedy this problem Booth laid out a carefully planned network of institutions designed to take the unemployed and homeless, wean them from strong drink, minister to their souls and teach them useful work and self-respect. Other kinds of practical welfare services, such as a bank that would accept a few pennies at a time, free legal advice and a kind of assisted immigration service, were suggested as well.

During the preparation of *In Darkest England* Catherine Booth died of breast cancer on 20 October 1890 at Clacton-on-Sea. The book was dedicated to her. Although William Booth lived more than two decades after the death of his wife, the period of his innovation and even that of his effective daily leadership was over. He was surrounded by persons whom he regarded, as they regarded themselves, not as associates but as subordinates. Even his own children, who became Army officers and were decorated with inflated titles (one daughter was 'the Consul', one son 'the Marshall'), ceased to think of him as a mere parent. Booth became isolated and lonely without the wise counsel and encouragement of Catherine. He became a ceaseless traveller and featured speaker at Army gatherings around the world, leaving the actual administration of the Army in the hands of his eldest son, Bramwell Booth, who as 'Chief of Staff' had the second-grandest Army title of all. William Booth died on 20 October 1912 at the family home at Hadley Wood, outside London.

Bibliography
H. Begbie, *The Life of General William Booth, the Founder of the Salvation Army*, 2 vols. (London: Macmillan, 1920); St J. Ervine, *God's Soldier: General William Booth*, 2 vols. (London: Heinemann, 1934; New York: Macmillan, 1935); R. J. Green, *Catherine Booth: A Biography of the Co-founder of the Salvation Army* (Grand Rapids: Baker Book House, 1996); R. Hattersley, *Blood and Fire: William and Catherine Booth and Their Salvation Army* (London: Little, Brown, 1999; New York: Doubleday, 2000).

E. H. McKinley

■ **BOREHAM, Frank William** (1871–1959), Australian Baptist pastor and writer, was born on 3 March 1871 at Tunbridge Wells, Kent, England, first son of Francis, solicitor's clerk, and his wife, Fanny. Reared in a devout Anglican home, Boreham was educated at Grosvenor United School in Tunbridge Wells, where he became a pupil teacher, aged twelve. In December 1884 he began work as junior clerk at the local brickworks, but a year later was severely injured in a locomotive accident in which he lost his right foot. He subsequently walked with a limp and a walking stick, and through the years endured frequent falls and breaks to his leg and hip. But young Boreham's observant eye, extraordinary memory and vivid imagination partly compensated for his physical loss.

Boreham moved to London late in 1887 to work as a clerk and was converted to Christ, attending Emmanuel Church, a Countess of *Huntingdon's Connexion church. He began open-air preaching and in 1890 was baptized at Stockwell Baptist Church, which belonged to the Old Baptist Union, a small group of evangelical Arminian churches founded in 1880. This church practised laying-on of hands at the time of baptism and, as Boreham later recalled, 'it did really seem to me that a gracious tide of spiritual power poured itself into my soul'. Boreham applied to Spurgeon's College to train for the Baptist ministry. He regretted that he was, he thought, the last student personally admitted by *Spurgeon, who had died before Boreham began studies in August 1892. Boreham had already had articles printed, and in 1891 he had published a booklet, a symbolic interpretation of Genesis 24 entitled *Won to Glory*, for which F. B. *Meyer wrote a gracious introduction. Boreham became student pastor at Theydon Bois, Essex, where he met Estelle (Stella) Cottee, who would later become his wife.

After only two years at Spurgeon's, Boreham agreed to become pastor at Mosgiel, a small town near Dunedin in the south island of New Zealand. Thomas Spurgeon, son of the famous preacher, had been active in Australia and New Zealand, and at his request the college had selected Boreham to join the numerous Spurgeon's graduates who served in Australasia. From the Antipodes Boreham was to earn a reputation as a writer and preacher of universal appeal.

Boreham was inducted at Mosgiel on 17 March 1895, and on 13 April 1896 he married Stella, who subsequently appeared in his writings as 'The Mistress of the Manse'. Mosgiel, a rural community mainly of Scottish settlers, provided Boreham with rich pastoral experiences and delightful characters who feature in his essays. He developed his unique preaching style, using only a few words of notes, though he delivered carefully constructed sermons, rich in quotations and illustrative stories. His preaching, though avoiding theological terminology, was always evangelical in purpose. His church grew steadily, but he also participated in wider community and church life, serving as president of the Baptist Union of New Zealand in 1902, and he was a vigorous campaigner for temperance in the liquor polls of 1905 and 1906.

Boreham began publishing sermons in the Mosgiel newspaper, *The Taeri Advocate*, and soon afterwards he became editor of the monthly *The New Zealand Baptist* (1899–1906). His colourful and whimsical style made even reports of Baptist conferences entertaining reading. He also began writing editorials for the major regional paper, *The Otago Daily Times*. While at Mosgiel Boreham published in London a collection of eleven sermons, *The Whisper of God and Other Sermons* (1902).

In 1906 Boreham accepted a call to the Hobart Baptist Tabernacle in Tasmania, and with his unique style of preaching and sensitive leadership he saw the church grow rapidly. He preached series of sermons, many of which later appeared as essays in his books. Among the more memorable was a Sunday evening series on 'Texts that Made History', which grew into 125 sermons and five books. Boreham also edited the Tasmanian section of *The Southern Baptist* and later made regular contributions to *The Australian Baptist* (commenced in 1913) and *The Australian Christian World*. He also began writing weekly editorials for *The Hobart Mercury* in 1912, and over the next forty years he produced over 2,500 editorials for this paper and *The Melbourne Age*. This was a unique contribution by a minister to secular papers. Boreham's columns generally avoided strongly religious themes and were biographical, topical or seasonal in focus, and they were extraordinarily popular. In Tasmania he served as president of the Baptist Union of Tasmania from 1910 to 1911. His busy pastoral and community work did not affect his annual publication of a book of essays.

Boreham moved to the Armadale Baptist Church in suburban Melbourne in 1916, enjoying the larger church with its competent leaders. His sensitive pastoral care, especially during the difficult war years, was memorable, with his carefully drafted letters being treasured by grateful recipients. He loved to learn of people finding faith through his preaching, and regularly wrote letters encouraging people to faith and baptism.

Boreham retired from Armadale in 1928 and toured Britain and America, where he was in great demand as a preacher. He was awarded an honorary DD from McMaster University, Canada, in 1928. On a later visit to Scotland in 1936, the moderator of the Church of Scotland introduced Boreham as 'the man whose name is on all our lips, whose books are on all our shelves, and whose illustrations are in all our sermons'. Boreham was a passionate lover of cricket. His entry in *Who's Who* claimed he was 'never absent from the Melbourne Cricket Ground when a match was in progress except when his house was on fire'.

For eighteen years (1937–1955) Boreham preached at a crowded Wednesday lunchtime service in Scots Church, Melbourne. He was appointed OBE in 1954 for his 'services to religion and literature as preacher and essayist'. When evangelist Dr Billy *Graham was in Melbourne in 1959 he made a special point of visiting Boreham at home, acknowledging his debt to his books.

Boreham published over 90 works and sold over a million copies. His writings were positive and refreshing, simple in style and characterized by humour and a deep love of history and literature, including Australian authors. They often began from simple everyday happenings, which always created a warm human interest. The most popular titles included *Luggage of Life* (1912), *Mountains in the Mist* (1914), *Mushrooms on the Moor* (1915), *Faces in the Fire* (1916) and *A Bunch of Everlastings* (1920). Most of his books ran to several editions. In addition to his sermons and essays, he wrote novels, a biography of Bishop George Selwyn (1911) and an autobiography *My Pilgrimage* (1940). His books remain popular, not only with an older generation; and *A Frank Boreham Treasury* was published in 1984. The Broadbanks Dispensary in Bengal was established by Boreham from proceeds of his writings and commemorates one of his Mosgiel characters, John Broadbanks, whom most regard as possibly Boreham himself.

Boreham died in Melbourne on 18 May 1959 and was survived by his wife, son and three of their four daughters.

Bibliography

T. H. Crago, *The Story of F. W. Boreham* (London: Marshall, Morgan & Scott, 1961); I. F. McLaren, *Frank William Boreham (1871–1959), A Select Bibliography* (Parkville: Whitley College, 1997).

K. R. MANLEY

■ **BOSTON, Thomas** (1676–1732), Church of Scotland minister and author, wrote *Human Nature in Its Fourfold State* (1720, 1729), a popular work of evangelical Calvinist orthodoxy explaining 'man's natural estate' and 'Christ the remedy for man's misery'. Boston inherited the basic structure from Augustine, who in his *Treatise on Rebuke and Grace (De Correptione et Gratia)* distinguished between the grace God gave Adam to be able not to sin (*posse non peccare*) and the grace he gives glorified saints to be unable to sin (*non posse peccare*). Medieval theologians used this distinction to identify four conditions of humanity, which Boston termed the states of Innocence, Nature, Grace and Eternity. His innovation was to use these four categories to organize his preaching, and thus to provide a simple, practical and memorable theological framework for his largely uneducated parishioners.

The *Fourfold State*'s emphases on the misery of depravity, the necessity of regeneration, the centrality of union with Christ and the reality of heaven and hell made it a formative text in the rise of evangelicalism in Britain and America. During the Great Awakening evangelical ministers often recommended the book to new converts, and Boston's *Fourfold State* became an eighteenth-century bestseller, going through more than one hundred editions in Scotland, England and America. The discovery of a few pages from the book led to revival on a Virginia plantation. Jonathan *Edwards liked it 'exceeding well' and considered its author 'a truly great divine'. George *Whitefield also appreciated Boston's work, claiming to find it 'of much service to my soul'. John *Wesley went so far as to include an abridgment of the *Fourfold State* in his Puritan library. Much later, a section of Boston's material on 'The New Birth' found its way into *The Fundamentals* (1910), thus confirming its author's evangelical bona fides.

Thomas Boston spent nearly all his life in the Scottish Borders south of Edinburgh. He was born on 17 March 1676 at Duns, Berwickshire. One of his earliest memories was visiting the prison where his father had been jailed for Nonconformity. Boston himself was converted in the summer of 1687 through the open-air preaching of another Nonconformist, the covenanter Henry

Erskine. He matriculated at Edinburgh University in 1691 and received his MA in 1694. He proceeded to study divinity at Edinburgh for four months, receiving the balance of his theological training under the supervision of his local presbytery.

In 1699 Boston was ordained to pastor the remote little parish of Simprin, also in Berwickshire, where he remained until his removal to Ettrick, the village usually associated with his name. During his first year at Simprin, Boston married Katharine Brown (on 17 July 1700), a devoted wife who struggled with chronic physical and perhaps psychological problems. In addition to the ordinary trials of parish ministry, Thomas and Katharine suffered the loss of six children in infancy (four survived to adulthood). Through his many sorrows, Boston learned to pray for each 'loss to be made up by the presence of the Lord'.

When Boston moved to Ettrick in 1707, he found his new parish to be as illiterate as his former one, and equally immoral: full of 'self conceit, a divisive temper, and sins of uncleanness'. His pastoral work in both communities was characterized by what he termed 'a heart exercised unto godliness'. In addition to preaching twice on the sabbath and lecturing once in midweek, he covered one hundred square miles on horseback to visit every household in his parish twice annually for spiritual conference and catechetical instruction. Although he was prone to melancholy and suffered from a variety of physical ailments, he never missed a week in the pulpit in more than three decades of public ministry. He preached his final sermons from his deathbed, with the members of his congregation gathered around the window of his manse. Thomas Boston died on 20 May 1732 and was buried in the Ettrick kirkyard.

Although reluctant to engage in controversy, Boston's theological scruples landed him at the centre of several disputes. One was political: Boston refused to sign the Oath of Abjuration (1712, 1719), by which allegiance was sworn to the English Crown, because as a Presbyterian he opposed the Anglican Church's episcopalian form of church government. Boston's refusal was made at some risk to his liberty and property, but it also served to enhance his popularity in the Scottish countryside.

Two other disputes were more explicitly ecclesiastical. Boston was one of the principal combatants in the Marrow Controversy (1717–1723). In the cottage of one of his parishioners at Simprin, he had discovered a copy of *The Marrow of Modern Divinity* (1645), a compendium of Reformed and Puritan writings first published in London. On Boston's recommendation, the book was republished in 1718. Among its distinctive emphases were evangelical doctrines such as the free offer of the gospel, assurance in Christ as the essence of faith, and sanctification by grace, which Boston described as the 'true spring of evangelical obedience'. In 1720 and again in 1722 (following an appeal by Boston and others) the General Assembly banned *The Marrow* on the mistaken assumption that it favoured antinomianism. For their part, the Marrow Men were determined to prevent Calvinism from degenerating into legalism, and they continued to preach the book's evangelical doctrines. After Boston's death, some of the Marrow Men and their followers initiated the First Secession from the Church of Scotland (1733).

Boston also opposed John Simson (1667–1740), a divinity professor at the University of Glasgow who twice was convicted of heresy: once for Arminianism (1717) and once on suspicion of Arianism (1726–1729). Simson's theological speculations were harbingers of Scottish rationalism and liberalism, developments that Thomas Boston was quick to detect and determined to prevent. When the professor's second trial resulted merely in censure, Boston protested that for the honour of Christ, Simson should have been deposed from the ministry.

Boston's own theological convictions were shaped by his broad exposure to the literature of international Calvinism, especially the writings of the Westminster Divines and other English Puritans. Boston preached in the plain style of the Puritans, and through his sermons he became a prolific author in his own right, with his *Complete Works* (1854, 1980) running to twelve volumes. He was a notable exponent of covenant theology, writing both *A View of the Covenant of Grace* (1734) and *A View of the Covenant of Works* (1772). Here his contribution was to prove that the covenant of redemption (between the Father and the Son) and the covenant of grace (between God and the elect) are one and the same: the Father makes a gracious covenant with the Son, who represents the elect in its fulfilment. Boston was also a careful student of the Old Testament and published a treatise (long since discredited) defending the inspiration of the accentuation in the Hebrew Bible (*Tractatus stigmologicus, Hebraeo-Biblicus*, 1738). His other works include a three-volume exposition of the Westminster Shorter Catechism (1773), a practical treatise on divine providence (*The Crook in the Lot*, 1737), and an intimate spiritual autobiography (*Memoirs of the Life, Time and Writings*, 1776). Although not published until long after his death, one of his earliest manuscripts was *A Soliloquy on the Art of Man-fishing* (1773), a small classic on evangelistic preaching.

The theology of Thomas Boston has sometimes been viewed as an attempt to moderate the doctrines of Reformed scholasticism. It is better understood as a vigorous exposition of the orthodox, gospel-centred Calvinism that nourished the first evangelicals in Britain and America.

Bibliography

W. Addison, *The Life and Writings of Thomas Boston of Ettrick* (Edinburgh: Oliver & Boyd, 1936); D. C. Latchman, *The Marrow Controversy, 1718–1723: An Historical and Theological Analysis* (Edinburgh: Rutherford House, 1983); A. T. B. McGowan, *The Federal Theology of Thomas Boston* (Carlisle: Paternoster, 1997); P. G. Ryken, *Thomas Boston as Preacher of the Fourfold State* (Carlisle: Paternoster, 1999).

P. G. RYKEN

■ **BOUNDS, Edward McKendree** (1835–1913), pastor, evangelist and author, was born in Shelby County, Missouri on 15 August 1835. His parents were Hester A. and Thomas Jefferson Bounds from Kentucky, who moved to Missouri in the 1820s seeking financial prosperity. Thomas Bounds helped to organize Shelby County and was elected to public office as county clerk. He died in 1849. A few years later, Edward began studying law, and on 9 June 1854 passed his bar examinations, earning a license as a Missouri lawyer. At the age of eighteen he began a flourishing practice in Monroe and Shelby Counties, impressing people with his sharp mind and communication skills.

Bounds' law career was brief. He had been a lifelong Christian, baptized and confirmed in a Methodist Episcopal Church, South (MECS). He believed in Christ for his salvation and tried to live morally. Yet in 1859 he experienced a keen sense of spiritual renewal. Bounds was transformed by a new understanding of God's grace and love, and from that time he lived out his conviction that 'no man does much for God who does not rise above the age in which he lives'. Bounds renewed his commitment to Christ and dedicated himself to a life of full-time ministry. Astonishing friends and associates, he forsook his law practice. By the latter part of 1859 he was preaching in a MECS and in 1860 was licensed to preach with the Hannibal Station Quarterly Conference. He was installed as a deacon and sent to Brunswick, Missouri, to begin a pastorate.

In the midst of the secessionist crisis and the impending Civil War, President Abraham Lincoln deployed troops in Missouri in order to prevent secession from the Union. Because Bounds was a minister in the pro-slavery MECS, he was imprisoned by Union troops in 1861. Since he opposed Union confiscation of church property, he was branded a traitor. Though he never pledged allegiance to the Confederacy, he ministered to his embittered rebel counterparts during his year-and-a-half of incarceration.

Finally, Bounds was released by order of Major General Samuel R. Curtis and expelled from Missouri until the war's end. As part of a prisoner exchange that left him in Arkansas, he was denied the opportunity to swear loyalty to the United States. So he travelled to Port Gibson, Mississippi, where he became the chaplain of the Third Missouri Volunteer Infantry Regiment. He won admiration from his fellow Missouri soldiers for his courage and compassion. During the Battle of Franklin, Tennessee, on 30 November 1864, Bounds was again taken prisoner. This time he took an oath of allegiance to the Union in exchange for his freedom and eventually went back to Franklin, where he helped to bury the Confederate soldiers who lost their lives there. He served briefly as interim pastor for the Methodist Episcopal Church at Franklin;

then he became an elder in the conference and devoted himself to healing the wounds the war had inflicted on Southerners. Eventually he became the official pastor of the church, remaining there until he was reassigned to a church in the Selma, Alabama, conference two years later.

In Selma Bounds met Emma Elizabeth Barnett. Their courtship turned into a long-distance romance when Bounds relocated to St Paul's Methodist Episcopal Church in St Louis. In September 1876 they were married, and they settled in Missouri. In November 1877 they welcomed their first child, Celeste. Bounds assumed the pastorate of First MECS of St Louis in 1879. His new congregation was affluent, prestigious and housed in a stately edifice. Bounds' desire for simplicity led to a clash with some church members, and he returned to the humbler St Paul's congregation in 1881. By then the Bounds family included another daughter, Corneille. The Methodist conference summoned Bounds once again, and in 1883 he became the associate editor of the St Louis Conference's official paper, *The St. Louis Advocate*.

The joy of the birth of Bounds' first son, Edward, was shattered by Emma's untimely death on 20 February 1884, probably due to cancer. She passed away at her parents' home in Alabama, leaving Bounds with a broken heart and the responsibility of raising three young children. In October 1887 Bounds fulfilled his promise to the dying Emma and married Harriet (Hattie) Elizabeth Barnett of Washington, Georgia. Hattie was Emma's first cousin, and though she was almost twenty-two years Bounds' junior, her family thought them well suited for one another. Bounds took his new bride to St Louis, where she gave birth to Samuel Barnett in 1888. Bounds then accepted the position of associate editor of the Nashville *Christian Advocate*, the official paper for the entire denomination. Unfortunately, Bounds' joy in his writing and the birth of Charles Rees in 1890 were overshadowed by the sudden death of Edward at the age of six. Charles also died unexpectedly in 1891, but Hattie gave birth to Osborne Stone and Elizabeth in 1892 and 1893.

At the *Christian Advocate*, Bounds used his editorials to fight the liberal 'New Theology'

in the MECS of the post-war period. He spoke against the lethargy caused by prosperity, calling ministers to integrity and sound teaching. He left the denomination when it abolished the office of evangelist, to which he felt a strong calling. Upon leaving the MECS he transferred his family to Georgia, where they lived with Hattie's parents, and began a life of writing, speaking and prayer. He rose at four o'clock every morning to praise and to pray; often the family joined him. At seven he ate breakfast; then he spent the remainder of the day writing, interceding and studying Scripture. Often he would become so consumed with his work that he would forget to come to dinner, even when called. Bounds received fewer speaking invitations from Washington than in former days; he was regarded as an outsider by the native Southerners, who were suspicious of those raised outside Georgia's boundaries. But he was asked to speak frequently at camp meetings during the summers. He considered all invitations in prayer and accepted them only if he felt led to do so. He relied upon God's direction for every decision. Two more children, Mary Willis and Emmie, were born in 1895 and in 1897. In 1902 Bounds published *Preacher and Prayer* (later *Power Through Prayer*) with Marshall Brothers in England.

Bounds became friends with Homer Hodge after he was invited to speak at Hodge's church in Atlanta. Bounds was grateful to have an eager pupil and instructed Hodge in the ways of biblical prayer and effective discipleship. *The Resurrection*, which turned out to be the last volume Bounds would publish during his lifetime, appeared in 1907 with the MECS in Nashville.

E. M. Bounds died on 24 August 1913 at his home in Washington, Georgia. He had been bedridden for several days. His legacy is his books: three that he published during his lifetime and eight that Hodge published after his death. Hodge also formed the 'Great While Before Day Prayer Band', a group of believers committed to waking at an early hour for extended times of prayer.

By the mid 1920s eleven of Bounds' works were in print, and eight of these, on prayer, are still in print. His most widely known book is *Power Through Prayer*, which currently appears as *Preacher and Prayer*. Bounds' devotional writings explore such topics as the Bible, family, heaven, money and materialism, the Holy Spirit, the resurrection of the body, revival and Satan. His writing on prayer forms the greater part of his literary output. Other titles that are still in print include: *Purpose in Prayer* (1920), *The Possibility of Prayer* (1923), *The Reality of Prayer* (1924), *The Necessity of Prayer* (1929) and *The Weapon of Prayer* (1931). Several of Bounds' devotional writings, originally composed for late nineteenth-century Methodist newspapers, may be found in Lyle W. Dorsett's *E. M. Bounds: Man of Prayer* (1991).

Bibliography

L. W. Dorsett, *E. M. Bounds: Man of Prayer* (Grand Rapids: Zondervan, 1991).

T. L. COOPER

■ **BOURNE, Hugh** (1772–1852), co-founder of the Primitive Methodist Connexion, was born at Fordhays, in Staffordshire, on 3 April 1772, on a moorland tenant farm, and into a pious family. The most powerful influence on his religious development was his mother, Ellen Bourne. The family moved in 1788 to a bigger farm in Bemersley, in the desolate and isolated countryside of North Staffordshire, which, although in the parish of Norton-in-the-Moors, was a marginal area, devoid of the pastoral provision of the established church. Shortly afterwards, Hugh began work with his uncle as an apprentice wheelwright. Bourne was largely self-taught; he studied Greek, Latin and Hebrew. Like many adolescents of the time, he was concerned with matters of faith and doubt, and struggled for spiritual awareness. As a result, however, of his reading of Quaker and Methodist texts, in particular John *Wesley's Sermons and John *Fletcher's *Letters on the Spiritual Manifestation of the Son of God*, Bourne experienced conversion. He joined the Wesleyan Methodists in 1799.

The seemingly providential emergence of Primitive Methodism on Christmas Day 1800 occurred when Bourne, now with his own business, travelled to the nearby mining village of Harriseahead to purchase timber. There he met a cousin, Daniel Shubotham, who had experienced similar religious struggles. It was while Bourne was engaged in 'conversation preaching' with this troubled collier and renowned pugilist that Shubotham was converted. That event, together with Bourne's initiation of cottage prayer meetings, caused a revival in the village. By 1804 the revival had spread southwards to the towns of Tunstall and Burslem, culminating in the conversion among others of William Clowes, an infamous reprobate. However, the revival was initiated without the official sanction or supervision of the Burslem Wesleyan circuit authorities, who looked with suspicion upon such untypically quiet means of conversion. They were also alarmed by the use of the popular practice of holding camp meetings, introduced from the American frontier by the visit to England of the charismatic and eccentric evangelist, and harbinger of republicanism, Lorenzo *Dow. The first camp meeting was held at Mow Cop, on the border of Staffordshire and Cheshire, on 31 May 1807. It symbolized the distinction between the increasingly industrializing bureaucrats of Wesleyanism and the simpler agricultural lay evangelists of Harriseahead. Within the context of war in Europe and the rise of radical beliefs and political tensions at home, the Wesleyan Conference was keen to stress its loyalty to the establishment by suppressing seemingly dangerous forms of popular gathering, excessive lay involvement and aggressive revivalism. Bourne's apparent rejection of the authority and the alienating policies of the Wesleyan Conference resulted both in mass expulsions, including that of Bourne himself, by the Burslem Quarterly Meeting in June 1808, and the formation, out of the Camp Meeting Methodists and Clowesites, of the Primitive Methodists in 1811. A movement of the labouring people, and with a strong lay participation, the Primitive Methodists sought to re-ignite the popular revivalism of John Wesley's original movement. They encouraged the expression of religious enthusiasm and community affiliation, connecting with the first democratic aspirations of the working classes within a rapidly industrializing society. A revival spread throughout Staffordshire, Derbyshire and Cheshire in the second decade of the nineteenth century and, after 1819, through Yorkshire and East Anglia. Bourne called the first Conference in Nottingham in 1819, and initiated the denominational *Primitive Methodist Magazine*. He also encouraged the circuits to make use of female preachers.

Bourne managed, through being financially independent, to spend a good deal of his life travelling, moving from circuit to circuit, symbolically uniting virtually autonomous and disparate groups around the country, and witnessing the growth of the largest new denomination in England since the birth of Old Methodism. A great patriarchal figure, he was obliged to retire, against his own wishes, in 1842 (aged seventy). In 1844 Bourne travelled to Canada and the United States, to engage in mission and repay his debt to Lorenzo Dow. A renowned abstainer, Bourne became active in the temperance movement in his final years, preaching teetotalism around the country. He wrote widely and prolifically, on such topics as baptism and present salvation. He compiled and edited *A Collection of Hymns for Camp Meetings, Revivals, &c. for the Use of the Primitive Methodists* (1832), an ecclesiastical history, the first connexional history of the Primitive Methodists, entitled *History of the Origins of the Primitive Methodists, Giving an Account of Their Rise and Progress up to the Year 1823* (1835) and an autobiography. He was also editor of *The Primitive Methodist Magazine* for over twenty years.

Being a timid and shy individual (he remained unmarried throughout his life), Bourne never possessed the populist, extrovert evangelistic techniques and preaching style of his contemporary, and co-founder, William Clowes; his gifts were for administration, organization and conversation preaching. Bourne died at Bemersley, Staffordshire, on 11 October 1852. At his funeral procession more than 16,000 were present in and around Tunstall. Bourne was buried at Englesea Brook in Cheshire.

To give an account of Hugh Bourne's life is to tell the story of the Primitive Methodists. Yet because of its more democratic organization, Primitive Methodism was able, unlike its parent body, to survive the death of its great leader without experiencing schism, faction or organizational turmoil.

Bibliography
J. Walford, *Memoirs of the Life and Labours of the Late Venerable Hugh Bourne*, ed. W. Antliff, 2 vols. (London and Burslem: 1855–6); J. T. Wilkinson, *Hugh Bourne, 1772–1852* (London: 1951).

W. J. JOHNSON

■ **BRADFORD, William** (1590–1657), Pilgrim Father and second governor of Plymouth Colony, was born in March 1590 in Austerfield, Yorkshire, England, the son of William Bradford and Alice Hanson. His father died in 1591, and his mother remarried in 1593. As a consequence, Bradford was raised from the age of four by his grandfathers and uncles.

From an early age, Bradford demonstrated a keen interest in religion. He came under the influence of the Nonconformist rector of Babworth, Nottinghamshire, Richard Clifton (or Clyfton), and began to attend meetings of the Separatist congregation that met in the home of William Brewster in nearby Scrooby. He subsequently became a full member at the age of sixteen. When the congregation moved to Amsterdam in 1607 to escape persecution, Bradford went too. Bradford and several other members of the original Scrooby congregation left Amsterdam in 1609 to form the congregation in Leiden of which John *Robinson was pastor.

In Leiden, Bradford was apprenticed to a Huguenot silk weaver, and earned his living in the textile trade. He was married in 1613 to Dorothy May. While in Leiden, Bradford read a great deal of theological literature. In 1620 he joined the members of his congregation who, with the encouragement of John Robinson, emigrated to the New World, sailing on *The Mayflower*. Bradford was a signatory to the Mayflower Compact, which provided for the government of the new colony. The party landed in Massachusetts in November 1620, and Plymouth Colony was established.

The winter of 1620–21 was a hard one, and nearly half the colonists died, including the governor, John Carver, and Bradford's wife. (He remarried in 1623, to Alice Carpenter Southworth.) After Carver's death in 1621, Bradford was elected governor, and except for the years 1633, 1634, 1636, 1638 and 1644, he served continuously in that office until 1656 (without pay until 1639).

Shortly after leaving the office of governor for the last time, he died in Plymouth on 9 May 1657.

As governor, Bradford forged an alliance with the native Wampanoag nation, and his policy towards them resulted in several decades of relative peace. He also established a close relationship with the neighbouring Massachusetts Bay Colony, but he resisted its efforts to absorb Plymouth. Although there were many similarities between the two colonies, particularly with respect to theology and church polity, they were never able to agree on what their relationship to the Church of England should be.

Under Bradford's leadership, Plymouth Colony did not enforce rigid religious uniformity, unlike Massachusetts Bay Colony. In general, Baptists were not barred (though Roger *Williams was expelled in 1636), and Quakers were not executed. Even a visiting Catholic, the Jesuit Father Druillette, was received with courtesy in 1650. Nevertheless, Bradford did block an attempt in 1645 to write religious toleration into the law, and in 1650 he participated in the drafting of legislation that was aimed against the Quakers.

Bradford wrote a history of the Colony, *Of Plimouth Plantation* (left in manuscript form at his death, and published only in 1856), which was composed over a period of twenty years. It is one of the most significant chronicles of the early European settlement in North America, written from a theocentric point of view and including a providential interpretation of events. Bradford began writing the account in 1630, and Book I was completed in 1631–1632, taking the narrative to the landing at Plymouth. Book II, which carried the narrative to 1646, was written between 1646 and 1650. Bradford wrote chiefly from memory, supplemented by correspondence and journal notes.

Bradford supported himself as a farmer and trader and was probably the ablest and best educated among the Plymouth colonists. He possessed a large library, was well versed in Reformed theology and towards the end of his life even sought to learn Hebrew. He was a moderate (rather than extreme) Separatist. Bradford sought to maintain fellowship with all Reformed churches, and represented Plymouth at the Cambridge Synod of 1647. However, he was a layman throughout his life and never held a spiritual office. Bradford had a balanced approach to religious toleration, though without holding to it in principle. He believed it was arrogant for any one church to claim that it alone knew all that the Bible taught. Bradford's lasting contribution, however, was his history of Plymouth Colony, which has given us the designation 'Pilgrims', and serves as the most compelling account of both the English settlement in the New World and the Separatist vision for a Christian society.

Bibliography
W. Bradford, *A History of Plymouth Plantation, 1620–1647*, ed. W. C. Ford, 2 vols. (Cambridge: The Massachusetts Historical Society, 1912); B. Smith, *Bradford of Plymouth* (Philadelphia: Lippincott, 1951).

N. S. AMOS

■ **BRADSTREET, Anne** (c. 1612–1672), poet, was the first British-American to have her poetry published. She was born in Northamptonshire, England, to Puritans Thomas and Anne Dudley. The family moved in 1619 to Sepringham, where Thomas Dudley served as the steward to the Earl of Lincolnshire. In 1621 Bradstreet met her future husband, Simon Bradstreet, a Cambridge graduate who came to help Thomas Dudley with the management of the earl's estate. The couple were married in 1628, and in 1630 both the Bradstreets and the Dudleys emigrated to the Massachusetts Bay Colony. Beginning in Charlestown, the Bradstreets moved several times within Massachusetts; in 1631 they moved to present-day Cambridge, and in 1635 to Ipswich. Between 1638 and 1644 they moved to Andover, where Bradstreet would live until her death in 1672. During the period between 1633 and 1652 Bradstreet bore eight children. The Bradstreets and the Dudleys played prominent roles in the life of the Puritan colony; both Simon Bradstreet and Thomas Dudley served as governors.

Bradstreet's poetic reputation rests on the publication of two volumes of verse, neither of which she prepared or approved for publication. The first volume, *The Tenth Muse* (1650), was brought to England for publication by a family friend. The second volume, *Several Poems* (1678), was published after her death. Her poetry addresses a wide variety of subjects, from personal to public concerns, reflecting her roles as daughter, mother, wife, poet and teacher. While the poems in *The Tenth Muse* display a breadth of learning and knowledge of the styles of English poets such as Spenser and Sidney, more critical attention has been given to the works in *Several Poems*, with their more personal and expressive style.

Bradstreet's poetry has tended to surprise readers who expect the work of Puritans to be dour and constricting. Many critics have commented on the ways in which internal conflicts between belief and doubt characterize her work. Debate on her work has thus centred on whether her poems accurately reflect a Puritan sensibility or if they represent a rebellion against that tradition. A strong argument can be made for the claim that her poetry falls firmly within the Puritan tradition of viewing the Christian life as a pilgrimage. Bradstreet's own purpose in her poetry was to erect for her children an 'Ebenezer', or memorial stone, of her own pilgrimage. As Jeffrey A. Hammond has noted, 'because her family readers needed to see that the pilgrimage was difficult, she not only described the pilgrim way but dramatized it through a speaker who is unquestionably conflicted but potentially redeemed in the very honesty with which she confesses that conflict'. The fact that publication of her poetry was not only tolerated but encouraged by members of the Puritan colony suggests that her work might form the basis of a re-evaluation of Puritan culture.

Bibliography

J. A. Hammond, *Sinful Self, Saintly Self: The Puritan Experience of Poetry* (Athens: University of Georgia Press, 1993); R. R. Rosenmeier, *Anne Bradstreet Revisited* (Boston: Twayne, 1991); E. Wade White, *Anne Bradstreet, 'The Tenth Muse'* (New York: Oxford University Press, 1971).

J. NORDLOF

■ **BRAINERD, David** (1718–1747), Presbyterian missionary to Native Americans, lived a short but intense life amid the fury of the First Great Awakening. He was born and raised in Haddam, Connecticut, a farming village along the Connecticut River. Brainerd

experienced conversion in July 1739. Two months later, he began as a student at Yale College and set his sights on becoming a Congregational minister and scholar. He was intelligent, passionate but a little imprudent, and his Yale career came to an abrupt halt when he supposedly accused one of his tutors of having no more grace than a chair. Expelled in early 1742, Brainerd remained convinced long after that his treatment had been excessively harsh and unjust.

Still interested in pursuing the ministry, Brainerd spent the summer of 1742 studying with Congregational pastor Joseph *Bellamy and gaining a licence to preach. Little did he know when he evangelized Indians along the Housatonic River near the New York–Connecticut border in August that this work would be a preview of his future career. Later that autumn, Presbyterian pastor Ebenezer Pemberton invited him to New York City to meet the colonial commissioners of the Society in Scotland for Propagating Christian Knowledge. That interview generated a job offer to work as a missionary to Native Americans. Brainerd accepted but privately expressed more gloom than excitement about his calling, a reaction explained largely by his melancholic spirit, lack of self-confidence and ongoing disappointment over unfulfilled scholarly ambitions. Furthermore, he realized that going among Indians meant moving not only to the geographic margins of colonial society but also to the religious margins of the colonial church.

Following six weeks of supply preaching to white Christians on Long Island and observing first-hand the poverty of the neighbouring Indians, Brainerd was sent further north to work among a small group of Mahican Indians at Kaunaumeek, New York. He served there for twelve months (spring 1743 to spring 1744) under the tutelage of John Sergeant, missionary to the Indians at Stockbridge, Massachusetts, about twenty miles away. Sergeant taught him many of the standard strategies English missionaries traditionally employed in evangelizing Indians. Brainerd, however, would later find many of them useless, including his arduous efforts to learn one Algonquian dialect which could not be understood by the Algonquian and Iroquoian speakers of New Jersey and Pennsylvania among whom he spent most of his career. Conversely, his contact with Mahicans taught him several valuable lessons of lasting relevance, including their claim that Indians living further into the American interior would be more resistant to Christianity.

Brainerd found that claim to be all too true when he took up residence in eastern Pennsylvania in May 1744. Ordained the following month by the Presbytery of New York, he began to labour among the smattering of Delaware Indians who still lived near the forks of the Delaware and Lehigh Rivers. They were often willing to hear him preach but remained strongly attached to 'the customs, traditions, and fabulous notions of their fathers'. Brainerd carried on there for a year with few tangible results. Two missionary trips deeper into Pennsylvania to visit native towns along the Susquehanna River saw him encounter Indians even more hostile to the Christian message. Brainerd was quick to blame such unpromising responses on Native American wickedness, but he also agonized over God's purposes and his own worthiness. Out of his dark night of the soul came a new understanding of what it meant to be a successful missionary: selfless execution of missionary duties was an appropriate criterion for judging his or any other evangelist's success, even in the absence of an impressive tally of converts. Brainerd's example and words would later inspire several generations of nineteenth-century missionaries to embrace a similar definition of missionary achievement.

In June 1745 Brainerd visited another group of Delaware Indians at Crossweeksung, New Jersey. There he found an audience much more receptive to the gospel, and within six weeks a spiritual awakening had dawned among his native listeners. Brainerd poured himself into the work of pastoring and catechizing the new believers. He quickly sensed the need for a more permanent home for his emerging congregation, and he set about acquiring lands to create a Christian Indian town. In the following May he helped them move to Cranberry, New Jersey, where he spent the next six months overseeing the community's spiritual and temporal concerns. Then, fighting ever worsening tuberculosis, he left Cranberry in November 1746, hoping to recuperate in New England so that one day he could return to his people. But apart from a brief visit the following March, Brainerd never again saw his congregation.

Both before and during his sixteen months among the New Jersey Delaware, Brainerd relied heavily upon his Indian interpreter, Moses Tatamy. With little or no facility in the Delaware languages and committed to a brand of Christianity dominated by words rather than images, symbols or rituals, Brainerd rightly saw his missionary effectiveness as directly dependent on his translator. As Brainerd's first baptized convert and a native already familiarized with English ways, Tatamy came to represent precisely the kind of Christianized and Anglicized Indian Brainerd set out to create. Most of his other Delaware converts were not so eager to become settled English farmers, but Brainerd still presented a number of them as models of sinners saved by grace and living in faith in his published journal of 1746. Brainerd used their awakening as an apologia for moderate evangelicalism, much as Jonathan *Edwards would use Brainerd's own story three years later when he edited for publication the young missionary's private journal.

That spiritual autobiography became Edwards' most popular work. He presented Brainerd to eighteenth-century readers as a dedicated Christian servant willing to persist in the face of severe trials. Modern readers will more likely notice Brainerd's self-absorption and intense spiritual introspection, which sealed him off from others, especially alien Indians. How wilful or deliberate Brainerd was in shielding himself from any Indian influence is difficult to say. Interestingly, however, his journal gives hints that whether he knew it or not, he felt the native touch and was changed by it. For example, as Delaware words and actions made him aware that concepts of sin, guilt, divine anger and eternal punishment were especially foreign to their vocabulary, he made concerted efforts to preach a 'milder gospel', one devoid of terror and focused instead on the 'compassion and care of the Lord Jesus Christ'. Their responsiveness in the summer of 1745 prompted him thereafter to reorient his message towards those themes natives preferred to hear.

Brainerd spent most of his last year housebound in Elizabethtown, New Jersey, and Northampton, Massachusetts. Though nursed by his fiancée, Jerusha Edwards

(Jonathan's daughter), he fought losing battles with physical affliction and emotional depression. Still, he had occasional moments when he felt well enough to talk about those things he considered most vital to the colonial church. High on his list was promoting Indian missions. Brainerd's original desire may have been to be a scholar, but once he became a missionary, evangelizing Indians and watching God's kingdom descend among them became his central concerns. His legacy among Native Americans was seen in the work of Joseph Peepy, Samuel Moore, Tobias and other Delaware men who served key roles as cultural mediators and assistants to later missionaries.

Bibliography
J. Conforti, 'David Brainerd and the Nineteenth-Century Missionary Movement', *Journal of the Early Republic* 5 (1985), pp. 309–329; J. Edwards, *The Life of David Brainerd*, in N. Pettit (ed.), *The Works of Jonathan Edwards*, vol. 7 (New Haven: Yale University Press, 1985); R. W. Pointer, '"Poor Indians" and the "Poor in Spirit": The Indian Impact on David Brainerd', *The New England Quarterly* 67 (1994), pp. 403–26; also appears in A. T. Vaughan (ed.), *New England Encounters* (Boston: Northeastern University Press, 1999).

R. W. POINTER

■ **BRAMWELL, William** (1759–1818), Methodist revivalist preacher, was born in the village of Elswick, near Preston, Lancashire, in February 1759, the tenth of the eleven children of George Bramwell, a farmer. His parents were both devout Anglicans, and William received a strict religious upbringing. Endowed with 'a fine mellow voice', he sang in the church choir from an early age but received only a limited formal education at the village school. When at the age of fifteen he went to live with his eldest brother, a Liverpool merchant, in preparation for a commercial career, he found the 'dissipated manners of the place', which strongly 'militated against his religious pursuits', uncongenial, and he was consequently bound as an apprentice to a currier in Preston. He attended worship at Preston Parish Church, where he was converted 'while receiving the sacred elements', but he was subsequently deeply affected by Methodist preaching, declaring 'these are the people with whom I am resolved to live and die!' After meeting John *Wesley on his visit to Preston on 24 May 1781, he 'received a clearer manifestation of the love of God, and was more fully established in the way of the Lord'. He became a class leader and an exhorter, establishing prayer meetings in various parts of the town 'in which great numbers were awakened and brought to God', and was soon appointed a local preacher, sometimes riding forty miles or more on Sunday and preaching three or four times a week in the open air throughout the Fylde countryside. He then spent several months assisting in the expanding Liverpool circuit, before returning to start a business in Preston, where he acquired a house and shop following his engagement to Ellen Byrom, 'a pious young lady, who had been converted to God under his preaching'.

However, Bramwell began 'to feel a powerful conviction that he was called to the exercise of the ministry', and several months later responded to repeated requests by Thomas *Coke to relinquish his business and itinerate in the Kent Circuit, where 'such a revival as had not been witnessed for many years occurred'. In July 1787 he returned to Preston, where he married Ellen Byrom, who bore him a son in September 1788; he continued his ministry in the nearby Blackburn (1788–1789) and Colne (1789–1791) circuits. In 1791 he moved to the West Riding, serving successively at Dewsbury (1791–1793), Birstall (1793–1795) and Sheffield (1795–1798) where, with the assistance of Ann Cutler, a handloom weaver from Macclesfield who had been converted under his influence at Preston, he inspired the great Yorkshire revival. The revival was a major contributory factor to the most rapid membership growth in the history of Wesleyan Methodism and established Bramwell's reputation as the connexion's most popular preacher and its most effective soul-winner in the late eighteenth and early nineteenth centuries.

Bramwell, although he also travelled in the midlands and south of England, remained throughout his ministry, as John Kent has observed, 'the focal point of a group of highly self-conscious revivalists in the north of

England'. His convert and first biographer, James Sigston, the Leeds schoolmaster, compared Bramwell with the American revivalist Charles *Finney, who has sometimes been regarded as the pioneer of mass revivalism. Kent has maintained, however, that Bramwell's technique, with his emphasis on the role of prayer in conversion and the necessity of an immediate personal response to the preaching of the gospel, had a closer affinity with that of John Wesley. However, Bramwell nearly severed his links with Wesleyanism on at least two occasions. In May 1797 he engaged in secret discussions with Alexander *Kilham at Sheffield, but Bramwell's ultimate decision to remain with the Old Connexion was a crucial factor in enabling Wesleyanism to survive its first major secession. Later, in the summer of 1803, after canvassing support for a revivalist union embracing the Leeds 'Kirkgate Screamers', the Manchester Band Room Methodists and the Macclesfield Christian Revivalists, he was finally persuaded to remain with the Old Connexion, although he continued to complain about rich and powerful Wesleyans who 'too frequently usurp improper authority, which damps too much the living flame among the simple'. He remained, moreover, sympathetic to the employment of women preachers and unsuccessfully opposed Conference moves in 1803 and 1804 to exclude them. He had worked closely with Ann Cutler in the Yorkshire revival and Mary Barrit in the Nottingham revival of 1799–1800, maintaining that he 'never knew one man so much blessed as this young woman is in the salvation of souls'. Generally, however, Bramwell's political quietism attuned well to the attitudes of the Wesleyan connexional leadership during the French Wars. He eschewed political discussion at Methodist gatherings, insisting that 'the attention of the company was directed exclusively to the great concerns of their present and eternal salvation'.

Bramwell's own life was characterized by humility and self-denial. A 'constant predisposition to corpulence' led him to institute a rigorous system of fasting and dieting, sometimes 'seldom tasting anything but turnips and a little bread'. He was a habitual early riser, and after washing all over in cold water, he 'generally spent a considerable portion of time in fervent prayer and in reading the Holy Scriptures'. Indeed, his breeches were often threadbare at the knees from his praying for hours on coarse sand. He promoted Wesley's doctrine of 'entire sanctification', and his success as an evangelist derived not only from the impact of his preaching but also from his assiduous pastoral visiting and his other strategies for sustaining revival. His acute spiritual foresight was evident even in his prophesying of his own death, which occurred suddenly outside his biographer James Sigston's academy in Leeds on 13 August 1818.

'Multitudes from all parts of the country' travelled to Westgate Hill, near Leeds, where Bramwell was buried in the chapel graveyard with a headstone proclaiming the text of his first sermon as a local preacher: 'Prepare to meet Thy God'. On 6 September 1818 the popular local preacher William Dawson of Barnbow preached a memorial sermon to a congregation of almost 10,000 near the place in Leeds where Bramwell died, paying tribute to 'the fire of his genius' which 'never blazed so bright as when he was addressing the sinner' or offering 'the arch of salvation' in Christ 'over which sinners may safely pass from darkness to light, from guilt to pardon, from bondage to liberty, from Satan to God, from earth to heaven'.

A genial and popular preacher, Bramwell exercised a wide and enduring influence. One of his converts, a young émigré French marquis, returned to evangelize Normandy during the Napoleonic Wars. The new revivalism was viewed by some early nineteenth-century Primitive Methodists as a return to the 'good old ways of Bramwell', and their founder, Hugh *Bourne, not only taught his missionaries to emulate Bramwell's methods but also published Bramwell's *Life and Death of Ann Cutler* as a testimony to the effectiveness of female preaching. Thomas *Cooper, the Primitive Methodist Chartist, claimed to have received 'entire sanctification' after reading Sigston's memoir of Bramwell, and William *Booth, the founder of the Salvation Army, named his eldest son after the evangelist. Moreover, James *Caughey's revivalist campaign in 1857–1858 evoked memories of Bramwell at Sheffield, and as late as 1863 a threepenny sketch of Bramwell's life enjoyed a wide circulation within Primitive Methodism.

Bibliography

J. Sigston, *Memoir of the Venerable William Bramwell* (London: James Nichols, ³1821–1822); T. Harris, *A Memoir of the Rev. William Bramwell* (London: Charles H. Kelly).

J. A. HARGREAVES

■ **BRENGLE, Samuel Logan** (1860–1937), Salvation Army speaker and author, was born 1 June 1860 in Fredricksburg, Indiana. After his father died, his mother remarried and the family moved several times, settling near Olney, Illinois, in 1872. There Samuel was converted in a Methodist revival at the age of twelve. He attended high school, had private tutoring for several years and attended Indiana Wesleyan University (later renamed DePauw University) from 1877 to 1883.

Intelligent and ambitious, Brengle made the most of his opportunities for learning, drawing on his family's few books, scholarly people who took an interest in him, and his formal education. Although a bookish man who remained an avid reader all his life, Brengle was a cheerful, generous and fun-loving person, active and gifted with an attractive personality.

A sincere Christian since his childhood conversion, Brengle became active in local church affairs in college. He reflected seriously on his own spiritual development. In 1882, to the disappointment of friends who were ambitious for him, Brengle felt called to preach. After college he spent a year as a Methodist minister on circuit. Hoping for a good career in the pulpit and anxious to see more of the world, he attended Boston Theological Seminary from 1884 to 1885. During this period he associated with the Octagon Club, a small group of students who studied and prayed for the experience of 'holiness', which they understood as the cleansing of self and full surrender to the Holy Spirit. Brengle himself, after much soul-searching and prayer, had this experience on 9 January 1885.

Brengle soon fell in with the pioneer Salvation Army in Boston. He was impressed at once with their commitment to evangelism and holiness, and with their fearless and unorthodox means of spreading the good news; their sermons, he remembered years later, had 'fire and bite in them'. He married Elizabeth Swift (1849–1915), a wealthy lay Salvationist, in May 1887, and the next month went to London for training as a Salvation Army officer.

William *Booth, the Army's founder, treated Brengle coolly at first, fearing that Brengle's education and years of independent life would make him unsuitable for Army discipline. Booth was soon impressed with his humble spirit and speaking skill. After six months in a varied training programme, which included much practical experience, Brengle returned to the USA as a captain.

Although he served three brief terms as a corps officer (pastor of a local congregation), Brengle believed even before his Army career that his particular calling was to be an evangelist and preacher of holiness. He freely admitted that he had no administrative skill and indeed, despite his cheerful willingness to take on any work assigned to him, Brengle's Army superiors soon realized that his usefulness was in speaking and writing. After several brief staff appointments, Brengle was made National Spiritual Special (national evangelist) in August 1897. But for a few unimportant temporary assignments, Brengle remained as the Army's official evangelist and expositor of doctrine for the remainder of his life. Despite having no administrative duties Brengle achieved high rank in the Army, retiring in 1931. He died in May 1936.

In addition to an extensive schedule as a speaker and an active role in counselling, Brengle was a prolific writer for Salvation Army periodicals, primarily *The War Cry*. He authored eight books, six of them anthologies of previous articles. His books are still in print, and widely read. In 1947 the Salvation Army established an annual spiritual seminar for officers called the 'Brengle Institute' in his honour.

Brengle's strength, in addition to his gentle personality and transparent sincerity, was in his practical approach. Despite being well educated, he believed theological subtlety missed the point of the gospel: salvation and sanctification were provided in the atonement of Christ, and were appropriated by simple faith, consisting of confession, repentance and trust. He was equally practical in his descriptions of the life of the consecrated Christian, and counselled discouraged Army personnel effectively, whether individually or in groups. To Brengle the critical virtues were humility, patience and love, and to keep one's mind on the big picture: the everlasting gospel and the Army's soul-saving work.

Bibliography
C. W. Hall, *Samuel Logan Brengle: Portrait of a Prophet* (Chicago: The Salvation Army Supply and Purchasing Dept., 1933); S. L. Brengle, *The Way of Holiness* (1902); R. D. Rightmire, 'Samuel Logan Brengle and the Development of Salvation Army Pneumatology', *Wesleyan Theological Journal* 27.1 and 2 (spring–fall 1992), pp. 104–131; E. H. McKinley, *Marching to Glory: The History of the Salvation Army in the USA, 1880–1992* (Grand Rapids: Eerdmans, ²1995).

E. H. McKINLEY

■ **BRIGHT, William Rohl** (1921–), founder of Campus Crusade for Christ, was born on 19 October 1921 to Forest Dale and Mary Lee Rohl Bright on a five thousand acre ranch owned by his father near Coweta, Oklahoma. Bright's mother was devout and took her seven children to church, but his authoritarian father was not religious. Although 'Bill' Bright was baptized at the age of twelve in a Methodist church, he found little use for religion, which he associated with women and children. After attending elementary school in a one-room schoolhouse, Bright became a student at Coweta High School. At graduation, he received an award for being the 'best all-around student'. In autumn 1939 Bright entered Northeastern State College in Tahlequah, Oklahoma, where he was elected president of his class, became editor of the school yearbook, was made president of the student body and was selected as the college's most outstanding student. After receiving his bachelor's degree in 1943, Bright repeatedly attempted to enlist for military service but was denied because of an ear injury. After a short period spent teaching extension students at Oklahoma State University, Bright moved to California in 1944 to seek his fortune.

After finding a flat owned by a devout elderly couple, Bright began a successful business selling gourmet fruits, nuts and brandies under the name Bright's Epicurean Delights (later Bright's California Confections and Bright's Brandied Foods). Bright's landlords repeatedly urged him to attend the famed evangelical Hollywood First Presbyterian Church where Louis Evans Sr was pastor and Henrietta *Mears was director of Christian education. When Bright attended a church-sponsored party at the home of a movie star, he was impressed by the successful and attractive people he met and surprised that these Christians were as ambitious and goal-oriented as he. He later declared, 'In one evening my notion that Christianity is appropriate only for women and children was really shaken.' Bright became a regular at 'Hollywood Pres.' where he was profoundly influenced by Mears. After hearing Mears speak at a young adult group about the conversion of the apostle Paul, Bright was converted to Christianity in the spring of 1945.

In 1945 Bright began corresponding with Vonette Zachary, a sophomore at Texas State College for Women, who, though five years younger, had attended school with him in Coweta as a child. When a business trip took Bright to Dallas, he arranged to meet with Zachary and asked her to marry him on their first date. They became engaged that weekend but waited three years to marry so that Zachary could finish college.

Feeling a need for theological training, Bright began attending Princeton Theological Seminary in 1946. He transferred to the recently founded Fuller Seminary in Pasadena, California, one year later in order better to attend to his confectionary business. In June 1947 Bright, along with Mears and two others, initiated a series of 'briefing conferences' designed to 'brief' college students about the need to 'win the world for Christ'.

In 1951 Bright became convinced that God wanted him to start a student ministry. He left the seminary and sold his business in order to launch Campus Crusade for Christ (CCC) at the University of California (Los Angeles). Within a year, Bright had enlisted six others to minister on three local campuses. From the outset, CCC focused on training Christians to evangelize others rather than simply on providing evangelistic services for non-believers. In the summer of 1956, after hearing a sales consultant emphasize the importance of simplicity and repetition in sales pitches, Bright revised a simplified presentation of the gospel on which he had been working since 1952 called 'God's Plan for Your Life'. Bright insisted that all CCC staff members memorize this presentation and use it as an evangelism technique. By 1958 Bright had refined this method into a set of 'Four Spiritual Laws'. One, 'God loves you and has a wonderful plan for your life'; two, 'man is sinful and separated from God'; three, 'Jesus Christ is God's only provision for man's sin'; and four, 'we must individually receive Jesus Christ as Saviour and Lord; then we can know and experience God's love and plan for our lives'. In 1959 Bright began introducing his technique to churches through his Lay Institute for Evangelism (LIFE) programmes. By the time his influential summary of the Christian message was first published in 1965, it had been in use for almost a decade on college campuses and had been adopted and adapted by many other ministries. Though it was often criticized as overly simplistic and formulaic, Bright defended his technique as an effective way to get individuals to make an initial faith commitment without their having first to learn theological jargon.

By 1960 CCC had 109 staff members operating on forty campuses in fifteen states, with additional offshoots in South Korea and Pakistan. In 1961 Bright raised two million dollars to purchase the once-fashionable Arrowhead Springs resort in the San Bernardino mountains as headquarters for CCC. Always seeking new ways to promote the gospel, Bright added the illusionist André Kole to his staff in 1963. In 1966 he launched not only a music ministry but also ministries to high school students, to military personnel and a 'ministry to jocks and their fans' called Athletes in Action. CCC sponsored a well-publicized, week-long 'blitz' at the University of California (Berkeley) in 1967, in which 600 'Crusaders' attempted to present the gospel to every one of the 27,000 students on campus. Despite the growth of CCC, some staff found Bright to be dictatorial, theologically rigid and unable to respond effectively to the new student counterculture, causing some prominent staff to leave the organization in the late 1960s. Bright also received criticism for prohibiting his staff from openly espousing the charismatic movement or speaking in tongues.

In 1972 Bright organized Explo '72, an evangelism training rally in Dallas, Texas, in which 85,000 participated. Explo '74, held two years later in Seoul, Korea, attracted 330,000 people. Bright attempted to saturate the United States with the gospel in 1975–1977 with his 'Here's Life, America' campaign, which proclaimed the tag line 'I found it!' in 246 cities. An international version of this campaign was later initiated.

In 1979 CCC released its heavily promoted *Jesus* film, based on the Gospel of Luke. By the end of the century it had been translated into 656 languages and viewed by more than 4 billion people. In 1980 Bright led 'Washington for Jesus', a gathering of one million people for prayer in the nation's capital. Five years later he sponsored Explo '85, which offered evangelism training simultaneously to groups in sixty-eight countries through satellite technology. Bright announced his ambitious New Life 2000 plan in January 1987, which aimed to present the gospel to every person on earth and gain a billion conversions by the end of the century.

Starting in the 1970s, Bright increasingly advocated a conservative political agenda and aligned himself with the New Christian Right. In 1991 the headquarters of CCC was moved to Orlando, Florida. Bright began a series of prayer and fasting gatherings in 1994 to combat moral decline. He formed alliances with Catholic, Orthodox and mainline Protestant leaders to advance his causes. He received the Templeton Prize for Progress in Religion in 1996. By the end of the century, CCC was operating in 181 countries with a full-time staff of more than 20,500.

In 2001 Bright announced that he was dying from pulmonary fibrosis and transferred the leadership of CCC to his long time associate Steve Douglass. Connected to an oxygen tank, Bright undertook numerous farewell appearances and even co-authored a series of suspense novels with spiritual themes.

Bibliography

M. Richardson, *Amazing Faith: The Authorized Biography of Bill Bright* (Colorado Springs: Waterbrook Press, 2000); R. Quebedeaux, *I Found It! The Story of Bill Bright and Campus Crusade* (San Francisco: Harper & Row, 1979).

D. K. LARSEN

■ **BRISCOE, D(avid) Stuart** (1930–), pastor, author and conference speaker, and **Jill Pauline Ryder** (1935–), author and conference speaker, played an important role in post-1960s evangelical circles, continuing a long tradition of interaction between British and American evangelicalism. Stuart Briscoe was born in Millom, Cumbria, England, in 1930, the son of Stanley and Mary Wardle Briscoe, who had a grocer's shop in the town. The family were members of an 'open' Brethren group, and although Stuart honoured his family's legalistic piety, as he grew older he became increasingly impatient with rigid fundamentalism. After completing secondary school he worked in a bank and took night classes with a view to a career in banking. At the age of seventeen he began to preach and work with local youth groups. Enlisted by the Royal Marines in 1948, he became a commando but spent the balance of his two years' service as part of the Marines' rugby team. After his discharge he returned to banking, eventually becoming a bank inspector in Manchester. Hearing of Major Ian Thomas' plans to work among ex-Nazi youth, he was involved in the beginnings of Thomas' Torchbearers' youth centre at Capernwray Hall near Carnforth. Through his involvement there, Briscoe met Jill Ryder, a Liverpool school teacher.

Jill Ryder was born in Liverpool in 1935, the daughter of William and Peggy Pont Ryder. Raised in modest middle-class comfort from her father's income as a car salesman, she was brought up in a nominally Presbyterian family. After finishing secondary school, she attended Homerton College at Cambridge University. While there she became ill, was converted through conversations with her roommate in hospital and became involved with the Cambridge Inter-Collegiate Christian Union. After earning her teacher's certificate, she returned to Liverpool to teach in a primary school in one of the city's poorer neighbourhoods. Concerned about the poor home lives of her pupils and their older siblings, she joined with others in establishing a youth centre and coffee house. Soon she was holding regular meetings for 150 teenagers; her account of this period was later published as *There's a Snake in My Garden* (1975). It was on a retreat with this group at Capernwray that she met Stuart Briscoe. They were married in July 1958 and later had two sons and a daughter.

For a short time the couple continued with their careers and working with young people at Capernwray. In 1959 Thomas invited Briscoe to become the Torchbearers' treasurer and a part-time Bible teacher. It was the latter work that quickly took up most of his time. A gifted preacher with a keen sense of humour, his teaching reflected the influence of Keswick holiness theology, but in his prescription for the Christian life he emphasized grace and avoided legalism. Soon he was in demand as a speaker, and Thomas encouraged him to embark on a three-month speaking tour in the United States. Soon afterwards Briscoe relinquished his financial duties and became a full-time emissary for the Torchbearers, leaving Jill to raise their young family while running a nursery school and working with young people at Capernwray.

In 1970, while on a trip to North America, Briscoe was asked to speak at the church of Bob Hobson, a Milwaukee pastor who had just resigned his pastorate to take a position at Capernwray. Elmbrook Baptist Church in Brookfield, Wisconsin, was a twelve-year-old independent Baptist congregation of about 700; impressed with Briscoe, the congregation offered him Hobson's former position. To the surprise of his wife and associates in Britain he accepted, resigned his position with the Torchbearers and moved his family to the United States.

Briscoe's first months with the new congregation were difficult and he seemed destined to fulfil the evangelist Alan Redpath's prediction that he could not last a year in the pastorate. Most controversial was Briscoe's insistence that the church would never be able to reach the Milwaukee area's predominantly German-Polish-Czech Lutheran and Catholic population as a Baptist church. The church decided to recognize the prior baptisms of prospective members, although it lost some of its existing membership as a result. The Elmbrook Church that Briscoe began to fashion was centred on his preaching but also featured an informal worship service with more upbeat music and tolerance for broad differences of doctrinal opinion. Members were expected to participate actively in the church's growing array of activities, and home Bible studies played a major role in the life of the congregation. For four years the church held additional services in a former cinema. By the mid-1970s the congregation had grown significantly and moved into a new building. Sunday morning attendance was over 2,000; a bookshop had been opened, and tapes of sermons were available; a radio programme ('Telling the Truth') was heard locally on a major station and on many other stations across the country; and a television programme ('In Reality') was broadcast in Milwaukee. Briscoe's reputation also spread through his speaking engagements and books dealing with church life and Christian discipleship, such as *Where Was the Church When the Youth Exploded?* (1972), *Getting Into God* (1975) and *What Works When Life Doesn't* (1976). In 1979 he served as the vice-chairman for Billy Graham's Milwaukee Crusade.

After an initially difficult period of adjustment to being a pastor's wife, Jill Briscoe determined to resume her work with children. In 1971 she founded a club, the 'God Squad', for junior high-school-aged children at Elmbrook. Increasingly, however, she found that her new role as a pastor's wife brought her invitations to speak at women's functions and local Bible study groups. Her natural speaking skills, sharp wit and ability to apply biblical teachings to the practical struggles of marriage and motherhood added another dimension to Elmbrook's appeal. In the early 1970s Jill began a Thursday morning Bible class for housewives at Elmbrook that soon attracted hundreds, as well as a Monday evening Bible study for working women. In addition, she quickly gained a good reputation as a conference and retreat speaker, which was enhanced by tapes from Elmbrook and occasional broadcasts of her talks on 'Telling the Truth'. By the early 1980s she had relinquished all her responsibilities with the church's youth work and was focusing on her ministry to women.

During the 1980s and 1990s Elmbrook Church continued to grow, with weekly attendance nearing 10,000. As the church grew, Stuart Briscoe encouraged efforts by members in different parts of the Milwaukee area to form new congregations, such as Westbrook Church in Delafield; in all, eight new churches had emerged from Elmbrook by the turn of the century. Throughout this period both Stuart and Jill spent considerable time travelling and speaking. In North America the Briscoes were increasingly perceived as a team; they often spoke to groups such as the National Association of Evangelicals, Focus on the Family and PromiseKeepers. Jill served on the board of *Christianity Today* magazine and World Relief. In Britain, Stuart enjoyed considerable popular influence, especially through his visits (almost every year) to the Keswick Conference Centre. Both Briscoes continued to write. Stuart concentrated on popular exposition of the Bible, in books such as *The Fruits of the Spirit: Cultivating Christian Character* (1993). Jill meanwhile concentrated on books aimed at women, such as *Renewal on the Run* (1992) and *De-Baiting the Woman Trap* (1994), launched *Just Between Us*, a magazine for women involved in ministry either as wives or leaders, and wrote a series of interactive children's books on biblical characters. Both Briscoes supported Christians for Biblical Equality, which did not endorse the ordination of women but argued that 'women as well as men exercise the prophetic, priestly and royal functions'.

In 2000 Stuart resigned after thirty years as Elmbrook's Senior Pastor, and both he and Jill assumed roles as ministers-at-large. Through their broadcasts, tapes, speaking and writing they continued to cultivate a large following within evangelical circles. The success of Elmbrook Church, with its informal style and broadly evangelical ecumenism, made it one of the earliest and most influential models of the 'megachurch' phenomenon, particularly for churches in regions of the United States where evangelicals were in the minority. Moreover, the Briscoes' example as a well-loved husband-and-wife team did much to break down resistance among moderate American evangelicals to the concept of women in prominent leadership and teaching roles within the church. Their major influence, however, was among the tens of thousands of evangelicals who looked to them for practical biblical exposition and guidance for living the Christian life.

Bibliography
J. Briscoe, *There's a Snake in My Garden* (Grand Rapids: Zondervan, 1975); J. Briscoe, *Thank You For Being a Friend: My Personal Journey* (Chicago: Moody Press, 1999); S. Briscoe, *What Works When Life Doesn't* (Wheaton: Victor Books, 1976); S. Briscoe, 'In This Together', Interview, *Leadership* XXII.2 (spring 2001), pp. 62–68.

L. ESKRIDGE

■ **BROWNE, Robert** (c. 1550–1633), English Separatist, was born at Tolethorpe near Stamford, Lincolnshire. He was educated at Corpus Christi College, Cambridge and there came into contact with Thomas *Cartwright and other Puritans who were campaigning for a Presbyterian form of church government. After leaving Cambridge in 1572, he spent three years teaching, but his outspokenness over the state of the church led to his dismissal. He went home and then later returned to Cambridge and lodged at Dry Drayton with the well-known Puritan leader Richard Greenham. While he was with Greenham, he began to question the authority of the bishops and to argue that a bishop had no right to appoint pastors; each local congregation, he claimed, had the right and duty to elect its own leadership.

Browne advocated congregational church polity, arguing that authority in the church rested, under Christ, with the whole company of believing Christians. He insisted that bishops had no right to license preachers, and when his brother obtained two preaching licences for him, 'he lost one and burned another'. In the early stages of his career, Browne, as a Puritan, defined the church in Matthew 18:15–17 not as a company of believers, but as ministers and elders chosen out of the congregation. By 1581 he was a Separatist who rejected episcopal authority and with it the established church.

Believing that those who were members of the pure church should separate themselves from the uncommitted, in 1581 Browne established an independent congregation in Norwich. This Separatist congregation was organized on the basis of a covenant in which the members 'gave their consent, to join themselves to the Lord, in one covenant and fellowship together, and to keep and seek agreement under his laws and government: and therefore did utterly flee and avoid such like disorders and wickedness, as was mentioned before' (A. Peel and L. H. Carlson [eds.], *The Writings of ... Robert Browne*, p. 422).

Browne was nicknamed 'Troublechurch Browne' by one of his contemporaries, and not without cause. He became so outspoken for Separatist views that he was imprisoned for his beliefs, and freed only after a relative, Robert Cecil, Lord Burleigh, Lord Treasurer of England and chief minister to Queen Elizabeth I, intervened on his behalf.

Like many others, Browne fled with his congregation to the continent; they settled in Middelburg in the Netherlands. Here he published several works, including *A treatise of reformation without tarying for anie* (1582) and *A book which sheweth the life and manners of all true Christians* (1582). As the title suggests, the first book was an ardent appeal for reform without delay. The latter work was an exposition of Browne's theology of the church, which was based on the idea that a Christian community was a congregation which had covenanted together to obey divine law. Browne, like his Puritan predecessors, sought to make his appeal on the basis of Scripture. He believed, however, that the reformation of the church would be based on the renewal of the covenant between God and his people. He held a 'mutualist' or conditional view of the covenant; although God in his mercy has made an agreement with his people 'that if we keep his laws, not forsaking his government, he will take us for his people and bless us accordingly', the people are to live in obedience to his laws (*Writings*, p. 257).

This conditional view of covenant was not the view held by contemporary Puritans, and the source of Browne's understanding of covenant is not certain. He may have taken it directly from his reading of Scripture, or from William *Tyndale or John *Hooper, who both wrote about covenant. But Browne seems to have been the first to have made this view the framework for a congregational polity.

Browne argued that the church is a voluntary association of believers who have covenanted together to walk in the ways of Christ. Under the final authority of Christ, members of the church have the right to govern themselves. The true church is the visible manifestation of the kingdom of Christ, and the local body of believers is obliged to separate from those who are not committed and to remove from their congregation any who are inconsistent in their Christian profession.

Although he believed firmly in the congregational way and insisted on the practice of discipline within the church, Browne was not willing to bow to the wishes of his congregation. He was temperamental and argumentative, and after a disagreement with members of his congregation in Middelburg, he went to Scotland in January 1584. He was imprisoned there for a time and later returned to England. In 1585 he made a formal submission to the Church of England, in which he accepted the authority of the Archbishop of Canterbury and recognized the church of the Elizabethan settlement as the true church. He became master of St Olave's School in Southwark in 1586.

In spite of Browne's promises to be faithful to the established church, it appears that while at Southwark he continued to minister to Separatist congregations. In 1588 he was accused of spreading Separatist views and of failing to take the sacrament at his parish church. In 1591 he received episcopal ordination and became the rector of Thorpe-cum-Achurch in Northamptonshire. In 1617 he was accused of failing to conform to the ceremonies prescribed in the Book of Common Prayer. He was suspended from his duties and excommunicated in 1631. A troubled man, he died in October 1633 in Northampton Gaol after he was arrested for assaulting a village police constable.

Although Browne was scorned by Separatists as an apostate from their cause, he was recognized as a pioneer theologian of the Separatist tradition, so much so that its early adherents were often called Brownists. His lasting contribution was his attempt to formulate a consistent doctrine of the church based on the idea of a mutual covenant between God and true believers.

Bibliography
B. R. White, *The English Separatist Tradition, from the Marian Martyrs to the Pilgrim Fathers* (Oxford Theological Monographs, 1971); C. Burrage, *The True Story of Robert Browne* (Oxford: 1906); A. Peel and L. H. Carlson (eds.), *The Writings of Robert Harrison and Robert Browne* (London: 1953).

K. E. SMITH

■ **BRUCE, Frederick Fyvie** (1910–1990), biblical scholar, was born in Elgin, Scotland on 12 October 1910, and educated at Elgin Academy (1921–1928) and the Universities of Aberdeen (1928–1932, MA), Cambridge (1932–1934, BA, MA) and Vienna (research student in Indo-European philology, 1934–1935). His early studies were in Greek and Latin, following in the tradition of Sir William M. Ramsay and Alexander Souter (his teacher at Aberdeen). He graduated at the top of his class at Cambridge. Aberdeen University honoured him with an honorary DD in 1957. He also obtained the MA in Hebrew language and literature from Manchester University in 1963.

Bruce's first academic post was that of assistant lecturer in Greek at Edinburgh (1935–1938), from which he went on to be lecturer at Leeds University (1938–1947) and then head of a new department of biblical history and literature at Sheffield University (1947–1959, Professor 1955–1959), even though (tradition has it, because) he had no formal training in theology or biblical studies. In 1959 he was appointed to the John Rylands Chair of Biblical Criticism and Exegesis at Manchester (1959–1978), where he distinguished himself by supervising more PhD students in biblical studies than any other scholar of his generation. Author of more than fifty books, numerous translations and editions, hundreds of essays and literally thousands of reviews, he was the doyen of evangelical scholars for his generation.

From his childhood Bruce possessed a love of the Bible and languages that would stay with him throughout his life. His father, Peter Fyvie Bruce, was an itinerant evangelist among the Christian (also known as Plymouth) Brethren and exerted a strong influence on his personal life. Bruce once commented that he had a sense of his father's looking over his shoulder when he wrote, especially in his early years; in his autobiography, he says, 'I have never had to unlearn anything I learned from him.'

Bruce mastered all of the ancient languages

necessary for the study of the Bible and the classics, as well as the modern European languages in which material of scholarly significance or general Christian interest was published, along with the Celtic languages of his ethnic heritage. For twelve years he edited *Yorkshire Celtic Studies* (1945–1957). He was a voracious reader, building a huge personal library that was eventually willed to the John Rylands University Library of Manchester. He was elected to the presidency of many academic societies, including both the Society for Old Testament Study (1965) and its sister, the Society for New Testament Study (1975), being one of only two individuals to serve as president of both.

In his early years as a scholar, he tended to limit his travels to the UK and Europe, generally to give lectures, preach or attend the meetings of learned societies. He edited *The Palestine Exploration Quarterly* for many years (1957–1971), but his first visit to Israel was with a group of colleagues in 1969. However, from the late 1950s, Bruce began to travel widely to give lectures in the USA and Canada, Australia and New Zealand, and east Africa (where his daughter and her family lived from 1965 to 1974) as well as in Europe. He drew unusually large crowds to his scholarly lectures. Most were thrilled at the opportunity to hear the great man whose writings they had enjoyed, but wondered how such an interesting writer could be such a dull speaker. He was dull when reading from a manuscript, which was his usual style, but when he spoke extemporaneously, especially when answering questions from the audience, he was spell-binding. The succinct answers to questions about the Bible and contemporary church life that he offered monthly in a popular Christian magazine (1952–1972), a selection of which were published in *Answers to Questions* (1972), were a brilliant model of effective communication.

Bruce was above all a biblical theologian. Although he edited *The Evangelical Quarterly*, a journal founded 'for the defence of the Reformed faith', for more than thirty years (1949–1980), he was not 'Reformed' in a sectarian or ideological sense. When people asked him about a particular theological position, he generally responded by asking what particular passage of Scripture they had in mind. Then, he would offer an interpreta-

tion of that text for their edification. He was well known as an evangelical, being an enthusiastic supporter of the Inter-Varsity Fellowship (now the Universities and Colleges Christian Fellowship) and all of its ministries and also a contributing editor of *Christianity Today* (1956–1978), but even in this respect he was by no means a party man. When asked whether he would describe himself as a 'conservative evangelical', he replied that he preferred to be 'an unhyphenated evangelical', one who is wholeheartedly committed to the message of good news about Jesus Christ but who did not wish to narrow this message in a manner that would separate him from either the whole counsel of God or the broader community of believers (*Answers*, p. 204). Some of his views, he said, might be described as 'liberal'; others, as 'conservative'. He chose to hold them because he thought them to be true, not because they fitted a particular mind-set or theological tradition. His sympathies were made clear by his choice of title for the British edition of his *magnum opus* on Paul: *Paul, Apostle of the Free Spirit* (1977), published in North America as *Paul, Apostle of the Heart Set Free*.

Bruce's knowledge of the Bible was prodigious. He seemed to have had the whole Bible, both in the original languages and in several translations, committed to memory. When asked a question about the Bible, he did not have to look up the text. He would sometimes take off his glasses, close his eyes as if he were scrolling the text in his mind, and then comment in such an exact manner that it was clear he was referring to the Hebrew or Greek text, which he either translated or paraphrased in his answer. If the context were academic, he might refer directly to the original language; in speaking to students who were not necessarily theologians, he would normally use a contemporary translation; in church, he would use the translation familiar to the majority of his hearers, whether RSV, NIV, NEB, KJV or, in conservative Brethren circles, JND (The New Translation by John Nelson Darby), again, normally quoting exactly from memory. He also seemed to know all of the hymns of the classical and evangelical Christian traditions by heart as well as a large body of secular poetry, English, Scottish, Greek and Latin.

Bruce had a simple filing system for the information he needed to write his books and essays, based on the verses of the Bible, from Genesis 1:1 to Revelation 22:21. His natural way to think of everything was in reference to the general flow of Scripture. He did not think topically, but according to chapter and verse. His mind was fundamentally exegetical.

Bruce's first major work was a commentary on the Greek text of the Acts of the Apostles (1951; ³1990), which heralded the resurgence of evangelical biblical scholarship associated with the work of the Tyndale Fellowship for Biblical Research, in the founding of which he had been a driving influence and to which he gave important leadership for more than four decades. The commentary was highly technical; the emphasis was historical and linguistic rather than theological. The learning displayed was immense, and the care with which Bruce wrote was a model of lucid brevity. He published a second commentary on Acts, in the New London/New International Commentary series (1954; ²1988), which was much more expositional and theological, intended for pastors rather than scholars. These two works together set the pattern for the burgeoning commentary series that were to be produced by an increasing number of evangelical Bible scholars during the next half century.

Bruce wrote commentaries on every Pauline letter and nearly all of the books of the New Testament. In addition to those on Acts, his major commentaries were on Hebrews (NICNT, 1964), Colossians (NICNT, 1957, to which Ephesians and Philemon were added in 1984), and Galatians (NIGTC, 1982). Smaller but also influential commentaries included those on Romans (TNTC, 1963) and 1 and 2 Corinthians (NCB, 1971). In 1965 he published *An Expanded Paraphrase of the Epistles of Paul*, in which he translated the letters in the order he believed them to have been written and set them in their historical context.

His earliest book, *The New Testament Documents: Are they Reliable?* (1943; revised many times and translated into many languages), grew out the talks he was invited to give to university student groups when he was still a lecturer in Greek. His history of the early church, *The Spreading Flame* (1953), and *The Books and the Parchments* (1950),

grew out of the lectures he had to give in Sheffield. His classic textbook on *New Testament History* (1969) was the first volume in a new series of theological texts and remains in print today, long after all of the other volumes in the series have gone out of print. Each book was revised regularly throughout his life, and most remain in print today.

Bruce was at home at the highest levels of academic life, but he was equally at home among ordinary lay believers, as well as seekers, whether they were undergraduate students, educated or uneducated church members, the vast array of people who came to hear his lectures in the UK or on his visits to Canada and the USA, Australia and New Zealand, and Uganda, or members of his home church in Stockport.

Bruce was an evangelical who focused on the centrality of Christ and the heart of the evangel (good news) rather than the doctrines or customs of a section of the Christian community. He believed that there was no incompatibility between the confession of historic Christianity and modern biblical criticism. Studying the Bible critically was simply an attempt to use one's God-given mind and all the tools provided by contemporary historical and literary scholarship in order to understand the Bible accurately.

If Bruce had a theological hobby-horse, it was the principle of liberty, which he regarded as the heart of the Pauline gospel. 'I find it hard to understand,' he commented, 'that some people simply do not wish to be free. They are afraid of liberty. They are afraid of having too much liberty themselves; and they're certainly afraid of letting other people … have too much liberty. … It seems much better to move in predestinate grooves' (Gasque, unpublished notes). He took his cue from Paul, 'who had an exceptional insight into the mind of Christ and realized that in Christ and nowhere else is true freedom to be found. Among all the followers of Christ, I suppose there has never been a more emancipated soul than the soul of Paul' (Gasque, unpublished notes). In spite of his Plymouth Brethren tradition, he became a champion of women in ministry and biblical egalitarianism (cf. his comments in his commentaries on Gal. 3:26–28; 1 Cor. 11:2–16; 1 Cor. 14:33–35; Eph. 5:21–33; 1 Tim. 2:8–15).

Bruce towered over British biblical scholarship for fifty years. He commended a moderate, intelligent and contemporary evangelicalism to his academic colleagues and he set an example of scholarship, balance, integrity, humility and ecumenicity for his evangelical brothers and sisters to follow. Younger scholars flocked from around the world to study with him, many of whom are teaching in colleges, universities and theological schools today.

Bruce demonstrated the importance of studying the New Testament within the context of the Graeco-Roman world, using all the resources of classical and hellenistic literature, archaeology and geography, and the results of more than a century of revolutionary historical research, to illuminate its text and, indeed, that of the Old Testament.

Bibliography

Journal of the Christian Brethren Research Fellowship 22 (Nov. 1971), pp. 21–47; F. F. Bruce, *In Retrospect: Remembrance of Things Past* (Exeter: Paternoster Press; Grand Rapids: Eerdmans, 1980).

W. W. GASQUE

■ **BRYAN, William Jennings** (1860–1925), politician and editor, was an outspoken leader of American fundamentalism in the early twentieth century. Bryan was born in Salem, Illinois, on 19 March 1860. His father, Silas Bryan, was a circuit court judge of Scotch-Irish descent. His mother, Mariah Jennings Bryan, was a member of a prominent Illinois family. Both parents were devout Christians. Silas Bryan was an active Baptist, who opened sessions of his court with prayer. Mariah Bryan was a Methodist, who encouraged her son to attend Methodist Sunday school each Sunday morning and Baptist Sunday school in the afternoons. Bryan's paternal grandfather, William Bryan, was active in the Baptist church near his home in the Blue Ridge Mountains of Virginia. The Bryans attended various weekly church services and conducted family devotions in their home. William Jennings Bryan was converted at fourteen years of age and joined the Cumberland Presbyterian Church.

Silas Bryan was a member of the Democratic Party who passed on his love of politics to his son and pointed him towards legal training. William Jennings Bryan received the BA degree from Illinois College in 1881, having majored in classics. He then entered Union College of Law, Chicago, graduating in 1883. His first law practice was in Jacksonville, Illinois, where most of his cases involved the sale of insurance and the collection of debts. On 1 October 1884 he married Mary Baird, the daughter of a prominent local merchant. After they were married, Mary Baird Bryan enrolled in Union College of Law, the only woman in her class, and graduated third among a group of seventeen students. The couple then moved to Lincoln, Nebraska, in 1887, where Bryan continued to practise law and to hone his public-speaking skills.

In 1891 Bryan was elected to the US House of Representatives, where he served two terms. After an unsuccessful campaign for the US Senate, he became editor of *The Omaha World-Herald*, a position he held from 1894 to 1896. Through his editorial work at the paper Bryan continued to address issues of his day, including populism and the concerns of farmers, exemplified in their effort to apply 'free silver' to the American monetary system over against the monopoly of the gold standard. He also developed a reputation as a popular speaker at political gatherings and church meetings around the state. Bryan's rhetorical skills and agrarian populism combined to produce his famous 'cross of gold speech', delivered at the Democratic National Convention in 1896. In this, his most famous address, he asserted: 'Having behind us the producing masses of this nation and the world, supported by the commercial interests, the laboring interest, and the toilers everywhere, we will answer their demand for the gold standard by saying to them: "You shall not press down upon the brow of labor the crown of thorns, you shall not crucify mankind upon a cross of gold."' It was classic advocacy on behalf of the weak, which set the rural farm culture of the Midwest against the corporate eastern establishment. After the speech Bryan was nominated as the Democratic candidate for president; he was only thirty-six years old. This was the first of Bryan's three Democratic nominations for the presidency, each of which ended in defeat, twice to William McKinley (1896, 1900) and once to William Howard Taft (1904). Yet even after these multiple defeats, Bryan remained a stalwart of Democratic politics. President Woodrow Wilson named him Secretary of State in 1913, but he resigned in 1915 in protest against what he saw as Wilson's efforts to develop alliances that would lead America into the war in Europe. His political influence soon declined, and he failed to be chosen as a delegate to the 1916 nominating convention. He represented Nebraska Democrats one more time, at the 1920 convention, but with limited influence. In 1921 the Bryans moved to Florida, where Bryan was elected as a delegate to the Democratic Convention of 1924; his election gave him some chance of standing for election to the Senate in 1926. At the Convention he promoted party unity by opposing a resolution that attacked the Ku Klux Klan by name (the resolution failed by one vote), but was willing to split the party over the election of a 'dry' (prohibition-supporting) presidential candidate. His support for the candidacy of William McAdoo was unsuccessful, and some in the crowd heckled his speeches. He reluctantly gave his support to John Davis, who was defeated for the presidency by Calvin Coolidge. Bryan's health broke and his political career was over.

Bryan was known as the 'Great Commoner', and his political idealism and religious conservatism led him to support a variety of progressive and reactionary positions. He supported direct election of United States senators, women's suffrage, prohibition, a national income tax, establishment of a cabinet Department of Labor, corporate funding of national political campaigns, and greater government regulation of monopolies such as meat-packing and railways. He played a leading part in the passage of the Eighteenth Amendment to the Constitution, which instituted the prohibition of alcohol in 1920. He also supported a single term of six years for American presidents, the abolition of the electoral college in favour of a single national vote for president, and the nationwide abolition of unsigned newspaper editorials. He called for the establishment of a national minimum wage, and national referendums on war except in cases of direct invasion. Bryan himself was perhaps a 'quasi-pacifist', who opposed war at every turn but who, in 1898 organized a military regiment from Nebraska to serve in the Spanish American War. At the end of the war, however, he immediately resigned his commission in protest against developing imperialism. He was also an outspoken supporter of the League of Nations. On racial issues Bryan's progressivism was tempered by his political support in the South, yet as a Democrat he was at least concerned to find ways of encouraging African Americans to desert the Republican Party. He urged African Americans to better themselves morally and educationally in order to improve their ability to integrate themselves into American society. Bryan was also a lifelong opponent of the use of alcohol, signed a temperance pledge and insisted that biblical references to wine, including those in the account of Jesus' miracle at Cana (John 2), were actually to non-fermented grape juice. Bryan was also a strict Sabbatarian who insisted that, while practices might vary, every citizen should be guaranteed a day of rest with sufficient peace and quiet to provide for relaxation and reflection. Although he would speak at church events on Sundays, he refused to give political addresses.

As the famous 'Controversy of the Twenties' developed in American religious life, Bryan was recognized as a thoroughgoing Presbyterian fundamentalist. He was convinced that the Bible was divinely inspired and its text totally without error on every matter it discussed. He affirmed the need for conversion to Jesus Christ, and that Christ's atoning death and bodily resurrection provided salvation for those who believed. Like many Presbyterian intellectuals, he chose not to enter into the debate over Christ's return and affirmed that debates over the premillennial or postmillennial second coming were matters of interpretation rather than inspiration. His progressivism found its way into church life in his advocacy of church loan funds to aid those who were in temporary economic difficulty, his consistent advocacy of pacifism and his relatively optimistic view of human nature. His view of the human condition was closely related to his opposition to evolution. Bryan believed that Darwin's views not only challenged the veracity of the Bible, but also replaced the idea of human progress and achievement with that of the 'survival of the fittest', which implied incessant violence. This idea, in his view, undermined the possibility of redemption, not simply for the individual, but for the entire race. Such challenges to orthodoxy would result in divine judgment upon those who undermined the truth revealed in Jesus and the Bible.

For Bryan, the fundamentalist opposition to evolution and other aspects of theological liberalism was yet another great crusade like those he had waged against the gold standard and the alcohol industry. For fundamentalists, Bryan was a superb spokesperson whose Christian commitments and oratorical brilliance could be used to respond to the liberal onslaughts. From 1902 until his move to Florida in 1921, Bryan was a ruling elder in the Westminster Presbyterian Church in Fairview, Nebraska. In Florida the Bryans joined the First Presbyterian Church of Miami, where he began to give 'Bryan Bible Talks' each Sunday, many of which were direct attacks on liberalism. The talks became so popular that they were moved outdoors in order to accommodate the crowds of two to six thousand people who attended each Sunday. Many of these talks were published. Indeed, Bryan wrote more than thirty books, most of which dealt with political issues and events. Several volumes dealt with religious topics, especially matters related to the fundamentalist/modernist debates. These included *The Prince of Peace* (1909), *The Bible and Its Enemies* (1921), *In His Image* (1922), *Orthodox Christianity versus Modernism* (1923), and *Christ and his Companions* (1925). His *Memoirs*, jointly written with Mary Baird Bryan, were published in 1925.

Bryan believed that the truth of the Bible was being challenged by liberal views on evolution and the historical-critical method of biblical interpretation. He labelled higher critics 'men without spiritual vision, without zeal for souls, and without any deep interest in the coming of God's kingdom'. Most of his fundamentalist activities were in the Presbyterian Church, although in 1922 he spoke at meetings of both the Southern Baptist Convention and the Fundamentalist Federation of the Northern Baptist Convention. In 1923 he stood for election as moderator of the Presbyterian Church, US, but was defeated by Dr Charles F. Wishart, president of Wooster College in Ohio, a school where the teaching of evolution was part of the curriculum. This was his last effort to secure elected office in any capacity. During this period, however, he was named as chair of the so-called 'Fosdick Committee', appointed to examine the theological positions of Baptist preacher and theologian Harry Emerson Fosdick, who although not a Presbyterian was preaching minister at First Presbyterian Church, New York City. The committee called for Fosdick's resignation, which was ultimately secured. Bryan also helped to write legislation for the state of Florida (1923) and other southern states that prohibited the teaching of evolution in state-supported schools. His attacks on Darwin, especially his lecture, 'The Menace of Darwinism', delivered and then published in 1921, made him a favourite of the fundamentalist leadership. 'Evolutionists', he told the West Virginia state legislature, 'rob the Savior of the glory of virgin birth, the majesty of His deity and the triumph of His resurrection. They weaken faith in the Bible by discarding miracles and the supernatural and by eliminating from the Bible all that conflicts with their theories. They render that book a scrap of paper.' He told state legislatures and denominations that professors who advocated the theory of evolution were free as American citizens to espouse their views but not at taxpayer or church expense. He argued that 'As long as Christians must build Christian colleges in which to teach Christianity, atheists should be required to build their own colleges if they wish to teach atheism ...'

The scene was thus set for a confrontation between Bryan and the evolutionists in the trial that would caricature both his life and the anti-evolutionist movement. In the summer of 1925 Bryan became involved in what became known as the Scopes Monkey Trial in Dayton, Tennessee, an event that would in many respects define his place in popular American history. John Scopes, a teacher in Dayton, was enlisted by the American Civil Liberties Union to challenge Tennessee's anti-evolution law, which forbade the teaching of Darwin's views in state schools. Charges were brought, and the ACLU secured the services of Clarence Darrow, one of the country's best-known jurists and agnostics, to provide Scopes' defence. In response, the supporters of the law invited Bryan to represent the prosecution. Bryan, who had not accepted a case for some twenty-eight years, was at a low point in his public career and desperately in need of a political, if not a religious, success. He readily agreed to take the case. Fundamentalist leaders such as Texas Baptist J. Frank Norris, evangelist Billy *Sunday and Canadian conservative T. T. Shields praised Bryan's decision and promised support but did not attend the gathering. Bryan, the Great Commoner, was left alone with 'the people' to defend the Bible and Christian truth.

The scene in Dayton resembled a carnival. Baptist evangelist T. T. Martin held a tent revival, hawkers sold souvenirs, and crowds packed the airless courtroom. H. L. Mencken, the secular columnist, portrayed the Scopes Trial as an example of the ignorance of religionists in general and southern fundamentalists in particular. Twenty-two telegraph operators were required to handle the 168,000 words sent out daily to newspapers around the world. There was a banner above the judge's bench that declared 'Read your Bible daily', until Darrow's call for its removal finally prevailed. The pivotal moment in the trial came when Bryan agreed to take the stand as a 'witness' to biblical authority. This action was contrary to his own comments several years before: 'I know of no reason why the Christian should take upon himself the difficult task of answering all questions and give to the atheist the easy task of asking them.' None the less, Bryan took the stand and was compelled to acknowledge that the 'days' mentioned in the Genesis account of creation did not refer to six twenty-four-hour periods, but perhaps to millions of years. This concession was of course a significant contradiction of the literalist interpretation of the Genesis account. Shaken and humiliated, Bryan stayed up most of the night writing an address that he hoped would help him to regain momentum. Unfortunately for Bryan, the judge ended the deliberations and sent the case to the jury, who declared Scopes guilty and fined him $100, which he never paid. Bryan returned to his rooms broken and exhausted and died in Dayton five days later on 26 July 1925. His funeral was conducted at the New York Avenue Presbyterian Church in Washington, DC.

Bryan's life was the subject of innumerable evaluations. His character was written into the play and then the film *Inherit the Wind*, a dramatization of the Scopes trial. Some suggest that L. Frank Baum used Bryan as the character for the Cowardly Lion in *The Wizard of Oz*, a children's book that mourned the defeat of populism to McKinley and the Republican machine. The lion, like Bryan, could roar loudly and eloquently, but with little success.

Bibliography

P. W. Glad (ed.), *William Jennings Bryan: A Profile* (New York: Hill & Wang, 1968); L. W. Koenig, *Bryan* (New York: Putnam's, 1971); C. A. Russell, *Voices of American Fundamentalism* (Philadelphia: Westminster, 1976).

B. J. LEONARD

■ **BUCER (Butzer), Martin** (1491–1551), Protestant Reformer, was leader of the Reform in the city-state of Strasbourg (1523–1548), and in his last years was influential in England while professor in Cambridge (1549–1551). Bucer is not easily classified in any one of the main categories of sixteenth-century Protestants, but he was more Reformed than Lutheran.

Bucer was born the son of a cooper in Sélestat in Alsace, where he benefited from the fine humanist-influenced grammar school before entering the local Dominican convent (1506/7). Here he not only was deeply exposed to the works of Thomas Aquinas, the Dominicans' leading theologian, but also encountered some by Erasmus, the dominant biblical humanist of the day, including his Latin/Greek New Testament.

Promoted by the Dominicans to their house in Heidelberg (1516/17), Bucer was ready to be won over by *Luther's disputation at the general chapter of the Augustinians in Heidelberg in April 1518. This experience was his evangelical conversion. He wrote enthusiastically of Luther's devotion to the Bible, and recognized, for all their agreement, that Luther was more explicit than Erasmus. He quickly came to appreciate Luther's commentary on Galatians, 'a treasury full of the dogmas of pure theology'.

Early in 1521 Bucer finally left the Dominicans, and in April gained release from his monastic profession on technical grounds. His marriage in mid-1522 to Elizabeth Silbereisen, an ex-nun, led to his excommunication. After a period of unsettled movement around and beyond Alsace, he was given asylum in May 1523 in Strasbourg, where the Lutheran gospel had been gaining ground for a few years. Within months he won approval for his Latin lectures on John's Gospel and then for his preaching in the cathedral. In 1524 he was elected pastor of the parish of St Aurelia and rapidly became the de facto leader of the city's Reformation. The mass was abolished in 1528, and synods of 1533–1534 approved brief doctrinal articles and a new church order, responding to challenges posed by the variety of reforming Radicals attracted to the city.

Bucer and his fellow pastors experienced intermittent friction with the city councils, which ultimately controlled the implementation of Reform. Unlike *Calvin in Geneva, Bucer never achieved a system of church discipline independent of the city government. Like other magisterial Reformers, Bucer inherited, and perhaps never seriously questioned, the socio-political pattern of medieval Christendom, in which church and civil community were viewed as coterminous. The populace as a whole was required to conform to the new religious order, and infant baptism was mandatory (Bucer having overcome his early biblicist doubts about it). The frustration of promoting spiritual renewal within the comprehensive bounds of the whole city community, without free exercise of pastoral discipline, provoked Bucer in the mid-1540s into experimenting with small discipleship cells of those who voluntarily submitted to mutual oversight, with confirmation often as the focal point of commitment. Bucer was one of the leading draughtsmen of a new evangelical service of confirmation.

The fortunes of Protestant Reform in Strasbourg were not immune from wider political upheavals in central Europe. The defeat of the Protestants' Schmalkaldic League by the Emperor Charles V in 1547 was followed by the imposition of the Augsburg Interim (1548) on Strasbourg. This compromise settlement was intolerable to Bucer, who chose Archbishop Thomas *Cranmer's invitation to England among several offers of exile. His presence as regius professor of divinity at Cambridge, together with that of other refugees, including Peter Martyr Vermigli at Oxford, represented the weightiest contribution of continental Protestant personnel to the cause of England's Reform. His years in England were not his happiest, but he influenced the 1552 revision of the Book of Common Prayer, drew up for Edward VI The Kingdom of Christ (1550), the most comprehensive charter for the evangelical reform of the whole body politic produced in sixteenth-century Protestantism, and initiated a new tradition of theological lecturing through exegesis with his Ephesians course of 1550–1551.

No church tradition or theological succession perpetuated Bucer's name. His works are belatedly appearing in modern editions, but as yet little exists in English translation. As a first-class second-rank Reformer he has been known chiefly for his influence on others, especially on Calvin during the latter's exile in Strasbourg during 1538–1541. Much in the Reformed pattern of Protestantism, which is more broadly based than Calvinism, reflects Bucer's formative contribution through Calvin and others: the four orders of apostolic ministry – pastor, deacon, elder and doctor (teacher, lecturer; the Strasbourg academy of 1538 inspired the Genevan one of 1559, which in turn was a model for post-Reformation universities such as Edinburgh); pastoral church discipline (which Bucer, like Vermigli and *Knox but unlike Calvin, made a third mark of an authentic church alongside word and sacraments); the importance of firm ordering of the church reformed; the vision of the Christian society and much else. Bucer was a prolific drafter of Reformed 'church orders' (Kirchenordnungen) for cities in Germany.

Bucer's evangelical theology and practice, though not without distinctives, were largely the common property of mainstream Protestantism in its regional and confessional varieties: rigorous biblicism; drawing profusely on Augustine on sin, grace and predestination, and treating the tradition of the early Church Fathers as largely pure; zeal for preaching and lecturing on whole books of the Bible; the pursuit, through pastoral discipline (the main theme of *The True Care of Souls*, 1538, perhaps the best pastoral treatise from any Reformer), of the fruit of the gospel in godly lives; and the holding up of Jesus Christ as sole Mediator and Saviour and as Lord of all human life.

Buceran distinctives clustered in good measure around the flexible unifying role he pursued, notably in the 'supper-strife' among Protestants from the late 1520s onwards. After Luther and *Zwingli failed to agree at the Marburg Colloquy in 1529, Bucer with relentless (some said, unprincipled) versatility created with *Melanchthon the Wittenberg Concord (1536) on the Lord's Supper (which satisfied Lutherans more than the Swiss). Bucer's own mature interpretation of the Eucharist defies brief exposition; it affirmed that by 'a sacramental union', as bread and wine are ingested by the mouth, so Christ's body and blood are received by faith, for above all else the intention of the supper is life-giving communion in the whole Christ.

Bucer was similarly a leading player in colloquies with reform-minded Catholics in Germany during 1539–1541. Agreement was reached even on justification by faith at Regensburg in 1541, through the development of Augustine's emphasis on 'faith working through love' (Gal. 5:6) as distinct from faith as bare trust. Bucer also taught a two-fold justification, for good works are rewarded by God even though they are really God's work in the believer. This teaching was reflected in a strong ethical concern, and a major emphasis from almost his earliest publication, *That No One Should Live for Himself but for Others* (1523), on service of the neighbour in love as the fruit of true faith.

Bucer's stature as an independent source of Protestant evangelicalism can only grow as more of his works become accessible. Calvin applauded the excellence of his *Romans* (1536), one of the very greatest, and most learned, of Reformation commentaries. He was also an expert Hebraist, as he shows in commenting on the Psalms. He exemplifies the richly biblical, theological and pastoral sixteenth-century roots of the evangelical tradition.

Bibliography

H. Eells, *Martin Bucer* (New Haven: Yale University Press, 1931); D. F. Wright (ed. and tr.), *Common Places of Martin Bucer* (Appleford: Sutton Courtenay Press, 1972); W. P. Stephens, *The Holy Spirit in the Theology of Martin Bucer* (Cambridge: Cambridge University Press, 1970); A. N. Burnett, *The Yoke of Christ: Martin Bucer and Christian Discipline* (Kirksville: Sixteenth Century Journal Publishers, 1994); D. F. Wright (ed.), *Martin Bucer: Reforming Church and Community* (Cambridge: Cambridge University Press, 1994).

D. F. WRIGHT

■ **BUCHMAN, Frank** (1878–1961), initiator of the Oxford Group and Moral Re-Armament, was born on 4 June 1878 in Pennsburg, Pennsylvania, of Pennsylvania Dutch parents. He graduated from Muhlenburg College in 1899 (MA 1902, Honorary DD 1926), and then attended the Lutheran theological seminary at Mount Airy in Philadelphia (1899–1902). In 1901 he was much influenced by a visit to the Northfield Student Conference in Massachussetts. In 1904 he set up a hospice for orphan boys in Philadelphia, but in 1907 left after a bitter dispute with his sponsors. Buchman's life was then radically changed during a visit to the Keswick Convention in England in 1908, where he gained a personal understanding of the cross. He was subsequently YMCA secretary at Penn State University (1909–1915), and worked with the YMCA in India in 1915–1916. In 1916 he was made Extension Lecturer in Personal Evangelism at Hartford theological seminary. On visits to China in 1916 and 1917–1918 he sought to bring a Christian experience to the Chinese nationalist leadership, but came into conflict with the local missionary community.

Buchman increasingly sought new ways of working. He resigned from Hartford in 1922, and thereafter never had a paid position. On his visits to Cambridge and Oxford in 1921 the non-denominational First Century Christian Fellowship was created, which from 1928 was known as the Oxford Group. The Oxford Group spread rapidly, often through house parties, and was possibly the most influential movement of Christian renewal in inter-war Britain. In addition, it had considerable impact in Scandinavia and South Africa. Buchman was also influential at Princeton University in the mid-1920s, although his direct approach to personal evangelism aroused fierce opposition there. His work had various by-products: Alcoholics Anonymous owed much to Buchman and his methods.

In his approach to 'personal work' Buchman was much influenced by John R. *Mott, Jessie Penn-Lewis, F. B. *Meyer, Henry B. Wright, and the earlier Henry Drummond. He encouraged people to listen to God, in order to receive God's 'guidance', and to measure their lives against the four absolute moral standards of honesty, purity, unselfishness and love. He emphasized the need for 'surrender' to God and an experience of 'change', and suggested that people make restitution for past wrongs where possible. Those involved in the Oxford Group were encouraged to be part of small 'sharing' groups, where they could be accountable for their spiritual lives. The Oxford Group were taught that God had a plan for their lives and for the world, and that a living faith should have a real impact on society. Buchman assumed that people would get theological training from their own churches, and the Oxford Group was widely supported by church members. However, some believed that it paid insufficient attention to doctrine and that its emphasis on 'sharing' could be misused.

Buchman hoped for a world 'governed by men governed by God'. In 1938, in response to the deteriorating world situation, he called for a programme of 'moral and spiritual rearmament'; henceforth the Oxford Group came to be known as Moral Re-Armament (MRA). He called for spiritual revolution and 'God-led' leadership in national and international life. He declared that people needed to have an 'experience of the Cross' as well as an understanding of it, and in 1946 he called for a worldwide 'revolution under the Cross of Christ'. At the same time, Buchman believed that the Holy Spirit was at work in people from other religious traditions, and felt that people with different faiths could sometimes work together in doing God's will; MRA increasingly embraced people from different religious backgrounds.

After 1945, in spite of ill health, Buchman developed a global strategy to establish moral and spiritual values in international life. MRA conference centres were established at Mackinac Island, Michigan (1942), and Caux-sur-Montreux, Switzerland (1946). The Caux centre became a notable focus for Franco-German reconciliation, and Buchman was himself recognized by both the French and the German governments for his contribution in the field. Buchman and his colleagues were also much involved in Africa and Asia in the post-war decades, seeking to heal distrust between Western countries and their former colonies, and to foster a 'God-guided' leadership in the newly independent countries. In general, Buchman sought to express traditional Christian truths in contemporary form: for example, during the Cold War, MRA presented itself as an ideology superior to communism and Western materialism; and much use was made of plays and films, written to present moral and religious experience in an accessible way.

Following Buchman's death on 6 August 1961 in Freudenstadt, Germany, MRA was led by the English journalist Peter Howard (1908–1965). It continued to be widely active, and in 2001 was renamed Initiatives of Change. Some of Buchman's speeches are available in Frank Buchman, *Remaking the World* (London: Blandford Press, 1961).

Bibliography
T. Spoerri, *Dynamic out of Silence* (London: Grosvenor Books, 1976); G. Lean, *Frank Buchman: A Life* (London: Constable, 1985); E. Luttwak, 'Franco-German Reconciliation: The Overlooked Role of the Moral Re-Armament Movement', in D. Johnston and C. Sampson (eds.), *Religion, the Missing Dimension of Statecraft* (New York: Oxford University Press, 1994), pp. 37–63.

P. C. BOOBBYER

■ **BULLINGER, Johann Heinrich** (1504–1575), Zurich Reformer, was one of the formative influences on the Reformed tradition. He was born on 18 July 1504 in Bremgarten, a small town in Canton Argau, 20 km west of Zurich. His father was the parish priest, whose marriage to his mother therefore lacked legal status until after the Reformation was introduced in 1529. Heinrich, who had four older brothers, started school locally in 1509, and then in 1516 left home to go to a school at Emmerich. There he was educated according to the principles of Renaissance humanism. In 1519 he moved on to the University of Cologne, where he gained his BA the following year. At Cologne the dominant ideology was the 'old way' of Thomas Aquinas and Duns Scotus rather than the 'new way' of Ockham and Biel. But Bullinger maintained his interest in the humanist approach, although this had as yet made little impact on the university. Stimulated by the controversy over *Luther, whose books were burned at Cologne, he turned to theology, especially the study of the early Church Fathers. This turned him away from the medieval scholastics to Luther. In 1522 he gained his MA, by which stage he had decided definitively for the Reformation.

Bullinger returned to Bremgarten and continued to study both the Fathers and Luther and *Melanchthon. In 1523 he became head teacher at the school of the Cistercian monastery at Kappel, introducing humanist and Reformed ideas. In due course the mass was replaced by a Protestant service and many of the monks became Reformed ministers.

In 1523 Bullinger met Zwingli and Leo Jud at Zurich. He found that he agreed with *Zwingli on many matters, especially on his rejection of the real presence. His relationship with Zwingli deepened. In 1525 he joined him in disputations with the Anabaptists, through which he developed his covenant theology. He also accompanied Zwingli to the disputation at Bern in 1528, where he met other Reformers such as *Bucer.

Also in 1528 Bullinger became part-time pastor of a village near Kappel. The following year he became the Reformer of Bremgarten. His father had belatedly embraced the Reformation earlier that year and had helped to initiate reform in his parish. His son carried on the work and brought it to fruition that summer. Because of his involvement with the Reform, he rejected the opportunity to accompany Zwingli to the Marburg Colloquy. That summer he married Anna Adlischwyler, a former nun, by whom he had eleven children.

In October 1531 Zwingli was defeated and killed on the battlefield at Kappel. One of the terms of the ensuing peace treaty was Bullinger's exile from Bremgarten. He set out for Zurich in November that year and was soon being sought for church office in Basel and Bern as well as Zurich. He opted for Zurich, and in December took over Zwingli's role as chief minister of the city, where he was to remain until his death in 1575.

Zwingli's death raised the issue of the relative authority of the pastors and the magistrates. Bullinger reached an agreement with the city council that guaranteed the freedom of the pastors to preach God's word in its fullness, but also laid down that the pastors should not meddle in the affairs of the magistracy. He saw moral discipline as the task of the magistrate and resisted Leo Jud's attempt to introduce a church court with the power of excommunication. The city council also had ultimate control over church finances and a major role in the Synod that was responsible for the appointment and discipline of clergy.

Bullinger was involved in ongoing controversy with both Anabaptists and Lutherans. He also played an important role in the development of Reformed theology and church life. He co-authored the First Helvetic Confession of 1536 and thirty years later wrote the fuller Second Helvetic Confession, one of the most influential of the Reformed confessions, which was accepted far beyond Switzerland. He was concerned to promote unity between Reformed Christians. He had close relations with *Calvin, with whom he did not agree on all points. He was out of sympathy with the Genevan approach to church discipline. Although he shared with Calvin a commitment to the Augustinian doctrine of unconditional election, he was not happy to go beyond this to talk of positive predestination to damnation. Most importantly, he reached a common agreement with Calvin on the Eucharist, the 1549 *Consensus Tigurinus* (Zurich Agreement). This was the fruit of some years of negotiations and involved an element of compromise on both sides. Bullinger helped to develop the idea of a conditional covenant between God and his people, which was to be very influential within Reformed theology.

Bullinger had a significant role to play in the English Reformation. During the reign of Queen Mary (1553–1558), Zurich played host to a number of leading Protestant exiles. These maintained their contact with Bullinger after their return to take up positions of leadership in the Elizabethan church, giving rise to the 'Zurich Letters'. Also, Bullinger's *Decades*, a selection of fifty sermons on Christian doctrine, became a standard theological textbook in Elizabethan England.

Bullinger was a prolific author, leaving behind many published works. He wrote New Testament commentaries, doctrinal treatises and polemical works against Anabaptists and Lutherans especially. His collected correspondence includes more than twelve thousand letters sent and received by him.

Bibliography
J. W. Baker, *Heinrich Bullinger and the Covenant: The Other Reformed Tradition* (Athens, Ohio: Ohio University Press, 1980).
A. N. S. LANE

■ **BUNTING, Jabez** (1779–1858), Wesleyan Methodist minister, was born in Manchester on 13 May 1779, the only son of William Bunting, a Manchester tailor, and his wife Mary Redfern. His mother was a model of Wesleyan piety; his father was a radical who sent him to two Unitarian schools and apprenticed him to Thomas Percival, a leading Unitarian doctor in the town. Though Bunting ultimately declined Percival's offer of professional medical education in favour of the Wesleyan ministry, he served happily with him for four years, and named his third son after him.

Taken on trial for the ministry in 1799, Bunting began to preach among revivalists, and was still looking to revival when appointed to Macclesfield in 1801. It was this appointment that fundamentally changed his views and made him the authoritarian figure he subsequently remained. He had trouble with a group who were preparing to separate as Christian Revivalists and join up with others of like mind in Leeds and Manchester. Henceforth Bunting was a ferocious exponent of church order and discipline, and an implacable opponent of revivalism. But he was also a notable preacher (he was commissioned in 1812 to produce a sermon on justification by faith as a doctrinal standard), and his preaching led to his stationing in all the best large town circuits in the connexion. Bunting also rapidly acquired a reputation as an administrator: his first London appointment in 1803 carried special responsibility for putting the accounts of the foreign missions and the connexional Book Room in order; he became assistant secretary to the Conference in 1806, and secretary in 1814. Administration and discipline went closely together in Bunting's mind, where discipline 'equally with the dispensation of the word and sacraments [was] an institution of Christ'.

The appeal of this doctrine was never greater than in the immediate aftermath of the Napoleonic wars. The rapid multiplication of married preachers with claims for the support of wife and children, combined with the sudden increase in the real burden of chapel debts occasioned by the post-war deflation created a tremendous financial crisis, which compounded the effects of social unrest and popular suspicion of government. Bunting, who had been an outspoken opponent of Luddism and had led the successful opposition to Lord Sidmouth's attempt to limit the Toleration Act in 1811, secured the primacy among the Wesleyan ministers by his willingness to fight their battles on a platform they could understand. Order, including financial order, enforced from the centre, and circuit discipline enforced by the ministry, was the way to salvation. The ideals underpinning this programme Bunting established in his first presidency (1820) in the *Liverpool Minutes*. These set out a conception of the ministry as evangelical and evangelistic, pastoral and efficient, paternal and single-minded. Bunting's friends, especially Richard *Watson and John Beecham, gave a doctrinal basis to this conception by developing the high Wesleyan theory of the Pastoral Office. On this view, Conference embodied the sovereign power which Wesley had exercised over the connexion; district committees maintained his daily oversight; and superintendents maintained locally his watch upon the flock. Moreover this Methodist ecclesiology was rooted in the New Testament. Christ had filled the whole Pastoral Office and transmitted his authority to his ministers. The pastor, wholly given up to the work, must feed and rule the flock; his authority could not be shared with those who were not pastors, even if, like local preachers or class leaders, they performed valuable spiritual functions. Bunting adapted practice to the theory; seminary training (1834–1835) and a Mission House (both with himself at the head) were followed by ordination by imposition of hands (1836) and the trappings of priesthood; ministers began to wear gowns and celebrate weddings.

These developments, theoretical and practical, greatly radicalized the views of those who would not accept them. In a number of great northern urban circuits that were crucial to connexional finance, suburban migration had deprived propertied Methodists of their influence in old city centre chapels and left the ministry with little backing other than its newly polished claims to authority, and the support of Bunting at the centre. The first great conflict came in Leeds, where disputes over the division of the Sunday school finally came to a head over the proposal to install an organ in the Brunswick chapel. Bunting's repeated intervention against all the local authorities except the trustees was unwise and probably illegal, and led to the expulsion of large numbers of members without trial before a Leaders' Meeting from which guilty verdicts could not have been obtained. To the Leeds Protestant Methodists (as the expelled called themselves) the key to Methodist reform was now the defence of circuit rights against the centre. They located authority in the circuit Quarterly Meeting which had the right to elect ministers for a year at a time. Thus power was to rise from below rather than descend from above, a notion anathema to the high Wesleyans. The hostility of the 'low' Methodists to the new institutionalization was compounded by their fondness for Sunday schools, their adoption of teetotalism (another undenominational cause), their vision of Methodism as an evangelistic outpouring of grace, and their political liberalism rooted in the rising of the British provinces against the centre. Would the Pastoral Office as Bunting conceived it be able to contain this alternative model of Methodism?

The event proved that in important respects it would not. In the 1830s there were a number of small secessions, and a bigger one led by Dr Warren, who contested Bunting's taking over of the Theological Institution.

The social strains of the 1840s took a heavier toll. The old connexion seemed to run out of steam, while the Primitive Methodists were still expanding rapidly. There was a general sense that new policies were required, but no agreement as to what they should be. And when in 1849 three ministers, Everett, Dunn and Griffith, were expelled on suspicion of pamphleteering against 'Dr Bunting's whole system of government', they took with them 50,000 members and scores of Sunday Schools, and for a few years so damaged the morale of the old connexion and its ability to recruit normally that total membership fell by a third. Bunting, the preachers' champion, was due for his fifth turn as president in 1852, but in this crisis he could no longer be thrown into the fray, and was hastily retired. He died on 16 June 1858.

There is no doubt that the strain of exercising the authority he had assumed took its toll of Bunting as it did of many of his colleagues. He ceased to write, preached less and, in pulpit as in Conference, often resorted to mere vehemence. His wife Sarah Maclardie, whom he married in 1804, and by whom he had three daughters and four sons, was a lively woman, but she died in 1835. In 1837 Bunting made a happy second marriage with a minister's widow, Mrs Martin, but she could not replace the life and soul of the family. Bunting's personality was increasingly absorbed in his office. Moreover, his policies all failed. In the early 1830s Bunting gambled heavily on the intuition that the Church of England would not be disestablished, and stood aloof from the campaign against it; his reward was to be vilified by the Tractarians. In Scotland he backed *Chalmers in the hope of finding a supporting role for Methodism under an evangelical establishment; at the time of the Disruption he foreswore his past by expressing the wish in Conference that 'two thousand clergymen would leave the English Church in the same way'. He contested the endowment of Maynooth on Protestant grounds and failed publicly again. Repeated attempts to enforce a union of Canadian Methodists under English, as distinct from American, leadership ended in acrimony. Bunting's doctrinaire attempt to substitute the Pastoral Office for older Methodist empiricism asked more of the Pastoral Office than it could provide.

Bibliography
T. P. Bunting, *The Life of Dr Bunting* (London: Longmans, 1859); W. R. Ward, *The Early Correspondence of Jabez Bunting 1820–1829* (London: Royal Historical Society, Camden Series, 1972); *Early Victorian Methodism: The Correspondence of Jabez Bunting 1830–1858* (Oxford: OUP, 1976).

W. R. WARD

■ **BUNYAN, John** (1628–1688), Nonconformist writer and preacher, is best remembered as the author of the English classic *Pilgrim's Progress* and about sixty other popular theological and devotional works. Born into a working-class family, child of the second of his father's three wives and trained by him to be a brazier ('tinker'), he went to grammar school only briefly. Such literacy as he attained later was shaped primarily by his reading of the Bible and books of devotion as a young adult. Following the death of his mother, his father's remarriage and his own service as a young man with *Cromwell's parliamentary army at Newport Pagnell from 1645 to late 1647, Bunyan married, at the age of nineteen, an unnamed wife. (Their first daughter Mary, born blind, was baptized 20 July 1650.) This first wife, of whom little else is known except that she was as poor as he, brought into the marriage two books that she and Bunyan read together. *The Plain Man's Pathway to Heaven* (1601) pictures the Christian life as a journey, employs dialogue and is essentially a Calvinist guide to self-examination for evidences of grace. Lewis Bayly's *The Practice of Piety* (1612), printed twenty times already by 1630 and more controversial on account of its author being a Church of England bishop, was deeply indebted to Puritan sources as well as to the Catholic spiritual meditations of Juan Luis Vives (Ludovicus). In his own effort at Puritan spiritual autobiography, Bunyan seems to credit these two books with helping to awaken in him a conviction of sin.

Grace Abounding (1666), though a classic of spiritual autobiography, is an insufficient source for Bunyan's life. Even though Bunyan revised and reissued it at least twice (c. 1673; 1680), he added nothing to its substance. Further, most of the events recorded fall between 1650 and 1656, the

period of his most intensive spiritual struggles, and throughout 'the chronology is at best imprecise, at worst chaotic'. Among the spiritually formative events there recounted are Bunyan's narrow escape from death in combat through his agreeing to take another soldier's place on a night patrol, his habitual playing of games then thought unsuitable on the Sabbath, an inordinate affection for bell-ringing and a penchant for colourful invective; all are recollected as occasions for repentance and confession. His scruples are typical of Calvinist confessional literature, except that sexual sin seems not to have been a serious temptation, and he evidences the mystic's instinctive capacity to sublimate his desires (as in his response to an early sermon on Song of Solomon 4:1) into a requited love of the soul for Christ as bridegroom.

Of Bunyan's own two marriages little intimate is recorded. His first wife having died in 1658 leaving him with three children, he married a second, Elizabeth, in 1659. She appears to have been a more active collaborator, pleading eloquently before the judges at Bedford and moving Sir Matthew Hale to sympathy (albeit ineffectual) for her imprisoned husband. She survived Bunyan, as did his children Thomas and Joseph from his first marriage and Sarah from his second.

Of central interest in the life of Bunyan is the evolution of his approach to Scripture. Clearly, Calvinist theology is his basic *modus* in interpretation from his early writings. At the same time, he is resistant to the subjectivism of some among his Calvinist contemporaries, and an important balance to his own intense and imaginative, almost visionary, spirituality is afforded by his growing confidence in what may be seen as a basic Augustinian orthodoxy. When he turned for theological guidance to great biblical interpreters of the past, it was for him a happy moment when he chanced upon *Luther's commentary on Galatians. Luther's parallel psychological experiences and his sense of liberty for the 'wounded Conscience' affected Bunyan deeply. Not that Bunyan's doubts and temptations were over: his darkest hours (in which he feared obsessively that his was the fate of Esau rather than that of Jacob) were yet to come. Yet in the end, like Luther, he overcame, believing that the 'Word of the Law and Wrath must give place to the Word of Life and Grace', and because, as Wakefield has it, 'the Scriptures became the keys of the Kingdom of heaven to him'.

As a direct result of his confidence in the Bible as perspicuous and self-interpreting, Bunyan came to believe that 'preaching the Word was second only in importance to the Word itself'. His preaching was not of the intertextual, learned, scholarly type that characterized earlier Elizabethan Puritanism. His low social origins and modest education generated a more direct, less theologically nuanced approach to the biblical text. Whereas the earlier Puritans theologized, Bunyan dramatized and allegorized with existential urgency. When he joined the Bedford Separatist Congregation in 1655 he was immediately noticed for the power and eloquence of his prayers; subsequently he was invited to offer 'a word of exhortation'. Soon he was an itinerant preacher in such great demand that he could no longer serve properly as deacon in his own congregation.

In Bunyan, sermons give rise to theology, rather than vice versa. His theological works can readily be seen as extended sermons of the sort that he preached against the Quakers and that issued in the tract *Some Gospel Truths Opened* (1656). Bunyan firmly resists the Quaker doctrine of the 'inner light' and insists upon an essentially objective reading of Scripture as the Christian's sole dependable guide. Here too he shows himself a worthy successor to John Gifford, his Bedford pastor, who was an essentialist regarding Scripture and resisted divisions over 'externals', though little is known of Bunyan's actual relations with the man who was probably his mentor in preaching.

There appear to have been many contemporary Dissenting preachers who gained their daily bread by means of manual labour. The charge that Bunyan was a 'mechanik preacher' was not levelled only at him, though few others could draw, as he did in Southwark and London, crowds of up to three thousand on a Sunday or as many as 1,200 for a 7 a.m. weekday sermon. Bunyan claimed, honestly no doubt, that his Bible and his concordance were his only library. He was not in the least ashamed that he knew no biblical languages; Pontius Pilate, he remarked wryly, could speak Hebrew, Greek and Latin. Bunyan's early Bible was the Geneva English translation with its useful marginal commentary; only later did he adopt the King James Version, which is cited in his later writings. Bunyan had little sense of (or interest in) the historical context of the text; nor was he greatly preoccupied with its literal sense. His was an instinctively spiritualizing, allegorizing imagination, and strangely, many of his typical 'readings' would have been more welcome among later medieval Catholics than among the putatively literalist Lollards who were his more direct ecclesial forebears. Yet there was above all a rich, text-centred freshness in his preaching, and it drew crowds from the start of his ministry. Even when, in the early years, his own spiritual wrestlings led to sudden urges to break into voluble blasphemy when in the pulpit, what his congregations apparently heard was vivid expository preaching in the 'language of Canaan'. Though evidently a gifted natural orator, Bunyan was not a garrulous man. He was observed by his first biographer (and editor), the Southwark comb-maker Charles Doe, to be 'in his conversation mild and affable, not given to loquacity or much Discourse in company'. Clearly, he had learned by middle age how to preserve the vital distinction between authoritative discourse and mere talkativeness. The distinction is one he later allegorizes as a contrast, at the gates of Vanity Fair, between the simple confession of Faithful and the overbearing ramble of Talkative, 'who hath only what lieth on his tongue, and his religion is to make a noise therewith' (*Pilgrim's Progress*).

Bunyan was a Baptist of sorts, though some historians are content to regard him merely as an unspecified Independent. He may have been re-baptized when he joined Gifford's Bedford congregation, but if so there is no record. Two of his children were baptized as infants, and he says he did not regard either baptism or the Lord's Supper as 'the fundamentals of our Christianity, nor ground or rule to communion with saints'. In his 1672 application for a preaching licence he put down his ecclesial identity as 'congregationall', and in two pamphlets of that period (*A Confession of My Faith* ... and *Difference in Judgement about Water-Baptism no Bar to Communion*) he makes clear both that church affiliation was a question on which some people wanted his answer and that, for him, the 'one baptism' of Ephesians 4:5 (baptism not by water but of the Spirit) was the baptism most needful. He had no liking for water baptism of either kind 'done in a Legal Spirit'.

Bunyan's understanding of the predominant Calvinist covenant theology of Puritanism is softened by the influence upon him of the text of Galatians and Luther's commentary (*The Doctrine of the Law and Grace Unfolded*). Righteousness is God's, not ours, his gift, not our attainment. Conflicts between Paedo-Baptists and Believer's Baptists were thus perilously 'old-covenant' in character; 'As for me,' Bunyan wrote, 'I hope I am a Christian ... and as for those factious titles of Anabaptists, Independents, and Presbyterians, or the like, I conclude they came neither from Jerusalem nor Antioch, but rather from Hell and Babylon; for they naturally tend to divisions – "you may know them by their fruits".'

Because he was not in any sense a systematic theologian, Bunyan is more difficult to categorize on many points than some would wish. Most of his ventures into doctrinal controversy were the result of a debate or conflict he could not avoid. Thus, though he was deeply committed to the fellowship of believers, he articulates no formal doctrine of the church other than to say (e.g. in *Christian Behaviour* [1663] and *Pilgrim's Progress, Part II*) that the healthy church resembles a well-kept garden, in which the planting and tending of the gardener is everywhere evident. It is clear in his controversial writings, however, that the resistance he shows to uncontrolled freedom to 'testify in the spirit' among the Quakers and the eccentric and biased biblical interpretation of some other Nonconformists (e.g. Ranters, Levellers) at least implies a belief that the gathered church should function as a constraint on untoward individualism. In a similar vein, he believed that prayer without the Spirit is blasphemy, that it must be 'with faith and understanding', i.e. in the vernacular. Glossolalia was for him as much a violation of this principle as the Latin of the mass.

Bunyan's treatise *I Will Pray with the Spirit* (1663) was, however, directed against the *Book of Common Prayer* of the Church of England, and, with other offences, his critique led to his imprisonment. He had first been arrested under an old Elizabethan act against conventicles as early as 1660; in January 1661 he was tried by Sir John Keeling (later Lord Chief Justice), and it is clear in the deposition that his opposition to the re-introduction of the Book of Common Prayer at the Restoration was already the most important issue, though Bunyan's lack of a Church of England licence to preach was also significant. At first he was allowed books in his cell, including *Foxe's *Acts and Monuments* (*Book of Martyrs*), and his second wife, Elizabeth, may have benefited, along with his congregation and some as far away as London, when he was let out occasionally to travel and to visit, especially after 1663. After being re-imprisoned for preaching, his conditions grew more harsh.

From the Act of Uniformity (1662) onwards, by which hundreds of ministers who refused to accept the Book of Common Prayer or episcopal ordination were ejected, the legal constraints upon Nonconformists grew steadily more severe; anyone taking part in an unauthorized service was subject to heavy fines and imprisonment. In 1665 the Five Mile Act forbade Nonconformist ministers from coming closer than five miles to their former churches. But Bunyan himself, in jail since the very beginning of the persecutions, experienced few of these additional measures directly. The period of his first imprisonment was, moreover, one of his most fruitful as a writer, yielding (in addition to the works mentioned already) *The Holy City* (1665), *One Thing is Needful* (1664) and *Resurrection of the Dead* as well as his *Prison Meditations* (1665).

Towards the end of his imprisonment Bunyan read and responded to a book by the ex-Puritan turned Anglican Latitudinarian Edward Fowler. Bunyan's reply, *A Defence of the Doctrine of Justification by Faith in Jesus Christ ...* (1672), is one text in which the usual serenity of his discourse gives way to turbulent insult. It occasioned a swift reply in kind, Fowler's *Dirt Wip't Off: A Manifest Discovery of the Gross Ignorance, Erroneousness and Most UnChristian and Wicked Spirit of One John Bunyan*. Fowler was not gratified when Bunyan (along with many Quakers) was released from prison on 15 March 1672 by a Royal Declaration of Indulgence. Bunyan then published several new works: *The Barren Fig Tree* (1673); *Light for Them that Sit in Darkness* (1675; another work against the Quakers); *Instruction for the Ignorant* (1675; a catechism); and *Saved by Grace* and *The Strait Gate* (both 1675). Both the last two works include character studies and dialogue.

Bunyan returned to his congregational preaching, something of a hero. But with the repeal of the Declaration of Indulgence in 1675 a warrant against him was issued and eventually he was imprisoned again for about six months (December 1676 – June 1677), the best efforts of his friends notwithstanding. John *Owen interceded for him, and along with two others offered bail for his release. It is thought by some that *Pilgrim's Progress* (1678) was written, or at least brought to completion, during this second internment. One of the evident ironies of Bunyan's life is that his enemies afforded him, in effect, a series of enforced sabbaticals; it is highly unlikely that his normal pastoral duties would have permitted him to accomplish nearly so much of his most enduring writing without these periods of incarceration.

Pilgrim's Progress is indisputably his greatest work, and also one of the most influential works in all English literature. Writers as diverse as Coleridge, George Eliot, Christina Rossetti and D. H. Lawrence have been influenced by it; among the radical Christians of the Taiping rebellion in China it served as a revolutionary 'red-book'; today it is still widely read in translation around the world. The lines of Valiant-for-Truth 'Who would true valour see ...' have been turned into the hymn, 'He who would valiant be / 'gainst all disaster', a hymn now sung more often by Anglicans than by Baptists. More importantly, the fictional structure of *Pilgrim's Progress* places it not only in the main tradition of Western 'grand narrative' epic (Homer, Vergil, Dante) but also in that particularly biblical reworking of the epic seen in works as diverse (and yet similar) as Augustine's *City of God*, Chaucer's *Canterbury Tales* and Langland's *Piers the Ploughman*. The governing element in all these works is an educational pilgrimage towards fulfilment and blessedness. Bunyan's text, with its allegory of the persevering journey of Christian to the Celestial City, commences, as do Dante's and Langland's, with a walk off the straight path,

'through the wilderness of this world', a falling asleep and the dreaming of a dream. The conventions of dream-vision as a means of inscribing the truths of revelation into human fiction, associated with the Bible and familiar through analogies in several medieval European vernaculars, are invoked by Bunyan almost as though he knew the relevant texts. As for Augustine, Chaucer and Dante's characters, the goal of Bunyan's faithful and persevering pilgrim is the New Jerusalem; like Chaucer, Bunyan begins, so to speak, in Southwark, the City of the World, and travels through a process of spiritual education in which his pilgrim develops a capacity for full repentance and dependence upon grace, which enables entry into a Holy City. But for Bunyan, no earthly Canterbury, Florence or Rome can be this city's sign or symbol.

Pilgrim's own city (the world) will be burned like the Troy of Aeneas or the Babylon of the biblical captivity. He is shown the way not by poetry (Vergil) or philosophy (Wisdom) but by Evangelist, who gives him the Good News, by Interpreter, who helps him understand it, and by Faithful, a redeemed fellow traveller and symbol of the true church. Ideas dressed up as people, however archaic, have a literary advantage; the objective, impersonal form of such allegory presents an otherwise probably dated intrusion of the self into a story intended to bear witness to a gracious redemption that is in fact communal. As a result the tale retains relevance. Few modern writers, one suspects, could have as effectively as Bunyan sublimated the rigours of their own bitter experience, or become so fruitfully self-effacing in their witness to the burden dropped off, the soul set free.

The book was not seen this way by all Bunyan's readers. Least impressed were some of the Baptists. One of them, 'T.S.', undertook to publish his own Part II, because he felt that Bunyan had given inadequate attention to church life and the sacraments, and that there were too many passages containing 'lightness and laughter'. He was a General Baptist, and disliked also what he took to be Bunyan's stress on a particular call to salvation for Christian. After *The Life and Death of Mr. Badman* (1680), about an inveterate liar who poses the question of Psalm 73, 'Why do some of the wicked prosper, seeing God is just?', and the eschatological historiography, *Holy War* (1682), Bunyan succumbed to the pressure to write a sequel of his own, *The Pilgrim's Progress, Part II* (1684). Ostensibly the story of Christian's wife's pilgrimage, it commences with her conversion upon his death. Theologically, it is an exploration of the meaning of God's pardon; literarily it is inferior, and, as it is a psychopharmicon, its audience is presumably different. As Milo Kaufmann puts it, 'While in the first part Bunyan is concerned to disturb the comfortable, ensuring a close examination of the reader's own calling, in the second part his concern is plainly to comfort the disturbed.'

There have been those who in every century since his death have wished to characterize Bunyan himself as among the disturbed. Most recently, John Stachniewski has portrayed him, much as many commentators have seen William *Cowper, as a psychically disordered victim of a despair-inducing Calvinism. Christopher Hill famously sees him as a hero of the social warfare in which his class was the perennial victim. Richard Greaves and Isabel Rivers see him as one player among many, albeit a formidable one, in the emergence of a vital democratic polity with its formative sources in the broader doctrines of English Nonconformity.

There is truth in all these views, but even so Bunyan is a giant in the devotional literature of English Christianity. In Gordon Wakefield's judgment, 'Bunyan's pilgrims, in spite of their joyous dances, are always in some sense the walking wounded.' There is for them no 'perfection' in this world (contra *Wesley); they must travel to the Celestial City for fulfilment. Bunyan does indeed side with the socially downtrodden, those maltreated by the rich and powerful. But his is neither an incipient liberation theology nor a call to arms; he promotes rather the virtues of active suffering. For Bunyan's pilgrim, it is the way of the cross that leads home.

Bunyan went one night through cold rain in response to a pastoral call to effect reconciliation between a father and his son. He caught a chill that led to pneumonia. Ten days later, on 31 August 1688, he died at the house of his friend Strudwick, a grocer. He was buried in the Dissenters' graveyard at Bunhill Fields.

Bibliography

J. Bunyan, *Grace Abounding to the Chief of Sinners*, R. Sharrock (ed.) (Oxford: Oxford University Press, 1962); J. Bunyan, *The Miscellaneous Works of John Bunyan*, R. Sharrock (ed.), 12 vols. (Oxford: Oxford University Press, 1960); J. Bunyan, *The Pilgrim's Progress*, J. B. Wharey and R. Sharrock (eds.) (Oxford: Oxford University Press, 1960); R. Greaves, *John Bunyan and English Nonconformity* (London: Hambledon, 1992); C. Hill, *A Tinker and a Poor Man: John Bunyan and his Church 1628–1688* (New York: A. Knopf, 1989); N. H. Keeble (ed.), *John Bunyan: Conventicle and Parnassus* (Oxford: Clarendon Press, 1988); I. Rivers, *Reason, Grace and Sentiment: A Study of the Language of Religion and Ethics in England, 1600–1780* (Cambridge: Cambridge University Press, 1991); J. Stachniewski, *The Persecutory Imagination: English Puritanism and the Literature of Religious Despair* (Oxford: Clarendon Press, 1991); W. Y. Tindall, *John Bunyan: Mechanik Preacher* (New York: A. Knopf, 1934); G. Wakefield, *Bunyan the Christian* (London: HarperCollins, 1992).

D. L. JEFFREY

■ **BURNS, Robert** (1789–1869), Presbyterian minister in Scotland and Canada and active proponent of the Free Church, was one of four brothers who entered the ministry, influenced by the evangelical faith of their father. They were part of the surging growth of evangelicalism in the Church of Scotland in their generation. Robert Burns became minister of St George's, Paisley, when only twenty-two years of age, and remained there for thirty-two years; then after the Disruption of 1843 he was minister of Free St George's until 1845. An able man, he was in the mould of the far abler Thomas *Chalmers. He engaged actively in parish evangelism; he was acutely concerned with urban poverty, which he believed could be effectively addressed only by the ministrations of the national church; his intellectual interests made him a diligent member of various philosophical and literary societies and secured him a DD from Glasgow University; and he strongly opposed Roman Catholicism. Amid his multifarious parochial pursuits his evangelical activism led him to be a founder and long-term secretary of the Glasgow Colonial Society. This was a voluntary organization that sought to assist in providing Church of Scotland ministers for the British North American colonies. Its work included fund-raising, sharing its vision with theological students, making arrangements for the emigration of ordained ministers and providing a measure of financial support, sometimes for a considerable period of time. This work, and his network of contacts, led the Free Church of Scotland, upon its inception, to send Burns as part of a delegation to North America to solicit sympathy or gain adherents as appropriate.

As a result of this visit, Burns was to emigrate to Canada at fifty-six years of age, remaining there until his death, and becoming one of the most powerful forces in the dynamic Presbyterian Church in Canada in connexion with the Free Church of Scotland. In 1843 Burns spent a significant amount of time in Upper Canada (Ontario), where he did much to secure the adherence of congregations and ministers to the Free Church, even though ministers by such adherence forfeited their claim to an annual stipend from the Clergy Reserves. The next year Burns was again in British North America, travelling all the way from Niagara to Halifax, rousing support for the Free Church. Following the success of these ventures, Burns accepted in 1845 a call to be minister of Knox Church, Toronto, which had been founded in 1820 as the first Presbyterian congregation in the town, with a mixed body of Presbyterians owning no relation to any British denomination. When St Andrew's in connexion with the Church of Scotland was formed there was a significant exodus, but when the Disruption occurred in Canada, the Free Church supporters who seceded from St Andrew's joined the original congregation, which was weak in numbers but rich in property. Burns ministered here until 1856, again displaying the activism of his years in Paisley. He made many missionary journeys from Toronto for the purpose of establishing new Free Church congregations; several Presbyterian congregations are still named after him. He was also active in the anti-slavery movement, being a strong supporter of the Buxton mission in south-western Ontario which established a community for those who successfully reached Canada by means of the Underground Railroad. In addition, he persuaded John Black to go to minister to the Selkirk settlers at Kildonan, north of present-day Winnipeg, where they had lived for thirty-nine years without a Presbyterian minister. His pastoral and social concern also made him an advocate of teetotalism.

In spite of Burns's accomplishments there was another side to his life. He had an overbearing manner which made personal relationships difficult, and by 1856 he had alienated so many of his congregation that he had to resign. In kindness he was invited to teach church history and apologetics to ministerial students at Knox College, which he continued to do until 1864, but he was far past his prime. In spite of his failures he did much to make evangelical Presbyterianism a powerful force in mid-Victorian Canada.

Bibliography

R. F. Burns, *Life and Times of the Rev. R. Burns, D.D.* (Toronto: James Campbell & Sons, 1871); B. J. Fraser, *Church, College, and Clergy: A History of Theological Education at Knox College, Toronto, 1844–1994* (Montreal and Kingston: McGill & Queen's University Press, 1995); R. W. Vaudry, *The Free Church in Victorian Canada, 1844–61* (Waterloo: Wilfrid Laurier University Press, 1989).

I. S. RENNIE

■ **BURWASH, Nathanael** (1839–1918), Canadian Methodist minister and educator, was raised on a farm in central Ontario. Burwash at an early age was exposed to strong evangelical influences by his parents, both of whom had converted in their youth to Methodism. In 1852, with the intention of entering the ministry, he enrolled as a preparatory student in the Methodist Victoria College, located in nearby Cobourg. The following year he took part in a large college revival and became a member of the Wesleyan Methodist Church in Canada. Graduating with a BA in 1859, he continued to be profoundly influenced by the college's curriculum of common-sense thought, and by the balance between piety and scholarship modelled by its president, Samuel Nelles.

Appointed a probationer in 1860, thanks to the growing need for educated ministers, he found himself stationed in some of central Canada's oldest Methodist urban churches: Belleville (1861–1863), Toronto East (1863–1864), and after his 1864 ordination, Hamilton (1865–1866). In 1866 he was asked to return to Victoria College, and following a few months spent at the Sheffield Scientific School of Yale College, assumed the recently vacated chair in natural science. Here, thanks to his careful adherence to the Baconian inductive method, he was able to avoid taking a position on such controversial matters as Charles Darwin's evolutionary thought.

A brief but intense struggle with religious doubt during his ministry had made him especially concerned to help ministerial students to face the challenges to faith posed by new thinking in science and biblical studies, and to that end he began to offer several courses in theology to arts students. In 1870, anticipating the establishment of a faculty of theology at Victoria, he enrolled in the Methodist Garrett Biblical Institute in Evanston, Illinois, from which he received a BD in 1871 and an STD in 1876. When in 1873 a faculty of theology was established, he was appointed professor of systematic and biblical theology, and the faculty's first dean, a position he would retain until 1900. Upon the sudden death of his mentor, Samuel Nelles, in 1887, he was also appointed chancellor and president of Victoria University, formed in 1884 through the union of Victoria College and Albert College in Belleville.

As the denomination's leading theologian, Burwash was able to exercise significant influence through his many addresses and writings, including several major publications, all of which became part of the ministerial reading list: *Wesley's doctrinal standards* (1881), a study of *Wesley's standard sermons, Handbook of the Epistle of Paul to the Romans* (1887) and a two-volume *Manual of Christian Theology on the Inductive Method* (1900). When in 1890 and again in 1906 complaints led by the denomination's more conservative general superintendent, Albert *Carman, were made over the teaching at Victoria of the new 'higher criticism', it was Burwash's moderate stance that ultimately triumphed. At the General Conference of 1910, he was able successfully to argue that any attempt to limit Methodist ministers to a literal interpretation of Scripture was contrary to Wesley's own position. Moreover, in future, doctrinal disciplinary cases were to be tried by a small committee of ministers 'of good repute for their knowledge of questions of doctrine', rather than by the General Conference.

Burwash's own gradual and selective acceptance of the higher criticism was mediated by a scholarly piety which found its way into the classroom in practical theology. In a modified version of the inductive method, students were encouraged to analyse and appropriate the experimental evidence offered by such Methodist doctrines as 'the witness of the Spirit' and 'Christian perfection'.

Progressive in his attitude to new developments in science and biblical studies, Burwash took a conservative position on any doctrinal changes that undermined Methodism's evangelical message. His strong views on infant depravity and the need for conversion of the young as a condition for church membership brought him into conflict with a number of colleagues more favourable to the theological shift towards childhood innocence. Although he was able to ensure that the denomination formally retained its traditional emphases, by the time of his death some of the younger ministers considered these outdated.

Burwash's desire to balance both old and new positions was not without ambiguous results. Methodist Social Gospel proponent and politician James Shaver Woodsworth, for example, was able to draw on his teacher's progressive spirit to articulate the principles of a new social Christianity, while at the same time rejecting traditional Wesleyan spirituality. A similar ambiguity can be detected in Burwash's support of the church union movement in Canada. When in 1904 formal negotiations began to unite three of the country's largest evangelical denominations, the Presbyterians, Congregationalists and Methodists, he was appointed president of the subcommittee on doctrine. In that capacity, and as the designated spokesman presenting the union case in the denominational paper, *The Christian Guardian*, he was able to exercise a decisive influence in ensuring that the proposed Basis of Union's doctrinal statement reflected the central tenets of evangelical belief. Although his own denomination by 1912 had voted to accept the Basis, considerable dissension within the Presbyterian Church and the concerns of war delayed the consummation of union until 1925. By that date the postmillennial optimism which had led Burwash and many of his generation to assume the imminent triumph of evangelicalism had waned, and the new United Church of Canada found itself casting about for new theological moorings.

More enduring would be Burwash's decision as newly appointed president and chancellor of Victoria to enter into federation with the secular University of Toronto. Though negotiations between the provincial government and Ontario's major universities had begun in 1881, opposition within the Methodist denomination delayed the proclamation of a Federation Act passed in 1887. Burwash as one of the key negotiators of the Act was convinced, unlike some of its Methodist critics, that the proposed division of labour assigning the teaching of the sciences to the university, and that of the humanities and theology to the denominational colleges, would protect evangelical moral and religious influences. Thanks to a $230,000 bequest in 1889 conditional on Victoria's moving to Toronto, criticism was overcome, and the Act was proclaimed in 1890. After the move in 1892, Burwash fought hard to safeguard the terms of the Act, as well as exercising vigilance over students' moral behaviour, a task facilitated by the construction in 1903 of a women's residence, Annesley Hall, and in 1913, a men's residence, Burwash Hall.

Throughout his life Burwash experienced much support from his wife, Margaret Proctor, a quiet strong-minded woman whom he had married in 1868. Of their twelve children, only four survived to adulthood, and in one week in 1889, three sons and a daughter succumbed to diphtheria. Despite tragedy, the family continued to exercise hospitality, and Aboriginal and foreign students from the mission fields were especially welcomed. Upon Burwash's retirement in 1913, in response to a request by Victoria's graduates in foreign missions, the couple undertook an extended tour to Japan, where he delivered lectures at the Tokyo Imperial University and

the Kwansei Gakuin, a Canadian Methodist school near Kobe.

At Burwash's death in 1918 after a brief illness, his eulogist claimed that 'no man in Canadian Methodism has influenced and guided the thinking of the ministry of the church to so great an extent'.

Bibliography

M. Van Die, *An Evangelical Mind: Nathanael Burwash and the Methodist Tradition in Canada, 1839–1918* (Montreal and Kingston: McGill–Queen's University Press, 1989); R. J. Taylor, 'The Darwinian revolution: the responses of four Canadian scholars' (PhD thesis, McMaster University, Hamilton, Ontario, 1976).

M. VAN DIE

■ **BUTLER, Josephine Elizabeth** (1828–1906), British feminist and campaigner for the civil rights of prostitutes was a lifelong member of the Church of England, whose name appears in the Anglican Calendar of Saints on 30 December, the anniversary of her death.

Josephine Butler was born on 13 April 1828 in Millfield, Northumberland, the seventh of nine surviving children of John Grey and his wife Hannah Annett. John Grey was an agricultural reformer and leading Liberal in the English border country adjacent to Scotland. The Greys were passionate supporters of the anti-slavery campaign and taught their children about this and other contemporary social issues, although Josephine's education was otherwise sporadic. Her childhood home in Dilston, Northumberland, was extremely happy, and the siblings remained close, even after marriage took them abroad.

The Grey family regularly attended the Anglican church of St Andrews in Corbridge, near their home, but they also maintained family ties to Nonconformity. Hannah Grey had received a Moravian education and employed a Methodist governess, who took Josephine and her sister to Wesleyan services. One of John Grey's sisters married a leading evangelical Presbyterian minister. Throughout her life Josephine Butler was notably ecumenical, attending services in a wide variety of Protestant churches and numbering many Nonconformists among her closest friends. 'Evangelical' was not a term that the Grey family appear to have used, but it is an accurate description of their beliefs. Josephine reported an experience of religious crisis in her late teens, which may have been a conversion, and during her early adult years she spent many hours daily in prayer and Bible study, keeping a spiritual diary that described several occasions upon which, she believed, Christ had 'manifested' himself directly to her.

In 1852 Josephine married George Butler, the son of the Anglican Dean of Peterborough, and moved to Oxford. George was ordained into the Church of England in 1853, but chose to work in boys' schools, Cheltenham College (1857–1865) and Liverpool College (as principal, 1866–1882), before becoming a canon of Winchester Cathedral on his retirement. In Oxford the Butlers 'rescued' the first of many prostitutes whom they housed and for whom they cared. Three sons were born to them and then a daughter, Eva, who was tragically killed in 1864, at the age of five, in a fall from the first-floor landing of their Cheltenham home. Still grieving, the Butlers moved in 1866 to Liverpool, where Josephine began a ministry of preaching to the imprisoned women of the 'Bridewell' in Liverpool workhouse, where she went to 'find some pain keener than my own'.

In 1866 Butler became president of the North of England Council for the Higher Education of Women and in 1869 accepted the far greater demands of the campaign to repeal the Contagious Diseases Acts. These Acts of 1864, 1866 and 1869 allowed the police to detain any woman suspected of prostitution in naval and military towns, to examine her for venereal disease on pain of imprisonment if she refused and to detain her in a certified hospital if she were found to be diseased. Butler and her supporters were horrified by this infringement of the civil rights of women (for any woman might legally be detained under the Act). Butler became the secretary of the Ladies' National Association campaigning for the repeal of the Acts, despite the cost to her family life, her health and even to her social status, since convention decreed that it was unacceptable for a respectable woman to speak publicly on such a taboo subject. She waged a courageous campaign of pamphlet- and letter-writing, parliamentary lobbying, petition-gathering and nationwide speaking that lasted until 1886. Although she gave evidence before a Royal Commission in 1871, one of the first women to do so, the majority of MPs were unmoved by her arguments. The final repeal of the Acts in 1886 owed much to the efforts within Parliament of James Stansfeld MP. *Personal Reminiscences of a Great Crusade* (1896) is Josephine Butler's account of the campaign.

From 1874 onwards Butler extended her campaigning activities to include the treatment of poor women and prostitutes on the European continent, especially in Paris, Geneva and Brussels. She demanded the right to inspect state brothels and challenged the activities of the police charged with regulating them. She objected particularly to the open involvement of city councils in the licensing of prostitution, arguing, for example in *Une Voix dans le Desert* (1875), that all citizens were thereby implicated in the maintenance of an evil system. The British and Continental Federation for the Abolition of Government Regulation of Prostitution was formed in 1875, with Butler as joint secretary. This campaign had some success, including the exposure of the traffic in young girls from England to Belgium in 1880.

In 1885 Butler became involved in W. T. Stead's hard-hitting campaign against child prostitution in London, which was conducted through his newspaper, *The Pall Mall Gazette*. Although Stead was eventually arrested and imprisoned as a result of the campaign, the sensational headlines ensured that the facts of child prostitution became public knowledge, as he and Butler intended.

Butler's campaigns for 'purity' began in the early 1870s, when she spoke of 'the necessity of purity of life in all who would join us'. In 1886 she joined the newly formed National Vigilance Association for the Repression of Criminal Vice and Immorality, but soon found that its methods (repressive action against 'immoral' individuals) were different from her own favoured approach of preaching personal morality.

In all these campaigns, Josephine Butler had the support of her husband, despite the presumed damage to his career. After his death in 1890, she had no settled home and travelled and wrote more than ever. She died on 30 December 1906 at the home of her son George Butler, in Northumberland and is buried at Kirknewton.

Josephine Butler's religion has, until recently, received less attention than her feminism from historians. The two were intimately connected, however, since her Christian faith provided the inspiration for her feminist crusade. She believed that Jesus had treated women as of equal importance to men and had 'liberated' them, and this liberation became her model for the treatment of women in her own day. Her conviction that she too had been 'liberated' by Christ and learned truths directly from God empowered her to speak out, to 'prophesy', against any opposition. Her belief in her right *as a woman* to stand up for her convictions made her theology explicitly feminist. She found few contemporary examples of the Christian woman she was trying to be, but drew inspiration from the life of the fourteenth-century Italian saint, Catharine of Siena. Butler's biography of Catharine (1878) depicts a woman who was, like herself, both a practical reformer and a contemplative mystic, who believed herself called by God to be a leader of both men and women.

Josephine Butler was a remarkable woman, described by Millicent Garrett Fawcett as 'the most distinguished Englishwoman of the nineteenth century'. In her courageous campaign she was a true Victorian, fighting with the zeal of a *Wilberforce against the sin of 'white slavery'. The feminist aspects of her Christian thought were radical in her own day and anticipate in some respects the Christian feminism of the twentieth century.

Bibliography

J. Jordan, *Josephine Butler* (London: John Murray, 2001); H. Mathers, 'The Evangelical Spirituality of a Victorian Feminist. Josephine Butler 1828–1906', *Journal of Ecclesiastical History* vol. 52.2 (April 2001), pp. 282–312; J. Walkowitz, *Prostitution and Victorian Society: Women, Class and the State* (Cambridge: Cambridge University Press, 1980).

H. MATHERS

■ **BUXTON, Sir Thomas Fowell** (1786–1845), the leading figure in the movement to abolish slavery in the British Empire, was born in Earls Colne, near Colchester in Essex, England, on 1 April 1786. Buxton was the eldest son of Thomas Fowell Buxton, who at one time served as High Sheriff of Essex. His father died when he was six, leaving Buxton and his five siblings to be raised by his mother, Anna (née Hanbury), who always treated him as an equal and taught him to think and act for himself. Like his father, Buxton had a passion for hunting, shooting and fishing. He grew to be tall and strong; at six foot four he was an imposing figure, and appropriately nicknamed 'Elephant Buxton'.

Following his education in private schools at Kingston and then Greenwich, his mother urged him to attend Trinity College, Dublin, in the hope that he might inherit an Irish estate. Following her advice, he entered Trinity in 1803, graduating as a gold medallist with several university prizes in 1807. Before going to university Buxton had become engaged to his cousin Hannah Gurney, of Earlham Hall, Norfolk, who was three years his senior. In 1807 they married at Tarsburgh Friends Meeting House, both families being members of the Society of Friends (Quakers). His brother-in-law, Samuel Hoare, from a wealthy Irish Quaker banking family, became Buxton's closest friend.

In 1808 the Buxtons moved to London as the hopes for an Irish estate faded. Here he became involved in the management of the Truman and Hanbury Brewery in Brick Lane, Spitalfields, a Quaker-owned business in which his uncles, Sampson and Osgood Hanbury, had an interest. By 1811 he was on the firm's board of directors and the company was renamed Truman, Hanbury and Buxton. The Buxtons lived for a time in Brick Lane and attended a Quaker Meeting House nearby. In 1811, however, Buxton was urged by Anglican friends to visit the Anglican Wheler Street Chapel in Spitalfields, a weaving village on the eastern edge of the City of London. The attraction here was the preaching of the Revd Josiah Pratt, the clerical secretary of the Church Missionary Society. Buxton took the advice and his life was revolutionized. During a serious illness in 1813 he experienced a profound deepening of his faith. It was at Wheler Chapel that he imbibed evangelical doctrine, thus gaining a missionary vision for the evangelization of Africa and a deep concern to see the abolition of slavery.

Buxton saw no conflict between his association with the brewing industry and his evangelicalism. Indeed, a number of the wealthiest brewers at the beginning of the nineteenth century were noted evangelicals (among them Arthur Guinness and Robert Hanbury). Buxton reorganized the brewery's business methods and implemented modern methods of book-keeping. While he eventually gave up being general manager, he always maintained general oversight of the enterprise.

In 1815 the Buxtons moved their family of four children from Spitalfields to Hampstead, a more fashionable area of London. In 1820, after losing four of their children, including their oldest son, the family moved away from London, and eventually Buxton built Northrepps Hall near Overstrand in Norfolk. About the same time Buxton and Hoare told their sister-in-law, Elizabeth *Fry, that they wanted to be involved in her efforts for prison reform. In 1818 Buxton was elected Tory MP for Weymouth, though he eventually crossed the floor of the Commons to become a Whig, feeling that the Whigs were more supportive of his desire to promote prison reform. In the same year of his election to Parliament Buxton published an essay entitled *An Enquiry whether Crime and Misery are produced or prevented by our present System of Prison Discipline*, in which he identified objectionable practices needing reform: in particular, the incarceration alongside hardened criminals of those not yet tried, the imprisonment of debtors, and the incarceration of people for trivial offences. The book was translated into French and was widely read abroad. Buxton's chief aim was to remove from the statute book the penalty of death for all crimes apart from murder.

Buxton's election to Parliament led to a developing friendship between himself and William *Wilberforce. In May 1821 Wilberforce wrote to Buxton inviting him to take up the leadership of the abolitionists; a year later Buxton agreed. He and his allies, both inside and outside Parliament, employed the same tactics to fight for the abolition of slavery as had been deployed in the earlier effort to suppress the slave trade. These included various techniques of public agitation such as the circulation of petitions and the monthly reporting of facts relating to the slave trade in *The Anti-Slavery Reporter*, edited by Zachary *Macaulay. The advent of a Whig government in 1830, the first in forty years, helped speed up the pace of abolition which was finally achieved in August 1833. Wilberforce thus died, on 29 July 1833, knowing that Buxton had successfully completed the task that had been entrusted to him.

In 1837 Buxton lost his parliamentary seat and declined many offers from other constituencies; he devoted the final period of his life to the cause of Africa. Although the slave trade had been officially renounced by Britain, it continued to be prosecuted in both West and East Africa by other nations. While evangelicals insisted that the British navy be employed in enforcing the letter of the law as regards British ships and citizens, Buxton and others were anxious to eliminate the underlying causes of slavery and to employ international agreements and other strategies to do so.

Buxton's vision for Africa included an expedition up the River Niger under the auspices of the 'African Civilization Society' to prepare for 'agricultural, commercial and missionary settlements' which could bring to Africa the benefits of Western civilization. This aim reflected Buxton's conviction that 'It is the Bible and the plough that must regenerate Africa.' In the spring of 1838 he outlined to the British cabinet his ideas on the way to suppress the traffic in slaves, and in December he was assured of British Government support. In 1839 Buxton published *The Slave Trade and Its Remedy*, which described both the horrors of the trade and his proposals to promote legitimate commerce as an economically viable alternative. In March 1840 he could write to one of his sons, 'The project for overturning the Slave Trade by civilization, Christianity and the cultivation of the soil, is no longer in my hands; the government have adopted the principle and taken the task upon themselves.' A model farm was established at Lokaja on the Niger, and the British public lavishly supported the expedition. In the midst of this climate of optimism Buxton was honoured for his public service by being created a baronet on 7 July 1840.

The Niger Expedition, however, was soon

to end in disaster. In late August 1840 three steamships provided by the British government entered the Niger, but an outbreak of fever devastated the expedition. Forty-one of the 145 Europeans involved died; all 108 Africans survived. Unfortunately, the treaties signed by African leaders to end slavery proved unenforceable, and government support was withdrawn. Buxton was forced to abandon the venture and its failure disgraced him; it was the major factor in his retirement from active politics. Yet his vision for the opening up of Africa to Christianity and the displacement of the slave trade by legitimate commerce had been passed on to David *Livingstone, who was a young medical student in London when he heard Buxton speak in 1840.

Buxton died at Overstrand, Norfolk, England, on 19 February 1845 at the age of fifty-nine. A statue in his honour was erected in Westminster Abbey and financed by public subscription with some fifty thousand Africans and West Indians making contributions. His eldest son, Sir Edward North Buxton, inherited the baronetcy on his father's death and proved to be an equally ardent evangelical. The Buxton family has since produced many politicians, evangelical clergy and missionaries.

Bibliography

T. Binney, *Sir Thomas Fowell Buxton Bart* (London: James Nisbet, 1853); C. Buxton, *Memoirs of Sir Thomas Fowell Buxton* (London: J. M. Dent, 1925); M. M. Hennell, *Sons of the Prophets* (London: SPCK, 1979); E. Stock, *History of CMS* (London: CMS, 1899).

D. M. LEWIS

■ **CALVIN, John** (1509–1564), French Protestant Reformer, was the leader of the Reformation in Geneva, fountain-head of the Calvinist tradition of theology and chief source of the Reformed pattern of Protestant Christianity. None of the sixteenth-century Reformers has been as influential as Calvin in the shaping of evangelicalism in the English-speaking world. Lutheranism still displays a special reverence for *Luther, but no Reformer is so widely read by pastors and theologians as John Calvin.

Calvin was born at Noyon in Picardy in northern France. During his time at the universities of Paris, Orléans and Bourges (which included a second period at each of the first two), Calvin studied the humanities, theology and law (c. 1523–1533). Several important details of his educational career remain uncertain, especially dates, but it is clear that Calvin was attracted to the new humanist learning, the study both of the classical languages (he also began to study Hebrew) and of the civil law code of the Christian Roman Empire. The identity of some of his teachers is known for certain, such as Melchior Wolmar in Greek at Orléans and the celebrated Italian humanist jurist Andrea Alciati at Bourges. Other teachers, such as the Scot John Major or Mair at Paris, may or may not have taught him. Determining which currents of traditional philosophy or theology impressed him is not easy.

Some of Calvin's fellow-students, friends and teachers are known to have been influenced by Lutheran teachings, which had already fallen under the ban of the Sorbonne. The Cop family, Calvin's cousin, Pierre Robert Olivétan (whom he would soon be assisting in translating the Bible into French), Wolmar, the young *Beza (later his successor in Geneva), members of the movement for biblical and spiritual reform led by Jacques Lefèvre d'Étaples (Faber Stapulensis) and Guillaume Briçonnet, Bishop of Meaux just east of Paris, and others must have introduced him at this time to the new Lutheran gospel. But Calvin was reticent about his personal life ('about myself I am reluctant to speak'), so the sudden (or, unexpected) conversion by which God 'subdued me to teachableness', of which he wrote years later in the preface to his Psalms commentary, is variously dated by scholars. Some place it before 1530, but most prefer the early 1530s, perhaps 1532/3. Calvin's first published work, a commentary on the Roman Stoic moralist Seneca's *De clementia* (April 1532), throws light on his aspirations as a humanist scholar but not on his evangelical allegiance.

Overt expressions of Protestantism in Paris from late 1533 provoked increasingly repressive measures. Calvin fled south, spending some months with Louis Du Tillet, a pastor near Angoulême, where he began work on his *Institutes*. He associated with groups of believers around Poitiers, preaching and sharing in a simple Lord's Supper. In late 1534 Calvin and Du Tillet left France via Strasbourg for Basel. During the next eighteen months, Calvin got to know many of the Reformers and teachers in the Swiss cities (and may even have met Erasmus in the Dutchman's last months), issued his first Protestant writing (a foreword to Olivétan's French Bible [June 1535]) and published the first (Latin) edition of his *Institutio* of the Christian religion (March 1536). The book sold quickly, and Calvin soon began work on a revised edition.

After visits to Ferrara in Italy and finally to Paris during a brief amnesty, Calvin had to stay overnight in Geneva unexpectedly, while en route to study in Strasbourg. Here Guillaume Farel, leader since 1532 of a reform movement that had succeeded in persuading the entire Genevan community to vote in May 1536 to 'live by the gospel', pressurized Calvin into staying to assist the Reformation. In September 1536 Calvin began to lecture on Paul's epistles in Latin, and within weeks he was working as a pastor. The rest of his life, even during his years of exile spent mostly at Strasbourg (1538–1541), was inextricably linked to the sometimes difficult progress of evangelical reform in Geneva. Henceforth, he seldom travelled far afield, although he eventually exercised a role of Europe-wide influence. Geneva, a city of some 10,000 people with little claim to distinction (it had no university, no major printing house and no leading industries or financial institutions) but strategically placed for trade and communications, became through the Reformation a centre of international importance in religion, higher education and publishing. This transformation is a measure of Calvin's achievement.

Geneva's adoption of the Reformation went *pari passu* with the winning and consolidating of its political independence from its prince-bishop and the duchy of Savoy. This revolution was accomplished only with the military assistance of Berne. The city's continuing dependence on Berne brought pressure on the council to adopt a Lutheran model of church reform, more conservative than that favoured by Farel and Calvin. Their *Articles concerning the Organisation of the Church and of Worship in Geneva*, which

were approved in early 1537, required not only an individual city-wide subscription to a new *Instruction and Confession of Faith*, the first catechism of the Genevan reform, but also a system of district wardens to report on residents' misdemeanours, which, unless subsequently amended, would be punished by exclusion from the Lord's Supper. Resentment at this wholly unprecedented level of intrusiveness stiffened the council's resolve to accede to Berne's demands (e.g. for the observance of four major Christian festivals). The result was the ministers' enforced departure, initially to Basel, in April 1538.

Calvin's renewed commitment to scholarly endeavours was again overborne, this time by Martin *Bucer's urgent summons to Strasbourg. There, in September 1538, Calvin assumed charge of a new French refugee congregation, and early in 1539 he began lecturing on the New Testament in the new academy. The Strasbourg years were both productive and formative for Calvin. The second Latin edition of the *Institutes* (1539) and the first French one (1541), his first biblical commentary, on Romans (1540), and an exemplary *Short Treatise on the Lord's Supper* (in French, 1541) were his main publications. In August 1540 he married Idelette de Bure, a widowed ex-Anabaptist with two children, whom Calvin undertook to raise when she died in 1549. Their only child, a son, died soon after birth in 1542.

Calvin not only observed closely the progress, and the frustrations, of Strasbourg's reform and engaged in theological discourse with Bucer and others but also had his horizons broadened regarding the wider Reformation movement and its political entanglements. He got to know *Melanchthon and took part in the colloquies with reformist Catholic representatives in Haguenau, Worms and Regensburg (1540–1541). He seized opportunities to champion the cause of France's persecuted evangelicals with sympathetic Protestant rulers.

Yet Calvin did not forget Geneva, nor it him. The possibility of his return was widely canvassed. It fell to Calvin in 1539 to send a *Reply to Sadoleto*, one of his most impressive writings, when Cardinal Jacopo Sadoleto addressed an attractive appeal to the Genevans to return to the Catholic fold. Eventually, after much agonizing, Calvin arrived back in

Geneva in September 1541, having in effect negotiated terms to his satisfaction. Within two months the councils had approved the *Ecclesiastical Ordinances*, his key demand for the ordering of the Reformed church, including the four orders of ministry (pastor, deacon, elder and doctor/teacher/lecturer) adopted in Strasbourg. The councils made some damaging revisions to the final text, which led to repeated wrangling over the right of excommunication until the company of pastors, which Calvin chaired, won independent control in 1555.

The introduction of the Reformation in Geneva redirected rather than pacified the factions that dated from the struggle for the city's independence. Parties rallied under pro-Bernese (or pro-Swiss) and pro-French banners, with the established Genevan families resenting the French incomers. The pastors were nearly all French, and the city attracted thousands of French Protestant refugees, some bringing significant resources, such as the Estienne (Stephanus) printing houses. The enfranchisement of the newly registered aliens (Calvin was one himself) was a sensitive issue. These forces of social and economic change interacted with resistance to the doctrinal and moral norms of the Reformed church, with the result that Calvin's ministry was rarely free of conflict and controversy, even after the critical election of 1555 that produced a pro-Calvin majority among the councillors for the first time. When Servetus was executed in 1553 for anti-trinitarianism and Anabaptism, the decision was taken by a council with a majority unsympathetic to Calvin, although Calvin supported the verdict.

Among Calvin's multifarious activities in Geneva (his legal training, for example, made him useful on diplomatic and constitutional matters), which have bequeathed to later Reformed evangelicalism not only a huge corpus of theological, biblical and controversial writings but also models of public worship, church polity and disciplinary oversight, his fourfold service of the Word of God must hold pride of place. He preached in French, about ten times a fortnight, at least from 1549 when his sermons began to be recorded by one Denis Raguenier and so preserved. The style was that of a homiletic commentary; Calvin worked verse by verse

through a biblical book by *lectio continua*, as long as the clock allowed, without notes, extempore, with only the Greek or Hebrew text before him. He employed the same method for the Latin lectures (*praelectiones*), delivered midweek to students and others, especially pastors in training for ministry in France, long before such teaching was formalized in the Academy of Geneva in 1559. From Calvin's lectures came several of his Old Testament commentaries, whereas those on the New Testament were specially written as such.

A third form of the ministry of the Word, of which few examples have survived, was the introductory exposition given in the ministers' weekly Friday Bible study known in French as the *congrégation*. The evidence suggests that often Calvin chose for this exercise a book on which he was writing a commentary or preparing to lecture. The fourth form has become clearly recognizable only with the recent publication of the minutes of the weekly Thursday consistory for disciplinary cases; most hearings ended with a biblical admonition delivered by Calvin. Calvin thus displayed remarkable fluency and versatility in making the meaning of Scripture as plain as possible. As he said in the preface to his Romans commentary, 'almost the only duty [of the commentator] is to lay open the mind of the writer whom he has undertaken to explain'. His disciplined approach made 'lucid brevity' the 'chief virtue of the interpreter'. Such qualities have made Calvin's commentaries more usable by modern expositors than any other sixteenth-century writer's.

Given the volume and comprehensive biblical coverage of his sermons and commentaries, to say nothing of the range of his individual treatises, from relics to God's eternal election, Calvin has too often been known as 'a man of one book': the *Institutes*. Nevertheless, the significance of this work among Calvin's corpus as a whole and its merits as a magisterial *summa* of Protestant theology are undeniable. It grew from the six chapters of the 1536 edition (basically a catechism with an apologetic preface to the French king Francis I, which made it almost a confession of faith) through four revisions to the massive four books of the definitive 1559 edition. All apart from the first were followed by French editions, which marked an important advance in the development of the language for use in serious works of theology or philosophy.

The *Institutes* grew, and its contents were reordered, in response to many factors, among which Calvin's engagement with Catholics, radicals such as Servetus or supposedly erring mainstream teachers such as Osiander was probably the weightiest. A point would need clarification, or Calvin's knowledge, for example of the early Fathers, or his understanding of a particular theological topic, would expand, perhaps as a result of lecturing or preaching on a part of Scripture. Rarely were the *Institutes* revised because Calvin had changed his mind.

The work is supreme as an ordered, lucid and comprehensive exposition and defence of the evangelical faith, of which the main elements inspired the whole Reformation. Its systematic character as a tightly and logically regimented presentation in the manner of late medieval scholastic theologies has been grossly exaggerated. Calvin was above all a biblical theologian. Atempts to identify one focal point around which the massive bulk of the *Institutes* is organized, or one dominant central motif that informs the complete work, are generally judged ill-advised. Certain themes were, however, particularly important for Calvin and distinguished him from other Reformers, individually or severally. These include the glory of God, scrupulous reliance on what God has revealed and rejection both of all speculation about divine mysteries and of all human fabrications in the worship of God, union with Christ, the so-called third use of the law of God (its defining of God's will for the life of his church), the practical usefulness of true theology, and the sovereign providence and election of God. But undergirding everything were the central evangelical affirmations of the Reformation: Scripture alone, Christ alone, grace alone, faith alone. These, Calvin claimed, were the convictions of the apostles and of the early Catholic Church; major distortion intruded only in the Middle Ages.

Calvin's achievement lay in combining his massive contribution in biblical exposition and theology (which included also the Genevan catechism, and the Reformed order of worship he brought back from Strasbourg to Geneva, which, translated into English and promoted by *Knox's Scotland, served the whole Presbyterian tradition) with a firmly ordered church polity (the essence of which was known subsequently as Presbyterianism), as successful an implementation of reform ideals as could be found anywhere in Reformation Europe, and a programme that sought the conformity of all aspects of human life in society to the will of God. With only a degree of exaggeration he has been called the founder of a civilization.

The terms 'Calvinist' and 'Calvinism' are used in a variety of senses, perhaps least often in direct reference to Calvin's own reforming or theological work. The term 'Calvinian' is applied increasingly to Calvin himself, but the Geneva reform movement that he led is often called the 'Calvinist Reformation'. 'Calvinist' and 'Calvinism' are frequently used for later phases of theological traditions, church polities or patterns of Christian society or culture that to different degrees claim inspiration from or fidelity to Calvin. Questions of the continuity between Calvin and later Calvinists remain keenly debated, but the historical Calvin was too complex to serve comfortably as the eponymous patron of most later Calvinisms.

Bibliography

W. de Greef, *The Writings of John Calvin: An Introductory Guide* (Leicester: Apollos, 1993); F. Wendel, *Calvin: The Origins and Development of his Religious Thought* (London: Collins, 1963); W. Walker, *John Calvin: The Organiser of Reformed Protestantism* (New York: Shocken, 1969); E. W. Monter, *Calvin's Geneva* (New York: Wiley, 1967); M. de Kroon, *The Honour of God and Human Salvation: A Contribution to the Understanding of Calvin's Theology according to his Institutes* (Edinburgh: T. & T. Clark, 2001); B. Cottret, *Calvin: A Biography* (Edinburgh: T. & T. Clark, 2000); R. S. Wallace, *Calvin, Geneva and the Reformation* (Edinburgh: Scottish Academic Press, 1988); R. A. Muller, *The Unaccommodated Calvin* (New York: Oxford University Press, 2000).

D. F. WRIGHT

■ **CAMPBELL, Alexander** (1788–1866), religious innovator, was the key leader in an indigenous American movement to restore original Christianity, expressed today in three major groups: Disciples of Christ, Churches of Christ and Christian Churches/Churches of Christ. He was a noted author, editor, debater and college educator, founding Bethany College in 1840 and serving as its president until his death. He proclaimed the authority of Scripture, and promoted independent elder-ruled congregations, non-credalism, believers' immersion, weekly observation of the Lord's Supper, and the appointment of ministers by local congregations.

Alexander Campbell was born in County Antrim, Ireland, on 12 September 1788, and died in Bethany, West Virginia, on 4 March 1866. He was the son of Thomas Campbell, who was born in County Down, Ireland, on 1 February 1763, and died in Bethany, West Virginia, on 4 January 1854. His mother was Jane Corneigle, of Huguenot descent. Thomas Campbell, whose father was an Anglican, joined the Anti-Burgher branch of the Seceder Presbyterian Church, attended the University of Glasgow, and then trained for the ministry at Whitburn. He worked as a schoolteacher, and served the North Ireland Ahorey Seceder church from 1798 to 1807. With others, he helped to form the ecumenical Evangelical Society of Ulster. In 1807, because of ill health, Thomas Campbell visited America and decided to stay.

Alexander Campbell's father and uncles organized his early education. He attended the University of Glasgow from 1808 to 1809. John Locke's writings on epistemology and government, and the publications of the Scottish Common-Sense Realists, made a deep impression upon his later thinking. At Glasgow, having been exposed to the Haldanean Scottish Independents, Campbell decided to break with the Anti-Burgher Seceders.

After coming into conflict with the Anti-Burgher Synod in Pennsylvania, Thomas Campbell and several Presbyterian lay people, founded the Christian Association of Washington, to promote Christian unity, forbearance and the preaching of the pure gospel. In 1809 the elder Campbell authored a major statement, *The Declaration and Address*, on behalf of the Society. Upon arriving in America in 1809 with the rest of his family, Alexander Campbell discovered that both he and his father were *persona non grata* among the Presbyterians. Alexander preached his first sermon in 1810 in a house gathering, and 100 further sermons over the next year. He married Margaret Brown in 1811, and was given a farm in Bethany, West Virginia, by his father-in-law, where he lived for the rest of his life. With Margaret he had eight children. After she died in 1827 he married Selina Bakewell and had six children, but only four of the fourteen outlived Campbell. In 1818 he established Buffalo Seminary for Boys, in which he himself taught. He determined at an early age never to accept payment for preaching.

The Washington Association formed a church at Brush Run, Pennsylvania, in 1811, and Campbell was ordained to the ministry on 1 January 1812. Father and son, having decided on baptism by immersion in 1812, entered the Redstone Baptist Association in 1813, but their churches were expelled in 1826–1827. After 1823, the Wellsburg church in which Campbell held membership was part of the Mahoning Baptist Association of Ohio. The Mahoning Association was dissolved in 1830. By that year the Campbell reformers had in effect separated from the Baptists.

By 1815 Alexander Campbell had emerged as the chief leader of the movement. His first noted address to the Redstone Baptist Association, in 1816, was designated the 'Sermon on the Law'. In this sermon he argued that later covenants in Scripture cancelled earlier ones; for example, the new or Christian covenant superseded the Mosaic covenant. This view differed from the typical Calvinist position, embraced by both Baptists and Presbyterians, that the covenant of grace, as against the covenant of works, commenced with Abraham.

Campbell gained additional importance among the Baptists as an effective debater. Religious debates were commonplace at the time. In his earliest debates Campbell defended baptism by immersion and human freedom to respond to the gospel. His first public debate was with John Walker, a Presbyterian, on the subject of baptism, at Mount Pleasant, Ohio, in 1820. After the proceedings were published, Campbell became increasingly convinced that debates could significantly further his cause. He debated with William McCalla, another Presbyterian, in 1823 at Washington, Kentucky. In his most famous debates, Campbell represented not so much his own religious affiliation, but Protestantism generally, first with Robert Owen, on the truth of Christianity (Cincinnati, 1829), then with Archbishop Purcell of Ohio (Cincinnati, 1836), on the infallibility of the Church of Rome. His lengthiest debate was in 1843, with N. L. Rice, at Lexington, Kentucky, on the distinctives of the *Stone–Campbell movement. Debates reflected Campbell's own religious understanding, since he perceived faith as 'intelligent belief in divine testimony'. He therefore marshalled detailed and powerful evidence from the Scriptures, early Christianity and contemporary scholars.

Campbell also became widely known through his journals. He founded *The Christian Baptist* in 1823, in which he focused especially upon the ancient church and how it differed from contemporary manifestations. In 1830 Campbell launched *The Millennial Harbinger*, and he served as editor until his death in 1866. Campbell was a postmillennialist, convinced that signs of progress, both secular and religious, heralded the coming millennium. He also edited and published a translation of the New Testament, *The Sacred Writings of the Apostles and Evangelists of Jesus Christ* (1826), also called *Living Oracles*, and *The Christian System* (1839). Campbell undertook extended preaching tours through most of the settled regions of the United States, and in 1847 toured the United Kingdom.

Campbell founded Bethany College in 1840 and continued as president until his death. The curriculum followed the example of leading Scottish universities in its science and practical agriculture courses, anticipating future developments in American higher education. Campbell was also a pioneer in offering courses on the Bible for credit.

In 1832 the Campbell reformers initiated a merger with the Christian churches throughout the Ohio Valley, among whom Barton W. Stone was the most respected leader. Campbell questioned Stone's emphasis upon the conversion experience, and his non-traditional views on the Trinity, Christology and the atonement. But Stone was undeterred, and with help from Campbell reformers in Kentucky brought about a merger of most of the churches further west. Many Stone churches in Ohio, Kentucky and further east, however, did not merge and formed the Christian Connexion.

Campbell listed the foundations of his platform in his 'Prefatory Remarks' to the 1850 *Millennial Harbinger*: (1) 'The Bible, the whole Bible, and nothing but the Bible', (2) 'Jesus Christ himself being the chief corner stone', (3) 'on this rock I will build my church', (4) the voice of the 'Messiah and his Apostles' (that is, the New Testament), and (5) 'organized effort' (that is, churches working on joint projects). At the time of Campbell's death in 1866 there were more than 200,000 people in the movement. Its heirs now total approximately five million worldwide.

Bibliography

R. Richardson, *Memoirs of Alexander Campbell*, 2 vols. (Philadelphia: J. P. Lippincott, 1868, 1870); J. M. Seale (ed.), *Lectures in Honor of the Alexander Campbell Bicentennial, 1788–1988* (Nashville: Disciples of Christ Historical Society, 1988); R. F. West, *Alexander Campbell and Natural Religion* (New Haven: Yale University Press, 1948).

T. H. OLBRICHT

■ **CAMPOLO, Anthony (Tony)** (1935–), Baptist author and speaker, is Professor Emeritus of Sociology at Eastern University in St Davids, Pennsylvania.

Born on 25 February 1935 in Philadelphia to a devout Italian-American family, Campolo was baptized at the age of twelve. A neighbourhood Bible study group was a decisive factor in his early decision to dedicate himself to full-time church work. A lifelong Baptist, Campolo served as a pastor for seven years following his ordination in 1957 and served a term as vice-president of the American Baptist Convention. Campolo received his Masters in theology at Eastern Baptist Theological Seminary in 1961. Four years later his life changed direction with his appointment as professor of sociology at Eastern College (now Eastern University). Campolo's teaching career at Eastern College, during which he also spent ten years as adjunct professor of sociology at the University of Pennsylvania and three years as adjunct professor at Eastern Seminary, became the launching pad for his energetic involvement in speaking, writing and ministry leadership.

One factor that contributed to Campolo's academic diligence was his parents' moving the family to a predominantly Jewish neighbourhood because serious study was the norm there. (In high school, Campolo's achievements in science won him two weeks of study with Albert Einstein at Princeton.) As a pastor, Campolo remained drawn to academic life. He went on to earn a PhD in religion with a minor in sociology from Temple University in 1968 and has since received seven honorary doctorates.

Campolo's attraction to sociology was linked to his emerging understanding of Christian mission as a two-fold calling: inviting individuals to enter the kingdom of God through a relationship with Jesus Christ, and working in Christ's name to transform the world into God's kingdom. Campolo grew increasingly interested in sociology in the service of mission. To change the world, he says, one has to understand the world.

Campolo acknowledges three significant influences on his theology. One was Jack Wertzen, a fundamentalist preacher whose evangelistic zeal Campolo admired. The second was Dr Jitsuo Morikawa, an American Baptist theologian who defined evangelism as the invitation to participate in God's transforming work. Campolo agreed with Morikawa that the primary purpose of evangelism is not simply getting people ready for heaven, but making people available to Christ as instruments of justice and love in *this* world. A third influence has been Campolo's long-term membership in an African American congregation, Mt Carmel Baptist Church in Philadelphia, where he currently serves as associate pastor. Black churches, in his experience, demonstrate the compatibility of evangelical faith with social action. Campolo describes his approach to ministry as a blend of Wertzen's passion for evangelism, Morikawa's emphasis on justice and the Christian social vision of Dr Martin Luther King, Jr.

Campolo's worldview came of age during the era of civil rights and social protest. As a faculty member at the University of Pennsylvania in the 1970s, Campolo embraced the anti-war movement, mobilizing students in favour of reform and running for congressional office. His campaign failed, but with a record percentage of the vote for a Democrat in the district.

In 1969 Campolo founded the Evangelical Association for the Promotion of Education (EAPE), with the goal of helping to 'build the Kingdom of God by combining evangelism and social justice in the name of Jesus'. EAPE serves as an umbrella agency for several organizations founded by Campolo, including UrbanPromise and Beyond Borders, as well as several adopted programmes. EAPE-supported groups have established schools, universities, literacy centres, tutoring programmes, orphanages, AIDS hospices and urban youth work in the developing world and American cities. Campolo's son Bart has continued this work with Mission Year, which equips urban youth ministry.

Campolo's speaking and writing ministry has focused on raising evangelical churches' awareness of issues of justice, encouraging mainstream churches to revitalize their evangelism, inspiring deeper surrender to the kingdom of God and enlisting Christians (particularly young people) in programmes of Christian service. His busy speaking schedule has brought him to a wide range of gatherings; he has delivered the distinguished Staley lectures (1974), addressed the convention of the National Evangelical Association (1987) and spoken at the Shadow Convention (a leftist alternative to the 2000 Republican Convention). His media opportunities have included two weekly television shows and a weekly radio programme in the United Kingdom. Nominated by *Time* Magazine as one of the best preachers and speakers in America, Campolo's popularity derives in part from his lively blend of humour, storytelling and hard-hitting confrontation.

Campolo's thirty books include *It's Friday, But Sunday's Comin'* (1984), based on a famous sermon; *Twenty Hot Potatoes Christians Are Afraid To Touch* (1988), an exploration of controversial social and moral issues; *The Kingdom Of God Is a Party* (1990), explicating Campolo's kingdom-oriented theology; *Sociology Through The Eyes of Faith* (1992); *Is Jesus a Republican or a Democrat?* (1995), calling for a progressive political middle way; and *Revolution and Renewal: How Churches Are Saving Our Cities* (2000), promoting faith-based approaches to social problems. In addition he has published over 500 articles. Campolo's wife, Peggy, whom he married in 1958, has served as a partner in his writing; she has edited all his books (except one edited by his daughter Lisa).

Campolo has often provoked controversy within Christian circles for his theological and political views; he has supported the ministry of women pastors, defended civil rights for homosexuals and advocated environmental protection. Another cause of contention is his divorce of Christian orthodoxy from political conservatism. Campolo has denounced the Christian Right for its alleged neglect of the poor and for what he sees as its uncritical acceptance of Republican principles. In turn, he has been criticized for his sympathies with liberal causes. There has also been an underlying conflict over the proper definition of the term 'evangelical'. Calling himself a 'neo-evangelical', Campolo has pleaded for a definition embracing a wider range of theological, social and political opinion within a basic orthodox framework, while acknowledging that many evangelicals are unhappy about being identified with him.

Two events in particular provoked intense controversy. In 1985 the Evangelical Free Pastors of Illinois objected to Campolo's planned appearance at a large youth conference. They claimed that his book *A Reasonable Faith* (1983) displayed an alarming universalism, in statements such as 'Christ lives in all human beings, regardless of whether they are Christians', and 'Jesus is the only Savior, but not everybody who is being saved by Him is aware that He is the one who is doing the saving'. The Christian Legal Society was allowed to mediate by convening a panel of prominent evangelical leaders to examine Campolo's theology. *Christianity Today* reported the finding of this so-called 'heresy trial': that Campolo, although possibly mistaken on some points, was 'entirely orthodox'. Nevertheless, many fundamentalists continue to regard him as 'a theological liberal and a radical political socialist whose teachings are heretical at best and blasphemous at worst'.

A second crisis arose in 1998 when, in the midst of the Monica Lewinsky sex scandal,

President Bill Clinton asked Campolo to serve as one of his spiritual advisors. Campolo's relationship with Clinton was strongly criticized by conservative evangelicals who considered the president anathema to Christians. Despite the cost in terms of funding for ministry and invitations to speak, Campolo persisted in what he saw as a pastoral responsibility to an errant brother in Christ. Hostilities were intensified by a front page *New York Times* article that erroneously described Campolo as a 'liberal Baptist, who advocates that Christians accept homosexuality'. (Campolo's *wife* has been an outspoken advocate on behalf of homosexual Christians; Campolo himself maintains that homosexual eroticism and gay marriage are unbiblical.)

Despite the controversies (and to some degree, because of them) Campolo has continued to have a profound influence through books, videos, lectures, sermons and classes. In April 2001, he suffered a stroke, which interrupted his intense schedule. He continues, however, to stimulate the church with his call to zeal for the kingdom of God.

Bibliography

W. Gallagher, *Spiritual Genius: The Mastery of Life's Meaning* (New York: Random House, 2002); K. Kantzer, 'A Man of Zeal and Contradiction', *Christianity Today* 29:13 (1985), pp. 36–38.

H. R. UNRUH

■ **CAREY, George Leonard** (1935–), Anglican archbishop, was born on 13 November 1935 in Bow in the East End of London, the eldest of five children. At the outbreak of the Second World War the family moved to Dagenham in Essex, where George's father worked as a hospital porter. After failing his eleven plus examinations, Carey attended Bifrons Secondary Modern School in Barking, leaving at fifteen to become an office boy with the London Electricity Board. Through the witness of Christian friends and the Anglican evangelical church in Dagenham, he was converted to Christ in May 1953.

Between 1954 and 1956 Carey undertook National Service, working as a radio operator in the Royal Air Force, based in Egypt and Iraq. After demobilization he returned to the

London Electricity Board but decided to seek ordination. Intensive study for O-level and A-level qualifications was followed by four years' theological training at the London College of Divinity, which included reading for a degree at King's College, London (where he was to be made a fellow in 1993). He graduated with a BD in 1962 and was ordained to a curacy at St Mary's, Islington in north London. Carey lectured at Oak Hill Theological College from 1966 to 1970 and at St John's College, Nottingham (where the London College of Divinity had relocated under the leadership of Michael Green) from 1970 to 1975. He gained a doctorate in 1971 from London University for a thesis on 'Church Order in the Shepherd of Hermas', which led him to the conviction that there was authentic continuity between early Catholicism and the New Testament.

In his only period in direct charge of a parish, Carey served as vicar of St Nicholas', Durham from 1975 to 1982. During this time the church experienced 'charismatic renewal' and undertook a programme of expansion, recounted in *The Church in the Market Place* (1984). In addition to fulfilling his parochial duties, Carey acted as chaplain to a youth custody prison and to the Durham branch of the RAF Association. In 1982 he was appointed principal of Trinity College, Bristol and soon became an honorary canon of Bristol Cathedral and an elected member of General Synod, serving on some of its major committees. Due to his stature as an 'evangelical charismatic' leader, Carey was chosen as Bishop of Bath and Wells in 1987, and he introduced and conducted a series of teaching missions across the diocese.

To the surprise of the nation, Carey was appointed to succeed Robert Runcie as Archbishop of Canterbury in 1991. A junior bishop in a minor see, he became the youngest Archbishop of Canterbury in the twentieth century, with the least previous episcopal experience. Perhaps a sign of sociological change within the higher echelons of the Church of England, he reached this position without the ecclesiastical background and social privileges enjoyed by most of his predecessors and was the first Archbishop of Canterbury since the Middle Ages not to be a graduate of Oxford or Cambridge University. In an age of 'spin doctors' Carey was

noted for his lack of concern with public image.

Carey's archiepiscopate witnessed some significant developments within the Church of England and the wider Anglican communion. He was a vocal advocate of the ordination of women to the presbyterate, which was finally authorized by the Church of England's General Synod in an historic vote in November 1992. None the less, he was keen to hold within the church those who did not agree with this decision, so he supported the controversial Act of Synod that allowed for extended episcopal oversight by Provincial Episcopal Visitors or 'flying bishops'. Opponents of the Act argued that it created the theological nonsense of 'two integrities' within one church. Equally contentious were debates throughout the 1990s on the church's attitude to human sexuality, particularly homosexual practice, about which Carey engaged in public dispute with Jack Spong, the notoriously liberal Bishop of Newark, New Jersey. Under the archbishop's leadership, the 1998 Lambeth Conference passed significant conservative resolutions on this subject.

Amongst other developments, at the start of the 'Decade of Evangelism' (the 1990s) Carey launched Springboard, an evangelistic initiative headed by Michael Green and Bishop Michael Marshall. In July 1992 the church was rocked by the revelation that, due to mismanagement and unwise property speculation, the Church Commissioners had sustained huge financial losses, rumoured to be as high as £800 million. This disaster was a catalyst for the establishing of the Turnbull Commission (chaired by Michael Turnbull, Bishop of Durham) to review the finances, structure and organization of the Church of England, including the bureaucracy of General Synod. The Commission's report, 'Working as One Body' (1995), recommended increased centralization of decision making powers and the foundation of the Archbishops' Council, which met for the first time in January 1999. Carey retired as archbishop in October 2002, being succeeded by Rowan Williams.

A keen ecumenist, Carey frequently laments the many divisions within Christendom. He defended the documents of the Anglican–Roman Catholic International

Commission (ARCIC) in General Synod, and in *The Meeting of the Waters* (1985) appealed for unity between the Church of Rome and the Protestant churches of the Reformation. During his visit to Pope John Paul II in Rome in 1996 the two bishops issued a joint declaration recommending closer cooperation between their churches and observing that 'our divisions obscure the gospel message of reconciliation and hope'. For this reason Carey strongly opposed the Anglican Mission in America (AMiA), set up in August 2000 to counteract what it considers to be apostasy in the Episcopal Church (ECUSA). When Archbishop Yong of South East Asia and Archbishop Kolini of Rwanda consecrated bishops for the AMiA, he rebuked them for their 'schismatic' action.

Carey's ecumenical vision and belief that the comprehensiveness of the Church of England is to be cherished have led him to distance himself from 'evangelical' as a term of self-description. He has moved theologically from his early evangelical roots, particularly on ecclesiology and the sacraments, and attracted criticism for questioning the Pauline authorship of the Pastoral Epistles. Although he acknowledges that 'I owe to evangelicalism my very soul', he none the less describes himself as someone 'whose heart beats in time with the evangelical love of Jesus and a deep devotion to the biblical tradition, but whose head cannot go along with received evangelical teaching'. Carey criticized modern evangelicalism for being 'too constricting intellectually, too narrow academically and too stifling spiritually' ('Parties in the Church of England', *Theology*, 91 (July 1988), pp. 269–270). In 1994 he stated: 'My theological colouring has changed. I started out from a very definite, conservative, evangelical, Protestant, Anglican church, and I'm nowhere near that now ... no one will ever hear me calling *myself* an evangelical' (Loudon, *Revelations*, pp. 252–253).

Carey's other works include *I Believe in Man* (1977), on the doctrine of humanity, *The Gate of Glory* (1986), on the cross of Christ, *The Great God Robbery* (1989), a Christian apologetic, and *Canterbury Letters to the Future* (1998), an introduction to the Christian faith. Collections of his sermons and addresses have been published as *I Believe* (1991) and *Sharing a Vision* (1993). In 1960 Carey married Eileen Hood, a nurse, who later wrote *The Bishop and I* (1998) about the lives of bishops' wives from around the Anglican communion.

Bibliography
G. Carey, *My Journey, Your Journey* (Oxford: Lion, 1996), pp. 22–33; G. Carey, *The Church in the Market Place* (Eastbourne: Kingsway, ³1995); E. Carpenter and A. Hastings, *Cantuar: The Archbishops in their Office* (London: Mowbray, ³1997), pp. 546–560; M. Loudon, *Revelations: The Clergy Questioned* (London: Hamish Hamilton, 1994), pp. 239–276.

A. ATHERSTONE

■ **CAREY, William** (1761–1834), Baptist missionary, is often, but rather misleadingly, termed 'the father of modern missions'. As the principal founder of the Baptist Missionary Society (BMS), he pioneered a movement that led to the formation of similar evangelical voluntary societies in Britain, Europe and North America, and played a large part in the transformation of Christianity into a truly global religion. However, his own missionary vision owed much to the earlier achievements of the Moravian Brethren. Carey did not so much initiate a new movement as introduce to Britain a concern for overseas missionary action by Protestants whose roots lay in continental pietism and the subsequent evangelical awakenings in central Europe: Lutheran Pietist missionaries had been working in Tranquebar, south India, since 1706.

William Carey was born on 17 August 1761 in the small Northamptonshire village of Paulerspury, the eldest of the five children of Edmund Carey and Elizabeth Wells. His father, originally a weaver, became in 1767 parish clerk and village schoolmaster, giving Carey access to a wide range of books. At the age of about fourteen, he was apprenticed to a shoemaker. Through the influence of a fellow apprentice, John Warr, he began to attend a dissenting prayer meeting and, from 1779, the Congregationalist chapel in the next village of Hackleton. On 10 June 1781 he married Dorothy Plackett of that village. Having been persuaded of the invalidity of infant baptism, Carey was baptized as an adult by John *Ryland, junior, in the River Nene at Northampton on 5 October 1783. While continuing to practise as a shoemaker, he began preaching to the Particular (Calvinistic) Baptist congregation at Earls Barton, and studied Latin, Greek and Hebrew in his spare time. In 1785 he assumed the pastorate of the Baptist church at Moulton, where he supplemented his meagre stipend by shoemaking and schoolmastering. While at Moulton, he developed close links with the leaders of the growing evangelical movement among the Particular Baptist churches of the East Midlands, notably Ryland in Northampton, Andrew *Fuller in Kettering (the movement's theologian) and John Sutcliff in Olney. In May 1789 Carey moved to the pastorate of Harvey Lane Baptist Church in Leicester, where in 1791 he was formally ordained to the Baptist ministry.

Carey's interest in the condition of the non-European world was awakened, perhaps as early as 1784, by reading the accounts of the South Sea voyages of Captain James Cook. He began writing a pamphlet urging the obligation of Christians to spread the gospel beyond the frontiers of European Christendom and insisting that endeavours to bring the gospel of Christ to the 'heathen' were nothing new. The pamphlet, *An Enquiry into the Obligations of Christians to Use Means for the Conversion of the Heathens*, published on 12 May 1792, is a classic statement of a moderate Calvinist theology of mission, arguing that the missionary obligation of the church is of permanent validity and grounded in the sovereign redemptive purpose of God.

The publication of this pamphlet was followed by Carey's famous sermon on Isaiah 54:2–3, preached on 30 May 1792 before the annual meeting of the Northamptonshire Association of Baptist Churches in Nottingham (the association covered the whole of the East Midlands). In the plight of exiled Judah, apparently forgotten by God her husband, Carey saw a picture of the barren and desolate church of his day, and in the promise of a new and wider destiny for Judah lay the promise of countless new children in the Christian family to be drawn from all the earth. However, God's promise was also his command. God was about to do great things by extending the kingdom of Jesus throughout the globe, and for that very reason Christians were bound to attempt great things by spreading the gospel overseas. Hence Carey's celebrated and oft misquoted slogan 'Expect great things from God. Attempt great things for God'. Although the text of the sermon has not been preserved, it is probable that what Carey actually said was simply 'Expect great things. Attempt great things'; the words 'from God' and 'to God' appear to be later textual interpositions, but ones that fully reflect Carey's meaning. The governing assumption of Carey's sermon was that the expectation of great things from God is theologically and chronologically prior to the attempting of great things for him. The role of the Holy Spirit was, therefore, central in Carey's theology of mission. The final section of the *Enquiry* begins with an exposition of the fact that all human means used in mission will be ineffectual without the '*fervent and united prayer*' of the people of God: 'If a temple is raised for God in the heathen world, it will not be *by might, nor by power*, nor by the authority of the magistrate, or the eloquence of the orator; *but my Spirit, saith the Lord of Hosts*.' In that statement Carey repudiated reliance on the two false sources of confidence that were to prove the undoing of missions over the next century: the leaky umbrella of imperial power (the authority of the magistrate) and the Enlightenment expectation that Christian rational apologetic would convince people of the superiority of Christianity.

The *Enquiry* (even though it sold few copies) and the Nottingham sermon led directly to the formation of the 'Particular-Baptist Society for Propagating the Gospel among the Heathen' (later known as the Baptist Missionary Society) in Kettering on 2 October 1792. Andrew Fuller was appointed secretary. Carey was present at the meeting, but was apparently too poor to contribute anything to the society's opening subscription list, from which his name is missing. At the society's third meeting, on 13 November 1792, Carey offered to accompany a former East India Company surgeon, John Thomas, on his return to Bengal as a missionary of the society. The first BMS party accordingly arrived in Calcutta in November 1793. The absence of any funds from England compelled Carey to accept a position as manager of an indigo factory owned by

George Udny at Mudnabati near Dinajpur (in what is now northern Bangladesh). Carey was criticized by some in England for this involvement in commercial activity, but it conformed to his understanding, derived from Moravian missionary precedent, that Christian missions should wherever possible be economically self-supporting.

Carey soon learnt the Bengali and Hindi languages and began to preach in the vernacular and to translate the Bible into Bengali. In 1800 he moved south to the Danish settlement of Serampore, north of Calcutta, following the refusal of the East India Company (which then ruled British India and was highly suspicious of evangelical missions) to grant permission to reside in its territory to a party of BMS recruits who had just arrived in Bengal. Among the recruits were Joshua Marshman, an educationalist, and William Ward, a printer and newspaper editor. The 'Serampore Trio' of Carey, Marshman and Ward built up the work at Serampore to a level which attracted widespread admiration in Britain and did much to popularize the idea of missions. The first Hindu convert, Krishna Pal, was baptized at Serampore amid great rejoicing in December 1800, but the rate of conversion was slow. The caste system proved a more formidable obstacle to conversion than Carey had anticipated. From 1804 onwards the Serampore mission established a network of subsidiary stations, radiating outwards through Bengal and up the Ganges valley into north India. By the end of 1821 some 1,407 converts had been baptized at Serampore, but half of these were Europeans or Anglo-Indians. In such circumstances it was easy to lose heart. 'When I first left England', Carey wrote in 1794, 'my hope of the conversion of the heathen was very strong; but among so many obstacles it would utterly die away, unless upheld by God, having nothing to cherish it.' Carey found his resources for endurance and encouragement in the promises of God in Scripture and wrote, 'Yet this is our encouragement, the power of God is sufficient to accomplish everything which he has promised, and his promises are exceedingly great and precious respecting the conversion of the heathens.'

The expectation of the Serampore missionaries was that India could never be won for Christ by Europeans, but only by Indians.

This conviction lay behind the foundation in 1818 of Serampore College with the primary purpose of training Christian Indians to be evangelists to their own people. The principal medium of instruction was Bengali rather than English, and the curriculum was wider than theology; it included both Western science and the study of oriental languages, supremely of Sanskrit, which 'the Trio' rightly held to be the key to understanding Hindu culture and learning other Indian languages. Controversially, however, the college also admitted Hindu and Muslim students, on the grounds that such a breadth within the student body would provide fruitful missionary experience for Christian students. In 1827 the college was awarded a charter by the Danish crown empowering it to award degrees; it remains to this day the degree-awarding body for all Protestant theological institutions in India.

Probably Carey's most enduring and remarkable achievement was as a Bible translator and linguist. He and his Indian pandits were jointly responsible for the translation of the entire Bible into six Indian languages (Bengali, Oriya, Sanskrit, Hindi, Marathi and Assamese), and of parts of it into a further twenty-nine languages. Although some of the translations were far from perfect (the first edition of the Bengali New Testament was almost unintelligible in places), they laid the foundations for all subsequent biblical translations in these languages. Carey also produced grammars of Bengali (1801), Marathi (1805), Sanskrit (1806), Punjab (1812), Telinga (1814) and Bhotia (1826), and compiled dictionaries of Marathi (1810), Bengali (1815) and Bhotia (1826). With Marshman he also began to translate the Hindu epic the *Ramayana* into English; three volumes had been published by 1810. Such attention to a Hindu text again attracted criticism, but for Carey and Marshman serious study of Hindu culture was indispensable to effective missionary communication.

Carey's expertise in Indian languages soon made him invaluable to the East India Company and thus guaranteed the political survival of the mission, which had initially been much in doubt. In 1801 the Company appointed him as professor of Sanskrit, Marathi and Bengali at its Fort William College in Calcutta. The Serampore missionaries were able to use their developing reputation to put pressure on the East India Company to outlaw the inhuman practice of *sati* (the forcible burning of widows on their husbands' funeral pyres). Lord William Bentinck's abolition of *sati* in Bengal in 1829 probably owes more to Carey than to any other single individual.

Carey was working on a universal dictionary of all Indian languages derived from Sanskrit when in 1812 a fire destroyed all his manuscripts and a large collection of printing fonts and paper, to the value of 70,000 rupees. In human terms it was a shattering disaster. Carey estimated it would take twelve months' hard labour to replace what had been lost. Yet in reporting the fire to Fuller, Carey described the fire as a 'providence' and rapidly passed from detailing the losses to a list of eight 'merciful circumstances' attending the fire, for which he wished to give thanks. The fire was in fact crucial in publicizing the mission's work and hence in attracting new support in Britain.

Carey's encouragement of the Bengali language was of lasting significance in establishing a corpus of Bengali literature and contributed to a Bengali cultural renaissance. Carey is thus one of the earliest examples in modern history of a missionary whose work has proved supportive, rather than destructive, of indigenous culture. He was in addition a highly accomplished botanist, being elected a fellow of the Linnaean Society of London in 1823. He edited for publication William Roxburgh's *Hortus Bengaliensis* (1814; a catalogue of the plants in the East India Company's Calcutta garden) and his *Flora Indica* (1832). These became the standard works on Indian botany. Carey also took a keen interest in Indian agriculture and questions of land reform. His understanding of his missionary vocation was thus considerably broader than that of many of his evangelical successors.

Carey's later years were marred by deteriorating relationships with the Baptist Missionary Society, culminating in the separation of the Serampore mission from the BMS in 1827, a bitter split that caused Carey much sadness and was not healed until 1837. Ostensibly the argument was over matters of property, but what was really at stake was the question of whether control of mission policy should be in the hands of a committee of businessmen and ministers in London, responsible to the subscribers who provided the funds, or vested in those who were on the spot in India, an issue that has proved of lasting importance in Christian mission.

Carey's first wife, Dorothy, had been unwilling to go to India, and soon after her arrival in Bengal developed acute mental illness, having to be kept under continual physical restraint owing to her deranged and violent condition. She died in 1807. Carey married twice more. In May 1808 he married Charlotte Emilia Rumohr, daughter of a Danish count and official in the Danish East India Company; she died in 1821. Carey married his third wife, a widow named Grace Hughes, in 1823; she outlived her husband, dying in 1835. William and Dorothy Carey had seven children, of whom two died in infancy. Three of their sons, Felix, William and Jabez, also became missionaries.

Carey died at Serampore on 9 June 1834. His grave bears the characteristically self-effacing inscription 'A wretched, poor, and helpless worm, on Thy kind arms I fall'.

Bibliography

M. Drewery, *William Carey: Shoemaker and Missionary* (London: Hodder & Stoughton, 1978); T. George, *Faithful Witness: The Life and Mission of William Carey* (Leicester: IVP, 1991); E. D. Potts, *British Baptist Missionaries in India: The Story of Serampore and its Missions, 1793–1837* (Cambridge: CUP, 1967); B. Stanley, *The History of the Baptist Missionary Society 1792–1992* (Edinburgh: T. & T. Clark, 1992).

B. STANLEY

■ **CARMAN, Albert** (1833–1917), Canadian Methodist minister and educator, was a great-grandson of loyalists who had settled in Matilda Township, Upper Canada, and his paternal ancestors were among this rural area's first converts to Methodism. After attending a local elementary and grammar school, he enrolled in Victoria College in Cobourg. In this strongly Methodist institution he was converted in 1854, and joined the Methodist Episcopal Church of his parents.

Graduating in 1855, Carman became principal of his old grammar school, and two years later, now a candidate for the Methodist Episcopal ministry, was appointed a teacher at the recently opened Belleville Seminary, a co-educational Methodist Episcopal preparatory school. Ordained in 1864, and appointed principal when the institution was awarded degree-granting rights in 1866 as Albert College, Carman was in the unusual position of never having served on a circuit. Although he would in later years become an ardent champion of the ministerial settlement system, it was as an educator and prudent administrator that he first made his mark. By 1868 he had initiated the creation of Alexandra College for women interested in pursuing a diploma course, and in 1870 he established a faculty of divinity.

Despite these advances in higher education, it had become apparent that with its central Canadian and largely rural base, his church's future was precarious. Costly attempts at church extension in cities and in the recently acquired Canadian northwest resulted in disappointment and increased debts. In union negotiations with the other Methodist bodies, begun in 1868, Carman was a strong defender of the episcopacy and resistant to lay representation; his views on these issues kept his denomination from entering the larger Methodist Church of Canada, formed in 1874.

Elected and ordained bishop in 1874, Carman became sole head of the denomination at the death of James Richardson, who since 1858 had occupied the episcopate. When in 1878 his General Conference approved lay representation and it became apparent that many within the denomination favoured union, he worked hard to safeguard his church's distinctive episcopacy. The acceptance in principle by the Methodist Church of Canada in 1882 of a strong general superintendency facilitated the union process. In 1883 a Basis of Union, which provided for two general superintendents, was adopted by the representatives of the various Methodist groups, including the Bible Christians and Primitive Methodists, who had also remained outside the 1874 union. When the new Methodist Church, Canada's largest Protestant denomination, was formally inaugurated in 1884, Carman became general superinten-

dent. Initially sharing the position, after the death in rapid succession of his two elderly colleagues he ruled alone from 1889 to 1910, when the General Conference elected Samuel Dwight Chown to share the position. Carman retired in 1914 as general superintendent emeritus at full salary.

Carman's thirty-year general superintendency spanned a crucial period in the development of Methodism in Canada and was not without controversy. His administrative skills strengthened and centralized the denomination's ability to take a leading role in moral reform and assert a Protestant and British hegemony within an ethnically and religiously divided country. Along with other evangelicals he was outspoken in resisting 'Romish aggression' and the extension of separate schools in Manitoba and the northwest.

One of the defining moments in Carman's career resulted from his opposition in 1898 and in 1909 to the teaching of the new biblical criticism in Victoria University. Carman's defence of 'the doctrine of the Divine inspiration of the Holy Scriptures' and his trenchant criticism of wealthy laymen who had brought from Britain the progressive George Jackson as professor-elect of English Bible at Victoria were well publicized in the secular and denominational press. In the end he had to acquiesce to the decision of the 1910 General Conference that any attempt to insist on a literal interpretation of Scripture was contrary to the Methodist standards of doctrine.

Concern that wealth was undermining Methodist polity and piety frequently surfaced in Carman's addresses. For him moral reform was not to be defined by the emerging social gospel but by the old evangelical agenda of sabbatarianism and prohibition. Conservative and dogmatic, he spoke for those who looked back to a simpler time when revivalism had been the denomination's distinguishing mark. Upon his death in Toronto on 3 November 1917 eulogists remembered a man of integrity, uncompromising in his leadership in a denomination which during his final decades had moved beyond him.

Bibliography

G. A. Boyle, 'Higher Criticism and the Struggle for Academic Freedom in Canadian

Methodism' (ThD thesis, Victoria University, 1965).

M. VAN DIE

■ **CARMICHAEL, Amy** (1867–1951), missionary and writer, was born on 16 December 1867, in Millisle, Northern Ireland. The eldest of seven children, she was descended on her father David's side from Scottish Covenanters, and on her mother Catherine's from a family friendly with their persecutors, a combination which their daughter regarded as significant. As a child Amy was physically adventurous and full of life, acting as the ringleader in various forms of mischief. In the Carmichael family there was strong discipline, fun and a lively faith, with regular family prayers. Having initially been educated at home, she was sent at the age of twelve to board at Marlborough House, Yorkshire, which she detested. Towards the end of her stay there, however, at the age of fifteen, she was converted at a Children's Special Service Mission rally at Harrogate. Soon afterwards she returned home due to her father's financial difficulties, which contributed to his early death in 1885, at the age of fifty-four.

By this time the family had moved to Belfast, where Amy became involved in various religious activities and missions, yet felt a spiritual lack in her own life. In September 1886, while visiting friends in Glasgow, she had a significant spiritual experience at a meeting linked with the Keswick Convention, which led to many connections with that movement. In particular, a friendship developed between the Carmichaels and one of the Keswick founders, Robert Wilson.

One venture that she had initiated in Belfast, work with factory girls (or 'shawlies'), continued to grow and develop. In January 1889 a new hall for the mission was opened. Through this she developed the principle of praying for financial supply, rather than asking or fund-raising, which was to remain her approach later in India. Later in the same year Amy and her mother moved to Manchester, where she had been invited to carry on work among factory girls. When illness prevented her continuing, she moved to live with Robert Wilson, taking the place of his daughter who had died. It was assumed that she would stay with the family until his death, but early in 1892 she sensed a clear call to mission with the words 'Go Ye'. Despite the distress of leaving both her mother and Robert Wilson, she eventually sailed for Japan via China in March 1893.

Amy spent only a year in Japan, during which time she was involved in missions to villages, with some positive results. After becoming ill, however, she left for a visit home and a short spell in Ceylon. Being advised that the climate in Bangalore was healthier, she set out for India, arriving there on 9 November 1895. Then came the tedious business of language learning, and struggling to get on with her fellow-missionaries. She eventually went to a missionary couple, the Walkers, in Tinnevelly district, for help in learning Tamil. The resulting friendship proved to be a strong and useful support to her for many years.

Initially, as in Japan, she was involved with village work, this time under the auspices of the CMS Zenana mission, although as before her financial support came from the Keswick conference. There were some conversions, and children in particular were attracted to the meetings she held. An unexpected incident, however, involving Pearl, a girl who had run away from a Hindu temple, changed the direction of her missionary efforts. Amy became convinced that she should devote herself to the work of rescuing girls from temple prostitution, although she herself never named the evil she was working to avoid. So in 1901 a small home for children was established, and this became the nucleus of the future Dohnavur Fellowship. Within a few years, as the nature of her work changed, she came to a parting of the ways with CMS, but continued to be supported by Keswick and an ever-widening circle of supporters.

In the early stages, mistakes were made, for instance when several young babies died. As time went on, however, more and more girls were added and found love and security in their new home. Many stayed on as adults to form the nucleus of the community as it grew. From 1909 the plight of boys involved in the dramas that accompanied Hindu worship led to a parallel boys' work being developed. A medical branch of the work was also established, led by Murray Webb-Peploe. In 1928 the first payment was made on land for a hospital for people from the surrounding areas, and the hospital was completed some time later. By the time of Amy's death, there were over 900 people in her 'family'. Such a growing community had many needs: food, education, opportunities for fun for the children. In all these matters, they strove to trust God, and people around the world supported the venture with finance and prayer. 'Amma', as she was known, was the driving force and the inspiration for the growing family in all its aspects.

In the midst of the busy life of the Fellowship, Amy found time to write books charting their experience of provision, and of the difficulties and joys they encountered in their work. These books brought fresh publicity for the Fellowship, and new supporters. *Gold Cord* (1932), which described the early days of the community, was followed by other works such as *Windows* (1937), which told the story of the financial provision for Dohnavur. Other books included some intended to encourage believers in their everyday lives, such as her thoughts on illness, *Rose from Briar* (1933) and *His Thoughts Said, His Father Said* (1941). In total, Amy wrote over thirty-five books, many of which are still in print.

Amy Carmichael's spirituality is revealed in these books. Initially shaped through a Presbyterian upbringing, this was given fresh direction through the Keswick movement. The emphases of Keswick, especially surrender and sacrifice, became her themes too. She also drew for inspiration on an eclectic mix of earlier believers from various traditions, ranging from Thomas à Kempis and Francis Xavier to Samuel *Rutherford, Ellice Hopkins and Josephine *Butler, and this richness informed her writing. Her beliefs in the centrality of Jesus and of prayer, in the necessity of unity within the Dohnavur community, and the high standards of service she set herself and others, mark her style of spirituality. According to some, she was autocratic and high-handed, and on occasion her style did lead to difficulties when newcomers failed to fit in to her way of working and left, causing pain to all concerned. Many others, however, found a permanent home in the Fellowship.

In October 1931 'Amma' was visiting a house in a town some miles away to which some members of the community were due to move, when she fell, breaking her leg and damaging her spine. She became an invalid from that time until her death, increasingly confined to bed. From her 'Room of Peace', however, she continued to read, write and direct the work at Dohnavur as far as possible. She often wrote letters to encourage the children and other members of the Fellowship. Amy Carmichael died on 18 January 1951, after over fifty years in India.

Bibliography
E. Elliot, *Amy Carmichael: Her Life and Legacy* (New Jersey: Fleming H. Revell, 1987; Eastbourne: Kingsway, 1988); F. Houghton, *Amy Carmichael of Dohnavur: The Story of a Lover and Her Beloved* (London: SPCK, 1953).

L. WILSON

■ **CARNELL, Edward John** (1919–1967), American theologian and apologist, was one of the brightest intellectual lights in the 'neo-evangelical' movement in the United States after the Second World War. Born in Antigo, Wisconsin, and raised in Albion, Michigan, Carnell was the son of a pastor in the highly sectarian General Association of Regular Baptist Churches. E. J. Carnell, however, would epitomize the transition of many intellectuals from the subculture of fundamentalism into a distinctly more cosmopolitan evangelicalism in the mid-twentieth century.

Edward Carnell graduated in philosophy from the evangelical Wheaton College, Illinois, in 1941. While at Wheaton, he came under the influence of the rationalist apologetics of Presbyterian professor Gordon Clark. This approach, which emphasized the intellectual coherence of the Christian faith as a mark of its veracity, Carnell carried with him into his studies at Westminster Theological Seminary. There he was most impressed with Cornelius *Van Til's 'presuppositionalism', a radical form of apologetical theology claiming that only the Christian worldview offered a sound basis for any thought; all other forms of thought could, at least theoretically, be shown to be incoherent and insufficient to account fully for reality. Carnell would combine these appeals to internal coherence with a classic appeal to external evidences in a distinctive blend that was attractive to many evangelicals.

Carnell joined a number of wartime and post-war fundamentalists in pursuing doctoral degrees at front-rank universities. Some sought merely to beard the liberal lion in his den; others, such as Carnell, genuinely engaged non-evangelical thought. Carnell earned a doctorate in theology from Harvard Divinity School (1948) and then a philosophy doctorate from Boston University (1949), with dissertations on Reinhold Niebuhr and Søren Kierkegaard respectively.

Having served briefly as a Baptist pastor in Boston while attending Harvard, from 1945 until 1948 Carnell taught philosophy and religion at Gordon College and Divinity School in Boston. In 1948 he moved permanently to the new Fuller Theological Seminary, founded the previous year in Pasadena, California. The leaders of this seminary, named after radio preacher Charles *Fuller, intended it to lead a renaissance of evangelical theological scholarship in America. Carnell was among the young talents whom they hoped would realize their dream.

The year 1948 figured large in Carnell's life for yet another reason. While still a doctoral candidate at Harvard, he published his first book, *An Introduction to Christian Apologetics*. This volume won a $5000 prize offered by the William B. Eerdmans publishing company of Grand Rapids, Michigan, the publisher that, more than any other, furnished the 'new evangelicals' with both resources and a platform for their ambitious intellectual agenda.

Setting out Carnell's characteristic combination of rationalist and evidentialist apologetical strategies, the *Introduction* purported to show that Christianity both demonstrated superior coherence to all other worldviews and adhered best to the relevant empirical evidence. It came to be ranked with Carl *Henry's *The Uneasy Conscience of American Fundamentalism* (1947) and Bernard *Ramm's *The Christian View of Science and Scripture* (1954) as the most significant and influential books of the new evangelicalism.

The breezy, even boastfully confident, tone of this book (perhaps the bluster of the nervous evangelical overcompensating for his lack of status in the academy, as controversial Carnell biographer Rudolph Nelson

would have it) softened into more discreet cadences in subsequent works. Carnell continued to write volumes that asserted the superiority of the Christian faith, but on the grounds that Christianity best offered happiness with the least regret (*A Philosophy of the Christian Religion*, 1952), or best explained moral phenomena (*Christian Commitment*, 1957), or best met human psychological and relational needs (*The Kingdom of Love and the Pride of Life*, 1960). His tone became more humble and subtle, less dogmatic and assertive. These themes and this posture were highly unusual from the pen of an American evangelical academician, and perhaps as a result the books never attained the popularity of Carnell's first work.

Carnell also distinguished himself as an interpreter of Reinhold Niebuhr (*The Theology of Reinhold Niebuhr*, 1951) and Søren Kierkegaard (*The Burden of Søren Kierkegaard*, 1965). Based on his doctoral dissertations, these books were perceptively critical of both subjects. Carnell placed himself, however, among the few evangelicals of his generation to suggest in print that Niebuhr and Kierkegaard each had something to teach evangelicals. Carnell again, that is, transgressed the boundaries of fundamentalism in his willingness truly to engage and profit from other points of view.

Carnell wrote one work that brought him far more attention than he had sought, not by transgressing fundamentalist boundaries but by openly scorning them. In the late 1950s the Westminster Press sponsored a trilogy of books setting out three dominant positions in contemporary American Protestant theology, and asked the liberal Harold J. DeWolf and the neo-orthodox William Hordern to contribute volumes. E. J. Carnell had come to their attention as one among the vanguard of evangelicals, and he accepted their invitation to introduce the evangelical viewpoint in *The Case for Orthodox Theology* (1959). This book, to the horror of Carnell's fundamentalist acquaintances, distinguished evangelicalism decisively from fundamentalism, referring to the latter as 'orthodoxy gone cultic'. To many readers, in this book Carnell was more interested in denouncing fundamentalism than in setting out a robust and articulate programmatic alternative to the liberal and neo-orthodox books in the series.

Carnell had nailed his colours to the mast, and he received a torrent of negative mail in response from those to his theological right. Those to his left adopted him as their favourite fundamentalist-cum-evangelical (he was the lone evangelical invited to interview Karl Barth publicly during his historic visit to the University of Chicago in 1962). To Carnell's mounting dismay, however, the mainstream theological academy rarely interacted seriously with his theological proposals.

Carnell was generally revered at Fuller as an exciting and unpredictable teacher. He served unhappily, however, as president of the seminary for a short time (1954–1959), clearly out of his element as a creative and controversial academician trying to be the administrator of a young and vulnerable institution. He returned to the teaching ranks as a man collapsing under obvious personal strain; depression, anxiety and insomnia dogged him. In fact, Carnell dedicated his book on Freud, *The Kingdom of Love*, to his psychiatrist. Students were increasingly taken aback by his emerging eccentricities, while many none the less lionized him as one of Fuller's most esteemed professors.

Carnell met his premature end mysteriously. Preparing an address to an ecumenical audience (sponsored by the Roman Catholic Diocese of Oakland), he took what the coroner called a 'moderate overdose' of the sleeping pills prescribed by his psychiatrist and collapsed in his hotel room, never to revive. Some have interpreted this episode as Carnell's intentional escape from the pincer of fundamentalist fury on the one hand and the disappointing indifference of the theological academy on the other. Others, however, see it simply as a tragic accident that took from American evangelicals one of the pioneers of their post-war intellectual resurgence.

Bibliography

G. M. Marsden, *Reforming Fundamentalism* (Grand Rapids: Eerdmans, 1987); R. Nelson, *The Making and Unmaking of an Evangelical Mind: The Case of Edward Carnell* (Cambridge: Cambridge University Press, 1987); J. A. Sims, *Edward John Carnell: Defender of the Faith* (Washington: University Press of America, 1979).

J. G. STACKHOUSE, JR

■ **CARTER, James Earl ('Jimmy'), Jr** (1924–), American president and Southern Baptist lay leader, was born in the rural community of Plains, Georgia. His father, James Earl, Sr, was a farmer and small businessman, and his mother, Lillian Gordy Carter, a nurse. He grew up in an environment dominated by the extended family, local congregation and traditional values, and from his earliest youth Plains Baptist Church was the centre of his life. At the age of eleven, he professed faith in Christ, was baptized and joined the church, and before long he became a Sunday school teacher. Finishing high school in 1942, he enrolled in the US Naval Academy at Annapolis and was commissioned as a navy officer four years later. After graduation he married his childhood sweetheart, Rosalynn Smith. He served on a battleship and later aboard submarines, and in 1950 was assigned to the new atomic submarine programme. Its leader, Admiral Hyman Rickover, instilled in the young man a drive for hard work and excellence that would prove to be a hallmark of his character throughout his life. When the elder Carter died in 1953, Jimmy resigned from the navy and returned home to Plains to manage the family enterprises, a farm supply store and peanut warehouse.

Jimmy Carter rapidly became a successful businessman, while at the same time being actively involved in the life of the church and community. He was a teacher and deacon in the Baptist church and served on the school, library and hospital boards. He was also an outspoken advocate of racial justice and civil rights, which was not a popular role in Georgia at the time. In 1962 he entered state politics; he served two terms in the Georgia senate but was defeated in his attempt to become governor in 1966. Although his political career seemed to be over, he rededicated his life to Christ and became convinced that God was leading him to a vocation as a public servant. In 1970 he stood again for election as governor and this time was victorious. Following one term in office, he entered the arena of national politics as a virtual unknown and sought the Democratic nomination for president in 1976. He believed that he could provide the country with strong moral leadership at a time of national uncertainty in the wake of the Vietnam War disaster and the

Watergate scandals that had driven Richard Nixon from office. Within a few months he had edged out his rivals in the party for the nomination, and he narrowly defeated incumbent president Gerald Ford in the autumn election.

Carter promised to bring to the presidency a sense of integrity, self-discipline, orderliness and fiscal responsibility as well as a commitment to social justice, values derived from his understanding of Christianity, which were set forth in his campaign autobiography *Why Not the Best?* (1975). He openly acknowledged his belief in Christ, accepting without equivocation the label of 'born again', and demonstrated a remarkable knowledge of the Bible. He had a devout prayer life, and both as private citizen and president he witnessed to others about his faith. His early mentors were the prominent Southern Baptist teachers and ethicists who, through the Sunday school literature they had written, instilled in him sensitivity to the social implications of the gospel and the need for civil rights for all citizens, regardless of their race. Also he read widely in theology and contemporary thought and admitted that he was inspired by such figures as Reinhold Niebuhr, Dietrich Bonhoeffer, Robert Bellah and Martin Luther King, Jr. Another important characteristic resulting from his Baptist roots was an unshakeable commitment to separation of church and state. Thus the same person who confessed that faith in Christ played a large role in his political life stressed that he would not formulate public policy on the basis of his personal beliefs. He consistently opposed state aid to church-related schools and amendments to the Constitution to ban abortions or permit government-sponsored prayer in the state schools. Rather than holding special worship services in the White House, as Nixon had done, Carter regularly attended First Baptist Church in Washington and on occasion even taught an adult Sunday school class.

The Carter presidency has received mixed reviews from media commentators and presidential scholars, most of whom do not comprehend how deeply his faith motivated his actions. At the outset he brought a new moral tone to politics, emphasizing the need for discipline and sacrifice for the common good. He clearly wanted to export American morality, but in a noninterventionist way. He established human rights as a basic tenet of US foreign policy, mediated the historic peace agreement between Egypt and Israel in 1979, turned the Panama Canal over to Panamanian control, and improved relations with China. But his efforts to resolve the worsening oil crisis failed, while spiralling inflation and interest rates, Soviet adventurism and the seizure of the US embassy in Tehran by Iranian extremists led to an uneasy, ill-defined feeling that American power was on the wane. His effort to sound a prophetic note in his appeals for nuclear weapons control and energy conservation fell on deaf ears. Carter became increasingly isolated and was under fire from critics on all sides as his presidency drew to a close. Even the evangelicals, whose beliefs were closest to his, largely repudiated their president because he would not implement the social programmes that they advocated. They were won over in large numbers to the Republican party by the political preachers and television evangelists of the New Religious Right, and they formed the backbone of Ronald Reagan's support in the 1980 election. Like most other Americans, evangelicals preferred Reagan's politics of nostalgia for the bygone America of limitless plenty and power.

After leaving office in 1981, Carter became the most energetic former president in American history. Nearly all his endeavours centred on his church and his intense passion for social justice. He worked with Habitat for Humanity building houses for the poor, established The Carter Center in Atlanta as a place where scholars and activists could meet and discuss political and social issues, travelled incessantly on missions of reconciliation to countries around the world and as a member of election observer teams and diplomatic delegations, and wrote a dozen books on inspirational and political topics along with the autobiographical works *Keeping Faith: Memoirs of a President* (1982) and *An Hour before Daylight: Memories of My Rural Boyhood* (2001). Bitterly disappointed about the fundamentalist takeover of the Southern Baptist Convention, he formally broke with the denomination in October 2000 because of the leadership's implementation of changes in the Baptist Faith and Message (1963) regarding the role of women in the church, and endorsed the moderate Cooperative Baptist Fellowship.

Bibliography

R. V. Pierard and R. D. Linder, *Civil Religion and the Presidency* (Grand Rapids: Zondervan, 1988); P. G. Bourne, *Jimmy Carter: A Comprehensive Biography from Plains to Post-presidency* (New York: Scribner, 1997); B. I. Kaufman, *The Presidency of James Earl Carter, Jr.* (Lawrence: University of Kansas Press, 1993); K. E. Morris, *Jimmy Carter: American Moralist* (Athens: University of Georgia Press, 1996); R. Troester, *Jimmy Carter As Peacemaker: A Post-presidential Biography* (Westport: Praeger, 1996).

R. V. PIERARD

■ **CARTWRIGHT**, Peter (1785–1872), American Methodist preacher, was an important transitional figure as mid-nineteenth-century Methodism moved from the margins of American culture to the mainstream. He was born on 1 September 1875 in Amherst County, Virginia. His father, a pioneer farmer and Revolutionary War veteran, brought the family to Kentucky in 1790, and three years later they settled in Logan County. Cartwright's limited early education was provided by his Methodist mother. In 1801, after a day of frolicking at a wedding, Cartwright experienced a sudden depression, which led him to three months of agonizing soul-searching. Then, at a post-Cane Ridge camp meeting in his neighbourhood, he had an ecstatic experience of divine forgiveness, and immediately joined a Methodist class meeting. A year later he was licensed as an exhorter and in another year had become an itinerant. His meteoric rise through the Methodist hierarchy continued; in 1806 Francis *Asbury ordained him as a deacon, two years later William McKendree ordained him elder, and in 1812 he was named a presiding elder, a position he held in various locations for the next fifty years. In 1816 he was elected to the General Conference and served as a delegate to thirteen successive conferences. In the midst of this activity, on 18 August 1818, he married Frances Gaines, who strongly supported her husband throughout his ministry. The couple had seven daughters and two sons. In 1824 the family moved to Illinois, losing a daughter

in an accident on the way and taking a pay cut from $238 a year to $40. Working as both farmer and preacher, Cartwright remained in Illinois for the rest of his career.

Cartwright became the archetypical pioneer preacher, relishing his role as 'croaker' in his opposition to fashionable innovation. Theologically orthodox and thoroughly Arminian, he was comfortable with the rough culture of frontier settlements and was not above resorting to physical force in dealing with camp meeting disruptions or using coarse insults in his theological controversies with Presbyterians. He was equally content with the emotional manifestations of Methodist enthusiasm, and he paid attention to what he regarded as instantaneous inspirations of the Holy Spirit. He provided a sympathetic (and one of the best recorded) description of 'the jerks', a camp meeting exercise which served, in his mind, as a necessary levelling process. He routinely condemned worldly ostentation and opposed pew rents because of the social stratification they represented. His defence of Methodist egalitarianism was legendary; he remained an outspoken proponent of the class meeting and plain dress for preachers long after both had fallen from fashion.

As consistent as Cartwright's opposition to spiritual and social complacency was, however, he was also supportive of the respectable, upwardly mobile aspirations of his parishioners, as long as their efforts remained circumscribed by Methodist discipline. Despite early protestations against collegiate theological training, he became a tireless proponent of higher education, helping to promote three Methodist colleges in Illinois: McKendree (Lebanon), MacMurray (Jacksonville), and Illinois Wesleyan (Bloomington). He also encouraged the self-educated religious life of his Methodist audiences in his distribution of devotional and theological literature. At the same time, Cartwright eschewed quietism for political activism; besides performing his conference duties, he was very active in Democratic politics. In 1828, allegedly encouraged by Andrew Jackson, he ran successfully for the Illinois legislature and was re-elected in 1832, beating Abraham Lincoln in the process. Fourteen years later, however, Lincoln avenged his defeat when he beat Cartwright in an election for the United States House of Representatives. In both the ecclesiastical and the political arenas Cartwright worked for centrist unity and opposed any radical position that tended to alienate the mainstream. Although he originally left Kentucky because of his anti-slavery views, he rejected the abolition position and fought hard to prevent the division of the denomination in 1844 in the controversy over Bishop James Andrews' slave-holding.

Cartwright's real genius, however, continued to lie in his preaching ministry, where the majority of his energy was always directed. It is estimated that he delivered over 15,000 sermons and baptized 12,000 converts in the decades he worked in Illinois. In 1856 he published his autobiography, which championed the traditions of Primitive Methodism as he had experienced them. Often feted as 'living folklore' and celebrated as 'God's Plowman', Cartwright preached well into his eighties. He died on 25 September 1872 in Pleasant Plains, Illinois, where his church still functions as an active congregation as well as a heritage landmark of the United Methodist Church. On Cartwright's tombstone are inscribed the words of Isaiah 26:4, from which he preached his first sermon, 'Trust ye in the Lord forever; for in the Lord Jehovah is everlasting strength.'

Bibliography

T. L. Agnew, 'Methodism on the Frontier', in E. S. Bucke (ed.), *The History of American Methodism*, 3 vols. (New York: Abingdon Press, 1964), pp. 488–545; P. Cartwright, *Autobiography of Peter Cartwright, the Backwoods Preacher*, ed. W. P. Strickland (New York: Carlton & Porter, 1857).

W. R. SUTTON

■ **CARTWRIGHT, Thomas** (1535–1603), English Puritan reformer, was one of the chief advocates of a full reformation of the English church in the late sixteenth century. Though Cartwright's career was no doubt limited by periods of exile and imprisonment, he became a model agitator for perhaps the key point of reform among early Puritans: the establishment of a presbyterian polity within the state church.

Cartwright was probably born in 1535 in Royston, England, to a farming family, close to Cambridge University where he would become a celebrated and notorious polemicist. In 1550 Cartwright became a student at St John's College, Cambridge, and despite the accession of Queen Mary in 1553 and the subsequent fleeing of many leading Puritans to the Continent, he stayed on and received his BA in 1554. Cartwright then spent some years studying law until the accession of Elizabeth I in 1558, when he returned to Cambridge as a fellow of St John's College; he later became a fellow of Trinity College. By 1564 he was already prominent enough at Cambridge to take a leading role in debates before the queen, and in 1565 he found his way into debates over clerical garments, speaking especially against the wearing of the surplice. Soon afterwards Cartwright left Cambridge briefly to become a domestic chaplain in Ireland, but in 1567 he received a BD and was elected a university preacher.

In 1569 Cartwright took the Lady Margaret professorship of divinity, in which position he began to advance his most controversial arguments for the presbyterian system. Cartwright believed that the Bible had laid out in unambiguous terms the model for church polity, and that that model was best exemplified in the simplicity of the early church. Because he took this primitivist approach to church polity, he argued that the episcopal offices of archbishop, bishop, dean and archdeacon should all be abolished, and the government of local churches be given over to local presbyteries, ministers and deacons. He also insisted that ministers should be elected by their own congregation.

Cartwright immediately fell foul of the university authorities, who saw these views as threatening the very foundations of the established church, and he was removed from his chair by the end of the year. He made his way to Geneva, where he was received as one of the leading spokesmen for the cause of full reformation in the church. Cartwright had developed a following among young preachers and scholars at Cambridge, however, and in 1572 he made an attempt to resume his duties there, but he was soon removed again by the authorities, particularly through the agency of John Whitgift (later Archbishop of Canterbury), with whom Cartwright became engaged in a pamphlet war. Whitgift in 1572 had written a reply to the famous Puritan tract *An Admonition to Parliament*, and Cartwright weighed in against his rival with his own *Reply to ... Doctor Whitgifte* (1573). In it Cartwright reaffirmed his appeal for a church fully reformed according to the primitive model. These and other works deeply troubled both the church and crown and were one cause of the suppression of the Puritans and their writings in 1573. Cartwright was identified as one of the chief troublemakers and a warrant for his arrest was sent out in December 1573. Cartwright took refuge again on the Continent.

After his departure, Cartwright moved frequently until his return to England in 1586. He spent time at the reformed universities at Heidelberg and Basel, where he produced his *Explicato* (1574), which served the international reformed community as an authoritative statement on presbyterian church discipline. By the late 1570s Cartwright had moved on to the reformed mercantile community in the Low Countries and served at the English Church in Antwerp for at least two years, as well as at a church in Middleburg, before finally returning to England as master of a charitable hospital in Warwick. Cartwright again fell foul of the monarchy and Ecclesiastical Commissioners, and in late 1590 his continued agitation led to his imprisonment in the Fleet Prison for about a year and a half. In 1595 Cartwright moved away from Warwick for six years to serve as a chaplain in Guernsey, returning to Warwick in 1601 and dying there in 1603.

Bibliography

B. Brook, *Memoir of the Life and Writings of Thomas Cartwright, B.D.* (London: Snow, 1845); A. Peel and L. H. Carlson (eds.), *Cartwrightiana* (London: Allen & Unwin, 1951); A. F. S. Pearson, *Thomas Cartwright and Elizabethan Puritanism, 1535–1603* (Cambridge: Cambridge University Press, 1925).

T. S. KIDD

■ **CASSIDY, Charles Michael Ardagh** (1936–), evangelist and social activist, was born on 24 September 1936 in Johannesburg, South Africa. A lifelong Anglican, Michael Cassidy is best known as founder and president of Africa Enterprise (AE), an evangelistic agency based in Pietermaritzburg, South Africa, which has been active across Africa since 1962. Under Cassidy's leadership it expanded its area of concern to include social action and work for political reconciliation. Cassidy is widely known in and beyond Africa for his work as a preacher, evangelist and writer.

Cassidy was born in South Africa but grew up in Maseru (in what is now Lesotho). He was educated at the South African schools of Parktown in Johannesburg and Michaelhouse in Natal, but read Modern and Medieval Languages at Cambridge University. He was converted as a student at Cambridge and embraced the conservative evangelicalism of the Cambridge Inter-Collegiate Christian Union. An equally strong influence was Billy *Graham. It was after attending one of Graham's meetings in New York in 1957 that Cassidy began to feel a call to an evangelistic ministry.

After studying Divinity at Fuller Theological Seminary, Pasadena, California, Cassidy returned to South Africa and with three others began AE in 1962. It sought to do for Africa what the Billy Graham Association was doing in America and beyond. AE concentrated on city-wide missions across Africa, preaching a 'pretty straightforward, down-the-line, true-blue evangelical' gospel. Cassidy sought to work with all churches that were broadly orthodox in faith and that stressed the importance of inter-racial partnership. Based in Pietermaritzburg, AE was active in South Africa and throughout the continent. In 1969 Cassidy met and married Carol Bam, with whom he had three children. AE was effective, notwithstanding substantial difficulties; in 1973 Cassidy was expelled from Uganda by Idi Amin, who wished to discourage missionary activity. AE rapidly expanded in size and importance, organizing the Pan African Christian Leadership Assembly in Nairobi in 1976. AE's growth was all the more striking given the decline of many older mission agencies.

In 1973 AE organized the South African Congress on Mission and Evangelism in Durban. This reflected a growing interest in charismatic and Pentecostal Christianity, confirmed when Cassidy himself had a profound experience of spiritual renewal in

1977. Thereafter he worked to build bridges between conservative evangelical and charismatic Christianity, a policy justified in his book *Bursting the Wineskins* (1983).

Cassidy was now a significant figure within the world of evangelicalism and was included on the Lausanne Committee for World Evangelization. Under his leadership AE built up strong support in Britain, America and Australia, and he led missions in a number of centres outside Africa. Cassidy had always opposed apartheid and promoted racial harmony, working in close partnership with Festo Kivengere, the Archbishop of Uganda. However, in its early years AE concentrated primarily on evangelism. In the 1970s, and especially in the 1980s, Cassidy began to stress the importance of political, economic and social change in South Africa. In 1985 he founded the National Initiative for Reconciliation, which drew together church leaders of various denominations and races to promote reconciliation. Heavily involved in bringing political opponents together in dialogue, Cassidy and AE helped to ensure that the elections of 1994 and 1996 passed relatively peacefully, particularly in the province of KwaZulu-Natal, where Cassidy and AE are based. This shift of emphasis has been reflected in his written work, which has increasingly addressed social and political themes, notably in *The Passing Summer* (1989) and *A Witness For Ever* (1995). None the less, Cassidy remains passionately committed to the central tenets of evangelicalism and to evangelism. In 1992 he led a large evangelistic campaign, 'From Africa with Love', to South Africa, conducted amid the difficult transition out of apartheid.

Michael Cassidy, mainly through his leadership of AE, had a significant impact on the evangelizing of Africa, and especially South Africa, in the latter half of the twentieth century. His work was important both for the success of AE's evangelism and for the manner in which that evangelism evolved. AE's increasingly ecumenical nature and readiness to embrace social action and the need for political reconciliation have drawn fire from both conservatives and radicals. Cassidy's advocacy of a 'biblical holism', combining evangelism with social and political work, has also been widely influential. Cassidy combines an emphasis on conservat-

ive evangelicalism with an ability to adapt to rapidly changing contexts.

Bibliography

M. Cassidy, *Bursting the Wineskins* (London: Hodder & Stoughton, 1983); M. Cassidy, *The Passing Summer: A South African Pilgrimage in the Politics of Love* (London: Hodder & Stoughton, 1989); M. Cassidy, *A Witness for Ever: The Dawning of Democracy in South Africa – Stories behind the Story* (London: Hodder & Stoughton, 1995).

D. J. GOODHEW

■ **CATHERWOOD, Sir Henry Frederick Ross** (1925–), industrialist and politician, was born on 30 January 1925 in Moyola Cottage, Lough Neagh, Northern Ireland. 'Fred', as he was known, became a leading industrialist and entered politics in later life, eventually becoming vice-president of the European Parliament. He has always been active in evangelical circles as a writer and speaker and by his involvement with various evangelical bodies. He was knighted in 1971 and has received honorary doctorates from Queen's University, Belfast, and the University of Surrey.

Fred Catherwood was born in the Ulster countryside but grew up mainly in Belfast. His family were staunch members of the Brethren, whose egalitarian culture always remained with him. The religion of Shrewsbury public school, where he was educated, was not wholly congenial to him, but his time at Clare College, Cambridge, drew him into contact with the Cambridge Inter-Collegiate Christian Union and the work of E. J. H. *Nash, which deepened Catherwood's commitment to conservative evangelical Christianity.

After going down in 1946 he trained as an accountant in London, where he attended the Congregationalist Westminster Chapel and was deeply affected by the ministry of Dr Martyn *Lloyd-Jones. Catherwood became close to Lloyd-Jones, especially after he married the latter's daughter, Elizabeth, in 1954. Then followed a succession of posts in industry, alongside involvement in the Inter-Varsity Fellowship (IVF). Inspired by Oliver Barclay, he wrote *The Christian in Industrial Society* (London: Tyndale, 1964). This volume represents one of the first examples of the revival of an evangelical social consciousness in the later twentieth century. In it Catherwood stressed that while personal faith was of paramount concern for evangelicals, social action was of great value because of the intrinsic worth of helping the community conform more closely to God's laws, because an awareness of God's standards was a precondition for human repentance, and because Christian lifestyle 'precedes and provides the occasion for the testimony of our message'. Catherwood illustrated these beliefs with detailed discussion of the value of work and wealth and the nature of management and government. Although he was to write a number of other works, this was his most influential.

In 1964 Catherwood became Chief Industrial Advisor to the new Labour government and in 1966 director-general of the National Economic Development Council. Here he played a central role in national life and began his involvement with European affairs. After leaving this post in 1971 he occupied a variety of positions in industry and management including, from 1974 to 1976, chair of the British Institute of Management. In these years Catherwood had a significant role in a number of national events such as the miners' strike of 1974 and the 1975 campaign over EEC membership. At the same time, he was increasingly active in evangelical organizations, being chair of the IVF Council between 1971 and 1977, a period in which IVF expanded its work, shifted its base to Leicester and changed its name to the Universities and Colleges Christian Fellowship (UCCF). In 1977 he was president of the Fellowship of Independent Evangelical Churches, and he was also heavily involved in the International Fellowship of Evangelical Students.

In 1979 he was elected Member of the European Parliament for Cambridgeshire, standing as a Conservative, having rejoined the party after some years' absence in 1978. Ideologically he was not on the right of the party and was deeply hostile to Thatcherite economics and to Euro-scepticism, seeing the real threats to British identity as moral collapse and materialism. From the mid-1980s he was much involved in attempts to broker peace in Northern Ireland. On occasion he lent support to individual Christians and churches, notably those against which the Greek and Turkish authorities discriminated. Between 1989 and 1991 Catherwood was vice-president of the European Parliament, in which role he did much work on the Common Agricultural Policy and in building links with Eastern Europe. In 1992 he became president of the Evangelical Alliance, where he strongly promoted the value of social action by evangelicals, especially via 'Christian Action Networks'.

A committed Christian throughout his adult life, Fred Catherwood has played a leading role in business, government and church affairs. As a speaker and writer he has done much to persuade evangelicalism in Britain to renew its concern for wider social issues.

Bibliography

F. Catherwood, *At the Cutting Edge* (London: Hodder & Stoughton, 1995).

D. GOODHEW

■ **CAUGHEY, James** (1810–1891), Methodist evangelist, was born in the north of Ireland. Very little information about his exact place of birth or his family is available. He wrote of himself as being of 'Scotch ancestry', almost certainly meaning that his family was Presbyterian. When he was in his mid-teens he emigrated with his family to the United States, and by the late 1820s he was working in a flour mill in Troy, New York. About this time he joined the Methodist Episcopal Church and was 'soundly converted to God in Christ'. Troy was part of what had become known as the 'burned over district' on account of the numerous revivals that had broken out in the area. As Methodism was very much committed to these revivals, it is not surprising that Caughey speaks of how he was caught up in 'a powerful revival of religion', and from that revival came his call to the ministry. In the early 1830s he was admitted to the rank of a preacher on probation, and in 1836 he was ordained into the Methodist ministry. He conducted his first revival services in Montreal and Quebec in Canada; some two hundred conversions were recorded and fifty believers were 'sanctified'. These revival services set a pattern that Caughey would follow for the next thirty years of his active, itinerant and revivalist ministry. He saw his congregations as made up of three kinds of people who needed specific and pointed preaching to meet their spiritual need. The lost needed to be converted; the backsliders needed to be restored; and, as a convinced Wesleyan, Caughey passionately advocated the view that all believers needed to be entirely sanctified.

Responding to what he believed to be a clear call from God, Caughey set sail for the British Isles and arrived in Liverpool in July 1841. This visit involved him in a growing controversy with the hierarchy of English Methodism. Although he brought to England a certificate from the Troy District confirming that he was a preacher in 'good standing', he had not been officially invited either by the Wesleyan Conference or by any other influential Methodist group. His revivalist services were not welcomed by conservative 'high church' Wesleyans like Jabez *Bunting, and Caughey's open attacks on ministers who were not engaged in 'soul-saving' did not endear him to the Wesleyan establishment. For the next six years, Caughey preached in Wesleyan chapels all over the north of England. Everywhere his powerful, pointed and passionate evangelistic preaching resulted in hundreds of public conversions. Caughey preached directly on the great issues of sin, repentance, saving faith, conversion, heaven and hell, as well as messages directed to Christians who, he believed, needed to move beyond conversion and be 'sanctified wholly' and enabled to live a life of victory over sin this side of heaven.

Caughey's letters recorded that in sixteen weeks of preaching in five Wesleyan chapels in Sheffield, 3,266 people had been 'justified' and 1,435 had been 'sanctified'. In every service, immediately after the preaching, Caughey encouraged the people to remain for a prayer meeting, and it was there that the 'saving work' was done. Caughey moved among the people, urging them to move up to the communion rail as 'penitents', and there the local preachers who assisted the evangelist counselled and prayed for them. In this way every penitent received personal attention, and careful record was kept of the transaction. Caughey was the first evangelist of note in Britain to make use of the 'penitent form', and among those who responded in

Nottingham was the teenage William *Booth, who later modelled his own evangelistic preaching style on the American's. Caughey's habit of keeping numerical records enabled him to give the precise numbers of those justified and sanctified in every service at which he preached. At the close of his six-year visit in 1847 he claimed that 20,000 sinners had been justified and 9,000 Christians had been 'entirely sanctified'.

Caughey's fame as a revivalist was enormously enhanced by reports of his British 'triumphs', ecclesiastical opposition and the very rapid sale of his Letters (1844–1847). Between 1848 and his second visit to Britain in 1856, Caughey was in constant demand, especially in New England and Canada. In eight years of unflagging revivalist preaching and soul-winning, he could not meet all the requests for his services.

On his three subsequent visits to Britain, while Caughey never quite achieved the huge congregations and impressive statistics of his first visit, his revival preaching was effective and fruitful. Ill health forced his retirement in 1866, and he died in Highland Park, New Jersey, on 30 January 1891.

Caughey published five volumes of Letters, and his half-dozen books mostly comprise records of his revival services and his travels in the British Isles and Canada, advice on soul-winning and many hortatory addresses. They include The Triumph of Truth, Arrows from my Quiver and Glimpses of Life in Soul Saving.

Bibliography

J. Caughey, Letters on Various Subjects, 5 vols. (London: Simkin Marshall, 1844–1847); R. Carwardine, Transatlantic Revivalism: Popular Evangelicalism in Britain and America, 1790–1865 (London: Greenwood Press, 1978), pp. 102–133; J. Kent, Holding the Fort: Studies in Victorian Revivalism (London: Epworth Press, 1978), pp. 77–87; 171–196; 311–324; D. Wise, 'Sketch of the Life of Rev. James Caughey', in Earnest Christianity Illustrated (Boston: J. P. Magee, 1855), pp. 9–19.

H. McGONIGLE

■ **CHADWICK, Samuel** (1860–1932), Wesleyan Methodist minister and college principal, was born into a Methodist family in Burnley, Lancashire. At the age of fifteen he felt a call to ordained ministry. At that time he was working in a cotton mill. A year later he began lay preaching. When he was twenty-one, he became a full-time lay evangelist in the Methodist Bacup circuit, where for two years he exercised a very successful ministry. Josiah Mee, the superintendent of the Bacup circuit, was a powerful encouragement to Chadwick, and Mee inculcated in the young trainee both the evangelistic nature of preaching and also the importance of the Methodist message of 'entire sanctification'.

The power of the traditional Methodist teaching about entire sanctification, also described as full salvation, captivated Chadwick in 1883 when he heard the preaching of the Methodist minister J. D. Brash, who successfully promoted the message of holiness through the periodical *The King's Highway*. Chadwick's subsequent personal experience of sanctification transformed what he contemptuously called his 'barren preaching' dramatically. It was in this period that he entered Didsbury College to train for Methodist ministry. Didsbury provided him with a solid theological education. During his first year at college, he heard a Methodist evangelist, Thomas Cook, preach and saw hundreds respond to Cook's evangelistic appeal. Cook provided Chadwick with a model for his own ministry.

In 1886 Chadwick completed his training and began ministry in Edinburgh, thereafter moving to Glasgow. From 1890 to 1893 he had a significant evangelistic ministry as superintendent of the Leeds Methodist Mission. His time there was described as one in which revival swept the neighbourhood. During this period he married. The services in Wesley Chapel drew a wide variety of people. Chadwick then spent a year in London but was recalled to Leeds to take charge of Oxford Place Chapel. It was a large building, but congregations had declined to the point where there were 1,000 empty seats each Sunday. Through Chadwick's outward-looking ministry from 1894 to 1907 the chapel was crowded every Sunday. By 1907, 2,000 people were enrolled in class meetings. A new building was erected. Many evangelistic organizations were established, which reached into all parts of the life of the city.

Chadwick became well known in Wesleyan Methodism. In 1906, at the Wesleyan Methodist Conference, H. J. Pope, who had arranged through the Wesleyan Home Mission Department the purchase of Cliff College, Derbyshire, as a training centre for evangelists, proposed that Chadwick be appointed tutor in biblical and theological studies at Cliff. This appointment may seem surprising, as Chadwick was more of an evangelist than a lecturer. However, he was a keen reader with a sharp mind. Cliff also trained lay evangelists, a task to which Chadwick was well suited. Thomas Champness, a Wesleyan Methodist evangelist, had begun training lay evangelists in the 1880s. The leadership of this operation had passed to Thomas Cook, and from 1906 the training was conducted at Cliff. In 1907 Chadwick joined the Cliff College staff. Thomas Champness had also launched a weekly paper entitled *Joyful News*, which reached a circulation of 30,000, and Chadwick took over the editorship in 1903.

In 1912, as a result of Cook's early death, Chadwick became principal of Cliff College. For the next twenty years he dominated the Wesleyan Methodist holiness movement and became well known among holiness groups outside denominational Methodism. The vision that he espoused was that through 'earnest prayer, living testimony, impassioned enthusiasm, and intense spirituality', Methodism would 'spread Scriptural Holiness throughout the land, evangelise the world, and reform the nation'. Cliff students, who were mostly aged between 18 and 25, constituted a vital part of this vision. The training they received was more practical than academic, although they were expected to be dedicated to their studies. On leaving Cliff, roughly one third normally went into lay circuit work in Methodism, one third into evangelistic work and one third into other ministry. About seventy were trained each year. Chadwick had a profound influence on the students. He ran the college in a highly disciplined way and moulded it according to his wishes.

The teaching at Cliff College was evangelical. Although Chadwick accepted the Bible unequivocally as the record of the revelation of God through the Holy Spirit, he proposed that the Spirit, not the Bible itself, defined inspiration. In his view a mechanical concept of the nature of the Bible, without an understanding of the Spirit, resulted in bibliolatry. Chadwick was also careful to affirm the place, as he saw it, of proper biblical criticism. He was influenced by biblical criticism during his early ministry in Scotland, and he gave lectures on the subject at Cliff College, believing that it had contributed to a saner conception of biblical inspiration.

From 1913 until his death in 1932, Chadwick was also president of the Southport Convention. This was started in 1885 in order to 'make more vital the traditional faith of Methodism'. Thomas Cook was the organizer of the first convention and was secretary and then president, using it as a vehicle for the presentation of the holiness message. Although Southport had no official standing in any of the Methodist denominations, it shared with Cliff College a significant constituency within popular Methodism that was dedicated to keeping alive the atmosphere of past holiness revivals. Annual Whitsun meetings were held at Cliff, and up to 15,000 people made their visit a kind of pilgrimage; the meeting became the best attended event in the Methodist year. Chadwick was also in demand for other large events and spoke at camp meetings in America.

Although Chadwick's own motto, which became that of Cliff College, was Christocentric ('Christ for All: All for Christ'), he strongly emphasized the work of the Holy Spirit and Christian perfection, as in two of his four books, *The Way to Pentecost* and *The Call to Christian Perfection*. For Chadwick, the weakness of the Christianity of his time was that thousands of believers had not personally experienced the power of Pentecost. This conviction led Chadwick to take a position that was similar to some of the views found in Pentecostalism. 'The Lord the Healer', said Chadwick, 'still gives to men the gift of healing by His Spirit ... quite apart from medical knowledge', and he asserted that 'the age of miracles is not past'.

It seems that Chadwick's expectation of impending revival, through the power of the Spirit, was heightened during his year as president of the Wesleyan Methodist Conference. In his presidential address in 1918, Chadwick spoke on 'The World Crisis and the Age', arguing for a renewed Methodist consecration to evangelism. Cliff College students soon became involved in what were termed 'revivals'. Chadwick pursued his revival theme as president of the National Council of Evangelical Free Churches, a post he held in 1922. At Whitsun 1925 Chadwick announced his determination to enlist Methodist Friars to evangelize England, and from 1926 these 'Cliff Trekkers' went out in bands each year to attempt the task.

Chadwick was unusual among the holiness leaders of his period in his commitment to the centrality of the eucharist and to some 'High Church' practices. As a young minister in Scotland he introduced Passiontide services, including a three-hour vigil on Good Friday, and he did the same in Leeds. He believed that a 'Real Presence' of Christ was available through the bread and wine, and he defended those within Methodism who leaned in a strongly sacramental direction. 'The theology of the Methodist', said Chadwick in a summary of his *credo*, 'is Catholic; the religion of the Methodist is Evangelical; the experience of the Methodist is distinctive.'

Bibliography

N. G. Dunning, *Samuel Chadwick* (London: Hodder & Stoughton, 1953).

I. M. RANDALL

■ **CHAFER, Lewis Sperry** (1871–1952), dispensationalist and seminary founder, was born in Rock Creek, Ohio, on 27 February 1871. He was the youngest of three children and second son of Thomas Franklin Chafer (an Auburn Seminary graduate and pastor of New School Presbyterian and Congregational churches) and Lomira Sperry Chafer.

Chafer's youth was marked by his conversion at the age of six during his father's first pastorate in Rock Creek, his father's death five years later from tuberculosis after years of suffering, and Lewis's commitment to ministry at the age of fourteen, at the prompting of an evangelist named Scott, who was also tubercular. When Thomas died, the family moved to New Lyme, Ohio, for the further education of the two eldest children at the Northern Collegiate Business Institute (known as the New Lyme Institute). After finishing his preparatory education, Lewis also entered the Institute.

In 1888 the family moved to Oberlin so that the two elder children could attend the college there. After a year in the pre-college course, Lewis enrolled for three semesters in Oberlin's Conservatory. His education was interrupted, however, by the increasing demands of his ministry as soloist and choir organizer with the Congregational evangelist A. T. Reed. Chafer never graduated; nor, apparently, did he enrol in theology courses at Oberlin. His ministry with Reed, which began in 1889, continued until Chafer married Ella Loraine Case, whom he met at Oberlin, in 1896. They formed their own evangelistic team and, for ten years, Lewis preached and sang while Ella accompanied him. Initially working in Ohio, Pennsylvania, New York and New Jersey, they later ministered in southeastern states as well. *True Evangelism* (written in 1901 and published in 1911) summarizes Chafer's convictions on the subject. He decries the widespread emphasis on emotional and commercial methods, calling instead for a restrained, Spirit-dependent approach.

After a year as assistant pastor of First Congregational, Buffalo, New York, Chafer was ordained in the Congregational Church in April 1900. In 1901 he moved to Northfield, Massachusetts, to participate in D. L. *Moody's summer conferences. He continued his revival ministry, especially in the winter months, but also became increasingly involved in the music at Northfield. He assisted in the founding of the Southfield Conference in Crescent City, Florida, in 1904, presiding over it in 1909. From 1906 to 1910 Chafer taught Bible and music at the Mount Hermon School for Boys and in 1907 published *Elementary Outline Studies in the Science of Music*.

The Northfield Conferences included the type of Bible exposition developed at the Niagara Bible Conferences and featured 'victorious life' teaching. There Chafer met F. B. *Meyer, G. Campbell *Morgan, W. H. Griffith *Thomas, Reuben *Torrey, James *Orr, James M. *Gray, A. C. *Gaebelein, Harry A. *Ironside, A. T. *Pierson and Charles Trumbull.

C. I. *Scofield was the most important influence on Chafer's theology and ministry. Scofield lived at Northfield from 1895, when not travelling to do research for, and write,

his Reference Bible. He presided over the Northfield Bible Training School and was the pastor of Trinitarian Congregational Church, which was attended by Moody. Having few revival meetings scheduled in 1901, Chafer attended the Bible School. He later recalled, 'Until that time, I had never heard a real Bible teacher ... My first hearing of Dr. Scofield was a morning Bible class at the Bible School. He was teaching the sixth chapter of Romans. I am free to confess that it seemed to me at the close that I had seen more vital truth in God's word in that one hour than I had seen in all my life before. It was a crisis for me. I was captured for life' ('What I Learned from Dr. Scofield', *Sunday School Times*, 4 March 1922, p. 120). The teacher–student, even father–son, relationship between them grew closer over time despite Scofield's frequent moves.

At Scofield's urging, Chafer became a Bible teacher. He published *Satan*, composed with Scofield's assistance and featuring Scofield's foreword, in 1909, the same year as Scofield's Reference Bible appeared. Chafer became increasingly involved with Scofield's itinerant teaching ministry. Through the major Bible and prophetic conferences, his books and articles, and his teaching in short-term Bible institutes, Chafer rose to prominence.

Scofield founded the Scofield (later New York) School of the Bible in New York City in 1911, appointing Chafer as director of the Department of Oral Extension. This agency distributed Scofield's Bible correspondence course (written in 1892) and coordinated conference activities. In this role Chafer travelled widely, teaching at conferences and holding seminars called 'Bible institutes'. He helped Scofield to establish the Philadelphia School of the Bible in 1914, serving on the faculty and apparently developing the curriculum. He and Ella moved to East Orange, New Jersey, in 1915, to be closer to the two schools.

Chafer continued his Bible teaching ministry until Scofield's death (1921), working out most of his theology and publishing most of his books during this period: *The Kingdom in History and Prophecy* (1915; with a Scofield foreword); *Salvation* (1917); *He That Is Spiritual* (1918); *Grace* (1922; dedicated to Scofield). In 1922 he became pastor of Scofield's former church, the independent

First Congregational, Dallas (renamed Scofield Memorial Church in 1923). He also served as general secretary of the Central American Mission, founded by Scofield in 1890. Chafer had transferred his ordination to the Presbyterian Church in the USA (Troy presbytery, synod of New York) in 1906, and then, because of his growing work in the south, to the Orange presbytery of the Presbyterian Church in the US (1912). He transferred to the Dallas presbytery in 1923.

During his speaking tours in 1912, Chafer interviewed ministers and students about theological education and visited a number of seminaries. He conceived the idea of a theological seminary that would embody the Bible conference movement's devotional and applied, as well as philological, Bible teaching and train ministers as Bible teachers. Like the Bible conferences, it would be non-denominational, training ministers from a broad range of churches. After considering other cities, Chafer, William M. Anderson (the pastor of First Presbyterian, Dallas), and the Anglican theologian W. H. Griffith *Thomas founded a college in Dallas. At Griffith Thomas' suggestion they gave it a British-style name, the Evangelical Theological College. It was renamed Dallas Theological Seminary in 1936.

Chafer served as president and Professor of Systematic Theology at the seminary from 1924 to 1952; he resigned his post as mission director in 1925 and his pastorate in 1926. He travelled widely, teaching in churches and at Bible conferences, and contributed frequently to The Sunday School Times and Our Hope. He compiled Major Bible Themes (1926) from a series in The Sunday School Times (April–December 1925), supplemented by new material.

Chafer opposed the direct solicitation of funds, insisting that the school live by the 'faith principle' of George *Müller, Hudson *Taylor and the China Inland Mission. His strict interpretation of Müller's policy resulted in chronic shortages and accumulating debt (in contradiction to Müller's principle); operating expenses and salaries were unpaid, and litigation from creditors and staff brought increasing pressure.

The seminary acquired Bibliotheca Sacra in 1933. When his elder brother Rollin died in 1940, Chafer succeeded him as editor. Much of his Systematic Theology (1947–1948), the first premillennial and dispensationalist theology, originally appeared as instalments in the journal.

Though he shared the doctrinal convictions of fundamentalism and left the Congregational church, following Scofield's lead, Chafer was not militant. He spoke at the inaugural World's Christian Fundamentals Association meeting, but later distanced himself from the association and strident, sensationalist leaders such as J. Frank Norris and William Bell *Riley. He decisively opposed theological liberalism, but emphasized the exposition of Scripture rather than the refutation of liberalism.

From the mid-1930s considerable controversy surrounded 'Scofieldism' in Presbyterian circles, especially in the south. Critics alleged that at certain points the teaching contradicted that of the Westminster Confession. In his Dispensationalism (1936; first in Bibliotheca Sacra, then issued separately) and elsewhere, Chafer charged his critics with misinterpreting his views and subordinating Scripture to confessional standards. Defending his teachings as biblical, he suggested that if the Westminster Confession excluded dispensational views, it should be revised. Chafer remained within the southern Presbyterian church, but an increasing number of his students were excluded. An advisory study committee report on dispensationalism (1944) concentrated on Chafer's views, finding them confessionally unacceptable, though this view was not binding on presbyteries. The report reinforced the independent, non-denominational orientation of Chafer's ministry. Many Baptists also adopted his teachings on dispensationalism and the spiritual life, ignoring his paedobaptist views.

Chafer's character, behaviour, and relationship with his students profoundly influenced them. They displayed extraordinary admiration and loyalty, especially because of his piety and graciousness. His personal impact reinforced his clear, persuasive teaching style.

In 1935 Chafer suffered a heart attack, partly due perhaps to financial pressures and threatened lawsuits by unpaid staff. His health problems recurred in 1945 and 1948, and he died of heart failure in August 1952 while in Seattle. Chafer's theological legacy is his *Systematic Theology*, the formal theological elaboration of Scofieldian dispensationalism. His vision for 'an entirely new departure' in seminary theological education 'institutionalized the Bible Conference movement' (Hannah, p. 145).

Bibliography

J. D. Hannah, 'The Social and Intellectual History of the Origins of the Evangelical Theological College' (PhD thesis, University of Texas at Dallas, 1988); R. T. Mangum, 'The Falling Out between Dispensationalism and Covenant Theology: A Historical and Theological Investigation of Controversies between Dispensationalism and Covenant Theologians from 1936 to 1944' (PhD thesis, Dallas Theological Seminary, 2001).

S. R. SPENCER

■ **CHALMERS, Thomas** (1780–1847), Scottish minister, was born in the royal burg of Anstruther Easter, a small fishing and coastal trading village on the south-east coast of Fife, on 17 March 1780, the sixth child of John and Elizabeth Chalmers. The family business was in decline, but Thomas was brought up in a comfortable middle-class home. A precocious child, he was sent to St Andrews University at the age of eleven. In 1803 he was appointed to the rural parish of Kilmany, not far from St Andrews. He became a controversial figure, deserting his parish during the week to teach mathematics and chemistry at the university. In the months following his thirtieth birthday he experienced an evangelical conversion, and the change in his conversation and preaching attracted attention. He became an enthusiastic supporter of Bible societies and took an interest, at first guarded, in Baptist and Moravian missions. In 1812 he married Grace Pratt. Their marriage was happy, and their six daughters helped to form a lively and hospitable household.

After a contested election, in 1815 Chalmers responded to a call to the Tron church in central Glasgow. He embodied an unusual blend of political and religious attitudes. He had never been at home with the Moderate Party even before his conversion, and he had links with evangelical Whigs such as Andrew Thomson that were political

before they were religious, yet he remained Tory in his instincts. Moderate friends encouraged him to read more theology, but his success as a preacher lay in his relating social and scientific questions to a personal faith in which a high value was placed on the atonement. In Glasgow his reputation soared following a series of midweek sermons on astronomy. In London and Edinburgh he drew huge crowds. As his fame increased he was distracted by civic responsibilities and concerned that his middle-class congregation was not touching urban poverty. When the city council erected the new parish of St John's, he negotiated to take pastoral responsibility for it as a self-contained area in which to demonstrate his developing social theories.

Chalmers believed that poor-rates generated expectations that outstripped the funds they made available. His answer to middle-class fears of an aggressive, immoral and irreligious underclass was to try to create an idealized parish community in defiance of population growth, mobility and structural unemployment. He defended his conviction that a poor parish could support its own poor without a poor-rate long after it was clear that his sums were wrong. Probably the issue of support was not the most important one. With a remarkable team, Chalmers built schools, invigorated elders, put social work in the hands of deacons and provided information on mission overseas to stimulate mission at home. His elders included William Collins, whose publishing he financed with profits from his astronomical sermons.

St John's was divided into 'proportions', and Chalmers, his elders, deacons and Sunday school teachers visited homes systematically and set up local Sunday schools. The deacons were determined to keep poor-relief within the funds provided by church offerings. Each situation was investigated and the possibilities of help from families and friends explored. Charity was a neighbourly obligation, before it was a church or city council responsibility.

Chalmers believed that he avoided poor-relief becoming an impersonal right and that if people were encouraged to give even small amounts to good causes they were less likely to succumb to poverty. It was a vision many wanted to believe, whatever the evidence that it could not solve the large-scale social problems around them. Chalmers' notion of the economic independence of the city parish was never realistic. Visiting deacons and their investigations were more personal than official handouts, but those investigations were not the intimate relationships of a rural parish. Despite Chalmers' efforts, his Sunday congregation came largely from outside the parish.

Yet the 'St John's Experiment' had considerable merits. Chalmers did grow a church. He helped people educationally, spiritually and socially. He made the mission of the church much more than the activity of its minister, however much people were attracted by his fame as a preacher. His 'case-work' approach became part of the history of social work. He inspired other churches to face the challenge of poverty through a process of visitation and social investigation. He was no armchair theorist and was hardly the last person to describe a church in terms of his vision rather than the reality.

In 1823 Chalmers left Glasgow to teach moral philosophy at St Andrews University. Many were surprised that he deserted a project that still needed his direction. Others were alarmed that he was giving up his ministry to teach secular subjects. The university hoped that his popularity would attract students. It did. Students were awed by his passionate integration of economics, ethics, philosophy and theology, and soon stimulated one another to Christian commitment, including commitment to overseas mission through town and student mission societies. Joshua Marshman and Robert *Morrison came to visit and brought fresh news from India and China. The theories and practices of the Moravians and Baptists and societies such as the LMS and CMS were compared. From among Chalmers' students came the first Church of Scotland missionaries to India, including Alexander *Duff. Duff and others took with them the conviction that all truth was God's truth, and that Christian faith should be actively related to all of society.

Chalmers' relationship with his students was deep, lifelong and rewarding, but his relationship with many of his colleagues soon soured. St Andrews was in a measure corrupt, and Chalmers saw the corruption with uncomfortable clarity. In 1828 he accepted the Chair of Divinity in Edinburgh. In 1832 he was moderator of the Church of Scotland, and he was soon regarded as leader of the Evangelical Party. Scotland's cities were expanding, and as an established church the Church of Scotland expected government support for new churches. However, the increase in the franchise from the Reform Act of 1832 made it difficult for the government to aid one church and not another. Chalmers was not alone in failing to take adequate account of changing political realities.

From 1834 Chalmers realized that as well as lobbying the government for finance, the church would have to raise its own funds for church extension, and in six years he and his committees financed over 200 new churches. Meanwhile disputes developed with the courts and the government, and within the church. The Evangelical Party in the Church of Scotland had gained a majority in the General Assembly and had moved to give greater authority to parishes over the choice of minister. They also gave votes in church courts to ministers in chapels. As these changes bore upon property rights some doubted whether the General Assembly had the authority to make them, and a number of Moderates started to challenge church decisions. As the cases worked their way by appeal to the House of Lords, a sequence of court decisions implied that the Church of Scotland was a creature of the state. Evangelicals sensed that their work was under threat and that they could not trust moderate presbyteries and patrons not to impose moderate ministers on evangelical parishes. Because of their defiance of court decisions, Evangelical leaders, including Chalmers, were regarded as lawbreakers. Both sides claimed the high moral ground, and those in the middle found it difficult to advance an alternative position. Members of Parliament sitting in England had little understanding of Scottish commitment to the spiritual independence of even an established church, and less still of how far Scots are capable of going on matters of principle.

The 1830s saw a mixture of cooperation and conflict. Evangelicals and Moderates were at first united in church extension at home and in mission overseas. As court cases pitted them against each other, each stereotyped the weaknesses and failures of the other. Chalmers was brilliant as an organizer and a preacher, but unreliable as a negotiator. Reading about the Covenanters and the Scottish Reformation, he developed a strong sense of the need to take a stand. Despite a passionate, if ironic, belief in the benefits of established churches (it was better for poor-relief not to be provided by the government, but spiritual needs required state assistance), he came to the view that the church might need to sever its connection to the state.

By early 1843 successive governments had failed to resolve the issue. English incomprehension was practically total and Scots opinion was divided. Chalmers had long shown himself quite capable of defying authority, and on 18 May he was the leading figure in the Disruption, in which over a third of the ministers and lay people resigned from the Church of Scotland to form the Free Church. In the same year he became Principal and Professor of Theology at New College, Edinburgh.

Chalmers retained his belief in the value of a national church able to evangelize the whole nation, and strove to make the Free Church of Scotland a national church independent of government support. He welcomed the possibility of cooperation and even incorporation with like-minded churches. His fund-raising skills, oratory and personal stature were essential to the success of the Free Church, but it was soon clear that his vision was broader and his theology more flexible than those of many other Free Church leaders. In his retirement he put his energies into an impoverished area of Edinburgh, and continued his travelling, speaking and correspondence. He died at home in Edinburgh on 30 May 1847. His funeral was a national event, drawing thousands from across the still fresh divisions of Scottish life.

Chalmers' popularity transcended those divisions. People who rejected his social analysis acknowledged him as the greatest preacher of his time. His efforts were often admired when his conclusions were not followed. Some criticize him for failing to save the church from the tragedy of the Disruption. For others he was the hero who led those prepared to sacrifice their own security in order to save the church from a fatal compromise.

Chalmers wrote extensively on 'political economy', and taught it at St Andrew's University, but he is not remembered for any notable achievement in economics. Even so his writings in this area have been republished. His theology, however, has been neglected, partly because of the assumption of some that real theology is only about classic Christian doctrines such as the Trinity, predestination and the atonement. In other ways the neglect is understandable. After his conversion Chalmers had prayed to be delivered from systematic theology. (He also prayed to be delivered from mathematics!) He was less enthusiastic about the arguments surrounding particular doctrines than about the practical application of what he believed the Christian message to be. Someone who later taught his students that they were not to preach Calvinism (by which he meant predestination) would not be preoccupied with rethinking its finer points. He supported Catholic emancipation while opposing Catholicism.

When an American visitor discussed *Calvin with him, Chalmers could not find a copy of the *Institutes* on his shelves, and they are not listed in his library catalogue. He had devoured philosophy in his youth, and there was nothing lightweight about his ongoing theological study, but he left others to read German theology. His emphases were conventional, reflecting a strong interest in natural theology and Christian evidences. His emphasis on external evidences troubled critics and his views shifted as he wrestled with the issues. He supported diverse causes with enthusiasm, but selected them carefully. He encouraged others in their causes, but some (e.g. legislative Sabbatarianism) held few attractions for him. He was familiar with the social problems associated with alcohol but did not accept teetotalism as a solution. He gave evangelical warmth to the orthodoxy of his teacher George Hill, whose theology lectures he used as a text for his own students despite his having criticized them when younger. The need of sinful humanity and the provision for that need in Jesus Christ provided the basic framework of his theology, and he was greatly concerned for the sensitive preaching and passionate illustration of these themes. Overly pious language made him cringe; in his own Christian mission he aimed to be both practical and prayerful.

An important theme in the theological history of nineteenth-century Scotland is the weakening of traditional Calvinism. Often judged to be heretics, Erskine of Linlathen, Edward *Irving and John McLeod Campbell are seen as representatives of the future, for good or ill. They all had close associations with Chalmers. Irving had been Chalmers' assistant at St John's; Chalmers corresponded with McLeod Campbell and was a good friend of Erskine. A surprisingly liberal and selective attitude towards the Westminster Confession is clear in Chalmers' writing, correspondence, teaching and preaching. Many referred to the large-heartedness of his spirit. His beliefs and values proved more enduring than those both more and less conservative.

Chalmers believed in a free gospel. He was excited by science. In his view the inspiration of the Bible related 'not to the thing recorded, but the truth of it', and church government was a matter of human preference, not of divine ordinance. He saw the expression of theology as historically conditioned. He was able to identify the most important questions of his time. One of his closest friends never came to faith. He was influenced by Methodists and Moravians, and was a friend of Anglicans, Baptists, proto-charismatics, Quakers, a good number of Moderates and a few judged by others to be heretics. His association with one of the great divides in Scottish ecclesiastical history should not obscure the significance of the way in which he took seriously and influenced people of such diverse religious convictions.

Chalmers' identity as an evangelical has never been in doubt. His contribution to evangelical identity is also significant. He embodied ideals from both the church parties that split at the Scottish Disruption: the socially liberal Evangelicals, and the politically conservative Moderates. His preaching, social concern, parish experiments and interest in Bible societies and missions made him famous in Britain, well known in North America and respected in France. His holistic philosophy and experimental approach to mission were reproduced and expanded by his students, who became missionaries, educationalists and church leaders around the world.

Bibliography

S. J. Brown, *Thomas Chalmers and the Godly Commonwealth in Scotland* (Oxford: Oxford University Press, 1982); A. C. Cheyne, *The Practical and the Pious: Essays on Thomas Chalmers (1780–1847)* (Edinburgh: Saint Andrew Press, 1985); J. Roxborogh, *Thomas Chalmers Enthusiast for Mission: The Christian Good of Scotland and the Rise of the Missionary Movement* (Edinburgh: Rutherford House, 1999); D. F. Wright and G. D. Badcock (eds.), *Disruption to Diversity: Edinburgh Divinity 1846–1966* (Edinburgh: T. & T. Clark, 1996).

J. ROXBOROGH

■ **CHAMBERS, Oswald** (1874–1917), teacher, minister and author, and **Gertrude** ('Biddy') (1883–1966), compiler, were responsible between them for a substantial body of biblical writings, of which one, *My Utmost for His Highest*, has become a devotional classic. Oswald was the eighth of nine children born to Clarence Chambers, a Baptist minister, and his wife, Hannah. Born on 24 July 1874 in Aberdeen, Scotland, Chambers grew up in Perth, where he studied at Sharp's Institution and exhibited an early talent in art.

After his family moved to London, the fifteen-year-old Oswald declared his allegiance to Christ while walking home with his father after hearing Charles Haddon *Spurgeon preach. He joined Rye Lane Baptist Church and became an active participant in Bible classes and evangelistic outreach meetings. Chambers' poems written during this time reveal a sensitive, deeply spiritual young man with a great love for art and music.

After two years of study at London's National Art Training School (later the Royal College of Art), Chambers sensed a call from God to 'strike for the redemption of the aesthetic Kingdom of the soul of man – Music and Art and Poetry'. At the age of twenty-one, he entered the University of Edinburgh for a two-year course in fine art. His curriculum, which included classical archaeology, moral philosophy, logic, ethics and psychology, stimulated his keen mind. In local churches, he feasted on the preaching of Alexander Whyte and George Matheson.

But before completing his course of study, he responded to an even stronger sense of call to study for the ministry.

In February 1897 Chambers left Edinburgh and entered Dunoon Training College near Glasgow, where he studied theology under the principal, Duncan MacGregor, who became Chambers' mentor and great friend. In 1899 Oswald was ordained to the Baptist ministry. Later, he sought and obtained ordination in the Presbyterian Church as well.

At Dunoon, Chambers passed through a four-year period of spiritual crisis. His dark night of the soul ended in November 1901 when, as he stated it: 'By an entire consecration and acceptance of sanctification at the Lord's hands, I was baptized with the Holy Ghost, and unspeakable joy and peace have resulted, ever deepening since.' Chambers never looked back on this spiritual experience with the smug satisfaction of having arrived, but always spoke of it as a new beginning.

During his years at Dunoon, Chambers began an association with the Pentecostal League of Prayer, founded by a prominent London barrister, Reader Harris. The League was 'an interdenominational union of Christian people, who conscious of their own need, would join in prayer: 1. For the filling of the Holy Spirit for all believers; 2. For revival in the Churches; 3. For the spread of Scriptural holiness'. In 1906, after nine years at Dunoon College, Chambers left to teach in Japan at the Tokyo Bible School, founded by Charles and Lettie Cowman. In company with the evangelist Juji Nakada, Chambers travelled to the United States, where he spent six months teaching at God's Bible School in Cincinnati. After reaching Japan, he stayed for a month; then he returned to England in November 1907 to become full-time travelling representative of the League of Prayer.

For the next two and a half years, Chambers travelled throughout Britain, maintaining a prodigious speaking schedule at League meetings and church services, often giving as many as ten addresses a week. His striking vocabulary and riveting delivery on the platform were balanced by his winsome personality and easy going humour in social settings.

In May 1910 Chambers married Gertrude Hobbs, to whom he gave the affectionate nickname 'Biddy'. They spent their honeymoon in the United States, where Oswald spoke at camp meetings as he had during the three previous summers. On their return to Britain, they helped to establish the Bible Training College in London under the auspices of the League of Prayer.

Chambers' experience in Dunoon and at God's Bible School in Cincinnati had given him a vision for a residential college where he could pour himself into men and women who wanted to serve Christ. He once said: 'When people refer to a man as a "man of one book", meaning the Bible, he is generally found to be a man of multitudinous books, which simply isolates the one Book to its proper grandeur. The man who reads only the Bible does not, as a rule, know it or human life.'

During the next four years, Oswald and Biddy gave themselves to a family of twenty-five residential students plus a growing number of day students who came for one or two classes. Chambers also marked papers for some 300 correspondence course students. Biddy, a trained court stenographer, attended Oswald's classes and took verbatim shorthand notes of his lectures. From these, the book *Biblical Psychology* was published by God's Bible School in 1912. *Studies in the Sermon on the Mount* appeared in 1915. On 24 May 1913 Oswald and Biddy's only child Kathleen was born, bringing a new and joyful dimension to the college family.

The outbreak of the First World War in August 1914 led to the closing of the college a year later, when Oswald volunteered for service as a chaplain with the YMCA in Egypt. In October 1915 he took up his duties at Zeitoun Camp just outside Cairo, where he was joined by Biddy, Kathleen and several students from the Bible Training College, who came as civilian volunteers.

To the great surprise of Oswald's superiors, 400 soldiers came to hear his first talk, entitled 'What Is The Good of Prayer?' In Chambers the men sensed a no-nonsense approach to life that was firmly grounded in the Bible and redemption through Jesus Christ. Oswald and Biddy created community with soldiers through their ministry of hospitality. But Chambers refused to use food as bait for the gospel. After every free tea, he dismissed the men, then taught the Bible at a subsequent meeting in an adjacent tent.

In late October 1917 Chambers underwent emergency surgery for a ruptured appendix. Two weeks later, on 15 November, he developed a blood clot in the lungs and died at the age of forty-three. He was buried with full military honours in the British Military Cemetery in Old Cairo.

Biddy and Kathleen, along with several of the Bible Training College students, remained at Zeitoun until the end of the war. A month after Oswald's death, Biddy printed one of his sermons and sent it as a gift to the troops in Egypt. Receiving numerous requests for more, the YMCA began sending 10,000 copies of a different sermon each month to soldiers in Egypt and France. The response led to Biddy's sense of calling to give her husband's words to the world.

After returning to England in 1919, Biddy began to compile and publish books from her notes of Oswald's lectures and sermons. All money received from sales went into the next publication. During this time she supported herself and Kathleen by keeping a boarding house for university students in Oxford, doing her 'work of the books' when she could make time.

In 1927 Biddy published a book of daily readings titled, *My Utmost For His Highest*. It has become an enduring bestseller, has stayed continuously in print and has been translated into more than a dozen languages. The readings come primarily from Oswald's lectures at the Bible Training College from 1911 to 1915, and at Zeitoun from 1915 to 1917. Many readers would echo the words of the late Dr Richard C. Halverson, pastor and former Chaplain of the United States Senate: 'No book except the Bible has influenced my walk with Christ at such deep and maturing levels. Nor has any influenced my preaching and teaching so much. The book's strength lies in its stubborn insistence on the objective reality of redemption as the only secure foundation. Through the years Chambers has kept me on course by bringing me back to Jesus.'

Before Biddy Chambers died in 1966, she had published fifty books bearing Oswald's name but never mentioned her own. He spoke the words; she wrote them down; and the resulting legacy to the world gave credence to Oswald's oft-spoken statement: 'When the heart sees what God wants, the body must be willing to spend and be spent for that cause alone.'

Bibliography

G. H. Chambers, *Oswald Chambers: His Life and Work* (London: Simpkin Marshall, ³1959); D. W. Lambert, *Oswald Chambers: An Unbribed Soul* (London: Marshall, Morgan & Scott, ²1996, and Minneapolis: Bethany House Publishers, ²1997); D. C. McCasland, *Oswald Chambers: Abandoned to God* (Grand Rapids: Discovery House Publishers, 1993).

D. C. McCASLAND

■ **CHARLES, Thomas** (1755–1814), leader of the second generation of Welsh Calvinistic Methodists, was born on 14 October 1755 at Llanfihangel Abercywyn, Carmarthenshire. The son of Rees Charles, a well-to-do farmer, and his wife Jael, and the grandson of David Bowen of Pibwr Lwyd, the sheriff of Carmarthenshire in 1763, he was educated at a village school in Llanddowror before proceeding to the Dissenting academy at Carmarthen in 1769. During his time there he visited Llangeitho, Cardiganshire, and on 20 January 1773, as he listened to Daniel Rowland preach, he was converted. In 1775 he matriculated at Oxford and attended Jesus College. During his college days he came into contact with several evangelicals, among them John *Newton and William Romaine. He graduated BA in 1779.

Ordained deacon on 14 June 1778, two weeks before leaving Oxford, he was appointed the curate of Sparkford, Somerset, in September, having preached his first sermon at Llanfihangel Abercywyn on 16 August. Priested on 21 May 1780, he was given the curacy of South Barrow in September 1782, but by this time he was eager to return to Wales. He left Somerset on 23 June 1783, and on 20 August married Sally Jones, the daughter of a shopkeeper at Bala in north Wales, whom he had met during a visit to the town with a fellow student, Simon Lloyd, in the summer of 1778. Making Bala his home, he encountered difficulty in obtaining a living due to his Methodist tendencies, but in January 1784 he was appointed curate of Llanymawddwy. Due to his support for the Methodists, he was dismissed on 18 April, and thus ended his career as a Church of England clergyman.

Having aligned himself fully with the Methodist cause by joining one of their societies in July, Charles went on to make Bala the centre of their activities in north Wales. Deeply interested in Christian education, he established circulating schools similar to those of Griffith Jones fifty years earlier, and trained teachers to work in them. These schools were, in time, to develop into Sunday schools, and thus to become central to the development of Calvinistic Methodism in this period. Though not the founder of the Sunday school in Wales, Charles more than anyone, through his firm leadership and gift for organization, secured a reliable foundation for it.

Out of his educational activity grew his literary work, which ranged from catechisms for children (1789) to a Bible dictionary (4 vols., 1805, 1808, 1810, 1811) that would provide the Methodist converts with the means to develop their understanding of the Christian faith. To weld the movement together he began publishing a periodical in 1799; *Y Drysorfa Ysbrydol* (The Spiritual Treasury) appeared intermittently until 1827 but was then superseded by *Y Drysorfa*. Among Charles's English-language publications were *A Short Evangelical Catechism* (1801) and *Welsh Methodism Vindicated* (1802).

A shortage of Welsh Bibles at the end of the eighteenth century led Charles to investigate the possibility of providing a cheap edition of the Scriptures for his people. It was as a result of this investigation, and his attendance at the meetings of the Religious Tract Society in London, that the British and Foreign Bible Society was established in 1804. One of its first achievements was to publish a new edition of the Welsh Bible, and Charles was charged with the responsibility of preparing the text and supervising the printing.

Following the expulsion of Nathaniel Rowland for misconduct in 1807, Charles became the foremost Welsh Methodist leader, and it was he who reluctantly led the movement to secede from the Church of England in 1811 by ordaining its own ministers. He therefore represents the transitional period during which Welsh Methodism developed from a Revival movement into a Dissenting denomination; he was amply qualified to undertake the challenge and succeeded in striking a balance between emotion and understanding, and between enthusiasm and organization.

Charles died on 5 October 1814 and was buried at Llanycil church near Bala. His wife died on 24 October. They were survived by two sons, Thomas Rice and David Jones.

Bibliography

D. E. Jenkins, *Life of Thomas Charles*, 3 vols. (Denbigh: Llewelyn Jenkins, 1908); R. T. Jones, *Thomas Charles o'r Bala* (Cardiff: University of Wales Press, 1979).

G. TUDUR

■ **CLARKE, Adam** (c. 1760–1832), Wesleyan Methodist minister and biblical commentator, was born about 1760 at Moybeg, County Londonderry, son of the Revd John Clarke, a minister of the Church of Ireland. John Clarke, a graduate of Glasgow University and Trinity College, Dublin, was a schoolmaster; his wife, a Maclean of Mull, was a Presbyterian who later became a Wesleyan Methodist.

Family poverty and frequent changes of residence perhaps accounted for Clarke's undistinguished career at school, but after a very slow start, he began to develop his considerable intellectual powers. He joined the Methodist society at Coleraine in 1778 and, following a brief spell working with a linen draper, began to preach in June 1782. His superintendent drew him to John *Wesley's attention, and Wesley offered him a place at Kingswood School. Clarke therefore travelled to England in August 1782, but spent only one unhappy month at Kingswood, because Wesley summoned him to Bristol for an interview and appointed him without further training to the Bradford-on-Avon circuit. He was received into full connexion with the Conference in 1783. While in the Bradford circuit Clarke met Mary Cooke of Trowbridge; they married on 17 April 1788. Of their twelve children, six died in infancy or early childhood. Their son, Joseph Butterworth Bulmer Clarke, was ordained in the Church of England in 1825 and died as a prebendary of Wells Cathedral.

The demands of Wesleyan itinerancy took

Clarke to Norwich (1783), east Cornwall (1784), Plymouth (1785) and the Channel Islands (1786–1789). Thereafter, apart from one year in Dublin (1790–1791), Clarke's appointments revolved around the major Methodist centres of Bristol, Manchester, Liverpool and London. He served in London from 1795 to 1798 and then from 1805 to 1815, before moving to Millbrook, near Liverpool, for seven years. The last ten years of his life were spent at Haydon Hall, Pinner. In later life, through his books and his wife's inheritance, Clarke achieved a measure of prosperity and an established social position, numbering the Duke of Sussex among his acquaintances.

As a circuit minister, Clarke was a conscientious pastor and an effective preacher. During his first appointment in London he estimated that he walked 7,000 miles in three years fulfilling his pastoral duties. He preached without notes, drawing on his wide reading, and a regular listener recalled that he seldom repeated a sermon. The effect of his oratory was 'overwhelming'; his sermons were expository, concentrating on the love of God and the challenge of the gospel. Clarke valued the Methodist discipline of the class meeting, enrolling himself in a class as a private member. He regularly added 'Mind your class' as a postscript to his letters, and his advice to young preachers included the exhortation 'Be much in private prayer; shun tea-drinking visits, rise early ... preach a full salvation, exhort those who are justified to look for all deliverance from sin now.'

In the Wesleyan connexion Clarke was a prominent, if controversial, figure. He was elected president of the Conference three times (1806, 1814 and 1822). He worked to establish the Preachers' Annuitant Society on a firm legal basis, and advocated the provision of accommodation for superannuated preachers and ministers' widows. He canvassed support for the theological training of Wesleyan preachers several decades before the connexion established its Theological Institution. In the controversy over Wesleyanism's evolving relationship with the Church of England in the years after Wesley's death, Clarke was involved in the abortive quasi-episcopal 'Lichfield Plan' of 1794 and opposed Joseph Benson and the Bristol 'Church' Methodists. Nearly twenty years later his initially positive response to Lord Sidmouth's proposals to restrict the activities of dissenting preachers was such as to provoke the judgment of a recent historian that Clarke 'combined massive theological learning with political naivety'. His relationship with Jabez *Bunting was sometimes strained: Clarke disagreed privately with Bunting over the Leeds organ controversy of 1827, and his establishment of schools in Ireland outside the control of the British Conference was officially censured in 1831. It would seem that Clarke was made supernumerary against his express wishes by the 1831 Conference. He died of cholera in London on 27 August 1832.

Clarke's massive erudition developed alongside his circuit ministry. He began studying Hebrew in his first circuit, encouraged by Wesley. In Plymouth he was lent a copy of Kennicott's recently published edition of the Hebrew Bible, and during his years in Plymouth and the Channel Islands he expanded his linguistic range to include Syriac, later adding Arabic, Persian and a reading acquaintance with Ethiopic and Coptic. It was estimated that by the end of his life he knew twenty languages or dialects, and his gifts were put to good use by the Bible Society, which petitioned the Wesleyan Conference in 1807 to allow Clarke to extend his stay in London to assist the Society's work. Clarke's depth and breadth of scholarship was acknowledged by membership of many learned societies, including the Antiquarian Society, the Royal Irish Academy and the Geological Society, and by the award of MA (1807) and LLD (1808) degrees by the University of Aberdeen. In 1808 Clarke was appointed by the Public Records Commission to revise Thomas Rymer's *Foedera*, a twenty-volume collection of state papers published in the early eighteenth century. Clarke worked on the collection, codification and editing of documents for ten years, publishing two volumes in 1818 before relinquishing the task. In addition to his literary and linguistic abilities, he was also interested in chemistry, mineralogy, astronomy and alchemy, and he had the practical skill to mend a pair of shoes, dismantle, repair and reassemble a watch, and build a haystack.

Clarke's publications were extensive, including a six-volume bibliographical dictionary

(1802–1804) and his *Memoirs of the Wesley Family* (1823). His major work, however, was an eight-volume commentary on the Bible, which he began in May 1798 and completed in March 1825. Clarke hoped that the *Commentary* would be published by the Wesleyan Book Room and be endorsed by the Conference, but when this did not take place, he arranged for publication in instalments by his brother-in-law, the law publisher and Methodist MP Joseph Butterworth. This delayed the appearance of the first volume until 1810. Besides his knowledge of biblical languages, Clarke also demonstrated considerable critical acumen as a commentator. His awareness of the importance of internal evidence, seen, for example, in his discussion of the authorship of the Psalms, anticipated later critical scholarship, and was in clear distinction to the approach of his contemporaries. Clarke's methodology, however, attracted far less attention than his suggestion that the tempter in the Garden of Eden was a baboon or orang-utan, rather than a serpent, while his long-standing and privately held denial of the eternal sonship of Christ, now reflected in print in his remarks on Luke 1:35, drew critical responses in the connexion and provoked a magisterial reply from Richard *Watson.

Bibliography

M. L. Edwards, *Adam Clarke* (London: Epworth Press, 1942); J. W. Etheridge, *The Life of the Revd Adam Clarke, LL.D., F.A.S., M.R.I.A., etc.* (London: John Mason, ²1858); N. W. Taggart, *The Irish in World Methodism 1760–1900* (London: Epworth Press, 1986).

M. WELLINGS

■ **CLARKSON, E. Margaret** (1915–), Canadian hymn-writer and author, was described by Donald P. Hustad, scanning the twentieth-century North American scene, as 'our one outstanding hymnist, in the classical sense of that term, because of both the quantity and the quality of her writing'. Although born in Saskatchewan on a hopeful but brief family foray to the west, she was the embodiment of the traditional, dominant culture of southern Ontario. With a Protestant Ulster Irish father and a mother of Scottish descent,

she settled happily in Toronto when the family returned there. From her earliest years she revelled in poetry, music and prose, and this natural inclination was given a Christian direction through the family's regular attendance at St John's Presbyterian Church. Here she delighted in the singing, the organ, the choir and the Book of Praise of the Presbyterian Church in Canada, which she frequently read as a child when the sermons seemed tedious, and of which she memorized many parts. At St John's the foundations of her Christian life, which are evident in everything she wrote, were laid through the expository sermons, her memorizing of the entire Westminster Shorter Catechism, and the missionary vision of John McPherson Scott, with his special concern for the Jewish people (his memorial is the inner-city Scott Mission). And it was here that she absorbed much of the best of British evangelical hymnology from the eighteenth and nineteenth centuries.

In one of her books, *Grace Grows Best in Winter*, Clarkson has a page of sources and acknowledgments, on which are listed the models of her hymnody and Christian prose. She recognizes a few medieval figures, acknowledging like many thoughtful evangelicals some common elements of spirituality, in spite of doctrinal disagreement. She does not mention the sixteenth-century Reformers, with their heavy theological tomes, but assumes that the essence of their work has been transmitted in simplified form by subsequent Protestant generations. She includes a few references to such seventeenth-century giants as *Milton, *Rutherford and *Bunyan, but from the Evangelical Awakening of the eighteenth century there are more names, including Tersteegen and *Watts, Charles *Wesley, John *Newton and Augustus Toplady. From the nineteenth century she lists even more, such as James Montgomery, H. F. Lyte, Horatius *Bonar and W. W. How, Ann Cousin, Anna Waring, Frances Ridley *Havergal, and the American, Fanny *Crosby, whose style was as close to that of the gospel song as Clarkson was prepared to go. Hymnology is broader than ideology, so Clarkson recognizes writers in the Catholic tradition such as H. W. Myers, F. W. Faber and Christina Rossetti. These influences prepared her for her work and stimulated her to write. At the age of ten she submitted a poem to Toronto's *Evangelical Christian*, which to the consternation of her family was published. Throughout her schooldays she continued to write Christian poetry, and at least a few of her poems were published. Others, years later, would be reworked into hymns.

When Clarkson was twelve a culture war began in St John's. A large number of young Irish immigrants had arrived in the east end of Toronto during the 1920s, seeking to escape the upheaval accompanying the partition of their homeland. Many found their way to St John's, a number bringing the eager faith of those touched by the contemporary Ulster revival. Their enthusiasm, premillennialism and enjoyment of the newest gospel songs seemed like extremism to some, and as a result the church was divided. The Clarksons followed the new minister, Mr Nisbet, and joined the new congregation, which came to be known as Calvary Church. Although Clarkson did not particularly enjoy the more populist worship, she found herself in a vital movement that kept her traditional evangelical theology and spirituality alive, at a time when many of her generation were diluting or abandoning them altogether. It also helped to prepare her for some difficult years ahead.

In 1935 this very introverted person was driven into isolation, as the only teaching position that she could find in the depth of the Depression was in the logging hamlet of Barwick in the Rainy River Valley of far north-western Ontario. After two years she moved to the larger but even more isolated mining community of Kirkland Lake, 400 miles north of Toronto. Amid the lack of biblical preaching, vital worship and Christian fellowship, she was forced to take responsibility for her own spiritual life, and found it being renewed. Much of what she wrote at this time testified to the greatness, sovereignty and grace of God in appropriate and beautiful words. Two themes seem to have been predominant in her work: faith and assurance, and the glory of the first advent.

Clarkson returned to Toronto in 1942. Although arthritis and migraine often restricted her activity, she received there some much-needed encouragement. Stacey *Woods and the Inter-Varsity Christian Fellowship was a source of understanding support, as was William Fitch and the congregation of Knox Presbyterian Church, and A. W. *Tozer

of the Avenue Road Church of the Christian and Missionary Alliance. It was in this environment that her first widely known hymn was written. Asked to write a hymn that could be used at the first IVCF missionary conference (the precursor of Urbana), which was held in Toronto, she composed 'We Come, O Christ, to Thee'. This was the first of her missionary hymns, which would eventually comprise one-quarter of her hymn corpus. During the next decade or so, despite all the demands of her teaching career, she produced about one hymn a year: a children's song (e.g. 'I Set My Life by God's Great Clock'), a communion hymn (e.g. 'Savior, I Seek Your Face'), an anticipation of the second advent (e.g. 'Rejoice, Rejoice, for Our King Shall Come') or frequently, a missionary hymn (e.g. 'So Send I You').

In the early 1960s Clarkson reached her peak, publishing five hymns in 1963 and nine in 1964, including 'Sing Praise to the Father, Creator and King', but the later 1960s, in which she struggled with increasing ill health and other pressures, were largely fruitless, save for 'One is the Race of Mankind', sung at the World Congress on Evangelism in Berlin in 1966. Early retirement in 1972, however, unleashed a new burst of creativity. For the Lausanne Congress on World Evangelization in 1974, she wrote 'Praise the Lord, Sing Hallelujah'; for Urbana '73, 'Lord of the Universe, Hope of the World'; for Urbana '76, 'Our God is Mighty'; for Urbana '79, 'Proclaim the Savior's Name'; and for the General Assembly of the World Council of Churches in Vancouver in 1983, 'Lord Jesus, Life of All the World'. 'Regents of Our Lord and Savior' was written for Regent College, Vancouver in 1979, and 'God of the Ages', written for a *Christianity Today* hymn competition in 1981, was adopted by Tyndale College and Seminary in Toronto in 1994 for their hundredth anniversary. And after all this she wrote some eighteen hymns between 1984 and 1990, including 'Ours Is a Living Lord'.

In addition to hymns Clarkson also wrote seventeen books, some of which have been translated into up to eight languages. Two are for parents and children: *Suzie's Babies* (Eerdmans, 1960), which uses a classroom hamster to explain reproduction, and which went through many printings; and *Growing*

Up (Eerdmans, 1962), for slightly older children, dealing with the issue of maturity. Two address the subject of suffering: *Grace Grows Best in Winter* (Zondervan, 1972; repr. Eerdmans, 1984), which includes no references to psychology or the social sciences, but which quickly went through four printings; and *Destined for Glory: The Meaning of Suffering* (Eerdmans, 1983). In 1987 Clarkson produced *A Singing Heart* (Hope Publishing), which contained the text of all her hymns published up to that point, with a number of illuminating biographical fragments. Subsequently she has published a few more hymns, bringing to a close a remarkable Christian literary career of some sixty-five years.

I. S. RENNIE

■ **CLIFFORD, John** (1836–1923), Baptist pastor, writer and campaigner for religious freedom, has been labelled by several authors 'an ardent evangelical', though one who exercised a liberalizing influence among his fellow Baptists. Similarly his principal biographer judges that 'For sixty years he held high place in the Evangelical movement' (Marchant: xii), and he is recorded as happy to be associated with the work of the Evangelical Alliance. Absolutely committed to personal evangelism, he also believed that there was necessarily a social dimension to Christian commitment and that integrity of mind involved new accommodations of both scientific understanding and critical method.

In many respects Clifford represented the opposite extreme within the Baptist denomination to that represented by *Spurgeon, yet it is important to recognize that there was no personal antipathy between the two men. Authoritative sources have indicated that Spurgeon declined to rank Clifford among Baptist heretics, while Clifford testifies to Spurgeon, saying to him in an interview in January 1888, 'As you know, we differ but we hold vital evangelical truth in common: still I do not like your last book.'

Clifford was the most articulate of the New Connexion General Baptists, who were Arminian in theology and born out of the experience of the Methodist revival, rather than out of the systematics of an older Puritanism. Clifford focused their position in what

became known as his three universals: 'the universality of the love of God to man, the universality of the redeeming work of the Son, and the universality of the convincing work of the Spirit'. Not surprisingly, Clifford was seen as the champion of this tradition by Particular Baptists, notwithstanding the fact that Marchant claims that John's father was 'a stern man, a hard disciplinarian, a Chartist and a Calvinist', and his New Connexion mother as of 'Puritan stock'. Clifford himself contradicts this by suggesting that his father's family was Methodist and his mother's Baptist; 'Baptist' of course meant East Midland New Connexion General Baptist.

Committed throughout his life to the evangelistic imperative ('Our first business is to make men see Christ'), it was in fact during a debate on this topic, in which Clifford had intended speaking, that he died at Baptist Church House on 20 November 1923. At the end of his life he confessed, 'Christ has been to me the centre of intellectual repose, as well as the guide and inspiration of my life, my Saviour and Master, Leader and Companion, Brother and Lord': however, 'with his centre so firmly fixed in Christ, Clifford's circumference could be wide'.

While Spurgeon's background was in rural Essex, Clifford's background was in the embryonic lace factories on the borders of Derbyshire, Nottinghamshire and Leicestershire, in which from the age of eleven he, following his father, experienced long hours of monotonous factory employment. Born at Sawley, Derbyshire, on 16 October 1836, his earliest associations were with the General Baptist New Connexion Chapel there, at whose day school he began his education. All three of his mother's brothers were New Connexion ministers, one serving as minister/schoolmaster in Sawley. Within a few years the Cliffords moved to Beeston on the outskirts of Nottingham, where again they associated with the New Connexion Chapel, though John attended first a Wesleyan School, then a Baptist School at Lenton, and finally the National School in Beeston. In November 1850 he experienced conversion, which he described in the Bunyanesque language of securing freedom from a great burden of guilt and misery: 'the fetters seemed to be broken by one stroke'. Assured of forgiveness, seven months later he was baptized at Beeston by the Revd Richard Pike and saw the ceremony as essentially his personal witness to commitment to the service of Christ in full dependence upon God. His call to the ministry was followed by study at the Midland Baptist College, first in Leicester but then in Nottingham.

During the early years of his only pastorate, at Praed Street, Paddington (subsequently Westbourne Park), London, Clifford successfully completed his studies in arts, science and law through London University (BA, Classics, 1861; BSc, Geology, 1864; MA, 1864; LLB, 1866; Hon DD, Bates, 1883, Chicago, 1911). Of the new church erected in 1877, he argued that it was not erected merely for worship or the administration of the sacraments but mainly 'as a meeting place, drill ground and working centre of a community of men "whose heart the Lord has touched", and who will be better themselves as Christian men and citizens, and do better work in the world by means of their fellowship in the Gospel of Christ'. Under Clifford's leadership such aspirations were abundantly fulfilled in the large, intelligent and influential membership of Westbourne Park.

Clifford's *The Inspiration and Authority of the Bible*, first published in 1892, sought to show guarded evangelical openness to reverent criticism, over against theories of verbal inspiration. Thus he wrote, 'We cannot suffer the Redeemer to be deposed from His throne in favour of the late and post-Reformation dogma which lifts the letter of Scripture into the position of inerrancy claimed for the Pope.' Whatever Clifford's intention, the book provoked a conservative reaction in the foundation of a Bible League to defend Scripture against what it took to be new views of inspiration, infallibility and the sole sufficiency of the word of God, which courted support from what Bebbington calls 'the Baptist fringe, around Spurgeon and the boundary with undenominational revivalism'.

Clifford first used the language of 'social gospel' as a campaigning slogan in addressing the Baptist Union in 1888. Later he was to write tracts for the Fabians, arguing on the basis of a theology of the kingdom of God for the urgency of social involvement. While this argument represented an expansion of the horizons of many Nonconformists, it did not detach them from their evangelical roots. For Clifford, sacred was not to be separated from secular; rather, he saw God's sovereignty extended over the whole realm of human activity, acknowledging that every social problem had a spiritual dimension. Some of these problems (e.g. drunkenness) called for stronger personal discipline, but this had to be accompanied by structural change in the fabric of society, which required government action. Nevertheless the church was not to be taken over by socialist utopianism: political change could do so much for humankind but could never do all that was needed. Evangelicalism's influence, however, should not be impaired by its having to 'run in blinkers'.

Clifford's contribution to national life is to be found within the annals of the Liberal Party, which he saw as the most viable political instrument for the exercise of the Nonconformist Conscience, in terms of both a moral policy abroad and issues of social purity at home. The latter included both matters of policy and the behaviour of those elected to political leadership; Nonconformist influence worked in favour of Gladstone but against Dilke and Parnell. Clifford's name will always be associated with Nonconformist hostility to rate-supported confessional education, and in particular with the leadership of the Passive Resistance movement to the payment of the educational rate for this purpose.

Clifford insisted that the gospel imperative concerning redemption of the individual was not to be compromised. Critical of theologians who thought they could exhaust the meaning of the atonement in wordy definitions, worked out in their 'verbal controversies and creed-fights', he nevertheless rejoiced in 'the free and full pardon it offers and the hope it creates'. Anti-sacramentalist and espousing only a modest ecclesiology, Clifford clearly stood in the believers' church tradition: 'the possession of the regenerate life is the indispensable condition of admission to the privileges of Church membership'.

Clifford believed that the churches' reticence in evangelism, which he could barely comprehend, shamed them and contributed to their failure to make a significant impact on outsiders. He challenged the Free Churches through the National Free Church Council to a campaign for a revived sense of individual responsibility for evangelism. For its part the Council had, from 1897, been employing

Gypsy Smith as its full-time missioner. Clifford soon became one of Smith's close collaborators in united Free Church missions up and down the country, including the very important Simultaneous Mission of 1901, first in London and then in the provinces. In 1921, in the context of post-war uncertainty, Clifford was even more convinced of the importance of personal evangelism and set up a Free Church campaign to this end. To ensure its success he lobbied and cajoled with articles, pamphlets, letters to every Free Church minister in the country, attendance at conferences and diligent committee work, even though he was by now over eighty, with fragile health and defective sight. Forbidden by his doctors to attend the National Free Church Council Conference in Liverpool in 1922, he nevertheless sent a message on 'The Aims of Personal Evangelism'. Not opposed to mass (or what he called 'shaking the tree') evangelism, he championed personal (hand-picking) evangelism, because he believed it had a profound impact not only upon the spirituality of those evangelized but also upon that of the would-be evangelist, spelling out to him or her the very essence of Christian discipleship.

Created one of the first Companions of Honour in 1921, Clifford was a prolific writer of more than seventy books, including *The Attitude of Men of Science to Christianity* (1874), *The Future of Christianity* (1876), *Socialism and the Teaching of Christ* (1884), *Christianity, the True Socialism* (1885), *The Inspiration and Authority of the Bible* (1892) and *God's Greater Britain* (1899). From 1869 he was for some fifteen years the lively editor of *The General Baptist Magazine*, which gave him wide influence throughout the connexion, from which position of advantage he campaigned successfully for the full integration of the work of the New Connexion with that of the Particular Baptists within the life of the Baptist Union.

Bibliography

Baptist Handbook (London: Baptist Union, 1925); C. T. Bateman, *John Clifford, Free Church Leader and Preacher* (London: National Council of the Evangelical Churches, 1904); Sir J. Marchant, *Dr John Clifford, C. H., Life, Letters and Reminiscences* (London: Cassell, 1924); G. W. Byrt, *John Clifford, A Fighting Free Churchman* (London: Kingsgate Press, 1947); M. R. Watts, 'John Clifford and Radical Nonconformity, 1836–1923' (DPhil thesis, Oxford University, 1966); D. Thompson, 'John Clifford's Social Gospel', *Baptist Quarterly* (January 1986), pp. 199–217.

J. H. Y. BRIGGS

■ **COGGAN, Frederick Donald** (1909–2000), Anglican archbishop and academic, was an international figure as leader of the Anglican Communion, spoke on radio and television, and faced, as churchman and unwilling politician, the social changes of the 1960s and 1970s that affected Anglicans in Britain and the rest of the world.

Coggan was born in Highgate, north London, on 9 October 1909. His father, Cornish Arthur Coggan, was a successful businessman and local politician and, although he was frequently away from home, his conservative evangelicalism had a profound effect on the future archbishop; what observers describe as Coggan's 'austere and dour evangelicalism' and 'puritanical streak' were characteristics of his father. Coggan was not, however, an exact copy of his father; he was called 'the layman's archbishop' because of his 'kindness, charm, warmth and humility', and many British Anglicans believed that his hope and confidence in the face of the malaise caused by problems such as workers' strikes, inflation, and violence in Northern Ireland strengthened the morale of the Church of England at a time when other institutions of society provided little hope.

Prior to 1956 Coggan was an academic, teacher and administrator. He received a BA from St John's College, Cambridge, in 1931 (taking a double first in oriental languages) and an MA in 1935; he won seven awards for his undergraduate work, including the Jeremie Septuagint, Tyrwhitt and Mason prizes in Hebrew. In 1931 Manchester University offered Coggan an assistant lectureship in Semitic languages and literature, and he held that position until 1934. From 1934 to 1937 he was a curate at St Mary's, Islington, London; this role gave him his only experience of parish ministry. In 1936 Coggan was invited by Moore College, Sydney, to become the vice-principal and by Wycliffe College,

Toronto, to become Professor of New Testament; he turned down the first offer and accepted the second on the understanding that he would not take the position until 1937. Coggan remained at Wycliffe until 1944, obtaining a BD from there in 1941 so that he would be better prepared to teach theology (and an honorary DD in 1944). Then he was invited to become the principal of the London College of Divinity, where he remained until 1956.

Coggan's appointment to the see of Bradford on 25 October 1955 marked a definitive and substantial change in his career; even though he was later pro-chancellor of two universities, York (1962–1974) and Hull (1968–1974), received seventeen honorary doctoral degrees and was made honorary fellow at St John's (1961) and King's College, London (1975), he was from then onwards a bishop first and an academic second. Coggan's success in revitalizing the clergy, reordering the services and raising money for church buildings in the diocese led to his appointment as Archbishop of York; a mere five years after his consecration as a bishop on 25 January 1956, he was enthroned as a primate and metropolitan on 13 September 1961. The announcement of Coggan's appointment as the 101st Archbishop of Canterbury on 14 May 1974 was a surprise in that he was a mere five years younger than his predecessor Michael Ramsey and so, many Anglicans assumed, would be simply a caretaker. Harold Wilson, however, believed that no-one was better qualified for the task.

Although commentators have noted Coggan's 'naïve approach' to national and international problems (he frequently identified the cause of political and social problems as moral, a lapse in individual and personal spirituality), his capacity for hard work and his ability to pursue an objective energetically resulted in several important changes during his archiepiscopates in the operation of the Church of England. Although most of the credit should go to Ramsey, the unity of the archbishops on the creation of General Synod (1970) and the ministry of women, as seen in the correspondence between them, made synodical government and the ordination of women almost inevitable. (Women's ordination to the priesthood was not approved until 1992, but Coggan probably supported it from 1929, when he witnessed Catherine Booth-Clibborn leading an evangelistic mission in Cambridge.) Coggan was a central figure in the creation of the Crown Appointments Commission (1976), a body that gave the church a much larger involvement in the process of choosing bishops, and in the completion of the Alternative Service Book (1980), which, according to The Times, created a liturgy 'biblical and essentially traditional but in language modern and untheatrical, just as he was'.

Partly due to his time spent in Canada, but also because of his belief in the importance of worldwide evangelism, Coggan brought an international perspective to his work as a bishop. He became an executive member of the Church Missionary Society in 1956 and travelled extensively on its behalf; he did the same for the Church Army and, in recognition of his efforts, the society made him its first life president in 1981. Coggan's Who's Who entry lists travel and motoring as hobbies; while Archbishop of York, he travelled to all five continents at least twice and had ample opportunity to indulge his hobby until his retirement. Coggan's involvement with and then leadership of the Anglican Consultative Council, the Anglican Primates and the Lambeth Conferences of 1968 and 1978 demonstrate the importance he placed on the development and stability of the Anglican Communion.

Coggan's influence was not limited to the Church of England or the Anglican Communion. Perhaps his greatest contribution to Christianity was as chairman of the Joint Committee on the New Translation of the Bible; Coggan was the third chairman and, though no-one could have complained if he had resigned the position when he became Bishop of Bradford, he saw the project through to its completion in the New English Bible (1970). Coggan was also interested in the distribution of Bibles throughout the world; he became a vice-president of the United Bible Societies in 1956 and a president in 1973.

The key to understanding Coggan was his evangelicalism. His evangelical faith was the foundation of his writing, preaching and life; as he said on more than one occasion, he was proud to be called an evangelical. At Cambridge, Coggan was 'an enthusiastic member' and officer of the evangelical Cambridge Inter-Collegiate Christian Union, and the first book published under his name, *Christ and the Colleges* (1934), was a history of the Inter-Varsity Fellowship, an evangelical society for university students. The only full-length biography Coggan wrote, *Cuthbert Bardsley: Bishop, Evangelist, Pastor* (1989), was of a like-minded evangelical and friend who, with Coggan's help, persuaded Archbishop Ramsey to create the Archbishops' Council on Evangelism. Although a brilliant linguist, Coggan generally ignored academic questions in his preaching and writing; his injunction to readers of the commentary *Psalms 73–150* (1999) that they should not look for logic but 'listen for a heartbeat' is typical of his approach. In his life, service to God was paramount, and he famously called himself 'a slave of Christ'. In his enthronement sermon on 24 January 1975 he called for more people to put themselves forward for ordination.

Coggan's interest in evangelism (the energy he put into planning for the first 'Decade of Evangelism', a nationwide series of locally based evangelistic projects in the 1990s, was typical) and his concern that Christianity should appeal to ordinary people is reflected in his published works. *Paul: Portrait of a Revolutionary* (1984) may be the closest to an academic work, though *These Were His Gifts: A Trio of Christian Leaders* (1974), the Bishop John Prideaux Lectures, and *Mission to the World: the Chavasse Memorial Lectures 1981* resulted from lectures given in an academic setting. Coggan's comment in *Five Makers of the New Testament* (1962) 'that we cannot do enough to help those people, clerical and lay, who week by week, in pulpit and in classes of various kinds, set themselves to the task of teaching and evangelism' is the principle underpinning *Preaching: An Essay in Co-operation* (1963), *Sinews of Faith* (1969), *The Heart of the Christian Faith* (1986) and *The Servant-Son, Jesus Then and Now* (1995).

Coggan announced his resignation on 5 June 1979 and retired on 25 January 1980. He received a life peerage at this time (he was already a Privy Counsellor [1961]) and became Lord Coggan of Canterbury and Sissinghurst. He continued to write and travel; his retirement was quiet only in the sense that he was no longer on the national stage. He and his wife Jean, whom he had married on 17 September 1935, became involved in various activities, including those of the local retired people's association, and had more opportunities to see their daughters, Ruth and Ann. Coggan died in Winchester on 17 May 2000.

Bibliography

M. Pawley, *Donald Coggan: Servant of Christ* (London: SPCK, 1987).

K. A. FRANCIS

■ **COKE, Thomas** (1747–1814), Anglican clergyman, American Methodist bishop and missionary pioneer, was born at Brecon on 28 September 1747, the third but only surviving son of Bartholomew and Anne Coke. There were several clergymen in Coke's family tree; his father was an apothecary. Coke was educated at Christ College, Brecon, proceeding to Jesus College, Oxford, as a gentleman commoner in April 1764. He subsequently graduated as BA (1768), MA (1770) and DCL (1775). Converted from deist sympathies by reading Bishop Sherlock's *Trial of the Witnesses of Jesus*, Coke was ordained deacon in 1770 and priest in 1772, serving as curate at South Petherton from 1771 until 1777. Coke progressed from being an earnest and conscientious curate into a supporter of Methodism through reading *Alleine's Alarm to the Unconverted and the works of John *Wesley and John *Fletcher. He first met Wesley in August 1776 and was urged to persevere with his parochial duties, but local opposition drove him from South Petherton the following Easter. He became a Methodist preacher and trusted assistant to Wesley, a role which provoked a measure of suspicion and hostility from older and well-established figures in the connexion, including Charles *Wesley. Coke's legal expertise was important in the drafting of the 1784 Deed of Declaration, which defined the Wesleyan Conference as the connexion's governing body after Wesley's death.

Coke's long association with America began in September 1784 when, in a decisive break with Anglican usage, Wesley ordained him as 'superintendent' of the growing Methodist work in the newly independent

United States. Coke travelled there nine times between 1784 and 1804. On his first visit, he met the American preachers at the 'Christmas' Conference at Baltimore, which organized the Methodist Episcopal Church, and ordained Francis *Asbury as fellow-superintendent. The title 'bishop' was adopted four years later, to Wesley's dismay. Coke's attempts to discharge his responsibilities in America while maintaining an active involvement in British Methodism led to strained relations with Asbury and the American preachers, and ultimately proved impossible to sustain.

Coke was in the United States when Wesley died in 1791. Contemporary and later critics alleged that he hoped to take Wesley's place in the connexion, and that these hopes were dashed by the refusal of the Irish and British Conferences to elect him to the presidency. Although Coke's social standing as an ordained clergyman and the holder of an Oxford DCL tended to encourage him to assume a position of leadership, which in turn fostered resentment among his colleagues, the persistent charge of personal ambition is not borne out by his actions. He held office as secretary of the Conference for much of the period 1791–1813, and was elected president in 1797 and 1805. He also played a full part in the debates about the emerging polity of Wesleyanism, proposing the abortive quasi-episcopal 'Lichfield Plan' in 1794 and drafting the 1795 Plan of Pacification which resolved disputes about the administration of the Lord's Supper by Wesleyan preachers. In 1811 Coke and Adam *Clarke were consulted by Lord Sidmouth over his proposals to restrict the activities of dissenting preachers; although they were persuaded of Sidmouth's good intentions, others in the connexion saw the potential threat to the structure of Methodism inherent in the legislation.

In addition to his ministry in America, Coke was the earliest and most persistent advocate of Methodist overseas missions. His first proposals were put forward in 1783–1784. In 1786 he secured support for work in the West Indies, America, the Channel Islands and northern Scotland. He was an assiduous fundraiser for the cause of missions, and from 1798 was officially designated superintendent of the missions. His plan to extend Methodist work to the East Indies led to his persuading the Conference to

sanction an expedition to India in 1813. Coke led the party, but died at sea during the voyage east on 4 May 1814.

In addition to various sermons, pamphlets and extracts from his journals, Coke published *A Commentary on the Holy Bible* in six volumes between 1801 and 1807. This production, based almost entirely on the work of other scholars, was stigmatized by Adam Clarke as 'no great task even for a blockhead'.

Coke was married twice, first in 1805 to Penelope Goulding Smith, who died in 1811, and secondly later in the same year, to Anne Loxdale, who died in 1812.

Bibliography

J. Vickers, *Thomas Coke: Apostle of Methodism* (London: Epworth Press, 1969).

M. WELLINGS

■ **COLSON, Charles Wendell** (1931–), American Baptist prison evangelist, reformer and author, was born in Boston, Massachusetts, the son of a comfortably middle-class, Episcopalian family. Educated in private schools, he graduated from Brown University in 1953 and married Nancy Billings; the couple had a son and a daughter. Colson spent the following two years in the United States Marine Corps, where he attained the rank of captain.

Following his discharge, Colson spent a year working for the Assistant Secretary of the Navy, and in 1956 became the youngest administrative assistant on Capitol Hill when he joined the staff of Massachusetts Republican Senator Leverett Saltonstall. While working for Saltonstall, Colson began legal studies at George Washington University, receiving the JD with honours in 1959. He remained on Saltonstall's staff until 1961, when he joined the Boston law firm of Gadsby and Hannah. Colson quickly became a partner in the firm, winning a reputation as a tough, win-at-all-costs attorney. In 1964, following a lengthy separation, he divorced his wife of eleven years and married Patricia Ann Hughes; the couple later had one son. Throughout this period, Colson cultivated a number of friendships and connections within the upper reaches of the Republican Party. He was rewarded in 1968 by being named as a member of Republican presidential candidate

Richard M. Nixon's 'Key Issue' committee. After Nixon narrowly won the election, he appointed Colson to the position of special counsel to the president. In this position Colson gave advice to the president on the political ramifications of various policies and decisions as well as being given special oversight to track the actions of designated political opponents on the notorious 'White House Enemies List'. As the 'hatchet man' for Nixon's 'dirty tricks' he soon won a reputation as a ruthless, unscrupulous political opponent. Colson's attitude was best characterized in his own famous admission 'I would walk over my grandmother if it would reassure the re-election of the President.' As part of the effort to re-elect Nixon in 1972, Colson attempted to discredit Daniel Ellsberg, a former member of the Defense Department staff who had leaked the infamous 'Pentagon Papers' to the *New York Times* and the *Washington Post*, by ordering a break-in to his psychiatrist's office. He also helped to organize the special 'Plumber's Unit' involved in the ill-fated burglary of the office of the Democratic National Committee at the Watergate building in Washington in June 1972.

As pressure began to build upon the Nixon administration, Colson resigned as special counsel in March 1973, opting to become a senior partner in his own Washington firm of Colson and Shapiro. Increasingly, however, Colson was plagued by his own conscience and was deeply dissatisfied with the man he had become. During that summer he was counselled by an acquaintance who had become a convinced Christian. Greatly influenced by a reading of C. S. Lewis's *Mere Christianity*, Colson underwent a conversion experience in August 1973. Immediately he began to tell others of the change in his life and his new Christian perspective. Seeking to be reconciled with former political enemies, Colson was taken under the wing of a Capitol Hill-based Christian prayer group that included members of both parties.

When news leaked out about Colson's religious commitment the story was greeted with a mixture of ridicule and disbelief. Many sceptical members of the Washington press corps believed that it was nothing more than a brilliant Colson dodge to avoid, or minimalize, pending legal actions connected to his involvement with the Nixon White House. In a number of interviews in the press and for television (often accompanied by Democratic Iowa Senator Harold Hughes, a devout evangelical and former political enemy) Colson insisted on the reality of his new-found faith before a wide public audience. In March 1974 he was indicted on counts related to both the Watergate and the Ellsberg break-ins. After a plea-bargain through which the Watergate charges were dropped, Colson was found guilty in June 1974 on one count of conspiracy to violate civil rights in the Ellsberg case, fined, and sentenced to one to three years in prison.

Colson's entry into Maxwell Federal Prison in Alabama in July 1974 inadvertently launched him into a career in Christian ministry. Appalled by the conditions and the dehumanizing effect of incarceration upon prisoners, Colson resolved to do something to address the situation. After serving seven months of his sentence, Colson was released in January 1975. Later that year he formed Prison Fellowship, which sought to evangelize prisoners and their families and to seek ways to promote a more just and humane prison system.

In 1976 Colson's autobiography, *Born Again*, was published, which detailed his rise to political power, his conversion and his discoveries about the deleterious characteristics of the prison system. A bestseller in both Christian and secular bookstores (sales of more than two million copies) it was made into a full-length feature film in 1978. Overnight, the book made Prison Fellowship well known within evangelical circles and gave credence to Colson as a bold new spokesman for the conservative, evangelical movement. Coupled with the election of the self-confessed 'born again' Democrat Jimmy *Carter as president, Colson's book made 1976, in the terms of *Newsweek* magazine, 'The Year of the Evangelical'.

During the rest of the 1970s and the early 1980s Colson threw most of his efforts into Prison Fellowship, quickly turning it into the largest and most visible prison ministry in the United States. One of his major emphases was on the need for Prison Fellowship to serve as an agent of reconciliation among offenders, within their families, and between felons and their victims and communities. Additionally, the organization worked with local, state and federal law enforcement and legal officials to institute, when practical, programmes based on the biblical principle of restitution. Besides evangelistic and discipleship programmes for prisoners, Prison Fellowship also organized programmes that dealt with the stresses of prison life, as well as educational and developmental programmes that helped inmates to ready themselves for life outside prison, including classes in job and interviewing skills, and marriage and parenting. Prison Fellowship estimated that in 2000 it held approximately 2,300 in-prison seminars involving over 80,000 prisoners, while over 100,000 enrolled in the regular weekly Bible studies it sponsored. In addition to its seminars and training, Prison Fellowship also published *Inside Journal*, a bimonthly newspaper distributed throughout the nation's prisons. A penfriend programme matched Christian volunteers with nearly 30,000 inmates. Perhaps the organization's biggest public success has been its 'Angel Tree' ministry. Begun in 1982, the programme enlists volunteers in local churches to purchase toy and clothing gifts at Christmas-time on behalf of inmates. In 2000, volunteers in 14,000 churches purchased and distributed gifts to nearly 600,000 children through the Angel Tree programme.

While work with prisoners has remained Colson's main activity through the years, he has played an increasingly important role within the American evangelical community as a voice in cultural, political and theological matters. As a speaker, frequent guest columnist and author of a number of books, Colson has addressed various topics of concern. His books, which have sold more than five million copies, have discussed a wide variety of issues including abortion, the church's role in society, the relationship of church and state, American cultural decline, the persecuted church around the world, and the economy and government regulation. In 1991 he launched *BreakPoint*, a daily syndicated radio programme commenting on political and cultural issues; by 2000 it was being broadcast on over 1,000 radio stations across the United States. One of his most controversial activities has been his leadership role in ecumenical dialogue between evangelicals and Catholics. With former Lutheran cleric

and Catholic convert Richard John Neuhaus, Colson was the co-author and co-editor of *Evangelicals and Catholics Together*, a cutting-edge 1993 document and collection of essays that explored the growing theological, cultural and political affinity between the two groups.

Colson's work with Prison Fellowship and his balanced calls for evangelical civic and cultural participation have made him one of the most respected American representatives of evangelical Christianity, both inside and outside the evangelical community. His awards include the Freedom Foundation's Religious Heritage Award (1977), the Layman of the Year award by the National Association of Evangelicals (1983), the Salvation Army's 'Others Award' (1990) and the million dollar Templeton Prize for Progress in Religion (1993).

Bibliography

C. W. Colson, *Born-Again* (Old Tappan: Chosen Books, 1976); C. W. Colson, *Kingdoms in Conflict* (New York: W. Morrow, 1987).

L. ESKRIDGE

■ **COOK, Thomas** (1808–1892), pioneer of the modern tourist industry, was born on 22 November 1808 in Melbourne, Derbyshire. When he was four years old his father died, and when he was ten his schooling came to an end. He was subsequently apprenticed as a woodturner. Cook's maternal grandfather, Thomas Perkins, had been a New Connexion General Baptist pastor. In 1824 Joseph F. Winks became the minister at Melbourne's General Baptist church and soon became a major influence on the young man. Winks baptized Cook on 28 February 1826. In autumn 1828 Cook began work for his denomination as a village missionary in Rutland and some other Midland counties. In the following year he travelled 2,692 miles in the course of his duties, 2,106 of them on foot. In 1831, however, the General Baptist Missionary Society found itself unable to fund Cook's salary. He returned to his trade, moving to Market Harborough, where he joined the General Baptist church and was soon superintendent of the adult Sunday school. On 2 March 1833 he married

Marianne Mason. They had a son, John Mason, and a daughter, Annie.

The young couple became committed to teetotalism, and work on behalf of this cause, including printing and selling temperance literature, began to supplant woodturning. While contemplating a forthcoming gathering of the South Midlands Temperance Association, Cook hit upon the idea of promoting temperance through the novelty and attractiveness of travel by rail. This idea led him to organize a highly successful train excursion from Leicester to Loughborough on 5 July 1841: 485 people went on this first outing, and thousands of people greeted them upon their arrival. Cook led the excited crowd in a cheer 'for Teetotalism and Railwayism!'

Cook then moved to Leicester, where he went into business as a printer. He founded various short-lived publications, *The Children's Temperance Magazine*, *The Temperance Messenger*, *The Anti-Smoker*, *The National Temperance Magazine* and *The Cheap Bread Herald* (a free trade publication). In 1853 he also opened a temperance hotel, which Marianne managed, and an impressive Temperance Hall.

Cook continued to organize train outings as well, and this part of the business gradually built up steam. In 1843 he took 3,000 Sunday school children on a trip to Derby in order to remove them from the morally dangerous atmosphere of racing week. Cook's trips to various parts of England, and then also Scotland, became frequent events. In 1855 he began trips to the continent. Cook pioneered the 'package' tour in which food and accommodation, as well as travel, are included in the price. Tours to America came next.

By 1869 Cook was ready to pursue his long-held, religiously motivated, desire to make it possible for middle-class people to tour the lands of the Bible. John Mason Cook, who was now in charge of the business, did not welcome his father's tendency to make use of the company in order to serve spiritual ends. Cook complained to Marianne about their son, 'He does not like my mixing Missions with business: but he cannot deprive me of the pleasure I have had in the combination.' Numerous ministers and devout lay people, on the other hand, were grateful for Cook's Holy Land tours. The fact that he ensured that there was no Sunday travelling

did not appear to hurt the business. The round-the-world tour came in 1873.

Cook died in Leicester on 18 July 1892. Throughout his life he had supported numerous religious and philanthropic causes, most notably his own denomination, the New Connexion of General Baptists, and the temperance movement. He built a schoolhouse for his local church, Archdeacon Lane, and served as president of the Leicester Temperance Society. One of the most important of his achievements was the founding and funding of the General Baptist mission in Rome in 1873. During the winter of 1855–1856 he supervised the feeding of 15,000 needy people in Leicestershire, and he later organized relief during a potato famine. He built fourteen cottages for the elderly in his native Melbourne.

Thomas Cook brought tourist travel to the masses. His name became a household word during his lifetime and, through the continued success of the company he founded, it still is today in Britain and beyond. Ironically, Leicester has also chosen to remember him by giving his name to a public house.

Bibliography

P. Brendon, *Thomas Cook: 150 Years of Popular Tourism* (London: Secker & Warburg, 1991); R. Ingle, *Thomas Cook of Leicester* (Bangor: Headstart History, 1991); T. Larsen, 'Thomas Cook, Holy Land Pilgrims, and the Dawn of the Modern Tourist Industry', in R. N. Swanson (ed.), *The Holy Land, Holy Lands, and Christian History*, *Studies in Church History* 36 (Woodbridge, Suffolk: The Boydell Press for the Ecclesiastical History Society, 2000), pp. 329–342.

T. LARSEN

■ **COOKE, Henry** (1788–1868), Irish Presbyterian minister, was born at the Grillagh, near Maghera, in County Derry on 11 May 1788, the fourth and youngest child of John Macook, a tenant farmer, and his second wife, Jane Howe. He was to drop the 'Mac' from his name and add an 'e'. Educated in local hedge schools and at Glasgow University (1802–1807), without taking a degree, he was ordained and installed in Duneane in County Antrim by the Ballymena presbytery on 10 November 1808. If his university education had been undistinguished, his first pastorate was inauspicious, ending in resignation after two years. This discouragement was short-lived, however, and on 29 January 1811 he was installed in nearby Donegore, where his gifts as a preacher blossomed, and marriage in 1813 to Ellen Mann of Toome gave his life a new stability.

An indulgent congregation allowed him to spend some time in further study, and while studying in Dublin he found a spiritual home in the Mary's Abbey congregation, which was at the centre of the growing evangelical movement in the capital. One of the congregation's ministers, James Carlile, was a founder of the Irish Evangelical Society, formed in 1814 to evangelize in the south and west of Ireland, and under its auspices Cooke preached regularly in Carlow and Stratford-on-Slaney, where moribund Presbyterian congregations were being revived.

After seven years in Donegore he was called to Killyleagh in County Down, where he was installed on 8 September 1818. In Killyleagh he came under the influence of an ardent evangelical elder in the congregation, Captain Sidney Hamilton Rowan, son of the local landlord, Archibald Hamilton Rowan. Cooke's son-in-law and biographer, J. L. Porter, considered that 'it would be impossible to estimate' Captain Rowan's influence on the young minister. In Killyleagh, encouraged by Rowan, Cooke emerged as a determined opponent of theological radicalism. The Synod of Ulster had long been divided by theological tensions between Old Lights, who held to the traditional Calvinism of the Westminster formularies, to which ordinards were supposed to subscribe, and New Lights, some of whom were Arians, who opposed subscription as a test of faith. In 1821 the visit to Killyleagh of an English Unitarian missionary and the appointment of a self-confessed Arian, William Bruce, to the chair of Hebrew and Greek in the recently founded Belfast Academical Institution, where many of the Synod's ordinands were being educated, drew Cooke into the public arena as a champion of orthodoxy. At the Synod's annual meeting in 1822 he launched his campaign against Arianism with the call to arms 'We must put down Arianism, or Arianism will put us down.' Cooke contended that the doctrine of the Trinity was not, as the Arians claimed,

merely speculative theology, but the foundation of the vital Christian doctrines of the incarnation and atonement, that any question-mark over Christ's divinity undermined the basis of salvation.

Cooke wanted a veto for the Synod over relevant professorial appointments in the Institution, but in this he failed. The Institution refused to concede any such veto, and the Synod decided that its moderator's membership, *ex officio*, of the college's governing body, gave it all the influence it needed. Dispirited, Cooke fell ill and, seeking medical aid in Dublin, he found spiritual renewal in an encounter with a Swiss Reformed pastor, César Malan. Malan had been influenced by the Scottish gentleman evangelist Robert *Haldane, and had been involved in a revival of evangelical religion and a campaign against Unitarianism in Geneva.

Cooke resumed his crusade against Arianism with renewed enthusiasm, and the open acknowledgment of Arian opinions by the clerk of the Synod, William Porter, and other prominent ministers in the course of a government inquiry into the Belfast Institution, enabled him to make a direct attack on the Arians in the Synod. He persuaded the Synod, at its annual meeting in 1827, to reaffirm its Trinitarian faith, in spite of the impassioned appeal for liberty of opinion by the urbane Arian leader, Henry Montgomery. The oratorical exchanges between Cooke and Montgomery were memorable features of the conflict in the Synod. Isolated in 1827, the Arians were put under further pressure in 1828 when the Synod instituted a theological examination committee to test the orthodoxy and spiritual experience of future ordinands. They drew up a Remonstrance against these 'innovations' and when it was rejected by the Synod, withdrew to a Remonstrant Synod, which became the nucleus of a small Non-Subscribing Presbyterian Church in Ireland.

Cooke now stood on a pinnacle of popularity and influence in the Synod of Ulster. A fine new church was built for him in May Street in Belfast, and from its pulpit and on political platforms he proclaimed a combination of belligerent Protestantism and political Unionism. The conflict in the Synod had had political overtones: Henry Montgomery and the Arians were identified with liberalism in politics as in theology, and Cooke became an

Orange hero, though he was never an Orange-man. As he became increasingly associated with conservatism in politics, championing the cause of the established church in Ireland as a bastion of Protestantism and opposing tenant farmers in their struggle with their landlords, many Presbyterians who had supported him theologically opposed him politically, though most of them were with him in his opposition to Daniel O'Connell's campaign to repeal the union. Cooke became one of the founding fathers of Unionism, which he personified in his anti-Catholicism and romantic veneration of Britain as the champion of Protestantism and political liberty.

Most Irish Presbyterians continued to honour him as their Athanasius whose victory over Arianism led to the union of the Synod of Ulster and the Secession Synod (which had come into existence as a conservative protest against the ascendancy of New Light in the Synod of Ulster in the eighteenth century) to form the General Assembly of the Presbyterian Church in Ireland, ushering in a creative period of outreach at home and abroad.

Honours were heaped upon him. Twice moderator of the General Assembly, he was appointed first president of the Presbyterian College, opened in Belfast in 1853, in which he was Professor of Sacred Rhetoric and Catechetics. He received honorary doctorates from Jefferson College (1829) and Dublin University (1837). When he died in Belfast on 13 December 1868 the *Belfast News Letter* described his civic funeral on 18 December as 'in all respects like a royal or imperial demonstration'.

A devoted husband and father, he lost his wife six months before his own death; a son and three daughters survived him. The first edition of J. L. Porter's *Life and Times of Dr Cooke* appeared in 1871. A number of Cooke's sermons and speeches were published, and he contributed 800 notes to the 1844 edition of Brown's *Self-Interpreting Bible*. His statue in the centre of Belfast was erected in 1876 by his political admirers.

Bibliography
J. L. Porter, *The Life and Times of Dr Cooke* (London: Murray, 1871); R. F. Holmes, *Henry Cooke* (Belfast, Dublin, Ottawa, Christian Journals, 1981).

F. HOLMES

■ **COOPER, Thomas** (1805–1892), popular apologist, was born in Leicester on 20 March 1805, but grew up in Gainsborough. His father died when he was four years old, and his mother, who worked as a dyer, raised him in straitened circumstances. He was given some local schooling, and he supplemented it with an insatiable appetite for reading and informal learning, which quickly revealed his exceptional intellectual gifts. When Cooper was fourteen, some Primitive Methodist evangelists came to town and, following an intense spiritual struggle, he was converted. After developing obsessional spiritual habits, however, he transferred his loyalty to the less emotionally charged Wesleyan Methodists.

In June 1820 he began work as an apprentice shoemaker. Before and after working hours, Cooper was a driven student of many varieties of knowledge: classical languages; natural history; literature; and, notably in the light of future developments, Christian evidences. He drove himself to a breakdown at the age of twenty-two. A change of vocation followed. Cooper established himself as a schoolmaster, a position which he held for eight years, but he was disappointed to discover that the poor did not consider it necessary for their children to learn Latin, and that the children concurred with the views of their elders.

He went for a time to an Independent church and a local parish church, but he reverted to the Wesleyans, where he endeavoured to appropriate 'the witness of the Spirit' and entire sanctification, but he found that spiritual highs were followed by lows. Nevertheless, in 1829 he became a Wesleyan local preacher. Cooper was a talented, popular, arrogant young preacher who clashed with his superintendent, making a move to Lincoln seem expedient. The superintendent, however, sent a negative report on to his colleague there, and Cooper then felt compelled to withdraw from the Wesleyans altogether, a move which marked the beginning of his drift into scepticism. In February 1834 he married Susanna Chaloner. Susanna had a miscarriage early in their marriage, and the couple remained childless.

Cooper next embarked upon a new vocation as a journalist, writing for local papers. In 1840 *The Leicestershire Mercury* sent him to report on a meeting of working-class political radicals, the Chartists. Cooper was politicized by this encounter, which resulted in his being fired, and he went into business as an editor of Chartist papers. Known as 'the General', he made the Leicester Chartists one of the most important local branches of the movement and developed a national reputation as a Chartist leader. He was intensely loyal to the fiery Chartist leader Feargus O'Connor, and a supporter of the strategy of 'physical force': direct action.

In August 1842 Cooper addressed a crowd of striking miners and potters in Hanley, Lancashire. The men rioted shortly thereafter, and Cooper was arrested and charged with seditious conspiracy. He was convicted and spent two years (ending in May 1845) in Stafford Gaol. While in prison he wrote his book-length poem *The Purgatory of the Suicides* (1845), which was well received, securing him encouraging words from Benjamin Disraeli, Charles Dickens and Thomas Carlyle.

Cooper then began a career as an author, editor and popular lecturer. His time in prison had deepened his religious scepticism, and he emerged as the most popular lecturer on freethought in London plebeian circles. He was convinced by D. F. Strauss's *Leben Jesu* (which George Eliot had recently translated into English), a work which argued that the gospel accounts of Christ's miracles were mythical rather than historical, and he popularized this teaching on the platform and in his *Cooper's Journal*, a weekly publication which he began in 1850.

Slowly, however, he began to feel the limitations of a sceptical approach and to re-examine the case for orthodoxy. In particular, he became convinced that there was no basis for morality without belief in a 'Divine Moral Governor'. In January 1856 he dramatically blurted out a confession to this effect when he was scheduled to lecture on 'Sweden and the Swedes' in a London freethinking hall. He then went through an extended period of wrestling with issues of faith and doubt. The author and Anglican clergyman Charles Kingsley became his spiritual adviser and confidant. Cooper wrote to him in June 1856, 'I read the New Testament, and *will* read it – but how often it all looks like a bundle of fables! Shall I ever come to read it with a feeling of the solid *reality* of what I

read? ... Can you tell me what to do – anything that will help me to Christ. *Him* I want. If the Four Gospels be half legends I still want him ... But how is it, then, that I am still so full of doubts?'

Ultimately, these doubts were banished. Cooper was baptized as a believer on Whit Sunday 1856 in a New Connexion General Baptist church in Leicester. He maintained this denominational identity for the rest of his life.

As he had been one of the most prominent leaders of popular freethought in England, Cooper's reconversion was a sensation. He continued his speaking career, and dramatic, well-attended debates followed, including one with his friend, the secularist leader G. J. Holyoake, and another with the rising atheist leader Charles Bradlaugh. Cooper came to find these clashes unproductive and emotionally draining, however, and decided to focus purely on lecturing. For the rest of his working life he criss-crossed the country as a 'Lecturer in Defence of Christianity', motivated by a desire to see unbelievers converted and Christians struggling with doubts strengthened in their faith. Unpublished ledgers he kept record that he delivered 4,292 lectures and 2,568 sermons in this final phase of his life. Many political radicals, old Chartists and plebeian sceptics would come to hear the celebrated leader, author and orator.

He published five volumes of popular apologetics which sold very well: *The Bridge of History Over the Gulf of Time* (1871), *God, the Soul and a Future State* (1873), *The Verity of Christ's Resurrection from the Dead* (1875), *The Verity and Value of the Miracles of Christ* (1876), and *Evolution, the Stone Book, and the Mosaic Record of Creation* (1878). He also published a Christian sequel to his popular poem *The Paradise of the Martyrs* (1873), two volumes of sermons, *Plain Pulpit Talk* (1872) and *The Atonement* (1880), and a miscellany which included Christian pieces, *Thoughts at Fourscore and Earlier* (1885). The book which is best remembered today is his autobiography, *The Life of Thomas Cooper, Written by Himself* (1872), which is often read for insights into the lives of working-class Victorians, but which also offers a detailed account of his religious development.

Cooper's apologetic works reveal his voracious reading: they may serve as a guide to all the important works of Christian evidences and scepticism from his own time and the century before. Rather than choosing one line of argument as the most convincing, Cooper would employ them all in turn: notably, the argument from design, the a priori argument and the moral argument. The argument from design allowed him to display his extensive knowledge of natural history, to the delight of working men hungry for 'useful knowledge', but he found the moral argument the most compelling personally, as his reconversion narrative indicates. His most popular book *The Bridge of History Over the Gulf of Time* presented his own, homemade attempt to answer Strauss and thus undo the earlier work he had done. His technique in this volume is to pay careful attention to the details offered in the Gospel narratives, highlighting their verisimilitude. Cooper continued on the lecture circuit until he was approaching his eightieth year. In 1884, when he was still very much alive and had more than a handful of years left in him, the General Baptists of Lincoln decided to erect the Thomas Cooper Memorial Church. When he died on 15 July 1892, Thomas Cooper's memorial service was duly held in Thomas Cooper Memorial, and the church still exists, albeit under the abbreviated appellation 'TCM Baptist Church'.

Bibliography

R. J. Conklin, *Thomas Cooper, the Chartist* (Manila: University of the Philippines Press, 1935); T. Cooper, *The Life of Thomas Cooper, Written by Himself* (1872; repr. Leicester: Leicester University Press, 1971); T. Larsen, 'Thomas Cooper and Christian Apologetics in Victorian Britain', *Journal of Victorian Culture* 5.2 (autumn 2000), pp. 239–259.

T. LARSEN

■ **COTTON, John** (1584–1652), Puritan minister, was born in Derby, England, in December 1584. A bright young student, Cotton came to Trinity College, Cambridge, at the age of thirteen and took his BA there in 1603 and his MA in 1606. At Cambridge Cotton was exposed to some of the greatest preachers and theologians of the Puritan movement in the Elizabethan era, including William *Perkins and Richard Sibbes. At first Cotton found Perkins's preaching on predestination offensive, but in 1609 he was converted under the preaching of Sibbes on the imputed righteousness of Christ. Cotton stayed on as a fellow at Emmanuel after taking his Master's degree and developed skills as a remarkable preacher and skilled debater in the plain style of Puritanism. Cotton's preaching at Cambridge undoubtedly helped to convince many of the saving work of Christ, but his most notable convert was John Preston, later master of Emmanuel. The sequence of conversions from Sibbes to Cotton to Preston demonstrates the power of personal connection and influence within the Puritan movement, and in fact one recent analysis places this Cambridge group at the centre of a submovement within Puritanism that emphasized pure grace and the role of the affections over the more rationalistic and legalistic preparationism of William *Ames and others. Cotton received Church of England ordination in 1610, and in 1613 he received the BD.

In 1612 Cotton, by then the most celebrated preacher at Cambridge, took a position as Vicar of St Botolph's in Boston, Lincolnshire. While there Cotton developed a reputation among friends and enemies as one of the leading pastors among the Puritans as he pushed for a fully reformed church polity and preached uncompromising Calvinist doctrine. In 1615 Cotton addressed the problem of how to distinguish a separate group of the elect within a state church by identifying those with assurance of salvation and having them covenant together 'to follow after the Lord in the purity of his Worship'. For this and other controversial moves Cotton faced brief suspensions in 1615 and again in 1622, as non-Puritan bishops grew tired of his agitation for reform.

During the 1620s more and more Puritans in England began to entertain the idea of emigration as a means of escaping growing persecution and of practising a fully reformed faith in freedom. Cotton developed close ties with the group led by John *Winthrop which departed for New England in 1630, and in fact he preached their stirring farewell sermon, *God's Promise to His Plantation*

(1630). Soon after the Winthrop fleet's departure, Cotton himself began seriously to think of leaving, especially as he began to hear rumours that he would be called before William Laud to be tried for his agitation in the church. Cotton went into hiding in 1632, leaving Boston and moving to London. After considering a number of options, including fleeing to Holland, Cotton gathered his family and left for New England in June 1633.

Cotton arrived in Boston in September 1633 and was soon asked to become the teaching pastor of the church there. He almost immediately became involved in trying to persuade the maverick minister Roger *Williams of Salem to take a more orthodox line with regard to liberty of conscience and the nature of the gathered church; their argument would continue even after Williams' banishment from Massachusetts in 1635. Then in 1636–1638 Cotton found himself in the uncomfortable position of defending a group accused of antinomianism. The group, led by John Wheelwright, Henry Vane, and most ominously, Anne *Hutchinson, downplayed good works as evidence of salvation and began to criticize some of the New England clergy's teaching as legalism, perhaps a natural tendency for those associated with Cotton's Cambridge circle. Since his conversion under Sibbes, Cotton had always insisted on the total passivity of the redeemed in receiving grace, and on salvation as completely an inner working of the Holy Spirit, depending not at all on outer conformity to the law or the church. But the rest of the leading ministers and magistrates strongly opposed the Wheelwright group with a developing New England orthodoxy that emphasized the value of good works as preparatory to and evidence of salvation. Though both Wheelwright and Hutchinson claimed Cotton as a source of inspiration for their teaching, Cotton eventually disassociated himself from their teachings, and in celebrated trials Hutchinson and Wheelwright were banished from Massachusetts in 1637 and 1638. Cotton's reputation and power allowed him to survive the controversy, but his disappointment lingered and he continued to defend a relatively radical position on grace in later writings such as A Treatise of the Covenant of Grace (1659). After the antinomian controversy, Cotton resumed his role as one of the chief defenders of the developing New England Congregational polity. On one hand, he defended Congregationalism against separatist attacks from Roger Williams and others, and in response to Williams' The Bloudy Tenent of Persecution (1644), which attacked Massachusetts' heavy-handed suppression of dissent, Cotton defended Congregational authority in The Bloudy Tenent, Washed and Made White in the Bloud of the Lamb (1647). But Cotton also defended New England's tendencies towards exclusive demands for church membership against critics in England, for example, in his The Way of the Churches in New-England (1645). Cotton was one of the chief architects of New England's dominant ecclesiology, which attempted to cut a middle path between the Presbyterianism gaining favour among reformers in England and the separatism finding a home in many towns of southeastern New England and springing up among some in the ferment and liberty of the English Civil War.

Cotton spent his later years in the normal duties of ministry in Boston, helping to develop Massachusetts' celebrated Bay Psalm Book (1640), and writing a catechism for children called Milk for Babes: Drawn out of the Breasts of Both Testaments (1646) and Singing of Psalms a Gospel-Ordinance (1647). Cotton died in December 1652, in conjunction with the appearance of a comet which contemporaries took as an ominous sign for the future of the church in New England.

Cotton was one of the key figures in English Puritanism, establishing himself as an influential leader on both sides of the Atlantic. He had a strong sense in his preaching and theology of the omnipotence of God in salvation and in history. He displayed a deep interest in eschatology, rooted in his sense that God controlled the fate of humans. Cotton also cultivated connexions within international Protestantism that perhaps tempered his sense of New England's chosenness compared to that of some of his contemporaries. He remained convinced that God's work in human history was coming to a climax, not just in the reformed polity of New England but across the known world. As a leader of the Puritan movement with a special interest in the power of God and the powerlessness of humans, Cotton's theology ultimately hinged on the work and person of Christ: 'In the Gospel ... all the promises are given to Christ, and all the conditions are fulfilled in Christ, and the revealing of both is by the revealing of Christ given of grace freely to the Soul.'

Bibliography

E. Emerson, *John Cotton* (Boston: Hall, 1990); J. Norton, *Abel Being Dead yet Speaketh: Or, The Life and Death of ... Mr. John Cotton* (London: 1658); L. Ziff, *The Career of John Cotton: Puritanism and the American Experience* (Princeton: Princeton University Press, 1962).

T. S. KIDD

■ **COWPER, William** (1731–1800), poet and hymn-writer, was born on 15 November 1731 in the Rectory House, Berkhamsted in Hertfordshire. His father was John Cowper, an Anglican clergyman; his mother was Anne Cowper. He was the fourth child, but his three siblings had died in infancy. His mother died just before his sixth birthday.

At Dr Pitman's boarding school he was bullied. At the age of ten he moved to Westminster School in London, leaving at the age of seventeen. In 1750, when staying with his uncle, he was articled to a Mr Chapman and began to study law. Attending church with his female cousins, he fell in love with one of them, Theodora Cowper, and though her father would not allow them to marry, their relationship continued throughout their lives.

Called to the bar in 1754, Cowper took chambers in London's Middle Temple in 1757. Facing the possibility of a public examination for the post of clerk to the House of Commons he had a nervous breakdown and attempted suicide. Calling out, 'O Brother, I am damned,' he gave voice to an insidious sense of oppression. He regarded himself as being under God's wrath, the greatest sinner on earth. His Bible was thrown away as being of no further interest to him. Fortuitously, Martin Madan, a chaplain of the Lock Hospital, 'pointed him to the blood of the Saviour'.

In an asylum, run by Dr Cotton in St Albans, Cowper began on the path to recovery. He started to read the Bible again and doing so brought him to the point of conversion, his psychological healing running hand in hand with his spiritual enlightenment.

He went to convalesce in Huntingdon, staying with the Revd Morley Unwin and his wife, Mary. The Unwins were committed Calvinists and supportive of the evangelical revival. Morley Unwin died in 1767, and Cowper moved, with Unwin's family, to Olney in Buckingham to live at Orchard Side. John *Newton was the curate at Olney, and he encouraged Cowper in the work of evangelism. Clearly he saw Cowper as a convert, educated and well prepared by his life's experience for this task, but he proved too frail for it.

After Cowper's recovery, his religious fervour was diminished, though he collaborated with John Newton in producing a collection of religious poetry, the *Olney Hymns* (1779). Cowper contributed sixty-six texts to this collection of 348 pieces. Most of his hymns were written in 1771 and 1772, when he became engaged to Mary Unwin. In 1773 he suffered a relapse and the engagement was broken off. In a tribute to Cowper in 1800 Greatheed spoke of a 'presentiment of this sad reverse' and said that 'during a solitary walk in the fields, he composed a hymn'. Bernard Braley sees 'God moves in a mysterious way' as, in some way, a manifestation of Cowper's condition. He observes that in this text we catch a vivid picture of the storm-battered mind with which Cowper craved a divine presence. William Rossetti wrote that 'The daylight of his manhood was not without its clouds'. Today he would probably have been diagnosed as clinically depressed.

Cowper struggled with Calvinism and arrived at the conviction that he was predestined to damnation. Writing to John Newton he said, 'The future appears as gloomy as ever; and I seem to myself to be scrambling always in the dark, among rocks and precipices, without a guide, but with an enemy ever at my heels, prepared to push me headlong. Thus have I spent twenty long years.' He goes on to state that death will come before another twenty are out, and that the 'enemy of Mankind' has had such an interest in him that 'even God's omnipotence to save is a consideration that affords me no comfort, while I seem to have a foe omnipotent to destroy'.

These experiences, together with Cowper's grasp of language, led him to write some of the finest hymnody on the subject of desolation. These texts are still well known, while his poetry has sunk largely into obscurity. His words are poignant, born of experience. They focus particularly on doubt and uncertainty yet, like the psalmist, his words are undergirded with faith so that, even as he anticipates damnation, he sees affliction as being part of God's will with the power to work for good. His words often seem contradictory, saying at one moment, 'The saints should never be dismayed', while at another giving voice to a sense of desperation, 'Send none unhealed away'. Cowper's God is one to whom people can come when they are 'Deep-wounded souls', but his sense of personal unworthiness is always evident:

The Lord will happiness divine
On contrite hearts bestow;
Then tell me, gracious God, is mine
A contrite heart, or no?

Throughout all his lamenting and searching there is the reassurance that God 'proclaims his grace abroad!' and changes hearts of stone, so that, on turning to God, 'calm content and peace we find'. Even when we are lost in 'blind unbelief ... God is his own interpreter / And he will make it plain', and though our 'love is weak and faint', we should seek grace to love God more, so that, in the end, we might echo the words of a hymn fragment which, both in language and rhythm, urges us to progress to our ultimate goal:

To Jesus, the Crown of my Hope,
My soul is in haste to be gone:
O bear me ye cherubims, up,
And waft me away to his throne!

There is, perhaps no more enigmatic writer, who feels at once the senses of divine providence and damnation so intimately intermingled; who feels hope and despair in equal measure; who cries to the God whom he believes cannot accept him in spite of that selfsame God's immense grace. His words speak of a whirlwind of change and uncertainty, of the inward struggle for faith: 'Where is the blessedness I knew / When first I saw the Lord'. In the end, the melancholic seems to win. For this reason he still speaks to our despair.

Cowper moved into the vicarage with John Newton to get away from the bustle of the Market Square and stayed from Easter until the late spring of the following year. He returned to Orchard Side in May 1774. His recovery was gradual. He was diverted by keeping hares and making hutches for them. In 1776 he again began to write to his friends. In 1780 Newton departed for London, having first introduced Cowper to William Bull, an independent minister, who, more than once, persuaded him not to tear up his writing. Though yearning for solitude, he found it difficult to live with himself. He resumed composing poetry. At Mrs Unwin's suggestion he wrote 'The Progress of Error'. 'Truth', 'Table Talk' and 'Exposition' were also written between December 1780 and March 1781. The flow of writing continued with 'Conversation' and 'Retirement'. This was a more optimistic period. Early in 1782 a collection of his work was published, which was little noticed.

In 1783 he published 'The Journey of John Gilpin', a successful ballad based on a story told to him by Lady Austen, a widow who lived on the first floor of the vicarage, let to her by the new incumbent, the Revd Thomas *Scott. She suggested that Cowper should write about a sofa. This theme developed into his principal work, 'The Task', which was published in 1785. He had become a distinguished minor poet.

In 1784 he moved to Weston, a nearby village, and began translating Homer. The translation was published in 1791 and he received £1,000 for the copyright. His health again began to suffer, and by 1795 he needed financial help from relatives. Eventually he moved with Mary Unwin to East Dereham in Norfolk, to live near a cousin. Mary, who had had a stroke in 1792, died in 1796. Cowper watched her decline and sank into a depression from which he never recovered. He died on 25 April 1800.

Some have said that his poetry lacked 'music', but the weight of his evangelical thought, and its application to the resolution of his own state of mind, marked him out as a profound theologian. He gave expression to his theology through the verse of a mere sixty-eight hymns.

Bibliography
J. King, C. Ryskamp, *The Letters and Prose Writings of William Cowper*, 5 vols. (Oxford: Clarendon Press, 1979–1986); B. Braley, *Hymnwriters*, vol. 1 (London: Stainer & Bell, 1987), pp. 28–53.

A. E. PRATT

■ **CRANMER, Thomas** (1489–1556), English Reformer, was the first Protestant Archbishop of Canterbury during the tumultuous reigns of Henry VIII, Edward VI, and Mary I.

Born in Aslockton, Nottinghamshire, to Thomas and Agnes Cranmer, the younger Thomas entered Jesus College, Cambridge in 1503 at the age of fourteen; he later received the BA (1511–1512), MA (1515) and DD (1526). Around 1515, shortly after he was appointed to a fellowship at Jesus College, he relinquished it following his marriage. After his wife's death in childbirth, he resumed his fellowship.

At Cambridge Cranmer was trained in Renaissance humanism, which predisposed him to assiduous study of the Bible as well as patristics. No substantial evidence exists to show that Cranmer was influenced by the new, radical, evangelical theology of the 1520s. In fact, the annotations in his copy of John Fisher's confutation of *Luther show that he was clearly unconvinced by the German Reformer's attack on the papacy and the doctrine of works. Cranmer was ordained priest in the early 1520s and continued as a reader in divinity at Jesus College as well as a university examiner in divinity until the summer of 1529, when his quiet academic life came to a sudden end.

In 1529 both Oxford and Cambridge universities were involved in legitimating Henry's impending divorce and subsequent second marriage, and Cranmer assured Henry that since Catherine of Aragon was the widow of his older brother, Arthur, his marriage had never been lawfully consummated according to canon law. This claim evidently assuaged Henry's apprehensions, and soon Cranmer moved to Durham House, the London home of the Boleyns. In January 1530, at Henry's behest, Cranmer was sent on a diplomatic mission with the Earl of Wiltshire's embassy to Pope Clement VII and to the Holy Roman Emperor Charles V at Regensburg, from which he returned in September 1530. Despite the best efforts of the English to persuade Clement VII to declare Henry's marriage to Catherine invalid, the Pope was understandably reluctant; he was under great political pressure from Charles V, who had not only sacked the papal city of Rome, but was also the favourite nephew of Catherine. Cranmer became archdeacon of Taunton in 1530, and while staying in Nuremberg in 1532, he married Margaret, niece of the famous Lutheran theologian Andreas Osiander. In so doing he broke his priestly vow of celibacy, revealing an inclination towards the Protestant faith. The Cranmers' marriage was to remain a secret for fifteen years.

In 1532 Henry appointed Cranmer, despite his protestations, as Archbishop of Canterbury; he was consecrated on 30 March 1533. His rise to ecclesiastical prominence had been very rapid. One of his earliest tasks as primate of all England was to find theological justification and historical precedents for the rejection of papal jurisdiction and supremacy in England. He adhered strictly to the doctrines of the 'godly prince' and the royal supremacy over both the political and the ecclesiastical realms. His dislike of papal supremacy, which dated from his time in Cambridge, was complemented by his enthusiastic support of Henry's royal supremacy. Cranmer cautiously promoted reform of the Church of England. *The Ten Articles of Faith* (1536) and *Bishops' Book* (1537) resembled the Lutheran *Wittenberg Articles*; the standards of faith were declared to be the Scriptures and three (not seven) sacraments, and the article on justification affirmed the Lutheran principle of *sola fide*. Cranmer was also convinced of the need for a vernacular Bible in order quickly to disseminate the evangelical faith. *The Great Bible* was published in 1539 and a second edition only a year later.

After the accession of Edward VI in 1547, Cranmer began more freely to express his desire for reform and to implement it more vigorously. He had a leading role in the writing of the first eucharistic liturgy in English (1548), the first two versions of *The*

Book of Common Prayer (1549 and 1552), the Book of Homilies (1547) and the Forty-Two Articles (1553). His Defence of the True and Catholic Doctrine of the Sacrament (1550) was severely criticized by the conservative Bishop of Winchester, Stephen Gardiner, but expressed his mature understanding of this contentious issue. Cranmer first abandoned his belief in transubstantiation in favour of the Lutheran doctrine of real presence, and then embraced the Calvinian doctrine of spiritual presence under the influence of Nicholas *Ridley in about 1546; he affirmed this doctrine during the Lords' debate on the sacraments in December 1548. The first Edwardian Prayer Book won measured approbation from Catholic conservatives such as Gardiner but was condemned as a woefully inadequate expression of Protestant religion by evangelicals such as John *Hooper, Bishop of Gloucester, Peter Martyr Vermigli and Martin *Bucer, who were unhappy with its apparent affirmation of real presence. In the second Edwardian Prayer Book of 1552, the mass was renamed 'Holy Communion', and the orientation of the service became more Protestant.

When Charles V declared the Augsburg Interim in June 1548, it put an end to Martin Bucer's indefatigable efforts for reformation in Strasbourg. Cranmer invited him and his associate Paul Fagius to England, appointing them as Regius Professor of Divinity and Regius Professor of Hebrew at Cambridge during the Michaelmas term of 1549. He also invited the Italian Reformer Peter Martyr Vermigli, whose exegetical works and Loci Communes had become prescribed reading for Protestant theological students, to become Regius Professor of Divinity at Oxford. Cranmer thus added great theological weight to the two English universities. Moreover, he welcomed many Protestant refugees to London and allowed them to form 'stranger churches', with the Polish Reformer Jan Laski as superintendent, to the chagrin of the bishop of London, Nicholas Ridley. He was thus hailed by Heinrich *Bullinger as 'the especial patron of the foreigners'.

As the eucharistic debate perpetuated the division between Zwinglians and Lutherans, Protestants were alarmed by the Catholic renewal movement and backlash against Protestantism at the Council of Trent.

Cranmer wrote to Bullinger, *Zwingli's successor at Zurich, to *Melanchthon, lieutenant of Luther, and to *Calvin in 1552, calling for a pan-Protestant synod to promote unity and to reach agreement on the sacrament.

Many of the great hopes of Cranmer and his like-minded colleagues were brought to nothing by the unexpected and premature death of the fifteen-year-old Edward VI, who had made the Church of England more Protestant. After the succession of Mary Tudor to the throne, the mass was reintroduced. On 13 September 1553 Cranmer was imprisoned in the Tower of London because of his denial of a cardinal doctrine of the Queen's Catholic faith and his attempt to put Lady Jane Grey on the throne immediately after Edward's death. Tried for treason two months later, he was declared guilty on all counts. In March 1554 the Council ordered Cranmer, Ridley and *Latimer to be sent to Oxford. While their execution was delayed due to Mary's marriage to Philip of Spain and Wyatt's peasant rebellion in Kent, Cranmer undertook an intensive study of the Eucharist to prepare for his confrontation with Gardiner and his supporters. On 16 April 1554, in what Cranmer had hoped would be a genuine debate, he was instead tried for heresy, convicted and excommunicated. Since he was an archbishop, the English ecclesiastical authorities had to wait for official approval from Rome. Finally, on 4 December 1555, Paul IV excommunicated Cranmer, who was then stripped of his orders. Under intense pressure from Mary's Commission in February and March 1556, Cranmer temporarily recanted six times his non-Catholic views on the Eucharist and his repudiation of papal supremacy. However, when no pardon was granted, Cranmer went to the flames on 21 March 1556 defying both the Marian and papal authorities. He renounced his earlier recantations, and held his right hand in the fire as a symbol of his rejection of the Marian regime and his own complicity in it.

The verdict of historians on Cranmer has ranged from the very positive to the very negative. But it is beyond doubt that he made a major contribution to the worship and theology of the Church of England, as a liturgist in the writing of the Book of Common Prayer, as a supporter of the vernacular Bible, as a proponent of Protestant ecumenism and patron of evangelical refugees, and finally as an adherent to the principle of royal supremacy.

Bibliography

P. Ayris and D. Selwyn (eds.), *Thomas Cranmer: Churchman and Scholar* (Woodbridge: Boydell Press, 1993); G. W. Bromiley, *Thomas Cranmer, Theologian* (London: Lutterworth Press, 1956); P. N. Brooks (ed.), *Cranmer in Context: Documents from the English Reformation* (Minneapolis: Fortress Press, 1989); D. MacCulloch, *Thomas Cranmer* (New Haven: Yale University Press, 1996).

P. C-H. LIM

■ **CROMWELL, Oliver** (1599–1658), Puritan statesman, was born in Huntingdon, the son of a country gentleman. He was educated at Huntingdon Grammar School and went to Sidney Sussex College in Cambridge in 1616. In 1617, however, his father died, and he returned home to run the family estate. In 1620 he married Elizabeth Bourchier, the daughter of a city merchant. During the next decade he farmed at Huntingdon and St Ives, served as a JP and sat as an MP for Huntingdon in the 1628 Parliament. In the late 1620s or early 1630s he experienced a spiritual and emotional crisis followed by a powerful conversion experience. In a letter of 1638 he wrote to a correspondent, 'My soul is with the Congregation of the firstborn, my body rests in hope ... You know what my manner of life hath been. Oh, I lived in and loved darkness, and hated the light. I was a chief, the chief of sinners. This is true: I hated godliness, yet God had mercy on me. Oh the riches of his mercy!'

Cromwell's conversion turned him into a zealous Protestant, a 'Puritan', and instilled the personal assurance that remained with him throughout his career.

In 1640 he was elected MP for Cambridge. In the Long Parliament he strongly supported the hard line taken by the parliamentary leader, John Pym. He spoke in favour of 'Root and Branch' reform of the church and against episcopacy, and was one of the first to contemplate armed resistance to the king. In 1642 he helped to secure Cambridge for Parliament and fought at the battle of Edgehill. The Civil War was to make his reputation. He became an outstanding cavalry commander and created his own regiment, later nicknamed the 'Ironsides'. Controversially, Cromwell encouraged members of the religious sects to join his regiment and became strongly identified with the Independents in their dispute with the Presbyterians. He wanted 'godly honest men' who were entirely committed to the Parliamentarian cause, and cared little about outward forms. In a letter to Parliament in 1645 he rejoiced in the ecumenical unity in the army and condemned the conservative Puritan drive for an enforced uniformity: 'Presbyterians, Independents, all had here the same spirit of faith and prayer ... They agree here, know no names of difference; pity it is it should be otherwise anywhere. All that believe have the real unity, which is most glorious because inward and spiritual ... As for being united in forms, commonly called uniformity, every Christian will for peace sake study and do as far as conscience will permit; and from brethren, in things of the mind, we do look for no compulsion but that of light and reason.'

In 1645 Cromwell played a central role in the organization of the New Model Army, of which he was made Lieutenant-General. He commanded the cavalry in the decisive Parliamentarian victory at Naseby in June 1645 and was present at the Royalist surrender in June 1646.

In 1647 Cromwell participated in the search for a constitutional settlement, though he tended to follow the advice of his son-in-law Ireton and was wary of the radical proposals made by the Leveller movement. When the king allied with the Scots Engagers to precipitate the Second Civil War in 1648, Cromwell defeated the Royalist forces at the battle of Preston in September. The war persuaded Cromwell that Charles I could not be trusted, and after an army purge of Parliament in December, Charles was put on trial and executed in January 1649. The regicide was followed by the abolition of the monarchy, and England was formally declared a commonwealth. The new commonwealth had many enemies, particularly in Ireland and Scotland. In 1649 Cromwell took the army to Ireland, and in a notorious campaign he struck terror into the Irish. After sieges at

Drogheda and Wexford, his troops slaughtered many hundreds of people, including civilians. For Cromwell, this was 'a righteous judgement of God upon these barbarous wretches', who had 'imbrued their hands in so much innocent blood' during the massacres of Protestants in 1641. In 1650 he turned his attention to the Scots Covenanters, whom he defeated at the battles of Dunbar (September 1650) and Worcester (September 1651).

Cromwell was now the most powerful figure in the land, but as Lord General of the army he was still a servant of the Rump Parliament. In April 1653, however, he marched troops to the House of Commons and forcibly dissolved the Rump because it had failed to fulfil hopes of reform and a new constitutional settlement. Instead of seizing power for himself, he supported the establishment of a Nominated Assembly in July 1653, nicknamed the 'Barebones Parliament' because it contained a significant number of Puritan radicals like Praise-God Barebones. In a fervent opening speech to the Assembly, Cromwell wondered if it might help to usher in the millennium, but deep divisions among its members soon led to its dissolution. In December 1653 Cromwell himself was made Lord Protector under a new constitution, the Instrument of Government. He remained head of state until his death and was offered the crown in 1657, an offer he refused due to opposition from the army and his own conviction that God had providentially destroyed the title of king. As Lord Protector, Cromwell enjoyed greater control over the entire British Isles than had any previous English ruler, and under him England once again became a major military power, enjoying significant victories over the Dutch and the Spanish.

In England itself, however, Cromwell was less successful. Even among Puritans he had many enemies. The Presbyterians had never come to terms with the regicide or with his tolerant Independency, while radical groups like the Fifth Monarchists, the Levellers and the Commonswealthmen viewed Cromwell as a power-hungry tyrant. The majority of the population resented the Puritan drive for godly reformation and hankered after the old 'Merrie England', with its monarchy, maypoles and Prayer Book Anglicanism. Cromwell's efforts to instil godliness through the rule of the Major-Generals in 1655–1656 were an abject failure. When he died in September 1658, his son Richard succeeded him as Lord Protector, but Richard lacked the personal charisma and authority of his father. Within twenty months of Oliver's death the monarchy was restored.

Although Cromwell was often accused of hypocrisy during his lifetime, most historians are persuaded that devout and sincere religious commitments were the key to his career. His politics were intensely providentialist; he saw his military victories as evidence that God was on his side, and during political crises he spent whole days seeking guidance from God through private prayer and biblical meditation. His outlook was closest to that of Calvinist Independents like John *Owen and Thomas Goodwin, but he was also suspicious of party labels and sympathetic to Protestant piety wherever he found it. Throughout his career, one of his great passions was the protection of the godly. Both as a military commander and as Lord Protector, he championed religious toleration, fearing that persecution would destroy the saints even when it was aimed at heretics and blasphemers. He shared the bitter anti-popery of his contemporaries, but during the 1650s he was remarkably lenient towards English Catholics. On his deathbed he was reported as having repeated the same sentence thrice over to his son: 'Richard, mynd the people of God and be tender of them.'

Evangelicals, especially Victorian Nonconformists, often celebrated Cromwell as a great Puritan statesman and a defender of civil and religious liberty. This is hardly surprising, for arguably Cromwell was one of the creators of modern Anglo-American evangelicalism. More than any other single individual, he was responsible for ensuring that English-speaking Protestantism became unusually pluralistic; under his protection movements like the Baptists and Congregationalists enjoyed space to organize and take root. He also pioneered the kind of evangelical ecumenism that was to be so central to the identity of later evangelicals. For Cromwell, one's denomination was neither here nor there. What mattered was whether people possessed 'the root of the matter': belief in 'the remission of sins through the blood of Christ and free justification by the blood of Christ'.

Bibliography
W. C. Abbott (ed.), *The Writings and Speeches of Oliver Cromwell*, 4 vols. (Oxford: Oxford University Press, 1937–47); J. Morrill (ed.), *Oliver Cromwell and the English Revolution* (London: Longman, 1990).

J. R. D. COFFEY

■ **CROSBY, Frances (Fanny) Jane** (1820–1915), hymn-writer, was born in Southeast, a village in Putnam County, New York, on 24 March 1820. Her parents, John and Mercy Crosby, came from old Puritan stock. The family traced its American roots to 1635, when Simon and Ann Crosby arrived in the Massachusetts Bay Colony. The Crosby family grew and prospered in the New World. Fanny's branch was descended from Simon's son, Thomas, who graduated from Harvard College in the 1650s and became a preacher and businessman in Sandwich, Cape Cod. In the 1760s his descendants moved across Connecticut to the frontier between the Hudson River and the Connecticut border.

John and Mercy both came from this Crosby lineage and lived among the tight-knit Crosby clan. Fanny was their only child. When she was six weeks old the mistreatment of an eye infection blinded her. Later in 1820 John Crosby died. Blind and fatherless, Fanny spent her early childhood with Mercy and Mercy's parents, Sylvanus and Eunice. They dedicated themselves to helping her to learn and be self-sufficient. The family spent long winter evenings reading from their small library of English poetry and literature. Fanny memorized whole books of the King James Bible. The Crosbys attended the local Presbyterian church. Mercy Crosby sometimes hired herself out as a housekeeper, and she and Fanny spent months boarding with families in nearby towns. While her mother worked, Fanny made the acquaintance of local artisans. She accompanied one to his Methodist class meeting, where she first heard the hymn singing for which *Wesley's followers were known. She learned plain speech among Quakers in northern Westchester County, and such contacts broadened her growing understanding of her Protestant world.

In 1835 Mercy enrolled Fanny as a student in the New York Institution for the Blind (NYIB). Still in its infancy, this experimental school was dedicated to providing basic education and job skills for the visually handicapped. A new programme of state scholarships enabled Fanny to attend. Though she never mastered Braille and disliked mathematics, Fanny thrived in courses in English, history, music and poetry. She manifested an unusual ability to express herself in extemporaneous poetry, and she often welcomed visiting dignitaries, such as General Winfield Scott or James Russell Lowell, with a spontaneous declamation. Her music teacher, George Root, gave her the opportunity to publish words to his music. Though she made no money, in the 1850s she contributed lyrics to successful cantatas and popular songs such as 'Rosalie the Prairie Flower' and 'Hazel Dell'. She also published three small volumes of poetry. Meanwhile, Mercy remarried and bore two more daughters.

In November 1850, during revival services at Thirtieth Street Methodist Church in Manhattan, Fanny Crosby's childhood faith came to life in an experience of conversion. During the singing of *Watts's 'Alas, and Did My Saviour Bleed?' Crosby made a personal commitment to Christ. She joined a class meeting but also continued regularly to visit various other churches, Episcopalian, Dutch Reformed and Presbyterian. Her distant cousin, Howard Crosby, was an influential Manhattan pastor, whose sermons at Fourth Presbyterian Church Fanny particularly enjoyed.

After completing her studies, Fanny remained at the NYIB as a teacher until her marriage in 1858 to Alexander van Alstyne, an NYIB graduate eleven years her junior. A native of upstate New York, van Alstyne had some college training and was a successful music teacher, church organist and composer. The two moved briefly to Queens, then returned to Manhattan in the early 1860s. During the Civil War, Crosby (who retained her maiden name) contributed generously to the outpouring of poems and songs that supported the union. Intensely patriotic, she frequently attended Henry Ward Beecher's Plymouth Church in Brooklyn, where this staunch opponent of slavery became her friend and favourite preacher.

At the Dutch Reformed Church on Manhattan's 23rd Street Fanny made the acquaintance of the pastor, Peter Stryker, who in 1864 recommended her to William Bradbury. One of the city's pre-eminent music publishers, Bradbury was also a noted evangelical hymn-tune composer and singing school teacher. Advertisements for his Bradbury Pianos appeared widely in religious periodicals, and in the 1870s one of the pianos graced the Hayes White House. Bradbury had already composed the common tunes for 'Just As I Am' and 'Jesus Loves Me', and he was part of a circle of people who wielded extensive influence over the religious music of the day. Pleased with Crosby's obvious poetic ability, Bradbury employed her to provide his company weekly with two hymns at a salary of $2 per week. Crosby wrote some of these hymns to specific tunes, but many were simply poems suitable for use as hymns. These she dictated as opportunity permitted, editing them in her mind and drawing on the vast store of Scripture and poetry she had memorized as a child. Crosby remained under contract to Bradbury and his successors, Bigelow & Main, until her death in 1915. In her old age they provided her with a modest, steady income without demanding a regular supply of lyrics.

Bradbury launched and sustained Crosby's career as a hymn-writer, but her most enduring hymns resulted from her collaboration with others, notably William Doane and Phoebe Palmer Knapp. Doane, a Baptist tune-writer and wealthy businessman, became Crosby's lifelong friend and business partner. Together they produced such gospel songs as 'Safe in the Arms of Jesus' (1868), 'Pass Me Not, O Gentle Saviour' (1868), 'To God Be the Glory, Great Things He Hath Done' (1875), 'Rescue the Perishing' (1869), and 'Jesus, Keep Me Near the Cross' (1869). Doane copyrighted his tunes with Fanny's texts and routinely refused permission to publish tune or text separately. Phoebe Palmer Knapp, a prominent Brooklyn socialite, Methodist stalwart, and daughter of holiness evangelists Walter and Phoebe *Palmer, wrote the music for one of Crosby's best-known texts 'Blessed Assurance' (1873). They also produced many hymns for Sunday schools and social meetings.

The changing religious scene facilitated Crosby's work as a hymn-writer. The growing Sunday school movement created a market for texts that taught basic morals and Christian doctrine set to simple, singable tunes. Crosby collaborated with her husband and others to produce hundreds of these. Their topics ranged from plain statements about God to injunctions to personal hygiene. Other Crosby texts supported the efforts of Protestant-based voluntary associations such as the Women's Christian Temperance Union in their efforts to prohibit the sale of alcohol. But most significantly, Crosby came to the attention of evangelist Dwight L. *Moody and his musician, Ira D. *Sankey.

During the 1870s and 1880s Moody and Sankey took Britain and America by storm. Sankey provided music to support Moody's evangelistic work. Songs of invitation, exhortation and testimony were particularly appropriate in the huge urban evangelistic campaigns that marked Moody's and Sankey's combined efforts. Sankey's solos and the music he introduced through the mass choirs he directed offered accessible texts and tunes to the masses. Some quickly gained popularity inside and outside the meetings, and urgent demand for their compilation and publication resulted ultimately in the publication of Gospel Hymns 1–6. Cited by its British publisher, Morgan & Scott, as one of the most valuable literary products in the world, this collection generated millions of dollars in royalties, which Moody and Sankey poured into evangelistic and educational work. Sankey found Crosby's hymns particularly appropriate to his efforts, and his use of them in crusades as well as in his hymnals assured their rapid spread across the English-speaking world. Many were immediately translated and became an integral part of the era's worldwide missionary endeavours.

A popular speaker, Crosby charmed audiences at Chautauqua Conventions, Christian Endeavor meetings, YMCA gatherings, Northfield Conventions and many churches. Though she travelled only in the north-east, the national secular and religious press hailed her for her winning personality and her enormous contribution to popular religious life. Though critics found her poetry mediocre, much of the Protestant public embraced her voice as their own.

By 1900 both Fanny and her husband needed care. A family in Brooklyn tended Alexander van Alstyne, suffering from cancer, and Fanny went north to make her home with her stepsisters in Bridgeport, Connecticut. Van Alstyne died in 1902. Fanny lived until 1915, making frequent trips to New York and elsewhere in the north-eastern United States. She wrote hymns until the day before her death on 12 February. Part of a group of text- and tune-writers who provided a new style of religious song for growing popular religious movements, Crosby is the most prolific American hymn-writer to date. Active in many evangelistic endeavours, she exemplified the Protestant sense of duty, purpose, faith and mission that characterized many of her evangelical cohorts.

Bibliography

E. L. Blumhofer, *Fanny J. Crosby: A Protestant Life* (Grand Rapids: Eerdmans); F. J. Crosby, *Memories of Eighty Years* (Boston: J. H. Earle, 1906); B. Ruffin, *Fanny J. Crosby* (Philadelphia: United Church Press, 1976).

E. L. BLUMHOFER

■ **CROWTHER, Samuel Adjai** (c. 1807–1891), CMS missionary and first African Anglican bishop (Bishop of the Niger), was born in Oshogun in modern Nigeria as a member of the Egba section of the Yoruba people. His African name is often rendered today as 'Ajayi'. Like many young West Africans he was captured by slave traders and put on a ship for the Americas. By then a British naval squadron was seeking to intercept the traders and their cargoes off the coast. Adjai was captured from the Portuguese ship *Esperanza Felix* in 1822. He was landed, with other captives, in Sierra Leone, the 'province of freedom'. Here he became a Christian and was baptized with the name of Samuel Crowther, an eminent evangelical clergyman of the day who was a supporter of the Church Missionary Society (CMS). He had a great aptitude for learning and in 1827 became the first pupil to be enrolled in Fourah Bay College, a CMS foundation that aimed to train able Sierra Leoneans for missionary service; in 1876 the college was affiliated to the University of Durham to enable it to grant degrees. Crowther became a tutor at Fourah Bay and married another captive from the same slave ship, Susan Thompson. He was appointed as a teacher at Regent in Sierra Leone in 1829, where he was assistant to the CMS missionary J. W. Weeks, later bishop of the colony (1855–1857). In 1841 Crowther was a member of the Niger expedition, which aimed to advance T. F. *Buxton's plan to introduce 'commerce and Christianity' into West Africa as an antidote to the slave trade; it was expounded in Buxton's *The African Slave Trade and its Remedy* (1840). Crowther's *Journal of an Expedition up the Niger in 1841* (written jointly with J. F. Schön) was published in 1843.

Crowther became a missionary to his own Yoruba people. He was ordained in England in 1843 after preparation at the CMS training college in Islington and worked with the influential CMS missionary Henry Townsend in Abeokuta from 1846. Here he was reunited with his mother, whom he had last seen in 1821, and who was baptized by her son in 1848. Crowther gave himself to the essential missionary task of translation. He produced a grammar and vocabulary of the Yoruba language in 1843 and was encouraged by Dandeson Coates, secretary of CMS, to translate Luke, Acts and the letter to the Romans. Coates' successor at CMS, Henry *Venn, established a strong personal relationship with Crowther and promoted his work through consultations with Professor Lee, the leading English authority of the day on orthography, and the great German linguist Professor Lepsius. As well as producing a Yoruba New Testament, Crowther translated the Book of Common Prayer in 1849–1850. He collected Yoruba proverbs on his travels and produced primers in Igbo and Nupe. Although he participated in further expeditions in 1854 and 1857, he regarded these as unwelcome interruptions of his real work of translation for his own and neighbouring peoples. Many of his resources for translating the Pentateuch and his collections of Yoruba and other proverbs were destroyed by fire in 1862, a disaster he met with admirable resolution; 'as soon as I am collected a little, I hope to sit down to work again' he wrote to Venn.

Henry Venn, who was secretary of CMS from 1841 to 1872, sought to establish churches that were indigenous; 'self-supporting, self-governing and self-extending'. Fundamental to this 'three-selfs' strategy was an indigenous ministry, with an indigenous bishop as its 'crown'. Venn had hoped for many years that Crowther would become such a bishop, but Crowther resisted the proposal. Confronted eventually by urgent appeals from the ageing Venn to grant him his wish, Crowther reluctantly agreed. He became 'Bishop of the countries of Western Africa beyond the Queen's dominions' (effectively bishop of the Niger mission stations, with no Europeans to oversee) and was consecrated at Canterbury on 29 June 1864 as the first black Anglican bishop.

Crowther's episcopate has attracted a great deal of scholarly attention and debate among both Nigerian and other historians, which has raised issues of racism and injustice on the part of CMS, European missionaries, commercial figures such as Sir George Goldie of the Royal Niger Company and the high imperialism of the 1880s, with its recurrent distrust of indigenous leadership in different parts of the world. Crowther was not working among his own people, the Yoruba, and he used other Sierra Leoneans who, like himself, were foreigners where they were working. His episcopate included some genuine missionary achievements, however, not least the work of J. C. Taylor at Onitsha, and the bishop was a pioneer in establishing friendly relationships with Muslims. Some members of his staff did not achieve his own high standards of Christian life and conduct, and one (W. F. John) was convicted of cruelty leading to the death of a slave girl. European critics later used this incident and others to accuse the bishop of being lax in discipline. Some of the white missionaries of the time were very willing to condemn others, perhaps as a result of a hyper-spirituality associated with the Keswick convention. This was reflected especially in the life of G. W. Brooke, a young lay missionary with CMS, whose influence was excessive in relation to his age and experience. After supporting Crowther for many years, until long after Venn's death, CMS finally gave way to the critics and put the administration of the diocese into European hands. The bishop himself bore his trials with humble dignity, offered his resignation to CMS in 1884 and wrote that Europeans were 'better managers'.

As a sad result of Crowther's experience, his able son, Archdeacon Dandeson Crowther, who had served the diocese from 1876,

decided in 1892 to secede and form the Delta Pastorate Church, which was independent of CMS and European missionaries. Crowther was succeeded by a European bishop and became 'a symbol, not only of African leadership but also of the supposed failure of African leadership', so that 'for half a century or more Africans were considered insufficiently "mature" for leadership in the church' (B. Sundkler, *The Christian Ministry in Africa*, pp. 46f.). But whatever shortcomings may have counterbalanced the undoubted achievements of his episcopate, Bishop Crowther remains 'one of the greatest and most loveable personalities in nineteenth century African Church history' (B. Sundkler and C. Steed, *A History of the Church in Africa*, p. 225).

Bibliography
J. F. A. Ajayi, *Christian Missions in Nigeria 1841–1891: The Making of a New Elite* (London: Longmans, 1965); J. Page, *The Black Bishop* (London: Hodder & Stoughton, 1908); T. E. Yates, *Venn and Victorian Bishops Abroad* (London: SPCK, 1974); B. Sundkler and C. Steed, *A History of the Church in Africa*, (Cambridge: Cambridge University Press, 2000); B. Sundkler, *The Christian Ministry in Africa* (London: SCM Press, 1960).

T. E. YATES

■ **CUNNINGHAM, Loren** (1935–), evangelist, missionary and founder of Youth With a Mission (YWAM), a prominent interdenominational charismatic mission organization sponsoring thousands of young people in evangelistic and relief work in over a hundred countries, was a notable evangelical leader in the second half of the twentieth century through his books, his preaching and the worldwide influence of his organization. Loren Cunningham was born in Taft, California, in 1935, the son of Thomas Cunningham and Jewel Nicholson, ordained Assemblies of God pastors. He and his siblings grew up travelling; their parents were itinerant preachers and served as pastors in various small churches, mostly in the southwestern United States. Cunningham's early childhood experiences of vivid spiritual visions, and dreams and other such experiences later in his life, are recorded in his autobiography. Divine guidance and supernatural experiences became significant themes in his life and ministry.

Cunningham sensed a call to ministry at the age of thirteen, after hearing his mother preach at a family reunion in Springdale, Arkansas. He recalled how he knelt at the altar and bold letters appeared before his eyes saying, 'Go ye into all the world and preach the gospel.' When he shared this vision with his mother, she confirmed his call to the ministry and bought him a pair of expensive new shoes symbolizing 'the feet of those shod with the preparation of the gospel of peace' (Ephesians 6:15, KJV). Soon afterwards, he preached his first sermon in his parents' church, and he has ever since regarded this as his inauguration into ministry. He was later ordained by the Assemblies of God and served in that denomination until he withdrew to begin his own mission organization in 1964.

Cunningham had one of his most vivid experiences, which further altered the course of his life, in 1956 in Nassau, the capital of the Bahamas Islands. He was there on a mission trip with a group of young Americans. One night, while staying in a missionary's home, he looked up at the ceiling from his bed and saw a vision of a map of the world with waves crashing against the shores of every continent; the waves were composed of throngs of young people reaching every part of the earth with the gospel. Cunningham believed that this vision was a call to a lifelong mission of recruiting, training and mobilizing young people to go all over the world preaching the gospel and conducting innovative mission work.

In 1963 Cunningham married Darlene Scratch, who became his lifelong partner in ministry. They had two children. Cunningham attended Central Bible Institute and Seminary (Central Bible College) in Springfield, Missouri and received a BA in Bible and Theology and a BA in Christian Education in 1957. He also received a BA in Religion and Philosophy from the University of Southern California in 1958 and an MS in Administration and Supervision of Education in 1979.

Cunningham is credited with developing a creative strategy for enabling large numbers of young people to participate in effective short-term projects; it was used later by many other organizations. His approach maximized the involvement of college-age young people and various other volunteers, and employed large numbers of full-time workers in raising their own support. The theological foundation for YWAM's ministry was conceived by Cunningham as a practical implementation of the basic commands of Christ to love God and love the neighbour. These commands define the mission of the organization as understood and articulated by its workers. His inspirational leadership style enabled Cunningham to present cross-cultural mission as a desirable opportunity for young people.

In the early years of his movement Cunningham hoped to keep it under the authority of the Assemblies of God. He reluctantly faced the possibility of independence only when he learned that he could not fully realize his vision within the denomination. In 1964, after an important meeting with the Assemblies' General Superintendent, Thomas *Zimmerman, he resigned.

Cunningham soon thereafter incorporated an independent, nondenominational mission organization called Youth With a Mission. It grew rapidly to become one of the largest evangelical organizations in the world, with a staff of over 15,000 from more than 130 countries. More than three million students, volunteers and staff have served with YWAM. The organization is currently based in over 135 countries, with more than 30,000 active volunteers, and over 200,000 workers in short-term projects. To train his workers Cunningham established an educational institution, The University of The Nations, in Kona, Hawaii, and hundreds of satellite programmes worldwide. Training centres were also established in Holland, Australia, Switzerland, Germany and several other nations, with extension programmes in over 100 countries.

Cunningham developed a creative relief effort utilizing ocean liners and other ships; heading the fleet was the *Anastasis*, which became the largest floating hospital of its kind in existence. He also equipped *The Good Samaritan* and other sea vessels for major relief work. These ocean vessels were commissioned as 'mercy ships' providing medical care, food and other basic assistance, mostly to countries in the developing world.

In 1972 YWAM missionaries gained international attention following a tragedy at the summer Olympics in Munich. Several Israeli athletes were taken hostage and killed, and the international media featured hundreds of YWAM workers reaching out and providing a calming presence in the difficult international climate. These events gave Cunningham and YWAM a positive image that opened doors throughout the world for years to come and made YWAM one of the most significant evangelical organizations during the second half of the century.

Cunningham's personal journey of faith is told in his widely read devotional autobiography, *Is That Really You God?* He has also written *Making Jesus Lord*, *To Live on the Edge: The Adventure of Faith and Finances*, and *Why Not Women?*

Bibliography
L. Cunningham, *Is that Really You God?* (Seattle: YWAM Publishing, 1984).

D. HEDGES

■ **DABNEY, Robert Lewis** (1820–1898), southern Old School Presbyterian pastor and theologian, was born in Louisa County, Virginia, to an English Presbyterian family. His father, Charles, was a ruling elder, and just before his death in 1833 was elected to the state legislature. Like most genteel Virginians, the family owned slaves. Dabney studied at Hampden-Sydney College (1836–1837) and the University of Virginia (1839–1842) and received his theological education at Union Theological Seminary (1844–1846).

His letters from this period reflect both a strong sense of loyalty to Virginia and a patronizing attitude towards the Scots-Irish farmers' sons who attended Union Seminary. He considered them worthy, perhaps, to pastor the small rural congregations of the backcountry, but they should not, he thought, be considered for influential urban congregations. After brief service as a supply preacher, he was ordained by Lexington Presbytery on 16 July 1847 as pastor of Tinkling Spring Church near Staunton, Virginia, where he ministered until 1853. He married Margaret Lavinia Morrison, daughter of a nearby Presbyterian minister, in 1848. They had six sons, three of whom died in childhood.

In 1853 Dabney was appointed Professor of Ecclesiastical History and Polity at Union Theological Seminary (the seminary was operated by the synods of Virginia and North Carolina), switching to systematic theology in 1859. From 1858 to 1874 Dabney also served as co-pastor with Benjamin M. Smith of the College Church in Hampden-Sydney. He received several calls to other service, such as the 1859 call to Fifth Avenue Presbyterian Church in New York City, and the 1860 call to the chair of ecclesiastical history at Princeton Seminary, but Dabney was committed to Union Seminary and the cause of theological education in the South, and particularly in his beloved Virginia.

While he made several efforts at conciliation prior to 1861 (and viewed South Carolina as almost as much of a nuisance as the North), Dabney was convinced of the righteousness of the southern cause; and when Virginia seceded, Dabney served as a military chaplain in 1861 and then as a major under General 'Stonewall' Jackson in 1862, serving as his chief of staff. Following the death of Jackson in 1863, Dabney wrote the *Life and Campaigns of Lieutenant-General Thomas J. Jackson* (1866) as well as his famous *A Defense of Virginia (and Through Her of the South)* (1867). In 1864–1865 he served as an *ad hoc* missionary to the army as it retreated through Virginia, before returning to Union Seminary.

While northern aid helped to restore the seminary, Dabney became convinced that the 'better sort' were moving out of Virginia due to increasing 'northern ascendency' in the state and considered joining a southern exodus to Brazil or Australia. He feared that the southern Presbyterian Church would either be swallowed up by the northern church or face 'ecclesiastical amalgamation with negroes'. But during the 1870s, as Virginians began to regain control of the state, he determined to stay.

The 1870s were a prolific decade for Dabney. He published his lectures on *Sacred Rhetoric* (1870) and his *Syllabus and Notes of the Course of Systematic and Polemic Theology* (1871), along with *The Sensualist Philosophy of the Nineteenth Century* (1875) and several articles in the *Southern Presbyterian Review* and *The Central Presbyterian* (among other journals).

While Dabney was a staunch supporter of Old School Presbyterianism, he was more southern than Old School. Both the New School and the Old School (who had parted company in 1837) had divided along sectional lines in 1857 and 1861 respectively. During the war, in 1863, the tiny southern New School (the United Synod of the South) was accepted by the much larger southern Old School (the Presbyterian Church in the Confederate States of America), mainly due to Dabney's argument that the merger would ensure that all New School candidates would attend Old School seminaries, thereby preventing the spread of New School theology and creating a united southern Presbyterian Church.

In 1869 northern Presbyterians reunited, and in 1870 they made overtures to the southern church with proposals to move towards merger. Dabney, as moderator of the southern General Assembly that year, vigorously opposed any such union, but as the 1870s progressed, Virginia Presbyterians sought closer ties with the North and increasingly distanced themselves from Dabney's southern isolationism. In 1883, as Dabney's health was deteriorating, he received an invitation to become the Professor of Moral and Mental Philosophy at the newly formed University of Texas. In Austin he helped to found Austin Theological Seminary, where he taught from 1884 to 1895. By 1890 he had lost his eyesight, but continued to lecture at both institutions. During these years he published *Christ Our Penal Substitute* (1897), *The Practical Philosophy* (1897), and his massive *Discussions* (4 vols., 1890–1897), along with numerous articles.

Dabney's theology was largely that of the Westminster Confession and the Genevan theologian Francis Turretin (1623–1687) and is quite comparable to that of Charles *Hodge. Dabney differed from the Princeton theologian with respect to the doctrines of original sin and imputation, suggesting that Hodge was too narrow in his understanding of the Christian's federal union with Christ. Also Dabney, with many other southern Presbyterians, viewed baptized children as 'unregenerate' and insisted that they were to be viewed neither as members of the invisible church nor as subjects of church discipline until they personally professed faith in Christ.

Dabney was convinced that religion was primarily a rational matter. Therefore he objected to revival preaching as appealing too much to the emotions, and he urged preachers to focus on the rational presentation of the truths of the gospel. An advocate of Scottish common-sense realism, Dabney claimed that the truth of God's existence is not a primary intuitive truth but requires deduction from such truths as the existence of an external world, cause and effect and the existence of the soul.

Dabney tended to be suspicious of natural science, and from 1873 he engaged in a debate over the relationship between science and theology with James Woodrow (uncle of Woodrow Wilson), professor at Columbia Theological Seminary. Dabney professed to be open to most geological views but desired theistic scientists to acknowledge that God might have created the universe with the appearance of age.

Frequently writing on social and political matters, Dabney believed in a republic governed by an aristocracy of intellect and character rather than a democracy, and he feared the influence of money over virtue. He penned a thoughtful critique of industrial capitalism and the dangers of allowing capital to control labour. In the 1890s he defended the single currency standard and argued that the interests of farmers were being overlooked by the 'money oligarchy'. His 1894 article 'Economic Effects of the Former Labor System of the Southern United States' defended the economic benefits of slavery.

Convinced also that public education infringed upon the right and duty of parents to educate their children, Dabney inveighed against the establishment of universal common schools, calling for a modified antebellum plan which would allow for a segregated literary fund by which white and black parents could establish and operate their own schools, with white money paying for white schools and black money paying for black schools. In the 1850s he had objected to the Old School Presbyterian attempt to establish parochial schools on the same ground of parental rights.

Dabney also argued that Virginia should establish high qualifications of property and intelligence for the vote, thereby eliminating most blacks and many whites. Universal education and universal suffrage, in his eyes, could result only in the sort of 'blind ignorance and brutal passion' that he believed the North had exhibited in the Civil War. As the New South was emerging, Dabney remained entrenched in the antebellum era.

Bibliography
T. C. Johnson, *The Life and Letters of Robert Lewis Dabney* (Richmond: The Presbyterian Committee of Publication, 1903); D. H. Overy, 'Robert Lewis Dabney: Apostle of the Old South' (PhD thesis, University of Wisconsin–Madison, 1967).

P. J. WALLACE

■ **DALE, Robert William** (1829–1895), Congregational theologian, was born in London on 1 December 1829. His mother and father, a dealer in hat trimmings, were members of Moorfield Tabernacle; the minister there during Dale's childhood was John Campbell, the most outspoken rearguard activist for Calvinism in a denomination that was rapidly relegating that theology to its past. Dale was converted at the age of fourteen. A year or so later, in 1845, he started preaching and contributing to Christian magazines and then produced a very precocious book entitled *The Talents*, published in 1846. In 1847 he began training for the ministry at Spring Hill College, Birmingham; so it was that at seventeen years of age he settled in the city which remained his home for the rest of his life. John Angell *James, minister at Carrs Lane, the principal Congregational church in Birmingham, appreciated Dale's qualities and chose him as his assistant when he completed his studies in 1853. A year later he was ordained as co-pastor. He took over leadership of the church when James died in 1859, and at the time of his own death there, on 13 March 1895, he was still leading a large congregation that had resisted the decline that was by then starting to overtake other inner-city churches.

R. W. Dale was the most prominent of the group of ministers who made up an informal collective leadership for the Congregational Union in his generation. That he was elected its chairman for 1869, before his fortieth birthday, is a sign of this prominence, and his status was sealed towards the end of his life by his selection as president of the first International Council of Congregational Churches (1891). He was prominent on the political scene too, not only locally in Birmingham in association with Joseph Chamberlain, but also in national Liberal circles, where he made his mark especially in the fraught education debates of his time.

The awareness and respect this prominence brought Dale helped in gathering an audience for his theology. Another contributory factor was the shortage of theological work of any quality being done around him. He was unusual in late nineteenth-century Nonconformity simply in preserving the ideal of a theological system. (Even C. H. *Spurgeon wrote, 'Angels may, perhaps, be systematic divines; for men it should be enough to follow the word of God, let its teachings wind as they may' [*The Sword and the Trowel* 4 (1868), p. 102]). But having an ideal is one thing, achieving it quite another; Dale confessed in 1880 that at the age of fourteen he had known more theology than he did then (*The Evangelical Revival and Other Sermons* [London, 1880, p. 263]). During his theological studies his early Calvinism failed to withstand the transcendental critique of George Dawson (whose church he attended) and the searing heat of Thomas Carlyle's brand of Romanticism; Dale said of Carlyle that 'He was more to us for a while than all our tutors; more to us than all the theologians and fathers of the church' ('Thomas Carlyle', *Congregationalist* 10 [1881], p. 210). But replacing it with anything like as comprehensive in the end proved beyond him, despite gallant efforts.

Dale always felt that his evangelical heritage was an expression of authentic Christianity, though one in need of radical reworking (he habitually distinguished between permanent 'substance' and transitory 'form'). He had a grand view of the scale of the task, believing that the collapse of Protestant scholasticism was bringing to a close the entire theological cycle that began with the Reformation. An entirely new system was needed, though he believed it would preserve all the great evangelical doctrines. He thought the process would be lengthy, proceeding at the rate of a doctrine or two per generation.

His own theology was thus an attempt to contribute to that process by combining his evangelical heritage with new Romantic emphases: on human moral freedom; on the divine power of conscience in interpreting the 'eternal law of righteousness', as he termed it; and on direct intuition of God (which he concluded was the 'ultimate principle' of Protestantism). At the heart of the new matrix of ideas lay an ethical system, broadly Kantian and set in a vocabulary Dale borrowed from Coleridge, and the difficulty Dale had in system-building has much to do with his struggle to resolve the dualism between this ethical track and his evangelical spirituality.

The crucial question for Dale was the relationship between the two authorities, God and the 'eternal law', and their respective mediators, Christ and conscience. In his earlier thinking he rejected both the Calvinist understanding of the law as the expression of God's nature and the Grotian view that it was an expression of his will. Instead, his conscience (with a little help from John Stuart Mill) dictated his conclusion that the law was independent, necessary and eternal, and that God himself was righteous only because he was true to it, thereby paying it homage ('The Expiatory Theory of the Atonement', *British Quarterly Review* 46 [1867], pp. 484–487). Later he backed away from the implication that the law was over God and progressively transferred his emphasis from the former to the latter; he was stimulated to this transfer by his growing opposition to what he observed to be the results of ethical liberalism when it lacked his compensating evangelical spirituality. Henry *Wace's idea that righteousness is a relation between persons helped him in this change of emphasis. But in his later theology he hesitated between separation and integration of the two authorities: at times he maintained that God and the law are distinct and equal authorities, the latter operating in the sphere of conscience and the former in that of the will (e.g. *The Atonement*, [7]1878, pp. 363–373); but on other occasions his language belies this: God is 'the living law of righteousness' (*The Epistle to the Ephesians*, p. 66), and Christ is 'the Eternal Law of Righteousness incarnate' (*Laws of Christ for Common Life*, 1884, p. 283).

But who is this incarnate Christ? Dale shared the Romantic predilection for internal over external authority; the picture of Christ in the Gospels could be verified and authenticated only to the extent that spiritual experience confirmed the written accounts. He thus shared in the liberal search for an experiential grounding of spiritual faith that would be proof against any assault from biblical criticism, in the process arguing for the mutual autonomy of the two realms (something to which he did not in practice fully adhere). Though he called Christ an 'objective conscience' (*Laws of Christ*, p. 281), the Christ to whom he could entrust himself fully resembled more a subjective conscience. And Dale's appeal to the authority of experience did not escape the characteristic weaknesses of such an apologetic: inability to escape all dependence on external authority and a naïve belief that all religious experience witnesses to the truth.

Dale's busy and many-sided ministry left him time for just one major theological project, a study of the doctrine of atonement. After important preliminary articles published in the 1860s, his main effort was presented as the Congregational Union Lecture for 1875, published as *The Atonement*. He shared the concern of John McLeod Campbell among others that the end product of atonement should be a genuine righteousness and not the 'fictitious imputation' of the traditional substitutionary theory. He rejected purely subjective theories, and also wished to preserve the principle of retributive justice in some way, an aspect of traditional thinking his conscience affirmed.

The focus of the first of the four points in which Dale summarized his work on the theory of atonement is on acknowledgment of the righteousness of the law. Christ's action here is twofold: firstly (as in Campbell's theory), he acknowledged the righteousness of sin's penalty; but secondly (going beyond Campbell), Jesus actually submitted to that penalty, God-forsakenness and death. Dale did not equate this submission to the penalty with punishment; he believed the latter is only possible where there is actual sin and guilt. This action of Christ's *can* relate to us because of the original and ideal relationship between Christ and humanity; Christ is the root of humanity, and his life is in us when we trust and submit to him. It is that underlying fact that made incarnation possible. For this thinking Dale's principal debt is to F. D.

Maurice. Christ's action *does* relate to us when we ask God to accept both his attitude and his act as our own homage to the righteousness of the law.

In his second point Dale's focus is on the reality of reconciliation between God and humanity or, in his language, on the retention or recovery of the original and ideal relationship that was spoilt by sin. Our problem is that sin has so changed our perspective that we cannot see how Christ's relationship to the Father can have any relevance to our own situation of alienation. But Christ solves this problem by putting himself right where sin had brought us in relation to God, thereby enabling us to see that we can approach God and retain or recover our relationship with him. This point is, therefore, a version of the subjective theory of atonement, which Dale considered inadequate on its own.

The third point is concerned with the righteousness of humanity, for Dale was convinced that genuine righteousness, not just a righteous status, had to be the outcome of atonement. The death of Christ involves the actual destruction of sin in those who through faith recover their union with him. This comes about because of the mystical relationship with him that is discussed in the first point.

The last point seeks to vindicate the righteousness of God. Dale wished to affirm the principle of retribution but to deny its application; how then could God be acting justly? Dale's answer was that the moral significance of retribution lies in its cost to the judge; the cost to both Father and Son of the Son's suffering the penalties of sin was greater than that of inflicting them on the guilty, so the principle of retribution thereby received greater recognition than would have been achieved by its implementation.

With typical modesty Dale accepted that these points did not amount to a complete theory. The stronger part of the lectures may actually be the careful and detailed work on the text of the New Testament that formed the majority of their content. The cumulative argument for an early church doctrine of expiatory sacrifice that emerged from this put a formidable obstacle in the way of any attempt to ground a purely subjective theory in the New Testament. *The Atonement* was considered by R. C. Moberly to have been the

book on the subject most familiar to members of the Church of England in the last quarter of the nineteenth century. A seventeenth edition came out shortly after Dale's death, and the book's rate of sale was then on the increase. But Moberly himself may have borne some responsibility for its rapid eclipse after the dawn of the twentieth century, in part through the popularity of his own work. He also pronounced a limited life expectancy for *The Atonement* in calling it 'a real and solid contribution to the faith and goodness of [Dale's] own generation', while suggesting that the earlier and lesser-known work of McLeod Campbell was philosophically and theologically in advance of Dale. It is unfortunate that Moberly's most prominent criticism was entirely erroneous; he understood Dale's belief that Jesus suffered the penalties of sin to mean that he suffered its punishment.

In contrast to his struggle to innovate in his work on atonement, Dale stood firmly in the mainstream of the Congregational tradition in his ecclesiology. His writing in this area is, however, noteworthy for the exceptional power and clarity of his high Congregationalism, which stood out all the more because he lived in a time when it was unusual, squeezed out by a combination of inattentive evangelical pragmatism and liberal rejection of its premise of a clear division between the converted and the unconverted.

The Atonement apart, most of Dale's publications are journal articles and collections of sermons and addresses. Among the most significant for an understanding of his theology are *The Living Christ and the Four Gospels* (London: Hodder & Stoughton, 1890) and *Fellowship with Christ and Other Discourses Delivered on Special Occasions* (London: 1891).

Dale's theology is marked by a mixture of elements drawn from older Protestant sources and those of newer, liberal inspiration. Both worlds attracted him, and his attempt to find some way of bringing them together was the most serious in English nonconformity in his generation. Yet it failed; his 'new evangelicalism' was as unstable and impermanent as the better known 'liberal evangelicalism' of the next generation. Firmly ensconced in one of the two worlds Dale tried to straddle, Spurgeon alluded to the unresolved tension in inimitable style: 'He is too gracious ever to become a success as a heretic.'

Bibliography
A. W. W. Dale, *The Life of R. W. Dale of Birmingham* (London: 1898); M. T. E. Hopkins, *Evangelical and Liberal Theologies in Victorian England: Nonconformity's Romantic Generation* (Carlisle: Paternoster, forthcoming); M. D. Johnson, *The Dissolution of Dissent, 1850–1918* (New York: Garland, 1987).

M. T. E. HOPKINS

■ **DARBY, John Nelson** (1800–1882), Brethren writer and itinerant preacher, was born on 18 November 1800 in Great George Street, Westminster, London, the youngest son among nine surviving children. He received his second name in honour of Lord Nelson, under whom an uncle, Admiral Sir Henry D'Esterre Darby, had commanded. His father, John Darby (1751–1834) of Markly, Warbleton, Sussex, was a merchant and an austere, taciturn individual who apparently profited as a naval supplier during the Napoleonic Wars. In 1823 on the death of Henry, Darby's father inherited Leap Castle, King's County (later County Offaly), Ireland. Darby's mother was Anne Vaughan (d. 1847), the daughter of a merchant and plantation owner in the Americas. Darby was baptized in St Margaret's Church, Westminster, on 3 March 1801, and from 1812 until 1815 he was educated at Westminster School, London, where his career appears to have been unremarkable. In 1815, at the age of fourteen, he entered Trinity College, Dublin, and he graduated as the classical gold medallist in 1819. In this last year he was also admitted to King's Inn, Dublin, and then to Lincoln's Inn, London, but continued to receive his legal training in Dublin. He was called to the Irish bar in 1822 but, according to his contemporary F. W. Newman, did not practise, concerned that 'he should be selling his services to defeat justice'.

About 1820 Darby had an experience of 'salvation and peace'. Apparently in 1824, longing 'for complete devotedness to the work of the Lord' and to the annoyance of his father, he determined to seek ordination. He was admitted to deacon's orders in 1825,

being ordained the following year and was appointed to the rural district of Calary, County Wicklow, which was evidently then a missionary charge. There he devoted himself to his duties, spending long evenings travelling among the poverty-stricken local people and eating the food they offered, with the result that (again according to Newman) he 'might have vied in emaciation with a monk of La Trappe'. Darby's churchmanship had been high; he later described himself as being in this period 'a conservative by birth, by education and by mind; a Protestant in Ireland into the bargain'. In 1827 the Irish Archbishops of Armagh and Dublin petitioned Parliament against Catholic emancipation, and the latter then imposed oaths of allegiance on Roman Catholic converts within his province. With others, Darby blamed these actions for stopping the flow of conversions then in progress, and he wrote a pamphlet, which was circulated privately, critical of the church's Erastianism. Late in 1827 his knee was severely injured when his horse crushed it against a doorpost, and until February 1828 he retired to recuperate at the home in Delgany of his sister, Susannah, and her husband, Edward Pennefather, later Lord Chief Justice of Ireland. During his compulsory retreat he came to an understanding of union with Christ through which he was 'forced to the conclusion it was no longer this wretched "I" which had wearied me for six or seven years in presence of the requirements of the law'. In 1863 he described his new understanding as being 'the absolute, divine authority and certainty of the Word, as a divine link between us and God, if everything (church and world) went; personal assurance of salvation in a new condition by being in Christ; the church as His body; Christ coming to receive us to Himself; and collaterally with that, the setting up of a new earthly dispensation, from Isaiah xxxii ...'

Doubtless this account makes his earlier experience appear too tidy, but he was evidently able to detect in it the central themes of his later theology in germ. It was also while in Dublin that he influenced two of the Pennefather children's tutors: Joseph C. Philpot, later a prominent Strict Baptist minister, and Francis W. Newman, then a fellow of Balliol College, Oxford.

It is uncertain how much influence Darby

had on the origins of the Brethren movement about this time. The participants' accounts, all written much later, are hard to reconcile, and opinion among historians tends to be correlated to their degree of admiration for Darby. According to one of his own statements, four individuals who were searching for Christian unity, had been visiting him: 'I proposed to them to break bread the following Sunday, which we did.' The event is variously dated by him, but it is clear that he was only fitfully present at the group, which, according to his contemporary at Trinity, J. G. Bellett, met in Dublin from 1829. Darby resigned his curacy, but he did not immediately secede; instead he itinerated, preaching in Anglican churches in his clerical robes. In 1830, at the invitation of Newman, he visited Oxford, where he was introduced to B. W. *Newton and impressed him. He supported his new Oxford friends in theological controversy and (possibly with one of them, George V. Wigram) visited Scotland to investigate the Clydeside prophesyings but was unimpressed. With Wigram and Newton, in 1832 Darby was responsible for establishing a new congregation at Plymouth, where he claimed, 'I have not met the children of God dwelling so much together in unity', and he apparently began to promote its order in his itinerancy. From 1831 conferences for the discussion of prophecy had been held at Powerscourt House, near Dublin, the home of Theodosia Wingfield, the widow of Lord Powerscourt. According to oral tradition, Lady Powerscourt and Darby considered marriage, but his itinerancy counted against it. Darby took a leading part in the Powerscourt discussions, and by 1833 it would appear that his separatist prophetic scheme was being formulated more firmly. A further impetus to secession was his continuing dissatisfaction with Anglicanism. He criticized in print the support the new anti-evangelical Archbishop of Dublin gave to the Irish education measures of 1832, which left religious education largely to the children's own churches. In 1833 the Irish Home Missionary Society was suppressed because of its ecclesiastical irregularities, and Darby responded with a pamphlet critical of the way in which, in his view, the institutional church repressed the action of the Holy Spirit, a point made more forcibly in an unpublished pamphlet of this period 'The Notion of a

Clergyman Dispensationally the Sin against the Holy Ghost'.

In 1835 Darby visited Switzerland. During his return visit of 1837 he made contact with groups of *dissidents* who were the product of the *réveil* of the previous decade, and on his next visit he stayed in Switzerland from 1839 until 1843, with the exception of a brief excursion into France in 1842. Initially he helped with pastoral and theological problems, but his lectures at Geneva in 1840, *The Hopes of the Church of God*, gave the most systematic exposition of his eschatology to date. Darby was developing his theory that the church was 'in ruins'. Israel and the church were allocated to different dispensations (divine modes of administration), and Christians would be removed from the earth before the public return of Christ and the reinstatement of Israel. Groups began meeting in the Brethren manner in several of the cantons, and Darby became embroiled in a pamphlet war with various protagonists. He now maintained that the church should not be restored but that Christians should meet in informal groups for the Lord's Supper. At a stormy meeting in 1842 with its pastors Darby finally broke from Swiss *Dissidence*. He gathered a group of men about him whom he taught and who then spread his principles in Switzerland and France. His Swiss experience confirmed Darby in his attitude to other evangelicals, the rightness of his teaching and his capacity for autonomous leadership.

In England Newton was also establishing a sphere of influence in which the new developments in Darby's premillennialism were rejected. After further visits to France and Switzerland, in March 1845 Darby returned to Plymouth, where he accused Newton of attempting to form a sect. In December, after several bitter oral and written exchanges which widened the conflict to include Newton's ecclesiology and behaviour, Darby began a separate congregation. After the publication in 1847 of a lecture by Newton containing unorthodox Christological statements, Darby proclaimed him a heretic and later refused to accept his retraction. When in 1848 two members of Newton's former congregation applied for membership at Bethesda Chapel, Bristol, Darby widened the schism to its pastors, George *Müller and Henry Craik because they did not condemn Newton's errors in the manner that he required. Henceforth, Brethren were divided into 'Exclusive' and 'Open' sections, the former following Darby's unofficial leadership in excluding the latter. Otherwise, Darby continued to practise an open communion for fellow evangelicals free from known sins and errors, although the latter qualification and intensifying separatism would increasingly make this openness one in principle only.

For the remainder of his life Darby continued itinerating. In Europe he spent most of his time in Britain, Switzerland and France. Brethrenism had spread from Switzerland to France. Darby apparently spent most of 1849–1850 there and made several other visits, pioneering, evangelizing and teaching, mainly in the south of the country where the movement spread most widely. From at least 1843 onwards he also visited the Netherlands, where various individuals had been won over to Brethren thinking, but here Darby's own activities were hampered by his lack of fluency in speaking Dutch. His first visit to Germany in 1853 was at the request of Christians in the Prussian Rhineland who had become Brethren, and on later visits he travelled elsewhere in the country, mainly in the north-west. He also visited Milan and Turin at least twice, in 1860 and 1871. However, although he influenced the Italian Free Churches through his translated writings, Exclusive Brethrenism had little success in Italy. In addition to the rather literal translation of the New Testament that he made from Greek into English (1868), he also made translations into German (NT, 1854; OT, 1871) and French (NT, 1859; OT, 1885). His best-known work, *Synopsis of the Books of the Bible* (1857–1867), ran to five volumes and was originally written in French. Darby's presence was not always welcomed by government officials, and the political conditions of continental European countries were unstable at times during his visits. He was aided by his stamina and ability to endure privations. In 1854 he reported from Westphalia, 'In these villages no question of meat in four out of six places, but rye bread and vegetables and a slice of bacon. One night I slept on chairs, another on straw.'

In 1868–1869 he also visited the West Indies, where Brethren evangelism among the Afro-Caribbean population had produced converts. Earlier, in 1862, he had journeyed to North America to visit French and Swiss Brethren immigrants, and in the following fifteen years he made a further six visits. He was very critical of what he believed to be the materialism of American society and the worldliness of its churches; a Calvinist in theology, he complained of 'what is the pest of the United States, the substitution of work for Christ'. On his initial visit he remained mainly in Ontario, Canada, and the annual Brethren conference in Guelph subsequently remained an attraction, but on later visits he travelled more widely. After 1872, in cities such as Chicago, Boston and New York, he began to have a wider influence on church leaders who were impressed by his biblical knowledge. He met D. L. *Moody, whom he dismissed as 'the active man at Chicago'. However, although a number of influential individuals, including Moody, accepted his eschatology, Darby was disappointed by his failure to gain many for the Brethren. On his 1875 visit to America he travelled to San Francisco and from there to New Zealand. In New Zealand he consolidated the task, begun by his loyal lieutenant Wigram, of bringing the Brethren there into conformity to Exclusive principles with regard to separation from other Christians, forcing several congregational schisms in the process. In 1876 Darby returned to America via Melbourne, where he spoke at a Brethren conference, and Sydney.

In 1858 Darby had commenced publication of some papers on Christology which maintained that there was an aspect of Christ's sufferings which was non-atoning due to his identification with Israel, an idea similar to that for which he had condemned Newton. As a result, several longstanding associates seceded from him in 1866. More serious was the 'Ramsgate' division of 1878–1881 forced by the 'New Lumpists', a faction whose members felt that ecclesiology was being neglected in favour of evangelism. It was decided that Edward Cronin, one of the Dublin founders, had been too precipitate in acknowledging a new assembly, and he was excommunicated. In the ensuing schism Darby supported the judgment, but his most able disciple, the scholarly William Kelly, who had edited his *Collected Writings*, went with the dissenters.

Darby was a complex personality. A learned individual, he was familiar with theology from the Church Fathers to contemporary authors and wrote works dealing with many of the religious controversies of the day. His influence was wider than Brethrenism. Robert Pearsall *Smith, the holiness teacher, was convinced by Darby's exegesis of Romans, and consequently it passed into Keswick teaching. Dispensationalism, which was systematized and popularized by C. I. *Scofield in his *Reference Bible* (1909), became orthodoxy within Protestant fundamentalism. Yet many of Darby's writings are impenetrable, rapidly written and unrevised. Disputatious with his peers, he enjoyed the company of the poor and was capable of considerable tenderness. 'Christ preferred the poor; ever since I have been converted so have I,' he wrote. Once, in the United States, he realized that the meal some poor people were offering him consisted of their child's pet rabbit. Darby refused to eat and afterwards spent an hour playing with the little boy. Family legacies had left him financially independent, but he was careless of personal appearance, as noted by F. W. Newman in his description of Darby in 1827: 'A fallen cheek, a bloodshot eye, crippled limbs resting on crutches, a seldom shaven beard, a shabby suit of clothes, and a generally neglected person, drew at first pity, with wonder to see such a person in a drawing-room.'

One critic, Open Brethren historian F. R. Coad, wrote of him, 'It would be trite to see his deplorable actions only as the fruit of a subconscious drive for power ... Somehow, beneath it all, there was also the force of a genuine and intense devotion to Christ' (*A History of the Brethren Movement* [Exeter: Paternoster Press, ²1976], p. 162). In 1881 Darby suffered a bad fall at the railway station in Dundee from which he never fully recovered. He died on 29 April 1882 at Sundridge House, Bournemouth, the home of a friend.

Bibliography
H. H. Rowdon, *The Origins of the Brethren 1825–50* (London: Pickering & Inglis, 1968); E. R. Sandeen, *The Roots of Fundamentalism: British and American Millenarianism 1800–1930* (Chicago: University of Chicago Press, 1970); T. C. F. Stunt, *Radical Evangelicals in Switzerland and Britain 1815–35* (Edinburgh: T. & T. Clark, 2000).

N. DICKSON

■ **DAVIES, Samuel** (1723–1761), Presbyterian revivalist, church-planter and educator, was born in New Castle County, Delaware, on 3 November 1723. His mother, Martha, who with his father was of Welsh descent, directed Samuel Davies' early education. When she moved from a Baptist to a Presbyterian church, she followed the guidance of the local Presbyterian minister and enrolled Davies in the classical academy of the Revd Samuel Blair in Fagg's Manor, Pennsylvania. Through Blair, a renowned teacher as well as a supporter of George Whitefield, Davies was connected to his era's rising tide of evangelicalism.

Shortly after Davies finished his study with Blair, he was licensed for the ministry by the New Side (or revivalistic) Presbytery of New Castle on 30 July 1746. In February of the next year he was ordained by his presbytery as an evangelist to Virginia, where there were no ministers not sanctioned by the colony's Anglican establishment. Davies spent one month in the spring of 1747 travelling through Hanover County, but not before he obtained a licence to preach from the Virginia General Court. This effort was cut short by illness, but he returned the next year, again taking care first to obtain a preaching licence, and established a permanent ministry. On 4 October 1748 Davies married Jane Holt, sister of the Virginia printer John Holt, who later published some of his books. (Davies was earlier married briefly to Sarah Kirkpatrick, who died in childbirth.) Five of the children of Samuel and Jane Davies survived to adulthood.

In a Virginia career of barely ten years Davies was a marvel. Before he left the colony in 1759, seven Presbyterian churches had been founded, a presbytery organized, and Presbyterian preaching stations established at several locations in Virginia and North Carolina. Davies was particularly effective in obtaining legal rights for non-Anglicans. His success came about in part through his skill at negotiating with the governor, the legislator and the Anglican clergy. In particular, he argued that rights granted to English

Dissenters by Parliament's 1689 Act of Toleration were just as valid in the colonies as in the mother country. A tremendous asset in Davies' effort to legitimize Dissent, however, was his dedicated service to the British cause during the Seven Years' (or French and Indian) War. During this conflict, which began in the colonies in 1754, Davies preached several memorable sermons that roused Virginians to defend their lands and freedoms against an enemy he described as a vicious blend of Roman Catholic bigotry and Native American savagery. In these sermons Davies did call upon his listeners to repent of their sins before God, but that repentance was pictured in utilitarian terms as a prerequisite for receiving the divine blessing upon British military efforts. Davies thus joined together themes of liberty, patriotism and Christian faith that, one generation later, his American successors turned against British rule.

Davies' preaching was famous even more for its effective gospel message than for its patriotism. As a New Side Presbyterian, Davies' regular sermons emphasized the main themes of revivalistic Calvinism: the desperate condition of sinners before God; the mercy of divine grace in rescuing needy humans from the bondage of sin; and the high privilege of living for the service of God. For example, a sermon from February 1757 on Christ as 'the only foundation' directed pointed questions to his listeners: 'Have you been formed into proper stones for this spiritual temple? Has God hewn you ... by his word, and broken off whatever was rugged, irregular, and unfit to be compacted into the building? ... Do you feel this divine architect daily carrying on this work in you, polishing you more and more into a resemblance of Christ?' (*Sermons on Important Subjects* [New York: Robert Carter & Brothers, 1849], vol. 2, p. 39). Davies' skills as a pulpit orator combined with his obvious devotion to the well-being of Virginians to make him a beloved figure. His abilities as a speaker also had an impact beyond the strictly spiritual realm. The young Patrick Henry, who would later lead Virginia in revolt against Britain, often heard Davies preach and later claimed to have modelled his own impressive rhetoric on that of the Presbyterian minister. Many of Davies' sermons were printed in his lifetime,

and eighty were gathered together into a much-reprinted collected edition.

Davies' activity as poet and hymn-writer extended the reach of his evangelical influence. Over the course of his life he published eighteen hymns, along with a number of poems. The hymns were the first American compositions taken up by the numerous hymnals published in the wake of the evangelical revival. At least one of them is still in use today:

Great God of wonders! all thy ways
Are matchless, godlike, and divine:
But the fair glories of thy grace
More godlike and unrival'd shine:
Who is a pardoning God like Thee?
Or who has grace so rich and free?

Davies' influence in Virginia grew also from his educational efforts. For several young men he provided an evangelical classical education like the one he had received from Samuel Blair. He was awarded the MA degree by the largely Presbyterian College of New Jersey in 1753. From November 1753 to February 1755 he undertook a fund-raising trip to Great Britain on behalf of this college, accompanied by Gilbert *Tennent of New Jersey, another stalwart of New Side Presbyterianism. During this trip the two Americans were forced to defend themselves against inflammatory statements about settled ministers that Tennent had made a decade earlier in the first flush of the colonial Great Awakening. They made this defence successfully and raised enough money to enable the college to move to Princeton and construct its first major building. Davies also enjoyed personal meetings with John *Wesley and Charles *Wesley, George *Whitefield and many other noteworthy figures. The character of Davies' evangelical Calvinism is suggested by the fact that after he returned to America he maintained a friendly correspondence with the Arminian Wesleys.

Among his generation, Davies was notable for his special care in trying to educate African American slaves and Native Americans. While Davies owned at least one or two slaves himself, he none the less was dedicated to evangelizing, educating and encouraging these marginal members of colonial society. In a sermon published in 1754 he went out of his way to defend the full humanity of African Americans at a time when others were expressing doubts on the subject. During his time in Virginia he baptized well over 100 slaves. For Davies, it was a particular pleasure that converted African Americans and Indians enjoyed singing his hymns and other hymns of the evangelical revival. It was primarily for slaves that Davies obtained shipments of hymnals from the Wesleys.

In August 1758 Davies was called to become the president of the College of New Jersey in Princeton, a call he accepted despite the outcries of his parishioners. Davies lived in Princeton only nineteen months, but he showed there the same promise for educational leadership as had marked his ecclesiastical career in Virginia. At the college he laid new stress on oratory and English composition, he trained graduates for the ministry, he wrote odes (on 'Peace' and 'Science') for his two commencements, he urgently pressed home the need for the New Birth, and he provided personal encouragement to several students who later became notables in Revolutionary America (including the nondenominational Philadelphia physician and signatory of the Declaration of Independence, Benjamin Rush, whom Davies guided to medical study in Edinburgh). Throughout his adult life Davies had never been entirely free from consumptive symptoms, and ardent labours at the college soon weakened an already feeble constitution. He died in Princeton on 4 February 1761, one month after preaching a memorable sermon on the same text that his predecessor, Aaron Burr, had chosen for the first Sunday of the year of his demise, Jeremiah 28:16, 'This year you shall die.'

Bibliography

L. F. Benson, 'The Hymns of President Davies', *Journal of the Presbyterian Historical Society* 2 (1903), pp. 343–373; G. W. Pilcher (ed.), *The Reverend Samuel Davies Abroad* (Urbana: University of Illinois Press, 1967); G. W. Pilcher, *Samuel Davies: Apostle of Dissent in Colonial Virginia* (Knoxville: University of Tennessee Press, 1971).

M. A. NOLL

■ DAWSON, Sir John William (1820–1899), scientist, author and educator, was the first British North American to be trained as an exploration geologist. A man of enormous energy and vision, he shaped the educational systems and curricula of Nova Scotia and the Protestant community in Quebec, transformed struggling McGill College into a world-class university, and he was an internationally recognized palaeontologist and Christian anti-Darwinian.

Born to Scottish immigrant parents, James Dawson and Mary Rankine, in Pictou, Nova Scotia, John William Dawson (known as William) grew up in 'genteel poverty' as his family weathered the economic storms of 'boom and bust' from the 1820s to the 1840s. The Dawson family's devout Presbyterianism greatly shaped the worldview of young William. He received an excellent education at the Pictou Academy, under the able direction of the Reverend Thomas *McCulloch, and graduated with competence in classical languages, Hebrew, physics and biology. He was especially drawn to McCulloch's interest in science and collected local specimens and traded them with other naturalists in the colony.

In the autumn of 1840 Dawson began work at the University of Edinburgh, where he took courses in geology and taxidermy and advanced his skills in microscope investigation. In fact, he pioneered the latter field in Canada. In the spring of 1841 he returned to Pictou due to financial problems at home. The next year Dawson met Charles Lyell, one of the founders of modern geology, and introduced him to the coal deposits in Pictou. This encounter stimulated Dawson's interest in geology to the point that he began to publish his findings and carry out contract work for mining entrepreneurs in Nova Scotia. In 1847 he returned to Edinburgh to marry Margaret Ann Young Mercer, with whom he had carried on a transatlantic courtship since 1841, and to enrol in a course in applied chemistry to further his contract work.

Returning to Nova Scotia in 1847, Dawson supplemented his geological work with teaching at the Pictou Academy and Dalhousie College. In 1850 he was persuaded by friends in the House of Assembly to assume the newly created position of superintendent of education for Nova Scotia. Although he was ultimately frustrated by the Assembly's slow response to his proposals and resigned two years later, he was instrumental in creating a Normal School (teachers college) in Truro in 1855. He also wrote several influential school texts in the area of science and agriculture that were used in the Maritimes and Quebec.

In 1854 Dawson became an elected fellow of the Geological Society of London and also completed one of his best-known works *Acadian Geology* (1855) that explored the geology and economic potential of Nova Scotia, New Brunswick and Prince Edward Island. In the light of his growing reputation as a gifted scientist, Dawson was seriously considered for a teaching position at the University of Edinburgh. Although the position was not offered to him, he did receive a firm offer to be the fifth principal of McGill College in Montreal, which he accepted in 1855. The McGill College that Dawson inherited consisted of a number of poorly maintained buildings, a serious funding shortage and a 'moribund faculty of arts'. The only bright spot was a well-functioning faculty of medicine. In spite of these challenges, Dawson was in agreement with the board of governors who believed that academic education at McGill College needed to be strongly practical and directed towards creating professionals to meet the growing needs of colonial society. Towards that end, he established the McGill Normal School in 1857, where he taught and served as principal for thirteen years, and at the same time he offered a variety of science courses at McGill College. In addition, he transformed the campus from a 'cow pasture' into a graceful environment conducive for study and put the institution on a stronger financial footing.

The academic reputation of the college continued to grow as Dawson added strong faculty members in the sciences and engineering. His own notability as a geologist spread in North America as he became the president of the Natural History Society of Montreal, worked with members of the Geological Survey of Canada and (through his activities and writing) established Montreal as an internationally known centre for the study of geology. In spite of administrative and teaching duties, Dawson continued to do field research in the summer and to publish his findings and debate current theories in academic periodicals.

In 1860 Dawson wrote a very critical review of Charles Darwin's *On the Origin of Species* in the *Canadian Naturalist and Geologist* in which he challenged Darwin's use of the fossil record and declared it to be incomplete. If Dawson had reservations about evolution from the perspective of science, he also rejected the theory on religious grounds. As a devout Christian, Dawson was convinced of the harmony of truth, believing that there must be fundamental agreement between the findings of the Bible and those of science. He advanced these views in the books *Archia* (1860) and *The Origin of the World, According to Revelation and Science* (1877). Perhaps his most mature reflection on these themes is found in *Modern Ideas of Evolution* (1890), in which he argued that evolution logically pointed not only to a godless understanding of nature but also a godless understanding of humans who, consequently, had no moral basis for living together. Tireless in his criticism of evolution, Dawson gave countless public addresses and wrote popular articles in order to educate ordinary people about the relationship between science and the Scriptures.

Dawson's popular writings and lectures brought him fame as an apologist for the faith in the face of philosophical materialism. However, his critique of Darwin damaged his academic reputation as a serious scientist, especially among the younger generation of scientists. However, this damage did not alter Dawson's conviction of the unity of knowledge and that science was the study of God's world, though it did lead some scientists who came after him to disregard or undervalue his scientific achievements.

If Dawson's faith led him to defend orthodox Protestant Christianity, it also prompted him to be an advocate of Protestant education in Quebec. As an instructor of teachers at the McGill Normal School and active member of the Protestant Board of School Commissioners for Montreal and the Protestant committee of the Council of Public Instruction, Dawson promoted educational reform built on liberal and Christian principles in order to produce a population who would be effective in building the new nation of Canada (founded in 1867). He did not believe that his vision for education could be accomplished by working together with the French-speaking Roman Catholics who were in the majority in the province of Quebec. He was also an advocate of the Sunday school movement and wrote lessons for Sabbath school teachers. In addition, he supported and served for a time as president of the Montreal division of the British and Foreign Bible Society.

In 1878 Dawson was invited to become president of the College of New Jersey, which was in the midst of debate over evolution and faith. This appointment would have been a promotion from McGill, but Dawson chose to stay in Montreal to continue to advance the cause of Protestant education and build a museum of natural history. Other distinctions were bestowed on Dawson, such as the Lyell Medal for outstanding achievement in geology in 1881. The next year, he served as president of the American Association for the Advancement of Science that met in Montreal and, in 1886, the British Association for the Advancement of Science named him as president. He was the only person ever to be president of both of these organizations.

On 19 November 1899 John William Dawson died after a lengthy illness in Montreal. He was remembered as an ambitious man of conviction and faith who successfully negotiated the challenges of faith and science, teaching and research, university administration and public service, and who contributed greatly to the development of education in Canada while at the same time being recognized as a world-class scientist.

Bibliography

S. Sheets-Pyenson, *John William Dawson: Faith, Hope, and Science* (Montreal and Kingston: McGill–Queen's University Press, 1996).

D. GOODWIN

■ **DENNEY, James** (1856–1917), Scottish theologian and New Testament scholar, was born in Paisley on 5 February 1856 into a working-class Reformed Presbyterian family and grew up in Greenock. At the age of eighteen he began a brilliant career at Glasgow University, earning a rare 'double first' in classics and philosophy upon graduating with an MA in 1879. That same year he continued his distinguished student career, under the direction of professors such as the New Testament scholar A. B. Bruce, at the Free Church College in Glasgow, a natural choice for his theological studies since most of the Reformed Presbyterian Church had united with the Free Church of Scotland in 1876. Denney received his BD in 1883 and spent the next three years as a missionary at Free St John's Church in Glasgow.

He was ordained in 1886 when he was called to become the minister of the East Free Church of Broughty Ferry, a suburb of Dundee. Later that year Denney married Mary Carmichael Brown. While the marriage produced no children, it did have a lasting effect upon Denney's theology. Through her own convictions and example, and especially by introducing him to the works of the pre-eminent English Baptist preacher C. H. *Spurgeon, Denney's wife encouraged him to move away from the kind of 'broad churchism' championed by Bruce towards a more distinctively evangelical approach.

Although Denney carried out his parish duties, including the conduct of regular church prayer meetings, with care and conviction, his primary gifts were as an expositor and preacher. Two series of sermons for his congregation in Broughty Ferry were the basis of his earliest publications, *The Epistles to the Thessalonians* (1892) and *The Second Epistle to the Corinthians* (1894), which appeared in the Expositor's Bible series of commentaries edited by his friend Sir W. Robertson Nicoll. Chicago Theological Seminary recognized Denney's broader theological abilities by granting him a DD and issuing an invitation to deliver a series of lectures in 1894, which were published as *Studies in Theology*.

In 1897 Denney returned to academic life full time when he accepted an offer to become Professor of Systematic and Pastoral Theology at the Glasgow Free Church College. Two years later he succeeded Bruce as Chair of New Testament Language, Literature and Theology, and in 1915 Denney was elected principal of the college by acclamation of the United Free Church General Assembly. He was by no means the only outstanding evangelical scholar on the faculty. During his tenure, James *Orr succeeded him to the theological chair, and George Adam Smith taught Old Testament. Noted for his clear and epigrammatic writing style, Denney published extensively throughout his academic career, particularly in the periodicals *The Expositor* and *The British Weekly*. His primary works include The Expositor's Greek Testament commentary on *Romans* (1900), *The Death of Christ* (1902), *The Atonement and the Modern Mind* (1903), *Jesus and the Gospel* (1908), *The Church and the Kingdom* (1910) and *The Christian Doctrine of Reconciliation* (1917).

Despite this prodigious scholarly output and his reputation as a teacher as demanding upon himself as upon his students, Denney remained an active churchman throughout his life. On most Sunday mornings and evenings he could be found filling a pulpit somewhere in Scotland. He participated in the negotiations that led to the union of the Free Church and the United Presbyterian Church in 1900 and later served as Convenor of the Central Fund of the resulting United Free Church, helping to raise the minimum stipends of its ministers. Denney was also an ardent advocate of the evangelical social cause of prohibition during the First World War, writing and speaking on behalf of the Scottish Temperance League. By no means narrow in his outlook, he took great delight in literature, occasionally writing and lecturing on his favourite authors: Shakespeare, Dickens and Robert Burns.

After collapsing while lecturing to one of his classes in February 1917, Denney died from respiratory complications on 11 June 1917 at the age of sixty-one. His extensive influence was summed up on a memorial plaque in what is now Trinity College, Glasgow: 'supreme alike as scholar, teacher, administrator, and man of God, to whom many owed their souls'.

Denney's relationship with evangelicalism has been somewhat ambivalent on both sides, with Denney expressing reservations about elements of evangelicalism, and evangelicals questioning aspects of Denney's thought. His commitment to seeing people enter into a life-transforming relationship with Jesus Christ was central to his life and theology: 'I haven't the faintest interest in any theology which doesn't help us to evangelize' (Taylor, *God Loves Like That!*, p. 29). Thus he could use the Westminster Shorter Catechism as a basis for a Bible class because it was excellent 'for evangelizing' and hold American evangelists D. L. *Moody and Ira *Sankey in high

regard. Yet Denney resisted being categorized as a Calvinist or even as 'orthodox'. He adopted this position in part because he suspected all theological and metaphysical systems, conservative and liberal, of obscuring Christ and becoming an obstacle to heartfelt faith. None the less, he seems to have made what he viewed as radical theologians and biblical scholars, particularly Albrecht Ritschl, the primary targets of his critiques.

Denney did not defend traditional interpretations of Scripture because he was a traditionalist, but because he believed they were true to the texts and could lead people to faith in Christ. He was always more comfortable as an exegete than as a theoretician, taking an inductive approach to theology that sometimes led to seemingly contradictory positions. While he strongly affirmed the authority of Scripture in practice, he rejected verbal inerrancy and infallibility because of his limited acceptance of some findings of biblical criticism, yet he did not provide any coherent alternative doctrine of inspiration.

Similar tensions emerge when examining Denney's work on the atonement, the centrepiece of his theology and scholarly writing and the primary basis of his enduring reputation. While he affirms traditional understandings of human sinfulness, divine wrath, propitiation and the penal and substitutionary nature of Christ's death, he resists the casting of these in terms of 'a transfer of merit and demerit, the sin of the world being carried over to Christ's account, and the merit of Christ to the world's account, as if the reconciliation of God and man ... could be explained without the use of higher categories than are employed in book-keeping' (*The Death of Christ* [London: Hodder & Stoughton, 1902], p. 194). Particularly in his final work, *The Christian Doctrine of Reconciliation* (1917), Denney seems to emphasize the subjective influence of the atonement more than its objective basis in the death of Christ, reflecting the views of his fellow countryman J. McLeod Campbell. None the less, Denney's ultimate conclusions are thoroughly orthodox and evangelical: 'The Christian attitude to [the Cross] is not that of repeating it; it is that of depending upon it, believing in it, trusting it to the uttermost. We are saved ultimately by what happened on the Cross as we trust the Saviour who bore our sins in His own body on the tree' (*The Christian Doctrine of Reconciliation* [London: Hodder & Stoughton, 1917], pp. 284–285).

Bibliography
J. R. Taylor, *God Loves Like That! The Theology of James Denney* (Richmond, Virginia: John Knox Press, 1962); T. H. Walker, *Principal James Denney: A Memoir and a Tribute* (London: Marshall Brothers, 1918).

D. A. CURRIE

■ **DODDRIDGE, Philip** (1702–1751), Nonconformist pastor, educator, mathematician and spiritual writer, was born the twentieth child of a London shopkeeper. Doddridge was nurtured in a love for Scripture and a conviction that it was the indispensable ground of all faithful Christian practice. His family had deep Puritan and Reformation roots. His paternal grandfather, John Doddridge, had resigned as vicar at Shepperton-on-Thames rather than accept the terms of the Act of Uniformity (1662), and his maternal grandfather was exiled from his native Bohemia (in 1626) on account of his visible support of the local Protestant church. Doddridge was educated at St Alban's by Nathaniel Wood and trained for the Nonconformist ministry by John Jennings at Kibworth. He soon came under the influence of Isaac *Watts and Samuel Clarke, who set him to reading John Locke in his eighteenth year. Three years later, Doddridge took his first pastoral charge (at Kibworth). He founded and operated one of the largest and most successful of the Dissenting Academies, at Northampton, from 1729 to 1750, and from 1730 to his death he was pastor of the Independent Church at Castle Hill.

Doddridge's importance as an educator can scarcely be overestimated. One of the first to introduce lecturing in English rather than Latin, he also adapted a system of shorthand to enable verbatim dictation by students. More than two hundred prominent figures completed their education under his tutelage; included among them are the educators John Aiken (Warrington Academy, and father of Anna Laetitia Barbauld), Caleb Ashworth (Daventry) and Andrew Kippis (London), but also Gilbert Robertson and James Robertson, both of whom became professors at Edinburgh. Baptists, Presbyterians, and conformists to the Church of England were all represented among those who came to him for study, and they went on to careers as diverse as medicine, law, business and the military, but also, in significant numbers, to the Dissenting ministry.

Like many of the leading figures of English Dissent, Doddridge was something of a polymath, superbly well read in several disciplines. Though a theologian (of Calvinist persuasions) primarily, he was also a competent mathematician, intimately familiar with current texts such as Sir Isaac Newton's *Principia Mathematica*, a work which had some influence on his *Course of Lectures on the Principal Subjects in Pneumatology, Ethics, and Divinity* (1794). For example, he cites Newton's proposition eleven on mechanics (on inertia), and proposition six on the conservation of energy, to buttress his argument for the finitude of creation and a necessary moment of origin. He presented formal papers on pendulums and collision of bodies to the Northampton Philosophical Society, and it is clear from the class notes circulating among his students, as well as from later testimony from pupils such as Andrew Kippis, that his teaching in mathematics, geometry and general physics was of a very high order.

Doddridge held a very high view of Scripture, but he was not an inerrantist. While attributing inconsistencies and small errors to various biblical writers, he nevertheless regarded the New Testament as authoritative for faith and life and held the Greek text to be 'in the main such as it came out of the hands of those by whom the several pieces in it were written' (*Course of Lectures*, 1.412–414). A moderate Calvinist, he believed there could be no contradiction between Scripture and natural philosophy (science) when each was rightly understood.

Amongst Doddridge's several works, the most important is his *The Rise and Progress of Religion in the Soul* (1745). Although not now so well known, this book was regarded by evangelicals more than a century after its publication as 'the safest, completest, and most effectual manual for anxious enquirers' into Christianity (*British and Foreign Evangelical Review* [1857]); it was soon translated into Welsh and French, and in the nineteenth century into Scots Gaelic, Italian, Tamil and Syriac. Large numbers of readers were converted through reading this book, among them the statesman and anti-slavery advocate William *Wilberforce. The idea for this work of broad apologetics was actually that of Doddridge's early mentor, Isaac Watts, who devised the original plan and, for the first sections, something more than that. Poor health made it impossible for Watts to write what he had intended, and he urged his younger friend to take up the task.

Doddridge's own style, nevertheless, thoroughly characterizes the work. The prayers and meditations that close each chapter are distinctly his innovation, and they help to make the book less a work of formal apologetics than a source for the reader's reflective and repeated meditation. His implied reader is a nominal Christian, not a cheerful pagan, and the argument moves from a tutorial, academic style in the opening sections to clear pastoral exhortation by the final sections, where he speaks of disciplines of the spiritual life and the growth to maturity of the faithful Christian.

Doddridge's moderate Calvinism left considerable room for evangelical outreach in a variety of directions. He founded a school for impoverished students and a county infirmary, and he was an earnest advocate of foreign missions, for 'the propagation of the gospel ... among the distant nations of the heathen world'. He also wrote hymns, among the best known of which are 'O Happy Day that Fixed my Choice' and the communion hymn 'My God, and is Thy Table Spread'.

The Correspondence and Diary of Philip Doddridge, DD, compiled and edited by his great-grandson John Doddridge Humphreys (5 vols., 1829), is an invaluable guide to his pastoral methods as well as to his personal character. He had a high regard for women, nurtured from his childhood by his own mother, to whom after he left home he continued to write confidences of the most intimate character. At the age of nineteen, after confessing to her his growing ardour for a member of the opposite sex, he concluded: 'But madam, I leave it entirely in your breast, and must only add, to prevent being mistaken, that though I am in so much haste for a mistress, I can stay seven years for a wife.'

He corresponded in a lively fashion with several young women, with most (but not all) in a spirit of cheerful disinterestedness, and, at twenty-eight, he married an orphan, Mercy Maris (22 December 1730). Theirs was a union notable in its time for intensity of friendship and frankness in affection.

Doddridge was renowned for his intellectual honesty and personal integrity alike. In his final years he contracted tuberculosis, the symptoms of which were extreme enough by the early summer of 1751 that he was persuaded to travel to Lisbon where, on 26 October 1751, he died, leaving behind his wife and four (of nine) surviving children.

Bibliography
M. Deacon, *Philip Doddridge of Northampton, 1702–51* (Northampton: Northamptonshire Libraries, 1980); G. Nuttall, *Calendar of the Correspondence of Philip Doddridge, D.D. (1702–1751)* (London: Her Majesty's Stationery Office, 1979); J. Orton, *Memoirs of the Late Reverend Philip Doddridge* (London: 1765).

D. L. JEFFREY

■ **DOOYEWEERD, Herman** (1894–1977), Dutch Calvinist philosopher and professor of law, dedicated his life to the development of a distinctly Christian philosophy based on creation ordinances (the 'Philosophy of the Law-Idea'; Dutch: *Wijsbegeerte der Wetsidee*). Influential in North America and South Africa as well as in his native Netherlands, Dooyeweerd received accolades from outside his own Reformed community. On his seventieth birthday the chair of the Royal Dutch Academy of Sciences called him the most original philosopher produced by the Netherlands, Spinoza not excluded.

Dooyeweerd's life and thought are inextricably intertwined with the Dutch Neo-Calvinist revival led by Abraham *Kuyper. He was born in Amsterdam on 7 October 1894, only two years after the union of two major Reformed churches: the Pietist Secession group (*Afscheiding*) and the culturally aggressive Kuyperian group (*Doleantie*). Dooyeweerd's mother was a Pietist from the Secession group, and his father was a devoted follower of Kuyper. Later, Dooyeweerd would attribute his characteristic emphasis on the *heart* as the centre of human existence to the influence of Kuyper. But this emphasis may in fact represent a creative blending of the two religious streams in the Dutch Reformed community, which were embodied in Dooyeweerd's parental home.

After completing his gymnasium (secondary school) education in Amsterdam, in 1912 Dooyeweerd followed his father's advice and enrolled in the law faculty at Kuyper's Free University of Amsterdam. His own inclination had been to pursue a career in the arts, probably in music. He completed his studies in 1917 with a doctoral dissertation on 'The Role of the Cabinet in Dutch Constitutional Law'. His academic work impressed upon him the necessity of a distinctively Christian philosophy. Though Kuyper had addressed some philosophical issues, no complete system had yet been developed by any Reformed Christian thinker. This need was confirmed for him when his understanding of Christian commitment was challenged at the [Dutch] Society for the Philosophy of Law.

After taking a number of government jobs, in 1922 Dooyeweerd was appointed as Assistant (to Dr Hendrik Colijn) Director of the Kuyper Institute in the Hague, which had been established to undertake legal and political research for the ruling Christian political party, the Antirevolutionary Party (ARP), of which Colijn was the leader. With his renaissance mind Dooyeweerd was well suited for such a post, and he declined the opportunity of active political service. As part of the appointment process, Dooyeweerd sent a memo to the board of the Kuyper Institute concerning the necessity of a well-developed Neo-Calvinist worldview as a basis for political and legal action.

It was during his time at the Kuyper Institute that Dooyeweerd rediscovered the piety of Kuyper himself, which was reflected in his numerous volumes of meditations. It was as much in these meditations as in Kuyper's more theoretical-theological works that Dooyeweerd discerned Kuyper's understanding of the heart as the existential centre of the human person. He described this discovery as a turning-point in his personal and intellectual pilgrimage. Dooyeweerd also helped to found, and served as the first editor of, *Antirevolutionaire Staatkunde*

(*Antirevolutionary Statecraft*), the monthly journal of the Kuyper Institute.

In 1926 Dooyeweerd returned to the Free University as Professor of Jurisprudence and Philosophy of Law, a position he held until his retirement in 1965. In 1935, with his colleague and brother-in-law D. H. T. Vollenhoven, he founded the international Society for Calvinist Philosophy. At the same time Dooyeweerd produced his major philosophical work, the three-volume *Wijsbegeerte der Wetsidee* (1935–1936), which was later revised and expanded into the four-volume English *A New Critique of Theoretical Thought* (1953–1958). Dooyeweerd's philosophical system, the 'Philosophy of the Cosmonomic Idea', anticipates a number of late twentieth-century philosophical trends, including postmodern critiques of Enlightenment rationalism.

At the core of Dooyeweerd's Christian philosophy is a revelation-based epistemology which challenged all forms of rationalism, and an ontology rooted in the Christian notion of creation ordinances or law. Reflecting a strong Augustinian sense of spiritual antithesis, Dooyeweerd followed Kuyper in insisting that all theorizing was rooted in religious presuppositions. In his judgment, the Enlightenment ideal of a religiously neutral, rational system of thought (a prejudice against prejudice) is impossible to achieve and is itself rooted in personal commitments.

There are clear parallels between Dooyeweerd's philosophy and contemporary postmodern thought, especially when the latter is directed to the goal of emancipation. Liberationism shares with Neo-Calvinist philosophy the conviction that nothing is neutral, all thought is engaged and interested. However, while liberation analysis focuses on a shared commitment to the sociopolitically oppressed and marginalized, Neo-Calvinism emphasizes religious presuppositions; the heart commitment of scholars and the religious basis of all scholarship. Dooyeweerd also does not ask whether particular ideas arise from or contribute to liberating praxis but begins with an analysis of theoretical thought itself, an analysis he calls a 'transcendental critique'. This Kant-inspired critical method, put to use as a means of Christian critique, is truly one of Dooyeweerd's most creative and significant intellectual accomplishments.

Rather than simply *asserting* on external grounds that thinkers are biased, Dooyeweerd insists that an immanent examination of thought itself reveals its religious presuppositions. Consideration of the necessary conditions of thought, he contends, discloses its supratheoretical or religious starting point. Philosophy's concern about meaning directs all thought to questions of origin, and these questions cannot be answered by theoretical thought itself. Awareness of the limits of theoretical thought forces the philosopher to confront the integrating capacity of the human ego or, in biblical terms, the heart. Self-knowledge is thus the basis of all epistemology, and pure presuppositionless rationality is an impossibility. According to Dooyeweerd, whether its role is acknowledged or not, religion is the integrative basis of all thought.

Dooyeweerd's ontology is rooted in the Christian conviction that creation is meaningfully diverse and structured by God's law; hence his philosophical system is called 'Philosophy of the Law-Idea'. This conviction is grounded on Abraham Kuyper's notion of *sphere-sovereignty*: the idea that physical and social reality exhibits an irreducible diversity that is grounded in divine creation ordinances. Kuyper utilized this doctrine primarily for political purposes (to free social structures such as the family and the school from the hegemony of the state), but Dooyeweerd expanded it into a full ontology based on what he calls *modal aspects*. These aspects of created reality (numerical, spatial, biotic, psychical, lingual, economic, jural-legal) are the investigative areas of the special sciences. The task of philosophy is to examine and explain how the modalities relate to each other.

Dooyeweerd's emphasis on the doctrine of creation entailed a positive attitude towards human culture and history. Strongly affirming Calvin's and Kuyper's doctrine of *common grace* (God's non-saving favour towards all humanity), Dooyeweerd articulated a philosophy of history that was very appreciative of cultural development. Cultural products and social institutions were perceived as unfolding organically and becoming differentiated from their creational roots. This differentiation and cultural diversity are to be respected.

A 'Dooyeweerd Center for Christian Philosophy', which publishes Dooyeweerd's works in English and stimulates the study of his thought, was opened at Redeemer College, Ancaster, Ontario, Canada in 1994.

Bibliography
L. Kkalsbeek, *Contours of a Christian Philosophy: An Introduction to Herman Dooyeweerd's Thought* (Toronto: Wedge, 1975); C. T. McIntire, 'Herman Dooyeweerd in North America', in D. Wells (ed.), *Reformed Theology in North America* (Grand Rapids: Eerdmans, 1985), pp. 172–185; *The Legacy of Herman Dooyeweerd* (Lanham: University Press of America, 1985). This volume contains a series of explorations on Dooyeweerd's thought by the faculty of the Institute for Christian Studies, Toronto, Ontario, Canada. It also contains a thorough bibliography.

J. BOLT

■ **DORSEY, Thomas Andrew** (1899–1993), celebrated African American 'father' of the gospel blues, composer of some 1,000 gospel songs, Chicago choir director, music publisher and collaborator with such well-known gospel singers as Sallie Martin and Mahalia Jackson, was born in Villa Rica, Georgia, some thirty miles east of Atlanta. His father, Thomas Madison, was an itinerant preacher and farmer, his mother, Etta, an organist. In 1908 the family, struggling with poverty, sought better opportunities in a move to Atlanta, where, despite his family's piety, the younger Dorsey heard the blues of Ma Rainey and Bessie Smith as well as the more sanctioned spirituals and sacred harp music.

In 1916 Dorsey joined the swelling African American migration out of the South to seek a better life in northern cities. Dorsey's destination was Chicago, where he was to make his home base for the rest of his life. As a blues pianist Dorsey accompanied singers such as Ma Rainey during the twenties and as 'Georgia Tom' teamed up with slide guitarist 'Tampa Red' (Hudson Whitaker) between 1928 and 1932. His best-known song from this era was 'Tight Like That'.

Dorsey experienced an initial conversion in 1921 at a Baptist convention, as a result of

W. M. Nix's singing of the (white) gospel song, 'I Do, Don't You?' (after which Dorsey wrote the first of his own sacred songs) and, following a period of depression, he renewed his faith commitment in 1928. Dorsey legend tends to relate that suddenly, at some climactic point in the twenties, he abandoned secular music for sacred, but the truth seems to be that he needed to make a living, and as long as secular compositions sold while his gospel pieces did not, he continued writing and playing his 'lowdown' blues. In the early thirties, however, two developments turned him to sacred music exclusively: his first wife died in childbirth (along with the baby), eliciting a crisis of grief that produced Dorsey's most famous gospel song, 'Precious Lord, Take My Hand' (1932); and Dorsey made a series of significant career moves that committed him to gospel. In 1932 he became director of the Gospel Choir at Pilgrim Baptist Church in Chicago, and in the same year he joined Theodore R. Frye, Sallie Martin and Marion Pairs in the founding of the National Convention of Gospel Choirs and Choruses. He also started touring with Sallie Martin (1932–1939); later he would travel the United States with Mahalia Jackson (1939–1944). Both singers would perform his gospel songs and help to promote the sale of sheet music and eventually recordings of Dorsey songs.

After the 1940s, Dorsey gradually cut down on touring and performance in favour of composition, lecturing and administrative duties connected with the church and gospel organization. He lived long enough to receive recognition from an admiring white world and from the small but growing group of historians of gospel music, and his charming personality was captured in the well-known 1982 film directed by George Nierenberg, *Say Amen, Somebody*. One might say he lived long enough to help to shape his own legend.

One part of the legend has been addressed above, that is, that Dorsey suddenly forsook the secular blues for the gospel blues. Indeed, Dorsey never condemned the blues he had played earlier, and in *Say Amen, Somebody* a glint in his eye suggests that he lived remarkably easily with his earlier reputation as 'Georgia Tom'. The gulf between black sacred and secular music has been exaggerated by both black and white observers; many

composers and performers have moved quite flexibly between the two genres. In fact, the 'line' between the two types of music has often been blurred.

Another part of the legend suggests that Dorsey suddenly introduced a bluesy form of the gospel song (or indeed that he introduced gospel music itself) into a musical void. In fact, blues elements had for several decades been incipient in the gospel songs of black composers (Charles A. *Tindley and William Henry Sherwood, for instance), and certainly performers had been known to 'swing' the early gospel songs. Dorsey furthered this earlier development, worked to institutionalize it through the gospel convention and publishing, and put it on stage with his superb selection of singers to popularize and promote his songs. Probably Dorsey's earlier reputation as a bluesman and accompanist to singers such as Ma Rainey helped to dramatize the considerable blues and popular music elements in gospel songs.

Yet another part of the legend is the assertion that the gospel blues needed to overcome an immense amount of resistance from black church people, both ministers and congregations. *Say Amen, Somebody* has Dorsey declaring that he was thrown out of some of the best churches. To an extent this allegation of opposition is true, especially when made against Baptist and Methodist middle-class congregations striving for respectability and acceptance by white society. But on the other hand, the musical culture of black churches provided plenty of contexts for gospel singing other than 'formal' worship: prayer meetings, denominational conventions, 'songfests' etc. Having demonstrated its popularity and its spiritual power, the gospel song gradually made inroads into Sunday worship. Acceptance or rejection of gospel songs was not always as absolute as portrayed in the legend.

But gently to question Dorsey's iconic status is not to doubt his enormous impact on the history of gospel music in the United States and indeed the world. In the African American community, Dorsey's songs became so well known that gospel songs in general were given the name 'dorseys'. Many white musicians and music publishing houses embraced his compositions as well; Red Foley and Elvis Presley enjoyed hits with Dorsey's 'There Will Be Peace in the Valley For Me', and Dorsey found common ground and friendship with Billy *Sunday's musical collaborator, Homer Rodeheaver, famous for his 'white' gospel creations.

Moreover, Dorsey created more 'down-home' songs than, for example, his forerunner Charles A. Tindley. His lyrics were closer to the colloquialism of the city street and farm; he abandoned the inversions and victorianisms of Tindley phrases such as 'when the dreary road you tread'. The natural character of Dorsey's lyrics is apparent even in his titles, for instance, 'If You See My Savior, Tell Him That You Saw Me'.

In addition to 'Precious Lord' and the other songs mentioned above, Dorsey's best-known compositions include 'It's a Highway to Heaven', 'I'm Gonna Live the Life I Sing About in My Song', 'Search Me, Lord', and 'Old Ship of Zion'. Over the decades, the Dorsey songs have been rendered in numerous arrangements, performance styles and venues, and in that sense their creation and recreation is ongoing.

Bibliography

H. W. Boyer, 'Take My Hand, Precious Lord, Lead Me On', in B. J. Reagon, *We'll Understand It Better By and By* (Washington: 1993); M. W. Harris, *The Rise of Gospel Blues: The Music of Thomas Andrew Dorsey in the Urban Church* (New York: Oxford University Press, 1992).

V. L. BRERETON

■ **DOW, Lorenzo** (1777–1834), American revivalist, was born on 16 October 1777 in Coventry, Connecticut. His father, Humphrey, and mother, Tabitha Parker, were of English ancestry, and Lorenzo was the fifth of six children. At the age of fourteen he was converted through the ministrations of Methodist itinerant Hope Hull, a charismatic figure renowned for his powerful preaching and prophetic gifts. Dow's conversion was quintessentially evangelical; after a long night of despair over his unrighteous condition, he dreamed that Jesus had intervened to save him from the condemnation he justly deserved. Overwhelmed by the consciousness of divine mercy, Dow proceeded to share his experience with family, fellow believers and unconverted neighbours. In the following years he began to preach locally, and in 1798 the Methodist annual conference admitted him on trial, with Francis *Asbury personally licensing him. From his earliest years as a preacher, however, Dow felt compelled to follow internal spiritual promptings rather than the instructions of Methodist officials. He made three unauthorized trips to England and Ireland between 1799 and 1818 and journeyed widely through the western wilderness of North America. Personifying the indefatigable itinerant of Methodist lore, he travelled 10,000 miles during 1805 alone, enduring harsh conditions with little material sustenance, in order to preach the gospel. Through his heroic efforts and powerful preaching, Dow was among the most successful revivalists of his time.

'Crazy' Dow was an anomalous figure, invariably described by contemporaries and historians as eccentric in the extreme. Many observers commented on his perceived effeminacy (his slight figure, unfashionably long hair, and physical frailty), and his journals are full of references to his impending demise due to sickness or exhaustion. At the same time, however, his audiences tended to attribute his eccentricities and preaching power to his 'manly independence', and countless children were named in honour of him. Just as he was prone to burst into tears at the psychic suffering of sinners striving for divine grace, he was also capable of issuing fearless challenges to threatening crowds and, in this manner, exemplified the androgynous nature of Primitive Methodism. His profoundly ascetic disposition was well documented, but it was located in his remarkable self-discipline, not in any sense of obligation to established authority or in socially enforced humility. And even though he was recognized as one of the most influential itinerants in America, he was always marginalized by the Methodist hierarchy.

Despite his tenuous official connections to the power structure, Dow never forsook Methodist doctrine. His basic message that human sinfulness and divine justice demanded the atonement provided by Christ's death and resurrection was pure orthodoxy, and his insistence that the divine economy required individuals to choose or reject that atonement, with eternal consequences, was undiluted Arminianism. In all his emotionally charged yet carefully reasoned preaching, Dow strongly opposed emerging cultural systems of privilege: social, political, ecclesiastical and intellectual. He heeded dreams and visions and at times exhibited psychic gifts, and his rough spirituality and unabashed supernaturalism challenged restrained respectability and the tightly rationalized theology of both Enlightenment sceptics and Calvinist apologists. His well-documented curse on St Stephens, Alabama (where he prophesied the town's ultimate destruction, so as to be fit only for roosting bats and owls) was only one instance in which Dow, confidently and with great effect on his audiences, invoked the supernatural to support his evangelical message.

As the archetypical populist, Dow singled out all aspects of aristocratic entitlement for contempt and ridicule, defining true Christianity in contradistinction to the material and social benefits enjoyed by the comfortable. Recognizing the spiritual temptations of wealth, he steadfastly refused to profit financially from any of his religious contacts and insisted upon a personal code of ascetic denial that served to bolster the legitimacy of his ministry in the eyes of common folk. In this light, he paraphrased *Wesley's famous dictum defining stewardship by urging his audiences to 'save all you can and give all you can, that the things of this world may prove a blessing and not a curse'. Dow also manifested this opposition to privilege in his embrace of the godly anarchy of camp meetings and his disdain for the alleged spiritual deadness of trained clergy. Of the unconventional revivalist himself, it was said that he was 'not learned but very intelligent'. For Dow, the legitimacy of a revivalist depended on valid personal spirituality and the ability to convey that experience to audiences, with the power to change lives.

Besides his remarkable popularity and success as a preacher, Dow's career was marked by controversy with the Methodist hierarchy. From his early refusal to remain on his appointed circuit, he proved impossible for ecclesiastical authorities to control. When he promised to bring his frontier style of revivalism to England in 1805, for instance, American Methodist leader Nicholas Snethen, referring to Dow as a spiritual 'imposter', urged British officials to deny the revivalist

preaching credentials. In the face of this opposition, however, Dow preached to enthusiastic crowds anyway, inspiring in the process Hugh *Bourne, founder of the Primitive Methodist movement in England. In spite of Snethen's opposition, Dow was sympathetic to his and other reformers' calls for the democratizing of Methodist organization in the United States. When New York Methodists under William Stilwell rejected fashionable renovations and political interventions in a dispute over increased worldliness in the John Street Church and founded their own Methodist offshoot in the early 1820s, Dow signed on as general missionary, deacon and elder. The Stilwellites, with Dow's support, supported racial and gender equality within Methodism, and Stilwell's subsequent willingness to ordain the leadership of the fledgling African Methodist Episcopal Zion denomination fitted in well with Dow's own friendliness towards black Methodists.

Like many Americans in the early republic, Dow easily conflated religion and politics. He attributed the establishment of the United States to providential intervention and interpreted its creation as the fulfilment of millennial expectations, in a manner similar to that of later restorationists such as Alexander *Campbell and Joseph Smith. His attraction to prophetic interpretations of current events led him to denounce Roman Catholicism as the author of all threats to liberty in national and international affairs. He was forthrightly Jeffersonian in his celebration of republican ideology, and he sprinkled his sermons with quotations from radical leveller Thomas Paine. He rejected the notion that political authority properly belonged to the wealthy or well-born and trusted the decision-making abilities of the common people for theological as well as social reasons. Throughout his career he publicly condemned those whose sense of 'distinction' and 'pride' proved only, in Dow's words, that they knew 'not God nor his worship'.

On 3 September 1804 Dow married Peggy Holcomb; the couple had one child who died in infancy. A fascinating figure in her own right, Peggy Dow recorded her story of co-labouring in Lorenzo's revival efforts in an appendix to Dow's autobiographical work *History of Cosmopolite*. Dow's autobiography was only one of more than twenty works he authored, appearing in over seventy editions during his ministry. After his controversial trip to England in 1805, Dow came back to North America, preaching extensively for the next decade throughout the United States and Canada. In 1818 he undertook a third trip to England, where he further encouraged the Primitive Methodists, returning to continue his itinerancy without interruption. On a trip to Washington, DC, to warn Congress of undue Catholic influence in political affairs, he became ill and died in Georgetown on 2 February (some sources say 7 February), 1834. Even after his death, Lorenzo Dow's counter-cultural rejection of privilege remained a vital though increasingly residual tradition within the development of American Methodism in the nineteenth century.

Bibliography

L. Dow, *History of Cosmopolite; or the Four Volumes of Lorenzo Dow's Journal Concentrated in One, Containing His Experience and Travels, from Childhood to Near His Fiftieth Year. Also His Polemical Writings* (Wheeling, Virginia: Joshua Martin, 1849); N. Hatch, *The Democratization of American Christianity* (New Haven: Yale University Press, 1989); C. Sellers, *Lorenzo Dow: The Bearer of the Word* (New York: Milton, Batch, 1928).

W. R. SUTTON

■ DRUMMOND, Henry (1851–1897), Scottish writer, left an indelible impression on the latter half of the nineteenth century as a writer, evangelist, scientist, teacher, minister, and explorer. Born in Stirling, Scotland on 17 August 1851, he entered the University of Edinburgh at the age of fifteen and began theological studies at New College at the age nineteen (in 1870). Although he was a devoted member of the Free Church of Scotland, he was unsure whether he was called to the ministry. He found his real vocation when he interrupted his theological studies to assist Dwight L. *Moody and Ira D. *Sankey in their first great mission to Britain (1873–1875). Drummond organized follow-up, spoke at student meetings and had numerous one-to-one conversations with seekers in the enquiry room. His evangelistic work was so effective that Moody invited him to join his ministry team in America. Drummond declined, although he assisted Moody again when the famous evangelist returned to Britain (1882–1884). Moody later said of Drummond: 'He is the most Christ-like man I ever knew.'

Drummond served briefly as assistant minister of the Barclay Church in Edinburgh and later continued his ministry among the working-class people of Glasgow at the Possil Park mission. He also pursued scientific studies and taught natural science at the Free Church College in Glasgow. His *Natural Law and the Spiritual World*, published in 1883, was a bestseller, revealing the subtlety of a fine scientific mind. Drummond became a major voice in the international debates on science and religion as he sought to interpret the Darwinian theory of evolution in the light of his evangelical Christian faith. He later pursued his theme further in his Lowell Lectures, which were delivered at Boston in 1893 and published the following year as *The Ascent of Man*. Although Drummond's synthesis of Christianity and evolution was criticized by both scientists and theologians, he was a pioneer in serious evangelical engagement with modern science.

Drummond's interest in the natural world also led him into a geological exploration of Africa. A report of his exploration of Lakes Nyasa and Tanganyika was published in his book *Tropical Africa* (1888). Like David *Livingstone before him, Drummond was repelled by the African slave trade and called on the British government to act against it. Gladstone and other members of the Liberal Party were impressed with Drummond's gifts and attempted to recruit him to stand for Parliament. He declined, claiming that he could do more 'for every cause of truth and righteousness' through his evangelistic and writing ministry.

Drummond is best remembered today as the author of a devotional commentary on 1 Corinthians 13, *The Greatest Thing In The World*. This essay was based on an extemporaneous talk first given to a group of Christian workers in England in 1884, when Drummond was persuaded by Moody to take his place on the platform. Moody was so impressed by what he heard that he insisted that Drummond repeat the talk to audiences in America. Drummond edited it for publication in 1887. *The Greatest Thing In The World* soon became a best-selling devotional classic. Before Drummond's death, it had been translated into nineteen languages and widely distributed throughout the world. In fact, *The Greatest Thing In The World* has never been out of print. Its practical message of love, seen as the fruit of the Holy Spirit and focused on the person of Christ, is a model of biblical exposition and evangelical piety at its best.

In his three visits to the United States (1879, 1887, 1893), Drummond was warmly welcomed at Chautauqua and Ivy League institutions, including Harvard, Yale and Princeton. His appearance at Harvard was likened to that of a comet which 'had flashed upon the view and had left a trail of light as it sank below the horizon'. A convincing speaker, Drummond also presented a convocation address to the fledging University of Chicago. At Moody's insistence, Drummond spoke at the famous evangelist's summer conference at Northfield, Massachusetts. His appearance there brought a storm of criticism because of his controversial views on evolution. Moody was advised not to let Drummond speak, but he said to the critics: 'I have been shown that he is a better man than I am, and, therefore, he should speak.'

Drummond's influence was not limited to Great Britain and North America. He was an eagerly sought-after speaker on the international evangelical circuit. He travelled extensively and was well received wherever he went: in France, Germany, Scandinavia, Australia, New Zealand, China, Japan and Africa. Deeply devoted to the work of the Boys' Brigade, he promoted this special ministry among children in his many travels.

Drummond's life was cut short by a painful illness and he died at the age of forty-five in 1897. In an exchange with Sankey near the end of his life, Drummond reaffirmed his long-held beliefs in atonement through the cross of Christ, the forgiveness of sins, the hope of immortality based on Christ's resurrection, and the necessity of personal conversion. Drummond experienced first-hand many of the cultural and intellectual cross-currents of the age in which he lived. He traversed with rare equipoise the worlds of science and religion, reason and revelation, the academy and the church. He spoke to Britain's elite at special religious meetings arranged by Lord and Lady Aberdeen at Grosvenor House in London and, with equal ease, he shared the message of Christ with the lowly down-and-outs who flocked to Moody's meetings. Although he never lost the common touch, his impact on college students was phenomenal. Many of his student friends became missionaries. Others became leaders in the Student Christian Movement, Inter-Varsity Fellowship and similar organizations. He seemed to embody many of the virtues prized by the rising generation of his day: sincerity, decorum, eloquence, manliness, idealism. Drummond was captivated by the pervasive power of love at the heart of the Christian message. The great theme of his life was to know Jesus Christ and to make him known to others.

Bibliography

T. E. Corts (ed.), *Henry Drummond: A Perpetual Benediction* (Edinburgh: T. & T. Clark, 1999); J. W. Kennedy, *Henry Drummond: An Anthology* (New York: Harper, 1953); J. R. Moore, 'Evangelicals and Evolution: Henry Drummond, Herbert Spencer and the Naturalization of the Spiritual World', *Scottish Journal of Theology*, 38 (1985), pp. 383–417; J. Y. Simpson, *Henry Drummond* (Edinburgh: Oliphant, Anderson & Ferrier, 1901); G. A. Smith, *The Life of Henry Drummond* (London: Hodder & Stoughton, 1899; a shortened version published by The Drummond Trust, Stirling, 1997); M. J. Toone, 'Evangelicalism in Transition: A Comparative Analysis of the Work and Theology of D. L. Moody and His Proteges, Henry Drummond and R. A. Torrey' (PhD thesis, St Andrews University, 1988).

T. GEORGE

■ DU PLESSIS, David Johannes (1905–1987), international Pentecostal spokesman and ecumenical leader known as 'Mr Pentecost', was born on 7 February 1905 at Twenty-four Rivers, a small community near Cape Town, South Africa, to Afrikaaner parents of French Huguenot stock. The family entered the Pentecostal movement through the ministries of John G. Lake and Thomas Hezmalhalch, American missionaries with ties to the Christian Catholic Apostolic

Church of John Alexander Dowie in Zion City, Illinois, and the Azusa Street Revival in Los Angeles, California, who arrived in South Africa in 1908. In 1916 the family moved to Basutoland (now Lesotho), where the senior du Plessis, a lay preacher, worked as a carpenter and helped missionaries to construct a mission station. A year later they moved to Ladybrand in the Orange Free State (now part of the Republic of South Africa).

The younger du Plessis testified to conversion in 1916 and was baptized in water a year later in the Apostolic Faith Mission (AFM), the denomination of his parents, which traced its origin in part to Lake. He received the post-conversion 'baptism in the Holy Spirit' with glossolalic utterance at the age of thirteen in 1918. He began his ministry in the AFM as a teenage street preacher, and then worked at the denomination's print shop in Johannesburg for a short time before returning to Ladybrand. He then completed secondary school and enrolled at Grey University in Bloemfontein for two years of study in order to become a school teacher. A shortage of funds, however, forced him to withdraw and work for a railway. After several years of pastoral work, du Plessis received ordination at the age of twenty-five in 1930. In 1927 he married Anna Cornelia Jacobs; the couple were to have seven children.

Rising quickly in the ranks of the AFM, the largest and most influential Pentecostal denomination in the country, he edited its magazine, *Trooster* (*Comforter*), worked in several regional judicatories, and eventually served from 1936 to 1947 as general secretary, the second highest office in the organization. It was in 1936 that the British Pentecostal evangelist Smith *Wigglesworth, the main speaker at the AFM annual conference in Johannesburg, prophesied to du Plessis that he would play a key role in a coming revival and that his ministry would assume global proportions. At the establishment of the Pentecostal World Conference (PWF) in Zurich in May 1947, du Plessis was appointed organizing secretary and resigned his AFM office. Since the Conference provided no budget or office expenses for the secretary, in 1948 du Plessis chose to move his family to the United States, where for several years he travelled widely in Pentecostal circles. He served as an instructor in

missions at Lee College (now University) in Cleveland, Tennessee (1949–1951) and as pastor of Stamford Gospel Tabernacle, Connecticut (1951–1952), and worked with the Far East Broadcasting Company (1952–1954) and as organizing secretary of the Voice of Healing association in Dallas, Texas (1956–1959). In 1955 he transferred his ministerial credentials from the AFM to the Assemblies of God (AG). His work with the PWC came to an end following its 1958 gathering in Toronto. In 1968, David and Anna gained US citizenship.

In 1951, while living in Stamford and still the secretary of the PWF, du Plessis made an unannounced visit to the headquarters of the National Council of Churches of Christ in the USA (NCC) in New York City. Expecting to be coldly received, he instead found a warm welcome; he was able to meet leaders of the NCC and, soon afterwards, leaders of the World Council of Churches (WCC). Having formerly criticized mainstream churches and their leaders, his attitude was now transformed. He became friends with John A. *Mackay, president of Princeton Theological Seminary and chairman of the International Missionary Council (IMC), and other ecumenical leaders such as Willem Visser 't Hooft and Lesslie *Newbigin. Among these new friends, du Plessis discovered a sincere faith and dedication to working towards Christian unity.

Despite growing criticisms from fundamentalists, leaders in the National Association of Evangelicals and officials of Pentecostal denominations, du Plessis began to move widely in ecumenical circles; this activity cost him his PWC leadership post. His widening circle of relationships enabled him to be a living witness to Pentecostal spirituality. He attended the first six assemblies of the WCC, lectured on the movement to influential theological audiences in the United States and Europe, and addressed the IMC meeting in 1952 at Willingen, Germany. He later served as an unofficial Pentecostal observer during the third session of the second Vatican Council (1963–1965) and became friends with three pontiffs (John XXIII, Paul VI, John Paul II). For church leaders of many traditions, du Plessis was the first Pentecostal they had met; he provided them with a window into a worldwide and dynamically growing movement. He received numerous honours including the Pax Christi award conferred by St John's University, Collegeville, Minnesota, in 1976 and the Benemerenti award from John Paul II in 1983.

Du Plessis was an icon of Pentecostalism as a renewal movement. When the charismatic movement began in the mainstream Protestant and Roman Catholic churches in the 1960s and swept across ecclesiastical and conciliar barriers in the following decades, he encouraged participants to remain in their churches as witnesses to the revitalizing work of the Holy Spirit. His activities in ecumenical circles, however, finally prompted AG leaders to revoke his ministerial credentials in 1962; these were restored to him in 1980. In the intervening years he retained membership at First Assembly of God in Oakland, California, where the family lived. Despite his estrangement from denominational officials, Bethany College of the Assemblies of God in Santa Cruz, California, conferred an honorary DD on him in honour of his contributions to the Pentecostal and charismatic movements.

The significant growth of Pentecostalism, especially in nominally Roman Catholic countries, and the emergence of the charismatic movement contributed to the establishment of the international Roman Catholic and Classical Pentecostal Dialogue in 1972. Though du Plessis was no longer a designated spokesperson for the PWC, his international stature enabled him to work with Fr Kilian McDonnell, OSB, in setting up annual meetings for dialogue under the auspices of the Pontifical Council for Christian Unity and an international self-regulating committee of Pentecostals. The latter has included official representatives of classical Pentecostal denominations and unofficial participants. The ongoing theological and missiological conversations and reports represent du Plessis' crowning ecumenical achievement.

Du Plessis communicated his activities to supporters by means of a newsletter, and the influence of his preaching ministry was multiplied around the world through the circulation of audiotapes of his messages. He published autobiographical reflections in *The Spirit Bade Me Go* (1961, 1970) and *A Man Called Mr. Pentecost* (1977), and practical spiritual teachings in *Simple and Profound* (1986).

David J. du Plessis died on 2 February 1987. His papers are held at the David J. du Plessis Center for Christian Spirituality at Fuller Theological Seminary, Pasadena, California.

Bibliography
A. Bittlinger, *Papst und Pfingstler: der römisch katholisch-pfingstliche Dialog und seine ökumenische Relevanz* (Frankfurt am Main: Peter Lang, 1978); M. Robinson, 'To the Ends of the Earth: The Pilgrimage of an Ecumenical Pentecostal, David J. du Plessis (1905–1987)' (PhD dissertation, University of Birmingham, 1987); B. L. Rutherford, 'From Prosecutor to Defender: An Intellectual History of David du Plessis, drawn from the stories of His Testimony' (PhD dissertation, Fuller Theological Seminary, 2000); J. L. Sandidge, *Roman Catholic/Pentecostal Dialogue (1977–1982): A Study in Developing Ecumenism* (Frankfurt am Main: Peter Lang, 1987).

G. B. McGEE

■ **DUFF, Alexander** (1806–1878), Scottish missionary to India, was born at the farm of Auchnahyle in the parish of Moulin in Perthshire on 25 April 1806. Duff was brought up as a native speaker of the Gaelic language. His family, particularly his father, had been deeply influenced by the evangelical revival in Moulin in 1798.

After attending Perth Grammar School, Duff went on to study at St Andrews University. He attended the Arts course at the United Colleges from 1821 to 1825. The classes in logic, rhetoric and moral philosophy played a major role in Duff's intellectual formation. He was a member of the St Andrews University Missionary Society committee during Professor Thomas *Chalmers' presidency. The society provided an important forum for student discussion on mission.

In late 1825 Duff began the study of divinity at St Mary's College. The curriculum was built around the orthodox Calvinist theology of the late eighteenth century. This theology was profoundly influenced by the Scottish Enlightenment, and in class lectures a strong emphasis was laid on the role of rationality in Christian belief.

On 30 July 1829 Duff married Anne

Scott Drysdale, who would accompany him throughout his mission service in India. The couple had five children, two of whom died in infancy.

At the conclusion of his divinity studies in 1829 Duff was appointed first superintendent of the General Assembly's new educational institution in Calcutta by the Church of Scotland's Committee on the Propagation of the Gospel Abroad. The convener of the committee, the Revd John Inglis, was instrumental in the preliminary planning and financing of the scheme. Since 1814 the General Assembly had been receiving regular reports on social and urban development in Bengal through its representative James Bryce, Presbyterian chaplain to the East India Company. In 1823 Bryce had suggested that the Church of Scotland establish some form of educational institution in Calcutta. Arriving in Calcutta in May 1830, Duff spent his first months observing the quickening social change in the city, brought about by the impact of Westernization. In July 1830, with the help of Ram Mohun Roy, leader of the Hindu reform movement the 'Brahmo Samaj', Duff opened a school for boys as a response to the increasing desire of the local Brahmin elite for Western learning.

Duff, however, was committed to the use of a wide range of mission methods. Students at Hindu College, the training institute for the Bengal Civil Service in Calcutta, had been engaged in a protracted dispute with the college authorities since 1829. Duff established contact with their leaders, and in December 1831 he invited them to attend a series of apologetic lectures on the evidences of the Christian faith. At the conclusion of Duff's public lectures four of the student leaders were converted to Christianity. Duff saw in these events a microcosm of the Christian revolution to come, first in Bengal, then throughout India. Thereafter, he was convinced that an Indian education system combining science and biblical study would provided a secure foundation for future Christian apologetic. While not the originator of mission education as a methodology, Duff became the most articulate exponent of its role in promoting the development of civil society in India.

Invalided home in July 1834, Duff embarked on a programme of tours throughout Scotland to publicize the General Assembly's work and to raise the necessary funding for its continuance. He fully endorsed Sir William Bentinck's Act of March 1835 establishing English as the language medium of higher education in India. In a series of Assembly addresses, speeches, pamphlets and books, he advocated Western education as an effective tool in Christian missions. Marischal College, Aberdeen, awarded him the honorary degree of DD in 1835. In 'Missions: the Chief End of the Church', a series of addresses later published (1839), Duff made a highly original contribution towards an understanding of the missionary nature of the church. He was probably the first mission theorist to set out the notion that the church exists for mission. The public lectures he gave in Edinburgh in 1839 on Indian missions were later published as 'India and Indian Missions'.

Following his return to Calcutta in 1840, Duff took part in vigorous opposition to the plans of the Governor General, Lord Auckland, for religious neutrality in State education. In 1843, along with the other Church of Scotland missionaries, Duff left the established church and joined the Free Church. By 1844 he had set up a new educational institution for the Free Church in Calcutta. In accordance with his understanding of the nature of the church and its mission, he suggested to the leaders of the infant Free Church that there be a chair in missions and education at the new Free Church college.

In 1849 Duff accepted an invitation by the Free Church to return to Scotland to organize its rapidly developing mission commitments. At the Free Church General Assembly of 1850 he advocated the development of mission associations throughout the presbyteries of the Free Church. He was elected moderator of the Free Church Assembly in the following year. During the parliamentary discussions in 1853 concerning the statutory renewal of the East India Company Charter, Duff gave evidence on the importance of education in India to the Select Committee of the House of Lords. His influence was crucial in securing the Educational Despatch of 1854, which laid the foundations for a modern educational system in India. In the same year he was sent by the Free Church Foreign Missions Committee to the United

States and Canada to promote the work of overseas missions. During the visit to the USA, the University of New York conferred on him the honorary degree of LLD.

Duff returned to Calcutta in 1856. In the years following the Indian Mutiny, he oversaw the further building work and established a new female school. He also devoted more time to the support of education in the vernacular languages of Bengal. Duff laboured for the founding of the University of Calcutta, and in 1863 he was invited to be its first vice-chancellor. Due to a period of severe illness, however, he was invalided home, leaving India for the last time in December 1863. Returning to Scotland, he was appointed convener of the Free Church Foreign Missions Committee once again. Anne Duff died on 22 February 1865.

While he was still concerned with the practical problems of establishing a new mission to the Gonds of Central India, throughout 1865 he continued to advocate the establishment of a chair of evangelistic theology, a missionary institute and a journal of missions within the Free Church. In 1867 the Free Church General Assembly finally approved the professorship in evangelistic theology, and Duff was appointed to the chair.

As convener of the Foreign Missions committee, Duff oversaw the establishment of a new mission in the Lebanon in 1870, and three new missions in south-east Africa. He toured Syria to examine the educational facilities among the Druse, Maronite and Greek communities. Duff had always been an advocate of interdenominational cooperation in missions, and he was once again elected moderator of the Free Church General Assembly in 1873 during the discussions on a proposed union with the United Presbyterian Church. He died in Edinburgh on 12 February 1878.

Bibliography

M. A. Laird, *Missionaries and Education in Bengal, 1793–1837* (Oxford: Oxford University Press, 1972); O. Myklebust, *The Study of Missions in Theological Education*, 2 vols. (Oslo: Egede Institute, 1955); G. Smith, *Alexander Duff, DD, LLD*, 2 vols. (London: Hodder & Stoughton, 1879).

I. D. MAXWELL

■ **DUFFECY, James Alfred Cave** (1912–1983), evangelist, was born in Newtown, New South Wales, his father a nominal Roman Catholic and his mother a nominal Anglican. Later the family moved to the beachside suburb of Coogee. There Duffecy was attracted to and began attending an open-air Sunday school run by an Open Air Campaigners (OAC) team, which led to his conversion in 1924 aged twelve. Throughout his formative teenage years he continued to attend Bible study, testimony meetings and open-air meetings, and he became a leader of the Coogee team. Thus began his lifelong connection with OAC.

Leaving school, he worked as an engraver with *The Sydney Morning Herald*, maintaining a consistent Christian witness in the workplace. However, at a Katoomba Convention meeting, while still a teenager, he responded to a call for full commitment and determined to become an evangelist. Continuing his association with OAC, he learned to conduct children's meetings, became a leader of the Voluntary Workers, and spoke at open-air meetings, especially the well-attended one on Sunday evenings in the central business district of Sydney.

In 1940 OAC invited him to become a full-time evangelist, a role he was to fulfil until his death. During the Second World War he was OAC welfare officer in military camps for three and a half years. After the war he was a staff evangelist before being appointed field director for Australia. His leadership and energy saw OAC begin work overseas and the organization expand, initially to New Zealand in 1954, and then to North America, England and Europe.

In 1956 Paul Smith, son of Pastor Oswald *Smith of the People's Church in Toronto, invited Duffecy and a team to revive open-air evangelism in Canada. The work soon spread to the United States where he became North American director; the USA was to be the centre for international development. As a result, local OAC branches began in Germany in 1962, in Britain in 1968, and in Italy in 1969. Today OAC operates in twenty-one countries, albeit as a loose fellowship; the organizational ties have not developed. As well as making trips to England and Australia, Duffecy travelled widely throughout the USA, mainly along the eastern seaboard and in the middle states, where he frequently spoke at Bible colleges, such as Columbia, Moody and Prairie, that had an evangelistic focus. In 1964 he opened the New York City OAC branch during the World Fair there, and was named New York director. In 1966 he was appointed international director at the first International Conference of OAC, and in 1978 he became the international president.

In 1936 Duffecy married Joyce Mayhew. They had three sons, Hugh (who died in a plane crash in the USA in the 1970s), Peter and Christopher, and two daughters, Lynne and Susan. The family joined him in 1957 shortly after he moved to the USA. He died on 17 November 1983 in Toronto, active to the last.

Duffecy was a Sydney Anglican but moved easily in interdenominational circles. His theology was very conservative, as was his exegesis, but he was not a militant fundamentalist, avoiding theological and ecclesiological controversy. He was a warm-hearted man, who was genuinely interested in people, even strangers. He had a great memory for details and always remembered people's names. He had a good sense of humour, with a self-deprecating lack of pretension. People of all ages and from a variety of social and educational backgrounds were attracted by his winsome, loving personality.

Duffecy was a great talker who conversed easily and directly with people, whether on a one-to-one basis or when speaking to audiences in many environments. He was almost inseparable from his sketchboard and paints, which he used to illustrate his message. The sketchboard method became characteristic of OAC's evangelistic methods. But, most of all, it was his personal qualities that shaped his contribution as an evangelist and as a leader. They shone through his ministry and first love, open-air preaching. Whether speaking in factories or wharves or the street or cathedrals, his messages were always down to earth, simple but powerful, and mostly evangelistic. As might be expected, his four books were also on the theme of evangelism: *Another Sherlock Holmes in England*; *Sketchboard Sermons*; *Sketchboard Sermons No 2*; and *The Truceless Warfare Advances* (a history of OAC).

He held a number of leadership positions with OAC, but was not a good administrator. His leadership was effective, though, mainly because of his energy and the personal interest he showed in people.

Bibliography

J. A. Duffecy, *Truceless Warfare Advances* (Citrus Springs, Florida: OAC, 1983).

D. PAPROTH

■ **DWIGHT, Timothy** (1752–1817), Congregational theologian, clergyman, poet and educator, was born in Northampton, Massachusetts, his mother being one of the daughters of Jonathan *Edwards. He graduated from Yale College at seventeen and became headmaster at Hopkins Grammar School (1769–1771) and then a tutor at Yale (1771–1777). While at Yale, Dwight began experimenting with the curriculum by emphasizing the study of classics and poetry. He helped to found, along with other tutors and students, the 'Connecticut Wits', which is thought to have been the first American school of literary criticism. During the Revolutionary War he served as a chaplain in the army, and after the war he worked in Greenfield Hill, Connecticut, as a pastor and head of an academy (1783–1795). During this period he began several of his important works, including a series of doctrinal sermons entitled *Theology, Explained and Defended* (published posthumously in 1818–1819). In 1795 he was called to the presidency of Yale College, and despite becoming functionally blind (most likely suffering from moderate to severe myopia), he served successfully as its eighth president until his death in 1817.

One of America's earliest men of letters, Dwight wrote long, patriotic poems and travel narratives, including *The Conquest of Canaan, a Poem in Eleven Books* (1785), *Greenfield Hill, a Poem in Seven Parts* (1794) and *Travels in New England and New York* (1821–1822). Politically, Dwight was a conservative federalist; he saw revolutionary France as an example of the social catastrophe that he believed would inevitably follow in the wake of the 'infidel philosophy' of Enlightenment deism and scepticism. Thus he strongly supported federalist attempts to protect the Connecticut Congregationalist churches from disestablishment at the hand of what he perceived to be deistically leaning

Jeffersonian Baptists, earning himelf the mock title, 'the Pope of Federalism'.

The revolutionary 'infidel philosophy' was fashionable among Yale students when Dwight arrived as their new president. To counter what he perceived to be their superficial attachment to the French Enlightenment deism of Voltaire, Rousseau and D'Alembert and their American counterparts, Jefferson and Thomas Paine, Dwight launched a two-pronged attack. First, through public debate, he sought to restore confidence in Scripture. For example, he purposely based the annual debate at Yale for 1795, the first year of his presidency, on the following question: 'Are the Scriptures of the Old and New Testament the Word of God?' Secondly, he offered a four-year cycle of sermons designed to communicate the essentials of the faith (which was later published as *Theology Explained and Defended* and used as an essential text in theological schools until the mid-nineteenth century). In these sermons, he maintained that God rules 'by motives addressed to the understanding and affections of rational subjects, and operating on their minds, as inducements to voluntary obedience. No other government is worthy of God: there being, indeed, no other, beside that of mere force and coercion.' He thus moved theology in a distinctly federalist direction. In 1802 there was a revival at Yale, in which a third of the 225 students were converted. Dwight has often been credited with stimulating the Second Great Awakening in New England through his successful preaching to students at Yale College. However, the most recent research into the revivals at Yale, and in New England as a whole (e.g. Shiels), suggests that the revivals among Yale students were a product rather than the cause of the Second Great Awakening.

Theologically, while Dwight affirmed the broadest outlines of Edwards' Calvinism, he was an early advocate of New Divinity theology and regarded its most important distinctives (e.g. on original sin and the Half-Way Covenant) as helpful developments of his grandfather's theology. Yet pastoral experience taught him that, if pressed too far, the problems of New Divinity theology outweighed its advantages. For example, whereas the New Divinity theologians such as *Bellamy and *Hopkins stressed the role of logic, Dwight erected his theology on the conviction that unbounded reason (the Enlightenment's unconditional commitment to the canons of reason) inevitably produced theological distortions.

Thus Dwight sought a middle ground of compromise. He echoed the teaching of his grandfather Edwards when to do so served his greater goal of promoting practical morality. Yet when he sensed the dangers of inflexible systems, he preached against the New Divinity. Though resort to compromise had previously served his professional ends (e.g. in his educational reforms at Yale), theologically, at least in this case, it led to middle-of-the-road mediocrity that failed to generate consensus or to restate and re-apply the Edwardsean tradition for nineteenth-century America. Thus as pedagogue, poet, politician, preacher, pundit and president Dwight was an important yet transitional figure in the development of American Christianity, as an inheritor of Edwards' Calvinism and its interpretation in the New Divinity, and as a forerunner of the New Haven theology of his student Nathaniel *Taylor.

Bibliography

S. Berk, *Calvinism Versus Democracy: Timothy Dwight and the Origins of Evangelical Orthodoxy* (Hamden: Archon Books, 1974); C. Cunningham, *Timothy Dwight (1752–1817), A Biography* (New York: Macmillan, 1942); J. Fitzmier, *New England's Moral Legislator: Timothy Dwight, 1752–1817* (Bloomington: Indiana University Press, 1998); R. D. Shiels, 'The Second Great Awakening in Connecticut: A Critique of the Traditional Interpretation', *Church History* 49 (1980), pp. 401–415; K. Silverman, *Timothy Dwight* (New York: Twayne Publishers, 1969).

J. HENSLEY

■ **EDWARDS, Jonathan** (1703–1758), Congregationalist minister, theologian and intellectual leader of the Great Awakening, was the only son of the eleven children born to the Revd Timothy Edwards, pastor of East Windsor, Connecticut, and his wife, Esther Stoddard Edwards, daughter of Solomon *Stoddard. Surrounded by the vibrant piety of his family, and influenced by the intellectual rigour of his father, Edwards was raised in an atmosphere that emphasized a strong 'experimental' (i.e. experiential) Calvinist theology. As a youth Jonathan imbibed his family's piety yet was unable to accept its Calvinist teaching. 'From my childhood up', Edwards wrote later, 'my mind had been full of objections against the doctrine of God's sovereignty ... It used to appear like a horrible doctrine to me.'

Showing remarkable intellectual potential, Edwards entered Yale College in September 1716, just before his thirteenth birthday. There he was introduced to the prevailing intellectual currents of the day, including John Locke's empiricism, Newtonian science, Continental Rationalism and Cambridge Platonism. This exposure significantly impacted his later thought, for by it he was able to interpret conservative Reformed orthodoxy in the categories of newer philosophies. He received his BA in 1720, graduating as valedictorian, and his MA three years later.

While he thrived at Yale intellectually, he struggled somewhat spiritually. While affirming notional beliefs about Jesus Christ as Saviour, he recognized that he lacked a true, heartfelt submission to God, and he disdained the doctrine of God's absolute sovereignty in salvation. In the spring of 1721, however, he came not only to a conviction of this teaching, but to a 'delightful conviction'. While meditating upon 1 Timothy 1:17, 'Now unto the King eternal, immortal, invisible, the only wise God, be honour and glory for ever and ever,' Edwards found his mind and heart turning to God: 'As I read the words, there came into my soul, and was as it were diffused through it, a sense of the glory of the Divine Being; a new sense, quite different from any thing I ever experienced before. Never any words of Scripture seemed to me as these words did. I thought with myself, how excellent a Being that was, and how happy I should be, if I might enjoy that God, and be rapt up to him in heaven; and be as it were swallowed up in him for ever!' From then on Edwards rejoiced in God's sovereignty, for to him it became an integral part of the beauty of God's glory. The importance of this turn of events in his spiritual life cannot be overestimated. Not only was it his conversion to Christ, as he later came to recognize, but it also would impress upon

his theology of conversion the experimental Calvinist aesthetic that later became the hallmark of his theology.

The 1720s were important years of vocational formation for Jonathan Edwards. During them he cultivated the intellectual disciplines and ministry skills that laid the foundations for his theology and life as a pastor. Between 1721 and 1726, Edwards received his MA, tutored students at Yale and briefly pastored two congregations, one in New York, and another in Bolton, Connecticut. As a bachelor with a voracious appetite for theological reflection and holiness, he spent much of his free time during these years in study and religious devotions. His fervent piety is reflected in both his *Resolutions*, a series of spiritual commitments intended to focus his life upon God and holy living, and his *Diary*, which he used for self-examination to monitor his growth in grace. Intellectually, he channelled his scholarly energy into a series of notebooks containing philosophical, theological and biblical reflections. These notebooks became a sort of theological workshop for his thinking, a place where he could test ideas, sharpen previously formulated arguments and construct his vast and intricate theological system over decades of reflection. Some of them, such as *The Mind and Natural Philosophy*, dealt with issues of metaphysics, philosophy and the natural sciences. These notebooks provided Edwards with the philosophical setting of his theology, yet were discontinued after a number of years. Other notebooks, such as the *Miscellanies*, *Notes on Scripture*, and the 'Blank Bible', were begun in the 1720s and continued throughout his life. In these he had written thousands of exegetical and theological essays by the time he died, many of which he cross-referenced and indexed. Through them we see the mind of a dynamic biblical theologian at work.

The year of 1727 brought personal and vocational changes to Edwards' life. It was the year when he married seventeen-year-old Sarah Pierrepont of New Haven, a young woman who had manifested an extraordinary piety at an early age. Their marriage would be one of unusual happiness and fruitfulness. A year later they would welcome into the world young Sarah, the first of their eleven children. Also in that year Edwards was ordained in

Northampton, Massachusetts, to assist the ministry of his ageing grandfather Solomon Stoddard. Stoddard's long pastorate (fifty-seven years), his vigorous personality and powerful leadership had transformed Northampton into the most influential New England pulpit outside Boston. During his apprenticeship Edwards learned his grandfather's powerful preaching techniques, skills that would have an enormous impact on the young minister's preaching. By the time of Stoddard's death in 1729 Edwards was a seasoned preacher, an acute theologian and the sole minister of Northampton's influential pulpit.

In the 1730s Edwards matured both as a defender of Reformed theology and as a keen observer of religious experience. The growing popularity of 'reasonable' Christianity among English divines was spreading throughout New England and threatening orthodox Calvinism. This newer Christianity exalted free choice, downplayed the effects of original sin and reduced the Christian life to morality. Edwards called this theology 'Arminianism' and vigorously opposed it from his pulpit and in his first published sermons God Glorified in Man's Dependence (1731) and A Divine and Supernatural Light (1734). It was not until he preached his sermon series on Justification by Faith in 1734 that hundreds of people in his town came under a deep conviction of sin. During this time Edwards shepherded many across the great divide of conversion, and thus became skilled in judging whether or not a religious experience ought to be considered a genuine conversion. He recorded his observations of the revival in A Faithful Narrative of the Surprising Work of God (1737), a book published both in New England and in England by Isaac *Watts and John *Wesley.

The 1740s was a decade of stark contrasts in Edwards' ministry, for while he was celebrated abroad as one of the many heroes of the Great Awakening, at home he was reviled as a villain in his own congregation. When the American Awakening began in 1740, sparked by the itinerant ministries of George *Whitefield and Gilbert *Tennent, Edwards immediately judged it to be a true work of the Spirit of God: in his estimation, thousands of individuals all across the eastern seaboard were coming under conviction of their sin through the preaching of the gospel and coming to a saving knowledge of Christ. Edwards himself promoted the work of the Awakening by preaching in nearby pulpits, his most famous sermon being Sinners in the Hands of an Angry God, in Enfield, Connecticut, on 8 July 1741. Yet as the Awakening progressed, excesses increased. The emphasis placed on the immediate experience of the Holy Spirit encouraged a rejection of traditional authority. If all that mattered was the experience of the Holy Spirit, then the church, a learned ministry and even strict morality could be deemed unnecessary to Christian living. This tendency, known as antinomianism, evoked a strong reaction from many New England ministers, who largely rejected the emotional components of the revivals. Edwards found himself between these two extremes, arguing his case in three treatises: The Distinguishing Marks of a Work of the Spirit of God (1741), Some Thoughts on the Revival of Religion in New England (1742), and his masterpiece on religious experience, A Treatise Concerning Religious Affections (1746). When the Holy Spirit works saving grace into an individual, Edwards argued, his work is always accompanied by a change in the person's affections. The soul intimately feels the divine truths that it beholds: just prior to conversion it knows the terror of what it is to be under the just wrath of God, and upon trusting Christ it is overjoyed at the beauty, glory and grace of God revealed in the gospel. Thus true Christianity is not simply an affair of morality but a loving communion with the sovereign creator. Yet true grace in the soul never bypasses the need for holy living or the church but will always tend towards certain patterns of behaviour: true humility before God, a deep love for Christ, a holy life and a respect for the order established in the community of faith. These alone are the true signs of a converted life. Any manifestation of antinomianism in one's life Edwards held to be an acceleration of sinful principles in the heart, or possibly an indication of the absence of saving grace. In 1749 Edwards published the Life and Diary of David *Brainerd, a young missionary to Native Americans in New Jersey, to illustrate the type of vital Calvinist piety he advanced in his revival treatises.

In contrast to his favourable reputation

abroad, Edwards experienced enormous troubles as a pastor at home after the Awakening ended in 1742. Through several pastoral misjudgments, he came to be regarded as overly authoritarian by many in his congregation, who were breathing the new air of liberty that was beginning to blow across the colonies. These tensions flared into controversy in 1748 when he showed a reluctance to continue his grandfather's practice of open communion. Stoddard had argued that the Lord's Supper is best understood as a 'converting ordinance'. In his view all the means of grace have an evangelistic component to them, and therefore the Lord's Supper is to be open to all baptized individuals, including those who have not experienced a work of regeneration. Stoddard's prestige and energetic promotion of the doctrine in the late seventeenth century convinced the Congregational churches of the Connecticut River valley, and by the 1740s open communion was a tradition enjoyed by two generations of Northamptonites. Edwards gradually became convinced that the practice engendered a false sense of security in his unconverted parishioners, and upon reconsideration he concluded that the Lord's Supper is a closed ordinance restricted only to true believers who evince the signs of gracious affections. Once Edwards went public with his position, controversy enveloped his congregation, leading to his dismissal in 1750.

In 1751 Edwards moved his large family to the frontier town of Stockbridge in western Massachusetts, where he served as pastor of a small congregation while labouring as a missionary to the local Native Americans. His seven years there were far from peaceful, for he had to resist a group of powerful townsmen who were exploiting the Indians, cope with debt (he could not sell his Northampton house), battle with an extended illness (probably malaria) and deal with the constant anxiety caused by the French and Indian Wars, which raged around his exposed frontier town. In spite of these pressures, Edwards waged a war of his own against Arminianism, deism and other ideas that threatened the principles of orthodox Calvinism. In 1754 he published his well-known *Freedom of the Will*, in which he argued that human willing is an instrument or function of the mind's strongest inclination. Divine sovereignty operates at the level of an individual's inclinations and affections. This teaching affirms both personal freedom, for an individual will always act in accordance with what is viewed as the greatest good (i.e. one will always do what one wants), and God's sovereignty, for he alone determines what a person values as the greatest good. Edwards next turned his attention to his *Two Dissertations* (published posthumously in 1765). In the first, *A Dissertation Concerning the End for which God Created the World*, Edwards argued that while God is self-sufficient, part of his infinite fulness is an inclination to communicate his internal glory externally to a finite creation. God pursues his own glory in creation by pursuing the happiness of the elect, because their conscious delight, praise and happiness in God *is* the fulness of God's own glory externally manifested in creation. In the second work, *A Dissertation on the Nature of True Virtue*, Edwards built an ethical theory upon the teleological and ontological structures established in the first dissertation. Lastly, Edwards wrote *The Great Christian Doctrine of Original Sin Defended* (1758), in which he argued that human beings are justly imputed with Adam's sin because God has constituted the entire human race as one entity. As the leaves and branches of an oak tree are in union with and participate in the nature of the acorn from which they grew, so all human beings are in union with and participate in Adam's nature and consent to his act of disobedience. Because of this Adam's sin is truly our sin, and hence his guilt and punishment are truly ours as well.

Edwards planned to write other works, such as *A History of the Work of Redemption* and *A Harmony of the Old and New Testament*, but he did not live long enough to complete them. In early 1758 he was called to the presidency of the College of New Jersey (later Princeton University). But just weeks after taking up the appointment he received a tainted smallpox inoculation, dying from complications on 22 March at the age of fifty-four.

Edwards' historical and theological influence has been immense, primarily because of the multifaceted nature of his ministry and writings. His New Divinity followers revered him as their spiritual father who established the groundwork for a more 'consistent

Calvinism', which combined revivalist activism, experiential piety and intellectual rigour. Their endeavours converted the majority of New England congregations to an Edwardsean theology by the turn of the nineteenth century, even though they modified significant aspects of Edwards' thought. Outside New England, Edwards was honoured as a traditional, albeit progressive, Calvinist divine, first by his supporters in the Church of Scotland, such as the *Erskines, in the eighteenth century, and later by the Princetonians in the nineteenth century. Many American evangelicals esteemed Edwards as both a giant of evangelical piety (thanks to the wide circulation of his *Resolutions*), and as a doctor of revival, admired by Lyman *Beecher and Charles *Finney. The nineteenth-century missionary movement honoured Edwards for two reasons: first, because his *Freedom of the Will* was the book that persuaded William *Carey to reject hyper-Calvinism and the necessity for missionary activism; and secondly, because his *Life of Brainerd* was cherished as an inspiring devotional book, second only to the Bible, by virtually every American missionary in the nineteenth century. Today, Edwards' vision of God, intellectual precision and intense piety still appeals to and challenges a wide variety of evangelicals.

Bibliography

G. Marsden, *Jonathan Edwards* (New Haven: Yale University Press, 2003); P. Miller, *Jonathan Edwards* (New York: William Sloan Associates, 1949); I. H. Murray, *Jonathan Edwards: A New Biography* (Edinburgh: Banner of Truth; Carlisle, Pennsylvania: Banner of Truth, 1987); P. J. Tracy, *Jonathan Edwards, Pastor* (New York: Hill & Wang, 1979).

R. W. CALDWELL III
D. A. SWEENEY

■ **ELIOT, John** (1604–1690), Puritan missionary in New England, was hailed by his admirers the 'Apostle to the Indians'. Eliot was born at Widford, Hertfordshire, to Bennett and Lettye Eliot. He was baptized on 5 August 1604 in the parish church of St John the Baptist. Bennett was a yeoman farmer with considerable land holdings in Essex and Hertfordshire. During the Lent term of 1618, Eliot entered Jesus College, Cambridge as a pensioner, and he received his BA in 1622.

Not much is known about Eliot's ministerial training or career in England. After graduation, he served for some time as usher at a school in Little Baddow, near Chelmsford, Essex, where the famous Puritan Thomas Hooker had been the schoolmaster. It is likely that Eliot's Nonconformist leanings developed here; they eventually led him to board *The Lyon* for its journey to Boston in New England in 1631. Although it is unclear whether Eliot was ordained while still in England, his ready acceptance as interim 'minister' at the First Church, Boston, in 1631 suggests that he was.

In 1632 Eliot refused the invitation to be John Wilson's assistant at the First Church of Boston, where he had taken Wilson's place during the latter's visit to England. Instead, Eliot chose to be the first minister of the Congregational Church at Roxbury, where he was installed in November 1632 and remained for fifty-eight years until his death. Meanwhile, in October 1632 he married Hanna Mumford, who had followed her fiancé to Boston.

Eliot, along with Richard Mather and Thomas Weld, translated the Psalms into English and published them in the so-called *Bay Psalm Book* (1640), which was the first book to be printed in America. After ministering in Roxbury for fifteen years, Eliot initiated a new phase of his ministry in 1646. His first experience in Native American evangelism was at the wigwam of a chieftain named Waban at Nonantum (near Newton, Massachusetts) on 28 October 1646. His sermon, lasting over an hour, focused on the fall of humankind, the resulting universal wrath of God and the gracious provision of reconciliation through Christ. Eliot was accompanied by Thomas Shepard, the minister at Cambridge, Daniel Gookin and John Wilson, pastor of the Boston church. He had not been commissioned by the Roxbury Church, nor was he sent by the colonial government in response to a Macedonian call from the Native Americans, even though the Puritans of Massachusetts Bay were supposedly committed to working among them.

Eliot's biweekly evangelistic visits to the Native Americans bore considerable fruit.

During these meetings, he first catechized young children, then preached a sermon and finally took questions on the sermon or any other topic relating to the Christian faith. In his effort to Christianize the Native Americans, Eliot urged them to forsake the pow-wows (medical consultations with shamans), observe the Sabbath and adopt a settled lifestyle. In 1652 the first professions were recorded by Eliot's associates, and in 1659 eight Native Americans, after satisfactorily confessing their faith before the elders of the Roxbury Church, were admitted as members.

More systematic Christianizing of the Native Americans was initiated in Natick, Massachusetts, where on 6 August 1651 an autonomous Native American civil government, commonly known as a 'praying town', was formed. It was structured according to the biblical precedent in Exodus 18 (one ruler of a hundred, two of fifty, and ten of ten were chosen) and entered by a mutual covenant. By 1675, just before the outbreak of King Philip's War, fourteen 'praying towns' had been founded as a result of Eliot's indefatigable and persistent ministry. At the height of Eliot's missionary activity, there were an estimated 3,600 Native American Christians in New England. The praying towns were intentionally situated at a distance from the English settlers so as to obviate any potential territorial, economic and moral conflicts, and also at a distance from the 'non-praying' Native Americans. They were self-consciously theocratic and theocentric in their life, faith and polity. In addition to preaching biweekly in various Native American villages, Eliot trained native evangelists and leaders; he was convinced that the indigenous pastors were best suited to sustain a long-term ministry among the Native Americans. By 1690 there were twenty-four trained Native American preachers serving their community.

Although Eliot did emphasize justification by grace through faith alone to the Native American Christians, he also unhesitatingly asserted that justifying faith never stood alone, but was accompanied by the fruit of faith, sanctification. Thus, following *Calvin's teaching on the third use of the law, Eliot claimed that Sabbath observance and keeping the Ten Commandments were tests of faith. Although he was Calvinistic in his theology, like other New England Puritan

pastors, in his sermons to the Native Americans he expounded the simplicity and wonder of the solution he believed God had provided to the problem of human sinfulness.

Much of Eliot's work was supported morally and financially by his English friends, especially those from the Society for the Propagation of the Gospel in New England, formed under the auspices of the Long Parliament in 1649. In the early period of the New England Company, Eliot received over £12,000 from his English supporters for his work among the Native Americans.

Criticism of and opposition to Eliot's work came from three main sources. The Native American shamans had lost prestige and income from their work of exorcism and healing. Some English settlers, including some clergy, had a shockingly low view of the Native Americans, especially their anthropological and spiritual character, and were sceptical regarding Eliot's claims to be the agent of a genuine work of God. The language barrier and the lack of willing and competent evangelists were a formidable challenge.

Eliot's zeal for evangelizing the Native Americans was matched by his desire to give them the Bible, without which, he was convinced, true and vibrant faith could not grow. Well-trained in the classical theological languages (Greek, Latin and Hebrew), Eliot demonstrated both the aptitude and the persistence required for Bible translation. He began studying the Algonquian language at the age of forty-five with a household servant in Dorchester, Cockenoe of Long Island. No books in Algonquian had been published before, nor any grammar of the language. Eventually, in 1663, the first edition of the Bible in Algonquian was published; it was also the first Bible printed in America and was funded almost entirely by the Society for the Propagation of the Gospel in New England. Eliot's Native American Bible had been preceded by a catechism, published in 1653, and some selections from Psalms in 1658. Most first edition copies of the Indian Bible were destroyed during King Philip's War (1675–1677), and a second printing was required. Despite the great reluctance of the New England Company to provide the finances for this great project and the unrelenting criticism of some New England ministers, the second edition was printed in 1685. It was the last significant landmark in Eliot's career.

Eliot translated and disseminated the works of English pastoral theologians, such as Richard *Baxter's *Call to the Unconverted* (1664) and Lewis Bayly's *Practice of Piety* (1665). He also wrote *The Christian Commonwealth* (London, 1659), in which he explained his eschatological perspective, which was the major motivation for his work among the Native Americans.

Eliot's missionary work faced its first great test during King Philip's War (1675–1677), when hostility among English settlers towards the Native Americans, irrespective of their religious beliefs, intensified. Despite Eliot's protests in October 1675 the General Council in Boston ordered the removal of 'praying Indians' to Deer Island in Boston harbour. When the Native Americans were released in 1677, Eliot sought to revive the moribund Christian convictions of the 'praying Indians'. Although four praying towns were rebuilt, the Native American mission never fully recovered its fervour after King Philip's War.

Numerous extant letters to and from Eliot and his English friends and supporters, such as Richard Baxter and Robert Boyle, provide helpful insights into the progress of the Native American mission, as well as the financial, ecclesiological and theological issues facing it. In addition, a number of Eliot's letters to English Christians were published in a series of 'Indian tracts' between 1648 and 1675.

Eliot was a product of his time and culture, and he frequently confused English cultural norms with Christian ones, with what seem to modern historians to have been alarming and tragic results. Nevertheless, his concern for the Native Americans was beyond question. Eliot died on 20 May 1690 in the parsonage at Roxbury, and was buried in the parish tomb. His wife Hanna predeceased him by three years, and he outlived five of his six children. His last words were 'Welcome, Joy'.

Bibliography
R. Cogley, *John Eliot's Mission to the Indians Before King Philip's War* (Cambridge: Harvard University Press, 1999); S. Rooy, *The Theology of Missions in the Puritan Tradition* (Delft: W. D. Meinema, 1965);

O. E. Winslow, *John Eliot "Apostle to the Indians"* (Boston: Houghton Mifflin, 1968).

P. C-H. LIM

■ **ELLIOT, Elisabeth Howard** (1926–), missionary and author, and **Jim** (1927–1956), missionary martyr, met in the autumn of 1945 at Wheaton College, Wheaton, Illinois, USA, where both were undergraduates majoring in Greek. Elisabeth was born on 21 December 1926 in Brussels, Belgium, daughter of Americans Philip E. Howard, Jr, and Katherine Gillingham Howard, members of the Belgian Gospel Mission. When Elisabeth, the second of six children, was five months old, her father returned to the United States to become associate editor of *The Sunday School Times*, an independent religious newspaper founded by Elisabeth's great-grandfather, Henry Clay Trumbull. Family piety in the Howard home was shaped by the values of northern fundamentalism, including Keswick holiness teaching, of which Elisabeth's great-uncle, Charles G. Trumbull, was the foremost twentieth-century American proponent. Missionaries were frequent visitors, with more than forty-two countries represented in the family guest book. During her high school years, Elisabeth was introduced to the writings of Amy *Carmichael. Carmichael's books and poems, the Howard family and her relationship with Jim Elliot were the formative influences in Elisabeth's life.

Jim (Philip James) Elliot was born on 8 October 1927 in Portland, Oregon, the third of four children. His father, Fred, was a travelling evangelist and a 'commended' (recognized) teacher for Plymouth Brethren assemblies who had served his apprenticeship with Bible teacher Harry A. *Ironside. Jim's mother, Clara, was a chiropractor. The Elliot home also was steeped in piety. Fred Elliot read the Bible to his children and prayed with them daily, religious gatherings were a central part of family life, and the Elliots, too, offered hospitality to missionaries. Jim displayed a precocious spirituality, 'preaching' to his playmates from a garden swing when he was only six or seven. In high school, Jim played football, starred in several school plays and was known as a fervent Christian. At Wheaton College, from 1945 to 1949, he was a top student, an outstanding wrestler and a leader in the campus Foreign Mission Fellowship.

In January 1948 Welsh evangelist Stephen Olford came to the Wheaton campus for a week of special religious meetings. As a result of his preaching, both Elisabeth Howard and Jim Elliot began spiritual journals. Jim would maintain his journal until his death eight years later, filling four notebooks with more than 800 handwritten entries. The entries, later published as *The Journals of Jim Elliot* (1978), reflect the concerns of an unusually articulate young man, passionately committed to God and absorbed with spiritual realities. They also demonstrate the extent to which Plymouth Brethren influence had shaped his piety. Jim's radical separation from the world, which led him to register for the draft as a conscientious objector, to look askance at the rituals surrounding church weddings and to struggle with a complicated and deeply ambivalent attitude towards the simple pleasures of life, had Brethren roots. The many reflections during the early years of the journals on death as a sign of absolute commitment to God echoed not only a strong evangelical tradition of missionary heroism, but also the centrality of the Lord's Supper and its remembrance of Christ's death to Brethren spirituality. The journals reveal Jim as a nonconformist who valued his independence before God and who seemed to have little need for any Christian community beyond his family and a few good comrades in the faith. The entries downplayed the fun-loving side of Elliot's personality, including his love of practical jokes.

In May 1948, a few weeks before Elisabeth's graduation, Jim Elliot and Elisabeth Howard declared their love for one another. Jim, however, had committed himself to the life of a celibate, pioneer missionary. The two began an unusual, and mostly undeclared, courtship that lasted for five years until Jim felt free before God to marry, which he and Elisabeth did in a civil ceremony in Quito, Ecuador, on 8 October 1953, Jim's twenty-sixth birthday. After college graduation, Elisabeth had continued her preparation for the mission field by attending the Summer Institute of Linguistics in Norman, Oklahoma, and the Prairie Bible Institute in Three Hills, Alberta, Canada. Jim graduated in June

1949 and spent about a year in Portland, seeking God's guidance for the future. In 1950 he attended the Summer Institute and there sensed a calling to missionary work among the Quichua Indians in Ecuador. In February 1952 Jim and missionary partner Peter Fleming sailed for Ecuador. After six months of language study, they travelled to the eastern jungles to work among the lowland Quichua. Elisabeth had arrived in Quito in April 1952 *en route* to an assignment among the Colorado Indians at the foot of the western slopes of the Andes. All three were independent missionaries, supported by Plymouth Brethren assemblies and under the umbrella of Christian Missions in Many Lands. After Elisabeth and Jim married, she joined him in the Quichua work. Their daughter Valerie was born in February 1955.

In mid-September 1955 Mission Aviation Fellowship pilot Nate Saint and Jim's Wheaton classmate Ed McCully, whom Elliot had recruited to work in Ecuador, spotted a small settlement of Huaorani (Waorani, Waodani, 'Auca') Indians living in the jungle about fifteen minutes by air from the mission station where McCully and his wife lived. Elliot, McCully, Fleming and Saint all wanted to take the gospel to the Huaorani, an unreached people feared for their tenacity in defending their territory against all outsiders. Elliot, McCully and Saint launched what came to be known as 'Operation Auca', a secret, three-month effort to cultivate contacts with the Huaorani through gifts dropped or lowered from a small plane. The project ended in early January 1956, when the three men, with Fleming and a fifth missionary, Roger Youderian, attempted a face-to-face encounter with the Indians. After an initial peaceful contact, all five were speared to death on the afternoon of Sunday 8 January, at their campsite on the Curaray River.

The search for the five men and then the story of their deaths became front-page news in the United States and around the world. A photo essay that appeared in *Life* magazine on 30 January 1956 was syndicated, and versions appeared in the *Picture Post* (Britain), *Epoca* (Italy) and the *Paris Match*, as well as in other publications worldwide. Subsequently, two best-selling books by Elisabeth Elliot, *Through Gates of Splendor*

(1957) and *Shadow of the Almighty: The Life and Testament of Jim Elliot* (1958), helped to make the story of the 'Auca martyrs' the defining missionary narrative for North American evangelicals during the second half of the twentieth century and an inspiration to evangelicals worldwide. Although Elisabeth preferred not to describe her husband and his colleagues as 'martyrs', except in the most basic sense of 'witnesses' to Jesus Christ, her books helped to establish the men, especially Jim, as paragons of evangelical piety. Their lives challenged a generation of young evangelicals who came of age in the 1960s and 1970s to sacrificial living and missionary service. 'He is no fool who gives what he cannot keep to gain what he cannot lose' and other aphorisms Elisabeth selected from Jim's journals, came to represent the Christian commitment and idealism of the five slain men. At the time of writing (2001) *Through Gates of Splendor* remains in print.

After Jim's death, Elisabeth remained in Ecuador. On 8 October 1958 she and Rachel Saint, Nate Saint's sister, made friendly contact with the Huaorani through the mediation of Rachel's language informant Dayuma and two other Huaorani women Elisabeth had befriended. Elisabeth lived among the Huaorani for a total of about two years. *The Savage My Kinsman* (1961), her third book, documented in text and photographs Elisabeth's life since her husband's death with particular emphasis on her first year among the Huaorani. The book was innovative in its use of photography and provocative in its reflections about missionary service. Elisabeth left the Huaorani work permanently in December 1961, in part due to differences with Rachel Saint. Elisabeth and Valerie returned to the United States in 1963.

As a speaker, missionary legend and prolific author, during the next four decades Elisabeth Elliot became an influential, if sometimes controversial, figure in American evangelicalism. She has published more than twenty-five books, served as an adjunct professor at Gordon-Conwell Seminary and as a writer-in-residence at Gordon College, both in Massachusetts, and hosted a daily radio programme. On 1 January 1969 Elliot married Addison H. Leitch, a professor of philosophy and religion. He died of cancer on 18 September 1973. On 21 December 1977 she married Lars Gren, who subsequently became her agent.

Elliot's books have dealt with missions, evangelical spirituality, the meaning of Christian womanhood and manhood, marriage and sexual purity. Throughout her work she has emphasized the theme of obedience to God no matter what the cost or results may be. Her most controversial book on missions, the novel *No Graven Image* (1966), raised questions about evangelical missions through a character who learned obedience after being the unwitting agent of the death of one of the Indians she had come to save. In the 1970s Elliot stimulated further controversy with *Let Me Be a Woman: Notes on Womanhood for Valerie* (1976). Written during the period of the women's movement of the 1970s, the book affirmed a hierarchical view of marriage. Among Elliot's other well-known books are *A Slow and Certain Light: Some Thoughts on the Guidance of God* (1973); *These Strange Ashes: The First Year as a Jungle Missionary* (1976); *Passion and Purity: Learning to Bring Your Love Life Under Christ's Control* (1984); and *A Chance to Die: The Life and Legacy of Amy Carmichael* (1987).

Bibliography
'Interview of Elisabeth Howard Gren by Robert Shuster', Collection 278, Tape #T2, Billy Graham Center Archives, Wheaton College, Wheaton, Illinois, USA; E. Elliot, *Shadow of the Almighty: The Life and Testament of Jim Elliot* (New York: Harper & Brothers, 1958; London: Hodder & Stoughton, 1958); D. Howard, 'Heaven Soon: Jim Elliot', in J. Woodbridge (ed.), *More Than Conquerors* (Chicago: Moody Press, 1992).

K. T. LONG

■ **ENGLISH, Donald** (1930–1998), British Methodist minister, was a leader of the evangelical movement within Methodism for much of his ministry. He was a well-known Bible expositor and much in demand as a preacher and evangelist both inside and outside Methodism. He was president of the British Methodist Conference in 1978 and 1990. He was the founding chairman of Conservative Evangelicals in Methodism, but probably became best known within Methodism as general secretary of the Methodist Home Mission Division from 1982 to his retirement in 1995. He also served on the World Methodist Council (WMC) Executive for many years, and he chaired the WMC from 1991 to 1996. He played a prominent role in British political life, meeting with the Queen, taking Bible studies for Members of Parliament and addressing groups of High Court judges and barristers, and he was also a regular broadcaster on the radio. For services to his country he was made a Commander of the Order of the British Empire in 1996.

Donald English was born in Consett, County Durham, in 1930 into a Methodist family. He attended the Leadgate Infant School and the Delves Lane Infant and Junior School (1935–1940) and went up to the Consett Grammar School in 1941. During the ministry of the Revd Frank Ward (1942–1947) he felt the challenge of the gospel. On hearing the testimonies of 'Big' Bill (a coal clerk) and Matt Wigham (both local preachers), he was impressed by their experiences, especially those during the war. At a Boys' Brigade enrolment service led by the Revd Benjamin Drewery English made his commitment to follow Jesus.

When English was eighteen he entered University College, Leicester, where he read history. As a member of the Christian Union (CU) his faith developed and he embraced a conservative evangelical theological position. He was particularly influenced by the books published by the Inter-Varsity Fellowship (IVF, now UCCF).

His formal Methodist preaching began in 1949 when he was home from college, under the tutelage of Drewery. Back at university, he gained experience preaching in the Leicester South Circuit and the open-air services in the market place.

English was the mission committee chairman when the CU invited the Revd Ronald Lamb, an IVF travelling secretary, to lead a mission. Lamb was an ordained Methodist minister who introduced the students to the Methodist Revival Fellowship (MRF), an evangelical movement within Methodism, which English joined. In 1952 English also became the Midland representative of the Executive Committee of the IVF. These were

movements to which English would remain committed for the rest of his life.

He graduated and went on to complete teacher training. While at university he also trained with Leicester City FC who, together with Sunderland FC, were interested in offering him a position as a professional player. He was called to a trial for the England International Amateur Team but, as the event was on a Sunday, he declined.

On completing National Service, English became a travelling secretary for the IVF, working in the Midlands and the north of England. He visited colleges, conducted missions and enjoyed a successful ministry. It was during this time that he felt called to be ordained in the Methodist Church and began the process of becoming a candidate. On acceptance, he was sent to Wesley House, Cambridge. It was during this time that he made contact with John *Stott and I. Howard Marshall. He graduated two years later after successfully sitting the Cambridge Tripos.

On leaving Cambridge, English was appointed assistant tutor at Wesley College, Headingly (1960–1962). From 1962 to 1965 he was tutor at the Union Theological College at Umuahia in Eastern Nigeria. Here he led his students in missions to various circuits. On returning from Nigeria, he worked as a circuit minister in the Broadway Church in Cullercoats until 1972, when he was appointed to Hartley Victoria College in Manchester. He was moved, the following year, to Wesley College, Bristol, to teach practical theology and Methodism. In 1982 he became general secretary of the Methodist Home Mission Division.

He was constantly in demand worldwide as a Bible teacher throughout his ministry. He received recognition for his academic scholarship from several universities in the UK and abroad that awarded him honorary degrees. He always insisted, however, that his knowledge was never merely academic but rather, as one commentator on his life has said, that it involved 'a personal and intimate passion for Jesus'.

English is remembered for his contribution in a number of areas. He was an international figure making a great impact as a statesman for Christ. But to him the following would appear to be the main areas of his vocation that he valued most. Firstly, he was glad to be valued as a evangelist, preacher and biblical expositor. His starting point was the discovery of the impact a passage had on those who first heard its teaching or read its message. He tried to get into their hearts and minds. He also knew that a preacher needed to apply his message to the context of those who heard it. He took much trouble over making his message relevant to all those who heard him preach. He expected there to be a response every time he preached. During his presidential years Methodists once more became accustomed to 'the altar call'.

Secondly, he was glad to be valued as a writer. Leslie Griffiths (a past president of the Methodist Conference) in his obituary for English in *The Guardian* newspaper suggested that writing was not his strong point. Others, even those who were his warmest champions, would not place him among the greatest of creative theologians. But these assessments miss the point of his work. English wrote because there was a gospel to proclaim. He did not seek to create something new, because for him the gospel was timeless. Much of his time was spent making this gospel accessible to people through tracts and pamphlets. Even these are characterized by mature wisdom and sound theological reflection. As one colleague put it, 'sadly, in recent years, there have been precious few popular mediators of the tradition of the quality of Donald English'. Christ exhibited the art of communicating simply, and English, who strove to imitate his master, aspired to transmit his message with simplicity. He had a great deal of respect for learning, yet coupled this with an evangelical passion. He was capable of works of scholarship but was always committed to making scholarship palatable to ordinary readers.

Of his many publications, the following are of special interest. His *The Message of Mark* (1992) is a good example of both his scholarship and his skill as a biblical expositor. It is here particularly that he reveals his ability to apply genuine scholarship, as the publishers put it, in a 'readable and non-technical way, applying the message to the issues of everyday life'. In *Into the 21st Century* (1995) English challenges Christians to offer a response to our fast changing society. English saw the need to address current issues so as to reveal the timeless relevance of Christ to every

situation. He called for a true dialogue between the Bible and the world and for dialogue with people of other faiths and no faith, claiming that if we take this challenge seriously, 'we may well find the footprints of Jesus Christ ahead of us'.

An Evangelical Theology of Preaching (1996) has been regarded as the pinnacle of English's achievements as a writer and 'brings together the fruit of a lifetime's reflection upon the nature and context of preaching'.

Bibliography

R. W. Abbott (ed.), *Donald English: An Evangelical Celebration* (Ilkeston: Moorley's, 1999).

D. R. OWEN

■ **ERSKINE, Ebenezer** (1680–1754), founder minister of the Original Secession Church, was born on 22 June 1680, the son of the noted covenanter Henry Erskine and the elder brother of fellow-seceder Ralph (1685–1752). Ebenezer Erskine was ordained to the post-revolution and hence presbyterian Church of Scotland in 1703, being inducted to the charge of Portmoak in Fife. Here he quickly made his mark as a minister of the evangelical (as distinct from the more liberal 'moderate') wing of the church.

Thomas *Boston of Ettrick found and recommended to like-minded friends a seventeenth-century text by the Puritan Edward Fisher, *The Marrow of Modern Divinity*. As a result it was republished in Scotland in 1718 and became a manifesto for dissent within the church. The republication of this work, which was written in the form of dialogues between people of different theological persuasions, was condemned by the Assembly of 1720 as promoting the antinomian heresy. A defence of the book at the Assembly of 1722 by a group led by Ebenezer Erskine was dismissed, and the twelve ministers involved were censured. Thereafter known as the 'Marrow Men', they formed a nucleus of evangelical dissent within the church.

Erskine's ministry in Portmoak was affected by his own ill health, the loss of several of his children and the death of his first wife. As a result, by 1729 he was ready for a change and was approached to become the third minister of Stirling, the other ministers being

Alexander Hamilton, an elderly evangelical, and Charles Moore, a younger moderate. It is said that Erskine's admiration for Hamilton was the main factor in his accepting the call.

Having been promised the principle of independent calling of ministers by the Revolution Settlement of 1690, the Church of Scotland strenuously opposed the reintroduction of patronage by the Act of Parliament of 1709, an act which was *ultra vires* of the recently united British Parliament. Erskine was one of a majority of ministers who formally protested at every General Assembly for several years. For a while Crown patronage in particular was exercised with respect for local opinion, but after 1725 patronage became increasingly politicized under the influence of Lord Islay. In 1732 the Assembly tacitly accepted the fact of patronage by enacting the Riding Acts, by which unpopular choices by patrons could be inducted by 'riding committees' against the wishes of local congregations. Erskine minuted his dissent at the Assembly and continued to protest at the opening of the Synod of Perth and Stirling, of which he was moderator. His sermon on that occasion, on Psalm 118:24, re-emphasized his belief in the rights of a congregation to call its own minister with such force that he was formally rebuked by the Synod and called to the bar of the Assembly the following year. This in turn led to the meeting at Gairney Bridge of four like-minded ministers who founded the 'Associate Presbytery', which became the Secession Church. Repeal of the acts by the General Assembly in 1734 and an invitation from the Presbytery of Stirling to become moderator were to no avail; the Secession Church was seen as a separate entity by 1736, although it was not until 1740 that Erskine was actually excluded from the parish church in Stirling. Thereafter he had a new church built for his burgeoning congregation.

During the period between the break from the established church and being excluded from the parish church in Stirling, Erskine had enjoyed the support of the local town council, who were also patrons of the charge. The whole affair became enmeshed in the political history of the time; Walpole's government, led in Scotland by Lord Islay, was vulnerable, and the vote of Stirling was important to its majority.

Stirling's choice for MP, James Erskine of Grange, a former judge and the brother of the Jacobite and exiled Earl of Mar, was not in fact elected MP for the Stirling group of Burghs but became MP for the neighbouring seat of Clackmannanshire. Erskine of Grange, a distant kinsman of Ebenezer Erskine, was one of the few members of the Edinburgh legal establishment to be evangelical in inclination, albeit with reputedly unevangelical morals. Ebenezer Erskine's supporters in Stirling were also Grange's political supporters, and a political riot in Stirling in 1734 was in fact blamed on Ebenezer Erskine.

When the town council took offence at Ebenezer Erskine's criticism of an act of council that made a profit for some of its members, it was to Grange that they appealed, asking him to use his influence to keep Erskine out of matters that they thought should not concern him. Grange gave a suitably neutral answer which suggested that the council had a responsibility not to give the impression of trying to make personal profits, but the incident showed the beginning of Erskine's marginalization in the town.

On the approach of the Jacobites to Stirling in 1745, Erskine led the resistance and raised a company of volunteers to guard the town. He was persuaded to flee for his own safety when the Jacobites took Stirling and Stirling Castle, but on the defeat of the Jacobites he received thanks from the government. The significance of this response was that for the first time it became accepted that religious dissent could go hand in hand with political loyalty, and that dissenters were not automatically a danger to the State. Sadly, the other effect of the end of the Jacobite Rising was the split in the young Secession Church into Burgher and Anti-burgher factions according to attitudes to the Burgess Oath imposed by the Government. This split was more bitter and more divisive than the original secession had been, and one of the Anti-burghers in Stirling was reprimanded for having 'dishonoured the Lord by listening to Mr. Erskine preach'.

Ebenezer Erskine died on 2 June 1754, being succeeded by his nephew James Erskine, son of his brother Ralph, and he was buried within his church.

The Secession Churches, Burgher and Anti-burgher, later split into New Licht and Auld

Licht factions, and as result of later processes of reunion and reabsorption only a small remnant survives separately as the United Free Church of Scotland, although many Church of Scotland churches owe their constitution to a Secession ancestry. The influence of Ebenezer and Ralph Erskine also survives in the United States, where the small, conservative Associate Reformed Presbyterian Church of the southern states is a direct descendant. In the Dutch Church Erskine's preaching is still studied. The text of many of their sermons is now available on the Internet.

Bibliography

D. Fraser, *The Life and Diary of the Reverend Ebenezer Erskine, A.M., of Stirling, Father of the Secession Church* (Edinburgh: William Oliphant, 1831); A. L. Drummond and J. Bulloch, *The Scottish Church 1688–1843* (Edinburgh: Saint Andrew Press, 1973). Website: http://www.puritansermons.com/erskine/erskindx.htm

A. T. N. MUIRHEAD

■ **ERSKINE, John** (1720/1–1803), Church of Scotland minister and leader in the evangelical party, was born in Edinburgh into a distinguished family. His father, also named John, was a prominent lawyer and professor of law at the University of Edinburgh. As a young boy he was given to the study of Scripture and to devotional exercises. Initially following his parents' strong desire that he also study law, John felt compelled to switch to divinity. He trained at the University of Edinburgh from 1734 to 1743, where he acquired a thorough classical education and engaged in extended academic discussions with many of the subsequent leaders of Scottish society. Licensed by the Dunblane presbytery in 1743, he was ordained in the following year and served successive pastorates at Kirkintilloch (1744–1753), Culross (1753–1758), New Greyfriars Edinburgh (1758–1767) and Old Greyfriars Edinburgh (1767–1803). He married Christian Mackay in 1743. In 1766 he was awarded the DD degree by the University of Glasgow. He died on 19 January 1803 while still active in ministry, although at a reduced level.

As a student he anonymously published a closely reasoned objection to various points in Professor Archibald Campbell's critique of deism. In it he relied on some of Bishop Warburton's arguments and sent him a courtesy copy; they remained in contact. Warburton later indicated his disappointment that Erskine had seemingly lost interest in this important issue.

Erskine's evangelical identity was shaped by the Awakenings in Britain and America. He shared John Willison of Dundee's negative assessment of Scotland's spiritual condition, followed with appreciation accounts of the 1735 Awakening in New England, debated with fellow students the work of the *Wesleys and George *Whitefield and promoted the 'concerts of prayer' which preceded the 1742 Cambuslang revival in Scotland. In 1742, while still a student, he published *The Signs of the Times Considered*, which heralded the spiritual stirrings in America and in western Scotland as 'a prelude of the glorious things promised to the church in the latter ages'. His evangelical convictions were firmly established by the time of his ordination, and they governed the remainder of his life and work. By the century's end he was leader of the evangelical party in the Church of Scotland.

As a pastor Erskine received respect and affection from his people. They esteemed his piety, learning and prominent social position, and his devotion to his duties won their hearts. He attended to their spiritual needs, offered them ready encouragement and counsel, and he was distinguished for his benevolent spirit. His preaching was thoughtful and timely, if not always gripping, and was memorialized in chapter 37 of Sir Walter Scott's *Guy Mannering*. Throughout his ministry he read avidly in many areas and was highly regarded for his knowledge of civil and social as well as theological issues.

Erskine was prominent in Church of Scotland assemblies, where he championed evangelical causes and opposed the positions of the moderate party. In his first charge he invited George Whitefield to preach from his pulpit and successfully withstood censure by the Synod of Glasgow and Ayr. From an early stage he resisted the theology of the Wesleys, objecting to their positions on free will, perfectionism, perseverance of the saints and divine election. The limited influence of Methodism in Scotland is credited to his resistance. Thoroughly Calvinistic in orientation, he opposed hyper-Calvinism and rallied support for missions by many means, including his 1765 edition of Jonathan *Edwards' An Account of the Life of the Late Rev. David *Brainerd and his extensive service on the board of the Scottish Society for Promoting Christian Knowledge. When opposition to missionary outreach threatened to prevail in the General Assembly, he rose to defend the biblical basis for evangelism, exclaiming to a fellow delegate, 'Rax [Hand] me that Bible!' In the late 1770s he led the General Assembly in opposing indiscriminate removal of penal statutes against Catholics. He argued that while Socinians and deists should not be 'deprived of the common privileges of society' because they were no threat to civil order, Roman Catholics represented a system that desired 'to restrain, disturb, or endanger their fellow subjects in the exercise of their natural or legal privileges' (A Narrative of the Debate in the General Assembly ..., 1780, p. v). His published account of Assembly debates on the matter popularized a position between those of liberal moderates and hard-line reactionaries and contributed to the ascendancy of thoughtful, irenic evangelicalism as the dominant religious influence in late eighteenth-century Scotland. His several tracts advocating a lenient, understanding attitude towards American colonial grievances were less successful in affecting public policy and popular opinion.

Erskine's published sermons emphasize the practice of discipleship (warning against lukewarmness and advocating self-denial, the maintenance of vital Christianity and faithfulness in personal responsibilities), civic-mindedness (warning against anarchy, supporting those in public office and advocating morality as the basis for national well-being), the high calling and duties of pastors, cardinal doctrines related to Christ and his atonement, and social responsibility (advocating education for poor children).

New Greyfriars Edinburgh was a collegiate pastorate, which Erskine shared with Dr William Robertson, principal of the University of Edinburgh and leader of the moderate party. Despite their differences, they were friends who respected each other. On one occasion Erskine persuaded a mob incensed at Robertson's views on the Catholic question to disperse. His funeral sermon for Robertson dates their friendship from their student days in 1737, when 'fondness for the same studies soon produced intimate familiarity and impressions of mutual regard'. It nevertheless acknowledges that they disagreed on matters of church government, on the American Revolution, on public policy regarding Roman Catholics, and even on the appropriate emphases in preaching.

Erskine made enduring and substantial contributions in ecumenical relations. He maintained a lively, informed interest in British, European and American civic and religious affairs. His correspondence with leaders in all three places runs to hundreds of letters, in which he passed on information and which were usually accompanied by several volumes of recently published works. His two-volume Sketches and Hints of Church History (1790 and 1797) introduced and translated the ideas of some of his contacts. His editions of the sermons of Revd Thomas Prince of Boston and several writings of Jonathan *Edwards, most notably A History of the Work of Redemption, contributed substantially to the rise of evangelical missionary and awakening activity towards the end of the century. Samuel Miller of the Princeton Seminary faculty regarded Erskine as 'one of the most pious and public spirited men of his day'. The number of Erskine's American correspondents ran to more than three dozen, and in 1804 the Princeton board of trustees adopted a resolution recognizing his unusual service to the school. Among eminent British contacts were Lord Kames, Sir David Dalrymple and Bishop Hurd. Ever interested in matters theological, he learned the Dutch language late in life in order to follow more closely religious developments in the Netherlands; he died on 19 January 1803 while reading a recently received book in Dutch.

Irenic, charitable, informed, John Erskine elevated evangelical Calvinism to a new level of respect in Scotland and beyond. His influence was spread through more than two dozen works of his own and another twenty that he edited or for which he provided prefaces.

Bibliography

H. M. Wellwood, An Account of the Life and Writings of John Erskine, D.D. (Edinburgh:

private publication, 1818); *A Biographical Dictionary of Eminent Scotsmen*, vol. 2 (Glasgow: Blackie & Son, 1855), pp. 266–273.

J. A. DE JONG

■ **EVANS, Christmas** (1766–1838), Welsh Baptist preacher, was born in Llandysul, Cardiganshire, on 25 December 1766 to Samuel Evans, a shoemaker, and Joanna (née Lewis), his wife. The family were Dissenters, Samuel being Presbyterian and connected with the Pen-rhiw church, Drefach, which was even then moving towards Unitarianism, while Joanna belonged to the Calvinistic Independents at Pant-y-creuddyn. Although the tendency among the Older Dissent of eighteenth-century Wales was towards a fairly sturdy financial independence, Samuel was not particularly well off. The family situation deteriorated markedly with Samuel's death in 1775, which necessitated Christmas's being sent to work for his uncle, James Lewis, who farmed land nearby. Despite being a member of the Pant-y-creuddyn congregation, Lewis was 'a cruel, selfish and drunken man' whose appalling treatment of his nephew served permanently to blight Evans' memories of his childhood.

Relief came with his transferral to work on a neighbouring farm, that of Castell-hywel, owned by the Presbyterian schoolmaster David Davis. 'Mr David Davis of Castle-howel', reported the Unitarian magazine *The Monthly Repository*, 'is an Arian and is greatly respected in his neighbourhood as a scholar, preacher and excellent man.' Evans experienced great kindness from his new employer, who not only treated him with care and respect but also sought to redress his educational deficiencies by teaching him the rudiments of literacy at the school that he ran at his home. As well as farming and school-teaching, Davis pastored the church at Llwynrhydowen, whose services Evans began to frequent. It was there, during a local revival in about 1780, that he made his first serious religious commitment: 'I cannot deny that this ... was the day of grace on my spirit,' he wrote. Sensing the young man's calling to ministerial service, Davis encouraged him to study and to begin preaching, and before long Evans was being invited to exhort local

Dissenting congregations, both Presbyterian and Independent. His interaction with the Llandysul Baptists at their church at Pen-y-bont challenged him to consider the question of baptism, and following due consideration he presented himself for immersion at the Aberduar church, to the north of Llandysul, in 1788.

Keen to be of ministerial service, Evans attended the meetings of the Baptist Welsh Association at Maes-y-berllan, Brecknock-shire, in 1789, where he met representatives from North Wales who were anxious to secure ministerial support for their struggling cause. The young preacher accepted their invitation to accompany them home and was ordained at Ty'ndonnen church, at the tip of Caernarfonshire's Llŷn Peninsula, in the summer of that year.

It was there that a huge transformation occurred in the mode and effectiveness of Evans' preaching. Previously unremarkable, from now on his ministry displayed all the marks of the revivalist spirit. 'Great power accompanied his ministry in those days,' it was said. 'His hearers would weep, wail and jump as though the world were igniting round about.' The Presbyterian decorum of his upbringing had given way to Baptist exuberance of a most dramatic kind, while Arminian moralism was replaced by an evangelical Calvinism which emphasized God's sovereignty in the salvation of souls.

Evans moved from Caernarfonshire to Anglesey in 1791, where he was to remain for the next thirty-five years. The revivalist spirit soon permeated the island's congregations, while membership increased from 150 at the beginning of his ministry to over 1,000 at its end. Overt revivalism came in two waves, the first in 1791–1792 and the second in 1815–1816, both of which signified the wholesale revitalization of Welsh Dissent through the energies of a popular evangelicalism. Although this caused a reaction through the secession of the influential preacher J. R. Jones of Ramoth to form a Sandemanian movement among the North Wales Baptists, it was revivalism which retained its popular appeal with Evans being accounted its undisputed leader.

As well as labouring in Anglesey, Christmas Evans embarked on an annual preaching tour which took him throughout Wales. By the early nineteenth century his reputation as an orator and evangelist of exceptional ability was secure, though his ministry at home was not devoid of tensions. In 1826 he left Anglesey for the pastorate of Ton-y-felin, Caerphilly, in Glamorgan, moving two years later to Tabernacle, Cardiff, and thence in 1832 to Caernarfon, North Wales. He died at Swansea while on a preaching tour in July 1838, and was buried in the cemetery of the Bethesda church.

Although he contributed to the theological controversies of his day, it is as a preacher and revivalist that Christmas Evans deserves to be remembered. His use of allegory in the service of the biblical revelation allowed his hearers to respond to the challenge of the gospel in a most effective way, while his sermons were regularly accompanied by revivalist fervour. He transcended the divide between the Older Dissent and the Evangelical Revival and helped consolidate the influence of the latter on the former. Along with the Calvinistic Methodist John Elias and the Independent William Williams of Wern, he remains one of the three most effective Welsh Nonconformist preachers of his generation.

Bibliography

D. R. Stephen, *Memoirs of the Late Christmas Evans, of Wales* (London: Alyott & Jones, 1847); D. D. Morgan, *Christmas Evans a'r Ymneilltuaeth Newydd* (Llandysul: Gwasg Gomer, 1991); D. D. Morgan, 'Christmas Evans and the Birth of Nonconformist Wales', *Baptist Quarterly* 34.3 (1991), pp. 116–124.

D. D. MORGAN

■ **FAIRFAX, John** (1805–1877), newspaper proprietor and philanthropist, was born on 24 October 1805 in Warwick, England, to evangelical Dissenters William and Elizabeth Fairfax (née Jesson). In his youth he was especially influenced by his mother's faith, and on completing an apprenticeship in 1825 spent two years in London working in a general printing office and as a typesetter for the *Morning Chronicle*. In 1827 he returned to Warwickshire, entering into a happy marriage with his childhood friend Sarah Reading, which lasted forty-eight years and produced five children, Charles (1829),

Emily (1831), James (1834), Richard (1838) and Edward (1842). In 1828 he produced his first newspaper, the *Leamington Spa Sketch Book*, and was co-proprietor, then proprietor, of the *Leamington Chronicle and Warwickshire Reporter* from 1835. Fairfax helped to establish the Congregational Spencer Street Chapel in Leamington, where he was a deacon, Sunday school superintendent and lay preacher. However, disaster struck in a series of libel suits. Though Fairfax was acquitted, legal costs bankrupted him and he emigrated to Sydney in New South Wales (NSW) with his family in 1838. After working as a typesetter for *The Sydney Herald* and a librarian, in 1841 Fairfax, with *Herald* reporter Charles Kemp, was assisted to buy the *Herald* by his fellow deacons at the Pitt Street Congregational Church. Seizing their opportunity, in five years of hard toil they established (from 1842) the *Sydney Morning Herald* as the benchmark for colonial journalism. In 1853 Fairfax bought out Kemp, and in 1856 his sons Charles and James joined him to form John Fairfax and Sons. Lasting five generations (until 1990), Australia's greatest entrepreneurial dynasty had begun.

Fairfax oversaw the *Herald* with a rare combination of literary, managerial, technical and financial skill. He attracted quality journalists and editorial staff and maintained technical superiority over his rivals. In 1854 the Revd John West, a Congregational minister, historian and anti-transportation activist, joined the *Herald* as editor, forming an intimate commercial and spiritual alliance with Fairfax. Boosted by the discovery of gold, by 1856 the *Herald* had a daily circulation of 6,600, a figure exceeded in the British Empire by only *The Times* and *Telegraph* of London. Indeed, Fairfax likened the *Herald* to gold, claiming, 'the *Herald* is the best mine'. Fairfax fought off able challengers, including James Macarthur's *Australian* in the 1840s and Henry Parkes' *Empire* in the 1850s. Crucially, the *Herald* kept the support of the business community and its advertising revenue. John Fairfax became Australia's first press baron and a prominent figure on the Sydney commercial scene. In 1849 he was a foundation director of the Australian Mutual Provident Society (chairman in 1859), and he held directorships of other major banking, insurance and commercial concerns, including the

Australian Gaslight Company. He was appointed to the Council for Education in 1871 and the NSW Legislative Council in 1874.

In Australian historiography the *Herald* of Fairfax's period is usually stereotyped as 'conservative' (even 'Tory'). This stereotype reflects a confounding of support for manhood suffrage, which the *Herald* opposed, with liberalism. It also reveals a failure to appreciate that while socially and morally conservative by choice, Nonconformists like Fairfax and West were fierce, theologically and philosophically principled advocates of the freedom of the conscience from state control. The *Herald* vigorously expounded the tenets of classical liberalism. It abhorred state interference, such as state aid to churches or trade tariffs, and witheringly denounced proposals to enforce temperance and Sabbath observance. In contrast, it strongly supported calls for voluntary moral renewal and self-improvement, advocated national schooling, championed the anti-transportation movement and was among the few to defend the rights of Chinese workers assaulted in the Lambing Flat riots of 1861.

John and Sarah Fairfax were deeply committed to the Pitt Street Congregational Church. From 1840 John was one of a diaconate of godly merchants, including his close friend David Jones, another famous name in Australian commercial history. A prayerful, earnest, active and influential congregation, it had a Savings Bank to encourage 'provident and economical habits', a Christian Instruction Society, and a 'City Missionary' and 'Bible Woman' for urban mission, and facilitated church planting in the colony and mission to the South Pacific.

Fairfax's evangelicalism was characteristic of the era: warm, energetic, disciplined, prayerful, Bible loving, Christ focused, cross-centred, optimistic and outward looking. With a strong sense of vocation, he viewed journalism as his God-given opportunity to influence society and generate wealth. In an 1856 address to the NSW YMCA, of which he was foundation president, he described the Christian who 'is early at church, but late in business' as an 'enigma' and one who 'belies the Christian profession he makes'. His nonsectarian evangelicalism was also seen in efforts on behalf of other interdenominational agencies, such as the Sydney Ragged Schools.

John and Sarah Fairfax's faith is most poignantly preserved in spiritual appeals to their children. At his fiftieth birthday celebration, John told his children 'some of you have decided for Christ, and are fellow pilgrims to Zion ... I beseech you suffer nothing to stand in the way of an early surrender ... to Him, who is both able and willing to save'. Sarah in a letter to their son James in 1855 implored him to 'secure those lasting treasures which Christ alone can bestow', while John assured James that as 'we have an interest in the love of Christ we are safe in travelling the pilgrimage of life'. John and Sarah also knew real personal grief. Their son Richard died in infancy in 1839, and their eldest son Charles and only daughter Emily were both killed in accidents, aged thirty-four and forty respectively. On Charles's death, John wrote of the 'hopes of ... parents, wife and children' being 'laid in the grave' and how their 'poor broken hearts come with trembling faith to Him who wept at the grave of Lazarus'.

Part of a close network of Nonconformist businessmen, Fairfax was untiring in his support of Christian ministry and served on a host of committees. He was particularly generous in financial support of the Pitt Street Church and its various societies, contributing £3,285 towards church extensions completed in 1868 and leaving a property to the church in his will. He also gave £600 to his former church in Leamington in 1852 and land for a church in Newtown, Sydney, in 1856, and helped establish Camden Theological College from 1863. He built a fine home, 'Ginahgulla', which became a synonym for hospitality, entertaining leading inter-colonial and British visitors, including the prominent English Congregationalist the Revd Thomas Binney. A man of broad association, Fairfax was a personal friend of NSW Premier Sir Henry Parkes, the poet Henry Kendall and the artist Adelaide Ironside. Many of his descendants, particularly his son Sir James (1834–1919, knight bachelor 1898), Mary Fairfax (1858–1945), Sir Warwick Fairfax (1901–1987), Caroline Simpson (1930–), and James Fairfax (1933–), became significant patrons of the fine arts and community groups, while the Family Foundation established by Sir Vincent Fairfax (1909–1993) exemplifies the philanthropic legacy of John Fairfax.

In 1875 Sarah Fairfax died, having displayed in John's words a 'beautiful exhibition of cheerful trust in Christ'. On 16 June 1877 John Fairfax, 'the Father of Australian journalism', died. A few days earlier he said 'I am looking up. I am going home.' A massive funeral bore testimony to his life and faith.

Bibliography
G. Souter, *A Company of Heralds* (Melbourne: Melbourne University Press, 1981).

S. B. JOHNSON

■ **FALWELL, Jerry F.** (1933–), Baptist preacher and television evangelist, was born in Lynchburg, Virginia, where his family had settled before the Civil War. His father, Carey Falwell, was a prosperous businessman and agnostic, who became an alcoholic and died of cirrhosis of the liver in 1948, a few days after a deathbed conversion, and his mother, Helen Beasley Falwell, was a housewife and devout Baptist. Jerry and his twin brother Gene, their youngest children, were born on 11 August 1933. Jerry was a bright but rowdy youth who showed little interest in religion, and after graduation as high school valedictorian attended Lynchburg College. In January 1952, after hearing a Charles *Fuller 'Old-Fashioned Revival Hour' programme on the radio, he visited a local church, Park Avenue Baptist, where he was converted. He also fell in love with the piano player there, Macel Pate, whom he married six years later.

Nurtured by the pastors of the church, Falwell became an earnest Christian, and within two months he decided to enter the ministry. The pastors encouraged him to transfer to Baptist Bible College in Springfield, Missouri, a recently founded and unaccredited school that trained pastors for their denomination, the separatist-fundamentalist Baptist Bible Fellowship. Falwell enrolled in the autumn, dropped out after two years to work at home for a while, and then returned to finish college in 1956. During the last year he was a part-time young adults' minister at a large BBF church, Kansas City Baptist Temple. Graduating with a degree in theo-

logy, Falwell left formal education and went back to Lynchburg. Against the wishes of the denomination's leaders, he agreed to pastor a new church that some disgruntled people from the Park Avenue congregation wanted to plant. On 27 June 1956 he met with thirty-five of them in an empty building that had formerly housed a soft drink bottling company to form the Thomas Road Baptist Church. This congregation would henceforth be the centre of his life's work.

The twenty-three-year-old pastor embarked on an aggressive programme to build up his small congregation, utilizing the motivational and entrepreneurial skills that would so characterize his career. He and his church members knocked on doors and used various gimmicks to persuade people to attend the church; then in September 1956 he started a radio broadcast on a local station and three months later a television broadcast as well. Within a short time, the growing congregation had enough money to purchase and expand its humble premises. Later the Thomas Road Baptist Church established a shelter for alcoholics, a youth camp, a halfway house for the rehabilitation of prison inmates and a maternity home for unmarried mothers. In 1964 the church moved into a new 1000-seat building, and in 1967 Falwell opened the Lynchburg Christian Academy.

A typical southern white preacher, Falwell was a segregationist. He opposed the civil rights movement, and in a sermon entitled 'Ministers and Marches', preached in March 1965 two weeks after the dramatic events in Selma, Alabama, he criticized the civil rights legislation passing through Congress. He denounced ministers and church workers who participated in marches and demonstrations and added: 'Believing the Bible as I do, I would find it impossible to stop preaching the pure saving gospel of Jesus Christ, and begin doing anything else – including fighting communism, or participating in civil rights reforms.' This sermon was quoted against him after he became a political activist. In 1964 the church itself was targetted by civil rights protestors, and the Christian school was clearly a 'segregation academy'. However, Falwell's views on the race issue gradually changed; the church and school began accepting blacks, and he later repudiated the 1965 sermon, the text of which, unlike that of nearly all his other early messages, had not been destroyed.

The burgeoning church, which, thanks to its practice of bringing in children by bus, now had one of the ten largest Sunday schools in America, built a larger 3,800 seat building in 1970. In the 1980s it claimed to have 20,000 members and 8,000 people attending its five services. The television broadcast had become 'The Old-Time Gospel Hour' and was seen in millions of homes across the nation. In 1971 Falwell founded Lynchburg Baptist College, which eventually became Liberty University, and he acquired a large piece of property outside the town, which he renamed 'Liberty Mountain', as a location for his college and other enterprises. He now resorted to all sorts of creative financing to pay for this growing empire, and in 1973 the Securities and Exchange Commission sued the Thomas Road Baptist Church for fraud and deceit in the sale of bonds. A Federal judge cleared Falwell and the church of wrongdoing, but Falwell had to adopt corporate methods of cost-efficiency, public relations and fund-raising to put his work on a firmer footing. Thereafter critics scrutinized his financial operations and the vast income flowing into his work; by his own testimony nearly $100 million was received in 1986–1987.

In the mid-1970s Falwell became concerned about abortion and the leftward drift of the country in general, and his preaching assumed a political character. During the 1975–1976 bicentenary of the American Revolution he sent students from his college on a nationwide tour, on which they performed I Love America, a glitzy 'civil religion' musical by the evangelical composer Don Wyrtzen. Falwell also supported anti-homosexuality campaigns, sent another musical team around the country to perform the political work America, You're Too Young to Die and launched a 'Clean Up America' campaign. This attracted the attention of several New Right Republican politicians, who saw the voting potential of conservative Christians. Following a high-level meeting with them, Falwell in July 1979 announced the formation of the Moral Majority.

This movement transformed Falwell into a national political as well as religious figure, and he travelled around the country mobilizing grassroots support and encouraging the usually apolitical fundamentalists to vote. He claimed that the Moral Majority was not a religious organization as such but one that enlisted people of all faiths to reclaim American values from the moral decline caused by liberal policies and church-state separation. Its news magazine, Moral Majority Report, had a wide circulation, and Falwell's name became a household word. Because of the group's key role in Ronald Reagan's electoral victory in 1980, Falwell was regularly invited to the White House and Republican gatherings. He had succeeded in converting moderate fundamentalists and conservative evangelicals into a formidable political force, and they quickly became a pillar of the Republican Party. Their impact was exemplified by George W. Bush's capturing 80% of the white evangelical vote in 2000.

However, Falwell was competing with several other luminaries of the Christian Right for popular acclaim, and he and his organization attracted hostile, even hysterical, media attention. 'Moral Majority' became a generic term for any narrowly intolerant group, whether or not it was associated with him. Moreover, the movement's moral agenda was a highly truncated one: opposition to abortion, the Equal Rights Amendment, pornography, homosexuality and an American nuclear freeze; support for prayer in schools; and criticism of failures in education and left-wing forces in Nicaragua. Public interest and the income that came with it began to decline, and in January 1986 Falwell dissolved the Moral Majority and replaced it with the Liberty Federation. The media ignored the new group, and it achieved nothing of note. Finally, Falwell announced his withdrawal from political life and in June 1989 closed down the Liberty Federation, claiming that it had accomplished its goal of activating the religious right.

The sex and money scandals that plagued some high-profile figures eroded public confidence in televangelists generally. As a result, Falwell was less of a presence on the political scene, and during the Bill Clinton years he focused on his organizations. He even joined the Southern Baptist Convention, which now had come under fundamentalist control. When he tried to reassert his influence by blaming the terrorist bombings of 11 September 2001 on the pagans, pro-abortionists, feminists, homosexuals, American Civil Liberties Union and others 'who have tried to secularize America', the Bush White House rebuked him sharply and he issued an apology.

Falwell repeatedly expressed his unqualified support for the state of Israel and was highly rewarded by its leaders, although his statements about God not hearing the prayer of unredeemed Jews and identifying the coming Antichrist as a Jew caused dismay in Jewish circles and had to be modified. His attempts to link fundamentalists with evangelicals were resented by some in separatist circles, and Bob Jones, Jr called him 'the most dangerous man in America'. The softening of hard-line fundamentalist ideas in his best-selling books *Listen, America* (1981), *The Fundamentalist Phenomenon* (1981), *If I Should Die before I Wake* (1986), *Strength for the Journey* (1987) and *The New American Family* (1992) reflected the impact of their ghostwriters, who were moderate conservatives, but the works were promoted as representing his views. Possibly more than anyone else in his time, Falwell secured the re-entry of fundamentalists into American public life.

Bibliography

D. D'Souza, *Falwell Before the Millennium: A Critical Biography* (Lake Bluff: Regnery-Gateway, 1984); W. R. Goodman and J. J. H. Price, *Jerry Falwell: An Unauthorized Profile* (Lynchburg: Paris, 1981); S. F. Harding, *The Book of Jerry Falwell: Fundamentalist Language and Politics* (Princeton: Princeton University Press, 2000); M. Simon, *Jerry Falwell and the Jews* (Middle Village: Jonathan David, 1984); D. Snowball, *Continuity and Change in the Rhetoric of the Moral Majority* (Westport: Praeger, 1991).

R. PIERARD

■ **FARADAY, Michael** (1791–1867), eminent scientist, was born at Newington Butts on 22 September 1791 to Margaret Faraday (née Hastwell) and her blacksmith husband, James. Owing to financial pressures his parents had recently moved from a small village near Clapham in Yorkshire where his father had joined the Sandemanian church.

As a child and young man Michael Faraday regularly attended the Sandemanian meeting house in Paul's Alley, Barbican, and through it he became acquainted with Sarah Barnard, the daughter of Edward Barnard, one of the elders and a wealthy silversmith. Michael and Sarah married on 12 June 1821.

Faraday was admitted to the church some five weeks later, having demonstrated to the congregation his faith in the saving grace of God and his willingness to live his life in imitation of Jesus Christ. His moral integrity must have impressed the community, who elected him deacon on 1 July 1832 and elder on 15 October 1840. For the next three and a half years he played a leading role not only in the London meeting but also in national and international Sandemanian affairs. However, on 31 March 1844 he was excluded from the sect owing to a schism within the church over the role and authority of the elders. Faraday's exclusion brought him 'low in health and spirits'. However, having expressed his sincere repentance, he was readmitted on 5 May 1844 and was reappointed elder in October 1860.

In contrast to his very private religious life, which he shared with about a hundred London Sandemanians, Faraday was widely recognized as the leading physical scientist of his generation. As a lecturer he attracted large and enthusiastic audiences including members of the Royal Family. Although he never used his public position to disseminate his sect's specific religious beliefs, he often evoked religious imagery and appealed to design arguments in his lectures. Moreover, as one listener commented, Faraday conveyed 'the deepest sense of religion, and ... was one of those happy mortals "who could read" sermons in stones, and good in everything'.

Faraday's reputation rested not only on his success as a lecturer but also on his innovative researches. Having served his apprenticeship as a bookbinder, he became Humphry Davy's assistant at the Royal Institution and was trained primarily in the manufacture and use of chemical apparatus. Much of his early research was directed to chemistry, but new possibilities became apparent after Hans Christian Oersted discovered that electricity passing through a wire affects a neighbouring magnetic needle. Soon after news of this exciting phenomenon was published Faraday extended the same line of investigation with his discovery of electromagnetic rotations (the basic principle of the electric motor) in 1821; in 1831 he detected electromagnetic induction. In the early 1830s he identified the laws of electrochemistry, and among his later investigations were extensive research into the magneto-optical effect, diamagnetism and paramagnetism. Although often celebrated primarily as an experimentalist, Faraday was a sophisticated theoretician, but he made little use of mathematics since he rejected the view that God's creation could legitimately be expressed by mathematical formulae.

Many of his scientific investigations were predicated on the assumption that nature is a divinely ordained system in which the total amount of 'force' (approximating to what we call 'energy') is conserved. Thus, when electricity is produced by chemical action (in a battery) he conceived the chemical force as being transformed into electrical action. As he stated in an 1846 lecture, the properties of matter 'depend upon the power with which the Creator has gifted such matter'. By the early 1840s he adopted the notion of force fields and rejected the standard Newtonian matter theory that postulated small particles with attractive or repulsive forces acting at a distance. His view of force fields was likewise endowed with theological significance since he denied that God would have permitted empty space (as required by the Newtonian theory).

The prolific marginal notes to his family Bible show that Faraday was deeply immersed in Bible study. Like other Sandemanians his exhortations consisted almost entirely of biblical quotations with a minimum of linking material. When Ada, Countess of Lovelace, enquired about his religious beliefs he characterized his position thus: 'I am of a very small & despised sect of christians known, if known at all, as Sandemanians, and our hope is founded on the faith that is in Christ.' By the time of his death on 23 August 1867 he was widely recognized as the 'Christian philosopher' *par excellence*.

Bibliography

G. Cantor, *Michael Faraday: Sandemanian and Scientist* (London: Macmillan; New York: St Martin's Press, 1991); D. Gooding and F. A. J. L. James (eds.), *Faraday Rediscovered: Essays on the Life and Work of Michael Faraday, 1791–1867* (London: Macmillan, 1985; New York: American Institute of Physics, 1989).

G. CANTOR

■ **FARNINGHAM, Marianne** (1834–1909), author and hymn-writer, was a household name in many evangelical families during her lifetime. When she was first introduced to the well-known preacher C. H. *Spurgeon, he commented, 'So this is the famous Marianne Farningham.' Through her contributions to Christian newspapers and her book sales, her influence reached into thousands of homes.

Marianne, who was the eldest of five children, was born Mary-Ann Hearn on 17 December 1834. She later took the name of her native Kent village, Farningham, as a pseudonym. Her parents, Joseph and Rebecca Hearn, attended a Strict Baptist chapel in the nearby village of Eynsford. Marianne joined the church at the comparatively early age of fourteen and wrote in later life of her happy memories of chapel. Her family also had regular prayers together that, Marianne commented, were 'as little likely to be omitted as breakfast or supper'. Her mother died young, and as a result Marianne had to spend time helping her father, who was the village postmaster. The combination of this work and the lack for some years of a local Nonconformist school led to a rather haphazard education, something she always regretted. She was, however, eager to learn and took every opportunity to read, 'burning the midnight tallow', as she expressed it, because the family could not afford oil.

In 1852 she had a brief spell teaching in Bristol and loved the city. After only a year, however, she returned to Farningham to nurse one of her sisters, who was dying. For some time Marianne had been writing poetry, and she passed the time at her sister's bedside writing verses, encouraged by her pastor, Jonathan Whittemore, who was involved in publishing. When he founded the evangelical weekly *The Christian World*, Marianne became a contributor. From the first edition of 9 April 1857, for over fifty years, her work appeared regularly in the newspaper. Initially she combined writing with other work, moving to Northampton in 1859 to be head of the infant department of a school. Here she joined College Street Baptist church, where she took a girls' class for many years, a responsibility she thoroughly enjoyed.

In 1867 she was thrilled to be invited to give up teaching and join the full-time staff of *The Christian World*, and from that time she earned her living as a writer. The paper had a circulation of 130,000 at its peak in 1880, and Marianne's name would have become familiar in many households. Her various contributions to the paper were collected and published at regular intervals by James Clarke & Co., the paper's publishers. Simple little prose or verse pieces about nature or the life of faith and stories intended for children formed much of her writing, and there are indications that they were very popular. She also wrote for another evangelical paper, *The Sunday-School Times and Home Educator*, first published in January 1860. For twenty years from 1885 she was also its editor, a task that, as she commented, was not an easy one.

From time to time her pieces were published in book form, the first being a collection of poems, *Lays and Lyrics of the Blessed Life* (1860). Several other volumes of verses followed, the final one being *Songs of Joy and Faith* (1909), published posthumously. Her poetry was very simple with a tendency towards sentimentalism. She also wrote hymns, and even now her writing can occasionally be found in some hymnbooks. Some of her serialized fiction was published in novel form, for instance, *A Window in Paris* (1898), an account of the Franco-Prussian War designed to demonstrate the tragedy of war. She acknowledged, however, that she was not a novelist. Some of her publications were aimed at encouraging young people to follow a life of faith, including *Girlhood* (1869), *Boyhood* (1870) and *Homely Talks about Homely Things* (1886). Her constant longing that young people would grow up to become lifelong followers of Jesus was couched in Victorian terms of usefulness and duty.

At the same time as her varied work for James Clarke, she wrote biographies and edited poetry books for Walter Scott & Co. under the different pseudonym of Eva Hope.

She was first approached to write a biography of Grace Darling (1875), which has been described by one critic as 'bad beyond belief'. Under this name she also edited poetry books and wrote other biographies including accounts of President Lincoln, Queen Victoria and General Gordon. Altogether, under both pseudonyms, she wrote over forty-five books. One of the best is her autobiography, *A Working Woman's Life* (1907), which contains many interesting stories and insights from her childhood and working life. In it she explains that she found the single life to have many compensations, and stresses the satisfaction of God-given work, the many friends she made and the enjoyment of being able to travel.

Much of Marianne's writing betrays a Victorian sentimentality about the home and a belief that domesticity and mothering was natural for women. Yet at the same time she had a firm belief that single women such as herself should be financially independent. She also asserted that women were men's intellectual equals and should take degrees, and that even married women could work as doctors and preachers as long as their domestic responsibilities allowed. She also admired those who had broken new ground on behalf of women. In *Queens of Literature* (1886), written under the name of Eva Hope, she described the lives of several women, including Frances Cobbe, Harriet Martineau and Mary Somerville. The latter, she asserted, had 'demolished, once for all, the idea that a woman's brain is less strong than that of a man's'. Marianne's attitudes towards women thus reveal a mixture of traditional and newer attitudes. For her there was no contradiction, as all her beliefs stemmed from her faith. Given her wide readership her views probably influenced many evangelicals.

In common with many of her contemporaries, her life was affected by Keswick spirituality. She discovered through the Brighton Convention in May 1875, a precursor to Keswick, what she understood as a new experience of the 'higher Christian life', the love of God, the constant presence of Christ and surrender to him. This influence is evident in her later writing. She also shared the general optimism of the nineteenth century, finding herself increasingly sympathetic to universalism.

For several years from 1877 Marianne delivered winter lectures. These were always well attended. Although she describes herself as initially 'shy and retiring', she came to enjoy speaking in public. Her first series on 'The Women of To-day' was extremely popular. The profits from her lecturing enabled her to buy a house in Northampton, which she shared with her father and later with one or other of her nieces. She was also, for six years, the only female member of Northampton School Board, where she was very conscious of the difficulties of being a woman in a public role.

Towards the end of her life Marianne bought a holiday retreat in Barmouth, North Wales, which gave her much pleasure. She died there on 16 March 1909. The memorial plaque in her church in Northampton declares that 'as Writer, Teacher and Friend she did more than can be told for the enrichment of many lives'.

Bibliography
S. Burgoyne Black, *A Farningham Childhood* (Sevenoaks: Darenth Valley Publications, 1988); M. Farningham, *A Working Woman's Life* (London: James Clarke & Co., 1907); L. Wilson, 'Marianne Farningham: Work, Leisure and the Use of Time', in R. Swanson (ed.), *Studies in Church History*, vol. 37 (Woodbridge, Suffolk: Boydell, 2002); L. Wilson, '"Afraid to be Singular": Marianne Farningham and the Role of Women, 1857–1909', in S. Morgan (ed.), *Women, Religion and Feminism in Britain, 1750–1900* (Basingstoke: Palgrave MacMillan, 2002).

L. WILSON

■ **FEE, Gordon Donald** (1934–), New Testament scholar and Pentecostal minister, was born on 23 May 1934 in Ashland, Oregon, a college town in the state's southwestern corner. That same year his father, the Revd Donald Fee, left the small Pentecostal body in which he had been ordained, the Open Bible Standard Church, to join the Assemblies of God, America's leading Pentecostal denomination. That decision led the Fees to Port Angeles, Washington, a bustling port on the Olympic peninsula, where Gordon's father became pastor of a local Assemblies of God church while his mother taught in the public schools.

Fee attended Seattle Pacific University, where he earned the BA and MA degrees (1956, 1958). University training, though relatively rare among Pentecostals of Fee's generation, came naturally to the son of a schoolteacher and an academically inclined pastor. Like his father (who would leave the pastorate in 1953 to join the faculty of Northwest College in Kirkland, Washington), the younger Fee combined the pastoral and the academic life. After completing his Master's degree in 1958, he took charge of an Assemblies of God congregation in picturesque Des Moines, Washington, on Vashon Island in Puget Sound, and was ordained the following year.

For the next four years Fee combined a local pastorate with part-time teaching while contemplating a future in foreign mission. When the latter did not materialize, he opted for a mission of a different kind. Moving to Los Angeles, Fee enrolled at the University of Southern California, where in 1966 he received his PhD in New Testament textual criticism. So began the 'mission' that would define him for evangelical audiences thereafter: as an evangelical missionary to the world of biblical scholarship, and a scholarly missionary to the world of evangelicalism.

After taking his degree, Fee joined the faculty of Southern California College (now Regent University), an Assemblies of God-related institution southeast of Los Angeles in Costa Mesa, California. Three years later, in 1969, he left Costa Mesa for one of America's flagship evangelical institutions, Wheaton College in Wheaton, Illinois. In 1974 Fee turned to the challenge of graduate research and professional training, accepting a position at Gordon-Conwell Theological Seminary in South Hamilton near Boston. That move also placed Fee in the dynamic intellectual climate of the Boston Theological Institute, a consortium of schools that included (in addition to Gordon-Conwell) Harvard Divinity School, Weston Jesuit School of Theology, Episcopal Divinity School, Andover-Newton (Congregational), Boston College (Roman Catholic) and Boston University (Methodist), among others. For the next twelve years Fee took his place among the cadre of New Testament scholars of international repute resident at these several institutions.

Finally, in 1986, Fee returned to the Pacific Northwest of his youth, joining the prestigious faculty of Regent College in Vancouver, British Columbia (most closely associated, perhaps, with the name of J. I. *Packer), where he has served as Professor of New Testament, Dean of Faculty and, following his retirement in 2002, Professor Emeritus of New Testament.

Over the course of his long and distinguished career, Fee has made numerous contributions to biblical scholarship in general and to evangelical scholarship in particular. He first gained a reputation as a textual critic and patristics expert, through his early work on Papyrus Bodmer II and Codex Sinaiticus and his research on Origen and Chrysostom. As an editor of the New Testament in the Greek Fathers series, Fee continued to play an influential role in these disciplines, in which he emerged as one of the leading defenders of 'reasoned eclecticism' (a model for resolving text-critical difficulties by reference to all available evidence, internal and external, and on a passage by passage basis) as opposed to either 'thoroughgoing eclecticism', which relies exclusively on internal evidence, or the 'documentary' or 'majority text' model, which relies exclusively on external evidence.

For the greater part of his career, however, and for the greater part of the evangelical public, Fee has been known first as an astute and imaginative, if sometimes controversial, exegete and commentator. His commentary on 1 Corinthians, in particular, broke new interpretive ground and influenced later scholarship on the Corinthian correspondence. Fee's most enduring legacy within evangelical circles, however, may prove to be the hermeneutic that has undergirded his exegesis. Whether in the conduct of his biblical scholarship or in the course of debates over highly emotive topics such as the nature of Scripture and the role of tradition, Fee has consistently integrated the implications of a thoughtful but unapologetic piety with an appreciation for, and a judicious use of, the insights of historical criticism. Furthermore, his commentaries have balanced contextual or historical-critical imperatives with spiritual or theological concerns, an approach that has since been widely adopted, as for example by Zondervan's NIV Application Commentary Series.

As noted above, Fee has been an evangelical missionary to the world of biblical scholarship as well as a scholarly missionary to the world of evangelicalism. Through leadership in professional organizations such as the Society for Biblical Literature, he has functioned as something of an ambassador, representing evangelical scholarship to the academy at large and raising, Fee quips, a 'sane' evangelical voice in the main centres of international biblical studies.

According to Fee, his sense of calling to an academic career was clarified by his reading the uncharitable remarks of a fellow Assemblies of God minister. His colleague had written a letter to Christianity Today in which, after disparaging the 'egghead' Christianity of the editor (the evangelical theologian Carl F. H. *Henry), he boasted that he would rather be 'a fool on fire than a scholar on ice'. Recognizing a faulty dilemma when he saw one, the young Fee determined to realize the first of the two unmentioned options, that of being 'a scholar on fire'. (That of being a 'fool on ice', of course, he left to others.) Fee's subsequent knack for building scholarly bridges and for perceiving a third way between competing extremes, then, flowed naturally from a personal history that has revolved around bringing the insights and commitments of his Pentecostal upbringing to bear on academia in general and biblical scholarship in particular.

Indeed, Fee has addressed the problem of the relationship between scholarship and spirituality throughout his career (witness the title of a recent book and article: 'To What End Exegesis? Reflections on Exegesis and Spirituality'), and he has always cultivated the role of churchman as well as that of scholar. His commitment to the practical relevance of Christian scholarship and his understanding of its place as a servant to the church have led him to accept a daunting schedule of public speaking at conferences, retreats and local churches, and to make frequent appearances as a consultant and guest lecturer at international theological institutions such as the Far East Advanced

School of Theology in the Philippines and the East Africa School of Theology in Nairobi.

Throughout his career Fee has remained an ordained Assemblies of God minister. Although he is generally held in very high esteem within his own denomination, his work has provoked some controversy both in the Assemblies of God and in Pentecostal circles generally. His ecumenical activities have been coolly received in some quarters, as has his openness to aspects of higher criticism. Also controversial has been his inductive hermeneutic with its implications for the classical Pentecostal view that glossolalia is the sole and necessary evidence of initial baptism with the Holy Spirit.

Fee is co-founder, with Earle Ellis and Gerry Hawthorne, of the Institute for Biblical Research and a founding member of the Society for Pentecostal Studies. He has published over fifteen books and more than 100 articles, and has edited or co-authored numerous additional volumes. His books include *To What End Exegesis? Essays Textual, Exegetical and Theological* (2001), *Listening to the Spirit in the Text* (2000), *God's Empowering Presence: the Holy Spirit in the Letters of Paul* (1994), *New Testament Exegesis* (1993), *Gospel and Spirit: Issues in New Testament Hermeneutics* (1991), *Paul's Letter to the Philippians* (1995) and *The First Epistle to the Corinthians* (1987).

Bibliography

S. Soderlund and N. T. Wright (eds.), *Romans and the People of God: Essays in Honor of Gordon D. Fee* (Grand Rapids: Eerdmans, 1999).

R. G. ROBINS

■ **FINNEY, Charles Grandison** (1792–1875), evangelist, educator and theologian, is generally considered the father of modern urban revivalism. Famous for his early campaigns in northern New York State and in cities along the Mohawk River in the 1820s, he built an international reputation, preaching extensively in New York City, Boston and Philadelphia and in Great Britain on two lengthy tours. At Oberlin, Ohio, beginning in 1835, in addition to his teaching and presidency of Oberlin College (1851–1865), Finney served as pastor of First Congrega-

tional Church, although his ongoing evangelistic career involved lengthy annual revival campaigns, usually in eastern cities. His published writings, especially *Lectures on Revivals of Religion* (1835) and his *Memoirs* (posthumous, 1876), remained influential among evangelicals on both sides of the Atlantic throughout the twentieth century.

Finney was born in Warren, Connecticut, on 29 August 1792 to Sylvester and Rebecca Rice Finney, modest landowners who made their living farming. Following a trend in the new Republic which has been called 'the refinement of America', he was named after the fashionable character in Samuel Richardson's novel *Sir Charles Grandison*. The family joined the New England migration to New York State in 1794, moving to Oneida County in 1794 and to Henderson, Jefferson County, on the north-eastern shore of Lake Ontario when Charles was sixteen. Finney minimized any religious instruction he may have received when growing up, stating that his parents were not 'professors of religion', although they did go to church. The first published version of his *Memoirs* (edited by Oberlin College president James Fairchild) includes the statement, 'I seldom heard a sermon', but the modern critical edition restores the sentence from the manuscript: 'I seldom heard a Gospel sermon from any person, unless it was an occasional one from some travelling minister.' Finney as a youth heard plenty of sermons but held himself critically aloof from dry doctrinal Presbyterian preaching and the ranting of unlearned Baptists. Educated in common schools, at Warren Academy (Connecticut) and possibly (according to family tradition; there is no record of his enrolment) at Hamilton College, he was a schoolteacher in Henderson, New York, and in New Jersey until 1818, when he returned north to Adams, New York, to work as a lawyer's apprentice. In Adams he also became the music director of the Presbyterian church under pastor George W. Gale and, with revival blazing in the villages throughout the region, he began to study the Bible. On 10 October 1821 he experienced a spiritual and vocational crisis; his soul was converted, and he sensed a call to the ministry of the gospel.

Finney was converted, ironically, not in an evangelistic meeting but when he retreated alone to a wooded grove outside the town. At the age of twenty-nine he determined that 'if I am ever converted, I will preach the gospel'. His was an emotional conversion, beginning with his desperately taking hold of the promises 'with the grasp of a drowning man', continuing with penitential tears during prayer in the office, and concluding in the experience of 'a mighty baptism of the Holy Ghost' in which 'it seemed to me that I should burst. I wept aloud with joy and love.' This was an experience that he sought to replicate in others through his preaching. He began witnessing to his new faith immediately, explaining to a client, as he later recounted, 'Deacon Barney, I have a retainer from the Lord Jesus Christ to plead his cause, and I cannot plead yours.' The St Lawrence Presbytery accepted Finney as a candidate for the ministry and, instead of directing him to attend Princeton or Andover Seminary, assigned George Gale as his instructor in theology. Finney was critical of Gale's more conservative Calvinism, but he was indebted to Gale for his conversion and for guiding him rapidly towards ordination. The St Lawrence Presbytery licensed Finney to preach in December 1823; the Female Missionary Society of the Western District of New York commissioned him as an evangelist in March 1824; and the presbytery ordained him on 1 July 1824. In October 1824 he married Lydia Root Andrews, with whom he had six children and who collaborated in his ministry by leading women's prayer, missionary and social reform groups.

A number of influences shaped Finney's early revival preaching in the north country of New York State. Theologically, as a New School Presbyterian he inherited much from the school of New England Calvinism known as the New Divinity developed by students of Jonathan *Edwards such as Samuel *Hopkins. New Divinity taught that individuals are 'moral agents', fully responsible for their own sin, and portrayed the atonement not as satisfaction of the penalty due to God for Adam's sin but as the establishment of God's 'moral government' by which sinners could be forgiven. Sanctification was described as a life of 'disinterested benevolence', full and free obedience to God's law, doing good just because it is good. In the 1820s Yale professor Nathaniel William *Taylor further modified Calvinism in his New Haven Theology by giving more room for human involvement in the experience of salvation, in ways that opponents labelled 'Arminianism'. Taylor's ideas moved in a Methodist direction and gave Finney the theological basis for his revival preaching. His sermons blended lawyer-like argumentation with Baptist- and Methodist-style extemporaneous directness, always ending with the call for immediate repentance and conversion to Christ: 'If there is a sinner in this house, let me say to him, Abandon all your excuses ... Will you submit to God tonight – NOW?' Finney appropriated the emotional power of the radical wing of the Second Great Awakening to bring such experiences as falling down 'in the Spirit', tearful conversions, shouting, and 'holy laughter' into staid Presbyterian and Congregational churches.

In 1825, the year the Erie Canal linked Buffalo with Albany and New York City, Finney moved his ministry south to the new commercial cities of central New York State. George Gale, who now lived in Oneida County, invited Finney to preach in his church, and it was in concert with a league of New School Presbyterian pastors that Finney extended the revival from Utica and Rome to the entire Mohawk Valley. In 1826 he went to Auburn, seat of the New School Presbyterian seminary, and then east to Troy, where the Mohawk River joins the Hudson. The evangelistic methods employed by Finney and his colleagues in these 'western revivals' (the call for immediate conversion, prayer for sinners by name, women's testimony in mixed meetings, emotional responses in worship) came under fire from Old School Presbyterians and more restrained New England evangelicals like Lyman *Beecher and Asahel Nettleton. These methods and this style had come to be known as 'Finneyism'. His first publication, A Sermon Preached in the Presbyterian Church at Troy, March 4, 1827, dismissed revival opponents as 'luke-warm' and no better than 'impenitent sinners'. To resolve the crisis, important to New Englanders because of the 1801 Congregational–Presbyterian Plan of Union, Lyman Beecher organized the New Lebanon Convention in July 1827, as a result of which Finney rose to national stature and began to receive invitations from larger eastern cities.

Finney preached in and around Wilmington, Delaware, and Philadelphia in 1828. His success, although not as dramatic as in central New York, was remarkable in the light of the dominance in the area of Old School Presbyterianism. Then in 1829 he preached for the first time in New York City, established there in a Free Presbyterian Church by reform-minded evangelical businessmen with New England roots. The period from September 1830 to June 1831 saw Finney in Rochester, New York, where he directed what is often called the greatest revival in American history. With the support of Presbyterian, Baptist, Methodist and Episcopal churches as well as business and civic leaders, the revival effectively transformed the social fabric of the city and surrounding area by linking conversion to Christ with the temperance movement. Here Finney employed not only his usual 'new measures' but also the 'anxious seat' (a more immediate means of prayer for penitents than the older 'inquiry meetings') and 'protracted meetings' in nearby villages. Throughout his career, Finney appealed most readily to the business and professional classes of the communities in which he preached; his approach was to convert civic and social leaders and assume that their influence would extend to others.

Following his success in Rochester, his New York City patrons brought Finney back as pastor at the renovated Chatham Street Theater. These philanthropist-reformers, including Arthur and Lewis Tappan, pressured him to link revival not only with temperance but also with the abolition of slavery. While Finney never put social reform above evangelism and was averse to more radical forms of abolitionism, he zealously condemned slavery as a sin, banned slaveholders from sacramental fellowship and allowed his church to be the Antislavery Society's headquarters. He suffered a breakdown, however, under the weight of attacks on his theology, anti-abolition mob vandalism of his church and a bout of cholera. During a miserable voyage to Europe intended to be therapeutic, his spiritual crisis ('my soul was in utter agony') was resolved when, he believed, 'the Spirit of prayer' came upon him as 'never before to such a degree'. This was one of several episodes in his life which he identified as spiritual turning-points. He

returned to New York City to begin a new phase of his career, in 1835 publishing *Sermons on Various Subjects* and *Lectures on Revivals of Religion*.

In the *Lectures* Finney stirred more controversy with his thesis that 'A revival of religion is not a miracle' but the 'purely philosophical result of the right use of the constituted means'. Although he also insisted that every conversion was empowered by the Holy Spirit, his emphasis on the sinner's ability to turn to Christ and his teaching of the efficacy of 'prevailing prayer' made him the enemy of orthodox Calvinists. Heresy trials were becoming common in the Presbyterian Church, and in 1836, as his patrons installed him in the new Broadway Tabernacle, Finney avoided indictment by becoming a Congregationalist. In 1835–1836 the Oberlin Collegiate Institute, the first college in America to admit blacks and women and founded by the same men who supported his ministry, called Finney as professor of theology, and he divided his time between New York City and Ohio. In 1837 he resigned his Broadway Tabernacle pastorate, devoting himself to teaching and serving as pastor at Oberlin and to annual evangelistic campaigns in eastern cities.

At Oberlin Finney, President Asa *Mahan and other faculty members moved further in the Wesleyan direction, although never giving up their Reformed identity, by embracing and developing the doctrines of 'entire sanctification', the 'second blessing', the 'higher Christian life', and 'perfection'. Through the periodical *The Oberlin Evangelist* and such books as *Lectures to Professing Christians* (1837) and *Views of Sanctification* (1840) Finney became a major theologian of the emerging holiness movement, thus alienating many Congregationalist and New School Presbyterian friends. He also came to lament the individualism of the earlier revivals ('the Church has been neglected'), now seeing the need for teaching and spiritual growth within the Christian fellowship. He published *Skeletons of a Course of Theological Lectures* (1840) and two volumes of *Lectures on Systematic Theology* (1846, 1847). The tone of Finney's theology was further defined in 1847 when, through the ordeal of his wife's fatal illness, he experienced what he called a 'fresh baptism of the Holy Spirit'.

Finney married Elizabeth Atkinson, a wealthy Rochester merchant's widow, who managed a women's academy, in November 1848. Capable and ambitious, she oversaw the college's women's department and encouraged Finney to expand his ministry in new directions, specifically in Great Britain, where *Lectures on Revivals* was a bestseller. Invitations from Congregational and Baptist missionary societies came through Potto Brown, a Nonconformist lay leader, merchant and evangelical philanthropist. Finney preached in Brown's church in Houghton near Huntingdon and St Ives, but he soon moved to large churches in London, Birmingham, Worcester and other cities, where Elizabeth furthered the revival with large women's meetings. In London Finney preached at the meeting of the Congregational Union and, from May 1850 to April 1851, at two churches served by John Campbell, George *Whitefield's Tabernacle and Tottenham Court Road Chapel. Upon the Finneys' return to Oberlin that summer the Oberlin trustees named Finney president of the college.

When the Finneys returned to England in January 1859, his theology came under attack from some of his earlier supporters, although invitations continued to come from Baptists, Methodists, Congregationalists and James *Morison's Evangelical Union in Scotland. While the second British tour was less satisfactory than his first, his continued popularity illustrates the transatlantic nature of evangelicalism. Finney was sixty-eight in the autumn of 1860 when he returned from Britain, and the United States was on the brink of civil war. While the town, church and college at Oberlin, heavily involved in the underground railroad, were a national symbol of abolitionism, Finney's days of national leadership were coming to an end. A participant in the national awakening of 1857–1858 known as the Businessmen's Revival (he preached mainly at Park Street Church in Boston), Finney limited his activities in the 1860s to his duties at the college and church and to writing. Following the death of Elizabeth in 1863, he retired from the presidency in 1865 and married Rebecca Allen Rayl, widowed assistant principal of the college's female department. In his last years he completed his *Memoirs*, wrote against Freemasonry and continued an active correspondence. Finney

died at Oberlin on 16 August 1875. At his memorial service, his longtime colleague Professor John Morgan said, 'There was in him, in prayer, the most remarkable power that I have ever seen in any human being.'

Finney's well-organized urban campaigns and his methods of evangelistic preaching appropriated earlier revival traditions from the First and Second Great Awakenings in New England and from the camp meeting tradition and created the culture from which emerged Dwight L. *Moody and the great evangelists of the twentieth century. His role in the holiness movement and emphasis on Holy Spirit baptism contributed to the more radical religious expectations which gave rise to Pentecostalism. At the same time, progressive elements in his theology and involvement in the temperance, women's education and anti-slavery movements strengthened the reformist impulse of American evangelicalism, which led to the Social Gospel movement.

Bibliography

C. G. Finney, *Lectures on Revivals of Religion*, ed. W. G. McLoughlin, Jr (Cambridge, Massachusetts: Harvard University Press, 1960); C. G. Finney, *The Memoirs of Charles G. Finney*, eds. R. A. G. Dupuis and G. M. Rosell (Grand Rapids: Zondervan, 1989); C. E. Hambrick-Stowe, *Charles G. Finney and the Spirit of American Evangelicalism* (Grand Rapids: Eerdmans, 1996); K. J. Hardman, *Charles Grandison Finney (1792–1875): Revivalist and Reformer* (Syracuse: Syracuse University Press, 1987).

C. E. HAMBRICK-STOWE

■ **FLETCHER, John William [Jean Guillaume de la Fléchère]** (1729–1785), Methodist clergyman and author, was born c. 12 September 1729 to an aristocratic and wealthy Swiss family in Nyon. Educated at home and enjoying an active childhood, he enrolled at Geneva University in 1746 to study 'Belles Lettres'. Considering himself unworthy of the calling of a minister, he rejected a career in the church and trained as a military engineer. After unsuccessful attempts to seek service, he came to England around 1750, where from 1752 he was tutor to the sons of Thomas Hill, MP for Shrewsbury.

Always a person of religious sensitivity, Fletcher reacted against elements of his native Calvinism, such as predestination, when young. He probably associated with French Protestant churches in London when first in England and experienced an evangelical conversion in January 1754, coming under the influence of Methodists. In March 1757 he was ordained into the Church of England and commenced preaching and ministering in London and occasionally in Shropshire. He became intimate with the *Wesleys (especially Charles) and the Countess of *Huntingdon.

In 1760 he accepted the living of Madeley, Shropshire, a parish at the heart of the industrial developments in East Shropshire and with social problems, reputedly renowned for the drunkenness and vice of the population. His ministry was typified by preaching and assiduous pastoral care. After some early successes, Fletcher met with opposition, particularly when he attempted to foster cottage meetings in the industrial settlements. Despite Wesley's criticism of his lack of discipline, his influence was considerable.

From 1765 Fletcher increasingly preached beyond his parish, in the West Midlands and further afield. He preached in evangelical parishes as well as for the Wesleys and Lady Huntingdon, becoming in 1768 visiting superintendent of her college at Trevecca, Wales. His visits were characterized by spiritual renewal. He also stipulated a comprehensive curriculum for the students and secured the appointment of the gifted young Joseph Benson (then classics master at Wesley's Kingswood School) as an effective head. Following Lady Huntingdon's disavowal of Wesley's 'Minutes' in 1771, Fletcher resigned. He wrote a *Vindication* of Wesley's doctrines, followed by the *Checks to Antinomianism*.

The *Checks* were an extensive promulgation of Arminian doctrine, setting out the case for the necessity of good works and for human free will and supporting the Wesleyan doctrine of Christian perfection. Fletcher's final contributions to the debate make it clear that he viewed Arminianism as a counterbalance, not an alternative, to Calvinism. Through the 'Controversy' he was strongly opposed by the *Hill brothers, and by Augustus Toplady, who none the less respected

him as a person and for the courtesy, clarity and learning of his writing.

In 1770 Fletcher travelled to France, Italy and Switzerland with his friend and patron James Ireland, a Bristol sugar merchant. During the 'Controversy' he continued to devote himself to his busy parish, but due to the strain occasioned by his writings he had a breakdown of health in 1777. Suffering from consumption, he spent periods convalescing in London and Bristol, then returned to Switzerland (1778–1781) to recover his health. He had previously returned to continental Europe only in 1770. At Nyon his ministry was initially welcomed but later restricted; he then wrote his acclaimed *Portrait of St Paul*, directed to Swiss pastors. It appeared in translation only after Fletcher's death.

Following his return to England, Fletcher married Mary Bosanquet (1739–1815) on 21 November 1781. Born of a wealthy London Huguenot banking family exactly ten years after Fletcher, she was led to faith through a Methodist servant. Rejecting the social life of her class, she left home and with other women formed a Christian community, caring for the poor and fostering local Methodist societies. She moved to Yorkshire in 1768 and started a similar community at Cross Hall, near Morley, which was visited and much admired by John Wesley and others. Wesley accepted that she had an 'extraordinary call' to preach, although she was never included among his itinerant preachers.

John and Mary Fletcher ministered together in Madeley and visited Dublin in 1783. In 1784 Fletcher opposed Priestley's Unitarianism, writing in defence of trinitarian theology. During an outbreak of typhoid in the summer of 1785, he contracted the illness while visiting the sick and died on 14 August. His last words were recorded as 'what shall become of my poor?', and he was deeply mourned in his parish and beyond.

While Fletcher did not travel extensively as a preacher, his ability was reckoned to be second only to that of *Whitefield. He drew crowds by his compelling personal manner and power of argument. His central theme was always the immeasurable love of Christ for humanity made real through the outpouring of the Spirit. He was clearly familiar with the hardship and dangers of the mines and ironworks in his parish, and he concentrated his efforts around the new industries. He cooperated with the Quaker Abiah Darby in forming early Sunday schools in the parish, and he influenced others, including Charles *Simeon. His particular concern was always for the poor, and his home was constantly open to those in need.

Fletcher played a leading part among Wesley's Methodists but refused John Wesley's suggestion that he be nominated as Wesley's successor. The Wesleys and their followers regarded him highly, particularly after the 'Controversy'. Despite his long association with them he was steadfastly non-partisan. During the debate around Wesley's Deed of Declaration at the 1784 Conference, Fletcher was able to reconcile the opposing parties by his irenic interventions.

Fletcher attempted to form a union of evangelical clergy in the West Midlands in the 1760s and also to remain on terms of fellowship with antagonists in the 'Controversy'. In 1775 he reworked a proposal by Joseph Benson to form the Methodists into a daughter church within the Church of England. In Madeley Methodism remained within the Church of England well into the nineteenth century.

Fletcher was considered a saint during his lifetime, and veneration for him grew after his death. He is reported to have claimed to have experienced entire sanctification in 1781, but his experience of 'perfect love' and his holiness of life were reached after long searching and a disciplined life of self-denial. In his writings he offered doctrinal support for the Wesleyan tenet of entire sanctification. He was a gifted scholar, pastor and preacher, and his prayer life was an inspiration to others.

Bibliography

J. Benson, *The Life of the Rev. John W. de la Fléchère* (1806); L. Tyerman, *Wesley's Designated Successor* (1882); P. P. Streiff, *Reluctant Saint* (London: SCM, 2001); B. Trinder, *Industrial Revolution in Shropshire* (Chichester: Phillimore, [3]2000).

P. FORSAITH

■ FLETCHER, Lionel Bale (1877–1954), evangelist and pastor, was born in Maitland, New South Wales, on 22 May 1877, into a godly family. His father was headmaster of a local school and a Methodist lay preacher who saw all of his seven sons become preachers; his mother was descended from Huguenots; and a great-grandfather was appointed a Methodist preacher by John *Wesley. A strong-willed and rebellious boy, Fletcher ran away from home at the age of ten. His parents sent him to study at Newington College in Sydney, but when he was sixteen he went to sea as an apprentice aboard the sailing ship *Macquarie*. The captain was a devout Christian and had a positive influence on the intelligent, cheerful but quick-tempered Fletcher, and advised him against a career at sea.

Fletcher then worked on his brother Henry's farm in western NSW, where the influence of his brother and the Methodist minister led to his conversion in 1896. He returned to Sydney, where he joined Christian Endeavour and, when attending the evangelical Petersham Conference, had a second, formative religious experience which resulted in his deciding to become a minister.

On 24 January 1900 he married Maud Bashan. She was a capable musician and speaker and was to be a true helpmeet for the fifty-four years of their life together; he always paid tribute to her as an exceptional, gifted and devoted wife. The Methodist church required four years probation but did not offer financial assistance. Fletcher therefore went to Charters Towers in Queensland, where he worked as a miner and a journalist. He showed a talent for religious journalism, preached, and taught a Bible class and in Sunday school. It was a valuable period which saw him develop facility in communication, especially to men.

In 1905 he returned to Sydney and transferred his allegiance to the Congregational Church, which gave him an opportunity to minister and maintain his wife and child while he studied part-time. He was appointed minister at Campbelltown church; in addition he preached at other places round Sydney. He soon displayed the characteristics of his later ministry: energetic pastoral ministry, evangelistic preaching, and a desire to reach young men with the gospel. He was ordained in the Pitt Street Congregational Church on 24 May 1908, when he was thirty-one.

His energy and ability were soon noted, and he was called to the Port Adelaide church to succeed the prominent social reformer Revd J. G. Coles. At Port Adelaide his vigorous preaching and forthright ministry were appreciated, and when he left in 1915 the church had the largest membership of any Congregational church in Australia. He also ventured beyond the parish boundaries, taking part in the Chapman–Alexander Mission in 1909 and conducting evangelistic campaigns. Invitations flooded in, and he resigned to lead the interdenominational mission to South Australia in 1915.

His growing reputation led to an invitation to become pastor of the Wood Street Church in Cardiff, which possessed the largest Congregational church building in the British Empire. The church could seat 3,000 but had only 265 members, mostly poor working-class people, and was £3,000 in debt and ready to close its doors. Despite the constraints of the war years, Fletcher quickly restored the fortunes of the church, energetically engaged in evangelistic work throughout the UK, and took a leading role in the YMCA and Christian Endeavour. He was Christian Endeavour president for Great Britain and spoke at the International Christian Endeavour Convention at Des Moines in 1923.

In 1924 he became pastor of the Beresford Congregational Church in Auckland. He repeated his Cardiff experience by reinvigorating a moribund church and saw its membership grow to 800 by 1932. He extended his ministry by being the first in New Zealand to give gospel broadcasts over the radio; he also continued to engage in itinerant evangelism, in New Zealand and beyond, including campaigns in London and America. He was elected Chairman of the New Zealand Congregational Union and World Vice-President of Christian Endeavour.

In 1932 he accepted an invitation from the World Evangelization Trust to become 'Empire Evangelist'. As such he was based in London and engaged in successful evangelistic campaigns in the UK, South Africa and Australia.

In 1941 he returned to Sydney, still a star in the evangelical/Congregational firmament, and in his remaining years continued to preach in Australia and New Zealand. In 1951 the Bible Institute of Los Angeles conferred on him an honorary DD. He died in Sydney on 19 February 1954.

Fletcher's three main pastorates – Port Adelaide (1909–1915), Wood Street, Cardiff (1916–1922), and Beresford Street, Auckland (1924–1932) – were all very successful. In addition to his pastoral and evangelistic endeavours, he spoke forthrightly about temperance and other social issues, was an enthusiastic supporter of Christian Endeavour and the YMCA, wrote popular books on evangelism, sermons and prayer, and in meetings for men only, encouraged manly responsibility. His life was marked and energized by daily prayer and Bible study, a desire to win souls, especially men's, an open and friendly personality and a commitment to 'Spirit-filled' living.

A lightly built active man, there was a certain gravity and flexibility about Fletcher. He was eloquent, speaking with a quiet penetrating voice, and had a sense of the dramatic. J. Edwin Orr referred to Fletcher as 'The outstanding evangelist of the between Wars period'. His evangelicalism was robust, albeit somewhat populist. His biographer claims that he was responsible for 250,000 conversions, but he left no institution or legend.

Bibliography

C. W. Malcolm, *Twelve Hours in the Day* (London: Marshall, Morgan & Scott, 1956).

D. PAPROTH

■ FORD, Leighton (1931–), evangelist and spiritual director, was adopted at birth (22 October 1931) by Charles Richard and Etta Olive Shankland Ford of Ontario. Richard owned a jewellery store, where he worked diligently to provide Olive with the lavish lifestyle she desired. Olive, a proper, pious woman, made substantial donations to foreign missions and oversaw the care and instruction of the various foster children that passed through their home.

Young Ford experienced a strict religious upbringing. Every morning he knelt at a specially made prayer bench where Olive taught him to pray. He began a regular practice of memorizing Scripture while he was still a toddler. His conversion occurred at the age of five when, in a children's meeting at Canadian Keswick, he repeatedly insisted that he was ready to make a decision for Christ, despite the teacher's initial scepticism. Olive developed clinical paranoia, which disrupted the Ford family, but Leighton continued at school, excelling both as a student and as an athlete.

A service at Blue Water Bible Conference marked the beginning of Ford's personal devotional life. After that meeting, his life seemed infused with a new spiritual vitality. The Canadian Youth Fellowship elected him president at the age of fourteen, and he met Billy *Graham when he booked him for a local youth rally.

At Graham's suggestion, Ford attended Wheaton College and graduated in 1952 with a BA in philosophy. He graduated *magna cum laude* with his Masters of Divinity from Columbia Theological Seminary in 1955.

On 19 December 1953 he married Jean Coffey Graham, Billy Graham's sister, and they eventually had three children: Deborah Jean, Leighton Frederick Sandys Ford, Jr (Sandy) and Kevin Graham. Ford was ordained through the Presbyterian Church in May 1955. He also started work for the Billy Graham Evangelistic Association that year, assuming the title of Associate Evangelist. Though he intended to stay with the BGEA for one year, he stayed for thirty-one and by the end of his term was vice-president and the regular second speaker for the crusades. An adept manager and powerful preacher, he thrived in his position. Graham offered Ford his own crusade team in 1962, the same year that he was awarded a Doctor of Divinity degree from Houghton College. He was awarded an honorary Doctor of Laws from Gordon College in 1973.

By 1980 Ford was considering career options beyond the BGEA. The following year, his son Sandy, who suffered from Wolfe-Parkinson-White syndrome, died during heart surgery. His son's loss, combined with the aging of many prominent evangelical figures of the time, prompted him to divert his energies to the development of young Christian leaders. Leighton Ford Ministries, founded in 1986, provided him with an avenue for imparting his expertise to junior leaders. The Arrow Leadership Program was designed to promote Christ-like character and an effective, Christ-centred philosophy in up-and-coming ministers. As the programme grew, Ford noted the significant impact of mentor relationships on the learners, particularly those that included mutual sharing of life experience.

Ford's 1992 sabbatical turned his life in yet another direction. During this time, his newly discovered spiritual activities, drawing and painting, taught him to pray more fervently and effectively. In 1993 he began practising and teaching *lectio divina*, repeatedly and prayerfully reading a scripture passage to discern divine direction. In 1998 he passed the leadership of Arrow to Carson Pue, a graduate of the programme, and took up spiritual direction. He now spends his time praying, cultivating spiritual friendships, reading books on spiritual mentoring, and visiting his own spiritual director, Father David Valtiera. He has written ten books, including the award-winning biography of his son, *Sandy: A Heart for God*, and his latest, *The Power of Story*.

Ford has been socially active, working against racism, poverty and world hunger. He received the 'Two Hungers Award' in 1990 as a result of his efforts in satiating the physical and spiritual hunger of people throughout the world. He has spoken to millions of people in forty countries on every continent. The 'Clergyman of the Year' award given by Religious Heritage of America was presented to him in 1985, and The National Presbyterian Center named him Presbyterian Preacher of the Year. He chaired the Lausanne Committee for World Evangelization from 1976 to 1992, and serves as Honorary Lifetime Chairman. He also served on the boards of World Vision US, Gordon Conwell Theological Seminary and the Duke University Cancer Center. Ford lives in Charlotte, North Carolina with his wife Jean.

Bibliography
N. B. Rohrer, *Leighton Ford: A Life Surprised* (Wheaton: Tyndale House Publishing, 1981); L. F. Winner, 'From Mass Evangelist to Soul Friend', *Christianity Today* (Oct. 2000), pp. 56–60.

T. L. COOPER

■ **FORSYTH, Peter Taylor** (1848–1921), Scottish Congregationalist theologian and minister, while delivering the 1907 Lyman *Beecher lectures at Yale University (later published as *Positive Preaching and the Modern Mind*), offered the following reflection on his intellectual and spiritual development: 'There was a time when I was interested in the first degree with purely scientific criticism. Bred among academic scholarship of the classics and philosophy, I carried these habits to the Bible ... [but] It also pleased God by the revelation of His holiness and grace, which the great theologians taught me to find in the Bible, to bring home to me my sin in a way that submerged all the school questions in weight, urgency, and poignancy. I was turned from a Christian to a believer, from a lover of love to an object of grace. And so, whereas I first thought that what the churches needed was enlightened instruction and liberal theology, I came to be sure that what they needed was evangelization, in something more than the conventional sense of that word.'

This was an extraordinary and modest confession of faith from someone who had, by this point in his career, earned a reputation as (in the words of Horton Davies) 'Dissent's greatest twentieth-century theologian'. The relationship between Forsyth's spiritual conversion and work as a theologian is complex. Following his conversion (which seems to have taken place over a period of time) he continued to develop and mature considerably as a theologian and biblical exegete. But after his conversion his basic theological insights were expressed differently and acquired a new character. On the occasion of his passing, J. K. Mozely adjudged that the 'death of the Principal of Hackney College has bereft English Christianity of its most powerful, its most challenging, and, perhaps, its actually greatest theologian in the sphere of dogmatics'. This article will outline Forsyth's life, ministry and theology with a view to understanding the distinction accorded to him within Victorian and modern British church history.

P. T. Forsyth was born on 12 May 1848 in Aberdeen, Scotland, the first-born son of Isaac Forsyth and Elspet MacPherson. The family had only modest means; the relative poverty of Peter's childhood was only partially eased by his mother's decision to take in university students as boarders. Although Peter was financially poor and suffered from chronic stomach disorders, he thrived intellectually and won numerous academic awards throughout his grammar school education. In 1864 he left school with first-class honours and won the gold medal for that year. In October of the same year, Forsyth entered the annual Bursary Competition of the university and was placed twenty-first out of a total of 204 students, winning the Cargill Bursary. This scholarship provided him with the only means by which he could ever have secured a university education.

At the age of sixteen Forsyth entered the University of Aberdeen, where he not only continued to win academic honours, but also gained a reputation for rhetorical elegance, intellectual courage, passion and aesthetic discernment. A severe illness at the close of his third year at Aberdeen forced him to leave early. His academic performance in the final year (1869) of his MA degree at King's College was so strong, however, that he tied for first prize in moral philosophy and was awarded outstanding first-class honours in the Department of Classical Literature. After spending the academic year of 1871–1872 as a Latin tutor, he travelled to Göttingen in Germany to study for a semester with the renowned theologian Albrecht Ritschl. The semester in Germany gave him not only a facility with the language but also a set of theological commitments that he would retain for many years to come. After his return from Göttingen, Forsyth entered Hackney College (later New College), London, in preparation for a life of pastoral ministry. But he contracted a serious illness during the second year of his course that forced him, once again, to withdraw from study.

It was difficult for the theologically liberal Forsyth to secure a position within the Congregational Union. Without the patronage of J. Baldwin Brown, who had himself demonstrated an independent spirit by championing the cause of a younger and more moderate generation of men in the Union, Forsyth would probably not have been given a Congregational pulpit. Nevertheless, in 1876 Forsyth was appointed to the working-class Congregational church in Shipley, Yorkshire, and was subsequently ordained to the ministry.

The Shipley church was an 'irregular' congregation; it had failed to win the confidence of the meticulously orthodox Yorkshire Congregational Union. Forsyth's participation in the notorious 1877 Leicester Conference did little, however, to allay the suspicions of the Union. Their worries were increased by a sermon delivered by Forsyth to the Shipley congregation and entitled 'Mercy the True and Only Justice'. This sermon reveals Forsyth's dependence upon the theology of his Göttingen teacher, Albrecht Ritschl. Forsyth acquired from Ritschl an antipathy towards legal or forensic models of the atonement, which led him to offer a *moral* reading of the doctrine of reconciliation, in which divine love, mercy and the kingdom of God were the *decisive* theological categories. Not surprisingly, his emphasis upon Christ's death as an expression of divine love and moral obedience led many to believe that he had failed to uphold a properly substitutionary account of Christ's work. But in speaking of divine justice and love Forsyth aimed to offer a corrective to an influential view of the atonement that was (he believed) too deeply influenced by a rigid Augustinian Calvinism and therefore mistaken.

In the year after his arrival in Shipley, Forsyth was married to Minna Magness (an Anglican). After four years of ministry in Yorkshire, he moved on to St Thomas' Square, Hackney, London. The years between 1880 and 1885 were remarkably important for Forsyth's ministry and development as a Christian theologian; it was during this period that his interest in religious art, music, theatre, politics and even the composition and delivery of children's sermons began to flourish.

In 1885 Forsyth began his third pastorate, at Cheetham Hill Congregational Church, Manchester. In its austere industrial setting many of the social, economic and moral problems associated with poverty were very acute. Forsyth offered a series of lectures on religious art (later published as *Religion in Recent Art*) to local workers. His commitment to questions of social and political justice issued in his vigorous support of the great dock strike of 1889. In the same year, he moved on to Clarendon Park Congregational Church, Leicester.

It was here that Forsyth began to distinguish himself as a theologian. His theological work had by this time won the approval of one of the most important English theologians of the late Victorian period, the Congregationalist R. W. *Dale. After reading Forsyth's essay 'Revelation and the Person of Christ', Dale declared that Forsyth had 'recovered for us a word we had all but lost – the word "grace".' This essay, published in the volume *Faith and Criticism* (a collection of essays that performed the same function for the Congregational movement – theological self-definition – as *Lux Mundi* had for Anglo-Catholicism), revealed the distance between Forsyth's position and the dominant trends in both liberal and conservative theology. Forsyth believed that one of the most problematic characteristics of liberal theology was its separation of the 'principle' of divine sonship (e.g. Kant's notion of Jesus as a moral 'archetype') from the concrete person of Jesus Christ. He held that an adequate doctrine of atonement must include the objective redemption of humanity, in and through the act of obedience to the Father of Jesus Christ, the Son of God. Forsyth was not entirely alone in this belief; his articulation of the doctrine bears a family resemblance to that of R. W. Dale, whose focus on the cross was reflected in Forsyth's later theological work, such as the essays, 'The Cross as the Final Seat of Authority' (1899) and 'Christ's Person and His Cross' (1917), and the monographs, *The Cruciality of the Cross* (1909) and *The Work of the Christ* (1910).

Forsyth's eventual break with liberal Protestantism resulted from the growing incompatibility between his own understanding of Christian life and theology and that of Ritschl. For the latter, the Christian faith was to be conceived as an ellipse with two foci (the kingdom of God and the cross). Like many others within nineteenth-century German liberal Protestantism, he reduced the religious life of faith to a largely moral enterprise by his emphasis on the 'kingdom of God'. In time, notwithstanding the influence of Kant and Ritschl, Forsyth was able critically to assess the strengths and weaknesses of this tradition and eventually to assert that the cross alone ought to stand at the centre of Christian faith and practice. As a result, his doctrine of atonement became increasingly objective.

In 1893 Forsyth was grieved by the death of his friend R. W. Dale. This loss was acutely felt throughout the Congregational Union, which was left without the kind of leadership required for its continued success. Forsyth was pressed hard to assume Dale's position of leadership among the Congregational churches. With reservations, he left his ministry in Leicester in 1894 to take up duties at the Emmanuel Congregational Church in Cambridge. Whereas his previous pastoral work may be regarded as parochial ministry, the call to Cambridge was an appeal to assume ministry at a national level.

Soon after arriving at Emmanuel, Forsyth was overwhelmed by the sudden illness and the death of his wife. His recovery was uncertain but he eventually began to make progress, due largely to the loving nurture and care of his new church and his marriage to Bertha Ison in 1897. Bertha was devoted to the wellbeing of her husband. Her energy, care and devotion established the basis for the most theologically vigorous and rewarding years of Forsyth's life.

By 1898 Forsyth had recovered far enough to deliver a sermon entitled, 'The Holy Father and the Living Christ' at the Leicester meeting of the Union. This address secured Forsyth's reputation as an evangelical preacher of the first order. His commitment to locating the meaning of the Christian faith and human freedom in the person and work of the crucified and risen Lord was fully expressed with rhetorical force and clarity. The confidence and esteem of the Union was reflected in his invitation to address an international assembly of Congregational churches in Boston. His address on that occasion was entitled, 'The Evangelical Principle of Authority' and, as in Leicester, he sought to focus the attention of his hearers upon what he had come to regard as the decisive event at the centre of reality, the death of Christ.

In 1901 Forsyth was elected principal of Hackney College, London. During his tenure of this post, he produced the most significant and creative theological work of his life. His commitment to ecclesial, moral and political life remained unbroken throughout this period. While continuing to administer the college, offer leadership to the Congregational Union, write and deliver lectures, attend conferences and preach, he also continued to reflect on all these responsibilities *theologically*.

Those familiar with Forsyth's work have sought to express the significance of his theology by referring to him as a 'prophet'. The term points to the original and prevenient character of his dogmatics. As a biblical theologian, for instance, he was unwilling to engage in extended reflection upon the atonement apart from the entire life and teaching of Jesus. His approach was based upon the conviction that Jesus Christ is, according to the biblical narrative, the primary agent of his own self-disclosure: 'Christ interprets his own action ... It is the whole Biblical Christ that is the truly and deeply historical Christ.' He persisted in reflecting on the identity and significance of Jesus Christ both exegetically and dogmatically; he sought to maintain the centrality of the cross while not allowing it to distort his reading of the whole text of Scripture. Through this approach he was able to understand how the gospel can be said to have taken up concrete residence within history (i.e. 'realized eschatology').

Forsyth's commitment to the task of understanding reality *through* the concrete, present activity of the person Jesus Christ has led many to think of him as a 'Barthian before Barth'. Forsyth, like Barth, understands divine revelation in terms of the gracious and reconciling activity of God in Jesus Christ. But for Barth, the Chalcedonian definition is essential to the task of understanding and speaking faithfully of the full divine and human identity of the person Jesus. Forsyth, however, adjudges this ancient Christology to be far too Hellenic (i.e. ontological) and therefore of no contemporary significance or authority. In its place, he proposes a 'metaphysic' of conscience. Forsyth allows his dogmatic conclusions on the atonement to determine his view of the incarnation; Barth does not countenance their separation. Forsyth's ready dismissal of the Chalcedonian motif of a 'unit-in-difference' sharply distinguishes his Christology and doctrine of the triune God from those of Barth; many would regard them as less adequate.

On 11 November 1921, P. T. Forsyth died in his sleep, aged seventy-three. He was an uncommonly gifted individual, a moral and political activist, intellectually curious, artistic in disposition, lyrical in prose and evangelical in theological conviction and proclamation. His work is well deserving of considered reflection if for no other reason than this: Forsyth was a theologian who found his way to the end of modernity by the light of the gospel. *Per crucem Christi ad lucem.*

Bibliography

A. P. F. Sell (ed.), *P. T. Forsyth: Theologian for a New Millennium* (London: The United Reformed Church, 2000); T. Hart (ed.), *Justice the True and Only Mercy: Essays on the Life and Theology of Peter Taylor Forsyth* (Edinburgh: T. & T. Clark, 1995).

M. HUSBANDS

■ **FOXE, John** (1516–1587), martyrologist and moderate English Puritan, was born at Boston, Lincolnshire, and educated at Oxford, where he was a fellow at Magdalen College (1539–1545). He married Agnes Randall in February 1547.

Ordained deacon in 1550, Foxe held several positions as private tutor during the later years of Henry VIII (reigned 1509–1547) and the reign of the Protestant boy-king, Edward VI (1547–1553), but on the latter's death he went into exile to escape the re-Catholicization programme of the new queen, Mary, and its attendant persecution. He had in any case been dismissed, because of his Protestant convictions, by his employers, the Catholic Howard family.

It was this exile which was to be the making of Foxe's career. Already interested in Christian history as a result of his friendship with John Bale, the scurrilous Protestant pamphleteer and Edwardian Bishop of Ossory, Foxe turned his attention to accounts of Christian martyrdom, both past and present. He had also joined the English refugee congregation at Frankfurt-am-Main by late 1554, and participated in its celebrated 'troubles' the following year, in which he sided with John *Knox's more stern, austere faction, which removed itself to *Calvin's Geneva.

Foxe, however, moved instead to Basel, where he continued his writing. The following year he published an apocalyptic drama, *Christus Triumphans*, followed in 1557 by another Latin work, pleading for an end to the persecution of Protestants in England. Unlike almost all of his contemporaries, however, Foxe was opposed to persecution (or at least to lethal forms of it) *per se*, rather than merely to the suppression of his favoured brand of religion. He was later, in 1575, to plead with the Protestant Queen Elizabeth for the lives of Dutch Anabaptists whose views he abhorred, and at least one historian has argued that he had done the same (with equal lack of success) for Joan Bocher, who was burned by Edward VI's government in 1550. This opposition in itself is enough to mark out Foxe as highly unusual (for one who was not himself a religious radical) in the age in which he lived.

Despite Queen Mary's death in 1558 and the succession of her Protestant half-sister Elizabeth, Foxe did not immediately return to England. Instead, he remained in Basel to complete (at least for the time being) his martyrology, which was published there in Latin the following year as *Rerum in Ecclesia Gestarum*.

In the autumn of 1559 Foxe returned to England, and he was ordained by his friend Edmund Grindal (now Bishop of London) in 1560. His objection to wearing the surplice, the symbolic target (as representing 'the rags of popery') of the infant Puritan movement, denied him any hope of high ecclesiastical position. Though he was eventually given a stipend as prebend of Salisbury Cathedral, he spent the rest of his life in London, working on extensions of his *magnum opus*.

The public records were thrown open to Foxe, and all who had personal knowledge or experience of the Marian persecution of Protestants were encouraged to submit their documentation to him. The first English edition of the *Actes and Monuments*, generally known as the *Book of Martyrs*, appeared in 1563. It was a massive work, but the new edition of 1570 was larger still, running to two volumes of a combined 2,312 pages. The 1576 and 1583 editions contained yet more material. The last of these was the final version to be published during Foxe's own lifetime, and he died in 1587, being buried at St Giles, Cripplegate in London.

It is almost impossible to exaggerate the influence of Foxe's work upon the English national and religious consciousness during the following three or four centuries. In Stuart England only the English Bible was more widely read; only a few illiterate people were unfamiliar with its themes and stories or untouched by its outlook.

The *Book of Martyrs* provides a catalogue of Christian martyrdoms from the earliest times of Christianity to Foxe's own day. The first sections, therefore, provide well-known accounts of early church martyrdoms. In covering the Middle Ages, however, Foxe is at pains to stress the persecuting nature of the official (and of course Roman) church itself. In covering the late medieval period, his more specific polemical purpose becomes clear. Most of the martyrs are English Lollards, the followers of John *Wyclif (c. 1329–1384), who might legitimately be seen as Protestants *avant la lettre*.

The culmination of his work, however, is the exhaustive accounts of the Marian persecution of Protestants from 1553 to 1558. Foxe supplies countless narratives of the interrogations and correspondence of the prisoners, both those who were martyred and those who, for one reason or another, were spared. In this, he is both copious in factual detail and polemical in his comments. His arch-villain is Edmund Bonner (c. 1500–1569), the Bishop of London ('bloody Bonner', 'bite-shepe Bonner').

Foxe is generally accurate in his accounts of the lives and deaths of his heroes, however much he colours them. His propagandist sins against strict accuracy are not generally sins of commission, but of omission. He is known to have left out details of individual cases that might have been damaging to the cause of state-church Reformed Protestantism. In particular, some of the prisoners whose stories he tells were, in fact, religious radicals, distant fellow-travellers with Anabaptism; but Foxe omits to mention key details in such cases, and sometimes coyly supplies only a person's initials.

In addition to its vast general influence upon English society, *Actes and Monuments* injected four major elements into English popular thought. In the first place, generations of readers were left in no doubt that Roman Catholicism was inextricably bound up with sinister and vindictive religious persecution. The all-pervasive influence of the *Book of Martyrs* thus played its part in shaping the visceral anti-Catholicism of English life that endured down to the early twentieth century.

In the second place, Foxe supplies a specifically nationalist religious vision. God has never been without his Englishmen who will serve the cause of the gospel, come what may; Catholicism is a foreign creed; Elizabeth is a new Deborah (the Old Testament prophet), come to lead the people of England, who are, in a sense, the people of God. This vision, apart from giving English Protestantism a peculiarly nationalist slant, was to bear fruit in later centuries in 'British Israel' theories.

Thirdly, Foxe believed that Protestants would consummate world history in a successful crusade against the papal Antichrist. In so doing, he injected an element of apocalyptic instability into the normally very stable amillennialism of the Protestant state church. In the seventeenth century, postmillennialism emerged as a result of this instability and played an important part in the unfolding events of the civil war and interregnum.

Fourthly, Foxe's accounts of ordinary laymen and women taking action as plain Christians against a godless government had a further unintended effect. They provided inspiration for a wide range of religious dissidents, beginning with the Separatists, to break with the Church of England and found new, pure churches. In so doing, they saw themselves as emulating the people whom Foxe held up for admiration, the Marian martyrs.

Foxe was no great ecclesiastical statesman, nor a theologian. But, through his vastly influential book, he proved the fountainhead of ideas that had greater long-term effects than did those of many thinkers who are more widely recognized and acclaimed.

Bibliography
W. Haller, *Foxe's Book of Martyrs and the Elect Nation* (London: Ebenezer Baylis & Sons, 1967); J. F. Mozley, *John Foxe and His Book* (London: SPCK, 1940).

M. PEARSE

■ **FRANCKE, August Hermann** (1663–1727), leading German Pietist of the second generation, founded the Orphan House and other institutions at Halle/Saale now known as the *Franckesche Stiftungen*. He was born on 22 March 1663, the son of a Lübeck lawyer, Johannes Francke, and his wife Anna, the daughter of the Syndicus and later Bürgermeister of the town. From 1666 until his death in 1670 Johannes was a counsellor to Duke Ernst the Pious of Saxe-Gotha, so that August Hermann was introduced in early life to the atmosphere of Lutheran Reform orthodoxy and the problems of reconstruction after the Thirty Years War. Destined by his family for theology, August Hermann was educated at the Gotha gymnasium and, very briefly, the University of Erfurt, before going on to Kiel in 1679 to study under the church historian Christian Kortholt, an orthodox theologian of the Arndtian style, who stood close to *Spener. Francke's education was supported by the Schabbel foundation, an endowment for the training of theologians created by his mother's forebears and now administered by her brother. This endowment bound Francke not merely to strictness of life, but also to strict conformity to the Lutheran symbols. However, his pursuit of philological and historical equipment appeared to his uncle to breach the terms of the endowment, and in 1682 he withdrew the grant. This setback decisively influenced Francke's career. For two months he was educated free of charge in Hebrew by Esdras Edzardus, the celebrated Hamburg orientalist. Edzardus could not tolerate Francke's asceticism, quarrelled with him, and sent him back to his mother's house in Gotha. Francke, however, later based the philological training of the Halle theologians upon Edzardus's method.

The second consequence of the setback was that in 1684 Francke was compelled by financial necessity to go to Leipzig to give private instruction in Hebrew, living in the house of a theology professor, Adam Rechenberg, Spener's son-in-law. The following year he took the master's degree, which carried the right to give philological and exegetical lectures on the Bible. He and Paul Anton were encouraged by Carpzov, another theology professor, to start a Collegium Philobiblicum for young masters and to fill one of the gaps in a university theological curriculum that was confined to dogmatic and polemical theology. This proved popular, but caused a personal crisis for Francke which came to a head in 1687. Teaching theology seemed to create a conflict between seeking professional distinction and seeking to serve others. To promote the former his uncle restored his Schabbel

stipendium on the condition that Francke took instruction in biblical exegesis from Superintendent Sandhagen in Lüneburg. Here he underwent a vivid conversion experience. It began with anxiety as to whether the Christian claims for the authority of the Bible were any more reasonable than those of Jews for the Talmud and of Turks for the Koran. In a way that became normative for evangelicals, these doubts were resolved with the aid of *Luther's Preface to the Romans, with its doctrine that faith was a transforming work of God in humans; certainty was derived from an immediacy of experience which required no further evidence. Yet Francke's problem of intellectual uncertainty was not Luther's problem of forgiveness of sin, and while conversion resolved his dilemma of whether to serve others or scholarly reputation, it cut him off from the characteristic concerns of the Enlightenment. Francke's experience also led him to an elaborately structured view of conversion in which the penitential struggle (*Busskampf*) was central. This led *Zinzendorf cheerfully to claim to be (on Francke's principles) an unconverted person. It also stiffened in Francke a pugnacity that had been foreign to the character of Spener. Returning to Leipzig, he gave the class-meetings there a popular and anti-clerical character which angered the Orthodox clergy and faculty, and produced violent hostilities between them and those they dubbed 'Pietists' over much of north Germany.

Francke was expelled from both Leipzig and Erfurt, but through Spener, Brandenburg was now providing a haven for persecuted Pietists, not least in the new University of Halle/Saale, which it was building up in direct competition with the Saxon and Orthodox University of Leipzig. Francke's first appointment there, however, was to the squalid and drunken parish of Glaucha, outside the walls; his university theological chair did not come until 1698. In Glaucha he proved himself one of the great organizers of Christian history, but many of the institutions connected with his famous Orphan House sprang from failures in his parish policy. Finding ignorance rife, he gave poor children money for the town school; they took the money but did not appear at school. Starting a poor-school of his own, he gave them textbooks; they sold them. The solution, he decided, must be residential schools adapted to every order of society. By the time of his death some 180 teachers were instructing over 2,200 children, and the Orphan House was one of the biggest buildings in Europe. This vast effort was funded partly by state privileges with a cash value, partly by carefully calculated appeals to European charity (it was by this means that Francke's cause was taken up by the SPCK in England), partly through the profits of the press, which speedily became one of the most important in Germany, and most of all through the dispensary, which marketed public health kits for provinces and towns throughout Protestant Europe. The whole system was designed to promote 'true godliness' and 'Christian cleverness' through the cardinal virtues of love of truth, obedience and industry.

When Francke resigned his parish in 1713 it was a respectable but still not a godly place. In his *Great Essay* Francke projected a Utopia built on his methods; this also was beyond his grasp, but he created training schools that produced valuable citizens, bureaucrats, soldiers and clergy for the Prussian state. Moreover, Halle even after Francke's death was still acting as a valuable agent of Prussian foreign policy in succouring Protestant minorities oppressed by the Habsburgs in Silesia, Hungary and Bohemia. But even before Frederick the Great succeeded to the Prussian throne, Hallesian Pietism was never quite a Prussian state religion. Prussia had no interest whatever in the notable support Francke provided for the Danish mission on the Tranquebar coast, or that of his successors for the German migration to Pennsylvania, and was actively hostile to his other favourite cause, that of the Protestant interest in Russia.

It was the same story with Francke's reform of theological study at Halle. He put biblical exegesis of the original texts at the centre and did not scruple to propose improvements to Luther's translation. But because he sought to interpret the Old Testament Christologically, he had to assume that there was a mystical sense of the Scripture behind the literal sense and indeed that the general meaning of Scripture was accessible only to the regenerate. To such a point could study descend when practical piety was preferred to learned theology.

Nor was this the only price for Francke's intense inner-worldly asceticism. As early as 1694 he needed a helpmate to share his burdens, and he chose one in Anna Magdalena von Wurm (1670–1734), seven years younger than himself. To all appearances they made a happy and successful marriage. Yet in mid-life they were alienated from each other when Anna was tempted by spiritualism, on which view all Francke's institutions were models of an outward Christianity that betrayed the inner life of the spirit. He died, mourned by thousands, on 6 June 1727. His wife survived him.

Bibliography

G. Kramer, *August Hermann Francke: Ein Lebensbild*, 2 vols. (Halle/Saale: Francke-Buchhandlung, 1880–1882); E. Beyreuther, *August Hermann Francke. Zeuge des lebendigen Gottes* (Marburg: Francke-Buchhandlung, 1956); K. Deppermann in M. Greschat (ed.), *Gestalten der Kirchengeschichte* (Stuttgart: Kohlhammer, 1982), vol. 7, pp. 241–260; M. Brecht (ed.), *Geschichte des Pietismus* (Göttingen: Vandenhoek & Ruprecht, 1993–), vol. 1, pp. 440–539; K. Deppermann, *Der hallesche Pietismus und der preussische Staat unter Friedrich III (I)* (Göttingen: Vandenhoek & Ruprecht, 1961); C. Hinrichs, *Preussentum und Pietismus* (Göttingen: Vandenhoek & Ruprecht, 1971).

W. R. WARD

■ **FRY, Elizabeth** (1780–1845), Quaker prison reformer, was born at Earlham Hall near Norwich, England, on 21 May 1780, the daughter of John Gurney, a wealthy Quaker banker, and his wife Catherine Bell. Catherine Gurney was a descendant of the influential seventeenth-century Quaker minister and writer Robert Barclay, and the Gurney home was a centre for travelling Quaker ministers and elders from the British Isles and North America. One of Elizabeth's younger brothers was Joseph John *Gurney (1788–1847), one of the most influential Quaker ministers in England in the nineteenth century and her associate in her prison reform work. Her sister, Hannah Gurney (1783–1872), married Sir Thomas Fowell *Buxton, the evangelical reformer and Member of Parliament.

Although the Gurneys were related to many of the oldest and most influential families in the London yearly meeting of Friends, the Gurney children had an upbringing that was, by Quaker standards, 'worldly'. They did not wear the usual Quaker 'plain dress' or use the Quaker 'plain language' of 'thee' and 'thy'. They often joined in dances and parties at the homes of gentry neighbours. In 1798, however, Elizabeth came under the influence of William Savery, an American Quaker minister. Under his guidance, she had a conversion experience and also commited herself to observing Quaker peculiarities, cutting off most of her social contacts with 'the world'. On 19 August 1800, she married Joseph Fry, a member of a wealthy Bristol Quaker merchant family. After their wedding, they settled in London. Elizabeth entered into marriage only after a struggle; she feared that it would interfere with the increasingly powerful religious vocation she was experiencing. A few years later the couple moved to the Fry estate at Plashet in Essex.

Joseph and Elizabeth (Gurney) Fry had eleven children, born between 1801 and 1822. All but one lived to adulthood. By her own account, Elizabeth was not enthusiastic about the management of her household, preferring to give her energies to her ministry. Often her relations with her children were tense, as they rebelled against the strict Quaker regimen that she tried to impose on them. Only one remained a Friend.

In 1809 Elizabeth Fry began to speak in Quaker meetings for worship, and in 1811 she was recorded as a Quaker minister. In that capacity she travelled widely in England, and also made several journeys to the continent of Europe. Like her brother, she attempted in her preaching to move Quakerism in a more evangelical direction, emphasizing the atoning sacrifice of Christ, the necessity of a definite conversion experience and the authority of Scripture.

While still a teenager in Norwich before her marriage, Fry was moved to try to aid the poor, particularly the inmates of the house of correction there. She formed a school for the education of the children of the poor and was often engaged in visiting the sick and poor.

Fry's best-known work began in 1813 when, at the urging of fellow London Friend William Forster, she began to visit the female prisoners at Newgate, the largest and most notorious of the city's prisons. Conditions were abysmal. Over three hundred women, many accompanied by their children, were crowded into a few large cells, the innocent awaiting trial mixed with convicted felons. Although they were given no bedding and slept on the stone floors, a tap allowed them gin whenever they desired it. No employment was provided, so many spent their time in gambling, drinking and fighting. Fry was so appalled that she would not allow unmarried women to accompany her. 'The begging, swearing, gaming, fighting, singing, dancing, dressing-up in men's clothes were too bad to be described, so that we did not think it suitable to admit young persons with us,' she later told a Parliamentary inquiry. One of her companions remembered that 'the railing was crowded with half-naked women, struggling together with the most vociferous violence, and begging with the utmost vociferation. I felt as if I were going into a den of wild beasts'.

Between 1813 and 1816 Fry gathered information on the condition of women prisoners all over England and, with her brother-in-law Samuel Hoare, visited the Coldbath-Fields House of Correction. She returned to Newgate in 1816, and over the next few years transformed the women's prison. She began by making provisions for decent clothing for the prisoners. She was able to obtain the appointment of a matron to oversee them. She helped to open a school, to educate both illiterate prisoners and their children. An association was formed for this purpose and to introduce women prisoners 'to a knowledge of the Holy Scriptures, and to form in them, as much as possible, those habits of order, sobriety, and industry which may render them docile and peaceable whilst in prison, and respectable when they leave it'. Fry's greatest influence, however, may simply have been her presence and character, her simple Bible readings and messages of comfort and hope. 'Two days ago I saw the greatest curiosity in London, aye, and in England too,' wrote the American ambassador. 'I have seen Elizabeth Fry in Newgate, and I have witnessed there the miraculous effect of true christianity upon the most depraved of human beings. And yet the wretched outcasts have been tamed and subdued by the christian eloquence of Mrs. Fry.'

As the fame of Fry's work at Newgate grew, so did her influence all over Europe. She corresponded with the Russian empress dowager, and was received at the courts of France and Prussia. She helped to reform conditions in the penal settlements of New South Wales. She became involved in other charities, such as those providing shelters and soup kitchens for the homeless. Her husband's bankruptcy in 1828, however, reduced her resources for such work, although not her reputation. She died at Ramsgate on 12 October 1845.

To her contemporaries, and for most Quakers and evangelicals since, Elizabeth Fry was a saintly figure who combined earnest piety with a commitment to confronting the evils of her society. It is certainly possible to see in her work certain limitations. Her desire to separate the 'worthy' from the 'unworthy' poor, and to instill 'order, sobriety, and industry', may be judged harshly today. For hundreds of prisoners, however, Elizabeth Fry's ministry was a transforming experience.

Bibliography

K. Fry and E. Creswell, *Memoir of the Life of Elizabeth Fry, with Extracts from Her Journal and Letters*, 2 vols. (London: Charles Gilpin, 1847); J. Rose, *Elizabeth Fry* (London: Macmillan, 1980); A. Van Drenth and F. De Haan, *The Rise of Caring Power: Elizabeth Fry and Josephine Butler in Britain and the Netherlands* (Amsterdam: Amsterdam University Press, 1999).

T. D. HAMM

■ **FULLER, Andrew** (1754–1815), Particular Baptist theologian and minister, was born on 6 February 1754, at Wicken, Cambridgeshire. His parents, Robert Fuller and Philippa Gunton, rented and worked a succession of dairy farms. Particular Baptists by conviction, both of his parents had been born into Nonconformist homes. His maternal grandmother, Philippa Stevenson, for instance, was among the founding members of the Particular Baptist Church at Soham, Cambridgeshire, where Fuller would later have his first pastorate.

When Fuller was seven, his parents moved to the village of Soham, about two and a half miles from Wicken. Once settled in Soham, they joined themselves to the Particular Baptist Church in the village. The pastor of this small congregation was John Eve, who had been a sieve maker before becoming pastor of the church in 1752. Eve was a High Calvinist, that is, according to Fuller, one who 'had little or nothing to say to the unconverted'. The sovereignty of God in salvation was so prominent a theme in English High Calvinist circles that it seriously hampered effective evangelism.

Nevertheless, in the late 1760s Fuller began to experience a strong conviction of sin, which issued in his conversion in November 1769. He was baptized in April 1770 and joined the Soham church. Over the course of the next few years, it became very evident to the church that Fuller possessed definite ministerial gifts. Eve left the church in 1771 for another pastorate. Fuller, who was self-taught in theology and who had been preaching in the church for a couple of years, was formally inducted as pastor on 3 May 1775. The church consisted of forty-seven members and met for worship in a rented barn.

The year following Fuller's induction as pastor he married his first wife, Sarah Gardiner (d. 1792), who was a member of the Soham church. The couple had eleven children, of whom eight died in infancy or in early childhood.

Fuller's pastorate at Soham, which lasted until 1782, when he became pastor of the Baptist church in Kettering, Northamptonshire, was a decisive period for the shaping of his theological outlook. It was during these seven years that he began a lifelong study of the works of the New England divine Jonathan *Edwards, his chief theological mentor after the biblical writers. It was also in this period of time that he made the acquaintance of Robert Hall, Sr, John *Ryland and John Sutcliff, who would later become his closest ministerial friends and colleagues. Finally, it was during his pastorate at Soham that Fuller decisively rejected High Calvinism and drew up a defence of his own theological position in *The Gospel Worthy of All Acceptation*, though the first edition of this book was not published until 1785.

Due to the fact that John Eve's preaching was essentially the only homiletical model Fuller had ever had, he initially preached like Eve and did not urge the unconverted to come to Christ. Increasingly, though, he was dissatisfied with High Calvinist reasoning and its perspective on evangelism. He began to sense that his 'preaching was anti-scriptural and defective in many respects'. Robert Hall, pastor of the Particular Baptist Church in Arnesby, Leicestershire, suggested that he read Jonathan Edwards' classic work on divine sovereignty and human responsibility, *A Careful and Strict Enquiry Into the Modern Prevailing Notions of the Freedom of Will* (1754). Hall was convinced that this work would help to clarify some of Fuller's thinking about the power of sinful men and women to obey God.

Fuller also immersed himself in the works of the Baptist author from the previous century, John *Bunyan, and *A Body of Doctrinal Divinity* by John *Gill, the doyen of eighteenth-century Particular Baptist theologians. Fuller found much that was helpful in Gill's systematic work but was deeply troubled by the evident differences between Gill and Bunyan. Both were ardent Calvinists, but whereas Bunyan recommended 'the free offer of salvation to sinners without distinction', Gill did not. Initially Fuller wrongly concluded that though Bunyan was 'a great and good man', he was not as clear as Gill regarding the gospel.

However, as Fuller studied the writings of other sixteenth- and seventeenth-century authors, in particular those of the Puritan theologian John *Owen, he noted that they too 'dealt ... in free invitations to sinners to come to Christ and be saved'. In other words, Fuller discerned that with regard to preaching there was a definite difference not only between Bunyan and Gill, but more broadly between sixteenth- and seventeenth-century Calvinism and that of the early eighteenth century. This then was the context in which *The Gospel Worthy of All Acceptation* was written.

A preliminary draft of the work was written by 1778. In what was roughly its final form it was completed by 1781. Two editions of the work were published in Fuller's lifetime. The first edition, published in Northampton in 1785, was subtitled *The Obligations of Men Fully to Credit, and Cordially to Approve, Whatever God Makes Known, Wherein is Considered the Nature of Faith in Christ, and the Duty of Those where the Gospel Comes in that Matter*. The second edition, which appeared in 1801, was more simply subtitled *The Duty of Sinners to Believe in Jesus Christ*, a title that well expressed the overall theme of the book. There were substantial differences between the first and second editions, which Fuller freely admitted and which primarily related to the doctrine of particular redemption. The work's major theme remained unaltered, however: 'faith in Christ is the duty of all men who hear, or have opportunity to hear, the gospel'. This epoch-making book sought to be faithful to the central emphases of historic Calvinism while at the same time attempting to leave preachers with no alternative but to drive home to their hearers the universal obligations of repentance and faith.

The book was a key factor in determining the shape of Fuller's ministry in the years to come. For instance, it led directly to his wholehearted involvement in the formation of the Baptist Missionary Society in October 1792 and the subsequent sending of the Society's most famous missionary, William *Carey, to India in 1793. Fuller also served as secretary of the society until his death in 1815. The work of the mission consumed an enormous amount of Fuller's time as he regularly toured the country, representing the mission and raising funds. On average he was away from home for three months of the year. Between 1798 and 1813, moreover, he made five lengthy trips to Scotland for the mission as well as undertaking journeys to Wales and Ireland (1804). He also carried on an extensive correspondence on the mission's behalf.

In 1813 a major threat to the mission's existence in India arose when the charter of the East India Company, which managed British interests and possessions in India, came before Parliament for renewal. Those who were opposed to the presence of the Baptist missionaries in India sought to use this charter to prevent the legal toleration of these missionaries in Bengal. Fuller succeeded in having a clause inserted in the charter that gave the Baptist Mission, and other missions, legal standing.

Fuller's commitment to the Baptist Missionary Society was rooted not only in his missionary theology but also in his deep friendship with Carey. Fuller later compared the sending of Carey to India as his lowering into a deep gold-mine. Fuller and his close friends Sutcliff and Ryland had pledged themselves to 'hold the ropes' as long as Carey lived.

However, The Gospel Worthy of All Acceptation also involved Fuller in much unwanted controversy. Not long after the publication of the book, Fuller was assailed in print by two London High Calvinists, the Baptist pastors William Button and John Martin. While writing a response to Button, Fuller found himself under attack by a representative of the other end of the theological spectrum, namely the General (i.e. Arminian) Baptist Dan Taylor (1738–1816). Later, Fuller was to describe his own theological position, which some dubbed 'Fullerism', as 'strict Calvinism'. He sought to differentiate it from High Calvinism, which was 'more Calvinistic than *Calvin' and 'bordering on Antinomianism', and from moderate Calvinism, which was essentially the theological perspective of the Puritan Richard *Baxter (1615–1691) and which Fuller considered as 'half Arminian'. Fuller reckoned strict Calvinism to be 'the system of Calvin'.

The critical role played by Fuller in this controversy did not preclude his engaging in other vital areas of theological debate. In 1793 he issued an extensive refutation of the Socinianism of Joseph Priestley, The Calvinistic and Socinian Systems Examined and Compared, as to their Moral Tendency. Due to the vigorous campaigning of Priestley, Socinianism, which denied the Trinity and the deity of Christ, had become the leading form of heterodoxy within English Dissent in the last quarter of the eighteenth century. Fuller's attack on Socinianism well displays the Christocentric nature of eighteenth-century evangelical thought. Fuller ably argued that the early church made the divine dignity and glory of Christ's person 'their darling theme'.

In 1800 Fuller published The Gospel Its Own Witness, the definitive eighteenth-century Baptist response to deism, in particular that of the popularizer Thomas Paine. This work was one of the most popular of Fuller's books, going through three editions by 1802 and being reprinted a number of times in the next thirty years. William *Wilberforce, who admired Fuller as a theologian and who once graphically described him as 'the very picture of a blacksmith', considered it to be the most important of all Fuller's writings. The work has two parts. In the first, Fuller compares and contrasts the moral effects of Christianity with those of deism. The second part of the book aims to demonstrate the divine origin of Christianity from the general consistency of the Scriptures.

Yet another vital controversy in which Fuller engaged was that with the Sandemanians, the followers of Robert Sandeman, who distinguished themselves from other eighteenth-century evangelicals by a predominantly intellectualist view of faith. They became known for their cardinal theological tenet that saving faith is 'bare belief of the bare truth'. In a genuine desire to exalt the utter freeness of God's salvation, Sandeman had sought to remove any vestige of human reasoning, willing or desiring in the matter of saving faith.

In his Strictures on Sandemanianism (1810) Fuller makes two major points. First, if faith does concern only the mind, then there is no way of distinguishing genuine Christianity from nominal Christianity. A nominal Christian mentally assents to the truths of Christianity, but those truths do not grip the heart and reorient his or her affections. Secondly, knowledge of Christ is a distinct type of knowledge, involving far more than knowing certain things about him, such as the fact of his virgin birth or the details of his crucifixion. It involves a desire for fellowship with him and a delight in his presence.

But Fuller was far more than an apologist and mission secretary; he also exercised a significant pastoral ministry at Kettering. During his thirty-three years there, from 1782 to 1815, the membership of the church nearly doubled (from 88 to 174) and the number of 'hearers' was often over a thousand, necessitating several additions to the church building. Fuller's vast correspondence (today housed in the Angus Library at Regent's Park College in Oxford) reveals that Fuller was first and foremost a pastor.

And though he did not always succeed, he constantly sought to ensure that his many other responsibilities did not encroach upon those related to the pastorate.

Two documents well display Fuller's pastoral heart. After he died, there was found among his possessions a small book entitled 'Families who attend at the Meeting, August, 1788'. In it he wrote: 'A Review of these may assist me in praying and preaching'. Then, among his letters there is one dated 8 February 1812, which was written to a wayward member of his church. In it Fuller lays bare his pastor's heart when he writes: 'When a parent loses ... a child nothing but the recovery of that child can heal the wound. If he could have many other children, that would not do it ... Thus it is with me towards you. Nothing but your return to God and the Church can heal the wound.'

In addition to his apologetic works, Fuller also published two series of expository sermons, one on Genesis (1806) and one on Revelation (1815), a good number of sermons and evangelistic tracts, and numerous essays and articles on a wide variety of theological topics, which appeared in various journals. When his second wife, Ann Coles, whom Fuller had married in 1794, once told her husband that he allowed himself no time for recreation, Fuller answered, 'O no: all my recreation is a change of work.'

One other of Fuller's literary works deserves mention. His *Memoirs of the Rev. Samuel Pearce* (1800) recount the life of his close friend, Samuel Pearce of Birmingham. In some ways modelled after Jonathan Edwards' life of David *Brainerd, it recounted the life of one whom Fuller regarded as a model of evangelical spirituality. Through the medium of Fuller's book, Pearce's extraordinary passion for Christ, which led to his being known as the 'seraphic Pearce' by contemporaries, and his zeal for missions had a powerful impact on his generation.

Fuller had remarkable reserves of physical and mental energy, which allowed him to accomplish all that he did. But it was not without cost to his body. What he called a 'paralytic stroke' in 1793 left him rarely free of severe headaches for the rest of his life. And in his last fifteen years he was rarely well. Taken ill in September 1814, his health began to decline seriously. By the spring of the following year he was dying. He preached for the last time at Kettering on 2 April 1815 and died on 7 May. He was sixty-two.

Fuller's funeral was attended by a crowd of perhaps 2,000 people. At Fuller's request, his old friend John Ryland preached the funeral sermon. Based on Romans 8:10, it included a brief account of Fuller's final days and a declaration made by Fuller in his last letter to Ryland. 'I have preached and written much against the abuse of the doctrine of grace,' Fuller wrote, 'but that doctrine is all my salvation and all my desire. I have no other hope than from salvation by mere sovereign, efficacious grace through the atonement of my Lord and Saviour.'

The importance of Fuller's theological achievements was noted during his life and after his death. The Colleges of New Jersey (1798) and Yale (1805) awarded him DDs, both of which he declined to accept. Charles Haddon *Spurgeon did not hesitate to describe Fuller as 'the greatest theologian' of his century, while A. H. Newman noted that 'his influence on American Baptists' was 'incalculable'. Without a doubt, he was the greatest theologian of the late eighteenth-century transatlantic Baptist community.

Bibliography

E. F. Clipsham, 'Andrew Fuller and Fullerism: A Study in Evangelical Calvinism', *The Baptist Quarterly*, 20 (1963–1964), pp. 99–114, 146–154, 214–225, 268–276; P. Morden, 'Andrew Fuller: A study in evangelical Calvinism' (MPhil. thesis, Spurgeon's College, London, 2001); J. Ryland, Jr, *The Work of Faith, the Labour of Love, and the Patience of Hope, illustrated in the Life and Death of the Rev. Andrew Fuller* (London: Button & Son, ²1818).

M. A. G. HAYKIN

■ **FULLER, Charles Edward** (1887–1968), radio evangelist, was a pioneer in religious broadcasting, hosting what was for a number of years the only national fundamentalist religious programme. Millions listened weekly to his 'Old Fashioned Revival Hour', giving it better ratings than virtually every secular programme on the air. Fuller wielded great influence by mid-century, helping other evangelical ministries and even creating his own seminary, actions that continue to have relevance today.

Fuller was born in Los Angeles and never strayed far from, nor stayed long outside, his beloved southern California. Raised in the orange groves that were coming to characterize the region, he majored in chemistry at Pomona College in order to work in the orange industry, graduating in 1910. The following year he married Grace Peyton, who became his partner and advisor in his lifelong work. In 1916, upon visiting the Church of the Open Door in downtown Los Angeles to hear boxer-turned-preacher Paul *Rader of Chicago, Fuller committed himself to fundamentalist Protestantism, seeing it as the heir to the highly religious background in which he had been raised. Leaving his lucrative position as a packing-house manager, he attended the Bible Institute of Los Angeles, graduating in 1921. Within four years he had helped to start and was leading an independent, non-denominational church in Placentia, California, and occasionally preaching on the institute's radio station.

By the late 1920s Fuller had realized the evangelistic potential of radio, having linked his services to a local station via telephone lines. Expanding his radio ministry, he began broadcasting several programmes from stations around Los Angeles and Orange Counties. Unhappy with a minister so distracted from his duties by radio work, his church forced him to resign in 1932. He flung himself completely into radio, just as the Great Depression reached its peak. Only with the faithful support of local fundamentalists did his 'Gospel Broadcasting Association' survive, broadcasting as many as seven separate shows.

Fuller's break came in 1936, when he joined the fledgling Mutual Broadcasting System with their skeleton network of fourteen stations. Forced to grow with the network or risk losing its prime Sunday air time, Fuller's 'Old Fashioned Revival Hour' and 'Pilgrims' Hour' (a teaching programme that ran until 1947) paid for themselves each week, as thousands of listeners across the country sent money, often coins taped to letters of testimony. Within two years, the programme was being broadcast on 128 stations and heard by an estimated five million people.

As Americans became increasingly concerned with the war in Europe, Fuller's programme offered particularly soothing entertainment. Drawing on local Hollywood talent, he put together a show in which the first thirty minutes was dedicated to music, using either a choir or a men's quartet to sing many of the old revivalist standards, often stylized to appeal to a new generation of evangelicals. And although he preached a gospel that identified sin and hell as the fate of depraved humanity, his was not the usual style of the sawdust trail. Rather, both Charles and Grace (who read listeners' letters on the weekly programme) employed a genteel, grandparently manner that attracted rather than repelled listeners.

Their tone bore handsome dividends in terms of ratings. By 1944 the programme was being broadcast on 575 stations worldwide, with over twenty million listeners. Fuller adapted the show's religious ritual to appeal to frightened soldiers overseas and their concerned families at home. Receiving nearly ten thousand letters each week, many from soldiers abroad, the Fullers made their programme a conduit for religious communication among family members, as Grace Fuller read letters from servicemen to their wives, parents and children, and letters from those at home whose brothers, sons and fathers were listening overseas on short-wave radio. Extant letters indicate that the programme appealed to conservative Protestants of all kinds (fundamentalists, Pentecostals, mainstream conservatives) and across ethnic and racial divides.

All was not easy for Fuller, however, during this period of growth. He endured scathing attacks from mainstream church leaders, who believed that conservative Protestant preachers, who were already ineligible to receive the free 'sustaining' radio time that mainstream churches enjoyed, should not be allowed to buy time on networks. Today the principle of free speech could be invoked against such opposition, but in wartime America fears abounded regarding anything seen as not the norm. Using the powerful Federal Council of Churches to pressure the major networks, mainstream Protestants, Catholics and Jews hoped to push Fuller off the airwaves. Conservatives rallied around the programme. The controversy became one impetus for creating the National Association of Evangelicals in 1943, in the hope that it would become an effective lobby in Washington, DC, and save Fuller's and others' programmes. It was not enough. Mutual Broadcasting dropped Fuller from their network in September 1944, despite the fact that one-eighth of their income came from the Gospel Broadcasting Association.

From the other side, Fuller faced fierce attacks from ultra-right-wing fundamentalists for his failure to advocate separatism. Indeed, Fuller believed strongly that conservatives needed to put aside differences and work with all like-minded Christians, even staying in mainstream denominations if necessary to effect change from within. Carl *McIntire became the leading voice of opposition to Fuller among the conservatives, publishing diatribes against him and protesting against his revival meetings in various cities.

Despite major setbacks, Fuller pressed on with his work. He reverted to his original policy of syndicating his programme, a now common practice he had helped to develop during the 1930s before joining Mutual. During the next five years he signed contracts with hundreds of local stations, some with powerful short-wave transmitters, in order to keep his global ministry alive. In 1949 he signed for ABC in order to regain his live programme from Long Beach, California, and he stayed with that network until 1963. Meanwhile, he was among the first preachers to experiment with television. Having broadcast briefly to the few sets in Los Angeles in 1941, Fuller agreed in 1950 to produce a television version of his immensely popular radio programme for ABC. Despite its popularity, Fuller decided not to renew the contract for a second year, as the programme was costly, and television stole from him his winning spontaneity that made him a religious radio superstar.

Meanwhile, Fuller worked with Harold John *Ockenga, the first president of the National Association of Evangelicals and pastor of Boston's famed Park Street Church, to found Fuller Theological Seminary in Pasadena, California. It was a compromise between the two leaders, one popular, the other intellectual. Fuller had long dreamed of a training institute for evangelists; Ockenga hoped for an evangelical answer to Princeton.

Using Fuller's fame and what was left of his father's fortune (the seminary is named after Henry Fuller), Ockenga hired some of the top evangelical scholars in the world. And although the school inclined towards the more academic vision of Ockenga, Fuller was pleased to see so many graduates enter the pulpit or travel overseas as missionaries. Fuller exhorted each class with the words of Paul, 'Do the work of an evangelist!'

Throughout the 1950s, Charles E. Fuller remained the elder statesman for a movement that was transforming itself from 'non-separating fundamentalism' to 'the New Evangelicalism'. He acted as mentor to Billy *Graham on numerous occasions during the latter's rise to prominence, and lent his substantial support to such institutions as the Navigators, New Life, Wycliffe Bible Translators and Youth for Christ. Finally, in 1958, the seventy-year-old Fuller ended the live, hour-long programme despite its continued popularity. Although he searched for someone to replace him, he could never release the reins to another. The taped half-hour version of the programme went off the air in 1968 on Fuller's death. At that time it still had an audience in the millions, being broadcast on over five hundred stations worldwide.

Although the memory of Charles E. Fuller seems to have faded, his influence on the evangelicalism of the twentieth-century was immense. One national news magazine recognized his importance at his death, calling him the greatest American evangelist 'between the two Billy boys', *Sunday and Graham. Over the years, approximately half a million people wrote to him describing conversions that resulted from listening to his programme. But his significance went far beyond that of an evangelist. He laid the foundation for today's numerous religious radio and television programmes, developing the contemporary practice of syndication, using religious entertainment to attract listeners, and preaching a broad message to consolidate his audience rather than dividing it. Moreover, Fuller Seminary is now the largest non-denominational seminary in the hemisphere, and boasts nearly 15,000 graduates worldwide. Many of the evangelical leaders of the late twentieth century studied under Fuller, including Billy Graham, Jerry *Falwell, Bill *Bright and Jack Chick.

Bibliography
D. E. Fuller, *Give the Winds a Mighty Voice: The Story of Charles E. Fuller* (Waco: Word Books Publishers, 1972); J. Carpenter, *Revive Us Again: The Reawakening of American Fundamentalism* (New York: Oxford University Press, 1997); G. Marsden, *Reforming Fundamentalism: Fuller Seminary and the New Evangelicalism* (Grand Rapids: Eerdmans, 1987); P. Goff, 'We Have Heard the Joyful Sound: Charles E. Fuller's Radio Broadcast and the Rise of Modern Evangelicalism', *Religion and American Culture: A Journal of Interpretation*, 9:1 (Winter, 1999), pp. 67–96.

P. GOFF

■ **FYFE, Robert Alexander** (1816–1878), Baptist pastor, educator and denominational leader, was born in Laprairie, Lower Canada on 20 October 1816. Robert Fyfe was raised in a solidly Calvinist home, converted in his late teens and baptized in 1835 by John Gilmour, a leading Montreal Baptist. After a year of preparatory studies in the Baptist academy in Hamilton, New York, Fyfe enrolled in the new Canada Baptist College, Montreal. A series of revivals in the Ottawa Valley during his school years profoundly shaped his religious values, and placed him within a milieu greatly influenced by the Haldanes. One such revival, in Osgoode in 1839, resulted in his call to the ministry and, subsequently, to his enrolment in Newton Theological Institute in Massachusetts. Fyfe struggled with doubts, however, and his uncertainty led to a profound spiritual crisis. The crisis proved to be a powerful experience that reaffirmed his call and led him back that summer to the Ottawa Valley as an itinerant evangelist. Though the rest of his life's work would be primarily in institutional leadership, Fyfe always maintained that his greatest loves were evangelistic preaching and encouraging churches.

After graduation in 1842, Fyfe returned to Canada and organized a church in Perth, Canada West. He served as pastor for a year, left, and returned in 1848–1849. Fyfe was also the pastor who firmly established a Baptist presence in Toronto. He was twice pastor of what would later become Jarvis Street Baptist Church, first when it was March Street Church (1844–1848), and later when it was Bond Street Church (1855–1860).

Deeply committed to uniting the disparate Baptist groups in Canada, Fyfe spent six years in self-imposed exile in the United States, frustrated over their continuing theological battles. Although he personally favoured closed communion, he refused to be drawn into the disputes over communion. Mission was his priority. He served a church in Warren, Rhode Island from 1848 to 1853, followed by one in Milwaukee, Wisconsin, in 1854–1855. While in Wisconsin, Fyfe helped the local Baptist Association to resolve a controversy over the issue of slavery, served on the board of the Wisconsin Baptist Education Society and chaired a committee for the American Baptist Missionary Union. He was also appointed in 1854 as the first president of Wayland University, where he developed a productive, lifelong friendship with the educator Francis Wayland. Fyfe returned to Canada only in 1855, when the theological strife seemed to be subsiding.

Remembered primarily as an educator, Fyfe began his teaching career in 1843–1844 as interim principal of Canada Baptist College, Montreal. He later served as the guiding force behind the Canadian Literary Institute, Woodstock, acting as president from its opening in 1860 until his death. This was a much more realistic educational project, as it met the real needs of the Baptist community. Rather than attempting to be a college, it was from its inception a co-educational preparatory school with a theology department. Here Fyfe did much of the teaching and fundraising. Although the fundraising was stressful, he was glad of the opportunity it afforded to encourage the churches and enlarge their vision. Fyfe also sat on the senate of the University of Toronto from 1863 until his death, where he continued to agitate for university reform, arguing especially for fairer treatment of institutions such as his own.

In addition to his work in education, Fyfe was also involved in political agitation and played a key role in drawing Baptists out of their narrow isolationism. First he defended his legal right to perform marriages; later he championed such political causes as non-sectarian universities and state schools and attacked the privileges of the Church of

England, particularly its control of King's College, Toronto. Fyfe's work slowly brought Baptists into the public arena.

Fyfe also possessed a tremendous sense of mission; he led outreach into western Canada and was instrumental in the formation in 1870 of the Regular Baptist Foreign Missionary Society of Canada. He recognized the need for a denominational paper to promote this vision. So in 1859 he formed a group that assumed control of *The Christian Messenger* (subsequently renamed *The Canadian Baptist*). He served briefly as its editor until 1862 and remained a regular contributor.

In recognition of Fyfe's widespread contribution to the Baptist cause, he was awarded an honorary DD in 1858 from his alma mater, Madison College, Hamilton, New York. He died in Woodstock, Ontario on 29 August 1878.

Bibliography

T. T. Gibson, *Robert Alexander Fyfe* (Burlington: Welch Publishing Co. Inc., 1988); J. A. Wells, *Life and Labours of Robert Alexander Fyfe, D.D.* (Toronto: W. J. Gage & Company, 1885).

D. A. GOERTZ

■ **GAEBELEIN, Arno Clemens** (1861–1945), premillennialist prophecy writer, was born on 27 August 1861 in Thuringia, Germany. He had what he described as a 'definite experience' of conversion at the age of twelve, and during his early teenage years he often felt 'a longing to become a foreign missionary, to preach the Gospel to those who know it not'. At the age of eighteen he emigrated to the United States, both to avoid military conscription and to satisfy his youthful wanderlust. Within months of his arrival, on 31 October 1879 in Lawrence, Massachusetts, Gaebelein found himself profoundly moved while reading the New Testament, causing him to surrender his life anew to Christ's work and dedicate himself to a life of ministry. Gaebelein soon met other fervent German Christians, who introduced him to the German Methodist Episcopal Church, of which he became a member in 1880. Within a year Gaebelein was not only studying for the ministry but also serving as a supply pastor for a Methodist mission in Bridgeport,

Connecticut. After doubling the size of that congregation, Gaebelein pastored another in Baltimore, Maryland (1882–1884), where his ministry also prospered. In 1884, after receiving his ordination as a deacon, Gaebelein was transferred to a church in Harlem, New York, where he met and married Emma Grimm, the daughter of a respected Methodist minister.

Gaebelein was ordained as an elder in the Methodist Episcopal Church in 1886, and a year later he was assigned to pastor a large German Methodist church in Hoboken, New Jersey. This pastorate significantly altered the course of Gaebelein's ministry. On the encouragement of a converted Jew within his new congregation, Gaebelein began to focus his attention on the evangelization of Jewish immigrants. Gaebelein had shown a facility with Semitic languages in his ministerial training, so he was soon able to preach in Hebrew. Gaebelein claimed that learning Yiddish likewise presented few problems: 'I literally massacred my good classical German and acquired the "Yiddish".' Gaebelein began preaching regularly at a Hebrew Christian Mission in New York and soon declared himself convinced 'that the Lord wanted me to turn aside from the regular ministry and devote myself to work among God's ancient people'. The messianic expectations of the orthodox Jews who gathered to hear him preach led Gaebelein to re-examine his views on prophecy and eschatology. After earnestly searching the Scriptures, Gaebelein became convinced that he had been guilty of 'spiritualizing' prophetic references to Israel by interpreting them as referring to the church rather than to the Jewish people. In consequence, Gaebelein rejected the postmillennialism that was then typical of evangelicals and became a convinced premillennialist and an ardent believer in the eventual restoration of the nation of Israel.

In 1891 Gaebelein asked the bishop of the East Conference of the Methodist Episcopal Church to allow him to devote himself fully to preaching the gospel among the Jews of New York. This permission was granted, and Gaebelein moved to New York's East Side with his wife and two young sons, where he began preaching services aimed at Jews every Saturday at the Allen Street Memorial Methodist Episcopal Church. These services were often attended by more than a thousand people, who were generally contentious and unreceptive to Gaebelein's message. Even so, there was a strong demand for materials in Yiddish and Hebrew, so Gaebelein wrote more than a dozen tracts in these languages, and in 1893 he began to produce a free Yiddish periodical, *Tiqweth Israel – The Hope of Israel Monthly*, that proved so popular that circulation increased from 5,000 to 15,000 within a year. The desperate social conditions experienced by many Jewish immigrants from Russia and Eastern Europe appeared to Gaebelein to offer 'a grand opportunity to show them the practical side of Christianity', and he opened a dispensary in his church that made food available to poor families. By 1893 Gaebelein's ministry had grown to such an extent that the New York City Church Extension and Missionary Society of the Methodist Church was no longer able to provide adequate financial support for it, so he was allowed to seek support beyond the confines of the denomination, using a new name, 'The Hope of Israel Movement'. In 1897 Gaebelein formally made the ministry non-denominational by refusing further support from the Methodist City Mission.

In July 1894 Gaebelein began publishing *Our Hope*, an English-language magazine directed at Christians, focusing on biblical prophecy. *Our Hope* soon became influential among the emerging fundamentalist movement. The magazine helped to shape fundamentalist attitudes towards Jews by avidly supporting Zionism, by maintaining that 'Israel is the key to all prophecy as well as to all history', and by regularly rebuking the church for its triumphalist stance with regard to the Jewish people. The magazine also anticipated the later Messianic Jewish movement by initially insisting that Jewish converts should observe the Mosaic law, an opinion that Gaebelein later renounced under the influence of other premillennialists in 1899. *Our Hope* continued to be published for a dozen years after Gaebelein's death until it merged with *Eternity* magazine in January 1958.

Publishing *Our Hope* brought Gaebelein into the orbit of like-minded fundamentalist teachers of biblical prophecy, and he soon became a regular and popular speaker on the fundamentalist prophecy conference circuit. By the turn of the century, Gaebelein had all but abandoned his New York mission to Jews in order to attend to his new non-denominational national ministry among fundamentalists, which he called his 'new commission'. *Our Hope* reflected this change by focusing more on expository Bible studies and prophecy than on Jewish missions.

In 1899 Gaebelein severed all connections to his Methodist denomination after its leaders refused to censure advocates of biblical criticism and modernism within the denomination. While many of his fundamentalist colleagues warned Gaebelein that an unaffiliated minister would not receive a hearing, this move in fact broadened his base, and he spent the rest of his life preaching among not only Methodist but also Presbyterian, Congregationalist, Baptist, Reformed, Lutheran, Brethren, Mennonite and Nazarene congregations throughout the United States and Canada.

The famed dispensationalist C. I. *Scofield told Gaebelein, 'I sit at your feet when it comes to prophecy', and he asked Gaebelein to interpret prophecy for the 1909 Scofield Reference Bible, the authoritative text for premillennial dispensationalists. In 1914 Gaebelein contributed the main prophetic essay to *The Fundamentals*, the series of articles that earned fundamentalism its name. Gaebelein avidly promoted the Stony Brook School for Boys, a Christian preparatory school that was founded in 1922 by his son Frank, who also served as an associate editor of *Our Hope*. In 1924 Gaebelein helped Lewis S. *Chafer found the Evangelical Theological College in Dallas, which later became Dallas Theological Seminary. He mounted an unsuccessful attempt in 1925 to prevent the union of the Canadian Presbyterian, Methodist and Congregational denominations into the United Church of Canada. He was outspoken in his opposition to both Communism and Nazism.

Gaebelein authored numerous books, the great majority being expositions of biblical books based on materials that had been previously published in *Our Hope*. Gaebelein considered his most significant work to be his nine-volume *Annotated Bible* (1912–1922), which consisted of a dispensational interpretation of the entire Bible that ran to more than 3,000 pages. Gaebelein died of heart failure on Christmas Day 1945 at the age of eighty-five.

Bibliography

A. C. Gaebelein, *Half a Century: The Auto-biography of a Servant* (New York: publication office of *Our Hope*, 1930); D. A. Rausch, *Arno C. Gaebelein, 1861–1945: Irenic Fundamentalist and Scholar*, Studies in American Religion, vol. 10 (Lewiston: Edwin Mellen Press, 1983).

D. K. LARSEN

■ **GARRETTSON, Freeborn** (1752–1827), Methodist preacher and missionary, was born to a prominent Church of England family in Harford County, Maryland. His parents were third generation English settlers who had acquired considerable farm land, a store and slaves. His mother died when he was ten, and his father in 1773, leaving him heir to the family holdings. Garrettson's education was above average for the time and place. He stayed in school until the age of seventeen, studying mathematics, bookkeeping, surveying and astronomy.

As a young man Garrettson attended the Church of England, but his faith was first actively awakened under the preaching of a number of early Methodist preachers, including Robert Strawbridge, a fiery Methodist local preacher from Ireland, and Francis *Asbury, who came to America in 1771. Garrettson attended both his parish church and Methodist preaching for about three years before experiencing conversion in June 1775. After joining the Methodists, Garrettson freed his slaves and preached and wrote against slavery for the rest of his life.

Garrettson began his career as a Methodist itinerant preacher in 1775. A fervent preacher, he soon became one of Asbury's most trusted assistants, travelling 100,000 miles between 1776 and 1793. During the American Revolution, Garrettson, like all Methodist preachers, was suspected of loyalist sympathies. He refused to bear arms or to take an oath of allegiance as a matter of conscience. As a result, between 1778 and 1780 he was beaten, nearly shot, threatened with hanging and thrown into jail. Yet Garrettson continued to travel and preach in Maryland, Virginia and Delaware. In preparation for the so-called Christmas conference of 1784 at which the Methodist Episcopal Church was created, Garrettson rode 1,200 miles in six weeks summoning preachers across the south to the event. At the conference, which organized an American church independent of its British counterpart, Garrettson was ordained an elder and assigned to Nova Scotia, along with James O. Cromwell. Under Garrettson and Cromwell, the movement grew rapidly in Nova Scotia. In 1787 John *Wesley apparently devised a plan to appoint Garrettson General Superintendent of Methodism for the British North American provinces and the West Indies. But the plan fell through, largely because Garrettson did not want to cut his ties with the American church. Instead, Garrettson spent the 1787 conference year supervising a district of important circuits on the Delmarva Peninsula (divided between the states of Delaware, Maryland, and Virginia, hence the name).

In 1788 Asbury sent Garrettson to New York to revitalize the church there, which had been disrupted considerably by the war. Asbury also intended Garrettson to continue on to New England, but Garrettson quickly realized that the needs of New York were more than enough to occupy his energies. As he preached across upstate New York, Garrettson encountered opposition from the entrenched Dutch clergy, some of whom claimed that the Methodists were British agents come to incite another war, while others warned that Methodist preachers threw blue spiders on their hearers. On one of these preaching tours, Garrettson fell in love with Catherine Livingston, whose politically powerful family owned 750,000 acres along the Hudson River. Despite opposition from her family, the two were married on 30 June 1793. Under Garrettson's leadership, New York Methodism expanded from 442 members and two circuits in 1787 to 3651 members and twelve circuits in 1791.

Though Garrettson consistently supported Asbury, he had a more democratic view of the church. One of the hallmarks of episcopal authority in early American Methodism was the bishop's power to appoint preachers to their circuits without appeal. At the 1792 General Conference, Garrettson initially supported James O'Kelly's attempts to limit this authority by giving the conference the right to overrule the bishops. Although it initially enjoyed widespread support, O'Kelly's motion eventually lost, at least in part because a majority of the preachers came to believe that he intended to use the provision to usurp authority over the southern Virginia circuits. Garrettson, willing to abide by the conference's decision, joined a committee assigned to formulate an agreement with O'Kelly. Their efforts failed, and O'Kelly left to form the Republican Methodist Church.

Like many Methodists of the time, Garrettson attached great importance to prophetic dreams, visions and supernatural impressions, seeing in these a means of divine guidance. In 1773, even before his conversion, Garrettson prayed for his brother John who was 'dangerously ill'. 'Instantly the disorder turned', and he soon recovered. While itinerating in Pennsylvania and the Jerseys in 1779, Garrettson noted that many 'thought the Methodists would work miracles'. Indeed, only a few months earlier, in Delaware, he had prayed for rain to end 'a great drought' with the result that 'a few minutes after the congregation was dismissed, the face of the sky was covered with blackness, and we had a plentiful shower; which greatly surprised and convinced the people'. Catherine shared her husband's mystical bent, and her own dreams and visions were no less vivid. During their courtship they read each other's journals and even had dreams in common.

For the 1793 conference year Garrettson was appointed presiding elder of the Philadelphia Conference. He and Catherine arrived in Philadelphia in July 1793 in the midst of a yellow fever epidemic. They stayed only until the spring of 1794, when Catherine's pregnancy prompted their return to Rhinebeck, New York. There they purchased a modest Dutch farmhouse, where their only child, Mary Rutherford, was born in September 1794. Mary suffered from chronic ill health, including scoliosis, an abnormal curvature of the spine. For five years, beginning in 1794, Garrettson served as presiding elder of the New York District. Relying on money from Catherine's inheritance, in 1799 the Garrettsons built a substantial mansion at Rhinecliffe, overlooking the Hudson River. At this estate, known as 'Wildercliffe', or 'Traveler's Rest' as Asbury later dubbed it, the Garrettson's welcomed weary circuit riders, entertaining them in a way that few Methodist households could match.

In 1799 Garrettson was once again appointed presiding elder over the Philadelphia District for one year. He returned to New York in 1800, where he served as a presiding elder and conference missionary for the next fifteen years. Thereafter he remained active in church affairs, mostly as an at-large missionary in the New York Conference. His daughter later wrote that all that was precious to her father lay at Wildercliffe. Yet Garrettson felt guilty in retirement, believing that he ought to travel and preach while strength remained. He died in New York City, shortly after preaching there, and was buried at Rhinebeck. Portions of Garrettson's journal were published as *The Experiences and Travels of Mr. Freeborn Garrettson, Minister of the Methodist Episcopal Church in North America* (1791), and were widely read by early Methodists. Garrettson also published an anti-slavery tract entitled, *A Dialogue Between Do-Justice and Professing Christian* (1805), and a spirited answer to a tract by Lyman *Beecher, entitled *A Letter to the Rev. Lyman Beecher containing Strictures and Animadversions on the Pamphlet entitled 'An Address of the Charitable Society for the Education of Indigent Pious Young Men for the Ministry of the Gospel'* (1816).

Bibliography

R. D. Simpson, *American Methodist Pioneer* (Rutland: Academy Books, 1984); N. Bangs, *The Life of the Rev. Freeborn Garrettson* (New York: J. Emory & B. Waugh, 1832).

J. H. WIGGER

■ **GEE, Donald** (1891–1966), British Pentecostal leader, began and ended his life in London, but spent much of his adulthood travelling the globe as a spokesman for, and organizer of, worldwide Pentecostalism. He was a leading light of the British Assemblies of God and one of its ablest and most prolific authors, producing more than thirty books and countless articles. His writings exuded a combination of humanity, balance and real intelligence, at once committed to Pentecostal distinctives (he consistently and vigorously defended speaking in tongues as initial evidence of Spirit baptism) and to healthy self-criticism. As an example of the latter, he decried the tendency to highlight the sensational and spectacular, and to make 'the abnormal the regular pattern. The Christian life is walking with God ... not a system of jerks along the upward way.' Similarly, he urged Pentecostal preachers to prepare written sermons of real weight, rather than delivering poor fare under the excuse of 'Spirit inspiration', and he was likewise critical of unrealistic views of Christian ministry, often perpetuated by 'heroic' missionary biographies ('the worst examples of unctuous flattery'), for encouraging 'false ideals and ideas' about Christian work in general and about missions in particular.

Gee became controversial in later life for his willingness to engage with non-Pentecostal and even non-evangelical church bodies, as well as for his desire to foster a World Pentecostal Fellowship. In the former enterprise he was associated with David *du Plessis, who like him advocated participation in the World Council of Churches but found the way blocked by opposition from his fellow Pentecostals. Again like du Plessis, Gee both welcomed and encouraged the early charismatic movement within the historic denominations. He was self-educated rather than formally schooled and counselled the Protestant charismatic leaders against temptations to anti-intellectualism: 'many of you are trained theologians with a good academic background. Do not, now you have tasted spiritual gifts, become fanatical in your repudiation of consecrated scholarship ... Some of us [i.e. Pentecostals] in our early folly set a premium upon ignorance.'

The son of a sign painter who died when Gee was nine years old, he was converted in 1905 in a London Congregational chapel, in circumstances that were part of the ripple effects of the Welsh revival of that year. He was briefly a Baptist, before embracing a Pentecostal experience in 1913. The First World War broke out eighteen months later, and Gee, a conscientious objector, was required to work on a farm as an alternative to military service. There he began his career as a Pentecostal leader in a small rural fellowship. From 1920 to 1930 he pastored a church near Edinburgh, but he was already becoming known further afield, partly through his articles in Pentecostal magazines and partly through his compilation in 1924 of the Redemption Tidings Hymn Book.

From 1928 onwards he began to teach and to lecture all over the world, beginning with Australia, New Zealand and the United States. Back in Europe, he taught annually in the 1930s in the Danzig Bible Institute, which had been founded using American funds by Gustav Herbert Schmidt in 1930, and which trained Christian workers from wide areas of Eastern Europe until forced by Nazi pressure to close. Gee also taught in the Bible School in Stockholm. Indeed, he acquainted himself with Pentecostal movements all around the Baltic, reporting back, both before and after the Second World War, on the conditions of the churches he found in the various countries he visited.

From 1934 to 1944 he served as vice-chairman of the British Assemblies of God, and was chairman from 1945 to 1948. He was one of the organizers of the European Pentecostal Conference at Stockholm in 1939 and, with du Plessis, of the first World Pentecostal Conference at Zurich in 1947. In that year he was appointed founding editor of *Pentecost* magazine, which continued publication until his death in 1966. In 1950 he was appointed the first principal of the Assemblies of God College at Kenley, in Surrey, an institution which had existed as a Pentecostal Missionary Union Bible School since 1921 but which had only just come fully under denominational control.

In the early part of Gee's career, his burden had been to build up Pentecostalism and to call Christians 'out of worldliness, out of formality, out of lukewarmness, out of half-heartedness'; in a word, out of the historic denominations into Pentecostal fellowships. Many of those early Pentecostals who had sought to remain in their churches had found themselves in painful situations involving church division, expulsion or a gradual spiritual retreat from their charismatic experiences into conformity to the patterns of their churches. Gee had no doubts as to what constituted the lesser evil in such circumstances. 'There are times', he wrote in 1930, 'when division is a sign of life, and union a sign of deterioration and death ... Steps towards "Union" among older bodies of believers, though vaunted as great spiritual conquests, are often in reality only a sign of decay. It is possible to "freeze" together.' This was not a stance he maintained during the latter part of his life. His own wide travels awakened him to the huge diversity of practice within Pentecostalism itself, and this in turn made him more open to the possibilities of engagement with other Christians. Indeed, in the two decades after the Second World War Gee used his position as editor, educator and Pentecostal elder statesman to advocate greater integration, both among Pentecostals themselves and also with other churches. However, his attempts at both the first and second World Pentecostal Conferences (in Zurich in 1947 and in Paris in 1949) to establish a World Pentecostal Fellowship were decisively rejected. Reflecting on this, Gee's friend du Plessis lamented in 1952 that fortunes were 'being spent fruitlessly in foreign lands' because Pentecostals would not coordinate their missionary strategies.

Gee was further criticized by his fellow Pentecostals for his involvement with Billy *Graham's evangelistic campaign in Harringay, London, in 1954. (Such problems were not unique; at the other end of the evangelical spectrum, the *Banner of Truth* magazine was equally urging non-cooperation with Graham.) It was a similar story in respect of engagement with the ecumenical movement. Gee had reversed his earlier criticisms of ecumenism, and was now himself criticized for attending the World Council of Churches' Faith and Order Commission in Scotland in 1960. He faced decisive pressure to decline his invitation to attend the Assembly of the World Council of Churches in New Delhi the following year.

Despite these setbacks, Gee's influence in weaning Pentecostals from their isolation was enormous. His metamorphosis was, perhaps, a prototype for a new breed of self-assured, non-defensive Pentecostals that has become more familiar since the 1960s. The author of two histories of the British Assemblies of God, as well as *Wind and Flame*, which described international Pentecostalism, Gee developed a calm, clear and unthreatened sense, less usual then than now, of Pentecostal identity. It was that assurance that enabled him to adopt a less polemical, more openhanded stance towards outsiders, while not compromising on distinctive Pentecostal beliefs.

His friend Walter Hollenweger (one of the foremost historians of worldwide Pentecostalism), described Gee's thought as constituting 'an average fundamentalist Pentecostal theology', but remained full of admiration for the balanced, thoughtful and nuanced way in which Gee sought, throughout his life, to apply that theology.

Bibliography

J. Carter, *Donald Gee: Pentecostal Statesman* (Nottingham: Assemblies of God Publishing House, 1975); W. J. Hollenweger, *The Pentecostals* (London: SCM, 1972), pp. 208–213; B. R. Ross, 'Donald Gee: Sectarian in Search of a Church', *Evangelical Quarterly* 50 (1978), pp. 94–103.

M. PEARSE

■ **GEORGE, David** (c. 1743–1810), black Baptist pastor and church planter, was born a slave in Sussex, Virginia, and was owned by a local sheriff whom George described as 'a very bad man to the Negroes'. George received 'rough and cruel' treatment but his most painful experience was seeing his mother and brother brutally whipped. At about the age of nineteen, he escaped and fled south, but he was captured first by the 'Creek Indians' in Georgia and then by the 'Nautchee [Natchez] Indians', who eventually sold him to a white fur-trader who worked for George Galphin. Galphin had a large trading outpost in Silver Bluff, South Carolina, and for three years George served him as a frontiersman transporting cargoes of deerskins hundreds of miles to the outpost. Afterwards, Galphin granted George's wish to move to Silver Bluff to 'wait upon him' there. Four years later George was married.

Slaves were allowed to hold church services on Galphin's property, and George began attending soon after the birth of his first child. Through the ministry of itinerant Baptist preachers, George, his wife Phillis and six others were converted and baptized. They were formed into a congregation (c. 1773), becoming the earliest known black Baptist church in America. With encouragement from itinerant preachers George began to pray and 'exhort' in services and became an elder. He asked some white children to teach him to read and soon rejoiced, 'I can now read my Bible, so what I have in my heart, I can see again in the Scriptures.' In between visits by itinerants, George preached to the congregation of thirty, and when the outbreak of the American Revolution restricted the movements of travelling preachers, he became the first black Baptist pastor in colonial America. After the British took Savannah, Georgia and pressed further inland, Galphin fled and left the slaves to fend for themselves. George and his flock left Silver Bluff and joined the British. At the end of the Revolution, George, Phillis and their children were evacuated with thousands of British loyalists.

Of the 3,550 black loyalists who landed in Nova Scotia, 1,500 of them settled in the Shelburne area, south of Halifax. As soon as George arrived, he began to hold outdoor meetings and recorded that the 'people came flocking to the preaching every evening for a month, as though they had come for their supper'. He baptized the converts, formed them into a congregation and erected a church building, establishing the first black Baptist church in Canada. But white opposition developed, and George was attacked by unemployed soldiers and forced to take refuge in the nearby all-black settlement of Birchtown. In 1784 he returned to Shelburne, where he reclaimed his meeting house and ministry. As George's fame spread he was regularly invited to preach in distant towns. He went to St John, New Brunswick, 200 miles away, to preach and baptize. When opposition erupted, he obtained a licence from the governor 'to instruct the Black people in the knowledge and exhort them to the practice of the Christian religion'. He founded as many as seven churches, and some say that he had a larger following among the blacks than any other preacher, white or black.

But the black loyalists were increasingly dissatisfied because of their poor living conditions. Only one third of them had received promised land grants, and these were often much smaller than those given to whites. Blacks also received fewer promised government provisions. So the black settlers sent Thomas Peters, a black loyalist who had been a sergeant with the British, to England to plead their case. The Sierra Leone Company, in England, took an interest in his petition. This Company was a philanthropic organization committed to the abolition of slavery and had recently unsuccessfully tried to establish a slave-free colony in Sierra Leone, West Africa. It was led by many outstanding evangelicals such as Henry *Thornton, Thomas Clarkson, Granville Sharp and William *Wilberforce, who saw Peters' appeal as an opportunity to try once more to realize their vision. Petitions were made to the government, which agreed to pay the costs of shipping free blacks to Sierra Leone. The Company appointed Lieutenant John Clarkson, a brother of Thomas Clarkson, to go to Nova Scotia and oversee the embarkation and voyage to Africa.

When Clarkson arrived in Halifax in October 1791 he advertised the invitation to Sierra Leone, hired ships and travelled to settlements to invite black settlers to make the journey. The results were greater than expected, and within weeks hundreds of blacks had come to the Halifax harbour; by mid-December more than a thousand had arrived. George, who would play a key role in the new colony, chose to emigrate, and most of his congregation followed his lead. So did three other black pastors (one a Wesleyan Methodist and two from the Countess of Huntingdon's Connexion) and some members of their congregations. Clarkson appointed George, whom he now described as his 'steady friend', to be one of three loyalists handling the concerns of those arriving in Halifax. On 15 January 1792 fifteen ships carrying 1,196 blacks finally sailed for Sierra Leone. This was the largest transatlantic migration of free blacks in history, comprising one third of the total black loyalist population in New Brunswick and Nova Scotia.

Landing at Freetown, George immediately began holding services. His evangelistic preaching resulted in conversions, baptisms and the building of a simple meeting house, the first Baptist church in Africa. At the end of the first year George was given the opportunity to visit England. During his six-month stay he met Christian leaders, stayed briefly with John *Newton, who described him as a 'good man', and spoke in many Baptist churches. John *Rippon published a fascinating report of an interview with George in his *Baptist Annual Register*. This stirring story provides a unique first-hand account of the horrors of slavery in colonial America. On returning to Africa, George became the major link between Baptists in Sierra Leone and England, and his letters were published in the *Register*. This correspondence inspired the Baptist Missionary Society in England to choose Sierra Leone as their first African mission field. The first missionaries, James Rodway and Jacob Grigg, arrived in 1795, but the venture failed within two years. Rodway was often ill, and the governor, Zachary *Macaulay (later associated with the Clapham Sect in England), ordered Grigg to leave Africa because of his meddling in politics.

Unfortunately, the early years in the settlement were marked by ongoing tension caused by the inclement weather, the death of settlers and government officials, delays in assigning property to the settlers, and controversial government policies. George, who often sided with the governors, used his influence to suppress periodic insurrections in the colony. Yet this suppression caused the more radical settlers to leave the Baptist church, and when George died in 1810 the Baptists had slipped from being the largest denomination in the colony to being the smallest. Although the exodus to Africa was not as successful as was anticipated, today Nova Scotians revere David George for his pastoral leadership and his ability to overcome many obstacles.

Bibliography

G. Gordon, *From Slavery to Freedom: The Life of David George, Pioneer Black Baptist Pastor* (Hantsport, Nova Scotia: Lancelot Press, 1992); G. A. Rawlyk, 'David George (1743–1810): Black Nova Scotian New Light Baptist', in *The Canada Fire: Radical Evangelicalism in British North America, 1775–1812* (Montreal: McGill–Queens University Press, 1994), pp. 33–43; J. Walker, *The Black Loyalists: The Search for a Promised Land in Nova Scotia and Sierra Leone, 1783–1870* (New York: Africana and Dalhousie University Press, 1976).

G. GORDON

■ **GILL, John** (1697–1771), Particular Baptist theologian and pastor, was a prolific writer and one of the most influential English Nonconformist leaders of the eighteenth century. He was born in Kettering, Northamptonshire, on 23 November 1697. Though converted at the age of twelve, he postponed baptism until he was almost nineteen, whereupon he began to exercise his gifts as a preacher and expositor of the Scriptures. Young Gill was an ardent student, mastering the rudiments of Latin and teaching himself both Greek and Hebrew. His ministerial labours were noted by London Baptist leaders, who supported his studies through a grant from the Particular Baptist Fund. In 1718 Gill married Elizabeth Negus, who shared the labours of his ministry for more than forty-six years. They had three children who survived infancy, one of whom, Elizabeth, died at the age of twelve.

On 22 March 1720 Gill was installed as pastor of the church meeting at Goat Yard, Horslydown, Southwark. A notable Particular Baptist congregation founded by Benjamin Keach in 1672, this church called Gill amid controversy and on a split vote. The anti-Gill faction protested that women members had been allowed to vote in the calling of the new pastor contrary to church custom. The dispute resulted in a schism, followed several years later by another secession led by disaffected members of the Keach family. Gill survived these challenges and enjoyed a pastoral tenure in the congregation of more than fifty years. When, as an old man, he tendered his resignation, the church refused to sever its pastoral relationship with him.

Gill was the first Baptist to develop a complete systematic theology and also the first Baptist to write a verse-by-verse commentary on the entire Bible. His *Exposition of the New Testament* (1748) filled three large volumes, while his *Exposition of the Old Testament* (1766) was a six-volume project. In 1769 he published in two volumes *A Body of Doctrinal Divinity*, followed in the next year by *A Body of Practical Divinity*. Gill also wrote treatises on the Trinity, justification by faith and baptism. Gill opposed the rising tide of rationalist thinking within evangelical ranks and wrote against Arianism, deism and latitudinarianism. He also engaged in a polemical exchange with John *Wesley on the doctrines of predestination and perseverance.

Among his best-known writings was *The Cause of God and Truth*, a classic defence of Calvinistic soteriology, published in four parts between 1735 and 1738. Like many of Gill's writings, this polemical work was originally delivered as a series of weekly lectures at Great Eastcheap, a theological forum sponsored by several Dissenting churches in London. It was designed as a response to Daniel Whitby's *Discourses on the Five Points*, considered by some the definitive critique of Calvinist thought. The first two parts of *The Cause* consist of detailed considerations of the scriptural passages used by each side in the debate concerning the doctrines of grace. Part three examines the philosophical arguments for these doctrines and seeks to refute the charge of Stoic fatalism made against them. Part four of *The Cause* is a historical excursus drawing especially on the writings of the Church Fathers. By quoting from these sources Gill intended to show that the doctrines related to predestination had patristic support as well as biblical warrant. The Gill–Whitby exchange was widely discussed and deserves to be counted among the classic debates on the doctrine of election.

The quantity of Gill's writings earned him the nickname 'Dr Voluminous', and the quality of his scholarship, especially in Hebrew and rabbinics, gained him the honorary degree of DD, an award conferred by Marichal College of the University of Aberdeen in 1748. His writings are interlaced with numerous classical and patristic references, as well as allusions to the Reformers, Puritan divines and contemporary writers. Gill is best seen as an English Baptist contributor to Reformed scholastic orthodoxy. He was well acquainted with continental dogmatics as well as Puritan theology, and he helped to edit the writings of the Dutch Covenantal theologian Herman Witsius. His writings circulated widely among Baptists in America as well as those in England and helped him to gain his reputation as a leading spokesman for the Baptist interest on both sides of the Atlantic.

Not everyone in the Baptist tradition, however, approved of Gill's theology. On one occasion, the Welsh evangelist Christmas *Evans remarked to Robert *Hall that he wished Dr Gill's works had been written in Welsh. To this Hall replied, 'I wish they had, with all my heart, for then I should never had read them. They are a continent of mud, sir.' While this remark may reflect distaste at Gill's pedantic style, it also indicates the divergent ways in which he has been interpreted in the history of dissent. Gill has frequently been interpreted as a hyper-(or High) Calvinist who so emphasized the sovereignty of God in salvation that he went beyond the teaching of John *Calvin, the mainline Puritans, and earlier Particular Baptist pioneers such as John *Bunyan and Benjamin Keach. In this respect, Gill's theology has often been contrasted with that of Andrew *Fuller, his younger contemporary, whose treatise *The Gospel Worthy of All Acceptation* (1785) provided the basis for the Baptist missionary awakening associated with William *Carey.

In recent scholarship the extent of Gill's hyper-Calvinism has been challenged by some historians who have pointed to the essential similarity between Gill's theology and that of George *Whitefield, the apostle of the Great Awakening. Although Gill disliked the practice of making 'offers' of the grace of God, he did believe that the gospel should be proclaimed indiscriminately to all people. It has also been shown that Gill did not teach true antinomianism, even though he was charged with this view in his own day. He taught, in fact, that the moral law of God did apply as a rule of conduct even to believers under grace. In other respects, however, it is difficult to exempt Gill from the charge of hyper-Calvinism. While not denying the necessity of conversion as a personal experience of grace, he did defend the doctrine of eternal justification in contrast to the clear teaching of the Second London Confession (1677). Gill's works were also cited by later hyper-Calvinists who denied the doctrine of 'duty faith', that is, the teaching that the Bible requires repentance and faith from all people, and not from the elect only. Charles Haddon *Spurgeon, one of Gill's pastoral successors, confronted this view in his own London ministry and responded to it with a clarity lacking in Gill, though Spurgeon held his famous predecessor in high esteem.

On balance, it seems that Gill did not intend to exalt so highly the initiative of God in salvation as to pre-empt the requirements of repentance, faith and conversion. His own theology should not be read in the light of the later Gillite–Fullerite debates, nor should the source of 'false Calvinism' (Fuller's phrase) be located in Gill himself. Still, Gill's theology did move in the direction of hyper-Calvinism.

He was so preoccupied with defending the gospel from rationalism and Arminianism on the left that he did little to check the rigid restrictivism and anti-missionary impulses on his right.

Gill is buried in the famous Nonconformist cemetery at Bunhill Fields. On his tomb is a Latin inscription describing Gill as 'a sincere disciple of Jesus, an excellent preacher of the Gospel, a courageous defender of the Christian faith'. His personal and pastoral gifts have been overshadowed by the controversies surrounding his theology, but an elegy published shortly after his death sums up his life and ministry well: 'Zion was his delight, his whole design was to adorn the church, and make her shine.'

Bibliography

J. Rippon, *A Brief Memoir of the Life and Writings of the late Reverend John Gill, D.D.* (London: 1809); G. M. Ella, *John Gill and the Cause of God in Truth* (Eggleston, Co. Durham: Go Publications, 1995); M. A. G. Haykin (ed.), *The Life and Thought of John Gill (1697–1771): A Tercentennial Appreciation* (Leiden: Brill, 1997).

T. GEORGE

■ **GILLESPIE, Thomas** (1708–1774), Scottish Presbyterian minister and founder of the Relief Church in Scotland, was born in 1708 near Edinburgh.

Gillespie was converted through the preaching of Thomas *Boston, a prominent Church of Scotland minister and author. The experience led him to enter the University at Edinburgh in 1732 and prepare himself for ordination to the Christian ministry. Gillespie appears to have completed his three-year course in philosophy and to have been nearing the end of his further three years study in divinity, when he left the university in 1738. Gillespie left Edinburgh to attend the newly formed secession divinity hall in Perth where William Wilson had been appointed the theological tutor. Gillespie did not find the theological atmosphere at Perth one in which he could live; indeed, he left after only ten days. Two years later, in 1740, Gillespie entered Philip *Doddridge's Academy at Northampton for the completion of his theological education.

Gillespie was licensed at Northampton as a preacher of the gospel on 30 October 1740 and ordained on 22 January 1741. After a short ministry in an Independent congregation at Hartbarrow in Lancashire, he returned to Scotland and became the minister of Carnock in Fife on 4 September 1741.

In 1742 Thomas Gillespie became involved in the revival movement in the neighbouring parishes of Cambuslang and Kilsyth. He believed that it was one of the most remarkable effusions of the Spirit in any part of Scotland since the Reformation. He was so much respected that James Robe, minister of Kilsyth, asserted that 'of all others, the Rev Thomas Gillespie, Minister of the Gospel at Carnock, was most remarkably God's send to me'.

Around this time Gillespie wrote his *Essay on the Continuance of Immediate Revelations of Fact and Future Events in the Christian Church*. In this work he expressed his concern lest an acceptance of immediate revelations and other strange phenomena should lessen the authority of Scripture. Gillespie was convinced that all extraordinary gifts of the Holy Spirit had ceased to exist following the death of the apostles and the completion of the canon of Scripture.

From 1749 until 1752 Gillespie, along with other members of the evangelical party in the presbytery of Dunfermline, opposed the imposition of a new minister under the patronage system. The General Assembly of 1752 passed a motion that one of the six ministers of the presbytery of Dunfermline who had refused to induct the new minister to Inverkeithing should be disciplined, and the majority voted for Gillespie to be deposed from the ministry.

Gillespie ministered to his congregation in Carnock until the autumn, when the congregation moved to Dunfermline. Following further disputed settlements, Thomas Boston, minister of Jedburgh, joined Gillespie at the induction of Thomas Colier to the newly formed congregation at Colinsburgh in Fife. On 22 October 1761, following the induction services, the three ministers and an elder from each of the three congregations met together and constituted themselves into the Presbytery of Relief. They believed that each individual, regardless of economic background or educational attainment, was of equal value in the eyes of God and should have a voice in the affairs of the church, including the selection of the minister. The church should not be controlled by the Crown or aristocratic patrons.

The final years of Gillespie's life witnessed the growth and consolidation of the Presbytery of Relief. From the three congregations which existed in 1761, the presbytery grew to nineteen congregations by the time of his death.

Gillespie exercised a significant pastoral and preaching ministry for thirty-three years, and the pressures and responsibilities which he bore were enormous. He was nearly sixty-six years of age when he died. He married Margaret Riddell on 19 November 1744; they had no children. The burden of caring for family and church affairs consumed all his physical, mental, emotional and spiritual resources. On 19 January 1774 he died 'with undiminished serenity of mind, and ... enjoyed a good hope through grace of a blessed and glorious immortality'. Following his death, the Relief Church continued to expand and grow. In 1800 it had sixty congregations and 36,000 members, and by 1847 it had grown to 136 congregations. In May 1847, when it joined with the United Secession Church to form the United Presbyterian Church in Scotland, it became the largest single denomination in Glasgow and accounted for slightly under one-fifth of church-goers in Scotland.

Bibliography

K. B. E. Roxburgh, *Thomas Gillespie and the Origins of the Relief Church in Eighteenth Century Scotland* (Bern: Peter Lang, 1999); W. Lindsay, *Life and Times of the Rev. Thomas Gillespie* (Edinburgh: 1849).

K. B. E. ROXBURGH

■ **GOFORTH, Jonathan** (1859–1936) and **Rosalind (Bell-Smith)** (1864–1942), Canadian Presbyterian missionaries, formed an unlikely couple. Jonathan was born on 10 February 1859 and raised on a farm near Thorndale, Ontario. He felt a call to China after hearing G. L. Mackay, the Presbyterian missionary to Formosa, and reading Hudson *Taylor's China's Spiritual Need and Claims*. He enrolled in Knox College, Toronto. Rosalind was born in London, England on 6 May 1864 and came to Montreal at the age of three, later moving to Toronto to study art. There, on a visit to the Toronto Union Mission, she met Jonathan. For two years they worked together among the urban poor. They also attended the Niagara Bible Conferences and became committed premillennialists. They were married in 1887. When Jonathan graduated from Knox College fellow students pledged enough money to send them to China.

Arriving in China in 1888 as part of the Canadian Presbyterian team, the Goforths were assigned to the province of Honan, where the people were very hostile to foreigners. This assignment immediately brought them into conflict with Hudson Taylor, who had been attempting for ten years to establish a base there. But after meeting Goforth, Taylor blessed their mission.

The Goforths did none of the contextualization work considered essential in modern mission. Jonathan never attempted to build bridges or find points of contact with Chinese religion or culture, yet his work grew remarkably. He was able to engage with people, establish a church, train leaders, entrust the church to them and move on to another place, all within a few months. A pioneer, he was also stubborn, totally convinced that he heard God correctly and deaf to all objections, including Rosalind's. His sense of urgency was greatly accentuated after he survived a vicious sword attack during the couple's escape from the Boxer uprising of 1900.

Rosalind and Jonathan practised open house evangelism. They countered negative perceptions of missionaries by allowing everyone free access to their home in continuous guided tours, which included proclamation of the gospel.

In 1902 Jonathan decided to take his whole family on his evangelistic journeys, making them part of his message. They spent a few months in each city and then moved on to the next. During the day Jonathan preached outside the house, while Rosalind, at home with the children, invited women to visit and preached to them. Joint meetings were then held in the evening. The toll on the family was enormous, and the exposure of the children to disease aroused controversy. Heavily influenced by the writings of A. J. Gordon and

A. B. *Simpson on the theme of healing, Jonathan believed that the only safe place for him and his family was where God wanted them. This belief was not shaken by the fact that only six of the couple's eleven children survived childhood.

In 1904 Jonathan was encouraged by accounts of the Welsh revival to begin an indepth study of the work of the Holy Spirit. He read books by Charles *Finney, A. J. Gordon and S. D. Gordon. Then he was exposed to revival on a visit to Korea in 1907. During his return journey through Manchuria, he held impromptu meetings at the railway stations. These were followed by a tour in 1908. The subsequent Goforth/Ting (Ting Li Mei, a young graduate of Shandong College) revival focused on public confession of sin, forgiveness and a cathartic, emotional experience of release. Manchuria made Jonathan the focus of worldwide Christian interest. He returned to North Honan a celebrity, and revival followed there. Canada, however, was not so open to his message; Presbyterians were fearful of the emotionalism of the revivals, associating it with Pentecostalism. Rosalind did not have the deep spiritual experience prescribed by Jonathan until 1916.

Following the Manchuria revival, Jonathan was never able to work as a settled missionary. Full-time itinerant evangelism was his passion, and in 1918 the presbytery released him.

On furlough in 1900, Jonathan became aware of the issues surrounding higher criticism and entered the debate. Once back in China, he accused a fellow missionary of heresy. Jonathan opposed the Church Union of 1925 and launched the new China mission of the continuing Presbyterian Church in Canada, which was established in Manchuria. This new mission was patterned on the China Inland Mission; it refused to solicit funds and relied on prayer alone.

Near total blindness finally forced Jonathan off the mission field at the end of 1934. He died in Toronto in 1936. Rosalind survived until 1942, writing Jonathan's biography and her own autobiography during those years. Both the Goforths published extensively.

Bibliography
R. Goforth, *Goforth of China* (Grand Rapids:

Zondervan, 1937); R. Goforth, *Climbing: Memories of a Missionary's Wife* (Toronto: Evangelical Publishers, 1940).

D. A. GOERTZ

■ **GRAHAM, William Franklin, 'Billy'** (1918–), evangelist, was born on 7 November 1918 near Charlotte, North Carolina. His parents, William Franklin and Morrow Coffey, raised him on a 400-acre farm with a well-managed and successful dairy. The farm had been passed down to Billy's father and his uncle, Clyde Graham, from their parents. Billy Graham grew up with three younger siblings: Catherine, Melvin and Jean. The four children enjoyed parents who provided love, strict discipline and a moral upbringing. The family attended church regularly. First they belonged to the fundamentalist Associate Reformed Presbyterian Church, and later to the mainline Presbyterian Church in Charlotte, which was less strict and separatist but markedly evangelical. By almost any social measurement for the two decades before the Second World War, the Graham family was upper middle-class. Despite losses of savings and cuts in the profits of the dairy and farm during the great depression of the 1930s, William F. Graham, Sr always brought in an excellent income. And even though Billy and his siblings worked long hours on the farm, they ate well and had better clothing than most North Carolinans, and the family enjoyed luxuries such as a large brick house, indoor utilities and plumbing, as well as good cars, a house maid and a small group of hired hands for farm and dairy.

A mark of the Grahams' affluence was in the children's education. They were encouraged to attend the state schools full-time, and received an education well beyond the national average for the depression and war years. To be sure, Billy's father was not certain that any man should go to college, believing that a real man should earn a living with his hands. Nevertheless, Mrs Graham encouraged Billy to go to college; indeed, she had a love for books and education. She had encouraged Billy as a youth to memorize the Westminster Shorter Catechism, and she encouraged him in his love for reading books by plying him with volumes of biography and missionary history.

With college on his mind and a mother nudging him along, Billy seriously considered enrolling at the University of North Carolina. But his mother feared he would lose his Christian faith if he went to the state university. He had been baptized as an infant and confirmed in the Presbyterian Church, and she urged him to consider a Christian college.

While Billy was weighing the advantages and disadvantages of various colleges advertised in *Moody Monthly* (one of Mrs Graham's favourite periodicals), an important event took place just prior to his sixteenth birthday. Mordecai Ham, an independent evangelist, arrived in Charlotte to preach a series of sermons. A so-called 'fire and brimstone' preacher, he challenged people to recognize their sinfulness and cry out to Jesus Christ for mercy before they perished and spent eternity in hell. During one of these nightly meetings, Billy Graham made an unemotional but deliberate 'decision', as he expressed it, to confess his sinfulness, seek mercy and dedicate himself fully to God's will.

In the wake of this decision, Billy began to sense a deeper commitment to Christ, but he had no sense of calling to ministry. Nevertheless, when another travelling preacher named Bob *Jones came to Charlotte the next year, he persuaded Billy's father that the unaccredited Bible college he had founded, named Bob Jones College, was an ideal place for a Christian man with educational ambition to study. Billy graduated from high school in 1936. Then he went to Cleveland, Tennessee with his family's blessing and financial support, but he stayed only one semester at Bob Jones College. By January of 1937 he had become uncomfortable with the narrow fundamentalism and rigid rules of the college. During this semester of discomfort, a series of circumstances led him to visit Florida Bible Institute in Tampa, Florida in December 1936. He enrolled there in January 1937 and graduated three and a half years later in the spring of 1940.

The period Graham spent at Florida Bible Institute proved to be one of the most significant of his life. The institute accommodated just under a hundred students a year at that time. The environment was conservatively evangelical, yet there was a joyous freedom that did not exist at Bob Jones College. In the Florida school, founded by a former Christian and Missionary Alliance (CMA) pastor, Billy Graham met students, staff and guest preachers from a much wider range of the evangelical world. CMA people, Methodists, Baptists and a host of others studied history, theology, Bible and hermeneutics together. While a student in Florida, Graham received numerous calls to preach and speak in Rescue Missions as well as in CMA, Methodist and Baptist churches. During this time, he not only gained a much wider view of the church universal; he also sensed a definite call from God to devote his life to full-time ministry as a preacher of the gospel. In 1939 Graham was baptized as a believer and ordained by the Southern Baptist denomination. Soon his giftedness as a preacher became apparent to many thoughtful men on the institute's faculty, as well as to leading Christian ministers who went to Tampa for sunshine, rest and rejuvenation.

One man who heard Graham preach in 1939 was Paul Fischer, a man with strong ties to Wheaton College in Illinois. Fischer urged Graham to get a degree from Wheaton as preparation for a career in ministry. He even promised to pay for his first year's tuition. Consequently, Graham applied, was admitted, and graduated with a BA in anthropology in 1943.

The Wheaton College years (1940–1943) were extremely important to Graham. He met students and staff from many evangelical traditions, broadening his ecumenical vision even more. The liberal arts education expanded his worldview, and thanks to encouragement from Dr V. Raymond Edman, president of Wheaton, he renewed his commitment to ministry and became pastor of a multidenominational independent church in Wheaton, the United Gospel Tabernacle. While at the college and preaching at the church, Graham met Ruth Bell, the daughter of missionaries recently home from China, Dr and Mrs L. Nelson Bell. Billy and Ruth courted at Wheaton, became engaged, graduated together in June 1943 and married on 13 August 1943 at Ruth's parents' home community in Montreat, North Carolina.

Ruth Bell Graham was raised on the China mission field. A lifelong Presbyterian, she became a devoted wife to Graham, supporting him despite his frequent travels and absence from the family. From the beginning of their marriage, even when he pastored a small Baptist church in Western Springs, Illinois, she willingly endured his continuous schedule of out-of-town speaking. Ruth Bell Graham bore five children (Virginia born in 1945; Anne Morrow in 1948; Ruth Bell in 1950; William Franklin III in 1952; and Nelson Edman in 1958), provided a nurturing home in the mountains near Montreat, North Carolina, and eventually developed her own ministry of speaking and writing.

Immediately after his honeymoon in 1943, Graham began faithfully to serve the congregation at First Baptist Church in Western Springs, Illinois, a southwestern suburb of metropolitan Chicago, but it soon became obvious that the young pastor's heart was not truly in pastoral ministry. He loved to preach, and he could not stay in one place long enough for either home and hospital visitation or committee meetings. The small church grew increasingly resentful of his absences for out-of-town preaching obligations. An influential deacon, Robert Van Kampen, defended Graham to the board by pointing out that he was markedly gifted as an evangelist and that their pastor was destined to be the next D. L. *Moody or Billy *Sunday. Van Kampen's words proved to be prophetic. Within eighteen months Graham realized he needed to be free to itinerate. He resigned from First Baptist in 1945. His ministry had built up the church's membership and budget, and he departed on good terms with everyone. After leaving he devoted more time to travelling, preaching and the Chicago radio gospel programme he had been hosting part-time.

Widespread exposure through radio and preaching vaulted Graham into the inner circles of the so-called 'new' evangelicalism, a growing movement of conservative Christians who eschewed the separatist stance of fundamentalists, but retained an uncompromising view of biblical inerrancy along with a passion for communicating the claims of Jesus Christ through home and foreign missions.

Increasingly Billy Graham drew away from narrow denominationalism and sectarianism. He fitted well among the interdenominational organizations that proliferated after 1945 with the express purpose of spreading the gospel in league with all sects and groups that believed the only way to peace with God was through the mediation of Jesus Christ. Indeed, Graham, before he was thirty years old, found himself as a leader among people who celebrated a more ecumenical mood among conservative Christians.

Upon leaving Western Springs Baptist Church, Graham took up evangelist Torrey Johnson's offer to help him and a group of other young evangelicals to reach the young people and military personnel at home and abroad. Graham became charter vice-president of Youth For Christ (YFC) International, based in Chicago, a position he held until 1950 while continuing itinerant evangelism. With YFC he preached throughout Europe and North America, emerging as one of the most gifted evangelists of his generation from the English-speaking world.

During his service with YFC, Graham also took on the presidency of Northwestern College, Bible School and Seminary in Iowa. Serving in that position from 1947 to 1952, he played a role in raising funds and helping young people to find educational programmes to equip them for full-time ministry. In 1950, two years before he resigned from Northwestern Schools, he brought together a group of directors, including his song leader Cliff Barrows, Ruth Graham and his lifelong friend Grady Wilson and formed the Billy Graham Evangelistic Association (BGEA). Incorporation of BGEA signalled a formalizing of Graham's calling. According to bylaws he was 'to spread the gospel by any and all means'.

The 1949 Los Angeles crusade launched Graham into the national limelight as crowds numbering in total over 350,000 attended his meetings night after night for two months. Then in early 1950 over 105,000 people came to hear his fiery preaching in Boston. In Columbia, South Carolina, nearly 200,000 attended a Graham crusade in less than a month, and in city after city across the United States for the next three years his meetings attracted phenomenal numbers. Millions of people filled auditoriums and arenas to hear him, with well over 100,000 coming forward in response to his invitations to 'inquire' about Christ's call on their lives.

In early 1954 Graham went to London, where over 2 million people came to hear the gospel in three months. From there he did a tour of northern and western Europe, before going back to America at the end of the year. In 1955 he went to dozens of cities all over Europe, where over 4 million witnessed him call forward over 100,000 inquirers.

The crusades in the 1950s were a prelude to nearly a half-century more of worldwide evangelistic preaching. Indeed, by the end of the century Graham had preached to more people in live audiences than any evangelist in history. He spoke live to over 210 million people in almost 190 countries and territories, and he reached countless millions more through television, radio, video, film, books and tracts. His preaching ministry was complemented by a weekly radio programme, 'Hour of Decision'. The BGEA also produces an official magazine, *Decision*, which has a monthly circulation of $1\frac{3}{4}$ million in over 150 countries. The BGEA also oversees World Wide Pictures, which has produced nearly 140 films. Graham himself has written scores of evangelistic tracts, which have been published by BGEA, and he has written eighteen books, many of which have been best sellers.

Graham attributes his phenomenal success as an evangelist to the Holy Spirit. He has remained extremely humble during a half century of preaching to millions, meeting with the heads of government in dozens of nations, including every US president from Harry Truman to the second George Bush. His face has adorned major magazines, and he is consistently selected as one of the 'Ten Most Admired Men in the World'. All of his closest associates have observed for over fifty years that he truly wants God to be glorified by his ministry. He has tried to avoid the typical trappings of success by living simply, taking a modest salary from the BGEA, refusing all gifts and honoraria above his salary and passing on book royalties to the BGEA. No hint of scandal, financial or sexual, has touched his life. Except for Mother Teresa, no twentieth-century Christian enjoyed such international celebrity status without provoking charges of corruption.

To be sure, Graham has his critics. He has been roundly attacked by Protestant fundamentalists for working alongside Roman Catholics and even having priests sit on the platform with him during crusades. His 1988 trip to the Republic of China brought a barrage of criticism from some quarters because he refused verbally to confront the Communist leaders and worked in concert with the Three Self Church in China. He was also the brunt of right-wing criticism when he accepted invitations in the mid 1980s to preach in other communist-bloc countries, notably the USSR and Romania. The most conservative Calvinist theologians and ministers are extremely critical of Graham because he is in the tradition of evangelists such as John *Wesley, Charles *Finney, D. L. Moody and Billy Sunday, believing that people can make a 'decision' to follow Christ and therefore encouraging them to do so.

Perhaps Graham is his own most thoughtful critic. One of the reasons for his lasting popularity is his transparency and willingness to admit mistakes. On numerous occasions he has said that he wished he had studied more and preached less, bemoaning his limited education and his neglect of his family as a result of his continuous travel and preaching. He also admits that he enjoyed to a fault the company of politicians, even to the point of being tempted to seek political office. Likewise, he acknowledges that during the 1950s and 1960s he too often identified American foreign policy objectives with God's will for the world.

Billy Graham is arguably the most successful evangelist of modern times. The modern world is different because of his ministry.

Bibliography
W. Martin, *A Prophet With Honor: The Billy Graham Story* (New York: Morrow, 1991); B. Graham, *Just As I Am: The Autobiography of Billy Graham* (San Francisco: Harper, 1997).

L. W. Dorsett

■ **GRANT, George Munro** (1835–1902), Canadian Presbyterian minister, author and educator, remains best known as Principal Grant, the dynamic leader who more than any other person contributed to the building of Queen's University in Kingston, Ontario, between 1877 and 1902. A man of many talents and broad influence, Grant was also 'the acknowledged giant among giants of

Canadian Presbyterianism' in his day, an influential proponent of British imperialism in Canada and a public moralist. In those roles, he helped to guide the Presbyterian Church in Canada in the late nineteenth century away from theological divisiveness and towards an 'accommodating evangelicalism'. He also helped to forge a broad and enduring ethic of Christian responsibility for, and service to, the Canadian nation.

George Monro Grant was born on 22 December 1835, the third child of James Grant and Mary Monro, in Albion Mines (Stellarton), Pictou County, Nova Scotia. James and Mary struggled financially, but they managed to raise their children in an atmosphere of intense Presbyterian piety within the Scottish, Gaelic-speaking, Highland tradition of their family. Mostly through Mary, George and his siblings also learned energetically to pursue lofty goals, and had fostered within them a good measure of common sense.

In spite of his family's lack of financial means, George received an excellent education. Having studied first at Pictou Academy under the well-known educator and humorist, Thomas *McCulloch, the young Grant moved on to a Presbyterian seminary at West River (Durham) in 1851. In both places, he was shaped by a Lowland, Dissenting evangelical Presbyterian tradition. At the seminary, in particular, he was also imbued with a strict Calvinism.

With the help of a scholarship from the Church of Scotland, Grant furthered his theological studies at the University of Glasgow from 1853. There he was heavily influenced by a moderating Church of Scotland movement that was more optimistic than traditional Calvinism in its view of human nature and the coherence of reason and revelation, and that rejected such doctrines as double predestination and limited atonement. It was in Scotland that Grant also developed a strong social conscience. The young Nova Scotian was deeply moved by time spent in city missions in the slums of Glasgow. Having reflected on his experience through the writings of Thomas Carlyle, Grant adopted a lifestyle of disciplined austerity and charitable giving, and aligned himself early in his life with the tradition of Old Testament prophetic calls for justice.

After concluding his studies with the obligatory tour of Europe in 1860, Grant returned to Nova Scotia as an ordained Presbyterian minister. Assigned the task of missionary for the Church of Scotland to remote communities in Nova Scotia and Prince Edward Island, he soon attracted attention in wider circles, and was called in 1863 to 'the largest and wealthiest Presbyterian Congregation in the Maritimes', St Matthew's Church in Halifax. Having married Jessie Lawson, the daughter of a leading Halifax merchant, on 7 May 1867, Grant used his new-found prominence to stir his comfortable congregation into action on a wide range of social concerns, including the School for the Blind and the Halifax Industrial School. A man of astounding energy, he was called by a Halifax friend 'a steam engine in trousers'.

Grant also began to establish himself as an influential voice in national politics and church affairs. Having absorbed as a student a strong Christian ethic of service to the nation, Grant threw himself into the confederation debates in 1867, firmly on the side of a broader union. In 1872, one year after British Columbia entered confederation, Grant's nationalist concerns led him to join a member of his congregation, Sandford Fleming, in an over-land railway survey expedition to Victoria, BC. The result of his 5,000-mile journey was a popular book, *Ocean to Ocean* (1873), a follow-up cross-country tour in 1883, again with Fleming, and *Picturesque Canada*, another romantic endorsement of confederation published in instalments between 1882 and 1884. Grant became a well-known nation-builder, one committed to the development of a Christian Canada within what he considered to be the blessed imperial framework of Great Britain. For Grant, politics and public life were primarily moral in character, and he considered the British political system, with its careful balance of liberty and authority, to be the most Christian in the world.

Grant's commitment to nation-building was, in fact, closely linked to his commitment to church-building. By the mid-1870s, the Nova Scotian minister was becoming one of the most influential voices in Canadian Presbyterianism. His most passionate cause was the union of Canada's several Presbyterian denominations into one great Presbyterian

Church of Canada, a union that was achieved in 1875. Grant's drive for church union was informed by the conviction that the newly united Canadian nation could be best served by one united, national, established church (an idea he had embraced during his studies in Glasgow). In subsequent years, Grant worked hard for a further union between Presbyterians and other denominations.

Shortly after his successful drive for Presbyterian union, Grant accepted an invitation (1877) to take the position of principal and primarius professor of divinity at Queen's College in Kingston, Ontario. He then devoted all of his considerable powers to the expansion of the struggling Presbyterian college, taking its enrolment from under 100 students to over 800 by the turn of the century. Greatly expanding Queen's facilities, Grant also worked hard to endow its graduates with a deep, broad-minded commitment to service of the nation. In his time and after, Queen's would be known as a formative centre for future men of public affairs, including many of the architects of Canada's welfare state.

As principal of Queen's, Grant continued to wield influence beyond the doors of his university. He was elected moderator of the Presbyterian Church of Canada in 1889, was a founding member of the Royal Society of Canada in 1882 and its president from 1890 to 1891 and spoke on behalf of Canadian Protestantism at the Congress of Religions at the 1893 World's Fair in Chicago. He also continued to publish articles in theological and scholarly journals such as *The Andover Review* and *The American Journal of Theology* and completed several books, including *The Religions of the World* (1894). The latter was recommended as the best short introduction to the subject as late as the 1940s, by John R. *Mott, founder of the World's Student Christian Federation.

Grant was evangelical in his theological convictions, but the term should be applied to him with caution. In the context of the recent historical debate about the secularization of Canada in the Victorian age, Grant has been called both a 'liberal modernist' and a 'romantic evangelical'. That broad range of theological categorizations can be at least partially ascribed to Grant's slippery mediating position between what have since become well-defined twentieth-century theological poles. Exposed as a student to common-sense realism, a Lowland, Dissenting evangelical Presbyterian tradition, a strict Calvinism and what might be called a moderating, 'accommodating evangelicalism', Grant became an accommodating evangelical himself. By his mid-twenties, it seems, he had fleshed out a theology that was biblical, not scholastic. An evangelical at heart, he was also convinced of the historical evolution of faith and theology, and open to the results of the 'new' scientific approach to biblical scholarship, historical criticism.

Grant, then, was neither a typical nineteenth-century orthodox Calvinist nor a twentieth-century modernist. Paul and *Luther were his most important theological influences, and under their inspiration he attempted to combine the 'old orthodoxy' with the best results of recent scholarship in the sciences and humanities. Within the Presbyterian Church, Grant was known as 'an influential champion of liberal theological and political views'. At the same time, however, he was an admirer of the great American revivalist, Dwight L. *Moody, and a supporter of the Salvation Army. He also continued to emphasize personal conversion, a heartfelt faith, the reality of 'original sin', and justification by faith as central components of Christianity. As his most recent biographer, D. B. Mack, has argued, 'Grant's target was false, externalized religion and self-righteous legalism, against which he set a living faith of the heart and mind and soul.'

Mack has argued, in fact, that as an accommodating evangelical and one of the most influential Canadian Presbyterians of his day, Grant helped to steer his denomination between the conservative Presbyterianism of Charles *Hodge's Princeton and the liberal modernism of advanced biblical critics. 'The one class believes nothing but what is old,' Grant wrote, 'the other believes nothing but what is new.' Neither, in his opinion, had a monopoly on the truth. As a result of the moderation exhibited by Grant and other Canadian Presbyterians in his day, the Presbyterian Church of Canada avoided the schisms and controversies that occurred south of the Canadian border.

Exhausted from years of astonishing labour and repeated bouts of illness, George Monro

Grant died in Kingston, Ontario, on 10 May 1902. He was deeply loved and revered within his beloved Queen's, and was recognized as one of the most important churchmen and citizens of late-nineteenth-century Canada.

Bibliography
R. Cook, *The Regenerators: Social Criticism in Late-Victorian Canada* (Toronto: University of Toronto Press, 1985); D. B. Mack, 'George Monro Grant: Evangelical Prophet' (PhD dissertation, Queen's University, Kingston, Ontario, 1992); D. B. Mack, 'Of Canadian Presbyterians and Guardian Angels', in G. A. Rawlyk and M. A. Noll (eds.), *Amazing Grace: Evangelicalism in Australia, Britain, Canada, and the United States* (Montreal-Kingston: McGill-Queen's University Press, 1994), pp. 269–292.

G. R. MIEDEMA

■ **GRAY, Asa** (1810–1888), Professor of Botany at Harvard and American defender of Darwin, was born to Moses and Roxanna Gray on 18 November 1810 in Sauquoit, near Utica. He went to Fairfield Academy in 1825 and transferred from there to Fairfield Medical School. He graduated as Doctor of Medicine in 1831, but never practised. After 1828 he was drawn to botany and spent the next eleven years developing his botanical career. He taught science at Utica from 1832, and from 1835 was curator at the New York Lyceum of Natural History. During this period he studied the flora in New York State and beyond. In 1836 he was appointed botanist to the Wilkes expedition but resigned shortly before the expedition departed. He worked with the botanist Torrey on the *Flora of North America* (1838–1843). In 1838 he was appointed Professor of Botany at the University of Michigan, but he never assumed his duties. From 1838 he spent a year in Europe to obtain books and to study typespecimens in European herberia.

In 1842 Gray was appointed Professor of Natural History at Harvard University, where he spent the rest of his life. He became the foremost botanist of his day. His herbarium at Cambridge, Massachusetts, grew to be the best in the country. He travelled much, not least to Europe (1850, 1855, 1868, 1880 and 1887), and met Darwin on several occasions. In 1848 he married Jane Lathrop Loving, who supported him in his work and edited his autobiography and letters. From 1835 until his death, Gray wrote copiously on botany. His most important work, *Manual of the Botany of Northern United States* (1848), has gone through numerous editions.

Gray is also important as the propagator of Darwin's ideas in the USA after 1859. He made them acceptable to many Protestants and is sometimes called 'Darwin's Retriever' in contrast to 'Darwin's Bulldog', Huxley. He first met Darwin in England in 1851 and frequently corresponded with him. In 1857 Darwin sent him a précis of his theory, and in 1859 a copy of *The Origin of Species*. In 1860 Gray facilitated the publication of an American edition and reviewed Darwin favourably in the *American Journal of Science* and *Atlantic Monthly*, interpreting his theory theistically. Darwin and Gray discussed the 'theology' of *The Origin* in letters (see M. B. Roberts, *Science and Christian Belief*, 9 [1997], pp. 113–127). At the end of *Variation under Domestication* (1868) Darwin made it clear that he could not accept Gray's theology and wrote, 'However much we may wish it, we can hardly follow Asa Gray in his belief "that variation has been led along certain beneficial lines"' (vol. II, p. 428).

Gray's religious training in childhood led him to 'a rather vague acceptance of an unexciting Presbyterian Church'. At Bridgewater in 1831 he encountered Jeffersonian deism and in 1835 joined the Presbyterians at Bleeker Street Church, who were orthodox but downplayed predestination. While in New York he taught in a negro Sunday school and later shared his passionate anti-slavery views with Darwin. In 1842 he transferred to Albro's Congregational Church in Cambridge, though his wife remained a Unitarian. Gray described himself as 'one who is scientifically ..., a Darwinian, philosophically a convinced theist, and religiously an acceptor of the "creed commonly called the Nicene" as the exponent of the Christian faith' (*Darwiniana*, p. 5). He retained his Nicene orthodoxy despite his long career at Unitarian Harvard.

Gray's faith was irenic, and he reckoned that Darwin was no more an atheist than he himself. He wrote, 'I don't believe the Bible teaches science' and believed that evolution could 'be held theistically or atheistically'. He was equally irenic when he reviewed Charles *Hodge's *What is Darwinism?* for *The Nation* in 1874, gently but firmly challenging Hodge's answer, 'It is atheism'. In 1874 Gray became acquainted with G. F. Wright, who persuaded him to publish *Darwiniana*, which included both his 1860 articles and several important later writings. In 1881 Gray gave lectures to Yale Divinity School, published as *Natural Science and Religion*, which caused no controversy because of the accommodation that had been achieved between evolution and Protestantism. That accommodation survived largely intact until the Scopes trial in the 1920s.

Noll and Livingstone aptly describe Gray as 'a fairly conservative, relatively traditional Christian'.

Bibliography

A. H. Dupree, *Asa Gray* (Cambridge: Belnap, 1988); J. R. Moore, *The Post-Darwinian Controversies* (Cambridge: Cambridge University Press, 1979).

M. B. ROBERTS

■ **GRAY, James Martin** (1851–1935), Reformed Episcopal rector and second president of the Moody Bible Institute, was born in New York City and raised in a Protestant Episcopal home. He experienced conversion at the age of twenty-two and joined the newly formed Reformed Episcopal Church two years later. The details of his education and ministerial training are obscure, but by 1876 he was ordained. Soon after he embarked on a series of rectorships including the Church of the Redemption, Greenpoint, New York (1878), the Church of the Cornerstone, Newburgh, New York (1879), and finally the First Reformed Episcopal Church in Boston (1880), which he held for fourteen years. While in Boston, Gray cultivated broad civic and ecclesiastical ties, largely through his presidency of the Ministerial Alliance of Boston, his prohibition activities and his participation in the Committee of One Hundred (a local civic organization formed to promote separation of church and state, largely in response to fears of Roman Catholic influence).

While in Boston, Gray also began a Bible teaching ministry. In 1889 he began a fifteen-year association with Adoniram J. Gordon's Missionary Training School teaching the English Bible. Three years later he accepted a lectureship on the English Bible at the Reformed Episcopal seminary and started teaching occasionally at the Moody Bible Institute in Chicago. A year later he spoke at Dwight L. *Moody's influential Northfield conferences and began giving evening public lectures on the Bible. By 1894 he had resigned from his church to pursue his Bible teaching full time. He taught a series of general Bible classes associated with the YMCA beginning in 1897 and participated in Bible and prophecy conferences throughout the country.

The substance of Gray's system of biblical interpretation, termed the 'synthetic method', had a significant influence on evangelicalism. Codified in his work *How to Master the English Bible* (1908), the system was closely connected with dispensational theology. Books of the Bible were to be studied in a predetermined historical order, starting with Genesis, so that the reader would grasp the overall flow and story: 'a single thread running through the whole – a pivotal idea around which all the subsidiary ones revolve'. This 'history' also included biblical prophecy, which was seen as a clear, infallible prediction of future events. The result was a complete, if complex, hermeneutical structure that mapped the entire scope of human existence within the Bible. Not surprisingly, Gray was selected as an editor of the *Scofield Bible* in 1909.

In 1898 Gray took the summer deanship of the Moody Bible Institute, the first step on the path to his eventual leadership of the organization. At the behest of the then-president Henry Crowell, Gray became permanently associated with the Institute in 1904. A year later he became dean of students and by 1908 was fully in charge of day-to-day operations (though the title of president was not given to him until 1925). Gray played a key role in transforming the Institute into one of the major fundamentalist institutions of the twentieth century. Along with Crowell, he sought to improve the academic standards of the institution without straying from the essentially pragmatic end of training Christian lay-workers. His dispensational-influenced synthetic method replaced the institute's earlier, less systematic, relational interpretation of the Bible. In addition, he brought a moderate Calvinism (essentially a simplified and softened version of Princeton theology) to the institute, which weaned it from its early roots in holiness theology and directed it more towards the idea of 'victorious living' embodied in the Keswick movement. In short, his systemization crystallized the institution both doctrinally and administratively. His template was not only maintained at the institute until well after his death in 1935, but also imitated by countless other Bible institutes throughout the country.

Gray also took an active role in the fundamentalist-modernist controversies. He launched a number of pointed written attacks against Harry Fosdick and other modernists, often using his editorship of *The Moody Bible Institute Monthly* (1907–1935) as his base of operations. Gray also contributed to *The Fundamentals* (1910–1915) and was highly suspicious of cooperative ventures such as the Federal Council of Churches. At the same time, he went to great lengths to distance the institute from denominational infighting and the appearance of sectarianism. He made a concerted effort to attract students from various denominations to the institute, and sought to keep his formulation of 'the fundamentals' generic enough to be acceptable among most conservative Protestants.

Bibliography

J. D. Hannah, *James Martin Gray, 1851–1935, His Life and Work* (ThD thesis, Dallas Theological Seminary, 1974); W. M. Runyan, *Dr. Gray at Moody Bible Institute* (New York: Oxford University Press, 1935).

T. GLOEGE

■ **GRIBBLE, John Brown** (1847–1893), missionary to Aborigines, was born to parents partaking in the exodus of Cornish miners to Australia. The infant Benjamin John Brown Gribble and his five sisters arrived at Port Phillip from England in 1848 with his parents, Benjamin Gribble and Mary (née Brown). They settled in Geelong, where John was educated and where he married Mary Ann Elizabeth Bulmer on 4 February 1868. Both he and his sisters had large families

(John and Mary had nine children), providing him with a network of relatives and friends in most of the eastern states of Australia.

Converted at the age of fourteen, Gribble dedicated his life to preaching the gospel. He was first admitted into the ministry of the United Free Methodist Church in 1876, but was drawn by the 'jackeroo parson' vision of J. J. Halley into the Congregational Union of Victoria, engaging in wide-ranging home missionary activities from the towns of Rutherglen and Wahgunyah on the Murray River. Gribble was not the only Methodist whom Halley brought in to build Congregationalist frontier work. In general, Gribble's success, like that of Moravian missionaries in Australia, was built on the difficulty traditional denominations with fixed parish structures had in coming to terms with the vastness of Australia. There was no alternative to the ministry of such people. After becoming the first resident minister in Jerilderie, Gribble showed his character in a legendary encounter with the bushranger, Ned Kelly, who held up the town in 1879. Gribble accosted the armed criminal, demanding and receiving back his stolen watch.

His location on or near the Riverina bought Gribble into close contact with aboriginal people, stirring him to 'compassion for them in their suffering, and anger at the injustice meted out to them'. In his book *Black but Comely*, he linked this sympathy to an occasion when he became lost as a child in the crush of crowds celebrating the separation of the new colony of Victoria from New South Wales (NSW). 'The small John Gribble was rescued by a kind aboriginal woman called Biddy, who took him back to her camp and looked after him until his frantic parents finally located him.' He made friends with Daniel and Janet Matthews, visiting their Maloga Mission on the Murray River. Determining to follow their example, he published his *Plea for the Aborigines of NSW* (1879). The following year, John and Mary Gribble opened their Warangesda Mission on the banks of the Murrumbidgee at Darlington Point. In the antagonistic setting of nineteenth-century Australia, his decision was perhaps even more courageous than confronting an armed bushranger: 'The flesh said "Stay where you are; why impoverish your wife and family and isolate them from all society?" But the spirit said – "Go and rescue the perishing! Go and build them a home in the wilderness."'

Despite opposition from local white settlers, and having to fund the mission themselves, 'they constructed the typical mission village – cottages for married couples, boys' and girls' huts, mission house, sheds and outbuildings'. News of the mission spread, and soon aboriginal people from all over the expanding frontier of western NSW were seeking it out as a refuge. In 1880 the Church of England bishop of Goulburn, Mesac Thomas, visited Warangesda and found that many Aborigines had already become Christians. He baptized nineteen, decided to assist the mission and made Gribble a stipendiary reader in the Church of England. Gribble was ordained deacon (1881) and priest (1883) by Thomas. This support, together with an annual government subsidy of £90, relieved the mission's financial difficulties, although it soon had over a hundred residents and was 'frequently reduced to the deepest poverty'. Nevertheless Gribble wrote, 'God interposed for us in every season of want ... we have endeavoured, in season and out of season, to win them to him "who is able to save to the uttermost" and we rejoice in the knowledge that the gospel of Christ has proved itself to be the very power of God unto salvation, even in the case of those whom, so many regard as little more than animals.' Gribble took a long sea voyage to England in 1884 to recuperate from illness and to write Black but Comely, his description of Aborigines and the Warangesda Mission, which he published in England with the assistance of the Archbishop of Canterbury.

In the west, the Anglican Bishop Parry was faced with the challenge of building a vast diocese with few resources. His efforts from 1878 to obtain a mission reserve led in 1884 to the reservation of 150,000 acres in the Murchison and Gascoyne area of the colony and an invitation to the Gribbles to develop it. The Gribbles arrived in Carnarvon late in 1885. Gribble immediately set out on a long inspection of the region, and quickly discovered the reason for the bishop's concern. The lack of a convict labour system in the west had led to the systematic use of forced labour ('which differed little from slavery') in the pearling, fishing and sheep-farming indus-

tries. Returning to Carnarvon, Gribble named his mission 'Galilee' and set about constructing buildings on the Gascoyne River about 4 km out of town. His evangelical fervour and high principles were roused when an aboriginal runaway sought refuge on the mission. Gribble found himself in immediate confrontation with the local farmers, telling the 'owners' that aboriginal people were not slaves but free subjects of the Queen. Gribble was attacked in public meetings held in Carnarvon, and a petition was sent to Perth calling for his withdrawal. Calling his seventeen-year-old son Ernest to help on the mission, Gribble went to Perth to defend himself before church dignitaries. He delivered a public lecture entitled 'Only a Blackfellow, or the Conditions and Needs of Our Aborigines', in which he strongly criticized the mistreatment of aboriginal people at the hands of the pearlers and farmers. Back in Carnarvon he found himself ostracized and publicly vilified. After further public meetings, the newspaper The West Australian took up the farmers' cause, reporting on the dispute and condemning Gribble. Parry was in a difficult position. The northern farmers were influential supporters of the Church of England, and so in February 1886 the diocese of Perth's mission committee restricted Gribble to his mission.

In June 1886 Gribble's book Dark Deeds in a Sunny Land took the story to a larger public. 'Even in Australia, under its sunny skies, deeds – the most dark and horrible in their nature – have been committed and are still being practised.' His details of atrocities, which became fuel for debates that continued in Australia for more than a century, created a furore. The diocese, concerned about its public position and funding, withdrew Gribble's license. The West Australian described Gribble as 'a lying, canting humbug'. Enraged, Gribble sued the newspaper. The Gribbles lived in dire poverty on the outskirts of Perth, awaiting the trial. In June 1887 Justices Onslow and Store found in favour of the newspaper. Penniless and unable to pay his legal costs, Gribble left Western Australia (WA) a broken man.

Back in the east, despite the best efforts of sympathetic bishops, Gribble was never happy. After several parish appointments, he cashed in his life assurance policy and selected a site not far from Cairns, in Queensland, where he began to construct what was to become Yarrabah Mission. There, within a few months, Gribble became seriously ill. Just before his death he wrote, 'I have given my life and substance to defend the blackman of Australia; I have walked hundreds of miles for his benefit and endured many hardships that I might serve him; I have sacrificed my worldly interests for his good but, oh, I don't regret it. Would that I had fifty lives that I might spend in such service.'

After calling his son Ernest Gribble to take over Yarrabah, John Brown Gribble died on 3 June 1893. His funeral oration by Martin Simpson, an aboriginal Christian, was based on the text Gribble himself had chosen for his first sermon on the Aborigines: 'Lift up thy prayer for the remnant that is left' (Isaiah 37:4). On his tombstone in Sydney's Waverley cemetery Gribble is called 'The Blackfellow's Friend'. He was survived by his wife, four sons and five daughters, among whom Ernest became the longest-serving missionary to Aborigines in Australian Anglican history.

Church historians, embarrassed perhaps at the church's treatment of Gribble, have generally suggested that he was too impetuous, outspoken and ill-tempered, and that he might have achieved more by acting with more tact, diplomacy and self-restraint. But Gribble himself wrote, 'If I am to work as a missionary, it must be on lines of justice and right to the Aborigines of this land, in opposition to the injustice and wrong-doing of ... unprincipled white men. This is my decision and by it I stand or fall.' His friend and loyal supporter, Bishop Mesac Thomas, wrote, 'John Brown Gribble was ... a man of earnest piety but ... impetuous temperaments. Nevertheless we like him, for he has done good work.'

Bibliography

J. Harris, *One Blood, 200 years of Aboriginal Encounter with Christianity: A Story of Hope* (Sutherland, NSW: Albatross Books, 1990); S. Hunt, 'The Gribble Affair: A study in colonial politics', *Studies in Western Australian History* (Dec. 1984): European/Aboriginal Relations in Western Australian History, pp. 42–51.

M. HUTCHINSON

■ **GROUNDS, Vernon C.** (1914–), theologian and counsellor, helped to shape twentieth-century American evangelical thought. Born on 19 July 1914 in New Jersey to John and Bertha Grounds, Vernon Carl Grounds grew up the youngest of three children. Though his father was a train engineer, young Vernon showed little interest in anything mechanical, but in his early education he distinguished himself as a student in many fields. At Rutgers University he read widely, loved poetry and sang in the glee club. He graduated BA from Rutgers in 1937 with Phi Beta Kappa honours.

During these college years his childhood Christian (Lutheran) faith was challenged. During his first year he seriously questioned Christianity's truth claims. The following summer (1933), while at home in Clifton, New Jersey, he listened one Sunday to a gospel quartet composed of his high school friends. After the church service members of the quartet invited him to a home to discuss Christianity. Thinking that they might offer him a psychological insight or two, he went with them. But in conversation with them that evening he was struck profoundly by the fact that they had experienced something genuine. Half sceptically, half seriously, as members of the group were praying aloud, one after the other, Grounds prayed too, asking God, if he was real, to show him that Jesus Christ could be his saviour too. This was the beginnings of his personal faith.

Two books were especially helpful to Grounds in the early years of his new faith. Thomas Mann's novel *The Magic Mountain* raised issues of perennial concern. Mann offered no solutions but starkly revealed that without the gospel all culture, philosophy and experience reach what Grounds called 'a self-destructive impasse'. James *Orr's *The Christian View of God and the World* gave the young Grounds specific help in reconciling faith and reason. This book, Grounds explained, 'freed me from the haunting suspicion that belief in the gospel must be maintained by faith alone in defiance of learning and logic'.

Grounds soon joined his friends in the gospel quartet, not only as a singer but also as a preacher. Later, a pianist called Ann Barton joined the group, and later still, in June 1939, Vernon and Ann were married. Grounds' first extended ministry as a pastor was at the Gospel Tabernacle in Paterson, New Jersey. During his decade there (1934–1945) the congregation grew from 25 to 300. During these years he also taught at the American Seminary of the Bible and at King's College, and earned his divinity degree at Faith Theological Seminary in Wilmington, Delaware. His classmates included Francis *Schaeffer, Kenneth *Kantzer, Arthur Glasser, Joseph Bayly and Jack Murray, all later regarded as American evangelical leaders.

Grounds' full-time teaching career began in 1945, when he became Dean and Professor of Theology and Apologetics at Baptist Bible Seminary in Johnson City, New York. There his concern for the students led him into the practice of counselling, in which he was to engage for the rest of his life. In 1951 Grounds moved to Denver to assume responsibilities as Academic Dean of the fledgling Conservative Baptist Theological Seminary. Five years later he became president of the Denver seminary, just as it was being swept into controversies sparked by the Billy *Graham crusades and the reform of American fundamentalism.

Grounds' public speaking ministry was simply exceptional for a seminary professor. It helps to explain his thousands of friends in American evangelical circles and his vast sphere of influence. He accepted numerous engagements outside the seminary: college chapels, convocations and graduations; Baptist denominational meetings; scholarly addresses; and weekend conferences in churches and schools around the nation. Often he would use his journeys to and from the airport and his hours on the aeroplane to counsel a student or write an article.

After keeping to this heavy schedule for years, Grounds finally completed his doctoral dissertation from Drew University in 1960, twenty years after starting it. It was entitled 'The Concept of Love in the Psychology of Sigmund Freud'. He later testified that his frequent reading of Søren Kierkegaard's *Works of Love* convinced him of the 'multi-dimensionality of love in biblical faith'.

During his deanship and presidency the Denver seminary grew from thirty students to nearly 400. It also moved to another part of Denver, built a campus and gained national accreditation. When he retired from the presidency in 1979, Vernon Grounds was named

Chancellor and retired to his library of twenty thousand books, continuing to teach, travel, speak and write until well into his eighties.

Bibliography

K. W. M. Wozniak and S. J. Grenz (eds.), *Christian Freedom: Essays in Honor of Vernon C. Grounds* (Lanham: University Press of America, 1986); B. L. Shelley, *Transformed by Love: The Vernon Grounds Story* (Grand Rapids: Discovery House, 2002).

B. L. SHELLEY

■ **GUINNESS, Henry Grattan** (1835–1910), preacher and writer, was a grandson of Arthur Guinness, who founded the famous Dublin brewery in 1759. The Guinnesses belonged to the Protestant minority in Ireland, and some became ministers of the established church. Henry's home was decidedly evangelical (and teetotal), but his parents were not committed Anglicans. His father, Captain John Guinness, became an evangelical while serving in the Indian army. His mother, Jane Lucretia D'Esterre, was converted after her first husband was killed in a duel with the politician Daniel O'Connell. They were married in 1829 and Henry, born in Kingstown (Dun Laoghaire), was the eldest of four children. The family led a nomadic life, and shortly after Henry's birth they moved back to Cheltenham, where they attended the Congregational Chapel.

When he was fourteen Henry was offered an apprenticeship in the Dublin brewery. He rejected the offer; he was interested in finding a more adventurous life. From the ages of seventeen to nineteen he served as a midshipman. His brother Robert was converted while at sea, and in 1854 Robert's story resulted in Henry's conversion. Henry was still intent on seafaring, but a serious illness altered his plans. In 1855 he returned to Ireland to work on a farm. However, his restlessness and Christian commitment made him change direction again. He became an itinerant preacher in Ireland, where his evangelism provoked strong hostility, and then in Britain where he became widely known and many regarded him as another C. H. *Spurgeon. He returned to Ireland and preached to vast crowds during 1859, the year of 'the Great Revival'. At the end of

1859 he left for the USA and Canada, where his intensive preaching schedule almost ruined his health.

Back in the British Isles, in October 1860 Henry married Fanny Fitzgerald, a member of the Brethren. He became involved in the movement himself, but his restlessness persisted. In 1861 he and Fanny left for the USA, but amid the Civil War fever his pacifism earned him bitter criticism. Henry and Fanny went to Canada, where their first child, also Henry Grattan ('Harry'), was born. Early in 1862 Henry and Fanny were back in England, but not for long; they set off for a tour of the Middle East. Their second child, Mary Geraldine ('Minnie'), was born in 1862.

Henry resumed the work of an itinerant preacher in England and Scotland. However, the response to his preaching was much less favourable than it had been a few years earlier. The prospect of his becoming another Spurgeon seemed unlikely to materialize. He was not helped by newspaper reports of accusations that he bribed his 'converts' with Guinness money. Actually Henry and Fanny lived in very difficult material circumstances. Far from having any Guinness money at his disposal, Henry had given away a legacy that was due to him. Never at any time did he ask for or accept money from the family firm.

From 1864 to 1868 Henry and his family lived in Ireland. Henry became an elder in Merrion Hall, the well-known Brethren Assembly in Dublin. In 1868 Henry and Fanny, now with three children (Lucy Evangeline was born in 1865), settled in Paris. Henry engaged in open air preaching and also set up a chapel in the centre of Paris. Another son, Gershom Whitfield (grandfather of Os Guinness), was born in 1869, and another daughter, Phoebe, in 1870. However, the Franco-Prussian War brought their time in France to an end. The dramatic events of 1870–1871, particularly the unification of Germany and the destruction of the Papal States, made Henry even more convinced that a divine plan was unfolding. His interest in biblical prophecy, a marked feature of Brethrenism, greatly increased.

Henry and Fanny eventually settled in London with their six children (Agnes was born in 1871). Henry had a vision for the establishment of an interdenominational missionary training college run on the same faith principles as Hudson *Taylor's CIM. In 1872 the Guinnesses opened their college in Stepney Green, in London's East End. Henry believed that work among the capital's poorest and most brutalized people was important in the training of prospective missionaries. A year later Henry and Fanny acquired Harley House, in Bow and the institute was moved. In 1875 they acquired Cliff House in Derbyshire and decided to establish another college. At Cliff College students had not only theological but also practical training, as they were involved in the renovation and maintenance of the property and were given experience of farming. The students of Harley House and Cliff were accepted on the basis of their suitability regardless of age, sex, denomination, background, nationality, colour or financial circumstances. They were not expected to pay fees. In everything Henry and Fanny (who had the difficult task of keeping the books) lived by faith. Within a few years former students were found in many different parts of the world, and they sent back letters which further stimulated missionary enthusiasm. The 1870s were a decade of great acts of faith and major accomplishments by Henry and Fanny. They became friends with, among others, Amy McPherson, C. H. Spurgeon, William *Pennefather, William and Catherine *Booth, the Earl of *Shaftesbury, and D. L. *Moody (Henry also had a hand in the founding of Moody Bible Institute). The Guinnesses were involved not only in training but also in extensive missionary and philanthropic work among the people of London (they were very closely connected with *Barnardo's work). They were involved in equipping and running a missionary ship, *The Evangelist*, acquired in 1876.

Biblical prophecy was never far from Henry's mind, and he became an internationally known authority on the subject. He was very much in demand as a speaker all over the world. His *The Approaching End of the Age* (1879) quickly became a bestseller. It was followed by *Light for the Last Days* (1887) and *The Divine Programme of the World's History* (1888). In the 1870s and 1880s the arrival of large numbers of Jews fleeing from the pogroms of Eastern Europe stimulated his interest in the future of the Jewish nation. His studies took him into the realm of astronomy. He was convinced that the timescales of

Daniel and Revelation could be related to astronomical cycles and convergences. Such was his expertise that he became a fellow of the Royal College of Astronomers and the Royal Geological Society. Henry did not attempt to calculate the date of the second coming, but he did pinpoint 1917 and 1948 as years of special significance for the Jews. Among those whom Henry influenced was Arthur Balfour (famous for his 1917 'Declaration').

Henry travelled extensively, sometimes with Fanny, and he continued to take an interest in missionary work around the world. John R. *Mott was one of the many people whom he influenced in the course of his travels. Henry and Fanny were particularly interested in the work of their own children. Harry worked as a doctor in London and in the Congo. Minnie married Howard Taylor and they worked in China, where Gershom also worked. Lucy married a German missionary, Karl Kumm, and worked with him for a time in the Sudan.

Fanny died in 1898, and in 1903 Henry married Grace Hurditch, who bore him two sons. He continued to travel and to preach to the end of his life. He died and was buried in Bath. All the major newspapers carried obituaries.

Bibliography

M. Guinness, *The Guinness Spirit: Brewers and Bankers, Ministers and Missionaries* (London: Hodder & Stoughton, 1999).

M. J. DOWLING

■ **GUINNESS, Howard Wyndham** (1903–1979), evangelist, student worker and Anglican minister, came from an Irish family with an extensive history of involvement in evangelism and missions (and, ironically, brewing). The Brethren background of his grandfather, the famed international evangelist Henry Grattan *Guinness, prefigured the interdenominationalism that would dominate the lives of both Howard and his father. In the late 1850s the *Daily Express* wrote of Grattan: 'Such a preacher is a great power, prepared and sent forth by God, and as such Mr. Guinness has been hailed by all denominations'. His Brethren emphasis on the role of the Holy Spirit in biblical interpretation,

his premillennialism and his interest in science (particularly astronomy) were also reflected in the life of Howard, who was able in later years to capitalize on the networks, reputation and influence his grandfather had developed in Canada and the USA and throughout the British Commonwealth. Grattan's contribution to the study of biblical prophecy, his connections to *Spurgeon and *Moody and his founding of the East London Training Institute also located the family in the developing anti-modernist circles that would become 'fundamentalism' in the 1920s. Howard's ministry, however, was also heavily influenced by the Anglican evangelist Bryan Green, through whom he was converted in 1917. He adopted Green's evangelical Anglicanism and his emphasis on young people, schools and sport.

Howard was the sixth son of Henry Guiness and Annie Reed. Following secondary education at The Leys School, Cambridge, where he became active in student Christian evangelism, he entered St Bartholomew's Hospital, London in 1922 and completed his studies in 1928 (MRCS, LRCP), though he never practised medicine. His medical interests were linked to his family's background in missions and quickly led him into the evangelical student groups that were developing in response to the perceived 'liberalization' of university Christian organizations such as the Student Christian Movement. 'An active sportsman with a warm, friendly personality, an engaging laugh, genuine interest in people, and above all with a zeal to win other students for the Kingdom of God, Guinness was soon recognized as an outstanding Christian leader' (Braga, *ADEB*). He was a founding member of the London Inter-Faculty Christian Union in 1923, and successively its head and vice-chair of the Inter-Varsity Fellowship after its foundation in 1928. Under the influence of people such as Norman Grubb, Keswick holiness, Protestant mysticism and faith missions became central to the Inter-Varsity movement. In response to a plea for help from Canada, the Inter-Varsity leaders Howard Gough, Guinness and Douglas *Johnson, decided that Gough would work in England, Johnson would administer the Fellowship and Guinness would go into the world. They collected what little money they had, sold various items (including their sports equipment) and bought a one-way ticket to Canada.

Guinness arrived on 6 November 1928 with £14 in his pocket. He visited various university campuses and began drawing the Christian Unions together to reinforce one another. This process resulted in the founding of the Inter-Varsity Christian Fellowship of Canada in September 1929. The next year, Noel Palmer became general secretary, leaving Guinness free to travel across the rest of Canada, establishing branches and incorporating existing evangelical agencies into the Fellowship, and establishing the first of what would become a national network of Inter-School Christian Fellowships. In July 1929 Guinness had also initiated the Pioneer Camps with thirty campers and counsellors at Doe Lake, Ontario. Guinness wrote in his diary: 'it is a necessarily small camp this year; we have only twenty to thirty boys at a time. But this is Pioneer work and will develop into something really worthwhile and big.' By the 1990s the camps had become a national institution; some 7,000 young Canadians per year were attending ten Pioneer Camps across the country. The camps were extended to the United States and then beyond by the children's evangelistic agency 'Teen Ranch'.

While in British Columbia, Guinness received a telegram from the prominent Australian Brethren businessman J. B. Nicholson, who invited and paid for him to come to Australia. Arriving in January 1930, Guinness visited the Katoomba convention, modelled on Keswick, where he met members of the small Sydney University Bible League, which later became the Sydney University Evangelical Union. Through other contacts, he inspired the founding of the Crusader Union in private schools and Inter-School Christian Fellowships in state schools. Speaking at a public engagement on 7 April, Guinness challenged over 300 students to experience the power of the 'indwelling Christ'. Journeying to Melbourne, he gathered students out of the existing Student Christian Movement and formed the first two branches of the Australian Inter-Varsity Fellowship of Evangelical Students; its constitution and doctrine were taken directly from the British IVF. A 'DPM' (Daily Prayer Meeting), public meetings and Bible studies were instituted in imitation of the CICCU and LIFCU, which greatly influenced the Anglican evangelicalism that developed in Australia's largest cities. Guinness's own mystical and spiritual approach, however, was challenged when a group in the Sydney EU, influenced by certain missions, began to espouse sinless perfectionism. The group was defeated, and the leaders of the victorious party (e.g. John Hercus, Donald Robinson, Marcus Loane, Paul White) would lead Sydney student work and hold positions of denominational leadership until the 1970s. Sydney Anglicanism, influenced by another Irishman, T. C. *Hammond, embraced an anti-experiential rationalism against which Guinness would struggle in his later years. Guinness made two trips to Australia in the 1930s (1930–1931 and 1933–1934, the latter in response to calls for help against the influence of Moral Rearmament in the Evangelical Unions), when he also visited South Africa, New Zealand, India and Europe.

Guinness realized, in the light of his global travels and his marriage to Barbara Green in 1939, that he would never practise medicine but could not rely on his student ministry to support him. Moreover, travel became more difficult as international tension increased in the 1930s, and Guinness began to study for ordination. His decision reflected an ongoing debate in Inter-Varsity circles: what was the relationship of student work to local churches? Different movements came to different conclusions, but Guinness discouraged the treating of IVF as an alternative church and paid the price. As an interdenominational, evangelical, non-ecclesial structure, IVF was always underfunded, and its officers struggled for recognition from both churches and missions.

Despite Guinness's keen intelligence and natural giftedness with people, ordained ministry could not replace student missions in his heart. Having trained at St Aiden's College, Birkenhead, he served as a curate for Leslie Wilkinson at Worthing, before becoming an Army chaplain in the RAF Volunteer Reserve (1942–1946). On demobilization he returned to university life, serving in Oxford (1946–1949), where he continued to encourage innovative evangelistic outreach with leading British Christians such as C. S. Lewis. The university setting suited him.

In 1949 the social reformer R. B. S. Hammond, rector of St Barnabas, Broadway died. Archbishop Howard Mowll, a former CICCU president and missionary, invited Guinness to take over the parish, which included Australia's largest university. Guinness used it as a base for building up student work among the rapidly expanding post-war student population, and for university missions across the country. In the early 1950s he built the largest university congregation in Australia, a distinction that was to remain with 'Barnies' (due to the impact of the Billy Graham Crusade in 1959) long after Guinness transferred to St Michael's, Vaucluse, in 1957.

Guinness's transfer to St Michael's was sudden and confusing to some, but by the early 1950s he was suffering from a mysterious soreness of the throat, which led him to seek a respite from the constant round of conferences and preaching in large churches. He sought healing and investigated and reported positively on the visit to Sydney of the Pentecostal healing evangelist A. C. Valdez Jr. Guinness found speaking increasingly difficult, but his published works spoke for him. Several, such as *Sacrifice* (1936) and *The Sanity of Faith* (1950), became classics and were reprinted in many countries to support Inter-Varsity work. Others, such as *I Object to Billy Graham* (1959), written in a populist style and illustrated by Australia's leading political cartoonist, Benier, demonstrated his soapbox debating style, developed from years of arguing with students. Others, such as *The Seekers*, demonstrated his willingness to go where he believed the Bible led him rather than following the party line. His annihilationism and belief in the power of the love of God were unpopular in Sydney, though they had a long history in evangelical circles (from George Grubb in the 1890s, or even earlier). Guinness became increasingly isolated as many of the men he had strengthened in their Christian service through his student work rose to prominent positions in the church. His throat ailment was diagnosed as lymphatic cancer, but despite successful treatment in 1960 his voice continued to deteriorate, and he retired in 1971. He lived in a bushland setting in Wentworth Falls until his death in 1979, still writing and speaking whenever he could.

Guinness's autobiography, *Journey Among Students*, is a testimony to his energy and testified to the international impact of Inter-Varsity around the world. If J. I. *Packer and others promoted a recovery of evangelical scholarship, and Billy *Graham led a renewed global evangelistic outreach, it was the houseparties and student groups begun by Guinness, Gough and Johnson that nurtured and discipled the scholars and converts. The combination of tough-minded faith based on personal relationship with Christ, orientation towards missions and Keswick holiness, which marked evangelical student work in Australia at least into the 1970s and elsewhere for much longer, reflected Guinness's own synthesis. While his writing has become dated, Guinness was an example of the impact that a highly committed Christian life could have on the lives of generations of believers. His achievements were effected almost entirely through personal relationships. As he wrote in *Total Christian War* in 1945: 'Fellowship is the keynote of this belief; such a deep fellowship with God through Christ as shall inevitably lead to a deep fellowship with others of His children. The revival of the Christian Church will surely come only through the disciplined and creative fellowship of surrendered Christians; for such a fellowship in Christ is God's supreme weapon for the evangelization of the world (1 John 1:5–7 and John 17:22–23). The isolated Christian is an anomaly.'

Bibliography
National Library of Australia, BIOG, Biographical Clippings on Howard Guinness, Rev. Dr; Guinness Papers and taped interview with Barbara Guinness, CSAC Archives, Robert Menzies College.

M. HUTCHINSON

■ **GURNEY, Joseph John** (1788–1847), Quaker minister and reformer, was born at Earlham Hall near Norwich, England, on 2 August 1788, the son of John Gurney, a wealthy banker, and Catherine Bell, a descendant of the seventeenth-century Quaker minister and theologian Robert Barclay. Although the Gurneys had a long Quaker history, John Gurney's family was more open to the outside world than were many contemporary Friends. For example, one sister, Hannah, married Sir Thomas Fowell *Buxton, the well-known evangelical MP. Another sister was the prison reformer Elizabeth *Fry.

Gurney received his early education in Anglican boarding schools near Norwich, although on the understanding that he would be allowed to attend a nearby Friends meeting. Between 1803 and 1805 he studied at Oxford with a private tutor, since as a Dissenter he was ineligible for a degree. His studies included not only the classical languages but Hebrew as well. At seventeen he returned to Norwich to enter the family bank, and Earlham Hall remained his home for the rest of his life.

In 1811 and 1812 Gurney went through a period of profound spiritual searching that culminated in the decision to devote his spiritual life and energy to Quakerism. He began to wear the distinctive Quaker plain dress, keeping on his hat in fashionable gatherings, and eventually cutting most of his social ties with non-Quaker neighbours. He became active in Quaker affairs, serving on numerous committees and as a manager of a variety of Quaker schools and institutions. In 1818 he was formally recorded as a Quaker minister.

Gurney's emergence as a Quaker coincided with his commitment to advancing humanitarian reforms. He was an associate of Thomas Clarkson, William *Wilberforce and his brother-in-law Sir Thomas Fowell Buxton as an advocate of the abolition of slavery. He worked actively with his sister Elizabeth Fry as a prison reformer and as an opponent of capital punishment, both in England and on the continent of Europe. He supported movements for popular education. His work with the Norwich Bible Society won him the close friendship of Charles *Simeon, one of the leaders of the evangelical party in the Church of England until his death in 1836.

Gurney, through his preaching and writing, had a profound impact on contemporary Quakerism. He published a number of books and pamphlets, and several of his sermons found their way into print. Most influential were his *Observations on the Religious Peculiarities of the Society of Friends* (1824, revised ed. 1834) and *Essays on the Evidences, Doctrines, and Practical Evidences of Christianity* (1825). He affected Quakerism

in at least three important ways, all of which moved Friends in the British Isles, and a majority of those in North America, in a more evangelical direction. First, Gurney urged Friends to become more open to ties and contact with non-Quakers, along the lines of Gurney's own relations with evangelicals such as Charles Simeon. Secondly, Gurney encouraged a significant change in Quaker views of the Bible. For previous generations of Quakers, the foundation of their faith had been belief in the guidance of the 'Inward Light' of Christ in the soul. Although Gurney did not publicly discard this doctrine (he privately questioned it), he argued that the light shed by the Bible was far superior to the Inward Light, and that Scripture must be the basis of Quakerism. Finally, Gurney gave Friends a new understanding of justification and sanctification. Since the late seventeenth century, Quakers had seen the two as inseparable; they believed that one could be justified, or saved, only through the achievement of sanctification, or holiness, through the guidance of the Inward Light and obedience to the Holy Spirit. This achievement was a gradual process, often the work of a lifetime. Gurney taught Friends to separate justification and sanctification; to see justification, or conversion, as a single, instantaneous experience, followed by a long process of sanctification.

Although Gurney's vision of Quakerism won the support of most Friends in Great Britain and America, it also made him an extremely controversial figure. More traditional Friends feared him, believing him to be a crypto-Anglican or Presbyterian who was undermining the foundations of Quakerism. When Gurney sought the approval of the London Yearly Meeting of Friends for a visit to North America in 1837, the meeting was badly divided over issuing him with the necessary credentials, and critical letters pursued him across the Atlantic. In the United States, Gurney found Friends already divided into Hicksite and Orthodox parties because of a split in the 1820s. English Friends recognized the Orthodox as the legitimate body of Friends, endorsing their views of the authority of Scripture and the divinity of Christ, and Gurney limited his official contacts and visits to them. But even many Orthodox Friends, particularly in Philadelphia, New England

and Ohio, denounced Gurney. Eventually, these differences would lead to further separations in America.

Most American Friends hailed Gurney, however, and his influence on them was substantial. He visited almost every Quaker neighbourhood, advancing his views on doctrine and reform, and encouraging the formation of Sunday schools and Quaker educational institutions. He also reached beyond the Quaker world, debating with the divinity students at Andover, meeting with President Martin Van Buren and other public officials and winning the friendship of Whig party leader Henry Clay. To Clay, Gurney addressed a series of letters describing the success of the abolition of slavery in the British West Indies.

Gurney returned to England in 1840, his influence among British Friends enhanced by the enthusiastic reception he had received in America. He continued to pursue his interest in religious and educational work until his death at Earlham Hall on 4 January 1847.

Gurney was married three times and was twice widowed. In 1817 he married Jane Birkbeck, who died in 1822. She was the mother of Anna and John Henry, who alone among his children survived infancy. In 1827 he married Mary Fouler, who died in 1835. In 1841 he married an American Quaker minister, Eliza Paul Kirkbride, who survived him.

Bibliography

J. B. Braithwaite (ed.), *Memoirs of Joseph John Gurney*, 2 vols. (Philadelphia: Lippincott, 1854); D. Swift, *Joseph John Gurney: Banker, Reformer, and Quaker* (Middletown: Wesleyan University Press, 1962).

T. D. HAMM

■ **HADFIELD, Octavius** (1814–1904), Anglican missionary to New Zealand, was born on 6 November 1814 in Bonchurch on the Isle of Wight to a highly respectable family. The youngest of ten children, he suffered from consumption in his childhood and youth, and was educated in Europe by a private tutor, apart from a brief period at Charterhouse and two years at Pembroke College, Oxford. He was converted to Christ at Pembroke College, writing later 'I first learnt to put my trust in Christ, and my life into his hands, whether I lived or died.'

Hadfield's background had much in common with that of the High Church bishop of New Zealand G. A. Selwyn. He applied to the Church Missionary Society (CMS) on 11 September 1837 without knowing where they might send him. He sensed a call to missionary service. 'I became very impressed with Jesus' last command to his disciples "to go into all the world and preach the gospel to all men". It seemed to me that if this was among his last instructions, then they must be among the most important.' It was a most surprising career for one bred in polite society. His original intention was to do medical work, but he was sent out on 23 February 1838 to Australia to be ordained (the Bishop of London declined to ordain a man with an unfinished degree). He was ordained deacon in Sydney on 23 September 1838, was sent to New Zealand in 1838 and was priested at Paihia in the Bay of Islands on 6 January 1839, the first person of any denomination to be ordained in New Zealand.

Hadfield's initial duties were at the Waimate North School for missionary children. Then in 1839 he was offered an opportunity to do directly evangelistic work at Waikanae and Otaki, at the southern end of the North Island. When the twenty-five-year-old Hadfield, tall, pale and sickly, was taken to Waikanae in November 1839, he found an audience already enthusiastic towards Christianity, but facing a serious crisis. The chief Te Rauparaha had invaded the area some years earlier and had defeated the local occupants just a month before Hadfield arrived. Meanwhile English settlers arrived at nearby Wellington at about the same time. Hadfield rose to the challenge, declaring: 'I never felt happier or more contented and composed in my life, or ready to endure and bear whatever the Lord may call me to do.' He based himself in Waikanae and organized the erection of a large church there. Maori liked him and called him 'Harawera'. Hadfield became a confident Maori speaker and wrote *A Spelling Book for the Use of Maori Children* in 1852. As a single man he chose to live in the local Maori village, not in the fenced European cottages that kept missionaries in the north separate from their converts. He purchased no land for himself, and thus earned the affection of Maori. His deliberate defiance of the laws of *tapu* led to a breakthrough for Christianity.

Unfortunately, after four years Hadfield's illness recurred, and he was obliged to live in Wellington from 1844 to 1849. Others of lesser calibre took his place until he was able to return. He did not marry until 19 May 1852, when he was aged thirty-eight. His wife was Catherine (Kate) Williams, the daughter of Henry *Williams, the senior CMS missionary; she died in 1902. They had ten children.

After Hadfield's return to the coast, he based himself at Otaki, slightly further north. It was a much larger centre of Maori population, and the death of Te Rauparaha in 1849 ensured his welcome. A huge wooden church, Rangiatea, was built there to symbolize the triumph of Christianity over the forces of tradition.

Hadfield's long-term strategy for mission was to develop an indigenous church. Although, like other CMS missionaries, he was very slow to baptize Maori, he showed the utmost trust in those who had been baptized, appointing as catechists Riwai Te Ahu and then Rota Waitoa. He urged the ordination of Maori to the priesthood and persuaded Selwyn to ordain then as deacons. For many years Waikanae was distinctive in its recognition of Maori clergy. In race relations Hadfield was a conservative integrationist; he was happy for the government to reduce the authority of the chiefs and wanted to extend the rule of English law to Maori. He urged Maori to register as voters and consistently honoured the authority of the chiefs, even those pilloried by other Europeans.

Meanwhile, within New Zealand as a whole the early cooperation between Maori and Europeans was collapsing. Hadfield grieved over the affray at Wairau in the South Island in 1843, and he lectured the governor on the unrighteousness of European incursions into Maori territory. His concern reached its zenith when war began in 1859. The tribes of the Kapiti Coast, led by Wiremu Kingi Te Rangitake, returned to their Taranaki lands in the late 1850s and were outraged when the governor purchased the lands they were seeking to reoccupy from other Maori who had squatted on them. The Waitara incident that resulted provoked the Taranaki war. Hadfield defended the Maori action and was bitterly criticized as a result. He responded with a series of pamphlets, the first of which was entitled *One of England's Little Wars*. It was a masterly work that made Hadfield the most unpopular man in New Zealand. Yet he kept the Kapiti Coast free from the warfare and tension that erupted in many other parts of the North Island.

Hadfield's involvement in public affairs continued for the rest of his career. Yet to call him a 'political parson' is misleading. In many ways he was politically naive, motivated by a sense of Christian justice, determined that truth should prevail regardless of the consequences. His interest in education reflected these values; he opposed the secular system, determined that the church would not lose its tradition of public service and concern with the public agenda.

Hadfield declined the position of bishop when the diocese was created in 1858, although he served as rural dean from 1844 and as archdeacon of Kapiti from 1849. He was consecrated the second Bishop of Wellington on 9 October 1870. As the senior New Zealand bishop he was primate briefly, from 1890 until his retirement in October 1893. He gave priority to the church, thus annoying the CMS committee in London. Some suspected that he had abandoned his evangelical convictions. Judge Chapman commented that 'Mr Hadfield used to be very evangelical but the bishop has archdeaconised him'. These suspicions were unfounded. Certainly Hadfield represented a new generation that was not embarrassed about the church. Consequently, Bishop Selwyn, who was emphatically High Church, was able to work with him. But Hadfield had no liking for tractarian innovations and remained a convinced Protestant. He admired *Simeon as a churchman and a moderate. He was a staunch defender of the special role of Anglicanism and felt it ought not to be mingled too much with Protestant Dissent. So he was somewhat ambivalent about the validity of Methodist baptisms, despite having attended Methodist meetings as a boy. His view of Anglicanism as a distinct entity did however tend to inhibit the development of a vigorous and distinctive evangelical tradition within the New Zealand church.

Hadfield was also a scholarly defender of

the faith. In a series of sermons and published tracts he staunchly defended the faith against the intellectual challenges of the day, including scepticism, liberal Bible criticism, evolution and freethought. In many respects he was somewhat alienated from modern secular society, but he was committed to his church and his Lord.

Bibliography

C. Lethbridge, *The Wounded Lion* (Christchurch: Caxton Press, 1993); B. Macmorran, *Octavius Hadfield* (Wellington: private publication, 1969).

P. J. LINEHAM

■ **HAGIN, Kenneth** (1917–), teacher, writer and educator, has helped to shape the charismatic branch of Christianity over several decades. Hagin's emphasis upon the 'faith message' generated a grassroots movement known as 'Word of Faith'. Denominationally independent, 'Word of Faith' churches have been established throughout the world, originating from the Rhema Bible Training Center in Tulsa, Oklahoma, founded by Hagin in 1974.

Hagin was born in McKinney, Texas on 20 August 1917, and his early life was beset by unusual hardship. He was born prematurely, weighing less than two pounds. His father abandoned the family when he was six. Hagin and his mother moved in with her parents when he was nine. Diagnosed with 'a deformed heart and an incurable blood disease', Hagin was confined to bed just before his sixteenth birthday. Experiencing partial paralysis and other complications, he was given no chance of survival by his doctors.

On 22 April 1933 Hagin's heart stopped beating, and three times he felt himself leaving his body and descending into hell; each time he was brought back to life. Convinced that he was unconverted, on his third ascent from hell he prayed for Christ's forgiveness and the new birth and experienced a sense of peace with God.

Even though his family had planned his funeral, Hagin now desired to be healthy. While reading the New Testament, he discovered the verse (Mark 11:24) that would transform his life. He applied the words of Jesus to his own desire to be healed: 'Therefore I say unto you, "What things soever ye desire, when ye pray, believe that ye receive them, and ye shall have them."' By August 1934 he had become convinced that one could have what one desired the moment that one's faith became real, even before its results were visible. Armed with this new conviction, Hagin reasoned with himself. 'You believe that you are healed. If you are healed, then you should be up and out of that bed.' Three days later he was able to walk to the breakfast table to join his family. After sixteen months in bed, he began to engage in a full range of physical activity. Hagin's doctor examined his heart, and could find nothing wrong with it.

After his high school graduation, Hagin became the pastor of an interdenominational community church. He served this church for two years, but found himself drawn to Pentecostalism because of its belief in 'divine healing'. He overcame his opposition to speaking in tongues and received the experience known as 'baptism of the Spirit' in 1937. That same year, Hagin made the transition to Pentecostalism by becoming a licensed minister of the Assemblies of God (AG). He was a pastor in AG churches until 1949. In 1950, after a dramatic experience (he claimed that Jesus appeared to him in order to anoint him for a special ministry of healing), Hagin began working as a healing evangelist. He travelled extensively during the waning years of the Healing Revival movement, which had captured the attention of Americans in the 1940s and early 1950s.

Hagin adapted to changing times as the Healing Revival dissipated. Despite his work in healing evangelism, he had known since 1943 that his primary gift was that of a teacher, and from 1952 he regarded prophecy too as part of his 'true ministry'. The nature of his message began to distinguish Hagin from other leaders. His distinctive message was rooted in the convictions concerning faith that he had adopted as a teenager on the basis of his reading of Mark 11:24. For the remainder of his ministry he followed one vocation: 'Go teach My people faith.'

Hagin laboured in relative obscurity for years, but his influence began to increase in 1967. No longer affiliated with the AG, he had organized his own Kenneth E. Hagin

Evangelistic Association in 1963. In 1966 he had moved his offices to Tulsa, Oklahoma; this strategic move inaugurated a new era of growth. That year he began teaching his faith message regularly on the radio. To meet the need among his listeners for study materials, the Rhema Correspondence Bible School was formed in 1974. The need for a residential school became apparent that same year, and Rhema Bible Training Center was established in order 'to teach the principles of faith to those preparing for the ministry'. The school moved to spacious surroundings in a Tulsa suburb, Broken Arrow, in 1976.

Fifty-eight students from the first intake graduated from Rhema in 1975. More than 22,000 Rhema graduates are currently living in some 110 nations. Graduates have planted 1,490 churches worldwide. Rhema Bible Training Centers have been founded in fourteen countries. Hagin remains Rhema's president, while his son, Kenneth Jr, serves as executive vice president. Another key to the expansion of Hagin's ministry is literature; he and his son have written 147 books, and more than 65,000,000 copies have been distributed around the world. The *Word of Faith* magazine has a circulation of more than 400,000 a month.

Hagin has greatly influenced the charismatic community. The 'Word of Faith' movement has gained a life of its own, though it has not been without its critics. Hagin's teachings have been fiercely attacked by some leading evangelicals, who have alleged that it contains heretical elements and components derived from non-Christian spiritual traditions. Others have suggested that 'naming and claiming' whatever one desires is dangerous and results from presumption, not faith. Yet 'faith teachers' such as Hagin stand firm in their view that the potential results of faith are limited only by the words of Jesus and the promises of Scripture.

Bibliography

K. Hagin, *I Believe in Visions* (Tulsa: The Faith Shield, 1984); K. Hagin and K. Hagin Jr, *Look What The Lord Has Done!* (Tulsa: The Faith Shield, Faith Library Publications, 1992); Rev. and Mrs K. Hagin, *Kenneth E. Hagin's Fifty Years in the Ministry* (Tulsa: The Faith Shield, 1984).

D. W. DORRIES

■ **HAGUE, Dyson** (1857–1935), Canadian Anglican clergyman, enjoyed great advantages in early life. His father (from Yorkshire) was for many years general manager of the Merchant's Bank of Toronto and was a serious Bible student. Hague was educated at Upper Canada College and the University of Toronto (BA, 1880; MA, 1881), and studied theology at the recently founded Wycliffe College, Toronto, which combined evangelical conviction and missionary spirit. He married May Baldwin, from one of Canada's most distinguished families, with an Irish evangelical Anglican heritage and strong links to the Cronyns and the Blakes. Hague served a curacy at St James's Cathedral, Toronto, and then became first rector of St Peter's, Brockville, renowned as the largest congregation between Toronto and Montreal. He was rector of the oldest Protestant congregation in Canada, St Paul's, Halifax, for eleven years, and then at forty years of age was appointed professor of liturgies, apologetics and pastoral theology at Wycliffe. Remarkably, this man who exuded confidence left Toronto for London, Ontario, where for eleven years he was rector of Bishop Cronyn Memorial Church and became a canon of St Paul's Cathedral. Returning to Toronto in 1912, he became first rector of the Church of the Epiphany in the growing west end of the city, where he conducted an effective and widely recognized ministry. He also became lecturer in liturgics at Wycliffe, where he was not merely a part-time adjunct, but the guardian of the original Wycliffe vision. He resigned from both congregation and college in 1933.

Hague was an utterly committed evangelical Anglican, with a particular love for the Book of Common Prayer. Much of his writing dealt with the Prayer Book; his first volume was *The Protestantism of the Prayer Book*, published in 1890 and going through six printings, with Bishop J. C. *Ryle of Liverpool providing the preface for one and H. C. G. *Moule of Ridley Hall, Cambridge the preface for another. This was probably Hague's best work and would be normative for all that he would write on the subject. His purpose was 'to demonstrate the essential Protestantism of the Book of Common Prayer ... the services of the Prayer Book were drawn up by Protestants in the true sense, and intended for the establishment of Protestantism'. In *The Story of the English Prayer Book* (1926, 1930) he affirmed: 'The Prayer Book was the product of an Age. That Age was the Reformation. The men who produced it were the Anglican Reformers. They were scripture-inspired, spirit-led men.' With his conviction and ability he was famous for reading the liturgy 'with beauty and drama', and then for preaching 'with power and clarity'. He took an active part in the work of the general synod of the Church of England in Canada, particularly in regard to Prayer Book affairs, leading the successful opposition to a proposed revision in 1902, and playing a very active part, along with his close friend Samuel Blake the lawyer, in the preparation of the accepted Revised Prayer Book of 1911.

Hague also represented what may be termed Anglican protofundamentalism, which emerged in the Church of England in the late 1820s and the 1830s. In contrast with the optimism of much of Protestantism, it was dominated by fear, of liberalism in theology and society, of Roman Catholicism, and then of the emergence of tractarian Anglo-Catholicism in the Church of England. It sought to maintain the theology of the Reformation, to resist much contemporary biblical criticism, to enunciate a premillennial eschatology that appeared to make sense of difficult times, and to uphold Christendom with its close linkage of church, state and society. A considerable number of Church of England evangelicals adopted this point of view, and naturally it spread to Canada. As the position of Hague and his friends became more difficult in the 1920s, he turned increasingly to the study of his model and mentor, Bishop Maurice Baldwin of Huron diocese, whose biography he wrote in 1927. In *The Story of the English Prayer Book* he insisted that 'The need of the hour is no new Reformation. We must not change the character of the Church of England.' Although the evangelical Anglicans did not join sectarian fundamentalism in describing all the major denominations as apostate and calling for withdrawal, Hague was fearful that such a step might be forced upon him. In the same volume he expressed his apprehension: 'The new wine of a revived Arianism or Unitarianism, commingled with the strange wine of a revamped medievalism, will surely burst the bottle of our Anglican Church unity.' In the light of this apprehension it was unsurprising that Hague took an active part in the production of *The Fundamentals*, providing the very first article on 'Higher Criticism', one on the theology of the early chapters of Genesis and another on the atonement.

Hague was one of the last prominent and staunchly conservative evangelicals in Canadian Anglicanism, until the recent appearance of a new generation of evangelicals, less dominated by fear, well represented by *Essentials*.

Bibliography
Who's Who in Canada, 1931; The MacMillan Dictionary of Canadian Biography.

I. S. RENNIE

■ **HALDANE, Robert** (1764–1842), Scottish Independent preacher, was born on 28 February 1764 in Cavendish Square, London, the son of Captain James Haldane, a wealthy landowner in Scotland.

By the time Robert was ten his parents had died, and along with his younger brother, James, he was brought up under the care of his grandmother. The two boys attended the Grammar School of Dundee and the High School of Edinburgh. After spending a very short time at Edinburgh University, early in 1780 he joined *HMS Monarch* as midshipman under his uncle, Captain (afterwards Viscount) Duncan. Next year he was transferred to *The Foudroyant*, commanded by Captain Jervis, afterwards Earl St Vincent. While on board he saw some active service against the French.

Haldane spent time at Portsmouth, where he came under the influence of David Bogue of Gosport. Bogue was a fellow Scot, the minister of an Independent congregation and tutor of a ministerial academy. On leaving the navy in 1783 Haldane spent some time under Bogue's tuition and then returned to Edinburgh University, where he remained for two sessions, following up his studies by making 'the grand tour' in the spring of 1785. In 1786 he married Kathlene Cochrane, daughter of George Oswald of Scotstown, and settled down in his ancestral home of Airthrey, where for ten years he led a country life. The outbreak of the French Revolution led him to take a keen interest in politics and express an interest in the politics of the Revolution. This led to his being viewed as a republican sympathizer. But he was dismayed by the eventual impact of the Revolution, and consequently became more and more engrossed in religious issues; he was converted in 1795. However, as late as 1800, in order to vindicate himself from various rumours, he published a pamphlet entitled 'Addresses to the Public by Robert Haldane concerning his Political Opinions and Plans lately adopted to promote Religion in Scotland'.

In 1796 he devised a project for founding a mission in India; he himself was to be one of the missionaries and to supply all the necessary funds. He proposed to sell his estates and to invest £25,000 for the permanent support of the work. His friend Bogue agreed to accompany him to India, and a body of catechists and teachers and a printing press were to be taken. But the East India Company refused to permit the mission to be planted on any part of its territory, and the scheme was abandoned. From 1796 to 1804 Haldane was a director of the London Missionary Society.

About 1798 he made a plan for bringing twenty-four children from Africa to be educated and sent back to teach their compatriots, and promised to bear the entire cost of their transport, support and education, estimated at £7,000. The children were brought to Britain, but for some reason they were not placed under Haldane's care, though he had arranged for their accommodation in Edinburgh.

Robert Haldane and his younger brother, James, became itinerant evangelists in 1797, having an interest and involvement in evangelism in Britain and overseas. As members of the established Church of Scotland they developed ecumenical contacts with leaders in the Church of England such as Charles *Simeon, as well as with Independents like David Bogue, believing that the success of evangelism depended on Christians co-operating in the propagation of the gospel message. Robert began to use his wealth to establish the Society for the Propagation of the Gospel at Home.

In 1798 Robert Haldane sold a large part of his Airthrey estate near Stirling to finance the work of home evangelism and began to open preaching centres where evangelicals of different denominations preached to the poor. The Haldane connexion grew rapidly. By 1805 there were twenty-five congregations in existence, and by 1808 the number had grown to eighty-five. Those who attended the services were encouraged to return to the established church to receive the Lord's Supper. The first building to be opened was the Edinburgh 'Circus', in Little King Street. The building drew crowds of more than two thousand, and in 1801 they moved to larger premises at the head of Leith Walk, 'Scotland's most capacious church building', with seating for over three thousand people, the average attendance for a Sunday evening service being about 3,600. For some time people were being converted as a result of every sermon, sometimes as many as ten to fifteen each Sunday. To provide pastors Haldane founded academies for the training of catechist-preachers in Glasgow, Edinburgh, Dundee and Elgin, whom he maintained at his own expense. It is said that in the twelve years from 1798 to 1810 he expended over £70,000 on his schemes for the advancement of religion in Scotland.

In 1803 Haldane adopted some Glasite views. Along with his brother he became increasingly committed to restoring the conditions of the early church within the congregation. The church began to 'break bread every Lord's Day', to practise mutual exhortation and to exercise discipline, and appointed a plurality of elders, although they did not adopt the holy kiss. As in some Glasite congregations, these issues caused division on more than one occasion. Indeed, the Tabernacle was the source of at least eight other churches in Edinburgh, most of them owing their origins to internal divisions.

Both brothers became Baptists in 1808. Although a considerable number left the church at this time and formed an Independent congregation, the Haldane brothers never made baptism an issue which barred people from communion or membership. This did not mean that Robert would not try to help individuals to understand his view of the meaning and purpose of baptism, but he never coerced anyone into being baptized. Haldane's involvement with Christians from various denominations, working alongside them in the furtherance of the kingdom of

God, led him to focus upon the more fundamental issues at the heart of religious life.

In 1816 Haldane went to Geneva and began a remarkable work of continental evangelization. A large number of students from the university came to him daily for instruction, and he gained over them a profound influence. In 1817 he moved to Montauban and procured the printing of two editions of the Bible in French, amounting to sixteen thousand copies in all, which he circulated along with a French translation of his 'Evidences' and a commentary on the epistle to the Romans in the same language, and many tracts.

In 1819 he returned to Scotland to an estate at Auchingray, Lanarkshire, which he had purchased. By the end of 1824 he had become involved in a controversy regarding the circulation by the British and Foreign Bible Society of the Apocrypha with the Bible. Although this policy was reversed, Haldane was instrumental in founding the alternative Trinitarian Bible Society in England and the Edinburgh Bible Society in Scotland.

Haldane died in Edinburgh on 12 December 1842, and was buried in Glasgow Cathedral.

Bibliography
A. Haldane, *The Lives of Robert and James Haldane* (London: Hamilton, Adams & Co., 1852).

K. B. E. ROXBURGH

■ **HALL, Christopher Newman** (1816–1902), Congregational minister and author, was born on 22 May 1816 at Maidstone, the fourth son of John Vine Hall, proprietor of *The Maidstone Journal*, and his wife Mary. His father was a reformed drunkard, a Congregational layman and the author of a popular gospel tract, *The Sinner's Friend*. Hall claimed that his earliest memory was of sitting on his mother's knee while she endeavoured to teach him John 3:16. This idealized vision of his early childhood was probably prompted by the homesickness and cruelty he experienced from the age of eight at boarding schools. From the age of fourteen he was an apprentice to his father for seven years, rising from manual work to journalism.

Hall experienced conversion when he was sixteen years old. He considered the ministry but struggled for some time over whether or not he had a true call. Having conquered this doubt, he quickly gained the support of his local minister and congregation. In September 1837 Hall entered Highbury College, a Congregational institution for ministerial training. While he was there, Highbury developed a relationship with the University of London, and he was awarded a London BA in 1841. He accepted a call from the newly founded Albion (Congregational) Church, Hull, to be their first minister and was ordained on 13 July 1842. During the twelve years in which he served that congregation, the membership grew from forty-two to around 700, with 768 children enrolled in Sunday school programmes.

In 1848 Hall wrote his enormously popular gospel tract *Come to Jesus*. Sixty-four pages long, it made almost no references to any authors or facts outside the Bible. Moreover, the prose was littered with biblical quotations, which comprised perhaps a quarter of the total, and each short section ended with biblical references for suggested further reading. The contents were a straightforward evangelistic appeal supported by basic evangelical teaching. One section was entitled 'Hell Awaits You – Come to Be Saved', and the question of one's future state runs unabashedly through the volume. In the section 'Ye Who Are Young Come', Hall writes, 'Perhaps you think, "I am too young to be religious yet; let me enjoy the world a little; I have plenty of time before me." Too young to be religious? But you are not too young to sin, or too young to die, or too young to be cast into hell.' During Hall's own lifetime, *Come to Jesus* was printed in forty different languages, some four million copies being issued.

Hall claimed as an old man that he had never delivered a sermon 'without the Cross being the keynote' and that he had never preached without aiming to provide an answer to the question 'What must I do to be saved?' His friend Charles *Spurgeon wrote to Hall in 1888, 'In these days, we are two of the old school. Our experience has taught us that, both for conversion and edification, the doctrine of Christ crucified is all-sufficient.' Nevertheless, in some ways Hall sided with the new school of evangelicals. On the three occasions during his ministry when a Congregational minister was accused by his peers of departing from evangelical doctrine (the controversy in 1846 over Edward White's *Life in Christ*, a volume that argued for conditional immortality; the 'Rivulet' controversy of 1855, in which T. T. Lynch's published hymns were censured by some as tending towards pantheism and suspiciously devoid of touchstone doctrines; and the 1859 controversy over J. Baldwin Brown's *The Divine Life in Man*, a volume that moved away from traditional evangelical notions regarding the atonement), Hall invariably defended and befriended the accused. His actions are partially attributable to his irenic nature and lifelong yearning for Christian unity. Nevertheless, he clearly indicated that White's annihilationist view had convinced him, and he also acknowledged that he did not believe in the verbal inspiration of the Scriptures.

In 1854 Hall accepted a call to Surrey Chapel, Blackfriars, London, a congregation founded by Rowland *Hill. He served this congregation for the rest of his long ministry, gaining a considerable reputation as a prince of the Victorian pulpit. He led the congregation through an ambitious building project, which resulted in 1876 in an extravagant neo-Gothic building, Christ Church, Westminster Bridge Road, costing £64,000. Lest anyone should miss the rise in Dissenting status that it put on display, Hall could not resist casually noting that the Archbishop of Canterbury's 'palace garden extends immediately under our steeple'. From a variety of clues, it seems probable that one of Hall's weaknesses was a tendency towards vanity.

During the American Civil War, Hall took a lead in endeavouring to rally support in Britain for the cause of the North; he tirelessly toured the country lecturing on this issue and wrote for publication on the subject, and privately to Gladstone. He toured the American North to great acclaim in 1867; he was invited to preach to a joint gathering of both Houses of Congress on a Sunday, and even the New York stock exchange ceased business for a few minutes in order to hear him speak. Hall dubbed the proposed steeple for Christ Church 'the Lincoln Tower' and raised money for it in America. When completed, the 220 foot high steeple was decorated with structural stars and stripes in red stones upon white, and it was opened on 4 July. We are not told what the archbishop thought of it.

In 1846 Hall had married Charlotte, the only child of Dr William Gordon, a man whom Hall greatly admired. In 1868 Charlotte began an affair with Frank Richardson, a livery stable keeper, leading to her permanent separation from her husband in 1870. Hall began a suit for divorce in 1873 but later withdrew it, partly out of fear that the publicity would hamper fundraising for Christ Church. When he again sought a divorce in 1879, Hall made legal history by establishing the precedent that a person who had withdrawn a divorce suit was still at liberty to make another attempt later on the basis of the same evidence. Following a well-reported trial, Hall secured his divorce on 17 February 1880. A month later (29 March 1880) he married Harriet Knipe, an Anglican woman he had met on a Cook's tour of the Holy Land in 1870, which he had taken as a way of dealing with the strain caused by the breakdown of his first marriage. His marriage to Harriet was a happy one.

Curiously, Hall decided when he moved to London to pursue a law degree. He obtained a London LLB in 1856. He was also awarded honorary DD degrees from Amherst (1864) and Edinburgh (1892). In 1866 Hall served as the chairman of the Congregational Union of England and Wales, the highest honour his denomination had to bestow. Throughout his career he published numerous (mostly small) volumes. To mention a few: *The Scriptural Claims of Teetotalism* (1846) expressed his lifelong commitment to that cause; *Divine Socialism* (1851) was a tribute to the influence of Christian Socialism upon his thought; and *Follow Jesus* (1856) was a sequel to his most popular work. His many other publications include biographical studies of his father and his first father-in-law, and an autobiography (which, with true Victorian reticence, did not mention his first marriage).

In the 1860s Hall began a relationship with W. E. Gladstone, who came to use him as a sounding board for Nonconformist opinion. In the 1870s Hall began to host in his own home meetings between the great Liberal leader and prominent Nonconformists, especially ministers. For example, a meeting in 1875 at which 'Papal decrees and Disestablishment' were discussed had at least fifteen guests, including the Congregational minister R. W. *Dale, the Wesleyan minister William *Arthur, the peace advocate Henry Richard, and the celebrated missionary Robert *Moffat. Undoubtedly, Hall deserves part of the credit for the strong loyalty to Gladstone which the Nonconformist community developed in those years, and, in our less evangelical age, when Hall is still remembered by scholars it is usually for his invitation to come to Gladstone rather than his invitation to come to Christ.

As if to solidify his reputation as an evangelical, in 1856 Hall published *Sacrifice; or Pardon and Purity by the Cross*, republishing it towards the end of his life as *Atonement: The Fundamental Fact of Christianity* (1893). Moreover, when he retired in 1892 he was delighted to secure as his successor at Christ Church F. B. *Meyer, who not only was a worthy heir in terms of the eminence that he would attain as a preacher and popular Christian author, but also would prove to be a leading standard-bearer for conservative evangelicalism.

Bibliography
N. Hall, *An Autobiography* (London: Cassell & Co., 1898); T. Larsen, 'Sex, Lies and Victorians: The Case of the Revd Newman Hall's Divorce', *Journal of the United Reformed Church History Society* 6 (May 2001).

T. LARSEN

■ **HALL, Robert, Jr** (1764–1831), Baptist clergyman, was the son of Robert Hall of Arnesby, a distinguished clergyman who advocated a moderate form of Calvinism and contributed to the doctrinal discussions concerning the Trinity in the late eighteenth century. The senior Hall was author of the widely circulated *Help to Zion's Travellers* (1781). Robert, Jr, was born at Arnesby, Leicestershire, on 2 May 1764, the youngest of fourteen children. He was a frail son of the manse who exhibited unusual learning capabilities as a child. At the age of three he is said to have learned to read by using the gravestones in his father's churchyard. He was educated in various academies, including that of the celebrated Baptist divine John *Ryland of Northampton, who taught him

Greek and Hebrew. At first terrified at Ryland's overpowering demeanour, Hall later attributed his love for liberty to Ryland. He attended Bristol Baptist Academy from 1778 to 1784, being much influenced by Hugh and Caleb Evans, leaders of the evangelical movement among Baptists in the West Country. An outstanding student, he received an award under Dr John Ward's Trust to continue his studies at the University of Aberdeen, where he enrolled in King's College and graduated with an MA. While a student at Aberdeen, he met Sir James MacIntosh, later to become one of the most celebrated scholars of the nineteenth century. They frequently discussed issues of philosophical importance and read classical authors together, thus establishing a lifelong friendship.

One of the best-educated Baptists of his era, Hall returned to Bristol Academy in 1785 as a tutor in classical studies. After five years he was ordained to the gospel ministry in 1790 at Arnesby, where his father delivered the sermon. In 1791 he succeeded Robert Robinson as Baptist minister at Cambridge, where he laboured until 1806. While in Cambridge, he suffered ill health and looked for a better climate. For the remainder of his life he suffered from bouts of depression. In 1807 he embarked upon a pastoral ministry at Harvey Lane Baptist Church in Leicester, which became the high-water mark of his ministry. While in Leicester he wrote his famous tract *Terms of Communion* (1815), and advocated a policy of open communion in his congregation. Feeling that the transition would be harsh for many in the congregation, Hall was supported by his church in the formation of a second congregation practising mixed communion, concurrent with his service at Harvey Lane. Twice the church built new facilities under Hall's pastorate, finally in 1811 providing space for a thousand worshippers. Following the death of John Ryland, Hall went to Broadmead Baptist Church in Bristol, where he finished his ministry.

Theologically, Robert Hall, Jr, was a progressive Calvinist in an era of theological change. In his youth he much appreciated the position of Jonathan *Edwards in the United States and would have considered himself an evangelical Calvinist. Similar to Dan Taylor of the New Connexion of General Baptists, and slightly more open than

Andrew *Fuller at Kettering, Hall led Baptists to a less deterministic theology at the beginning of the nineteenth century. As time passed, he developed an Arminian understanding of the atonement, and this had implications for his practice of ministry. From his reading of original texts in several languages, he compared biblical materials with other sources, notably Plato and Dante. Hall's strong and lifelong advocacy of relations with other Christians than those of his own denomination set him apart from mainstream Particular Baptists. For those who affirmed his work, he was the herald of the union between General and Particular Baptists finally realized in 1891. But for those who anathematized his thought, he was the *cause célèbre* for the growth of hyper-Calvinism and the Strict Baptist movement in Britain.

Robert Hall was an important advocate and spokesman for the Particular Baptists. His numerous tracts include works on 'Infidelity' in the context of the French Revolution (1800), 'War' against the background of Napoleon's rise to power (1801), education (1810) and church polity (1815). A moderate pacifist, he opposed international conflict because of the injustices it promoted and the misery it created. He wrote an important treatise against slavery in 1824; on this issue he was well ahead of others in his denomination. An ardent supporter of various types of education, he extolled the advantages of learning in Sunday schools for the labouring classes, and he favoured the establishment of the Baptist 'academical' institution for aspiring Baptist ministers at Stepney in 1810. He was popular among American Baptists due to his support for American ideas of liberty. Several editions of his works were printed in the United States. For his overall literary and scholarly achievements, Marischal College at Aberdeen University awarded him the Doctor of Divinity degree in 1817.

Between 1814 and 1820 Hall was engaged in a literary debate with Joseph Kinghorn, pastor at the Baptist Church in Norwich, over closed and open communion. The practice of open communion reflected a significant theological move for Baptists on both sides of the Atlantic. Hall was considered a leading liberal thinker and much in tune with the future of the emerging denomination. In his classic tract *Terms of Communion*, which he patterned on the work of John *Bunyan and Robert Robinson, Hall dealt with the question of whether the acknowledged unbaptized person ought to be allowed to take communion at the Lord's Table, unravelling Abraham Booth's classic work *An Apology for the Baptists* (1778). Hall contended that no person or council had any right to make the terms of communion different from those of salvation. Further, he found no warrant in the early church for closed communion and believed that it destroyed the unity of the Body of Christ that the New Testament prized so highly. Kinghorn responded with his tract *Baptism a Term of Communion at the Lord's Supper* (1816). In his retort to Kinghorn and Strict Baptists Hall referred to closed communion as 'a pestilential evil still cherished and retained in too many British churches'. He found that the zeal of the opponents of open communion was out of proportion to that of his own following and that those who opposed his position sought to embarrass and discredit him. Throughout the exchange Hall remained on close personal terms with Kinghorn and enjoyed Kinghorn's support for his advocacy of press freedom.

Hall was remembered as a great orator and oft-quoted conversationalist. It is said that his extemporaneous pulpit style was so effective as to cause his hearers to lean forward on the pews to catch his every word. He referred to the eminent John *Gill's works as a 'sea of mud' and taunted his Calvinistic hearers with gibes about predestination. He referred to John *Wesley as the 'quiescence of turbulence' and to John *Owen as 'intolerably heavy and prolix'. In 1784 Hall was one of the observers present at G. F. Handel's Commemoration in Westminster Abbey when King George III stood up to honour the performance of *Messiah*. Hall remarked that 'it seemed like a great act of national assent to the fundamental truths of religion'.

From his childhood Hall suffered from a painful recurring condition diagnosed posthumously as a build-up of kidney stones. In his youth his brothers often had to carry him around during attacks. As an adult he was not allowed a full night's rest by the pain and suffered extended setbacks. By 1826, seeking to alleviate his misery, he had developed an opium dependency. Hall died at Bristol on 21 February 1831. He was averse to any portrait being made of him during his lifetime, but a statue stands near his Leicester church.

Bibliography

R. Brown, *The English Baptists of the Eighteenth Century* (Didcot: Baptist Historical Society, 1986); O. Gregory (ed.), *The Works of Robert Hall, A.M.* (New York: Lippincot, 1848); A. C. Underwood, *A History of the English Baptists* (London: Carey Kingsgate Press, 1947).

W. H. BRACKNEY

■ **HAMMOND, Thomas Chatterton** (1877–1961), evangelist, apologist and theological educator, was born in Cork, Ireland, on 20 February 1877, the youngest child of Colman Hammond, a farmer and retired sailor, and his second wife, Elizabeth. When his father died six years later the family moved from their farm to the city, where Hammond was educated at the Cork Model School. Straitened family circumstances required that he leave school at the early age of thirteen and take a post as a railway clerk. About the same time he became an active member of the Cork YMCA. In this setting he was converted under the influence of John McNay, whose sister, Margaret, he later married (1906). Almost immediately Hammond began taking part in open-air gospel meetings in the streets of Cork. Amid scenes of bitter sectarian recrimination he was soon notorious among Catholics as 'the Boy Hammond'.

In 1895 Hammond entered the Training School of the Irish Church Missions (ICM) in Dublin. After two years' training, he worked as an itinerant evangelist for the Missions in the western half of Ireland (1897–1899). During this time he decided to seek ordination in the Church of Ireland. Following a year's private study, he entered Trinity College, Dublin, in January 1900. Three years later he graduated with a first-class degree and a gold medal in philosophy. His education added intellectual rigour to his naturally clear mind and caused his subsequent approach to theology to be philosophical.

At the end of 1903 Hammond was ordained and began work in the lower-middle-class parish of St Kevin's, Dublin, where he served as curate for seven years before succeeding the rector in 1910. He led the parish in an increasingly vigorous Protestant and evangelical life. At the same time he became well known further afield as a popular preacher and sound 'Protestant', aggressively evangelizing and opposing Catholicism in both its Anglican and Roman forms. His reputation led in part to his selection as superintendent of the ICM early in 1919. His tenure coincided first with the Irish war of independence and civil war, and then with the economic hardships and Roman Catholic hegemony of the Irish Free State. Under these difficult conditions Hammond toiled unflaggingly for the Missions. He guided their welfare and educational work to new levels of achievement. The evangelistic and apologetical work he spearheaded resulted in the reception of some 500 Catholic 'converts' into the Church of Ireland, including twenty-five priests. Hammond's humanity and fairness in controversy won wide respect on both sides of the sectarian divide.

Alongside his practical activities Hammond was always a prolific author, mainly of pamphlets and booklets. Conditioned by their sectarian setting, his writings articulated a theology of opposition. *The One Hundred Texts* (1939) in particular codified Protestant opposition to Roman Catholicism. Hammond's reactions to events were expressed in *The Catholic*, which he edited during these turbulent years. A Unionist disappointed at Ireland's abandonment by Britain in 1922, he persisted in the belief that the nation needed spiritual more than political freedom.

Hammond's work and reputation led to increased work abroad. Each year he travelled around England on deputation work for the ICM, which he also represented at Keswick. He was an early supporter of the Bible Churchmen's Missionary Society in its revolt against CMS. As a member of the Fellowship of Evangelical Churchmen, he contributed to *Evangelicalism* (1925), its response to liberal evangelicalism and the wider theological unsettlement of the day. In 1926 he toured Canada and Australia to speak against revision of the Prayer Book. His work among students led naturally to support for the nascent IVF, which invited him on to its theological advisory committee. From this connection came an invitation to write an introductory handbook of doctrine for students. Emphasizing the importance of the mind in the life of faith, *In Understanding Be Men* (1936) became an evangelical best-seller, passing through five editions over the next fifty years. It was soon followed by similar works on ethics and apologetics, *Perfect Freedom* (1938) and *Reasoning Faith* (1943). Neither was as successful as the first, but all three contributed to the post-war intellectual revival of evangelicalism.

Although almost sixty years old, Hammond embarked on a new career when he was appointed principal of Moore College in Sydney late in 1935. At a low ebb when he took over, the college was transformed under his leadership. He worked closely with Archbishop Howard *Mowll to pay off a large debt, restore and augment the buildings, and raise academic standards. But his greatest contribution was as teacher and pastor to the students, whose numbers grew markedly, particularly after the Second World War. The moderate Calvinism and strongly objective theology he imparted to these men left a lasting impression on the diocese of Sydney.

In other ways too Hammond was a force in the diocese. Simultaneously with his post at Moore College he held the important city rectorship of St Philip's, Church Hill. He was a frequent and powerful speaker in the synod, to whose standing committee he was elected. Preferment came quickly: he was made Rural Dean of Balmain (1936), Canon of St Andrew's Cathedral (1939) and archdeacon without territorial jurisdiction (1949). Notoriously unable to say 'no' to invitations, he spoke widely in the parishes. Behind the scenes he was theological adviser to Archbishop Mowll, most notably in dealing with 'the Memorial' (a protest by some fifty clergy against the trend towards a strictly conservative evangelical churchmanship in the diocese), and president of the Anglican Church League, which sought to control diocesan elections.

Hammond also participated in the affairs of the wider Australian church and community. He represented Sydney in the Anglican General Synod, where for almost twenty years, during the preparation of a national church constitution, he argued for the independence of the separate dioceses. He persuaded Sydney to accept the final version as the best that could be achieved. Characteristically opposed to Catholic teaching and unauthorized ritual in the Church of England, he led the way in court action against the 'Red Book' of Bishop A. L. Wylde of Bathurst (1943–1948). He served as president of the NSW Council of Churches, wrote regularly for *The Australian Church Record* and *Evangelical Action*, and travelled widely throughout Australia and New Zealand to speak for the IVF and at Keswick-style conventions. At Sydney University he encouraged the Christian students by debating effectively with the influential atheist philosopher, John Anderson. He also fiercely opposed the sinless perfectionism that was popular in the Evangelical Union in the 1930s. Hammond maintained contact with Irish Australian Protestants as a member and office holder of the Loyal Orange Lodge of NSW and the Federated Loyal Orange Grand Council of Australasia. But he was best known for his weekly 'Principles of Protestantism' broadcast on Sydney's Radio 2CH, in which he often argued against the views of the Roman Catholic apologist Bishop Leslie Rumble, expressed on the rival station 2SM.

With his powers beginning to fail, Hammond resigned the principalship of Moore College at the end of 1953. He continued with his other ministries for another eight years. Then the good health he had enjoyed throughout his life broke down. After a short period of illness he died of a cerebral haemorrhage on 16 November 1961. An energetic and compassionate man with an impish sense of humour, he had been much loved by his friends and supporters, and at least respected by his opponents. At a time when leaders of his intellectual calibre were rare, his life of proclaiming and defending the evangelical gospel had made a considerable impact on evangelicalism in Australia and Britain.

Bibliography

S. Judd and K. Cable, *Sydney Anglicans* (Sydney: Anglican Information Office, 1987); W. Nelson, *T. C. Hammond* (Edinburgh: Banner of Truth, 1994); Hammond Papers (Moore College); *Australian Dictionary of Evangelical Biography*, pp. 150–153.

G. R. TRELOAR

■ **HARFORD-BATTERSBY, Thomas Dundas** (1823–1883), founder of the Keswick Convention, grew up in an evangelical home, but while studying for the Church of England priesthood at Balliol College, Oxford, came under the influence of John Henry Newman and the Oxford Movement. For Harford-Battersby, Newman and his circle were committed to a high standard of holy living in the Church of England, and this he found attractive. Harford-Battersby served his first curacy at Gosport in Hampshire with a rector of High Church sympathies. However, as he studied theology more deeply, he became increasingly dissatisfied with the High Church way of thinking.

In 1849, after two years at Gosport, Harford-Battersby moved on and exchanged High Churchmanship for the broad churchmanship of St John's, Keswick, as curate to Frederick Myers. He found in Myers 'a guide and a prophet', but in due course was dissatisfied again, and it was not long before he found himself returning to the evangelical fold of his upbringing. Myers died two years after Harford-Battersby's arrival in Keswick, and Harford-Battersby replaced him as vicar of St John's.

Harford-Battersby was respected and liked by all the citizens of Keswick. He promoted a scheme to supply the town of Keswick with pure water from the nearby mountain of Skiddaw. He also established a local library in St John's parish hall, which was later amalgamated with the Country Library, and he was heavily involved in the activities of the Mechanics Institute, an adult education centre for working men in the town, which encouraged the reading of good literature and organized topical lectures and discussions. The lecture hall he founded as the venue for these activities was subsequently named after him (Battersby Hall).

Harford-Battersby's activities and interests were not limited to the town of Keswick itself. In 1859 he took the lead in forming the Lay and Clerical Evangelical Union for the Diocese of Carlisle. He also organized and promoted the work of the Church Missionary Society throughout Cumberland and Westmoreland. The Bishop of Carlisle made him an honorary canon.

Yet Harford-Battersby was not wholly content. In 1874 he wrote of lacking the peace and joy and love promised by Christ. Through reading books by the American holiness teachers Robert and Hannah *Pearsall Smith, he decided he must seek further spiritual blessing. From 29 August to 7 September 1874 Harford-Battersby attended a conference at which he heard an address by Evan Hopkins, an Anglican clergyman, which changed his understanding and transformed his life. Hopkins spoke on the difference between 'seeking faith' and 'resting faith'. The revelation to Harford-Battersby of the right to act in complete dependence on the full sufficiency of Christ (resting faith) brought him peace. Harford-Battersby returned to his parish in Keswick to explain, in the emerging vocabulary of the holiness movement, that God had enabled him to make a 'full surrender' of his life.

In 1875 Harford-Battersby, together with his Quaker friend Robert Wilson from Broughton Grange, Cockermouth, participated in very large holiness meetings (attracting up to 8,000 people) in Brighton. They decided at Brighton to hold similar meetings in Keswick, and Robert and Hannah Pearsall Smith were invited to lead and speak. The only available dates in their diary were at the end of June, just three weeks after the conclusion of the Brighton meeting. The Convention in Keswick was therefore planned to commence on 29 June and run for three days to 1 July. An invitation was circulated headed 'Union Meetings for the Promotion of Practical Holiness'.

In the event the Pearsall Smiths returned unexpectedly to America, but Harford-Battersby secured the services of speakers such as Prebendary H. W. Webb-Peploe, who was to become a well-known leader of the Keswick Convention. Between three and four hundred attended the first Keswick Convention, meeting in a tent with a capacity for six hundred. At this first Convention the text, 'All One in Christ Jesus' was hung above the platform, and this became the motto of the Convention.

Much controversy surrounded these and other similar meetings, and the whole holiness movement was subjected to violent criticism from many evangelical Christians, who saw it as teaching perfectionism. To assuage evangelical concerns, the leaders changed the description of the Convention from 'Meetings for the Promotion of Practical Holiness' to 'Meetings for the Promotion of Scriptural Holiness'. Until his death in 1883, Harford-Battersby was chairman of the annual Keswick Convention, a gathering that was destined to grow in the early twentieth century, becoming the most significant annual meeting for evangelicals in Britain.

Bibliography

J. C. Pollock, *The Keswick Story* (London: Hodder & Stoughton, 1964); C. Price and I. M. Randall, *Transforming Keswick: The Keswick Convention, Past, Present and Future* (Carlisle: OM Publishing, 2000).

I. M. RANDALL

■ **HARPER, Michael Claude** (1931–), English charismatic Anglican then Orthodox priest, was educated at Cambridge University, where he read law. He was converted during a communion service in King's College Chapel in 1950 and went on to train for the ministry at Ridley Hall. He was ordained deacon in 1955 and priest in 1956, and he became curate of St Barnabas, Clapham Common. During this time he married Jeanne, whom he had first met on an Inter-Varsity Fellowship student mission in Norwich in 1952. From 1958 to 1964 he served on the staff of All Souls, Langham Place, under John *Stott, for whose ministry he had the utmost respect. He was 'baptized in the Spirit' in May 1962 while preparing for a speaking engagement. In 1964 Harper resigned his position at All Souls and established the Fountain Trust in order to extend charismatic renewal among the churches. As the organization's first full-time general secretary, he visited with his wife over forty cities and towns in the British Isles in its first year, organizing informal conferences. In 1966 Harper edited the first edition of *Renewal*, a magazine that has continued to be a major influence in spreading charismatic Christianity. In the period from 1964 to 1970 the Harpers travelled over 100,000 miles in the British Isles. In 1971 Harper organized the Guildford Conference centred on the cathedral. It was the first time anywhere in the world that Roman Catholics, Pentecostals and other Protestants shared the same platform. In the words of one leading participant,

'the charismatic movement was now firmly on the map'.

In 1975 Harper resigned from the Fountain Trust, of which he had been director since 1971, feeling that he should focus on international teaching and give himself to a sustained period of writing. This issued in the publication in 1977 of *Let My People Grow*, which was to have a significant impact on many charismatic churches. In 1978 Harper convened a charismatic conference for Anglicans at Canterbury immediately before the Lambeth Conference of Bishops. Over 300 leaders and thirty bishops met together to pray for renewal in the Anglican Church. The conference ended with a Series Three eucharist, presided over by the Archbishop of Cape Town, Bill Burnett, which was noted for dancing bishops, 'glorious singing', 'holy chaos', 'powerful preaching from Colin Urquhart' and the ministry of healing.

The Canterbury conference led to the formation of SOMA, Sharing of Ministries Abroad, which was born in July 1978. One of its aims was 'to facilitate the sharing of the gifts and spiritual resources God gives within the body of Christ everywhere'. SOMA began to organize a series of major conferences in different parts of the world. The first was in February 1979. In 1986 Michael Harper was the principal organizer of ACTS 1986, a major charismatic conference held at the National Exhibition Centre in Birmingham with 7,300 delegates from over forty countries. There were more than twenty speakers including Michael Green, John *Wimber and Tom Forrest, the international director of Catholic Charismatic Renewal. A further major conference was sponsored jointly by SOMA and Anglican Renewal Ministries in the summer of 1991.

In much of his ministry Harper was supported by his wife, Jeanne, particularly in the early days of the Fountain Trust. As an accomplished musician who had trained at the Royal Academy of Music, she was influential in promoting renewed worship. In the early 1970s she worked with Betty Pulkingham to produce the song book *Sounds of Living Waters*. In 1976 Jeanne was the leader in England and Wales of the Lydia Prayer Fellowship. She also founded what became known as the Caring Professions Seminars with the aim of harnessing the spiritual resources in the caring professions.

Michael and Jeanne, although firmly rooted in the evangelical tradition, had a long-standing and deep attachment to the Catholic faith. When, therefore, on 11 November 1992 the General Synod decided by a two-thirds majority to ordain women to the priesthood, Harper wrote, 'I knew that my remaining time in the Church of England would be short.' In March 1995 the Harpers joined the Orthodox Church, Michael writing, 'we came home'. He was ordained later the same year by bishop Gabriel Saliby at the Greek Orthodox church in Paris, and subsequently became the first dean of the new British Antiochian Orthodox Deanery. He also continued as chairman of the International Charismatic Consultation on World Evangelisation.

Harper is a gifted writer, and in addition to editing *Renewal* he has produced a steady stream of thoughtful devotional books. Among the more significant have been *Power for the Body of Christ* (1964), *Walk in the Spirit* (1968), *Spiritual Warfare* (1970), *None Can Guess* (1971), *Let My People Grow* (1977), *The Love Affair* (1982) and *The True Light* (1997). Michael Harper is a gracious man of deep spirituality with an intellectual grasp of renewal. He was a courageous leader at a time when charismatic renewal was scorned by most in positions of authority in the evangelical world. He proved himself a brilliant organizer who saw the best in everybody and displayed a real ability to encourage potential leaders. There is no doubt that he has been a major influence in the promotion of charismatic evangelicalism in the Church of England and in the UK. On the world stage he has certainly been an influential statesman, whose management skills have helped to establish charismatic Christianity as a global phenomenon.

Bibliography
The Charismatic Movement in the Church of England (CIO Publishing, 1981); K. Hylson-Smith, *Evangelicals in the Church of England 1734–1984* (T. & T. Clark, 1988); *Renewal*, 77 (October/November 1978), 95 (October/November 1981), 185 (October 1991).

N. A. D. Scotland

■ **HARRIS, Howel(l)** (1714–1773), founder of Welsh Calvinistic Methodism, was born at Trevecca, Breconshire, on 23 January 1714, the son of Howell and Susannah Harris. He was educated locally at Talgarth and Llanfihangel Tal-y-llyn before progressing to the Dissenting academy at Llwyn-llwyd near Hay-on-Wye in 1728, and it was intended that he should enter holy orders, but his father's death in 1731 interrupted his education and led to his employment as a schoolmaster at Llangorse. Converted in 1735 through the ministrations of the church and his discovery of devotional literature, he embarked on an itinerant lay ministry that soon evolved into preaching and the forming of small devotional groups or 'societies'. These developments incurred the wrath of both his parish clergyman and his bishop, and though Harris repeatedly applied for ordination, he was rejected on account of his religious 'enthusiasm'. His activities as a revivalist also prevented him from receiving a university education; though he matriculated at Oxford in November 1735, he remained there for less than a week and returned to Trevecca to resume itinerating.

As the months went by, his sphere of activity expanded, and in 1737 he met Daniel Rowland of Langeitho. During the same period, he became acquainted with Howell Davies and William *Williams of Pantycelyn; both were converted under his lay ministry. Together these four men were regarded as the leaders of the Revival in Wales.

Though Harris was an Anglican, the Dissenters took a keen interest in his early activities. Congregational and Baptist ministers invited him to preach in various parts of southeast Wales, and cooperation lasted until the beginning of the 1740s, when disagreements about doctrine and personality clashes drove them apart. By then Harris had met his contemporaries in England; between March and June 1739 he had struck up friendships with George *Whitefield and both John and Charles *Wesley. The English and Welsh revivals, which had until then been developing independently, now merged. Thereafter, Harris often travelled to London to assist at Whitefield's Tabernacle, and in 1745, following John Cennick's defection to the Moravians, he found himself at the head of the Calvinist branch of the work, and remained there until Whitefield's return from America in 1748. Though there were theological differences between him and the Wesleys, relations remained amicable between them throughout Harris's life.

The period between 1739 and 1745 was one of consolidation for the Welsh Methodists. As the societies multiplied, monthly, quarterly, half-yearly and annual conferences were established, and these 'Associations' were responsible for regulating the activities of the movement around the country. As Harris was the mainspring of the process of organization, he was appointed 'Superintendent' of all the societies in 1743 in recognition of his contribution.

By 1745 it was becoming apparent that changes were taking place in Harris; the stresses and strains of leadership were beginning to take their toll. Fearing that the revival was coming to an end, he began to emphasize the need for discipline among the converts, and set standards within the societies that others found impossible to attain. Censures and expulsions followed, and when Daniel Rowland began accepting the offenders back into fellowship, Harris assumed that he was trying to undermine his authority because he was a layman.

At the same time, changes were also taking place in his theology. Harris had always preached the blood of Christ as the means of salvation, but when he began to refer to it as the 'Blood of God' many were uneasy because of the Patripassian connotations. Despite being warned to be more guarded in his statements, Harris persisted, and on 1 October 1746 his doctrine was called into question by the exhorters during an Association meeting. This dispute further heightened the tension within the movement as Harris now believed that the exhorters, through their challenge, were rebelling against God.

The situation deteriorated rapidly, and when Harris began travelling the country in the company of Sidney Griffith, a married woman from north Wales, claiming that she possessed prophetic powers, an air of nervousness could be discerned among the other revival leaders, both English and Welsh. In 1744 Harris had married Anne, the daughter of John Williams of Skreen in Radnorshire, and though he insisted that the new relationship was platonic, they decided to

distance themselves from him. The final breach came on 7 June 1750. Harris and a small group of supporters decided that they could no longer work with the 'carnal' clergy. Welsh Methodism was divided, and was to remain so for over a decade.

Though Harris campaigned tirelessly to muster support for his party, he soon realized that few were willing to join him, and by 1752 he recognized that the battle was lost. He therefore turned his attention to the establishment of a religious community at Trevecca in which he and Sidney Griffith could serve God together. The old house was partly demolished in April and the foundation laid for a new building; over the years, several other buildings were to be erected to accommodate those who would join them. However, on 31 May 1752 Sidney Griffith died of tuberculosis in London. Harris was devastated and withdrew from the work of the revival.

During 1756 the outbreak of the Seven Years' War brought fears of foreign invasion, and Harris was invited by the Breconshire gentry to accept a commission as ensign in the militia. Though at first hesitant, he decided to accept on condition that he be allowed to preach. Military service took him no further than Great Yarmouth, and when the regiment was disbanded at the end of 1762, he returned to Trevecca.

His discharge coincided with an invitation from Daniel Rowland and William Williams to return to his former position within the Methodist movement. The years following his retirement had been difficult ones for the other leaders, and Harris's skills as an organizer and disciplinarian had been sorely missed. He decided to accept, and for the first time in more than a decade, an Association meeting was held at Trevecca in 1763.

By then, a new revival had begun in Wales. Harris was eager to participate in its activities and resumed itinerating, but despite his best efforts, it cannot be said that he was as successful during these years as during the period 1735–1750. Not only was he an older man, but also a new generation had emerged during his absence who had taken over the reins of the movement, and as Harris moved among them, emphasizing the need for discipline, there was friction. Trevecca imposed further demands; with over a hundred people to support, the Countess of *Huntingdon, eager to establish a college in a nearby building (which she did in 1768), Harris was again in danger of over-stretching himself.

Following Anne Harris's death in March 1770, Harris complained of bouts of pain which restricted his involvement in the revival work. His health began to deteriorate, and he died on 21 July 1773 and was buried at Talgarth. His contribution to the revival had been immense, and though he came close to destroying what he had helped to create, the Welsh Calvinistic Methodist tradition has always recognized its debt to him.

Bibliography

G. Tudur, *Howell Harris: From Conversion to Separation, 1735–1750* (Cardiff: University of Wales Press, 2000); G. F. Nuttall, *Howel Harris: The Last Enthusiast* (Cardiff: University of Wales Press, 1965); H. J. Hughes, *Life of Howell Harris* (1892, repr. Hanley: Tentmaker Publications, 1996).

G. TUDUR

■ **HATFIELD, Mark Odom** (1922–), politician and author, served his home state of Oregon for nearly five decades as a United States Senator, Governor, Oregon Secretary of State, State Senator and State Representative. Described as 'the most prominent politician among the nation's 40 million evangelicals' by United Press International's Wesley Pippert, Senator Hatfield embodied a progressive evangelicalism that set him apart from both his co-religionists and his fellow Republicans.

The son of a railway blacksmith and a school teacher, Hatfield attended a Conservative Baptist church during his youth. After graduating from Willamette University (BA, 1943), he served as a Navy lieutenant in the Second World War, in which he witnessed 'some of the bloodiest operations' of the entire conflict, 'including Iwo Jima and Okinawa'. These experiences, along with a visit to Hiroshima 'after the bomb', led Hatfield to rethink his views on war and peace, bringing him 'very close' to pacifism.

After earning a master's degree from Stanford University in 1948, Hatfield worked as political science professor and dean of students at Willamette. In the midst of his time as dean, he had a conversion-like 'encounter with Jesus Christ' in 1954. The years at Willamette also marked the beginning of his career in state politics, witnessing his election to the State House of Representatives (1950), the State Senate (1954) and the Secretary of State's office (1956).

As Governor of Oregon (1959–1967) Hatfield took his place on the national political stage. As keynote speaker at the 1964 Republican Convention he criticized both the conflict in Vietnam and the 'extremism' in his own party. (Hatfield later estimated that as many as one-third of the 1964 delegates belonged to the ultra-conservative John Birch Society.) At the 1966 meeting of the National Governors' Association, Hatfield was the sole opponent of a resolution supporting President Lyndon Johnson's policies in Vietnam.

Despite his maverick views, by the mid-sixties Hatfield had emerged as a major figure in American politics. Elected to the United States Senate in 1966, Hatfield was suggested as a potential running mate for Republican presidential candidate Richard Nixon in 1968 (by Billy *Graham) and for Democrat George McGovern in 1972. He went on to become one of the most outspoken critics of the Nixon administration's policies in Southeast Asia, co-sponsoring the Hatfield-McGovern Amendment in 1970 (a measure that would have cut off money for the war) and condemning the bombing of Cambodia.

In opposing the Vietnam War, Hatfield parted company with the vast majority of American evangelicals, many of whom questioned his patriotism. In spite of such criticism, Hatfield urged his co-religionists to re-evaluate their support for the war. At Fuller Seminary in 1970 he criticized the 'theological "silent majority" in our land who wrap their Bibles in the American flag', arguing that 'our modern faith in superior fire-power' flies in the face of 'our national motto, "In God We Trust"'.

During his long career in the Senate, Hatfield never once voted in favour of a military authorization bill. Called the Republican Party's 'most notorious dove' by *Washington Post* columnist Mary McGrory, Hatfield led the fight against the Vietnam War, the MX missile, the B-1 bomber, nuclear testing and the Persian Gulf War. In 1982 he co-sponsored the Kennedy-Hatfield resolution calling for a nuclear freeze, and was instrumental in securing passage of the Underground Test Ban Treaty in 1992.

Undergirding Hatfield's dovish stance was a personalist vision of politics that political scientist Robert Booth Fowler has called the 'politics of love'. Rejecting the 'artificial polarization' between the 'Social Gospel' and 'individual conversion', Hatfield argued that the 'mission of peace cannot be severed from the task of evangelism'. The 'politics of love' profoundly shaped Hatfield's thinking on issues of poverty and inequality. Although many mainstream evangelicals distrusted the state, Hatfield believed in the power of government to help the poor, speaking out on behalf of education, housing and anti-hunger initiatives.

At the same time, Hatfield tempered his support for government programmes with a critique of the centralizing of American life, lamenting the growing power of big corporations and the federal government. Advocating a greater role for small businesses, community development programmes and neighbourhood government, he used a 1972 speech (recorded in Wesley Pippert's book *Faith at the Top*) to call for the decentralization of 'political and economic power'. Though his agenda often alienated many in the Republican party, Hatfield saw himself as an exponent of the 'Radical Republicanism' of the 1850s, noting that 'the founders of our party were for small business, education, cutting the military budget'.

Though a liberal on peace and justice issues, Hatfield was a strong opponent of abortion. Unlike most evangelicals, he linked the defence of the unborn with opposition to war, poverty and capital punishment, earning a high approval rating from JustLife, a consistent life ethic organization, in the late 1980s. In 1994 Hatfield wrote an article in *Christianity Today* calling for moral and ethical reflection in the area of biotechnology, arguing that 'these issues cut straight to the core of how we as a society perceive the sanctity of life'.

From his days as a campus advisor to the Inter-Varsity Christian Fellowship chapter at Willamette University, Hatfield maintained close ties with the evangelical subculture. In his book on evangelical politics, Robert Booth Fowler linked Hatfield to a 1970s cohort of 'reform-oriented evangelicals', a group that included such figures as Congressmen Paul Henry and John B. Anderson, sociologist David Moberg, philosopher Richard Mouw and theologian Ronald Sider. While in Washington, Hatfield attended both the Fourth Presbyterian Church (of which the late Richard C. Halverson was pastor) and Georgetown Baptist Church. He has also been a strong supporter of the Council for Christian Colleges and Universities, Evangelicals for Social Action, World Vision and Bread for the World. He served as a trustee of Willamette University, George Fox University, Western Conservative Baptist Seminary and Dag Hammarskjold College.

Over the course of his political career, Hatfield published his reflections on faith and public life in books such as *Not Quite So Simple* (1968), *Conflict and Conscience* (1971), *Between a Rock and a Hard Place* (1976), *Confessing Christ and Doing Politics* (1982) and *Against the Grain: Reflections of A Radical Republican* (2000).

Once known as 'Saint Mark' by his colleagues, Hatfield's reputation was tarnished somewhat by a series of ethics investigations in the 1980s and 1990s. In 1992 the Senate Ethics Committee rebuked Hatfield for failing to report $43,000 in gifts and travel expenses, stopping short of an official censure. In a written statement, he accepted personal responsibility for his 'mistakes'. Despite these acknowledged lapses in judgment, he was widely admired by his colleagues.

Citing the 'high price' of public life, Hatfield retired from the Senate in 1997, along with moderate Republicans William Cohen and Nancy Kassebaum. President Bill Clinton spoke at his retirement event, noting that 'because he has tried to love his enemies, he has no enemies'. Since retiring from the Senate, Hatfield has served as the Herbert Hoover Distinguished Professor at the evangelical George Fox University (Hoover's alma mater). He is married to the former Antoinette Kuzmanich. They have four children: Elizabeth, Mark Odom, Jr, Theresa and Charles Vincent.

Bibliography

R. Eells and B. Nyberg, *Lonely Walk: The Life of Senator Mark Hatfield* (Portland: Multnomah Press, 1979); M. Hatfield and

D. Solomon, *Against the Grain: Reflections of A Radical Republican* (Ashland: White Cloud Press, 2000); R. B. Fowler, *A New Engagement: Evangelical Political Thought, 1966–1976* (Grand Rapids: Eerdmans, 1982); W. Pippert, *Faith at the Top* (Elgin: Cook, 1973); M. Hatfield, *Conflict and Conscience* (Waco: Word, 1971).

J. SCHMALZBAUER

■ **HAVERGAL, Frances Ridley** (1836–1879), Anglican author of hymns, poems and devotional books, was born in her father's rectory at Astley, Worcestershire, England. Frances was the youngest of six children born to Jane Head and the Revd William Henry Havergal, who were both in their early forties when she was born on 14 December 1836. Her parents and siblings cherished her for her bubbly personality, golden curls and precocious intelligence. The family was in many ways a sterling example of Victorian evangelicalism. William Havergal secured an early appointment through the ground-breaking evangelical bishop Henry *Ryder; he toured on behalf of the Church Missionary Society; and he co-edited the anti-Romanist *Protestant Warder*. The family kept a strict Sabbath and held daily household prayers; they disapproved of novels, theatre and various amusements. Yet theirs was a large, hospitable and stimulating home in which a mix of tutors, curates, students, relatives and suitors engaged in lively conversation. It was also a home in which accomplishment in music, languages, history and theology was encouraged. William Havergal had begun building a large library in his Oxford days and had published hymns and musical compositions and harmonized tunes before Frances' birth. After her arrival he also contributed to the revival of Elizabethan church music by re-publishing works of psalmody. So important was public education to the Havergals that one-quarter of the family's sizeable income was set apart for the work of the Society for the Promotion of Christian Knowledge.

Frances was clearly her father's favourite from birth, but because she was the youngest girl in such a tumultuous nineteenth-century household, the shape of her childhood education was not premeditated. Yet before the age of three she was found in corners reading to herself, and as a child learned European languages by overhearing her siblings' home tutorials. She revelled in her family's musical culture, sitting on her father's shoulders as he played the seraphine organ during family worship, and wrote her first poetry at the age of seven. She eventually enjoyed her own tutors, but was given no formal education and musical training until her adolescent years, after her mother's untimely death in 1848. But she was educated early in the ways of rectory daughters by her sisters. Frances began a career of Sunday school teaching at the age of nine, and was soon accompanying her indefatigable sisters in constant rounds of parish visitation.

After her mother's death, Frances' education was given more attention. As her three sisters had been, she was sent in 1850 to Campden House (by now in Belmont), a select residential school that prepared its young ladies for respectable drawing rooms. The formidable Mrs Teed, a sound evangelical, had dispensed with dancing instruction, but exalted modern languages. French only was to be spoken by students in the course of the day. Mrs Teed taught the Thirty-Nine Articles, gave typological lectures on the Bible, and inculcated the theology of the atonement and the need for an experiential conversion. As it was the last term before Mrs Teed's retirement and the closing of the school, the mood of urgency affected Frances. Though by her later admission she had long resisted the urgings of her older sisters to declare her own conversion to faith in Jesus Christ, she now thought much about it. Soon after, at the urging of Caroline Cook, formerly on the staff of Campden House, she joyfully committed her soul to Christ, though she later could not put a precise date to her conversion. Within months her father had married Miss Cook, twenty years his junior. In August 1851, Frances departed for another term at school, this time at Powick Court, a school of more moderate evangelical views. She excelled at her studies, but within the year was forced to withdraw by illness. During an extended trip to Germany (1852–1853) for the sake of her father's health, Frances received her last formal schooling. She attended a strict Prussian Gymnasium in Dusseldorf and received high honours amongst native German speakers.

As she approached her twentieth year, Frances's future was unclear to her. Her relationship with her stepmother was deteriorating, and she had no clear sense of vocation. By 1860 she had begun to contribute verse to *Good Words*. She stayed for some time with her sisters and brothers, though family harmony had been somewhat strained by the growing Anglo-Catholic sympathies of her two brothers, both priests. But she was far from idle. In her father's and her siblings' households Frances pursued her own theological education, worked at her Hebrew, Greek and Latin, continued the study of modern languages and pursued advanced musical education. She assisted in parish visitation and various missions and for a time served as a governess. In the 1860s she began singing seriously, serving as soloist for the Kidderminster Philharmonic Society. In 1869 she published her first book of verse, entitled *The Ministry of Song*, the result of ten years of writing.

It is the last decade of her life for which Havergal is most recalled. It was the crisis prompted by the death of her father in 1870, and her other personal crises and experiences in the 1870s (including a typhoid attack in 1874), that inspired almost all of the literary and musical contributions for which she is remembered. Her increasingly difficult relationship with her stepmother increased her incentive to travel, and to assist in missions of various kinds. The intervention of the Revd C. B. Snepp allowed her to become her father's *de facto* literary and musical executor, and made her more widely known.

Although Havergal was cautious about the holiness movement, her experience of consecration on Advent Sunday 1873 was the most important one of her life; 'What is seen,' she said later, 'can never be unseen.' It focused her hymn-writing, helping her to produce hymns such as the still popular *Take My Life* (1874). Others flowed from her pen in the same year; among them were *Like a River Glorious* and *I am Trusting Thee, Lord Jesus*. A few years and many hymns later she wrote *Who is on the Lord's Side?* (1877). Although the music of these hymns sounds sentimental to some people today, Havergal's melodies were fresh and spiritually fitting in her own day. The elevated language of the 'higher life' appealed immediately to many evangelicals.

From their first appearance Havergal's hymns had both an international and an inter-denominational appeal, though no-one could have predicted that they would so soon find their way around the world and into Anglo-Catholic hymnals.

But Havergal's enormous appeal did not rest on her hymns alone. Her association with the Mildmay and Keswick conferences and the *Moody and *Sankey missions in England made her more popular. The many devotional books and booklets she wrote in the last decade of her life, such as *Kept for the Master's Use* (1879), and her participation in many missions of various kinds (during which she sang and played a number of her own hymns and music), led many people to seek her advice. For some time she attempted to respond to a hundred letters a month, and soon had to take refuge in frequent visits to the Swiss Alps, which she climbed with enthusiasm. She also turned down the last of her marriage proposals. It was without a doubt both the most trying and the happiest period of her life.

Frances Ridley Havergal's sudden demise during an attack of peritonitis was widely mourned. Always friendly to her Anglo-Catholic brother Francis, she requested the sacrament from his hand just before her death (3 June 1879). Her *Memorials*, published the year after her death by her unmarried sister Maria, were widely read. By the 1920s some 2,000,000 copies of her works were in circulation in English. But her hymns, of all her works, have best endured to the present. Their power can be attributed to the lifelong discipline of her considerable gifts and to deep spiritual experience honestly expressed.

Bibliography

T. H. Darlow, *Frances Ridley Havergal: A Saint of God* (New York and Chicago: Fleming H. Revell Company, 1927); J. Grierson, *Frances Ridley Havergal: Worcestershire Hymnwriter* (Bromsgrove: The Havergal Society, 1979); M. V. G. Havergal, *Memorials of Frances Ridley Havergal* (New York: A. D. F. Randolph, 1880).

P. FRIESEN

■ **HAYFORD, Jack Williams, Jr** (1934–), pastor, author and educator, was born in Los

Angeles, California, to Jack and Dolores Hayford. Raised in evangelical Protestant churches in the Oakland, California, area, he joined the International Church of the Foursquare Gospel (ICFG), a small Pentecostal denomination with headquarters in Los Angeles. He attended the denomination's Bible college, LIFE (Lighthouse of International Foursquare Evangelism). There he met and married fellow student Anna Smith, from Nebraska, a lifelong participant in the Foursquare denomination and a capable partner in her husband's many endeavours. The Hayfords had four children. Following their graduation in 1956, the couple moved to Indiana, where they served a Foursquare congregation and discovered a passion for youth ministry. In 1960 they returned to Los Angeles, where Hayford became National Youth Director for his denomination. In 1965 he accepted an appointment as dean of students and faculty member at LIFE.

The small Pentecostal denomination that provided the context for Hayford's development had been established by evangelist Aimee Semple *McPherson (1890–1944). Its core message reflected the four pillars of her Foursquare Gospel: Christ is saviour, baptizer in the Holy Spirit, healer and soon-returning king. In the overall context of American evangelicalism its efforts were modest. Its distinguishing features were its vigorous missionary programme and a broader openness to interdenominational cooperation than classical Pentecostals often manifested. Every Foursquare sanctuary displayed Hebrews 13:8: 'Jesus Christ, the same yesterday and today and forever.' This legacy both shaped Hayford and continued to provide the context for his work. In 1969 he accepted a call to the pastorate of a dwindling congregation of eighteen known as the First Foursquare Church of Van Nuys. An initial temporary commitment soon became a full-time passion. Hayford moved from the classroom to the pulpit and refocused his administrative gifts on the local church. Renamed 'The Church on the Way', Hayford's congregation grew to include over 10,000 active members before his retirement in 2000. During these busy years, he found time also to serve as president of LIFE Bible College (1976–1982).

Hayford's growing influence was not limited to the ICFG. He rose to prominence at a time when Christianity in many forms was being stirred by renewed interest in the 'filling' of the Holy Spirit. Devoted to the traditional Pentecostalism of his formative years, Hayford also embraced what came to be known as the charismatic movement. He brought practical experience to constituencies eager for guidance in charismatic worship. Speaking and writing opportunities propelled Hayford to fame in the growing movement. He quickly gained an international reputation, and The Church on the Way attracted crowds of visitors as well as well-known Californians such as the singer Pat Boone. Speaking and teaching engagements have taken Hayford to more than forty countries. He leads popular study tours to Israel and the Middle East. A broadcaster, he can be heard on radio or television in all fifty states and many foreign countries. Hayford is also a talented song writer. Perhaps the best known of his hundreds of hymns is 'Majesty', written in 1981. Hayford has strong views about worship and spiritual gifts, and he is widely respected as a teacher and mentor to pastors in part because of his long experience in the pulpit. His book The Beauty of Spiritual Language (controversial among some Pentecostals because it does not insist on speaking in tongues as evidence of the baptism of the Holy Spirit) is perhaps the best presentation by a practitioner of the meaning of this Pentecostal practice. In 1987 Hayford founded The King's College, an interdenominational Bible training centre. The Jack W. Hayford School of Pastoral Nurture, established in 1997, serves senior pastors with week-long intensive seminars. Shorter Regional Schools of Pastoral Nurture bring encouragement to pastors across the country. The King's Seminary, established in 1999, exists to prepare leaders for 'the Spirit-Formed Church' of the twenty-first century. Living Way Ministry produces and distributes teaching cassettes that circulate around the globe.

Over the years, Hayford has gained renown in his denomination, the international Pentecostal community, the charismatic and independent Pentecostal movements and various evangelical circles. He has spoken on behalf of organizations such as the Lausanne II Congress on World Evangelization, the National Religious Broadcasters' Association, the Pentecostal World Conference, the National

Association of Evangelicals, the Gospel Music Association, the Billy *Graham Evangelistic Assocation's Schools of Evangelism, the Full Gospel Business Men's Fellowship International and Promise Keepers. In his capacity as senior editorial advisor for *Ministries Today* and *Christianity Today*'s *Leadership Journal*, Hayford reaches a wide audience of pastors. He is also general editor of the popular Spirit-Filled Life publications list released by Thomas Nelson Publishers. Tireless and passionate, Hayford has built an extensive network of organizations at the intersection of traditional Pentecostalism and charismatic Christianity. He wields enormous influence within this international evangelical subculture and is widely recognized as a responsible spokesman for its interests.

Bibliography
J. W. Hayford, *The Church on the Way: Learning to Live in the Promise of Biblical Congregational Life* (Old Tappan: Fleming Revell Co., 1983).

E. BLUMHOFER

■ **HENRY, Carl Ferdinand Howard** (1913–), American theologian and church leader, was born the son of German immigrant parents in New York City on 22 January 1913, and grew up on Long Island in Central Islip, New York. Educated in state schools, Henry showed great promise as a student of journalism. He worked as a reporter for several major newspapers including *The New York Times*, later becoming editor of the *Smithtown Star*, a major weekly paper on Long Island.

Although baptized and confirmed as an Episcopalian, Henry considered himself a virtual pagan prior to his personal conversion to Christ in the summer of 1933. Two years later, Henry enrolled as a student at Wheaton College, where he came under the influence of Presbyterian theologian Gordon Clark, whose emphasis on propositional truth and the rationality of belief in God shaped his thought. At Wheaton he also met his wife, Helga Bender, whose parents had been Baptist missionaries to the African Cameroons. Another fellow student at Wheaton was Billy *Graham, a Youth for Christ worker who would become Henry's partner in shaping the post-Second World War evangelical movement. After graduating from Wheaton (BA, 1938), Henry studied theology at Northern Baptist Theological Seminary in Chicago, eventually receiving a ThD there (1942), while also earning the MA from Wheaton (1941). Through his study of the Scriptures, Henry became a convinced Baptist. He was immersed as a believer at his home church on Long Island and served as student pastor of the Humbolt Park Baptist Church in Chicago, where he was also ordained to the gospel ministry in 1941.

For several years Henry taught theology at Northern Baptist Seminary while pursuing yet another doctoral degree, the PhD in philosophy at Boston University. His dissertation there under Edgar S. Brightman, completed in 1949, would later be published as *Personal Idealism and Strong's Theology* (1951). In this work, Henry criticized the eminent Northern Baptist theologian of an earlier generation, Augustus H. *Strong, whose mediating theology based on the philosophy of ethical monism could not withstand the inroads of modernism in his day. Near the end of his life, Strong had sided with the fundamentalists in the struggle with the modernists in his denomination, but Henry believed that Strong's inadequate doctrine of revelation contributed to the collapse of the very orthodoxy he affirmed. Henry's life's work was to provide a sturdier theology for the evangelicals of his generation than Strong had been able to provide in the early decades of the twentieth century.

1947 was a pivotal year in Henry's development. In that year he was invited by Harold John *Ockenga and Charles E. *Fuller to help launch a new evangelical seminary in Pasadena, California. A member of the founding faculty of Fuller Theological Seminary, Henry taught theology, philosophy and ethics. He also served for some time as dean of the emerging institution. For nearly ten years Henry was a key leader at Fuller, his role made even more important by the frequent absence of Ockenga, the seminary's first president.

Also in 1947 Henry published his first major work, *The Uneasy Conscience of Modern Fundamentalism*. Although it was only a brief tract compared to his later voluminous productions, this little book had a tremendous impact on the nascent movement dubbed by Ockenga as 'neo-evangelicalism'. Henry had been a founding member of the National Association of Evangelicals, a coalition of conservative Protestants formed in 1942 to offer a constructive alternative to the liberal mainstream church establishment on the one hand and anti-intellectual sectarianism on the other. In *Uneasy Conscience* the new evangelicals found a basis for positive engagement with society and culture without the theology of the 'social gospel' movement. Like Ockenga, Henry promoted the ideals of unity, education, evangelism and social ethics while maintaining the absolute truth claims of historic Christian orthodoxy. This combination would become a mark of Henry's leadership in many other evangelical ventures across the years.

Uneasy Conscience was the first of a series of books that flowed from Henry's prolific pen. Other key titles over the next twenty years include *Remaking the Modern Mind* (1948), *Giving a Reason For Our Hope* (1949), *Fifty Years of Protestant Theology* (1950), *The Drift of Western Thought* (1951), *Christian Personal Ethics* (1957), *Basic Christian Doctrines* (1962), *Christian Faith and Modern Theology* (1964), and *Jesus of Nazareth: Savior and Lord* (1966). Through these and other writings Henry gained influence as the leading theological voice of the evangelical movement in North America. Henry was preoccupied with the doctrine of God and the doctrine of Scripture, affirming biblical theism and an error-free, authoritative Bible. He occasionally clashed with fellow evangelical theologians, especially those of a more evidentialist bent. Henry's primary theological method was deductive, based on presuppositions derived from God's special revelation in Scripture, interpreted in the light of Jesus Christ and the consensual confessions of the church through the ages.

Henry gained national prominence in 1956 when he was called from his post at Fuller to become the founding editor of *Christianity Today*, a new magazine founded by Billy Graham and Graham's father-in-law, L. Nelson Bell. *Christianity Today* was intended to provide an articulate alternative voice to the *Christian Century*, a left-leaning journal published since 1900 by liberal, main-stream Protestants. Under Henry's vigorous leadership, *Christianity Today* soon eclipsed its rival in circulation, which grew to more than 170,000 during his twelve-year term as editor. In his lengthy editorials and articles, Henry gave definition and direction to the emerging evangelical movement. He sounded the note already set forth in *Uneasy Conscience*, encouraging evangelicals to move from the 'rearguard' to the 'vanguard' in efforts to apply Christian values and principles to every area of society. Henry also wrote about the importance of prayer and the disciplines of the spiritual life, but he rejected outright the kind of quietism and interiorized piety that left Christians disengaged from the world and its pressing needs.

Well aware of the fissiparous tendency of fundamentalism, Henry wanted *Christianity Today* to become a unitive force for evangelical Christians. Thus, although Henry was Reformed in theology and a Baptist in his view of the church, he published a wide variety of opinions ranging across the breadth of the evangelical spectrum. He also regularly published interviews and articles by outstanding European theologians such as G. C. *Berkouwer, Emil Brunner, Helmut Thielicke and Karl Barth.

Henry was enormously successful as an evangelical networker, bringing together thinkers, activists, evangelists and church leaders. His concern for a united, worldwide evangelical movement led to the 1966 World Congress on Evangelism in Berlin, an event chaired by Henry with Billy Graham as honorary chairman. This gathering of evangelical leaders from around the world was a precursor of the even more influential International Congress on World Evangelization at Lausanne in 1974. Henry's call for evangelicals to establish a national Christian university was less successful. However, he worked closely with theological seminaries and colleges, encouraging them to train students to think in terms of the Christian worldview across the various intellectual disciplines. To this end, in 1968 Henry helped to launch the Institute for Advanced Christian Studies.

Henry's editorship of *Christianity Today* was never an easy role. He was criticized by some Christians on the left for not taking a more aggressive, prophetic stance during the civil rights struggle and the conflict over the war in Vietnam. Others on the right, including the powerful businessman J. Howard *Pew, a major financial backer of *Christianity Today*, were unhappy that Henry was not more critical of the liberal political and economic policies of the National Council of Churches. On 1 July 1968 Henry was forced to leave his position as editor of *Christianity Today* due to a bitter conflict with the board. Following a sabbatical year in Cambridge, England, Henry returned to a teaching post at Eastern Baptist Theological Seminary (1969–1974).

In 1976 the first two volumes of *God, Revelation and Authority* were published. In six volumes, this was Henry's *magnum opus*, the most sustained theological epistemology produced by any evangelical theologian of the twentieth century. *God, Revelation and Authority* shows the breadth of Henry's expansive mind and his ability to interact with competing and opposing theological perspectives. For example, in this work he deals extensively with secularism, naturalism, existentialism and various forms of contemporary atheism. He also shows a close familiarity with theological views he considers deviant and misdirected, including liberation theology, radical feminism, and process views of God and the world.

In some ways, however, Karl Barth is the figure always standing behind Henry's shoulder. Henry met Barth in Europe and corresponded with him on several occasions. He also met Bultmann and could not appreciate his work, but he applauded Barth for his protest against liberal theology and his strong defence of the virgin birth of Christ, the Trinity, an orthodox Christology, and other doctrines. However, Henry warned his fellow evangelicals against following Barth's theological method too closely. Barth, Henry believed, had conceded too much to the Enlightenment. This left Barth with a weak doctrine of revelation, seen in his view that the Bible 'becomes' the Word of God in existential encounter, rather than being the Word of God itself. Barth's doctrine of revelation was not sufficient, Henry believed, to withstand Bultmann's efforts to demythologize biblical events and miracles, nor indeed many other forms of radical theology, including 'the death of God' movement of the 1960s; some of its advocates cited Barth as an inspiration for their work.

In recent decades, Henry has gained an undisputed status as a theologian of stature and senior evangelical statesman. His global connections have been put to good use in his role as lecturer-at-large for World Vision International (1974–1986). He also rendered valuable service as a member of the board of Charles *Colson's Prison Fellowship Ministries. Henry's writings have been translated into many languages, and he has continued to travel and speak in every continent. His concern for both personal and social ethics, based on an orthodox evangelical theology, is reflected in his involvement with contemporary issues such as the sanctity of human life, the duties of Christian citizenship, and proper stewardship of the environment.

In 1986 Henry published a revealing autobiography, *Confessions of a Theologian*. Since then, he has continued to travel extensively and speak widely on issues of importance to the evangelical movement. Concerned that evangelicals were fragmenting over secondary issues such as the precise definition of biblical inerrancy, the charismatic gifts of the Spirit and the role of women in ministry, Henry co-chaired with Kenneth *Kantzer a conference on Evangelical Affirmations in 1989. In recent years, Henry has been cited as a major influence on the conservative renewal in the Southern Baptist Convention, America's largest Protestant denomination. At the same time, Henry has been critical of an 'unbalanced preoccupation with inerrancy'. He has said that 'the mark of New Testament authenticity is first and foremost proclamation of the crucified and risen Jesus as the indispensable and irreplaceable heart of the Christian message.'

Despite the growing success of the evangelical movement, of which Henry himself is a major shaper, he has been increasingly concerned that the movement may lose its identity by uncritical accommodation. Henry was an early critic of the 'new hermeneutics', which has since blossomed into full-blown theories including theological revision and postmodern deconstruction. Some of Henry's concerns are reflected in the title of a book he published in 1988, *Twilight of a Great Civilization: The Drift Towards Neo-Paganism*. But Henry is also a person of hope, and he has consistently challenged his fellow evangelicals to theological fidelity and apologetic clarity. These themes are reflected in the Rutherford Lectures he delivered at Edinburgh in 1989, *Toward a Recovery of Christian Belief* (1990).

Today some younger evangelical theologians dismiss Henry and his theological achievement as a relic from the past. Some find Henry's emphasis on propositional revelation and his stress on the cognitive character of theological assertions unhelpful in today's theological debates. But the influence of Henry's defence of biblical authority and his practice of Christian apologetics cannot be gainsaid. Henry's stature within evangelicalism rivals those of Karl Barth in neo-orthodoxy and Karl Rahner in Roman Catholicism. Henry is the only theologian who has served as president of both the Evangelical Theological Society (1967–1970) and the American Theological Association (1979–1980). The world evangelical movement owes much to his legacy of personal devotion to Christ, strategic evangelistic thinking, cultural and ethical engagement and theological consistency and faithfulness across several generations.

Bibliography
G. Fackre, 'Carl F. H. Henry', in M. Marty and D. Peerman (eds.), *A Handbook of Christian Theologians* (Nashville: Abingdon, 1991); R. A. Mohler, Jr, 'Carl F. H. Henry', in T. George and D. S. Dockery (eds.), *Theologians of the Baptist Tradition* (Nashville: Broadman & Holman, 2001); B. E. Patterson, *Carl F. H. Henry* (Waco: Word Books, 1983); J. D. Woodbridge, 'Carl F. H. Henry: Spokesperson for American Evangelism', in D. A. Carson and J. D. Woodbridge (eds.), *God and Culture: Essays in Honor of Carl F. H. Henry* (Grand Rapids: Eerdmans, 1993).

T. GEORGE

■ **HILDEBRAND, Henry Peter** (1911–), educator, was born in the Mennonite village of Steinfeld in southern Ukraine. He emigrated with his parents to southern Manitoba on the Canadian prairies in 1925, when they, like many other Russländer Mennonites, fled the persecution that followed the October Revolution of 1917 and the rise to power of the communists.

Although living among emigrant Mennonites in Manitoba and attending a rural Mennonite Brethren church, Hildebrand was educated in English with other Canadian children from the age of fourteen. In the spring of 1929 he learned 500 verses for the Bible memorization contest of the Canadian Sunday School Mission (CSSM), and thereby earned a free week at summer camp on Lake Winnipeg. It was there that Hildebrand experienced an evangelical conversion. Fired by his experience at camp, he enrolled at the Winnipeg Bible Institute. While there he was inspired by the teaching of Simon Forsberg, a graduate of Dallas Theological Seminary, whom he was later to consider one of the most important influences on his life. Hildebrand went to a Mennonite Brethren church during his first year in Winnipeg, but later he attended the nondenominational Elim Chapel because of its proximity and the famous preachers who came to speak there. Elim Chapel in these years was one of the centres in a network of fundamentalist strongholds across North America. Hildebrand's summers were devoted to working with the CSSM as an itinerant rural evangelist.

Fully assimilated to the fundamentalist ethos through these connections, Hildebrand was well prepared for the call in 1935 from the members of a small nondenominational gospel assembly in southern Saskatchewan to be their pastor and to start a Bible school. Significantly, the call came from a businessman named Sinclair Whittaker, who had been himself converted by Lloyd Hunter of the CSSM. The school Hildebrand and Whittaker established in 1935 was the Briercrest Bible Institute, and it was in many ways modelled on Winnipeg Bible Institute. Hildebrand kept up his links with the CSSM, and soon the pattern of students doing Sunday school work and Sunday school converts going to Bible school was established at Briercrest. In 1937 Hildebrand took over as the provincial superintendent of the Sunday School Mission. This was also the year in which he was married to Inger Soeyland, an emigrant from Norway, whom he had met in Winnipeg.

Briercrest was one of many Bible schools begun on the prairies during these years. The pattern of independent gospel chapel, local nondenominational Bible school and itinerant Sunday school work in the surrounding area was repeated in towns across the west. On a small scale, this pattern reflected the relationship between Moody Church, Moody Bible Institute and the American Sunday School Union in the American Midwest.

Hildebrand became known to many during these years as the radio pastor of the popular 'Young People's Hour', which at its height was broadcast across Canada on twenty-two stations. However, Hildebrand's significance as an evangelical leader is linked principally to the growth of the Bible Institute he founded. Student numbers dropped during the Second World War, but climbed sharply afterwards when in 1946 Whittaker arranged for the purchase of the Caron airbase, which had been used during the war to train RAF pilots. The school moved, and the H-huts became dormitories for students, and the dance hall a chapel. The institution expanded dramatically through these post-war years. Despite a period of decline in the late 1960s, it reached a high of nearly 800 students in the 1980s and remains one of the largest Bible colleges in North America. Under Hildebrand's leadership the institution began an extensive process of curriculum revision, accreditation, faculty development and building work, a process that was carried on by Hildebrand's successor, Henry Budd. Hildebrand retired as president in 1977 but continued to live on the college campus as chancellor until 1992. In recognition of his work as an educator, he was awarded the Order of Canada in 1979.

Hildebrand has made a significant contribution to evangelical Christianity as a pioneer evangelist of the prairie west and as an educator, training thousands of young people for work as pastors and missionaries, and for other forms of Christian service. His autobiography illustrates clearly the way in which evangelicalism can function as an agent of ethnic assimilation, and also the way in which someone raised in the Anabaptist tradition can find a home within interdenominational evangelicalism. His use of radio and the entrepreneurial style of his leadership illustrate further the keen sense of contemporaneity within fundamentalism in its heyday. Hildebrand was a fundamentalist concerned with mission, not with the militant defence of Christianity against its ideological enemies. He himself would probably wish to be remembered chiefly as a Bible teacher.

Bibliography

H. Hildebrand, *In His Loving Service* (Caronport: Briercrest Bible College, 1985).

D. B. HINDMARSH

■ **HILL, Rowland** (1744–1833), preacher (known as 'Roly'), the sixth son of Sir Rowland and Mary Hill, was born at Hawkstone Park, near Wem, Shropshire, on 23 August 1744. Hill was educated at Shrewsbury School and Eton College, and was converted through his elder brother Richard. While a pupil at Eton and a student at St John's College, Cambridge, Hill formed religious societies for outreach, fellowship and good works. He graduated BA in 1769 (MA in 1772). Much to the concern of his parents, Hill spent the four years after leaving university as an itinerant preacher. Apart from his brother and sister, George *Whitefield and John Berridge most influenced him. They helped to shape his strongly held Calvinistic convictions and encouraged his preaching ministry. But to which denomination could Hill align himself? He was too Calvinistic for the Methodists, too much of an itinerant for the Church of England, and too hot-tempered for the Countess of *Huntingdon! Although six bishops refused to accept him for ordination, in June 1773 he was ordained deacon by the Bishop of Bath and Wells. Hill became a curate at Kingston, near Taunton, on a stipend of £40 a year. But since he continued to exercise an itinerant ministry, he could not find a bishop to ordain him priest. Thus within the eighteenth-century revival he remained something of an anomaly: part Anglican (he was ordained deacon but not presbyter and continued to use the Book of Common Prayer in his chapels) and part Nonconformist (he continued to itinerate). This dual association helped to make him deeply committed to the promotion of evangelical unity and, as he put it, to lowering the walls between the denominations, so 'that we may shake hands a little easier over them'.

In May 1773 Hill married Mary Tudway and they settled at Wotton-under-Edge,

Gloucestershire. There he built a chapel, an adjoining schoolroom and dwelling-house, an almshouse (rebuilt in 1883) and a woollen mill in which to employ the poor. The chapel, which seated 700 people, was rebuilt in 1851 and closed in 1973. Rowland and Mary Hill had no family of their own, but he loved children and wrote hymns, prayers and books for them. His London base was Surrey Chapel, Blackfriars, and he opened other chapels in Cheltenham and Leamington Spa. He generally spent the summer months in Gloucestershire and the rest of the year at Surrey Chapel. During his absences both Anglican and Nonconformist ministers officiated in his chapels. Throughout the year he continued to itinerate and described himself as the 'Rector of Surrey Chapel, Vicar of Wotton-under-Edge, and curate of all the fields, commons etc. throughout England and Wales'.

Surrey Chapel was the largest of its kind in London and could accommodate 3,000 people. It was the centre of Hill's missionary and philanthropic activity, and his congregation included both the rich and the poor. There was a Sunday school for 3,000 children and numerous programmes for social welfare. There was also a Dorcas Society for poor married women, an almshouse for poor women and a school of industry for poor girls. In Gloucestershire Hill became associated with Dr Edward Jenner and thoroughly involved with his vaccination programme, and he personally vaccinated thousands of people in London, Gloucestershire and Pembrokeshire. Hill promoted outreach among the poor, and was one of the promoters of a floating chapel on the River Thames. He was supportive of the London Missionary Society, the Religious Tract Society and the British and Foreign Bible Society.

Hill was one of the leading preachers of his generation and, like Whitefield, could attract immense crowds of people. For example, on one of his preaching tours in Scotland he addressed an estimated fifteen to twenty thousand people. His preaching was arresting, a combination of humour, pathos and vivid illustration. He wrote, or contributed to, a number of publications the most popular being his fictional work *Village Dialogues*, and composed a number of hymns, some of which were revised by William *Cowper.

Hill was a larger-than-life character, an aristocratic eccentric, with a good sense of humour. He remained active for most of his life and well into his eighties still preached six or seven times a week. He died in London on 11 April 1833 and was buried beneath the pulpit of Surrey Chapel.

Bibliography
W. Jones, *Memoirs of the Rev. Rowland Hill MA* (London: Bennett, 1837); E. Sidney, *The Life of the Rev. Rowland Hill MA* (London: Wertheim, 1861).

A. F. MUNDEN

■ **HODGE, Archibald Alexander** (1823–1886), Old School Presbyterian theologian, was born to Charles *Hodge and his wife, Sarah, in Princeton, New Jersey, the year after Charles was appointed to serve with Archibald *Alexander on the faculty of Princeton Seminary. Although he never had a 'conversion experience', Hodge made a profession of faith in the First Presbyterian Church in Princeton in 1842. He graduated from the College of New Jersey (1841) and, after a two-year period as a tutor in the college, from Princeton Seminary (1846).

Hodge was ordained by the Presbytery of New Brunswick in 1847 as a missionary to Allahabad and, recently married, embarked that summer for India with his wife, Elizabeth Holliday of Winchester, Virginia. His three years in India gave him an enduring zeal for foreign missions, and also gave him an appreciation for the British aristocracy that led to his critical stance towards American democracy.

Three years and two children later, Hodge and his family returned to the United States due to ill health. Over the next fourteen years he pastored three Old School Presbyterian churches: Lower West Nottingham, Maryland (1850–1855), Fredericksburg, Virginia (1855–1861), and Wilkesbarre, Pennsylvania (1861–1864), the last move being occasioned by the outbreak of the Civil War. His Sunday evening lectures to his Fredericksburg congregation resulted in his *Outlines of Theology* (1871), which succinctly translated his father's systematic theology into a more accessible form.

From 1864 to 1877 he served as professor

of didactic theology in Allegheny Seminary, Pennsylvania, where he continued to preach regularly, pastoring North Church, Allegheny, from 1866 to 1877. During this period he wrote a study of *The Atonement* (1867) and an *Exposition of the Confession of Faith* (1869), and contributed to such theological journals as *The Princeton Review*.

In 1877 Hodge was called to assist his father in the chair of didactic and polemic theology at Princeton Seminary, which he occupied after his father's death in 1878 until his own death in 1886. While generally agreeing with his father in theology, in the debate between immediate versus mediate imputation Hodge sided with Robert L. *Dabney, declaring that the whole distinction was invalid. His biography of his father, *Life of Charles Hodge* (1880), reveals his twin emphases on evangelical piety and orthodox theology, but also demonstrates a shift away from the revivalist emphases of the early nineteenth century towards more emphasis on Christian nurture.

From 1880 to 1883 Hodge served as co-editor with Charles Briggs of *The Presbyterian Review*, a journal devoted to bringing together recently united New School and Old School Presbyterians. With B. B. *Warfield, Hodge wrote a famous article entitled 'Inspiration' in the 1881 *Presbyterian Review*, which articulated the classic Princeton doctrine of inerrancy, namely that the original autographs of the Scriptures were completely free from error. The authors claimed that although apparent discrepancies exist, and difficulties in interpretation abound, no true contradiction can be found in Scripture. This doctrine would be endorsed by the General Assembly of the Presbyterian Church in its Portland Deliverance of 1892 and again in the Five Point Deliverance of 1910; it was hotly debated during the fundamentalist–modernist controversy.

Although not as involved in ecclesiastical politics as his father was, Hodge spoke at the first conference of the World Alliance of Reformed Churches in 1877, arguing that orthodox Reformed theology was needed for a secure foundation of law, education, politics and public life. Indeed, only such Calvinist convictions as the sovereignty of God, the total depravity of humans and the Lordship of Christ over every sphere of life could preserve

society from the anarchy and atheism of secularism. For Hodge, the separation of church and state should not entail the isolation of religion from public life. Rather, as a fervent postmillennialist, he argued that religion should be an integral part of every social institution. In his *Popular Lectures on Theological Themes* (1887) Hodge argued that only a thoroughly Reformed theology could provide an adequate foundation for public institutions.

In 1874 Hodge joined the National Reform Association's effort to obtain a constitutional amendment that would acknowledge God's authority over the United States, but without success. While supporting public education, he objected to a national system in the hope that local and state education could retain more religious teaching. Given the secularizing trends of the nation, the claims that education was 'neutral' could not be defended. Education must be either biblical or naturalistic, Christian or anti-Christian.

Bibliography

C. A. Salmond, *Princetoniana: Charles & A. A. Hodge* (New York: Scribner & Welford, 1888); G. S. Smith, *The Seeds of Secularization: Calvinism, Culture, and Pluralism in America, 1870–1915* (Grand Rapids: Christian University Press, 1985).

P. J. WALLACE

■ **HODGE, Charles** (1797–1878), Old School Presbyterian theologian, was born in Philadelphia to Hugh Hodge, a Scots-Irish physician, and his wife, Mary Blanchard, who was of English and Huguenot descent. Reared within the Second Presbyterian Church of Philadelphia, under the ministry of Ashbel Green, Charles never knew his father, who died in 1798 from the effects of yellow fever. The family lived comfortably for a time due to the income that came from their owning a portion of the Philadelphia shipping yards, but after Thomas Jefferson's embargo and the war of 1812 cut off their livelihood they were reduced to poverty, which may partially account for Hodge's lifelong attachment to the anti-Jeffersonian Whigs. In 1812 the Hodges moved to Princeton, where Mary took in boarders in order to provide an education for her two sons at the College of New Jersey. Hugh, the elder brother, became a physician like his father and frequently assisted Charles financially.

In 1813 Mary Hodge's boarders included the widow Mrs Bache and her three children. Hodge fell in love with the eldest, fourteen-year-old Sarah (a great-granddaughter of Benjamin Franklin), and they married in 1822 after a long friendship and courtship. Eight of their children survived infancy, two of whom, Casper Wistar and Archibald Alexander *Hodge, later taught at Princeton with their father.

Hodge studied at the College of New Jersey (1812–1815) under Ashbel Green, who came to Princeton as president of the college in 1812. Having always trusted in God, in 1815 he made a public profession of faith by joining the Presbyterian Church in Princeton, which started a revival among the college students. After a year of travel and study, Hodge entered Princeton Theological Seminary, where he studied from 1816 to 1819 with Archibald *Alexander and Samuel Miller, who trained him in the theology of the seventeenth-century theologian Francis Turretin and the Westminster Confession of Faith, together with Scottish common-sense realism and the devout piety from the tradition of the First Great Awakening. Even while Hodge was a student Alexander took a special interest in him, and in many ways served as a father figure for the young man. While at Princeton Seminary, Hodge formed his lifelong friendship with John Johns, afterwards Bishop of the Episcopal Church in Virginia. Throughout his life, Hodge was particularly noted for establishing and maintaining close personal friendships.

Licensed by the Presbytery of Philadelphia in 1819 and already being groomed for a professorship at Princeton, Hodge studied Hebrew in Philadelphia and preached regularly as a supply preacher in three parishes outside the city. In 1820 he travelled to New England, where he met Moses Stuart of Andover Seminary and Nathaniel W. *Taylor of the Yale Divinity School, with whom he would later engage in debate regarding the nature of original sin and the atonement. From 1820 to 1822 he was employed as a teacher of Greek and Hebrew at Princeton Seminary and was ordained in 1821 by the New Brunswick Presbytery as a minister supplying the First Presbyterian Church of Trenton.

In 1822 Hodge was elected Professor of Oriental and Biblical Literature at Princeton Seminary by the General Assembly, in which chair he remained for eighteen years. His inaugural address emphasized the importance of piety among the qualifications for interpreting Scripture, a theme to which he frequently returned. Having established himself in his calling, he and Sarah Bache were married that summer. Three years later he founded The Biblical Repertory, commonly known as The Princeton Review, which he edited until 1871, contributing no fewer than 142 articles on theology, biblical criticism, psychology, philosophy, ethics, politics, science, church polity and most current issues in the church. His annual review of the Old School General Assembly provided a running commentary on the state of the church from 1835 to 1867 (except 1841).

From 1826 to 1828 he studied in France and Germany in order to gain an acquaintance with the latest European biblical and theological scholarship, leaving his classes in the hands of John W. *Nevin. While approving his course of study, Alexander, his mentor and colleague, warned him against 'the poison of Neology', which dominated much of German theological scholarship. In Paris Hodge studied French, Arabic and Syriac, and in Halle he studied biblical criticism with Wilhelm Gesenius and theology with August Tholuck, one of the leaders of the mediating school of German theology, with whom he struck up a lifelong friendship. The last year he spent in Berlin studying with Ernst Hengstenberg, whose approach to Old Testament studies would influence Princeton for nearly a century, and Johann Neander, a leading church historian. During this time he became involved with a circle of German scholars, pastors and politicians who were seeking to respond to the inroads of rationalism in the German church and society. He heard Friedrich Schleiermacher preach several times, and while he would frequently inveigh against Schleiermacher's theology over the next fifty years, he always insisted that Schleiermacher's piety was evident. Ever interested in the natural sciences, he also regularly attended scientific lectures in Berlin.

After a tour of Switzerland, England and Scotland, he returned home.

Having gained one of the finest theological educations of any scholar in America, Hodge quickly established himself as an exegete and theologian. Despite being confined to his bed with 'rheumatism' in his leg for most of the 1830s, he continued to write and teach. Writing regularly in *The Princeton Review* against the development of the New Haven theology of Nathaniel W. Taylor, Hodge was a staunch defender of the traditional Calvinist doctrines of original sin, total depravity and the imputation of Adam's sin. His *Commentary on the Epistle to the Romans* (1835, 1864) was largely a response to New School exegetes, such as Moses Stuart and Albert Barnes. Hodge rejected the idea that sin consisted simply of an individual's own sinning, but taught that Adam had acted as the covenant head of all humanity, and therefore that each individual is guilty of Adam's sin. He eventually published commentaries on 1 and 2 Corinthians (1857) and Ephesians (1856) as well.

Hodge followed Alexander and Miller in maintaining a moderate stance towards those holding New School beliefs in the Presbyterian Church, and even after his colleagues had sided entirely with the Old School, Hodge disagreed privately about the wisdom of the 1837 General Assembly's act of excluding three synods which it believed were infected with New School theology, though he granted the propriety of excluding the fourth synod, which consisted almost entirely of Congregational churches. Hodge argued that certain New School beliefs were consistent with the system of doctrine contained in the Westminster Confession. If a minister 'holds that all mankind, since the fall of Adam, and in consequence of his sin, are born in a state of condemnation and sin, whether he accounts for that fact on the ground of immediate or mediate imputation, or on the realistic theory, he was regarded as within the integrity of the system. If he admitted the sinner's inability, it was not considered as a proper ground of discipline that he regarded that inability as moral, instead of natural and moral.' On the other hand, Hodge believed that Taylor's views, which denied that humanity was born in a state of condemnation and sin, and asserted that 'sinners have plenary ability to do all God requires of them', were inconsistent with the Confession and therefore should not be allowed in the church.

In the wake of the Old School / New School controversy, he published his *Constitutional History of the Presbyterian Church in the United States* (1839–1840), which challenged the received opinion that the revivals of George *Whitefield and Gilbert *Tennent were an unmixed blessing. Alexander was a firm supporter of the eighteenth-century revivals, but Hodge believed that the evidence did not support his mentor's view. Although he approved of the revivals in general, he objected to the manner in which they were conducted; he took the same attitude towards the revivals of his own day. As he demonstrated in his review of '[Horace] Bushnell's Discourses' in *The Princeton Review* (1847), Hodge was convinced that an overemphasis on revival would result in a 'false or unscriptural form of religion'.

In 1840 Hodge was transferred to the chair of exegetical and didactic theology at Princeton in order to enable him to focus more on his theological work. Hodge engaged in theological polemics with theologians all around the United States, and regularly reviewed the major contributions of scholars from Britain and Germany in *The Princeton Review*. Many of these essays were republished in *Theological Essays* (1846) and *Essays and Reviews* (1857). In 1851 Archibald Alexander died, and Hodge succeeded him as professor of didactic and polemical theology.

Hodge maintained an office in his home, and during his invalid years his children would frequently assist him in obtaining books. He even removed the latch from the door of his study so that even the smallest children could push the door open and visit their father while he worked. On Christmas Day 1849 his wife Sarah died after twenty-seven years of marriage. In 1852 he married Mary Hunter Stockton, the widow of a navy lieutenant.

Hodge defended above all else 'an Augustinian picture of the human condition'. Any view, including those of Roman Catholicism, Friedrich Schleiermacher, the Oxford Movement, Charles *Finney and Horace Bushnell, that downplayed the sovereignty of God in salvation or overemphasized the moral capacity of human nature received his censure.

One of his most sustained debates occurred in the 1850s with Edwards Amasa Park of Andover Seminary on the relationship between 'the theology of the intellect and that of the feelings'. While Park argued that 'Calvinistic categories should be considered an emotional expression that did not correspond precisely to an external reality', Hodge insisted that such a view overturned not merely Calvinism but 'Catholic Christianity', by which he meant the whole Christian tradition. For Hodge, it is God and God alone who turns people to himself.

In 1848 he wrote a review entitled 'Doctrine of the Reformed Church on the Lord's Supper' in which he tried to refute his former student John W. Nevin, who had attempted to reformulate Calvin's doctrine of the Lord's Supper in the light of German idealist psychology. Although he shared the concern of the Mercersburg theologians regarding the revivalism that was sweeping America, he believed that German idealism would result in the destruction of traditional piety.

This concern for piety expressed itself in his writings for the laity, such as his popular introduction to the Christian faith *The Way of Life* (1841), which was addressed to young people considering religion. His sermons and pastoral counsel to his seminarians seen in his *Conference Papers* (1879) reflect his emphasis on personal piety.

Although Hodge was thoroughly conservative in his defence of traditional Calvinism, his conservatism enabled him to remain a moderate during a time in which American religion and culture were becoming more and more radical. At the urging of James Henley *Thornwell, in 1845 the Old School General Assembly declared Roman Catholic baptism to be invalid. Hodge objected that no other Reformed church had ever taken this position and that it violated the Reformed doctrine of the catholicity of the visible church. Likewise, Hodge refused to yield to the increasing zeal of the temperance movement by declaring all alcohol sinful.

In the same way, he opposed the radical abolitionists who insisted that slavery was inherently sinful and that slaveholders should not be allowed in Christian churches. Hodge believed that since the Bible does not condemn slavery, it could not be called inherently sinful. But Hodge did say that American slavery failed to meet biblical standards and therefore was indeed a great evil that needed to be eliminated. In several articles in *The Princeton Review* ('Slavery', 1836, 'West India Emancipation', 1838, 'Abolitionism', 1844, 'Emancipation', 1849, and 'Civil Government', 1851) Hodge called for the gradual emancipation of slaves and suggested that since it was unlikely that whites would treat blacks as equals, the freed slaves should be sent to a colony in West Africa. Not surprisingly, his repeated calls for moderation aroused increasing hostility in both the North and the South.

Predictably, when northern Presbyterians such as Gardiner Spring brought a resolution to the Old School General Assembly of 1861 requiring all Presbyterians (North and South) to affirm their support for the federal government, Hodge objected that this would require the church to decide a political question: namely, whether Americans owed primary loyalty to their state or to the federal government. Hodge was unwilling to make this a test of ministerial fellowship in the church, and after the war he objected to the Old School's policy of requiring southern ministers to repent of the sin of treason as a condition of returning to the northern church. But while urging moderation, Hodge was a fervent supporter of Abraham Lincoln and the Union, writing a glowing eulogy for Lincoln in 1865.

While many northern Presbyterians sought to reunite the Old and New School churches in the North, Hodge hoped to see a reunion first with the southern Presbyterian church. Concerned for the national testimony of the church, Hodge believed that a union with the New School would be detrimental to the health of the church unless the more conservative southern church was included as well. He thought that he espied in the New School some of the doctrines that he had decried for forty years. But in 1869 the Old and New School churches reunited.

Convinced of the rational grounds for the Christian religion, Hodge maintained a lively interest in the natural sciences. Believing that theology itself was a science, Hodge followed the Baconian method of induction and Scottish common-sense realism, saying in the first chapter of his three-volume *Systematic Theology* (1872–1873) that 'The Bible is to the theologian what nature is to the man of science ... In theology as in natural science, principles are derived from facts, and not impressed upon them.' But when science departed from this inductive method, as Hodge was convinced that Charles Darwin had done, it was no longer true science. In his 1874 volume *What Is Darwinism?*, Hodge answered his own question with a resounding 'It is atheism!' While he could accept the idea of animal evolution and even natural selection (properly understood), Hodge argued that what was distinctive to Darwin's view was the rejection of teleology, the rejection of purpose in the natural world. In his many years of service as the chairman of the board of trustees for the College of New Jersey, Hodge worked with college president James *McCosh to encourage a harmonious relationship between religion and science.

Although his *Systematic Theology* did not contain any treatment of the doctrine of the church, Hodge probably wrote more about the church than about any other subject, as is reflected in his collected essays on *Church Polity* (1878). Hodge called upon the church to consider how to minister more effectively to cities, warning against the danger of becoming a middle- and upper-class church and suggesting a plan of sustentation like that utilized in the Free Church of Scotland. In 1857 he noted the decline of infant baptism and urged the church to remember that all baptized children were truly members of the visible church. He supported the voluntary usage of Presbyterian liturgies in order to train pastors in public prayer, and defended Presbyterian polity against Episcopal and Congregational views.

Princeton Seminary had the most diverse student body of any American seminary, with students coming from every region of the United States and from several foreign countries, especially Britain and Canada. Among Hodge's more than three thousand students were more than fifty moderators of Presbyterian general assemblies and at least 170 foreign missionaries. James Pettigru Boyce (Southern Baptist) and Robert Watts (Presbyterian Church of Ireland) were among those whose study with Hodge was influential in denominations outside American Presbyterian circles.

Bibliography

A. A. Hodge, *The Life of Charles Hodge* (New York: Charles Scribner's Sons, 1880); A. W. Hoffecker, *Piety and the Princeton Theologians* (Grand Rapids: Baker, 1981); M. A. Noll, *The Princeton Theology, 1812–1921* (Grand Rapids: Baker, 1983); J. W. Stewart, 'Mediating the Center: Charles Hodge on American Science, Language, Literature, and Politics', *Studies in Reformed Theology and History* 3.1 (winter 1995).

P. J. WALLACE

■ **HOOPER, John** (c. 1499–1555), Bishop of Gloucester and martyr, was the main representative of the views of Ulrich *Zwingli and Heinrich *Bullinger of Zurich among the English reformers in the reign of Edward VI (1547–1553) and is often seen as a forerunner of later Puritanism.

Born some time between 1495 and 1502 in Somersetshire, Hooper was the only son of a man of some wealth. He received the BA from Oxford in 1519, but his college is unknown. At some undetermined time he became a Cistercian monk, entering Cleeve Abbey in Somerset, where he resided until the abbey was dissolved by Henry VIII in 1537. After a brief period at court in London, he was converted to a Protestant position through the writings of Zwingli and Bullinger. He returned to Oxford, where his new views were opposed as contrary to the Act of Six Articles of 1539.

Hooper found refuge as steward of Sir Thomas Arundel, who had him examined theologically by Stephen Gardiner, Bishop of Winchester, who could not dissuade him from his Protestant opinions. To escape arrest, Hooper eventually fled to Paris and then to Strasburg, where he had settled by January 1546. There he met a noblewoman from Antwerp, Anna de Tserclas, whom he married in Basel in March 1547. Hooper also received a doctorate of theology some time prior to 1550, probably from the University of Basel.

On 29 March 1547 Hooper and his wife were welcomed by Bullinger to Zurich. There he published his first works, including an answer to Gardiner's book on the Lord's Supper, and there his daughter Rachael was born (a son, Daniel, would later be born in

England). When the Hoopers left for England on 24 March 1549, he was hailed by the Zurichers as the future Zwingli of England.

Arriving in London on 16 May 1549, Hooper gave lectures that proved attractive to radicals and Anabaptists, but he was annoyed with their forthright opinions. In the summer of 1550 he would be sent into Kent and Essex to oppose the Anabaptists there. Meanwhile he was appointed to preach a series of seven sermons before the king in Lent 1550. In these he expounded the book of Jonah, applying it to the imperfections of the English Reformation.

Offered the bishopric of Gloucester on 7 April 1550, Hooper declined because of scruples over the required vestments. The king and council were willing to grant a dispensation, but Archbishop Thomas *Cranmer and Nicholas *Ridley, Bishop of London, refused to proceed. Opinions were sought from continental theologians then in England. Martin *Bucer of Cambridge and Peter Martyr Vermigli of Oxford, while disliking the vestments, regarded them as tolerable. John à Lasco of the Strangers' Church in London, which Hooper had helped to establish, supported Hooper's stand. The bitter conflict ran from October 1550 to February 1551, including a stay of three weeks for Hooper in the Fleet prison, and foreshadowed Anglican and Puritan differences in the Elizabethan period. For Ridley the question was one of church authority in matters of indifference, whereas for Hooper even adiaphora should be grounded in Scripture.

Once Hooper had yielded, he was consecrated Bishop of Gloucester on 8 March 1551. He proved to be an exemplary bishop, energetically improving the organization and education of his clergy, whom his visitation in 1551 revealed to be woefully ignorant of even the Lord's Prayer, the Ten Commandments and the Apostles' Creed. Preaching three or four times a day, he did much to improve the discipline of his diocese and that of Worcester, which was added to his see early in 1552.

With the accession of Mary Tudor, Hooper was arrested in September 1553 on the charge of a debt to the queen. After six months in the Fleet, he was tried in March 1554 for his views on marriage and against transubstantiation in order to deprive him of his bishopric. On 22 January 1555 he was tried for heresy.

When he refused to recant, he was excommunicated, degraded and turned over to the secular arm for execution. He was taken to Gloucester to be burned at the stake in his former diocese. On 9 February 1555, before a crowd of some 7,000, he remained constant in the flames for three quarters of an hour, while the wind and green faggots prevented the fire from swiftly ending his life, in an agonizing demise described vividly in John *Foxe's *Actes and Monuments* (*Book of Martyrs*).

Bibliography

E. W. Hunt, *The Life and Times of John Hooper* (c. 1500–1555) Bishop of Gloucester (Lampeter: Edwin Mellen Press, 1992); J. Opie, 'The Anglicizing of John Hooper', *Archiv für Reformationsgeschichte* 59 (1968), pp. 150–177; J. H. Primus, *The Vestments Controversy: An Historical Study of the Earliest Tensions Within the Church of England in the Reigns of Edward VI and Elizabeth* (Kampen: J. H. Kok, 1960).

W. S. BARKER

■ **HOPKINS, Samuel** (1721–1803), Congregational minister, Reformed theologian and abolitionist, was born on 17 September 1721 in Waterbury, Connecticut to Judge Timothy Hopkins and his wife Mary. The first of nine children, Samuel was sent to Yale College in 1737 to prepare for the ministry. Although he had made a profession of faith by his third year and joined his home church in Waterbury, he soon began to doubt his own salvation. In the autumn of 1740, his fourth year, religious revival engulfed the Yale campus as George *Whitefield and other evangelists stormed through New Haven preaching the necessity of conversion and warning against the dangers of an unconverted ministry. Hopkins heartily embraced the evangelical message of itinerants like Whitefield and Gilbert *Tennent, and after much spiritual agonizing, experienced conversion in the spring of 1741. At his graduation the following September, upon hearing Jonathan *Edwards' famous commencement sermon defending the revival, he resolved to join Edwards in Northampton,

Massachusetts to further his ministerial preparation.

In December 1741 Hopkins arrived at Edwards' 'school of the prophets' and studied intermittently with the great New Light theologian for the next year-and-a-half. Hopkins was ordained on 28 December 1743 at the Second Congregational Church of Sheffield in Housatonic (later named Great Barrington), amid the Berkshire Mountains in western Massachusetts. He served this parish for twenty-six years. On 13 January 1748 he married Joanna Ingersoll. She gave birth to five sons and three daughters. Controversy over his strict ecclesiastical policies (he rejected the Half-way Covenant and the practice of open communion) and theological peculiarities, as well as continued conflict with Dutch settlers who opposed his ministry from the outset, led to his dismissal in the winter of 1769. On 11 April 1770 Hopkins became pastor of the First Congregational Church in Newport, Rhode Island. His wife Joanna died on 31 August 1793. He was remarried on 14 September 1794 to Elizabeth West. In January 1799 Hopkins was stricken with paralysis, but continued his clerical duties until his death on 20 December 1803.

Hopkins was arguably Edwards' greatest disciple and the most significant divine of late eighteenth-century New England. Together with theologians such as Joseph *Bellamy, Jonathan Edwards, Jr, and Nathaniel Emmons, he developed the religious thought of Edwards into what became known as the New Divinity, one of the most important and abiding theological traditions in American history. This movement was derisively called 'New Divinity', 'Hopkinsianism' or 'Hopkintonianism' by doctrinal adversaries to suggest that Hopkins and his colleagues had deviated from traditional Reformed standards. But the New Divinity men preferred the labels 'Consistent Calvinists' or 'Edwardseans'.

Hopkins was a rigorous thinker and energetic controversialist who stoutly defended traditional Calvinism against the encroachments of Arminianism, antinomianism and Enlightenment naturalistic philosophy in New England. Yet he was not content simply to restate the traditional formulas of the Westminster Confession. The charge that he taught new doctrines stemmed from his bold, meticulously reasoned and sometimes provocative reformulation of Reformed theology. In reaction to Enlightenment and Arminian currents that encouraged a softening of such hard Calvinist doctrines as the divine decrees, original sin, irresistible grace, human depravity and eternal damnation, he pushed facets of these teachings to their logical extremes. Yet in doing so he appropriated aspects of Enlightenment discourse to rebut allegations that Reformed dogma was intellectually indefensible and morally repugnant. This approach resulted in a creative refashioning of Calvinism that responded to eighteenth-century cultural changes without being compromised by them.

In his first major work, *Sin, through Divine Interposition, an Advantage to the Universe* (1759), Hopkins tried to reconcile Reformed notions of sin and divine sovereignty with Enlightenment ideas of divine benevolence by arguing that God wilfully permitted and directed sin to produce the best possible universe. Indeed, the world was a *much better* place than if sin had never existed. Sin provided the occasion for the most complete display of divine love and grace in the cross of Christ and the salvation of sinners. It also furnished a means for God's power and wrath to be exhibited in the eternal punishment of sinners. To Hopkins, God's sovereignty was limited by his benevolence, which compelled him to act always to promote the greatest good of the whole system of being.

Hopkins' strident defence of Calvinist doctrines of divine sovereignty and human depravity led to a dispute over grace and the spiritual worthiness of unregenerate preparationist practices. In 1761 Jonathan Mayhew published two sermons insinuating that the sincere strivings of unregenerate sinners would be rewarded with salvation. Hopkins countered this Arminian threat with the release of *An Inquiry Concerning the Promises of the Gospel* (1765). He not only denied the spiritual goodness of unregenerate endeavours but insisted that unrepentant 'awakened' sinners who used the means of grace (i.e. Bible study, prayer, Sabbath observance) were more vile in God's eyes than the most wicked 'unawakened' sinners who neglected those means. Their continued impenitence in the face of increased gospel instruction simply aggravated their guilt and revealed the deep obstinacy of their hearts.

Hopkins' radical position appeared to under-cut the preparationist scheme of grace that lay at the heart of much New England church practice and embroiled him in a lengthy controversy with 'Old Calvinists' who accused him of teaching 'New Divinity'.

The debate over the nature of religious conversion was the stimulus for Hopkins to develop fully his understanding of Christian holiness, particularly as it related to the issue of self-love. To thwart what he thought was an increased acceptance of selfishness in New England church life and religious and ethical discourse, Hopkins articulated a morally stringent concept of holiness as universal or disinterested benevolence. In *An Inquiry into the Nature of True Holiness* (1773), he declared that true virtue was synonymous with obedience to the divine law, which required a regenerate, 'holy love' of God and all intelligent beings or the promotion of 'the highest good of the whole'. This demanded the surrender of one's own self-interest whenever it was inconsistent with the good of 'being in general'. Hopkins even conjectured that holiness entailed a willingness to be damned *if* God's glory would be promoted by one's consignment to hell. He spoke out so forcefully against self-love because he feared that Old Calvinist and Arminian concessions of self-interest as a motive for seeking salvation or as a starting point for genuine virtue undermined the doctrine of God's sovereign grace and encouraged selfish religious and moral behaviour.

Hopkins' summons to radical, self-denying love provided a powerful theological catalyst for the ethical and missionary activism of evangelicals well into the nineteenth century. In his own life the social implications of his teachings were clearly evidenced in his opposition to slavery. From his post in slave-trading Newport, he became one of New England's most forceful and articulate champions of abolitionism. In *A Dialogue Concerning the Slavery of the Africans* (1776), he called slavery the worst of America's sins, condemned the gross hypocrisy of the colonies' quest for freedom, and linked the eradication of slavery to the overall ethical purity of the revolutionary war. After the war he promoted the founding of a mission colony of freed slaves in Africa in order to spread the gospel and thereby bring some greater good out of the evil of slavery.

Perhaps Hopkins' greatest achievement was the publication of his eleven-hundred-page *System of Doctrines* (1793), the first comprehensive, indigenous, American systematic theology. His *System* defended biblical authority against deistic attack, codified New Divinity principles and provided a theological foundation for the training of future Edwardsean ministers.

Bibliography

E. A. Park, 'Memoir of the Life and Character of Samuel Hopkins, D.D.' in *The Works of Samuel Hopkins, D.D.*, vol. 1 (Boston: Doctrinal Tract and Book Society, 1852); S. West, *Sketches of the Life of the Late, Rev. Samuel Hopkins, D.D.* (Hartford: Hudson & Goodwin, 1805); J. Conforti, *Samuel Hopkins and the New Divinity Movement: Calvinism, the Congregational Ministry, and Reform in New England Between the Great Awakenings* (Grand Rapids: Christian University, 1981).

P. D. JAUHIAINEN

■ **HOUSTON, James Macintosh** (1922–), founding principal of Regent College, Vancouver, was born on 21 November 1922 in Edinburgh, Scotland. His parents, James and Ethel May Houston, served as missionaries to Spain. His father was an itinerant preacher to Glanton Brethren congregations in England and Scotland and lived by faith in the manner of George *Müller of Bristol.

At the age of eight or nine Houston was converted, and he was baptized at the age of twelve. Houston joined Inter-Varsity Fellowship at Edinburgh University, where he received the MA (with first-class honours) in 1944. Houston received the BSc (1947) and DPhil in geography (1949) from Oxford University.

He served as university lecturer in geography at Oxford (1947–1971), fellow of Hertford College, Oxford (1964–1971) and bursar of Hertford College (1967–1970). He published a standard university textbook, *The Western Mediterranean World* (1964), and edited over ten other works of historical geography. While at Oxford, Houston was the first secretary of the University Faculty Christian Fellowship and co-founder of the

Young Men's Bible Teaching Annual Conference and the Overseas Graduate Hostel, and helped to plant Northway Church. He belonged to the 'Open Brethren' of the Plymouth Brethren (1945–1989) and to the Baptist Union of Western Canada (1989–). On 20 March 1953 he married Margaret Isobel ('Rita') Davidson in Glasgow, Scotland. They had four children.

Before marriage, he shared a flat (1946–1953) with Nicolas Zernov, lecturer in Russian history at Oxford. A wide circle of Christian intellectuals (including C. S. Lewis) met regularly in their flat to present papers on religion. Lewis became a model for Houston of a serious lay theologian. In 1976 Houston and James Hiskey founded the C. S. Lewis Institute in Washington, DC to encourage believers 'to articulate, defend, and live their faith in personal and public life'.

Lewis's influence led Houston to abandon his own professional career at Oxford and accept the invitation to become founding principal of Regent College in Vancouver, Canada in 1970. Regent was the first evangelical graduate college affiliated to a major university to make as its focus the theological education of the laity. Originally Houston envisaged an institution that would produce lay thinkers like C. S. Lewis, who was able to reach millions in a way that clergy had not. Later the school included ministerial students. In 1978 Regent made a bold move by creating the first professorship devoted entirely to spiritual theology in any evangelical college or seminary in North America, and it gave this position to Houston when he stepped down as principal to become chancellor and concentrate on teaching spirituality. He retired from the Board of Governors' Chair in Spiritual Theology in 2001. J. I. *Packer argued that Houston's awakening of Protestants to the heritage of spirituality, of which they had been largely ignorant, was his 'greatest contribution to the life of the church'. Long before spiritual direction had acquired a following in evangelical circles, the pioneering Houston led evangelicals to an appreciation of spiritual guidance through his courses and personal guidance of students. During Houston's time at Regent College, it gained an international reputation as a centre for evangelical thinking and spiritual formation.

In his courses Houston emphasized the history of Christian spirituality in all its Catholic, Orthodox, Protestant and evangelical dimensions. John *Stott indicated the 'risk' Houston 'has been willing to take in inviting us [evangelicals] to explore the spirituality of Christian traditions other than our own'. To correct absent-mindedness about spiritual writers from past ages, Houston edited ten books in a series called *Classics of Faith and Devotion*.

Of all Houston's writings, two are particularly influential. *The Transforming Friendship* (1989), a book available in eight languages, about the practice of prayer based upon friendship with the triune God, advocated the social Trinity as a model for relationships and spiritual friendship. Prayerlessness results, Houston argued, not primarily from lack of discipline or technique but from lack of deep relationships. The rediscovery of the Trinity was Houston's way out of prayerlessness. *The Heart's Desire* (1992), written within an Augustinian framework, explores various symbols of the diverse conditions of the Christian life to lead the reader towards greater intimacy with God.

Bibliography
A. D. Thomas, 'James M. Houston: Pioneering Spiritual Director to Evangelicals', *European Journal of Theology*, 3 (1994), pp. 117–136; J. I. Packer and L. Wilkinson (eds.), *Alive to God: Studies in Spirituality Presented to James Houston* (Downers Grove: Inter Varsity Press, 1993); K. Pearson (ed.), *Alive to the Love of God* (Vancouver: Regent College Press, 1997).

A. D. THOMAS

■ **HOWARD, John** (1726–1790), English prison reformer, saw himself as an ordinary Christian and an English gentleman, whose 'hobby-horse' was prisons. His father, a miserly upholsterer in London, had apprenticed him rather than giving him an education, and all his life Howard turned to his friends to polish his prose. Inheriting wealth, the young Howard set up as a country gentleman in Bedfordshire, and was a model landlord. He was a Protestant Dissenter, but this did not stop him (as strictly by law then it should have) from serving as high sheriff of the county in 1773. In this role he had official charge of the prisons, and he was shocked to find that acquitted prisoners were not released because their jailors charged them fees they could not pay. He then visited the neighbouring counties to see if this practice was usual, and thus began his life's work. The prisons of Britain were a disgrace, with all categories of prisoner mixed together (lesser offenders such as debtors with hardened criminals) and always dirt, disease, financial malpractice and, when the prisoners had money, drunkenness and vice.

Howard went round collecting statistics of space and provision of air, water, exercise and food. He then went to the continent of Europe to make comparisons. Europe still officially used torture, but only Britain had jail-fever, and some countries, like the Netherlands, had very well-run prisons, with far fewer criminals, and those healthy and usefully employed.

As a reformer, Howard experienced little hostility, but rather compliments and then inaction. He inspected most of the prisons of Britain several times, and sometimes could report improvement. Acts of Parliament were passed based on his evidence-packed book *The State of Prisons in England and Wales, with an Account of Some Foreign Prisons* (1777). He was single-minded and ascetic, never seemed to need sleep, and was a strict vegetarian and teetotaller. He travelled tens of thousands of miles, went into every stinking dungeon he could find, and could quell a prison riot or beard an emperor. He moved on from prisons to hospitals (*An Account of the Principal Lazarettos of Europe* [1780]), and died while inspecting Russian army hospitals in the Ukraine.

Why this zeal? He had been in prison, as a prisoner of war taken by the French in 1756, years before he began his life's work. Twice widowed, his grief for his second wife made sitting at home unbearable. He was an eager Christian; his private papers throughout his life were filled with rhapsodic (rather than systematic) Calvinism, testifying to his own sin and the sufficient grace of God. An Independent when his minister at Bedford turned Baptist, Howard led out the minority and founded another Independent chapel. Characteristically, however, he stayed close friends with the minister and continued his subscription to his chapel. He accompanied his Anglican wives to the parish church, and many of his closest friends were Quakers or Unitarians. When the benevolent but rash despot Emperor Joseph II of Austria turned on the Catholic religious orders, Howard protested because he knew their work in prisons.

Howard was not a theorist of prison reform, and it is misleading to attribute to him, or to his Calvinist creed, the more rigorous and terrifying aspects of the model penitentiaries of the next generation, such as long solitary confinement. His own self-discipline made him sometimes unaware of how hard some others found discipline (such as his son, who went mad, not through Howard's fault). But his dry statistics were supplemented by many individual acts of kindness in jails. He always looked at the prisoners with sharp and loving eyes. The Howard League for Penal Reform was founded in 1866 in his memory.

Bibliography

J. Aikin, *A View of the Life, Travels, and Philanthropic Labours of the Late John Howard Esq. LL.D., F.R.S.* (Littleton, Colorado: Fred B. Rothman & Co., 1994); J. C. Freeman, *Prisons Past and Future* (London: Heinemann Educational, 1978); M. Ignatieff, *A Just Measure of Pain* (London: Macmillan, 1978).

A. F. MASON

■ **HOWELLS, Rees** (1879–1950), founder of the Bible College of Wales, was born on 10 October 1879 in Brynaman, Carmarthenshire, one of the eleven children of Thomas and Margaret Howells. His schooling was meagre, and he began work at the local tinplate mill at the age of twelve. He emigrated to Pennsylvania in the late 1890s, finding work in Pittsburgh, Martin's Ferry and later Connellsville, where he was converted in a tent mission led by Maurice Reuben, a converted Jew. Returning home in 1904 to work in the coal mines, he partook fully in the activities of the Welsh Revival, and a visit to the Llandrindod Convention in 1906 introduced him to Keswick-type holiness teaching, for which he became a keen advocate. While still employed as a coal miner, Howells spent the next four years locally in mission work, developing an extraordinary capacity for intercessory prayer accompanied by some eccentric ascetic practices. He married Elizabeth Hannah Jones, also from Brynaman, on 21 December 1910, and thereafter sought ordination into the Congregational ministry, undergoing training at the Presbyterian College in Carmarthen.

In the meantime, a vacancy had arisen for a married couple to undertake mission work with the South African General Mission. Feeling led to apply for the joint post, Howells and his wife were accepted and, following a period of preparation, at the Glasgow Faith Mission for her and through a medical course at Livingston College, London, and the City Road Hospital for him, they embarked in July 1915 for Rusitu, Gazaland, near the border of Portuguese East Africa. By this time Howells had abandoned his intention of becoming a Congregational minister, at least for the time being. Immediately following their arrival, scenes of revivalist fervour, reminiscent of the Welsh Revival ten years earlier, spread through the Mission's twenty-five stations in the Belgian Congo (Zaire), Angola and Mozambique and lasted two years or more. Having engaged in a preaching, pastoral and healing ministry along revivalist lines, the couple concluded their African sojourn and returned to Britain in December 1920.

During a journey to America in 1922, when the fundamentalist–modernist controversy was at its height, Howells was impressed by the Bible institutes that were being established there in opposition to the denominational seminaries that had been influenced by theological liberalism. He returned fired with a vision to establish a Welsh Bible institute, modelled especially on the Moody Institute in Chicago. Following the example of George *Müller, he refused to appeal for financial support but depended on faith alone. Considerable provision was forthcoming, which allowed him to purchase the Glynderwen estate overlooking Swansea Bay in Sketty, Glamorganshire for £6,150, and on Whit Monday 1924 the Bible College of Wales was opened with a complement of thirty-eight students and five tutors.

The venture, however, did not go smoothly. Even before it began there were signs of rivalry between Howells' institution and the South Wales Bible Training Institute founded simultaneously by the evangelical firebrand R. B. Jones at Porth in the Rhondda Valley. Soon after teaching commenced, the disciplinary regime within the college was criticized for extreme harshness, while Howells, as director, was accused of tyrannizing the students. He, in turn, charged them with worldliness and a lack of consecration. By October 1925 thirty-three students and three of the staff had resigned, many of them transferring to the rival establishment at Porth. Five years later the situation had been partially retrieved. There were by then thirty students in residence, most of whom were preparing for overseas mission work, along with an academic staff of four, and the college was consolidated by the purchase of the adjoining, handsome estate of Derwen Fawr in order to create a school for missionaries' children.

As well as providing a grounding in the Bible and Christian theology, the college, through its community, was drawn into the director's ongoing intercessory ministry. Prayer was offered for a plethora of issues: domestic, national and, as the 1930s progressed, international as well. The parliamentary debate over the 1928 Prayer Book, the abdication of Edward VIII, Mussolini's invasion of Ethiopia, the Munich crisis and much else besides, became matters of fervent supplication and profound concern. Howells' intense piety, which was highly subjective at the best of times, led him to claim what he believed was God's promise that war would be averted, and then, when hostilities were under way, the further 'promise' that victory over Germany would be secured by Whitsun 1940. The fact that both predictions were proved wrong did little to damage his credibility among pupils and staff, most of whom held him in high, if uncritical, esteem.

Howells died on 12 February 1950, passing on the college's directorship to Samuel Rees Howells, his son.

Bibliography
N. Grubb, *Rees Howells, Intercessor* (Cambridge: Lutterworth Press, 1952); N. Gibbard, *Taught to Serve: the History of Barry and Bryntirion Colleges* (Bridgend: Evangelical Press of Wales, 1996).

D. D. MORGAN

■ **HUBMAIER, Balthasar** (1480–1528), Anabaptist preacher and theologian, was born in Friedberg, near Augsburg. He went to the University of Freiburg, where he was taught by Johann Eck, later one of the leading Roman Catholic controversialists of the Reformation. In 1512, having already been ordained, he went to Ingolstadt to take his doctorate, which was awarded later that year. He served in the university as prorector until 1516, when he went to Regensburg to be the preacher at the cathedral. Becoming part of the anti-Semitic movement in the city, he was partly responsible for the Jews being driven out. He then became the chief preacher at a pilgrimage centre, the Church of the Beautiful Mary, which was built on the site of the synagogue.

In 1521 he went to become priest in one of the two parishes of Waldshut, a small town on the Rhine. It was there that he began to make contact with the humanist and reforming movement. He was increasingly drawn into the new way of thinking. In 1522 he was invited back to Regensburg, and returned to the same post as before, but did not stay. The parting seems to have been amicable, but it was becoming clear that he now belonged among the reformers. His explanation for why he could no longer do what he had done was that 'Christ was starting to sprout in me'. His position was similar to that of *Luther at this time; he emphasized preaching and wrote on the nature of the sacraments. In 1523 he took part in the October Disputation in Zurich. He agreed with *Zwingli on the meaning and place of the sacraments, but not on the speed of reform.

Back in Waldshut, Hubmaier became involved in a similar disputation, for which he wrote eighteen theses. These outlined a programme of reform. In 1524 the series of uprisings known as the Peasants' Revolt or War started, and Waldshut as a community committed itself to the peasants. Hubmaier's writings make it clear that he supported the peasants in their demands, but it is unlikely that he had much to do practically with the progress of the struggle.

In 1525 an Anabaptist preacher, Reublin, came to Waldshut from Zurich and invited people to be baptized. On Easter Sunday Hubmaier and sixty others were baptized. In the following days another three hundred were baptized. This was the beginning of a territorial Anabaptist congregation in Waldshut. However, in autumn 1525 the peasants were defeated, and Waldshut came under political pressure. By the year's end Hubmaier had fled to Zurich, and Waldshut had been re-Catholicized. Moreover, Zwingli had distanced himself from Hubmaier over baptism and the nature of the church. Without protection, Hubmaier was arrested and tortured, and recanted his baptismal theology. In 1526 he was freed, and left the city, going first to Nicolsburg, and finally to Moravia, where there was more religious freedom.

In Moravia he recommitted himself to Anabaptist views, and set up a congregation, as in Waldshut, under the civil authorities. In this case, the local prince was baptized, which gave the congregation protection. However, in 1527 the Habsburg authorities arrested Hubmaier. He was charged with rebellion and taken to Vienna for trial. On 10 March 1528 he was burned as a rebel and heretic.

Hubmaier's theological path is clear because of his publications. He wrote to defend his position and to educate others. His most significant writings deal with the nature of the gospel sacraments (and include orders of service for baptism and communion), the question of free will and the Christian understanding of the State. He taught a memorialist theology of sacraments, and linked baptism not just to joining the church, but also to a life of penitence and discipline. Communion included a 'pledge of love', an expression of congregational commitment. With regard to free will, he emphasized the nature of sin, but also the ethical responsibility of the Christian, arguing that in Christ a person can both desire and do what is good. On the State, his teaching differed from another strand of Anabaptist theology which taught pacifism and withdrawal, advocating instead the involvement of believers in the government of the community. He refused to rule out the use of violence. He provides a very distinctive voice among Anabaptist theologians.

Bibliography

T. Bergsten, *Balthasar Hubmaier, Anabaptist Theologian and Martyr*, trans. I. J. Barnes and W. R. Estep (Valley Forge: Judson

Press, 1978); H. W. Pipkin and J. H. Yoder, *Balthasar Hubmaier: Theologian of Anabaptism* (Scottdale: Herald Press, 1989).

R. GOULDBOURNE

■ **HUGHES, Hugh Price** (1847–1902), preacher and social reformer, was the most influential British Methodist in the late nineteenth century. His gifts as an evangelist, orator, reformist visionary and ecclesiastical statesman animated the Methodist 'Forward Movement' and transformed British Methodism and the other English Free Churches.

Hugh Price Hughes was born on 7 February 1847, in Carmarthen, Wales, to John Hughes, a doctor, and his wife Anne (née Phillips). Hughes' paternal grandfather, Hugh Hughes, was a prominent Wesleyan Methodist preacher in Wales. Hugh Price Hughes was sent as a boy to a Methodist school near Swansea, where he excelled in both sports and academics. At the age of fourteen, he experienced a conversion and decided to become a preacher. From 1865 to 1869, Hughes attended the Wesleyan seminary in Richmond, near London, where he became captain of the cricket team, chairman of the Student Missionary Society and, in 1868, one of the first Richmond students to earn a concurrent bachelor's degree from the University of London. In that same year, he fell in love with Katherine Barrett, the fifteen-year-old daughter of the governor of the college. After three years of enforced separation, their courtship was resumed, and they were married in 1873.

In accord with Methodist practice, Hughes was appointed to a succession of three-year appointments to various circuits: Dover (1869–1872), Brighton (1872–1875), Tottenham (1875–1878), Dulwich (1878–1881), Oxford (1881–1884) and Brixton (1884–1887). In 1887 he was appointed permanently as superintendent of the West London Mission (1887–1902). Hughes was admired throughout his career as a masterful preacher and orator. He appealed to both the emotions and the intellect, for he strongly believed that evangelism would increasingly depend upon its alliance with higher learning. Accordingly, he completed in 1880 a master's degree in modern philosophy from the University of London. His argumentative approach was popular with audiences. In a rapid and dramatic style employing short, pungent sentences, he presented himself as a barrister seeking to convince the jury to pass judgment in favour of Christ, or of some moral cause.

Deep involvement in the temperance movement and the campaign to abolish the Contagious Diseases Acts convinced Hughes that social and political reform was inextricably linked to preaching the gospel. In 1877 he emerged as the primary temperance spokesman within Wesleyanism. From 1876 to 1881, he served as editor of the *Methodist Protest*, a monthly journal produced by the Wesleyan Society for the Repeal of the Contagious Diseases Acts. Hughes denounced these Acts (which mandated inspection and treatment of prostitutes near military bases for venereal disease) as government approval of prostitution and as a state-sponsored attack on both the bodies and the souls of women. Political activism did not divert Hughes from evangelism. In 1876 he adopted the techniques of Dwight *Moody and became one of the most popular revival preachers in British Methodism. During his years as superintendent of the Oxford circuit, he emphasized evangelism, organizing openair revivals and encouraging undergraduates to preach the gospel in surrounding villages.

In subsequent years, Hughes discovered new ways to advance his unique blend of evangelism and social reform. In 1884 he declared himself a Christian Socialist and called upon all churches 'to do their long-neglected duty in caring for the social welfare of the people, and so doing bring back the alienated masses to the social brotherhood of Christ'. By 1885, Hughes' Forward Movement had taken shape and assumed its name. In that year he began publishing his weekly newspaper, *The Methodist Times: A Journal of Religious and Social Movement*. His primary goal was to transform Methodism from a sect into a full-fledged church that preserved the old principles of holiness and evangelism, but integrated into its calling a larger role as the conscience of state and society. To accomplish this goal, he advocated the practice of evangelism in concert with Christian social service and the promotion of Christian ideals in political life.

The centrepiece of the new movement was the West London Mission, which opened in

1887. Hughes chose west London because it was the home of the British government as well as a centre of prostitution and poverty. Hughes' wife Katherine organized the most distinctive feature of the Mission, the 'Sisters of the People'. These were unmarried, middle-class, full-time volunteers who made regular visitations in poor neighborhoods, assisted as lay preachers and developed projects including food and medicine dispensaries, an employment agency, a rescue home for prostitutes, a home for the dying and numerous clubs for mothers, boys, girls and disabled children. On Sundays, at St James's Hall, Piccadilly, Hughes typically delivered an afternoon address on the issues of the day, and preached in the evening a revival sermon after a concert by the mission's orchestra. He published four volumes of these addresses and sermons: *Social Christianity* (1889), *Philanthropy of God* (1889), *Ethical Christianity* (1892), and *Essential Christianity* (1894).

Hughes was best known by the general public for his articulation of the 'Nonconformist conscience' in public affairs, which for Hughes centred on combatting the great social evils of 'pauperism, ignorance, drunkenness, lust, gambling, slavery, mammonism, war and disease'. In 1890 Hughes and other Nonconformist leaders successfully demanded that Charles Stewart Parnell, the leader of the Irish Nationalist parliamentary party allied with the Liberals, resign from the leadership after he was unable to defend himself against charges of adultery. Hughes, in particular, was an avid supporter of the Liberal Party and Home Rule for Ireland, but for him 'social purity' was a higher priority. In denouncing Parnell, he famously declared that 'what is morally wrong can never be politically right'. This episode, along with the continuing debate about government subsidies for Anglican 'voluntary' schools, helped to ignite a movement towards greater unity among the free churches.

Hughes was an avid ecumenist. He believed that Christianity, like an army, would be strengthened spiritually and politically by unity and strong leadership. Accordingly, he championed the reunion of the various Methodist denominations and sought to build ties between Nonconformist denominations (Baptists, Congregationalists, Methodists,

Presbyterians and Quakers). He was instrumental in calling the first Free Church Congress in 1892; he later served as president of the Congress (1895–1896) and supervised its reorganization as the National Council of Evangelical Free Churches, of which he was the first president (1896–1897). He chaired the committee that drafted the Free Church Catechism in 1899. Between 1892 and 1895, he was a key participant in the Grindelwald (Switzerland) Reunion Conferences, which were organized by his protégé, (Sir) Henry Lunn, to seek the unity of British Protestantism.

Within Wesleyan Methodism, Hughes promoted greater power for the laity, and he pressed Conference to encourage the emergence of stronger leaders by abolishing the three-year limit on ministerial appointments, and by creating full-time district chairmen who would act as virtual bishops. Although laymen did attain much broader powers in the 1890s, his other proposals, including his effort to have women admitted as delegates to Conference, failed to win approval until after his death. His leadership in Methodism was recognized by his election for a year's term as president of the Wesleyan Conference (1898–1899). Shortly afterwards, his health began to decline steadily and he died of a stroke on 17 November 1902, at home in London.

Bibliography

C. Oldstone-Moore, *Hugh Price Hughes: Founder of a New Methodism; Conscience of a New Nonconformity* (Cardiff: University of Wales Press, 1999); H. S. Lunn, *Chapters From My Life* (London: Methuen & Co., 1918); D. P. Hughes, *The Life of Hugh Price Hughes* (London: Hodder & Stoughton, 1904).

C. OLDSTONE-MOORE

■ **HUGHES, Ray Harrison** (1924–), denominational executive and international Pentecostal leader, was born to Joseph Harrison and Emma Lou (née Cochran) Hughes in Calhoun, Georgia on 7 March 1924. Joseph H. Hughes was a pastor and former state overseer affiliated to the Church of God, the largest of the white Holiness-Pentecostal denominations in the United

States; its international headquarters was in Cleveland, Tennessee. The younger Hughes became a national evangelist with the Church of God (CG), gaining a ministerial licence in 1941. He came to national prominence in the Pentecostal movement in 1946 as the speaker at a mass youth rally at the Hollywood Bowl in Los Angeles. He was ordained in 1950. Pastoral appointments took him to Fairfield, Illinois (1945–1946) and North Chattanooga, Tennessee (1948–1952). In 1942 he married Marian Euverla Tidwell; the couple had four children.

A highly respected preacher, Hughes rose quickly in the ranks of the organization, becoming its best-known leader in the latter half of the twentieth century. Though always an evangelist at heart, he held many offices in the rotating hierarchy of the CG, including general director of youth and Christian education (1952–1956), state overseer of Maryland-Delaware and Washington, DC (1956–1960), president of Lee College (1960–1966, 1982–1984), state overseer of Georgia (1974–1976), president of the Church of God School of Theology (now CG Theological Seminary) (1984–1986) and chairman of the evangelism and home missions board (1990–1992). During the intervening years he served as third assistant general overseer (1966–1968, 1992–1994), second assistant general overseer (1968–1970) and first assistant general overseer (1970–1972, 1976–1978, 1986–1990, 1994–1996). As general overseer (1972–1974, 1978–1982, 1996), he challenged the CG to initiate new efforts in evangelism. He also served on the denomination's executive council at various times from 1956 onwards. During his time as speaker on the 'Forward in Faith' radio programme (1960–1963), its network of stations grew quickly from forty-two to 120 in thirty-seven states and five foreign countries.

As he became a national church leader, Hughes pursued higher education. He graduated with a BA from Tennessee Wesleyan University in 1961, and an MS in 1963 and an EdD in 1966 from the University of Tennessee; his dissertation was entitled, 'The Transition of Church Related Junior Colleges to Senior Colleges with Implications for Lee College'. During his earlier term as president of Lee College, the school increased its student enrolment and academic standing and developed its campus.

A prolific author, Hughes has written many books, including *Planning for Sunday School Progress* (1955), *Religion on Fire* (1956), *The Order of Future Events* (1962), *What Is Pentecost?* (1963), *Church of God Distinctives* (1968; ²1989), *Dynamics of Sunday School Growth* (1980), *Pentecostal Preaching* (1981), *Understanding the Holy Spirit* (1982), *Who Is the Holy Ghost?* (1992), *Lord, Show Us Thy Glory* (1997), *The Rapture & Revelation* (2000) and *The Cross Loves Necessity* (2000). He also edited the *State Overseer's Manual* (1972) and *Sermon Outlines on the Person and Work of the Holy Spirit* (1981). His best-known collection of recorded sermons is entitled 'The Anointing Makes the Difference'.

Hughes played a noteworthy role in the transition of the CG from the margin to the mainstream of American evangelicalism in the post-war period, a development evident in his service on the executive committee of the National Association of Evangelicals (1978–1989), as president (1986–1988) and later as a permanent member of the board of administration. Like other classical Pentecostal leaders, he kept his denomination at a distance from the charismatic movement, because of disagreements over doctrine, the nature of Christian unity and the content of a holy life. The priority of maintaining close relations with conservative evangelicals and eschatological speculations led Hughes and other CG leaders to refrain from making contacts with conciliar agencies (e.g. the World Council of Churches). Representing the CG among other Pentecostals, Hughes chaired the Pentecostal Fellowship of North America (1976–1978), worked on the international advisory committee of the Pentecostal World Conference and served as its chairman (1989–1998). His papers are held at the Hal Bernard Dixon, Jr, Pentecostal Research Center in Cleveland, Tennessee.

Bibliography

C. W. Conn, *Like a Mighty Army: A History of the Church of God, 1886–1976* (Cleveland: Pathway Press, 1977); M. Crews, *The Church of God: A Social History* (Knoxville: University of Tennessee Press, 1990); R. H. Hughes, 'The New Pentecostalism:

Perspective of a Classical Pentecostal Administrator', in R. P. Spittler (ed.), *Perspectives on the New Pentecostalism* (Grand Rapids: Baker Book House, 1976).

G. B. McGEE

■ **HUNTINGDON, Selina Hastings, Countess of** (1707–1791), leader of the Calvinistic Methodist movement bearing her name, was born Lady Selina Shirley, the second daughter of Earl Ferrers, at Astwell House, Northamptonshire. Little is known about her childhood other than that it was not easy; the family spent some time in Ireland in relative poverty, and the parents separated in 1712. Selina remained with her father and, from the evidence of spelling and grammar in her adult letters, seems to have received little education. Her marriage to Theophilus, ninth Earl of Huntingdon, in 1728 was probably a love match. She bore him seven children, of whom three (Francis, Elizabeth and Selina) survived childhood. Only Elizabeth outlived her.

Talented and charismatic, the Countess became the focus and director of a lively and influential evangelical movement, through her encouragement of students and preachers, possession of widespread estates on which to build chapels, ready use of private money and personal conviction and charm. Lady Huntingdon's charisma was as responsible as her wealth or rank in her success as a religious leader, but her wealth and rank none the less helped, as did her being widowed at a relatively early age. Although her husband had been in broad sympathy with her evangelical views, it was the freedom that widowhood uniquely brought to wealthy women of the era which enabled her to achieve so much.

Lady Huntingdon's commitment to evangelicalism predated her widowhood. Her close relationship with her half-sister-in-law, Lady Elizabeth Hastings, had brought her into contact with Moravianism, and she experienced conversion in 1739, the year of Lady Elizabeth's death. In the early 1740s she undertook various religiously inspired projects, as did many noblewomen, including the financing of a local charity school. She attempted to bring the servants of her household to conversion and also witnessed to high society, for example, when visiting Bath for her health.

By 1742 the Countess had met George *Whitefield and John and Charles *Wesley and had begun to invite preachers to her house. This began to make her a focus for evangelical religion, especially among elite society. The deaths of two of her sons in 1743, followed by that of her husband in 1746, provoked a spiritual crisis that resulted in her rejection of Wesleyanism and increasing commitment to Calvinism. By 1748 her relationship with the Wesleys had cooled, and she was committed to the doctrines espoused by Whitefield and Howell *Harris. Her religious activity began to be more intense and extreme. She closed her charity school, commenting that education was of little use without salvation. From this time, the central message that she endeavoured to promote through letters, personal exhortation and the direction of preachers was the need for the Christian to depend utterly upon God and his mercy.

In the 1750s the Countess of Huntingdon began large-scale patronage and protection of Methodist clergy and clerical students, paying for their training, supporting their cases against establishment bishops suspicious of their 'enthusiasm' and helping them to find livings. In 1761 she erected a chapel in Brighton, the first of many that she built in the subsequent three decades, exploiting a loophole in the law that enabled a peeress of the realm to attach to her private residence a chapel exempt from episcopal jurisdiction, without being obliged to license it as a Dissenting place of worship.

Already a focus for evangelical religion in her own social rank, Lady Huntingdon's building of such chapels, mostly in fashionable watering places, was an extension of her attempt to provide elite society with godly preaching, while offering patronage and protection to the preachers. Many would agree with her most recent biographer that her chapel-building programme was 'the most visible and most decisive step towards her final separation from the Church of England twenty years later' (Schlenther, p. 69). The reality is more ambiguous. On the one hand, Lady Huntingdon's stated aim was the rejuvenation of the Church of England from within. She had no desire to establish a separated church. On the other hand, her creation of alternative spaces for worship to those of the established church had begun much earlier. In the 1740s Lady Huntingdon had exerted her authority over the many clergy whom she patronized in her own home, and invited large numbers of clergy and laity to her home for preaching, teaching and the sacraments. The space for worship that she created there was largely under her own control.

The 1760s, although seeing her chapel-building programme inaugurated, were a difficult time for the Countess. There were ever-deepening doctrinal rifts between the Calvinistic Methodists and the Wesleyans, and Lady Huntingdon drew apart from her former favourite Howell Harris, as he became ever keener to forge links with the Moravians and she to sever them. She also suffered from a shortage of personnel for her chapels. Although she had three personal chaplains, Whitefield, William Romaine and Martin Madan, and some twenty evangelical clergy under her protection, they were not constantly available. She had already been entertaining the notion of her own ministerial college when, in 1768 six evangelical students whom she had been nurturing for ordination were expelled from St Edmund Hall, Oxford. Aided by Harris, the Countess established a college at Trevecca, near Brecon in South Wales, on Harris's own land. It was opened on her sixty-first birthday, 29 August 1768, with the Church of England Methodist John *Fletcher as occasional minister and overseer.

Trevecca failed to flourish as Lady Huntingdon had hoped. It never attracted large numbers of students and was undermined by her growing rift with Harris. Further problems were caused by the Countess's final split with John Wesley in 1771, following which Fletcher resigned. The college continued to attract students, who were well grounded there in theology, Latin and Greek, but their training was persistently disrupted by calls to go out preaching. Lady Huntingdon perceived the land to be in instant need of godly preaching and would not wait for a generation of students to be fully trained. That impatience may have been a root cause of the connexion's lack of long-term success.

A further cause was the dependence of the connexion on the person of Lady Huntingdon. This became increasingly problematic as she became more and more isolated from other leading evangelicals, especially after the deaths of Whitefield and Harris, in 1770 and 1773 respectively, and due to her increasingly extreme Calvinism. The Countess of Huntingdon was an emotional and volatile woman. The same warm and passionate temperament that could attract devotees could drive them away with equal force. Her characteristics and her convictions became more extreme with age. For example, her earlier extreme distaste for the Wesleyan doctrine of sanctification had become utter abhorrence by the 1770s. Her general distrust of others had, by then, become so great that she assumed almost complete control of Trevecca for some years.

Lady Huntingdon's decision to take up permanent residence at Spa Fields, London, in the late 1770s, caused serious problems for Trevecca, and for her chapels in the west. It had always been her personal presence that facilitated the flourishing of the connexion in any locality. By the mid-1780s Trevecca had dwindled to ten students, raw, untrained and financially ill provided for.

It was Spa Fields chapel that finally caused the Countess's secession from the Church of England. A former tea-house, it had been rented by an independent group of Calvinist Methodists and licensed as a Dissenting place of worship in 1777. It had a flourishing congregation, but ran into difficulties when the incumbent of the parish, Walter Sellon, successfully proceeded against two Church of England clergymen who preached in it. Against such a background, the Countess might have been wise to have hung back, but her impetuosity with regard to the acquisition of preaching stations won the day. She obtained possession of the chapel, had its Dissenting licence cancelled, and installed her own preachers, officially styled as her personal chaplains as they were in her many other chapels.

In fact, the Countess was by law entitled to maintain only two private chaplains, and although this fact had previously been overlooked, it was no protection against Sellon. For three years he determinedly campaigned for the removal of the Spa Fields preachers. On 7 January 1782 her reputation and integrity as a religious patroness within the Church of England seriously threatened, the Countess was finally obliged to register Spa Fields as a Dissenting place of worship. This in effect marked the connexion's secession, and that was confirmed in March 1783 when two of her chaplains ordained six Trevecca students at Spa Fields.

Not all of her preachers followed her into secession, and although the connexion was most likely to survive as an Independent church, it was ever more dependent on the person of its ageing leader. By the late 1780s, although it had 116 chapels, there was increasing confusion about how the connexion would be run after Lady Huntingdon's death. Constitution, formal procedure and hierarchy were all lacking, and the Countess's dominant personality had made it hard for an obvious successor to come forward. In 1789 a conciliar plan was drawn up, which might have had a chance of success, but the Countess was not keen on such an oligarchic method of running her connexion, and never approved it.

In 1790 she agreed to the connexion being taken over by four personal friends after her death: Lady Anne Erskine, John Lloyd and Thomas and Janetta Haweis. Haweis was one of the chaplains of the Spa Fields chapel and, paradoxically, had remained a clergyman of the Church of England after 1782. That fact enshrines the ambiguity that always lay at the heart of the Countess of Huntingdon's Connexion, and demonstrates the extent to which a religious movement could be both of, and separate from, the Church of England in an era of religious change and enthusiasm, informal worship-meeting and extempore preaching.

The other essential characteristic of the connexion was the extent to which it remained, both legally and psychologically, the Countess's own property. Its chapels were all hers, and its paid personnel were all paid by her. The property was bequeathed not to the connexion as a body, but to the four chosen leaders personally, which almost certainly hampered the growth of the connexion and, in other hands, might have caused corruption. The connexion did survive (it has twenty-five congregations today), but it was never as large as in the 1780s, and it lost its public prominence and influence when it lost its foundress. Thomas Haweis, the foremost of the four successors, died in 1820. There was then an attempt to implement the conciliar plan, but although this was partly successful, it was implemented too late to allow the connexion to flourish. It had been dependent on the person of one leader for far too long.

Lady Huntingdon died in 1791. It was striking that her death came within three months of John Wesley's, especially as the two were almost the same age. It seemed, in 1791, that an era had passed; the first phase of Methodism had ended with the passing of two of its major leaders. Both were characterized by a love of the Church of England and a disinclination to separate from it, by a lifetime of travelling and personal supervision of the chapels, meetings and people under their care, and by considerable personal charisma, leadership ability and popularity.

There can be no doubt that Wesley's significance on the long-term movement was much greater than Lady Huntingdon's, not least because he was a man, an ordained priest and a prolific and profound writer. It is perhaps surprising that the Countess published no writings. Her letter writing was certainly prolific. Lady Huntingdon's legacy to the historian, aside from her letters, lies largely in her reputation and in contemporary references and biographies. The fullest biography published in the generation following her death, by an anonymous 'member of the House of Shirley and Hastings', though quoting many of her letters, is flawed throughout, and its actual author, Arthur Seymour, had little claim to a family connexion.

The obscurity surrounding the Countess of Huntingdon, though irritating for the historian, mirrors to some extent her life and activity, especially in view of the roles that were open to women in the world of eighteenth-century British religion. Lady Huntingdon could not be ordained, and although there were some eighteenth-century female exhorters and even preachers, they were few in number and often surrounded by controversy. Lady Huntingdon was averse to female preaching all her life, and the nearest she came to public speaking was addressing the students at Trevecca.

Despite, or even because of, her avoidance of 'male' public roles, Lady Huntingdon's significance was remarkable. The roles she exercised (hostess, patroness and private spiritual exhorter) were acceptable for a woman of high rank, but she exercised them on an unparalleled scale, thanks to her combination of rank and wealth with an iron will and charismatic character. She thus acquired a degree of religious authority that was, for a woman, almost unprecedented. By hosting worship and preaching in her own home (a great mansion), she created an alternative space for worship from that of the established church. By giving her patronage to not one or two, but to hordes of preachers and clergy, she became, in one sense of the word, their bishop. Whitefield likened her to 'a good archbishop' in 1749, when she gathered clergy around her in her home (*The Life and Times*, vol. 1, p. 163). The simile would later become even more apt. She oversaw clerical appointments in her chapels, took a close interest in the behaviour and movements of her protégés and even directed their training and the content of their preaching.

The Countess of Huntingdon remained a shadowy figure in many ways, making her presence felt through her letters, through the words and actions of her protégés and in her own home. None the less, her influence was great and to a certain extent lasting, although there can be no doubt that her personal control of the connexion, and the consequent lack of formal office and hierarchy in it, ultimately undermined its long-term success. Although its character was due in part to her volatile character and increasingly extreme views, it was inevitable in a connexion that was led by a woman. She could not easily create a religious office for herself in an era in which women did not hold church office. It was in her own interests to keep the status and operation of the connexion vague and in her own hands. The formal creation of a separated church would have required the formal creation of a male church hierarchy, such a development, as became visible in mainstream Methodism after 1800, was characterized by the erosion of the leadership and preaching roles that women had exercised in the more informal early period. As the financer and literal owner of a religious connexion, Lady Huntingdon, though a woman, retained an unprecedented degree of control over it.

It would be unfair to claim, however, that the Countess was motivated by a desire for power. Her prime motivation (perhaps the only one that could have inspired her to such tireless activity) was religious. She was determined to do all in her power to advance the cause of the gospel and to maintain as many preachers and clergy as possible for this purpose. Like Wesley and so many other evangelical leaders of the era, Lady Huntingdon sought the conversion of the country and ultimately the world. In the 1770s she financed an unsuccessful mission to the East Indies and an orphanage in Georgia that Whitefield had bequeathed to her. The Countess of Huntingdon was, above all, a committed evangelical who took seriously the duty of the Christian to evangelize, and the duty of an aristocrat to influence, finance and direct those around and below her. Her achievements mark the summit of what a woman of high rank, when motivated by religious conviction, could do for her God and her people in eighteenth-century England.

Bibliography
B. S. Schlenther, *Queen of the Methodists: the Countess of Huntingdon and the Eighteenth-Century Crisis of Faith and Society* (Durham: 1997); [A. C. H. Seymour], *The Life and Times of Selina, Countess of Huntingdon, by a Member of the House of Shirley and Hastings*, 2 vols. (London: 1839–1840); E. Welch, *Spiritual Pilgrim: A Re-assessment of the Life of the Countess of Huntingdon* (Cardiff: 1995).

H. M. JONES

■ **HUS, Jan** (c. 1372–1415), leader of the movement of church reform in Prague in the early fifteenth century, was born in Bohemia, probably in about 1372. He began his studies at the University of Prague in 1390 and graduated BA in 1393 and MA three years later. In 1404, after teaching in the Faculty of Arts and also studying theology, he earned his BD.

In the same period, Jerome of Prague brought to Hus's attention works by John *Wyclif from England which attacked the corruption of the Catholic Church. These criticisms were in tune with the thinking of a reform group in Prague, which began to have as its focus the preaching of Hus in the

Bethlehem Chapel, a plain building founded in 1391 as a centre where people could hear preaching in the Czech language. Hus was committed to such preaching (he described Czech as being as precious to God as Latin), and from 1402, when he became the rector and preacher at the chapel, he eloquently addressed each week a congregation of 3,000 people.

Within the University of Prague there were tensions between the German and Czech leaderships. Through German influence, Wyclif's writings (which included attacks on transubstantiation) were condemned in 1403. This condemnation created resentment among the Czechs, and in reaction the German voting majority was eliminated. This development gave opportunity for Hus to exercise greater influence. In 1410, however, he was excommunicated by the Archbishop of Prague. Two years later Hus began to preach vehemently against the practice being promoted by Pope John XXII of selling indulgences to support his costly papal ventures, an issue that Martin *Luther would address a century later.

To add fuel to the theological fire, three young men who supported Hus (Martin, John and Stašek) were put on trial by Prague's city councillors for protesting against the sale of indulgences at St Vitus Cathedral, the Týn Church and St James, the three principal churches in Prague. Despite promises of leniency, the three were beheaded, which fanned the flames of unrest. The bodies were taken to the Bethlehem Chapel, with huge numbers of people processing and singing of the young men as saints. Hus sang a martyr's mass over them.

Pressure mounted on Hus, and he was excommunicated by Rome, with Prague being placed under a papal interdict (there could be no authorized church services) while he remained there. There were attacks on the Bethlehem Chapel. King Wenzel asked Hus to go into exile, and this he did for a time. During the exile he wrote his famous *The Church*, in which he argued that the true church had Christ as its head, not the pope. He took the view that it was right to rebel against a pope who erred.

A Council was called at Constance in Germany in 1414 to discuss reform of the church. Hus was invited to attend and given a promise by Emperor Sigismund that he would have completely safe passage. But a few weeks after he arrived in Constance he was arrested by soldiers and put in prison. It was regarded as justifiable to break a promise given to a heretic. The cell was next to the sewer system and Hus became violently ill. He was then transferred to a cage and was kept in dreadful conditions for about two months.

The trial of Hus began on 5 June 1415 and lasted for a month. Many of the charges, such as the assertion that he denied transubstantiation, were untrue. On 6 July 1415 Hus was brought into the cathedral in Constance. The bishop of Lodi preached a sermon in which he argued that to kill heretics was one of the works that was most pleasing to God. Hus was taken out to be burned and was asked whether he would recant. 'I shall die with joy', he affirmed, 'in the faith of the gospel which I have preached.' Jerome of Prague, who had come to Constance to support Hus, was arrested while returning to Bohemia, and he was later burned on the same spot as Hus.

Increasing numbers of people in Bohemia followed the teaching of Hus. Moderate reformers seeking to persuade the church to allow the laity to receive the wine as well as the bread had as their symbol the communion cup. They were given the name 'Utraquists', from the phrase *sub utraque* ('under both kinds'). A second Hussite branch became militant, and because they were located around Mount Tabor in south Bohemia they received the name 'Taborites'. In the 1420s Catholic and Hussite armies numbering over 100,000 fought each other. In the sixteenth century the Hussites, representing the earlier 'first reformation', made contact with Luther and the leaders of the 'second reformation'.

Bibliography
M. Spinka, *John Hus* (London: Greenwood Press, 1979).

I. M. RANDALL

■ **HUTCHINSON, Anne Marbury** (1591–1643), American religious leader, originally of London and Lincolnshire, arrived in Massachusetts Bay in 1634. Like many of the colonizing Puritans, she came to New England with her entire family to escape escalating persecution and to help build a new, godly country that would serve as an example to other nations. Upon arrival, Hutchinson and her husband William, an affluent and highly respected merchant, joined the Boston church and established themselves among Boston's leadership. As the daughter of Francis Marbury, a Dissenting cleric who valued erudition, Hutchinson had been carefully educated, and her scriptural knowledge and theological sophistication were greatly admired. In Boston she continued an English Puritan practice of private religious meetings in the home. These were initially established for Boston's women, but Hutchinson's remarkable charisma attracted large numbers, and the gatherings soon included many men. She was later said to have sponsored two meetings, one for women only and one mixed; at the peak of their popularity sixty-eighty people attended. Scarcely three years after her arrival, Puritan leaders judged Hutchinson to be a disturber of consensual order, and in November 1637 the colony banished her; in the following March the church of Boston excommunicated her. She moved with many of her followers to Rhode Island, and, after her husband's death, to Long Island, where, with six of her children, she was killed during an Indian-Dutch war in 1643.

The disturbances created by Hutchinson and her followers were social, political and theological. Although her opponents (and future historians) may have overstated the threat she posed, it is likely that the embryonic and therefore unstable state of the six-year-old colony exacerbated the damage she and her followers caused to the ecclesiastical and civil leadership. Since her followers had participated in efforts to discredit many clerics, and since she had spoken critically of most of New England's ministers, the General Court charged Hutchinson with sedition. Many men of high rank, including several magistrates, assembly members, and Governor Henry Vane supported her and formed a faction opposing the founding leadership. Additionally, as Hutchinsonians were Bostonians, who largely represented the interests and ambitions of merchants, their attitudes stood in opposition to those of the rest of Massachusetts Bay.

Moreover, both ministers and magistrates were troubled that growing authority and power were being granted by many Bostonians to a woman. They accused Hutchinson of teaching men as well as women, and they construed several elements of her behaviour, such as her successful leadership of the private meetings, as a crossing of gender boundaries. She failed to submit to her male superiors; she acted the part of a husband rather than that of a wife. She was known to be particularly helpful in the birthing chamber, and although she had once been credited with bringing women to salvation, she was later accused of seducing women, at moments of weakness, to follow her example. Such accusations were framed within a perception of women as intellectually incapable of deep, complex theological study and spiritually incapable of strength of character. Puritan writers sometimes argued that women who were not controlled by men were at risk of being seduced by Satan, so that they might seduce others. This conviction became especially apparent during Hutchinson's church trial, when some asserted that her theological explorations had led to heresies, which would, in turn, lead to sexual misconduct.

Theologically, two issues troubled the leadership. The first involved the relationship between human endeavour and salvation. The Calvinist doctrine of predestination, accepted by Puritans, placed salvation completely in the hands of God. Only faith in Christ as redeemer could justify the innately depraved soul, and faith was impossible except through the free, unconditional gift of divine grace. Once grace was offered and, perforce, accepted, confirmation of grace and salvation could be found in the sanctification of the believer's behaviour. In other words, the believer's gracious standing manifested itself in the saint's daily conduct.

Hutchinson's teachings challenged the clergy over the question of justification by faith through free grace and the significance of sanctified behaviour. Echoing her mentor John *Cotton, Hutchinson stressed the futility of human action, the passivity of the believer and absolute dependence upon God. Most New England clergymen judged this emphasis dangerous; such attitudes, in their view, led inevitably to heresy, irreligion and anarchy. While granting the arbitrary and unconditional nature of God's actions, Puritan ministers also understood the anxiety of believers desperate to discern some sign of their own salvation; thus preachers emphasized the hope that lay in sanctification. Many also promoted the notion that the potential saint could prepare for God's grace. Although affirming that no human effort could truly affect God's salvific work, ministers encouraged believers to study Scripture, attend church services, guard their conduct and pray so that they would be ready. Such efforts may well have kept believers from feeling powerless, but Hutchinson, along with John Cotton, found in preparationism hints of salvation through works. Two conferences between Cotton, Hutchinson and the clergy did little to assuage the concerns of either side. John Cotton was deeply concerned about the ministers' position, critical yet tactful, but Hutchinson attacked the ministers for preaching a legalistic covenant of works. The New England ministers addressed Cotton's concerns but denounced the Hutchinsons as antinomian or anarchic.

The second issue involved Hutchinson's conviction that she had received divine revelation. While many Puritans were inclined to reject such claims as delusional or blasphemous, arguing that the age for such miraculous communication was long past, the point remained debatable. The strength of Hutchinson's following indicated that a significant number of Bostonians were convinced of her spiritual gifts. During her trial, Hutchinson declared that she had received immediate revelations. This assertion, along with testimonies to her prophetic declarations, precipitated a prolonged debate upon the nature of revelation itself. Cotton, still an apparent Hutchinson supporter, argued that an expectation of the miraculous would be a delusion, but that anyone might justifiably have faith in special providence. Since further discussion did not resolve this problem and raised questions among laymen about Cotton's orthodoxy, Governor John *Winthrop closed the debate and organized the proceedings so that the Court banished Hutchinson for sedition.

Permitted to remain in Boston during the winter months but lodged in the home of a hostile minister, Hutchinson was frequently visited by ministers. Their avowed purpose was her repentance, but long conversations upon an extraordinary range of issues resulted in extensive testimony being delivered at her church trial. There Hutchinson was judged heretical on the grounds of several esoteric beliefs, most notably concerning the resurrection of the body, that had never been raised before, not even during her November trial. This fact was noted, and questioned, by Hutchinson as well as by one accuser, the magistrate Thomas Dudley. That the previous issues of preparationism, free grace and revelation were not raised indicates that one purpose of this trial was to bring John Cotton into alignment with the other clergy by avoiding debate on controversial tenets and convincing him, through the discussions of other matters, of Hutchinson's heresy and essential sinfulness. The strategy succeeded; Cotton joined others in their condemnation and excommunication of Hutchinson.

Later accounts, particularly the history written by John Winthrop, stressed the threat posed by Hutchinson's claim to revelation. During the state trial Hutchinson successfully countered ostensibly biblical arguments and still acceded to the demands that she cease all public activity, but a charismatic woman whose supposed experience of the divine was reflected in prophetic utterances undermined the established secular and sacred authority. Even silent, a woman claiming authority from God, authority recognized by the majority of her community, would have continued to represent a threat to the standing order. In the final analysis, although the ostensible cause for her banishment was sedition, the primary factors driving her accusers were her claims to prophetic revelation and the challenge these represented to their own magistracy and control.

Bibliography

E. Battis, *Saints and Sectaries: Anne Hutchinson and the Antinomian Controversy in the Massachusetts Bay Colony* (Chapel Hill: University of North Carolina Press, 1962); F. J. Bremer (ed.), *Anne Hutchinson, Troubler of a Puritan Zion* (Huntington: 1981); P. J. Gura, *A Glimpse of Sion's Glory: Puritan Radicalism in New England, 1620–1660* (Middletown: Wesleyan University Press, 1984); S. R. Williams, *Divine Rebel: The Life of Anne Marbury Hutchinson* (New York: Holt, Rinehart & Winston, 1981).

M. WESTERKAMP

■ **IRONSIDE, Henry ('Harry') Allen** (1876–1951), fundamentalist pastor and expositor, was born in Toronto, Ontario to Scottish immigrant parents. His father, a Brethren lay evangelist, died when Harry was two, though his mother and the numerous travelling evangelists whom she boarded perpetuated this religious heritage. Ironside was religiously affected at a young age. When the family moved to Los Angeles in 1886, he started his own Sunday school and preached on street corners. After his professed conversion at the age of fourteen, his energy was directed towards evangelistic activities within the Salvation Army, which he joined in 1890. Five years later, after serving in various posts throughout California and having achieved the rank of captain, he entered the Army's rest home, exhausted from overwork and doubtful of its holiness theology. After a short-lived crisis of faith, he came to reject the holiness teaching on sanctification known as the 'second blessing' and left the organization, an episode he later chronicled in his book *Holiness: The False and the True* (1912). In 1896 he returned to his religious roots by joining the Plymouth Brethren and entered into independent ministry. He maintained his association with the Brethren for the rest of his life, though he criticized them in his book *A Historical Sketch of the Brethren Movement* (1942), primarily for their sectarian tendencies. In 1898 Ironside married Helen Schofield, another former Salvation Army member and daughter of a Presbyterian minister. Two years later they settled in Oakland, though Ironside's increasing popularity as a speaker progressively reduced his time at home.

Ironside preached extemporaneous, exegetical sermons, filled with definite interpretations and sprinkled with telling anecdotes. Because of his unusual familiarity with the Bible and ability to formulate his theology in a manner that was accessible to laypeople, he was increasingly in demand as a speaker in conservative circles. What had begun as a California-based ministry soon became a nationwide one. True to his Salvation Army roots, he maintained an almost non-stop schedule. Between 1916 and 1929 he preached an estimated 6,500 times. During one particularly busy period he preached sixty-seven times in twenty-five days. Venues varied between small urban missions, centres for rural evangelism (particularly among Native Americans in Arizona, southern California and New Mexico), large Bible conferences (including the Keswick conference in England), and churches of all sizes. When he was not preaching, Ironside was often involved in personal evangelization, speaking with Roman Catholics, Jews, those without faith of any kind, saloon patrons and any other individuals he believed were in need of the gospel.

Though Ironside's formal education ended at elementary school, he had a natural curiosity that fuelled continuing self-education. He was a voracious reader on a variety of topics including philosophy and history (which he found to be of little use), literature, theology and biblical studies. Ironside was most influenced by J. N. *Darby and other Brethren writers, who led him wholeheartedly to embrace dispensational theology. Ironside was, however, primarily a man of one book: he read through the Bible numerous times and memorized large portions of it. In his later years, when cataracts made him practically blind, he reportedly was able to give a verse-by-verse exposition of a chapter of Revelation from memory after having it read aloud once.

Ironside's influence increased exponentially when he accepted his first and only pastorate at the non-denominational Moody Church of Chicago in 1930. For eighteen years he led one of the most prominent fundamentalist institutions and preached to capacity crowds at the 4,200-seat auditorium. Ironside's influence extended to other major fundamentalist and evangelical organizations. He served on the boards of Africa Inland Mission (also serving as its president in 1942), Bob Jones University, Dallas Theological Seminary (where he also occasionally taught biblical literature from 1925 to 1931), the Moody Bible Institute, Wheaton College and the Winona Lake Bible Conference. It is no wonder that he was called the 'Archbishop of Fundamentalism'.

Ironside was greatly concerned with the individual's personal relationship with Christ, an experience he saw as an act of the will that accepted on faith the resurrection of Christ, his promises of eternal life and the authority of the Bible. Regardless of the text, he always concluded his sermons with an evangelistic invitation. (He claimed that during his pastorate at Moody Church there were only two Sundays on which no one responded.) The idea of a personal relationship with Jesus Christ was so important to Ironside that he was willing to acknowledge the salvation of certain Roman Catholics even while maintaining virulent anti-Catholic rhetoric. Although Ironside held that those who did not adhere to his strict dispensational theology should be excluded from fundamentalist fellowships, his rooting of salvation in experience and his maintenance of 'theological essentials' in a denomination-neutral form were significant in diminishing the importance of traditional denominational differentiations within fundamentalism and evangelicalism.

Ironside was even more influential through his publishing efforts. Though beginning modestly (the Western Book and Tract Company he founded in 1914 to distribute his writings had significant financial problems in its early years), he proved to be a prolific and popular writer. He wrote fifty-one books, which sold well over one million copies. His book *Except Ye Repent* (1936) won an American Tract Society book contest for the 'best treatise on one or more essential evangelical doctrines of the Christian faith'. Most of his works, however, were stenographic recordings of his sermons, which he later edited into biblical commentaries. Ironside eventually published works on the entire New Testament, all of the Old Testament prophets and other selected books of the Bible. These commentaries quickly became the fundamentalist canon for biblical interpretation and remain popular in certain circles even today. Ironside also published numerous pamphlets and booklets on various theological topics. Finally, he guided a generation of Sunday school teachers with his weekly lessons published in the popular fundamentalist publication *The Sunday School Times*.

Ironside's main contributions to evangelicalism came by way of this extensive influence more than through any unique theological formulation. He was one of a group of Bible teachers who popularized dispensational theology beyond its origins in the Brethren sphere of influence. Ironside's theology, combined with his earlier negative experiences with holiness theology, also made him a vocal critic of Pentecostalism. He wrote several pamphlets highly critical of speaking in tongues and faith healing and played an influential role in the exclusion of the movement from participation in the wider fundamentalist sphere. At the same time, he did not reject God's present interruptive action altogether. Ironside spent most of his life 'living by faith' (that is, running his ministry without regular support or even telling anyone of his financial needs), a policy he modified only after accepting the pastorate of the Moody Church. The direct attribution of his daily sustenance to answered prayer (sometimes through vivid anecdotes of last-second provision) reinforced the belief in God's miraculous intervention in fundamentalist piety.

Ironside remained active to the end of his life. After the death of his wife in 1948 and his resignation from Moody Church a few months later, he married Annie Turner Hightower in 1949 and, with her help, continued his hectic preaching schedule. His death in Taupo, New Zealand three years later was in the midst of a worldwide preaching tour. His final book, *Expository Notes on the Prophet Isaiah* (1952), was published posthumously.

Bibliography

E. S. English, *Ordained of the Lord: H. A. Ironside* (Neptune: Loizeaux Brothers, 1976); H. A. Ironside, *Random Reminiscences from Fifty Years of Ministry* (New York: Loizeaux Brothers, 1939).

T. GLOEGE

■ **IRVING, Edward** (1792–1834), Scottish minister and forerunner of the Catholic Apostolic Church, was born on 4 August 1792 at Annan, near Dumfries. He studied at Edinburgh University, graduating MA in 1809. To support himself as a divinity student, he became a schoolmaster at Haddington and then at Kirkcaldy. Licensed to preach by the presbytery of Kirkcaldy in 1815, his preaching was not well received and he experienced difficulty in finding a ministerial position before becoming assistant to Thomas *Chalmers at St John's, Glasgow, in 1819.

Working in a deprived area, he won the affection of many parishioners.

In 1821 Irving received a call to the Caledonian Chapel in London's Hatton Garden. His forthright condemnation of the evils of contemporary society in his preaching, and the sincere concern that marked his praying, soon attracted attention. The church became crowded with hearers from all levels of society, and a larger one was opened in Regent Square, the 'National Scotch Church'. Irving's high view of the preaching office is evident in his famous *Ordination Charge* (1827).

Although he was concerned for evangelism and missionary work, Irving's idealism made him ill at ease in the annual fund-raising meetings then held by many societies. His sermon to the London Missionary Society in 1824, published in part as *For Missionaries after the Apostolical School* (1825), called for missionaries who would depend on God alone for support (cf. Matthew 10) and was perceived as an attack on the existing system.

Irving readily acknowledged that friendship with Samuel Taylor Coleridge (1772–1834) had influenced him in many ways; among other things, he acquired a pessimistic outlook on the future of church and society, evident in his eschatology. His eschatological framework was derived from James Hatley Frere, to whom he dedicated *Babylon and Infidelity Foredoomed of God* (1826). Adopting the 'year-day' approach to prophetic interpretation, Irving calculated that the second coming would occur in 1868. Coleridge, however, regarded his eschatological speculations as a delusion which would have dire effects on his character and usefulness, while Chalmers feared that interest in prophecy would 'unship him'.

The *Preliminary Discourse to the Work of Ben Ezra* (1827) was Irving's major eschatological work. In it he foretold judgment upon the Gentile church and the divine raising up of another 'ark of testimony', revival among the Jews and their restoration to Israel, and the personal return of Christ followed by the millennium.

Irving was also prominent among the circle of prophetic students (mostly radical evangelicals) that met annually from 1826 to 1830 at Albury Park near Guildford, the home of Henry Drummond. As well as affirming Irving's views, they concluded that the Christian dispensation would end in the same way that the Jewish dispensation had ended, with the destruction of the visible people of God. Their views on prophecy and other subjects found trenchant expression each quarter in *The Morning Watch* (1829–1833).

Christology was another area in which Irving's views were to prove controversial, and he expounded his views in *The Doctrine of the Incarnation Opened in Six Sermons* (1828) and *The Orthodox and Catholic Doctrine of Our Lord's Human Nature* (1830). Seeking to uphold Christ's full humanity, Irving portrayed him as sharing fallen humanity but preserved from sinning by the Holy Spirit. He wished thus to encourage believers by showing that Christ endured all that they had to endure, and to challenge them to overcome sin in the Spirit's power. During this period he, John McLeod Campbell and Thomas Erskine also began preaching that Christ died for all, not for the elect alone. In 1830 the Church of Scotland's General Assembly investigated the views of Campbell and others, condemning them in 1831 and threatening to proceed against Irving if he should appear in Scotland. When the Presbytery of London also moved to try him, he rejected their jurisdiction and, with his office-bearers, affirmed the orthodoxy of his Christology.

It was A. J. Scott, Irving's assistant, who guided him to a belief that the charismata could be restored to the church. When tongues, prophecy and healing were reported in Scotland in 1830, Irving welcomed the news. For him, belief in the gifts was a natural consequence of his Christological views (to which the gifts testified): if Christ performed his miracles as a human anointed by the Holy Spirit, then believers might do likewise.

In October 1831 the gifts were first manifested at a Sunday service in Irving's church. His decision to allow their public manifestation brought him into conflict with the trustees; since he would not accept that such practices contravened the trust deed, they appealed to the Presbytery of London. The presbytery considered the matter from 26 April 1832, rejecting the manifestations as unscriptural and contrary to the Church of Scotland's subordinate standards; it declared that Irving was to be removed as pastor. Up to

800 of his congregation followed him from Regent Square to form a new congregation, no longer part of the Church of Scotland.

A shift in Irving's ecclesiology was becoming increasingly evident. In spite of his expectation of the visible church's destruction, he had upheld the concept of an established national church. He now advocated a 'remnant' ecclesiology, urging believers to separate from the Church of Scotland as apostate because of its rejection of his theology. In March 1833 he was tried for Christological heresy by the Presbytery of Annan (which had ordained him in 1822) and deposed from the ministry. Soon afterwards the apostles of the new movement made him 'angel' (bishop of a local congregation) of his church in Newman Street, London.

For six months during 1831 and 1832 the solicitor Robert Baxter had exercised an immense influence on Irving and his congregation as a prophet, before rejecting the manifestations. Irving remained convinced that Baxter's gift had been genuine, and with his flock he continued to look for the fulfilment of his prophecies through the new movement, especially those concerning the raising up of apostles and prophets to lead the church. However, his relations with these individuals were often strained. While he submitted to the authority of the prophets, he often found it difficult to accept their pronouncements, partly because of his high view of the ministerial office and concern for his flock, and partly because some of the prophets were unstable characters. Yet he believed that God had restored these ministries to the church.

Prone to overwork, Irving became terminally ill. None the less, he insisted on making a preaching tour during the autumn of 1834, which brought him to Glasgow, where he died on 9 December. Buried in Glasgow cathedral, he is commemorated by a window depicting him as John the Baptist, an appropriate choice considering his sense of vocation as a preacher of repentance and his role as forerunner of the Catholic Apostolic Church.

Locating Irving theologically is not easy. His idealism has helped to ensure his being numbered among the radical evangelicals of the 1820s, but his high view of the church and the sacraments (which he found in the *Scots Confession* of 1560) and his vigorous condemnation of much contemporary evangelical religion ensured that his relationship with evangelicalism was problematic even before his Christological views began to attract attention. The centrality of ecclesiology in his thinking was partly due to Romantic influences, but equally important was the way in which ecclesiology and national identity were linked in post-Reformation Scottish thought.

Another problematic area is the nature and extent of the theological debt of the emerging Catholic Apostolic Church (the title was first used in 1849) to Irving. It claimed that through it God was restoring to the church the ministries of apostle, prophet, evangelist and pastor (Ephesians 4:11), in order to purify, re-unite and perfect Christendom in preparation for the second advent. The combination of 'High-Church' and restorationist elements in its ecclesiology undoubtedly owes much to Irving; however, the movement has consistently rejected the label 'Irvingite', partly because of the charismatic excesses that it believes were associated with his ministry, but also because it has sought to avoid exalting the role played by one human instrument in what it sees as 'the Lord's work'.

Bibliography
A. L. Drummond, *Edward Irving and His Circle* (London: James Clarke); M. O. W. Oliphant, *The Life of Edward Irving* (London: Hurst & Blackett, 1862); C. G. Strachan, *The Pentecostal Theology of Edward Irving* (London: Darton, Longman & Todd, 1973); H. C. Whitley, *Blinded Eagle* (London: SCM, 1955).

T. G. GRASS

■ **JAMES, John Angell** (1785–1859), Congregational minister, was born in Salisbury Street, Blandford, Dorset on 6 June 1785, the fourth child and eldest son of Joseph James, a draper and button maker, and Sarah James (née Blake). His parents were Dissenters who attended Blandford's Independent chapel, although Sarah, who claimed descent from Admiral Blake's younger brother, was a General Baptist.

James's education was characteristic of the rural middle-classes: day school, then small boarding schools (one of these, run by a Presbyterian minister, Robert Kell, was considerably better than the other), followed in 1798 by apprenticeship to a Dissenting draper in Poole. It was a mixed upbringing, in which Dissent exerted a powerful though as yet largely unseen influence: Arianism in tension with Methodism, an easy-going father and a prayerful mother, financial difficulty and unsuitable associates, healthily unacademic. (James's fists dealt suitably with the charge that he was a pug-nosed Presbyterian.) He became firmly evangelical.

Poole's Congregational chapel was the crucible for James's development: the contrasting ministries of the Whitfieldite, high Calvinist Ashburner and the warm Durant, pointed sermons by Sibree of Frome and Richard Keynes, James's future brother-in-law, and an informal young men's group at John Poole the cobbler's, where James learned confidence in prayer. Poole the cobbler had been influenced by William Huntington, and another associate, Tilley the tailor, became a Baptist, but James himself was steadfastly Independent; he was particularly influenced by Matthias Maurice's *Social Religion Exemplified* (1737). At Poole James taught in the Sunday school and became convinced that he was called to ministry, even though he had yet to become a church member.

James's father bought him out of his apprenticeship, and in 1802 he entered Dr Bogue's Gosport Academy, helped by an annual bursary of £30 raised by Robert *Haldane. At Gosport he was baptized and joined the church. His academic memories were mixed, but his student friendship with Robert *Morrison gave him a lifelong interest in overseas mission, especially in China.

James preached his first sermon in Ryde, Isle of Wight, and in 1804 he was introduced to the church at Carrs Lane, Birmingham, where his stated ministry began in 1805, being confirmed on 8 May 1806 by an ordination service five hours long. His denominational loyalties were both familial and confessional. A brother, a brother-in-law, two nephews, a nephew-in-law and a great-nephew became Congregational ministers, and family friendships and kinships brought him to Birmingham; he was connected by marriage to Joseph Phipson, a button maker and Carrs Lane deacon. None the less his prospects in Birmingham were uncertain; Carrs Lane was still recovering from the disruptive ministry of Jehoiada Brewer (1752–1817), who had taken much of the congregation with him.

James was left with an elderly remnant and a salary of £120. He made little progress. A fine voice and a gift for oratory could not compensate for his deficient training. Then came a change. In 1812–1813 Carrs Lane was renovated, and its people moved to Old Meeting, where James's old schoolmaster, Kell, now ministered. The move resulted in helpful publicity, and Carrs Lane began to make progress. The building now seated 800. In 1819–1820 it was rebuilt; the cost was £11,000. Membership rose dramatically; by the 1850s it exceeded 900. Giving also increased. In James's time what was neither a wealthy nor a socially elevated congregation raised £23,000 for church planting; its outgoings of £1,900 in 1851 point to an average annual giving of £2 per member. James's own giving was exemplary and he became known beyond English Congregationalism as a preacher and author.

There was much more to this success than the church's brief migration to Old Meeting or even a steady refinement of the minister's pulpit style. James had become an outstanding pastor. At one level he was authoritative, distant, formidably severe. In his youth, to his shame, he had attended an amateur 'mimic play' and an election ball. In his maturity his austerity was fabled. He opposed the theatre, novels, even the public performance of oratorios. He also refused to use the honorary degrees conferred by Glasgow, Princeton and Jefferson.

At another level James was immediately credible. The apprentice tradesman was now a professional man among professional men, his prestige bolstered by two excellent marriages. His first wife, Frances Charlotte Smith, a doctor's daughter whom he married on 7 July 1806, brought him a house. His second wife, Anna Maria Neale (née Baker), was wealthy and well connected. He was, therefore, financially independent, and lived accordingly on Hagley Row. His salary reached £300 in 1826, and he refused one of £1,000 from a London chapel. He was thus his deacons' minister, not their servant. Because they recognized his authority, he took them into his full confidence and held regular meetings to plan church business, acknowledging them as fathers and brethren in the church; they included his brother James. Their secular and church responsibilities increased as they assumed the leadership of Carrs Lane's proliferating weekday agencies. The church was a male-dominated community, rare among Congregational churches in that its deeds specifically limited the role of women. James disapproved but accepted the situation, for he had a creative belief in the 'separate spheres' of men and women. At Carrs Lane female responsibility was recognized and assumed, in its proper sphere.

This consolidation was itself consolidated by James's increasingly high profile in Birmingham life and by his practical writing on church life. The austere, naturally conservative puritan could escape neither his Dissent nor his consequent commitment to the painstaking application of first principles. His preference for merit over rank and his dislike of the complex implications of Establishment led him to a consistent and distinctive Whiggery. The intrepidly moderate leader who disliked pressure groups found himself in unexpected alliances: voting for Joseph Sturge and, years later, for John Bright; united in 1830 with the radical Baptists, F. A. Cox and J. P. Mursell, in opposition to what they regarded as Anglican presumption; in London in 1834 with the Dissenters' United Committee; supporting Catholic emancipation notwithstanding his horror of Rome, which he later graphically expressed in response to the 'Papal Aggression' of 1850; overcoming his suspicion of legislation if it fostered peace, Sunday observance or temperance or challenged slavery. A Nonconformist Conscience was forming in this examplar of an earlier evangelicalism.

James's writings were manifold. As Carrs Lane's historian put it, 'we find Young Men and Women Guided, Widows Directed, Families helped to Domestic Happiness, Christian Professors Counselled and Cautioned, Quarrels Settled, Servants Advised, and Scoffers Admonished' (A. H. Driver, *Carrs Lane 1748–1948* [Birmingham 1948], p. 44). James's *Sunday School Teacher's Guide* (1819), *The Christian Fellowship or the Church Member's Guide* (1822) and

Earnestness in Churches (1848) projected the world of Matthias Maurice into that of the institutional church. His *Autobiography* (1864) revealed a man with a sense of humour and proportion. He was also a man of wide horizons. James developed influential American friendships and an active interest in overseas mission, and he was both a denominational leader and an evangelical strategist.

James's Independency was naturally congregational. He was a companionable minister with friends in good Congregational places: William Jay of Bath, George Redford of Worcester, Joseph Fletcher of Stepney, the Wilsons of Highbury (Mrs Joshua Wilson and Anna Maria James were related). His prominence in national Congregationalism began with his Surrey Chapel London Missionary Society sermon on 12 May 1819, and it was confirmed by the major role he played in the formation of the Congregational Union of England and Wales in 1831 and the Declaration of Faith, Order and Church Discipline that it adopted in 1833. He was chairman of the Union in 1838. He was a lifelong promoter of a Ministers' Retiring Fund, providing the money which formed its basis, and he was a constructive governor of the theological college founded at Spring Hill, Birmingham (1838). He chaired its Education Board for twenty years, and his nephew, Joseph James (1828–1875), designed its fine buildings (1857).

James's undoubted but pragmatic theological conservatism, bolstered by his reputation in the larger evangelical world, made him a weighty conciliator in denominational disputes. His *Anxious Inquirer after Salvation, Directed and Encouraged* (1834), a classic of its genre, was a best-seller and was soon translated into six languages. Between 1842 and 1846 James played a role in the formation of the Evangelical Alliance akin to the one he played in the founding of the Congregational Union. He was the chief Congregational proponent of the Alliance.

Conciliation was less easy in the 1850s. James was disturbed by the 'Rivulet' and Davidson controversies, which seemed to some to signal a move within the denomination away from classic evangelicalism into theological liberalism. Carrs Lane was as full as ever, but it had ceased to be a young person's church (the secularist G. J. Holyoake, who was for five years in the Carrs Lane Sunday school, must be accounted its most notable failure). Even so, James's relationship with his remarkable co-pastor (from 1854) and successor R. W. *Dale shows him (and Dale) to great advantage. Dale was a man for the new age, but he also endorsed James's application of first principles.

John Angell James died on Saturday 1 October 1859. He was buried in a vault beneath the Carrs Lane pulpit, following a special dispensation from the Home Secretary.

Bibliography
R. W. Dale (ed.), *The Life and Letters of John Angell James: Including An Unfinished Autobiography* (London: James Nisbet, 1861); T. S. James (ed.), *The Autobiography of John Angell James ... with Additions By His Son* (London: Hamilton Adams, 1864); A. Peel, *These Hundred Years* (London: Congregational Union of England and Wales, 1931).

C. BINFIELD

■ **JEFFREYS, Stephen** (1876–1943) and **George** (1889–1962), prominent early leaders in English Pentecostalism, George the founder and leader of the Elim Foursquare Gospel Alliance (Elim Pentecostal Church) and Stephen a prominent evangelist, were the third and sixth of eight sons of a Welsh miner, Thomas Jeffreys, and his wife Kezia. During the Welsh Revival of 1904 both brothers committed their lives to Christ in Shiloh chapel, where the minister was Glasnant Jones. At the age of twelve Stephen went to work with his father in Caerau Colliery. George began his employment as a salesman in the Co-operative stores at Maesteg.

When the first waves of Pentecostalism reached Wales, the brothers were both sceptical. When, however, Stephen's son Edward spoke in tongues while on holiday in 1910, they began to see it differently and to pray in earnest for the baptism in the Holy Spirit. On 3 June George testified to 'the Spirit falling upon me, then speaking through me in other languages, according to the Bible evidence. Bless His Name', Stephen had the experience some time later.

Soon afterwards both brothers left secular employment to engage in full-time Christian work. George applied to join The Pentecostal Missionary Union (founded in 1910) in September 1912 and began a course of training under Thomas Myerscough in Preston. In January 1913 he responded to his brother Stephen's call for assistance with a mission he was conducting in Swansea. In May 1913 George held a series of meetings for Alexander *Boddy in Sunderland, after which he went to Ireland. There, in Monaghan in 1915, he established a group that became known as the Elim Evangelistic Band. The first Elim church was established in Belfast in 1916. Shortly after this, George received a legacy and was recommended to seek legal recognition for his group, which became known as the Elim Pentecostal Alliance. The first Elim church in England was established in 1921.

Stephen began to preach at Cwmtwrch, near Swansea, in 1912 with considerable success. He joined his brother on several mission trips and accepted the pastorate of Island Place Mission, near Llanelli, in 1913. Although frequently away on preaching trips, he retained this position until 1920, when he became pastor of Dowlais. At this time he joined his brother George's Evangelistic Band.

In 1924 the two brothers and a small team embarked on a tour of Canada and the United States, which lasted for five months. Early in 1926 Stephen became a full-time evangelist and for the next two years travelled extensively, working for the Assemblies of God, which had been established in 1924. In a variety of places, from Bishop Auckland and Sunderland in the north to Dover in the south, Stephen strengthened existing churches and established new ones. His preaching, which was said to be often accompanied by remarkable healings, led to a significant growth in the Assemblies of God. In 1928, following what seems to have been an unjustified attack on his integrity, he left England for the United States, where he held campaigns in Springfield, Missouri, and in Los Angeles. He continued on to New Zealand, Australia and South Africa. On his return home his health began to fail. His wife died in 1941, and he lived in relative quiet until his death in November 1943.

During the same period George also engaged in an intensive period of evangelistic work, which extended from 1925 to 1934.

His meetings were attended by huge crowds, and there were reports of remarkable healings. The most successful of his revival meetings was at the great Bingley Exhibition Hall in Birmingham, where *The Elim Evangel and Foursquare Revivalist* of 27 June 1930 reported 10,000 registered converts, more than a thousand cases of miraculous healing and over a thousand candidates immersed in baptism.

With the rapid growth of new churches, the need arose for a more structured organization. In 1925 the former Redemptorist Convent with four-and-a-half acres of land in Clarence Road, Clapham was purchased. It became the movement's headquarters and Bible College and George Jeffreys' home until his death in 1962. In 1926 the Elim Foursquare Gospel Alliance of the British Isles was founded with the expectation that it would become an umbrella for all Pentecostals in Great Britain. In the event only Elim members joined, and the name was subsequently changed to Elim Pentecostal Churches.

Up until 1934 George Jeffreys was the undisputed leader of the Elim movement, acting without any official structure or organization. It was then decided that there should be an executive committee, and Pastor E. J. Phillips (1893–1973) took office as its secretary. From this point forward the executive began to assume an increasing control over both the buildings, which had originally been managed by local trustees, and matters of doctrine and church government. Jeffreys' view of church polity, which was not always clear, was essentially a congregational one with strong lay representation, and he eventually parted company on this issue in 1939 with the denomination which he himself had founded. In a pamphlet entitled *Why I Resigned from the Elim Movement* he gave as two of his reasons that lay representation was a 'remote prospect' and that local churches 'had no control over the property which they had paid for'. In another essay George Jeffreys asserted that 'the local church is in grave danger' and that the Elim movement had become 'enslaved by a legalised system of Central Church Government that is decidedly Babylonish'. Fewer than ten ministers and about twenty churches left the Elim Alliance to follow Jeffreys. At a meeting held in Nottingham on 28 and 29 November 1940 they formed The Bible Pattern Church Fellowship. In 1944 Jeffreys signed over some fifty-six properties of which he was still a trustee to the Elim Trust Corporation. It was to the Bible Pattern Church Fellowship that George Jeffreys devoted his remaining years. Significantly, many of the changes for which he had contended were subsequently accepted by the Elim Conference.

The issue of church government was not the only controversy in which Jeffreys was involved. In the early 1920s he accepted British Israelitism. This was the belief that the power and influence of the British peoples and their empire could be explained by identifying them with the ten lost tribes of Israel. After a debate in 1933 in the conference of ministers the preaching of British Israelitism was banned in centrally governed Elim churches.

Despite the struggles of the 1930s, George Jeffreys continued to travel widely. He was in Switzerland between 1934 and 1936, where he made some 14,000 converts. He also campaigned in Sweden and was honoured as the keynote speaker at the European Pentecostal Conference in Stockholm in June 1939. His later years were spent largely away from the limelight, and he died at his home in Clapham on 26 January 1962.

Both brothers had played a major role in establishing the two great UK Pentecostal denominations, the Assemblies of God and the Elim Pentecostal Church. Both were distinguished revivalists and perhaps rank among the greatest British evangelists and exponents of Pentecostalism in the twentieth century.

Bibliography

G. Adams, *Stephen Jeffreys* (The Covenant Publishing Co., 1928); E. C. W. Boulton, *George Jeffreys: a Ministry of the Miraculous* (Elim Publishing House, 1928); D. W. Cartwright, *The Great Evangelists* (Marshall Pickering, 1986); W. J. Hollenweger, *The Pentecostals* (SCM Press, 1972); E. Jeffreys and S. Jeffreys, *The Beloved Evangelist* (Elim Publishing, 1946); G. Jeffreys, *Fight for the Faith and Freedom* (Crystal Publications Ltd, 1944); W. K. Kay, *Inside Story* (Assemblies of God Bible College, 1990); W. K. Kay, *Pentecostals in Britain* (Carlisle: Paternoster, 2000).

N. A. D. SCOTLAND

■ **JOHNSON, Douglas** (1904–1991), doctor and mission worker, was born on 31 December 1904 in Uckfield, Sussex, England. After training as a doctor, he worked for the Inter-Varsity Fellowship (IVF, later known as the Universities and Colleges Christian Fellowship), a conservative evangelical association seeking to evangelize British and Irish university students. As general secretary of the IVF (in which he was widely known as 'DJ') from 1928 until 1964 he helped to turn it into the most significant Christian organization in British universities and a major influence on Christianity in Britain and abroad. He was married to Dorothy; they had two sons and a daughter. Johnson died on 10 December 1991.

Educated at Uckfield Grammar School, Johnson was deeply influenced by an independent gospel hall, affiliated to the Brethren. The Brethren stress on conservative biblical theology and the priesthood of all believers indelibly marked his approach to faith; he ensured that IVF was conservative in doctrine yet allowed students great freedom of manoeuvre. In later life he attended a variety of churches, Presbyterian, Anglican and Methodist. Johnson always saw his Christianity as being above denomination, but he was most at home in the Presbyterian tradition. He retained strong links with key figures within the Brethren, such as Arthur Rendle Short. An emphasis on doctrine and a conservative view of the Bible were the foundation of his life and work.

Johnson read English at University College, London, and medicine at King's College, London. He managed to complete a course in theology at King's at the same time, and engagement with his lecturers, notably with less conservative figures such as Charles Gore, helped to clarify his theology. He was also extremely active within the London Inter-Faculty Christian Union and in promoting a wider student movement. Johnson was secretary to the Inter-Varsity Conference from 1924 and general secretary of the IVF from its foundation in 1928. His strategic vision was clarified by the rivalry between IVF and the much larger and more liberal Student Christian Movement. He believed that a lively evangelical orthodoxy could regain ground in the student world and beyond, and consequently displayed an adamantine determination not to allow the evangelical faith to be compromised. He was always wary of Roman Catholicism. After qualifying as a doctor in 1931, he spent a brief period practising medicine in Bristol and in a deprived area of London. Johnson began working full-time for the IVF in 1933.

The organization was small, and Johnson supplied organizational skill, the capacity to identify and cultivate the gifts of others, immense energy and great intellectual and strategic vision. He did much to draw intellectually capable speakers into IVF activities and to pursuade students and young graduates to accept responsibility. Johnson drafted the classic statement of conservative evangelical faith, *In Understanding be Men*, to which T. C. *Hammond gave his name after editing the drafts. Johnson actively built up international networks, culminating in the International Fellowship of Evangelical Students, founded in 1946 through a partnership with the independent preacher Dr Martyn *Lloyd-Jones.

Johnson was extremely well read and stressed the need for evangelicals to engage in intellectual debate if they were to be effective in evangelism. To this end, he was instrumental in the establishing of Tyndale House (a centre for conservative evangelical biblical scholarship in Cambridge), London Bible College and the publications arm of IVF (later Inter-Varsity Press), which greatly expanded its work during his time as general secretary. His deep involvement with the Christian Medical Fellowship and the International Congress of Christian Physicians, as secretary of both bodies, coincided with their rapid growth. Johnson's influence did much to recall evangelicalism in general from anti-intellectualism.

Johnson was intensely shy of publicity, always preferring to persuade others to give a public lead, and was almost phobic in his aversion to appearing in photographs. Yet he is, humanly speaking, the individual most responsible for the growth of the IVF. As such Johnson was crucial to the renaissance of evangelicalism among students in the twentieth century and has had a profound and lasting impact on Christianity in Britain and further afield. Little known outside IVF/UCCF circles, Johnson was one of the most significant Christians in twentieth-century Britain.

Bibliography

D. Johnson, *Contending for the Faith* (Leicester: IVP, 1979); G. Fielder, *Lord of the Years* (Leicester: IVP, 1988).

D. J. GOODHEW

■ **JOHNSON, Richard** (1755?–1827), first chaplain of New South Wales, Australia, was one of a coterie of Yorkshire Anglican evangelicals. He was educated at Hull Grammar School, which William *Wilberforce also attended, and may have been influenced towards evangelical faith by Joseph and Isaac Milner. A sizar at Magdalene College, Cambridge, he received his BA in 1784. He was made a deacon in 1783 and a priest in 1784, and served as a curate to the well-known London evangelical, Henry Foster.

The provision of a chaplain for the new settlement of Botany Bay appears to have resulted from William Wilberforce's friendship with Prime Minister William Pitt the Younger, as is suggested by a letter from Pitt to Wilberforce, dated 23 September 1786: 'The colony for Botany Bay will be much indebted to you for your assistance in providing a chaplain ... Seriously speaking, if you can find such a clergyman as you mention we shall be very glad of it; but it must be soon.'

On the evening of that same day, Johnson was offered the position. John *Newton bestowed on him the title, 'Patriarch of the Southern Hemisphere'. So the Botany Bay chaplaincy was the result of the fellowship of some of the best-known members of the evangelical movement. But their aspirations and optimism for the new colony were severely tested by their antipodean clientele. Preaching to the convicts, whom Johnson regarded as practical atheists, cannot have been easy, and although usually depressed and often unwell, Johnson had to force himself to do his duty. On board ship his hopes rose temporarily when, on preaching on the second sabbath to the convicts on the evil of swearing, he observed an abatement. But it proved only temporary, and he arrived in Port Jackson believing that his charges, both convicts and soldiers, were still in their sins, and that these included much vice and depravity. It was a dutiful rather than buoyant chaplain who presided at his first service under a 'great tree', beginning at 10 o'clock on 3 February 1788, a hot midsummer's day. Johnson chose as his text, 'What shall I render unto the Lord for all his benefits toward me?' (Ps. 116:12).

Newton consoled Johnson, declaring that NSW was 'an awkward, unpromising corner of the Lord's great house', and the first chaplain's own understanding of the situation did not change as he became more familiar with the convicts. Towards the beginning of his twelve years in NSW, he described his charges as the most godless people he had ever seen, and towards the end he characterized them as 'lost to all sense of virtue, and abandoned to every species of wickedness'. He tried to turn them primarily by preaching sermons 'upon the awful strain'. The first governor, Arthur Phillip, a stranger to evangelical religion, advised him instead to 'begin with *moral* subjects', advice which hurt the sensitive chaplain. Newton counselled Johnson not to disregard the governor's advice, 'though you and I know that it was like requiring you to cut down a large tree with a wooden hatchet'.

Attempts to enforce church attendance faltered under Phillip, and then, Phillip's successor, Francis Grose, assumed the easier task of enforcing non-attendance. The lengths to which Grose would go to humiliate Johnson were farcical: he ordered him to hold only one service on a Sunday, setting its time at 6am, limiting its duration to three-quarters of an hour, and insisting that the population be called to worship by a bell so small that it could not be heard beyond a hundred yards, while a larger bell especially sent out for the purpose was unhung and unrung. No church building was erected for over five years after the settlement was founded, and then it had to be built at Johnson's own expense and in the teeth of opposition and obstruction by Grose, who described Johnson as 'a very troublesome, discontented character'. In 1794 Johnson wrote to Wilberforce: 'No person dreads and hates disputes and differences more than I do, yet few seem to have ever been involved and pestered with these more than I have been of late. Whether I have brought these upon myself ... or whether they have come upon me whilst in my line of duty, others, not I, must be the judge.'

Despite the deprivation of the early years in the settlement, the vices of the convicts and the apathy or opposition of Phillip and Grose,

Johnson stayed at his post for thirteen years. He faced unusual pressures: he had to officiate at a burial almost every second day for the first five years, and his responsibilites at settlements distant from Sydney involved him in constant travel in all weathers at all times of the day and night, and the conducting of services in all manner of shelters and in the open air. He did not shirk the unpleasant, even unwise, task of visiting disease-ridden convicts in the hold of the *Surprise*, one of the ships of the Second Fleet. He looked on all (convict and free, Church of England and other) as equally entitled to his ministry, and he was determined to approach all equally 'as men and women, as intelligent creatures, possessed of understanding and reason'. In his 'affectionate' *An Address to the Inhabitants of the Colonies Established in New South Wales and Norfolk Island* (1794), dedicated 'especially to the unhappy prisoners and convicts', he wrote: 'The gospel ... proposes a free and gracious pardon to the guilty, cleansing to the polluted, healing to the sick, happiness to the miserable, light for those who sit in darkness, strength for the weak, food for the hungry, and even life for the dead' (pp. 11f.).

It is interesting that the only contemporary criticism of Johnson still extant is that of Grose. If the convicts criticized Johnson, their criticisms have not survived. His was an hospitable home, and his wife Mary (née Burton) communicated well with the convicts. Johnson does not appear to have gone out of his way to avoid contact with the convicts. He attempted to visit them when they were sick and to read to them, and he admitted to finding more pleasure in visiting the convicts from hut to hut than he did in preaching.

Perhaps few have proved as unequal to the task set them as Australia's first chaplain, but this is far more of a comment on the enormity of the task than on the feebleness of the instrument. He had to endure more persecution than most are called upon to bear. He had little of which to be ashamed: he was tolerant, loyal and dutiful, and if the convicts were not won to evangelical religion, neither were they turned from it by Johnson. He did not have to turn them; they were already turned.

Johnson's two surviving children were both born in Australia. His daughter's aboriginal name, Milbah, expressed his feeling for the indigenous inhabitants, while the name of his son, Henry Martin [sic], demonstrated his complete identification with the evangelical missionary cause. Returning to England in 1801, he was presented to the parish of St Antholin's in London in 1810, and died there in 1827.

Bibliography
Johnson Papers, Lambeth Palace Library; J. Bonwick, *Australia's First Preacher: The Rev. Richard Johnson, First Chaplain of New South Wales* (London: Sampson Low, Son & Marston, 1898); N. Macintosh, *Richard Johnson, Chaplain to the Colony of New South Wales: His life and Times, 1755–1827* (Sydney: Library of Australian History, 1978).

S. PIGGIN

■ **JONES, Bob, Sr** (1883–1968), fundamentalist evangelist and founder of Bob Jones University (BJU), was born on 30 October 1883 in Dale County in south-eastern Alabama. Robert Reynolds Jones became one of the leading and most influential fundamentalists of the twentieth century. He was converted in a revival meeting at the age of eleven and began preaching at fourteen. As a member of the Methodist Episcopal Church, South, he attended a denominational school then called Southeastern University, in Greensboro, Alabama, for three years but never graduated. The university is known today as Birmingham Southern. In 1908 he married Mary Stollenwerck from a prominent Uniontown, Alabama, family. The couple's only son, Bob Jones, Jr, was born in 1911. Jones was a full-time evangelist from 1900 to 1927, then founding president of Bob Jones College (BJC) from 1927 to 1947, when he relinquished the presidency to his son. He continued as an evangelist and fundamentalist leader until his death in 1968.

Jones's career as a full-time evangelist took place simultaneously with those of Billy *Sunday and Sam Jones. Aimee Semple *McPherson was also active during the later years of this period. All were influenced by the revivalistic methods established in the late nineteenth century by Dwight L. *Moody.

Sunday was the most prolific of these early twentieth-century evangelists and had a clear influence on Jones. The two appeared together several times, and Jones made Sunday's widow a trustee of BJC, eventually naming a campus building after her.

The fundamentalist–modernist controversy was crucial in Jones's development. He was active in the Winona Lake Bible Conference, co-authoring a 1920 resolution that required evangelists affiliated with the conference to shun meetings held under the auspices of theological modernists. He routinely preached against modernists, denouncing them for not adhering to the inerrancy of Scripture and for de-emphasizing the supernatural elements of the Christian faith.

As Jones preached against modernism, he became increasingly concerned about its influence in higher education. In 1926 he began to consider founding his own college. BJC opened the following year at College Point (formerly Longpoint) in the Florida panhandle. Motivated largely by Jones's desire to provide an alternative to both public and denominational colleges, BJC, in his own words, was to be a school to which 'no evolutionist need apply'. He also stipulated that the college creed never be altered, and to this day it has not changed. For financial reasons the college moved to Cleveland, Tennessee, in 1933, then again to Greenville, South Carolina, in 1947. In conjunction with the last move, Bob Jones, Jr, took over the presidency and the college became Bob Jones University. For decades the college's motto was 'the world's most unusual university'.

The founding of the college was motivated in part by separatism, which would eventually become the feature of fundamentalism most important to the Joneses. Jones's separatism developed gradually between 1927 and the early 1950s. While many northern Baptists and Presbyterians were leaving their denominations to form separate fundamentalist bodies, Jones stayed in the Methodist Episcopal Church, South until 1939. That year both Jones and his son left Broad Street Methodist Church in Cleveland, Tennessee, after the pastor allowed a modernist to preach. Jones transferred his membership to Trinity Methodist Church in Los Angeles, the church of the fundamentalist 'Fighting Bob' Schuler. Surrendering his ministerial

credentials in 1940, he was subsequently licensed to preach by the Gospel Fellowship Association, which he founded in the 1930s.

However, Jones chose affiliation with the more moderately fundamentalist National Association of Evangelicals (NAE) rather than the highly militant and separatist American Council of Christian Churches (ACCC), which was headed by the fundamentalist firebrand Carl *McIntire. Jones was one of the signatories of a 1941 letter that invited fundamentalists to the 1942 meeting in St Louis that resulted in the founding of the NAE. A principal biographer attributes Jones's choice of the NAE to the fact that, although he was militantly opposed to modernism, he was primarily an evangelist. By most accounts, the ACCC's primary motive was to shadow and fight against the modernistic Federal Council of Churches, while the NAE's programme was more positive and, therefore, more conducive to evangelism.

Jones's activities in the NAE put him in the mainstream of the emerging neo-evangelicalism, but he did not maintain this position. From the late 1940s Jones and his son came into increasing conflict with mainstream evangelicalism and eventually chose a more militant and separatist path. At least five factors seem to have contributed to Jones's alienation from mainstream evangelicalism. First, in 1949 the NAE declined an invitation to hold its annual meeting at Bob Jones University. While the stated reason was that the NAE feared appearing partial to one of the evangelical schools, the Joneses attributed the rebuff to personal jealousies. Second, the Joneses feared that the neo-evangelical emphasis on intellectual engagement might divert attention from evangelism and lead to elitism. Jones often made anti-intellectual statements. (For example, he once said that every time he hired a faculty member with a PhD, BJC had to hold a revival.) Neo-evangelicals looked askance at such attitudes. Third, Bob Jones University and everything affiliated with the college came increasingly under the influence of Jones, Jr, who was 'more aggressive and confrontational' than his father. The Joneses' most recent biographer has written that the younger Jones was 'less patient than his father and more willing to sever ties with those with whom he disagreed'. Fourth, at the same time as the

Joneses experienced increasing conflict with the NAE and seemingly all things connected with mainstream evangelicalism, there was an internal crisis at the college, where an assistant to the president was accused of fomenting resistance to Jones, Jr. This seems to have exacerbated Jones, Jr's, militancy and sense of institutional insecurity.

The final factor that pushed the Joneses into the highly separatist wing of fundamentalism was their experiences with Billy *Graham. Graham attended BJC briefly in 1936, finding the atmosphere there too stifling. Before Graham left for a Bible college in Florida and eventually Wheaton College, Jones, Sr, informed the young man that if he left, 'you'll never be heard from again'. After a brief rapprochement in the late 1940s while Graham was president of Northwestern Bible College, the Joneses were again critical of Graham in the fifties. In 1957, when Graham's New York crusade accepted the aid of modernist churches, the Joneses formally denounced Graham, with Jones, Jr, telling a group of fundamentalists that the most dangerous threat to the faith was no longer modernism but compromise with modernism on the part of Bible-believing Christians. In that Graham had become by the late 1950s the central figure in the rise of neo-evangelicalism, the Joneses' break with him signalled their emergence as, in their own words, 'ultra-fundamentalists'. They began openly to denounce neo-evangelicalism.

Jones, Sr, continued until his death as a fundamentalist evangelist, separatist advocate and ambassador for the college he had founded. For the last decade of his life he had no church affiliation. He is buried on a small island in the middle of a fountain on the campus of Bob Jones University. Each year on the anniversary of his death, the university celebrates his life in a Founders Day ceremony, paying tribute to the man who became the patriarch of the family that collectively might well be called the leading proponents of twentieth-century fundamentalist separatism.

Bibliography
M. T. Dalhouse, *An Island in the Lake of Fire: Bob Jones University, Fundamentalism and the Separatist Movement* (Athens: The University of Georgia Press, 1996); D. L. Turner and S. Skaggs, *Standing Without*

Apology: The History of Bob Jones (Greenville, South Carolina: Bob Jones University Press, 1997); M. Wright, *Fortress of Faith: The Story of Bob Jones University* (Grand Rapids: Eerdmans, 1960).

B. HANKINS

■ **JUDSON, Adoniram, Jr** (1788–1850), first Baptist foreign missionary appointed by a missionary society in the United States, was born on 9 August 1788 in Malden, Massachusetts, the eldest son of the Revd Adoniram Judson of Woodbury, Connecticut, a Congregationalist divine, and Abigail Brown Judson of Tiverton, Rhode Island. He learned to read at the age of three and showed an early facility for languages. An ambitious youth, he was valedictorian at Brown University (BA, 1807), where he adopted deistic views, much to the horror of his family. After graduation, he briefly opened a private academy in Plymouth and published *The Elements of English Grammar* (1808) and *The Young Lady's Arithmetic* (1808).

In the midst of a personal religious crisis in 1808, Judson entered the Theological Institution at Andover, although he did not profess a personal conversion and was not a candidate for the ministry. On 2 December 1808 he dedicated his life to God, and on 28 May 1809 he publicly professed his faith and joined the Third Congregational Church in Plymouth, where his father was the pastor. Judson graduated from Andover on 24 September 1810.

On 28 June 1810 Judson, along with fellow divinity students Samuel Nott, Jr, Samuel J. Mills, Jr, and Samuel Newell, submitted a request for support as foreign missionaries to the (Congregationalist) General Association of Massachusetts Proper. In response, the General Association created the American Board of Commissioners for Foreign Missions (ABCFM). On 19 September 1811 Judson, Nott, Newell and Gordon Hall were appointed missionaries 'to labor under the direction of [the ABCFM] in Asia, either in the Burman Empire, or in Surat, or in Prince of Wales Island, or elsewhere, as in the view of the Prudential Committee, Providence shall open the most favorable door.' Luther Rice was appointed on 27 January 1812, but he had to raise the money to pay for his own passage. The missionaries received ordination on 6 February 1812, the day after Judson's wedding to Ann Hasseltine. She was to bear three children; one was stillborn and the others died in infancy.

The Judsons embarked from Salem on 19 February with Samuel and Harriet Newell, and arrived in Calcutta on 17 June.

During the voyage, Judson became deeply troubled over the practice of infant baptism. By 31 August both he and his wife had rejected infant baptism on biblical grounds and adopted the Baptist position. On 1 September Judson wrote to the ABCFM to resign his appointment, and on 6 September the English Baptist missionary William Ward baptized the Judsons at the Baptist mission at Serampore. Luther Rice, who had sailed from Philadelphia with Gordon Hall and Samuel and Roxana Nott, underwent a similar change of sentiments and was baptized on 1 November.

The Judsons arrived in Rangoon (Yangon) on 13 July 1813. For health reasons, Rice was forced to return to the United States before reaching Burma. Immediately he began soliciting Baptist support for foreign missions, and on 18 May 1814 'The General Missionary Convention of the Baptist Denomination in the United States of America for Foreign Missions', also known as the 'Triennial Convention', was organized in Philadelphia. Judson became the Baptists' first missionary and Rice their American agent.

In Burma Judson studied Burmese language and culture. He learned Pali (the language of the Buddhist scriptures) in 1815 and completed his *Grammatical Notices of the Burmese Language* in 1816, although it was not published until 1842. By April 1819 Judson was finally able to preach in Burmese, so he built a *zayat* (a traditional Burmese meeting place) and used it to distribute tracts, meet enquirers, hold public worship and teach reading and writing in Burmese. On 27 June 1819 he baptized the first Burmese convert, Moung Nau. He completed the New Testament in Burmese in 1823 (revised 1829, 1837), along with an epitome of the Old Testament.

In December 1823 the Judsons moved to Ava, the imperial capital, to begin a mission, but on 8 June 1824, because of the outbreak of the first Anglo-Burmese War, Judson was imprisoned as a spy, first at Ava and then at Oung-pen-la. In November 1825 he was forced to serve the Burmese as an interpreter in the peace negotiations with British forces. On 21 February 1826, after more than twenty months of imprisonment and intermittent torture, he was released. He helped the British to negotiate the Treaty of Yandabo, and on 2 July 1826 he moved to the new British settlement of Amherst on the Tennasserim Coast. Meanwhile his first Burmese dictionary was published in Calcutta (1826).

Judson survived imprisonment because Ann Judson, despite her own illness and suffering, provided for his needs, nursed him through sickness and petitioned the Burmese officials for the mitigation of his sufferings. Meanwhile, she endured childbirth and cared for the sickly newborn, Maria. Ann Judson died in Amherst on 24 October 1826, while Judson was in Ava with a British embassy. Judson returned to Amherst on 24 January 1827, and Maria died on 24 April. Judson's personal asceticism, disturbing to many of his contemporaries because it was influenced by Thomas à Kempis, François Fénélon and Madame Guyon, became more extreme in the aftermath of these sufferings, and he cut off all social contacts not necessary to his work.

In 1830 and 1831 Judson tried unsuccessfully to evangelize in Rangoon and Prome. Returning to Maulmain, he made several preaching tours among the Karen in the jungle. He completed his first Burmese translation of the Old Testament in 1834 (revised 1835) and revised the whole Bible for a quarto edition in 1840.

On 10 April 1834 Judson married Sarah Boardman, veteran missionary to the Karen and widow of missionary George Dana Boardman. By 1845, weakened from frequent bouts of dysentery and having borne Judson eight children (five of whom survived to adulthood), Sarah Judson was gravely ill. They embarked for the United States in an attempt to save her life. She died on board ship in the port of St Helena on 1 September 1845.

Judson arrived in Boston on 15 October 1845. He was welcomed as a hero throughout the country, but he felt useless and out of place. His voice was weak due to illness, and he could no longer preach well in English. In

December 1845 he met Emily Chubbuck, a writer of popular fiction under the pen-name 'Fanny Forester'. At first Judson hoped merely to engage her to write a biography of Sarah Judson, but soon he proposed and they married on 2 June 1846. Five weeks later the newlyweds embarked for Burma. On 30 November 1846 the Judsons arrived in Maulmain. Emily was to bear two children, one of whom died at birth.

Judson was an affectionate, kind and compassionate husband, father and stepfather, always attentive to his family's spiritual and material needs. He nursed his wives and children in sickness and grieved deeply over their deaths. His surviving children were sent to the United States to be raised and educated by friends and family members.

Judson published *A Dictionary English and Burmese* (1849), the first volume of a projected two-volume work. He became seriously ill, and his doctor advised a sea voyage as his only hope. Judson died during the voyage on 12 April 1850 and was buried the next day in the Indian Ocean near the Andaman Islands. At his death the Burmese and English portion of the dictionary was left incomplete. Another missionary, E. A. Stevens, finished it, and the complete work was published under the title *A Dictionary Burmese and English* (1852). Judson's revision of his *Grammatical Notices* was published with the 1852 quarto edition of the dictionary under the title *A Grammar of the Burmese Language*. The dictionary has gone through many revisions and is still a standard reference work.

Judson's theological contributions include his famous sermon on 'Christian Baptism' (1812), which William *Carey said was the best he ever read on the topic. Judson's first tract, *A View of the Christian Religion, in Three Parts, Historic, Didactic, and Preceptive* (1816), the first account of Christianity ever printed in Burmese, revealed his triumphalistic postmillennialism. *The Threefold Cord* (1829), written in English, in which some see Roman Catholic quietism or a Buddhist influence in the emphasis on renunciation and self-denial, outlined his views on discipleship. *The Golden Balance* (1829), written in Burmese, offered a comparison of the Christian and Buddhist systems. Judson also wrote several poems and hymns, including 'Come, Holy Spirit, Dove Divine' (1829).

Judson's missiological views were very influential in shaping the strategy and administration of American Baptist missions. He always regarded himself as primarily a preacher, and he advocated evangelism through indigenization rather than Christianization through civilization. He believed that schools and hospitals, although necessary, were secondary to the work of preaching, planting churches and training indigenous leaders. He devoted himself to translation and *zayat* ministry because he believed they were direct and effective means of making the gospel indigenous.

According to Judson, the missionary calling was lifelong and demanded wholehearted devotion and self-denial. He believed missionaries should be totally dependent upon the mission board for support and disapproved of missionaries becoming involved in ancillary scientific and literary pursuits, even as hobbies. He disliked large mission stations and believed missionaries were more effective when they were widely dispersed in smaller groups, using indigenous assistants to extend their ministries.

Judson's strategy for church planting was to provide practical training and supervision for indigenous pastors and assistants. He viewed the Western model of seminary training as inappropriate for the needs of indigenous workers. He compiled the 'Septenary' or 'Seven Manuals' (1829) to aid his pastors in ministering to the churches. The manuals included a catechism written by Ann Judson, his *View of the Christian Religion*, guides for conducting public worship, baptisms, weddings and funerals and a teacher's guide for instructing converts. When Judson arrived in Burma there were no Burmese or Karen Christians. At his death there were nearly eight thousand Christians united in sixty-three churches.

Judson believed that Christianity was inherently superior to other religions and would be embraced by the Burmese people if fairly presented in an environment free of coercion. Consequently, he was a consistent if unsuccessful advocate for religious freedom in Burma.

Bibliography

C. Anderson, *To the Golden Shore: The Life of Adoniram Judson* (Boston and Toronto:

Little, Brown & Company, 1956; repr. Valley Forge: Judson Press, 1987); B. R. Pearn, *Judson of Burma* (London: Edinburgh House Press, 1962); F. Wayland, *A Memoir of the Life and Labors of the Rev. Adoniram Judson, D.D.*, 2 vols (Boston: Phillips, Sampson & Co.; London: Nisbet & Co., 1853).

K. P. MOBLEY

■ **KANTZER, Kenneth S.** (1917–2002), theological educator, administrator and editor of *Christianity Today*, was a key figure in the resurgence of Protestant evangelicalism in the United States during the second half of the twentieth century as a professor, editor, college and seminary administrator and senior statesman of the evangelical movement.

Kantzer was born in Detroit on 29 March 1917, and graduated as BA from Ashland College in 1938. Ruth Forbes, who became his wife on 21 September 1939, helped to lead him to Christ. He made a profession of faith for the first time in 1935, at her commencement, a Wheaton College baccalaureate service. After earning an MA at Ohio State University in 1939, he attended Faith Seminary in Philadelphia and graduated with an MDiv in 1942 and an STM in 1943.

Kantzer was ordained as a minister in the Evangelical Free Church in 1948. Having taught at The King's College while studying at Faith, he then taught Hebrew at Gordon Conwell Theological Seminary for two years while pastor of a church in Rockport. From 1946 to 1963 Kantzer taught and was chair of the department of Bible, Philosophy and Religious Education at Wheaton College. He completed a PhD in Philosophy and Religion from Harvard University in 1950 (his dissertation focused on the knowledge of God in the thought of John *Calvin) and undertook post-doctoral studies in Europe, at both Gottingen and Basel, in 1954.

In 1963, Kantzer became the academic dean of the new Trinity Evangelical Divinity College, which at that time had fewer than forty students. He gave up the opportunity to take a sabbatical and write a book on Barth's theology in order to take on the challenge of building a leading theological institution. He made a major contribution to the development of the divinity school into one of the leading evangelical theological seminaries in the world until 1978, when he was named 'Dean Emeritus'.

Beginning in 1978, Kantzer served for five years as editor-in-chief of *Christianity Today*, and in 1984 he was named senior editor and dean of the research institute of *Christianity Today*. From 1982 to 1983 he served as president of Trinity College and helped to rescue it from collapse by persuading it to re-affiliate with the Evangelical Free Church. After 1983, he served as chancellor of the college. From 1984 to 1991 Kantzer taught at Trinity Evangelical Divinity School, and he served as director of the PhD programme from 1986 to 1990.

Kantzer held four honorary doctorates (from Ashland Theological Seminary, Gordon College, John Brown University and Wheaton College) and served a term as president of the Evangelical Theological Society, in the leadership of which he played a significant role for many years. Kantzer was also a major figure in the work of the International Council on Biblical Inerrancy during the 1970s and 1980s. He edited several books, including *Evangelical Roots: A Tribute to Wilbur Smith* (1978), *Perspectives on Evangelical Theology: Papers From the Thirtieth Annual Meeting of the Evangelical Society*, with Stanley Gundry (1979) and *Applying the Scriptures: Papers From the ICBI Summit III* (1987). In addition to his many editorials in *Christianity Today*, he also wrote many popular articles and contributed to a number of edited volumes.

Kantzer sacrificed the opportunity to engage in scholarly research and writing himself in order to give leadership to the evangelical movement in various ways at different times. It is interesting to note that while building Trinity Evangelical Divinity School, he put in place one of the most generous sabbatical programmes offered by any seminary, thus allowing others to do what he had found himself unable to do because of the time pressures of administration.

Despite his unwavering advocacy of the doctrine of inerrancy as the hallmark of consistent evangelicalism, Kantzer exerted his considerable diplomatic skills and keen mind in an attempt to hold the evangelical coalition together. A word that readily comes to mind in thinking of Kantzer's work is 'irenic'. As editor of *Christianity Today*, he attempted to combine doctrinal orthodoxy with a keen sense of the priority of mission and warm-hearted, practical ministry.

Kantzer died on 20 June 2002 in Victoria, British Columbia.

Bibliography
J. D. Woodbridge and T. E. McComiskey (eds.), *Doing Theology in Today's World: Essays in Honour of Kenneth S. Kantzer* (Grand Rapids: Zondervan, 1991).

C. A. CARTER

■ **KEMP, Joseph W.** (1872–1933), Baptist minister, was born in Kingston upon Hull on 16 December 1872, and was orphaned at the age of nine. Converted at the age of fifteen, he embraced Keswick teaching and became a devoted and active church worker. As a result, he was offered the opportunity to study at the first, newly founded British Bible Institute, in Glasgow, between 1893 and 1895. On graduating, he became a Baptist and an itinerant preacher and was then offered a pastorate in Kelso. He served there from 1897 to 1898 before moving to Hawick. He married Winnie Binnie in 1897; the couple had two children. In 1902 the famous old Charlotte Chapel in Edinburgh invited Kemp to become its pastor, and under his ministry and the influence of the Welsh revival the church's fortunes were dramatically reversed. In 1915 he transferred, surprisingly, to Calvary Baptist Church in New York, later a famous centre of fundamentalism. His ministry there was not a success, and although he founded an independent Metropolitan Baptist Tabernacle in the city (the name recalled one of his heroes, *Spurgeon), by 1919 he had returned to the United Kingdom a sick and dispirited man. A recommendation from Graham *Scroggie led him to accept the pastorate of the Auckland Baptist Tabernacle, and he arrived in New Zealand in August 1920. His ministry was immediately successful, and it became profoundly significant for the formation of the evangelical cause in New Zealand; Kemp founded an evangelical magazine, a missionary convention and a Bible Institute. Above all, he changed the Tabernacle into a city-centre fundamentalist church, built on preaching, Bible study and gospel music and firmly resistant to social activities.

One writer on Kemp has described him as a translator of American fundamentalism into the New Zealand setting. There is some truth in this description, given Kemp's contacts in America. While in New Zealand Kemp kept abreast of American trends, corresponding with some key commentators, reading key magazines of the new movement and reproducing their contents in his strident magazine, *The Reaper*. Yet the description also requires some qualification. Kemp's time in America had been unhappy and had concluded painfully with a breakdown in his health. His greatest work had been at the mecca of Scottish Baptists, Charlotte Chapel in Edinburgh, and he came to New Zealand with a reputation as a restorer of an inner-city church. Charlotte Chapel represented an older version of evangelicalism linked with *Moody's formula for lay Bible training (without theological teaching), passionate evangelistic preaching and defensive apologetic preaching. Kemp followed this formula quite closely, and he is said to have been alarmed by what he saw of fighting fundamentalism in the United States during a sabbatical year in 1926. He was also an interdenominational evangelist, like many of the fundamentalists, and sponsored the introduction of a number of the major evangelical mission agencies previously unrepresented in the dominion. But he never sought to abandon the Baptist Union, and resisted the trend towards independency which was so evident in the United States and in Spurgeon's work in London, although in other respects Spurgeon was clearly a major influence on him. So, although Kemp had uncomfortable relations with the leading Baptist pastor J. J. North, he encouraged the Baptist College to begin its work in rooms in the Baptist Tabernacle (even though his much-beloved Bible Training Institute was next door) and served as president of the Baptist Union. As a result he did much to make the Baptist churches in New Zealand strongly evangelical.

Kemp was diagnosed with a brain tumour early in 1933 and died on 4 September. Six thousand people attended his funeral.

Bibliography
W. Kemp, *Joseph W. Kemp: The Record of a*

Spirit-Filled Life (London & Edinburgh: Marshall, Morgan & Scott); J. Simpson, 'Joseph W. Kemp: Prime Interpreter of American Fundamentalism in New Zealand in the 1920's', in D. Pratt (ed.), *Rescue the Perishing. Comparative Perspectives on Evangelism and Revivalism*, Waikato Studies in Religion, 1 (Auckland: College Communications, 1989), pp. 23–42.

P. J. LINEHAM

■ **KILHAM, Alexander** (1762–1798), founder of the Methodist New Connexion, was born on 10 July 1762 in the village of Epworth in Lincolnshire. The son of a Methodist weaver, Simon Kilham, and his wife Elizabeth, both devout 'Church Methodists', Alexander was baptized on 6 August 1762 and educated at home with his brothers in preparation for entry into the family linen manufacturing business. He rebelled against his father's attempts to compel him to 'attend public service' until at the age of eighteen he was converted and reconciled with his father during a religious revival at Epworth. He then engaged in village evangelism, preaching his first sermon at Luddington in 1782, before becoming an assistant to Robert Carr Brackenbury, the Methodist gentleman-preacher, on a pioneering missionary visit to the Channel Isles. He had apparently regarded himself as a Dissenter from the moment he had been obliged to register for a preacher's licence in 1784 under the terms of the Toleration Act, but became one of *Wesley's itinerant preachers in 1785, travelling mainly in the north. He married, with Wesley's permission, Sarah Grey of Pickering, in March 1788, and their first child, a daughter, was born in December 1788, followed by a son, in 1790, who died from inflammation of the stomach within a year. Kilham, displaying a growing antipathy towards the established church, had repeatedly declined to have the infant baptized by a clergyman.

As long as Wesley lived, Kilham believed it his duty 'to comply with his will … out of affection to him as our father in the Gospel'. However, as soon as Wesley died Kilham felt free to agitate for reform. He saw no reason why Methodists should be forced to rely on the Church of England for administration of the sacraments. He wrote his first pamphlet

to defend the veteran preacher Joseph Cownley's decision to celebrate the Lord's Supper in Hull in 1791, but his denial that 'Mr Wesley was infallible' resulted in a move by Thomas *Coke to expel him at the London Conference of 1792. However, he escaped with a censure and was sent to Aberdeen, where Wesley had reluctantly agreed to the participation of ministers in the administration of the sacraments in accordance with Presbyterian practice. Kilham's experience there only strengthened his resolve to agitate for changes in English Methodism. Moreover, it is now clear from his private correspondence that during this period his 'republican principles', support for parliamentary reform and antipathy towards Pitt's government were also reinforced, as well as his hostility towards episcopacy and the established church, and he congratulated the barrister who secured the acquittal of Hardy and Horne Tooke of charges of high treason in 1794.

Kilham lobbied the 1795 conference, but emerged from it dissatisfied with the Plan of Pacification, which he believed had failed to address fundamental issues of church government. He published his *Progress of Liberty* at Alnwick in the autumn of 1795, proposing more power for the laity in all aspects of connexional government, arguing that the Wesleyan hierarchy was emulating 'the conduct of persecuting Neros and all the bloody actions of the great whore of Babylon' and citing Robert Browne's radical dictum, 'the voice of the people is the voice of God'. He also levelled charges of financial peculation against the travelling preachers, which precipitated a major conservative reaction during the autumn and winter of 1795–1796, when the divergent elements within the connexional leadership closed ranks to deal 'a fatal blow to Methodist Jacobinism' and called for a district meeting in Newcastle to investigate Kilham's views. Undaunted, Kilham claimed that 'no government under heaven, except absolute monarchies, or the papal hierarchy' was as despotic and oppressive as that of the Methodists, and although he willingly apologized for 'improper expression', he ultimately refused to retract his controversial unproven allegations at his three-day trial at the London conference of 1796; he claimed that it infringed the sacred rights of Englishmen.

He was consequently unanimously expelled from the Connexion on 28 July 1796.

After his expulsion Kilham canvassed support through *The Methodist Monitor* and by preaching in northern towns, and on 9 August 1797, with the support of three other preachers, he founded 'the New Itinerancy' at the former Ebenezer Baptist Chapel, Leeds. Although the secession reduced Wesleyan membership by around 5%, it was less devastating in its impact than many had feared. The Methodist New Connexion, as it became known, appealed predominantly to a small clique of prosperous anti-clerical laymen and to a more numerous following of politicized artisans in the industrializing counties of Lancashire, the West Riding, Nottinghamshire and Staffordshire. Membership growth was steady rather than spectacular, and by the third conference at Nottingham in 1799 the total membership had risen to 5,700; this figure had nearly trebled to 16,962 by 1851.

Kilham was stationed at Sheffield in 1797, where he married Hannah Spurr, a former Quaker, some fourteen months after the death of his first wife. He moved to Nottingham in 1798, where he died at the age of thirty-six on 20 December 1798 from a burst blood vessel following an arduous journey to Wales. He was buried within the walls of Hockley Chapel, Nottingham, where a memorial tablet recorded how 'zealously he contended against priestly despotism against the rights of the people'.

Kilham has either been demonized by his conservative detractors as the Methodist equivalent of Tom Paine or venerated by his more liberal admirers and by Whiggish Methodist historians as a martyr to reform and the precursor of nineteenth-century Liberal Nonconformity. Revisionist historians, however, have sought to identify Kilham's political sympathies with older libertarian or Dissenting traditions. David Hempton, for example, has argued that 'the best way to understand Alexander Kilham is not as an anticipator of the future but as a man moulded by the past ... firmly within the old-fashioned tradition of the freeborn Englishman', but more in the style of Major Cartwright than Tom Paine. M. R. Watts, however, is also convinced that Kilham's radical and sectarian instincts were deeply rooted in the past, portraying him 'in his faith in the inspired common sense and hence political rights of the ordinary Christian believer' as 'both in temperament and doctrine the reincarnation of the eponymous Elizabethan Separatist Robert *Browne'.

A sympathetic (if unflattering) much-quoted contemporary account of Kilham's appearance and character describes him as a man of slight stature, with a 'countenance common almost to coarseness', a 'clumsy hobbling sort of walk' and a 'faltering' pulpit delivery, but then proceeds to underline the magnetism he achieved through 'a solemnity in his look, an earnestness in his manner, a richness in his matter, and an unction which accompanied his word, which more than compensated for every natural defect'. Indeed, even his sternest critics acknowledged his evangelical piety and his 'indefatigable labours in the work of the ministry'. He preached at least seven times a week, read voraciously and corresponded assiduously. However both contemporaries and historians have concluded that he was, in many respects, too brash, opinionated and precipitate in his actions to lead a successful reform movement in the anxious years following the death of Wesley and the outbreak of war with Revolutionary France.

Bibliography

D. Hempton, *Methodism and Politics in British Society 1750–1850* (London: Hutchinson, 1984); A. Kilham, *The Life of Mr Alexander Kilham* (Nottingham: C. Sutton, 1799); J. Blackwell, *Life of the Rev. Alexander Kilham* (London: R. Groombridge, 1838); M. R. Watts, *The Dissenters*, vol. ii, *The Expansion of Evangelical Nonconformity 1791–1859* (Oxford: Clarendon Press, 1995).

J. A. HARGREAVES

■ **KIRBY, Gilbert** (1914–), pastor, interdenominational leader and college principal, was born at Forest Hill, London, on 7 September 1914 and educated at Eltham College, London, and Cheshunt College, Cambridge, from which he graduated MA in 1937. At the age of thirteen he was converted and subsequently grounded in evangelical beliefs through the agency of Bromley Crusaders. An ordained Congregational minister, he served at Halstead Congregational Church,

Halstead, Essex (1938–1947) and Ashford Congregational Church, Middlesex (1945–1956). Following his appointment as general secretary of the Evangelical Alliance (EA), he became honorary pastor of Turner's Hill Free Church, Sussex, at that time part of the Countess of Huntingdon Connexion (1956–1970), and then of Roxeth Green Free Church, Harrow, Middlesex (1971–1983). After retiring from the principalship of London Bible College (LBC) in 1980, he served as moderator of Bushey Baptist Church (1983–1985), and from 1985 as an elder of Northwood Hills Evangelical Church, Middlesex.

As general secretary of EA (1956–1966), he played a key role in expanding its activities and influence and taking new initiatives. Of immense significance was the decision to extend membership of EA, hitherto confined to individuals, to local churches and whole denominations. Two Pentecostal denominations, Elim and the Assemblies of God, were among those which joined. In 1958 the overseas committee of EA merged with the Fellowship of Interdenominational Missionary Societies to form the Evangelical Missionary Alliance (EMA) with Kirby as secretary. EMA helped to end the isolation of the missionary societies and Bible colleges, which joined it in increasing numbers. *Crusade*, an interdenominational magazine, was launched by EA in 1959 to capitalize on the success of the Billy Graham Crusades of the 1950s, in which it had played so significant a role. An EA fund to assist refugees was developed into the Evangelical Alliance Relief Fund (1968), soon to become known as TEAR Fund, and one of the largest relief funds in the UK. Kirby's far-flung network of contacts crossed the Atlantic Ocean and included Billy *Graham, who frequently consulted him on European matters. He chaired the European Congress on Evangelism, 'Amsterdam 1971', giving a major address on 'Strategy for the Seventies'. For a time, Kirby served as international secretary of the World Evangelical Fellowship. Yet another of Kirby's initiatives was the National Assembly of Evangelicals (1965), which brought together 1,000 delegates from across the denominations. The assembly held in 1966, which was marked by a clarion call by Dr D. M. *Lloyd-Jones to evangelicals in

theologically mixed denominations to reconsider their position with a view to withdrawing, precipitated a crisis for EA. By then, Kirby had moved on to become principal of LBC.

Kirby's connection with LBC went back to its earliest years. In 1945 he had joined its consultative faculty, teaching English and homiletics part-time. (From time to time he also lectured at Redcliffe, Ridgelands and All Nations colleges.) In 1958 he joined LBC's board of directors, and in 1966 followed Ernest Kevan as principal. Kirby's very considerable pastoral gifts, earthed in local church ministry, made an enormous contribution to the well-being of the college. It was he who propelled LBC from the formal style of its early years to an informality appropriate to the closing decades of the twentieth century. He presided over the removal of the college from its original venue in central London to more commodious premises in suburban London. This facilitated the recognition of the college and its degree programme by the Council for National Academic Awards, thus releasing it from the tutelage of the external department of London University.

Ever the advocate of networking (for example, he had helped to initiate the Congregational Evangelical Revival Fellowship in 1948), Kirby brought into being an Association of Bible College Principals, which brought together UK Bible college principals for regular consultation, and spawned similar networks for other college officials. He was the architect of ALSO (an acronym representing four evangelical colleges in the London area: All Nations, London Bible, Spurgeon's and Oak Hill), which annually brought together faculty members for joint meetings.

Kirby's writings reveal his gift in mediating theology to the general public. Also notable is their lucid and irenical nature. Among them are biographies of his predecessor at LBC, *Ernest Kevan: Pastor and Principal* (London: Victory Press, 1968), and the Countess of *Huntingdon, *The Elect Lady* (privately printed, 1972); a survey of Protestant churches in Britain, *Why All These Denominations?* (Eastbourne: Kingsway, 1988); a survey of Christian ethics, *The Way We Care* (London: Scripture Union, 1973); an assessment of contemporary controversial issues, *Too Hot to Handle* (London: Lakeland,

1978), which in his hands lost much of their heat; and a collection of essays on the second coming which he edited, *Remember, I am Coming Soon* (London: Victory Press, 1964).

Kirby stands out as a man with firm evangelical convictions, far-sighted vision, keen pastoral insight, the ability to relate easily to people of every kind, wide sympathies, wry humour and a very warm heart.

Bibliography
S. Brady, 'Gilbert Kirby, an Evangelical Statesman: a Tribute and Profile', in S. Brady and H. Rowdon (eds.), *For Such a Time as This* (London: Scripture Union, 1996), pp. 1–20.

H. H. ROWDON

■ **KNOX, John** (c. 1514–1572), Scottish minister and Protestant reformer, was born in Haddington and studied at St Andrews University, perhaps encountering there the conciliarist John Mair. Ordained in 1536, Knox was employed as a notary public; he must have known Latin and some canon law. By the early 1540s, he had become tutor to the sons of some minor landowners near his home, and in 1543 he heard the ex-friar Thomas Gwilliam proclaim solafideism 'without great vehemency against superstitioun'. Knox's commitment to a Protestant position was more certainly established from December 1545, when he accompanied the itinerant preacher George Wishart on his brief tour around Leith and East Lothian. Bearing a two-handed sword on these travels, Knox acted as a bodyguard and assistant to Wishart, until in January 1546, suspecting a plot against himself, Wishart sent Knox back to his pupils, stating that 'one is sufficient for one sacrifice'. Knox does not appear to have attended Wishart's trial or execution in St Andrews, showing already an 'instinct for self-preservation' that would be evident throughout his career. He did, however, emulate the ministry of his mentor in energetic preaching and prophetic declarations, and embraced his scripture principle, sacramental memorialism and belief that the mass, images and other ceremonial activities were idolatrous.

The following May, Cardinal David Beaton was assassinated and his castle in St Andrews occupied by a group of pro-Protestant conspirators, who hoped for assistance from England. Shortly thereafter, a steady stream of individuals sympathetic to evangelical theology or alliance with England began to join them, including at Easter 1547 John Knox and his three pupils. Knox was soon asked by some fellow 'castilians' to begin preaching, but he declined; he was then publicly charged in a sermon by John Rough to take up this vocation, at which he 'byrst furth in moist abundand tearis, and withdrew him self to his chalmer'. Eventually, feeling it necessary to respond to a Catholic opponent of Rough, he preached his first public sermon, on Daniel 7, in Holy Trinity parish church.

This sermon revealed Knox's Protestantism clearly to an audience that included John Mair; it was said afterwards that while others clipped branches, Knox struck 'at the roote, to destroy the hole'. Knox not only decried indulgences, pilgrimages, enforced fasts and clerical celibacy as contrary to justification by faith alone, but also described them as blasphemous and declared the Pope to be an antichrist. Knox expounded the scriptural principle when called before John Winram, subprior of the Augustinians; he held that ceremonies that went beyond the express command of God, including the mass, were idolatrous. Moreover, he denied purgatory and articulated a doctrine of the true and false churches. Winram, evangelically minded himself, took no action; he may even have influenced Knox, particularly through a catechism he had written.

Knox's ministry in St Andrews, which culminated with a Reformed service of 'the Lordis Table', was short-lived, as the castle surrendered under a French siege on 31 July 1547. The castilians were taken prisoner aboard the galleys, and as the French did not consider Knox one of the 'principalles', he remained at the oars until his release in early 1549. During this period of 'torment', Knox not only fought severe illness, but also endured the agonizing sight of his homeland from on board, as his ship went twice to Scotland. However, in captivity Knox's position as a religious leader of the exiles was confirmed. Some wrote to Knox asking whether they could justifiably escape from prison; he answered that they could, so long as they did not shed blood. Henry Balnaves, imprisoned in Rouen, sent Knox a lengthy treatise on justification, which Knox annotated and forwarded to Scotland. This treatise offered a detailed defence of solafideism, as well as comments on vocation that supported obedience to all rulers, even wicked ones, so long as their commands were not contrary to the law of God; Knox, as he stated in his précis of the text, was in agreement with both positions.

After his release, Knox went to England, where he was given a small reward and made minister in Berwick and then in Newcastle. During this time he met his future wife, Marjory Bowes, with whom he would have two sons, and to whose mother, Elizabeth, he would offer lengthy pastoral advice. Continuing to preach as he had in St Andrews, Knox had to answer the Council of the North in 1550 for his attacks on the mass. In 1551, supported by the Duke of Northumberland, Knox was appointed a royal chaplain to Edward VI, but continued his ministry in the north until called to London in 1552. Preaching before King and council in September, Knox denounced as idolatry the practice of kneeling at communion, which was about to be established with the publication of the revised Book of Common Prayer. Knox's concerns were, however, overridden by *Cranmer; the 'Black Rubric' on kneeling in the 1552 prayer book reflects Cranmer's position on the practice rather than Knox's. A defiant Knox nevertheless refused to kneel at communion himself. In October 1552 Knox was nominated by Northumberland for the see of Rochester, but he declined the appointment, and his views on the episcopal order of church government have been much debated by scholars.

After Edward's death, Knox joined the flight from Mary Tudor, arriving in Dieppe in January 1554. Here he composed the *Admonition or warning*, the first of several epistolary publications written in exile that enjoined the 'small and dispersit flock of Jesus Chryst' to 'flie from idolatrie', meaning principally the mass. Since it was idolatrous, Christians should avoid the mass even if the ruler commanded participation, for they must obey God rather than men (Knox cited Acts 5). Like the *Faythfull admonition* published in July, this tract draws heavily on Old Testament examples, and casts its author in the role of prophet, proclaiming to rulers and realms the judgment of God in the wake of Edward's death.

From Dieppe, Knox went to various Swiss cities to consult with *Calvin, Viret and *Bullinger about questions of obedience and resistance, which would be the other major theme of his writing in exile. Knox at this stage enjoined patience under a hostile ruler; God would send 'one Jehu or other to execute hys vengeaunce uppon these bloudde-thyrsty tyrauntes and obstinate idolators'. Although Viret may have claimed for the lesser magistracy the right to resist an idolatrous monarch, Knox took to heart Bullinger's caveats regarding their potentially mixed motives in doing so.

In autumn 1554 Knox moved to Frankfurt-am-Main to minister to the Marian exiles there, among whose number were John *Foxe, John Bale, William Whittingham and Christopher Goodman, the last of whom would become Knox's closest male friend. Exile and persecution had not eradicated former controversies, and by the following spring Knox was again opposing elements of the 1552 Prayer Book that he considered idolatrous, particularly versicles and the litany. Countering Knox was Richard Cox, who promptly mentioned to the Frankfurt authorities that Knox's *Faythfull admonition* encouraged sedition against the Emperor; they requested Knox to leave, and on 26 March 1555 he was on his way to Geneva.

Geneva, where Calvin's influence had just reached its apex, seemed to Knox 'the maist perfyt schoole of Chryst that ever was in the erth since the dayis of the Apostillis', and there is no question that it was his experience of this city, where 'maneris and religioun' were 'so sinceirlie reformat', that clarified his vision of a society guided by godly discipline. To Knox, discipline thus administered constituted a third mark of the church, in addition to word and sacraments. His sojourn in Geneva was brief, however; he returned secretly to England in the autumn of 1555, in order to solemnize his marriage to Marjory Bowes.

From Berwick Knox decided to travel to Scotland, now governed by Mary of Guise, the queen mother. In Edinburgh Knox found to his surprise the existence of 'privy kirks', small groups of evangelicals meeting for Bible reading and prayer. He urged the leaders of these groups to reject the mass as idolatrous. Knox spent the following months staying with sympathetic nobles in Angus and the Mearns, Lothian and, after Christmas, Kyle; unlike the travelling preacher Wishart, Knox engaged primarily in secret instruction and the administration of the Lord's Supper in evangelical houses. Knox's work eventually became known to the Dominicans, who wished to try him, but he departed in July 1556, having received a request from the English congregation in Geneva for him to return; soon thereafter he was tried for heresy *in absentia* and burnt in effigy.

Back in Geneva, Knox and Marjory had two sons, and he served as minister to the English exiles. In 1558 he published new treatises concerning the right of revolt, of which the most infamous is *The First Blast of the Trumpet against the Monstrous Regiment of Women*, a scathing attack on Mary Tudor that called for a revolt on the basis of a broadly held aversion to female rule at the time. The English nobility, said Knox, should overthrow their queen, since the rule of a woman was a 'monstrous' violation of the law of God. The treatise was very badly timed; soon after its publication Mary died and Elizabeth took the throne, and despite Knox's protestations that his arguments were not meant to apply to her, he was not allowed to join the English exiles returning to their homeland. Knox would later complain that 'my First Blast hath blowne from me all my friends in England'.

However, other tracts from 1558, addressing Scotland, propose a programme so different that it is common to refer to 'two John Knoxes' at this time. To the Scottish lesser magistracy, Knox argued, applied the *ius reformandi*, and they should establish and defend Protestant worship even against Mary of Guise's wishes, provided that they did not make this an excuse for political revolution or personal gain. To the people belonged the right to demand godly ministry from their superiors, for all were equal in religious terms. The difference in tone between the tracts addressed to England and Scotland is partly explicable by their different audiences, but also reflects Knox's understanding of the covenanted nation. England had committed itself to godly principles, and hence had been punished for breaching them; the Scots, on the other hand, had not entered into such a covenant, and the Protestant nobility did not have the prerogative or duty of enacting justice upon an idolatrous monarch.

Knox was finally recalled to his homeland in 1559, after twelve years in exile. The religious and political situation had changed considerably, and shortly after his arrival on 2 May, Knox preached a fiery sermon in Perth that resulted in an iconoclastic riot; he also acted as a liaison officer with the English on behalf of the 'Lords of the Congregation'. In July Knox was appointed minister in Edinburgh with the approval of the town council, a well-paid position he would hold until his death. The following year, with Mary of Guise dead and English and French forces withdrawn, parliament outlawed the mass, abolished papal authority and established the Scots Confession of Faith. This confession was produced by a committee of 'six Johns', including Knox, and its dependence on the confessions of the Genevan students and of the English congregation in Geneva, reveals Knox's guiding hand. The same committee had begun work on the *(First) Book of Discipline* earlier in the year; this likewise reflects some of Knox's theological and ecclesiastical concerns.

These activities placed Knox on the national stage in 1560; in the same year his lengthy treatise on predestination was published, and his 'dear bedfellow' Marjory died in December. Although Knox saw the national events of 1560 as divinely arranged, he was not satisfied with the resulting situation. Not only was the new kirk not financed according to the programme in the *Book of Discipline*; the Protestant nobles were proving themselves as unreliable as Bullinger had warned that they might be. Knox did not hesitate to criticize their behaviour, eventually quarrelling even with the Earl of Moray, one of his closest allies.

The national situation deteriorated in Knox's eyes the following year with the return of the young widow Mary, Queen of Scots, from France. Particularly vexing to Knox was the fact that the Queen was allowed to hear mass at Holyrood, and thus idolatry and the right of resistance were central themes of his four heated meetings with her between 1561 and 1563. Knox did not manage to convince Mary to cease her Catholic practice, or the

Protestant political leadership to prohibit it. A lengthy debate followed at the 1564 General Assembly regarding the right of the people to revolt against an idolatrous monarch; Knox now saw Scotland as a covenanted nation, and believed that its people could enforce God's laws on the queen. Many of his compatriots in the Protestant ministry disagreed, however, and by this time it was clear that the new kirk was not made purely in Knox's image.

The sizeable population of Edinburgh made it a challenging ministerial charge, particularly since most of the population remained religiously conservative, and a second minister, John Craig, was appointed to the burgh in 1562. Knox never acted as moderator of the assembly or superintendent, though he did undertake various, and sometimes lengthy, commissions from the kirk, including a debate with a Catholic theologian, the adultery trial of a leading Protestant minister and some travels when the situation in Edinburgh became dangerous. Knox's publishing was curtailed after his ministry began, apart from some documents on church polity and liturgy (notably the *Forme of Prayers* or 'Book of Common Order' in 1564) and some brief polemical works, though he continued to work on his *History of the Reformation in Scotland*, which would be published posthumously (an incomplete version appeared in 1587). Knox was remarried in 1564, to the teenaged Margaret Stewart, with whom he would have three daughters.

Scandal and dissatisfied nobles finally accomplished what Knox could not, and in 1567 the queen was forced to abdicate in favour of her infant son James VI. Knox preached at the coronation of the young king, and in a hopeful sign Moray was appointed regent. Moray's assassination in 1570 discouraged Knox, and he suffered a small stroke later that year. As civil war intensified between the 'king's men' and 'queen's men', Knox had to leave for St Andrews, where although he had to be assisted in ascending to the pulpit, by the end of a sermon 'he was sa active and vigorus that he was lyk to ding that pulpit in blads'. Knox returned to Edinburgh in August 1572, and soon after installing his replacement at St Giles, he was taken ill and died on 24 November.

The degree of Knox's importance in Scotland, England and Geneva has been debated. In his *History* Knox did not hesitate to claim prophetic significance, but some historians have questioned whether he has received greater attention simply because of a lack of sources on other figures. However, Knox was without question regarded as important by his contemporaries. Mary Stewart considered him 'the most dangerous man in all her realm', while a Catholic opponent named him 'principle patriarch of the Calvinian court'. In death Knox has maintained a central position in Scottish historiography, having been analyzed not only by historians but also by writers from Robert Louis Stevenson to Thomas Carlyle to Hugh MacDiarmid.

Political influence in any case would have been difficult for Knox to attain given his characteristic refusal to compromise; eulogizing Knox, the Regent Morton said that he 'nather feirit nor flatterit anie fleche', and indeed at moments when his influence might have increased through even slight compromise, as when he was offered the see of Rochester, Knox almost invariably fell out with his allies, however powerful they may have been. His tactlessness and boldness should modify the view that he shrank from trouble. Perhaps Knox's greatest personal legacy lay with his congregations and the women with whom he corresponded. Although sometimes cast as the sixteenth century's most notorious misogynist, Knox's correspondence shows him to have been a sensitive and respected pastor to several women.

Knox was not a leading theologian or scholar, as his derivative and unreliable patristic references demonstrate. However, his writings on resistance occupy an important place in the development of resistance theory in the sixteenth century. Perhaps of more lasting significance was Knox's firm stand on the scripture principle and against idolatry, which made him a 'founding father of English Puritanism' as well as an influence on later Scots Protestantism. Knox left a legacy of Reformed theology for the kirk, in his preaching and especially in the liturgical materials he produced. Very few of Knox's sermons have survived, but contemporary accounts liken them to thunder and trumpets.

Often simply caricatured, Knox was nevertheless a complex figure living in complicated times. His context and contacts affected him, and he cannot be understood apart from the immensely varied situations in which he found himself. However, his basic motivations remained fairly consistent: a purified church, dependent on Scripture and eschewing idolatry; a prophetic witness to the governing authorities; and a godly and disciplined society. While Knox has been seen as more English than Scottish, he is perhaps best described as a 'Protestant internationalist'. Knox's writings and personal life have remained controversial, but the site of his grave is marked only with a plain brown tile in the car park behind St Giles, a memorial he would probably have found satisfactory.

Bibliography

J. Knox, *The History of the Reformation in Scotland*, vols. 1–2 of D. Laing (ed.), *The Works of John Knox* (Edinburgh: Wodrow Society, 1846–1868); R. Mason (ed.), *John Knox and the British Reformations* (Aldershot: Ashgate, 1998); E. Percy, *John Knox* (London: James Clarke, ²1964); J. Ridley, *John Knox* (Oxford: Clarendon, 1968).

M. H. DOTTERWEICH

■ **KUHLMAN, Kathryn Johanna** (1907–1976), evangelist, was born in rural Missouri near the town of Concordia on 9 May 1907, the third of the four children of Joseph and Emma Kuhlman. In 1911 the family moved to Concordia, where Kathryn's father, a self-styled 'backslidden Baptist', operated a livery stable and was elected mayor. Converted in a Baptist revival in 1921, Kuhlman began preaching in 1923, joining her sister and brother-in-law, Myrtle and Everett Parrott. Parrott, a graduate of Moody Bible Institute, itinerated in small-town middle America, but the Parrotts' troubled marriage made it impossible for Kuhlman to work with them for long. She set out on her own, accepting invitations to preach in Idaho, Utah and Colorado. In 1933 she settled in Denver, where she presided over the Kuhlman Revival Tabernacle. By 1935 she was operating from a 2,000-seat building known as the Denver Revival Tabernacle and had begun broadcasting on local radio. Her ill-judged marriage to Burroughs Waltrip, an evangelist who in 1938 divorced his wife to marry

Kuhlman, destroyed her prospects in Denver. The Waltrips moved to Mason City, Iowa, as co-pastors of Waltrip's short-lived Radio Chapel. The Chapel collapsed, bankrupt, in 1939. For the next few years, the Waltrips were travelling evangelists, first together, then separately. After eight years of marriage, the couple divorced and Kathryn Kuhlman reorganized her independent ministry.

Kulman's break came in 1946 in the town of Franklin in northwestern Pennsylvania. After months of services, several participants testified in 1947 to physical healings. Kuhlman had not preached on healing, and she concluded that the Holy Spirit healed directly, without healing lines or anointing oil. Kuhlman drew unprecedented crowds to the 1,500-seat Franklin Gospel Tabernacle, crowds that exceeded even those that had come a generation earlier to hear Billy *Sunday. Kuhlman began broadcasting on radio. In time, disagreements with the manager of the Franklin Gospel Tabernacle compelled her to move, and she chose to go to nearby Pittsburgh. In 1948 Kuhlman set up a base of operations in the city. Her first service in Carnegie Hall on 4 July 1948 filled the building and brought her press coverage. By 1951 local religious leaders were objecting publicly to her non-stop healing meetings, charging her with luring away their members. When they complained to the mayor's office, it sided with Kuhlman. Amid the public debate, *Redbook* magazine assigned Emily Gardner Neal to write a feature story on Kuhlman. The ensuing sympathetic account brought Kuhlman national prominence but also plunged her into theological controversy over healing. From this time she was challenged repeatedly and publicly to prove the authenticity of her healings. Wherever she went, people claimed miraculous healing, generally without the laying on of hands and vigorous praying that often accompanied prayers for the sick. Opposition led to further coverage, and wherever Kuhlman went, crowds flocked to so-called 'miracle services'. A growing following necessitated staff, and by the early 1950s Kuhlman was gathering around her the nucleus of loyal helpers on whom she was to depend for the remainder of her life.

With the dramatic growth of the charismatic movement in the 1960s, Kuhlman was besieged with invitations. In 1965 she accepted a call from Ralph Wilkerson, pastor of Anaheim Christian Center (later Melodyland). The Pasadena Civic Auditorium (capacity 2,500) proved too small, so Kuhlman moved to the Los Angeles Shrine Auditorium, where she conducted services regularly for the next decade. At the same time, she held regular meetings in Pittsburgh and began travelling within the network of the thriving Full Gospel Business Men's Association. This ministry brought her among the associates of evangelist Oral *Roberts as well as into more prominent roles in the global activities of Pentecostalism. Oral Roberts University awarded Kuhlman an honorary doctorate in 1972.

Kuhlman's emphasis on healing and spiritual gifts gave her ready appeal among charismatics. Until the charismatic movement emerged, she had not identified particularly with Pentecostals. She had briefly attended a Christian and Missionary Alliance Bible school in the Northwest, and there is some evidence that she attended Angeles Temple and perhaps the affiliated LIFE Bible College in the late 1920s. There she would have observed the colourful Pentecostal evangelist Aimee Semple *McPherson. But Kuhlman minimized her past associations and was known to deny what she preferred not to confront, and she admitted no influence from McPherson. Her admiring public was not easily convinced, however; comparison was natural. At any rate, Pentecostals objected to the circumstances of Kuhlman's marriage to Waltrip and to her subsequent divorce and wondered about her apparent disinterest in their distinctive practice of speaking in tongues. Kuhlman did claim to use the gifts of discernment and knowledge. Known for the ability to identify the ailments from which people were being healed, she also saw many who came forward fall down in her presence, a phenomenon known as being 'slain in the Spirit'.

Kuhlman appreciated the luxuries her growing popularity made possible: expensive clothing, first-class travel, elegant hotel apartments, jewellery and Cadillacs. But she was generous too. The Kathryn Kuhlman Foundation provided scholarships and help in crises. She assisted the fundraising efforts of charities, especially in western Pennsylvania, and promoted the drug rehabilitation work of David *Wilkerson and his Teen Challenge. A supporter of American participation in the Vietnam conflict, Kuhlman visited Vietnam in 1970. There she was received by South Vietnam's first lady and given a palace reception, and was awarded the Vietnam medal of honour, the highest award the military could bestow on a civilian. But most of the money she raised went either into her own growing media work or into the missionary work of the Christian and Missionary Alliance and the Assemblies of God.

By the 1970s Kuhlman was a best-selling author, with *I Believe in Miracles, God Can Do It Again* and *Nothing Is Impossible with God* reaching a vast readership. She wrote eight of her nine books with the popular charismatic author Jamie Buckingham. She conducted a television ministry, producing 500 thirty-minute broadcasts over ten years as well as thousands of radio programmes. Kuhlman's schedule was gruelling. She recorded programmes in California studios, preached regularly in Los Angeles and Pittsburgh and addressed congregations and conferences around the world. A private person, she chose not to reveal that she had a serious heart problem diagnosed years earlier by doctors in Washington, DC. As her schedule intensified, her heart problems increased. Her last public meeting was at the Los Angeles Shrine Auditorium on 16 November 1975. A few days of recordings followed, exhausting her diminished reserves of strength. Friends rushed her to hospital, first in Los Angeles, then in Tulsa, Oklahoma, where she had open heart surgery. Kuhlman died on 20 February 1976 at Tulsa's Hillcrest Medical Center.

The last year of Kuhlman's life had been marked by stressful controversy concerning her ministry. Her highest-paid associate took her to court over salaries and contracts, and articles in *The New York Times*, *The Los Angeles Times* and *People Magazine* questioned her integrity. Her choir director died, and her pianist broke with her amid allegations of interference in his private life and over consumption of alcohol. She had faced criticism before, of course, including sustained opposition in the Pittsburgh press and in Akron, Ohio. William Nolen MD launched an investigation into her healings, and criticized her in *McCall's* in the autumn of 1974 and in his book, *Healing: A Doctor in Search of a Miracle* (1974). Other doctors and many of the faithful countered with claims of authentic healings. Such challenges had begun almost as soon as Kuhlman began her healing ministry. But the attacks in 1975 were personal and came from within her organization, and they took their toll on her health as well as her spirit.

Kathryn Kuhlman was buried in Forest Lawn Cemetery, Glendale, California. Oral Roberts preached her funeral sermon in the cemetery's picturesque chapel.

Bibliography

J. Buckingham, *Daughter of Destiny* (Logos, 1976); W. E. Warner, *Kathryn Kuhlman: The Woman Behind the Miracles* (Ann Arbor: Servant Publications, 1993).

E. L. BLUMHOFER

■ **KUYPER, Abraham** (1837–1920), Dutch theologian and statesman, is important in the history of Reformed and evangelical Protestantism for having devised a comprehensive Christian response to the social and intellectual challenges of modernity. He joined the classic tenets of Reformed theology and habits of Dutch piety to a recovery of Calvinism's historic concern for public life, at the same time appreciating the religious pluralism of that life in modern society. His principal innovations thus consisted in calling the Dutch Reformed people to live by their full heritage without seeking official preferment or infringing on the rights of others.

Kuyper was born in Maassluis (in South Holland) on 29 October 1837 to Jan Frederik Kuyper and Henriette Huber. His father had risen above his family's shopkeeper status to become a minister in the Netherlands Reformed Church (Nederlandse Hervormde Kerk, or NHK) with the help of an evangelical English tract society for which he worked as a translator. Kuyper would be ambivalent towards such ecumenical evangelicalism and would break decisively with the complacency he saw in his father's career, but that career did bring the family to Leiden, where Kuyper completed gymnasium (1855), a BA in philology (1858), and a doctorate in theology (1862). In the course of his graduate work Kuyper won a national prize for scholarly research, but in the process overworked himself to the point of breakdown. Both the prize and the overwork were signs of things to come.

At Leiden Kuyper was impressed by the theologian J. H. Scholten, who sought to pass the Reformed confessions through a modernist prism to make Calvinism a scientific system. Kuyper's later writings suggest that he was also reading closely in German Romantic literature and philosophy at this time. This reading was part of Kuyper's struggle with faith. According to the conversion narrative he published in *Confidentie* (*Confidentially*, 1873), he moved from ethical idealism late in his university years to a more heartfelt faith upon reading *The Heir of Redclyffe* (1853) by novelist Charlotte Yonge, a devotee of the Oxford Movement. His conclusive move to Calvinist orthodoxy followed in his first charge at Beesd (in the Betuwe region of Gelderland), where the fixed conviction of some of his more 'difficult' parishioners contrasted sharply with the drift of the modernists and moderates he knew. In *Calvin's strict principles, Kuyper said, he found 'that shelter in the rocks which, being founded on the rock and being hewn from the rock of thought, laughs at every storm'.

At Beesd Kuyper began to connect religion to politics, arguing for greater lay control of local church affairs and, by extension, for more democracy in civil politics. To him, broadening the franchise was advantageous to the church as well as just, since the common people were typically the more religiously orthodox. Kuyper's leadership won him quick promotion to Utrecht (1867–1870), but he broke with the dominant conservatism there by advocating a plural school system geared to the nation's religious diversity. The uniform system that conventional conservatives wanted to keep, Kuyper insisted, violated rights of conscience while watering down the Christianity it supposedly maintained. Kuyper's stance on education shortened his stay at Utrecht but attracted the attention of working- and lower-middle-class Calvinists in Amsterdam, where he was installed as pastor in 1870. There, in the national capital, Kuyper became a national leader. He used the Amsterdam church council to promote the orthodox cause across the country. Taking over a religious weekly, *De Heraut* (*The Herald*), in 1871 and the next year adding to it the daily *Standaard*, he found in them an ideal context for mixing his gifts as scholar and agitator. Through these papers he mobilized a national movement and conducted a Calvinist 'night school for the masses' on the issues of modern citizenship.

Kuyper's increasing political involvement won him election in 1874 to the Second Chamber (lower house) of the Dutch States General. His election forced him to resign from the active ministry, although he continued writing weekly theological and devotional columns in *De Heraut*. Meanwhile, he inherited a political cause lacking in organization, strategy and unified vision. He tried to remedy those deficiencies by his own labours, only to overtax them. For relief he got involved in the holiness movement arising out of the 1873–75 *Moody-*Sankey revival in Great Britain. Its gathering at Brighton in June 1875 impressed him with its promise of ecumenical unity and 'endowment with power', so Kuyper began promoting the 'higher life' back in the Netherlands. The additional work and, perhaps, the discordance between this and his political project brought him to complete collapse by February 1876. Kuyper spent the next fifteen months recuperating abroad. When he returned, he resigned his parliamentary seat and reaffirmed his commitment to more traditional Reformed theology. Brighton led on to the Keswick movement; Kuyper gave himself to organizing Neo-Calvinism.

Kuyper began by organizing a petition against a bill, which the Second Chamber passed in 1878, secularizing public education and pricing religiously based schools out of the market. Although the measure received royal approval anyway, the 300,000 signatures garnered in the campaign identified a considerable constituency with which Kuyper could work. Simultaneously, he published a complete political programme (*Ons Program*, 1879) and formed a central committee to link programme with people. Thus, in two years he constructed the Netherlands' first mass political organization, the Antirevolutionary Party (ARP). Kuyper moved similarly and simultaneously in the area of education, organizing the petition-signers into leagues to support a separate Christian school system and a Reformed university. When this, the

Free University, was opened in 1880, Kuyper had a complete political, educational and communications network that gave his movement a clear identity and formidable mobilization capacity.

In the 1880s Kuyper worked to deploy the movement's power, beginning with church reform. The bad habits of official privilege, he said, had led the NHK to forfeit its autonomy to the state, its authenticity to the shell of national unity, and its confessional integrity to the corruptions of liberalism. A 'free church', liberated from bureaucratic hierarchy, would remove the shelter heresy had found in it and release the long-suppressed energies of local congregations. But Kuyper's manoeuvring prompted sharp counter-measures from church officials and alienated those conservatives who remained loyal to the idea of a national church as they had to that of a unitary state school system. When Kuyper was officially disciplined in 1886, some 10% of the NHK followed him out of the church in *Doleantie*, 'mourning' and 'aggrieved by' its faithlessness. Six years later these dissidents joined with most descendants of an earlier (1834) secession from the NHK to form a new denomination, the *Gereformeerde Kerken in Nederland* (the Reformed Churches in the Netherlands), pledged to following the heritage of Dort in polity, liturgy and confession. This traditionalism notwithstanding, Kuyper's programme drew some new ecclesiological distinctions. Against the *volkskerk* and its cloying uniformity, he posited the normative 'pluriformity of the church'. But although the formal church 'institute' of confession, worship and administration was to be freed from the state's embrace, the church as 'organism' was to be engaged in everything. The body of believers, living out of the word in their vocations and daily life, would be a leaven in and a lighthouse to the nation.

The crucial sector on the latter front was politics, and there Kuyper achieved lasting success by a daring move. Recognizing that Roman Catholics held views closer to those of his followers than did liberal Protestants, Kuyper turned the knob of party divisions ninety degrees and created a 'monster alliance' between staunch Calvinists and their ancient enemy. With the Reformed supplying most of the captains and the Catholics most of the troops, the coalition achieved its first majority in the Mackay cabinet of 1888–1891, and its second in the government that Kuyper himself headed from 1901 to 1905. In between, however, Kuyper was embroiled in intra-party strife over the question of democratization. The Christian Social Congress he convened in 1891 signalled his own radicalism as he castigated the exploitation of the poor in the process of industrialization. The economic depression of the time gave Kuyper's words added bite, but he was speaking from principle and not just expediency. The prophets, apostles and Christ himself 'invariably [spoke out] *against* those who were powerful and living in luxury, and *for* the suffering and oppressed', he declared (*The Social Question and the Christian Faith*, 1891). Although Kuyper resisted increasing state controls in response to economic need, he favoured directly empowering the poor instead, by lowering property qualifications for the suffrage. The more conservative members of the ARP baulked at this proposal, but Kuyper outmanoeuvred them, precipitating their departure into a separate party, the Christian Historical Union. Yet Kuyper's cause prevailed, and after suffrage was granted to all adult males in 1917 (and to women in 1919), his original insight was vindicated: Dutch 'democracy' gave seats to the religious coalition in every cabinet until the 1990s.

The 'antirevolutionary' label of Kuyper's party needs explication. He did not think revolution was necessarily wrong to resist civil authority, secularize public life or promote participatory government; Calvinism had supported revolution in pursuit of all these goals, to its lasting glory. Rather, he objected to the principles behind the French Revolution: replacing divine ordinance with human will, substituting ideological schemes for patterns of historical development, vaunting individual self-interest over mutual obligation. The same principles defined the Dutch parties of his own day, Kuyper added. Socialists and radicals, liberals and conservatives largely advocated variations on the theme of human autonomy, each according to its social class. To identify with the conservatives, as his constituency was wont to do, was thus to back the order of privilege, not that of divine justice; and to opt for free-market individualism, as did the 'liberals' of his day, was to live by the French Revolution, now the establishment, but no better than it had been on the barricades. Kuyper countenanced temporary, strategic coalitions with one or another of these groups, but he wanted his party to be distinct from the secular spectrum and to develop its own consciousness from the principle of divine sovereignty as refracted through Scripture and history.

This principle required two kinds of legislation. First, given the drive of every modernizing nation-state towards cultural integration, Kuyper thought it important that culture-shaping institutions, especially the school and university, should give due space to religious conviction. Equitable public funding for separate educational systems would do this, he believed, without violating the state's proper confessional neutrality. If cultural diversity were promoted over uniformity in the process, so much the better. From the church's point of view the policy would give faith a strong public presence in the future, and so deserved top priority. Secondly, Kuyper deemed it vital for the general welfare that the atomizing effects of the 'revolution' (the industrial-capitalist revolution as well as the French) be countered by strengthening communities and social bonds. Stronger government could not strengthen them, for in Kuyper's view the state was an 'artificial' response to sin, good at restraining evil but constricting of social vitality. 'Society', on the other hand, was organic and would thrive spontaneously if only relieved of the hegemony of individualism and concentrations of wealth. Thus Kuyper sought to address the labour-capital conflict by having the former organized as fully as the latter, with compulsory arbitration to resolve differences that the two sides could not negotiate themselves. He proposed a household, rather than individual, franchise in civil elections, and representation in one house of the States General for corporate entities such as localities, occupations and interest groups. His ideal state was a supervisor called in to redress grievances between one community or 'sphere' and another.

Kuyper's political thinking grew out of a sociological, indeed ontological, theory he called 'Sphere Sovereignty' (1880). The term signified that God in creation had ordained distinct domains of being and action, each of which possessed a delegated sovereignty to ward off encroachment by others. The spheres would flourish harmoniously if each followed its own innate principle of development. This theory manifested Kuyper's pronounced concern with restoring the honour of creation in Reformed theology. Over against the spiritualizing tendencies of Reformed pietism, Kuyper reasserted the primacy of creation for theological thinking, the continuing worth of creation after the appearance of sin, and the renewal of creation as the goal of Christian living in this world and its promise for the next. Moreover, Kuyper highly esteemed human cultural development *in toto* and in all its variations as testimony to the enduring image and purposes of God. The entrance of sin into the world had wrought distortions in and among the spheres, but did not negate their original promise or reduce the believer's calling to show it forth. Christians were always to remember, as Kuyper's most famous dictum put it, that 'there is not a square inch in the whole domain of our human existence over which Christ, who is sovereign over *all*, does not cry: "Mine!"'

God's work in redemption, however, drew a sharp divide across this landscape. Rejecting the promise of humanistic progress found in liberal theologies, Kuyper said that those on either side of the line of divine election lived in 'antithesis', inevitably saw the powers of creation in a different light and used them to different ends. God's sovereignty in 'common grace' modulated this divide by upholding creation and endowing the non-elect with virtues, talents and wisdom. For Kuyper these were especially apparent in the arts and cultural development, and useful in enabling Christians to work with others towards some common goals. It was best, however, that each community or confessional 'sphere' live by its own convictions, build its own body of institutions, and work, especially in scholarship, to elaborate its own worldview. Modern religious pluralism could not stop short of the university, the press, the party or any context of human endeavour.

Kuyper's scholarship always fed off his activism, and his activism off his scholarship. This mutual inspiration was especially evident in the 1890s, when he reached the peak of his powers. The decade began with his declamation in favour of democracy at the Christian Social Congress in 1891 and ended with his elevation to the office of prime minister in 1901. In between he delivered two magisterial addresses on the state of European culture ('The Obliteration of the Boundaries', 1892; 'Evolution', 1899), published his three-volume *Encyclopedia of Sacred Theology* (1894), and delivered his *summa, Lectures on Calvinism*, at Princeton in 1898 as part of his triumphant tour of America. The last twenty years of his life, in contrast, illustrated the trials of answered prayer. Kuyper's term as prime minister was disrupted by a railway strike, and though he pushed through his educational programme, the second term he had planned for social legislation never materialized. The rising generation in the ARP took over its leadership, leaving him to write from the sidelines. Write he did, relinquishing his editorial posts only on his deathbed. Death found him (8 November 1920), like Calvin himself, regretting how much remained undone. But what Kuyper had done – the 223 titles from his pen, the newspapers, party, university and reformed church – created a movement that sought a way for Christianity in the modern world between establishment and privatization. A significant group of evangelical thinkers are convinced that this agenda continues to be relevant in a postmodern context.

Bibliography

J. Bolt, *A Free Church, a Holy Nation: Abraham Kuyper's American Public Theology* (Grand Rapids: Eerdmans, 2001); J. D. Bratt, *Abraham Kuyper: A Centennial Reader* (Grand Rapids & Carlisle: Eerdmans, 1998); P. S. Heslam, *Creating a Christian Worldview: Abraham Kuyper's Lectures on Calvinism* (Grand Rapids & Carlisle: Eerdmans, 1998).

J. D. BRATT

■ **LADD, George Eldon** (1911–1982), American biblical scholar, was born in Alberta, Canada, on 31 July 1911, and raised in New England. Ladd attended Plymouth High School in Plymouth, New Hampshire (1924–1927), and Kent's Hill School (also known as the Maine Wesleyan Seminary) in Kent's Hill, Maine (1927–1928). Ladd was converted to Christianity in 1929, after hearing a young woman graduate of Gordon College of Theology and Missions in Massachusetts preach in his Methodist church. After taking a Bachelor of Theology degree from Gordon College (1933), Ladd attended Gordon Divinity School, where he received a Bachelor of Divinity degree in 1942. After two years at Boston University, Ladd enrolled at Harvard, where he studied under Henry J. Cadbury and received a PhD in Biblical and Patristic Greek in 1949. In 1950 Ladd joined the faculty of Fuller Theological Seminary in Pasadena, California, where he spent the remaining thirty years of his career. He suffered a stroke in 1980, and died in 1982.

Ordained in the Northern Baptist Convention (now American Baptist) in 1933, Ladd was pastor of three congregations before moving to California. He served the First Free Baptist in Gilford, New Hampshire (1934–1936), the First Baptist Church of Montpelier, Vermont (1936–1942), and Blaney Memorial Baptist Church in Dorcester, Massachusetts (1942–1945). While at Blaney Memorial, Ladd taught at both Gordon College and the Divinity School, rising to the rank of professor in 1949.

Ladd was one of the remarkable group of conservative evangelical scholars who rejected strict separatism and trained at elite American universities in the 1940s. Other members of this group, which included Carl F. H. *Henry, Kenneth *Kantzer, Edward John *Carnell, Glenn Barker, Bernard *Ramm and Paul King Jewett, became leaders in the resurgent evangelicalism of the post-war era, and were influential in the rise of the National Association of Evangelicals (NAE), Fuller Theological Seminary and Christianity Today. Ladd brought to this movement an intense desire for scholarly respectability in the broader academic world. This quest for credibility was an important theme in his life and work.

During the 1950s, Ladd focused his energies on correcting the hermeneutical excesses of dispensational premillennialism, the dominant theological system among American evangelicals and fundamentalists. Ladd learned dispensationalism in his first years as a Christian and at Gordon College, but his training at Harvard forced him to reexamine his beliefs. In his Crucial Questions

about the Kingdom of God (1952) and The Blessed Hope (1956), Ladd challenged the biblical basis for the interpretative framework of dispensationalism. Ladd's critique, unlike attacks from outside the evangelical camp, affirmed the supernatural character of the Bible and championed a classic form of premillennialism. Ladd argued that while dispensationalism had elements which were persuasive, only the true teaching of the Word of God could be the final authority. In 1958 Ladd published The Gospel of the Kingdom, an exposition of the biblical texts related to the kingdom of God, and a challenge to evangelicals to limit their understanding of this doctrine to the boundaries set in the biblical record. Ladd thus established himself at this stage of his career as a trusted, faithful defender of conservative belief, especially in the area of eschatology, even as he sought to correct crucial components of that belief.

In the early 1960s Ladd turned his attention to the influence of modern historical thought on evangelical theology. While other American theological traditions confronted the rise of historical consciousness at the turn of the twentieth century, many American conservative evangelicals simply denied its significance to the theological enterprise. Ladd sought to fill this gap by entering into the critical discussion of the historical nature of the resurrection of Jesus, which he did in a series of articles in 1962–1963. Ladd used the technical terms of historical interpretation to argue that the modern mind was not necessarily compelled to reject the historicity of the resurrection. He argued that the self-imposed limits of Historie, or scientifically proveable facts of history, by definition made it impossible to disprove the resurrection, which clearly found its full expression in the realm of Geschichte, or interpretations of historical events. Ladd's third way was not widely accepted, and exposed him to attacks from conservative scholars, who believed he had given up too much in his attempt to make the resurrection acceptable to modern scholars.

Ladd was also one of the first American evangelical scholars to engage critically the work of Rudolf Bultmann. In three articles and one short book, Ladd challenged Bultmann's unwillingness to allow for the possibility of God's intervention in historical processes. But Ladd's was not the shrill attack of a militant fundamentalist. Ladd recognized that Bultmann's influence was a direct result of the quality of his work and his willingness to wrestle with the issues raised at the intersection of faith and modernity. Evangelicals, according to Ladd, might match Bultmann's influence if they showed his diligence and passion for excellence in their work.

To that end, Ladd published *Jesus and the Kingdom* (1964), his long-awaited *magnum opus*, which he hoped would finally earn a measure of scholarly credibility both for him and for evangelical thought. Ladd went to great lengths to place this work before a broader audience, leaving Eerdmans, an evangelical publishing house, in favour of Harper and Row. The response was devastating. While most of the notices were generally positive, Norman Perrin (1920–1976), a British New Testament scholar, wrote a scathing review which was published in the biblical theology journal *Interpretation*. Particularly humiliating for Ladd was the fact that *Interpretation* represented the audience whose approval Ladd most craved. Perrin's criticisms, furthermore, attacked Ladd precisely at the point on which he was most vulnerable: his obsessive need for credibility, and his resulting tendency to align his views with convenient excerpts from better-known scholars. Ladd's response was to abandon his lifelong quest for scholarly credibility in the broader academy, and focus primarily on his evangelical audience.

In the late 1960s and 1970s Ladd continued to build his reputation as the dominant figure in evangelical New Testament studies. With *The New Testament and Criticism* (1967), Ladd introduced modern critical methods for studying the Bible to a conservative audience. Ladd's interest in eschatology also remained an important part of his work, and in 1972 he published *A Commentary on the Book of Revelation*, followed in 1974 by *The Presence of the Future* (a revision of *Jesus and the Kingdom*), and *The Last Things: An Eschatology for Laymen* (1978). Ladd's most influential book was his magisterial *Theology of the New Testament* (1974), a major work of evangelical scholarship, which was revised and reissued in 1993.

George Eldon Ladd was arguably the most important New Testament scholar of the post-war evangelical resurgence in North America. He engaged the major exegetical and theological issues of his day, while influencing generations of evangelical pastors and missionaries who trained at Fuller Seminary during his tenure. Ladd opened the door for evangelical scholars to use the critical methods of biblical research, making the credibility he desired possible for those who came after him. Ladd's standing among evangelical scholars was demonstrated by Mark Noll in his *Between Faith and Criticism* (1986); in a survey Ladd was placed second in influence behind only John *Calvin.

Bibliography

J. Carpenter, *Revive Us Again: The Reawakening of American Fundamentalism* (New York: Oxford University Press, 1997); G. Marsden, *Reforming Fundamentalism: Fuller Seminary and the New Evangelicalism* (Grand Rapids: Eerdmans, 1987); M. Noll, *Between Faith and Criticism: Evangelicals, Scholarship, and the Bible in America* (New York: Harper and Row, 1986).

J. A. D'ELIA

■ **LaHAYE, Tim F.** (1926–) and **Beverly Jean (née Davenport Ratcliffe)** (1929–), American leaders of the New Christian Right, have spent their lives campaigning for traditional nuclear families, though neither was raised in a two-parent household, having both experienced the death of a father at an early age. Tim LaHaye was born on 27 April 1926 in Detroit, Michigan, to Francis T. and Margaret LaHaye. When Tim was nine years old, his father, an electrician, died of a heart attack, forcing Tim, his mother, his five-year-old sister and his seven-week-old brother to live with relatives. His mother took a series of jobs to support her children while spending nine years completing a degree at Detroit Bible College. Tim's mother served as fellowship director at the family's Baptist church and his uncle was a Baptist preacher, resulting in a strongly evangelical home environment. Tim received scholarships to attend a church camp in Brighton, Michigan, by winning Scripture memorization contests at his Sunday school. Since he disliked secondary school, Tim instead attended evening classes until he graduated at the age of seventeen. From 1944 to 1946, he served in the US Air

Force, in which he attained the rank of sergeant. In 1946 he began to study for the ministry at Bob Jones University, a staunchly fundamentalist school in Greenville, South Carolina, where he met and married Beverly Davenport within a year.

Beverly Davenport was born on 30 April 1929, in a rural suburb of Detroit. Her father died suddenly when she was two years old, leaving the family so destitute that Beverly, her four-year-old sister Barrie and her mother were forced to move in with a kindly couple who had been their neighbours. Her mother worked at the Michigan telephone company in order to support her daughters. When Beverly was four, her mother married a forty-year-old bachelor who lived only a block away. After her mother became temporarily bedridden due to heart problems and a nervous breakdown, Beverly took time off from school to care for her and to run the household. Although her parents were not particularly religious, they began attending a missions-oriented church in Highland Park, Michigan, when Beverly was in secondary school. At the age of fourteen, Beverly decided to become a missionary. When she was eighteen, she left home for the first time in order to study at Bob Jones University. She struck up a friendship with Tim LaHaye soon after arriving there, and they were married at the end of their first year on 5 July 1947.

In 1948, during their second year of college, Tim accepted a pastorate at a country Baptist church in Pumpkintown, South Carolina. Beverly dropped out of college when she gave birth to their daughter Linda. After Tim received his bachelor's degree in 1950, the LaHaye family moved to Minneapolis, Minnesota, where Tim pastored a Baptist church for the next six years. During this period, Beverly gave birth to two sons, Larry and Lee. The entire family moved to California in 1956, when Tim assumed the senior pastorate of the Scott Memorial Baptist Church in El Cajon, a position that he would hold for the next twenty-five years. Two years later, the couple's last child, a daughter named Lori, was born.

Within a year of their arrival in California, the LaHayes began a weekly thirty-minute television programme called *The LaHayes on Family Life* that continued until 1959. Although this programme focused on marriage and family ministry, Tim LaHaye has described the couple's marriage during this period as 'going downhill'. Since they did not believe in divorce, the couple decided to make the best of their situation. Their marriage was unexpectedly revitalized in the mid-1960s under the influence of a Christian counsellor named Henry Brandt. The LaHayes distilled what they had learned into a series of Family Life Seminars, which they began offering in 1972 and presented more than 450 times in over forty countries during the next two decades.

Frustrated with the increasing secularism of the state school system, Tim LaHaye founded the Christian High School of San Diego in 1965. He later expanded it into the Christian United School System, consisting of a primary school and two secondary schools. Christian Heritage College was added in 1970 with the help of Henry M. *Morris, a leading creationist. In addition, LaHaye and Morris created the Creation Science Research Center in 1970 and the Institute for Creation Research (the most prominent creationist organization) in 1972. Feeling a need to bolster his academic credibility, Tim completed a doctorate in ministry at Western Conservative Baptist Seminary (Portland, Oregon) in 1977.

The LaHayes authored a series of popular psychology books that characterized individuals according to Hippocrates' four basic temperaments. The first, *Spirit-Controlled Temperament* (1966), was written by Tim and sold more than half a million copies in the decade after it was published. Although the LaHayes opposed sex education classes in state schools, the couple wrote many books addressing sexuality within marriage including *The Act of Marriage* (1976), an explicit sex manual that sold in the millions. Other books written by the LaHayes focused on such topics as prophecy, Bible study and women's issues.

Starting in the 1970s, the LaHayes were instrumental in creating the New Christian Right as a movement in opposition to abortion, feminism, homosexuality, pornography and the prohibition of prayer in state schools. In his manifesto for the Christian Right, *The Battle for the Mind* (1980), Tim argued that America's rejection of traditional morality could be traced to a single enemy, an atheistic worldview that he called 'secular humanism'. The skirmishes against this mindset continued with *The Battle for the Family* (1982) and *The Battle for the Public Schools* (1983).

Beverly launched Concerned Women for America in 1979 in order to counter feminists who claimed to speak for all women. This organization not only mobilized conservative women into a nationwide prayer network, but also lobbied actively for conservative causes. The organization claimed the allegiance of more than half a million individuals by 1984, declaring itself 'the nation's largest public policy women's organization'. Tim campaigned for 'traditional values' through involvement with the Moral Majority and by founding the Council for National Policy in 1981 and the American Coalition for Traditional Values in 1984. The couple moved to Washington DC in 1984 in order better to promote their views. Tim LaHaye's willingness to go beyond his evangelical base in mobilizing conservatives attracted criticism from evangelicals in the mid-1980s, when it was learned that he had accepted large amounts of money from Sun Myung Moon's Unification Church.

During the 1990s, the LaHayes continued to promote their conservative social agenda to millions of evangelicals through both radio and television programmes, including *Beverly LaHaye Live*, *Beverly LaHaye Today*, *Tim LaHaye's Capitol Report* and a revived version of *The LaHayes on Family Life*. In 1995, Tim LaHaye along with prolific evangelical author Jerry B. Jenkins, began producing the *Left Behind* series of premillennialist apocalyptic novels. This highly successful series sold more than thirty million copies by the end of the century, and the seventh and eighth of twelve projected volumes topped all major best-seller lists in 2000.

Bibliography

A. E. Christiansen and J. McGee, 'Beverly Davenport LaHaye', in K. Kohrs Campbell (ed.), *Women Public Speakers in the United States, 1925–1993: A Bio-Critical Sourcebook* (Westport, Connecticut and London: Greenwood Press, 1994), pp. 146–160; D. Garrison, 'Tim and Beverly LaHaye', in C. H. Lippy (ed.), *Twentieth-Century Shapers of American Popular Religion* (New York, Westport, Connecticut and London: Greenwood Press, 1989), pp. 233–240; R. Bush (ed.), 'Reflections on 50 Golden Years: July 5, 1947–July 5, 1997', *Family Voice* (6 June, 1997).

D. K. LARSEN

■ **LANG, John Dunmore** (1799–1878), Presbyterian minister, politician, educationalist and propagandist, was born in Greenock, Scotland. A centre of the rising world shipping trade, Greenock was pastoral enough to give Lang a lasting desire to recreate its agricultural virtues, which he saw as 'next to godliness', in the societies he influenced. It was also not far from Edinburgh, so Lang grew up in the midst of tensions between rationality and romanticism, ritualism and evangelicalism, republicanism and imperialism and the love of God and the love of money. Each of these contributed to the complex character that was so to exasperate conventional opinion in the colony of New South Wales (NSW). Lang idolized and 'rather feared' his domineering, church-going mother. Her influence inclined him to Calvinism, though his temperament and aspirations also made him pragmatic. His mother's emphasis on vocation made him certain of his special calling to the colonies.

Lang was affected by Enlightenment Scottish education in two important ways: through his reading of the classics, and through his pride at being a 'University-bred man'. His training in the classics and at the University of Glasgow helped to create in his mind a conception of himself as a writer, driving him to become an energetic propagandist throughout his life. At Glasgow, Lang was infuenced by the strongly evangelical Stevenson Magill and Thomas *Chalmers. Magill's example pointed to the identity of life and belief, and that of Chalmers to the unity of belief and action. Their influence explains, at least in part, the interpenetration of politics, theology and life in general in Lang's eventful career. Glasgow also made him fervently anti-Catholic, suspicious of Irish immigration and healthily respectful of self-help. By the time that Lang came to Australia, then, the basic elements of his social ideas were already in formation. Lang was licensed by the Church of Scotland presbytery of Irvine on 1 June 1820.

In 1823 Lang followed his brother's advice by emigrating to the colonies, away from a hidebound Scotland that offered little in the way of clerical advancement. He was later to claim to have come 'from decent people', like St Patrick, and to have struck out a path for himself, like St Paul. The Pauline aspect of his 'mission' was particularly pronounced in his writings, and the migration to NSW was his effort 'to follow the example of the great apostle of the Gentiles'. On the one hand, he was a religious man filled with 'the faith of his fathers' (or, at least, of his mother). He had a belief based on the Scriptures, a life shaped according to the theological goals of his Presbyterian education, and a sense of 'calling' to do great things. He believed that God's hand moved in history, stamping the same predestination upon its course as upon individual lives. The assurance of his own 'rightness' and 'righteousness' that this conviction gave Lang also made him a bigot, intolerant, ambitious and proud. Viewing himself as a saint on the Pauline model, he was also later to consider himself a martyr to the machinations of this world. Suitably, this 'martyr' image was matched by an idiosyncratic millenarianism. Combined with a naturally overbearing character, this conviction often burst forth in vitriolic declamation against the moral character of the age, and apocalyptic predictions of the fate reserved for his enemies. He was, not surprisingly, gaoled a number of times for libel.

While rigid in his beliefs, Lang was not 'other worldly' in action. At one time or another, he involved himself in almost every contemporary debate, in consequence of his early and developing involvement in colonial life. He arrived early in the 1820s, and his clerical position immediately catapulted him into politics; the central authority of the governor made all life political. At first, Lang fought for grants to build his church, and then for salaries and extra ministers. Even at this stage, his methods were overly abrupt and questionable. In a short time, he alienated the governor, Sir Thomas Brisbane, and drew upon himself charges of, at best, 'lack of scruple' and at worst, 'fraud'. For some time, his activities remained largely pastoral. As the debate over colonial schools intensified, however, Lang was led through his typically Presbyterian concern for education into

standing for the Legislative Council. During a long life, he supported the separation of Victoria and Queensland (successfully), immigration from the Protestant areas of Britain (as opposed to that of Irish Catholics), radical reform on the American model and numerous education schemes, including the separation of church and state in the establishment of church schools. The first Presbyterian minister on the mainland of Australia, he was personally responsible for the immigration of most of the Presbyterian ministers who came to NSW between 1824 and 1840, many of whom he brought out to teach in his Australian College, a school he eventually hoped would grow into a tertiary institution. Built by funds and labour Lang himself had imported, the college was intended by him to serve Presbyterians and colonists alike. It did well throughout the 1830s, but his neglect of its affairs allowed it to slip into decay, and it closed in 1854. He managed to antagonize many of those he imported to establish the church, featuring in a number of well-publicized rifts with his church from 1837 to 1865, over issues as wide ranging as moderatism, immorality and drunkenness in the clergy, property rights over Scots Church, Sydney, and the building of the Presbyterian College, St Andrews, at the University of Sydney. An active lobbyist at Whitehall, his failure to achieve the colonial church's independence from the Church of Scotland led him to travel through the United States and return to NSW championing the cause of voluntarism in religion and education. He naturally supported the Disruption of the Scottish church under his old mentor Thomas Chalmers.

Lang founded and produced three newspapers, *The Colonist* (1835–1840), *The Colonial Observer* (1841–1844) and *The Press* (1851), all of which he used to attack his enemies in politics and presbytery. He was a prolific writer, though seldom producing anything of high literary value among the some 13,000 pages of material he published, much of it repetitive and ill-organized.

Lang retired from active ministry in his church in 1872, his congregation giving him a pension on the basis of his promise not to become involved further in the management of the church. When his successor, Gilchrist, resigned in May 1877, Lang declared himself sole pastor. Members of the congregation locked him out, forcing him to gain entry with the services of a builder and several constables. The incident well summed up his life; legally he won, but in the process caused so much disruption and opposition that the victory turned out to be pyrrhic. Lang died at his home of apoplexy and was interred at Devonshire Street Cemetery. Historians have remained divided as to his importance, with some suggesting he was the most important public figure of his time, and others that he was little more than an historical irritant. He was, however, undeniably an important figure in the development of Australian Christianity, politics and social life.

Bibliography

D. W. A. Baker, *Days of Wrath: A Life of John Dunmore Lang* (Carlton, Vic.: Melbourne University Press, 1985); K. Elford, 'The Theology of Clerical Participation: John Dunmore Lang and Direct Clerical Participation in Politics', *Journal of Religious History*, 5 (1969); K. Elford, 'A Prophet Without Honour: The Political Ideals of John Dunmore Lang', *JRAHS*, 54.

M. HUTCHINSON

■ **LATIMER, Hugh** (c. 1485–1555), Bishop of Worcester, English Reformer and preacher, is perhaps most famous for his death at the stake in 1555 during the reign of Mary I. He was born around 1485 in Thurcaston, Leicestershire, the son of a yeoman-farmer, also named Hugh Latimer. He entered Clare Hall, Cambridge (now Clare College) in 1506 and received a BA in 1510, being elected to a fellowship at Clare that same year. In 1514 Latimer received an MA, and soon thereafter he was ordained priest in Lincoln.

As late as 1524, in his public oration for his BD, Latimer was staunchly opposing the supposed errors of Philip *Melanchthon and adhering to Catholic orthodoxy. However, by 1525 he was taking an increasing interest in evangelical faith, probably due to the influence of Thomas Bilney, whose intimate friend he remained. In 1525 he was brought to Thomas Wolsey, the papal legate, charged with Lutheran sympathies. Latimer denied the charges, and his licence to preach was renewed by the cardinal.

In February 1530 Latimer was selected as a representative of the University of Cambridge to study the Scriptures, canon law and patristic testimony and to determine a theological rationale for Henry VIII's annulment of his marriage to Catherine of Aragon and legitimation of his marriage to Anne Boleyn. He was known to be supportive of the king. On 13 March 1530 Latimer preached his first court sermon before Henry. Having won the king's admiration, Latimer was chosen in the same year as one of twenty-four divines from Cambridge and Oxford appointed to examine books allegedly propagating objectionable opinions. In 1530 Latimer received his first benefice, as Rector of West Kington, Wiltshire, which was offered to him by the king at the suggestion of Thomas Cromwell.

Despite a few strident complaints about his denunciatory preaching against 'all popes, bishops, and rectors who enter not by the door', and his subsequent appearance before the Bishop of London and convocation on 11 March 1532, Latimer continued his rise through the ecclesiastical ranks. During Lent 1534, he was given the privilege of preaching before Henry every Wednesday, and soon thereafter was made a royal chaplain. *Cranmer, now Archbishop of Canterbury, entrusted to Latimer in 1534 the authority to withdraw preaching licenses from non-preaching and negligent incumbents. Latimer's steady rise culminated in his appointment to the see of Worcester in September 1535. In 1539 the reversal of Henry's ecclesiastical policy resulted in the Act of the Six Articles, which affirmed transubstantiation, auricular confession, legitimacy of private masses, clerical celibacy, communion in one kind and the lawfulness of monastic vows. This conservative reaction, following the fall of Anne Boleyn in 1536, prompted Latimer to resign his bishopric on 1 July 1539.

Shortly after Latimer's resignation, Henry VIII ordered him to be held in the custody of Sampson, the Bishop of Chichester. In July 1540 he was set free, only to see his patron Cromwell sent to the block and his old evangelical friend Robert Barnes burned at the stake. He was ordered to move out of London, not to visit Oxford, Cambridge or Worcester, his old diocese, and to stop preaching. Not much is known about Latimer's life between 1540 and 1546.

When Edward VI succeeded to the throne in January 1547, Latimer was invited to reclaim the see of Worcester, but he declined it and chose rather to labour among people of the lower and disenfranchised class. He lived with Cranmer at Lambeth Palace and assisted him in reforming ecclesiastical law, in repressing heresy, in ensuring and enforcing the widespread use of the Edwardian Prayer Books and by preaching twice every Sunday, often before Edward. In these various ways he influenced the course of the Reformation in England. However, with the death of Edward, the so-called 'second Josiah', that Reformation came to an abrupt halt.

No sooner had Mary succeeded to the throne after Edward's premature death in July 1553 than Latimer was summoned before the Council, and on 13 September 1553 he was sent to the Tower of London. Subsequently Latimer was transferred to Oxford and imprisoned with Thomas Cranmer, Nicholas *Ridley and John Bradford. In April 1554 Cranmer, Ridley and Latimer held disputations with the commissioners from Convocation on transubstantiation and the sacrifice of the mass. On 28 September 1555 the commissioners examined the three men, excommunicated them as heretics and handed them over to the secular arm.

On 30 September 1555 Latimer, along with Ridley, was brought before three bishops at the divinity school, who demanded his recantation. Latimer did not yield under pressure, but pledged his allegiance to the true church catholic, in which, he declared, Rome had no share. On 16 October 1555 Latimer and Ridley were burned at the stake in front of Balliol College in Oxford. As the fire was lit and laid at Ridley's feet, Latimer is said to have encouraged his colleague with these memorable words: 'Be of good comfort, Master Ridley, and play the man; we shall this day light such a candle, by God's grace, in England, as I trust shall never be put out.'

Latimer's seven Lenten sermons before Edward VI were published as a collection in 1549, and other sermons were published in 1548, 1550 and posthumously in 1562 and 1571. In his Edwardian sermons he vigorously attacked the numerous wealthy landlords who had dispossessed tenant farmers, called for equitable stewardship and criticized the remnants of Catholic faith and practice in England. 'The Sermon of the Plough' is perhaps the best known of these sermons and typifies the evangelical fervour and spirit with which Latimer propagated the Reformation faith.

Bibliography

A. G. Chester (ed.), *Selected Sermons of Hugh Latimer* (Charlottesville: University of Virginia Press, 1968); G. E. Corrie (ed.), *The Works of Hugh Latimer* (Cambridge: Cambridge University Press, 1844–1845; repr. New York, 1968); D. Loades, *The Oxford Martyrs* (New York: Stein & Day, 1970).

P. C-H. LIM

■ **LAWS, Curtis Lee** (1868–1946), pastor and editor, was an active Baptist fundamentalist. Laws was born on 14 July 1868 in Aldie, Loudoun County, Virginia. His parents were John T. Laws and Laura J. Nixon. He received his early education at Dale Academy and Richmond College in Virginia, from which he received the BA degree in 1890. Laws then attended Crozier Theological Seminary in Chester, Pennsylvania, graduating in 1893. During this time the Crozier faculty was moving towards modernist approaches to biblical and theological studies, and Laws opposed these changes. His pastoral ministry began in the Northern Baptist Convention as pastor of the First Baptist Church, Baltimore, Maryland, a position he held for fifteen years. In 1908 he moved to Brooklyn, New York as pastor of the Greene Avenue Baptist Church. Five years later, in 1913, Laws became editor of *The Watchman-Examiner*, a combination of two Baptist periodicals, *The Watchman* and *The Examiner*. The journal published articles on Scripture and theology and was widely read by Baptists and other conservatives. Laws remained editor until his retirement in 1938. He married Grace Burnett on 25 April 1894. After her death he married Susan Bancroft Tyler on 14 February 1922.

As an editor, Laws expressed his concern about the rising tide of liberalism he observed in the Northern Baptist Convention. In 1917 he began to address doctrinal divisions among Baptists and other denominations through a series of articles that contrasted the 'Old and New Theologies'. He soon brought together a group of Baptist clergy and laity, including Earle V. Pierce and the Baptist missionary leader Lucy W. Peabody, who agreed to oppose what they believed to be their denomination's acceptance of liberal theology. In 1920 the group united with the conservative Texas pastor J. Frank Norris and the northerner William Bell *Riley to organize the Buffalo (New York) Conference on Fundamentals, a group of conservatives within the Northern Baptist Convention. Laws believed that the conference would allow conservatives to attack liberalism within the convention while remaining within it themselves. Also in 1920, in an article in *The Watchman-Examiner*, he became the first to use the word 'fundamentalist' to describe those whose response to modernism was based on commitment to the fundamentals of the faith. He wrote: 'We suggest that those who still cling to the great fundamentals and who mean to do battle royal for the fundamentals shall be called "Fundamentalists".' Throughout the fundamentalist/modernist debates Laws encouraged the Convention to affirm conservative positions while encouraging fundamentalists to remain in the denomination. He wrote that *The Watchman-Examiner* would 'not seek to be neutral. It stands frankly, openly, earnestly but good-naturedly for the conservative position.'

A thoroughgoing conservative, he none the less eschewed debates over premillennialism and the insistence of some fundamentalists that orthodoxy was dependent on one's theory of Christ's return. He welcomed people of different millennial perspectives to the movement as long as they were traditionally orthodox on such issues as the virgin birth of Christ and Christ's sacrificial atonement. Like Princeton theologians, he insisted that the truths presented in the Bible could be discerned by common sense. He declared that, 'The infallibility of the Bible is the infallibility of common sense, and of the experimental triumph within us.' The Bible's objective reality was confirmed by the power of inner experience. Laws' concern for confessional orthodoxy led him to support the founding of Eastern Baptist Theological Seminary in Philadelphia and the Association of Baptists for World Evangelism. He served on the board of trustees of several evangelical seminaries, including Eastern Baptist

Seminary and Gordon College. He was also a board member of the American Tract Society and the American Bible Society. Through *The Watchman-Examiner*, Laws responded to many of the great events of his times. In 1917, as the United States prepared to enter the First World War, Laws affirmed the importance of advocating peace, but he agreed with President Woodrow Wilson that the nation was forced to prepare for war. Laws firmly supported the war effort, but sought to avoid the extreme anti-German rhetoric of some other religious leaders.

Laws wrote numerous pamphlets including *Baptist, Why and Why Not* (1904), *The Fiery Furnace: Present Struggles of the Non-Conformists in England for Religious Liberty* (1904) and *Who and What Are the Christian Scientists?* (1899). Laws died 7 July 1946 in New York.

Bibliography

W. Brackney, *The Baptists* (New York & London: Greenwood, 1988); J. W. Bradbury, 'Curtis Lee Laws, D.D., LL.D.', *The Watchman-Examiner* (18 July 1946); G. M. Marsden, *Fundamentalism and American Culture* (New York: Oxford University Press, 1980).

B. J. LEONARD

■ **LINDSELL, Harold** (1913–1998), ordained Southern Baptist author, editor and educator, is most readily identified as the 'defender of the Bible'. A friend and colleague of evangelical 'giants' such as Carl F. H. *Henry and Billy *Graham, and author of over twenty books and numerous articles, Lindsell played a crucial role in the development of the new evangelicalism of the 1950s and 1960s, as well as in the conservative reaction to modern historical criticism in the 1970s and 1980s.

Lindsell was born on 22 December 1913 in his parents' apartment in the Bronx, New York City. His parents, Leonard Anthony and Ella Briggs (née Harris), were active and pious Presbyterians who sought to raise their three children in the Christian faith. Harold was a sickly child, but with the special encouragement and attention of his mother, along with her high expectations, he quickly excelled at reading and at school.

After omitting two grades, and graduating from high school at the age of sixteen, he learned his excellent administrative skills at a local business office. These skills would be evident throughout the course of his life and ministry.

At the age of twenty-one Lindsell left the business, where he had worked his way up from 'office boy' to office manager, in order to attend college. He obtained a BS at Wheaton College (1938), an MA at the University of California, Berkeley (1939), a PhD in history from New York University (1942) and an honorary DD from Fuller Theological Seminary in Pasedena (1964). His first teaching position was at Columbia Bible College (now Columbia International University) from 1942. It was here that he met his future wife Marion Bolinder. He also taught at Northern Baptist Seminary before joining the Fuller faculty in 1947.

Under the presidency of Harold John *Ockenga, Lindsell served as one of the founding faculty members of Fuller, along with Wilbur M. Smith, Everett F. Harrison and Carl Henry (his friend, whom he met at Wheaton College). He taught courses on missions and the history of Christianity, and was also registrar. He later became dean and vice-president of Fuller, and remained on the faculty until 1964. At Fuller he was supportive of attempts to forge a new evangelicalism, one that avoided the pitfalls of the American fundamentalist movement since the early part of the century. He was not supportive, however, of the desire to include within the definition of an evangelical one who held to what he perceived to be a diminished view of inerrancy. In 1964, when the faculty of Fuller was in turmoil over its statement of faith regarding the inerrancy of the Bible, Lindsell, concerned that the school was drifting from its traditional statement of faith, left to become associate editor of *Christianity Today*. He resigned from *Christianity Today* in 1967 in order to teach the Bible at Wheaton College, only to rejoin it as editor in 1968. He remained with the magazine until his retirement in 1978, and in the same year he was appointed editor emeritus.

Lindsell's most famous work, *The Battle for the Bible* (1976), was a call to arms over the issue of inerrancy. His concern was not the decline of belief in inerrancy in the mainstream or liberal churches, but the infiltration of anti-inerrancy views into the evangelical camp. He was convinced that evangelical educational institutions, denominations and organizations were departing from their original view of inerrancy. To support his claim that there was a 'widespread' move away from the doctrine, Lindsell gave various examples from the Lutheran Church, Missouri Synod, Fuller Theological Seminary and the Southern Baptist Convention, as well as from other evangelical colleges, publishing houses and individuals. In all these cases, he argued, there was the beginning of a move away from a view of Scripture that evangelicals had always held to be true. His conviction was that a departure from inerrancy would 'lead to disaster'. He wrote that abandoning inerrancy would bring about a 'loss of missionary outreach; it will quench missionary passion; it will lull congregations to sleep and undermine their belief in the full-orbed truth of the Bible; it will produce spiritual sloth and decay; and it will finally lead to apostasy.'

Lindsell used the terms 'infallible' and 'inerrant' interchangeably, and he used them to mean that 'the Bible [was] free from error in the whole and in the part'. His understanding of inerrancy was based primarily on his understanding of revelation. Lindsell argued that since the life, death and resurrection of Jesus, special revelation, that is, God's disclosure of his redemptive plan, had become 'inscripturated'. Consequently, there were two Words of God; the Word of God incarnate (Jesus Christ) and the Word of God written (the Bible). Just as Jesus was divine and human, so was the Bible. Just as Jesus was the Word of God, so was the Bible.

The way in which the Bible had become the Word of God was through the inspiration of the Holy Spirit upon and in the writers. Ascribing inerrancy only to the original autographs, Lindsell claimed that the process of inspiration ensured that the Bible was without error in any way. To deny this claim, he felt, was to deny the Bible's own teaching on its inspiration, and to erode the Christian's only sure foundation for religious knowledge.

In proclaiming his view of inspiration, Lindsell believed that he was being faithful to the historic position of the church. Only in the nineteenth and twentieth centuries, he wrote, with the rise of the historical-critical method, did the church stray from its long-held views on inerrancy. And it was only in the past few decades, he felt, that anti-inerrancy views had begun to spread within evangelicalism. His *The Bible in the Balance* (1979), written in response to his critics, further developed his original thesis that the spread of such views would ultimately lead to apostasy. In the years that followed, Lindsell actively championed the cause of inerrancy through his writing, speaking and service on committees. For example, during the discussion surrounding New Testament Professor J. Ramsey Michaels' *Servant and the Son*, Lindsell was the chair of the executive committee of Gordon-Conwell Theological Seminary that 'asked President Robert Cooley to begin a process to examine Michaels' writings on the Bible and to recommend action.'

Although many supported Lindsell's thesis, some of his closest friends and co-workers, such as Carl Henry, were critical of parts of his thesis and methodology. Attempting to form a broader conservative witness that avoided the pitfalls of fundamentalism, Henry felt that Lindsell's making of inerrancy a test of 'evangelical *authenticity*' was harmful. Henry claimed that it would 'sacrifice the enthusiasm and cooperation of one whole wing of the conservative theological witness today, precisely at a time when we need all the energies we can enlist in the battle'.

Although Lindsell's call to arms over the issue of inerrancy in the evangelical churches led to considerable debate in the church, especially in the Southern Baptist Convention, his writings addressed a wide variety of issues of major concern for both evangelicals and fundamentalists. He was concerned with the erosion of traditional Judeo-Christian values and influence, and with the growing influence of Roman Catholicism, warned against the communist threat from the Soviet Union and defended free enterprise. He also wrote on prayer (*When You Pray*, 1969), the Holy Spirit (*The Holy Spirit in the Latter Days*, 1983), discipleship (*The World, the Flesh, and the Devil*, 1973), missions (*A Christian Philosophy of Missions*, 1949; *An Evangelical Theology of Missions*, 1970) and eschatology (*The Gathering Storm*, 1980).

Lindsell was appreciated by many for his editing of the popular *Harper Study Bible* (1964, 1985) and the *Lindsell Study Bible* (1980). Both these works sold widely, and, part of Lindsell's impact in the 1970s was due to the popularity he had already achieved through the publication of the *Harper Study Bible* in 1964. A popular public speaker, Lindsell preached in churches within and outside the Southern Baptist Convention throughout his life. His constant contact with parishioners in the evangelical and fundamentalist community also contributed to his influence.

After a long illness, Lindsell died at the age of eighty-four on 15 January 1998, in Lake Forest, California. He was survived by his wife and four children.

G. L. HEATH

■ **LINDSEY, Hal** (1929–), author of best-selling prophecy books, was born in Houston, Texas, on 23 November 1929 to parents who were not especially religious. His mother occasionally went to church and took her son with her. At the age of twelve, Lindsey made his first religious commitment by responding to a church altar call. Although he joined the church and was baptized, Lindsey afterwards felt that he still did not know God. At the age of fifteen, while experiencing adolescent conflicts in his home and personal life, Lindsey again responded to an altar call, at a different church. He joined this church and was baptized a second time, but later said he felt 'no new reality of Jesus'. Moreover, his church's restrictions on sex, drinking, smoking and films began to make him feel that he had 'all the liabilities and none of the assets of this business of being a Christian'. At seventeen, he responded for a third time to an altar call at a new church and was baptized, but still he did not attain the religious experience he was seeking, so he decided to live his life his own way and 'started in big with booze and sex'.

He entered the University of Houston to study business but instead lived hedonistically. His poor academic standing made him eligible for enlistment for the Korean War, so he left the university after two years to enrol in the US Coast Guard. After a year of training in Connecticut, Lindsey was stationed for two years in New Orleans. After his discharge, he worked as a tugboat captain on the Mississippi River for almost four years. He married, but his wife soon left him for someone else. A narrow escape from a tugboat accident sent Lindsey back to the Bible to search for meaning in life. While reading a Gideon New Testament, Lindsey became convinced of his need to be born again. He followed the directions at the back of the Bible, and for the first time felt himself truly converted.

He returned to Houston, where he was introduced to the study of prophecy by a young minister named Jack Blackwell. Blackwell's premillennial dispensationalist approach to prophecy revolutionized Lindsey's understanding of the Bible, which was transformed into a key to understanding and predicting current events. Lindsey began to study the Bible for six to eight hours each day and soon convinced his parents to make religious commitments. After a year and a half of Bible study, Lindsey decided that he wanted to become a Bible teacher, but as his grammar was poor, he spent two nights each week for a year studying with a local schoolteacher. Although Lindsey had not completed college, he was admitted to the strongly dispensationalist Dallas Theological Seminary in 1958 by passing an IQ test and through the intervention of his pastor.

During his second year in seminary, Lindsey met Jan Houghton, a staff member with Campus Crusade for Christ, who was visiting the seminary for five days. Within two weeks Lindsey proposed to her, and they were married two months later.

In 1962 Lindsey received his master's degree in theology, having majored in New Testament and early Greek literature with a minor in Hebrew. Lindsey joined his wife as a staff member for Campus Crusade for Christ and became director of the Crusade chapter at the University of California (Los Angeles). Lindsey spent the next ten years speaking to college students throughout the United States, Canada and Mexico. In order better to communicate his message in the midst of the fomenting student unrest of the late 1960s, Lindsey learned to sprinkle his theology with contemporary slang and countercultural references. He also stressed the significance of current events in light of biblical prophecy. During this period, Lindsey became the father of three daughters, Heidi and twins Jenny and Robin. Lindsey eventually broke from Campus Crusade to form his own student ministry, the Jesus Christ Light and Power Company.

In 1969 Lindsey compiled his notes from his student lectures into a book with the help of Carole C. Carlson, an evangelical freelance writer. Published in 1970, *The Late Great Planet Earth* became an instant bestseller, and within months Lindsey went from being an obscure campus minister to the most well-known interpreter of biblical prophecy. The book sold more than 15 million copies during the 1970s, causing *The New York Times* to name it the highest-selling non-fiction book of the decade. It was made into a film featuring Orson Welles in 1978.

There was little that was original in the book's prophetic interpretations, for as one scholar has observed, 'Premillennialists have been writing books like it since the nineteenth century.' Yet Lindsey was adept at translating the intricacies of premillennial speculations into the contemporary vernacular. (In his hands, the rapture became 'the ultimate trip' and the Whore of Babylon 'Scarlet O'Harlot'.) Moreover, Lindsey's timing was impeccable as two of the three major preconditions for the second coming predicted by premillennialists had recently been fulfilled: the re-establishment of the nation of Israel in 1948 and the retaking of Jerusalem by Israel in June 1967. Lindsey argued that these two events made possible the final precondition: the rebuilding of the ancient Jewish temple. Even more tantalizing to readers was Lindsey's assertion (based on Matthew 24:34) that Jesus would return within 'a generation' of the founding of Israel, a period that he estimated as 'something like forty years'. As the world was destined for imminent apocalyptic destruction, the only hope for escape was the rapture, which would take all true believers in Christ to heaven before life on earth became really difficult.

In 1972 Lindsey again collaborated with Carlson to produce another bestseller, *Satan is Alive and Well on Planet Earth*, which warned of the dangers of the occult. During the next four years, Lindsey (sometimes with Carlson) authored six more prophecy books, which proved so popular that at one point he had three books on the *New York Times* bestseller list.

Lindsey lost some credibility among conservative evangelicals at the end of the 1970s when he divorced his second wife, but this did not prevent his 1980 book, *The 1980s: Countdown to Armageddon*, from becoming a bestseller with an initial printing of 500,000 copies. Although this book was largely an update of *The Late Great Planet Earth*, it included a new emphasis on political activism that reflected the concerns of the emerging New Christian Right.

During the 1980s and 1990s, Lindsey authored more than a dozen books on prophetic themes, including a 1996 apocalyptic novel *Blood Moon*. He served as pastor of the Palos Verdes Community Church in California and married his third wife, Kim. In addition, he hosted a weekly radio show, *Saturdays with Hal Lindsey*, that was broadcast on more than 100 radio stations in the late 1980s. In the 1990s, he co-hosted with Cliff Ford the live radio programme *Weekend Review* as well as producing the weekly television programme *Hal Lindsey* on the Trinity Broadcasting Network. These programmes both highlighted the prophetic significance of current events and promoted a conservative political agenda.

Bibliography
S. R. Graham, 'Hal Lindsey', in C. H. Lippy (ed.), *Twentieth-Century Shapers of American Popular Religion* (New York, Westport, Connecticut, London: Greenwood Press, 1989), pp. 247–255; M. Jeschke, 'Pop Eschatology: Hal Lindsey and Evangelical Theology', in C. N. Kraus (ed.), *Evangelicalism and Anabaptism* (Scottsdale: Herald Press, 1979), pp. 125–147; T. P. Weber, *Living in the Shadow of the Second Coming: American Premillennialism, 1875–1982* (Grand Rapids: Zondervan, 1983; repr. Chicago and London: The University of Chicago Press, 1987).

D. K. LARSEN

■ **LIVINGSTONE, David** (1813–1873), missionary and explorer, was born in the Lanarkshire village of Blantyre, Scotland. His family was originally of Highland origin, a factor in Livingstone's character and thinking that has often been under-emphasized in reference to his linguistic and cultural empathy with Africans.

Livingstone began work at the local cotton-spinning factory at the age of ten, but he also attended the local night school in an attempt to better his education. As a young man, his growing interest in missionary work led him to enrol in Anderson's College in Glasgow, where he began medical studies, while at the same time continuing to work at the mill. His family, though originally Presbyterian, had become associated with a local independent (Congregational) church, and David applied for service with the London Missionary Society (LMS). In 1838 he travelled to London to begin missionary training. He had originally hoped to work in China, but a combination of factors (the outbreak of the Opium War between Britain and China, and a speech by the LMS missionary Robert *Moffat) turned his thoughts towards Africa. He sailed for Africa in 1840, arriving in Cape Town early in 1841.

Livingstone worked briefly with Robert Moffat at Kuruman, before moving north in 1843 to found a series of mission stations at Mabotsa, Chonuane and Kolobeng. In 1845 he married Moffat's daughter Mary. Livingstone was keen to extend mission work to areas beyond European control, and in the late 1840s undertook several journeys to the north, including one to Lake Ngami, accompanied by his wife and young family. By the early 1850s, Livingstone was planning a much more extensive journey and decided to send his family back to Scotland: a controversial move, since none of them was familiar with the country. By now Livingstone was beginning to see his vocation as the exploration of Central Africa, as a way of opening up the continent to commerce, civilization and Christianity. In 1852 he began what was probably his greatest journey of exploration: his transcontinental expedition. Starting in Cape Town (from where he had sent his family to Britain), he travelled north to the country of the Makololo (with whom he was to establish a long-lasting and mutually respectful relationship). He then headed west, eventually reaching the coast at Luanda (in Angola). Refusing the possibility of a return to Britain on board a naval vessel because he had promised to return his Makololo companions to their homeland, he went east again. On this leg of the journey he eventually traversed Africa from west to east; in the latter part of the journey he attempted to follow the course of the Zambezi river.

On his return to Britain Livingstone was greeted as a national hero and published the first of his three books, *Missionary Travels and Researches in South Africa*, which combined scientific and linguistic observations with explanations of how he regarded the missionary task. The latter were reinforced in his famous Cambridge speech, delivered in the Senate Room at Cambridge University in December 1857, which finished with the words, 'I go back to Africa to try to open up a path for commerce and Christianity. Do you carry out the work which I have begun. I leave it with you.' Inherent in this speech were several of the basic missionary assumptions that motivated Livingstone's career. First, that the slave trade was 'an open sore' on the flesh of Africa; secondly, that the slave trade could be eliminated by the introduction of 'legitimate trade'; thirdly, that such trade could be facilitated by the introduction of limited numbers of British 'colonists' – not, it needs to be noted, as imperial conquerors, but as teachers of new technologies and skills.

As a result of Livingstone's appeal in his Cambridge speech for further missionaries for Central Africa, the Universities' Mission to Central Africa was established, supported by Anglicans at the universities of Oxford, Cambridge, Dublin and Durham, and led by Bishop Charles Mackenzie. The first party arrived in Central Africa in 1860, where Livingstone had arranged to meet them. He had returned to Africa in March 1858, this time at the head of a government-sponsored expedition to explore further the Zambezi river. By this time Livingstone had severed his connections with the LMS, who were not entirely in sympathy with his peripatetic understanding of his missionary vocation. Technically, therefore, he was no longer a missionary for the last fifteen years of his African career, though clearly he understood his vocation as God-given and his task as preparing the way for others. He described himself as a 'missionary-explorer'.

While the trans-Africa expedition may be seen as the high point of Livingstone's career, the Zambezi expedition may be regarded in many ways as the nadir. For the first time he travelled with a large entourage of Europeans, who included his brother Charles, the artist Thomas Baines and the botanist John Kirk (later to be British consul in Zanzibar), as well as the African companions of his previous journeys. He proved not to be a good manager of a diverse group of Europeans, and several of them were dismissed or resigned during the course of the expedition. In addition, during his previous expedition, Livingstone had taken a short cut across a major bend of the Zambezi, thus missing completely the Cabora Bassa rapids. As a result he greatly over-estimated the suitability of the river for navigation: a major drawback for an expedition that had carried a steamship with it, for the purposes of sailing it up what Livingstone had described as 'God's Highway'. The *Ma Robert* (named after the Makololo nickname for Mary Livingstone) was unable to pass up the rapids. One indirect advantage of this setback was that Livingstone diverted the boat into the Shire river, and eventually, in September 1859, reached Lake Malawi. Contrary to the myth, Livingstone did not 'discover' Lake Malawi (or Nyassa, as he named it). The lake had appeared on many European maps of Africa since the early eighteenth century, correctly positioned, and bearing the name 'Maravi', a variant of 'Malawi'. The importance of Livingstone's achievement, however, was that he carefully mapped and recorded his journey, and wrote about it in detail in his book *Narrative of an Expedition to the Zambesi and its Tributaries* (1866), thus opening up the possibility of further missionary involvement in the area.

Even before then, however, the Universities' Mission under Charles Mackenzie had arrived in the area, to be met by Livingstone, who guided them to Magomero, in the Shire highlands of modern-day Malawi, where they set up their first station. In the short term the mission was not a success. Both the climate and Mackenzie's activism against the slave trade caused early trouble. Within a couple of years Mackenzie and his fellow missionary, Burrup, were dead, and his successor, Tozer, had withdrawn the mission to Zanzibar.

In 1861 Mary Livingstone, depressed by her lonely life in Britain, travelled out to Africa to rejoin her husband. She travelled up the Shire river with a young Scottish clergyman, James Stewart, later to be the principal of the famous Lovedale Institute in the Eastern Cape of South Africa, and with Bishop Mackenzie's sister and Mrs Burrup. A few months after her arrival, she caught fever and died at Shupanga in Mozambique. Livingstone was shattered by her death, but his strong sense of purpose drove him to continue his exploration. By this time, however, the major achievements of the expedition were behind him, and the British government ordered his withdrawal in 1863.

Livingstone arrived back in England in July 1864. This time, however, he was not greeted with the same level of adulation as after his trans-Africa expedition. Nevertheless, he still had important supporters in both the religious and the scientific communities. Livingstone still believed deeply that the key to the Christian future of Africa lay in the exploration and 'opening up' of the main waterways into the interior. For this reason, and because of his scientific curiosity, he remained fascinated by the continuing controversy over where the source of the Nile really lay. With the help of a group of rich friends, and the support of the Royal Geographical Society, Livingstone returned to Africa in 1866 to try to discover the source of the Nile. For the next seven years he was to travel thousands of miles (mostly on foot) in circuitous meanderings through much of Central Africa, visiting many river systems and lakes in his ultimately unsuccessful search for the source of the Nile. For much of this time he was out of touch with Europe, giving rise to rumours that he was lost or even dead. These led to the launch of at least three search expeditions to 'find' Livingstone. By far the most famous of these was that undertaken by the Welsh-American journalist Henry Morton Stanley on behalf of the *New York Herald*. Stanley met Livingstone at Ujiji on the shores of Lake Tanganyika in late October or early November 1871 (the precise date is disputed) and greeted him with the famous words, 'Dr Livingstone, I presume?' Though the underlying motives for the *New York Herald* expedition were not as altruistic as is sometimes believed, Livingstone and Stanley did strike up a close and genuine relationship during their four months together; both Livingstone and Stanley, in fact, were to liken the relationship to that of a father and a son. Since Stanley was an orphan, and Livingstone's relationship with his own children (especially his son Robert)

was complex, the affinity is all the more poignant. Robert had been a vivacious and, to his parents, troublesome child. Yet he seems to have had a deep longing to get closer to his famous father. In 1863, as a young man of sixteen, he travelled out to Africa to try to join his father. Robert got only as far as Natal and did not have the funds to proceed further. The young man took ship to America, where he enrolled in the Union Army during the Civil War and, after being wounded, died in a prison hospital in December 1864 at the age of eighteen. It is likely that Livingstone felt a mixture of grief and guilt at the death of his eldest son, and may have seen Stanley (however temporarily) as some sort of replacement.

In spite of Stanley's attempts to persuade Livingstone to return home with him, the older man was determined to continue his explorations. By now, however, he was suffering increasing ill health, brought on by many years of travel and living in hostile conditions and pushing himself beyond what most people could have endured. By the beginning of 1873 he was growing increasingly weak and was having to be carried in a *machila*. Finally, his closest followers stopped at Chitambo's village in what is now northern Zambia, and here, on 1 May 1873, David Livingstone died, at the age of sixty. The story of how his remains reached England from Central Africa is well known, yet at the same time often undervalued. His immediate followers, Susi, Chuma, and Jacob Wainwright, determined not to leave his body where he died. Victorian prurience and romanticism recorded that David Livingstone's heart was buried in Africa, and this claim has been repeated in almost every account since. The reality was more mundane. In order to carry his body to the coast, Livingstone's followers had first to embalm it. They therefore disembowelled him, buried all his innards in a tin box and then sun-dried the corpse for a couple of weeks, before setting off on their epic journey of well over a thousand miles to the coast. In fact, the party that carried the body to the coast was more than eighty strong, and included several women, notably Ntaoeka and Halima. Though their achievement was never sufficiently recognized, it indicated the huge respect that Livingstone's followers had for him. Livingstone returned in death (as he had in life in 1856) as a national hero, and was buried in Westminster Abbey on 18 April 1874.

Though more than a century and a quarter has passed since Livingstone's death and burial, he is still often seen as the quintessential British missionary of the nineteenth (and perhaps any other) century. To some extent, this perception is due to the innate qualities of the man himself, but at the same time his reputation is partly based on something that in the modern world might be designated 'spin': the creation of the myth of the heroic missionary and the omission of the many faults and shortcomings of his character. It remains, therefore, to assess his achievement, and to give him his proper place, in the light of modern scholarship.

First, it is important to recognize that the Livingstone myth grew up (in the 1870s and 1880s) at a time when the modern colonial movement and the scramble for Africa were just getting under way. It was fostered by the large number of books and articles that appeared in the years immediately following his death, including *The Last Journals of David Livingstone*, edited by Horace Waller. Many of Livingstone's ideas on commerce and Christianity, on legitimate trade and on European settlement in Africa were used later to justify the wider colonial enterprise. Livingstone, however, had very specific projects in mind when he spoke of these things, and they were very different from the kind of European settlement that was taking place in South Africa and (later) Zimbabwe. For Livingstone, European settlement was a means of taking poor, skilled and God-fearing working-people from Britain and settling them in small numbers in parts of Africa such as the Shire Highlands of Malawi to encourage and instruct local farmers in the production of crops such as cotton. Today that idea may appear very paternalistic, and Livingstone's hope that the expansion of the African cotton trade could help to eliminate the slave trade was rather naive. Be that as it may, its basic motivation was the welfare of Africans themselves and should not be confused with a proto-colonialism.

Livingstone's attitude towards the Afrikaner (Boer) farmers in South Africa reveals his motivation. One of the reasons why he began his journeys in the 1840s was to get away from those areas where white settlers controlled Africans. In a little-known letter he compared the plight of the Xhosa in the Eastern Cape to that of the Magyars in the Austro-Hungarian Empire and affirmed the right of Africans to take up arms to defend their rights against European incursion.

Livingstone's attitude to Africans was much less racist than that of most other missionaries of his period and certainly than that of missionaries in the following generation. He had a deep interest in African languages; his notebooks are full of linguistic jottings, and he was critical of those Europeans who made little effort to learn African languages. Though his own Christian faith was deeply evangelical, he was not dismissive of African religiosity, as were many missionaries of the time. He records early in his first book an encounter with a local rainmaker; contrary to much missionary writing of the time, his concern seems to be, not the denigration of African 'superstition', but rather the accurate reporting of another's belief system.

Central to any understanding of Livingstone must be his own view of his missionary vocation and of the nature of the missionary task in general. Livingstone saw his task, partly at least, as preparing the way for others, yet never as a merely geographical task. As he himself said, 'the end of the geographical feat is but the beginning of the Missionary enterprise'. When, in 1865, he was debating whether or not to return to Africa on what appeared to be an entirely geographical expedition, he wrote to his friend Sir Roderick Murchison that he would feel it was worthwhile only if he could do some work as a missionary.

On the missionary task in general Livingstone had a broad view and his understanding broadened as his career progressed. Speaking of 'the Missionary enterprise' he declared: 'I take the latter term in its most extended signification, and include every effort made for the amelioration of our race, the promotion of all those means by which God in His providence is working, and bringing all His dealing with man to a glorious consummation.' Though the term did not come into common use for another century, we might say that Livingstone described and practised a form of *Missio Dei*.

Victorian biographies of David Livingstone (and indeed, many more modern studies) tended to be almost entirely hagiographic, ignoring the complex nature of Livingstone's character. He could be bad-tempered, stubborn and unreasonable, as can be seen most clearly in his treatment of several of his European colleagues during the Zambezi expedition, most notably the artist Thomas Baines, who was dismissed after being accused of dishonesty and was refused a fair hearing by Livingstone. He was driven by a will to succeed which made it difficult for him to admit that he was wrong, as in his stubborn attempts to drag the *Ma Robert* up the Cabora Bassa rapids. By modern standards (though not necessarily by those of his own day) his apparent subordination of the best interests of his family to his own agenda may well be open to criticism, and in particular his relationship with his eldest son Robert was tragic and may have troubled Livingstone himself. On the other hand, he was clearly deeply affected by the death of his wife Mary, and he had a close and loving relationship with his daughter Agnes.

As an explorer, he must rank among the foremost of the Victorian era, even though his attempts to find the source of the Nile were unsuccessful and based on wrong geographical premises. The information gleaned during his earlier expeditions hugely increased European knowledge of large parts of Africa, not least because of Livingstone's very careful notes, drawings and maps, prepared on an almost daily basis.

And what, finally, are we to make of Livingstone the missionary? Several recent biographies have criticized him as making only one convert during his entire missionary career: Chief Sekeletu. To think in these terms, however, is to misunderstand the nature of Livingstone's vocation. Even a cursory reading of his diaries will bring home the deep and personal Christian faith that he maintained throughout his time in Africa. Yet, as has been pointed out, he saw his vocation as that of preparing the way for others. In this respect his legacy is secure. Though the UMCA got off to an inauspicious start, and retired to Zanzibar, it eventually returned to Malawi in the 1880s. Immediately after Livingstone's death, both the Free Church of Scotland and the Church of Scotland set up missions in his memory: the former the Livingstonia mission (which eventually settled in northern Malawi) and the latter the Blantyre mission, in the south of Malawi. In addition several other missions, including what eventually became the Congo Balolo mission, were founded as a result of Livingstone's work. Moreover, countless thousands of Christians, both missionaries and supporters of mission, have been deeply influenced by David Livingstone and his legacy.

Yet there remains a sense in which Livingstone was diminished by the very myth created around him, for the myth created a Livingstone in the image of a later conception of 'the good missionary', playing down his radical political views and his pro-African stance and misinterpreting his ideas on colonization. As 'the real Livingstone', faults and all, is rediscovered, his continuing relevance for mission in the twenty-first century will be revealed.

Bibliography
W. G. Blaikie, *The Personal Life of David Livingstone* (London: John Murray, 1880); T. Jeal, *Livingstone* (London: Heinemann, 1973); A. C. Ross, *Livingstone: Mission and Empire* (London: Hambledon & London, 2002).

T. J. THOMPSON

■ **LLOYD-JONES, David Martyn** (1899–1981), preacher and theologian, was born in Cardiff on 20 December 1899. He was the second of three boys born to Welsh-speaking parents. In 1906 his family moved to Llangeitho, Cardiganshire, where his parents joined the local Calvinistic Methodist (CM) church, established by Daniel Rowland during the eighteenth-century revival.

The years from 1910 to 1916 were full of challenge for Martyn Lloyd-Jones. He won a scholarship to Tregaron County Intermediate School in 1911. In 1914 the family moved to London to run a dairy business and joined the CM Church in Charing Cross Road.

Matriculating at Marylebone Grammar School in 1916, Lloyd-Jones joined eighty-one other students, including his future wife, Bethan Phillips, to study medicine at St Bartholomew's Hospital, London. A brilliant student, by the age of twenty-five he had amassed a string of medical undergraduate and postgraduate qualifications: MB (distinction), BS, MRCS, LRCP (1921, London), MD (1923, London) and MRCP (1925).

Sir Thomas Horder, the king's physician, appointed Lloyd-Jones as his junior house physician in 1921 and his chief clinical assistant in 1923. Lloyd-Jones's post-doctoral research in 1924 focused on sub-acute bacterial endocarditis; he worked at Bart's Hospital till December 1926 and married in January 1927. Lloyd-Jones and his wife had two daughters, Elizabeth and Ann.

Although Lloyd-Jones was an active church member, his profession of Christianity was nominal until his early twenties. Conscious of sin and guilt before God, he was converted and given a stronger sense of call to the Christian ministry. Even prior to conversion, Lloyd-Jones had begun to believe that his future might lie in the ministry. Now the sense of call became irresistible. Contributory factors included his growing conviction of God's love in Christ, his belief that he was 'a debtor' responsible for preaching the gospel (Romans 1:14) and his view of his patients' spiritual needs. Despite their wealth and fame, many of them were dying, and Lloyd-Jones was convinced that their greatest need was the gospel.

Lloyd-Jones refused to undertake formal theological training, regarding his medical training with its diagnostic approach as valuable preparation for preaching. He also believed that a minister is primarily a preacher and pastor called and gifted by God, and that academic theological education could be harmful to divinely gifted preachers because of its emphasis on qualifications and the dominance of liberal theology in universities.

Lloyd-Jones's first pastorate was at a mission church, under the supervision of the CM or Presbyterian Church of Wales's Forward Movement, in Aberavon, Port Talbot, South Wales, where he exercised a powerful preaching ministry from February 1927 to the summer of 1938. Facing a large building debt, the church (of ninety-three members) had previously emphasized the social gospel. It was transformed by 'the Doctor's' biblical, Christ-centred and evangelistic preaching. Remarkable church growth took place as many locals were converted. In other areas of Wales thousands came to hear him preach.

From 1938 to 1943 Lloyd-Jones first assisted, then was co-pastor with, Campbell *Morgan at Westminster Chapel, London, and he succeeded him as sole minister in 1943. His influential London ministry continued until March 1968, when he underwent major surgery and formally retired. Until 1980 he exercised an itinerant preaching ministry and prepared some of his material, such as his sermons on Romans and Ephesians, for publication. Lloyd-Jones died on 1 March, St David's Day, 1981 in London. Two days before his death, he wrote for the benefit of his family, 'Do not pray for healing. Do not hold me back from the glory.'

In Lloyd-Jones's early years, the influence of the CM church of Wales upon him was evident in his consciousness of the glory of God and his doctrine of predestination. CM history, with its countless local, regional revivals, great preachers and theologians, stimulated his lifelong interest in theology, church history and revival. Later, Lloyd-Jones insisted that the term 'Calvinistic Methodist' appropriately expressed the essentials of Christianity. While the term 'Methodist' highlighted the important experimental aspect, the term 'Calvinistic' conveyed the necessary biblical, doctrinal content of the faith. The early New Testament Christians, according to Lloyd-Jones, 'were the most typical Calvinistic Methodists of all'.

Between 1925 and 1929 Lloyd-Jones 'discovered' the Puritans, George *Whitefield, Jonathan *Edwards, James *Denney and P. T. *Forsyth. In the war years (1939–1945) he studied the writings of Charles *Hodge, J. C. *Ryle and B. B. *Warfield; the latter strengthened his conviction of the need for doctrinal teaching.

In addition to reading the whole Bible annually, Lloyd-Jones read widely. He read many major theological volumes from people of different theological positions, such as Emil Brunner and Karl Barth, and from 1928 read the annual Bampton and Gifford Lectures. He singled out Kenneth E. Kirk's *The Vision of God* as having 'a great effect' on him; 'it made me think …' For Lloyd-Jones the purpose of reading was to stimulate thinking. Before embarking on a new series of expository sermons or Bible studies such as those on Romans, he read all the well-known commentaries, sermons and addresses that were available.

Lloyd-Jones was a conservative evangelical, a robust Calvinist, an able theologian and an informed preacher. It is impossible to understand 'the Doctor' apart from his Reformed, experimental theology. He saw divine sovereignty in creation, providence and salvation as 'the foundation doctrine of all Protestant and Reformed theology'.

By the late 1930s Lloyd-Jones's growing theological stature and compelling preaching gifts made him a likely candidate for an academic teaching post. In 1933 he lectured in his denomination's theological college in Bala, north Wales on preaching and pastoral work, and in the late 1930s many, including Lloyd-Jones himself, were disappointed when he was not appointed to a vacant chair there. 'The Doctor' was invited to become Principal of London Bible College before it opened in 1943, but he declined. He lectured and preached in numerous colleges over the years and, with others, was instrumental in establishing Tyndale House, a biblical research centre in Cambridge. His vision for theological reformation extended to the church at large and, as one way of achieving this, he encouraged publishing companies to make available old and new books to the Christian public.

Lloyd-Jones's long-term involvement with evangelical student work (with the Inter-Varsity Fellowship [IVF], now the Universities and Colleges Christian Fellowship) began in 1935 and was multi-faceted. He spoke at Christian Unions, university missions, and national and international conferences. From 1939 to 1942 and in 1952 he was IVF president. Strengthening the IVF doctrinal basis, safeguarding its conservative doctrine of Scripture, advising the IVF secretary Douglas *Johnson, helping to revive evangelical theology and challenging the dominant theological liberalism of his day were among his major contributions in the student world.

Lloyd-Jones also endeavoured to correct the anti-intellectual stance popular within the IVF and the view that it was more 'spiritual' to become a missionary or minister than to enter the professions. Lloyd-Jones was involved in the Christian Medical Fellowship and the International Fellowship of Evangelical Students (IFES), of which he was chairman from 1947 to 1957, then president until 1967. He provided IFES with a strong theological base and encouraged national leadership.

Lloyd-Jones took an active interest in the opening (January 1945) and continuing work of the Evangelical Library in London, the founding of the Banner of Truth Trust in 1957 and the emergence and development of the Evangelical Movement of Wales from the late 1940s. The first 'Puritan Conference' was held in his church in December 1950 (renamed 'Westminster Conference' from 1969), and Lloyd-Jones spoke annually. He was also instrumental in establishing the London Theological Seminary in 1977.

Another of Lloyd-Jones's major contributions was his pastoring of pastors by advising and encouraging them and preaching in their churches. He chaired the monthly Westminster Ministers' Fraternal from 1943 (a study group was first established in 1941), which was open to evangelicals of all denominations until 1967. In the 1960s up to 400 pastors met for one Monday a month.

But Lloyd-Jones's most outstanding gifts were as a preacher and evangelist. Described as 'the greatest preacher in Christendom', he saw expository preaching as 'the primary task of the church' and the greatest need of both the church and the world. His mature reflections on preaching are found in *Preaching and Preachers* (Hodder & Stoughton, 1971).

For Lloyd-Jones, preaching means delivering God's message, so it must be biblical, expository and Christ-centred. Authentic preaching influences people profoundly and involves the preacher's whole personality. Freedom and control by the Holy Spirit are of the essence of preaching. Seriousness, liveliness, zeal, a sense of concern, warmth, urgency and an element of pathos are also essential in preaching. This pathos arises from a love for the people and the recognition of God's love in Christ. Another vital feature of preaching is power, which is entirely God's gift, although it is the preacher's responsibility to pray and seek the Lord and his power.

Lloyd-Jones's powerful ministry in Westminster involved preaching aimed at believers on Sunday mornings and preaching aimed at unbelievers on Sunday evenings. He engaged regularly in mid-week itinerant preaching. In

1952 he terminated the existing Friday fellowship and discussion meeting in favour of a series of weekly lectures on biblical doctrines (published by Hodder & Stoughton in three volumes in 1996, 1997 and 1998 in the 'Great Doctrines Series'). From 1955 to 1968 Lloyd-Jones gave his magisterial exposition of Romans up to 14:17 (Banner of Truth Trust in twelve volumes; one more to be published).

'The Doctor's' more famous Sunday morning expositions included the *Sermon on the Mount* (commenced in October 1950; the first of two volumes was published by IVP in 1957), thirteen sermons on John 17 in 1952 (*Saved in Eternity*, Kingsway, 1988), *Faith on Trial*, an exposition of Psalm 73 in eleven sermons started in the Autumn of 1953 (IVP, 1965) and twenty-one sermons on *Spiritual Depression* (commenced in January 1954, Pickering & Inglis, 1965). His longest Sunday morning series was 260 sermons, from October 1954 to July 1962, on Ephesians (Banner of Truth, eight volumes).

Sunday evening evangelistic preaching by Lloyd-Jones sometimes took the form of an expository series, such as those on Acts (commenced in 1965; *Authentic Christianity: Acts 1–3*, vol. 1, and *Acts 4*, vol. 2: Banner of Truth, 1999) and Isaiah chapter 1, preached in 1963 (*God's Way, Not Ours*, Banner of Truth, 1998), and was sometimes based on individual texts (e.g. *Old Testament Evangelical Sermons*, Banner of Truth, 1995). Lloyd-Jones saw himself primarily as an evangelist but never gave an altar-call or appeal and refused to cooperate with the evangelist Billy *Graham in his 1954 mission to London. Lloyd-Jones had four major objections to Graham's practice; he believed that: (a) only God regenerates sinners; (b) responding to an appeal can be wrongly identified with conversion; (c) such a response confuses individuals concerning their spiritual standing before God; (d) Graham compromised the gospel by cooperating with 'liberal' and 'sacramentalist' church leaders.

At the second Assembly of the National Association of Evangelicals in London in October 1966 Lloyd-Jones called for a wide expression of evangelical unity (see 'Evangelical Unity: An Appeal', pp. 246–257; also 'The Basis of Christian Unity', pp. 118–163, in *Knowing the Times*, Banner of Truth,

1989). He did not want an evangelical denomination but rather a 'fellowship or an association of evangelical churches' committed to gospel unity. His primary burden was to uphold the uniqueness of the revealed gospel; he felt this concern most acutely with regard to ecclesiology.

Lloyd-Jones's concerns were five-fold: (i) the formation of the World Council of Churches in 1948, which presented 'an entirely new situation' worldwide in which denominations would further compromise Reformation, biblical teaching on gospel distinctives; (ii) the Evangelical Alliance's 'benevolent neutrality' in relation to the WCC; (iii) a major shift between 1954 and 1966 in the attitude of evangelicals towards ecumenism; (iv) the second Vatican Council's (1962–1965) favourable disposition towards Protestants and non-Christian religions; (v) the positive attitude of Anglican evangelicals towards ecumenism, expressed at the Keele Congress in 1967.

Lloyd-Jones taught, on the basis of his interpretation of John 17 and Ephesians 4:1–16, that Christian unity is the result of the Holy Spirit's activity in regenerating sinners and establishing their mystical union with Christ. The nature of Christian unity, therefore, is spiritual, not organizational; it is also characterized by fidelity to Bible teaching. The situation was opportune, in Lloyd-Jones's opinion, for a wide expression by Christians of evangelical unity in the gospel. How could evangelicals continue in denominations where those who modified and denied the gospel were not disciplined?

Failing to obtain this wide expression of gospel unity, including evangelical Anglicans, Lloyd-Jones turned in 1967 to the British Evangelical Council. Founded in 1952, the BEC is committed to the expression of gospel unity outside the ecumenical movement. Between 1967 and 1972 Lloyd-Jones gave the closing addresses at eight of the BEC annual conferences. Those addresses are published in *Unity in Truth* (Evangelical Press, 1991); the best known are 'Luther and his message for today' (1967), 'What is the church?' (1968) and 'Wrong divisions and true unity' (1970).

Within a Trinitarian framework, Lloyd-Jones distinguished between the 'general' and 'particular' work of the Holy Spirit. He insisted that regeneration was 'incomparably the most important doctrine of all'. He understood regeneration as part of the Spirit's particular work, 'the implanting of a principle of new spiritual life and a radical change in the governing disposition of the soul'. This initial, supernatural work by the Holy Spirit is inseparably related to union with Christ, conversion, assurance and sanctification. Lloyd-Jones taught that the Holy Spirit can come in power upon a preacher or individual Christian or church many times and without bestowing tongues or other gifts.

Lloyd-Jones's view of Spirit-baptism was expressed on three occasions: (a) in five sermons on Ephesians 1:13 in 1955, (b) in fifteen sermons on Romans 8:15–16 in 1960–1961, and (c) in twenty-four sermons on John 1:26, 33 in 1964–1965. Spirit-baptism is distinguishable from regeneration and conversion; it is personally and corporately recognizable; its purpose is for power in witness and preaching; it is not evidenced by tongues. Such baptism gives 'an unusual sense of the presence of God and divine glory', 'a sense of awe', a deep assurance of God's love to us in Christ as well as joy and love for God. Lloyd-Jones believed that in the New Testament being 'filled' with the Holy Spirit was synonymous with being 'baptized' with the Spirit (except in Eph. 5:18).

Lloyd-Jones regarded Spirit-baptism as independent of human agency; it is a sovereign, unconditional work of God. Revival and Spirit-baptism are aspects of the same divine work; the former is extensive and corporate while the latter is personal. Revival is, therefore, an extraordinary enlivening of believers by the Holy Spirit, the manifestation of his influence and power in unusual degree. And that, for Lloyd-Jones, is what made the church mighty in the past.

Bibliography

D. M. Lloyd-Jones, 'Knowing the Times', addresses delivered on various occasions 1942–1977 (Edinburgh: Banner of Truth, 1989); I. H. Murray, *D. Martyn Lloyd-Jones: The First Forty Years 1899–1939* (Edinburgh: Banner of Truth, 1982); I. H. Murray, *D. Martyn Lloyd-Jones: The Fight of Faith 1939–1981* (Edinburgh: Banner of Truth, 1990).

D. E. DAVIES

■ **LÖHE, Johannes K. W.** (1808–1872), German Lutheran theologian, was a strong proponent of Lutheran orthodoxy, church order and a high view of the pastoral office. Keenly interested in outreach, he promoted the training of men and women for mission and diaconal work in Germany and America.

Johannes Konrad Wilhelm Löhe was born on 21 February 1808 in Fürth outside Nürnberg, Germany. He attended gymnasium in Nürnberg before studying theology at Erlangen University. Although raised in the Reformed church, he became a Lutheran; the defence of Lutheranism was to be a hallmark of his career. An accomplished preacher, Löhe drew people to St Giles in Nürnberg with impassioned sermons, denouncing sin even among those in high positions and turning the civil authorities against him. In 1837 Löhe moved out of the city to become pastor in Neuendettelsau. Though it was little more than a village, it was to gain international attention through Löhe's social and outreach programmes.

In mid-century Löhe thought of seceding from the Bavarian territorial church, frustrated at its lack of interest in his ideal of purity in confession and lifestyle. Eventually he chose to stay, out of respect for the tradition and history of the church, flawed though it was. Löhe was outraged to see Reformed and Lutherans meeting at the same altar, ignoring their doctrinal differences and without formal union. But in 1852 Gottlieb Christoph Adolf von Harless, a friend of Löhe, was appointed by the Bavarian king to head the consistory and supervise the territorial church. Harless opposed both rationalism and doctrinal indifference, and pressed for the distinction between Lutheran and Reformed to be maintained. He introduced a new hymnal, which was decidedly Lutheran and traditional in spirit. Löhe took heart and stayed with the Bavarian church.

Löhe had made plain his support for traditional Lutheranism in his *Drei Bücher von der Kirche* (*Three Books on the Church*, 1845). He claimed that orthodox Lutheranism was complete; there was no need to revise or replace traditional beliefs and practices with something deemed more acceptable to the contemporary mind. Löhe believed that the role of the pastor was to guard and transmit true doctrine and encourage right living.

Löhe's view of the place and authority of the pastoral ministry, his high esteem for the sacraments and his emphasis on confession and absolution were unusual in Lutheran circles and aroused suspicions of Romanism, which were reinforced by his insistence that the church should strive for visible unity and purity. Yet his firm support for the Reformation doctrine of justification bound him to the Lutheran tradition.

But Löhe did more than advocate orthodox standards; he also worked hard to promote outreach and charitable work. In 1840 he began to prepare workers to minister among Germans emigrating to the American upper midwest. Friedrich Wyneken, a Lutheran pastor working among Franconians in Michigan, asked for help from Germany. Löhe answered his request with the so-called *Sendlinge*, the 'emissaries' or 'sent ones'. These men did not have a theological education such as Löhe had received from Erlangen, and were prepared to varying degrees for their work, but they were well enough versed in the basics of Lutheran theology to serve in the emergency until Lutheranism in America could be more firmly grounded. The *Sendlinge* themselves continued to mature and study in their new home. Löhe was understandably protective of his programme – these were *his* men – and he carefully monitored their work. They would eventually make way for others with greater formal training, but they were invaluable in establishing a Lutheran presence in the United States and rallying the German Americans around Lutheran doctrine before they could be scattered in the vast country. Like the Saxons in Missouri led by C. F. W. *Walther, the Franconians from Neuendettelsau played a major part in the formation of the Missouri Synod, a voice of conservative Lutheranism that was welcomed by many in the growing German population and by others attracted by its evangelical theology. Löhe exported Lutheran influence even further afield by sending workers to Australia. His training centre exists to this day and is still active in missionary education.

In 1849 Löhe turned his attention to home missions, and four years later he began to train deaconesses, who proved highly popular, serving in hospitals, charitable homes, asylums and vocational schools. Deaconesses too are still trained in Neuendettelsau.

Although known for his pastoral sense, Löhe's intense interest in Lutheran orthodoxy and in liturgy alienated some people. His lofty view of the pastor's office and authority eventually caused a rift with Walther and others in the Missouri Synod whom Löhe believed were diminishing the office under pressure from democratic culture. In the Bavarian church, with its weak confessional identity, Löhe did great work on behalf of evangelical theology. That work also proved crucial for establishing Lutheran identity in the United States, even though Löhe would eventually distance himself from the American scene, which he may not have fully understood. He died in Neuendettelsau on 2 January 1872.

Bibliography

E. H. Heintzen, *Love Leaves Home: Wilhelm Loehe and the Missouri Synod* (St Louis: Concordia Publishing House, 1973); J. L. Schaaf, *Wilhelm Löhe's Relation to the American Church: A Study in the History of Lutheran Mission* (ThD dissertation, University of Heidelberg, 1961); H. Kressel, *Wilhelm Lohe als Katechet und als Seelsorger* (Neuendettelsau: Freimund-Verlag, 1955); J. Gotz, *Wilhelm Lohe: Im Dienst der Kirche. Quellen und Urkunden zum Verstandnis Neuendettelsauer Art und Geschichte* (Neuendettelsau: Verlag der Buchhandlung der Diakonissenanstalt, 1933).

R. ROSIN

■ **LUTHER, Martin** (1483–1546), German Reformer, stands at the headwaters of that vast movement of ecclesial and spiritual renewal known as the Reformation. He was born on 10 November 1483 in the Thuringian village of Eisleben. He was the son of Hans Luder, a copper miner, and his respectable wife, Margaret Ziegler. He was named Martin because he was baptized on 11 November, the feast day of St Martin of Tours.

Although Luther later complained of the harsh discipline he received as a young boy, his parents recognized that he was a precocious child and provided for his early education at Latin schools in Magdeburg and Eisenach. In 1501 Luther matriculated at the University of Erfurt, where he received his baccalaureate (1502) and master's (1505) degrees. He then took up the study of law in accordance with his father's wishes.

In the summer of 1505, however, Luther's career underwent a dramatic change when, in the midst of a violent thunderstorm, he cried out in panic, 'Saint Ann, help me, I will become a monk.' To the chagrin of his friends and parents, Luther insisted on fulfilling his vow. He joined the monastery of the Observant Augustinian friars, a strict religious order in Erfurt. By all accounts, Luther was a conscientious monk and kept the rule of his order scrupulously. But his many prayers, vigils and fastings only made him more uncertain of his own salvation. At every turn he was frustrated in his quest to find a gracious God.

Luther was overwhelmed by his sense of God's sovereign power and holiness. After being ordained priest in 1507, Luther nearly fainted at the altar while presiding at his first mass. The idea that a finite creature could hold in its hands the very body of Christ terrified him. But Luther was troubled even more by his fallenness and falling short of God's standard. Could he be sure that he had remembered every single sin in the confessional? On one occasion Johann von Staupitz, Luther's confessor, admonished him to forget his scruples and simply love God. 'Love God?' retorted Luther, 'I hate him.' Luther experienced the dark night of the soul, when he seemed to tremble on the verge of the abyss, when the rustling of a mere leaf was enough to produce in him the terrors of hell. Luther later described these bouts of dread as *Anfechtungen*, times of testing and fierce assault from the devil.

Luther found relief only through his 'discovery of the Gospel', which he made after a long, arduous study of the Scriptures. In the preface to the collection of his Latin writings in 1545, Luther recalled this process: 'I did not learn my theology all at once, but I had to search deeper for it where my trials and temptations took me ... living, nay rather dying and being damned make a theologian, not understanding, reading or speculation.' Luther wrestled with the Bible, especially the Psalms and Paul's letter to the Romans. He stumbled over the phrase 'the righteousness of God' in Romans 1:17. This verse brought him no comfort so long as he interpreted the righteousness of God as the exacting justice by which God condemned sinners. By focusing on the atoning work of Christ on the cross, Luther came to believe that the righteousness of God to which Paul referred was the righteousness secured by Christ alone. On the basis of the righteousness secured by Christ, God declared unworthy sinners acceptable in his sight. On the basis of this insight, Luther developed his doctrine of justification by faith alone (*per solam fidem*).

Luther claimed to have made this major exegetical breakthrough while studying the Bible in the tower of the monastery. His insight into the gracious character of God, he said, was like being born again. Scholars debate the exact date of Luther's famous '*Turmerlebnis*' (tower experience), with suggested dates ranging from 1512 to 1519. They were probably two separate developments: an initial breakthrough and conviction of God's gracious mercy and salvation in Christ, and the later formulation of a mature doctrine of justification, a new standing with God based on the imputation of Christ's alien righteousness by faith alone. This teaching became the guiding principle of Luther's thought and the cornerstone of Reformation theology.

As early as 1509, Luther had begun to lecture on Peter Lombard's *Books of Sentences*, the standard medieval textbook in theology. At the behest of Staupitz, he completed the requirements for his doctorate in theology in 1512 and was appointed *Lectura in Biblia* at the University of Wittenberg, succeeding Staupitz himself. Luther was influenced by the prevailing nominalism of the day as well as by the German mystical tradition and currents of humanistic thought. However, it was his regular study of the Bible that led him to question the theology and practices of the medieval Catholic church. In the winter of 1512, Luther began preparation for his lectures on the Psalms (1513–1515), which were followed in turn by those on Romans (1515–1516), Galatians (1516–1517), Hebrews (1517) and Psalms again (1518–1519). He later remarked: 'In the course of this teaching the papacy slipped away from me.'

Luther's conflict with the church of Rome was the result of both his biblical studies and his pastoral labours in Wittenberg. Within the space of five years, Luther was catapulted onto the stage of European history.

The obscure monk became a famous theologian at the centre of an international movement that would leave the church in the West permanently divided.

On 31 October 1517 Luther posted on the door of the Castle Church of Wittenberg ninety-five theses protesting against the selling of indulgences and calling for a public debate on this issue. Luther was incensed because members of his own church had purchased indulgences from the Dominican Johann Tetzel. Luther attacked the assumption that forgiveness of sins or release from purgatory could be bought by such a monetary exchange. The sale of indulgences, Luther argued, undermined the sacrament of penance and reinforced a theology of cheap grace.

Using Erasmus' Greek New Testament of 1516, Luther interpreted *poenitentiam agite* ('do penance') in the original biblical sense of *metanoiete*, 'change you mind and heart; be converted'. Thus, in the first of his ninety-five theses, Luther declared: 'When our Lord and Master Jesus Christ said "Repent", he meant for the entire life to be one of repentance.' Other theses called into question the treasury of merits, the invocation of the saints, and the power of the papacy. Luther's call for an academic debate became an ecclesiastical *cause célèbre* as his ninety-five theses were disseminated far and wide.

The pope sent Cardinal Cajetan to Germany to persuade Luther to recant his teachings, but to no avail. In April 1518 Luther further clarified his views in the Heidelberg Disputation, at which time he also won over Martin *Bucer, later the Reformer of Strasbourg. On this occasion Luther challenged certain fundamental assumptions of medieval theology, which he called the theology of glory, in favour of a more Christocentric 'theology of the cross'.

In July 1519 Luther confronted John Eck at the Leipzig Debate. In this famous exchange Luther set forth the Reformation principle *sola scriptura*. He aligned himself with certain statements made by John *Hus, who had been condemned (unfairly, Luther thought) as a heretic at the Council of Constance in 1415. In the course of the debate, Luther denied both the infallibility of church councils and the primacy of the pope. Only the Holy Scriptures, Luther asserted, could be trusted as the normative rule for Christian belief and church policy.

At first the papacy was slow to react to Luther's challenge, thinking that the matter was just another quarrel among monks. By 1520, however, Luther's campaign had become a serious crisis. Luther set forth his ideas with passion and clarity in three famous treatises (1520). In *An Appeal to the Nobility of the German Nation* Luther exploited the rising national sentiment in Germany to demolish the 'three walls' that he believed the partisans of the pope had erected against true church reform: first, the claim that church officials were exempt from the authority of civil magistrates; secondly, the elevation of church tradition over Scripture; and, not least, the assertion that papal decrees took precedence over church councils.

On the Babylonian Captivity of the Church was published in October 1520. This treatise was a frontal assault on the medieval sacramental system. Luther found two, not seven, sacraments in the Bible. He denounced the mass as an abomination. And, finally, he redefined sacraments as visible signs of God's holy promises.

On the Freedom of the Christian, Luther's third great work of the year, further challenged the claims of the papal church system by emphasizing Christian liberty, the priesthood of all believers, the sufficiency of Scripture and the doctrine of justification by faith alone. This treatise also contained the basis of Luther's ethics: good works are to flow from faith as its fruit. God's grace is a radically free gift and cannot be earned by any merits of our own.

Luther was excommunicated in the papal bull *Exsurge Domine*, which he burned publicly along with the corpus of canon law in December 1520. He was then summoned to appear before the Diet of Worms, where he was asked to retract his writings. He refused to do so, claiming that his conscience was captive to the Word of God. Unless he was persuaded by reason and conscience, he said, he would not recant. His famous words, 'Here I stand, I can do no other', became the watchword of the Reformation.

The 1520s witnessed the consolidation of the Lutheran Reformation, culminating in the famous Augsburg Confession of 1530. Following his defiant stand at the Diet of Worms,

Luther had been taken secretly to the Wartburg Castle near Eisenach, where he lived in seclusion for several months under the protection of his territorial prince, Elector Frederick III. He spent his time wisely, however, translating the New Testament into German. His *Das Newe Testament Deutsche* was published in 1522. His work on the Old Testament took much longer, and his complete translation of the Bible appeared only in 1534. Luther's translation of the Bible influenced the development of the German language in the same way as the King James Version influenced English.

The year 1525 was pivotal in Luther's life and career. One of his most substantial theological works, *On the Bondage of the Will*, was published as a response to Erasmus's earlier attack on the doctrine of predestination, *On the Freedom of the Will* (1524). For Erasmus, humans, though fallen, remained free to respond to grace and thus to cooperate in their salvation. Luther, however, saw the human will as enslaved by sin and Satan. We think we are free, he contended, but we only reinforce our bondage by indulging in sin. Grace releases us from this enslaving illusion and leads us into 'the glorious liberty of the children of God'. God wants us to love him freely, but we can do this only when we have been freed from captivity to Satan and self. After this fierce debate, neither Luther nor Erasmus spoke or wrote to one another again. Many humanists who had earlier applauded Luther's attack on abuses in the church now went their separate way, unable to accept Luther's radical Augustinian theology.

Also in 1525 many of Luther's erstwhile followers abandoned his cautious approach to reform in favour of violent revolution (the bloody Peasants' Revolt) led by Thomas Müntzer and other radicals. One happy note in Luther's life at this time was his marriage to Katherine von Bora, a runaway nun, who brought stability, order and great joy into Luther's harried life. Luther and his 'Katie' established the tradition of the Protestant parsonage as they presided over a bustling family and numerous student boarders in the remodelled monastery that became their home in Wittenberg.

Luther continued to shape the Reformation through his sermons, letters, hymns, polemical treatises and commentaries. His sermons on Genesis and the Gospel of John circulated widely as models of good Protestant preaching. He himself regarded his 1535 commentary on Galatians (which he called 'my Katie von Bora') as his greatest work. It was a ringing affirmation of the doctrine of justification by faith alone, the 'article that makes or breaks the church'. In 1539 he published *Of the Councils and Churches*, which emphasized the catholicity of the Reformation and Protestant commitment to the trinitarian and Christological dogmas of the early church. Many of Luther's off-the-cuff remarks were recorded by his students and published in several volumes as his *Tischreden* (Table Talks). Among his several hymns, *Ein' Feste Burg* ('A Mighty Fortress') is best remembered, as the anthem of the Reformation.

As Luther grew older, his health began to fail. He was beset by numerous ailments, including kidney stones, gout, constipation, urine retention and depression. Near the end of his life, his attacks against his enemies became even more extreme. He excoriated the papacy, which he equated with the Antichrist. He was never reconciled with *Zwingli and his followers, whose memorialist doctrine of the Lord's Supper Luther regarded as a betrayal of the Christian faith. Most disturbing of all in the light of recent history were Luther's virulent attacks against the Jews, whose refusal to embrace the gospel led him to call for their banishment from Germany. Although Luther's disdain for the Jews had little in common with Hitler's racist policies, it is not surprising that the Nazis cited Luther as a precursor of their own antisemitism.

Luther's legacy does not lie primarily in the saintliness of his life. His faults were many; his vices were sometimes more visible than his virtues. Yet despite his foibles and sins and blindspots, he was able to conceive with remarkable clarity his belief in the paradoxical character of the human condition and the great possibility of human redemption through Jesus Christ. Luther's true legacy is his belief in the gracious character of God. 'What else was Luther,' asked Karl Barth, 'than a teacher of the Christian church whom one can hardly celebrate in any other way but to listen to him?'

Bibliography

R. H. Bainton, *Here I Stand: A Life of Martin*

Luther (Nashville: 1990); M. Brecht, *Martin Luther*, trans. J. L. Shaaf, 3 vols. (Philadelphia: 1985–1992); G. Ebeling, *Luther: An Introduction to His Thought*, trans. R. A. Wilson (Philadelphia: 1970); T. George, *Theology of the Reformers* (Leicester: 1990); H. A. Oberman, *Luther: Man Between God and the Devil*, trans. E. Walliser-Schwarzbart (New Haven: 1986); D. Steinmetz, *Luther in Context* (Bloomington: 1986).

T. GEORGE

■ **MACAULAY, Zachary** (1768–1838), a leading slavery abolitionist and governor of Sierra Leone, was born in Inverary, Argyllshire, Scotland, on 2 May 1768. He was the son of a Church of Scotland minister and younger brother of the evangelical Lieutenant-General Colin Macaulay, MP. Macaulay began working at the age of fourteen in the office of a Glasgow merchant. At sixteen he went to Jamaica as a bookkeeper, rising to become the manager of an estate. However, at twenty-four he returned home deeply repulsed by West Indian slavery. A year after his return, in 1793, he took up the suggestion of his brother-in-law, Thomas Babington, and went to West Africa to assist Thomas Clarkson in the management of Sierra Leone, a newly-founded colony where it was hoped that freed slaves would establish a model Christian community that would serve as a base for the evangelization of Africa. The Sierra Leone experiment was the brainchild of a group of wealthy and powerful evangelical Anglicans led by the indomitable William *Wilberforce and known by posterity as the 'Clapham Sect'. In this informal group Wilberforce was like a prime minister surrounded by a talented and powerful cabinet, with Macaulay and James *Stephen, MP, being responsible for developing the case against the slave trade, and Macaulay sharing with Hannah *More the portfolio for public relations.

In Sierra Leone, Macaulay soon replaced Clarkson as governor (1793–1799). This involved him in a wide range of activities: adviser, mediator, judge, clerk, educationalist, paymaster and preacher. Because the colony was managed by an underfunded private company with philanthropic aims, life was very difficult. The European slave trade had brutalized the natives; it was difficult to work with the freed slaves, who even threatened insurrection. In addition, the French briefly occupied Sierra Leone in 1794 and remained a threat. Furthermore, the malarial swamps of West Africa proved deadly to many Europeans; it was not unusual for people arriving from Europe to die within weeks of disembarking, as they lacked the immunity to the disease that many of the natives had developed.

In spite of all these difficulties, Macaulay stabilized the situation and brought the colony to a degree of prosperity. Eventually, however, his health broke down completely. He determined to book his passage home on a slave ship bound for the West Indies so that he could give first-hand evidence against the horrors of the slave trade. Once back in Britain, he did all that he could to end Britain's involvement in the trade.

An initial step towards this aim was to bring some twenty-five African children to London, where Macaulay hoped they could be educated and eventually become a black missionary force for the evangelization of West Africa. Most of them died, however, because they were unable to acclimatize to the cold and damp. In England Macaulay served as the secretary of the Sierra Leone Company until it came under the direct control of the British Government in 1808, thereby becoming a Crown colony rather than a Company colony. Macaulay also established a business which sought to develop legitimate trade with Africa; the strategy here was not primarily to make money but rather to model a viable economic alternative to the slave trade. In the end Macaulay's poor choice of a business partner and his own neglect lead to its collapse; he was rescued from financial ruin by his friend Wilberforce, who lent him £10,000.

Macaulay devoted much of his energies to three causes: anti-slavery, philanthropy and the strengthening of evangelicalism within the Church of England. His contribution to the research side of the abolition cause was enormous. Macaulay had a phenomenal memory and meticulous research skills; his hard work and attention to detail made him a walking encyclopaedia, so much so that when any fact was questioned, his friends said that they would 'look it up in Macaulay'. Despite being virtually blind in one eye, he had a photographic memory, allowing him to recall the minute details of long reports and then relate those facts to the larger issues involved.

Macaulay was not just a researcher; he also corresponded widely with abolitionist supporters in Britain and abroad. (Fluent in French, he was even sent by Wilberforce to France to try to enlist the French in the abolitionist cause.) Although not a public orator, he wielded his pen effectively by providing the public with accurate accounts, which included expositions of difficult details. He also had phenomenal powers of organization and sat on innumerable committees for various societies, such as the Anti-Slavery Society (which he helped to found) and the African Institute (1807–1812). He also wrote numerous anti-slavery pamphlets, which were crucial in bringing the cause before the British public, thereby mobilizing public support for the thousands of petitions presented to Parliament by the anti-slavery activists. The first great victory in the anti-slavery cause was achieved in 1807 when Britain prohibited the slave trade within its dominions. The second triumph was achieved considerably later (1833) when Parliament abolished slavery itself.

Macaulay was an intensely shy man who appeared austere and humourless to others; his great contributions to the anti-slavery cause were achieved behind the scenes. He was never a Member of Parliament, nor known as a public figure like other notables such as Wilberforce or James Stephen. Nevertheless, the significance of Macaulay's invaluable contribution to the cause can be measured by the degree of hostility with which his enemies treated him. He was the target of bitter invective doled out weekly by the periodical *John Bull*, the mouthpiece of the West India slave owners. In spite of the galling attacks, he never drew back from the anti-slavery cause.

Macaulay's philanthropic interests were wide-ranging and intertwined with his religious commitments. (In early nineteenth-century England the term 'philanthropist' was often regarded as synonymous with 'evangelical'.) Chief among these was his interest in education, which involved him in the promotion of Sunday schools (designed to bring literacy to the children of the poor) and

infant schools. Serving on the founding committee of the University of London, Macaulay also shared actively in its management. In 1815 he became involved in a scheme to send mathematicians and agriculturalists to Hayti (now Haiti) where they would aid King Henri Christophe in a scheme to educate Haitians. His other causes included prison reform and the regulation of public houses. As a commissioner on the Inquiry into the Administration of Public Charities, he was always ready to respond to requests to relieve individuals in distress who approached him. Macaulay was eventually honoured by his election as a Fellow of the Royal Society.

The third area of his activities was his labour on behalf of the fledgling evangelical grouping within the Church of England. He was founding editor of the *Christian Observer*, an influential periodical begun in 1802 by the Clapham Sect. Its aim was to commend a moderate and cultured evangelicalism to the middle and upper classes of England in the hope of capturing the Church of England from within for the evangelical cause. (Anglican Evangelicals were regarded by the Anglican establishment as untrustworthy enthusiasts, potentially disloyal because of their sympathy for non-Anglican evangelicals and therefore unworthy of senior appointments in the Church of England.) For fourteen years (1802–1816) Macaulay served as the *Christian Observer*'s unpaid lay editor, using it also to further slave trade abolition. Not only did he write many of its articles, but he also subjected everything in it to his editorial revision.

Macaulay was an important member of the three most important evangelical societies established at the turn of the century: the British and Foreign Bible Society, the Church Missionary Society and the Religious Tract Society. Being a devout Anglican, he instigated the Prayer Book and Homily Society designed to promote use of the Prayer Book and to emphasize the importance of the Thirty-Nine Articles of Religion as the theological basis of Anglicanism. He was involved with the Society for the Suppression of Vice, the Merchant Seaman's Bible Society and other societies. He also became active in efforts to promote Sabbath observance and to repress Sunday newspapers. In 1813 Macaulay was a key figure in the parliamentary campaign led by

Wilberforce to allow the entry of Protestant missionaries into British India. As a result of his efforts Parliament was flooded with thousands of petitions on a scale reminiscent of the anti-slave-trade agitation.

In 1799 Macaulay married Selina Mills, a former pupil of Hannah More, who had waited for him during his absence in Sierra Leone. Their son Thomas Babington Macaulay was a Member of Parliament, who became in the 1830s an important shaper of British policy in India. His grandson was Lord Macaulay, the famous British historian.

Macaulay had a deeply warm heart, which was obscured from public view by his eminently cool head. Hannah More maintained that Macaulay combined the characteristics of 'an enlightened statesman, a scriptural philanthropist, an orthodox and accurate divine, and a devout and practical Christian'. Macaulay died in London on 13 May 1838.

Bibliography
Viscountess Knutsford, *Life and Letters of Zachary Macaulay* (London: E. Arnold, 1900); *The Christian Observer* (1839), pp. 756–768 for obituary; Sir R. Coupland, *Life of William Wilberforce* (London: Collins, ²1945), p. 203; J. Pollock, *Wilberforce* (London: Constable, 1977).

D. M. LEWIS

■ **McCHEYNE, Robert Murray** (1813–1843), Scottish Presbyterian minister and major participant in the Scottish revivals of 1839–1843, was the youngest child of Adam (1781–1854) and Lockhart (1772–1854) McCheyne. He was born on 21 May 1813 at 14 Dublin Street, Edinburgh. Educated at the High School in Edinburgh, McCheyne showed an early aptitude for the arts, especially music and poetry. He was keen on sports, particularly gymnastics, a hobby that he was to retain into his adult ministry and that resulted in at least one accident that may have contributed to his early death.

The religion of the family was fairly typical of the Edinburgh middle class at the time, respectable and moral with little evidence of evangelical 'enthusiasm'. When McCheyne entered Edinburgh University in 1827, his brother David was the most earnest evangelical in the family. David's death on 8 July 1831 was to have a profound effect on his younger brother, who regarded that day as decisive in his own conversion.

On 28 September 1831 McCheyne presented himself to the presbytery of Edinburgh and was accepted to study divinity at the University of Edinburgh. It was here that he met his mentor, Thomas *Chalmers, Professor of Divinity. Chalmers was to become the pattern for his thought, life and ministry. Under Chalmers' influence McCheyne joined the Missionary Association and engaged in visitation of the poor in the needier districts of Edinburgh. He developed an interest in overseas missions, meeting several times with Alexander *Duff, the first Church of Scotland missionary.

After a short assistantship in Larbert, near Falkirk, McCheyne was inducted to the new charge of St Peter's, Dundee, in November 1836. St Peter's was built as part of the Church of Scotland extension programme initiated by Chalmers, and was situated in a rapidly expanding industrial area of Dundee. McCheyne did not appear to be ideally suited for his work. He was from a prosperous middle-class background with little experience of the industrial working class, his health was not good, and in many ways he seemed more suited to a rural parish. But his training under Chalmers and his experience in Edinburgh and in Larbert had prepared him for his new charge.

McCheyne's ministry in St Peter's was innovative and radical. Largely unhindered by tradition, he was able to build a team of leaders around himself and to initiate new work. He saw the prime need of the area as evangelism and acted accordingly. He was concerned that the church's services should be as attractive as possible and did his utmost to ensure that the singing was melodious and enthusiastic. He started psalmody classes and sometimes even led the singing himself.

His preaching was simple. He sought deliberately to keep his speech plain and to use plenty of word pictures. Sermons varied in length from twenty minutes to one and a half hours. He preached with authority, diligence and winsomeness. McCheyne liked to preach from the Old Testament, especially the Song of Solomon, but the majority of his extant sermons are from the New Testament.

He also engaged in an assiduous pro-gramme of pastoral and evangelistic visita-tion. Notes were kept of all his pastoral visits, with dates, descriptions and a record of the passages of Scripture read. As well as making full use of his elders and deacons he instituted a group of tract distributors and established a group of deaconesses whose job was to help with the visitation.

Under McCheyne, St Peter's became an active church with a large programme. As well as the regular Sunday services there was a Bible study on Thursday evenings. This was a less formal meeting for which the building was often full. (St Peter's was able to seat 1,100 people.) Smaller classes were taught by both the elders and McCheyne throughout the week. A church library was started to encourage reading and learning.

McCheyne's success is often attributed to his devotional life. He made prayer, medita-tion and self-discipline key aspects of his work throughout his life. His usual daily pattern was to rise at 6:30 a.m. and spend two hours in private prayer and meditation (including an hour devoted to the Jews). Between 8:30 and 10 a.m. he had breakfast and conducted family prayers. On Sundays his practice was to spend six hours in prayer and devotional reading. McCheyne felt so strongly about private and family worship that he devised a calendar for his people to enable them to read the Old Testament once and the New Testament and Psalms twice in a year. This calendar is still available and widely used today.

McCheyne had a particular missionary interest in the Jews. Consequently, after the 1838 General Assembly decided to appoint a committee to examine the state of the Jews and what could be done to address it, McCheyne was appointed as one of the members. The committee decided to send a deputation to Israel to investigate the condi-tion of the Jews there and throughout Europe. Dr Alexander Black (Professor of Divinity in Aberdeen), Dr Alexander Keith (minister of St Cyrus) and Andrew Bonar accompanied McCheyne. On 27 March 1839 they sailed for London. During the course of their six-month journey their letters home were pub-lished in the national and foreign press. The account of their journey, written by Bonar and McCheyne, was a bestseller.

Whilst McCheyne was in Israel, revival broke out in St Peter's under the ministry of William Chalmers Burns. As a result, McCheyne returned in November 1836 to a church that was packed nightly and had become the object of national press attention. Although he was extremely cautious in pro-nouncing anyone converted, McCheyne esti-mated that over 700 people had been 'savingly influenced' in St Peter's during this period. There were other centres of religious revival in Scotland at the same time, but St Peter's was seen as particularly important due to its being a city church extension. During the remaining four years of his life McCheyne was invited to other parts of Scotland to encourage spiritual revival and renewal. His unpublished papers contain notes and assessments concerning areas where he considered revival was taking place.

McCheyne was not a prolific writer. His devotion was expressed in more than fifty poems and hymns, of which *Jehovah Tsid-kenu* and *I am a Debtor* became the most famous. His only published book was a joint effort with Andrew Bonar, *The Narrative of a Mission of Inquiry to the Jews*.

In 1843 McCheyne was appointed as a commissioner to the General Assembly that was to result in the Disruption and the estab-lishment of the Free Church of Scotland, but in March he contracted typhus whilst visiting in the Hawkhill area of his parish. After two weeks of illness, and despite the church being full of people praying for his recovery every night, he died on 25 March. Over six thou-sand people attended the funeral. Immediately after McCheyne's death, Andrew Bonar, a close friend and colleague, wrote *The Memoir and Remains of Robert Murray McCheyne*. This book, widely regarded as a devotional and spiritual classic, has sold hundreds of thousands of copies, is still in print and has resulted in McCheyne's name still being known to a significant number of evangelicals in the Western and English-speaking world.

McCheyne was the right man in the right place. His spirituality, training, poetic and musical gifts, youth, and experience in the poorer areas of Edinburgh and Larbert made him an ideal minister for St Peter's. There he was able to put into practice the principles and methods of his mentor, Thomas Chalmers. Whilst the full extent of his ministry upon

Dundee has yet to be assessed, it is already clear that the combination of McCheyne and St Peter's was a powerful and potent one, the effect of which was felt far beyond the boundaries of the parish.

Bibliography

A. Bonar, *Memoir and Remains of Robert Murray McCheyne* (Edinburgh: 1844); A. Smellie, *Biography of R. M. McCheyne* (Fearn: 1995); L. J. Van Valen, *Gedreven Door Zijn Liefde* (Houten: 1993); R. M. McCheyne, *From the Preacher's Heart* (Fearn: Christian Focus, 1993); Web site: http://web.ukonline.co.uk/d.haslam/m-cheyne.htm

D. A. ROBERTSON

■ **McCOSH, James** (1811–1894), Presbyterian minister, philosopher and college president, was born to farming parents in Ayrshire in southwest Scotland on 1 April 1811. At just thirteen years of age he began studies at Glasgow University (1824–1829), which were followed by ministerial training at Edinburgh University (MA 1834). At Edinburgh he was formatively influenced, in his religious commitments and intellectual orientation, by two great Victorians: Thomas *Chalmers, then professor of divinity and the ascendent leader of the evangelical revival in Scotland, and Sir William Hamilton, the last major voice of the Scottish common-sense philosophical tradition. Subsequently McCosh served two Church of Scotland parishes to the immediate northeast of Dundee: Arbroath (1834–1839) and then Brechin (1839–1852). During his ministry in Brechin, Scottish evangelical protest swelled against state control, patronage appointments and the allegedly tepid spiritual condition of the established church. When the Disruption finally came in 1843, McCosh sided with his mentor Chalmers, marching with him in the famous procession that left Edinburgh's St Andrew's Church to form the Free Church of Scotland. Two years later he married Isabella Guthrie, the niece of Thomas Guthrie, another Scottish evangelical leader.

During his years as a parish minister McCosh stayed abreast of leading continental and British philosophical developments, always wary of what he once called 'the sophistries of infidel metaphysicians'. In 1843 John Stuart Mill's influential *System of Logic* appeared, a work that altogether excluded the supernatural from its empirical worldview. McCosh's first book, *The Method of the Divine Government* (1850), was an apologetic response to Mill's sceptical challenge. In it McCosh sought to demonstrate that nature, through both its external phenomena and its internal psychological evidences, points unmistakably to the supernatural reality of divine presence and intelligence.

On the strength of this publication McCosh was appointed professor of logic and metaphysics at Queen's College, Belfast (1852–1868). During his sixteen years in Ireland, McCosh produced some of his most important scholarly work. This included *Typical Forms and Special Ends of Creation* (1856), which he co-authored with the scientist George Dickie and which anticipated some of his later accommodations to Darwin's evolutionary hypothesis. He also wrote *The Intuitions of the Mind* (1860), in which he sought to defend, along the lines of Scottish realism (i.e. common-sense philosophy), the possibility of genuine epistemological certitude, and at the same time distance himself from what he considered Sir William Hamilton's near-fatal concessions to Kantian thought. (Near the end of his life McCosh published a revised and expanded version of this work under the title *First and Fundamental Truths* [1889].) If there was a distinct feature of McCosh's articulation of the Scottish philosophy, it lay in the manner in which he made explicit some of the chief ways in which this philosophy supported and legitimized theism and orthodox Christian belief. This approach is clearly in evidence in his *The Supernatural in Relation to the Natural* (1862) and in other works.

J. S. Mill's *An Examination of Sir William Hamilton's Philosophy* (1865) was widely regarded as having effectively discredited Hamilton's thinking. Though McCosh did not agree with Hamilton in every respect, he none the less interpreted Mill's work as a challenge to the fundamental optimism of Scottish epistemology and promptly wrote a polemical rejoinder entitled *An Examination of Mr. J. S. Mill's Philosophy* (1866).

In the same year McCosh toured the United States, lecturing in defence of evangelical orthodoxy, and the positive impression he made led to his appointment as the eleventh president of the Presbyterians' College of New Jersey (later re-named Princeton University) at a time when the theologian Charles *Hodge still served as chairman of its board. It was also a critical post-Civil War moment, when institutional resources were depleted and the college's recruitment base in the South had been lost. But McCosh's Free Church convictions and values were a particularly good fit for the ethos and opportunities of post-war America. During his two-decade tenure as president (1868–1888, emeritus 1888–1894), the institution was transformed from a fledgling, parochial college into a national university. The size of the faculty doubled, bright young alumni were groomed in European universities for future Princeton appointments, and student enrolment tripled. Buildings were erected and the curriculum expanded, especially in the empirical sciences, for which the Scottish common-sense philosophy was such a natural ally. However, McCosh's Princeton reflected his conviction that the training of the intellect was the primary method for transforming society and that philosophy in particular was the fountain of societal development, inevitably influencing all aspects of culture. At the same time, moral supervision of students was strict, course-work in biblical studies was mandatory and student revivals were encouraged.

The modest (by contemporary standards) size of Princeton, where enrolment, despite steady growth, remained in the hundreds, was undoubtedly a factor that enabled McCosh, a tireless administrator, also to remain active in scholarship and teaching. During his years as president he published *Christianity and Positivism* (1871), *The Scottish Philosophy* (1875), a magisterial historical survey of the tradition from its inception with Francis Hutcheson to its mutation at the hands of William Hamilton, *Psychology* (2 vols., 1886–1887) and *The Religious Aspects of Evolution* (1888). As a teacher he personally influenced a student body that included the future United States president Woodrow Wilson.

Debates within American Christianity over the Darwinian hypothesis were intense and divisive from the beginning. Although he refused to rule out the possibility of super-natural intervention(s) in the evolutionary process, McCosh none the less pursued a rapprochement between science and faith. His position, which was relatively accommodating in comparison to those of many evangelical contemporaries, was based on the critical distinction he drew between the truths of the biblical creation narrative and its literal form. Having thereby established the point, he believed, that Scripture is not necessarily discredited by judicious concessions to evolutionary theory, he maintained that evolution did not in fact deny the reality of God. On the contrary, the evolutionary process actually magnified the wonder and mystery of creation.

In 1870 he proposed the idea of an international Presbyterian alliance to promote Reformed ecumenicity and the spiritual vitality of the tradition, to resist continental unbelief, and to oppose the debilitating effects of state control of the church. Five years later he was elected president of the inaugural meeting of the World Alliance of Reformed Churches. He was also responsible for preparing a statement of defining principles that was adopted at the organization's Edinburgh Conference in 1877. While subscribing personally to the main contours of Reformed theology, McCosh also embraced the larger evangelical movement and actively supported the Evangelical Alliance.

McCosh died on 16 November 1894 at Princeton. His *Intuitions of the Mind* (1860) and *The Scottish Philosophy* (1875) may have been his most profound works. Throughout his career in three countries (Scotland, Ireland and the USA) he laboured to identify and refute any influences that might encourage subjectivity or scepticism in religious matters. In this effort he attempted to fuse a lively evangelical faith with the best of modern thinking, including a philosophy forged by the Scottish Enlightenment. Although McCosh failed to preserve Scottish realism among American intellectuals or to ensure a uniformly evangelical future for Princeton, he exercised a significant influence on American religious and intellectual life in his day.

Bibliography

J. D. Hoeveler, Jr, 'Evangelical Ecumenism: James McCosh and the Intellectual Origins of the World Alliance of Reformed Churches',

Journal of Presbyterian History, 55.1 (Spring 1977), pp. 36–56; J. D. Hoeveler, Jr, *James McCosh and the Scottish Intellectual Tradition* (Princeton: Princeton University Press, 1981); W. Sloane (ed.), *The Life of James McCosh: A Record Chiefly Autobiographical* (Edinburgh: T. & T. Clark, 1896).

G. G. SCORGIE

■ **McCULLOCH, Thomas** (1776–1843), Presbyterian cleric, author and educator, was born in Fereneze, Scotland, the second of nine children of Michael McCulloch and Elizabeth Neilson, and died in Halifax, Nova Scotia, British North America.

Coming from a Presbyterian family in the artisan class, in which his father was a master blockmaker for the printing of cloth, Thomas McCulloch was formed by his Calvinistic heritage, the Scottish Enlightenment and the rise of industry in the late eighteenth century. He graduated in logic from the University of Glasgow in 1792, with facility in languages and a strong interest in church history. Later, he began to study medicine but did not complete the course, choosing instead to read theology at the theological hall of the General Associate Synod in Whitburn, where ministers of the Secession Church were prepared for ministry. Licensed to preach by the presbytery of Kilmarnock in 1799, McCulloch was called to serve a church in Stewarton, near Glasgow. Shortly thereafter he married Isabella Walker, the daughter of the Revd David Walker.

In 1803 McCulloch sought to be dismissed from his pastoral charge, petitioned the General Associate Synod to be assigned to North America and was appointed to Prince Edward Island. He and his family arrived in Pictou, Nova Scotia, that November. In June 1804 McCulloch was inducted into the 'Harbour' church in Pictou; he never did settle on Prince Edward Island. Soon after his arrival McCulloch became outraged at the monopoly that the Anglican Church in Nova Scotia had over higher education. Their King's College in Windsor was the only institution for higher learning in the province, and its students were required to accept the Thirty-Nine Articles of Religion in order to graduate. This meant that the 80% majority was prevented from being granted a college degree from King's. The Anglican ruling elite, centred in the colonial capital of Halifax, believed that higher education should be reserved for their 'sons' and should exclude Dissenters, who were suspected of holding socially destructive 'republican' or 'democratic' notions of liberty. Coming from Scotland, where universities advocated a liberal education that accommodated students from a variety of denominational backgrounds, McCulloch spent much of his North American career trying to extend higher educational opportunities to Presbyterians and others. This commitment to education was buttressed by his conviction that Nova Scotia Presbyterians would never be adequately served by ministers trained in Scotland, and therefore he determined to train a native clergy.

McCulloch's first step towards achieving his educational goals for the colony was to start a school in his home, which was later moved to a school building and boasted thirty to forty students by 1814. Four years later Pictou Academy was founded with McCulloch as principal. Merging Christianity and education, and believing in the essential unity of knowledge, he made sure that his school provided instruction in the 'classical' and 'scientific' disciplines such as philosophy, mathematics and the physical sciences. In promoting his school, McCulloch highlighted the courses in physical and natural sciences and mathematics that were not offered at King's College. Nevertheless, McCulloch faced a variety of challenges in developing the Pictou institution. For example, although Dissenting groups such as the Baptists and Methodists were quite willing to work with McCulloch on petitioning for non-Anglican clergy to have the right to conduct marriages by license, they were less enthusiastic about supporting his non-denominational vision for higher education. So too were clergy from the Church of Scotland, or the Kirk, who carried long-standing old-world antipathies to the British colony that were not allayed by McCulloch, the undisputed and often intractable leader of the Seceders. (In Nova Scotia, the two Seceder branches, the Burghers and Anti-Burghers, united in 1817, forming the Presbyterian Church of Nova Scotia.) The Kirk viewed Pictou Academy as a 'local' concern, and when the Church of Scotland in Nova Scotia increased in popularity and political influence it did not support McCulloch's petitions to the government for financial aid to the fledgling school. The division of the 'Scottish' churches in Nova Scotia tended to undermine the view of Pictou Academy, advanced by McCulloch, as a place of religious liberty and reformist activity.

McCulloch's efforts were frustrated further by his failure, after a great struggle, to convince the Nova Scotia Assembly to grant the Pictou Academy college status, a nonsectarian board of trustees and a guaranteed annual grant for operating. Problems with finances were exacerbated further by McCulloch's clash with the Glasgow Colonial Society, which he had hoped would provide support for the struggling educational enterprise. However, in the face of these obstacles McCulloch sent his theological students to the University of Glasgow, where they took the qualifying examinations as one of the necessary steps towards ordination.

In 1834 McCulloch wrote to a friend that Pictou 'has very little appearance of being much longer the place for me'. Four years later the despondent McCulloch resigned from Pictou Academy, which was by then dominated by the Kirk and held little promise of ever being much more than a grammar school. On 6 August 1838 he was appointed president of Dalhousie College, in Halifax. Although originally envisaged as a nonsectarian college by Lord Dalhousie, political squabbling and denominational jockeying had made the college, by its founding, an educational institution dominated by the Kirk. Nevertheless, McCulloch assumed his administrative duties, and was appointed Professor of Logic, Rhetoric, and Moral Philosophy. During his presidency of Dalhousie College, he unsuccessfully tried to make the college a truly non-denominational institution and to introduce a Roman Catholic to the faculty.

If McCulloch did not always win his political and denominational battles, he did mentor a number of influential clergy who came to advance his cause of liberal reform in Nova Scotia during and after his lifetime. Furthermore, his considerable skill as a writer of sermons, theological works, satire and political critique made him one of the major Canadian writers of the nineteenth century. Although he authored religious tracts such as

Popery Condemned (1808), *The Prosperity of the Church in Troubled Times* (1814) and *Calvinism, Doctrine of the Scriptures* (1846), McCulloch is perhaps best remembered for his *Colonial Gleanings: William and Melville* (1826) and the 'Stepsure Letters', which were first serialized in the *Acadian Recorder*, beginning in the 22 December 1821 issue, and were later published as *The Letters of Mephibosheth Stepsure* (c. 1860). These enormously popular letters satirized the indolence and desire for upward mobility and recognition among Nova Scotia's rural folk and townspeople. Literary theorist Northrop Frye called McCulloch 'the founder of Canadian humour', highlighting his capacity for humorous writing based on an implicit understanding of the cultural context.

In keeping with his commitment to liberal education, McCulloch also published *A Lecture at the Opening of the ... Pictou Academical Institution* (1821), *The Nature and Uses of a Liberal Education* (1818) and a series of letters in the *Acadian Recorder*, beginning in 1823, that reflected his interest in science and desire that it be put to practical use. McCulloch spent much energy collecting specimens, such as rocks, birds, mammals and 'creeping things', that could be placed in his natural history museum at Pictou Academy. The collection was later sold in Britain.

Thomas McCulloch was driven by his Calvinism, philosophical liberalism and desire to transform Nova Scotia through a 'race of evangelical preachers' and liberal nonsectarian education. In many ways, he was a man before his time. However, his vision would be significantly implemented through the efforts of his former students, who became influential clerics, missionaries, educators, lawyers, politicians and scientists, and through his literary output.

Bibliography
W. McCulloch, *The Life of Thomas McCulloch, by his Son* (Truro, Nova Scotia: 1920).

T. Goodwin

■ **McGOWAN, Robert J. H.** (1870–1953), Australian Presbyterian minister, is best known for his unsuccessful attempts in the 1930s to have Samuel Angus (Professor of

New Testament Exegesis and Historical Theology at the Theological Hall, Sydney) tried for heresy. Born in Ballarat in Victoria on 25 August 1870, of Irish Presbyterian stock, McGowan first worked as a bank officer, but attended Ormond College from 1894 to 1896. Ironically, there was a minor delay in his being accepted as a ministerial candidate because he confessed in a letter to the presbytery of Melbourne North in April 1897 that he had some difficulties with infant baptism and other points of doctrine. These were quickly resolved, and McGowan was licensed on 1 July 1897 by the presbytery of Beechworth. After serving at Birchip (1899–1905) and Beaufort (1905–1907), he was called to the thriving church at Ashfield in NSW, where he was inducted on 11 October and ministered until his retirement in 1951.

Physically, McGowan was an imposing figure. His first wife, Jessie (whom he married in 1898), died suddenly on 8 March 1926. McGowan was granted nine months' leave of absence to go abroad, to visit India, Palestine, Asia Minor, Britain and the United States. He indulged his passion for archaeology and returned with a large collection of lantern slides. Regarded as 'hopelessly undomesticated', McGowan then married a widow, Mrs Fanny Franklin.

In 1905 the *Messenger* wrote that McGowan possessed 'a strong face and an evangelical heart'. Later, Alan Dougan was to remember McGowan as 'a plain and stolid preacher'. At the social to welcome him to Ashfield, McGowan stated that the four principles on which he proposed to base his ministry were the atoning death of Christ for sin, the trustworthiness of the Scriptures, the filling of the Spirit and united prayer.

Fearing worldliness, McGowan opposed short sleeves, the theatre and dancing, and supported Sabbath observance and temperance. On the other hand, the congregation formed a soccer team in 1925, and the young people played tennis on Saturday afternoons. When visiting people in need, McGowan often talked, prayed and left a pound note under the clock. At Sunday school picnics he appeared in a yellow silk coat, his clerical collar and the pith helmet he wore on archaeological trips.

An ardent evangelical, McGowan served as convener of the Foreign Missions Committee

for ten years (1909–1914, 1921–1926). In 1912 he visited South India to transfer the jurisdiction of the station at Sholinghur from the Church of Scotland to the NSW Church. In addition, he was convener of the Jewish Mission Committee (1918–1948) and served on the Council of the Presbyterian Ladies College, Croydon for forty years. He also lectured regularly at Croydon Missionary and Bible College.

From 1920 to 1924 Australian Presbyterians were asked to vote regarding a possible union with the Methodists and Congregationalists. McGowan was alarmed at the omissions from the proposed Basis of Union, and in 1920 he wrote *A Doctrinal Landslide*. In it he asserted that 'The great issue to-day is the Deity of Christ.' He feared the adoption of a creed that was only superficially orthodox. The NSW Church favoured union, but it was achieved only later, in 1977. In 1933 McGowan made the unlikely claim that the proposed union was rejected because *homoousion* was not in the doctrinal basis.

In 1931 McGowan was elected state moderator. He spoke of the crisis in church and society, claiming that 'The present day laxity in doctrine and morals is in a large measure due to the attitude of this generation to the Word of God.' He also urged compassion for the weak, and prayer for revival.

The following year a petition was presented to the NSW Assembly that called for the removal, on the grounds of heresy, of one of the professors at St Andrews. The Assembly simply reaffirmed its adherence to the doctrines of the evangelical faith. Always a reluctant leader, McGowan said that he wept like a child at the end of 1932 when he realized what was being taught at the college.

In January 1933 McGowan voiced his concern publicly by writing to the press in opposition to Angus. At the Sydney presbytery in March, McGowan asked that the NSW Assembly inquire into Angus's views. Using notes supplied by three students and Angus's own writings, McGowan raised six issues: the deity of Christ, the atonement, the resurrection of Christ, the Holy Spirit, the historicity of the gospels, and what Angus called the 'two Christianities' (the religion of Jesus and historic Christianity).

Angus responded shrewdly by affirming propitiation, the divine sonship of Jesus, and the resurrection as 'an objective, super-natural, historic fact'. Realizing that he had little support and threatened with civil court action, McGowan lost his nerve at the NSW Assembly of May 1933. He left the house just as he was about to introduce his motion. The Assembly stood to applaud Angus and voted 245 to 19 in favour of R. G. Macintyre's motion affirming tolerance. Seven men, including McGowan, dissented and appealed to the General Assembly of Australia (GAA). However, the GAA returned the case to the Sydney presbytery.

Now Angus became more aggressive and mocked McGowan, claiming that he represented 'the Presbyterian espionage system at its best'. Indeed, he said, on entering heaven McGowan would institute a heresy hunt against St Luke. Angus even said that he accepted the Scriptures 'without mental reservation', but only in the spirit, not the letter! The presbytery decided to proceed against Angus by judicial process. In *Truth and Tradition*, published in 1934, Angus mocked the God of Calvinism as the 'Divine Sultan' and repudiated the Trinity, the deity of Christ, substitutionary atonement and the bodily resurrection. At the same time he asserted, 'it is not in any ecclesiastical hands to expel me from my prophetic calling'.

McGowan affirmed the evangelical faith: 'It is at the Cross the Christian life begins.' He went on: 'The death of Christ propitiates God's justice, and is a satisfaction rendered to God's holy nature.' On the cross, he declared, God's justice and mercy were reconciled: 'The One who required the atonement was the One who provided it.'

In May 1934 McGowan told the NSW Assembly that Angus's view of Christ was worse than that of Arius in the fourth century, and claimed that the acceptance of Angus's theology would destroy the church. However, the Assembly decided by a two-to-one majority that the church was 'wide enough' to include people of different opinions. McGowan appealed to the judicial commission, but it only chastised Angus for being unwise in some of his expressions.

McGowan refused to give up his campaign, and the case came before the 1936 GAA, but the Assembly passed a unanimous and contradictory resolution that both criticized and supported Angus. McGowan was not present for this GAA as the presbytery of Sydney had refused to elect him as a delegate.

One of Angus's disciples, E. H. Vines, maintained that McGowan had not read Angus's books and did not understand his teaching. In fact, McGowan possessed a robust intellect and was quite well read in theology. At various times he cited Emil Brunner, Claude Montefiore and even the radical P. W. Schmiedel.

In the decades to come the issues raised by McGowan became less clear. Principal Alan Dougan imagined McGowan and Angus going for walks together in heaven. McGowan died on 14 January 1953, mourned by his student J. T. H. Kerr as 'a valiant soldier of Christ'.

Bibliography

S. Emilisen, *A Whiff of Heresy* (Kensington: NSW University Press, 1991).

P. BARNES

■ **McGREADY, James** (c. 1760–1817), Presbyterian pastor and revivalist, was born in western Pennsylvania to a Scots-Irish family, who moved to North Carolina before 1778. Raised within a devout Presbyterian family, at the age of seventeen he joined the Old Side Buffalo Church, which was pastored by David Caldwell, who had studied at the New Side College of New Jersey.

McGready returned to Pennsylvania in the early 1780s to study with John McMillan and Joseph Smith, Presbyterian ministers in Washington County, who taught orthodox Calvinist theology and the necessity of a conversion experience. Although McGready had always maintained a devout lifestyle, it was only then that he 'underwent a profound conversion experience that altered the way he approached eternity as well as his ministry on earth'. Licensed by Redstone presbytery in 1788, he returned to North Carolina, and in 1790 he was ordained by Orange presbytery as pastor at Haw River and Stony Creek. That same year he married Nancy Thompson.

Convinced of the importance of education in promoting revival, McGready opened a classical school in his home, also teaching in David Caldwell's nearby academy. Regularly preaching against the threat posed by deism to the revivalist view of the importance of conversion and to the stability of society, McGready also warned against the danger of becoming a 'christianized deist', who might attend an orthodox church but who did not truly believe the gospel. He antagonized many within his church, but as early as 1791 sparked a revival in the Carolina piedmont that produced a number of notable converts including Barton W. *Stone, William McGee and Samuel McAdoo, all of whom would take their mentor's teachings further than he wished.

By 1796 tensions within McGready's churches had reached the point of violence, and he hastily accepted a call from former parishoners in Logan County, Kentucky. McGready quickly set to work teaching the theology and piety of revivalist Calvinism, and by the summer of 1799 revival had broken out in the Red River congregation. In the summer of 1800 McGready encouraged people to camp around the church building, creating the first camp meeting (which largely followed the pattern of the traditional Scottish communion season, except that previously visitors had stayed with local church members). The communion at Gasper River in 1800 produced dramatic reactions such as swooning and crying out. That autumn McGready took the revival to various Tennessee and Kentucky communions. From 1801 to 1803 the revival spread back into the Carolinas and western Pennsylvania.

McGready defended the 'uncommon bodily exercises and agitations', such as falling, jerking, barking and dancing, as supernatural signs of the Spirit's working. He pointed to the change in morals that accompanied these exercises as confirmation of his view. The Presbyterian General Assembly of 1804 approved of the revivals in general, although the 1805 Assembly cautioned against 'irregular and disorderly' camp meetings.

As the revivals began to include Methodist and Baptist ministers, many Presbyterians began to raise concerns about Arminian preaching. In 1803 Richard McNemar and Barton Stone left Transylvania presbytery, after rejecting limited atonement, creeds and Presbyterian church order, and in 1804 they formed the Christian Church, with McNemar joining the Shakers shortly thereafter. McGready's Cumberland presbytery caused some concern between 1803 and 1805 by

licensing nearly thirty lay exhorters without regard to their educational background, and requiring them to accept the Westminster Confession of Faith 'only so far as they ... think it corresponds with the scriptures'.

When the Synod of Kentucky ruled against the revivalists in 1805, McGready had to choose between his associates and orthodox Calvinism. At first he attempted to convince his friends of the importance of Calvinist doctrine, but by 1806 he realized that they were moving towards Arminian doctrine. 'Having stepped to the edge of the precipice, McGready turned back, but had then to watch his students, friends, and spiritual children jump off the cliff.' In 1810 four revivalist ministers, including McGee and McAdoo, constituted themselves as the Cumberland Presbyterian Church, which followed Presbyterian polity, but rejected predestination and limited atonement.

In 1807 McGready moved to Henderson, Kentucky, where he continued to hold revivals at communion seasons and organized congregations throughout the west under the auspices of the General Assembly. Frustrated at the success of the Cumberland Presbyterians despite their (in his view) shallow doctrine, McGready remained convinced of the need for sound theology and fervent piety. More than forty of his sermons were published as the *Posthumous Works of James McGready* (1831).

Bibliography
P. K. Conkin, *Cane Ridge: America's Pentecost* (Madison: University of Wisconsin Press, 1990); L. E. Schmidt, *Holy Fairs: Scottish Communions and American Revivals in the Early Modern Period* (Princeton: Princeton University Press, 1989); J. T. Scott, 'James McGready: Son of Thunder, Father of the Great Revival' (PhD dissertation, The College of William and Mary, 1991).

P. J. WALLACE

■ **MACHEN, John Gresham** (1881–1937), fundamentalist Presbyterian theologian and educator, was the son of Arthur Webster Machen, a Harvard-educated lawyer, and Mary Gresham, and was raised in a socially prominent and wealthy Baltimore family. Machen's parents, moreover, were loyal

southerners and devout members of the affluent Franklin Street Presbyterian Church, a
congregation of the southern Presbyterian
Church.

After attending a private academy, Machen
matriculated in 1898 at the Johns Hopkins
University on a scholarship. Under the tutelage of the foremost American classics scholar
Basil L. Gildersleeve, Machen excelled in
Greek. In 1901 he earned his BA degree
with highest honours, graduating as the class
valedictorian. Undecided about what career
to pursue, he continued his advanced study of
Greek under Gildersleeve for another year
and even spent a summer studying banking
and international law at the University of
Chicago.

Although still undecided about his vocational aspirations, and despite his personal
misgivings about his suitability for the ministry, he decided to enrol at Princeton Theological Seminary in the autumn of 1902 for a
trial year of theological education. Given
Machen's background in the southern Presbyterian Church, his choice of Princeton,
which was affiliated with the northern Presbyterian Church, might seem odd. None the
less, Princeton probably attracted him for
several reasons. Princeton had longstanding
connections with the southern church, as
evidenced by the fact that several southerners
taught on the faculty. Moreover, the seminary's president, Francis Landey Patton, was
a friend of the Machen family. More importantly, Princeton enjoyed an international
reputation as the pre-eminent centre of scholarly Old School Presbyterian orthodoxy.
Established in 1812, Princeton's faculty had
included a distinguished list of conservative
theologians, including Archibald *Alexander,
Charles *Hodge and Benjamin Breckinridge
*Warfield. Like southern Presbyterianism, the
Old School Presbyterian tradition of Princeton espoused the conservative Reformed
orthodoxy expressed in the Westminster Confession of Faith and advanced a strict doctrine
of biblical inerrancy. Moreover, the Princeton
theology embraced the philosophy of Scottish
common-sense realism and the Baconian
method. Consequently, the task of theology,
according to the Princeton theologians, was
the orderly systematization of the 'facts' of
the Bible. However, there were certain differences between northern and southern Old

School Presbyterianism. Unlike the northern
church, the southern tradition advocated the
doctrine of the 'spirituality of the church',
which proscribed the church's direct involvement in civil affairs.

While a seminarian, Machen also enrolled
in an MA programme in the philosophy
department at Princeton University. He
earned an MA in 1904 from the university
and a BD in 1905 from the seminary. With
the encouragement of William Park Armstrong, his mentor in New Testament at the
seminary, and the largess provided by a
seminary prize that he had won in New
Testament studies, Machen determined to
spend the 1905–1906 academic year studying
in Germany. He hoped that the year would
afford him the opportunity to work through
his vocational options. Ironically, instead of
providing him with a time of quiet reflection,
the year precipitated a faith crisis.

As a student at the universities at Marburg
and Göttingen, Machen studied with three of
Germany's leading biblical scholars, Adolf
Julicher, Johannes Weiss and Wilhelm
Bousset. But it was Marburg's systematic theologian Wilhelm Herrmann whom
Machen found most challenging. Herrmann
had an engaging personality and a devout
liberal theology. According to Herrmann, the
essence of a genuine Christian faith lay in
one's experience of communion with God
through Christ. In direct contradiction to
Old School Presbyterian orthodoxy, Herrmann argued that science and faith were two
entirely distinct realms. Moreover, since the
Bible was subject to refutation by historical
research, he argued, Scripture could not provide a sufficient basis for faith.

Although unwilling to forge an intellectual
compromise between these two competing
visions of the Christian faith and still troubled
by unresolved vocational aspirations, Machen
was persuaded by William P. Armstrong in
1906 to accept a one-year appointment as an
instructor in New Testament at Princeton.
Over the next several years, Machen resolved
his intellectual qualms and embraced the Old
School faith of Princeton. His 1912 address,
'Christianity and Culture', reveals his vision
of supernatural Christianity in society.
According to Machen, the secularization of
American culture threatened the gospel. The
task of the church, therefore, was neither to

compromise with modernity nor to retreat from culture. Rather, its task was to engage the ideas of secular culture in order to transform them, to make them consistent with an orthodox Christian worldview.

After years of personal struggle with secular modernity, Machen had found his vocation. Machen's personal experience bolstered his commitment to combat modernism within the Presbyterian Church in defence of orthodoxy. He was ordained in the northern Presbyterian Church in 1914 and installed as an assistant professor the following year. In Machen's inaugural address, 'History and Faith', he responded to his former teacher Wilhelm Herrmann. Whereas Herrmann contended that the gospel was independent of history, Machen countered that the gospel was at its heart historical in nature because, he argued, Christ's resurrection was a historical event.

During the First World War, Machen served in the Young Men's Christian Association in France and Belgium. In 1921 he delivered the James Sprunt Lectures at Union Theological Seminary in Virginia, which were published that same year as *The Origins of Paul's Religion*. While many higher critics of the day held that the apostle Paul depended heavily upon Greek philosophy and taught a theology rather different from the simple teachings of Jesus, Machen attempted to demonstrate the theological continuity between Jesus and Paul. Unlike many fundamentalists, however, Machen eagerly engaged in critical scholarship. For this reason, the study was well received by both conservative and liberal scholars.

If *The Origins of Paul's Religion* substantiated Machen's credentials as a genuine scholar, his next major work, *Christianity and Liberalism* (1923), established his reputation as a leading fundamentalist polemicist. For more than a decade, conservative Presbyterians had attempted to stem the rising tide of theological liberalism within their church. To this end, the General Assembly of the Presbyterian Church approved in 1910 the Five Point Deliverance, which required all ministerial candidates to subscribe to five doctrines (the inerrancy of Scripture, the virgin birth of Christ, the substitutionary atonement, the bodily resurrection of Christ, and the miracle-working power of Christ) as essential beliefs of historic Christianity.

In 1916 and again in 1923, the church's highest ruling body reaffirmed the Five Point Deliverance.

Despite these efforts, theological liberalism continued to gain popularity within the church. Within this context, *Christianity and Liberalism* represented the Old School Presbyterian perspective on the theological conflict dividing the northern Presbyterian Church. According to Machen, liberal theology had sacrificed 'everything distinctive of Christianity' in its effort to preserve the faith's relevance to secular culture. Because liberals used traditional Christian language but denied the supernatural intervention of God into history, Machen accused them of dishonesty. To Machen, liberalism and Christianity were two distinct religions. Since liberalism was not Christianity, Machen contended, liberals ought to take the honourable course of action and withdraw from the church. Machen's stinging criticisms of liberalism's efforts to preserve its relevance by conforming to secular modernity won admiration from such cultural modernists as Walter Lippmann and H. L. Mencken. The liberal party within the northern Presbyterian Church, however, did not share the secular savants' appreciation for Machen's critique. In response to the Five Point Deliverance, liberal Presbyterians issued a protest statement, the Auburn Affirmation, in 1924. Without explicitly denying the Five Point Deliverance, the Affirmation contended that the five-point test for orthodoxy offered only one theory or explanation of these doctrines. There were other theories, the Affirmation declared, that were equally consistent with Scripture and the church's doctrinal standards.

In the midst of the growing fundamentalist-modernist controversy within the northern Presbyterian Church and in American culture at large, Machen played a leading role in fomenting conservative opposition to liberal innovation. He was a frequent speaker at Bible conferences, churches, colleges and seminaries. William Jennings *Bryan even invited him to serve as an expert witness in the Scopes Monkey Trial in Dayton, Tennessee, in the summer of 1925. Although critical of the scientific naturalism that guided a Darwinian view of creation, Machen, like Warfield before him, did not share the emerging Six Twenty-Four-Hour Days creationist interpretation of Genesis. Consequently, he declined Bryan's invitation.

As the fundamentalist-modernist controversy threatened to produce a schism within the northern Presbyterian Church, the General Assembly appointed a special commission in 1925 to ascertain the specific causes of the conflict and to propose a resolution. Machen was among those invited to share his perspective on the division at one of the commission's meetings. The commission's final report, which received official approval at the 1926 General Assembly, constituted a major defeat for the fundamentalists. To the chagrin of Machen and other conservatives, the report, echoing the position advocated in the Auburn Affirmation, opted for toleration of doctrinal diversity over strict confessionalism in order to preserve the unity of the church and its mission to American society.

For several years the fundamentalist-modernist controversy within the northern Presbyterian Church had divided the Princeton Seminary community. The majority of the faculty, led by Machen, remained committed to the institution's traditional confessional position. A minority of the faculty, led by president J. Ross Stevenson and practical theology professor Charles R. Erdman, were theologically evangelical but more willing to tolerate theological liberalism within the church. Growing tensions over these ecclesiastical matters were intertwined with personality conflicts, and to many observers Machen often stood at the centre of both. In 1925 the seminary's board of directors elected the conservative Clarence Macartney to the chair of apologetics. After Macartney decided to remain in the pastorate, the directors elected Machen to the position. There was so much friction within the seminary faculty that the 1926 General Assembly appointed a committee to address the situation. Not only had the General Assembly abolished the Five Point Deliverance, but now it had also handed Machen a personal defeat by deferring its required approval of his election to the chair of apologetics at the seminary until the special committee completed its investigation.

Although not explicitly mentioned during the floor debate at the 1926 Presbyterian General Assembly, Machen's opposition to prohibition probably played a critical role in thwarting the immediate approval of his election as the professor of apologetics. As popular support for the Eighteenth Amendment waned in the 1920s, many Protestant denominations, especially the northern Presbyterians and the Methodists, continued to champion the cause. The 1926 Presbyterian General Assembly adopted a resolution opposing any modification of the Volstead Act. While Machen advocated strict confessional standards, he was also a civil libertarian and sometimes outspoken opponent of what he perceived as growing government infringements upon individual freedom. Another source of Machen's opposition to prohibition lay in his commitment to the doctrine of the 'spirituality of the church'. Among both leading liberal and fundamentalist Presbyterians, Machen stood out as a lone opponent to the 'noble experiment'.

After nearly three years of testimonies, debates and delays, the majority report of the special committee proposed an administrative resolution to the theological crisis engulfing Princeton Seminary and the northern Presbyterian Church. Their solution, which the 1929 General Assembly approved, collapsed the seminary's separate boards of directors and trustees into one grand thirty-three-member board, which included two signatories of the Auburn Affirmation. Although no-one involved in the reorganization of Princeton aspired to make the seminary a bastion of theological liberalism, Machen viewed the efforts to give Princeton a moderate evangelical orientation as a compromise constituting nothing less than the abandonment of Princeton's Calvinist and scholarly heritage. The only reasonable course of action, in Machen's eyes, was to establish another institution to carry on the Old Princeton tradition. With the support of a number of former Princeton trustees and directors, as well as several younger members of Princeton's faculty, Machen helped to organize Westminster Theological Seminary in the autumn of 1929.

A frequent contributor to various religious radio programmes and popular publications, Machen wrote a number of collected works, including *What is Faith?* (1925), *The Christian Faith in the Modern World* (1936), and *The Christian View of Man* (1937). In 1930 Machen published a second major erudite work, *The Virgin Birth of Christ*. Machen had been working on this topic since his days as a seminarian, and delivered the Thomas Smyth Lectures at Columbia Theological Seminary in South Carolina in 1927 on the subject. In *The Virgin Birth*, Machen affirmed the historical reliability of the gospel birth narratives and yet, like liberal scholars, demonstrated a willingness to examine the historical origins of the doctrine. In the throes of the fundamentalist-modernist controversy, *The Virgin Birth* stood out as the last in a long line of conservative works that valued advanced learning and looked sceptically upon fundamentalists' popular interpretations of the Bible.

When Machen read the 1932 publication *Re-Thinking Missions: A Laymen's Inquiry after One Hundred Years*, it only confirmed his suspicions that theological modernism had come to dominate the northern Presbyterian Church's foreign mission efforts. In 1933 Machen headed a group of fundamentalists who organized the Independent Board for Presbyterian Foreign Missions. The following year, the General Assembly of the Presbyterian Church ordered independent board members to resign or face trial. Machen, however, refused to end his connection with the board because he interpreted the decision as another administrative effort to forge unity by bureaucratic centralization. In 1935 Machen was tried in ecclesiastical court and suspended from the ministry. After his appeal against the verdict failed in the 1936 General Assembly, Machen played a central role in organizing a new denomination, the Presbyterian Church in America (later the Orthodox Presbyterian Church). While on a trip to Bismarck, North Dakota, to generate support for the fledgling denomination, Machen contracted pneumonia and died in 1937. He never married.

Although one of the leading fundamentalist opponents to modernism, Machen's educational and social background, his obdurate commitment to Old School Presbyterian confessionalism, and his civil libertarian leanings, not to mention his lack of sympathy for certain central fundamentalist beliefs, such as premillennial eschatology, distinguish him from many other militant conservatives of the 1920s and 1930s. Machen's disciples included not only ultra-conservative fundamentalists, such as Carl *McIntire, who

formed his own seminary and denomination in 1937 after Machen's death, but also future leaders of the neo-evangelical revival of the 1950s, including Harold J. *Ockenga, Edward J. *Carnell and Francis A. *Schaeffer.

Bibliography

D. G. Hart, *Defending the Faith: J. Gresham Machen and the Crisis of Conservative Protestantism and Modern America* (Baltimore: Johns Hopkins University Press, 1994); B. J. Longfield, *The Presbyterian Controversy: Fundamentalists, Modernists, and Moderates* (New York: Oxford University Press, 1991); G. M. Marsden, 'Understanding J. Gresham Machen', *Princeton Seminary Bulletin*, 11 (1990), pp. 46–60; C. A. Russell, *Voices of American Fundamentalism: Seven Biographical Studies* (Philadelphia: Westminster, 1976); N. B. Stonehouse, *J. Gresham Machen: A Biographical Memoir* (Grand Rapids: Eerdmans, 1954); W. J. Westin, *Presbyterian Pluralism: Competition in a Protestant House* (Knoxville: University of Tennessee Press, 1997).

P. C. KEMENY

■ **McINTIRE, Carl** (1906–2002), militant separatist fundamentalist and anti-Communist crusader, was born in Ypsilanti, Michigan, on 17 May 1906. His father, Charles Curtis McIntire, was a Presbyterian minister, and his mother, Hettie, was a teacher and librarian. Soon after McIntire's birth, the family moved to Durant, Oklahoma, where his grandmother had been a missionary to the Choctaws. His father suffered from delusions and spent 1914 to 1919 in a mental institution, forcing Hettie McIntire to raise her four sons on her own. She sought a divorce in 1922, fearing for her own safety and that of her family, and eventually became dean of women at a college in Oklahoma. When Carl McIntire reached college age, he began to attend Southeastern State College in Oklahoma, but then transferred to Park College in Kansas City, Missouri, where he received his BA in teacher education in 1927. Although McIntire contemplated a law degree, he decided instead to study for the ministry and entered Princeton Seminary in 1928, where he was elected president of the entering class.

Princeton in the late 1920s was caught up in the fundamentalist-modernist controversy, and McIntire soon came under the influence of the renowned scholar and fundamentalist leader J. Gresham *Machen. When the Presbyterian Church placed Princeton Seminary under a liberal governing board in 1929, Machen left to found Westminster Seminary in Chester Hill, Pennsylvania. McIntire followed his professor and graduated from Westminster in 1931. Soon afterwards he married Fairy Eunace Davis of Paris, Texas. On 4 June 1931 McIntire was ordained into the Presbyterian Church and installed as pastor of the Chelsea Presbyterian Church in Atlantic City, New Jersey, which had been decimated by the suicide of the previous pastor. Through aggressive evangelizing and outdoor preaching on the ocean boardwalk, McIntire added almost 200 members within two years. On 28 September 1933 McIntire was called as pastor to the 1,000-member fundamentalist Collingswood Presbyterian Church in Collingswood, New Jersey, a position that he would hold for the next sixty-six years.

In 1934 McIntire became a member of the Independent Board for Presbyterian Foreign Missions, which Machen had created as an alternative to the increasingly liberal Presbyterian Board of Foreign Missions. The creation of a rival missions agency provoked the ire of the Presbyterian General Assembly, which brought McIntire, along with Machen and his followers, to trial for creating disorder. McIntire responded by broadcasting his evening services on a local Philadelphia radio station, giving full vent to his dispute with the Presbyterian Church. He began publishing *The Christian Beacon*, a weekly newspaper that chronicled his struggles, on 13 February 1936, and he continued to publish it for more than five decades.

On 15 June 1936 McIntire and the others responsible for the Independent Board were found guilty and ousted from the Presbyterian Church. Those expelled immediately formed the Presbyterian Church of America, but this new denomination was soon racked by internal conflicts. Two factions developed, one (represented by McIntire) that supported premillennial dispensationalism and another (represented by Machen) that accepted premillennialism but viewed dispensationalism

with suspicion. Machen managed to hold the denomination together until his death in 1937, but soon afterwards McIntire's followers formed the Bible Presbyterian Church, while those loyal to Machen formed the Orthodox Presbyterian Church. McIntire founded Faith Theological Seminary in July 1938 to train ministers for his fledgling denomination.

All but eight of McIntire's congregation voluntarily left the Presbyterian Church when McIntire was expelled, but as a civil court in 1938 refused to grant them ownership of the Collingswood Presbyterian Church property, they were forced to meet in a tent while a wooden 'Tabernacle of Testimony' was built, which served the congregation from 1938 until 1957. Denied the Collingswood Presbyterian Church name, the congregation changed its name to the Bible Presbyterian Church of Collingswood.

Ruthlessly insistent on doctrinal purity, McIntire formed the American Council of Christian Churches in 1941 and the International Council of Christian Churches in 1948 to oppose and offer an alternative to the ecumenical positions of the National Council of Churches and the World Council of Churches. McIntire's extreme separatism created a schism within the Bible Presbyterians that caused more than three-quarters of the denomination's hundred churches to disassociate themselves from him in 1956. The American Council of Christian Churches followed suit in 1968. However, McIntire was far from beaten by these struggles. He continued to pastor his large Collingswood church, maintained control of Faith Seminary and the International Council of Christian Churches and reached millions more through his radio broadcasts and *The Christian Beacon*.

On 7 March 1955 McIntire began broadcasting 'The Twentieth Century Reformation Hour', a thirty-minute radio programme on WCVH in Chester, Pennsylvania. He daily excoriated the twin threats of apostasy and Communism, and his message proved popular in the Cold War era. Within five years, he was heard on 600 stations throughout the country and was receiving almost two million dollars a year in contributions from an estimated 20 million listeners. These funds enabled him to buy several hotels in Cape May, New Jersey, which he turned into fundamentalist conference centres. In addition, he assumed control of Shelton College (formerly the National Bible Institute) in 1964. He founded a secondary school in 1968 and a primary school in 1973.

McIntire worked closely with Senator Joseph McCarthy and the House Un-American Affairs Committee to identify suspected Communist clergymen. He also regularly attacked the National Association of Evangelicals, Billy *Graham and other 'New Evangelicals' for their refusal to separate themselves from non-fundamentalists. His other targets included the Revised Standard Version of the Bible, the Roman Catholic Church and the Civil Rights movement. He used protest demonstrations at the meetings of groups he opposed to attract publicity. In 1970 and 1971 McIntire garnered national media attention by rallying at least 50,000 people for a series of 'Victory Marches' in support of the Vietnam War.

McIntire's influence waned greatly after 1971, and he faced insurmountable obstacles. In 1971 Faith Seminary was rocked by the departure of the institution's president along with all but two of its staff and half the student body in protest at McIntire's dictatorial style. McIntire fought the Federal Communications Commission for years over the licensing of his radio station WXUR. McIntire's conference centres in Cape May proved unsustainable when the city decided that they did not meet the requirements for tax-exempt status. Shelton College faced twenty years of struggles over accreditation with the state of New Jersey. McIntire attempted to move the school to Florida, but financial difficulties forced a return to New Jersey, where the accreditation struggles continued until they were settled by the US Supreme Court in favour of New Jersey in 1985. By that time, the school had been reduced to a handful of students.

Despite these obstacles and a near-fatal pancreatic disorder in 1978, McIntire continued to fight Communism and ecumenism well into the 1990s. Yet his situation worsened. His wife died in 1992 and a car crash almost killed him in 1993. *The Christian Beacon* ceased publication soon afterwards. In 1996 financial problems forced the sale of Faith Seminary, which according to some insiders had become a money-oriented diploma mill. In 1999 the Bible Presbyterian Church in Collingswood ousted McIntire after he refused to retire. The ninety-two-year-old McIntire responded by holding Sunday services in his home. Carl McIntire died, aged 95, on 19 March 2002.

Bibliography

J. Fea, 'Carl McIntire: From Fundamentalist Presbyterian to Presbyterian Fundamentalist', *American Presbyterians*, 72, 4 (1994), pp. 253–268; E. Fink, *40 Years ...: Carl McIntire and the Bible Presbyterian Church of Collingswood, 1933–1973* (Collingswood: Christian Beacon Press, 1973); C. McIntire, 'Fifty Years of Preaching in Collingswood, N. J.', *Christian Beacon* 48, 33 (1983), pp. 1–5, 7.

D. K. LARSEN

■ **MACKAY, John Alexander** (1889–1983), missionary and theologian, was born in Inverness, Scotland, on 17 May 1889 to parents who joined the newly formed Free Presbyterian Church of Scotland in 1893. 'I was a lad of only 14 years of age when, in the pages of the Ephesian Letter, I saw a new world ... "and you hath he quickened, who were dead in trespasses and sins". I had been quickened on a Saturday in July 1903 at the Preparation service in Rogart,' he wrote later. He studied for the ministry at Aberdeen University (MA, first-class honours Philosophy, 1912) and with his church tutors in Inverness (1910–1911) and Wick (1912–1913). In 1913 he went to Princeton Theological Seminary and graduated BD in 1915. He proceeded to Madrid to study philosophy under Miguel de Unamuno, the Spanish philosopher and interpreter of Kierkegaard. He developed a great understanding of Spanish thought, and it is not surprising that after marriage to Jane Logan Wells in 1916 he was sent by the Free Church of Scotland, which had now joined, to Lima, Peru, where he founded the Colegio San Andres. He was also the first Protestant holder of the Chair of Philosophy in the National University of San Marcos in Lima.

In 1926 Mackay went to Montevideo, then to Mexico City as Religious Work Secretary of the South American Federation of YMCAs, and travelled widely as an evangelist. He also, during study leave in Bonn, gave Karl Barth his first English lessons. In 1932 he was appointed Secretary for South America and Africa for the Board of Missions of the Presbyterian Church in the USA. For a time he was disillusioned with the institutional church, both because of the increasingly sectarian tendencies in the churches of his upbringing, and because of his study of the Catholic Church in Spain. But his calling did not leave him, and he rediscovered the church in its widest sense as he immersed himself in the work of the growing ecumenical movement. In 1937 he presided over commission V of the Oxford Conference on Life and Work, 'The Universal Church and the World of Nations', and for it coined one of his many memorable phrases. 'Let the Church be the Church' has been described as tautological but provocative. 'It must be her ceaseless concern to rid herself of all subjugation to a prevailing culture, an economic system, a social type, or a political order.'

In 1936 he was appointed president of Princeton Seminary and Professor of Ecumenics. He was able to restore stability after the difficult years of theological controversy, which had culminated in the secession of J. Gresham *Machen. He occupied several important offices during his years as president. He was a member of the central committee of the newly formed World Council of Churches from 1948 to 1954, chair of the International Missionary Council from 1947 to 1958, president of the World Alliance of Reformed Churches from 1954 to 1959, and moderator of the General Assembly of the Presbyterian Church in the USA in 1953. He was one of those instrumental in bringing about the merging of the WCC and the IMC, and was in the forefront of ecumenical activity. At Princeton he taught mission under the rubric of ecumenics.

His basic courses were always crowded. He often alluded to his Celtic blood and to the sacramental services in his native Highlands of Scotland. It was said of him that he preferred religious fanaticism to a cold and sterile intellectualism. Nels Ferré described Mackay's theological position as dynamic centralism, 'the opposite of fence-sitting'. Strongly in the Reformed tradition, he attempted to make the historic confessions

personal. He maintained, in line with his Calvinist heritage, that God's sovereign rule is the controlling factor in history. There were many other influences on his theology. His interest in Spanish thought never waned, and he could claim Teresa of Avila as 'his saint'. Kierkegaard and Dostoevsky also profoundly influenced him, and his Christocentric ecclesiology owed much to Karl Barth.

Although he did not become directly involved in political life, he nevertheless took a firm stand for an inclusive worldview at a time when the Cold War was influencing many American Christians towards isolationism. In 1950 he urged the USA to recognize the *de facto* government of China, and in 1953, at the height of the furore caused by the McCarthy hearings, he addressed his 'Letter to Presbyterians', which, it is said, 'turned the tide of public hysteria, mistrust and slander against their principal fomenter, the late Senator Joseph McCarthy of Wisconsin'. In this letter he maintained that the church has a prophetic function in every age and every society. The church is loyal to government but does not derive its authority from the nation but from Christ. Its supreme and ultimate allegiance is to Christ, its sole head, and to his kingdom, and not to any nation or race, class or culture. His statement was adopted unanimously by the 1954 General Assembly of the Presbyterian Church in the USA. Not surprisingly Mackay was attacked by fundamentalists such as Carl *McIntire, and he was portrayed as a crypto-communist and worse.

Mackay was an encourager of scholars and writers. With Henry van Dusen he founded and edited the Library of Christian Classics. By founding the successful Journal *Theology Today* he did a great service to American biblical and theological writing. His own thirteen books include *The Other Spanish Christ* (1932), *A Preface to Christian Theology* (1943), *Heritage and Destiny* (1943), *Christianity on the Frontier* (1950), *Ecumenism – The Science of the Church Universal* (1964), and his commentary on Ephesians, *God's Order, the Ephesian Letter and the Present Time* (1953). His memorable phrases, such as 'Splendour in the Abyss', 'In Unity for Mission' and 'The Form of a Servant' (a description of the church) have been absorbed into Christian discourse. He delivered around twenty-two series of lectures in various universities, from the Merrick Lectures on Prophetic Thinkers at Ohio Wesleyan University in 1932 to the Croall lectures in New College Edinburgh in 1952, from which his book on Ephesians emerged.

John Mackay retired from the presidency of Princeton Seminary in 1959, and in retirement taught Spanish thought at the American University in Washington DC. He continued to write and teach for many years and died at the age of ninety-three on 9 June 1983. He is described by former students as 'a warm, gracious, understanding, supportive, appreciative, sympathetic, loving person'. He was also 'sometimes austere'.

It is difficult to describe accurately Mackay's position on the evangelical spectrum. From his evangelical Highland background he absorbed elements of mysticism, which were strengthened in him through his study of Unamuno. When he went to Princeton, he was faced with the results of a fundamentalist division, and he was by nature hostile to any form of fundamentalism. In the 1959 special edition of *Theology Today*, the tributes to him are from neo-orthodox rather than evangelical theologians. Yet Mackay continued to consider himself an evangelical, albeit of the liberal and ecumenical variety.

In the obituary in *Theology Today*, 1984, it is said that 'he would have made a distinguished Secretary of the United Nations or a superlative Shakespearean Actor'. He and his wife Jane had four children, three daughters and a son.

Bibliography

Festschrift edition of *Theology Today*, 16 (1959), pp. 301–375; R. J. Graham and B. L. McCormick, in N. M. de S. Cameron, *Dictionary of Scottish Church History and Theology* (Edinburgh: T. & T. Clark, 1993), pp. 519–520.

D. B. MURRAY

■ **McLAREN (MACLAREN), Alexander** (1826–1910) (the double spelling of the name is occasioned by the fact that he used the form 'McLaren' when signing his name but 'Maclaren' in all his publications), Baptist preacher and expositor, was born on 11 February 1826 in Glasgow, where his father was a leader in a group who seceded from Ralph Wardlaw's congregation to form a Scotch Baptist church. The older McLaren became a ministering elder of this congregation until business concerns took him to Australia, where he became a founder of a Baptist work. The family remained in Glasgow, and the younger McLaren was baptized in 1840 whilst undertaking studies in Latin and Greek at Glasgow University alongside his more regular education at Glasgow High School.

The family having moved to London on the father's return from Australia, McLaren entered Stepney College in 1842, where he benefited from Benjamin Davies' reverent and painstaking Hebrew scholarship, on which so many of his later expository gifts depended. From Davies, McLaren also learnt the Augustinian emphases that characterized his theology: the majesty of God and the awfulness of sin.

McLaren graduated from London University in 1845, complete with a hard-won prize. Two influences on his life at this stage were the Congregationalist Thomas Binney, and his fellow Baptist Charles Stovel, who respectively instilled in him a love of preaching and a concern for freedom. It is no surprise, therefore, that he was present at the founding of the Liberation Society and was considerably influenced by Edward Miall, MP, the determining intelligence of the disestablishment movement. From his earliest days he hated all ecclesiastical pretension, bureaucracy and display, and had a Quaker-like disregard for the externals of ecclesiastical life, perhaps reflecting the parity of lay and ordained within his Scotch Baptist background.

In 1846 McLaren became pastor of Portland Chapel, Southampton. He dedicated the rest of his life to the Christian ministry, for which he developed a tremendous respect, affirming that the minister was 'neither priest nor philosopher, but messenger and proclaimer'. Portland Chapel had formerly been a Union Church with John Pulsford as pastor. But contrary to its constitution, internal dissension had arisen, which led in 1844 to its re-foundation as a Baptist church, with the Baptist interest buying out the others for some £1,350. The Southampton congregation waited a year for McLaren, until he finished his college course. The freshness of the young minister's approach (he could confine a sermon to twelve minutes) led some to question his orthodoxy, and *Spurgeon at one time thought him 'a dangerous man'. From the beginning, McLaren was not given to pastoral visitation but was diligent in his concern for his Sunday schools; for some twenty years he sent an exposition of the International Lesson of the week to the *Sunday School Times* in Philadelphia. He was soon a well-known figure in the Southampton Athenaeum, and the ethical implications of the gospel were very real to him, making him intolerant of a society that afforded privilege to some and consigned others to poverty. Thus he writes, 'We hear a great deal to-day about a "social gospel", and I am glad of the conception, and of the favour which it receives. Only let us remember that the gospel is social second and individual first ...' In later years he felt that he had been over-intellectual in his Southampton ministry, confessing on moving north to Manchester, 'I have abjured for ever the rubbish of intellectual preaching.' In March 1856 he married his cousin, Marion Maclaren of Edinburgh, who fully supported her husband, especially in temperance and mission work.

In 1858 McLaren accepted the call to what was to be his life's work at Union Chapel, Manchester, which all too soon proved too small for the congregation he attracted, so that in 1869 a new £22,000 sanctuary had to be built for his ministry. His church eventually secured a membership of 700 and a congregation of three times that number. Although described by Robertson Nicholl as possessing the looks of 'a Highland chieftain born to command', he was an essentially shy man, who found the anonymity of a large congregation easier to handle than the intimacy of a small one. Whilst he was perceptive with respect to human psychology, intimate relationships seemed always to worry him, and helped him maintain a quite genuine humility. To the work of Union Chapel he added the People's Institute in Rusholme in 1872, the planting of two churches in Gorton and the founding of three missions in downtown districts.

At Union Chapel worship was carefully and sensitively structured. In McLaren's preaching, which was always expository and theological, never sensational, all his wide reading, in English and German, was brought to bear upon the text he sought to expound, which he dutifully studied either in the original Hebrew or Greek, effortlessly eliciting its principal (normally three) parts. Beyond such technical homework was the power of his own prayerful preparation for the sharing of the Word of God, which he so aptly expressed and illustrated that it immediately took root within the lives of his hearers. For them he developed a peculiar sympathy, which one biographer calls an 'instinct for souls', whilst another author comments on his fruitful study of 'the living book of humanity'. He himself, in his famous late sermon on 'Evangelical Mysticism', described the emphasis of his later preaching like this: 'when so many brethren are speaking to the times, let one poor brother speak of eternity'. A fierce defender of all the supernatural elements in the Gospel record, from the virgin birth to the ascension, he once said: 'expunge any of these elements and you will not have much difficulty accounting for the rest, and it will not be worth the accounting for'. At the same time he was equally aware that 'it is possible to hide the Cross behind the cobwebs of doctrine, be it never so orthodox'. On eternal punishment, he found the New Testament affirmed both universal punishment and universal restoration, but he chose not to preach on this topic. Revelation could rightly be portrayed as progressive, 'measured by the moral and spiritual capacities of those who receive it', though to affirm this was not to deny the finality of revelation in Christ. In his preaching, a text, particularly one from the Old Testament, could all too easily be used as a prompt rather than as the basis of exegesis. Thus, for example, a sermon on 'See that ye hasten the matter' (2 Chronicles 24:5), after eighteen brief lines, says, 'we need not say anything more about Joash and his lazy Levites, but take these words as a very imperative and earnest exhortation to ourselves ... [in] whatever it be that God has entrusted to you'.

Acquaintance with the literary and artistic culture of his age, from Carlyle to Browning, helped McLaren to understand and preach to the contemporary mind. He accordingly counselled his fellow Baptists to heed 'the voices of their time', but not at the expense of their main task, 'the earnest and uncontroversial proclamation of the crucified Christ'. A principal of Owen's College went on record as regarding 'Dr McLaren's preaching as the chief literary influence, or if not absolutely the chief, certainly one of the chief literary influences in the city of Manchester.' From 1881 Union Chapel provided McLaren with pastoral assistants, the last of whom, E. J. Roberts, became his co-pastor. Marion McLaren died on Christmas Eve, 1884.

A moving force in the founding of the Free Church movement, he was twice president of the Baptist Union (1875 and 1901), presided over the first congress of the Baptist World Alliance in 1905 and was the recipient of honorary doctorates from Edinburgh, Manchester and Glasgow. He died in Edinburgh on 5 May 1910.

Bibliography

Baptist Handbook, 1911; J. C. Carlile, *Dr Alexander MacLaren, the Man and the Message* (1901); D. Williamson, *The Life of Alexander McLaren* (1910); E. T. McLaren, *Dr McLaren of Manchester* (1911); I. Sellers, 'Other Times, Other Ministries: John Fawcett and Alexander McLaren', *Baptist Quarterly* (Oct. 1987), pp. 181–199.

J. Y. H. BRIGGS

■ **McNICOL, John** (1869–1956), Canadian educator, author and Presbyterian minister, was best known as the principal of Toronto Bible Training School from 1906 to 1946. A broad-minded evangelical, McNicol dedicated his life to biblical education for Christian missions.

The first of eight children born to the family of a school teacher in Hanover, Western Ontario, McNicol spent most of his childhood in Ottawa, where his father worked in the civil service. There the young John became a member of St Andrew's Presbyterian Church. He remained a Presbyterian throughout his life.

As a young man coming to maturity in the 1880s and 1890s, McNicol was formed by a late-Victorian Protestant commitment to self-discipline, duty and service. While at the University of Toronto (1887–1901), he was an accomplished athlete in tennis and cricket, served for two years as the secretary

of the university YMCA, became a member of the 'Varsity' editorial staff and involved in the Student Volunteer Movement, and worked at the Elizabeth Street Mission of the Presbyterian Church. In those positions he was the peer and colleague of individuals who would form a future generation of public men, including a future prime minister of Canada, W. L. Mackenzie King. McNicol was also an outstanding student. In 1891 he received his BA from the University of Toronto with honours in classics.

During his undergraduate years McNicol had become convinced of the necessity of Christian mission. As a result, when the Student Volunteer Movement was at its height in 1892, McNicol offered himself for foreign missionary service to China, but was rejected by his denomination's Foreign Missions Board. Deciding quickly to enter the divinity programme at Knox College in Toronto, he received his BD with first-class honours in the largest class in the history of the college in 1895. The young Presbyterian minister was first posted to a charge in Aylmer, Quebec (1896–1901). While in Ottawa for a Student Volunteer Convention in January 1902, he was asked by the prominent Baptist preacher Dr Elmore Harris, to join the staff of the Toronto Bible Training School as instructor in the English Bible. Recently married to Louisa Maud Burpe, he accepted.

Toronto Bible Training School (TBTS) suited McNicol well. Founded by Elmore Harris in 1891, the school had been set up to train laymen and laywomen for service in everything from Sunday schools to city, home or foreign missions. Intended not to compete with seminaries and divinity colleges but to augment them, the school offered biblical training for those feeling called to Christian service, but who were not able to study for an extended period of time. Furthermore, TBTS also reflected the broad-minded evangelicalism of late-Victorian mainstream Protestantism with which McNicol had been imbued. The school was devotional, mission-minded and inter-denominational.

McNicol was a successful teacher and an effective leader. Humble, kind and extolled for his quiet but strong Christian character, he was appointed principal of TBTS for one year in 1906, then permanently two years later. In the position of principal, he continued to teach and lead at TBTS for the next thirty-eight years.

Clear principles, goodwill and an emphasis on the 'corporate headship of the Holy Spirit' characterized McNicol's approach to leadership and to controversial issues. Under his principalship, the board, faculty and student cabinet aimed for complete unanimity in decision making. Though a contributor to *The Fundamentals* in 1909, McNicol refused to be called a 'fundamentalist' when theological controversy began to rage in the 1920s. He maintained neutrality during schisms among Baptists in the late 1920s. Though under pressure to draw TBTS in a more separatist and dispensational direction, McNicol continued to insist on a broader Reformed and evangelical view of the Scriptures and of the church, one which emphasized the presence of the Holy Spirit at the centre of Christian corporate life. 'McNicol's gift was not theology but spirituality,' one scholar has noted. His emphasis was on prayer and holiness. He valued unity and looked for 'a middle between extremes'.

McNicol's approach to biblical studies was conservative, but not defensive. Although he did not ignore the 'modern scientific approach to the Bible with its methods of analysis', his approach to the Bible was exegetical and devotional. He preferred positive assertions of faith and avoided defensive polemics against liberal theology. The Bible, he argued, should interpret itself. As a scholar, he wrote articles for the *Biblical Review* and *The Evangelical Quarterly*. Inter-Varsity's *New Bible Commentary* included comments by him on Luke. He published *The Christian Evangel* in 1937, but was best known for his four-volume work, *Thinking through the Bible* (1944), a distillation of lectures developed over forty years of teaching.

Under McNicol's warm, broad-minded leadership, TBTS (later Toronto Bible College, Ontario Bible College and now Tyndale College and Seminary) grew to be one of Canada's most important evangelical institutions. Without children of their own, McNicol and his wife Louisa made the college community their 'family'. Their care and devotion contributed to a spirit of harmony and holiness which characterized TBTS in their day.

McNicol never lost touch with the wider ecclesiastical world outside of TBTS. In appreciation for his labours within the Presbyterian Church of Canada, he was awarded an honorary DD degree in 1935 by Knox College, Toronto. Tellingly, McNicol never lost his passion for missions either. Particularly after enthusiasm for missions waned in mainstream Protestant seminaries in the 1920s, he saw his college as an important missionary training ground. McNicol remained a member of the boards of the China Inland Mission and the Sudan Interior Mission until his death, and served as a governor of the British and Foreign Bible Society for sixty-five years.

John McNicol died of heart failure while recovering from a broken hip in Toronto in September 1956.

Bibliography

W. Charlton, 'Dr John McNicol and Toronto Bible College: A Research Paper' (the library of Tyndale College and Seminary, 1976); J. G. Stackhouse, Jr, *Canadian Evangelicalism in the Twentieth Century: An Introduction to its Character* (Toronto: University of Toronto Press, 1993).

G. R. MIEDEMA

■ **McPHERSON, Aimee Semple** (1890–1944), evangelist and founder of The International Church of the Foursquare Gospel, was born in Salford, a hamlet near Ingersoll, Ontario, on 9 October 1890. Her parents, James and Minnie Kennedy, made a comfortable living from their farm. James Kennedy identified with the local Methodist church that his first wife, Elizabeth, attended regularly. In contrast, Minnie Kennedy threw herself into the colourful pageantry of the early Ontario Salvation Army. Aimee knew both worlds, and both contributed to her future work.

As a child, Aimee manifested an ability to declaim and perform. She passed the qualifying examination and enrolled at Ingersoll Collegiate High School. When the local newspaper sponsored a subscription/popularity contest, she took first place and won her first trip out of the area, a visit to Toronto. Except for her intimate familiarity with the Salvation Army (where prayer meetings were 'knee drills' and dramatic expression played a central role), Aimee was a typical Protestant southern Ontario teenager.

Then, during the winter of 1907, a mission began near Ingersoll Collegiate High School, and Aimee prevailed on her father to take her to hear the evangelist. His name was Robert Semple. An Irish immigrant, he was in the town to promote Pentecostalism, a new and growing religious movement. At the heart of his message was the conviction expressed in Hebrews 13:8: 'Jesus Christ the same, yesterday, today and for ever.' For Semple this verse implied that New Testament Christianity, with its range of spiritual gifts, was available to all. He encouraged his hearers to pray earnestly for a definite experience of baptism with the Holy Spirit. They would know that they had received it, he said, when they spoke in tongues. Semple had only recently embraced this message himself. Part of a handful of people who identified with the Pentecostal movement in Toronto from the winter of 1906, Semple dedicated his energies to spreading the news that apostolic Christianity had been divinely restored.

Aimee found the message interesting and the preacher irresistible. Against the objections of her parents she began praying for the baptism with the Holy Spirit, with such focus that she neglected her school work. Before long she opted to attend prayer meetings instead of school. When her parents finally forbade her to associate with Pentecostals, she defied them, spoke in tongues, and then won them over to her point of view. On 12 August 1908, in a Salvation Army ceremony on the lawn of the Kennedy farm, she married Robert Semple.

The couple lived first in Stratford, Ontario, where Robert worked for the railway by day and preached at a small Pentecostal mission at night. After a few months, they moved briefly to London, Ontario, to begin a new Pentecostal mission. Next they moved to Chicago, and spent much of 1909 working in cooperation with a well-known Pentecostal evangelist and pastor, William Durham. Durham's mission on Chicago's North Avenue stood on a busy thoroughfare in a Scandinavian and German neighbourhood. Known among Pentecostals as a 'power house', the mission published an influential Pentecostal paper, The Pentecostal Testimony, and took advantage of its location at the heart of the nation's railway network to host conventions that gathered Pentecostals from far and near. After a year of intense ministry, the Semples returned to Canada to bid farewell to the Kennedys. They now felt called to devote their lives to missionary service in China. After an emotional farewell service at the Hebden Pentecostal Mission in Toronto, the Semples sailed for Ireland.

After a few weeks with Robert's family, the couple travelled among Pentecostals in England before embarking for Hong Kong. They arrived on 1 June 1910 to join a small group of Pentecostal missionaries who were looking longingly towards the mission field of the Chinese mainland. The Semples found a flat and hired a language teacher. Ten weeks later both lay gravely ill with dysentery and malaria in Matilda Hospital. Robert died on 19 August 1910, but Aimee clung to life. She recovered slowly, gave birth to a daughter, Roberta, in September, and then sailed for home. Her dreams shattered, she crossed the United States by train and was reunited with her mother in New York. Minnie was working temporarily at the Salvation Army headquarters in Union Square, and Aimee now donned the Army uniform too.

On 5 February 1912 in Chicago (where the couple took refuge from Minnie Kennedy's opposition) Aimee married Harold McPherson, a young entrepreneur. They set up house in Harold's home town, Providence, Rhode Island. On 23 March 1913 Aimee gave birth to their son, Rolf. Harold provided amply for his family and was devoted to Robert Semple's daughter, Roberta, but Aimee soon became restless. She feared that she had run from the divine call that she and Robert had set out to fulfil. In June 1915 she took her children and left Harold for her childhood home in Ontario. Her parents cared for the children while she made her way to a Pentecostal camp meeting. There, following an intense struggle, she found inner peace, and also found her calling. When she left the camp, she had her first engagement to preach at an evangelistic crusade, in Mt Forest, Ontario.

Harold came after his family and agreed to try to help Aimee to pursue her mission. For several years the family travelled up and down the east coast in a 'gospel car' emblazoned with Scripture texts and slogans. They purchased a tent, and Harold arranged its transportation and erection for meetings. Attendance at the crusades grew, and Aimee became an east-coast sensation. But Harold did not find the satisfaction that energized his wife. In 1918 he left her for good and returned to his work in Providence. They divorced quietly in 1922. Minnie Kennedy took Harold's place as Aimee's companion and childminder. She quickly manifested business acumen and undertook the daunting task of organizing Aimee's thriving outreach. By 1918, this included a monthly magazine, *The Bridal Call.*

Late in 1918 Aimee moved the base of her operation to Los Angeles. She drove across the country on a new network of roads, camped by the roadside, and distributed thousands of tracts along the way. In the next four years she crossed the country repeatedly and achieved stunning success as an evangelist. Audiences for her crusades overflowed the largest available venues in Denver, St Louis, Rochester (NY), Oakland, Baltimore and Winnipeg. In San Diego her outdoor services filled Balboa Park. In San Jose she preached in a huge tent. Billed as 'the female Billy *Sunday', she offered a straightforward evangelical message in an appealing narrative style. She acceded to popular demand to set aside time to pray for the sick. Clergy of all denominations graced her platform and applauded her obvious success. Particular Pentecostal experiences like speaking in tongues played no part in her public crusades. Those who 'sought the baptism with the Holy Spirit' did so in smaller, separate meetings. McPherson drew criticism from Pentecostals for refusing to permit people to use such 'utterance gifts' as prophecy and tongues in her crusades. While she regarded herself as Pentecostal, she stood somewhat apart from the movement because she made Hebrews 13:8 ('Jesus Christ, the same, yesterday, today and forever') rather than Acts 2:4 ('And they were all filled with the Holy Spirit and spoke in tongues as the Spirit gave them utterance') her starting point.

On 1 January 1923 McPherson dedicated Angelus Temple, a 5,300-seat domed structure at the intersection of Glendale and Sunset Boulevards. Directly opposite Echo Park, the commodious building included a prayer tower staffed twenty-four hours a day. Throngs lined the streets hours before services, which were broadcast to an overflow meeting in Echo Park. In 1924 McPherson purchased and began broadcasting on KFSG, the third radio station in Los Angeles. In 1925 she dedicated a building adjoining Angelus Temple as LIFE, the Lighthouse of Foursquare Evangelism. She had founded a Bible school a month after the Temple opened, and its growing appeal made adequate premises a priority. During her lifetime, this school enjoyed enormous popularity and trained thousands of missionaries, pastors and evangelists, male and female, to serve in McPherson's Echo Park Evangelistic Association. Its students joined Temple faithful in a massive campaign to invite everyone to the Temple. McPherson's illustrated sermons made the Temple a magnet for Sunday evening entertainment. Hailed by critics as the best shows in a show-crazed city, these elaborate productions featured stage sets built with advice from Hollywood's film set creators, costumed actors, live animals and more. McPherson spared no expense in producing the sermons, and the city responded by scheduling extra trolley buses to transport the crowds. Her flair for the dramatic and her oratorical skills caused her adoring public to generally regard her as the star of her own shows. She provided her people with her own gospel hymns and wrote several operas, which were produced at the Temple.

McPherson began formally calling her message the 'Foursquare Gospel' in 1923. 'Foursquare' was a word in common use in her day, describing something or someone perfect or complete. The KJV used 'foursquare' to describe the heavenly city. McPherson's Foursquare Gospel had four distinct but interrelated themes: 'Jesus, the Only Saviour; Jesus, the Great Physician; Jesus, Baptiser with the Holy Spirit; Jesus, the Coming Bridegroom, Lord and King.'

In 1922 McPherson travelled to Australia, where her efforts poured energy into the emerging Pentecostal movement. In 1926 she and her daughter Roberta visited the Semples in Ireland, and Aimee went on to the Holy Land. She left the Temple in the care of Paul *Rader, a former pastor of Chicago's Moody Church and a popular evangelist.

On 18 May 1926 a story announcing McPherson's disappearance shocked the nation. Her radio broadcasts and extensive preaching tours had made her a national celebrity, and an eager press fed public curiosity. McPherson mysteriously disappeared while on the Santa Monica beach. After weeks of intensive searching for her body, Minnie Kennedy attempted to end speculation by orchestrating an elaborate memorial service at Angelus Temple on 20 June. Then on 23 June, Aimee reappeared. She telephoned her mother from a hospital bed in Douglas, Arizona, claiming to have escaped from kidnappers. Even before she made a triumphal return to Los Angeles on 26 June, some people publicly expressed doubts about her story.

For the rest of 1926 the press exploited the drama of an unfolding grand jury investigation. When the district attorney failed to prove that he had a case, he dropped charges. The faithful complained that Los Angeles had invested millions of dollars in an unsuccessful campaign to smear McPherson rather than in a determined effort to find her kidnappers. Dissatisfied detractors murmured about suborning of the jury and a romantic tryst. Early in 1927 McPherson set out on a vindication tour, with appearances in New York City and Chicago as well as in smaller cities across the nation. She demonstrated the strength of her following, but after 1926 she faced a less appreciative press.

The late 1920s brought important changes to McPherson's organization. A public break with her mother over Angelus Temple affairs ended Minnie Kennedy's organizational oversight of her daughter's affairs. Her son Rolf dedicated himself to facilitating Aimee's work, but she was lonely and often ill. On 13 September 1931, a few months after Rolf's marriage to Lorna Dee Smith, Aimee married David Hutton, an aspiring singer eleven years her junior. The wedding had an element of the drama that Aimee loved. The couple flew to Las Vegas for an early morning ceremony and returned to Los Angeles in time for the morning service at Angelus Temple, where Aimee introduced her third husband to a full church.

Her marriage to Hutton lasted barely three years; the couple spent much of that time apart. The response to the marriage demonstrated at last the limits to her adoring public's tolerance. Her organization lost

clergy in local ministries who grew tired of the distractions caused by her decisions. Churches withdrew. Then in 1936 Aimee broke with her daughter during a struggle over the management of Temple affairs. Deprived of her mother's and daughter's protection and common sense, Aimee endorsed several ill-advised, short-lived money-making schemes such as films and a cemetery. By the 1930s the United States was suffering in the Depression, and the mood of the country differed sharply from that of the roaring twenties. Beset by ill health, McPherson travelled extensively. Her evangelistic campaigns in the 1930s were interspersed by surgery in Paris, a meeting with Gandhi in India, a visit to Charlie Chaplin at his villa in Spain and a brief, disappointing period in Broadway vaudeville. In the late 1930s, Aimee's advisors and the trustees of her institutions severely restricted her movements and worked to develop a religious organization that could survive the Depression.

During the 1930s the work of which McPherson was most proud was the Angelus Temple Commissary, an ambitious programme that fed and clothed thousands of hungry people in the city. Always a motivator, Aimee galvanized her audiences to help the needy and formed a programme that became a model for state and private relief work.

During the Second World War, McPherson turned her skills to the sale of war bonds. After a few years away from the limelight provided by her evangelistic crusades, she returned to it in a September 1944 crusade in Oakland. Apparently enthusiastic about her prospects, she rode in a parade and opened a series of meetings on 26 September, concluding with the promise to give her ever-popular rendition of her life story the next night. The next morning, her son Rolf found her unconscious in her hotel room. She had apparently accidentally taken a combination of drugs that soon proved fatal. On the evening of 27 September, California papers that had hailed her renewed energy announced her death.

McPherson's church family proved that her dramatic flair had not been wasted. They held her body for two weeks and scheduled her funeral for her fifty-fourth birthday, 9 October 1944. That date had long been special to her people. She always conducted a service that featured her ritualized rendering of the story of her life. Now her open coffin under the Angelus Temple dome drew some 50,000 mourners. The funeral was a three-hour series of tributes interspersed with the hopeful gospel music featured in her services. Two thousand held tickets for the 'private' committal service that followed at Glendale's magnificent Forest Lawn Cemetery.

Despite her tumultuous life, McPherson left behind institutions poised for growth. With its worldwide constituency, The International Church of the Foursquare Gospel has carried her vision forward. Foursquare churches around the world display in their sanctuaries the text that McPherson adopted as her theme: 'Jesus Christ, the same, yesterday, and today and forever.'

Bibliography

E. L. Blumhofer, *Aimee Semple McPherson: Everybody's Sister* (Grand Rapids: Eerdmans, 1993); D. M. Epstein, *Sister Aimee* (New York: Harcourt, Brace, Javanovich, 1993); A. S. McPherson, *This is That* (Los Angeles: Echo Park Evangelistic Association, 1919).

E. L. BLUMHOFER

■ **MAHAN, Asa** (1799–1899), Holiness theologian and educator, grew up in the revivalistic 'burned over district' of western New York, the son of Presbyterian parents, Samuel and Anna Mahan. He graduated from Hamilton College (1824) and from Andover Theological Seminary (1827). After seminary, he worked as a colporteur for the American Tract Society in South Carolina. His first pastorate was at Fourth Presbyterian Church in Rochester, where he married Mary Dix in May 1828. His next pastorate was at Pittsford, New York, where he hosted revival meetings led by Charles *Finney. In 1831 he was invited to Sixth Presbyterian Church in Cincinnati. Elected to the board of trustees of Lane Theological Seminary, he supported the abolitionist students against the rest of the board and their 'Old-School' Presbyterian supporters.

The abolitionist students selected Mahan as the first president of Oberlin College (1835). Finney was appointed, at the students' request, as the first professor of theology.

Oberlin became the model for many colleges. It enrolled the poor, women and African-Americans. It was a major centre for Holiness revivalism and abolitionism. Mahan's first book, written in response to students' questions about the degree of sanctification available to the believer, was entitled *Scripture Doctrine of Christian Perfection* (1839). It became the standard exposition of the Wesleyan doctrine of 'Christian Perfection'. A second edition was published later: *Christian Perfection* (1875). Other books grew out of Mahan's lectures, including *A System of Moral Philosophy* (1848), *Doctrine of the Will* (1845) and *Lectures on the Ninth of Romans* (1851). *System of Intellectual Philosophy* (1845) promoted Scottish commonsense philosophy; *Moral Philosophy* provided a social analysis based on the categories of the same intellectual tradition. Both passed through many editions. The *Doctrine of the Will* was intended to refute the view of Jonathan *Edwards.

Financial difficulties and Mahan's activist social agenda and administrative style led to his departure in 1850 for the new University of Cleveland. He had served Oberlin for several years without salary, but the college and its new president, Finney, worked to undermine the University of Cleveland (which went bankrupt in 1852) and refused to pay the percentage of Mahan's salary that it had promised. During the following period of unemployment, Mahan republished some of his books and wrote against spiritualism in *Modern Mysteries Explained and Exposed* (1855), a subject he also addressed in a later publication, *The Phenomena of Spiritualism Scientifically Explained and Exposed* (1875).

Mahan moved to Jackson, Michigan, as pastor of the Congregational Church (1855–1858) and received an honorary doctorate from Hillsdale College (1858). In 1858 he accepted a pastorate at the Plymouth Congregational Church in Adrian, Michigan. At his urging, the Wesleyan Methodist Michigan Union College moved to Adrian, renaming itself Adrian College, and Mahan became its president. While at Adrian he lost his son in the Civil War and his wife to disease. He married a widow, Mary E. Chase, in 1866. During the Michigan years he published *Science or Logic* (1857), *The Science of Natural Theology* (1867) and the influential

The Baptism of the Holy Ghost and the Enduement of Power (1870).

The Mahans moved to England in 1872 to claim an inheritance and to work with the revivalistic Mildmay Centre in London. Mahan participated in the Oxford (1874) and Brighton (1875) Conferences. In England he edited Banner of Holiness (1875–1876) and founded Divine Life and Missionary Witness, which became Divine Life and International Expositor of Scriptural Holiness. This periodical circulated throughout Europe, and many of its articles were translated into other European languages. Mahan also wrote books on Holiness, including The Promise of the Spirit (1874), The Natural and the Supernatural in the Christian Life and Experience (n.d.), and Life Thoughts on the Rest of Faith (1877). These and other publications were translated, wholly and in part, into various European languages. They were quite influential in the development of Holiness and Pentecostal thought throughout Europe. Mahan was also involved with the Bethshan Healing Centre and helped to awaken interest in divine healing throughout Europe.

Mahan died in Eastbourne, England, in 1889. He told his own story in his Autobiography: Intellectual, Moral and Spiritual (1882).

Bibliography

D. W. Dayton, 'Asa Mahan and the Development of American Holiness Theology', Wesleyan Theological Journal, 9 (1974), pp. 60–69; M. E. Dieter, The Holiness Revival of the Nineteenth Century (Metuchen: Scarecrow Press, 1980; ²1996); E. H. Madden and J. Hamilton, Freedom and Grace (Metuchen: Scarecrow Press, 1982).

D. BUNDY

■ **MAIER, Walter Arthur** (1893–1950), Lutheran radio evangelist, was born in Boston, Massachusetts, the son of a devout builder of organs and pianos who had emigrated from Germany in the early 1880s. A brilliant student, Maier spent six years at the Lutheran Church, Missouri Synod's (LCMS) Concordia Collegiate Institute in Westchester County, New York. After earning a combined high school and junior college degree in 1912, he took on a double academic load and completed his BA in just one year at Boston University. Desirous of entering the ministry, Maier enrolled at Concordia Theological Seminary in St Louis in the autumn of 1913, becoming particularly interested in Hebrew. Upon graduation in 1916, he received a graduate fellowship in Old Testament Studies at Harvard Divinity School. While a student, Maier was ordained to the ministry (May 1917), serving in his spare time as assistant pastor at Zion Lutheran Church in Boston. After the United States entered the First World War, Maier served as chaplain to several hundred interred German merchant seamen held on an island in Boston Harbor, spent several months as the Protestant chaplain at Camp Gordon in Georgia, and returned to Massachusetts as chaplain at Camp Devens and a nearby German POW camp. At the end of the war, Maier resumed his studies, switching to Harvard's Graduate School as his concentration turned towards Semitic languages. In 1920 he was awarded an MA and entered the doctoral programme. He was awarded the PhD in Semitics in 1929.

After receiving his MA, Maier turned down several offers to teach at the university level, opting instead for the newly created position of executive secretary of the LCMS' youth programme, the *Walther League. Moving to Milwaukee, Maier threw himself into the new position, which included editing its monthly periodical The Walther League Messenger, and travelled widely to promote interest in the League's work. Maier was responsible for targeting sub-groups such as college and university students and younger teenagers for specialized programmes, as well as relaxing the League's ethnic German identification which so marked the parent denomination. After two years at the helm of the Walther League, Maier accepted a position teaching Old Testament at Concordia Seminary in the autumn of 1922. Under his leadership, the Walther League had doubled its chapters to nearly 900, seen its membership double to 50,000, added several full-time staff, and moved into more expansive quarters in Chicago. In spite of his new duties, however, Maier remained vitally interested in the work of the League, retaining his position as the editor of the Messenger until 1945. By that time, the magazine had increased its 1920 circulation figure more than ten times to 80,000. In 1924 he married Hulda Eickhoff, his former assistant at the League; the couple had two sons.

Maier kept up his peripatetic activity during the rest of the 1920s, dividing his time between teaching, editorial responsibilities, his doctoral studies, and a growing interest in the new *wunderkind*, radio. Convinced that the new medium was an ideal way to evangelize and catechize the masses, Maier laid the groundwork for a LCMS-owned radio station in a series of *Messenger* editorials. He then approached Concordia's dean, John H. C. Fritz, about the idea. Fritz was enthusiastic and authorized Maier to take steps to making his vision become reality. With the backing of $7,000 donated by the Walther League and a matching amount from local laymen and the seminary community, Maier oversaw the purchase of a 500-watt transmitter and the construction of a makeshift studio in Concordia's attic. On 14 December 1924 KFUO (Keep Forward, Upward, Onward), 'The Gospel Voice', went on the air. The station was warmly received by Midwestern audiences, featuring a variety of programming that mixed religious programmes with classical music, drama and cultural discussions. From the beginning, Maier's hard-hitting, machine-gun-like delivery played a prominent role on the station; for example, he hosted a Sunday night vespers service and a Thursday evening 'Views on the News' programme. The station proved so successful that by May 1927 KFUO had its own building and up-to-date equipment, courtesy of the Lutheran Laymen's League.

By 1930 Maier was actively seeking to launch a coast-to-coast Lutheran radio presence over a national network. He found NBC unreceptive to requests for more than doling out an occasional share of some of the public service time it supplied to the liberal Protestant Federal Council of Churches (an organization to which the conservative LCMS did not belong). However, Maier found the CBS network more amenable to the idea of a major commitment through the sale of airtime. Taking his plan to the Lutheran Laymen's League at their May convention, he persuaded the group to raise $100,000 to back the new venture. On Thursday evening, 2 October 1930, the weekly half-hour broadcast of 'The Lutheran Hour' premiered on CBS' thirty-six-station network at a cost of $4,600 per week. Although 'The Lutheran Hour' received a weekly average of $2,000 in donations from its listeners, it proved too expensive an undertaking for the Lutheran Laymen's League, given the mounting effects of the Depression. By mid-June 1931 'The Lutheran Hour' was off the air, despite the fact that CBS had received more mail about it than about any other network broadcast.

During the next few years Maier busied himself with his duties at Concordia and with numerous speaking engagements and occasional radio appearances. However, reviving the dormant 'Lutheran Hour' was his foremost ambition. With a financial pledge from Chevrolet president William T. Knudsen, a devout LCMS layman, 'The Lutheran Hour' made its reappearance in February 1935 on a small network managed by KFUO, and on two powerful stations in Detroit and Cincinnati. When contributions from listeners exceeded Knudsen's financial pledge, the Lutheran Laymen's League agreed to sponsor the next season's worth of broadcasts on the new Mutual Broadcasting System. From that point in the 1930s and into the 1940s, 'The Lutheran Hour' expanded both its number of stations and its listening audience, becoming probably the second most popular religious radio broadcast behind only independent fundamentalist broadcaster Charles E. *Fuller's 'Old-Fashioned Revival Hour'. By 1940 the technological advance made possible by the use of 'electrical transcription' recordings meant that the programme was heard on over 170 stations in the United States, and was broadcast in Spanish on several shortwave stations in Central and South America and in the Philippines.

During this period Maier and 'The Lutheran Hour' became one of the leading combatants on behalf of conservative religious broadcasters. Maier's programme was the most visible component in the resistance to the Federal Council of Churches' attempts in the late 1930s to persuade the National Association of Broadcasters and the Mutual Broadcasting System to discontinue the sale of air time for religious broadcasts. Additionally, 'The Lutheran Hour', through the presence of Maier's Director of Radio Operations, Eugene R. 'Rudy' Bertermann, was also a major player in the formation of the National Religious Broadcasters (1942), an interest group that zealously promoted the interests of its conservative, and overwhelmingly evangelical, Protestant members.

'The Lutheran Hour' continued to grow during the years immediately following the Second World War. So demanding had its responsibilities become that in 1944 Maier took what became a permanent leave of absence from his teaching duties at Concordia. By 1949 the programme was being broadcast on nearly 800 stations in the United States, including nearly 200 new stations of the American Broadcasting System. Overseas, over 400 stations were broadcasting 'The Lutheran Hour' in thirty-six languages. Additionally, Maier had ventured into the fledgling medium of television with some experimental appearances on a local St Louis station, beginning on New Year's Day, 1948. At the peak of his ministry and in seeming good health, Maier suffered a series of heart attacks after Christmas 1949 and died in St Louis in early January 1950.

Walter A. Maier was a seminal figure in the early history of religious broadcasting, lending a needed aura of dignity and intellectual competence lacking in many fundamentalist broadcasters of the era. Indeed, Maier's positive emphasis upon the pan-Protestant truths of grace and biblical authority, unburdened by inflammatory attacks upon other denominations, the controversial marks of revivalism, or evangelical end-times speculation, gave 'The Lutheran Hour' a broad acceptance within the listening audience that no other programme, fundamentalist or liberal, could duplicate. Indeed, it is hardly surprising that the majority of Maier's listeners and contributors came from outside the LCMS. Maier's career also played an important role within his native denomination, helping to free it from the insular, ethnocentric attitudes that had been its traditional hallmarks. Through the irenic nature of his own preaching, his refusal to dwell upon doctrinal hairsplitting, and his determination to make common cause with responsible, evangelical broadcasters, Maier did much to bring the LCMS into a wider coalition of conservative Protestants that would play an increasingly important role within American culture in the following years.

Bibliography

P. L. Meier, *A Man Spoke, A World Listened: The Story of Walter A. Maier and the Lutheran Hour* (New York: McGraw-Hill, 1963); W. A. Meier, *The Best of Walter A. Maier* (St Louis: Concordia, 1981); M. L. Rudnick, *Fundamentalism and the Missouri Synod: A Historical Study of Their Interaction and Historical Influence* (St Louis: Concordia, 1966).

L. ESKRIDGE

■ **MARSDEN, Samuel** (1765–1838), chaplain to New South Wales (NSW) and missionary strategist to New Zealand and the South Seas, was born in Bagly, Yorkshire. His father's sons were named Samuel, John and Charles, recalling the *Wesley brothers. Marsden was a pupil of Joseph Milner at York Grammar School, and in December 1790 he entered Magdalene College at Cambridge as a sizar. He was supported by the Elland Society, a fund established in 1777 to which, among others, *Wilberforce and John and Henry *Thornton contributed. The Elland Society had been established to keep poor but able and zealous churchmen, who might consider entering the ministry of the Dissenters, in the service of the Church of England. At Cambridge, Marsden was further nurtured in his evangelical development by Joseph Milner's brother Isaac, president of Queen's, and by the vicar of Holy Trinity Church, Charles *Simeon. Thomas Thomason, later a chaplain in India, testified that 'Mr Marsden, you know, was [Simeon's] intimate friend, and had access to him in his most retired moments.'

In April 1793 Marsden married Elizabeth Fristan, niece of Thomas *Scott, the Bible commentator, destined to be the first secretary of CMS. The Marsdens may have exercised considerable influence in the convict colony of NSW through their modelling of Christian family life. Among the many reasons why the senior NSW chaplain, Richard *Johnson, and the Marsdens became exceptional farmers was that the wives were eager to provide for their children and delighted in their health as they responded to the plentiful produce. Marsden's own family was his major solace. He observed that his 'Situation would have been much more intolerable had I been a single Man. My Wife and Family in the Hour of Temptation and Trial have often procured an Asylum of Peace and Tranquility.'

On his arrival in the colony in March 1794, Marsden quickly came to grief at the hands of Francis Grose, the second governor, who frustrated his efforts to force the convicts to observe the Sabbath. Then at Parramatta, west of Sydney, he came into conflict, which proved lifelong, with the senior officer there, Captain John Macarthur, who dismissed his charge against a drunken emancipist. Wilberforce commended Marsden to Governor Macquarie with the words, 'He is a very worthy man and has a sound understanding and in general good principles.' But the increasingly hostile governor found that judgment hard to accept, as did successive governors, with all of whom Marsden quarrelled. He appears to have been motivated in all his battles by a desire to maintain the dignity of the clerical office, on which he thought the propagation of the gospel depended, and to establish the distinctness, if not the independence, of the church in a decreasingly penal society.

Historians argue, however, that Marsden, having suffered much at the hands of his enemies, who were legion, suffered far more at the hands of his friend, Governor Hunter, who appointed him a civil magistrate. Marsden served as a magistrate from 1795 to 1807, when he returned to England; then Macquarie appointed him to the bench from 1812 to 1818, when he dismissed him; finally Brisbane appointed him for less than a year in 1822. Neither the fact that the practice of appointing clerical magistrates was well established in England, nor the fact that it was difficult to find men of integrity to fill the office in NSW, could mitigate the dislike felt for clerical magistrates by convicts, and Marsden's undoubted severity in the role has been identified as a factor in the development of anticlericalism in Australia.

Marsden was the unrelenting castigator of blasphemy, Sabbath-breaking and immorality. His zeal to resist sin extended to the use of every available instrument, and he was adjudged even by the standards of his own day to be excessive in his severity. His opposition to Macquarie's policy of fully accepting emancipated convicts into society represented the strong evangelical desire for respectability

found among the upwardly mobile artisan classes from Britain. In contrast, Macquarie, through the definite if high Tory evangelicalism of his wife Elizabeth, together with the paternalistic evangelicalism of his mentor Wilberforce, felt that the doctrine of justification by the atoning blood of Christ, accompanied by the Anglican emphasis on absolution, meant that everyone was redeemable and should be given a second chance. Yet before concluding that Macquarie's legacy was more 'evangelical' than that of Marsden, we need to remind ourselves that, in supporting the drive for a post-convict, free, prosperous and progressive colony, Marsden came closer to aligning himself with evangelicalism's greatest early contribution to the development of Australia, the transformation of a convict society into a free nation.

Disappointed in his ministry to convicts and soldiers, Marsden sought consolation in farming, making a significant contribution to the wool industry, and to missions in the South Seas. In 1798 he extended hospitality to eleven LMS missionaries who had fled from Tahiti. In 1804 he was appointed LMS agent in the South Seas. On 17 February 1810 a second group of LMS missionaries arrived in NSW, also dislodged from Tahiti. Marsden encouraged them to persevere with the Tahiti Mission, and within a few years King Pomare became a Christian and the entire population converted to Christianity.

Among evangelicals the most honoured accolade which has been bestowed on Marsden is 'the Apostle to the Maoris'. As early as 1803 he had met Maoris at Parramatta. He pleaded for a civilizing mission to the Maoris before the CMS Committee on a visit to England in 1807. For three decades his name appears in the minutes of CMS with more frequency than that of any other individual. He consistently maintained that the establishment of commerce with the natives was critical to the success of any mission. In 1814 the mission was launched along lines recommended by Marsden with the appointment of two artisans, William Hall and John King. Marsden himself first set foot on the mainland of New Zealand at the still exquisite Matauri Bay on 20 December 1814. Elaborate preparations were made for a solemn ceremony to be held on the following Sunday, which was also Christmas Day. Marsden preached from Luke 2:10: 'Behold I bring you glad tidings of great joy'. The sermon was translated, or at least its drift explained, by an old Maori friend, Ruatara. Marsden made seven voyages to his New Zealand mission, his last when over seventy years of age, lame and almost blind.

Marsden was an untiring if not always efficient activist, with a strong desire to improve everything in sight, including his own reputation and fortune. He improved the ministries and facilities of the church; he sought to tighten the administration of justice and the supervision of public works around Parramatta, the largest town west of Sydney; he developed missions to New Zealand and the South Sea islands and attempted to protect natives from rapacious white traders by legislative action; he focused attention on the needs of Aborigines; and he dramatically improved NSW's agriculture and animal husbandry. The not entirely undeserved epithet of 'flogging parson' has stuck to him like a limpet, disqualifying him from any admiration in the popular history of Australia. But among the evangelicals, his counsel was always sought and his advice usually respected.

Bibliography

J. R. Elder (ed.), *The Letters and Journals of Samuel Marsden, 1765–1838* (Dunedin: Otago University Council, 1932); A. T. Yarwood, *Samuel Marsden, the Great Survivor* (Melbourne: Melbourne University Press, 1977).

S. PIGGIN

■ **MARSHALL, Catherine** (1914–1983), best-selling author, and **Peter** (1902–1949), Presbyterian minister and Chaplain of the US Senate, were one of the most celebrated evangelical couples in mid-twentieth-century America. Peter Marshall was born on 27 May 1902 in Coatbridge, Scotland. He grew up under the loving care of his mother (his father having died when Peter was only four years old) and in the Buchanan Street Evangelical Congregational Kirk. His love for the Bible was nurtured as a boy by his reading it to his blind grandmother. His great ambition was to go to sea, and at the age of fourteen, he left secondary school to join the British Navy. He was refused admission, however, because of his age. Rather than returning to school, he took a job with a firm of civil engineers and began attending the Coatbridge Technical School and Mining College in the evenings to study mechanical engineering, eventually becoming a machine operator at Stewarts and Lloyds Imperial Tube Works. Between 1916 and 1923, he made several further attempts to enter the navy, but none of them succeeded. Then, in the autumn of 1925, at the close of a church meeting, he publicly committed his life to full-time Christian service. Within a year, he sensed that God was calling him to America and into the ministry.

Marshall arrived in America on 5 April 1927 and lodged with an aunt from New Jersey. He took a job digging ditches and then as a moulder in a foundry. In August, at the suggestion of an old friend, he moved to Birmingham, Alabama, and secured a position in the circulation department of the Birmingham *News*. He joined the Old First Presbyterian Church and was soon made president of the Young People's Society and the regular teacher for the Men's Bible Class. Later that autumn he was examined by the Birmingham presbytery and accepted into Columbia Theological Seminary in Decatur, Georgia. After graduating in May 1931, he took a pastorate in Covington, Georgia, and two years later accepted a call to Westminster Presbyterian Church in Atlanta. During his four years at Westminster, he took the church from a state of 'almost closing' to 'bulging walls and sagging balconies'.

In the pulpit Marshall exuded an irrepressible vitality. He had an extraordinarily resonant speaking voice that was both clear and dramatic. One of those who came to listen to him was Catherine Wood, a student at nearby Agnes College. She was born Sarah Catherine Wood in Johnson City, Tennessee, on 27 September 1914 and grew up in the south, where her father was a Presbyterian minister. If the sea was Peter's passion, writing was Catherine's. Her hope was to pursue a career of writing and teaching after graduation, but this was not to be. As she listened to Peter, she grew more impressed with him, and in a letter to her parents dated January 1934, she unburdened herself: 'He's only [thirtyone] and has had just four years experience, but believe me, he's something already. I have never heard such prayers in my life. It's as if, when he opens his mouth, there is a connected line between you and God. I know this sounds silly, but I've got to meet that man.' The silliness lay in the fact that Peter Marshall was thirty-one and a clergyman, while Catherine was only nineteen and a college student. But later that year she found herself sharing the same speaking platform with Peter at a prohibition rally. On the way home, Peter surprised her by asking if he could see her again. Twelve months later, and just two days before Catherine's graduation in the spring of 1936, they were engaged.

In the autumn of that year, just prior to their wedding on 4 November, Peter received a call from the New York Avenue Presbyterian Church of Washington, DC. Although he declined the offer, the church continued to pursue him, and after several months he and Catherine decided to accept. On Sunday 3 October 1937 Peter delivered his first sermon at the historic Presbyterian Church. The expectations laid on both of them were formidable. Catherine was only twenty-two, and Peter had less than six years of ministerial experience. 'To say that a pastor's helpmate was expected to be gracious, charming, poised, equal to every occasion,' Catherine recalled, 'would be a gross understatement' (A Man Called Peter, p. 101). According to her own account, many God-directed changes in her life were required before she began to measure up to the expected standard. Peter, on the other hand, rose to the occasion with characteristic style, quickly developing a reputation as an eloquent and 'thrilling evangelical preacher'. Crowds formed queues at the door on Sunday mornings hoping to get a seat. At the core of his preaching, observed Catherine, was an imaginative faculty dedicated to Christ: most ministers aim to develop an idea in their sermons; Peter sought to paint a picture. 'Christianity is a matter of perception, not proof,' he was often heard to say.

With success came stiff challenges. Catherine spent the period from March 1943 to the summer of 1945 in bed with tuberculosis. It was for her a time of intense spiritual reflection, in which she came to believe that her illness and later its cure were 'spiritual as well as physical'. During this period of spiritual cleansing, as she described it, she began writing again. Then in March 1946, less than six months after Catherine had begun to recover,

Peter collapsed in the pulpit with a heart attack. He soon recovered, however, and shortly thereafter entered the most productive period of his life. He was elected chaplain of the US Senate on 4 January 1947, and quickly established a reputation among the senators for his 'spirited way of being spiritual' and for the brevity, pungency and sharp relevance of his prayers. 'Not without reason,' announced The Kansas City Star, 'are the prayers of the Rev. Peter Marshall attracting national attention ... Even the Senators are now listening to the prayers that open the session.' In addition to his duties at the church and Senate, Peter was now in constant demand as a speaker. His love for preaching made it difficult for him to refuse engagements, and in the end the strain took its toll. On the morning of 25 January 1949, Peter Marshall suffered another heart attack and died. 'The measure of a life,' he once preached, 'is not its duration, but its donation.'

Left alone to support herself and her six-year-old son, Peter John, Catherine soon discovered the true measure of Peter's donation. At the prompting of Fleming H. Revell publishers, she selected twelve of Peter's sermons and thirteen of his prayers and bound them together in a book entitled Mr Jones, Meet the Master. Published in the year of Peter's death, the book became a bestseller and stayed on the non-fiction bestseller list for nearly a year. Shortly afterwards, McGraw-Hill Book Company expressed interest in more published sermons. From this request came Catherine's biography, A Man Called Peter. The book was published in 1951 and within ten days reached the non-fiction bestseller list, remaining there for more than three years. Through the publication of Peter's sermons and prayers, Catherine not only kept the family afloat financially, but also began to realize one of her greatest dreams: to make a contribution to her generation through her writing. For both her literary achievements and her contribution to the 'reawakening of national interest in spiritual welfare', she received the 'Woman of the Year' award from the Women's National Press Club in 1953. In 1955 A Man Called Peter was made into one of the most successful films of the year.

From this early success, Catherine went on to a varied career. She wrote inspirational books, among them To Live Again (1957),

Beyond Ourselves (1961), the novel *Christy* (1967) and *Something More* (1974). In 1959 she married Leonard LeSourd, executive editor of *Guideposts* magazine. Together they established their own publishing company, Chosen Books. From 1958 to 1960 she served as editor for the *Christian Herald*, and from 1960 as roving editor for *Guideposts*. She spent her last years in Florida, where she died on 18 March 1983 on Boynton Beach.

Bibliography
C. Marshall, *A Man Called Peter: The Story of Peter Marshall* (New York: McGraw-Hill Book Company, 1951); C. Marshall, *Meeting God at Every Turn: A Personal Family History* (Grand Rapids: Chosen Books, 1980); K. McReynolds, *Catherine Marshall* (Minneapolis: Bethany House Publishers, 1999).

C. W. MITCHELL

■ **MARSHALL, Daniel** (1706–1784), Baptist revivalist, helped to carry the New England Great Awakening to the back country of the southern colonies. Born in Windsor, Connecticut, with roots in New England Puritanism, Marshall was converted at twenty years of age and became a deacon in the Congregational church. But during the Great Awakening in 1744 he seems to have questioned the practice of infant baptism and made himself, as one historian puts it, 'odious to the orthodox church in Windsor by preaching the Baptist doctrines'. After hearing George *Whitefield preach in 1745, he was moved to leave his farm for an itinerant preaching ministry.

In 1748, after the death of his first wife Hannah Drake, he married Martha Stearns, the sister of the revivalist Shubal *Stearns. By 1751 both men were convinced Separatists (revivalistic Congregationalists), and shortly thereafter Marshall with his family began travelling south. He settled briefly in Pennsylvania for a ministry to the Mohawk Indians, but then moved on to western Virginia. Settling near Winchester, he founded a Baptist church (Mill Creek Church) affiliated with the Philadelphia Baptist Association. He was himself baptized there and licensed to preach.

Meanwhile, Shubal Stearns, who had followed Marshall south, had halted at Opeckon in Berkeley County, Virginia. The two men joined company and settled for a time on the Cacapon river in Hampshire County, about thirty miles from Winchester. Marshall then joined Shubal Stearns in his two-hundred-mile trek to the piedmont region in North Carolina and a ministry on Sandy Creek.

Though not blessed with great talents, Marshall was an indefatigable preacher. In North Carolina he first evangelized at Abbott's Creek, about thirty miles from Sandy Creek. After a few months the church appealed to Sandy Creek, the mother church, for a constitution and for the ordination of Marshall as their pastor. Marshall accepted the call, but his ordination was problematic. It required a plurality of elders to constitute a presbytery (or ordination council), and Shubal Stearns was the only ordained minister among them. They found other Baptists in the area uncooperative because of Sandy Creek's revivalistic, 'disorderly' practices. Stearns finally found Marshall's brother-in-law, Henry Ledbetter, living somewhere in the southern colonies and enlisted his aid in the ordination.

After establishing the ministry at Abbott's Creek, Marshall continued to sally forth for revivalistic missions. He went first to Pittsylvania County in southern Virginia, where he was able to baptize several people, one of whom was a young man from Baltimore named Dutton Lane. Marshall's ministry sparked a revival, and he returned to preach in the area. On one of these return visits he baptized forty-two people. Then, in August 1760, Marshall helped to establish a church under the pastoral care of Dutton Lane, the early convert. This was the first Separate Baptist church in Virginia and, in some sense, the mother of all the rest. The church prospered under Lane's ministry with occasional visits from Marshall and Stearns. But Lane also often travelled with Marshall in his revival ministry and came to share his zeal, diligence and manners.

Later, Marshall moved to South Carolina and helped to establish seven churches, which formed the Congaree Association in 1771. That year he also found the Georgia field so promising that he left his home on Horse Creek, South Carolina, fifteen miles from Augusta, and moved to Kiokee Creek in the Georgia colony to preach the gospel there. Marshall had so much success in Georgia that

Lieutenant Governor Bull encouraged the Anglican minister in Augusta to preach in New Windsor, hoping that this would 'effectively put a stop to the progress of those Baptist vagrants, who continually endeavor to subvert all order, and make the minds of the people giddy, with that which neither they nor their teachers understand.'

In the end, Marshall was arrested, convicted and commanded to preach no more in the colony. But he was determined to preach. He was supported by his fearless wife, who quoted Scripture passages pronouncing woes upon those who hinder the preaching of the gospel. There the matter ended, except that the arresting constable, the magistrate who tried Marshall, and a witness named Cartledge were all converted to Baptist views as a result.

Marshall continued in ministry through the Revolutionary years and died near Augusta, Georgia, in 1784.

Bibliography

W. L. Lumpkin, *Baptist Foundations in the South* (Nashville: Broadman Press, 1961); R. B. Semple, *History of the Baptists in Virginia* (Lafayette: Church Research and Archives, 1976).

B. L. SHELLEY

■ **MARTYN, Henry** (1781–1812), East India Company chaplain and missionary scholar, was the first Protestant to develop a distinctive evangelistic approach to Muslims. Although never sent out by a missionary society, he saw his brief career in the East as a missionary vocation. His work left an important legacy for later generations of Christian missionaries to the Islamic world.

Martyn was born in Truro, Cornwall, on 18 February 1781, the third child of John Martyn, chief clerk to a merchant. He was educated at Truro Grammar School and St John's College, Cambridge, where in 1801 he obtained his BA as Senior Wrangler, the best mathematician in his year. He was elected a fellow of his college in 1802, and appeared destined for a brilliant university or legal career. Martyn had, however, experienced an evangelical conversion following the death of his father in January 1800, and came under the influence of Charles *Simeon,

vicar of Holy Trinity Church and leader of the Cambridge evangelicals. He also became firm friends with John Sargent, an evangelical student at King's College. Through Simeon's encouragement and reading Jonathan *Edwards' life of David *Brainerd, Martyn resolved to offer for missionary service to the newly founded Church Missionary (now Mission) Society, and prepared himself for ordination.

Martyn received little encouragement in his intention to become a missionary. He was told by a friend that he had 'neither strength of body or mind for the work'. Even his pious sister Sally disapproved, judging him to be deficient 'in that deep and solid experience necessary in a missionary'. Such lack of encouragement reinforced Martyn's natural tendency to self-criticism and introspection. His journal, kept in order to 'improve my soul in holiness', records agonizing struggles with pride, even, for example, on the day of his ordination on 23 October 1803. He became a curate to Charles Simeon and was given charge of a village church at Lolworth, near Cambridge. By early 1804 it was evident that Martyn's hopes of becoming a missionary were unrealistic, as he had assumed financial responsibilities for his family that could not be discharged on the basis of a missionary's allowance. Instead, on Simeon's recommendation, Martyn was introduced to Charles Grant, the evangelical director of the East India Company, who was searching for evangelicals to appoint as chaplains. Martyn accordingly left Cambridge at Easter 1805 and prepared to go to India.

Martyn feared that his impending appointment as a company chaplain, stationed among Europeans, and with a princely salary of £1,200 per annum, would prove too worldly a calling. His self-questioning was made more acute as a result of his falling in love with Lydia Grenfell, a young Cornishwoman six years his senior. Martyn travelled to Cornwall in July 1804 to say farewell to family and friends, but was torn apart by the 'direct opposition' between his 'devotedness to God in the missionary way' and his love for Lydia. His friends gave contradictory advice: many urged him to go to India as a married man; others, such as Simeon, urged celibacy. In the end, Martyn left for India in August 1805, leaving Lydia behind, she having neither agreed nor refused to marry him. Once in India, Martyn continued to agonize on the matter. Reading the life of the Jesuit missionary, Francis Xavier, in July 1806 convinced him of the virtue of celibacy, but within a week of reaching this conclusion, he had sent a letter to Lydia requesting her to join him. However, family ties prevented her from doing so. The couple continued to correspond for the rest of Martyn's life, but never met again.

Martyn arrived in Calcutta in April 1806, and was greeted by William *Carey. The Serampore Baptist missionaries made him welcome, and Martyn assisted them in translation work while awaiting a specific appointment from the Company. During the long voyage he had studied Bengali, Urdu and Arabic, as well as Persian, which he had begun to learn in Cambridge. In October 1806 Martyn took up his first posting at Dinapur (near Patna in Bihar), where he was responsible for the spiritual welfare of two regiments and a substantial body of company civil servants. He found his European flock indifferent to spiritual concerns, but increasingly turned his mind to the Muslim population of India, rather than to the Hindus, who had been the object of his original vision. He began to translate both the Book of Common Prayer and the New Testament into Urdu, assisted by an Arab convert from Islam, Nathaniel Sabat, who later collaborated with Martyn on Arabic and Persian translations of the New Testament. Martyn read everything he could find about Islam and engaged in debate with the local Muslim *ulema* (religious intellectuals and jurists).

In April 1809 Martyn was transferred to a new post at Kanpur (Cawnpore). Here he came into contact with a young Muslim scholar, Shaikh Salih. Attracted by Martyn's preaching, Salih secured employment as a copyist working with Sabat on the Persian New Testament. When Martyn completed his Urdu New Testament, Salih was given the job of binding it. He read it, and was convinced of the truth of Christianity. Initially he said nothing to Martyn. Martyn's health had rapidly deteriorated owing to tuberculosis, and he obtained leave of absence from the Company. Shortly before he left Kanpur, in October 1810, Salih confessed his faith and requested baptism. Salih then accompanied Martyn to Calcutta, where he was entrusted to the care of David Brown, a senior company chaplain and evangelical. Brown later baptized Salih, who adopted the name of Abdul Masih ('servant of Christ') and became a pioneer of Christian evangelism to the Muslim population of northwest India.

Martyn determined to return to England via Persia and Arabia. He had realized that his Persian and Arabic versions of the New Testament were gravely deficient, and that only residence in Persia and Arabia would suffice to improve them. He arrived in Shiraz in June 1811, and stayed for a year, retranslating the Persian New Testament and debating with the Sufi mystics. Martyn's ascetic devotion had a certain appeal to Sufi theologians. He left Shiraz in May 1812 for Tabriz, where the British ambassador, Sir Gore Ouseley, resided. Martyn hoped that Ouseley would enable him to present the completed New Testament to the Shah of Persia, but by the time he reached Tabriz, Martyn was too ill to see the Shah. The Ouseleys nursed him so that he was able to travel on towards Constantinople, but he got no further than Tokat (in Turkey). There he died on 16 October 1812, and was buried with great honour by the Armenian church. Ouseley fulfilled Martyn's wishes by presenting the New Testament to the Shah, and also secured its publication in St Petersburg in 1815.

Martyn's short life had a great impact, both through those he influenced, such as Abdul Masih, and through the spiritual model he presented to later generations. John Sargent published a biography in 1819 which went into numerous editions, and was preparing Martyn's letters and journals for publication when he died in 1833. This volume appeared in 1837, edited by Sargent's son-in-law, Samuel Wilberforce. Martyn's self-denying piety and apostolic zeal were admired, not simply by evangelicals, but also by the pioneers of the Oxford Movement in the 1830s. It might be said that he became the first saint of the evangelical movement.

Bibliography

C. E. Padwick, *Henry Martyn: Confessor of the Faith* (London: SCM Press, 1922); J. Sargent, *A Memoir of the Rev. Henry Martyn, B.D.* (London: Seeley & Burnside,

1819); G. Smith, *Henry Martyn: Saint and Scholar* (London: Religious Tract Society, 1892).

B. STANLEY

■ **MASON, Charles Harrison** (1866–1961), General Overseer of the Church of God in Christ, was born on 8 September 1866 on a farm on the northern outskirts of Memphis, Tennessee, in what is now the town of Bartlett. His parents, Jerry and Eliza Mason, were former slaves and members of the Missionary Baptist Church. In 1878 the family moved to Plumersville, Arkansas. Licensed and ordained among the Baptists in Preston, Arkansas in 1891, Mason married Alice Saxton. The marriage ended in divorce in 1893 when Alice opposed Mason's plans to enter full-time ministry. During the difficult days that followed, Mason happened to discover the newly published auto-biography of Amanda Smith, a popular and widely travelled black holiness evangelist. Her story inspired Mason to claim for himself the so-called 'second blessing' of entire sanctification.

In the autumn of 1893 Mason enrolled at Arkansas Baptist College, intending to pursue formal ministerial training. He soon found himself uncomfortable in the college environment, and in January 1894 he withdrew. In 1895 he met Charles Price Jones, a Mississippi Baptist, who shared Mason's fascination for Christ-centered holiness preaching. Jones wrote hymns and had also briefly attended Arkansas Baptist College. Both Mason and Jones knew Elias Camp Morris, founder of the college and first president of the National Baptist Convention. Jones enjoyed particular prominence among black Arkansas Baptists, who recognized his abilities as a preacher and offered him a succession of influential pulpits as well as the post of editor of *The Baptist Vanguard*.

During the 1890s, Mason and Jones became involved in serious conflict with Arkansas Baptists over their views on Christian perfection. The controversy began at Jones' local church, Mt Helm Baptist Church in Jackson, Mississippi, engulfed the Mississippi Negro Baptist Convention and eventually demanded the attention of the leaders of the newly formed National Baptist Convention.

In 1899 a court order to vacate the property of the Mt Helms Baptist Church made the separation of Jones, Mason and their followers from the Arkansas Negro Baptist Convention formal and final. Jones and Mason established a new group that came to be known as the Church of God in Christ, the first of the cluster of formal associations that came to constitute the tradition later known as the Sanctified Church. They instituted a periodical, *The Truth*, to serve their constituency. Mason claimed that the church's name had come to him from 1 Thessalonians 2:14, accompanied by a specific divine promise: 'If you take this name, there will never be a building large enough to house the people whom I will send to you.'

During the 1890s Mason worked as an evangelist, walking from town to town in northern Mississippi, western Tennessee and northeastern Arkansas. Whites as well as blacks responded to his preaching and identified with the 'sisters' and 'brothers' who formed his community of 'saints'. In 1905 in Jackson, Mississippi both Mason and Jones met William J. *Seymour, another son of slaves who had embraced the holiness message and felt the call to preach. The next year, Seymour accepted an invitation to Los Angeles, where he began proclaiming views he had learned from Charles Fox *Parham, a Kansas evangelist who had been holding meetings in Houston, Texas. Seymour taught that all Christians should pray for the baptism with the Holy Spirit, an experience that would be evidenced by speaking in tongues. He believed that Christ was about to return and urged sanctification and Spirit baptism as 'enduement with power for service' in spreading the gospel around the world. His meetings attracted a noisy following and moved from a house to an abandoned Methodist Church on Azusa Street.

Mason, Jones and other holiness Baptists heard reports of this revival and decided to evaluate it for themselves. Mason travelled to Los Angeles with J. A. Jeter and D. J. Young, where they had the experience known as baptism with the Holy Spirit and speaking in tongues on 19 March 1907. In Mason's words, 'I received Him, Jesus, my Lord in the Holy Ghost.' Mason and his friends spent some five weeks at Azusa Street and became firmly convinced of the validity of Seymour's message. They returned to Jackson and Memphis to endorse the Azusa Street revival, only to find Jones and others of their friends hostile to the association of speaking in tongues with the baptism in the Holy Spirit. After prolonged and sharp debate, Mason and Jones separated. For two years they fought in court over the name and property of the group they had built together. In the end, Jones reorganized his followers as the Church of Christ (Holiness) USA. Mason gained the legal right to the name 'Church of God in Christ'. In 1907 the organizing council of his Pentecostal faction elected him General Overseer and authorized a new periodical, *The Whole Truth*.

Mason worked tirelessly to spread his message and build an association of churches. Although most of his associates were black, a number of white workers joined the Church of God in Christ, and Mason was a popular speaker among white as well as black Pentecostals. Between 1910 and 1914, Mason helped southern white Pentecostals by granting Howard Goss, an associate of Charles Parham's Apostolic Faith Movement, permission to use his organization's name in the ordination of some white Pentecostal ministers, thus enabling them to obtain clergy rail discounts. Their ministerial credentials read 'The Church of God in Christ and in Unity with the Apostolic Faith Movement'. During the anti-German phobia of the First World War era, Mason's interracial contacts as well as his pacifism attracted the attention of the Federal Bureau of Identification. Allegations that he preached against the war led to his brief imprisonment in Lexington, Mississippi in 1918.

Mason's visit to Azusa Street marked the beginning of a series of new experiences in his personal life. At Azusa Street, he began seeing visions, and he claimed that he continued to do so. He now spoke publicly in tongues and interpreted his speech. He claimed that God 'taught him and gave him new songs' and that 'the Holy Ghost began all kinds of drawings and spiritual writings done without any thought of my mind'. Early Pentecostals called such unusual experiences 'manifestations', and, combined with his determination to keep alive the emotional intensity of his black religious heritage, they led some to see him as a bold and creative preacher.

Under Mason's leadership, the Church of God in Christ gathered annually for Holy Convocations, sacred weeks of renewal and community building held after Thanksgiving to allow farmers to harvest their crops and save the money to travel to Memphis. As Chief Apostle and General Overseer, Mason led his growing church in three weeks of constant preaching, prayer, testimony and song. Mason's personal charisma and his enthusiasm for commissioning workers greatly helped to sustain the spiritual and physical growth of the denomination. By 1934, the Church had 345 congregations and a membership of 25,000. Mason instituted a growth plan in the mid-1930s, consecrating five bishops in 1933 and appointing ten overseers in 1934 to supervise local extension. By the time Mason died in 1961, the Church of God in Christ claimed well over 375,000 members.

From 1912 Mason sent out male and female evangelists to spread his message, though he opposed the ordination of women to the pastorate. During the First World War the evangelists went especially to growing northern cities, following the black migration. Such outreach was facilitated by Mason's strategic decision in 1911 to organize a women's department. He thus mobilized a dedicated army of workers who oversaw children's ministry, prayer groups, sewing circles and home and foreign mission work.

Mason remained single until his divorced wife, Alice, died. In 1903 he married Lelia Washington, with whom he had eight children. She died in 1936. In 1943 he married Elsie Washington, a woman more than fifty years his junior, who survived him.

In 1946, the year of Mason's eightieth birthday, his grateful followers dedicated the 3,000-seat Mason Temple, at the time the largest black-built structure in the United States. By then, Mason had become an economic and civic force in Memphis. The street on which the temple stands is named in Mason's honour. (A few years after Mason's death in 1961, Martin Luther King Jr gave his last public address, on 3 April 1968, from the pulpit of Mason Temple in Memphis, Tennessee.) Mason, who died at the age of ninety-five in Detroit on 17 November 1961, is buried in a vault in the temple's foyer.

Bibliography

I. C. Clemmons, *Bishop C. H. Mason and the Roots of the Church of God in Christ* (Bakersfield: Pneuma Life Pub., 1996); G. A. Wacker, *Heaven Below: Early Pentecostals and American Culture* (Cambridge, MA: Harvard University Press, 2001).

E. L. BLUMHOFER

■ **MATHER, Cotton** (1663–1728), leading early American minister, was descended from two prominent New England families. His grandfathers, John *Cotton and Richard Mather, were spiritual and intellectual leaders of the first generation of New England Puritans. His father Increase, minister of the North (Second) Church in Boston, president of Harvard College and a power in the life of Massachusetts, married John Cotton's only daughter, and Cotton was their first child.

Early in life Mather came to believe that he was a member of a covenanted community divinely obligated to advance the kingdom of God and that he was destined for greatness. He benefited from the best education available in New England, beginning his formal studies at the Boston Latin School, and in 1674 entering Harvard College, the purpose of which was to give a liberal education. In addition to the classics, Mather completed the traditional required studies: logic, ethics, metaphysics, mathematics and natural philosophy, rhetoric, oratory and divinity. He was keenly interested in natural philosophy (science). During his student days the Aristotelian natural philosophy long taught at Harvard was being eclipsed by a new natural philosophy that culminated in Newton, whose *Principia Mathematica* (1687) appeared shortly after Mather graduated.

Mather had a speech impediment that led him to doubt whether he could enter the ministry, and for some time he studied medicine. He learned to overcome the imperfection, however, and by the time he graduated in 1678, he was well educated in the classics, the Bible, and Christian history and literature. Despite a mannered style, he wrote clear, fluent and graceful prose.

At the age of sixteen Mather experienced a religious conversion and was admitted as a member of the North Church. In 1681 he earned an MA degree from Harvard and a year later issued the first of his many publications. In September 1680 he had become his father's unordained assistant at the North Church. On 13 May 1685 he was ordained in the prestigious North Church, the largest in America; he served there until his death.

New England's spiritual crisis conditioned Mather's career. The earliest American Puritans had believed that they were God's elect nation engaged in a divine mission to build a holy commonwealth. A combination of unfavourable circumstances (natural disasters, the witchcraft mania, political adversity, including the Crown annulling the charter of 1629 under which Massachusetts had been a self-governing Bible commonwealth, and perceived religious declension) led Mather's generation to question the soundness of their inherited vision. Mather had to choose between viewing Massachusetts as simply another colony in the British imperial system, a choice that spelled catastrophe for the idea of a covenanted community, or as God's elect nation still engaged in a divine mission to open the last stage in human redemption and bring a blessing upon the entire human race.

Above all, Mather lived during a time of rapid intellectual change. When he was born the medieval worldview dominated the Western mind. It held that nature and the supernatural were one system derived from God, who rules the physical universe by first and secondary causes. The former were inscrutable divine decrees, and the latter the regular sequences of nature that could be understood by human reason. The medieval mind believed in a world of wonders that demonstrated the power of God (or Satan) to suspend the laws of nature. These age-old convictions were challenged by the scientific revolution that began with Copernicus and triumphed with Newton. The new model of reality retained a conventional belief in the Christian religion while employing the experimental method of observation and demonstration. Natural laws were seen as part of the law of God and capable of mathematical proof.

Mather was foremost among the New Englanders who remained committed Calvinists while adjusting to the new mentality. He did not entirely abandon ancient superstitions, and as a result he acquired a reputation as a bigot and reactionary. Actually, Mather was among the most progressive men of his generation in responding to intellectual advances. He embraced the new science without accepting a completely mechanistic universe.

Mather devoted his life to reinvigorating the Puritanism of the founders in the light of the best thought of the age. Beyond his ministerial duties, he took an active part in colonial political affairs and wrote prolifically, publishing more than 460 works during his life, mainly in history, science and theology, and leaving many thousand pages in manuscript.

Mather's most important publication was the *Magnalia Christi Americana: Or, The Ecclesiastical History of New England* (London, 1702). The idea for the work sprang from Mather's conviction that history was one of the ways in which to decipher the progress of God's plan for the redemption of humanity. The book interpreted the Protestant Reformation as the climax of the effort to bring heaven down to earth and the New England churches as the cutting edge of the Reformation.

Mather's *Biblia Americana* was an effort to produce an American commentary on the Old and New Testaments that would reconcile the scriptural text with what he regarded as scientific fact. He laboured on this work for years, producing a manuscript of six volumes of about a thousand pages each. This monumental and unwieldy treatise, never published, updated earlier glosses, and most of the material was available from British authors.

Mather was the first American to write a book dealing with all the sciences known at the time. *The Christian Philosopher: A Collection of the Best Discoveries in Nature, with Religious Improvements* (London, 1721) expounds the thesis of the harmony between science and religion within the framework of the argument from design, which holds that one may reasonably infer the existence of a purposeful Creator from the evidences of order in the universe. This ancient pagan idea was first reinterpreted by Christian apologists and later by English authors who elaborated the idea in terms of the new mechanical philosophy spawned by the scientific revolution. Mather's purpose in writing was to vivify piety. In closing he emphasized the mediatorial role of Christ in the divine plan of redemption. The book was a harbinger of the Enlightenment in America.

Mather's *Angel of Bethesda*, a lengthy manuscript first published in 1972, argued that there is a close correlation between spiritual health and physical well-being. Among his own books Mather's favourite was *Bonifacius* (Boston, 1710), best known as *Essays to do Good*. He wrote that the great end in life is to do good; thus he reduced charity to a system and planted the seeds for vast schemes of benevolence. Benjamin Franklin discarded the religious basis of Mather's idea in order to introduce it into the mainstream of American culture. Mather's *Manuductio ad Ministerium: Directions for a Candidate of the Ministry* (Boston, 1726), was a work on pastoral care. This manual for the training of ministers reflects the older Puritanism in discussing systematic theology, but it shows an indebtedness to recent thought by viewing religion more as a matter of practical conduct than one of abstract contemplation of the divine.

Cotton Mather, a mountain peak on the early American intellectual and theological landscape, has been burdened by a poor reputation. But the stereotype of a bigoted Puritan priest and a persecutor of witches is a bad caricature. Mather remained an orthodox evangelical Christian while accepting much of the new scientific outlook. His most important books have worked their way into American thought and culture.

Bibliography
D. Levin, *Cotton Mather: The Young Life of the Lord's Remembrancer, 1663–1703* (Cambridge, MA: Harvard University Press, 1978); K. Silverman, *The Life and Times of Cotton Mather* (New York: Harper & Row, 1984).

W. U. SOLBERG

■ **MAXWELL, Leslie Earl (L. E.)** (1895–1984), Bible school principal and teacher, was the founder of Prairie Bible Institute (PBI) in Three Hills, Alberta, Canada. Under Maxwell's leadership this nondenominational Bible school grew to be one of largest schools of its kind in North America, and gained a reputation in evangelical circles for its emphasis on missionary training. In addition to serving as a teacher and administrator at PBI, Maxwell edited two monthly periodicals, preached on the school's weekly Sunday radio programme and travelled extensively throughout Canada and the United States as an evangelist and conference speaker. Maxwell's single-minded goal in all of these activities was to motivate and train Christian men and women for missionary service. Although he deliberately avoided linking PBI with any particular denomination, Maxwell identified most closely with a strand of fundamentalism derived from the holiness theology of A. B. *Simpson and his Christian and Missionary Alliance movement. Although he made his home in Canada for sixty-one years, L. E. Maxwell retained his American citizenship throughout his life.

Maxwell was born and raised on a small farm just outside Salina, Kansas. His family had no connection to things Christian, and in his own words, he spent his childhood and teenage years 'playing ball, playing pool and playing the fool'. After completing his secondary school education, he moved to Kansas City, Missouri, and began working in a bank. Through the influence of a God-fearing aunt, Maxwell began attending a Presbyterian church, and shortly thereafter underwent a personal conversion to Christianity. He returned to Kansas City in May 1919, after serving with the American military forces in France during the last year of the First World War. In the autumn of the same year he enrolled in a small local Bible school founded by William Stevens, a teacher for many years at A. B. Simpson's Missionary Training School in Nyack, New York.

During his three years of Bible school training, under the mentoring of Stevens, Maxwell developed an understanding of his faith through the teachings of holiness theology. As a result he adopted three beliefs that provided the foundation for the school he founded in Canada. The first of these was the necessity for each Christian to undergo a personal crisis of spiritual brokenness, or 'yieldedness'. This was an experience following one's conversion, in which one came to a point of completely surrendering one's own will to God's authority. The second belief was the adequacy of the inductive method of studying the Bible for fully equipping the individual believer for the teaching of others. Thirdly, Maxwell became convinced that for any sincere Christian missionary service should follow naturally from this kind of formal biblical training.

In 1921, the year before Maxwell graduated from Bible school, Stevens received a letter from Fergus Kirk, a young farmer in Alberta, Canada, asking Stevens whether he knew of anyone who was qualified and available to come north and give biblical instruction to a group of local Christian young people. When Stevens approached Maxwell with the request, the young student had no interest in taking the position. Besides his personal fear of public speaking, Maxwell hated cold climates and rural living. By the end of his final year, however, Maxwell became convinced that Kirk's letter was indeed God's call to service. In September 1922 Maxwell headed north to Three Hills, Alberta, where he was warmly received by Kirk and several other local farming families.

That autumn Maxwell began teaching a series of Bible classes to eight local young people and three adults in an abandoned farmhouse, which had been hastily renovated to serve as a classroom. At the end of the academic year Maxwell concluded the term by holding a set of meetings which focused on the work of missions. As a result the small group of students raised $2,000 in support of evangelical missionary work. During the following spring and summer months Maxwell worked as an itinerant minister for a local Baptist missions board, frequently travelling on horseback to rural parishes in south central Alberta. In so doing Maxwell established a pattern of classroom education and active ministry that would become the norm for staff as well as many students in later years. This itinerant ministry also allowed Maxwell to recruit students for the coming academic year.

From these humble beginnings the school continued to grow, largely fuelled by Maxwell's tireless efforts and charismatic personality, both in the classroom and in the pulpit. As a teacher he was well liked by his students; as a preacher, both in school chapels and in other churches, he became known for his forceful messages on living the 'crucified life' and heeding the call to missionary service. Over the next twenty-five years PBI's enrolment grew to over 1,100 students, 800 of whom were enrolled in either a two-year or a four-year Bible school programme, as well as

300 other students who were part of a general education division (grades 1–12). From the outset, Prairie Bible Institute chose to remain non-denominational, but developed a doctrinal statement in line with fundamentalist evangelical theology. As a result it attracted students from across Canada and the northwestern United States who came from similar church backgrounds.

During these early years Maxwell started and edited a monthly periodical, *The Prairie Overcomer*, which by the early 1960s had a circulation of 60,000 subscribers. In the early 1930s he also began a weekly radio broadcast each Sunday evening over several Alberta radio stations.

As he had done in the school's first year, Maxwell continued to host a spring missions conference, which became the high point of each academic year. These eight-day conferences featured a variety of missionary leaders and other prominent evangelical figures. During the 1940s the radio preacher Charles *Fuller, and the editor of the *Sunday School Times* Philip Howard, were keynote speakers at PBI conferences. Although such speakers helped increase the school's popularity, the conferences served primarily as an opportunity for various missionary organizations to recruit candidates from the student body. The largest recruitment was for trans-denominational mission societies such as the China Inland Mission and the Sudan Interior Mission. As a result of this strong missions emphasis, PBI soon gained a reputation as one of the most effective missionary training institutions in North America.

From the mid-1940s to the mid-1950s Maxwell also found time to write three books while carrying on his responsibilities as a teacher, editor, radio preacher and itinerant speaker. These three books, *Born Crucified* (1945), *Crowded to Christ* (1950) and *Abandoned to Christ* (1955), formed a trilogy which summarized the holiness theology central to PBI's curriculum. Belying the stereotype of conservative evangelicals of his generation, Maxwell was a supporter of women exercising preaching and teaching ministries; his rationale for this position was expounded in his posthumous book, *Women in Ministry* (1987).

Beginning in 1975, Maxwell gradually began to relinquish leadership of the school to others. In 1977 he turned over the presidency of PBI to his youngest son, Paul Maxwell; and in 1981, at the age of eighty-six, he taught his final class in the Bible school. His teaching career spanned fifty-nine years. On 4 February 1984, at the age of eighty-eight, Maxwell died from Parkinson's disease. He was survived by his wife, Pearl, whom he had married in 1925, as well as five daughters and one son. At his death, over 2,000 PBI alumni were active missionaries in over eighty countries, and another 1,600 were serving as home missionaries and pastors in North America.

Bibliography

J. G. Stackhouse, Jr, *Canadian Evangelicalism in the Twentieth Century: An Introduction to Its Character* (Toronto: Toronto University Press, 1993).

J. C. ENNS

■ **MEARS, Henrietta Cornelia** (1890–1963), educator, was born in Fargo, North Dakota on 23 October 1890, the youngest of the seven children of Margaret and Elisha Ashley Mears. The granddaughter of Baptist ministers, Henrietta was reared in a home deeply affected by the Panic of 1893. Her father, a banker, lost his fortune. Shaped by her Baptist upbringing, Mears was deeply influenced by the Minneapolis Baptist fundamentalist William Bell *Riley. She enrolled at the University of Minnesota, from where, despite difficulties with her eyesight, she graduated in June 1913 with an outstanding academic record. She accepted a position as chemistry teacher and principal of the high school in Beardsley, Minnesota and began teaching in the Sunday school at the local Methodist church. She taught the next year in North Branch and then returned to Minneapolis, where she lived with her sister, Margaret, an arrangement that continued until Margaret's death in 1951. Margaret kept house, and Henrietta taught chemistry at Central High School. She also taught a class of young women in the Sunday school of Riley's First Baptist Church.

In 1927 Mears took a sabbatical from teaching and began seriously to consider resigning her high school teaching job to devote herself entirely to Christian education.

Following a suggestion from Riley, the Mears sisters went to Europe and then to California, where they visited Hollywood Presbyterian Church. A growing congregation, Hollywood Presbyterian Church was strongly committed to Christian education with an emphasis on young adults. At the end of her sabbatical Henrietta returned to Minneapolis with a pressing invitation to move to California as Director of Christian Education at Hollywood Presbyterian Church. In 1928 she resigned her teaching position. The Mears sisters sold their Minneapolis home and moved to California.

The Sunday school that Henrietta Mears undertook to lead had 450 on its roll in 1928. In two years Mears increased that number to 4,200. Mears attributed the dramatic growth to her 'purposeful action'. She insisted that each lesson should 'honor Christ' and attended closely to the curriculum and schedule of activities. Her aggressive attitude and willingness to work alongside her staff endeared her to the Sunday school workers and made recruiting easier. Under her direction, the Sunday school offered something for every family member. She tried to build a better, rather than a bigger, Sunday school. A graded curriculum and motivational guidance for teachers helped to promote what Mears described as 'contagious Christianity'.

Before long, people were enquiring about the secret of the success of the Sunday school at Hollywood Presbyterian Church, and Henrietta Mears was being invited to address Sunday school conventions around the country. Thousands packed large auditoriums to hear Mears' common-sense approach to Christian education through graded curricula.

Mears searched available resources, looking for attractive, 'biblically sound' material. She preferred a chronological approach to biblical history. Her work on the curriculum committee of the state schools of Minneapolis had taught her the importance of material graded to students' abilities. Her review of available Sunday school curricula led her to the conclusion that the Bible was for the most part poorly taught. That conviction launched the next phase of her career.

Mears and her staff decided to write their own Sunday school lessons, guided by a prospectus that outlined what they expected of students at different age levels. She recruited Esther Ellinghusen, a junior high school teacher, to write lessons. Ellinghusen began by exploring remedial reading in the Los Angeles school system. Next she reviewed vocabulary charts for schoolchildren and examined textbooks for font size, vocabulary and style. With this information before her, she began writing and became an invaluable partner in carrying forward Mears' vision for her Sunday school. The incessant demand for more and better copies of Mears' lessons led ultimately to the founding of Gospel Light Press. In 1933 Mears first copyrighted her materials and, with her staff, published twelve Sunday school courses. This series launched Gospel Light Press as a provider of Sunday school curricula. Mears' company was the first to offer lessons that corresponded to the grading she promoted in her Sunday school.

Wider dissemination of Mears' lessons combined with her growing speaking schedule to create a demand for teacher training workshops. From the outset, these proved immensely popular. Eventually they included week-long training courses at the Forest Home Christian Conference Center in the San Bernardino Mountains, for which Mears had the original vision in 1938. But shorter national and international workshops also brought her message and resources to local churches, large and small. Wherever she found opportunity she worked to inspire her followers to address American young people with the claims of the Christian gospel.

Mears influenced the evangelist Billy *Graham, who attended a conference at Forest Home with his friend Charles Templeton at a critical moment in his life. About to undertake his pivotal 1949 Los Angeles crusade, Graham wrestled with doubts exacerbated by Templeton's persuasive arguments against the authority of Scripture. His decision at Forest Home to embrace in faith what his reason could not comprehend proved a turning-point in his life.

For more than a decade after the death of her sister in 1951, Mears shared a large house with Bill and Vonnette *Bright, founders of Campus Crusade for Christ. Located across Sunset Boulevard from the UCLA campus, the house made possible Mears' direct involvement with students eager to share their faith. Its spaciousness made it a gathering place as well as a centre of ministry and facilitated the hospitality in which Mears delighted.

Mears' decision to move to Hollywood proved strategic for her future. It placed her among an eager group of evangelicals who shared her vision for an activist faith and were poised to emerge on the public stage. Many people whom she influenced assumed pivotal roles in the post-Second World War renewal of evangelicalism. The steadily expanding national influence of the pastors of Hollywood Presbyterian Church kept the church in the public eye and drew attention to Mears' extraordinary accomplishments. Her publishing company, Gospel Light, has expanded and offers its materials in many languages around the world. The influence of Henrietta Mears as a Christian educator persists in the expanding academic field of Christian education, which she helped to define. Her college degree and brief teaching experience proved invaluable as she brought principles from public education to bear on church curricula.

Henrietta Mears, indefatigable as ever in her seventies, died in her sleep on 19 March 1963.

Bibliography

B. Powers, *The Henrietta Mears Story* (Westwood: Fleming H. Revell, 1957); E. O. Roe (ed.), *Dream Big: The Henrietta Mears Story* (Ventura: Regal Books, 1990).

E. L. BLUMHOFER

■ **MELANCHTHON, Philip** (also Melanthon, humanist name of Philip Schwartzerdt, 1497–1560), German humanist and Lutheran theologian, was born on 16 February 1497 in Bretten, a city in the electoral Palatinate (present-day Kreis Karlsruhe, Germany). Melancthon was the eldest son of George, a respected armourer, and Barbara, daughter of a prosperous merchant. A prodigious child, he excelled as a student. A mural in the century-old Melanchthonhaus in Bretten depicts him as a lad, stopping travellers in the local marketplace in his thirst for information. After comprehensive studies in Pforzheim (1508–1509), Heidelberg (1509–1512) and Tübingen (1512–1518), and at the recommendation of Johannes Reuchlin, he received a call in 1518 to a newly established teaching position in Greek at the University of Wittenberg, where he encountered Martin *Luther. After participating in the Leipzig Disputation (1519), he became the leader of the Reformation movement in 1521, during Luther's confinement at the Wartburg. Subsequent years saw him immersed in Bible translation and commentary. During this time, he also implemented Luther's vision of public education in Germany, earning himself the title 'preceptor of Germany'. He was present at the Diet of Speyer (1529), the Colloquy of Marburg (1529) and, most crucially, the Diet of Augsburg (1530), and was the main author of the Augsburg Confession. He also signed the Schmalkaldic Articles (1537). In his latter years, Melanchthon oversaw the organization of the Church of Saxony and became embroiled in the Adiaphoristic and Cryptocalvinistic controversies.

Melanchthon's early intellectual formation was in humanism, and this shaped his entire theological outlook. In accordance with a common practice of the humanists, he translated his rather ordinary German name into its more elegant Greek version. He arrived in Wittenberg already in possession of a well-developed Christian philosophy, which included a theory of the liberal arts, an interest in epistemological issues and familiarity with Aristotelian dialectic, rhetoric and ethics. There Melanchthon came under Luther's influence (thus beginning a lifelong friendship) and began to study theology. The proclamation of God's grace freely given became the enduring mainstay of his life and thought. As the experience of grace penetrated his intellectual world, it led him to develop the first systematic presentation of Reformation theology, the *Loci communes theologicae* (literally 'common places', but best rendered 'basic concepts'), and through this a new genre in theological literature.

In the *Loci*, ordered by topics, Melanchthon gave organization and precision to Luther's fundamental ideas. Wedding a Renaissance approach to textual interpretation with a Reformation conviction concerning Scripture, Melanchthon's unique contribution to the history of Christian theology was to create a systematic theology derived *directly* from the Scriptures. Conceiving of Scripture within the classical canons of rhetoric and dialectic, he sought to uncover the basic themes (*loci communes* or *topoi*) of the text that provided the interpretative key for the whole. The proper *loci* consisted of sin, law and grace, and were derived largely from Paul's epistle to the Romans. These, especially the distinction between law and gospel, were his organizational principles. Thus Melanchthon inaugurated a form of Protestant scholasticism and foreshadowed the emergence of Lutheran orthodoxy.

Melanchthon was ever active intellectually, and his positions on key theological issues evolved throughout his life. Though he understood himself to be Luther's disciple, and though he remained within the theological trajectory inaugurated by Luther, his approach is clearly distinguishable. Melanchthon placed his own distinct emphasis on several key Reformation themes. With respect to human freedom, he eventually espoused the position that saving faith is the product of three elements: the preached word, the Holy Spirit and the cooperation of the human will, a view often called 'synergism'. For a time, he maintained that good works are 'necessary to eternal life', not as the basis of salvation but as its indispensable evidence. Regarding the Lord's Supper, he espoused a position midway between those of Luther and *Calvin, holding that Christ is given 'not in the bread, but with the bread', thereby stressing spiritual rather than physical reception. Finally, he viewed many Roman Catholic practices as 'nonessential' matters (*adiaphora*), a view vigorously attacked by some of his contemporaries. Perhaps his most radical departure from Luther's approach emerges in relation to Aristotelian philosophy. In the later editions of the *Loci communes*, Aristotle's thought is increasingly prominent, as Melanchthon takes it up as a useful tool for grounding, clarifying and ordering the biblical theology of Luther. For Melanchthon, faith is not merely the sinner's trust in God's fatherly mercy (as for Luther), but also an assent to a set of revealed truths. Therefore philosophy aids faith and is an essential tool of the theologian.

Philip Melanchthon may be considered the first systematic theologian and a central architect of the Protestant Reformation; indeed, in his own lifetime he was given the title, 'theologian of the Reformation'. Yet he is often overshadowed by his well-known contemporaries, Calvin and especially Luther, with whom he laboured throughout his adult life.

Though perhaps lacking their originality, Melanchthon's life and works were none the less profoundly influential, exceeding by common account those of Luther within their lifetimes. His life's work aimed at the formulation of clear, commonly accepted doctrine. Though he never completely achieved this goal, he was able to develop a sense for exact formulations and thus prepared the way for Protestant orthodoxy.

Melanchthon's historical significance may be seen chiefly in his recognition of the problem of the relation between humanism and the Reformation (that is, between the classical and biblical heritages in the history of the West), his coming to terms with the problem, and his introduction of his solution into the thought and organization of both ecclesiastical and educational reform in Germany. In this he avoided twin dangers, that the fledgling movement would be sidetracked into an anti-intellectual spiritualism and, at the opposite extreme, that philosophy would be imposed upon theology, knowledge upon faith and reason upon revelation. He retained both poles, uniting them in a single system founded upon the distinction between law and gospel. Through his writings, his influence extends beyond the Lutheran Church to all the major Protestant denominations. The authors of the Westminster Confession, and of the Dort and Heidelberg Catechisms, clearly consulted the Augsburg Confession; it is directly the source of the Anglican Thirty-Nine Articles and indirectly that of Methodism's twenty-five articles. Melanchthon also created a Christian and humanist educational system influential throughout the Enlightenment and into the modern period.

Bibliography
H. Scheible, *Melanchthon, Eine Biographie* (Munich: C. H. Beck, 1997); C. Manschreck, *Melanchthon, The Quiet Reformer* (New York: Abingdon Press, 1968); T. J. Wengert and M. P. Graham (eds.), *Philip Melanchthon (1497–1560) and the Commentary* (Sheffield: Sheffield Academic Press, 1997).

B. T. COOLMAN

■ **MELVILLE, Andrew** (1545–1622), Scottish educator and Presbyterian churchman, was born in Baldovie, Angus and lost both parents as a child. His eldest brother, Richard, who had studied at Protestant universities on the continent, sent Melville to grammar school in Montrose, where he began to study Greek. Melville went to the new foundation of St Mary's College in St Andrews in 1559, the same year that the burgh implemented a rapid Protestant reformation; he received his MA in 1563, with high praise for his scholarly abilities. The following year, Melville began studies at the Royal Trilingual College in Paris, where he studied semitic languages and was taught by the logician Peter Ramus, who had converted to Calvinism in 1562. After two years in Paris, Melville went to study law at Poitiers in 1566; he departed after the city was besieged by Coligny in 1568. With religious tensions high in France, Melville opted to go to Geneva, where *Beza gave him the chair of humanities in the city college and where he learned Syriac.

Eventually Melville accepted a call to return to Scotland, arriving in Edinburgh in July 1574, and soon accepted an appointment as principal of the University of Glasgow. Here he made dramatic changes, abolishing old curricula and educational structures in favour of a Ramist course of study dominated by the liberal arts and ancient languages, with specialist instructors. Melville himself taught divinity and oriental languages. The student population increased dramatically, and in 1577 Melville gained additional financial security from the benefice of the parish kirk of Govan, which required him to preach every Sunday. In 1580 Melville left Glasgow to become principal and professor of systematic theology at St Mary's College, St Andrews, recently transformed into a divinity school, where again his energies effected changes and improvements.

Soon after his return to Scotland, Melville also began attending general assemblies of the kirk, which at the time were struggling with the tenuous relationship between assembly and bishop defined by the Concordat of Leith (1572). In 1575 Melville declared that '[t]he words bishop and presbyter are interchangeably used in the New Testament', and that the prelacy of the former was a corruption of early Christian practice. He believed that all ministers were bishops, though he was prepared to allow some of them a visitation role. The Assembly agreed, and by 1580 it was

calling for all bishops to relinquish the title and accept ministerial charges. Meanwhile, Melville was appointed to the large committee that produced the Second Book of Discipline (1578), and acted as moderator of the general assembly four times between 1578 and 1594.

The presbyterian faction, for which Melville provided theological leadership, was ascendant in the kirk until 1584, challenging both archiepiscopal appointments in Scotland during this time. However, during the regency of James Stewart, Earl of Arran, the government established episcopacy through the 'Black Acts', and Melville, charged with sedition, fled south to England. He returned after Arran lost power in November 1585, but as James VI was now promoting episcopal polity, Melville was sent to the north until the autumn of 1586, when he returned to St Mary's. He accepted the rectorship of the university in 1590. Although forbidden to preach in English, Melville was on the kirk session of St Andrews from 1591 and a regular participant in the weekly 'exercise' for biblical study.

The presbyterian cause regained the ascendancy in the late 1580s, and in 1592 the 'Golden Act' was passed, which established the general assembly as the governing body of the kirk and gave no place to bishops, but still assumed royal supremacy. Melville held a 'two kingdoms' theory of church and state and was sharply critical of James's Erastian aims; he also criticized the king for preferring Catholic nobles. Most famously, confronting the king at Falkland in 1596, Melville informed him that he was not the head of the church but its chief member, and, grabbing James's sleeve, he told the monarch that he was 'God's sillie vassal'. James, in spite of his fondness for Melville's Latin poetry, began to limit his influence; in 1597 Melville was banned from presbyteries and assemblies and removed from the office of rector. Melville continued to comment on what he regarded as the failings of the kirk, however, and in 1602 he was confined to St Mary's. After signing a formal protest against episcopacy in 1606, Melville was summoned to London, where James now reigned, and was imprisoned in the Tower from 1607 to 1611. After his release he returned as an exile to France, where, under the protection of the

Edict of Nantes, he became professor of biblical theology at Sedan; he remained there until his death in 1622.

In many respects Melville was the father of Scottish Presbyterianism, championing the equality of ministers and the freedom of the assembly. At a time when the Scottish (and then British) state wanted very much to be involved in ecclesiastical affairs, Melville struggled to maintain a distinction between the two kingdoms and their two kings. This struggle inevitably brought him into conflict with the state, and his forthright confrontations with his monarch, along with his unwillingness to compromise, invite comparison with *Knox. However, Melville's opponents were a Protestant king and largely Calvinist episcopalians, and thus his struggles did not take on the apocalyptic dimension of Knox's career. Melville's legacy may be found both in the Presbyterian form of church government and in the educational revitalization of both Glasgow and St Mary's in the late sixteenth century.

Bibliography

T. M'Crie, *The Life of Andrew Melville*, 2 vols. (Edinburgh: William Blackwood, ²1824); R. Pitcairn (ed.), *The Autobiography and Diary of Mr James Melvill* (Edinburgh: Wodrow Society, 1842).

M. H. DOTTERWEICH

■ **MENNO SIMONS** (1496–1561), Anabaptist leader and theologian, was born in Witmasum, Friesland in northern Holland. As a child he was placed in a monastery, with a view to his training as a priest and monk. He was ordained as a priest in 1524, and sent to serve as one of the three priests in Pingjum, the next village to his home. He stayed there until 1531, when he was placed as parish priest in Witmasum. He served there until 1536, when he renounced his orders, was baptized as a believer and joined a group of radical Anabaptists under the leadership of Obbe Philips.

Menno's move into Reform was provoked first by questions over the nature of the eucharist, and then by a new and growing conviction about baptism. From his later accounts, it is clear that he had started to have doubts about the theology of transubstantiation as early as 1525, though the cause of these doubts is unknown. His discomfort with traditional teaching drove him to study Scripture for the first time, and he found a conflict between the authority of the Bible and the authority he had been taught to respect, of the early church Fathers and church tradition. He later wrote that in this struggle he found help in *Luther's writings, because of the distinction that Luther drew between divine and human commands. Over the next few years, although he did not leave his parish ministry, he began to teach a message which was more and more recognizably in line with Reformed rather than traditional thinking.

In 1531 a tailor called Snijder was executed for being rebaptized. As a result, Menno questioned for the first time the validity of infant baptism, the more so because he recognized Snijder as a man of integrity and commitment. As with the question of the eucharist, the issue sent him back to study the Bible. When, as he believed, he found no warrant for the baptism of infants there, he went first to his senior colleague, then to the Fathers, and finally to the leading Reformers to find justification for it. His colleague argued from tradition, which Menno had already rejected with regard to the eucharist. The Fathers argued infants needed to be cleansed of original sin through the rite of baptism administered by the church, a position that from Menno's point of view undermined belief in the cross as the answer to sin and guilt. The Reformers' arguments were based on reason rather than on the authority of Scripture to which Menno was now committed, and so he regarded these also as unsatisfactory. As a result of this exploration, he adopted a theology of believers' baptism, emphasizing the important distinction, which he was to draw later, between knowing and being born again. However, he remained within the old church for another five years, later claiming that he was in love with the 'secure and frivolous life' that he had there. Another reason for his slowness to withdraw may have been the absence of a coherent group with which to identify himself.

Although Menno had been helped by Luther's teaching on the eucharist, he differed from him over baptism. The groups with which he agreed on baptism were divided and in some areas confused. Scholarship is unclear about whether or not Menno was linked with the Hoffmanite community, which was shaped by the teachings of Melchior Hoffman. He clearly agreed with them in their insistence on believers' baptism, but his agreement is less clear on other issues. Hoffman's Christology, in which Christ did not take flesh from Mary but brought it with him from heaven, seems to have influenced Menno, though he developed his own version of it in later years. Hoffman's belief that there was a new age to come, and that it was the duty and right of the saved ones of God to cleanse the earth in preparation for it, does not seem to have been as important to Menno. It was, however, a very influential view, and together with certain other elements of radical religion, helped to shape the attempt to create an Anabaptist kingdom in the city of Münster in 1536. The defeat that followed, and the horror with which Anabaptism was henceforward regarded, seem to have provoked Menno's final break from his previous position.

Menno's brother had been involved in a community that was modelled on Münster, in which he was killed. This tragedy, together with his attempts to prevent people from his own parish from leaving for Münster, eventually caused Menno to leave the security of the Catholic church and acknowledge himself as one of the Anabaptists. He had been arguing with those who wanted to link themselves to the radical movements, and he had come to realize that he was no more committed to the community within which he was trying to persuade them to remain than to the community he wanted them to avoid. He also spoke of the impact of his brother's death, recognizing that he and those with him had been willing to give their lives for what Menno believed to be error, while he himself was not willing to risk his income for what he believed to be the truth.

Menno began to preach his true beliefs openly, and within months was excluded from his parish church. At this time he was baptized as a believer and publicly identified himself with the Anabaptist community. He moved to Leeuwarden, where Obbe Philips, a non-Münsterite Anabaptist, was leading a fellowship. The community was in significant danger of disintegration. Following the horrors of Münster, the Anabaptists who had not been involved, and in particular those who were committed to Philips' more quietest theology, had begun to develop a pattern of Nicodemism, that is, of taking part in public services and practising their own faith in private.

During the next year Menno travelled around Holland, visiting the now dispirited communities of Anabaptists. In the winter of 1536–1537, he was ordained as an elder by Philips, after urging by those he visited. He started an itinerant ministry of preaching and baptizing, at first locally in Gronigen and West Friesland. At this time he was married. He was soon recognized, both by local Anabaptists and by hostile authorities, as a significant leader, and some of those who sheltered him in his travels were executed as a result.

In 1541 Menno moved to Amsterdam, and continued his ministry in and around that city for two years. In 1543 he moved again, to East Friesland in Germany, and then in the next year he went to Cologne. When he arrived in Cologne, it was a relatively tolerant city, and he found a measure of freedom there. However, following the Smalcaldic war in 1546 the city was recatholicized, and Menno had to flee. He went to Holstein, an area under Danish rule, where once more he found a degree of freedom. He stayed in Holstein until his death, from natural causes, in 1561.

Much of Menno's importance for the development of the Anabaptist community resulted from his longevity. At a time when those who were known to be leaders in the Anabaptist fellowships might expect to live for eighteen months following public recognition, he survived for many years, and so was able to offer continuity and stability to the movement.

Menno also wrote, mainly short, straightforward works in which the thinking of the communities was propagated, and made available to those who were not trained theologians. He began writing during the struggle to prevent people from identifying with the Münster community, and much of his work followed a similar pattern of argument to that of his early material. His first major works include *Foundation of Christian Doctrine* (1539), *Christian Baptism* (1539) and *True*

Christian Faith (1541). In 1543 he wrote *A Brief and Clear Confession*, and his final major work, produced in 1552, was *Reply to Gellius Faber*, in which he dealt with the themes of ministry, baptism, the sacraments, the incarnation, the nature of the church and the ban as a disciplinary measure. Most of his writings address the same subjects, and can be divided into two groups: that which concerns the rebirth of the Christian and the meaning of discipleship, and that which concerns the church as the new community.

Menno's basic understanding of the world was profoundly dualistic, and this may have shaped the slightly unorthodox incarnational theology that he adopted. He argued that the life of the believer was centred on rebirth. This rebirth, brought about through the Spirit, involved the believer in the abandonment of the carnal life and commitment to a life in imitation of Christ, free from sin.

Menno conceived the church as a pure community, unspotted by sin and separated from the sinful world. It was, therefore, important that discipline was exercised in the church, and this was done by means of the ban; a miscreant was to be excluded from communion and also from all forms of fellowship and social interaction. Those Anabaptists who followed Menno seem to have transformed the early communities' desire to cleanse the earth into a desire to cleanse the Christian community.

Menno assumed that persecution was the normal state of the true church, and was in fact part of the life of the cross. The church would always be in conflict with the ruling authorities because it lived by a different set of rules. The church should, therefore, be completely separate from the secular community, and its members should not be involved in any form of government. This separatism included a commitment to pacifism. In fact, many Anabaptist and Mennonite communities survived because of the toleration of sympathetic authorities. They developed a community life in seclusion from the wider community, and were referred to as the *Stille im Lande*, the 'still in the land', quietists and separatists.

Having committed himself to a theology of believers' baptism, Menno then attacked the theology of infant baptism to such an extent that he came close to arguing that no form of baptism was important. He ceased to associate water baptism with the action of God, and regarded it as purely a matter of human witness and obedience.

Although Menno argued for a figurative understanding of the Old Testament, he developed quite a rigorous legalism based on a particular reading of the New Testament. Believers' baptism involved the commitment to lead an ethical life in imitation of Christ, by taking the teaching of the New Testament at face value. In 1554 a division emerged over church discipline: were those who were banned to be shunned, even by their family members and marriage partners? Anabaptists in Switzerland and southern Germany argued that they were not, and a bitter controversy developed. Menno argued for a policy of at least one warning before the ban was imposed, but held to the strict position otherwise. In 1557 conference agreed a more moderate position, which allowed for the continuance of family life and appealed to Menno, as one of the elder statesmen of the movement, to accept this position. However, he found himself unable to do so, although he did his best to maintain a mediating position between the two parties.

Menno Simons is important for the way in which he helped to rebuild a shattered community, and for his transmission of ideas, both through his clear writings and through the attractiveness of his personality. The Mennonites, a group that still exists, took their name from him.

Bibliography
H.-J. Goertz, *The Anabaptists* (London: Routledge, 1996); G. H. Williams, *Radical Reformation* (Missouri: Sixteenth Century Essays and Studies, 1992).

R. GOULDBOURNE

■ **MERLE D'AUBIGNÉ, Jean Henri** (1794–1872), historian of the Reformation and leader of the international Réveil, was born in Geneva to a prominent family. He was educated in the best schools in Geneva, pursuing theological studies. After a year of resisting the Scottish evangelist Robert *Haldane, in 1817 he was converted to an evangelical faith through being challenged to study Scripture, especially the letter to the Romans. Reacting against a curriculum strongly influenced by Enlightenment interests, he became part of the international evangelical revival, the Réveil movement. While some followers of the Réveil left the Church of Geneva, Merle d'Aubigné felt strongly committed to the Calvinist tradition, and worked to revive interest in the central orthodox doctrines of original sin, justification by faith, and the divinity of Christ, and the Reformed creeds of the sixteenth century. When he was twenty-three, on 3 July 1817, he was ordained a minister in the established Church of Geneva, and it appears that his evangelical spirit found full acceptance there.

Merle d'Aubigné had a large vision of the Christian church, and wanted to continue to study its history and place in society. He became interested in the newly established University of Berlin, and decided to go there to join the excitement. He attended the lectures of Friedrich Schleiermacher in theology and August Neander in ecclesiastical history. Both scholars had a lasting influence on his theological interests, even though he never accepted their particularly liberal ideas. His experience of diverse churches was expanded when he became the pastor of a French-speaking Reformed church in Hamburg (1818–1823), and then moved on to become the pastor of the prestigious L'Église du Musée in Brussels (1823–1830). This post allowed him to minister not only to some prominent families in Brussels, but also to foreign diplomats and businessmen. His position also made him chaplain to King Willem I of the Netherlands, who was influenced by his spiritual fervour for the gospel.

It was at this time that he first met the well-known Dutch royal historian Guillaume Groen van Prinsterer, who referred to Merle d'Aubigné as his 'spiritual father'. From this initial contact with the Dutch, and by continual instruction through his letters and writings, Merle d'Aubigné became one the most important leaders of the Réveil in the Netherlands, and his ministry bore fruit in spiritual and political renewal, through the free Reformed churches and the orthodox Calvinist 'Anti-revolutionary Party', which culminated in the leadership of Abraham *Kuyper. When the Revolution of 1830 shook Brussels, and Belgium broke away from Dutch control, Merle d'Aubigné decided

to return to his native Geneva to teach in the newly established Evangelical School of Theology. He also became one of the leaders of an evangelical congregation in the Church of Geneva called the 'Oratoire', also known as the 'place of preaching'. But the struggle between liberals and evangelicals in the Church of Geneva led to division, and eventually (1848) to a split within the church. With a strong commitment to what he called 'Evangelical catholicity', Merle d'Aubigné became a leader in the Evangelical Society (Société Évangélique) in Geneva and in the many chapters in France, Belgium, the Netherlands and the German lands. He became a well-known speaker in Britain as well, and was influential as a host to the Evangelical Alliance, which met in a large conference in Geneva in 1861. Through his leadership in practical initiatives, Merle d'Aubigné also supported the movement of Christian social care that became the foundation for the Red Cross.

Merle d'Aubigné was arguably the most important historian of the Reformation for English-speaking readers in the nineteenth century. Due to the dramatic increase in the size of the general reading public who had a great interest in history, and to the widespread desire to know about the origins of the Protestant faith, his books on the sixteenth-century Reformation found a very energetic audience. The first two volumes were translated into English within two years; the third was published simultaneously in French and English; and the fourth was written in English. It is difficult to imagine, given the plethora of literature available today, that very little was known about the Reformation in general, and especially about John *Calvin and the French-speaking, Reformed contributions to it. In addition to the Reformation histories, written in two sets of volumes, the first in five volumes (1835–1853) and the second in eight volumes (1863–1879), Merle d'Aubigné produced many other books and articles, almost ninety in number. A noteworthy contribution was his important study of Oliver *Cromwell. Many of his writings were translated into English, Dutch, German or Italian.

Merle d'Aubigné reconstructed a picture of the Reformers in their context with dramatic relief and colour. He called the history of Christianity a 'new field', because his focus was not only on the external details of institutions and events, but also on the work of God in human hearts and behind the external events. His style of writing was strongly influenced by the contemporary Romantic movement, which sought to reconstruct the past with such vividness that the reader could almost see the characters through a rich description of their full emotional engagement in the events recounted. Romanticism also connected the past and present through an organic bond, so that despite the passing of time and the uniqueness of each historic event, continuity was demonstrated. The study of the Reformation was not merely an erudite exercise, but offered a means of recovering the essential doctrines and beliefs of the past and translating them into contemporary forms.

Not only did Merle d'Aubigné offer a thorough account of the Reformation, but he also firmly believed that through history God's revelation could be seen. Though he did not waver in his firm commitment to a high view of the divine inspiration of Scripture, he is known for his principle: 'GOD IN HISTORY' (his emphasis). Through his study he came to the view that history was a field of constant divine activity; in fact, that it contained a soul (*âme*), a spiritual history of human action, feelings and thoughts. Knowledge of history allowed contemporary readers to understand how God worked in the world. Merle d'Aubigné's application of these general principles of historical study became very personal in his vision of the work of God in every Christian through conscience: 'Christian conscience is independent, in matters of faith, to all human power: it relies only on the Word of God, and does not submit to other control. No power is able to impose on them its yoke, neither tradition, nor pope, nor nobles, nor the state.' Conscience is a quality of God, innate in human nature, that allows communication, and by means of secondary causes, God's revelation can be known through history.

Bibliography

J. B. Roney, *The Inside of History: Jean Henri Merle d'Aubigné and Romantic Historiography* (Westport: Greenwood Press, 1996).

J. B. RONEY

■ **MEYER, Frederick Brotherton** (1847–1929), Baptist minister, was born on 8 April 1847 in Clapham, London, the son of Frederick Meyer, a London businessman. His mother was Ann, daughter of Henry Sturt, chief executive of Ward, Sturt and Sharp. Meyer's family attended Bloomsbury Chapel, an outward-looking Baptist church. Meyer was baptized as a believer at New Park Road Chapel, Brixton, in 1864. In part through the influence of William Brock, Bloomsbury's minister, Meyer felt called to Baptist ministry. In 1866 he began training at Regent's Park College and in 1869 graduated with a London University BA.

On 20 February 1871 Meyer married Jane Eliza Jones (1845–1929), from Birkenhead. They had one daughter. From 1870 to 1872 Meyer was assistant minister and then associate minister at Pembroke Chapel, Liverpool, as a colleague of C. M. Birrell. The biblical preaching and cultured style of Birrell made a profound impression on Meyer. He later came to feel, however, that such preaching was inadequate. His messages, he considered, should communicate his true self more fully. Personal revelations became a distinctive feature of his preaching.

During his first full pastorate (1872–1874), at Priory Street Baptist Church, York, Meyer came into contact with Dwight L. *Moody and his co-evangelist and singer Ira D. *Sankey, who were to become highly influential evangelists in Britain as well as in America. Through the impact of Moody's approach to evangelism, Meyer considered that he had been freed from traditional thinking about ministry. He also came to believe that evangelism should be his own priority. In 1874 Meyer moved from York to Victoria Road Nonconformist Church in Leicester, a respectable Baptist church, but found that his commitment to reaching those outside the orbit of church life, especially industrial workers, was not shared by the Victoria Road church leadership. He resigned after four years.

Although Meyer intended to leave Leicester, he was persuaded to stay by a number of those who were supportive of his ministry, and this group, which included several younger people from prominent Nonconformist families, formed a new church with Meyer as the minister. A new building, Melbourne Hall, was built on the outskirts of

Leicester. Melbourne Hall, which was constructed in a non-ecclesiastical style, was intended by Meyer to function as a centre for evangelism, educational and social activities and Christian teaching. Congregations quickly reached 1,500. Meyer was renowned particularly for his ministry to discharged prisoners. By 1888, when he left Leicester, Meyer had personally met over 4,500 prisoners who were being discharged from prison. He offered employment through two businesses he established, a firewood business and a window-cleaning service.

From Leicester, Meyer moved to London in 1888, to a ministry at the unusually upper-class Baptist church, Regent's Park Chapel. Meyer's urbane background fitted this congregation well. The remainder of his ministry was in London, at Regent's Park (1888–1892 and 1909–1915), and at Christ Church, Westminster Bridge Road, Lambeth (1892–1907 and 1915–1920). Christ Church was affiliated to the London Congregational Union, although Meyer moved it towards Baptist practice by installing a baptistery where baptisms by immersion could take place. Congregations at Christ Church grew from a few hundred to 2,500 in the evenings. Morning services were more liturgical in style, while the evening services incorporated the Moody and Sankey style of worship. Meyer's even more informal Sunday afternoon Brotherhood meeting attracted 800 working-class men, and he created a massive network of groups offering social services in Lambeth, one of the poorest areas of London. He became a prominent campaigner on behalf of 'social purity', and through his efforts over 700 brothels were closed between 1895 and 1907. Meyer also hired a disused factory, which he turned into a youth centre.

In the early twentieth century Meyer became involved in national political activity. With many other Free Church leaders in England, he opposed the Conservative government's Education Bill of 1902. Nonconformists saw this as discriminating against them. Meyer was one of the leaders of 140,000 people in a 1903 demonstration against the legislation in Hyde Park. Before the 1906 general election he campaigned nationally on behalf of the Liberal Party. From 1907 to 1909 Meyer acted as a travelling representative for the Free Churches, and

in 1910 he became honorary secretary of the National Free Church Council. Alongside his spiritual work, he campaigned against injustices, attacking, for example, the vested interests of the House of Lords. Meyer came to personify the 'Nonconformist Conscience'. In 1911 he opposed a world boxing title fight at Earl's Court. His belief was that because Jack Johnson, the title holder, was black and his challenger, Bombardier Wells, was white, the contest would be seen as a test of racial superiority. The fight was eventually cancelled by Winston Churchill, then home secretary.

Peace issues were important to Meyer. During the First World War, although not a pacifist, he assisted No-Conscription Fellowship members in their work on behalf of Conscientious Objectors (COs). He relayed to Asquith, the prime minister, the concerns felt about the ill-treatment of COs. Bertrand Russell supplied Meyer with material for a book about COs entitled *The Majesty of Conscience*.

From 1887 Meyer came to be regarded as the leading representative of the Free Churches in the Keswick holiness or higher Christian life movement. This movement drew its name from the convention, which drew up to 6,000 people, held annually in the Lake District. Keswick was predominantly Anglican in its early period. Meyer was important as a symbol of its inter-denominationalism (the Keswick motto was, and is, 'All One in Christ Jesus'), and he especially stressed the steps into the life of spiritual blessing. He spoke at twenty-six Keswick conventions as well as at important regional conventions, and encouraged Keswick teaching within the Baptist denomination through a Prayer Union, which attracted wide ministerial support.

As someone who revelled in travelling, Meyer became Keswick's leading international representative. His links with Moody were vital. In 1891 he spoke at Moody's annual conferences in Northfield, Massachusetts, and subsequently Meyer made nearly twenty visits to the United States and Canada. In 1908 he spent six months addressing meetings in South Africa, where he had discussions with Gandhi, and tours to the Middle and Far East followed. Following the Welsh Revival of 1904–1905, Meyer reported in Los Angeles on what he had observed in

Wales. His report encouraged future leaders of the Pentecostal movement, which was to spread from 1906.

In 1917 Meyer launched, with the support of several Keswick leaders, the Advent Testimony and Preparation Movement, which became a significant body within the evangelical scene promoting the view that Jesus Christ would soon return and inaugurate his millennial kingdom. Large meetings were held, most notably in 1927 in the Royal Albert Hall, where Christabel *Pankhurst was the speaker. Meyer had nurtured Pankhurst, who had been prominent in the women's movement and came to believe in the imminent second advent.

Meyer was twice president of the National Free Church Council. He was elected to the presidency of the Baptist Union, serving with distinction in 1906–1907. He was president of the World's Sunday School Association from 1907 to 1910, and in the 1920s was director and general secretary of the Regions Beyond Missionary Union. McMaster University in Canada awarded him an honorary DD in 1911.

The majority of Meyer's books were devotional in nature; many dealt with biblical characters. He wrote over seventy books and booklets, and by the time of his death five million copies were in print. Meyer's personality and experience were such that he was essentially transdenominational. His convictions were evangelical, but he drew from varied spiritual sources, especially those in the mystical tradition. He related well to different sections of evangelicalism, functioning as the most important bridge-builder in the evangelical world of his day.

Bibliography

W. Y. Fullerton, *F. B. Meyer* (London: Marshall, Morgan & Scott, 1929); I. M. Randall, 'The Career of F. B. Meyer (1847–1929)' (MPhil thesis, CNAA, 1992).

I. M. RANDALL

■ **MILTON, John** (1608–1674), poet and controversialist, was born in London and was taught by private tutors, among them the Dissenting Scots minister Thomas Young, before attending St Paul's School. His father was a scrivener (a kind of minor lawyer) and a successful composer. In his poem 'Ad Patrem' ('To My Father') the younger Milton thanks his father for encouraging him to study five languages, Latin, Greek, Hebrew, French and Italian. Milton's prodigious learning owed much to his early assiduousness. In 1625 he became an undergraduate at Christ's College, Cambridge, and graduated fourth highest in the whole university in 1629, becoming Master of Arts in 1632. During this time he wrote a number of Latin and English poems, including 'On the Morning of Christ's Nativity'. From 1632 Milton returned home, to 'studious retirement' at Hammersmith and then Horton. His first published poem, on Shakespeare, appeared in that year. His earlier work is full of concern about vocation; while an obvious choice would have been a preaching ministry, he complained in the 1640s of being 'church-outed' by the bishops, a hint that he would not have been comfortable with the increasingly dominant High Church tendency led by Archbishop Laud. However, his real vocation as an English Protestant Christian poet emerges clearly enough from these early writings.

After the death of his mother in 1637, Milton's situation changed. In that year he wrote *A Maske at Ludlow*, an entertainment for the Earl of Bridgwater, the new Lord of the Marches (the Welsh border). This is normally known as *Comus*, a title from the eighteenth-century editions. Its central theme is chastity. His monody 'Lycidas' first appeared in 1638 in a memorial volume for Edward King, a fellow-student who had drowned, and in it he openly questions the value of his ambitions to be a poet. It is also a swingeing attack on the 'blind mouths', the corrupted clergy of the time.

In the same year he went to Europe, to France and Italy. His visit was not a Grand Tour exactly, nor a pilgrimage, but he did meet Galileo and the Dutch scholar Hugo Grotius, and he was impressed by two academies he visited in Florence. He visited Rome and collected books and music. On his return in 1639 he began work on a British epic. He also took private pupils, and the breadth of reading he prescribed to them developed into the ideas in *Of Education* (1644), a prose tract on liberal education, addressed to the educational and scientific reformer Samuel Hartlib. At the same time he was drafting plans for tragedies in the Greek style. However, several years were to pass before he could begin work on long poems. For the next twenty years most of his work was in political prose, powerful, emotive and learned. *Of Reformation* (1641) is the first of a series of interventions in the pamphlet wars about liberty and the power and nature of the church.

In May 1642 Milton married Mary Powell, sixteen years his junior and from a Royalist family in Oxfordshire. After a brief period they separated for three years, but were reconciled in 1645 and had four children between then and 1652. During this period Milton was exploring ideas of Christian liberty in such works as *Areopagitica* (1644), a plea for unlicensed, uncensored printing, and *The Doctrine and Discipline of Divorce* (1643/4), the first of four divorce tracts, pleading for the grounds of divorce to include spiritual incompatibility. His *Poems* of 1645 consists of his early pieces as well as some of the political sonnets he continued to write while most of his effort went into prose. During the same period he began to have eye trouble; by 1652 he was completely blind.

In 1649 Milton took public office. He had argued for the possibility of regicide in *The Tenure of Kings and Magistrates*, perhaps his most important political work. After Charles I's execution, he was appointed Secretary for Foreign Tongues to the Council of State, a post which involved much Latin correspondence and the composition of texts in defence of the Council's position. The latter included *Eikonoklastes* (1649), an attack on the cult of King Charles as a martyr, and two Latin Defences of the English people (1650 and 1654), which circulated in Europe. The death of Oliver *Cromwell in 1658 precipitated the collapse of the republican government. As late as 1659–60, with *The Ready and Easy Way*, Milton was still arguing against the return of the monarchy. When Charles II was restored in 1660 he went into hiding; later he was briefly imprisoned, and then released on the payment of a small fine through the help of, among others, Andrew Marvell, fellow poet and supporter. *Eikonoklastes* was banned and burned.

In 1652 his first wife and his son died; he married Katherine Woodcock in 1656, but she died in 1658, along with her daughter. In 1663 he married Elizabeth Minshull, who survived him by fifty years. Contrary to legend, there is no evidence that Milton used any of his three daughters as amanuenses for his poems. However, there was friction between them and their father in later years.

He lived in retirement from 1660, but his greatest work, the epic poem *Paradise Lost*, appeared in a ten-book version in 1667, and in the twelve-book version in 1674. It was not until the illustrated edition of 1688, however, that it began to be noticed, and the story of Milton's celebrity as an epic poet is really an eighteenth-century one. *Paradise Lost* tells us it was written to 'justify the ways of God to man', and as an imaginative reconstruction of the first three chapters of Genesis, the temptation of Adam and Eve by the devil, it has had an enormous impact. After the discovery and publication of Milton's Latin *De Doctrina Christiana* in 1823–1825 readers have located some heterodox material about the relationship of the Father and the Son, and the nature of creation, in the poem. Milton's mortalism, his belief that the soul dies with the body until the last judgment, was shared by other radicals in the period.

Paradise Regained was published in 1671, together with *Samson Agonistes*. *Paradise Regained* is a short epic poem in four books, based on the temptations of Christ in the wilderness. It has a less cosmic frame of reference but it balances the emphasis of *Paradise Lost* on disobedience with a stress on Christ's obedience. Like its predecessor, it expounds, expands and makes explicit the biblical text. *Samson Agonistes* is in the form of a Greek tragedy, not written for performance (though there have been attempts). It is linked with the theme of temptation, as Samson is visited by his father and Dalila, among others, as he lies 'Eyeless in Gaza' just before his final act of destruction and self-destruction. More than are Milton's other Restoration pieces, this is a reflection on living with the experience of the defeat of one's cause. *The History of Britain* came out in 1670; a section on the Long Parliament was not published until 1681.

Milton died of heart failure in London on 8 November 1674. One way of looking at Milton's poetic career is to see him as taking hold of the major poetic genres, ranging from the sonnet to the epic, and reforming and recreating them according to radical Christian principles. Another is to link the poems with his prose, and see them as a means of establishing a more thorough Reformation in England: Protestant, patriotic and republican.

Bibliography

W. R. Parker, *Milton: a Biography*, 2 vols. (Oxford: Clarendon Press, ²1996); D. Danielson (ed.), *The Cambridge Companion to Milton* (Cambridge: Cambridge University Press, 1989); C. C. Brown, *John Milton, A Literary Life* (Basingstoke: Macmillan, 1995).
R. POOLEY

■ **MOFFAT, Robert** (1795–1883), missionary and Bible translator, was born on 21 December 1795 at Ormiston in East Lothian, Scotland, to Robert and Ann (née Gardiner) Moffat. His father was a lowly civil servant, and the family moved a number of times, finally settling at Inverkeithing in Fifeshire. In 1809 Moffat was apprenticed to the trade of gardener, and during his apprenticeship he learnt some Latin, the use of the anvil, and the violin. This was the sum total of his formal education when, at the age of eighteen, he was employed as an under-gardener in High Leigh, Cheshire and left Scotland.

In 1815 he came under the influence of the Methodist revival, was converted and felt called to missionary work. He met William Roby, a leading figure in the London Missionary Society (LMS), who organized work for him in the gardens of Mr Smith of Dunkinfield, near Manchester. This move enabled Roby to provide theological training for Moffat, and here he met and fell in love with Mary, the daughter of his employer. On his second application he was accepted by the LMS, and on 13 September 1816 he was ordained and set apart with eight other missionaries for work in South Africa.

The first four years in Africa were spent in language study and itinerant evangelism. After Mary received permission from her father, she sailed to Cape Town to join and marry Robert in December 1819. The newly-weds then moved north. Here Moffat began his work as the senior missionary amongst the Batswana at Kuruman on the edge of the Kalahari Desert at the age of only twenty-five.

He served in this post for fifty years with only one break in England (1839–1843).

Moffat was a charismatic man who had the uncanny ability to build relationships of mutual respect with a wide range of people, and numbered amongst his personal friends chiefs such as Afrikaner of the Nama, Waterboer of the Griqua, Mothibi of the Batlhaping, Makaba of the Bangwaketse, Sechele of the Bakwena, Moselekatse of the Matebele and Sir George Grey of the Cape Colony. He fathered ten children, five of whom died before him, three as infants in heart-breaking conditions. He was the father of one missionary (John Smith Moffat) and the father-in-law of three others (David *Livingstone, Jean Fredoux and Roger Price). His domestic relations were such that, Scottish patriarch though he undoubtedly was, he still created the space in which his wife Mary emerged as a strong and powerful frontierswoman and missionary in her own right. Their correspondence tells of a deep love and affection for each other.

Moffat lived on the edge of the Kalahari for fifty years. He was a large man with a great beard, and extremely hardy and tough. He was a hunter, a horseman, an explorer, a strategist and a frontiersman, who knew the African bush at first-hand and at very close quarters. He was a blacksmith, who could set up a forge almost anywhere and fix any part of an ox-wagon, spending days at the furnace if necessary. He was a farmer, who established the first use of irrigation in the interior of the subcontinent when he dammed the famous 'Eye' of Kuruman and dug irrigation channels for 5 km to carry water to his gardens. He was a miller, who built a corn-mill using the power of the water in his furrow. He knew thirst, hunger and the uncertainty of almost everything he set out to accomplish, and yet his deep personal faith in the loving God who, he believed, had called and sent him provided the courage to persevere for the sake of the gospel. Out of this faith and commitment Moffat was able to make three key contributions to the Christian faith in southern Africa.

The first was the development of the mission infrastructure and church community in the Kuruman river valley. The first years at Kuruman were a time of great difficulty owing to raiding bandits, warring parties and rumours of attacks. However, by 1829 the first converts were baptized, the school room was built, the translation of the first book of the Bible (Luke) was completed, and work on the church building commenced. By the start of the 1830s the infrastructure of the mission was well established, apart from the large chapel, which was completed in 1838.

The Kuruman station was a key factor in the development of evangelical missions into the interior of Africa and especially to Botswana and Zimbabwe. It was the base for the LMS in southern Africa for many years, from which the society's evangelism and educational work grew. It was the first home of David Livingstone in Africa, and provided a western bulwark against the land-encroachment of white settlers in South Africa. The mission continues to serve the church and community today.

Moffat's second key achievement, the translation and printing of the Setswana Bible, is perhaps his most astonishing. Having had only one year of formal education, he attained facility in Setswana, reduced the language to writing, developed the orthography and then set about translating the Bible. A small press was acquired, and Moffat and his helpers then began to print small items such as Scripture selections, school readers and Setswana grammars. He did not intend to print the full Bible in Kuruman, but after a lengthy stay in England to have the New Testament (and then the Psalms) printed there, he decided that it would be easier both to translate and to print in Kuruman. Working on the press, Moffat translated and printed the Old Testament by 1857 and a revision of the New Testament by 1867. This was the first Bible to be printed on the African continent. Moffat's work is recognized in a memorial window in the library at the Bible Society House in London, in which he features alongside *Tyndale, Jerome, *Luther and *Carey.

Moffat's third major achievement was the opening of the frontier between Kuruman and Matabeleland (Zimbabwe). Moffat made five visits to Moselekatse, chief of the Matabele. The first two (1829, 1835) were to his kraal near the site of present-day Pretoria, and the last three, undertaken after a nineteen-year hiatus, were near to the site of present-day Bulawayo in Zimbabwe (1854, 1857 and 1859). The visits secured a number of benefits

of general importance to the mission and wider community, such as assistance for scientific exploration, the support and follow-up of the work amongst the Batswana tribes of those called 'native teachers', the freeing of numerous captives taken by the Matabele and the delivering of supplies to David Livingstone further north on the Zambezi. However, from the perspective of the LMS, the key achievement of Moffat's relationship with Moselekatse was the establishing of a permanent mission station amongst the Matabele at Inyati near Bulawayo, which continues to this day.

In 1870 Robert and Mary retired to England. The death of his 'beloved partner' Mary a year later was a huge blow, yet with the support of his youngest daughter Jane, he continued in his service to Christ and the church. He oversaw the printing of the revised Setswana Bible (1871), hymn book and *Pilgrim's Progress* (1875), received a DD from Edinburgh University (1872), was present at the funeral of his son-in-law, David Livingstone (1874), had audiences with Queen Victoria on two occasions (1872, 1876) and received the freedom of the City of London (1877). He died on 10 August 1883, a few months before his eighty-seventh birthday.

Bibliography
R. Moffat, *Missionary Labours and Scenes in Southern Africa* (London: John Snow, Paternoster-Row, 1842); J. S. Moffat, *The Lives of Robert and Mary Moffat* (London: T. Fisher Unwin, 1886); C. Northcott, *Robert Moffat: Pioneer in Africa* (London: Lutterworth Press, 1961).

S. DE GRUCHY

■ **MOODY, Dwight Lyman** (1837–1899), evangelist and Christian educator, had an enormous impact on the character of evangelism, missions and church planting during his lifetime. Much of the work he did over a century ago still influences the goals and methods of Christian ministry.

D. L. Moody was born on a small farm in Northfield in rural northwestern Massachusetts on 5 February 1837. His parents (Edwin Moody and Betsy Holton) maintained a subsistence farm on hilly, rocky soil. Because the land was only marginally productive,

Edwin Moody supplemented his income by working as a stonemason. In 1841, when Dwight was four, Edwin Moody died unexpectedly, leaving Betsy with seven children and pregnant with twins. With an adult and nine children to be supported from a scrubby subsistence farm, life was extremely difficult. Betsy Moody held the family together, but when Dwight was still young he and his older brothers were required to live for several months each year on other farms as hired hands and helpers for local people in need of labourers.

By the time Moody was seventeen years old, he had acquired no more than four years of formal education. What little he did have he had gathered sporadically at the local one-room school. With his ability to read and write sorely underdeveloped and a vocabulary as limited as his social experience, the ambitious teenager determined to escape from the backbreaking drudgery of farm labour. He moved to the quickly growing coastal city of Boston and found employment in his uncle's shoe shop.

The Boston experience was catalytic. Moody's uncle, S. S. Holton, insisted that his nephew attend the Mt Vernon Congregational Church every week, thereby causing young Moody to enter into his first extended experience of practising Trinitarian Christians. Although there were churches in the Northfield area, the Moody family had a connection only to the Unitarian Church, and this was because the Unitarian pastor was the only churchman who reached out to help the impoverished widow and her nine children. Moody and his siblings were baptized by the Unitarians, but it was only at Mt Vernon Church that he began to worship formally each Sunday. In retrospect, he admitted that he did not know anything about the God he was supposedly praising, and he likewise had no understanding of the pastor's sermons. What did touch him was the kindness of Edward Kimball, his Sunday school teacher. One Saturday afternoon, 21 April 1855, Kimball felt led by the Holy Spirit to visit Moody at the shoe shop. Finding the young man alone wrapping shoes in the back room, Kimball talked with Moody about his need for a saviour. Then he led the shop assistant in a simple prayer of confession, repentance and request to Jesus Christ for mercy.

It was eleven months and several oral interviews later before the senior pastor and deacons were convinced that Moody understood the claims of Christ well enough to warrant membership of the church. Finally, in March 1856, he joined the church and began to reap some understanding and joy from his Bible reading and prayer time. Many years later, Edward Kimball recalled that no-one at the church would have ever dreamed that Moody, a decade and a half later, would be a spiritual leader throughout the English-speaking world.

The next steps in Moody's preparation for ministry took place in Chicago, Illinois. In autumn 1856 he left Boston and moved to the rapidly growing metropolis of the Great Lakes and upper Midwest, taking work in a thriving boot and shoe business. He also began investing his earnings in the lucrative real-estate market. During the next two years he earned a substantial income and made new friends, many of them committed Christians. Moody's landlady, 'Mother' H. Phillips, taught him much about prayer and daily devotions. A mature Christian companion, J. B. Stillson, became a spiritual father to him. Stillson taught him how to do personal evangelism. He also introduced him to George *Müller's autobiography, A Life of Trust, and to the Brethren denomination. Moody's heart increasingly turned towards the growing number of impoverished and neglected children in Chicago's slums. By 1858 he was spending many hours each week visiting the children and telling them about Jesus. Because the two local churches he attended (one Baptist and one Methodist) were not comfortable with the throng of street urchins he brought to church each Sunday, he rented a building on Sunday mornings and started a mission Sunday school for the waifs. Among his Christian friends who helped to teach and befriend these poorest of the poor was Emma Revell, an attractive young woman who had emigrated to the United States from her native England in 1849. Emma was six and a half years younger than Moody, but they delighted in each other's company and found joy in ministering to lonely and abused children.

Another new friend who joined Moody in the mission school was John V. Farwell. Born in New York in 1825, this brilliant entrepreneur, twelve years Moody's senior, had launched an extremely successful drapery business in Chicago in the early 1850s. Emma Revell was a Baptist and Farwell was a Methodist. Moody enjoyed worshipping at their churches and attended Sunday or mid-week services at both. He showed a remarkable propensity to work with Christians of any denomination if they wanted to reach out to people with the gospel.

In 1860, four years after moving to Chicago, Moody sensed a strong call to leave his lucrative secular employment and enter full-time evangelistic work. Despite the fact that he was earning more money annually than most workers could garner in fifteen years, he walked away from the shoe business and his real-estate investments. He began devoting all of his waking hours to evangelism and sleeping on two chairs in the local YMCA building. At first, he focused his attention on his Sunday mission services and classes, and on follow-up work among the children in their tenement neighbourhoods. He also volunteered his services to the YMCA, helping to organize daily prayer and devotional services.

In 1862 Moody married Emma Revell, and they served under the auspices of the US Christian Commission as missionaries to the Union soldiers in the American Civil War. They ministered to Union troops, Moody serving as a chaplain by preaching and praying before the men marched into battle. Perhaps his most important work was his service to the wounded and dying in the tent hospitals throughout the war-torn South. It was in these battlefield hospitals that Moody learned through practical experience the importance of personal work with one person at a time. Indeed, they became his most significant training ground for practical ministry.

Moody never had the advantage of formal theological training. Instead he bombarded his circle of educated and experienced pastors and evangelists with questions on doctrine and theology. He always talked to men of various traditions, listened carefully and took detailed notes. Besides picking the brains of educated ministers, Moody studied published sermons of Charles *Spurgeon and read books by men actively involved in the rescue and care of souls.

Moody also prayed for the Spirit to teach him. The result was that he pioneered a successful ministry (eventually imitated by people all over America) among poor children and their dysfunctional families. Through prayer and perseverance he led hundreds, and with the help of other workers he trained perhaps thousands, to Christ from the slums.

By 1864 Moody was quite well known in Chicago, YMCA and Union military circles. People were unconcerned that he had no schooling because seldom had anyone encountered a man who could work so well ecumenically, yet on sound and biblical principles, with such evangelistic effectiveness. Through friends like John Farwell, business leaders came to Christ and then supported evangelistic and discipling enterprises launched by Moody.

Before the Civil War ended in 1865, Moody planted a church that was evangelical, independent and the kind of place where the poor as well as the middle-class and wealthy felt welcome. It grew rapidly. He also made Chicago's branch of the YMCA one of the most effective in the United States in reaching and teaching the unconverted. Furthermore, he was a sought-after preacher who could attract the attention of crowds because he knew how to communicate Bible truths in the vernacular. By the end of 1865 he was president of the YMCA, leader of the Illinois Street Church and director of the Mission School for children.

During the next few years several events sharpened Moody for even more effective work. First, in 1867 he travelled to Great Britain, where he met Charles Spurgeon and George Müller. Both men encouraged Moody to pour himself into reaching the poor, preaching the gospel and equipping young people to serve in full-time ministry. Then in 1871 two women, W. R. Hawkhurst and Sarah Cooke, urged Moody to pray for the anointing of the Holy Spirit. At first he resented their insinuation that he was not already filled with the Spirit. Nevertheless, he solicited their prayers and began to sense that much of his ministry was motivated by his fleshly desires and ambition. For several months he agonized in prayer for the Spirit to come upon him with the fire of cleansing and empowerment. Nothing happened until he took a trip to New York City to raise funds for rebuilding a YMCA building that had been destroyed during a great Chicago fire. While walking along Wall Street Moody was suddenly overcome by God's presence. He found a place of solitude, and according to his own testimony, after an extended time of prayer received such an assurance of God's love and power that he was nearly overpowered. Indeed he had to beg the Lord to withdraw his hand for fear of death.

In the wake of this powerful experience, Moody's ministry became astoundingly effective. He took his family to Northfield, Massachusetts, for a time of rest and reflection, and then felt led to return to Great Britain. In 1873 he made yet another trip to Britain, this time with his ministry partner and music leader, Ira D. *Sankey. For over two years (June 1873–July 1875) they travelled in England, Scotland, Ireland and Wales. Moody preached the gospel to millions, and it was said that Sankey 'sang the gospel' to them. A great spiritual awakening swept the United Kingdom. An uneducated and, to British tastes, somewhat crude and boorish American led the way.

When Moody returned to America in 1875 he was internationally famous, and was invited to engage in speaking tours all over the United States. Rather than letting fame distract him, he surrounded himself with friends and advisers, and prayerfully sought guidance as to what steps to take next. For the next twenty-four years he continued to engage in evangelistic preaching throughout the US. He also returned to Britain, and fulfilled speaking engagements lasting weeks or months in Canada and Mexico. At least a hundred million people heard him preach; millions professed faith in Christ for the first time; countless souls returned to faith after drifting away; and millions more had their faith and ministry encouraged by his messages. Moody and Sankey also published a gospel song book that ultimately transformed Christian music for at least two generations.

To carry on this itinerating ministry and keep his family stable was no small task, but Dwight and Emma Moody managed to protect their family quite well. All of their three children (Emma b. 1864; William b. 1869; Paul b. 1879) were well adjusted and no more than normally rebellious. All three eventually married and lived long lives as devout followers of Jesus Christ. If Moody was in one

place for a year or more, the entire family accompanied him; the children were placed in local schools or privately tutored. During all his other trips, Moody left his wife with the children and wrote letters full of encouragement to each member of the family almost every day. Finally, the children were well disciplined and taught that it was a privilege for all of the family to make sacrifices to further their father's role in God's work. By these various means the Moodys succeeded in keeping the family healthy.

Moody's concern for his children was one manifestation of his sense of calling to serve all children and youth. Moody never had much schooling, but he longed to see economically disadvantaged people receive more education than he had been able to afford. Consequently, he brought together Christian business leaders, educators and clergy, and led the way in some significant educational endeavours. In 1879, with the help of many friends he had made during the Civil War and during his preaching tours, Moody opened the Northfield Seminary for young women. This was a college preparatory school for girls and young women from northern New England who could not afford the preparatory training required to enter college. Two years later (1881) he opened the Mount Hermon School for boys just across the Connecticut River from Northfield. Both schools were college preparatory institutions with strong Christian faculties and a determination to integrate faith and learning.

After opening these two schools, Moody launched a third educational enterprise in Chicago. This school, eventually called the Chicago Bible Institute (the Moody Bible Institute after his death), was designed to provide free ministerial training to men and women who felt called to home and foreign missions but had neither the education nor the money adequately to prepare for their work. Focusing on the English Bible, basic doctrine and theology, and practical pastoral theology and soul care, this school became an enormous success. Indeed, so many people sought access that Moody opened a fourth school, the Northfield Bible Training Institute, in Massachusetts. This latter school was for women only, and it served many women well until a few years after Moody's death.

Moody's vision to equip young people for rescuing and nurturing souls did not end with these four schools. He urged his brother-in-law, Fleming H. *Revell, to start a publishing company to generate all types of Christian literature. Revell's efforts were extremely successful and he became a pioneer in the field of Christian publishing. Revell did not share Moody's vision for publishing inexpensive paperback books, the Christian alternative to the ubiquitous 'Dime Novels'. Therefore, Moody launched the Colportage Association, which became the successful forerunner of today's Moody Press.

Besides his preaching, publishing and formal educational enterprises, Moody became an innovator in the field of Christian conferences for college men and women. He sponsored annual summer conferences at Northfield, to which speakers were brought from the United Kingdom and other states of the USA to teach Scripture and encourage young people to give their lives to full-time home or foreign missionary service.

Although Moody is best remembered in the popular imagination as a preacher, he believed that his most enduring works would be the educational institutions he set in place. He told his son just a few years before his death on 22 December 1899, 'I think I have some streams started that will flow on forever. What a joy to be in the harvest field and have a hand in God's work.' The schools, he mused, 'are the best pieces of work I have ever done'. It is arguable that no-one in the nineteenth century did more than Moody to reach non-Christians, make disciples, train a new generation of home and foreign workers and encourage others to commit their lives to gospel ministry.

Bibliography

L. W. Dorsett, *A Passion for Souls: The Life of D. L. Moody* (Chicago: Moody Press, 1997); J. F. Findlay, Jr, *Dwight L. Moody: American Evangelist, 1837–1899* (Chicago: University of Chicago, 1969); W. R. Moody, *The Life of Dwight L. Moody* (New York: Fleming H. Revell, 1900).

L. W. DORSETT

■ **MORE, Hannah** (1745–1833), author and educator, was during her lifetime renowned for her charm, famous for her writings, praised for her moral influence on all classes of society, castigated as a 'Methodist' and attacked as a 'bishop in petticoats'. Since her death she has been described as one of the 'Fathers [sic] of the Victorians', praised for helping to save Britain from revolution, criticized for her individualistic moralism, described as a paternalist who unwittingly subverted paternalism, and subjected to gender analysis as a woman who conformed to accepted patterns of womanly behaviour in order to subvert them.

Hannah More was born on 2 February 1745 at Fishponds, Stapleton, near Bristol. Her father Jacob, from a Norfolk gentry family, had become a schoolmaster under the patronage of Norborne Berkeley of Stapleton after losing his hopes of an inheritance and moving to the West Country. Here he married Mary Grace, a farmer's daughter. Hannah was the fourth of their five daughters. In 1758 the five sisters, who had been soundly educated by their father and others, opened a school in Trinity Street, Bristol. It moved to the newly built and fashionable Park Street in 1762 and remained in the sisters' ownership until 1790. They were all involved in running the school; Hannah taught and wrote stories, verse and drama for schoolroom use, including *Sacred Dramas* (published 1782) and the drama *The Search After Happiness* (published 1773), both written much earlier. The school became renowned for its religious and moral curriculum and common-sense ethos as well as its sound basic education, music, drama and dancing. At the same time Hannah became involved in Bristol literary and intellectual circles; her ability to captivate older men first showed itself here. One such admirer, Edward Turner of Belmont, near Wraxall, became engaged to her, but after postponing the wedding three times (apparently out of an inability to overcome his own shyness) he settled an annuity on her of £200 a year. Such a proceeding was not unusual in these circumstances, and it ensured her financial independence for the rest of her life.

After a stay near Weston-super-Mare, recovering from the nervous strain of these events, where she refused a proposal of marriage from John Langhorne, the Somerset poet, Hannah, with two of her sisters, made her first visit to London in 1774. These annual visits continued for more than twenty years. She quickly became well-known in theatrical and literary circles. The friendship of David Garrick and his wife Eva was particularly important to her; she appreciated their naturalness and spontaneity, qualities which marked Garrick's acting as well as his home life. The Berkeley connection introduced her into the Blue Stocking circle. She became a friend of Dr Johnson, being criticized for flattering him, although in fact she was not uncritical of him. She published *The Search After Happiness*, *The Inflexible Captive* (a tragic moral drama, 1774), *Sir Eldred of the Bower* and *The Legend of Bleeding Rock* (dramatic poems, 1776), and *Essays on Various Subjects, principally designed for Young Ladies* (1777), in which she argued that women's quick perceptions and delicate feelings should be used to civilize men. Her tragedy *Percy* played for twenty-one nights at Covent Garden under Garrick's direction in 1777–1778 and was praised for its emotion and elegance. *The Fatal Falsehood*, another tragedy, appeared in 1779 after Garrick's death and was unsuccessful. More was accused of plagiarism by Hannah Cowley and wrote no more plays. She and Eva Garrick lived together in seclusion for almost a year.

More then returned to society and continued to publish, exploring in several works the limits of appropriate 'sensibility' (the susceptibility to and expression of feeling): *Sacred Dramas* (1782), *Sensibility* (a poem, 1782), *Florio* (a poem inspired by her friendship with Horace Walpole, 1786) and *Bas Bleu* or *Conversation* (a poetic tribute to the London literary circle of the Blue Stockings, 1786). After this the focus of her life and work began to change. She had always professed a longing for country life and in 1785 bought a cottage at Cowslip Green near Wrington in Somerset. In 1784 she had been shown the work of the Bristol milkwoman Ann Yearsley, an unlettered poet. More constituted herself her tutor and patroness, but the relationship ended in acrimony in 1785 with a dispute over royalties. More characteristically wanted to administer the trust set up for the benefit of the Yearsley children, and did not appreciate her protégé's desire for independence. Other attempts at patronage also foundered when their recipients failed to come up to expectations. At the same time more profound changes were taking place in More's opinions and beliefs.

More had always been more pious than many of her London friends, being remarkable there, though not in Bristol, for her Sunday observance and dislike of opera. Faith to her was always a matter of feeling as well as of opinion and conduct. She was always socially conservative, believing that the upper classes had a duty to reform society by their example. From the mid-eighties, and still more after 1789, these attitudes took on a new significance. Boundaries in religion were redrawn by the emergence of Methodism as a separate denomination, while the cataclysm of the French Revolution changed the categories of politics for ever. At the same time More was coming into closer contact with the Clapham evangelicals. Her friendship with Captain Charles Middleton and his wife brought her into the campaign against slavery and thus into contact in 1787 with William *Wilberforce, who became a particularly close friend. In that year she wrote *The Slave Trade: A Poem* and began to urge her friends to boycott slave-grown sugar.

Deepening religious convictions gave rise to a new kind of writing. *Thoughts on the Importance of the Manners of the Great to General Society* (1788) can be read as a rather shallow critique of the corruption of servants' morals by the demands of their employers (Sunday working, polite lies, dependence on tips). It can also be read as a deeper attack on the self-regarding 'sensibility' of polite society. *Estimate of the Religion of the Fashionable World* (1790) was more explicit in its call for vital religion, uniting faith and morals, among the upper classes. Advice to the wealthy continued with *Strictures on the Modern System of Female Education, with a View to the Principles and Conduct of Women of Rank and Fortune* (1799). Women were to reform society by means of their influence on men, having themselves been transformed by religion which touches the heart and thus changes conduct. Although More adopts the conventional view of women as creatures of feeling, she advocates a system of education designed to increase their rationality (cultivation of plain language, history and biography rather than novels), thus subversively adopting 'masculine' norms for their mental formation. The ironic agreement with

Mary Wollstonecraft has not gone unnoticed. *Hints Towards Forming the Character of a Young Princess* (1805) was a specific development of these themes with reference to the heir to the throne, the Prince of Wales's daughter Princess Charlotte. It was More's friendship with Dr Robert Gray, Prebendary of Durham and later Bishop of Bristol, that led to her being approached to write this work.

Friendship with another highly placed member of society, in this case Bishop Porteus of London, led to a request to write a reply to Tom Paine's *Rights of Man* in a form accessible to the lower orders. The result was *Village Politics* (1792), cast as a dialogue between the village blacksmith and the stonemason. This was followed by *Remarks on the Speech of M. Dupont* (1793), in which she attacked French atheism. A further appeal from Bishop Porteus led to the inauguration of the Cheap Repository Tracts. The Tracts, short stories, ballads and Sunday readings, were in the same format as existing chapbook genres, with illustrative woodcuts, and sold at $\frac{1}{2}d$, $1d$ and $1\frac{1}{2}d$. It was no accident that More embarked on this project at the same time as her educational work in Somerset (see below). Teaching the poor to read made it possible to educate them in habits of duty and obedience if they had access to cheap and appropriate reading matter. The stories in the series contain vigorous action and are written in plain language. Their message is an advocacy of discriminating charity for the rich and hard work, sobriety and deference for the poor, the whole underpinned by an active religion which regards wealth and poverty alike as part of an immutable divine dispensation. Henry *Thornton acted as treasurer to the project, Wilberforce gathered subscriptions and Babington and Zachary *Macaulay acted as agents. Over two million copies were circulated in the first year. One hundred and fourteen tracts were produced between 1795 and 1798, of which More wrote forty-nine herself. It is impossible to estimate how many copies actually found their way into the homes of the poor (many were bought by the rich for distribution, and large numbers were sent to the colonies), but contemporaries judged them to have been deeply influential in combating revolutionary influences. Organizational difficulties led to the ending of the series in 1798, but the Religious Tract Society (founded in 1799), although disapproving of the Cheap Repository's theological inadequacy, paid it the sincerer compliment of imitating its methods.

At the same time that the Cheap Repository was in production, More was actively involved in the education of the poor. Following a visit from Wilberforce in 1789, she took up the challenge of 'doing something', first for Cheddar and then for other villages near her country home at Cowslip Green. She and her sisters visited the farmers who were the main opponents of schooling for the poor, combating their belief that education would ruin agriculture. They worked with sympathetic local clergy and bypassed uncooperative absentee incumbents. Building on the experience of Robert *Raikes and other founders of Sunday schools, they taught reading and Scripture but not writing. In three villages (Cheddar, Shipham and Nailsea) 'greater schools' were established, teaching domestic, industrial and agricultural crafts to children during the week as well as Scripture and reading on Sundays. In addition, Scripture reading classes for adults were held on weekday evenings. Women's Friendly Societies were established in these villages, paying benefits for sickness and childbirth. These villages were typical of many in which the parish system had become inadequate, in Cheddar through a succession of absentee incumbents, in Shipham and Nailsea through the population growth resulting from industry (calamine mining and glass manufacture). Other villages had 'lesser schools', offering only Sunday instruction and week-night Scripture reading. Every year the villages united for the Mendip Feast, at which Hannah More would deliver an address advocating the faithful discharge of paternalistic duties and responsibilities.

Contemporaries described a dramatic increase in social cohesion in the Mendip villages. Church attendance increased (from 50 to 700 in ten years in Cheddar) and crime decreased. In 1795 the curate and churchwardens of Blagdon begged More to open a school in their notoriously unruly village. She did so, with spectacular results. In 1798, however, Mr Bere, the curate, preached a sermon against the school, and in 1801 called for the schoolmaster's dismissal. The Blagdon controversy seriously damaged More's reputation. At its heart was the issue of control over the education of the poor. Mr and Mrs Younge, who were in charge of the Blagdon school, had already been removed from Wedmore because of a similar dispute. Bere attacked them for encouraging personal religious testimony at the evening Scripture reading sessions, allowing extempore prayer and giving spiritual guidance. Such practices were characteristic of Methodism; they took religious life away from the control of the parish clergy. In the bitter controversy More was accused of being a 'Methodist', a she-bishop and an abetter of immorality. After three years during which the school was closed, re-opened and closed again, the new Bishop of Bath and Wells accepted her explanation and the controversy abated. It had highlighted the problems associated with 'enthusiasm' and lay leadership in religious matters, the difficulty of obtaining suitable teachers for village schools and the threat posed to parish structures by help 'intruded' from outside, particularly at a time when traditional institutions were felt to be under threat because of events in France. Occurring at a time of general evangelical consensus, it both reached back into the past and foreshadowed the denominational controversies of later years.

In 1790, when the Park Street school was sold, the sisters had built themselves a house in Great Pulteney Street, Bath. More did not find Bath society particularly congenial, and attended the Presbyterian Chapel in Argyle Street on Sunday evenings (something which was held against her at the time of the Blagdon Controversy). In 1801 the sisters sold the house and the Cowslip Green cottage, and moved to Barley Wood, Wrington. Although this move was planned as a retirement, it did not prove to be such. More continued her writing and her involvement with the Mendip schools. In 1808 she published her only novel, *Coelebs in Search of a Wife*, in which the bachelor of the title finds the perfect wife in the well-educated Lucilla. Further moral and religious writings followed: *Practical Piety* (1811), *Christian Morals* (1812), *The Character and Practical Writings of St. Paul* (1815), *Moral Sketches* (1819), *The Feast of Freedom* (1821), *Bible Rhymes* (1821) and *The Spirit of Prayer*

(1825). In addition, the Cheap Repository Tracts were revived in 1817. The years from 1813 to 1819 were blighted by the deaths of her four sisters, and in 1828 the failure of her servants to care for her at Barley Wood led to her removal to Hotwells, Clifton, where she died in 1833. She was buried in Wrington churchyard with her sisters.

Hannah More's writing was hugely popular in her lifetime; subsequent generations found her contemporaries' praise inflated. She was criticized in her lifetime as being too eager to please, but more generally praised for her charm and vivacity, her generosity and goodness of heart and her singleness of purpose. Later generations criticized the narrowness of her evangelicalism and the individualistic moralism of her social analysis. Reading her ideas against the background of her own age reveals her as a gifted teacher and communicator. She was equipped as a writer by her upbringing, education and social setting, and from the mid-1780s onwards the driving force of her life and writing was her evangelical faith.

Bibliography
W. Roberts, *Memoirs of the Life and Correspondence of Mrs. Hannah More* (London: Seeley & Burnside, 1834); C. M. Younge, *Hannah More* (London: Allen, 1888); M. G. Jones, *Hannah More* (Cambridge: Cambridge University Press, 1952); C. H. Ford, *Hannah More. A Critical Biography* (New York: Peter Lang, 1996).

M. JONES

■ MORGAN, George Campbell (1863–1945), evangelist, was born in Tetbury, Gloucestershire, on 9 December 1863. His father was a Baptist minister, who resigned his pastorate because he was drawn to the views of George *Müller, although he never joined the Brethren. The family soon moved to Cardiff, and George attended Roath Road Wesleyan Church. He preached his first sermon at thirteen, and regularly thereafter, apart from two years during which he experienced a crisis of faith about the authority of the Bible. After being educated at The Douglas School, Cheltenham, he became a teacher at the Wesleyan Day School, Birmingham, and subsequently at the Jewish

Collegiate School from 1883 to 1886, where the principal, Lawrence Levy, who had trained as a rabbi, became a close friend and taught him much about Judaism. In 1883 Morgan attended D. L. *Moody's three-week mission in Birmingham and assisted in the 'enquiry room'.

The school closed just when Morgan had decided to commit his life to preaching. He first thought of entering the Salvation Army, and went to conduct a mission in Hull for two weeks, which eventually ran for thirteen months. Here he first met the evangelist Gipsy Smith. He became a lay evangelist for the Wesleyan Methodist Church in the Macclesfield district, and in 1888 offered himself for ministry, only to be rejected. In August 1888 he married his cousin, Annie. He was called to the ministry of the Congregational church at Stone, Staffordshire, in 1889, and was ordained to the ministry in 1890. He moved to Rugeley in 1891, and then to Westminster Road, Birmingham, in 1893. His first London ministry was at New Court Church, Tollington Park (1897–1901), where he was noted for his 'extraordinary eloquence'. He also spent a considerable time conducting evangelistic campaigns around the country.

Morgan first visited the USA in 1896, where he met Moody and was invited to preach at the Northfield Bible Conference. Moody described him as 'one of the most remarkable men who ever came to Northfield', and he was invited to the General Conference every year until Moody's death in 1899. In 1901 Moody's son invited him to become the Northfield Extension Lecturer, a post which involved leading Bible conferences all over the United States and Canada and developing the work of the YMCA. In 1902 Chicago Theological Seminary gave him a DD. His book The Crises of the Christ (1903) represented his approach to the life of Jesus.

Morgan returned to London in 1904 to become minister of Westminster Chapel. He raised money to renovate the building and revived a cause that had seemed almost lost, assisted by his friend the Revd Albert Swift. Here he established his reputation for biblical preaching, undoubtedly a consequence of his time in America; his weekly sermons were published in The Westminster Pulpit (repr. 10 vols., 1954–1956). His congregation included cabinet ministers and other leading social figures. He set up the Friday evening Bible School, from which came The Analyzed Bible (1907), and a new Sunday school, and established a sisterhood of women workers in the church. The Northfield pattern was imitated in summer camps at Mundesley in Norfolk, with a wide range of visiting preachers. He was president of Cheshunt College, Cambridge (1911–1914), spending the week in Cambridge and the weekend in London. He raised the money for the College's new buildings, but found the combination of tasks too much and resigned because of ill health. In August 1914 he was almost the only London minister in his pulpit when war broke out, and his preaching made him a national figure. After resigning from Westminster Chapel in 1917, he helped to train YMCA workers at the Mildmay Centre, and also undertook a temporary pastorate at Highbury Quadrant (1918–1919).

In 1919 Morgan returned to the USA, spending the next thirteen years in Bible conference work, concluding with a three-year pastorate at Tabernacle Presbyterian Church, Philadelphia (1930–1932). Here the opportunities open to a travelling evangelist, which were disappearing in Britain, were still considerable. The Great Physician (1937) contains fifty addresses from these tours. He returned to Westminster Chapel in 1932, as assistant to Hubert Simpson, and as minister from 1934. Dr Martyn *Lloyd-Jones joined him as assistant in 1938. The war years brought increasing frailty; Morgan retired in 1943, and died in London on 16 May 1945. His four sons all became ministers.

Campbell Morgan is usually described as an 'expository preacher'. His sermons were certainly primarily biblical in content, giving careful attention to marginal readings and different meanings of words. He preferred the American Standard Version (1901) to the Authorised and Revised Versions, and thought Weymouth's translation of the New Testament the most accurate. But he was not concerned with biblical scholarship in the technical sense. He was not interested in how the biblical books reached their canonical form; his Analyzed Bible is a preaching tool, which does not refer to source or form criticism, or even to textual criticism.

Morgan cannot properly be called a fundamentalist; he disliked the word and the related controversies. He did believe that 'the Scriptures, as originally committed to writing, were safeguarded in every word by the Holy Spirit'. There was room for 'devout and scholarly criticism' in the areas of translation and copying; thus, the longer ending of Mark was 'of somewhat doubtful authority'. For him Genesis was accurate history (because Christ accepted the accuracy of the Old Testament), and the theory of evolution 'could not account for man'. He accepted the Mosaic authorship of the Pentateuch (although he did not think it mattered) and the unity of authorship of Isaiah; he regarded the Gospels as having been written by those to whom they are attributed (but he did not defend the direct Pauline authorship of Hebrews). Although he believed in the priority of Mark, he thought Galatians was written before 1 Thessalonians.

Morgan avoided controversies over predestination, though he regarded the idea of the inevitable reprobation of certain souls as unscriptural. He believed that the baptism essential to salvation was that of the Holy Spirit, and that immersion was the appropriate form of water baptism; he and his children were all immersed. But he respected the conviction of parents who wanted their children baptized. He did not believe in 'a hell of literal fire', not thinking it essential to a doctrine of future punishment. Similarly he took a premillennial view of the second advent, but would not lay exclusive emphasis on it. Nor would he ever sign any declaration of faith drawn up by fallible human beings.

Morgan remained a friend of more liberal Congregationalists such as *Forsyth, Selbie, Jowett and J. D. Jones, and appreciation of his preaching does not depend on acceptance of his theology. However, he was never a 'denominational' man; Sidney Berry, general secretary of the Congregational Union, said that he managed to get Morgan on a Union Assembly platform only once, 'and when he got there he was not happy'. So it is not surprising that he was never chairman of the Union. Morgan was classically an evangelist in the tradition of Moody. Despite his various pastorates, he was happiest as a travelling preacher. Martyn Lloyd-Jones rightly called him 'the last of the great pulpit personalities'.

Bibliography

J. Harries, G. Campbell Morgan (New York: Fleming H. Revell, 1930); J. Morgan, A Man of the Word (London: Pickering & Inglis, 1951); J. Morgan, This was his Faith: the Expository Letters of G. Campbell Morgan (London: Pickering & Inglis).

D. M. THOMPSON

■ **MORISON, James** (1816–1893), Scottish preacher and theologian, was instrumental in the foundation of the Evangelical Union in 1843. He was born at Bathgate, Scotland, son of Robert and Jessie Morison. His father was minister of the Anti-Burgher branch of the United Secession Church in the town. James Morison was educated at Edinburgh University (1830–1834) and the Theological Hall of the Secession Church (1834–1839). Here he was tutored in the evangelical Calvinism of his denomination, in which the Westminster Confession and the Westminster Shorter Catechism predominated. A significant figure in his ministerial education was Dr John Brown, who had embraced broader views on some key issues within the Calvinistic scheme. As a student Morison demonstrated both a precocious theological talent and a propensity for controversy. In 1839 he was licensed by the Edinburgh presbytery of the United Secession Church. Perhaps a little suspicious of his theological views, they seconded him to work in the rural area around Elgin. His early ministrations in a series of isolated Secession congregations coincided with the revivals in Kilsyth and Dundee, the progress of which he followed with much interest. He was deeply influenced in 1839 by reading Charles *Finney's Lectures on the Revival of Religion (New York, 1835), declaring he had 'reaped more benefit from the book than from all other human compositions put together'. The effect of Finney's thought on Morison's subsequent ministry was marked, impressing on him an intense desire to win souls and encouraging him to make his sermons practical and often extemporary evangelical discourses, with urgent supplications to his hearers of their need for faith in Christ. He enjoyed considerable success in his evangelism, and preached to crowded congregations. His emphasis on the effort required of the individual hearer to believe brought him into conflict with the traditions of his denomination. He began to enunciate a belief in universal atonement, outlined in his tract, *The Question, 'What Must I do to be Saved?' Answered* (Edinburgh, 1840). Morison set out a governmental theory of the atonement in *The Nature of the Atonement* (Edinburgh, 1841), and Sandemanian views of faith were expressed in his *Saving Faith; or, The Simple Belief of the Gospel Considered* (Kilmarnock, 1842).

Although he considered becoming an evangelist, in October 1840 he received a call to the Clerk's Lane Secession church, in Kilmarnock, Ayrshire. The call was not unanimous, and his ordination and induction were shrouded in controversy. Doubts over his Calvinistic orthodoxy were quickly raised by his opponents, and he was summoned to appear before his presbytery to answer questions about his views. Although aged only twenty-five, and newly ordained, he was utterly convinced of the rightness of his position, and (perhaps naively) believed that he could convince his senior opponents of the unscriptural nature of their historic doctrinal formularies. Privately he was encouraged in his stance by others in the Secession Church who were also moderating their Calvinism. His hope that they would join him publicly in the cause was disappointed. The denomination was ready for no such doctrinal restatement, and just five months after his ordination and induction, Morison was suspended by his presbytery for his failure to retract or suppress the promulgation of his unorthodox views.

Morison appealed to the synod of the United Secession Church, and further explored his view of the universal love of God and a general atonement in *The Extent of the Atonement* (Kilmarnock, 1841), arguing that it was 'spurious Calvinism to hold that Christ died for the elect alone'. The appeal to synod, although unsuccessful, revealed an increasing divergence of opinion within the denomination on these matters. Morison was removed from office as a United Secession minister, but the verdict was defied by his Clerk's Lane congregation, which continued to function as a church disconnected from the United Secession denomination. Convinced that his doctrinal views were bringing great blessing to his ministry, Morison declared unflinchingly, 'I cannot make any compromise with regard to what I believe to be God's eternal truth.'

The fallout from Morison's removal from office as a minister of the United Secession Church was significant. His father and two other Secession ministers were suspended from office for supporting his views. In May 1843, two days before the Disruption in the Church of Scotland launched the Free Church, the deposed ministers formed an association called the 'Evangelical Union' for mutual countenance, counsel and cooperation in teaching the 'glorious, simple soul-saving and heart-sanctifying gospel of Christ'. Morison had by then completed the transition from Westminster orthodoxy to an Arminian system of doctrine. His views were adopted by the Evangelical Union, and were often termed Morisonianism. The Evangelical Union also adopted a Congregational church order, whilst retaining a plurality of elders, and an anti-credal stance; their doctrinal standard was the Bible alone. In 1897 the Evangelical Union, which had come to number ninety churches, merged with the Congregational Union. Morison was president of the Evangelical Union conference in 1845 and 1868.

When in August 1843 the newly formed Evangelical Union opened its own theological academy, Morison took on the role of tutor. By 1846 student numbers had reached thirty-three. His theological acumen was demonstrated in a series of scholarly commentaries, on Matthew (London, 1870), Mark (London, 1873) and on various chapters in Romans. He edited the Evangelical Union's periodical, the *Evangelical Repository*, from 1854 to 1868. For his scholarly labours he was awarded the honorary DD of Adrian College, Michigan, in 1862, and of Glasgow University in 1882. A. M. Fairbairn believed Morison typified the ideal of the scholar who never forgot he was a Christian, and of the Christian who never forgot he was a scholar.

Morison remained primarily a preacher and pastor. Although departing radically from Calvinistic orthodoxy, he embraced no commensurate political or social radicalism, although he became a committed total abstainer. He resolved to 'take no side in politics', submerging all lesser concerns under his desire to preach 'the one thing needful'. He contended that his confrontation with the United Secession Church came from a concern for the salvation of sinners. His pulpit ministry was highly fruitful; in his first three years of ministry at Clerk's Lane, 680 new members were added to the church. He also undertook regular evangelistic preaching tours, in which he often preached to large crowds in the open air.

In 1851 Morison was called to the Evangelical Union's Glasgow congregation, and in 1853 a chapel on North Dundas Street was built for the flourishing cause. His preaching was expository; the task of the preacher was to find out the mind of the Spirit in the words of Scripture, and then to exhibit it. The theme of an atonement for all was frequently part of his message. He resigned his pastorate in 1884 owing to ill health, but retained a link with the North Dundas Street Church until his death. James Morison married Margaret Dick in 1841, and they had three children. After the death of his first wife, Morison remarried in 1877.

By the time of Morison's death his doctrinal views, once considered heresy, had gained widespread acceptance in many Scottish denominations, although he did not share the increasingly negative stance of some regarding the authority of Scripture. Close adherence to the Calvinism of the Westminster Confession had largely given way to a theology emphasizing God's universal love.

Bibliography

W. Adamson, *The Life of James Morison, D.D.* (London: Hodder & Stoughton, 1898); O. Smeaton, *Principal James Morison* (Edinburgh: Oliver & Boyd, 1901); F. Ferguson, *History of the Evangelical Union* (Glasgow: T. D. Morison, 1876).

I. J. SHAW

■ **MORLING, George Henry** (1891–1974), principal of New South Wales Baptist Theological College, Sydney, Australia, was born on 21 November 1891 in Sydney, the third child of Charles Morling and Annie Hillman, who married on 6 April 1885. Both his parents had emigrated to Sydney from London in the early 1880s. Not long after his arrival in Sydney, Charles became a foundation member of Petersham Baptist Church (1882) and later secretary of the Ashfield Baptist Church, which became the family's home church. For George Morling, home life was strict but loving. His childhood was also marked by 'nervousness', fears and a speech impediment.

At the age of seventeen Morling confessed Jesus Christ as his Saviour and was baptized and received into the fellowship of the Ashfield Baptist Church. In July 1913 he was accepted to train for the Baptist ministry. Soon afterwards, he was sent to Tamworth, in rural New South Wales, for his pre-ministry experience. There he suffered great inner turmoil, but emerged from his struggles with a strong assurance of salvation. He was sent back to Sydney for 1914. There he suffered a breakdown but received from the Revd T. R. Coleman some teaching on the theme of the deeper things of God, which helped him to persevere in his training. The life of holiness or, as Morling called it, experimental religion was to become a major theme of his ministry.

A year at the Victorian Baptist College in 1915 was followed by a year at the newly formed New South Wales Baptist College in 1916. While studying Morling also engaged in pastoral ministry at Easthills and pioneered a work at Bankstown. As a result of his own time in training Morling adopted and propagated the view that both scholarly exactness and practical pastoral engagement were required of those who received God's high calling to ministry. An emergency in a country church circuit at Dungog/Thalaba led to Morling's transfer to that work in 1917. He was to complete his studies 'extra-murally'.

On 28 April 1917 Morling married Gladys Rees. She would be an integral part of his ministry, providing in their home a place of sanctuary from the demands of others, yet a place of warm hospitality to all. She would also act as his advocate to the college council when she saw him over-committing himself in ministry to the detriment of his health. Yet she readily accepted that her ministry was to release her husband from the home to exercise his ministry on state, national and international stages.

On 12 February 1918 Morling was ordained with five others, and in September that year members of the Annual Assembly noted with approval a speech by the young minister. He was transferred to a city pastorate commencing early in 1919. During his final service at Dungog/Thalaba Morling baptized fourteen people, evidence of his effectiveness as a preacher and evangelist. Effective preaching and evangelism would also be emphases of his training of ministerial candidates.

On taking up his appointment at Hornsby/Pymble in 1919, Morling initiated two innovations, the systematic exposition of books of the Bible and public lectures defending Christian faith in a public hall. Morling's abilities as a Bible teacher were brought to the attention of the wider Baptist community in 1928–1930 through a series of Bible teaching tours associated with his own presidential year and that of the Revd C. J. Tinsley. From 1932 he was a frequent platform speaker at two significant Bible conferences in Australia, Upwey (later Belgrave Heights) in Victoria and Katoomba in NSW, and from 1937 at Auckland in New Zealand. His association with Bible conferences continued until 1967.

Morling's long association with the NSW Baptist Theological College as a teacher began in 1919, when he first presented lectures in church history. In 1920 he was elected to the college council, later that year becoming its secretary. The sudden resignation of the college's principal at the 1920 Assembly led to Morling taking on the major responsibility for its administration. At the 1921 Assembly Morling was appointed acting principal on a full-time basis, despite the opposition of some who deemed him too young. The following year at the September Assembly he was appointed principal for a three-year term. He would remain in the position until his retirement in December 1960.

His early years as principal were marked by periods of frenetic ministry and total incapacity due to ill health. Early in 1924 he was hospitalized and instructed to cease work on his MA degree in history at Sydney University. However, he recovered his health and completed the work for his MA, which was granted in May 1925. The relationship between health and spirituality became an increasingly important theme in his personal life and later in his public teaching ministry. A conversation with Dr Graham *Scroggie at the Katoomba Convention of 1934 brought Morling a vital new insight, namely 'that the life of faith includes the deliberate offering of the body to God, with the expected outcome of improved health and greater effectiveness in service.' Morling later noted, as a consequence of that bodily surrender of himself

to God 'a continuance of health which makes spiritual rest easier and deeper'. Morling's small book *Quest for Serenity*, published in 1950 (revised and updated in 2002), brought together his mature reflections on the person and work of the Holy Spirit and the life of holiness, and included some comments on health and healing.

In addition to his college commitments, Morling's workload in the wider Baptist community was extensive. At times he acted as moderator for the Blackheath church, and between April and August 1939 was virtually pastor of the Ashfield church. His extra-collegial activities peaked in the years immediately following the Second World War. In 1947 he had major preaching and teaching commitments in Western Australia (where he delivered thirty-seven addresses in a little over a month), Victoria, Queensland and South Australia, and made a major preaching tour of rural New South Wales as part of the Christian Commonwealth Crusade. He also spent two weeks in New Zealand at various Baptist Union camps.

Within Australia his contribution beyond the Baptist denomination included an honorary appointment as lecturer in church history at Sydney University in 1938 and increasing involvement with university students through the Evangelical Union. In 1947 he was appointed chairman of the Inter-Varsity Fellowship. He was also an active participant in Evangelical Alliance proceedings.

The international aspects of Morling's career began in 1925 when he visited the mission fields of Bengal. This visit began a long association with the missionary enterprise in that country and his support of overseas mission. In January 1934 Morling began a world tour that gave him the opportunity to visit theological colleges in Britain and America, where he made significant contacts with Baptists from the wider world. He gave major addresses at the Commonwealth and Empire Baptist Congress in London in June 1951 and participated in the conference of principals of Baptist colleges that followed the Congress, his positive contribution being reported in the *Baptist Times*.

Following the Second World War, Australian Baptists debated joining the World Council of Churches. In 1949 Morling prepared publications detailing the cases both for and against. At a special Assembly in May 1950, NSW Baptists voted not to join the World Council of Churches. The waves of disquiet generated by Pentecostalism were also being felt in Baptist churches in NSW. It fell to Morling to present the official position of the executive of the NSW Baptist Union. In his booklet *Pentecostalism*, published in 1952, he strongly rejected the second-blessing teaching of Pentecostalism while firmly advocating the life of holiness developed through the indwelling person of the Holy Spirit.

After his retirement Morling served from 1960 to 1962 as ministerial vice-president of the NSW Baptist Union, and between 1962 and 1964 as president-general of the Baptist Union of Australia. In 1963 he was awarded an OBE for services to religion. He died in Sydney on 8 April 1974. At his memorial service on 10 April 1974 he was accorded many commendations by representatives of a wide cross-section of denominations. They commended him for his long and influential ministry, his teaching in many theological disciplines, particularly on the Holy Spirit and the deeper life, and his gracious Christ-like personality. His legacy lived on in theological education. At the time of his death five of 'Morling's Men' were engaged in ministerial training as principals, vice-principals and faculty members of Baptist and non-denominational theological colleges throughout Australia and internationally. The NSW Baptist Theological College is now called Morling College.

Bibliography

G. H. Morling, *Quest for Serenity* (Eastwood: Morling Press, 2002); E. R. Rogers, *George Henry Morling: The Man and his Message for Today* (Forest Lodge, NSW: Greenwood Press, 1995).

G. R. CHATFIELD

■ **MORRIS, Henry Madison** (1918–), father of modern creationism, was born on 6 October 1918 in Dallas to Henry Madison Morris and Emily Ida Hunter. His father was a land agent, and during the Great Depression poverty struck the family. Morris graduated in civil engineering from Rice Institute in 1939. He worked first as an engineer with the International Boundary and Water Commission at El Paso, and at the outbreak of war returned to Rice as an instructor. In 1946 he published his first book, *That You Might Believe*, advocating a recent creation and worldwide flood. In this book Morris allowed the possibility of the 'gap theory', but he soon came to regard it as unbiblical. He obtained his PhD from the University of Minnesota in 1950. He joined the American Scientific Affiliation (ASA) in 1949, the year the geologist L. Kulp attacked flood geology.

Until 1957 Morris was head of civil engineering at Southwestern Louisiana Institute; then he moved to Virginia to head the department of civil engineering at Virginia Polytechnic Institute. While there he co-authored *The Genesis Flood* (1961). In 1963 he cofounded the Creation Research Society, and his creationist work was soon absorbing an increasing amount of his time and energy. In 1970 he joined Tim *LaHaye at San Diego, becoming cofounder, Professor of Apologetics and vice-president for academic affairs at Christian Heritage College. From 1978 to 1980 he was president of Christian Heritage College and from 1970 to 1995 president of the Institute for Creation Research (ICR). Professionally he was a competent hydraulic engineer and wrote a standard textbook, *Applied Hydraulics in Engineering* (1963), but his significance for evangelicalism lies in his espousing of creationism. From small beginnings, creationism became a political and religious force in the USA, and activists challenged the teaching of evolution in many states, most notably Arkansas in 1981.

Morris professed conversion and was baptized at the age of eight at First Baptist Church, Corpus Christi, Texas. After his marriage in 1940 to Marie Louise Beach, they joined 'a sound Bible-preaching church', and he joined the Gideons in 1942. Marie and Henry had six children. One son, John, has continued Henry's work at ICR. Henry did much work in Rice Christian Fellowship, before it affiliated with the InterVarsity Christian Fellowship. After the publication of *The Genesis Flood*, he left his local Southern Baptist church because he considered that it was too liberal. With others he formed an Independent Baptist church, which soon joined the Independent Fundamental Churches of America. His theology was strongly inerrantist, literalist and dispensationalist, and he welcomed the description 'fundamentalist'. Initially he accepted the gap theory, 'in a sort of tentative way', but soon rejected it because of his growing conviction that the Bible taught a literal six-day creation and that the evidence for evolution was inadequate. He expounded these views in *Biblical Creationism*. In *Creation and the Second Coming* (1991) he relates his view of creation to prophecy and argued that the return of Christ was very near.

Morris has written many books, articles and contributions to ICR literature, such as *Acts and Facts*. Many are variations on the same theme, but one stands out as the most significant. *The Genesis Flood* is without question the most important creationist work ever written, and its influence on evangelical Christian thinking about science in the second half of the twentieth century cannot be overestimated. It has received equal measures of acclaim and derision. Whether or not its conclusions were right, its attempt to disprove evolution by insisting on a young earth and a universal flood was bold and very influential. In it Morris directly confronted the fundamentalist 'gap-theory' consensus on creation in the 1960s.

The book resulted from Morris's meeting with J. C. Whitcomb at an ASA meeting in 1953 and his concern over Bernard *Ramm's book, *The Christian View of Science and Scripture*. Morris and Whitcomb began to work together in 1957. Whitcomb provided theological reasons for interpreting Genesis literally, arguing that it teaches a six-day creation and a universal flood. Morris, who wrote the greater part of the book, provided the 'science', which was an adaptation of McCready Price's flood geology. (Price was a Seventh Day Adventist who wrote a number of books in the early twentieth century.) Morris argued that all sedimentary strata were deposited during the flood, that the theory of the geological column was based on circular argument, and that radiometric dating was flawed. Neither his criticisms of 'evolutionary science' nor his alternative scientific models have gained acceptance by mainstream scientists, including the majority of evangelical scientists in the ASA and Christians in Science. However, the arguments of *The Genesis Flood*, with modifications, have

formed the basis of all subsequent creationist thinking. Possibly the book's most important theological contribution is the Appendix, *Paleontology and the Edenic Curse*. The authors argue that to affirm the death of animals before the existence of humans on the basis of old-earth geology is to deny the doctrines of the fall and of the atonement. This soteriological argument gives creationism its strongest theological appeal; it was used as early as the 1820s by evangelicals such as George Bugg to challenge the implications of contemporary geology (*Scriptural Geology*, 1826).

Before publication Moody Press, the intended publisher, became hesitant about the book; it was finally published by Presbyterian and Reformed in February 1961. Despite the absence of acknowledgments, the book represented the theory of G. M. Price brought up to date. The ASA took three years to review it (critically), and secular scientists began to take note of it only in the 1970s as creationism made inroads into education, especially in schools. Most criticisms have centred on its scientific aspects; Whitcomb and Morris have often been accused of misrepresentation and misquotation. Theological criticisms from evangelicals are less common and harder to justify because of Morris's commitment to biblical authority and soteriology.

The work of Morris has spawned many creationist groups in North America, Britain and Europe as well as in the Far East and the former Soviet bloc. Many states in the USA have passed bills concerning the teaching of evolution, which have caused much controversy. As a result of his work six-day creationism has become the touchstone of orthodoxy for many evangelicals and is part of the basis of faith of some churches, colleges and parachurch groups.

Before 1961 creationism could be ignored as irrelevant, but since then it has had to be taken seriously, especially because Morris and others claim it to be both the traditional stance of the Christian church and the only tenable interpretation of both Genesis and science.

Morris has created controversy, but a discussion with Ken Miller emphasizes the sincerity and the motivation of his beliefs: 'Scripture tells us what the right conclusion is ... we have to keep working until we get the right answer' (K. Miller, *Finding Darwin's God*, 1999, p. 173).

Bibliography
R. L. Numbers, *The Creationists* (New York: Knopf, 1992); H. M. Morris, *History of Modern Creationism* (San Diego: Master Books, 1984).

M. B. ROBERTS

■ **MORRIS, Leon Lamb** (1914–), theological educator, biblical theologian and commentator, was born on 15 March 1914 in Lithgow, NSW, the first of four children of George Coleman Morris, an iron-founder, and his second wife, Ivy (née Lamb). Educated first at the Lithgow Public and Intermediate High Schools, as the Great Depression tightened its grip he was enabled to attend the University of Sydney by a teacher's scholarship. A degree in science (1931–1933) was followed by a year at Sydney Teachers' College, after which Morris entered the service of the NSW Department of Education.

From his parents Morris received a churchgoing upbringing. In his first year as an undergraduate his formal understanding of Christianity ripened into a personal commitment to Christ under the influence of R. B. Robinson, rector of All Souls, Leichhardt, and the Evangelical Union at the university. Sensing a 'call' to the ministry soon afterwards, Morris was obliged first to work out a five-year bond as a schoolteacher with the Department of Education. He used his spare time to teach himself Greek, and then to prepare as a private candidate for the Licentiate of Theology examinations of the Australian College of Theology. When he came first in the national list in Part II, the Anglican diocese of Sydney paid out the bond and arranged for his immediate ordination, even though he had had no formal preparation in a theological college. Morris learned the work of the ministry as curate (1938–1940) to Cecil Short, rector of St John's, Campsie.

In 1940 Morris realized a long-cherished hope of working with the Bush Church Aid Society when he went as priest in charge to the Minnipa Mission in South Australia. In *Bush Parson* (1995) he gives an account of his five years of itinerant ministry to an outback community struggling with difficult conditions aggravated by the effects of the Second World War. During this time he sought to deepen his understanding of Christianity by reading for the University of London BD (1943) and MTh (1946), often studying as he was driven about the mission by his wife, Mildred (née Dann), whom he had married in 1941. The possibility of an academic career arose in 1945 when Morris accepted an invitation to become vice-principal of Ridley College in Melbourne, a post he held until 1959, apart from two years' leave (1950–1951) taken to complete a Cambridge doctorate under the supervision of R. Newton Flew. This was his only theological study under the direction of a recognized teacher.

Following his return to Australia in 1952, Morris moved into what was to become an immensely productive career as an author by publishing his doctoral thesis. A careful study of the vocabulary of the atonement, *The Apostolic Preaching of the Cross* (1955) set the tone in method and content for his principal work as a biblical theologian. Its findings were developed and popularized in numerous subsequent works, most notably *The Cross in the New Testament* (1985) and *The Atonement* (1983). Intending to develop the classical doctrine of the substitutionary atonement by taking account of all the relevant biblical data, Morris used careful linguistic scholarship as the basis of an extended exposition of the salvific meaning of the death of Christ. For Morris there was nothing more important in Christianity, a conviction reflected in the attention given to the cross and its effect in his *New Testament Theology* (1986).

Morris's manifest regard for Scripture and the solidly exegetical quality of his early work soon attracted the attention of the evangelical community. As a result he was included in the team of scholars asked to write the Tyndale commentaries. His contribution eventually included the volumes on 1 & 2 Thessalonians (1956), 1 Corinthians (1959), Judges and Ruth (1968), Revelation (1969) and Luke (1974). He also wrote more substantial works on the Thessalonian correspondence (1959) and the Fourth Gospel (1971) for the New International Commentary series. Morris wrote on every New Testament book except Acts either at a scholarly or a more popular level. All his commentaries were characterized by attention to words and their meanings in their biblical and historical contexts; the commentary was the ideal medium for his characteristic approach. The details of scholarly debate and, in later years, more innovative methods of interpretation were of interest only in so far as they shed light on the meaning of the words in the text.

Morris supplemented the two principal strands in his writing by a steady stream of monographs, thematic and devotional studies, and articles for a wide range of church publications. For many years this literary output was sustained in addition to a heavy teaching and administrative burden. At Ridley College Morris was an exacting lecturer on doctrine and the Bible. After a period of study leave in the United States (1960–1961) he accepted an invitation to become Warden of Tyndale House, Cambridge, where he promoted evangelical biblical scholarship by building up and reorganizing the library. In 1964 Morris was recalled to Ridley as principal. An efficient and pragmatic administrator, he presided over a period of change and expansion. His initiatives included an ambitious building programme, recruitment of additional staff to allow the introduction of new courses and postgraduate degrees, and formalization of Ridley's status as a hall of residence of the University of Melbourne. Morris's achievement as principal was recognized in 1977 when he was made a member of the University Council.

Morris sought to participate in the wider church, believing in the importance of evangelical involvement. He travelled widely to teach and preach, throughout Australia, in the United States, Asia and South America. Although no controversialist, he would occasionally speak out on current issues, as when in *The Abolition of Religion* (1964) he rejected the 'religionless Christianity' popularized by J. A. T. Robinson's *Honest to God*. In Australia Morris served on the Anglican Doctrine Commission, a position from which he spoke out in favour of the ordination of women. For many years he served on the Council and Board of Studies of the Australian College of Theology. As president of the Evangelical Alliance in Victoria he was instrumental in setting up TEAR Fund in Australia. Morris was a ready supporter of

other evangelical agencies such as IVF, SU, CMS and the Bible Society. In many of his addresses to them he defended the authority of the Bible for Christian life and practice in the contemporary world; he explained his views on the subject systematically in *I Believe in Revelation* (1976). From 1964 he was a canon of Melbourne's St Paul's Cathedral, where he defended traditional evangelical standards and sensibilities; for example, he steadfastly refused to wear vestments. His underlying conviction of the need to bring the gospel to the people was reflected in his chairmanship of the committee for the 1968 Billy Graham crusade in Victoria.

An unpretentious man of deep but straightforward faith, Morris aimed always to serve God in the place of his appointment. Yet he welcomed retirement in 1979 as an opportunity to spend more time in his study. With more than fifty books now to his credit, he is one of Australia's most prolific Christian authors. Morris's writings over the years contributed to the worldwide rise of evangelical biblical scholarship following the Second World War. In Australia he was in its vanguard.

Bibliography

Taped interview, 8 August 1986, CSAC Archives; *Lucas* 25 & 26 (1999), pp. 185–216; D. J. Williams, 'Leon Morris', in W. A. Elwell and J. D. Weaver (eds.), *Biblical Interpreters of the Twentieth Century* (Grand Rapids: Baker, 1999).

G. R. TRELOAR

■ **MORRISON, Robert** (1782–1834), missionary to China, translator and Sinologue, was born in Morpeth, England, on 5 January 1782, but the family moved to Newcastle when Morrison was about three years old. Although his father James was an elder in the High Bridge Presbyterian Church in that city, and Robert attended that church in his youth and would remain a Presbyterian his entire life, his work in China as a missionary of the non-denominational London Missionary Society (LMS) took on an increasingly Protestant ecumenical character.

At the age of twenty Morrison felt God's call to missions, and in 1803 he entered Hoxton Academy in London. The following year he enrolled in the 'missionary academy' at Gosport, where he continued his studies for two and a half years. He also briefly studied medicine at St Bartholomew's Hospital in London and astronomy at Greenwich. When the LMS appointed Morrison a missionary, it was not to Africa, the country to which he had originally felt called. Rather, his destination was to be China, where his initial task would be to translate the Bible into Chinese to help prepare the way for future missionaries. Before leaving England, with a Chinese man in London named Yong Sam-tak, he began a study of a partial Chinese Bible manuscript in the British Museum. This was just the initial step that began a lifelong journey into the intricacies of the Chinese language.

Morrison sailed for China on 5 January 1807. Because of the East India Company's prohibition on missionaries in Canton, he travelled by way of the United States, where he arrived on 18 April. During the three weeks he was there, Morrison visited evangelicals in New York, Philadelphia and Boston. While he was in America, a merchant asked the young missionary if he really expected to 'make an impression on the idolatry of the Great Chinese Empire', to which Morrison replied, 'No, Sir, I expect God will.'

Leaving New York on 12 May, Morrison sailed for nearly four months, reaching Canton on 6 September 1807. For the next twenty-seven years (except for two years in England in 1824–1826), Morrison continued his work of translation and writing, fully aware of his role as a forerunner. He was never an evangelist in the mode of a missionary evangelist, and apparently fewer than a dozen Chinese became Christians as a direct result of his ministry.

In 1809 Morrison married Mary Morton, the daughter of a surgeon of the Royal Irish Regiment who was briefly in Macao with his family. The apparently happy marriage, although frequently marred by Mary's ill health and long periods of physical separation, produced two children who lived to adulthood: Mary Rebecca, later a missionary herself, and John Robert, who as a young man became quite significant in the history of British relations with China. When Morrison's wife Mary died in 1821, the two children returned to England, where they remained until 1826. In November 1825 Robert Morrison married Elizabeth Armstrong and the next year returned to China with his new wife, Mary Rebecca, John Robert, and a new son named Robert. The couple would have four more children in the next five years.

Also in 1809 Morrison began employment as a translator and interpreter for the East India Company in China, a position which gave him a legal basis for remaining in China and also provided him with an income sufficient to allow him to work almost independently of the LMS and its financial support. Morrison also served as interpreter and translator for two official British government delegations to China (the Amherst Mission in 1816 and the Napier Mission in 1834).

The main focus of Morrison's twenty-five years in Canton and Macao was translation and publication. By 1810 he had published his first translation of part of the Bible, the Acts of the Apostles. He and his co-worker William Milne continued to work on the Bible translation, completing it in 1819 and publishing the complete work in 1823. In addition to translating the Bible, Morrison published nearly forty other works in Chinese and English, plus many articles in periodicals. Perhaps his best-known literary work, other than the Bible translation, was his six-volume A Dictionary of the Chinese Language, which he published in Macao between 1815 and 1822. Morrison and Milne also published two periodicals, one in English (The Indo-Chinese Gleaner) and one in Chinese (The Chinese Monthly Magazine). Later Morrison and his son John Robert produced a short-lived periodical entitled The Evangelist and Miscellanea Sinica.

Morrison and Milne established the Anglo-Chinese College in Malacca in 1818. They designed the institution as a place for educating local boys, but they also wanted to provide training in the Chinese language for future missionaries. Always aware that more co-workers were needed, Morrison began to seek additional help very soon after his arrival in China. Milne was sent out by the LMS in 1813 and slowly others began to arrive at Malacca, Singapore, and other places to help in the work. But it was not until 1830 that another missionary arrived in China to assist Morrison directly. In that year, David Abeel, sponsored by the American Seamen's Friend Society, and Elijah Coleman Bridgman, appointed by the American Board of Commissioners for Foreign Missions, joined Morrison at Canton and Macao. By the time of Morrison's death four years later, there was a small but growing missionary presence on the China coast. Morrison's translation work earned him an international reputation not only as a missionary, but also as a leading Sinologue. Frequently recognized in evangelical circles, the missionary was also granted an honorary doctorate by the University of Glasgow and had an audience with King George IV in recognition of his work.

Robert Morrison died in Canton on 1 August 1834 and was buried in the Protestant cemetery in Macao alongside his first wife Mary (and first-born infant son James who had died at birth). The apparent reasons for his death were a fever from a cold, caught while in a squall on board ship between Macao and Canton, and exhaustion.

Although his Bible translation was revised, and although only a few conversions could be directly attributed to his ministry, Robert Morrison gave his life in the conviction that he was laying the necessary groundwork for later effective missionary work in China. His Bible, dictionary, grammar book and assorted other publications assisted future missionaries in learning the language and understanding more about Chinese culture. His pleas for more workers led directly to the appointment of both British and American missionaries to China. Despite his worldwide recognition as a Sinologue, Morrison remained at heart a missionary. No introduction to the history of Christian missions in China would be complete without mention of the contributions of Robert Morrison, the 'Father of Protestant Missions in China'.

Bibliography

M. Broomhall, *Robert Morrison: A Master-Builder* (London: The Livingstone Press, 1924); E. A. Morrison, *Memoirs of the Life and Labours of Robert Morrison, D.D.*, 2 vols. (London: Longmans, 1839).

J. B. STARR

■ **MOTT, John Raleigh** (1865–1955), evangelist and ecumenical pioneer, was one of the principal architects of the World Council of Churches. His long life spans several phases in the history of Anglo-American Protestantism, from the evangelical ecumenism of the Victorian era, through the more polarized ecclesiastical and theological configurations of the period after the First World War, to the efforts for international Christian reconstruction after 1945.

Mott was born in Sullivan County, New York state, on 25 May 1865. He was the third child and only son of John Stitt Mott and Elmira Dodge Mott. The family moved to Postville, Iowa, while he was still an infant. His parents were devout Methodists, and at the age of thirteen Mott made his first commitment to Christ. He was educated at Upper Iowa University and Cornell University, where he developed the University Christian Association into the largest and most active student YMCA group in the United States. While he was at Cornell, an evangelistic visit to the university in 1886 by the former Cambridge cricketer, J. E. K. Studd, played a part in leading Mott to consecrate himself entirely to God's service. He interpreted this new stage of personal commitment to Christ, in terms common within the holiness movement in American Methodism, as an experience of 'entire sanctification' or 'the higher life'. In July 1886 he spent a month at D. L. *Moody's summer school for students at Mount Hermon, Massachusetts, at which Mott and ninety-nine other students signed the pledge, promoted by Robert P. Wilder, to commit themselves, 'God permitting', to become foreign missionaries. The 'Mount Hermon Hundred' were the first-fruits of what was formalized two years later as the Student Volunteer Movement for Foreign Missions, of which Mott would be chairman for thirty-two years. It is estimated that by 1945 some 20,745 members of the volunteer movement had undertaken overseas missionary service.

On graduating from Cornell in 1887, Mott was appointed initially for a year as the intercollegiate secretary of the North American Student YMCA. He made such a success of this assignment that it was extended for a second year. He became senior student secretary of the American YMCA in 1890. In 1901 he was promoted to associate general secretary for the foreign department, a post he held until 1915, when he was appointed general secretary. He retired from his YMCA post in 1928. Mott combined his YMCA work with his role as chairman from 1888 to 1920 of the Student Volunteer Movement, which in the United States functioned as the missionary arm of the YMCA. In addition, he was from 1895 to 1920 the first general secretary of the World Student Christian Federation (formed to unite the various national student Christian movements founded in the early 1890s), and chairman of that body from 1920 to 1928. Mott was a man of irrepressible energy and travelled great distances in his work. In twelve months in 1890–1891 he covered 31,000 miles within North America. As his reputation spread, his travels became international; he visited Europe on numerous occasions, made seven trips to Asia, five to Russia, five to the Near East, three to Africa, two to Australasia and one to Latin America. It is estimated that he travelled 1.7 million miles in all, mostly by sea or rail. His first international flight was in 1946.

In 1891 Mott married Leila White, an English teacher. They had two girls and two boys. Leila accompanied her husband on many of his travels, and was his critic, editor and even secretary. She died in 1952. In 1953 he married Agnes Peter, a friend for many years.

Mott's contribution to the missionary movement centres on his role as chairman of the World Missionary Conference at Edinburgh in 1910. He was largely responsible for the character of the conference as a gathering of experts devoted to the scientific study of missionary problems rather than a large popular convention on the lines of the New York Ecumenical Missionary Conference of 1900. He chaired the first and most important of the eight commissions, which prepared material for the conference, on 'Carrying the Gospel to all the Non-Christian World'. Mott made a great impression on delegates by his firm chairmanship of the sessions, keeping all speakers to their allotted span of seven minutes each. His book *The Decisive Hour of Christian Missions* (1910) expounded the message of the conference, that the world stood poised at a moment of unique opportunity for missions. He published seventeen other books.

After the conference, Mott played a crucial part in the organizing of regional conferences of the Edinburgh Continuation Committee in India and the Far East. These conferences paved the way for the establishment of national councils of churches in Asia. The work of the Continuation Committee led to the formation of the International Missionary Council (IMC) in 1921. Mott served as its chairman until 1941. In that capacity he presided over the Jerusalem conference of 1928, when the divergences between the liberal and fundamentalist wings of evangelicalism became visible as the churches responded to the growing secularism of the West. Mott also presided over the IMC conference at Tambaram, Madras, in 1938.

In comparison with his prominent role in the IMC, Mott played relatively little part in the 'Life and Work' and 'Faith and Order' movements until steps were taken to bring the two movements together during the 1930s. In 1937 he was appointed a vice-chairman of the provisional committee of the World Council of Churches in process of formation, even though he feared that the impending world body might swallow up the IMC and neglect the missionary imperative, a fear that subsequently proved well founded. Nevertheless, at the inaugural assembly of the World Council of Churches at Amsterdam in 1948 Mott was named as honorary president. In 1946 he was awarded the Nobel Peace Prize for his contributions to the ecumenical movement.

For all of his stature as an ecumenist, Mott's unique gift was as an evangelist of university students. The Oxford University paper, the *Isis*, observed in 1908 that the source of his uncommon spiritual power was his 'life of quiet, simple, and unostentatious, but also quite absolute, devotion to the cause with which he has identified his whole being' (C. H. Hopkins, *John R. Mott*, p. 327). The earnest practical piety of the Holiness Movement in late nineteenth-century America shaped his spirituality for the rest of his life, which he devoted to the task of making 'Jesus Christ known, trusted, loved, and obeyed, in the whole range of one's individual life and in all relationships' (Hopkins, *Mott*, p. 629). The essence of his evangelistic appeals was a demand that students should become disciples of Jesus and thus become inwardly and morally just persons. R. L. Pelly commented in 1912 that Mott's appeal seemed to be 'entirely to the moral nature and there is no theology in it' (Hopkins, *Mott*, p. 385). His relative indifference to theology and broad ecumenical sympathies were characteristic of the holiness evangelicalism of the late nineteenth century, and his growing emphasis on the Social Gospel after the First World War was shared by many whose spirituality remained evangelical. He insisted that there was but one gospel which embraced both individual and social regeneration. Mott always described himself as an evangelical, and at the end of his life asked, 'when John Mott is dead, remember him as an evangelist' (Hopkins, *Mott*, p. 701). He died in Evanston, Illinois, on 31 January 1955.

Bibliography
C. H. Hopkins, *John R. Mott 1865–1955: A Biography* (Grand Rapids: Eerdmans, 1979).
B. STANLEY

■ **MOULE, Handley Carr Glyn** (1841–1920), Anglican bishop and academic, was one of the foremost New Testament scholars in the Church of England in the late nineteenth and early twentieth centuries.

Moule was born on 23 December 1841 in Dorchester, Dorset, the youngest son of Henry Moule, the long-time vicar of Fordington, a parish on the outskirts of Dorchester. Moule demonstrated the potential to become a scholar from an early age; before he was sixteen he had already memorized the Greek text of the letters to the Ephesians and Philippians. In October 1859 he matriculated at Trinity College, Cambridge (following his father and brothers) and began an association with the area which lasted until 1901. A distinguished undergraduate career included a first prize in the classics for writing a set of Latin hexameters (1861), the Carus Prize for Greek Testament (1862), two Sir William Browne medals for writing a Latin ode and Greek and Latin epigrams (1863) and second place in the list of students taking first-class honours in the classical examinations (1864).

Moule's academic and clerical career began in 1865 after he was elected a fellow of Trinity College and passed the theology examination. He accepted the post of assistant master at Marlborough College (1865–1867) in order to gain teaching experience.

Having undergone what he called 'a crisis' in the Christmas period of 1866, probably a conversion experience, Moule was ordained a deacon in 1867, the same year that he received his Master's degree, and a priest in 1868. While retaining his fellowship at Trinity, Moule assisted his father as a curate at Fordington (1867–1873 and 1877–1880) until he was asked to become a dean at Trinity (1873–1877), a position he gave up after the death of his mother so that he could again assist his ageing father. In June 1880 Moule was asked to become the principal of Ridley Hall, a college in Cambridge where graduates could train for holy orders; he accepted the post in October and remained there until 1899. While principal, Moule completed a BD (1894) and DD (1895) from Cambridge and made Ridley Hall a centre for evangelicalism (a development Moule attributed partly to the *Moody Mission held in Cambridge in 1882). In March 1899 Moule was elected Norrisian Professor of Divinity and in May fellow of St Catharine's; both positions were recognition of his stature as a preacher, minister and teacher of Cambridge students.

Moule married Mary Elliott in August 1881, and they had two children, Mary and Isabel, born in November 1882 and February 1884 respectively.

By 1899, although he did not realize it, Moule had surpassed the famous scholar J. B. Lightfoot, his first college tutor, as the standard commentator on the Pauline epistles. Moule had written on the letters to the Romans, Galatians, Ephesians, Philippians and Colossians, both in the Cambridge Bible for Schools series and in stand-alone commentaries. One of his commentaries had been translated into Dutch as *Christlijke Levenswandel* ('The Christian Life', 1895), and revised and updated versions of his commentaries had already been published, a process that continued until 1992 (*The Classic New Testament Commentary: Romans* published by HarperCollins). Moule's writing on biblical studies also included works on classic evangelical concerns such as salvation in *Justifying Righteousness* (1885) and overcoming sin in *The Christian's Victory over Sin* (1887).

Moule was more than a New Testament scholar. An essential component of his writing and his philosophy of life was his contemplative approach to Christianity. Moule was a spiritual man, in the sense that medieval mystics were spiritual, and a sensitive man in that he was able to sympathize with the fears and griefs of others; his poetry is the best expression of these characteristics. He had already published a poem privately in 1865, *Apollo at Pherae: A dramatic poem after the Greek model*, but after his ordination he regularly wrote religious poetry. In 1869 he won the prestigious Seatonian Prize offered by Cambridge University for the poem 'Christian Self-Denial', and he won it again for a dramatic poem called 'The Beloved Disciple' about the relationship between the apostle John and two Church Fathers, Polycarp of Smyrna and Ignatius of Antioch. (Moule also won the Seatonian in 1871, 1872, 1873 and 1876.) All of Moule's poetry is deeply reflective; a poem entitled 'In Memory of St. Anselm' ends with the lines:

'Tis Thine to bid the outcast find
His God within his breast,
And Thine to win an Anselm's mind
At Calvary's Cross to rest.

What Moule described as 'the call of Heaven' came in 1901; he was asked to become Bishop of Durham and was consecrated on 18 October in York Minster. In one sense the ending of his connection with Cambridge preceded the most productive period of Moule's life, and in another sense his nineteen years at Durham were, at best, a limited success; he was a good pastor and a poor administrator. As a minister, Moule was the ideal bishop. Clergy and laity alike saw him as a great spiritual leader and an approachable priest; he was much in demand as a counsellor and guide and wrote an average of thirty letters a day while he occupied the see. He continued to write and publish and was perceived as a scholar-bishop in the tradition of his predecessors, Lightfoot and Westcott. Nevertheless, Moule's kindness towards all and willingness to listen, which some interpreted as a desire to compromise, led to weak administration. His successor, Hensley Henson, complained frequently in his diary about the problems left festering, the poor placement of clergy and the allowing of Catholic practices such as masses, with which Moule, as an evangelical, could not have agreed theologically. Furthermore, Moule 'was not really at home', as one of his biographers puts it, in one of his most important responsibilities, that of member of the House of Lords.

Moule was better suited to what he called 'the wider world of the Church of England'. He was the Select Preacher at Cambridge in thirteen different years from 1880 to 1912, and he served as honorary chaplain to Queen Victoria (1899–1901) and Chaplain-in-Ordinary to Edward VII (1901). After some initial reticence, he became a regular speaker at the Keswick Conventions, an annual meeting of evangelicals, whose leaders stressed the importance of personal holiness, and spoke eighteen times at the Church Congress, an annual meeting for Anglicans, from 1886 onwards. He supported the work of missionary societies such as the China Inland Mission by sponsoring meetings, and he became the president of the Church Missionary Union in 1882.

Moule wrote more than sixty books and pamphlets as well as articles on religion for newspapers such as *The Guardian*. His commentaries, *The Epistle of Paul the Apostle to the Romans* (1879), *The Epistle to the Ephesians* (1886), *The Epistle to the Philippians* (1889) and *The Epistles to the Colossians and to Philemon* (1893) established his reputation as a scholar, but books such as *Veni Creator: Thoughts on the Person and Work of the Holy Spirit of Promise* (1890), *How Can the Individual Soul Approach God?* (1905) and *Concerning Them which are Asleep: Words to a Mourner from a Mourner* (1906) show him to be a thoughtful and caring pastor.

Moule died on 7 May 1920 at his brother's home in Cambridge (having preached his last sermon, before the King and Queen at Windsor Castle, the previous day).

Bibliography

J. B. Harford and F. C. Macdonald, *Handley Carr Glynn Moule, Bishop of Durham: A Biography* (London: Hodder & Stoughton, 1922); J. B. Harford (ed.), *Letters and Poems of Bishop Moule* (London: Marshal Bros., 1922); M. L. Loane, *Handley Carr Glyn Moule, 1841–1920* (London: Church Book Room Press, 1947).

K. A. FRANCIS

■ **MOWLL, Howard West Kilvinton** (1890–1958), Anglican missionary and bishop, was born in Dover on 2 February 1890 and died in Sydney, NSW, on 24 October 1958. He was educated at the King's School, Canterbury, King's College, Cambridge (BA, 1912) and Ridley Hall, and was ordained in the Church of England in 1913.

Mowll was a leader in the Cambridge Inter-Collegiate Christian Union (CICCU) in its breach with the Student Christian Movement and president in 1911–1912. He was responsible for the R. A. *Torrey Mission to Cambridge University in 1911, which led to a surge of spiritual life in Cambridge and strengthened the CICCU as a spiritual force in undergraduate circles. His spiritual outlook was dominated by the Keswick style, which he promoted vigorously all his life.

Mowll served on the staff of Wycliffe College, Canada, from 1913 to 1922, except for some months in 1918 as an army chaplain in France. In a series of long summer tours he held parish missions or visited isolated Wycliffe men, rather than engaging in scholarly writing.

On 24 June 1922 Mowll was consecrated as an assistant bishop for the diocese of West China, largely staffed by the Church Missionary Society (CMS). He resided at Cheng-tu in Western Szechwan, which was the home of the West China University, founded by missionary societies. In 1924 he married Dorothy Anne Martin. He tried hard to wrestle with the language, but mostly had to rely on interpreters, notably his wife. In 1926 he became Bishop of West China, responsible for CMS personnel in Western Szechwan and China Inland Mission workers in Eastern Szechwan. His ten years in China were crowded with travel, adventure and excitement; he and Dorothy were captured and held to ransom by brigands in 1925, robbed by river pirates, and clubbed and stabbed in 1931.

Mowll saw the need for a strong indigenous church. He fostered evangelistic work among students in the West China University. He led efforts to train Chinese clergy for leadership. He was responsible for the consecration of C. T. Song as an assistant bishop in Western Szechwan and Ho-lin Ku as an assistant bishop in Eastern Szechwan. He was the bridge from the paternal age to the progressive age of Chinese bishops as he transferred control from the missionary conference to the diocesan synod.

In 1933 Mowll was elected Archbishop of Sydney in succession to John Charles Wright, as the candidate of conservative evangelicals fearful of another leader tolerant of liberal tendencies. With enormous energy he had soon visited every parish and institution. He possessed a phenomenal memory and an amazing grasp of detail. He made good use of his height of six feet four inches (193 cm). He was especially concerned about CMS, which had not yet recovered from the Depression. No new missionaries had been sent out; it was in debt to the parent society; missionary vision was in decline. At Moore Theological College standards had fallen and finance was lacking. The Home Mission Society's vision had faded; its affairs were largely static. Mowll reinvigorated all three agencies and they were soon flourishing.

Mowll's election had bitter repercussions. Liberal evangelical clergy soon joined with other disaffected men to form the Anglican Fellowship (29 April 1933). 'The idea,' wrote Canon Garnsey, 'is to work against the power of the machine in Church politics and to consolidate the influence of those who love the light.' Their opposition coloured Mowll's first five years in Sydney. They felt that Mowll's policy was weighted against their interests, notably his choice of T. C. *Hammond as principal of Moore College. Many criticisms levelled against Mowll had little to do with him and more to do with the powerful conservative evangelical Anglican Church League (ACL). Nevertheless, they culminated in 1938 in a Memorial from the disaffected clergy asking for a conference. The Memorial caused Mowll acute embarrassment. He handled it poorly; there was prolonged delay, and he was badly advised by Hammond. Signatories were soon stripped of elective posts in the diocese by vengeful ACL leaders. By patience and kindness, Mowll eventually regained the respect and goodwill of surviving Memorialists, but the conservative character of the diocese of Sydney was reinforced.

All Mowll's latent strength was called forth with the outbreak of war, along with the devoted energies of his wife. Plans were set afoot at once to provide for the spiritual, moral and social welfare of men and women in uniform. The Church of England National Emergency Fund (CENEF) and the Sydney Diocesan Churchwomen's Association came into being. They organized the delivery of huts for rest and recreation to the cathedral grounds and to army camps, hostels to provide overnight accommodation for men and women on leave, mobile canteens to serve others on duty, special equipment for chaplains in the armed services, and a host of voluntary workers. CENEF was to maintain its great community service after the war through the CENEF Memorial Centre in the heart of Sydney. Meanwhile, in spite of the many clergy who were released to serve as chaplains and the falling numbers of men in training for ordination, Mowll continued his drive to strengthen the parochial and spiritual life of the diocese, demonstrated in his major effort to secure church buildings, however exiguous, which would serve out-lying districts. The motor car made many of these new churches unnecessary within a few decades. His emphasis on well-resourced and coordinated youth work yielded great dividends to the diocese for decades to come.

Having been denied the post in 1935 by suspicious High Church bishops, Mowll was elected Primate of the Church of England in Australia in November 1947. This office broadened his field of action as he strove to make it as effective as possible. He led the Australian bishops at the Lambeth Conference and was present in Amsterdam for the formation of the World Council of Churches in 1948. He arranged for Dr Fisher, the Archbishop of Canterbury, to visit Australia in 1950. He launched the South East Asia Appeal through the Australian Board of Missions and CMS in 1953. He travelled throughout Australia to encourage every diocese. He led a small delegation to the church in China in 1956. As Primate, he helped to guide the long-drawn-out efforts to achieve an acceptable constitution for the Church of England in Australia, despite the fears of ACL leaders that this would constrain the conservative evangelical character of the diocese of Sydney. Mowll rejoiced when his own diocesan synod gave its formal consent in 1957. The death of Dorothy Mowll in December of that year was the prelude to the breakdown of his own health, and he died a year later.

Mowll was a big man, with a big voice and a commanding presence, who was never afraid to accept the burden of responsibility, despite privately fearing that he might prove inadequate for it. His skill in personal relations and decision-making grew with experience. He was always a fertile source of new plans and ideas, and he had the gift of knowing how to translate them into practice, even though not all could be made to work. He was a totally committed evangelical in faith and churchmanship, always promoting Keswick spirituality. His gift for friendship and his hospitable spirit allowed him to cultivate cordial relations with those from whom he differed. He was appointed CMG in 1954.

Bibliography
M. L. Loane, 'Mowll, H. W. K.', in B. Dickey (ed.), *The Australian Dictionary of Evangelical Biography* (Sydney: Evangelical History Association, 1994); M. L. Loane, *Archbishop Mowll* (London: Hodder & Stoughton, 1960); S. Judd and K. Cable, *Sydney Anglicans* (Sydney: AIO, 1987); S. Piggin, *Evangelical Christianity in Australia* (Melbourne: Oxford University Press, 1996).

B. DICKEY

■ **MÜLLER, George** (1805–1898), philanthropist, pastor and preacher, is famed for the orphanages he established in Bristol, England, which he maintained without any direct appeal for funds. Müller's example of 'living by faith' proved inspirational for many other evangelical causes.

Müller was born in Kroppenstaedt, Prussia, on 27 September 1805. His father intended that Müller should become a clergyman, primarily to ensure that his son secured a comfortable living. Müller entered Halle University in 1825, so becoming entitled to preach in the Lutheran Church, notwithstanding the fact that his spasmodic attempts to reform himself had effected little change in the dissolute behaviour that had characterized his youth. A permanent transformation in Müller's lifestyle followed his conversion at a private prayer meeting in Halle late in 1825. Although deciding almost immediately that he should be a missionary, he completed his study but ceased to accept financial support from his father, who was infuriated by his plans. This experience of living without organized financial support was Müller's first. In February 1829 he left Berlin for London to train with the London Society for Promoting Christianity amongst the Jews, having with difficulty secured exemption for Prussian military service on health grounds through the intervention of sympathetic army officers.

Once in England, tension developed between Müller's desire to be free to preach the gospel as he felt led and the organizational requirements of the missionary society. His views were being influenced by those later recognized as founders of the Brethren movement, most significantly Anthony Norris Groves, a dentist who decided to sell his considerable possessions, abandon any links with a missionary society and go into the mission field simply trusting the Lord to meet his needs. Müller's missionary society was not amenable to his request that he be allowed a freer hand as to where and to whom he preached, and his connection with the society ended in early 1830. Within months, however, Müller had accepted an invitation to become minister of Ebenezer Chapel in Teignmouth, Devon.

By this time Müller was confident that God would provide for his material needs whether or not he was in receipt of a salary. In October 1830 he married Mary Groves, the sister of A. N. Groves, and shortly after their marriage they decided to 'live by faith'. Müller no longer accepted his salary on the basis that it was made up of pew rents which were socially discriminatory, that it might include monies that had not been given freely, and that being paid by the congregation might influence his teaching (he was shifting doctrinally at that time from infant to believer's baptism). Müller was also emulating other trends currently emerging within the embryonic Brethren group in Dublin. At Ebenezer Chapel he inaugurated a weekly celebration of the Lord's Supper, as well as open meetings that provided opportunity for lay members to offer exhortation or teaching, in recognition of the priesthood of all believers.

In May 1832 Müller accepted a call to be co-minister with Henry Craik of Gideon Chapel in Bristol, and within weeks a second congregation had begun meeting in the empty Bethesda Chapel in the heart of the city. Craik, like his friend Müller, had been powerfully influenced by Groves' attitude to possessions, and both Craik and Müller 'lived by faith' from the outset of their joint work. They were initially supported by way of voluntary donations placed in a box with their names above it at the back of the church, but even this arrangement was dropped in 1842 as they felt it could give the impression that they were the only 'ministers'. Thereafter, any gifts had to be brought to their homes or conveyed in some other way.

Müller's epithet, the 'Father of Orphans', grew out of his plan, formulated in 1835, to open an orphanage in Bristol. The institution was founded before the publication of Charles Dickens' Oliver Twist in 1837, which drew public attention to the plight of orphans, and at a time when private orphanages were still rare and regarded as somewhat revolutionary experiments. No more than a dozen had so far been founded in England, and all of these were in London or the Home Counties. While a student at Halle, Müller had lodged briefly in an orphan house built by the German Pietist, Auguste *Franke, but his desire 'to do something ... for the supply of the temporal wants of poor children' was matched by a perceived spiritual imperative. In his mind, the culture of the age was coloured by the scepticism of rational thought and scientific enquiry, which seemed to undermine the validity of orthodox Christianity's supernatural claims and led to a decline in popular belief. Müller's aim in founding an orphanage was to strengthen the faith of believers through 'a visible proof' that God was still the same as in the past. Providing for the care of orphans through organized philanthropic activity would not meet this purpose. Only miraculous provision in direct response to prayer would arouse confidence in a living and personal God. From 1836 the orphanage work expanded steadily until by 1870 five purpose-built orphanage buildings had been opened on Ashley Down, Bristol, housing 2,000 orphans. Notwithstanding periods of severe personal hardship for Müller, the entire work was undertaken without a commitment to finance it from any source, individual or corporate, and without ever soliciting funds or stating its needs. In 1865 Müller was visited by James Hudson *Taylor, an ardent admirer of Müller's principles, whose China Inland Mission (later Overseas Missionary Fellowship) would be run on similar 'faith' lines.

In addition to the orphanages, Müller had founded in 1834 'The Scriptural Knowledge Institution for Home and Abroad' to stimulate scriptural teaching in Sunday schools and other educational establishments and to distribute Bibles and support missionary work. Between 1875 and 1892 Müller himself undertook a series of extensive preaching tours within the British Isles and in Europe, North America, India, Australia and New Zealand. He remained active in Bristol until his death at home on 10 March 1898 in his ninety-third year.

Müller became a revered figure within the Brethren movement, which grew dramatically from the mid-nineteenth century. Bethesda Chapel, Bristol, was at the epicentre of the schism which divided the young movement in 1848. Müller and Craik were reluctant to allow their church to be drawn into the controversy which had arisen in the Brethren congregation at Plymouth between B. J. *Newton and J. N. *Darby, both learned and strong-minded leaders of the movement. This hesitation was interpreted by Darby (possibly the most influential Brethren figure at the time), who was of an impulsive nature, as tantamount to endorsing certain purportedly heretical doctrine, prompting him to declare excommunicated any Brethren congregations which refused to sever links with Bethesda Chapel. Darby's actions were highly provocative, and when he made a personal move to reopen the matter the following year Müller did not warm to his approach. The division of Brethren into so-called 'open' and 'exclusive' streams was sealed.

It is, however, primarily on account of his notable ministry among orphans that Müller is renowned. Although he was not the first to adopt the principle of 'living by faith' in modern times, the practical quality of his faith has frequently been commended as a model for Christian life and service.

Bibliography

N. Garton, *George Müller and His Orphans* (London: Hodder & Stoughton, 1963); G. Müller, *The Autobiography of George Müller* (London: J. Nisbet, ³1914); R. Steer, *George Müller: Delighted in God* (London: Hodder & Stoughton, 1975).

R. N. SHUFF

■ **MULLINS, Edgar Young** (1860–1928), Southern Baptist leader and theologian, set himself between fundamentalists who exalt an infallible and authoritative Scripture and modernists who discount all authority. In his intentionally moderate theological position, religious experience is the definitive characteristic of evangelicalism. While fundamentalists and liberals engaged in trench warfare during the early twentieth century, Mullins sought to hold an increasingly tenuous middle ground on this basis. In *Faith in the Modern World* (1930), he declared simply, 'I am an evangelical Christian.'

Born in Mississippi during the Reconstruction era, Edgar Young moved with his father, a Baptist farmer-preacher, to Corsicana, Texas, at the age of eight. He joined the inaugural class at the Agricultural and Mechanical College of Texas before experiencing personal conversion in 1880 at a revival in Dallas. Sensing a call to ministry, Mullins entered the Southern Baptist Theological Seminary in 1881 and received his only earned degree (a 'Full Graduate' diploma) from that institution in 1885. He subsequently pursued part-time studies at Johns Hopkins University in Baltimore and Newton Theological Institution in Boston. A gifted speaker, he was granted an honorary doctorate in 1895 by Carson-Newman College. Mullins married Isla May Hawley in 1886. Their two sons, Edgar Wheeler and Roy Granberry, died prematurely. Ordained a Southern Baptist pastor at the Harrodsburg, Kentucky, First Baptist Church in 1885, he led increasingly prominent churches at Lee Street in Baltimore (1888–1895) and Newton Centre in Boston (1896–1899). His first denominational service, at the Foreign Mission Board of the Southern Baptist Convention (SBC), ended summarily after personality conflicts with his superior (1895–1896).

Looking for a compromise candidate after the rancorous debate over Baptist origins between the 'high church' or 'Baptist successionism' Landmarkists and William Heth Whitsitt, a proponent of the case for a seventeenth-century origin for Baptists, the trustees of Southern Baptist Theological Seminary selected Mullins to be their new president in 1899. Mullins had written against Landmarkism, but his contributions went unnoticed. Originally assigned to teach church history, a field in which he had little expertise, Mullins gratefully gravitated to Southern's chair of theology after an opponent resigned that post. Mullins's amateur understanding of history did not, however, keep him from using historiography to redefine Baptist principles. Mullins also served as president of the SBC during the crucial years of the fundamentalist–modernist controversies (1921–1924) and as president of the Baptist World Alliance during its formative years (1923–1928).

Theologically, the Southern Seminary president was concerned with apologetics, freedom and authority, and systematic theology.

Mullins's first apologetic work *Why Is Christianity True?* (1905) identified four classes of facts favouring the Christian worldview, but it was the third, 'Christian experience', which he emphasized. Drawing on the religious psychology of William James and the personalist philosophy of Borden Parker Bowne, Mullins sought to reach the cultured despisers of Christianity in emulation of Friedrich Schleiermacher, but without embracing the latter's pantheism. Two decades later, apologetics again became a major concern for Mullins. In *Christianity at the Cross Roads* (1924) he responded to the debates over scientific evolution and historical criticism. His moderate conclusion was to separate science, philosophy and religion into autonomous spheres, whose experts respected disciplinary boundaries.

In his most popular work, *The Axioms of Religion* (1908), Mullins addressed the issue of freedom and authority by reinterpreting Baptist history. Having vilified the Landmarkists, with their high ecclesiology, as 'a Roman Catholic party among the Baptists', he now adopted their language of 'Baptist distinctives', redefining these in terms of modern individualism. Ranging between four and seven in number, these axioms included divine sovereignty over individuals, equal rights of access to God for all souls, equal privileges in the church, responsible and free morality, a free church in a free state, and a mild form of the Social Gospel. All of the axioms were encapsulated in a new term, 'soul competency', by which Mullins meant a pre-regeneration capacity in humans to deal directly with God apart from any human mediation. In *Freedom and Authority in Religion* (1913) Mullins interacted with the denial of all external authority by Auguste Sabatier, whose work he considered 'brilliant'. Mullins partially adopted Sabatier's programme, which opposed the freedom of the spirit inherent within man to the supposed tyranny of Roman Catholic credalism. To this inherent 'subjective' authority, Mullins added the 'objective' authority of the New Testament. It is in the subjective experience of the Christ of the New Testament that religious authority is found. Freedom and authority are perfectly correlated in Christ, who respects the basic human right of access to God. In an anthropocentric conclusion, Mullins makes humans the subject and God the object of this religious relation.

The Southern Baptist leader's systematic theology is detailed in his *magnum opus*, *The Christian Religion in Its Doctrinal Expression* (1917), and summarized in *Baptist Beliefs* (1912). Although its theological content was generally conservative, his methodological dependence on experience paralleled the employment of religious consciousness in the liberal agenda established by Schleiermacher. Mullins sought to ground doctrine first in personal experience but without denigrating Scripture. This subjective emphasis led him to reject some 'abstract theories' in the Calvinism he learned from the first president of Southern Seminary, James Petigru Boyce. Thus, an exalted anthropology with a strong sense of God's immanence permeated his work. He viewed the Bible as the authoritative literary source of theology, yet merely a record of the supreme authority, God's personal revelation in Jesus Christ. His short treatment of the Trinity in *Christian Religion* affirms both the immanent and economic trinitarian relations in the Godhead, but *Baptist Beliefs* offers a modalist interpretation. After reviewing various theories of the atonement, he settled on a holistic view incorporating elements from both the Godward and humanward theories. He denied that the atonement was limited in scope, and tried to balance the human and divine activities in salvation. Regeneration in Christ is correlated with 'self-realization', 'self-determination' and a Nietzschean 'will to believe'. Due to his distrust of human mediation and to his embrace of atomistic individualism, ecclesiology is entirely absent from his major work and receives only cursory treatment in the smaller book.

From his position as president of the premier Southern Baptist seminary, Mullins created an institutional and theological legacy still felt among Southern Baptists. He led the moderate party of the SBC in its efforts to steer a course between fundamentalism and modernism. In the 1920s, however, fundamentalism became dominant, and Mullins atypically found himself presenting a lengthy confession, *The Baptist Faith and Message*, to the 1925 convention. Paradoxically, his participation in denominational fundraising led to the creation of a powerful institutionalism in the SBC, in spite of his apprehension over ecclesiastical structures. Mullins's *Christian Religion in Its Doctrinal Expression* was used in Southern Baptist seminaries until the 1950s, and his *Axioms of Religion* was twice revised by his followers. In the SBC today, moderates and liberals consider his theological work as definitive, while conservatives are more comfortable with his institutional legacy.

Bibliography

W. Carrell, 'Edgar Young Mullins and the Competency of the Soul in Religion' (PhD dissertation, Baylor University, 1993); W. E. Ellis, *A Man of Books and a Man of the People* (Mercer University Press, 1985); I. M. Mullins, *Edgar Young Mullins: An Intimate Biography* (Nashville: Baptist Sunday School Board, 1929).

M. B. YARNELL, III

■ **MURRAY, Andrew** (1828–1917), Dutch Reformed minister, was born on 9 May 1828 in Graaff Reinet, South Africa, the second son of the Revd Andrew Murray, minister of the small Eastern Cape town. With his brother John he was sent to Aberdeen in Scotland at the age of ten for seven years. There they obtained MA degrees from Marischal College and were influenced by revivalists such as Thomas *Chalmers, Robert Murray *McCheyne and W. C. Burns, who led the 'disruption' of the Scottish state church in 1843. In 1845 the Murray brothers moved to Utrecht in Holland to study Dutch as well as theology. Murray was to receive honorary doctorates from Aberdeen in 1898 and Cape Town in 1907.

In 1845 Andrew Murray wrote to his father describing his conversion: 'I have been led to surrender myself wholly to Christ.' In Holland his views became firmly conservative and hostile to what he saw as the spiritual and moral stagnation around him. Although Murray was rooted in Calvinism and a conservative view of the Bible, he was able to appreciate those outside his tradition. In later life he named his home 'Clairvaux' after the Cistercian monk St Bernard of Clairvaux, was deeply influenced by the eighteenth-century Englishman, William Law, and left a biography of *Zinzendorf uncompleted at his death. Murray described Law as 'one of the most influential and inspiring authors on the Christian life with whom I have come into contact' and published six books of extracts from Law's works. It was the mysticism of these writers that touched Murray, agreeing with his own stress on the need for faith to be an inner reality in the believer's life.

In 1848 Andrew and John Murray were ordained into the Dutch Reformed Church (DRC) on Andrew's twentieth birthday and returned to South Africa. Because of his youth Andrew Murray could not have his own parish, but he was allowed to minister to the isolated communities across the Orange River, from a base at Bloemfontein. Murray ministered until 1860 across a colossal area, encompassing the modern Orange Free State, and showed concern where he could for communities in what is now the Transvaal. In 1856 he married Emma Rutherford, with whom he had eleven children. Murray assiduously travelled across the interior of South Africa, notwithstanding the threat of disease, a difficult climate, sporadic civil unrest and occasional difficulties with lions and snakes. In all this travelling his zeal was undimmed.

In 1860 the Murray family moved to Worcester in the Western Cape. There Murray experienced the revival for which he had often prayed. It occurred in a multi-racial prayer meeting of young people, and Murray's first response was to shout out, 'Silence ... I am your minister sent from God. Silence.' When no notice was taken of his commands, Murray eventually concluded that it was he who was in the wrong. In 1864 the Murrays moved to a Cape Town parish. In 1871 Murray was inducted at Wellington, where he worked until his retirement in 1906 and where he died, on 18 January 1918. Wellington provided a base from which he travelled extensively. Between 1879 and 1891 he conducted seven evangelistic campaigns in South Africa with great effect. Wellington was also the site for much of Murray's educational work. He modelled his Huguenot Seminary for women on the American Mount Holyoke Seminary, importing teachers from the latter and later opened a boys' boarding school. More widely, Murray was a great promoter of institutions; the South African General Mission, the YMCA in South Africa, the South African counterparts to the English Keswick Convention, the Student Christian Association and a Prayer Union were all either founded by Murray or owed a great debt to his work. Mission work in what is now Zimbabwe and Malawi owed much to Murray's prompting. Contemporary South Africa is closer to the USA than to Western Europe in the prominence it gives to Christianity. To the extent that this prominence can be attributed to the ministry of individuals, Andrew Murray is one of those most responsible for it.

In theology Murray was firmly, but never dryly, conservative. Amidst much conflict between conservatives and liberals, Murray proved an adept apologist. As moderator of the Synod in 1862, Murray found himself locked in conflict with another minister, J. J. Kotze, who questioned the Heidelberg Confession's stress on the sinfulness of humanity. Murray and the synod lost the resulting legal battle, but won the battle in the church as a whole. He was to be moderator of the DRC synod a further five times, in 1876, 1883, 1886, 1890 and 1894.

However, Murray's heart lay in devotional, not doctrinal, theology. His numerous writings are primarily devotional in character and his main contribution lay in his role within the holiness movement. After years of exhausting ministry in the interior of South Africa, Murray was painfully aware of an inner lack of peace which belied his outward fervour. A revival at Worcester in 1860,

events in Oxford and Brighton in 1870 and an unspecified evening in his study in Cape Town led him into a new depth of Christian experience, which caused him to affirm 'the possibility of unbroken communion with Jesus personally'. Just as justification was by faith, so holiness was by faith: 'We need not wait to enter heaven to have a noble, holy, great mind. It is attainable even here ... it may be ours through the indwelling of the Holy Spirit of God, through receiving Christ as our sanctification as well as our justification.' Murray came to believe in two distinct stages in the Christian life; belief was insufficient without the indwelling of the Spirit. Whether or not this second stage was called a 'baptism of the Spirit', something like it was needed in the life of the believer. The lack of the Spirit was the primary cause of the weakness of the church. Murray's personal life was characterized by a desire to seek concord and avoid confrontation: 'He had a very gracious way of getting rid of cranks without hurting them.'

Murray was well aware of developments in Europe and America, notably the writings of George *Müller, Hudson *Taylor, Broadman and Cullis. After a two year period in the early 1880s when illness left him unable to preach, Murray emerged more than ever convinced of the role of the Spirit, in which the believer's part was simply to have faith and wait upon the Spirit's work.

Alongside this teaching, Murray strongly emphasized providence. Prayer was crucial; God would answer and send his Spirit. Murray was a key figure in the DRC's practice of setting aside the ten days between Ascension Day and Pentecost to pray for a outpouring of the Spirit. From this view of providence in turn came an emphasis on healing, reinforced by his own experience of the work of Bethshan, a healing institution in London. Murray declared, 'Sick Christian, open thy Bible, study it and see in its pages that sickness is a warning to renounce sin, but that whoever acknowledges and forsakes his sins finds in Jesus pardon and healing.' Elsewhere, Murray could be less trenchant, but his views provided much support for those who saw sickness as simply due to sin and who saw healing as simply a matter of prayer and faith rather than of medical care.

Murray's influence through his holiness

teaching was extremely widespread. In five visits to Europe and two to the USA he influenced the important Keswick and North-field Conventions. The 1895 Keswick Convention was the only one in which he took a major role and was described as 'outstandingly that of Andrew Murray'. Murray's book *Abide In Christ* was published in 1882 and enjoyed immense sales. His teachings touched such diverse groups as the African Independent Churches, the Inter-Varsity Fellowship and Watchman *Nee. He acted as mentor for Pieter Le Roux, who was to be a key figure in the establishment of Pentecostalism in South Africa.

Murray has been accused of promoting a narrow pietism that both ignored the social conditions of his own day and encouraged Christians to accept, or not oppose, the racial intolerance of the twentieth century. Although Murray's views can be used to advocate political quiescence, his own life was not lived in detachment from the wider world. In his early ministry Murray was a friend of Boer leaders such as Potgieter and Pretorius, serving as interpreter (and informal arbitrator) at the Sand River Convention between the Boers and the British in 1852 and travelling to Britain in 1854–1855 to seek the retention of British authority over the Free State. Shortly before the Anglo-Boer War broke out in 1899 Murray appealed to British opinion to discourage conflict. By then he had grow more positive about Afrikaner nationalism: 'a more strongly developed national life in our half-slumbering Dutch population will afford a more vigorous stock for the Christian life to be grafted on'. Whilst deeply concerned for Afrikaner welfare during the war, Murray readily prayed with his Anglican counterparts and eschewed bitterness. In 1913 he had a prominent role in the unveiling of a monument to the Boer women and children killed during the war, but at the same time opposed the ultra-nationalist, D. F. Malan.

The 'racial problem' was seen primarily in Murray's lifetime in terms of the tension between the British and the Afrikaners. But Murray was not unconcerned with the black population. On the slavery question, his father had been a strong abolitionist, and Murray was concerned about the mal-treatment of black people. He was a great supporter of missionary work and hostile to colour prejudice, which jeopardized missionary progress. At the same time, he was willing to live with a DRC resolution of 1857 which allowed separate worship for whites and blacks as a necessary expedient, although he could not have envisaged how such worship would become the norm. Murray's close connections with the emerging Afrikaner nation meant that he was heavily involved in its social and political life. For social groups with whom he had fewer links, he was less active, even though during his lifetime major injustices were perpetrated against the black population. Murray's emphasis on evangelism, personal spirituality and irenic attitude offered resources with which to resist systematic racism.

Andrew Murray was one of the most remarkable Christians to be produced by South Africa. A man of enormous energy, he exercised a deep influence on the nature of the emerging country. His ministry, evangelism and promotion of welfare touched the whole of South Africa and other parts of Africa. The isolated communities of the early and mid-nineteenth century were often only nominal in their religious practice. Murray was crucial in strengthening the hold that the DRC developed on the Afrikaner people and on many others besides. Murray was far from indifferent to social and political issues, particularly as they affected the Afrikaner community. His voice was essentially irenic amid the conflicts of the times. Regarding the black population, his primary concerns were evangelism and, to a lesser degree, welfare. Murray's lack of concern for its growing political disabilities and the highly personal tone of his spirituality left an unfortunate legacy for twentieth-century South African Christians faced with apartheid. Yet whilst Murray might have done more to prevent racial abuses, he was not to blame for the way his successors misused his legacy. On a wider level, Murray was a significant figure in the Holiness Movement. By his speeches at conventions and by his writings he did much to popularize its insights and promoted the growth of many brands of Christianity besides that of his own DRC.

Bibliography

W. M. Douglas, *Andrew Murray and his Message: One of God's Choice Saints*

(London: Oliphants, 1926); J. Du Plessis, *The Life of Andrew Murray of South Africa* (London: Marshall, 1919).

D. J. GOODHEW

■ **MURRAY, John** (1898–1975), Scottish theologian, was born on a small croft near Bonar Bridge, Sutherlandshire. Murray was reared in a deeply pious home within the Free Presbyterian Church of Scotland and received his early education at Bonar Bridge Primary School and Dornoch Academy. He enlisted in April 1917 in the Royal Highlanders (Black Watch) and served in France, losing the sight of his right eye during the last German offensive. Following honourable discharge he studied at Glasgow University (MA 1923). After graduation, he began tutor-based training for the FPC ministry under Donald Beaton, who, in 1924, encouraged him to continue his studies at Princeton Seminary; its faculty then included such luminaries as Geerhardus Vos, J. Gresham *Machen and C. W. Hodge.

Murray proved an outstanding student ('Few students have maintained as high a level of scholarship' noted the *Princeton Seminary Bulletin*), but following his graduation in 1927 he found himself in difficulties of conscience over his views on the use of public transport *en route* to Sunday worship. Rather than pursue ordination he took advantage of the Gelston-Winthrop Scholarship he had won at Princeton to undertake graduate studies at New College, Edinburgh. Invited to return to Princeton, he joined the faculty in 1929, precisely the year in which Machen, with others (O. T. Allis, Robert Dick Wilson and the young Cornelius *Van Til and some fifty students) left to form the fledgling Westminster Seminary in Philadelphia, convinced that a theological malaise was destroying the old Princeton orthodoxy. Murray's sympathies lay with the new work, and in 1930 he joined the faculty in Philadelphia. There he remained until retirement in 1966. Returning to the family croft near Bonar Bridge, and having remained a bachelor until retirement age, he married his longtime friend Valerie Knowlton, a professor of anatomy at the Woman's Medical College in Philadelphia (and a former student). They had two children, the second of whom survived her father's death in 1975 by only a few months.

During his long tenure at Westminster, whose rigorous academic standards made it a seed-bed for new scholars, Murray came to be regarded as probably the most significant orthodox reformed theologian in the English-speaking world. Deeply influenced by *Calvin and the Puritan tradition, he married that inheritance to the orthodoxy of Princeton's Charles *Hodge and B. B. *Warfield within the context of Vos's biblical theology ('the most penetrating exegete it has been my privilege to know'). His lectures were heavily exegetical as he sought to recover a biblical way of doing systematic theology, in sharp contrast to the contemporary decline of the enterprise into a discussion of the views of the theologians. Thus he would later argue that systematic theology must be rooted in biblical exegesis, but also that 'biblical theology is regulative of exegesis. It coordinates and synthesizes the whole witness of Scripture in the various topics with which it deals'.

Like Warfield before him, Murray did not compile his own systematic theology, but saw his contribution as standing within the Calvin-Hodge-Warfield-Vos tradition, developing orthodox formulations in line with biblical teaching. His major contributions appeared in a series of monographs which were crowned by his impressive two-volume commentary on Romans (Grand Rapids: Eerdmans, 1960, 1965).

Covenant theology belongs to the central nervous system of classical reformed theology. Murray's Tyndale Lecture on this theme, *The Covenant of Grace* (London: Tyndale Press, 1954), sought to formulate it biblically by identifying the nature of divine covenants in Scripture. He distanced himself from the historical tendency to define a covenant in terms of contemporary usage as a compact or agreement. Rather, in Scripture it is a 'sovereign administration of grace and promise' (pp. 7–8). His conviction that 'covenant' has an essentially redemptive or restorative quality inevitably raised for him the question of whether the classical reformed dual covenant formulation (covenant of works/covenant of grace) was altogether consistent with Scripture.

A related topic was the focus of his monograph *The Imputation of Adam's Sin* (Grand

Rapids: Eerdmans, 1959). The topic had been one of ongoing interest in American Presbyterian theology since the time of Jonathan *Edwards. Murray himself had studied it under C. W. Hodge. Although Murray rejected the idea of an Adamic covenant ('covenant of works') and preferred the terminology 'the Adamic administration', he nevertheless vigorously contended, on the basis of exacting exegetical study, for the immediate (rather than mediate) imputation of Adam's sin to all of his posterity. Thus, while distancing himself from the classical reformed federal formulation, he espoused the most rigorous form of the doctrine of the imputation of sin.

Elements of his biblical-theological perspective had already emerged in a popular presentation of redemption which Murray had penned under the title *Redemption – Accomplished and Applied* (Grand Rapids: Eerdmans, 1955; London: Banner of Truth, 1961). The second part (redemption applied) had been written as a series of magazine articles, but the first part, written in a somewhat less popular style, focused on the nature of the atonement. Here Murray took up the biblical Adam-Christ parallel in stressing the importance of the obedience of Christ as the 'inclusive category in terms of which the atoning work of Christ may be viewed' (p. 24). Throughout his work a strong emphasis is found not only on both the active and passive obedience of Christ but also on the progressive nature of that obedience: not from imperfection to perfection, but from childhood through to maturity.

Within this context, Murray was a committed exponent of effectual redemption. While radically disagreeing with the views of his fellow Scot John McLeod Campbell (1800–1872) on the *extent* of the atonement, he recognized that the central issue at stake was, as Campbell had claimed, the *nature* of the atonement. Murray held equally firmly to 'limited' atonement and to the free offer of the gospel.

Murray's interest in the ethical dimensions of the gospel came to expression in a variety of publications. From 1946 to 1949 he contributed a series of articles to *The Westminster Theological Journal* (of which he was an editor) on the theme of the biblical teaching on divorce. Arguing that Scripture allowed divorce (and therefore remarriage) for Christians on only two grounds (adultery and the desertion of a believer by an unbeliever), he made the striking suggestion that in view of the current confusion in legislation in this area, the church should give serious consideration to providing recognition for divorce on biblical grounds. Equally striking is the fact that, flying in the face of the assumption that the Bible enables us to solve every human problem, in one of his illustrations Murray comments that 'we are not able to answer (concerning the legitimacy of remarriage) dogmatically one way or the other' (*Divorce*, Philadelphia: Committee on Christian Education, Orthodox Presbyterian Church, 1953, p. 115).

Murray's interest in ethics came to full expression in his Payton Lectures given at Fuller Theological Seminary in 1955. Published in expanded form under the title *Principles of Conduct* (Grand Rapids: Eerdmans, 1957), they expressed his 'attempt to apply to the ethic of Scripture something of the biblico-theological method, understanding "Biblical Theology" in the sense defined by Geerhardus Vos as "that branch of Exegetical Theology which deals with the process of the self revelation of God deposited in the Bible"' (p. 7). In particular, Murray demonstrated the basis for ethical action in the nature of creation and the creation ordinances established in the early chapters of Genesis, the continuing validity of the moral law, and the harmony between grace and law, law and love, and the indicatives and imperatives of the gospel.

A notable section in *Principles* sought to show how the New Testament's doctrine of union with Christ in his death and resurrection provided the dynamic required for the realization of the Christian ethic. Here Murray emphasized 'definitive sanctification', underlining the New Testament's stress on sanctification as an already accomplished reality with profound ongoing implications.

In *Principles* Murray also stated a conviction to which he gave, in the testimony of colleagues and students alike, rich personal expression: the fear of God is 'the soul of godliness ... the sum of piety'. (The echo of Calvin in the latter phrase is not accidental.)

Murray's combination of exegetical skills, theological acumen, biblical theology and personal godliness made him N. B. Stonehouse's choice to author the New International Commentary on Romans. This, alongside the posthumously published four volumes of his *Collected Writings* (Edinburgh: Banner of Truth, 1976–1983), provide the capstone to a theological contribution which widely influenced the resurgence of interest in classical reformed orthodoxy in the second half of the twentieth century.

Bibliography
I. H. Murray, *The Life of John Murray* (Edinburgh: Banner of Truth Trust, 1984).
S. B. FERGUSON

■ **NASH, Clifford Harris** (1866–1958), Anglican clergyman and founding principal of the Melbourne Bible Institute, was born in Brixton, London, on 16 December 1866.

Nash was educated at Oundle School in Northamptonshire. From there he won a classical scholarship to Corpus Christi College, Cambridge (BA 1888, MA 1900). His time at Cambridge (1885–1889) was crucial in the development of his evangelicalism. J. B. Lightfoot and B. F. Westcott had established a tradition of careful biblical scholarship that provided a viable alternative to scepticism and dogmatic assertion. In later life Nash said that he believed that the Cambridge scholars were critical in keeping Anglican evangelicals on track. He often referred to the influence that Westcott had on him.

Corpus Christi had by the 1880s become a stronghold of the evangelical movement. Its ethos had an impact on Nash. After Corpus Christi he studied for a year at Ridley Hall under H. C. G. *Moule, who influenced Nash in at least four areas: in scholarship (Nash's later teaching and preaching from the Greek text were reminiscent of Moule's daily expositions at Ridley); in holiness (Moule was closely associated with Keswick, and Nash with the Upwey, later Belgrave Heights, Convention); in pastoral counselling (through which Nash would be influential); and in the very Anglican character of Nash's evangelicalism.

After Cambridge Nash taught at Loretto School in Musselburgh near Edinburgh for eighteen months. He was ordained deacon in 1890 by Westcott at Durham and went to a curacy at St Peter's, Huddersfield, in York-shire. His curacy was interrupted by a world tour with a Cambridge friend, Robin Barclay of the Barclay's Bank family. On his return, he was priested by Bishop William Walsham How in Wakefield Cathedral on 26 February 1893 and settled down to a promising career. However, one evening in 1895 he impetuously tried to kiss the vicar's daughter. On being rebuffed, he apologized, insisting that he intended nothing more than a kiss, but her father over-reacted and refused to recommend him to another parish. Nash was devastated. (When asked later in life what had been the most significant influences on him Nash paused and said, 'my failures', but did not elaborate.) He resigned and sailed to Tasmania to begin a new life in the Antipodes. There he became superintendent of a settlement for unemployed men until February 1897, when Bishop William Saumarez Smith of Sydney invited him to resume his career. In Sydney he was curate of two churches and *locum tenens* of another, and in January 1899 he married Louise Mary Maude Pearse.

Nash's ability quickly drew people's attention, and at the end of 1899 he was offered the incumbency of St Columb's, Hawthorn, one of Melbourne's leading parishes. During his time at St Columb's (1900–1906), the parish continued to flourish, and he built up a reputation as a preacher and leading evangelical. He also engaged in a number of extra-parochial activities. He began home mission work in the Dandenong Ranges; he was involved in the founding of St Hilda's, a training home for deaconesses and female missionary candidates for the China Inland Mission; he was appointed a lecturer in (the diocesan) St John's Theological College; he was a founding member of the Parker Union, a society of evangelical clergy with scholarly interests; he was elected a member of General Synod; and he was made a canon of St Paul's Cathedral.

In September 1906 Nash became vicar of Christ Church, Geelong. A year later allegations concerning his friendship with a servant girl at Hawthorn were brought against him. In a split vote the Cathedral Chapter found him guilty of indiscretion and asked him to resign, which he did, though protesting his innocence. His resignation aroused strong opposition from clergy and laity to Archbishop Lowther Clarke; petitions were taken up and Christ Church renominated Nash a number of times in spite of Clarke's veto. A statutory declaration by the girl's mother refuting the charges and saying that Nash had at all times acted with propriety was published in the daily newspapers. While in England for the Lambeth Conference, Clarke tried to uncover details about Nash's supposed previous indiscretions, thus further exacerbating opposition to him; in fact he had to cable Melbourne that there was no substance to any of the allegations. Nash was completely exonerated but, while Clarke was prepared to give him a general license, he refused to license him to Christ Church. His actions were motivated by his personal animus against Nash and by his dislike of evangelicals. The Nash affair was one of the events that led to the founding of Ridley College in 1910, as an evangelical protest against an archbishop and a diocese from which they felt alienated.

In 1908 the evangelical Bishop Arthur Wellesley Pain of Gippsland invited Nash to become rector of Sale and archdeacon of Gippsland. Nash accepted the invitation and very soon became the outstanding clergyman in Gippsland, being elected or appointed to many committees, and had a fruitful ministry. However, Archbishop Lowther Clarke sued the editor of a tabloid newspaper for libel after a defamatory article against him. This led to Nash's alleged improprieties being discussed once more. Unable to defend himself, and not wishing to be a cause of division in the church, Nash once again resigned his appointment and license. He moved back to Melbourne, and in 1913 began a boys' preparatory school in Kew. Then the Congregational Church in Prahran invited him to become its pastor. He served as such for six successful years (1915–1920); he was glad to be back in the pastoral ministry, though he never felt completely at home in the Congregational Church.

At the end of 1919 the council of the China Inland Mission, of which he was a member, invited him to begin a Bible institute for the training of missionaries. Thus the Melbourne Bible Institute (MBI) began in 1920. Numbers grew quickly, and Nash resigned from the church, devoting himself fully to the fledgling institute until he retired in 1942. It was his life's work; there is a sense in which

everything before had been a preparation for this. He brought to the task a mature and tested leadership, remarkable teaching and preaching gifts, and qualities of personal holiness, all of which made a profound personal impact on his students. Nash, and MBI, provided a focal point of leadership and unity for the evangelical movement in Melbourne.

Nash also exercised a far-reaching influence through other evangelical enterprises. In 1929 he began the City Business Men's Bible Class. All of the evangelical lay leadership in Melbourne for a generation came out of this Bible class. Campaigners for Christ was also a product of the class, with Nash being a mentor to those who ran it. He was deeply involved with, and a frequent speaker at, the Upwey Convention. He was a member and first president of the Bible Union.

Nash was actively interested in missions. He was a member of the Council of CIM from 1916 to 1943, and after 1926, when Archbishop Harrington Clare Lees relicensed him, a kind of elder statesman to the Church Missionary Society (CMS). He helped to found the CMS League of Youth in Melbourne and had a great impact on it through his Bible studies. The story of conservative Protestant missions cannot be told apart from the profound influence that Nash and MBI had on them. Over 1,000 students went through MBI under Nash, half of whom served on the overseas mission field. Additionally, a number of missionary organizations, such as the Borneo Evangelical Mission, were founded at MBI or by MBI people.

After being relicensed, Nash was happy to assist in a number of parishes around Melbourne, and was frequently invited to Sydney by Archbishop Howard *Mowll to lead ordination retreats. Nash died at Royal Park, Melbourne, on 27 September 1958. He was given a funeral service in St Paul's Cathedral and buried at the seaside suburb of Dromana.

Under normal circumstances Nash would have been marked out for high office in the Anglican Church. He had outstanding gifts of leadership and communication. His educational credentials were good, and he had the knack of cultivating friendships with important people. He always thought of himself as a loyal son of the Church of England. But because he was forced to resign from the Anglican Church he was able to exercise a much greater influence through his leadership in wider, non-Anglican evangelicalism. His leadership was exemplified by his voice, personality and presence; his Cambridge education gave him a certain status and authority; his outstanding preaching and teaching gifts captivated his hearers; his pastoral gifts, which influenced many, were shaped by his personal experiences before he began MBI; and personal holiness was an important element in his character. Though Nash's friends and supporters deferred to him, he did not dominate them. Rather, he should be understood as a facilitator who enabled each of them to work and develop their own gifts, and to exercise their initiative. It was in large part because of his style of ministry that Melbourne evangelicalism was largely lay led rather than clergy led, as in Sydney. And it was the nature of Nash's personality and leadership that spared the evangelical movement in Melbourne from the conflicts and divisions that America and, to a lesser degree, Sydney experienced.

Bibliography

D. N. Paproth, 'C. H. Nash and His Influence' (PhD thesis, Deakin University, 1993).

D. N. PAPROTH

■ NASH, Eric John Hewitson (1898–1982), Anglican clergyman, affectionately known as 'Bash', was born at Maidenhead on 22 April 1898, the second of the three sons of the Revd Charles Hewitson and Frances Nash. After being educated at Maidenhead College, Nash worked for a London insurance company. In February 1917 he was converted on a train journey and five years later entered Trinity College, Cambridge, and graduated BA in 1925 (MA in 1929). After ordination training at Ridley Hall, Cambridge, he was ordained deacon in 1927 and priest a year later. He served two curacies, at St John's, West Ealing, London, and Emmanuel Chapel, Wimbledon. Between 1929 and 1931 he was the chaplain of the newly opened Wrekin College, Wellington, Shropshire.

He was unsuccessful in his application to work for Scripture Union in 1929, but in 1932 he began his thirty-three year ministry with the organization as a travelling secretary and missioner with the Children's Special Service Mission. His brief was to work among boys in the leading public schools. His vision was to evangelize 'key boys from key schools' who would become the future leaders in the church and nation. In April 1930 he led his first 'Varsities and Public Schools Camp' at Ashampstead, Seaford, Sussex. At first the 'camps' were under canvas, but soon they were being held in boarding schools during the school holidays. The camps were unashamedly elitist, developed their own jargon and were run on disciplined lines. The leaders were 'officers' under the direction of the 'commandant'. The model worked well, and was copied by other Christian organizations at home and overseas. Subsequent Easter and summer camps were held at various places until in 1940 they were settled at Clayesmore School, in the Dorset village of Iwerne Minster. After the Second World War the work greatly expanded, and other camps were held for boys at preparatory schools and independent day schools. A separate work, under the same auspices, was developed in the north of England. From 1956 separate camps for girls were led by the wives of Iwerne Minster officers, and more recently mixed camps for boys and girls have been held.

It is estimated that over 7,000 boys attended Iwerne Minster camps under Nash's leadership and many hundreds went to other camps. Generations of men who subsequently became evangelical leaders, particularly Anglican clergy or public school staff, attended what were generally known as 'Bash Camps'. These included Michael Green, Dick Lucas, John Pollock and John Wenham. John *Stott considered that Nash was one of the seven people who had exercised the most significant influence on his life and who had 'developed my appetite for the Word of God'. The aim of the camps was simple: to present the gospel in an uncomplicated and unemotional way, so that the hearers could commit their lives to Christ. Nash was unconcerned with academic questions and critical issues. He let the Bible speak for itself. The close pastoral supervision that was exercised on the camps was maintained beyond public school and university and extended through a network of lasting friendships. This was valued by those on the inside but widely criticized by those not directly involved in the movement.

Nash gave himself wholly to his camps. He was a gentle, softly spoken, humble man. He was an eccentric, a cautious, unassuming bachelor who was something of a hypochondriac. He was neither athletic nor adventurous, made no pretence to scholarship, and had little interest in music or art. But in spite of his limitations Nash had a sharp, penetrating mind and was a shrewd judge of character. He was a good listener and had a great sense of humour. Though shy and awkward with women, he was in his element when he was addressing a small group of boys or young men, whether they were sixth formers or undergraduates. Nash is still remembered by his friends for his prayer, his nurture and his correspondence.

Nash officially retired from Scripture Union in 1965 but continued to be involved with Iwerne Minster until the late 1970s. He died unmarried in Maidenhead, Berkshire, on 4 April 1982. Although he had no family, a large congregation attended his memorial service held on 15 June at All Souls' Church, Langham Place, London.

Bibliography

T. Dudley-Smith, *John Stott: The Making of a Leader* (Leicester: IVP, 1999); J. Eddison (ed.), *'Bash': A Study in Spiritual Power* (Basingstoke: Marshalls, 1982); T. Saunders and H. Sansom, *David Watson* (Sevenoaks: Hodder & Stoughton, 1992), pp. 29–36; J. Wenham, *Facing Hell* (Carlisle: Paternoster, 1998), pp. 40–44.

J. EDDISON
A. F. MUNDEN

■ **NEE To-sheng**, known as Watchman Nee (1903–1972), founder of the Local Church Movement (also called the Little Flock), was born in Swatow and raised in Foochow in the Fukien province of China. He has been widely recognized as a major Chinese theologian whose ministry of preaching and writing has significantly influenced the development of the Christian church in modern China. Many of his books have been translated into other languages.

Before Nee's birth, his mother, Lin Ho-p'ing, asked God to remove from her the frustration and shame of having no male child and promised to dedicate her son to lifelong Christian service if her prayer was answered. He was given the name 'To-sheng', which means 'the sound of bamboo gong', as a reminder of his dedication to be God's 'bell ringer' (watchman) for the Chinese church.

Nee's family background influenced the education he received. His father, Nee Wen-hsiu, was employed as a maritime customs officer, having successfully completed the second level of the civil service examination. His grandfather, Nee Yu-cheng, was a Congregational minister affiliated to the American Board of Commissioners for Foreign Missions. Confucian classics and Christian faith combined to shape the youthful mind of Watchman Nee.

The Chinese society in which Nee grew up experienced unprecedented turmoil. The Republic Revolution of 1911 under the leadership of Sun Yat-sen toppled the Ch'ing Dynasty and ushered in a new era in China's history. In the Provisional Constitution of the Republic, religious liberty was affirmed, and Christianity became a legal religion. The church's more favourable circumstances not only gave momentum to the emergent independent church movement, but also paved the way for a revival movement in the Chinese church, led by missionaries such as Jonathan *Goforth, Sherwood Eddy and John R. *Mott and Chinese preachers such as Ding Li-mei, Ch'eng Ching-I, Dora Yu, John Yang and Chang Yu-hsin.

In 1916 Nee entered Trinity College at Foochow, which was run by the Church Missionary Society and staffed by missionaries from Dublin, Ireland. The college consisted of five sections (primary, middle, high, normal and divinity school), but its Western style and strict discipline were not appreciated by Nee. His academic performance was excellent in all subjects except the Bible.

During Nee's years at high school, China plunged into political confusion. Following the establishment of the Republic, various political parties competed for power; their strife resulted in a period of Warlordism (1916–1928). Seizing the opportunity to further its imperialistic ambitions, Japan began to put pressure on China, issuing the Twenty-One Demands. In an atmosphere of growing patriotism, the famous May Fourth Movement (1916–1923) was launched, aimed at saving the nation from internal dissension and external invasion. The Christian community had to determine its response to these crucial events.

Nee was converted in 1920 at an evangelistic meeting led by Dora Yu and began immediately and enthusiastically to preach the gospel. A team of young evangelists gathered in Foochow, including Leland Wang, Simon Meek and Faithful Luke, but their cooperation was later undermined by personality conflicts. Nee's early Christian life was deeply influenced by Margaret E. Barber, a former Anglican missionary, who introduced to him various theological traditions of the Western church, such as the British Keswick movement and the Brethren movement. He immersed himself in the writings of Andrew *Murray, D. M. Panton, Jessie Penn-Lewis, Madame Guyon and J. N. *Darby.

During the 1920s a new movement swept across the country, attacking Christianity as foreign, unscientific and outdated. In response to its challenges, many church leaders gave their support to the indigenous church movement, seeking to make the church in China a Chinese church. Sharing this vision, Nee started the Local Church Movement in Shanghai. He was inspired by the Brethren movement in England, but later parted company with it because of its exclusive approach to church life. At the age of twenty-five Nee wrote *The Spiritual Man*, a three-volume work on theological anthropology that deals with various aspects of spiritual formation.

In the 1930s the Local Church Movement spread rapidly throughout the country, despite the unstable socio-political situation, and was even extended overseas. The movement was strengthened by the recruitment of Witness Lee; Simon Meek and Faithful Luke went to Manila and Singapore to plant churches. Nee advocated the principle of 'one locality, one church' as the solution to the problem of denominationalism in China. To him denominations were sinful; true Christians should leave their denominations to join the Local Church. Each Local Church was autonomous and directed by appointed elders in order to achieve its threefold goal of being self-supporting, self-governing and self-propagating. Nee and his workers (called 'apostles') travelled from place to place to assist local leaders in nurturing church

members. In 1938, a year after the beginning of the Sino-Japanese War, Nee attended the Keswick Convention and visited some European countries. His famous book *The Normal Christian Life* consists of a series of sermons delivered during the journey, expressing theological viewpoints taken from *The Spiritual Man* and insights gleaned from the Keswick tradition.

The war seriously unsettled the nation's economy and plunged the Local Church Movement into financial difficulties. Early in 1942 Nee accepted an invitation to be the chairman of his brother George's pharmaceutical company in Shanghai in order to raise money for the support of over 200 Local Church workers in his care. His business did well, largely due to the wartime need for medicine. Nee believed that he was 'tent-making', but to his colleagues his motives were suspect. Eventually Nee was forbidden by the local elders to preach at the Hardoon Road Church until he abandoned his business.

The rejection by his own church grieved Nee and caused him to re-examine his ecclesiology, especially his view of the structure of church leadership. In his previous book, *Rethinking our Mission*, he made elders of each Local Church completely independent of apostolic control. But according to Nee's new doctrine, elders were to obey the apostles who appointed them. When the war ended in 1945, Nee published *The Orthodoxy of the Church* and *Spiritual Authority* to explain his revised position. In 1947 Nee decided to transfer his company's profits and properties to the church, and was able, with the help of Witness Lee, to regain his position of leadership. The example of Nee inspired many Local Churches to hand over church assets and personnel to the central administration, but some were reluctant to conform. A new form of outreach ministry known as 'the Jerusalem Principle' was introduced. It involved establishing mission centres in large cities such as Foochow and sending out from them self-sustaining teams of Christians to live in particular areas and evangelize them. After more than twenty years of development, the Local Church became one of the most successful examples of indigenous church growth in China, with over 70,000 members and 700 assemblies.

After the communist takeover of Mainland

China in 1949, the Chinese church faced an uncertain future. Nee was confronted with the hard question of whether to go overseas to continue his ministry or to stay behind to lead the Local Church. He decided to stay, against the advice of some colleagues. In 1952, when Nee was on a journey to Shenyang, Manchuria, he was arrested by the Department of Public Security and, after a public trial, was sentenced to fifteen years' imprisonment. Still resolute in his Christian faith, he died in June 1972.

Bibliography

A. I. Kinnear, *Against the Tide: The Story of Watchman Nee* (Eastbourne: Victory, 1973); W. H. Lam, *The Spiritual Theology of Watchman Nee* (Hong Kong: China Graduate School of Theology, 1985).

W. H. LAM

■ **NEVIN, John Williamson** (1803–1886), German Reformed theologian and architect of the Mercersburg theology, was born in Pennsylvania, the oldest of nine children of Scotch-Irish parents, and was raised as a Presbyterian. At the age of fourteen he entered Union College, Schenectady, New York. Due to a recurring illness, which plagued him for more than half of his life, he was forced to spend two years on the home farm following his graduation in 1821. In 1823 he began a three-year course at Princeton. Between 1826 and 1828, he served as Professor of Hebrew Language and Literature at Princeton, while his former mentor Charles *Hodge studied in Europe. After his ordination in the Presbyterian church (1828), he was the preacher at Newville, Pennsylvania, for almost two years.

In 1830 Nevin was called to the chair of Hebrew and Biblical Literature at the newly formed Western Seminary in Allegheny, Pennsylvania. He remained there for ten years, during which time he pastored nearby congregations, edited a literary journal called *The Friend* (named after a publication by Samuel Taylor Coleridge), and received his Doctor of Divinity from Jefferson College, Canonsburg, Pennsylvania (1840). It was during this period that Nevin began his study of German theology and church history. His reading of Johann August Neander and other German scholars marked a major turning-point in his theological development.

In 1840 Nevin accepted a call from the German Reformed Church to succeed Professor Lewis Mayer at Mercersburg Theological Seminary in Mercersburg, Pennsylvania. There he enjoyed a brief but significant friendship with his colleague Frederich Augustus Rauch, who died in 1841. It was Rauch who first introduced Nevin to conservative, Hegelian psychology. Nevin took on, in addition to his own obligations, Rauch's duties as president of Marshall College until 1853. Both the seminary and the college were perpetually in need of financial support. As a result, Nevin laboured for years, with less than adequate compensation, in an attempt to stabilize the failing institutions. The arrival of church historian Philip *Schaff in 1844 provided some relief. Not only did Schaff reaffirm Nevin's interest in German theology, but Schaff's Romantic-idealist understanding of church history became an essential element of Mercersburg theology.

Nevin engaged in a number of controversies during the 1840s, which made him unpopular in some quarters. He recorded his opposition to 'New Measures' revivalism in *The Anxious Bench* (1843) by calling for a return to the Reformed system of catechism. He defended Schaff's 'heretical' inaugural address, which traced the development of Protestantism through the medieval Catholic Church. In 1846 he published one of his most controversial books, *The Mystical Presence: A Vindication of the Reformed or Calvinistic Doctrine of the Holy Eucharist*. Nevin's defence and enlargement of *Calvin's eucharistic doctrine, over against the symbolic-memorial view held by most Reformed churches, brought him into direct conflict with his former mentor, Charles Hodge. The dispute generated hundreds of pages of journal articles and drove a permanent wedge between Mercersburg and Princeton. In his *History and Genius of the Heidelberg Catechism* (1847) Nevin again expressed his high regard for Reformed confessionalism and challenged the church to uphold it. His most stinging polemic was contained in *Anti-Christ, or the Spirit of Sect and Schism* (1848). Here Nevin argued for a unified, catholic church. Schism is rooted in a heretical disregard for the incarnation. Discontinuity in the church is no more than practical Gnosticism.

Nevin's High Church tendencies continued to develop into the early 1850s as reflected by his journal articles in the *Mercersburg Review*. These included 'Catholicism', 'The Anglican Crisis', 'Early Christianity' and 'Cyprian'. There can be little doubt that Nevin came close to surrendering to Catholicism, at least on an intellectual level. This development accounts, in part, for his resignation from the seminary in 1851. The Protestants of his day were vehement in their criticism of the Roman church. To Nevin, who found strains of piety even in medieval Catholicism, this hostility was evidence of near total defection from the ancient life of the church.

Despite Nevin's 'Romanizing' tendencies, the synod in Lancaster gave him an overwhelming vote of confidence upon his withdrawal from the seminary. He continued to serve as president of Marshall College until it was moved to Lancaster in 1853. After himself moving to Lancaster in 1858, he joined the faculty of Franklin and Marshall College during the Civil War, serving as Professor of Philosophy, History and Aesthetics. In 1866 he was elected president and continued in that position for ten years. During that time he was involved in a major dispute over the nature and use of liturgy in the German Reformed Church. So far-reaching was this controversy, that it resulted in an exchange of lengthy journal articles between Nevin and the famous German mediating theologian I. A. Dorner.

In his remaining years Nevin's attention turned mainly towards the inspiration and interpretation of Scripture. He became intrigued by the hermeneutics of Emanuel Swedenborg, though he rejected many of his conclusions. Nevin's sacramental and even mystical view of Scripture was deeply rooted in his Presbyterian piety and Christian Platonism. Indeed, his later articles on sacred hermeneutics echoed many of the principles he articulated in his pre-Mercersburg writings. He died in Lancaster, Pennsylvania, at the age of eighty-three.

Nevin's Mercersburg theology is, above all else, a Christocentric system rooted in the incarnation. It is precisely for this reason that Nevin placed such great emphasis on the historic church, the sacraments and the Scriptures. It is in these that the life-power of the new creation is dynamically embodied. Theologically, Nevin's thought is a synthesis of German mediating theology (e.g. Karl Ullmann, I. A. Dorner, Richard Rothe) on the one hand, with English piety (e.g. John Howe, Henry Scougal, Archbishop Robert Leighton) and British Romanticism (e.g. S. T. Coleridge) on the other. Philosophically, it is an attempt to fuse Platonism and German idealism (e.g. G. W. F. Hegel, F. W. Schelling) with British empiricism (e.g. John Locke) and common sense realism (e.g. Thomas Reid). Despite the tremendous breadth of his scholarship, the Mercersburg doctor never strayed from the confessional theology of the Heidelberg Catechism and the orthodoxy of the Apostles' Creed. He regarded the Creed as the root all true theology because it comprised the substance of the apostolic faith and the hermeneutical matrix of biblical interpretation.

Though Nevin's historical impact on evangelical theology has been relatively slight, his relentless critique of American religion and culture has aroused ongoing interest in contemporary scholarship. By focusing exclusively on the atonement, American religion had all but set aside the historic doctrine of the incarnation along with its theological implications for creation, the church and the sacraments. Democratic individualism served only to extinguish the organic concept of the church, and biblical rationalism and religious subjectivism undermined the doctrine of the real presence of Christ in both the sacraments and the Scriptures. Finally, cultural materialism and common-sense realism obviated the possibility of an idealistic or spiritual Christian philosophy. Many aspects of Nevin's theology did move beyond standard evangelical convictions, but because his trajectory (from evangelicalism to sacramentalism) was a journey undertaken by several important evangelicals in the nineteenth century, and because his theology remained rooted in the Heidelberg Catechism (the most obviously evangelical of the classic Reformed Confessions), he is none the less an important figure in the history of evangelicalism, broadly considered.

Bibliography

T. Appel, *The Life and Work of John*

Williamson Nevin (Philadelphia: Reformed Church Publishing House, 1889); W. DiPuccio, *The Interior Sense of Scripture: The Sacred Hermeneutics of John W. Nevin* (Macon: Mercer University Press, 1998); S. Hamstra, Jr, and A. J. Griffioen (eds.), *Reformed Confessionalism in Nineteenth-Century America: Essays on the Thought of John Williamson Nevin* (Lanham: Scarecrow Press: 1995); J. H. Nichols, *Romanticism in American Theology: Nevin and Schaff at Mercersburg* (Chicago: University of Chicago Press, 1961); R. Wentz, *John Williamson Nevin: American Theologian* (New York: Oxford University Press, 1997).

W. DiPuccio

■ **NEWBIGIN, J. E. Lesslie** (1909–1998), evangelist, ecumenist and author, was born on 8 December 1909 in Newcastle-on-Tyne, within a year and a hundred miles of the Edinburgh 1910 world missionary conference from which the modern ecumenical movement is conventionally dated. Any attempt to drive a wedge, from whatever side, between ecumenism and evangelism is challenged by the life and thought of Lesslie Newbigin. From selling gospels at an anna each in the streets of Kanchipuram to holding distinguished lectureships in the universities of Europe and North America, Newbigin never ceased to commend Christ as Lord and Saviour. From negotiating and defending the union of Anglicans, Methodists, Presbyterians and Congregationalists in the Church of South India to frustrated attempts to achieve at home what had been achieved overseas, Newbigin never renounced the obligation to pursue visible ecclesial unity. In the heyday of the World Council of Churches Newbigin at different times occupied important positions in the commission on faith and order and in the area of mission and evangelism. He marched under the banners first hoisted by John R. *Mott, the pioneer of the Student Christian Movement and the Student Volunteer Movement and his senior by some forty-five years: 'Ut Omnes Unum Sint' and 'The Evangelization of the World in This Generation'. As a faithful disciple of Christ, Newbigin considered that he could do no less, for Jesus himself had prayed for his disciples, 'that they all may be one, so that the world may believe' (John 17:21).

Newbigin's ship-owning family was Presbyterian and prosperous, and he eventually went to school at Leighton Park, the Quaker institution in Berkshire, and from there in 1928 to Queens' College, Cambridge, where he read geography and economics (hearing the lectures of John Meynard Keynes). In his first long vacation from the university, he worked in a Quaker camp for the unemployed in South Wales, where one night he had a vision of 'the Cross spanning the space between heaven and earth, between ideals and present realities, and with arms that embraced the whole world'. At Cambridge he began to explore again the Christian faith, about which he had had doubts as an adolescent; he became active in the Student Christian Movement, met such luminaries as J. R. Mott, Jack Winslow (a missionary from India), John Mackey (a missionary from Peru) and William Temple, then Archbishop of York, and took part in evangelistic campaigns during vacations. Newbigin was confirmed into church membership at St Columba's Presbyterian and, while attending an SCM conference at Swanwick, sensed an inescapable call to the ordained ministry.

To finance his future theological education, Newbigin worked for two years after graduation as an SCM staff secretary in Glasgow, where he had as a colleague Helen Henderson, whom he would marry in 1936 and who remained his stay and support throughout their long lives. Returning from Scotland to Cambridge in 1933, he studied for three years at Westminster College under John Oman, Herbert Farmer and W. A. L. Elmslie. Crucial to his studies was work on the theme of atonement in the Old Testament, and a thorough immersion in the epistle to the Romans with the guidance of James *Denney's commentary in *The Expositor's Greek Testament*. In May 1936 the Newbigins were commissioned by the Church of Scotland for missionary work in India; in July Lesslie was ordained by the Edinburgh Presbytery; in September Lesslie and Helen sailed for Madras.

For the next twenty-three years, interrupted only by a serious motor accident and normal furloughs, Newbigin ministered in South India. Acquiring fluency in Tamil, he served as a missionary in Kanchipuram, where he toured his district for pastoral and evangelistic purposes, strengthened local leadership in the congregations, and engaged with a Hindu monastic community in a weekly study group devoted to the Svetasvara Upanishad in Sanskrit and John's Gospel in Greek. At the denominational level, he was a representative of the South India United Church in the final years of negotiation with Anglicans and Methodists before the successful inauguration of the Church of South India (CSI) in September 1947. At the age of thirty-seven, Newbigin was elected and consecrated among the first bishops of a church on which was fixed the attention of the whole ecumenical movement. He was appointed to the diocese of Madurai, a mill city in largely rural surroundings; he described his early years there in *A South India Diary* (1951). Newbigin's pastoral work was of such high quality that L. W. Brown, then a missionary colleague in South India and subsequently Archbishop of Uganda and finally Bishop of St Edmondsbury and Ipswich, would many years later declare, 'To see a true bishop, I look at Lesslie.'

As a young, intelligent, vigorous bishop in a newly united church, Newbigin was much in demand on the international scene. He was a consultant at the founding assembly of the World Council of Churches (WCC) in Amsterdam in 1948 under the banner 'Man's Disorder and God's Design', and then chaired the high-powered Committee of Twenty-Five (including Karl Barth) that prepared for the second assembly to meet at Evanston, Illinois, in 1954 on the theme 'Jesus Christ, the Hope of the World'. In the meantime, Newbigin played a vital role in 1952 at the conference of the International Missionary Council (IMC) in Willingen, Germany, where he showed himself a master draughtsman of reconciling but uncompromising ecumenical statements. In 1958 he was elected *in absentia* chairman of the IMC, but he gave up this position when the Church of South India seconded him to serve as general secretary of the IMC, in time to oversee the integration of the IMC with the WCC, which formally took place at the New Delhi assembly in 1961. As part of his work in these years on the faith and order commission, Newbigin was largely responsible for the famous paragraph adopted at New Delhi describing 'the unity we seek': it was a unity in the gospel and the apostolic faith, in baptism and the breaking of bread, in ordained ministry and corporate life, in prayer, witness and service, bringing together 'all in each place' and joining them with 'the whole Christian fellowship in all places and all ages'.

An efficient but reluctant bureaucrat, Newbigin stayed with the WCC for a few years as associate general secretary and first director of its division on world mission and evangelism, travelling globally in a strategic capacity. In 1965 he was glad to return to India, where he served for nine years as CSI bishop in the metropolitan city and diocese of Madras until his first retirement. He gathered his presbyters and women workers regularly for Holy Communion, at which he preached some remarkable pastoral homilies that were later published under the title of *The Good Shepherd* as the Archbishop of Canterbury's Lent book for 1977; he became active in civic life and urged the minority Christians to play a distinctive part in the social, industrial and commercial spheres; his energetic ubiquity caused his successor to refer to him as 'a bishop on the run'.

On returning to England in 1974, Newbigin taught mission and ecumenism at the Selly Oak Colleges in Birmingham, becoming engaged in a local controversy over religious education in the city schools. He was able to transpose his thinking on religious education from the context of officially secular but profoundly Hindu India to that of officially Christian but profoundly secular Britain. His Selly Oak lectures on mission were published as *The Open Secret* (1978; [2]1995). After his second retirement in 1979, Newbigin responded to a challenge he had set before the Birmingham District of the United Reformed Church by assuming for most of his eighth decade the pastorate of an apparently dying cause in the racially and religiously mixed neighbourhood of Winson Green, where he continued to practise direct evangelism and encourage ecumenism among the Christian congregations.

In 1992 Lesslie and Helen moved to southeast London to be nearer their children, but again the move was hardly a real retirement for Lesslie. He finally saw to fruition a national consultation on 'The Gospel as

Public Truth', on which he had worked as part of the '1984' project of the British Council of Churches; and he continued to travel, nationally and internationally (especially in continental Europe and in Scandinavia), in the principal cause that occupied him for the last quarter-century of his life, namely the encouragement of a 'missionary encounter' with modern Western culture. In late 1996 Newbigin was persuaded to attend, for the last time, a mission and evangelism conference of the WCC, at Salvador de Bahia, Brazil, where he delivered a powerful and moving address on 'Gospel and Culture', the theme of the meeting but one on which he put his own stamp. In the 1980s and 1990s, in fact, Newbigin had become gravely disappointed with the World Council of Churches, which he saw as drifting from the two principal concerns of the classic ecumenical movement: evangelization was yielding to the important but by no means equivalent interest of interreligious dialogue, and the churches were looking less towards organic unity than to much looser forms of association (what he had earlier called 'reunion without repentance'). Lesslie died on 30 January 1998, and Helen a year later.

Two of Newbigin's books have already been mentioned. He was in fact a prolific author, whose writings combine intellectual acuity, spiritual depth, theological competence, contemporary relevance, and a vivid style. His first book was written on the boat to India in 1936. Entitled *Christian Freedom in the Modern World* (1937), it was a critical response to John Macmurray's *Freedom in the Modern World*, which was enjoying a certain popularity in the British SCM but which seemed to Newbigin antinomian in tendency. (He also warned the church against the 'New Morality' of the 1960s, for the same reason.) Although they remained unpublished on account of wartime conditions, Newbigin's Bangalore lectures of 1941 on 'The Kingdom of God and the Idea of Progress' set the lines for all his future thinking on society, history and eschatology: faithful deeds were acted prayers, and God was able to preserve until the Day of the Lord what had been entrusted to him; but neither personal improvement nor social development could lead 'progressively' to the kingdom of God as the transcendent and final reality that alone gives history its meaning in both its individual and its communal dimensions. Further examples of Newbigin's teaching in India are his outstanding text-book *Sin and Salvation* (1956), which was originally written in Tamil as the bishop's aid for village teachers, and the addresses he gave to religiously mixed audiences at the Christian Medical College in Vellore: *Christ Our Eternal Contemporary* (1968) and *Journey into Joy* (1972).

In *The Reunion of the Church* (1948) Newbigin pugnaciously defended the South India plan of union by attempting to convince 'Protestant' critics of the need for apostolic continuity, which he himself had learned from A. M. Ramsey's *The Gospel and the Catholic Church* (1936), and to persuade (Anglo-)Catholic critics that the church remained a community of justified sinners with real corporate failings that were redeemed only by grace. A more serene ecclesiology is found in *The Household of God* (1953); its status as a classic was confirmed by its translation into several languages. In this book Newbigin set out a trinitarian doctrine of the church as 'Congregation of the Faithful', 'Body of Christ' and 'Community of the Holy Spirit', charged with participating in God's mission to the ends of the earth and to the end of time; and the striking of the pneumatological note, long muffled in the standard Protestantism and Catholicism of the West, gained attention for the book among Pentecostals and Eastern Orthodox.

Amid the Cold War on one side and decolonization on the other, Newbigin argued in lectures given at Harvard in 1958 that the unity of humankind could be found only in the atoning cross of Christ; these lectures were later published as *A Faith for This One World?* (1961). In the early 1960s Newbigin dallied briefly with the 'secular theology' then in vogue, but even in *Honest Religion for Secular Man* (1966), based on lectures given at the University of Nottingham in 1964, he never embraced radical reductionism, and his views are better captured by his later formulation of 'the public character of the Gospel'. His lectures at Yale in 1966, published as *The Finality of Christ* (1969), provided by anticipation an answer to the 'religious pluralism' that would swing into fashion in the 1970s.

The final phase of Newbigin's own theological career was concentrated on the engagement with modern culture that he saw to be necessary not only in the declining Christendom of the West but in every place where the tentacles of global capitalism and technology had reached. His key writings are the Princeton lectures of 1984, published as *Foolishness to the Greeks* (1986), and the Glasgow lectures of 1988, published as *The Gospel in a Pluralist Society* (1989). The church's chief intellectual task, he maintained, was to challenge the 'plausibility structures' of modernity and their false separation between public 'facts' and private 'values'. Stimulated by Hungarian scientific philosopher Michael Polanyi's *Personal Knowledge* (1958), Newbigin attacked the Cartesian priority of doubt in epistemology, arguing instead for the fiduciary basis of all knowledge and the place of tradition and community in its advance and transmission; he sought the recovery of the category of 'purpose', which had been displaced from large areas of life by the triumph of 'efficient causality' in the natural sciences. The resurrection of Jesus, said Newbigin, fits into no other worldview than that of which it is the foundation; it is the beginning of God's new creation. Christians engaging in various ways and at various levels in re-evangelizing the culture will need the fellowship of local congregations as communities of mutual responsibility in truth, hope, the praise of God and the service of the neighbour. In his final, co-authored book, *Faith and Power: Christianity and Islam in 'Secular' Britain* (1998), Newbigin held up a 'Christian vision for society' as an alternative to unbridled capitalism, the new paganism, and an Islam of the *shariah* law.

Newbigin's life was based on his daily devotions. The Scriptures were for him, as for *Calvin, the spectacles through which he saw the world. He was frequently invited to preach and lead Bible studies. (His long-maturing commentary on the Fourth Gospel was published in 1982 as *The Light Has Come*, and sessions he conducted in his last years at Holy Trinity, Brompton, were recorded on audio tape.) He had a strong sacramental sense and often presided on ecumenical occasions at celebrations of the Lord's Supper according to the rite of the Church of South India that he had helped to shape. According to many testimonies, his pastoral care was supported by prayer. He could be forthright in criticism but bore no grudges. His humour found expression in what he called 'the lowliest of art-forms', as the collection *St Paul in Limerick* (1998) shows.

For the range of his ministries both local and global, for his ecclesiastical statesmanship, for his theological acumen, and for his sheer stature as a man of God, Lesslie Newbigin merits comparison with the great bishop-theologians of the early church.

Bibliography

G. Hunsberger, *Bearing Witness of the Spirit: Lesslie Newbigin's Theology of Cultural Plurality* (Grand Rapids: Eerdmans, 1998); L. Newbigin, *Unfinished Agenda: An Autobiography* (Edinburgh: St Andrew Press, 1993); G. Wainwright, *Lesslie Newbigin: A Theological Life* (New York: Oxford University Press, 2000).

G. WAINWRIGHT

■ **NEWTON, Benjamin Wills** (1807–1899), preacher and writer, was born on 12 December 1807 in Devonport, Plymouth, ten days after the death of his father, also Benjamin, who was a draper. Until he was twelve, Newton lived with his maternal grandfather, Roger Treffry of Lostwithiel, Cornwall. A precocious child, Newton was educated at the grammar schools in Lostwithiel and, more briefly, Plymouth; from 1815 until 1824 he was tutored by Thomas Byrth, rector of Diptford, Devon. He matriculated at Oxford in 1824, was appointed a fellow of Exeter College in 1826 when eighteen and gained a first-class honours degree in classics in 1828, graduating the following year.

Although his family were Quakers, Newton intended to be ordained in the Church of England. At Oxford his friend Henry Bulteel, an Anglican curate, persuaded him to hear Robert Hawker, the Calvinist vicar of Charles, near Plymouth, and in 1827 Newton experienced assurance of salvation. He was stimulated by his former university tutor, Francis Newman, then an evangelical, to begin the study of prophecy. In 1830 Newman introduced Newton to John Nelson *Darby. Increasingly identified with more radical evangelicals, Newton helped to depose

J. H. (later Cardinal) Newman, Francis Newman's brother, from the Oxford secretaryship of the Church Missionary Society, and was visibly associated with Bulteel's university sermon of 1831 in which he protested against the condition of the Church of England. The apparent cause of Newton resigning his fellowship was his marriage in 1832 to Hannah Abbott, daughter of a Plymouth flour merchant, but he was, in fact, by then close to seceding from the established church.

Returning to Plymouth, Newton preached locally at cottage meetings, and he invited Darby there to preach in the churches. In 1831 George Wigram, a wealthy friend, had rented Providence Chapel, Raleigh Street, for lectures, but soon the Lord's Supper was being observed, at first privately but eventually publicly on Sunday mornings. Initially Newton attended various churches, and it seems likely that the new venture was intended to be transdenominational. However, it quickly became a separate congregation, which in 1840 moved to Ebrington Street. Newton was appointed an elder, and for a while he presided over the open worship at the Lord's Supper, stopping fruitless contributions. Along with others he also preached widely in the southwest, thereby founding other congregations of the 'Plymouth' Brethren in the region.

By the late 1830s, disapproving of association with other denominations and allowing only premillennialists to preach at Plymouth, Newton was also critical of Darby's sharp division between Israel and the church and his concept of a 'secret rapture'. He attempted to insulate the Plymouth congregation and its satellites from these new ideas, and letters he had written against them around 1840 were circulated in manuscript form before being published some five years later. His *Thoughts on the Apocalypse* (1843) also gave expression to his post-tribulationist premillennialism. When Darby returned to Plymouth in 1845 conflict ensued. His principal complaint was that Newton was establishing a separate sect, but he later also accused him of deceit over the publication of the letters. At the end of the year Darby instituted a new congregation, which eventually met in the Raleigh Street chapel. In 1847 J. L. Harris, one of Newton's former associates, published, with critical comments attached, unrevised notes of a lecture by Newton expressing the view that some of Christ's sufferings had been non-atoning, incurred under the federal headship of Adam. Although within the year Newton repudiated these ideas, Darby condemned him for heresy. Newton withdrew from Plymouth to avoid causing further embarrassment and thereafter moved outside the Brethren movement. Although the view of eldership that he developed at Plymouth was to be accepted by most Open Brethren, and the controversy with Darby was to mark the entire movement, once Newton left and with the shadow of heresiarch over him, he had no further influence on Brethrenism.

Newton's wife had died in 1846, and in 1849 he married Maria Hawkins, whose father had been in the Madras Civil Service; in 1855 their only child, Maria, died at the age of five. Newton, in later years a rigorous independent, continued to write, often on eschatological themes, and he preached for a number of years at a chapel built for his use in Queen's Road, Bayswater, London. In retirement, he lived successively in Orpington, near London, Newport, Isle of Wight, and Tunbridge Wells, Kent. He had a group of devoted followers, one of whom preserved his recollections and correspondence, and at present many of his writings are kept in print by the Sovereign Grace Advent Testimony. Towards the end of his life Darby reputedly said, 'Mr. Newton is the most godly man I ever knew.' Newton died at Tunbridge Wells on 26 June 1899.

Bibliography

H. H. Rowdon, *The Origins of the Brethren 1825–50* (London: Pickering & Inglis, 1968); T. C. F. Stunt, *From Awakening to Secession: Radical Evangelicals in Switzerland and Britain 1815–35* (Edinburgh: T. & T. Clark, 2000).

N. DICKSON

■ **NEWTON, John** (1725–1807), Anglican clergyman, hymn-writer and author, was born on 24 July 1725 (OS) in Wapping, London, the only child of John Newton, a ship's captain, and his first wife Elizabeth. Baptized at the Independent Chapel that his mother attended and where David Jennings was the minister, he learned the hymns of Isaac *Watts and was nurtured in the piety of Old Dissent. His mother died of tuberculosis when he was only seven. His father remarried after his mother's death, but his relationship with both his father and his stepmother was distant, and his religious training ceased. For two years (1733–1735) he was sent to a boarding-school at Stratford in Essex. Then, from the age of eleven, he went to sea with his father and made several voyages with him (1736–1742).

Newton recounts the story of his early life in his autobiography, *An Authentic Narrative* (1764), and he weaves together the stories of his religious conversion, his courtship and his seafaring adventures. On a journey to Kent he visited friends of his late mother, and fell immediately in love with their eldest daughter Mary Catlett ('Polly', 1729–1790), whom he would later marry. He prolonged his visit, evading his father's plans to send him to Jamaica to be set up in business. Returning at the end of 1743 from a voyage to Venice, during which he began his decline into 'apostasy', he again evaded his father's plans by a protracted visit to the Catlett family. Before another business opportunity could be found, he was press-ganged on board HMS *Harwich* in the tense days just before France formally declared war on England (during the War of the Austrian Succession, 1739–1748). Newton soon attempted to desert, but he was discovered, returned to the ship in disgrace and disciplined. As his ship left England at the end of 1744, bound for a five-year voyage to the East Indies, he claimed it was only his love for Mary that kept him from attempting to murder the captain or commit suicide.

The day before his ship was to leave Madeira he was transferred to a merchant vessel in the African slave trade. His behaviour during this period was openly coarse and immoral. After six months trading, he contrived to stay on the Guinea coast, hoping to make his fortune as an agent in the slave trade. Instead, during the next two years he suffered ridicule and near destitution as his master, a man named Clow, used him brutally. Newton always marked this point as the lowest in his spiritual experience.

His father had arranged for a ship to look out for his son. But meanwhile Newton's prospects in Africa had so improved that when the captain located him, he could barely be persuaded to leave. The ship, the *Greyhound*, returned to England via Brazil and Newfoundland, but encountered a harsh North Atlantic storm in the winter of 1748. On 21 March Newton was awakened in the middle of the night to find that the ship was in trouble and that a man had already been washed overboard. Newton found himself whispering a prayer for mercy. When the ordeal was over, the ship had survived the storm but was damaged. Even more seriously, the crew were left with very little food or water. Newton began again to read the Bible and other religious books. When, after many troubles, the ship reached Ireland, he considered himself no longer an 'infidel'. In his diary he would always remember 21 March as the anniversary of his conversion.

In terms of his later evangelical theology, however, this was his awakening of conscience more than his true repentance. He did not become a 'true believer' until six months later. Upon his return to England, he obtained a new position on a slave-trading ship bound for the Guinea coast and West Indies (1748–1749). He hoped to acquit himself well and make a proposal of marriage to Mary Catlett upon his return. However, it was on this voyage, in Africa, that Newton found himself unable to live up to his new spiritual and moral intentions. Only a violent fever recalled him to seriousness. Barely able to stand or walk, he struggled to an isolated spot on the island where the ship came to land and cast himself before God in an act of submission. From this moment, he claimed, he experienced a new sort of spiritual liberty. He returned to England and married Mary on 12 February 1750.

After his marriage he made three voyages as the master of a slave-trading ship. On his last voyage he met another captain, Alexander Clunie, who acquainted him with the progress of evangelical revival in England. Consequently, when a seizure caused Newton to leave the maritime trade in 1754, he attended religious meetings in London and was soon drawn into the revival associated with George *Whitefield and the *Wesleys. Gradually, through his contact with Dissenters and Calvinistic Methodism, and through his personal study, he became a convinced Calvinist himself.

Newton has sometimes been accused of hypocrisy for holding strong religious convictions at the same time as he was active in the slave trade. He was not, however, within the milieu of evangelicals such as John Wesley, who opposed slavery, until he had already left the sea. Later in life he had deep regrets and repented of his involvement in the traffic, supported William *Wilberforce in his abolition crusade, gave evidence to the Privy Council and wrote a tract supporting abolition, *Thoughts Upon the African Slave Trade* (1787).

In August 1755 he took up a civil service post in Liverpool, where his duties included inspecting import cargoes and checking for smuggled goods. Newton used all his spare time to pursue private studies in theology. Soon he was one of the leading evangelical laymen in the region, well known to 'awakened clergy' up and down the country. He was nicknamed locally 'young Whitefield' and soon hosted large religious meetings in his own home.

It was natural that in 1757 he began to have thoughts of entering the ministry himself. It was, however, seven frustrating years before he achieved ordination in the Church of England. In the end, his written draft of his autobiography acted as a curriculum vitae, which Thomas Haweis used to introduce Newton's case to the young evangelical nobleman, Lord Dartmouth. The Earl used his influence to help Newton, and he received holy orders in 1764. A little later that same year Newton's *Authentic Narrative* appeared in print. Much reprinted, it soon established his place as one of the leading evangelicals in the revival.

Newton became the curate-in-charge of Olney, a market town in Buckinghamshire. Newton's stipend was only £60 a year, but the wealthy evangelical merchant John Thornton allowed him an additional £200 a year for hospitality and to help the poor. During his sixteen years at Olney, Newton established a variety of popular services and society meetings. The church became so crowded that a gallery was added. With Olney as his base, Newton made forays into adjacent parishes too, to speak at cottage prayer meetings. His relationships with local Dissenters, such as the Independent minister William Bull of Newport Pagnell, were friendly for the most part. Yet while known for being tolerant of those with whom he differed, he rejected both the Arminianism and perfectionism of Wesley, and the high Calvinism prevalent among some Baptists in the region. He liked to call himself 'a sort of middle-man'.

In 1767 the poet William *Cowper, having recently come to evangelical convictions, settled at Olney to be near Newton. Cowper shared in the life of the parish, and in 1771 he and Newton began to work on a project to publish a volume of their collected hymns. It was to be a celebration of their friendship and spiritual ideals. With the onset of Cowper's third major episode of depression in 1773, however, the whole project was cast into doubt, for from that point Cowper wrote only a few more hymns. In the end, Newton decided still to publish what they had. Many of the *Olney Hymns* (1779) addressed specific situations in the parish, but the hymn-book quickly became popular more widely. Newton's most famous contributions include 'Glorious Things of Thee are Spoken', 'How Sweet the Name of Jesus Sounds!' and 'Amazing Grace'. The style and tone of these hymns fit somewhere between the sobriety of Old Dissent seen in Isaac Watts's *Hymns and Spiritual Songs* (1707) and the exuberance of Wesleyan Methodism found in the standard *Collection of Hymns, for the Use of the People Called Methodists* (1780).

Soon after Cowper's death in 1800, a long debate commenced over the causes of his mental illness. Some blamed the emotionalism of evangelicalism for aggravating his condition, while others laid the blame specifically on Calvinism. The belief that Newton's influence had served to undermine Cowper's sanity was long perpetuated by Robert Southey's *Life of Cowper* (1835). The debate continued throughout the nineteenth and early twentieth centuries, with very little fresh work in the sources and a great deal of bias. Newton's life has all too often been presented as merely an episode in the poet's melancholy. Although there were temporary breaches in their friendship, Newton continued to treat Cowper with tenderness, fulfilling the role of a spiritual counsellor. He wrote to Cowper in 1780, 'I know not that I ever saw you for a single day since your calamity came upon you, in which I could not perceive as clear and satisfactory evidence, that the grace of God was with you, as I could in your brighter and happier times.'

Indeed, it was at Olney that Newton emerged as a well-known spiritual writer. One historian has dubbed him 'the St. Francis de Sales of the Evangelical movement, the great spiritual director of souls through the post'. Although Newton published sermons and even a *Review of Ecclesiastical History* (1770) – which may have suggested to Joseph Milner the idea of his *History of the Church of Christ* – his favourite form of writing was the personal letter. In 1774 he collected and published twenty-six such letters, which had earlier been published in the *Gospel Magazine* under the pen-name Omicron. His three letters on growth in grace (originally written to John Thornton in 1772) have frequently been reprinted from the Omicron series as a compact essay on evangelical spirituality. Newton's later collection of more intimate letters, *Cardiphonia, or the Utterance of the Heart* (1780) established his place as the gentle casuist of the evangelical revival. Included in *Cardiphonia* is Newton's correspondence with Thomas *Scott, the biblical commentator, whom Newton helped to convert, after much debate, from Socinianism. Over 500 of Newton's letters of spiritual advice were published during his lifetime or shortly afterwards.

In 1780 Newton accepted the offer from John Thornton of the benefice of St Mary Woolnoth in London. This was an important city living, and at that time when William Romaine was the only other evangelical incumbent in London. Unlike his extensive parish ministry at Olney, Newton's work at St Mary Woolnoth was chiefly that of a preacher, since the church was located in the midst of a highly mobile population with little parochial identity. In 1786, during the Handel commemoration, Newton preached and published fifty sermons on the libretto of the 'Messiah'. Throughout his ministry in London people came from afar to hear him, and his congregations were large.

Newton increasingly gained the status of a patriarch within the emerging evangelical party, and his home was regularly crowded with younger ministers eager to glean wisdom from him. Richard Cecil and William Jay were present to take down notes of Newton's casual table-talk. William Wilberforce called on Newton for counsel during the crisis of his evangelical conversion in 1785. Claudius Buchanan, who later served as chaplain in India, was converted by a sermon at St Mary Woolnoth and later became Newton's curate. Newton visited Charles *Simeon in Cambridge and Hannah *More in Cowslip Green. He was also involved in the founding of the Eclectic Society (1783), which would become famous as the origin of the Church Missionary Society, and the *Christian Observer* magazine. He continued to represent an amiable evangelicalism within the Church of England, and his Calvinism became, if anything, more moderate as he grew older. He told William Jay that he used Calvinism in his ministry like sugar in his tea: 'I do not give it alone and whole; but mixed and diluted.' This statement is a good example of his epigrammatic wit and homely style in and out of the pulpit. Yet in the troubled 1780s he felt the need to defend his churchmanship in an *Apologia* (1784), in which he made clear his reasons for staying within the Church of England. It satisfied few of his Dissenting friends.

Newton's wife died in 1790 of cancer, and though he was able to preach her funeral sermon, his sense of loss was as deep as his love for her had been devoted. He published his *Letters to a Wife* in 1793, poignantly tracing his grief in meditations recorded in his own interleaved copy. Newton and his wife had no children of their own, but they adopted two of their orphan nieces on the Catlett side of the family. Elizabeth ('Eliza') Cunningham came into their home in 1783 but died while still a child in 1785. Elizabeth ('Betsy' or 'Eliza') Catlett had been adopted earlier, in 1774. After his wife's death, Newton depended upon Betsy. In 1801 she experienced a period of derangement and was confined to Bethlehem hospital, much to Newton's distress. After her recovery she married an optician named Smith but continued to take care of Newton as his sight failed and his health deteriorated. He died peacefully on 21 December 1807, and was buried beside his wife in St Mary Woolnoth; both bodies were reinterred at Olney in 1893.

Interpretations of Newton's life have varied. Almost every generation since his death has produced one or more inspirational biographies, and these have largely affirmed

Newton's sense that his life was a symbol of divine grace to hardened sinners. Richard Cecil's *Memoirs of the Rev. John Newton* (1808) was squarely in the tradition of Newton's own autobiography; Josiah Bull's more carefully researched *John Newton of Olney and St Mary Woolnoth* (1868) was equally reverent. These volumes are also the chief repositories of information and anecdotes about Newton. Though Newton has often appeared as an unsympathetic foil to William Cowper in biographies of the poet, historians have consistently portrayed Newton as a genial Christian and a devoted minister, one of a number of evangelical clergy who helped to raise the spiritual tone of the Church of England in the eighteenth century.

Bibliography

J. Bull, *John Newton of Olney and St Mary Woolnoth* (London: Religious Tract Society, 1868); D. B. Hindmarsh, *John Newton and the English Evangelical Tradition Between the Conversions of Wesley and Wilberforce* (Oxford: Clarendon Press, 1996); J. Newton, *Works of the Rev. John Newton*, 6 vols. (London: 1808).

D. B. HINDMARSH

■ **NOEL, Baptist Wriothesley** (1798–1873), Anglican clergyman then Baptist minister, announced his resignation from St John's, Bedford Row, a proprietary chapel in the west-end of London, sometimes described as 'the headquarters of the evangelical party in London', on 3 December 1848. Prior to his secession, and following such famous preachers as Richard Cecil and Daniel *Wilson, Noel ministered there to a large and well-to-do congregation that stood outside the regular parochial structure of the Church of England, by means of direct subscription in support of an explicitly evangelical ministry. On 9 August 1849 Noel, hitherto leader of London's Anglican evangelicals, was baptized as a believer at the neighbouring John Street Baptist Chapel, of which he became the pastor in September. Moreover, he clearly identified himself with the Baptist cause nationally in a way that his predecessor J. H. Evans, who himself had seceded from the Church of England as part of the so-called 'Western Schism', had never done.

Baptist Noel, sixteenth child and eleventh son of Sir Gerard Noel and Diana, Lady Barham, born on 16 July 1798 into a prominent Whiggish evangelical family, was educated at Westminster School and Trinity College, Cambridge. Against the wishes of his family he was ordained, serving St John's for some twenty-two years. In his early career the undenominational spirit of the 1790s lingered longer than elsewhere, developing eventually into a new search for Protestant unity within the Evangelical Alliance. In this Noel played a conspicuous part; non-churchmen attending the initial conference of the Alliance were invited to take communion alongside churchmen at St John's. Earlier, in 1824, his first public advocacy had been on behalf of the London Missionary Society, which also bridged the divide between church and dissent. In 1828 he lectured to the British Reformation Society on 'Protestant Unity in Fundamental Doctrines', and in 1836 published *The Unity of the Church, Another Tract for the Times, Addressed Especially to Members of the Establishment*.

Noel strenuously worked for unity in the 1830s when Anglican Evangelicals were polarized over their millenarian views, but in 1831 he opposed the admission of Unitarians to the committee of the Bible Society. A passionate advocate of overseas missions, he championed, more than any other individual, the cooperation of churchmen and Dissenters in the work of the London City Mission. An eloquent advocate of the work of the Ragged Schools movement, in 1836 he inspected schools in Ireland to ascertain the true condition of education there, and in 1840 investigated elementary schooling in England for the Privy Council Committee on Education. His recommendation that government take initiatives to improve standards upset Dissenters.

In 1841, in the midst of the Chartist agitation, his *Plea for the Poor*, the only contribution to the debate by an Anglican clergyman, attacked the operation of the Corn Laws. The plea appeared just as Noel was gazetted as a chaplain to the Queen, and consequently caused much controversy.

Noel attacked the increase in the grant to the Catholic College at Maynooth, not simply as a Protestant, but also because he believed that a government that was already funding

Protestant ministers became an instrument of irreligion if it also sought to subsidize Catholicism. The legitimacy of all establishment was called into question by his advocacy of Irish disestablishment. Although pressed to join and speak for the Liberation Society, he was hesitant to do so. Because he thought its objectives just, however, he allowed the society to use his publications.

The First Five Centuries of the Church; or, the Early Fathers, no Safe Guides (1839), revealed his awareness of developing Tractarian teaching, though he came to very different conclusions about baptismal regeneration. This Noel clearly rejected, thereby incurring episcopal censure. In fact, he was trying to interpret Prayer Book language in an evangelical way at the same time as the Tractarians were seeking to interpret it in a Catholic way.

Noel's secession, defended in his *Essay on the Union of Church and State* (1849), proved to be an isolated act, for it appears that only one Anglican clergyman followed his example. At John Street, however, he baptized as believers some 100 from his former congregation. He was an 'eloquent and earnest advocate of vital and personal religion', and his preaching has been described as 'plaintive and gentle', appealing to the heart rather than to the head; nothing could be allowed to stand in the way of his concern to call sinners to repentance. His evangelistic passion made him a keen collaborator with Lord *Shaftesbury in sponsoring outreach services in the Exeter Hall, though clerical action soon curtailed these.

Serving as chairman of the Baptist Union in both 1855 and 1867, in the 1860s he both berated the Jamaican authorities for their handling of the Governor Eyre affair, and sat on the committee of the London Emancipation Society in support of the North in the American Civil War. At home he took up the temperance cause and joined the Midnight Meeting Movement for the rehabilitation of prostitutes.

In 1864–1865 he protested against *Spurgeon's censuring of Anglican evangelicals reciting Prayer Book language about baptismal regeneration at the expense of their consciences, as unbrotherly and certainly a breach of that pan-evangelical 'Catholic Christianity' in which he had been raised. In writings and hymns he reinforced the views of those Baptists who held to an evangelical sacramentalism: 'As the confession of Christ is necessary to salvation, so is baptism to those who know that this is the appointed method of "confessing him"' (*Essay on Christian Baptism*, 1849, p. 99).

Bibliography
D. W. Bebbington, 'The Life of Baptist Noel', *Baptist Quarterly* 24 (1972), pp. 389–411; G. Carter, 'Evangelical Seceders form the Church of England, c. 1800–1850' (DPhil thesis, Oxford, 1990); K. R. M. Short, 'Baptist Wriothesley Noel', *Baptist Quarterly* 20 (1963), pp. 51–61.

J. H. Y. BRIGGS

■ **O'BRYAN, William** (1778–1868), founder of the Bible Christians, was born at Luxulyan, Cornwall in 1778, the son of William O'Bryan, a farmer and tinner, and his wife Thomasine. His parents were 'Church Methodists', and both William and his father served as churchwardens, but his mother's family also had a Quaker ancestry, and William retained an admiration for the Quaker 'plainness of dress and manner'. Another formative influence was William's introduction as a child to John *Wesley, who expressed the hope that he might be 'a blessing to hundreds and thousands'. By the age of eleven O'Bryan was attending Methodist band meetings, and his formal schooling, which ended when he was fifteen, was followed by a period of self-education in which he developed interests in painting, engraving, Roman history and the religious writings of Thomas à Kempis, John *Bunyan, John Wesley, Richard *Baxter and John *Fletcher. Under the influence of Adam *Clarke and other visiting preachers he became a Wesleyan local preacher in 1800. However, subsequently feeling 'a deep sense of duty laid on [him] to seek the wandering souls of men', he engaged in a wider ministry as an unauthorized itinerant evangelist in 1801, claiming 'to preach wherever God sent him' and establishing several promising societies across eight different parishes in northeast Cornwall.

O'Bryan married Catherine Cowlin, the daughter of a Callestick draper, in 1803, and they lived at the farm at Luxulyan that William had inherited from his father.

Following the loss of their son Ebenezer in 1808, O'Bryan was rejected for the Wesleyan ministry in June 1810, ostensibly because of his family responsibilities, but more probably, in the judgment of the Methodist historian Thomas Shaw, 'on account of his known inability to work with others'. His unauthorized evangelism, his increasing criticism of the Wesleyan itinerants and his radical proposals for connexional reform, which included a reduction of the financial obligations on members and the support of itinerants from voluntary contributions, led to allegations that he was 'tearing up Methodism by the roots'. Indeed, he was twice expelled from membership, in 1810 and 1815: on the former occasion for failure to attend his class meeting and on the latter occasion for his refusal to confine his missionary preaching within the Wesleyan circuit system. He declared defiantly following his initial expulsion: 'I had made up my mind to obey God rather than man and take all the consequences ... not all the men, nor all the fire and faggots on earth could have moved me.'

On 1 October 1815 O'Bryan established an independent circuit based on Week St Mary in northeast Cornwall, where the whole of the Wesleyan society joined him, and soon afterwards he formed new classes at Launcells and at Shebbear, across the Devon border. Popularly known as the Bryanites and later officially as the Bible Christians, the connexion had around 100 members by 1816, and held its first conference near Launceston in 1819 with O'Bryan as president. Many of O'Bryan's supporters were the sons and daughters of landed yeomen, in their early twenties, who were disillusioned with Wesleyan clericalism and connexionalism. By 1820 the connexion was poised for rapid expansion, with forty-three itinerants, no fewer than nineteen of whom were women, including O'Bryan's daughter Mary, 'the Maiden preacher', who as soon as she reached her sixteenth birthday began to assist in missionary activity as far away as Guernsey, where she preached in French in the open air. However, O'Bryan's autocratic style of leadership aroused opposition, which resulted in his emigration to North America with his wife and his effective withdrawal from the movement in 1829, although his journal

reveals continuing unsuccessful attempts to secure an annuity from the connexion. By 1851 the Bible Christians, concentrated largely in Cornwall, Devon and the Isle of Wight, numbered 13,324, and in 1907 they contributed over 32,000 members to the United Methodist Church, of whom nearly 7,000 were in Cornwall.

O'Bryan, who had travelled extensively in London and Kent as well as the West Country, remained a compulsive traveller, undertaking long journeys in North America and Canada and crossing the Atlantic thirteen times between 1831 and 1862. He preached wherever he went, but without the extraordinary impact of his preaching in England, and his journal in his declining years reveals a disappointed, querulous and tired octagenarian. He died in New York in 1868 and was buried in the Greenwood cemetery, Brooklyn, having reverted to the family name of Bryant.

Bibliography
T. Shaw, *The Bible Christians, 1815–1907* (London: Epworth Press, 1965).

J. A. HARGREAVES

■ **OCKENGA, Harold John** (1905–1985), American church leader and educator, was born in Chicago on 6 July 1905, the son of a transit worker and a devout Methodist mother. Converted in 1916, he graduated from Taylor University, Upland, Indiana, in 1926 with athletic and academic distinction. He went on to Princeton Theological Seminary, and when that school was reorganized in 1929, although recently elected president of the student body, he transferred to the newly founded Westminster Theological Seminary in Philadelphia, where he joined Professor J. Gresham *Machen and graduated with honours in 1930. Transferring from the Methodist to the Presbyterian Church (USA) on ordination, he was chosen by Clarence Edward Macartney to be his assistant at First Presbyterian Church, Pittsburgh, from which he went on to be minister (from 1931 to 1936) of Point Breeze Presbyterian Church, also in Pittsburgh. During that time he studied for a PhD in philosophy from the University of Pittsburgh, which he received in 1939. While there he met and married the socialite and artist Audrey Williamson in 1935. They had two daughters, Starr and Aldryth, and a son, John.

In 1936 a leading fundamentalist Congregationalist, A. Z. Conrad, who had been for over thirty years minister of the historic Park Street Church on the Boston Common, chose Ockenga to be his successor. With his striking good looks and his beautiful wife, Ockenga soon became known for his intellectual sermons, cultural sophistication, organizational genius and quick mind. He also had a gift for fundraising from wealthy patrons. By 1940 Ockenga was becoming a player on the national stage, attempting to make a fundamentalism battered by liberalism, anti-intellectualism and ecclesiastical separatism more positive and attractive. He helped to organize the National Association of Evangelicals, composed of both separatists and those who had, like Ockenga, remained in the larger mainline denominations, and was its first president from 1942 to 1944. At Park Street Church he developed new ministry initiatives, including from 1940 annual overseas missionary conferences, the outdoor Mayflower Pulpit, and radio broadcasts of both Sunday services, which reached a wide audience. Never afraid of controversy, he challenged Boston's Roman Catholic hierarchy, led by the redoubtable Cardinal Cushing, and also attacked the academic 'liberal' establishment represented by Harvard. There a significant number of evangelical graduate students came under Ockenga's mentorship, among them Edward John *Carnell, Carl *Henry, Kenneth *Kantzer, Paul King Jewett and Merrill Tenney. Ockenga inspired them with a positive, intellectually responsible and theologically orthodox vision for recapturing the intellectual initiative evangelicals had lost.

Such relationships were useful when Ockenga was approached by radio evangelist Charles E. *Fuller of the radio broadcast 'The Old Fashioned Revival Hour', who offered his inherited wealth for the funding of a theological seminary modelled on the pre-1929 Princeton Seminary of Charles *Hodge, Benjamin *Warfield and Gresham Machen. On 17 April 1947 Ockenga and Fuller with Wilbur Smith, author and self-taught scholar, founded Fuller Theological Seminary with a faculty of 'stars' who would model academic achievement and orthodox faith. Ockenga was to be president, commuting from Boston, where he would continue as pastor at Park Street Church, to Fuller Seminary, which would be located in Pasadena, in suburban Los Angeles. Ockenga was then forced out of the Presbyterian Church (USA) because of charges of divisiveness by the large and powerful Los Angeles presbytery. Before the academic year 1953–1954 Fuller Seminary, with a completed faculty, new buildings and large student body, asked Ockenga to be full-time resident president. Ockenga initially agreed but, under pressure from Park Street Church withdrew his acceptance and remained in Boston. Ockenga's protégé Edward John Carnell then became Fuller Seminary's second president.

In early 1950 evangelist William Franklin *Graham, invited to Boston by Ockenga after a successful Los Angeles campaign, created great excitement with a three-month series of meetings throughout the New England states. Ockenga and Billy Graham forged close bonds and were involved in many evangelical endeavours. One such enterprise was the magazine *Christianity Today*: Graham produced the idea; Ockenga was the first chairman of the board; and generous funding was provided by oil magnate J. Howard *Pew. According to Graham's initial statement, the periodical would 'plant the evangelical flag in the middle of the road, taking a conservative theological position but a definite liberal approach to social problems'. In December 1957 Ockenga was described as 'the originator of "the new Evangelicalism"', as distinct from neo-orthodoxy, modernism and fundamentalism. But tensions arose and increased. Edward John Carnell resigned as president of Fuller Seminary in 1959, faced with mounting criticism of his supposedly vacillating theological position. Ockenga was deeply distressed by Carnell's growing mental instability and by his tragic death in April 1967. A year later Carl Henry resigned after eleven years as editor of *Christianity Today*. Henry felt that Ockenga, as board chairman, had given him inadequate support in his conflicts with Pew, the politically right-wing patron.

In 1969, after almost thirty-three years at Park Street Church, Ockenga became president of the newly formed Gordon-Conwell Theological Seminary. The school represented an amalgamation (at Billy Graham's initiative) of Gordon Divinity School of Boston (founded 1889) and Conwell School of Theology of Temple University in Philadelphia (founded 1884). With the financial backing of J. Howard Pew, the seminary was situated in a former Carmelite seminary in north shore Boston. In his inaugural address on 22 October 1969, Ockenga declared: 'The time has come for us to re-emphasize the Christian virtues of purity, honesty, industry, charity and courtesy. We must allow Christian convictions to penetrate every aspect of our existence ... And in so doing, we must hold fast to an unchanging biblical standard of truth and virtue.' His gifts as a fundraiser were particularly challenged when Pew died suddenly in 1971 without leaving a legally binding obligation on the Pew Charitable Trust to support the seminary to the extent promised. Ockenga set up a Center for Urban Education, countering the drift of American evangelicals to the suburbs and fulfilling his vision for urban ministry. In April of 1976 Harold *Lindsell, Ockenga's biographer (1951) and chairman (from 1979 to 1992) of the board of Gordon-Conwell Theological Seminary, published the controversial The Battle for the Bible. Its claim that there had been a radical departure from historic orthodoxy on the part of some evangelicals made an immediate and divisive impact on the Ockenga circle.

Ockenga retired as president of Gordon-Conwell Theological Seminary at the age of seventy-four in 1979. In his later years he became increasingly a senior statesman for evangelicalism and took an advisory role in the 1966 Berlin Conference on Evangelism and the 1974 Lausanne Conference on World Evangelization. But the so-called 'network' that he administered was no longer unified and coherent. He had succeeded in raising the profile of evangelicalism, but the centre of the movement could not hold together amid the complexities and diversity of life in late twentieth-century America. Active to the end, though afflicted by the dimming of his once quick mind, he died in South Hamilton, Massachusetts, on 8 February 1985.

Bibliography

J. A. Carpenter, Revive Us Again: The Reawakening of American Fundamentalism (New York: Oxford University Press, 1997);
H. C. Englizian, Brimstone Corner: Park St. Church Boston (Chicago: Moody Press, 1948); H. Lindsell, Park Street Prophet (Wheaton: Van Kampen, 1951); A. D. MacLeod, 'A. Z. Conrad, Park St. Pioneer', New England Reformed Journal 16 (summer 2000), pp. 1–16; G. M. Marsden, Reforming Fundamentalism: Fuller Seminary and the New Evangelicalism (Grand Rapids: Eerdmans, 1987); R. Nelson, The Making and Unmaking of an Evangelical Mind: The Case of Edward Carnell (New York: Cambridge University Press, 1987); G. Rosell, 'The Ockenga Vision', Contact vol. 30, 1 (summer 2000), pp. 3–6, 10–11, 20–21.

A. D. MacLeod

■ ODEN, Thomas Clark (1931–), Methodist minister and theologian and professor at Drew University, was born on 21 October 1931, in Altus, Oklahoma. His father was a lawyer, and his mother a music teacher. In 1949 he enrolled in the University of Oklahoma and graduated with a BLitt in 1953. He began studying theology formally at Perkins School of Theology (Southern Methodist University), graduating with his BD in 1956. Ordained by the Oklahoma Conference of the United Methodist Church (deacon, 1954; elder, 1956), he served in varied parish ministries. Beginning in 1956 he studied at Yale University, and was awarded his MA in 1958 and his PhD in 1960. Hans Frei and H. Richard Niebuhr supervised his work. His doctoral dissertation was revised for publication as Radical Obedience: The Ethics of Rudolf Bultmann. One year of postdoctoral study followed at Heidelberg.

In 1958 he began his professional teaching career as an instructor at Perkins School of Theology. From 1960 to 1970 he was associate professor and then professor at Phillips University. In 1971 he became the Henry Anson Buttz Professor of theology at Drew University, where he taught until his retirement.

Oden was also a guest lecturer or visiting professor at Moscow State University, Oxford, Edinburgh, Duke, Emory, Princeton and Claremont. In addition he was consultant to the Ethics and Public Policy Center of Washington, DC, the White House Dialogue on Urban Initiatives (1985), and the Public

Information Office Briefings (1984–1986). Oden has published approximately forty books and eighty articles.

Following his *Agenda for Theology* (1978), republished as *After Modernity, What?* (1990) with four additional chapters and an introduction by J. I. *Packer, Oden described himself as an 'out-of-the-closet evangelical'. He continued to distance himself from the ethos of the institutions, images and 'isms' with which he was previously identified. His *Requiem: A Lament in Three Movements* (1995) is an anguished autobiography concerning the lethal stranglehold that totalitarian 'liberals' have on denominational bureaucracies, church conferences and seminary education. A former left-wing radical, he later affirmed the genuine *radix* of the Scripture-normed authority of the post-apostolic writers. His 'new' radicalism, inspired and measured by the gospel, led him to espouse out-of-step causes, such as the utter unreformability of the seminaries without the overhauling of the practice of tenure.

After his retirement, Oden became a contributing editor of *Christianity Today*. His position there magnified his influence enormously, as this magazine was the most widely read evangelical journal in North America.

Never backing away from rendering the judgments that he deemed gospel fidelity to enjoin, Oden made the rare move of publicly faulting another denomination in another country. He pronounced the United Church of Canada (Canada's largest Protestant denomination, formed in 1925 from Methodists, Presbyterians and Congregationalists) devoid of ecumenical identity; it was no longer 'properly to be called an ecumenical communion'; i.e. was no longer the church in that it had abandoned consensual teaching on creation, sin, covenant sexual fidelity and the blessings of marriage.

By his own admission every theological turn that Oden took, except the last, was a left turn. The 'turn' that 'righted' him, however, was not a right turn or a series of compensatory right turns but rather a turn back into the Fathers. Startled at the shallowness and virulence of 1960s radicalism, he looked for theological resources and discovered that patristic thinkers exhibited a profundity and pertinence that few modern authors could rival.

Oden described himself as an 'orthodox, ecumenical evangelical', whose orthodoxy 'is nothing more or less than the ancient consensual tradition of exegesis'. His work is designed to articulate, in the spirit of Vincent of Lerins, the faith of the universal church.

Its focus is the consensus of the first five centuries, since 'antiquity is a criterion of authentic memory in any historical testimony'. Oden's preoccupation with antiquity makes him refuse to renounce his 'zeal for unoriginality ... the apostles were testy with revisionists'.

Its mood is evangelical, reflecting throughout the gospel's particularity and inherent militancy. This mood contrasts sharply with a theological modernity the treachery of which has rendered evangelism impossible and orthodoxy unrecognizable. An evangelical invitation suffuses Oden's work as he urges readers to decide for Christ, warning them tenderly yet solemnly about the peril of procrastination: 'One who neglects an opportunity at hand may not have another.'

Its centre is the rediscovery of ancient ecumenical theology and the recovery of classical Christianity in Oden's evolving Wesleyan tradition.

Its target audience is the working pastor, since in Oden's view Christian teaching is healthy only where living tradition is embodied by an actual community. (See his several books on pastoral theology.)

Its orientation is that for which Oden commends *Arminius and those after Arminius – *viz.* 'the gradual Protestant retrieval of the ancient ecumenical consensus on grace and freedom'. Oden consistently disavows the predestinarianism of the later Augustine (even though for him Augustine remains one of the ecumenical giants) that emerged so very strongly in the work of the magisterial Reformers. Oden regards this deterministic misunderstanding of election as a departure and declension from the received faith. Characteristically the church has upheld the inviolability of the humanness of God's covenant partners. At the same time, Oden discerns and denounces the error of Pelagianism, together with the more subtle seductiveness of semi-Pelagianism. His work incorporates everywhere a nuanced discussion of *gratia operans/gratia co-operans* that, while strange to Protestants who are unacquainted with patristic thought, is crucial in any approach to him.

Its most recent expression is the *Ancient Christian Commentary on Scripture*, the purpose of which is the recovery of classical Christian exegesis. A major strength of this project, Oden maintains, is the re-presentation of texts so very old that they contain no trace of European imperialism (and, therefore, no inherent revulsion, for instance, for Asian and African Christians). These texts will therein prove singularly significant as they are brought to bear on the cultural formation of both West and East. In addition, ancient exegesis will expose readers to the intimate connection between prayer and study, to the relation of theology to vibrant Christian community, and to worship as the context in which Scripture is read. Oden hopes that Protestants especially will peruse the *Ancient Commentary*. Their doing so will remedy the theological one-sidedness that arises on account of Protestantism's neglect of pre-Reformation texts, and also reduce Pietism's extreme vulnerability to modern consciousness. Protestants can expect to be startled, for instance, by Nazianzen's theological power and Jerome's openness to the Spirit's energy.

Oden indicates repeatedly why he writes polemically and prolifically. Although theology as the inquiry into God is inherently the most engaging of all subjects, theologians have turned it 'into a yawning bore'. Contemporary theology is boring because it is so very destructive; heresy is treasonous, and when protracted, tedious. He is aware, however, of the presumption that threatens anyone claiming to be a corrective, and the stated aim of his three-volume *Systematic Theology* (1987, 1989, 1992) is to invite readers to test his own fallibility.

Oden sees all his work as setting a limit to the licence of 'guild' (i.e. academically appointed) theologians and exegetes, whose perfidy has summoned him to be 'someone to teach you the elementary truths of God's word all over again' (Heb. 5:12). For this reason his work as a whole and his systematic theology in particular re-visit the elemental, doctrinal 'building blocks' of the faith: specifically, theological matters that are articulated in the creed and that appear in the standard *regulae fidei*.

Oden's single largest work is his *Systematic Theology* (1,500 pages, 15,000 references to classical writings). Its purpose is 'to set forth an ordered view of the faith of the Christian community upon which there has generally been substantial agreement between the traditions of East and West, including Catholic, Protestant and Orthodox'. Unlike virtually all systematic theologians, however, Oden insists that the exposition of the traditional theological topics in his work serves primarily as an introduction to the annotations; i.e. the annotations embedded in the text are more important than the text itself. Aiming to be true to Scripture, to his native Wesleyanism, and to the Fathers, he regards God's holiness as the linchpin of the entire theological enterprise.

Oden's theological 'journey' brought him to this point after earlier starts that if not false were hesitant at least. He names five theological instructors who shaped his thought: Albert Outler, Rudolf Bultmann, H. Richard Niebuhr, Karl Barth and Will Herberg. Despite the apparent neo-orthodoxy of these men, Oden subsequently criticized neo-orthodoxy for its non-interest in worship, sacrament, pastoral care, the concrete tasks of ministry and the holiness of the church. His 'best' teacher was Outler, who introduced him to Augustine and *Wesley. Although his PhD dissertation was a comparative study of Bultmann and Barth, he soon repudiated the favoured Bultmannism that had first brought him to theological prominence and concentrated on Barth. In the 1960s Oden was concerned chiefly with the relation of theology to psychotherapy. Attentive now to the necessity, nature and integrity of human agency, he came to regard the Eastern Church Fathers as a corrective to Barth's one-sidedness.

Upon Oden's appointment to Drew University his friend and colleague Will Herberg persuaded him to ground his thinking in classical sources. Ironically, said Oden, a conservative Jew was his chief mentor in classical Christianity. With the arbitrariness and weakness of his earlier liberalism now exposed, and himself repulsed by his former support of the abortion platform, he abandoned situation ethics and with it the entire liberal worldview. Rejecting too his earlier notion that novelty is the task of theology, he jettisoned 'creativity', now convinced, thanks to J. H. Newman, that his responsibility was to *listen* to the deposit of truth already sufficiently given. Intrigued by the decisions of the ancient Ecumenical Councils, he plunged into patristics. Quickly he identified himself in terms of 'paleo-orthodoxy', an expression coined to indicate the distance now between him and neo-orthodoxy. By his own admission modern psychology had taught him to trust his experience, whereas ancient writers now taught him to trust that Scripture and tradition would transmute his experience.

Oden endeavoured to honour his theological parents by means of two books relating to Wesley. *Doctrinal Standards in the Wesleyan Tradition* (1988) assesses the nature, place and function of normative doctrine in the United Methodist Church specifically and in the churches of the Wesleyan family generally. It aims at healing the doctrinal amnesia that has largely afflicted mainline North American Methodists. *John Wesley's Scriptural Christianity* (1994) expounds Wesley's theology on all major points, beginning in the time-honoured way with God's attributes and concluding with eschatology. It is a contemporary exposition and interpretation of Wesley's thought, aiming always at fidelity to Wesley's text. Its subordinate purpose is to convey Wesley to other branches of the Christian family. Finding Wesley rooted in the patristic, Anglican, holy living and Puritan traditions, Oden sees Wesleyanism as a bridge between Protestants and Catholics, although it has profound affinities with the Eastern Church tradition. He deems Wesleyanism's characteristic resistance to cooperation at the hands of party or fad to be one of its major strengths.

Two areas of Oden's theology that seem problematic for evangelicals are his seemingly uncritical espousal of the Fathers and an 'ecumenical' view of baptism, that some may find indistinguishable from sacramental regeneration. Concerning the first matter Oden affirms repeatedly his agreement with the Fathers that in the 'theandric' (*sic*) One the humanity suffers but never the deity. Specifically, he denies that the Father suffers in the Son's crucifixion. Nowhere does Oden claim that the risen, exalted Lord continues to suffer. In the same vein the neo-Platonism of the Fathers goes unchecked. Concerning the second matter Oden, to be sure, insists that '... it is not baptism of itself that saves', yet he appears to undo this assertion throughout his discussion of baptism, as in his remark, 'The Holy Spirit through baptism offers, calls forth, and elicits regeneration in a spiritually blessed water in which the whole triune God is by grace effectively present', and 'The Spirit remains in those who have received the grace of baptism, who remain indelibly known to God.' He appears impelled to speak this subject much as the Fathers do.

Oden predicts that a sign of hope in twenty-first century Christian thought will be its preoccupation with the rediscovery of boundaries in theology: 'I would love to find a seminary where a discussion is taking place about whether a line can be drawn between faith and unfaith.'

Bibliography
T. C. Oden, *Requiem: A Lament in Three Movements* (Nashville: Abingdon Press, 1993).

V. SHEPHERD

■ **OLDHAM, Joseph Houldsworth** (1874–1969), missionary strategist and ecumenist, was born in Bombay, India, the son of George Oldham, a military engineer and lay evangelist. After schooling in Scotland, he entered Trinity College, Oxford, in 1892. During his first term he decided for Christ at one of D. L. *Moody's evangelistic meetings, and joined the evangelical Oxford Inter-Collegiate Christian Union (OICCU) and, soon, the Student Missionary Volunteer Union (SMVU). In 1894 he met John R. *Mott on the latter's first visit to Oxford, and became secretary of OICCU.

On graduating in 1896, Oldham took up a year's appointment as joint general secretary of the British SMVU and the Inter-Varsity Christian Union, and in 1897 began what he envisaged would be a lifelong missionary career by going to Lahore as Scottish YMCA Secretary. There in 1898 he married Mary Fraser, sister of his close Oxford friend Alex Fraser. Both had to be invalided home in 1901 after typhoid. Oldham's short Indian experience, however, was to prove decisive for the course of his life. His closest friendships had been with Indian Christians, notably S. K. Datta and K. T. Paul, through whom he quickly learned to see the Western missionary enterprise through Indian eyes, especially the problem of Christianity being the religion of 'the ruling race'.

Oldham then spent three years studying theology at New College, Edinburgh, and a year at Halle, Germany, with the pioneer missiologist Gustav Warneck. From 1906 he was secretary of the Mission Study Council of the United Free Church of Scotland, quickly proving his abilities as educator, writer and organizer. It was at John Mott's personal instigation that in 1908 he was appointed secretary for the International Missionary Conference being planned for Edinburgh in 1910.

Edinburgh 1910 is generally regarded as the birth of the modern ecumenical movement, for by setting up a Continuation Committee it produced the first structure accountable to churches and mission boards at the international level. Oldham was appointed secretary, and in 1912 founded the *International Review of Missions*, which he edited for many years. Hopes for increasing cooperation in world mission were frustratingly slow in being realized, however, and were all but dashed by the 1914–1918 war. German missionary leaders were embittered by what they felt to be their British and American partners' acquiescence in the confiscation of German missions in British territories. Oldham's efforts, through patient negotiation with the British Government, to ensure their long-term preservation and eventual return to German hands after the Versailles Treaty came to be seen as an outstanding example of ecumenical service and reconciliation.

A new beginning came in 1921 with the formation of the International Missionary Council (IMC), largely of Oldham's designing and of which he became secretary, based in London. A chief concern of Oldham was to ensure cooperative mission under the management of the indigenous churches, and he was instrumental in creating the Indian National Christian Council. He was also insistent that the mission agenda must embrace concerns as broad as race relations, economic justice and education. Throughout the 1920s he was himself deeply involved in campaigning for the rights of Africans in British colonial Africa, and in the development of a partnership between missions and government in education. He was the prime mover in persuading the British Government to set up in 1923 the Permanent Advisory Committee on Native Education in Tropical Africa, and with others founded in 1924 the International Institute of African Languages and Cultures. The climax of his African work came with his participation in the Hilton-Young Commission, which in 1928 visited east and central Africa and advised against the policy of 'closer union' which would have indefinitely entrenched white dominance. It was in the midst of this engagement with African issues that he wrote his most substantial book, *Christianity and the Race Problem* (1924), a pioneering study in the field.

By the late 1920s Oldham was increasingly dissatisfied with what he saw as the introverted and self-preserving attitudes dominating the missions boards. He was sceptical about the aims and methods of the Jerusalem International Missionary Conference (1928), and believed that greater value lay in smaller-scale but more focused work utilizing the 'best minds' on contemporary problems. 'Real life is meeting' became his motto, deriving from the personalist philosophy of Martin Buber, which he applied both to his understanding of society and to his methods of study in encounter groups. In the face of the yawning crisis within Western society and the rise of totalitarianism, he was progressively more attracted by the neo-orthodox theology of Karl Barth and Emil Brunner, especially with the onset of the German Church Struggle, during which he and his assistant at the IMC William Paton did their best to help the German missions threatened by the Nazi regime. He was greatly drawn to the 'Life and Work' movement and in 1934, somewhat to the dismay of John Mott, became study secretary for the conference on 'Church, Community and State' to be held in Oxford in 1937. Oldham effectively acted as organizer for Oxford 1937, especially its preparatory process, which drew together theologians, social scientists and political and literary figures from many confessions and (mainly Western) countries in the most enterprising attempt at international and ecumenical study hitherto undertaken.

Meanwhile, discussions were under way on the formation of a world body which would integrate the diverse strands of ecumenical work. Oldham was chief architect of the World Council of Churches (WCC), the constitution of which was agreed in 1938. The Second World War interrupted the process of formation of the WCC, but during the war years Oldham pursued his concerns through three main channels: 'The Moot', a high-powered discussion group including figures as diverse as Karl Mannheim, T. S. Eliot and John Baillie; his popular weekly *Christian News-Letter*; and the formation in 1942 of the Christian Frontier Council, which brought together lay people sharing a concern for engagement with the world through their secular occupations in politics, industry and academic life. Always central to Oldham was the role of lay people as the prime agents of mission. By the time of the inauguration of the WCC at its first Assembly in Amsterdam in 1948, Oldham had long since retired from any official ecumenical position but he remained an influential adviser, and it was he who coined the phrase 'the responsible society' which was taken up by the Assembly and remained in force for some twenty years as the key motif of ecumenical social thinking.

In old age Oldham remained alert to many contemporary issues, from atomic power to cybernetics. The title 'evangelical' might be thought questionable for one who had travelled so far from his student context. But Oldham retained many features of evangelicalism. His famous description of Christianity as 'not primarily a philosophy but a crusade' in his book on race is redolent of the campaigning *Wilberforce. He was a prolific writer, but his most widely used work was his little *Devotional Diary*, and prayers at breakfast remained his daily practice. As late as 1942 he could still write: 'To save society we have to begin by saving persons.' Significantly, his last substantial theological essay was entitled *Life is Commitment* (1953), while the one biography he wrote was of the evangelical Anglican missionary Florence Allshorn. His faith found outward expression in a remarkable self-effacement, not to mention a patient endurance of the almost complete deafness which afflicted him from middle life. 'A wily saint', many affectionately called him.

Bibliography
K. Clements, *Faith on the Frontier: A Life of J. H. Oldham* (Edinburgh: T. & T. Clark; Geneva: WCC, 1999).

K. CLEMENTS

■ **ORANGE, William A.** (1889–1966), New Zealand Anglican minister, was the most influential Anglican evangelical in the New Zealand church. He was born on 9 August 1889 into a large working-class family. He was converted when his family was living in Kaikoura, in the northern part of the south island of New Zealand, between 1899 and 1904. Back in Christchurch from 1904, he was deeply influenced by strict teaching on unworldly discipleship, which he received partly from Brethren sources, yet he turned to the Anglican Church for his ministerial training, enrolling in College House in 1914.

How Orange came to be the effective founder of the modern evangelical movement in the Anglican Church in New Zealand is something of a mystery. A modest evangelical contribution had been made previously, notably by the Church Missionary Society, the diocese of Waiapu and then the Nelson diocese, which had very close links with the strongly evangelical diocese of Sydney. Yet the overall tone of the denomination was High Church; the church was reluctant to see itself as purely Protestant or to cooperate with other churches, and its level of biblical literacy was low. Orange was ordained a deacon in 1919, having already engaged in several battles with workmates and churchmen over worldliness and ritualism. He served as a deacon at St Saviour's, Sydenham, and then at St Barnabas, Fendalton, but between his two curacies he travelled overseas with a friend. Priested in the Anglican Church in 1923, he became vicar of Waikari, a country parish in North Canterbury, in 1924, and here made his name by opposing dancing and bazaars as means of fundraising. His evangelicalism was now mature and conscious.

A crucial event in Orange's career was his appointment in 1930 as vicar of the Low Church parish of Sumner, a beach suburb of Christchurch; he remained there until 1946. These years at Sumner were remarkable. Less than six months after Orange's arrival Dr Howard *Guinness visited New Zealand as the missionary of the newly founded Inter-Varsity Fellowship, and founded both the Canterbury University College Evangelical Union and the Crusader Movement for boys and girls from state secondary schools. Orange at once gave his support to the new movements. At the same time, he continued the boys' Bible Class established by his predecessor on Sunday afternoons. It soon became very popular with intelligent young evangelical men. Students from many suburbs and denominations, including Brethren, began travelling long distances by tram or bicycle to Sumner to hear Orange's lucid expository teaching, often staying for the evening service at the church. His impact was reinforced by the frequent series of Friday evening expositions that he gave to the newly formed Evangelical Union at Canterbury University College. After a few years, members of this group, which numbered about eighty and had been moulded into a close fellowship popularly known as the 'Orange Pips', began to seek ordination and enter other forms of Christian service: mission, theological teaching and interdenominational work. Two of them, Maxwell Wiggins and Maurice Goodall, later became bishops. The group was remarkably influential, particularly in the Anglican Church.

Orange's own influence was based on his ardour as a biblical preacher. For him the text of Scripture was full of meaning, and he interpreted it in a passionately Protestant way. Dispensational eschatology was an important element in his teaching, and from the Brethren he adopted a typological interpretation of many parts of the Old Testament. He believed that literally every word of the Bible mattered and supported his belief by means of allegorical interpretation. He had an ability to inspire followers, to bring out the best in people, to develop evangelical ardour and deep commitment among people who were capable leaders in their own right. He made some impact in British and Australian evangelical circles on his several visits abroad. The 'Orange Pips' who were ordained in the Church of England were very capable, very certain of themselves, but (perhaps surprisingly) never unbalanced zealots, although some were sceptical regarding bishops and church structures. They were outstanding in the roles that they attained. Curiously, they showed greater wisdom than their mentor did in some of his decisions.

In 1946 Orange was persuaded by L. B. Miller, a prominent Brethren businessman, to escape from the pressures and minutiae of parish ministry in order to oversee a new evangelical study centre that would extend and focus his ministry. He was appointed warden of Tyndale House, which was based in a beautiful property on the Cashmere Hills in another part of the city. The appointment seemed to provide him with an extraordinary opportunity, but almost immediately it proved disastrous. Different concepts of work and ministry and different churchmanships proved irreconcilable. Within a year, and in sympathy for his predicament, the dean of the Cathedral, who was anything but Low Church, appointed him as acting and then permanent precentor of the Cathedral, which dominates the centre of the (very Anglican) city. He became an honorary canon in 1951, and in 1954 chaplain of the Cathedral Grammar School, where the boy choristers were trained. His churchmanship never altered, but it had been his love of Anglican liturgy that had kept him in the church from the beginning, and now he was able to enjoy that liturgy at its best. For their part, the other members of the Cathedral staff, even the colourful dean, Martin Sullivan, learned to appreciate the meticulous little man.

Meanwhile, Orange's vast library continued to grow, and he continued to have a significant influence, particularly in Scripture Union and the Inter-Varsity Fellowship, although he slowly came to seem rather archaic in the world of the new evangelicalism. His style of evangelical exposition did not translate well into the post-war world, but his influence was not limited to this, being built upon his personal Christian faith and commitment and his passionate love of Jesus Christ. He died on 28 June 1966, leaving behind a large personal library, which formed the basis of Latimer House, which was for the next forty years the centre of the evangelical Anglican community in New Zealand.

Bibliography

P. J. Lineham, *No Ordinary Union: The Story of Scripture Union in New Zealand*

(Wellington: Scripture Union in New Zealand, 1980).

P. J. LINEHAM

■ ORR, James (1844–1913), Scottish theologian and polemicist, was born in Glasgow on 11 April 1844. He was orphaned at an early age; subsequent apprenticeship (out of economic necessity) to a bookbinder and postponement of his university entrance until the age of twenty-one suggest a Spartan adolescence. He identified as a young man with the minority United Presbyterians (UPs) and their egalitarian tradition. He then studied at the UP Divinity Hall, Edinburgh (1868–1872), and Glasgow University (MA, 1870, BD, 1872, DD, 1885) where, under the tutelage of John Veitch (one of Scotland's last common-sense philosophers) and the Neo-Hegelians John and Edward Caird, he acquired a respect for reason's role in theology. After a pastoral ministry of seventeen years in the Scottish Borders town of Hawick, he delivered a lecture series that was published as *The Christian View of God and the World* (1893). This work, which proved to be his greatest, launched him on a prolific academic career. In the remaining two decades of his life, while serving first at the UP College in Edinburgh (1891–1900) and then at the United Free Church College in Glasgow (1900–1913), he wrote sixteen books, edited a magazine and a major reference work, contributed hundreds of articles and reviews, and frequently lectured in North America. The cumulative effect of these activities was that his voice seemed omnipresent in his day.

During the 1870s Orr was among those Presbyterians who campaigned for modified subscription to the Westminster Confession. He helped draft the UP Declaratory Statement of 1879, which qualified and effectively reduced the extent to which a minister was obliged to affirm the content of the church's subordinate standards. The UP approach was imitated by the other main wings of Scottish Presbyterianism, and served to undermine the rule of Calvinism in Scotland.

The central thesis of Orr's *The Christian View* (a thesis that later directly influenced American evangelical theologian Carl F. H. *Henry among others) is that there is inherent in the Christian faith a uniquely adequate and coherent interpretation of existence. Though Christianity is a religion and not a philosophy, it does offer among its benefits a supremely satisfying worldview. It is the coherence of the Christian worldview, its harmony with reason and moral experience, that makes it compelling. Thus the systematic presentation of evangelical doctrine (which is nothing other than the setting forth of this worldview) is in fact the most comprehensive apologetic for the Christian faith. Accordingly, *The Christian View* does not begin with an apology for Scripture and then proceed to confident deduction therefrom. The Christian system of belief is commended on the basis of its own intrinsic merits and the correspondence assumed to exist between its claims and humanity's capacity to recognize truth intuitively and rationally. In this sense, then, the Christian faith is self-authenticating.

Having retreated from a strict adherence to confessional Calvinism, Orr gave notice in *The Christian View* of what he considered the Christian faith to be, namely, a religion of personal redemption necessarily undergirded by the classic doctrines of evangelical belief. 'I do not believe,' he said, 'that in order to preserve [the Christian view] one single truth we have been accustomed to see shining in that constellation will require to be withdrawn'. This comment set the tone for Orr's subsequent theological contribution, which may best be described as a call for continued adherence to the central tenets of evangelical orthodoxy. In the course of his career, he urged such continuity in the face of challenges from Ritschlianism, Old Testament criticism, evolutionary theory and the quest of the historical Jesus.

Orr was one of the earliest and principal British critics of German liberal Albrecht Ritschl's thought. In his *The Ritschlian Theology and the Evangelical Faith* (1897) and elsewhere, Orr insisted that Ritschlianism was opposed to genuine Christianity and was intellectually untenable because of its limitation of the role of reason in Christian thought and experience. In *The Progress of Dogma* (1901) Orr tried to counter Ritschlian Adolf Harnack's negative verdict on the history of dogma by arguing that it has unfolded according to a recognizable inner logic. By regarding this logical movement as a manifestation of God's hand in history, Orr sought to vindicate the orthodox doctrines that the movement produced.

In *The Problem of the Old Testament* (1906), which was prompted partly by his Glasgow colleague George Adam Smith's advocacy of the documentary hypothesis, Orr argued for the 'essential Mosaicity' of the Pentateuch, and for a traditional construction of Old Testament history. Orr treated Charles Darwin's theory of humanity's origin as a serious threat to the Christian doctrines of humanity and sin. Initially he appeared comfortable with theistic evolution but later, in *God's Image in Man* (1905), he stressed the necessity of supernatural interruptions of the evolutionary process to account for the human being as a embodied soul and still later, in *Sin as a Problem of Today* (1910), he argued that the idea of moral evolution (as articulated by F. R. Tennant and others) undermined the seriousness of sin and humanity's accountability for it. Finally, he held firmly to orthodox Christological formulations in the face of alternative assessments of the historical Jesus. Among his reasons for doing so was his pragmatic conviction that nothing less would be sufficient to sustain the vitality of the church's practical religious life. In such works as *The Virgin Birth of Christ* (1907), he defended theologically as well as biblically the virginal conception of the mediator.

In the course of all these initiatives, Orr made allowances that later fundamentalists would view as unthinkable concessions. He welcomed Ritschl's emphasis on kingdom expansion; he made qualified allowance for evolutionary development; he was unconcerned to defend a literal interpretation of the early chapters of Genesis, and he took the view that an insistence on biblical inerrancy was actually 'suicidal' (see his *Revelation and Inspiration* [1910], p. 198).

None the less, a fairly widespread academic resistance to his views, combined with his own deep-seated populist instincts and common-sense convictions, led Orr in later years to direct his appeals primarily towards the Christian public (see, e.g., his *The Bible Under Trial* [1907], *The Faith of a Modern Christian* [1910] and his contributions to *The Fundamentals* [1910–1915]). His last great work as general editor of the five-volume *International Standard Bible Encyclopaedia* (1915),

according to its preface a reference tool 'adapted more directly to the needs of the average pastor and Bible student', constituted a substantial and enduring means of extending conservative orthodoxy's line of defence.

Orr's contribution was decisively shaped by the conviction that evangelical orthodoxy is ultimately self-authenticating, that truth comprises a unity or interconnected whole, and that genuine Christian belief implies a two-storey supernaturalist cosmology. The significance of Orr's theological contribution lies not in its pervasive originality, but in the breadth of his grasp of classic doctrine, the exhaustiveness of the reading upon which his conclusions were based and the vigour with which he defended and propagated his views. His personal emphasis on supernaturalism, as well as his populist sympathies, were certainly hallmarks of later fundamentalism; very rarely, however, were the breadth of his scholarship, or the firm but cordially inclusive tenor of his apologetic efforts, matched among his conservative successors.

Bibliography

G. G. Scorgie, *A Call for Continuity: The Theological Contribution of James Orr* (Macon: Mercer, 1989); A. P. F. Sell, *Defending and Declaring the Faith: Some Scottish Examples 1860–1920* (Exeter: Paternoster; Colorado Springs: Helmers & Howard, 1987).

Earlier versions of this article appeared in N. M. de S. Cameron, D. F. Wright and D. C. Lachman (eds.), *Dictionary of Scottish Church History and Theology* (Edinburgh: T. & T. Clark, 1993) and T. Hart (ed.), *A Dictionary of Historical Theology* (Carlisle: Paternoster Press, 2001).

G. G. SCORGIE

■ **OTTERBEIN, Philip William** (1726–1813), German Reformed pastor, was a leader of the United Brethren, a German-American evangelical movement. Otterbein enjoyed fellowship with non-Reformed evangelists such as the Mennonite Martin Boehm and the Methodist Francis *Asbury, oversaw missionary and church-planting work and, near the end of his life, ordained the United Brethren preacher Christian Newcomer. Although the United Brethren became a separate denomination, Otterbein never relinquished German Reformed membership. His career exemplified in eighteenth-century America continental Pietism's ideal of evangelical unity.

Born into a clerical family at Dillenburg, Nassau, Otterbein and his five brothers followed their father, grandfather and uncle into the ministry. Philip was educated at the University of Herborn, where Reformed confessionalism, as expressed in the irenic Heidelberg Catechism (1563), was combined with the devotion and methods of Pietism. After several preaching and teaching posts between 1748 and 1752, Otterbein responded to Michael Schlatter's call for pastors to serve the German Reformed of America. Following ordination, in 1752 he and five others were commissioned by the Reformed Synod in Amsterdam. Otterbein began his ministry in Lancaster, Pennsylvania, where the mystical communitarian Pietism of nearby Ephrata Cloister was influential. During his six-year Lancaster pastorate the congregation erected a stone building and adopted stricter 'rules of order', and Otterbein established his ministry on the evangelistic, as opposed to the liturgical, wing of the German Reformed Church. After two years as pastor in Tulpehocken, where he instituted small-group prayer meetings, he was called in 1760 to Frederick, Maryland, and, from 1765 to 1774, to York, Pennsylvania. In 1762 he married Susan LeRoy of Lancaster, who died childless six years later. Otterbein's one extant sermon, *The Salvation-Bringing Incarnation and Glorious Victory of Jesus Christ Over the Devil and Death*, published in German by Christopher Sauer in 1763, pointedly called for 'agony of heart' for our 'inner corruption' and offered grace – 'to be born again' with 'Christ in us'.

In his pastorates Otterbein travelled extensively to preach the gospel and bring the sacraments and pastoral care to rural congregations. At Pentecost 1767 he met the Mennonite evangelist Martin Boehm at a 'great meeting' ('grosse Versammlung') held at Isaac Long's barn in Lancaster County. These two- and three-day revival meetings, remarkably similar to the Scots-Irish 'sacramental season' gatherings that evolved into the American camp meeting, attracted German-speaking people from across the Lutheran-Anabaptist spectrum. After hearing Boehm preach, Otterbein embraced him and announced, 'Wir sind Bruder' ('We are brothers'). Otterbein's desire to hold together his Reformed Church and broadly evangelical allegiances was evident in his 1770 visit to Germany, where he reaffirmed old ties with his teachers and friends who were now pastors. And, as he carefully explained, when he accepted the call as pastor in Baltimore in 1774, the controversy that had already split the original church was not of his making, and his congregation was in full fellowship with the Reformed coetus. Further, his 'Pipe Creek conferences' in rural Maryland were aimed at the renewal of the Reformed Church through revival preaching and class meetings.

The German Evangelical Reformed Church of Baltimore, with Otterbein as pastor, became the centre of the United Brethren movement. Otterbein, Boehm and like-spirited preachers went on preaching tours together and supported an association of societies and churches throughout Pennsylvania, Maryland and Virginia. The Baltimore congregation's *Church Book* of 1785 referred to 'churches, under the superintendence of William Otterbein' which 'stand in fraternal unity with us'. Otterbein in 1774 began a close friendship with Francis Asbury, participating in his 1784 ordination as superintendent of the Methodist Episcopal Church. In response to criticism of his theology, Otterbein admitted that on predestination 'I cannot side with Calvin ... I believe that God is love and that he desires the welfare of all his creatures ... I believe in election, but cannot persuade myself that God has absolutely and without condition predestined some men to perdition.' Preachers associated with Otterbein and Boehm held a significant meeting at his Baltimore parsonage in 1789 and organized as the Vereinigte Bruderschaft zu Christo (United Brethren in Christ) in 1800. Although Otterbein continued to attend Reformed Church synod meetings with some regularity, it may be noted that after he died in Baltimore on 17 November 1813 no Reformed pastor attended the funeral.

The United Brethren denomination united in 1946 with the Evangelical Association (founded by Jacob Albright in the early 1800s) and in 1968 became part of the United Methodist Church.

Bibliography

C. Core, *Philip William Otterbein: Pastor, Ecumenist* (Dayton: Board of Publication, Evangelical United Brethren Church, 1968); W. Drury, *The Life of Rev. Philip William Otterbein* (Dayton: United Brethren Publishing House, 1884); J. S. O'Malley, *Pilgrimage of Faith: The Legacy of the Otterbeins* (Metuchen: Scarecrow Press, 1973).

C. E. HAMBRICK-STOWE

■ **OWEN, John** (1616–1683), English theologian, was without doubt not only the greatest theologian of the English Puritan movement but also one of the greatest European Reformed theologians of his day, and quite possibly possessed the finest theological mind that England ever produced. He was born in Stadhampton, near Oxford, in 1616, the second son of Henry Owen, the local vicar and a man of Puritan sympathies. Little is known of Owen's early upbringing, though when he was about ten years old he attended a grammar school in the parish of All Saints, Oxford, in preparation for studies at Queen's College. He matriculated at Oxford University on 4 November 1631 and graduated BA on 11 June 1632.

His time as a student at Oxford was characterized by extreme acts of self-discipline, such as taking only four hours sleep a night to allow more time for study, and by an equally competitive attitude to play; Owen apparently excelled at playing the flute and taking part in the long-jump and javelin throwing. He graduated MA on 27 April 1635, and was shortly thereafter ordained deacon and enrolled on the seven year course that would lead to a BD. While at Oxford his tutor was Thomas Barlow, an anti-Arminian philosopher whose metaphysics were to prove a formative influence on the thought of the young Owen.

Due to the increasing power of Archbishop Laud and his supporters in the university, Owen left Oxford and stayed in the household of John, Lord Lovelace, in Berkshire. On the outbreak of war in 1642, Owen moved to London; Lovelace was a Royalist, so clearly a man of Owen's political convictions could not comfortably have remained with him.

It was around this time that Owen went to Aldermanbury Chapel to hear the famous Edmund Calamy preach. On the day in question, however, Calamy was absent and a substitute preacher, whose name Owen could never remember, preached on Matthew 8:26. While Owen was at first intensely disappointed that Calamy was absent, the sermon none the less precipitated a kind of conversion experience in his life and, from then on, he enjoyed a new assurance of God's love and his own adoption as a son of God. His Puritan commitments were now combined with a vital, experiential piety that was to shape the rest of his life.

March 1642 saw the publication of Owen's first work, *A Display of Arminianism*. The work gave clear evidence of his sharp polemical skills, his firm grasp of contemporary theology and his astute understanding of philosophy. Not only did he cite contemporary Arminians, but he also showed an extensive awareness of the writings of patristic, medieval and contemporary Catholic authors. The catholicity of his reading and of his intellect was already apparent. The book made him something of a theological celebrity and, shortly after its publication, the Committee of Religion (to whom the book was dedicated) conferred upon him the living of Fordham in Essex. It was here that he married his first wife, Mary Rooke, who was to bear him eleven children, all of whom predeceased their father and only one of whom reached adulthood.

Owen was to remain in Fordham until 1646, when the right to appoint the minister reverted to the patron, who appointed another person to the charge. Just before he left, however, he was called to preach before Parliament on 29 April 1646. This invitation marked the start of Owen's long and significant public role in the politics of his day.

Late in 1646 Owen took up the charge of St Peter's in Coggeshall. At about the same time he read John *Cotton's book, *The Keys of the Kingdom*, and became as a result convinced of the correctness of the Independent position on church government over against that of the Presbyterians. As a result, Owen continued to minister at St Peter's while also gathering a church along congregational lines in the same place. In the context of the mid-seventeenth century, Owen's move to Independent convictions is highly significant, locating him on the more politically radical wing of Puritanism. This allegiance was to be significant for his future relations with Oliver *Cromwell.

Owen's political radicalism, evident in his writings on toleration, no doubt lay behind his invitation to preach before Parliament on 31 January 1649, the day after Charles I's execution. His sermon that day proved popular, and he returned to the capital to preach before the Commons on 19 April of the same year. In the audience on that occasion was Oliver Cromwell, who liked Owen's prophetic tone. As a result, he appointed Owen as his chaplain on his now infamous expedition to Ireland and then manoeuvred him into the position of vice-chancellor of Oxford University (1651–1657). During this period Owen also dedicated himself to combatting the rising threat of Socinianism, as evidenced in his large tome, *Vindiciae Evangelicae*, which was specifically commissioned by the government as a refutation of the works of the leading English Socinian, John Biddle.

In 1657 Owen's strong republican sympathies led him to fall out with the Protector Cromwell's consideration of an offer of the crown. He resigned the vice-chancellorship and, significantly, had no role the following year in Cromwell's funeral. In this year, however, he was involved, along with Thomas Goodwin and others, in composing the Savoy Declaration, a document that was essentially a reproduction of the Westminster Confession with relevant Independent modifications.

With the Restoration of 1660, Owen, along with other Independents and Presbyterians, saw his influence sharply diminished and, with the passing of the Act of Uniformity (1662), his ministry within the established church came to an end. Nevertheless, he continued to enjoy some personal influence at court (for example, Charles II occasionally gave him money to distribute to the poor) and was therefore cushioned from the harshest results of the king's anti-Puritan legislation. He also managed to give some limited help to Nonconformists who were less fortunate than himself.

While Owen's churchmanship was Independent, and his writings have a reputation for fearsome doctrinal precision, it must be remembered that the notion of orthodoxy in the seventeenth century was somewhat broader than that often imputed to the Puritans. Owen's writings are those of a theologian who was moving towards many of the ideas of toleration that were embodied in the political settlement of 1689. In addition, when he engaged with *Baxter in an attempt to find a theological basis for a united Nonconformist front against the Establishment after 1662, the negotiations broke down on the issue of the use of explicitly trinitarian creeds: Baxter believed that the Apostles' Creed was sufficient; Owen disagreed. The gap was ultimately too wide to bridge and negotiations broke down.

Denied a role in wider church politics, Owen produced massive theological works on the Holy Spirit and the letter to the Hebrews: these were the greatest legacy of his final years. In the nineteenth century edition of his works, the former occupies two volumes and the latter seven; they represent significant contributions to the history of pneumatology and the exegesis of Hebrews respectively.

To describe Owen's theology as 'Puritan' is to obscure almost as much as to clarify it, in part because of the problems inherent in such terminology. 'Puritanism' is notoriously difficult to define, and is probably best restricted to those within the Church of England who argued for a more Reformed ecclesiastical settlement prior to 1662 and desired an experiential piety. On this definition, Owen was indeed a Puritan, but he was also part of a much wider European movement of Reformed theology. He was indeed England's pre-eminent representative of Reformed Orthodoxy, that tradition of Reformed theologians who sought to give precise formulation to the theology of the Reformation, and to defend it against heterodox and Roman Catholic assault in the years after the initial reforming fervour had died down. His theology was thus developed in conscious dialogue with the best of the church's theologians, from the patristic era through the Middle Ages, to the Reformation and beyond. For example, his basic metaphysics represents an appropriation of the thought of Thomas Aquinas with certain Scotistic modifications. Then his formulations of sin, grace and predestination recall the work of Augustine but also appropriate elements from the medieval anti-Pelagian tradition and from contemporary Jansenist writers within the Catholic

Church. The references throughout his works, the marginalia and the contents of his library (as listed in the posthumous auction catalogue, *Bibliotheca Oweniana*) all reveal a man of catholic tastes in reading and vast knowledge of a wealth of different topics. He was as much an intellectual figure of the wider European theological scene as of the more parochial Puritanism.

Where Owen can be said to make truly significant contributions to the tradition is with respect to the doctrines of the Trinity and the atonement and to Christology. Driven to a large extent by the need to combat the rise of Socinianism within England in the 1640s and 1650s, Owen produced a number of writings which addressed germane topics, the most (in)famous of which was the 1647 essay, *The Death of Death in the Death of Christ*. Often caricatured today as arguing for limited atonement, the work actually represents both an extended reflection upon the implications of the inner-trinitarian life of God for the incarnation and atonement, and an attempt to draw out the implications of the Old Testament sacrificial context for understanding the events of Calvary. Indeed, the position of the treatise would be better described as 'particular redemption' than as 'limited atonement'. Owen's concern was to ask the simple question of whether Christ's death made salvation possible or actual. He affirmed the latter, arguing that Christ's death is part of his high priestly office resting upon his appointment as mediator. Therefore, both the death and the offering of that death are inextricably linked in Christ's mediatorial action.

In articulating this idea of atonement, Owen used the categories of federal theology, particularly that of the covenant of redemption between the Father and the Son; yet much of his argumentation is rooted directly in exegesis of biblical passages and careful reflection upon the relationship of the Old Testament to the New. With the basic trajectories of reflection set by Hebrews, Owen's understanding of Christ's saving work is driven above all by the need to work out the implications of its antitypical relationship to Old Testament priesthood and to relate this as a whole to the fact that God is Trinity, and that his external works find their counterpart in internal trinitarian relations.

Owen's own theology was constantly undergoing revision in the light of his biblical exegesis and the issues raised by contemporary polemics. Thus, for example, in 1647 he was happy to maintain that God could have forgiven sin without atonement had he so wished, but by 1653 he had rejected this position as incompatible with Scripture, as metaphysically incoherent and as a half-way house to a Socinian Christology. His arguments are developed in the highly technical *Dissertation of Divine Justice* (1653), which shows evidence of his extensive reading of contemporary Catholic authors, especially Francis Suarez, and increasingly rigorous commitment to Thomistic metaphysics.

Owen's most profound contributions to theology are no doubt to be found in his studies of Christology and pneumatology. In Owen's thinking, the two are intimately connected. His understanding of the incarnation focused on the importance of the Holy Spirit for the relationship between Christ's divine and human natures, with careful emphasis upon the anhypostasis of the latter. On this basis Owen was able to articulate an understanding of Christ's person that allowed him to stress both the very real humanity and human experiences of the mediator and his continual dependence upon God's Spirit, while yet safeguarding the absolute uniqueness of his person and office. In this context, Owen's Christology is both a careful defence of orthodoxy in the face of the relativizing tendencies of Socinianism, and an example of how the orthodox tradition could be exploited and developed in new controversial contexts.

Owen's defence of scriptural authority was also an important part of his work. His use of the terms *verbum agraphon* ('the unwritten word', i.e. the Logos) and *verbum engraphon* ('the written word', i.e. Scripture) allowed him to bring out clearly the connection between the Bible as the cognitive source of theology and God as the ontic source in a way that pre-empts the naive opposing of Christ-centred and Bible-centred theologies. In addition, he also stressed the role of the Holy Spirit in both the inspiration of the delivery of Scripture by the original authors and the illumination of later readers. He also defended the antiquity of the Masoretic vowel points against the critical work of Brian Walton in the London Polyglot, but his Hebrews commentary shows that he also used Walton positively and, indeed, was willing to amend the Received Text when he felt that textual evidence required a change.

In addition to his more strictly doctrinal and polemical works, Owen also wrote several important treatises on the power of indwelling sin within the believer's life. Again, these works are marked by careful distinctions, which facilitate a detailed theological and psychological analysis of the experience of sin by Christians. These represent perhaps the most sophisticated and articulate exposition of the Reformed position prior to the later critiques of nineteenth-century perfectionism by B. B. *Warfield.

The breadth of Owen's writing, his grasp of the wider tradition, and his ability to engage in informed polemic and theological construction at the highest level while still applying his theology to the layperson make him, along with Gisbertus Voetius of Utrecht, one of the two most acute Reformed theological minds of his day.

Owen died in 1683 and lies buried in the famous Nonconformist cemetery, Bunhill Fields, in London.

Bibliography

P. De Vries, *Die mij heeft liefgehad* (Heerenveen: 1999); S. B. Ferguson, *John Owen on the Christian Life* (Edinburgh: Banner of Truth, 1987); A. Spence, 'John Owen and Trinitarian Agency', *Scottish Journal of Theology* 43 (1990); P. Toon, *God's Statesman* (Exeter: Attic Press, 1971); C. R. Trueman, *The Claims of Truth: John Owen's Trinitarian Theology* (Carlisle: Paternoster Press, 1998).

C. R. TRUEMAN

■ **PACKER, James Innell** (1926–), Anglican theologian and educator, was born into a working-class, nominally Christian family in Gloucester, England. At the age of seven he suffered a near-fatal skull fracture after being chased from a school playground into the street, where he was hit by a passing bread van. The accident not only left him with a permanent dent in his forehead, but also helped to make him a reserved, solitary child, who found his enjoyment in reading. For his eleventh birthday, Packer received a typewriter (not the bicycle he had expected), which became his prized possession. At the age of thirteen, he was captivated by hearing on the radio Jelly Roll Morton's 'Steamboat Stomp'; this experience was the beginning of his lifelong love for Dixieland jazz.

After attending the Crypt School in Gloucester, Packer went up to Oxford University in 1944 to read classics at Corpus Christi College, having earned a prestigious academic scholarship. On 22 October 1944 he made a personal commitment to Christ at a service held at St Aldate's Church by an evangelical student organization, the Oxford Inter-Collegiate Christian Union (OICCU). Packer's spiritual growth was facilitated by prayer meetings and Bible studies associated with OICCU; he gave up playing the clarinet in a jazz band, The Oxford Bandits, in order to attend Saturday evening Bible expositions. In 1945–1946 Packer became dissatisfied with the doctrines of 'victorious living' and 'total consecration' being taught by OICCU preachers who were influenced by the Keswick holiness movement. Their emphasis upon 'reconsecration' as the chief means to sanctification seemed unrealistic and untrue to his own experience. During this personal struggle, Packer (a self-confessed 'bookworm') became junior librarian of OICCU when it received a large donation of classic Christian books.

While organizing this collection, he stumbled across the works of John *Owen, a major Puritan author, whose treatises *On Indwelling Sin in Believers* and *On the Mortification of Sin in Believers* made a profound impression upon him. This discovery of Puritan theology marked a turning-point in his personal and academic life; some forty years later, Packer would say that he 'owed more to the Puritans than to any other theologians he ever read'. As he became interested in ordained Christian ministry, he excelled as a classics student, receiving the BA degree in 1948.

Packer was a temporary lecturer in Latin and Greek (teaching also the Greek text of Ephesians) at an Anglican training college, Oak Hill, in London during the 1948–1949 academic year. This experience bolstered his confidence as a classroom teacher and led him to consider a career as a theological educator. In 1949 he returned to Oxford to begin studying theology at its evangelical theological college, Wycliffe Hall, in preparation for ordination. After obtaining a second BA in 1950, Packer moved immediately into doctoral research during 1950–1952, completing a dissertation, *The Redemption and Restoration of Man in the Thought of Richard *Baxter*, under the supervision of Geoffrey Nuttall, in 1954. Seeking to spread the influence of his Puritan heroes, Packer began publishing scholarly articles dealing with their thinking, and in 1950 he worked with Raymond Johnston to involve Martyn *Lloyd-Jones in the establishing of the Puritan Studies Conferences, held at Westminster Chapel in London. Ordained as a deacon in the Church of England in 1952, and as a priest in 1953, Packer served for two years as a curate at St John's, Harborne, in Birmingham. In 1954 he married 'Kit' Mullett, a nursing student from Wales. They adopted three children.

Between 1955 and 1961 Packer served as lecturer in theology at another evangelical Anglican college, Tyndale Hall in Bristol. He taught biblical theology, church history and Reformation studies, being acclaimed within evangelical circles as a cogent theological teacher. This recognition led to extensive involvement with local branches of the Inter-Varsity Fellowship (IVF) and with Christian Unions as a visiting speaker; many of Packer's lectures from IVF events eventually became published articles or chapters in books. Meanwhile, he and Johnston in 1957 edited a new edition of Martin *Luther's treatise *The Bondage of the Will*, in order to reinforce Reformation teaching within English evangelicalism. In 1958, also while teaching at Tyndale Hall, Packer wrote an article on 'fundamentalism' in Britain for a promising American periodical, *Christianity Today* (established just a year earlier). Thus began a lifelong association with what would become a major instrument of North American evangelicalism.

His first book, *'Fundamentalism' and the Word of God* (1958) emerged from a context in which conservative Protestant views were under attack, including those associated with Billy *Graham, whose evangelistic missions in England in the 1950s had caused controversy. The book was a detailed rebuttal of liberal criticism of evangelicals as obscurantist anti-

intellectuals who hold an inadequate view of Scripture. The book originated as a lecture to Christian students, which was expanded into a full-scale defence of the main tenets of evangelical Christianity and a forceful rejection of theological liberalism. According to Packer, evangelicalism's hallmark is an affirmation that 'the teaching of the written Scriptures is the Word which God spoke and speaks to His Church, and is finally authoritative for faith and life'. Packer explicates the inspiration of Scripture and its 'propositional revelation' in the terms used by Reformed thinkers such as Charles *Hodge and B. B. *Warfield. The immediate popularity of the book, both in Britain and North America, helped to establish Packer as a leading theological spokesman for evangelicalism.

Packer's second book, *Evangelism and the Sovereignty of God* (1961), according to the author's foreword, was 'a piece of biblical and theological reasoning, designed to clarify the relationship between three realities: God's sovereignty, man's responsibility, and the Christian's evangelistic duty'. The book not only provided a defence of the full compatibility of Calvinist understandings of divine sovereignty in salvation with the task of evangelism, but also argued that confidence in God's omnipotent grace is a necessary presupposition for evangelistic ministry. Packer's succinct definition of evangelism became well known in evangelical circles: 'To evangelize is to present Jesus Christ in the power of the Holy Spirit, that men shall come to put their trust in God through Him, to accept Him as their Saviour, and serve Him as their King in the fellowship of His Church.'

These early books exhibit important factors in Packer's widespread influence in English-speaking, transdenominational evangelicalism. They are readable volumes of rigorous and constructive theology. They are primarily theological exposition of the Scriptures, drawing upon the intellectual and spiritual depth found in the Calvinist tradition as interpreted by the Puritans. They display an unmistakable style marked by exacting linear argumentation, careful distinctions and remarkable economy of words ('Packer by name, packer by nature,' he said). Both early books, like most of his subsequent writings, emerged from his pastoral ministry and deal with specific needs and ecclesial controversies; for this reason, he called himself 'an accidental author'. (His short writings alone fill four full-length volumes, though he has also written over thirty books.) Moreover, they addressed topics at the heart of evangelical concern, defending the authority of Scripture and the propriety of evangelism in the face of criticism, and did so by elucidating central Christian doctrines in order to describe their relevance for evangelical life and witness.

Between 1961 and 1970, Packer served as librarian, then warden, of Latimer House in Oxford, an Anglican research institution intended as a strategic centre for advancing the evangelical cause within the Church of England. From this base, Packer was thoroughly engaged in central issues facing his denomination during the 1960s, during which time evangelicals were an isolated minority struggling for influence. Within the Anglican theological spectrum, Packer championed the Reformation inheritance found in the Thirty-Nine Articles and in Cranmer's Prayer Book, on the basis of which he affirmed that 'Anglicanism embodies the richest, truest, wisest heritage in all Christendom'. From this viewpoint, his pamphlet Keep Yourself from Idols provided a thorough theological critique of John A. T. Robinson's 'radical theology' in Honest to God (1963). Along with John R. W. *Stott, Packer was a major figure in countering Lloyd-Jones' argument that faithful evangelicals should leave the Church of England in favour of Free Churches rather than remaining within their denomination to strive for its reform. He also played a central role in organizing the National Evangelical Anglican Congress in 1967 at the University of Keele, an event which united and strengthened evangelical witness within the Church of England.

In 1970 Packer returned as principal to Tyndale Hall, where he was caught up in pressures surrounding the denominational reorganization of theological education. The college eventually merged with two other institutions, becoming Trinity College in 1972, where Packer served as associate principal until 1979. During this period, he published the celebrated book Knowing God (1973). The content of the book originated in a series of articles appearing over a five year period in The Evangelical Magazine. These articles were revised for publication in Britain and America as a 300-page volume. Written for an audience of intellectually curious laypeople, its success made Packer a luminary in evangelical churches, especially those in North America. The book was an international bestseller; over one and one-half million copies were sold in its first thirty years in print. It also became recognized as a contemporary classic, among the clearest and most compelling articulations of evangelical conviction and practical piety written in the twentieth century.

Knowing God is an extended study of the nature and character of God, based on what Packer called 'five foundation-principles of the knowledge about God which Christians have': 'God has spoken to man, and the Bible is His word ...'; 'God is Lord and King over His world'; 'God is Saviour, active in sovereign love through the Lord Jesus Christ ...'; 'God is Triune'; 'Godliness means responding to God's revelation in trust and obedience, faith and worship, prayer and praise, submission and service'. As the book's title indicates, Packer's supreme concern is to foster the Christian's knowledge of God, not merely to advance an intellectual knowledge about God: 'Our aim in studying the Godhead must be to know God Himself the better. Our concern must be to enlarge our acquaintance, not simply with the doctrine of God's attributes, but with the living God whose attributes they are.'

Finding an increasing receptivity to his ministry in North America, Packer moved to Vancouver in 1979 to become Professor of Historical and Systematic Theology at Regent College, a transdenominational graduate school of Christian studies, where he spent the rest of his career. He continued to be active in parish ministry as an honorary assistant at St John's Shaughnessy Church. During his teaching ministry at Regent, Packer travelled extensively across North America and internationally as a visiting lecturer at evangelical seminaries and as a conference speaker or symposia participant. He also played a central role in the leadership of Christianity Today as a senior editor and frequent essayist. Packer's previous writings on the doctrine of Scripture made him a leading figure in the 'Battle for the Bible' controversies in North America during the

1970s and 1980s, in which he played a central role on the International Council on Biblical Inerrancy. Once again, Packer's overriding concern was for Christian faith and practice; if the notion of biblical inerrancy was jeopardized, he believed, evangelicalism would be undermined, as Scripture would be hindered from exercising authority over the church. Packer understood 'infallibility' ('neither deceiving nor being deceived') and 'inerrancy' ('freedom from error of any kind, factual, moral or spiritual') as synonymous terms. '[We] accept as true what Scripture says' on the grounds that Scripture is infallible and inerrant because of its inspiration, that is, its 'God-breathed' origin. 'If we speak of Holy Scripture as altogether true and trustworthy, or as wholly reliable in its own terms, making no false assertions, claims or promises on its own account … we shall be expressing in formula terms exactly what these words mean' (God Has Spoken, Hodder & Stoughton, 1979, p. 110). Among Packer's most substantial writings from this period are Keep in Step with the Spirit (1984), a treatise on the doctrine of the Holy Spirit and the pursuit of sanctification which includes an extensive analysis and critique of the charismatic renewal movement, and A Quest for Godliness: The Puritan Vision of the Christian Life (1991), the culmination of forty years of research.

Throughout his ministry, Packer unwaveringly affirmed evangelical Protestantism as a stream of historic Christian orthodoxy, the church's 'Great Tradition'. This stance made Packer a valuable partner in ecumenical discussions, both in Britain and North America, and led him to become a signatory of two controversial documents prepared by Roman Catholic and evangelical leaders, 'Evangelicals and Catholics Together' (1994) and 'The Gift of Salvation' (1997). Although some evangelical theologians were severely critical of Packer's involvement, he advocated parachurch partnerships with Catholics on the basis of common ground, including shared support for the view that 'we are justified by grace through faith because of Christ'. In his own defence, Packer affirmed that 'evangelicals and Catholics who actively believe are Christians together' and that 'grassroots collaboration with Roman Catholics in ministry is the most fruitful sort of

ecumenism that one can practice' (Christianity Today, 12 December 1994, p. 35).

In 1989 Packer became Regent's first occupant of an endowed chair as Sangwoo Youtong Chee Professor of Theology. His inaugural lecture, 'An Introduction to Systematic Spirituality', expressed surprise at the realization that he had been talking and writing about what was being called 'spirituality' throughout his entire career as a systematic theologian: 'I should have known all along that I was writing spirituality, for the Puritan passion for application got into my blood quite early; I have always conceived theology, ethics, and apologetics as truth for people, and have never felt free to leave unapplied any truth that I taught, whether orally or on paper; and to speak of application of truth to life is to look at life as itself a relationship with God; and when one does that, one is talking spirituality' (Crux 26, 1990, p. 2).

J. I. Packer has been among the most influential figures in English-speaking evangelicalism during the latter half of twentieth century. He became the professional theologian most widely read and popularly respected, someone to whom the evangelical movement frequently looked for insight and guidance on matters of Christian belief and conduct. Although some evangelical leaders were disappointed that Packer did not use his formidable theological learning to produce more scholarly writing aimed at academic audiences, an astute observer described Packer as a 'scholar who found his vocation in popular communication, a popular communicator who never abandoned scholarship'.

As a thinker who has worked confidently within the Puritan tradition, Packer is a staunch Calvinist. For him, Reformed Christianity is 'evangelicalism in its purest form' and John *Wesley was a 'muddled Calvinist'. Never one to avoid controversial issues, throughout his career he engaged in polemics surrounding doctrines of importance to Calvinist orthodoxy (e.g. the limited atonement and eternal punishment). Packer has not charted new territory theologically, but rather has sought to dig deeply into the riches of his inheritance of classical Christian orthodoxy. Packer's prominence has been attributable not only to his powers of intellect and communication, but also to his advocacy of a biblically oriented form of Calvinism, which resonated with the outlook of a broad range of evangelicals.

Bibliography

A. McGrath, *J. I. Packer: A Biography* (Grand Rapids: Baker, 1997), also published as *To Know and to Serve God: A Biography of James I. Packer* (London: Hodder & Stoughton, 1997); J. I. Packer, 'What the Puritans Taught Me', *Christianity Today* (8 October 1990), pp. 44–47.

J. P. GREENMAN

■ **PALMER, Phoebe Worrall** (1807–1874), American Methodist theologian, revivalist and author, was born in New York City, the fourth of sixteen children of Henry and Dorthea Wade Worrall, nine of whom survived to adulthood. Her father had emigrated to America from England in the early 1790s; her mother was American born. Both parents were active in the fledgling American Methodist Episcopal Church. Phoebe joined the church as a young girl, and was an active member for the rest of her life.

In 1827 Phoebe married Dr Walter C. Palmer, a practitioner of 'homeopathic medicine', and like her a second generation Methodist. Phoebe and Walter's early life together was bittersweet; they had six children, but only three survived infancy and early childhood. These losses had a profound effect upon Phoebe, who interpreted them as acts of God, severing her from 'worldly' cares and drawing her into more devoted service to Christ. As a result of these losses, she resolved that 'the time I would have devoted to [these children], shall be spent in work for Jesus'.

Over time Phoebe Palmer became involved in various church activities, and soon emerged as an acknowledged lay leader among New York Methodists. Among her many activities was participation in a weekly prayer and Bible study group made up of women from two New York Methodist churches. This group began meeting in 1835 under the leadership of Phoebe's sister, Sarah Worrall Lankford. By 1837 it had begun to define itself as committed to the one goal of promoting the Wesleyan doctrine and experience of 'entire sanctification', 'perfect love', or 'Christian holiness', and had taken on the name 'The Tuesday Meeting for the Promotion of Holiness'. This shift in focus coincided with a time of rapid change in American Methodism. Many feared that distinctive elements of the Wesleyan heritage, especially the doctrine of Christian perfection, might be forfeited as Methodism expanded numerically and geographically.

The Tuesday Meeting largely followed the Pietist-Methodist model of small group meetings for spiritual nurture. Eventually including men as well as women, it provided a context where lay people and clergy, women and men, Methodists and non-Methodists could come together for the pursuit of a common spiritual goal. The meeting involved free discussion on equal terms, and included Bible reading, prayer and, above all, personal testimony. In time the Tuesday Meeting became a major vehicle for stimulating interest in Christian perfection within American Methodism and in other Protestant denominations as well. By 1840 Phoebe Palmer had taken over from her sister as leader of the meeting.

It was through the Tuesday Meeting that Palmer began to travel and to write. Her first 'preaching tour' outside New York City took place in 1840, and her first significant publication on holiness appeared a year later. In 1843 she issued her most widely read and influential book, *The Way of Holiness*, which passed through more than fifty editions during her lifetime.

From this time until her death in 1874, Phoebe Palmer was a tireless advocate of Christian perfection. She travelled thousands of miles speaking and teaching in churches, camp meetings, colleges and seminaries and public auditoriums. She crossed the United States and Canada several times, and travelled to Great Britain and (briefly) to the European continent. In the process she became one of the most widely recognized revivalists in the world.

Palmer also gained increasing fame as an author and editor. She published nearly twenty books, many of which went through multiple editions, and some were published in several languages. In addition, she edited an influential journal, *The Guide to Holiness*, for ten years (1864–1874).

Palmer also carried on correspondence by letter with hundreds of spiritual enquirers, and worked in a variety of projects serving the poor and needy. Though she was a life-long Methodist, her work quickly extended beyond Methodism into a large number of Protestant denominations, helping to fuel interest in Christian perfection, holiness and 'the higher Christian life' throughout much of English-speaking Protestantism.

It is as a theologian or religious thinker that Palmer has had her most profound influence. Not a 'professional' theologian, she was none the less a creative religious thinker who refashioned the Wesleyan Methodist view of Christian perfection or 'entire sanctification' in the process of attempting to defend and promote it.

Influenced by her own intense and pro-longed spiritual quest (she sought perfect love for eleven years before she could claim, in 1837, to have received it), nineteenth-century revivalism and the spiritual biographies of several prominent British Methodist lay leaders (notably Hester Anne Rogers and William Carvosso), and exhibiting a strongly pragmatic inclination, Palmer crafted a new understanding of Christian perfection. Her 'shorter way' theology provided seekers with a simple path to the 'second blessing' and emphasized the supposedly instantaneous nature of entire sanctification.

Palmer presented the path as involving a series of steps: (1) acknowledge God's require-ment of, and provision for, perfect holi-ness; (2) consecrate oneself entirely to God; (3) believe that God always keeps his promise to sanctify what is consecrated; (4) testify clearly to what God has done. With respect to the third step, Palmer developed what came to be known as her 'altar principle' or 'altar theology'. This was grounded upon her inter-pretation of Matthew 23:19, which she under-stood as a promise to a Christian believer who is seeking to be perfect as God is perfect. She reasoned that since the passage speaks of the altar of sacrifice 'sanctifying' the gift that is placed upon it, it promises to the seeker of holiness that the Christian's altar, Christ (Hebrews 13:10), will sanctify the gift of a life fully consecrated to him. For Palmer, the act of consecration and the reception of the blessing of entire sanctification were linked in a clear cause and effect relationship.

An essential part of Palmer's emphasis on a 'shorter way' to sanctification was her insist-ence that entire sanctification occurs in an instant and is available to the sincere seeker *now*. This was an element in John *Wesley's understanding of Christian perfection. How-ever, Wesley's teaching about the 'instant-aneous blessing' of entire sanctification was embedded in a larger doctrine of sanctifica-tion that strongly affirmed the continuous, progressive, ongoing work of divine grace from God's initial calling of a sinner, through repentance, to final glorification after death. Wesley insisted that entire sanctification is 'constantly both preceded and followed by a gradual work' of grace. Palmer did not deny the larger Wesleyan view of sanctification, but she clearly emphasized one particular element within it, the instantaneous blessing of entire sanctification.

Palmer's theology also helped to popularize the concept of the 'baptism with the Holy Spirit'. Early in her public ministry she did not teach this doctrine. However, in the middle and late 1850s it begins to appear in her writings, and by the end of her life it was a dominant theme.

Over time Palmer fashioned a doctrine of assurance that emphasized divine activity and objective 'evidence'. She found resources for this in the writings of British Methodist lay leaders such as Hester Anne Rogers. Rogers had been strongly influenced by the teaching of John *Fletcher, who identified entire sanc-tification with the disciples' experience at Pentecost. Palmer embraced Fletcher's under-standing, and eventually began to teach that the act of entire consecration results in the baptism of the Holy Spirit. This baptism is always attested by evidence. For her, this evidence was a passion in believers to bring others to faith in Christ. Christians not yet entirely sanctified were likely to be 'cold' in their concern for unsaved people.

Palmer's theological ideas, which she taught on her travels, through her books and through *The Guide to Holiness*, had a tremendous impact upon English-speaking Protestantism. They largely defined the 'holi-ness revival' or 'holiness movement' that grew from her work and that of other proponents of Christian perfection, Christian holiness and the higher Christian life.

In the United States Palmer's ideas were embraced by the National Camp Meeting Association for the Promotion of Holiness (organized in 1867), which aggressively championed the cause of Christian holiness following the American Civil War. Throughout the second half of the nineteenth century this organization spawned hundreds of local and regional groups that claimed holiness as their distinctive cause. These groups generally expressed their ideas about holiness in terms that closely echoed the teachings of Palmer.

In time these organizations gave birth to independent holiness churches and denominations, which continued to propagate Palmer's theological ideas into the twentieth century. These included the Church of the Nazarene and the Pilgrim Holiness Church (now Wesleyan Church). In addition, some older Methodist bodies, including the Wesleyan Methodist Church (now Wesleyan Church) and the Free Methodist Church, identified themselves with the holiness movement and embraced Palmer's teaching. So did some churches from well outside the Wesleyan movement, such as the Brethren in Christ Church, the roots of which were in the Mennonite tradition.

In England, Palmer introduced her ideas during an extended preaching tour between 1859 and 1863. Later, other American revivalists, notably Robert *Pearsall Smith and his wife Hannah Whitall Smith, and Asa *Mahan, followed up her visit, preaching versions of her theology throughout the British Isles. Their work led directly to the organization of the Keswick Conventions and the ongoing Keswick 'Higher Life' Movement among British evangelicals.

Palmer also influenced modern Pentecostal and charismatic movements. She taught that the baptism with the Holy Spirit cleansed the hearts of believers from sin and empowered them for Christ-like living and effective Christian witness. She herself never spoke in tongues nor advocated speaking in tongues. However, it is clear that her emphasis on Pentecost and the baptism with the Holy Spirit and her interpretation of the early chapters of Acts as primarily accounts of the imparting of divine power to Christian believers, laid the groundwork for much modern Pentecostal and charismatic thinking.

Palmer was an unusual nineteenth-century revivalist primarily because she was a woman. She was nearly alone as a female in a male domain. A very small number of women worked as travelling preachers or 'exhorters' in early and mid-nineteenth-century America and managed to cultivate very localized followings. Palmer, however, was the only female revivalist of her time to achieve national and international popularity.

Palmer was extraordinarily active as a travelling revivalist after 1840. She participated in more than three hundred revival campaigns and camp meetings. In later years (from 1859), she often travelled in the company of her husband, but in the beginning she almost always travelled alone. When away, she regularly wrote poignant letters home to her husband and three children affirming her love for them.

Surprisingly, Palmer encountered only limited opposition to her work as a highly visible female revivalist. However, there were enough undercurrents of criticism over the years that she eventually wrote a long, carefully reasoned defence of the ministry of women (*The Promise of the Father* [1859]), arguing her case on biblical, theological and historical grounds.

The central argument of the book is that the present age is the 'dispensation of the Spirit', which was inaugurated with 'signs and wonders' on the day of Pentecost. Chief among these signs and wonders is the power to 'prophesy', which Palmer understood to mean 'herald the glad tidings [of Jesus] to others' or proclaim 'to every creature the love of God to men through Jesus Christ'. This power is given to all believers, both women and men. In fact, this gift of power and its extension to female as well as male believers is 'a marked specialty of the Christian [i.e. Holy Spirit's] dispensation'. Churches that forbid the ministry of women thus violate one of God's primary means of calling the world to salvation in the 'last days'.

Mounting a strong argument for the right of women to minister, *The Promise of the Father* nevertheless avoids the issue of the ordination of women. However, the thrust of Palmer's argument for the ministry of women leaves little room for denying any form of ministry to women. Her logic in *The Promise of the Father* can easily be extended into arguments for the ordination of women. Such arguments were being advanced in the holiness movement well before the end of the nineteenth century, and almost all of the new denominations that grew out of it endorsed the ordination of women.

Palmer rarely discussed the status of women in society as a whole, and for the most part her social views were quite conservative for her day. However, she did assume roles that were not traditionally taken by women, and in doing so provided a highly visible model of female emancipation, at least in religious life. The outspoken nineteenth-century feminists Catherine *Booth of the Salvation Army and Frances *Willard of the Women's Christian Temperance Union both credited Palmer with a significant influence on their lives.

Finally, in addition to her many other avenues of ministry, Palmer invested substantial time and energy in works of compassion and humanitarian aid, and urged others to do likewise. For many years she exercised a ministry of prison visiting. She also served as secretary of the Female Assistance Society, a group of volunteers who aided poor people needing medical attention. She was a member of the board of directors of the Ladies Home Missionary Society of the Methodist Episcopal Church. In that role she was a principal founder of the Five Points Mission, an ambitious project in the heart of one of New York's poorest neighbourhoods. The mission, founded in 1850, provided a day school for children, low cost housing for a number of poor families, and clothing and food distribution. It was also connected with the Five Points House of Industry, a manufacturing enterprise that employed over five hundred people. The Five Points Mission was one of the earliest efforts by Protestant churches to address the problems of poverty, overcrowding, and crime in America's rapidly growing urban centres.

Palmer was also specially burdened for orphans, one of the most vulnerable groups in mid-nineteenth-century American society. Throughout her life she supported a 'Home for the Friendless', and often used her influence and connections to find permanent homes for the children who found their way there.

Devoted as she was to compassionate and humanitarian aid to those in need, Palmer was never a 'reformer' in the sense of one who works to change basic social structures or systems that encourage and perpetuate poverty or injustice. She was reluctant to speak out publicly about slavery in the United States. Her private correspondence makes it clear that she was appalled by the practice, but she refused to become involved in the Abolitionist movement because it challenged principles of American law and encouraged civil disobedience.

Bibliography

T. C. Oden, *Phoebe Palmer: Selected Writings* (New York: Paulist Press, 1988); H. E. Raser, *Phoebe Palmer, Her Life and Thought* (New York: Edwin Mellen Press, 1987); R. Wheatley, *The Life and Letters of Mrs. Phoebe Palmer* (1876); C. E. White, *The Beauty of Holiness: Phoebe Palmer as Theologian, Revivalist, Feminist, and Humanitarian* (Grand Rapids: Zondervan, 1986).

H. E. RASER

■ **PANKHURST, Christabel Harriette** (1880–1958), militant feminist and fundamentalist teacher, was born on 22 September in Manchester. She was the first child of Richard Marsden Pankhurst, a lawyer who supported radical causes, including women's suffrage, and his wife, Emmeline. Richard, who had been a member of a Congregational-Baptist union chapel, became a religious sceptic, and therefore religious education and church/chapelgoing were not regular features of Christabel's childhood. Richard died in 1898 while Christabel was still in her teens, but the family chose to continue his tradition of political activism. Emmeline and Christabel founded the Women's Social and Political Union (WSPU) in 1903. On 13 October 1905 Pankhurst and a loyal follower, Annie Kenney, disrupted a Liberal Party meeting and committed a technical assault on a policeman in order to necessitate their arrest. They became the first of the Suffragettes (the new, militant campaigners for votes for women) to spend a night in prison. This incident led into a decade-long campaign of civil disobedience that escalated into vandalism on a massive scale, including the systematic smashing of shop windows in commercial districts.

Although her mother was the titular head of the WSPU, Pankhurst was widely seen as its chief strategist. The Suffragettes proved adept at harassing government ministers; even banning women altogether from their political meetings did not ensure that ministers could speak without disruption. Meanwhile, Pankhurst also took advantage of a new opportunity for women to study law and was awarded an LLB with first-class honours from Victoria University, Manchester, in 1906. With the benefit of this legal training, when she was brought to trial for WSPU activities in October 1908, Pankhurst defended herself, and even subpoenaed Lloyd George (then Chancellor of the Exchequer) and cross-examined him personally to his considerable discomfort. When in 1912 the government finally decided to crush the movement by charging its leaders with conspiracy and imprisoning them all long-term, Pankhurst fled to Paris and continued to lead the WSPU from there. In 1913 her book, *The Great Scourge and How to End It*, was published. This was an anti-venereal disease tract that vehemently exposed and denounced male promiscuity, placing Pankhurst in a feminist tradition of campaigning for sexual purity notably exemplified by the evangelical Josephine *Butler.

When the First World War broke out a 'truce' was created between the Suffragettes and the government. Pankhurst came back to England and threw herself into the war effort with patriotic fervour. Emmeline Pankhurst developed a scheme for adopting children who needed homes, and one child, Elizabeth, was adopted by Christabel. Elizabeth is known to have been somewhat wild at university, but her ultimate fate has not been traced. Pankhurst never married; nor is there any evidence that she ever had a romantic or sexual relationship of any kind. A votes for women measure became law in 1918. Pankhurst ran for Parliament later that year, and received an impressive number of votes, but did not secure the seat (Smethwick).

Also in 1918 Pankhurst read a copy of Grattan *Guinness' *The Approaching End of the Age Viewed in the Light of History, Prophecy, and Science* (1879), a popular pre-millennialist work. This led to a conversion experience and a growing preoccupation with the notions that the second coming of Christ was imminent and that biblical prophecy provided a key for understanding and predicting the course of current events. Her spiritual journey was private until the summer of 1921, when she saw an advertisement in *The Times* for a meeting of the Advent Testimony Movement, a conservative evangelical organization that had F. B. *Meyer for its chairman. Although Pankhurst was just packing to go to America, she went to the meeting and then later wrote to Meyer from California.

In 1923 Pankhurst moved to Toronto to join her mother there. The noted fundamentalist leader A. B. Winchester was minister-at-large at Knox Presbyterian Church, and he arranged for Pankhurst to address the congregation. This invitation launched her into a popular preaching and teaching ministry in both North America and Britain. Meyer became a faithful supporter of her ministry. He wrote the foreword to her first book, 'The Lord Cometh': The World's Crisis Explained* (1923). This very successful volume was followed by *Pressing Problems of the Closing Age* (1924; published in America under the title *Some Modern Problems in the Light of Bible Prophecy*); *The World's Unrest: Visions of the Dawn* (1926); *Seeing the Future* (1929); and *The Uncurtained Future* (1940). For twenty-five weeks in 1926–1927 Pankhurst also wrote a column in *The Christian*, an evangelical newspaper published in London, for part of 1934 she published her own monthly journal, *Present and Future*, and she was a frequent contributor to the *Sunday School Times*.

Pankhurst repeatedly took her place on the great fundamentalist platforms and in the pulpits of the movement's flagship churches. In Britain, she toured nationally speaking for the Advent Testimony Movement (1926–1927), a journey that culminated in sold-out meetings in the Royal Albert Hall, and for the Bible Testimony Fellowship (1937–1938). In America, she repeatedly occupied John Roach Straton's pulpit at Calvary Baptist Church, New York, the centre of fundamentalism in the northeast at that time. She also spoke at Moody Bible Institute, the Bible Institute of Los Angeles (Biola), Winona Lake Bible Conference (1941), the third annual Fundamentalist Rally and Prophetic Conference in Atlantic City, New Jersey (1932), and numerous other such places and gatherings. Perhaps most interestingly of all, she was one of the main speakers at the annual conference of the World's Christian Fundamentals Association in 1931. There is no doubt that she was at one time a star of the fundamentalist circuit.

In her writing and speaking, Pankhurst continually reiterated her core message; the world's problems are insoluble by human effort, but the signs of the times indicate that Christ will return soon, and he will solve them all. For an apocalyptic preacher, she had a surprisingly upbeat message. Hell and judgment were absent from her teaching, although she attributed the evil, suffering and disorder in the world to Satan, absolving the Almighty. Her attempts to read the signs of the times allowed her to exercise her well-honed skills for interpreting political developments. Although they had been foes during the Suffragette campaign, she struck up a friendship in the early 1930s with Winston Churchill. (They were both convinced that another world war was on the horizon.) Her support for Zionism led to her speaking to Jewish groups, even giving an address in a synagogue. Pankhurst also read an impressive amount of serious contemporary thought, especially scientific, and put it to work in her efforts to teach the Bible and doctrine. She gave appeals at the end of some of her addresses, and was known as an evangelist as well as a teacher and preacher.

Although it is sometimes said that Pankhurst abandoned her feminism, in fact she went out of her way to tell fundamentalist audiences that she still believed in gender equality. Her frequent admission that she had learned that votes for women could not save society (something only Christ can do) has been misconstrued. In *Seeing the Future* she remarked, 'Emphatically, we are not disappointed in votes for women.' Moreover, some of her backers, such as Meyer and Straton, were also supporters of votes for women. Although Pankhurst always considered herself a member of the Church of England, fundamentalism offered her scope for ministry that could not be found in her own denomination. (At that time, women were not allowed to preach in Anglican churches.) Her own support for women in ministry was derived from the women at Christ's tomb, who are commissioned to bring the good news of the resurrection to the other disciples, thereby becoming women in ministry who 'make the men astonished' (a phrase of Pankhurst's based upon Luke 24:22).

In the New Year's honours list for 1936 Pankhurst was created a Dame Commander of the Order of the British Empire. In the late 1930s she moved to California, where she lived for the rest of her life. She died in her apartment in Santa Monica on 13 February 1958, at the age of seventy-seven. A local paper reported, 'Dame Christabel Pankhurst, militant campaigner for Christ and women's suffrage, is dead.'

Bibliography

T. Larsen, *Christabel Pankhurst: Fundamentalism and Feminism in Coalition* (Woodbridge: Boydell, 2002); D. Mitchell, *Queen Christabel: A Biography of Christabel Pankhurst* (London: Macdonald & Jane's, 1977).

T. LARSEN

■ **PARHAM, Charles Fox** (1873–1929), Pentecostal pioneer and architect of classical Pentecostal doctrine, was born on 4 June 1873 in Muscatine, Iowa, to William M. and Ann Maria (née Eckel) Parham, the third of five sons. The younger Parham suffered from physical weakness, first caused by a virus (probably encephalitis) when still a child and rheumatic fever at the age of nine, the latter probably stunting his growth and recurring at later stages in his life. In 1878 the family moved to Sedgwick County, Kansas, and prospered from the strong agricultural economy.

Though the family was largely unchurched, Parham's mother encouraged some measure of Christian devotion. In the same year as his first bout of rheumatic fever, he felt 'called' to be a minister, even before his professed conversion. A year after the death of his mother in 1885, he received assurance of his conversion and began to attend the local Congregational church. In 1890 he enrolled at Southwest Kansas College to prepare for ministry in the Methodist Episcopal Church, North. His surviving another attack of rheumatic fever renewed his commitment to ministry and convinced him of the availability of divine healing for physical maladies. Without finishing his studies, he left the college in 1893 to become the supply pastor at the Methodist Church in Eudora, Kansas. Although he achieved success there, he became restless, and his embrace of controversial Wesleyan holiness teachings and ardent belief in divine healing made his ecclesiastical superiors uneasy. In 1895 Parham relinquished his preaching licence to begin an independent ministry. In the following year he married Sarah Eleanor Thistlethwaite, of Quaker parentage. Five of their children survived into adulthood.

In 1898 the Parhams moved to Topeka, Kansas, and opened the Beth-El Healing Home as a hostel for seekers of divine healing. There Parham began to publish the bimonthly periodical *Apostolic Faith*. In the summer of 1900 he spent three months visiting important holiness centres, spending the last six weeks at Frank W. Sandford's commune and Holy Ghost and Us Bible School at Shiloh, Maine, and travelling with Sandford. Already influenced by holiness teaching on the 'latter rain' outpouring of the Holy Spirit and intrigued by the disciples' experience of speaking in tongues on the day of Pentecost, Parham was deeply impressed by Sandford's operation and vision for world evangelization. Both Sandford and Parham believed that the premillennial return of Christ would occur after a worldwide revival including unprecedented progress by mission agencies. Believing that the gift of speaking in known human languages (xenolalia) through the agency of the Holy Spirit was available to missionaries, and having learned of Jennie Glassey, a missionary who testified to this experience, Parham was fascinated when he heard speaking in tongues at Shiloh. By the time he returned to Topeka, his view of baptism in the Holy Spirit had developed significantly. He now taught that tongues would signal reception of Spirit baptism and provide linguistic expertise for 'Spirit-filled' missionaries, who could then bypass language school and preach immediately upon arrival on the mission field. Opening Bethel Bible School in October for the training of missionaries, he urged the students to consider his new understanding of Spirit baptism. Revival commenced on 1 January 1901 when Agnes Ozman experienced speaking in tongues; within a few days many other students and Parham himself had had the same experience. None the less, intense criticism and unexpected problems soon led to the closing of the school. Parham returned to the evangelistic circuit, and not until a revival in Galena,

Kansas, in 1903 did he achieve success again and move beyond obscurity.

In early 1905 Parham and several followers moved to Houston, Texas, where they held evangelistic meetings in the suburbs. At this time the Apostolic Faith movement, as the Pentecostal movement was originally known, began to experience considerable success as a loosely organized network of congregations emerged. In December Parham styled himself as the 'Projector' of the movement and opened another short-term Bible school that lasted for ten weeks. During this time, William J. *Seymour, an American of African descent and holiness evangelist, listened to Parham's lectures from outside the classroom, an arrangement determined by the segregation laws of the period.

In February 1906 Seymour left for Los Angeles, California, where he played a crucial role in the development of the Azusa Street revival (1906–1909), an event that quickly gave worldwide dimensions to the movement. In September 1906 Parham travelled to Zion City (now Zion), Illinois, founded by John Alexander Dowie, where his preaching received a warm response from hundreds of Dowie's former supporters. By the time he visited Seymour's Apostolic Faith Mission on Azusa Street in late October, the revival there had taken on its own identity. Seymour and most of his congregation rejected Parham's attempt to exercise authority over them and curb the religious enthusiasm of the services. Returning to Zion City, he faced another defeat when he failed to win control of the organization and worldwide network from Wilbur Glenn Voliva.

Parham's troubles continued to mount, and he lost his position of leadership after he was arrested for sodomy in San Antonio, Texas, in the summer of 1907. Although the details of the alleged incident are sketchy and the charges were dropped, his enemies, particularly those in Zion City, exploited the report and added to the innuendo. Denying any wrongdoing, Parham persevered in ministry, but his influence on the Pentecostal movement declined sharply, leaving him with only a few thousand followers at the time of his death in Baxter Springs, Kansas, on 29 January 1929. After 1907 Parham became increasingly embittered because of his diminished influence, racist in attitude and disillusioned with the movement that he had helped to shape. In the course of a few decades he became a forgotten figure until historians of Pentecostalism discovered his early role in the movement.

Parham defined the Pentecostal movement theologically by forging together the doctrinal tenets of salvation by faith, the Wesleyan-holiness understanding of sanctification, divine healing and premillennial eschatology, and baptism in the Holy Spirit as a work of grace subsequent to conversion and marked by xenolalic tongues. The latter served as the indispensable 'Bible evidence' (later called 'initial evidence') of Spirit baptism and provided empowerment and linguistic expertise to expedite the evangelization of the world. This theology gave classical Pentecostalism a separate identity from that of the Wesleyan-holiness and 'Higher Life' movements that preceded and contributed to it, and from that of the larger evangelical community, and generated a distinctive spirituality that has endured to this day. Thus, although Parham left little in terms of organization, his theological convictions fuelled one of the most vigorous movements in modern Christianity. Notwithstanding, Pentecostals did not accept his teaching uncritically; they rejected his annihilationism, Anglo-Israelism and views on the relevance of tongues for missionary evangelism. His written contributions include editorials and articles in the *Apostolic Faith*, *A Voice Crying in the Wilderness* (1902; [2]1910) and *The Everlasting Gospel* (1911); also his views are expounded in *Selected Sermons of the Late Charles F. Parham and Sarah E. Parham* (1941) and in *The Life of Charles F. Parham* (1930) written and compiled by Sarah E. Parham.

Bibliography

J. R. Goff, Jr, *Fields White Unto Harvest: Charles F. Parham and the Missionary Origins of Pentecostalism* (Fayetteville: University of Arkansas Press, 1988); G. B. McGee (ed.), *Initial Evidence: Historical and Biblical Perspectives on the Pentecostal Doctrine of Spirit Baptism* (Peabody: Hendrickson Publishers, 1991); G. B. McGee, 'Shortcut to Language Preparation? Radical Evangelicals, Missions, and the Gift of Tongues', *International Bulletin of Missionary Research* 25 (July 2001), pp. 118–123; G. Wacker, *Heaven Below: Early Pentecostals and American Culture* (Cambridge: Harvard University Press, 2001).

G. B. McGee

■ **PARKER, Joseph** (1830–1902), Congregational minister, was born in Hexham, Northumberland on 9 April 1830, the only child of Teasdale Parker, a stonemason, and Elizabeth (née Dodd). Both had relatives in better circumstances. The Parkers were Congregationalists, apart from a Wesleyan interlude provoked by dissension in their chapel. They were also politically radical. Thomas *Cooper, George Dawson, Edward Miall and Joseph Rayner Stephens were eagerly heard and critically assessed.

Parker's education suited his station: three schools of contrasting quality, run by Dissenters, followed at fourteen by apprenticeship to his father. That experiment failed. Parker was to be neither a mason, nor a surveyor, nor an architect. He became a teacher, establishing an ambitious school, Ebenezer, on chapel premises and marrying a Wesleyan farmer's daughter, Ann Nesbit, in Hexham's Congregational chapel in November 1851. Five months later he felt called to the ministry.

Parker's preaching had begun impulsively on Wall village green in June 1848. He became a Wesleyan local preacher (and thus met his wife) and discovered the potential of the temperance platform. Certain of his call, he wrote to Dr John Campbell of Moorfields Tabernacle, London. Campbell, Congregationalism's 'Bombastes, Furioso, Brag & Co', was controversial and influential in equal measure. His attitudes were instinctively conservative but he could judge character shrewdly. R. W. *Dale grew up in his congregation. Parker, the failed stonemason, impressed Campbell, the former blacksmith. Entry to theological college was deemed inappropriate (and was probably precluded by Parker's recent marriage), so Campbell gave Parker a crash course in preaching and theology, with practical experience as his assistant and an unimpressive taste of academe from lectures at University College. Nine months later, and having already published 'Chapters for Young Thinkers' in

Cassell's *Popular Educator*, Parker was called to the pastorate of Banbury Congregational church.

Parker's course as preacher, teacher and writer was thus set. He would excel in the first, make his mark in the second and achieve transient distinction in the third. A fourth role should be added; he became a denominational leader almost despite himself.

Parker had three pastorates: Banbury (1853–1858), Cavendish Street, Manchester (1858–1869) and what became the City Temple, London (1869–1902). Each was a secular and evangelistic success story.

At Banbury, silk-hatted and in 'a collar as high as Mr. Gladstone's', Parker revelled in a salary of £120 and confronted a congregation of fifty. He increased both. A new chapel was built to seat 600. Parker preached alfresco in the Bear Garden (in fact a cricket field); he lectured in the Corn Exchange, debated famously with G. J. Holyoake, wrote *Six Chapters on Secularism*, dispatched sermons to *The Homilist*, competed for a Glasgow essay prize and came second, and refused overtures from eligible churches.

In Manchester Parker inherited English Congregationalism's finest chapel and one of its grandest diaconates. They had turned to Parker when R. W. Dale refused to leave Birmingham. Their glorious building had 1,666 sittings, but in 1858 only 710 were filled. In three months another 240 applied, and in eleven years the membership of 344 tripled.

Parker took his time accepting Cavendish's call and imposed famous conditions ('I cannot visit for the mere sake of visiting'), but then Cavendish's minister was a national figure. He chaired Lancashire's powerful Congregational Union and Manchester's Congregational Board (as he would later chair London's Union and Board), and he wrote two well enough regarded books, *Ecce Deus* (1867, spurred by Seeley's *Ecce Homo*) and *The Paraclete*. He was awarded a Chicago DD in 1862, ten years before his first visit to the USA. In December 1864, a year after Ann's death, he married a Sunderland banker's daughter, Emma Common, who was attractive, a fine singer and well connected in Congregational circles. Her family joked that they were beauty and the beast. Parker protested that his wife was no beast.

In London Parker, already a national figure, became an international one. He took even more time to accept the call from Poultry Chapel ('the oldest Congregational Church in the greatest city in the world'), and his primary intention (to rebuild the church on a better site) was not achieved until 19 May 1874, when the City Temple was opened on Holborn Viaduct. It would become what the *Congregational Year Book* of 1903 described as 'the greatest and most powerful centre of Nonconformist teaching that London or England possesses'. The name had been prefigured in Parker's weekly published sermons at Poultry; it provided a Congregational balance in the City, just north of the Thames, to *Spurgeon's Baptist Metropolitan Tabernacle in the Borough, just south of the Thames. It had cost £80,000; it seated around 3,000 people; and its 'Great White Pulpit', from where Parker surveyed the world as far as the 'Rockies' (as the topmost galleries were nicknamed), was given by the City of London. Gladstone spoke in March 1877 at the packed midday service that Parker held each Thursday. Although the City's population steadily declined, the City Temple was consistently full for its Sunday and Thursday services and its writer-teacher preacher was in his element.

Parker the teacher has been unjustly forgotten. In Manchester he founded Cavendish Theological College, intended for older, less standard candidates. The concept was creatively re-applied in Nottingham by J. B. Paton. In London Parker founded an 'institute of homiletics'. It did not survive the move from Poultry Chapel, but its spirit continued in *The People's Bible* (25 vols.).

Parker the writer was quickly forgotten. He wrote over sixty books, ranging from novels to reminiscence. He should have been an instinctive journalist, given Campbell's coaching and, in later years, the friendship of W. Robertson Nicoll, but his style was seldom shaped or sustained, as *A Preacher's Life* (1899), written at Nicoll's urging, bears witness.

Parker the preacher, however, was unequalled. His appearance and voice helped magnificently. He was a master of timing. The electrifying impact of 'God damn the Sultan' (a reference to the German Emperor's visit to Turkey, inserted into a tercentenary commemoration of Oliver *Cromwell on 25 April 1899) depended on the pause that followed 'God'. His impact also depended on a constantly surprising use of language. His radical turn of phrase concealed a conservative turn of mind. His chairman's addresses to the Congregational Union in 1884 were memorably full of sharp humour and intelligent comment on current social and political issues, but although they were clearly capable of radical interpretation, their theology was conservative, however broad its scope: 'Ours is a four-square Faith: GOD, the Maker of all; CHRIST, the Saviour of all; INSPIRATION, the guide of all; IMMORTALITY, the heritage of all. With such a Faith we cannot have a little Ministry' (*Congregational Year Book*, 1885, p. 93). One of his later works, *None Like It: A Plea for the Old Sword*, was a riposte to R. F. Horton's moderate *Inspiration and the Bible* (1888).

This apparent and perhaps real ambivalence marked and perhaps strengthened Parker's denominational leadership. Parker was a wise Congregationalist if a poor Congregational minister. Stories of his pastoral autocracy were legion. He had a low view of deacons; he was not naturally gregarious; he could be a difficult colleague; he was thin-skinned; and his humour was too often taken literally. The City Temple was almost a parody of what a Congregational church should be. Its pews were full but its membership in 1902 seems to have been under a hundred. None the less, on (and behind) the national platform Parker was surprisingly often a moderating force, and he developed a bold but prophetic vision of how Congregationalism should develop in the twentieth century. The man who in 1876 witheringly criticized organized Congregationalism and in 1901 advocated a United Congregational Church (suggestively promoted in a joint session with the Baptist Union) was not in fact contradicting himself, and while it might seem surprising that the man who criticized R. F. Horton should choose one of the denomination's most theologically liberal thinkers, R. J. Campbell, as his successor, in doing so he ensured a future for the critical stimulus of the City Temple pulpit.

Parker twice chaired the Congregational Union (1884, 1901). The chairmanship was a rare honour, but on neither occasion was it uncontested, and for much of the 1890s Parker withdrew from Union affairs following his ill-judged criticism of its new secretary (W. J. Woods, a successor of Parker's at Cavendish, Manchester). His public prominence, however, remained unassailed. Although he had wisely decided not to stand for Parliament (for the City, on a platform embracing disestablishment and prohibition) in 1880, in 1902 he was preparing to support passive resistance in opposition to Balfour's Education Act, and in March 1902 he became president of the National Free Church Council.

Parker lived comfortably at Tynehome, 14 Lyndhurst Gardens, Hampstead. His wife's death on 26 January 1899 shattered him, and in 1901 his heart began to fail. He died on 28 November 1902, three weeks into the jubilee of his ordination. He left £27,000. He had no children.

Bibliography

A. Clare, *The City Temple 1640–1940* (London: Independent Press, 1940); W. Robertson Nicoll, *Princes of the Church* (London: Hodder & Stoughton, [4]1921); J. Parker, *A Preacher's Life: An Autobiography and an Album* (London: Hodder & Stoughton, 1899); A. Peel, *These Hundred Years* (London: Congregational Union of England and Wales, 1931).

C. BINFIELD

■ **PAYNE, Daniel Alexander** (1811–1893), African American minister, educator and historian, was a bishop of the African Methodist Episcopal (AME) Church and the first black president of Wilberforce University in Ohio, the oldest black college or university in the United States. An ardent opponent of slavery, he was a significant figure in the black church before, during and after the American Civil War, especially through his promotion of education.

Payne was born in Charleston, South Carolina on 24 February 1811, to free black parents who were themselves of interracial origin. After Payne was orphaned at the age of ten, he lived with a great-aunt, who saw that he regularly attended Methodist class meetings. His early formal education in Charleston included instruction in Greek,

Latin and French. Payne became an instructor and tutor; in 1828 he established a school in Charleston at which children were instructed during the day and adult slaves at night. In the wake of the publication of David Walker's *Appeal* in 1829 and Nat Turner's slave revolt in 1831 many southern whites prohibited the education of blacks, and Payne's school was closed in 1834. Payne left the South for the North in 1835 to study for the ministry but remained strongly committed to the education of blacks as an important means of elevation.

Payne received his formal theological education at the Lutheran Theological Seminary in Gettysburg, Pennsylvania between 1835 and 1837. In 1839 he was licensed to preach by the abolitionist Franckean (Franklin) Lutheran Synod in Fordsboro, New York. Although licensed by the Lutherans, Payne served as a pastor of a black Presbyterian congregation in upstate Troy, New York for two years (1837–1838). Afterwards he opened a school for African American children in Philadelphia while maintaining his connection with the Lutherans. Payne joined the AME Church in 1841 and was admitted to its Philadelphia Annual Conference in 1842. Once he made this move the school he had founded became affiliated to the Methodists. Payne was later pastor of AME congregations in the state of New York, Washington, DC and Baltimore, Maryland.

Payne was convinced that education was critical for the advancement of blacks in the United States. He vigorously advocated an educated ministry within the AME Church. His views on education and appropriate Christian behaviour also led him to question certain aspects of black folk religion, including those musical styles and exclamations that he considered too exuberant for public worship. The AME denomination eventually chose to have a formally educated ministry, and Payne influenced the shaping of its standards. As part of his commitment to education he also emphasized the importance of history; consequently, the AME Church made him its official historiographer in 1848. The extent of the growth of Payne's influence is evidenced by his election as a bishop in the AME Church on 7 May 1852 at the age of forty-one.

While Payne was presiding bishop of the second episcopal district of the AME Church,

with offices in Washington, DC, on 11 April 1862 the US Congress passed a bill abolishing slavery in the District of Columbia. Payne met with President Abraham Lincoln at that time and urged him to sign the bill, which he did on 16 April 1862. Once the new law was enacted, Payne wrote *Welcome to the Ransomed; or Duties of the Colored Inhabitants of the District of Columbia*, in which he celebrated emancipation and welcomed the newly freed slaves to the AME churches, where he claimed they would discover a new type of freedom in Christian living.

Payne's advocacy of education through his preaching and writings as well as his concern about clerical illiteracy contributed to the establishment in 1847 of Union Seminary, near Columbus, Ohio. The Ohio Annual Conference of the AME Church played a central role in this project. The school was housed in the basement of an AME church, provided basic education and acted as a trade school. Unfortunately, it suffered from limited and diffused support as well as competition from other more established institutions.

Meanwhile, in 1856 the northern and primarily white Methodist Episcopal Church (the Methodist Episcopal Church having split regionally into two denominations over the issue of slavery) established a school near Xenia, Ohio for training 'colored' missionaries and teachers. Payne was one of their four black trustees on a board of twenty-four, this arrangement being the result of the co-operative efforts of the Ohio conferences of the Methodist Episcopal and AME Churches. The institution was named Wilberforce University in honour of the British statesman and abolitionist Sir William *Wilberforce. The university's primary mission was to educate blacks.

In 1862 the Cincinnati Conference of the Methodist Episcopal Church determined that it could not continue to support and run Wilberforce University given its declining enrolment and increased debts and announced its closure. Under the leadership of Bishop Payne, the AME Church purchased it in 1863. Its acquisition by the AME Church made Wilberforce University the first college or university in the United States for African Americans to be owned and managed by a self-governing African American organization. The AME Church's struggling Union

Seminary was sold and its proceeds used to support Wilberforce University. Payne served as university president from 1863 to 1876, becoming the first black college president in the United States. Wilberforce University was formally incorporated in 1866. Its curriculum included industrial education, classical education and theological studies inaugurated by Payne. This combination of studies influenced the development of theological studies among blacks in other denominations. Growing out of the theology department, Payne Theological Seminary was established in 1894.

Payne was influential in the rapid growth of the AME Church after 1865. One of the results of the end of the American Civil War was that independent African American denominations, of which the majority of members lived in the North, embarked on an aggressive evangelism programme among blacks in the South. As part of this new wave of African American Christianity Payne returned to Charleston in 1865 after an absence of thirty years and organized a new AME South Carolina Annual Conference, which was illustrative of the aggressive expansion of the AME Church among the freed slaves.

In 1881 Payne was a delegate from the AME Church to the Ecumenical Methodist Conference (the precursor of the World Methodist Conference) held in London. He also participated in the first World Parliament of Religions in Chicago in 1893. Payne's writings include *Recollections of Seventy Years* (1888) and *History of the African Methodist Episcopal Church* (1891), which continues to be a valuable source for the history of the first seventy-five years of the denomination.

Throughout his life Payne saw being an educator as a central part of his vocation. He worked to create a more educated ministry in the AME Church through the establishment of reading courses and schools. In many ways Payne was a major organizational force in the AME Church and one of its most influential bishops. His own lifestyle expressed his dedication to the church, especially in his emphasis on scholarly achievement, positive morality, sacrifice, effort and responsibility. Payne was married to Eliza Clark Payne and became a father to her four children; they had

one child of their own. Payne died on 2 November 1893 in Wilberforce, Ohio.

Bibliography

C. Killian (ed.), *Daniel Alexander Payne: Sermons and Addresses, 1853–1891* (New York: Arno Press, 1972); C. E. Walker, *A Rock in a Weary Land: The African Methodist Episcopal Church During the Civil War and Reconstruction* (Baton Rouge: Louisiana State University Press, 1982).

E. D. APONTE

■ **PEAKE, Arthur Samuel** (1865–1929), Primitive Methodist biblical scholar, was born on 24 November 1865 at Leek, Staffordshire, the second son and third child of Samuel and Rosabella Peake. Peake's father was a Primitive Methodist minister and a gifted evangelist; his family was raised in what Peake later described as 'a rather narrow evangelicalism'. Although the demands of the itinerant ministry necessitated frequent changes of school, in 1883 Peake won a scholarship from King Henry VIII's Grammar School, Coventry, to St John's College, Oxford, to read classics. A disappointing third class in classical moderations led to the loss of his scholarship, but also encouraged him to transfer to theology, at which he excelled. In 1887 Peake was awarded a first-class degree, and he followed this with the Denyer and Johnson Scholarship (1888), the Ellerton Essay Prize (1890) and a fellowship at Merton College (1890), becoming the first Nonconformist lay person to gain a theological fellowship at Oxford. From 1890 to 1892 Peake combined his Merton fellowship with teaching at the newly founded Mansfield College, under A. M. Fairbairn. In June 1892 he married Harriet Mary Sillman at the parish church of Cowley St John. The Peakes had three sons.

In May 1891 Peake was introduced to W. P. Hartley, the Primitive Methodist industrialist and philanthropist. Hartley was anxious to improve the level of training offered to students at the Primitive Methodists' theological college in Manchester and, having discussed the situation with Peake, he promised to fund an additional tutor for at least five years. After a year's consultation, the connexion accepted Hartley's offer, appointed Peake as tutor and gave him a free hand to reform the curriculum. From a college with a single member of staff providing a one-year course, the institution expanded by 1908 to a faculty of five offering its students three years of training. Hartley's financial support for new staff and buildings was reflected in the decision to rename the institution 'Hartley College' (1906), but the guiding hand in teaching and ministerial formation was that of Peake, who remained at the college from 1892 until his death. Although never ordained, as the longest-serving and most eminent tutor at the Primitive Methodists' only college he exercised a decisive influence over the outlook and theology of the whole connexion.

In addition to teaching at Hartley, Peake also lectured at the Lancashire Independent College and at the United Methodists' Victoria Park College. He played a key role, moreover, in the establishment of the theology faculty in the University of Manchester (1904), where he served as the first dean, and he represented the faculty on the university senate from 1904 until his death. He was the first holder of the Rylands Chair of Biblical Exegesis (1904–1929), and was Pro-Vice-Chancellor of the University in 1925. His academic achievements were recognized in the award of honorary DD degrees by the Universities of Aberdeen (1907) and Oxford (1920).

Peake was hailed by W. F. Howard as 'the greatest biblical scholar of his generation'. His Oxford years coincided with the gradual acceptance of higher criticism by mainstream British scholars and, reflecting on his undergraduate studies, Peake acknowledged the varied influences of T. K. Cheyne, S. R. Driver, William Sanday, Edwin Hatch and A. M. Fairbairn. His own work encompassed an extensive list of publications on both Old and New Testaments, including an estimated twenty books and numerous monographs, articles and reviews. Notable works ranged from commentaries on Job (1905), Jeremiah and Lamentations (1910, 1912), Hebrews (1902) and Colossians (1903) to The Problem of Suffering in the Old Testament (1904) and A Critical Introduction to the New Testament (1909). In The Bible: Its Origin, Its Significance and Its Abiding Worth (1913), Peake set out his approach to biblical interpretation, and in The Nature of Scripture (1922) he

defended critical scholarship against conservative and fundamentalist attack. A founder member of the Society of Old Testament Study, and its president in 1924, Peake edited The People and the Book (1925) for the society. His chief literary legacy, the one-volume Commentary which bears his name, was published in 1919; in it he sought 'to put before the reader in a simple form ... the generally accepted results of Biblical Criticism, Interpretation, History and Theology'. Peake wrote one-eighth of the text himself and was reputed to have worked through the articles of the other sixty-one contributors ten times before publication. Besides his books, many of which were best-sellers, Peake made scholarship accessible to a wider public through a weekly column in the Primitive Methodist Leader and through his work from 1892 as literary editor of the Primitive Methodist Quarterly Review (Holborn Review from 1910); he became editor of the Review in 1919. His acquaintance with the leading British and European biblical scholars added personal insight to the Review's discussions of current literature. Although gifted with a capacity for sustained hard work and an ability to dictate books and reviews directly to his secretary, Peake's workload of teaching and popularizing contemporary scholarship meant that proposed major studies of Isaiah and Paul remained unwritten.

Peake's frank endorsement of, and enthusiasm for, modern biblical criticism made him a controversial figure. Graham *Scroggie described Peake's Commentary as 'sodden with infidelity', and Peake was a popular target for abuse in ultra-conservative circles. Among Primitive Methodists, however, he was accorded unfailing confidence and growing respect. In part, this may have been due to denominational pride in the connexion's possession of a scholar of international renown. To a large extent, however, it was due to Peake's combination of meticulous scholarship, lucidity of expression, deep humility and manifest personal piety. He was an advocate of higher criticism, not for its own sake, but because he believed that it enabled the Word of God to be more clearly heard. As a local preacher, his sermons were invariably Christocentric, simple and direct. A contemporary attributed Peake's empathetic understanding of Paul to his 'rich personal experience of the saving grace of the Gospel'. Another suggested that he 'represented the not impossible combination of Modernist and Evangelical'. In an oft-quoted tribute, the Wesleyan George Jackson credited Peake with saving English Christianity from a fundamentalist controversy, a judgment echoed by the Congregationalist C. H. Dodd.

Beyond the immediate academic sphere Peake was an active supporter of the National Council of the Evangelical Free Churches, serving as the Council's president in 1928. He represented the Primitive Methodists in the conversations on reunion (1922–1925) stimulated by the 1920 Lambeth Appeal. Above all, however, Peake played a leading part in the negotiations towards the reunion of the Primitive, Wesleyan and United Methodist connexions, which gathered momentum after the First World War. He was involved in drafting and amending the reunion scheme and in shaping the proposed doctrinal basis of the united church. His advocacy persuaded the Primitive Methodists to persevere with the scheme in the face of a decade of substantial opposition from the Wesleyans, and he addressed directly the doctrinal issues raised by the Wesleyan 'Other Side' in 1922. In response to Wesleyan allegations that the Primitives regarded their ministers as mere 'paid agents of the Church', Peake made it clear that his connexion did not denigrate the pastoral office, writing 'Be it ours to have a high doctrine of the ministry just because we have a high doctrine of the Church.' The necessary majorities were finally achieved in the three Methodist Conferences in the summer of 1928, but Peake did not live to see the Methodist Union Enabling Act and the Uniting Conference of 1932, dying in Manchester Royal Infirmary after a short illness on 19 August 1929.

Bibliography

L. S. Peake, *Arthur Samuel Peake: A Memoir* (London: Hodder & Stoughton, 1930); J. T. Wilkinson, *Arthur Samuel Peake: A Biography* (London: Epworth Press, 1971).

M. WELLINGS

■ **PENNEFATHER, William** (1816–1873), Anglican clergyman and evangelical ecumenist, was born in Dublin on 5 February 1816, the son of Richard Pennefather, a prominent Irish lawyer. He was educated at schools in Dublin and at Westbury on Trym near Bristol, and from 1832 to 1834 by a private tutor, William Stevens, at Levens parsonage in Westmorland, where he developed a deep love for the scenery of the English Lake District. In 1834 he entered Trinity College, Dublin, but had to leave because of ill health. He convalesced in Westmorland and at Portstewart on the north coast of Ireland, where he began to work among the local fishermen, reading and expounding the Bible to them and visiting the sick, work which he later regarded as the beginning of his ministerial life. In 1837 he returned to college and eventually graduated BA in 1840. Although he had developed a strong interest in foreign missions while a student, Pennefather felt called, at least initially, to work in Ireland. He began by working as an unpaid curate at Ballymachugh in County Cavan and was ordained in 1841. In 1844 he moved to the incumbency of Mellifont near Drogheda and was very active in relieving the mainly Roman Catholic poor of his parish during the famine of 1845–1847. In 1847 Pennefather married Catherine, the eldest daughter of Rear-Admiral James King of Angley in Kent, and the following year accepted the incumbency of Holy Trinity, Walton, near Aylesbury in England. The living was a new one, created in 1845 to secure an evangelical ministry within the town, and had only a small income. Pennefather remained at Walton until 1852, when he was offered the living of Christ Church, Barnet, where he worked for a further twelve years before accepting his final incumbency at St Jude's, Mildmay Park, Islington. Pennefather died in his ninth year of ministry at Mildmay on 30 April 1873.

Despite his often fragile health, the activity, creativity and success of Pennefather's ministry both in Ireland and in England qualify him for recognition as one of the outstanding pastors of his generation. He was notable both for the success he made of the recognized means of extending the influence of the church and for his willingness to innovate in the face of the particular challenges posed by the circumstances of his parishes. He was a powerful, affective preacher who was in considerable demand as an evangelist and seems readily to have attracted large congregations. He was so successful in this respect that it soon became necessary to enlarge the church buildings in Aylesbury, Barnet and Mildmay. He was also concerned to maximize the proportion of his parishioners who received communion in the church and organized special meetings for communicants in both large and small groups. The enlargement of St Jude's was prompted not just by the requirement for additional seats, but also by the need for a more commodious chancel to accommodate the communicants. Church services were supplemented by a regular prayer meeting that Pennefather regarded as the most important energizing element in the life of the parish.

Pennefather's parochial ministry was, however, dominated by his overriding perception that it was essential to take the gospel out to the people rather than simply seeking to attract them into the church. His first attempts, pioneered at Ballymachugh and Mellifont, which had relatively scattered Protestant populations, involved setting up a number of local stations for cottage lectures and Bible readings, at which he could meet with his parishioners in small groups and address their individual circumstances in greater depth than was possible at ordinary services. In England, faced by more densely populated urban parishes, Pennefather supplemented these activities with the full panoply of measures commonly employed by the evangelical incumbents of large parishes in the mid-nineteenth century. These included the purchase or building of mission chapels staffed by curates or paid lay workers and the organization of a large team of district visitors to supplement his own pastoral activity in the homes of the parish. He was particularly concerned about the education of his parishioners and rapidly built new or expanded existing accommodation for day schools and Sunday schools at Barnet and Mildmay. He fostered organizations for adult education and self-improvement and for the welfare of his parishioners, including soup kitchens for the poor during the winter and a public house that served coffee and other non-alcoholic drinks as a refuge for working men. At the same time, however, Pennefather seems to have been particularly concerned to build a Christian community in which the poor were full participants according to their means and not simply consumers or the objects of the ministry of others. Thus, according to his biographer, 'he was ... anxious that the work of the district visitors should never set aside the visit of the Christian neighbour, or the parochial machinery blight the outgoing love of the poor in their kindness to one another.' Pennefather's innovative approach to parish ministry is exemplified by his persistence, despite the common evangelical suspicion of sisterhoods, in establishing a community of deaconesses at Barnet and thereby pioneering deaconess work for the church as a whole. The first deaconess house was opened in 1860 and was subsequently transferred to Mildmay following Pennefather's move in 1864. The deaconesses were primarily involved in domestic visitation, both pastoral and evangelistic in nature, and gradually expanded their work to other parishes by invitation of their incumbents.

Pennefather's ministry was founded on his personal religion. He was a moderate evangelical, who combined an informal and approachable style with a reputation for an intense personal holiness and the depth of his relationship with Christ. He was deeply interested in the study and application of biblical prophecy, was a member of a prophetic society and convened a prophetic group in his own parish. According to his biographer, Pennefather 'always rejoiced to meet with those who were intelligently and practically looking for the coming King'. Pennefather's adventism thus encouraged his enthusiasm for evangelical ecumenism, the cause for which he became most famous. Pennefather was committed to the idea that the spiritual unity of the body of Christ ought to be made manifest. In 1856 he sent out invitations for a conference to be held at Barnet for the purpose of promoting 'personal holiness, brotherly love, and increased interest in the work of the Lord'. A second conference was held in 1858, and the conference became an annual event thereafter. The conferences transferred to Mildmay in 1864, and by 1867 the attendance had grown to such an extent that it was necessary to construct a 2,500 seat conference hall to accommodate the gathering. The conferences continued to be notably ecumenical, attracting a wide range of British evangelical speakers and also contributors from across the Atlantic. Pennefather was instrumental, for example, in introducing D. L. *Moody to Britain. Following Pennefather's sudden death in 1873, the conferences continued, initially under the inspiration of Catherine Pennefather, and while substantially eclipsed by the Keswick conventions remained into the twentieth century an influence on British evangelicalism, promoting a distinctive blend of intense piety and revivalism. Pennefather's other commitments left relatively little time for writing, and most of his publications were sermons and addresses. Particularly interesting is his *The Church of the First-Born: A Few Thoughts on Christian Unity* (London: J. F. Shaw, 1865), in which were reprinted many of the circular invitations to the conferences.

Bibliography

R. Braithwaite, *The Life and Letters of Rev. William Pennefather B.A.* (London: J. F. Shaw, 1878).

M. SMITH

■ **PERCEVAL, Spencer** (1762–1812), British prime minister, was born in London on 1 November 1762, the seventh son of John Perceval, the second earl of Egmont. He was educated at Harrow School and at Trinity College, Cambridge, where he graduated MA in 1781. Having only a small private income, Perceval opted to make his living in the law, a career in which his command of detail and notable skills as a speaker and debater, as well as his prominent connections, brought him success. He began his practice as a barrister in 1786, and in 1787 gained, through family influence, the office of deputy recorder of Northampton, which provided him with a modest but reliable income. In 1790 Perceval married Jane, the daughter of Sir Thomas Wilson, who three years previously had refused his consent because of Perceval's slender means, but who seems eventually to have consented after the young couple presented him with a *fait accompli* by eloping when Jane came of age. The marriage appears to have been a happy one and produced eventually a total of twelve children, six sons and six daughters.

The expenses of his household compounded Perceval's financial difficulties. However, a succession of minor appointments and, from 1792, a series of crown briefs enabled him both to survive and to build a reputation for advocacy that also boosted his private legal practice. In 1796 he was made a King's Counsel and was also for the first time offered public office, as chief secretary for Ireland, by the prime minister, William Pitt. Perceval felt obliged to decline the offer since he could not support his family on any salary that might be appropriately attached to the post. He did, however, enter Parliament as MP for Northampton in September 1796 and rapidly distinguished himself as a speaker for the government side. Following Pitt's resignation in 1801, Perceval finally entered office, first as solicitor general and then as attorney general in the Addington administration, where his debating skills were highly valued, and he continued in this post when Pitt returned to power in 1804. Following Pitt's death in January 1806, Perceval spent just over a year in opposition, though he remained an active parliamentarian and initiated legislation to improve the lot of curates in the established church. He was a leading member of the administration of the Duke of Portland from March 1807 to September 1809, serving as both chancellor of the Duchy of Lancaster and chancellor of the exchequer, and was successful in stabilizing the public finances as a basis for the continuing war against France. When Portland resigned in 1809, Perceval succeeded him as prime minister, and over the next three years he gradually strengthened an initially unstable government, not least by the force of his own debating prowess. His prospects of a lengthy period in office were, however, abruptly terminated on 11 May 1812, when he was assassinated in the lobby of the House of Commons by the deranged John Bellingham.

In politics Perceval was a conservative, firmly opposed to the principles of the French Revolution and to attempts to widen the parliamentary franchise to include Roman Catholics. He was, however, willing to sponsor cautious reform in a number of areas and was a firm supporter of the abolition of the slave trade.

In religion Perceval is best described as a moderate evangelical. He was firmly committed to the defence of the established church and intervened to protect its position in respect of popular education. At the same time, he was an enthusiast for the study of biblical prophecy and published anonymously *Observations Intended to Point Out the Application of a Prophecy in the Eleventh Chapter of the Book of Daniel to the French Power* (1800). He was also friendly with members of the evangelical Clapham Sect, including William *Wilberforce and Henry *Thornton. He promoted the evangelical Henry *Ryder, the brother of his close political allies Dudley and Richard Ryder, to the deanery of Wells and would have secured him a bishopric but for his own early death. However, his chief ecclesiastical advisor was the non-evangelical William Mansel, his old college tutor who had been made Bishop of Bristol through Perceval's influence. It is perhaps characteristic of his religion that while Perceval encouraged Mansel to provide him with advice on ecclesiastical policy, he provided the bishop with spiritual counsel.

Bibliography

D. Gray, *Spencer Perceval: The Evangelical Prime Minister* (Manchester: Manchester University Press, 1963); S. Walpole, *The Life of the Right Honourable Spencer Perceval* (London: Hurst & Blackett, 1874).

M. SMITH

■ **PERKINS, John** (1930–), community organizer and racial peacemaker, was born in a sharecropper's shack in New Hebron, Mississippi. His father had abandoned the family, and his mother died shortly after the birth of John, her youngest child. The baby was taken in and raised by his grandmother, aunts and uncles. After his oldest brother, Clyde, was shot and killed in a racial incident, the elder relatives sent seventeen-year-old John to California to save him from a similar fate in a rigidly white supremacist Mississippi.

From the 1920s to the 1970s the spread of mechanized agriculture and the desire for opportunity in the less racially discriminatory cities of the North and West caused the Great Migration of African Americans out of the South. A part of that mass movement, young John Perkins enjoyed upward mobility in the Los Angeles area as shop steward in a newly unionizing steel foundry. He was drafted into the army, sent to Okinawa, and discharged in 1951. Shortly thereafter he married Vera Mae Buckley. Living near Pasadena, and enjoying further upward mobility working in an expanding supermarket chain, he experienced conversion in 1957 after accompanying his six-year-old son Spencer to Sunday school.

Plunging into intensive Bible study with a Presbyterian missionary from Child Evangelism Fellowship, Perkins found that he too was attracted to missionary work. While subsequently evangelizing at a mountain institution for youth offenders, he was struck by the fact that many of the young men were black southerners like himself. Tracing the origins of the problems that had landed them in detention camp to the Jim Crow South, Perkins decided to move his expanding family back to the poverty and oppression of Mississippi, where he began work as an evangelist in 1960. He had been discipled by a white minister, and many of the early contacts he had developed were with white evangelical churches. It was they who supported him in his mission to African Americans in the Deep South.

While living among the impoverished people of the black section of Mendenhall, a county town in south central Mississippi, Perkins began to develop a distinctive style of mission that he called 'holistic'. He believed that the whole of the downtrodden life that blacks experienced in the South produced an ignorance and lack of self-confidence, coupled with a destructive anger and despair, that they carried with them as they migrated. Hence he directed his missionary work not merely to inner spiritual needs but to outer material ones as well. It was common for rural black preachers in the region to itinerate among a number of churches and not to reside in any of the communities in which those churches were situated. Perkins, however, moved into the community where he was ministering. Immediately their wants became his, and he found himself ministering to people according to their 'felt need'. In this respect his work resembles that of the social settlement house movement and that of the Catholic Worker, of which the Hospitality Houses minister to the urban poor.

In his pioneering work in Mendenhall Perkins addressed a range of needs: youth development and schooling and adult education, nutrition and health care, housing and employment. In looking for means of developing the community, he utilized whatever would do the job. He made use of federal programmes for housing, nutrition and health care. For his own support, for building work and expanding projects, he raised money from the white evangelicals in California who had initially supported him, and they led him to others, in whose churches and colleges he spoke around the country. During the 1960s, the years of the Civil Rights movement, Perkins educated conservative white evangelicals as to the worthiness and importance of the African American cause.

But Perkins did not want black communities to remain dependent on outside largesse. His ultimate goal was a healthy, self-supporting Christian community. It was to this end that he became involved in a cooperative movement, of which the principal regional organizer was a black Louisiana Catholic priest, A. J. McKnight. The two men procured Ford Foundation grants and created the Southern Cooperative Development Fund, which was for a time the largest black owned bank in the South. They were able to fund cooperatives in agriculture, housing and retailing that brought economic development, employment and ownership to Mendenhall and other poor rural areas.

In planting a church that became the hub of a number of closely related projects, Perkins set up a model of holistic faith-based development that he and others then introduced to other communities. African Americans developing their community in Mendenhall began to assert themselves in the broader context of town life. Under Perkins' leadership they became part of the Civil Rights movement, which was reaching its peak by the mid-1960s. They boycotted white-owned shops that refused blacks employment and issued demands for extension of city services to the black community. Perkins was challenging the whole structure of white domination, and he was ultimately successful. But like many other black leaders he paid a heavy price. He was ambushed by police following one of the Civil Rights marches, taken to a jail in another county, and beaten almost to death.

During his recovery, which took over a year, Perkins relinquished the Mendenhall projects to younger disciples, moved to Jackson, the state capital, and began a second set of projects much like those in Mendenhall, but adapted to Jackson's felt needs. At this time, as a result of his confrontation with white hatred, he began to redirect his work towards the goal of racial reconciliation. He brought in many white volunteers to work on housing renovation and in other projects, and he began to employ whites on his staff. Eventually this policy caused inter-racial friction due to the recurrence within the projects of culturally ingrained patterns of white domination. Perkins' eldest son, Spencer, led a movement in the 1980s and 1990s designed to overcome these old patterns and promote racial reconciliation.

The Jackson projects became the model for the teaching and spreading of 'Christian community development' throughout the country and abroad. Perkins' concept comprises what he calls 'the three R's': relocate to the community of need; reconcile across all lines of division; redistribute resources from affluent, educated and skilled people who move into the community to the indigenous people.

In 1982 Perkins relinquished the Jackson projects to another group of disciples and moved to an inner city neighbourhood in Pasadena, California, where he began the development process again. Vera Mae Perkins was instrumental in the Child Evangelism Good News Clubs, consisting of home-based spiritual and moral formation for the young, which formed the foundation of the other projects. In Pasadena the Good News Club became the seed of an elaborate after-school youth development programme now run jointly by the Perkins' third son Derek and Rudy Carrasco. The northwest Pasadena neighbourhood has also become the home of a college preparatory school, of which the principal is Karyn Perkins, Derek's wife.

In 1983 in Pasadena, Perkins and a number of associates from projects around the country established the John M. Perkins Foundation for Reconciliation and Development to support an expanding series of community development projects. In 1989 the foundation created the Christian Community Development Association, a confederation of what is now over five hundred faith-based community development organizations in locations throughout the United States and in other countries, including Haiti. Most of these organizations utilize the concepts first developed by John Perkins in Mendenhall.

Bibliography
S. E. Berk, *A Time to Heal: John Perkins, Community Development and Racial Reconciliation* (Grand Rapids: Baker Book House, 1997); J. M. Perkins, *Let Justice Roll Down* (Venture: Regal Press, 1976); J. M. Perkins, *Beyond Charity: The Call to Christian Community Development* (Grand Rapids: Baker Book House, 1993).

S. E. BERK

■ **PERKINS, William** (1558–1602), Puritan theologian, was born in Warwickshire in 1558. He matriculated at Christ's College in Cambridge, from where he graduated in 1581 and where he was to spend most of his adult life. While a student, he was tutored by Laurence Chaderton, who was the effective leader of the moderate Puritanism that characterized Cambridge at that time. Around the time of the completion of his MA degree (1584) he underwent a dramatic religious conversion, although its precise timing is unclear. Legend has it that prior to that time he was a byword among the townsfolk for drunkenness and loutish behaviour, though the anecdotal evidence for this can be dated back only to Thomas Brooks in the nineteenth century. After conversion he soon began preaching to prisoners in the town gaol and, shortly thereafter, he was appointed as lecturer (preacher) to Great St Andrew's Church, a post he held from 1584 to 1602. In addition he also held a fellowship at Christ's from 1584 to 1595, when he resigned after performing the marriage ceremony of Timothy Cradocke, college rules forbidding fellows to be married.

In 1587 Perkins began to object to the practice of kneeling for reception of the elements in the communion service and then, in 1591, he was summoned before the Star Chamber because of his role in a 1589 conference which sought to promote a presbyterian Book of Discipline, although it seems that his appearance was as a witness for the prosecution, not the defence. Indeed, there is no evidence in Perkins' writings of any strong presbyterian commitments on ecclesiology, and his overall position on this and related issues seems to have been at best a broadly pragmatic one.

Perkins died in 1602 while still a lecturer at Great St Andrews, where he had exerted one of the most influential preaching ministries of the day.

Perkins' theology is marked by many of the traits that characterize later English and Dutch Reformed theology. First, a clear catholicity is evident in his approach to sources; he cites patristic, medieval and contemporary authors. Puritanism as a theological tradition exhibited no sectarianism with regard to learning but drew widely on the whole Western tradition in a manner that reflected the university context from which it emerged.

Secondly, Perkins' practical, experiential concern is evident in his definition of theology as 'the science of living blessedly forever'. This practical definition foreshadows that of his influential pupil William *Ames and indicates an approach to theology that makes practical piety the goal of theological reflection. This was to be a hallmark of the writings both of later English Puritans and of the leaders of the Dutch Nadere Reformatie ('Second Reformation'). In Perkins it manifests itself specifically in the posthumously published *Whole Treatise of Cases of Conscience* (1606), which was one of the earliest Puritan attempts at casuistry, the branch of theology concerned with specific ethical questions and dilemmas. As the Reformation had focused more responsibility for personal salvation on the laity, so the need to deal with pastoral problems increased. Perkins' casuistry was one influential response to the new questions that Reformation theology had thrown up in its wake.

For Perkins, this emphasis upon the personal, affective aspects of theology is almost certainly the result of his experience as a pastor at Great St Andrews and the need to make Reformed theology relevant to the daily renewal of individual Christian lives. It was also undergirded by his perception of the state of the English national church. The English church had changed its broad theological allegiance several times in the sixteenth century, finally reaching the settlement under

Elizabeth whereby a rigidly enforced conformity was offered as the answer to the political and religious needs of the wider society. In this context, Perkins' work can be seen as a reaction against such formalism, stressing the need for personal renewal and reformation as of the essence of a vital church. Perkins' casuistry, his emphasis upon sanctification, and his somewhat open and pragmatic attitude to the details of church polity should all be read within this wider context.

Thirdly, Perkins' writings represent an attempt to grapple with the profound issues surrounding the relationship between God's eternal purposes, the historical reality of the incarnation, and the human experience of salvation in time. In *A Golden Chaine* (1590) Perkins famously attempted to schematize the Christian life in the context of God's eternal decrees of predestination. His scheme was summarized in the elaborate chart that he included in the book. Based on a similar chart in Theodore Beza's *Tabula Praedestinationis* (1555), the diagram shows in pictorial form Perkins' understanding of salvation. Much scholarly ink has been spilt over the significance of the chart, but three points need to be made. First, it is a significant elaboration of the Bezan original, subdividing the believer's life into far more component phases. Secondly, it has a central column dealing with Christ, which relates the believer's own life to that of the Messiah. It therefore represents a far more highly developed scheme than that offered by Beza and indicates that Reformed theologians, far from seeing theology as a static entity, were constantly engaged in theological reflection and development of their tradition. Thirdly, and most importantly, the Bezan chart (and its Perkinsian adaptation) is meant to be read from the bottom up, not the top down. It is an expression in visual form of the fact that each stage in salvation is comprehensible only in the light of what precedes it. It is emphatically not, therefore, an example of deducing salvation from the decrees, but quite the reverse, a point correctly noted by Karl Barth in his *Church Dogmatics* but missed by many of his followers. This point is important because it strikes at the very heart of the school of thought that sees Perkins as importing Beza's theology into England and turning Puritanism into a decretal system. Puritan theology was always too eclectic for

one man to effect such a change, and close reading of the documents in historical context reveals that this alleged decretalism never existed anyway. Perkins theology was vigorously anti-Pelagian and drew fire on that score from the Dutch theologian Jacob *Arminius, but it was not decretal in any simplistic deductive sense.

Perkins was doubtless the most influential English theologian of his time. Any account of the development of Reformed theology in either England or the Netherlands must place him at the centre of the intellectual narrative.

Bibliography
D. McKim, *Ramism in William Perkins' Theology* (New York: Peter Lang, 1987); R. A. Muller, *Christ and the Decree* (Grand Rapids: Baker Book House, 1986); P. R. Schaefer, 'The Spiritual Brotherhood on Habits of the Heart' (DPhil thesis, University of Oxford, 1994).

C. R. Trueman

■ **PERRY, Charles** (1807–1891), first Anglican bishop of Melbourne (1847–1874), was the son of a wealthy merchant who was also sheriff of Essex, and was educated at Harrow and Trinity College, Cambridge. He graduated BA in 1828 with first-class honours in both mathematics (senior wrangler) and classics (seventh) and was first Smith's prizeman. From 1829 to 1832 he studied law at the Inner Temple. In the same period he struggled with religious doubt, which left him with a deep sense of the duty of private judgment in matters of religion. It was on the basis of his own study of the Scriptures that he accepted the evangelical faith. Only then, through Edward Hoare and William Carus, Charles *Simeon's successor at Holy Trinity, Cambridge, did he become part of the evangelical network, making special friendships with Thomas Fowell *Buxton and Joseph John *Gurney. In 1832 he was appointed tutor at Trinity College. Thus confirmed in his religious beliefs and in his desire for ordination, he was made deacon by the Bishop of Gloucester in 1833 and was priested by the Bishop of Ely in 1836. He became assistant curate of Christ Church, Barnwell and St Paul's Newtown, and vicar of the latter from 1845. In 1841 he married Frances, a daughter of

Samuel Cooper, a Hull merchant. She was well-educated, of a sunny disposition and shared his evangelical convictions.

Perry was appointed Bishop of Melbourne on the advice of Henry *Venn, the Church Missionary Society (CMS) secretary. Venn had been impressed by Perry's interest in pre-ordination training and in CMS. He was consecrated Bishop of Melbourne at Westminster Abbey on 29 June 1847 along with bishops for Adelaide, Newcastle and Cape Town. His was considered the least propitious of the four sees, and on his arrival in Melbourne on 23 January 1848, the population of his diocese numbered only 43,000. Yet nearly half of these were Anglicans. He had very few clergy and most of these were from Ireland. Perry credited them with zeal and 'more or less of a wrong-headedness'. Controversially, he relied greatly on lay readers.

The discovery of gold in 1851 brought massive immigration to Victoria, completely transforming the colony and catapulting Perry into a key position in the Australian church. 'Gold! gold! gold!' wrote Frances Perry, '... we are gone mad with gold and what is to be the end of it no one knows ... Melbourne is left pretty nearly under petticoat government.' Together the Perrys toured the goldfields, where he preached in riding clothes and she reassured the wives of clergy, anxious about the bad influence that the goldfields might have on their children. Childless herself, she was distressed by the high rate of mortality in childbirth, and so established the lying-in hospital which in time developed into the prestigious Royal Women's Hospital.

At the first conference of Australasian bishops in Sydney in 1850, Perry argued for a view on infant baptism consistent with the Gorham judgment in England, which had declared that the denial of baptismal regeneration was not inconsistent with the doctrine of the Church of England. The five other bishops, with High Church convictions, led by the aged William Grant Broughton of Sydney, were disconcerted by Perry's evangelical convictions and their consequent inability to present a united view on what they regarded as a major issue of both doctrine and church–state relations. Perry acted consistently on the basis of his evangelical convictions and sought to exclude from his diocese any clergy who believed in the 'doctrine of Christ's presence,

in any sense whatever, in the *bread* and *wine* upon the Lord's table after consecration', in auricular confession or in private absolution. He tried hard, but failed, to stamp out chanting and surpliced choirs, since in his view they threatened to turn the liturgy into 'a mere musical performance'. He fought a losing battle against the influence of the Ecclesiological Society, since Melbourne now had a number of architects who understood its recommendations and used them to create neo-Gothic designs for church buildings.

The 1850 Sydney conference also explored the manner in which self-government might be granted to the new dioceses. Perry's legal training alerted him to the problems created by the inappropriate application of English ecclesiastical law to the new colony. Whereas Bishops Short (of Adelaide) and Selwyn (of New Zealand) sought to establish a constitution for their dioceses on the basis of consensual compact, Perry was convinced that an Imperial act was necessary for Melbourne. In 1854 a bill granting self-government to the Victorian Church of England was passed by the Victorian Legislative Council. This received the royal assent in the following year, and in 1856 Perry presided over the first legally authorized synod in the colonies. The dioceses of Sydney and Tasmania were to follow a similar procedure, while the then remaining dioceses of Newcastle, Adelaide and New Zealand followed the route of consensual compact without any reference to the legislature.

Perry presided over the establishment of the Melbourne Diocesan Grammar School (1849) and Geelong Grammar School (1857) which, he believed, because they were based on the principles of Thomas Arnold, were likely to produce the future leaders of society. Perry was also a councillor of the University of Melbourne from its foundation. In 1851, the year in which Victoria was separated from New South Wales and gold was discovered, Perry wrote, 'The creation of a people must always in a measure depend upon the means of education which are provided for them.' As principal founder of Trinity College, Melbourne (1872) he sought to recreate his Cambridge college, but of necessity the college had to develop differently in a more secular climate. He never managed to found a clergy training college in his diocese.

By 1869 the growth in the population and the church in Victoria was spectacular; there were 113 clergy, 162 churches and 75 parsonages. In 1873 a new diocese, Ballarat, was separated from the Melbourne diocese. Perry neither courted nor attained popularity. On his return to Britain in 1874, he was appointed canon of Llandaff Cathedral and continued to maintain his lifelong support of CMS, now as a vice-president. In 1881 Ridley Hall, Cambridge, was opened, his finest achievement in retirement. Some criticized his requirement that college councillors should subscribe to a doctrinal statement, but Perry insisted that such a barrier was needed against rationalism and ritualism.

On his retirement from the diocese of Melbourne in 1874 the *Church Times* berated his 'obstinacy and Puritanism' and concluded, 'What a disaster it is when a Presbyterian or Dissenting minister who has missed his way and got into the church is made a Bishop.' A cool and rational thinker and an uncompromising evangelical, Perry brought sound, analytical judgment to a colony where too often passion and partisanship determined policy. He laid the constitutional foundations of the Church of England in Victoria, presided over a rapidly growing diocese and facilitated the contribution of the laity to the life of the church. A severe personality limited the achievements of this ecclesiastical statesman of great ability. He meticulously observed proper legal procedures and was unfailingly courteous to his opponents. While his narrow churchmanship was often criticized, his fairness was never questioned.

Bibliography

G. Goodman, *The Church in Victoria during the Episcopate of Bishop Perry* (Melbourne: Melville, Mullen & Slade, 1892; M. Loane, *Hewn from the Rock: Origins and Traditions of the Church in Sydney* (Sydney: Anglican Information Office, 1976); A. de Q. Robin, *Charles Perry, Bishop of Melbourne: The Challenges of a Colonial Episcopate, 1847–76* (Nedlands: University of WA Press, 1967).
S. PIGGIN

■ **PEW, John Howard** (1882–1971), businessman and philanthropist, was born in Bradford, Pennsylvania, the son of Joseph Newton Pew, a partner in the People's Natural Gas Company in Pittsburgh and founder of what became the Sun Oil Company in 1890. The product of a devout Presbyterian household, Pew was educated at the Presbyterian Grove City College, receiving the BA at 18. He pursued graduate studies at the Massachusetts Institute of Technology for a year, but left in 1901 to join his father's efforts to develop a refinery in Marcus Hook, Philadelphia. As an engineer and researcher in his first several years with Sun Oil (by then based in Philadelphia), Pew made a significant contribution to the company's success, particularly with his development of refining processes that enabled the salvaging of low grade Texas crude oil. In 1907 Pew married Helen Jennings Thompson; the couple adopted two daughters and a son.

Pew was made a vice-president of Sun Oil in 1910 and subsequently became a member of the company's board of directors. When his father died in 1912, he was selected as the company's new president. Under Pew's leadership the Sun Oil Company entered the shipbuilding business during the First World War and gained a secure niche in the oil industry in the 1920s as a producer of high octane gasoline for cars and aviation fuel. Sun Oil became a publicly traded corporation on Wall Street in November 1925. By the end of the 1940s, Sun Oil had accumulated assets in excess of $3 billion dollars and was ranked as the eleventh largest American oil producer. Pew resigned from his position as president of the company in 1947, but maintained an active role in its operations, returning for seven years as the chairman of its board of directors after the death of his brother Joseph N. Pew, Jr in 1963.

From the 1930s Pew became increasingly identified with conservative politics. An outspoken critic of the New Deal, Pew was a staunch anti-communist and supporter of the free enterprise system. Pew and his brother Joseph were prominent supporters of the conservative wing of the Republican Party led by Ohio Senator Robert A. Taft. They both gave millions of dollars to back Republican candidates, and Pew personally provided substantial support for Barry Goldwater's 1964 presidential campaign.

Beyond his political interests, however, Pew was a committed Presbyterian layman concerned with upholding theologically conservative views and institutions. Pew was a major voice for conservatism within his own Presbyterian Church of the United States of America, serving as the president of its General Assembly's Board of Trustees from 1940 until his death. In 1967 he helped to launch the *Presbyterian Layman* magazine to promote conservative theology and piety within the denomination. Pew was also a major benefactor of his alma mater Grove City College, joining its board of trustees upon his father's death in 1912, and serving as president of the Grove City Board from 1931 until his death forty years later.

Pew also maintained a vital interest in supporting conservative religious forces outside his own denomination. One of his major efforts was an attempt to counter the liberalism of the Federal Council of Churches and its successor, the National Council of Churches (NCC). Pew became a major conservative voice within its ranks through his financial power and served as the chairman of the NCC's Lay Committee from 1950 until its dissolution in 1955. Pew eventually became disenchanted with the NCC as it continued to drift to the left, and concentrated his efforts on more conservative institutions and projects. Frequently approached by the leaders of various fundamentalist and evangelical causes, Pew played an important role in the financing of the 'neo-evangelical' movement in the 1950s and 1960s. Key to his support for conservative Protestantism was the Pew Memorial Foundation, which Pew, along with his brother and two sisters, formed in 1948. Funded by a gift of 800,000 shares in Sun Oil, the Foundation, in addition to supporting medical, educational and local (Philadelphia) charities, channelled much of its money into conservative theological education and evangelism. Among the diverse conservative religious causes he supported were Carl *McIntire's International Council of Christian Churches, Fuller and Gordon-Conwell seminaries, the Billy *Graham Evangelistic Association, and the founding of the evangelical journal *Christianity Today*.

Pew died in Ardmore, Philadelphia, in 1971. However, his philanthropic work was embodied in the Pew Charitable Trusts. Grants from the Pew Trusts played a significant role in the expansion of institutions for evangelical theological education, as well as providing support for American evangelical scholars in a wide variety of academic disciplines throughout the later decades of the twentieth century.

Bibliography

G. M. Marsden, *Reforming Fundamentalism: Fuller Seminary and the New Evangelicalism* (Grand Rapids: Eerdmans, 1987); M. Sennholz, *Faith and Freedom: The Journal of a Great American, J. Howard Pew* (Grove City: Grove City College, 1975).

L. ESKRIDGE

■ **PHILIP, John** (1775–1851), missionary, was born on 4 April 1775 in Kirkcaldy, Scotland. His concern for the welfare of the black community in South Africa brought him into frequent conflict with settlers and the state. His stance was so resented that even in the 1950s the apartheid prime minister Hans Strijdom could be found warning radical Christians 'not to do a Philip'. Philip continues to arouse strong emotions, being seen by some as a hero in Christian opposition to racism and by others as distorting Christianity by linking it to imperialism and capitalism.

Philip's Scottish upbringing marked him indelibly. He left school at eleven to work as a weaver. Aged twenty-three he became a clerk at factories in Dundee, where he was greatly disturbed by working conditions. Philip experienced an evangelical conversion in his mid-teens and in 1799 began to train for the Congregationalist ministry at Hoxton College, London. In 1802 he moved to Newbury, Berkshire, to be assistant minister of a congregation there.

In 1804 Philip became minister of the First Congregational Church in Aberdeen, described as 'the Mother Church of the Congregational Union of Scotland' and conducted a highly influential ministry in the northeast of Scotland. In 1809 he married Jane Ross, who was the mother of his seven children and his companion and partner in much of his work.

In theology Philip distanced himself from the sixteenth- and seventeenth-century confessions and the denominational divides within Scotland, stressing personal faith in Christ and commitment to evangelism. Philip had a deep interest in classical culture and admired its civilization; this admiration influenced his understanding of how evangelism and social action were related. Philip saw an analogy between the benefits of Roman civilization and those of British rule. Civilization was not a precondition for faith, but it was inextricably bound up with it. Thus in 1833 Philip wrote, 'The civilisation of the people among whom we labour in Africa is not our highest object; but that never can be secured and rendered permanent among them without their civilisation. Civilisation is to the Christian religion what the body is to the soul; and the body must be prepared and cared for, if the spirit is to be retained upon earth.' He also admired Scotland's pre-Christian culture; this admiration contributed to his respect for African culture prior to the arrival of missions.

In other respects Philip was a child of the Scottish Enlightenment. He supported the economic ideas of Adam Smith, but rather than leading him to renounce concern for society, these made him hostile to harsh factory discipline which, he believed, constrained the individual. Andrew Ross states that 'For Philip education, evangelical Christianity and freedom from feudal restraints had created the prosperity of the Scotland of his youth as Smith said it should. The same combination of factors could do the same for all humankind.' In common with many evangelicals of his time, Philip was deeply committed to the abolition of slavery, which was achieved in South Africa only in 1833. At the time most missionaries were not from the upper classes, and Philip's artisan background complicated by class tension his already difficult relations with more aristocratic state officials.

In 1819 Philip moved to Cape Town to begin the work that would occupy the rest of his life. His dramatic change of direction resulted partly from his long interest in missionary work, and partly from urgent and persistent appeals from the London Missionary Society (LMS), whose work in South Africa was near collapse. Philip was appointed with John Campbell as a two-man commission to assess the situation and plan reforms. Philip stayed on as resident director of LMS missionaries, based at the Cape.

Initially Philip's relations with the colonial authorities were good. He shared their hostility to the concerns of missionaries like James Read over white rule in South Africa. Philip became minister of the Congregational community in Cape Town, quickly learnt Dutch and became a spokesman for the settlers. But a series of incidents, including a visit to the mission station of Bethelsdorp to see Read's work for himself, changed his views. He became a strong, sometimes vituperative, advocate of the rights of black people.

Philip's main work at this time was explicitly religious. By 1825 he had reorganized the mission stations and restored their sense of purpose. Between 1819 and 1834 the number of LMS stations increased from five to eighteen. A station such as Bethelsdorp embodied for Philip the complementary nature of Christianity and civilization. In such conditions, he believed, a virtuous, free, hardworking community could be developed. Equal rights were both a necessity for such communities to thrive and the just reward for their good character.

By the mid-1820s Philip had both restored order to the LMS missions and become heavily involved in campaigns to ameliorate the treatment of black people in the Cape Colony. Between 1826 and 1829 he lived in England, forming a close relationship with Fowell *Buxton, the new head of the Anti-Slavery Society. It was at this time that he wrote his *Researches in South Africa*. These were much attacked as biased but have now been largely substantiated. Philip's thesis was that the Khoi and other free black people lacked civil rights and were oppressed as being cheap labour for whites. Buxton promoted this view, and in 1829 Ordinance 50 was promulgated by the British Parliament. This represented a substantial bulwark for black rights in the Cape and was, in part, the result of Philip's lobbying.

Philip returned to South Africa in 1829, being increasingly seen as the 'Protestant Pope', overseeing not just the work of LMS, but also that of the Paris Evangelical Mission, the Rheineschen Missionsgeseellschaft and the American Board of Commissioners for Foreign Missions. However, the white community now hated him for Ordinance 50 and *Researches*. In 1830 he lost a libel case to one William Mackay and was saved from financial ruin only by evangelical supporters in Britain who paid his costs. A new vagrancy act was passed in South Africa in 1834 but Philip, using his contacts in England, was able to block its implementation.

He continued to rely on the power of London after 1834, even though his influence there was declining. Philip in the 1830s was increasingly concerned about the Xhosa people, living beyond the Cape frontier but liable to encroachment from the colonists. Amidst frequent frontier clashes, Philip worked with Buxton to persuade the central government to restrain the local governor, D'Urban. Philip encouraged the central state to annex further tracts of land, such as the Transkei, and advocated the separation of black and white people in the hope that it might protect the indigenous population. He urged black people within the colony to be loyal to the state. Between 1836 and 1838 Philip was again in England to lobby the government, albeit to limited effect.

From 1833 a band of settlers began what became known as 'the Great Trek' into the interior of Southern Africa, seeking to escape the restrictions of colonial rule. Philip strongly opposed such moves, fearing that the settlers would mistreat black people and destabilize groups such as the Griqua, whom he saw as an example of what Christianity could do for a African people. Between 1838 and 1841 Philip was absorbed with internal problems within LMS and his congregation in Cape Town, but from 1838 he campaigned for the annexation of Natal, hoping that by this means the trekkers could be controlled. He also encouraged the governor to support the Griqua against the settlers and acted as a intermediary between the Sotho chief, Mosheshwe, and the governor. Further upheavals within LMS led him to resign his ministry in 1841, although he took it up again in the following year.

In the 1840s Philip became a beleaguered figure. Personal bereavements, the waning of the humanitarian lobby in Britain, divisions within LMS and the ever-growing power of the settler lobby eroded his position. Some missionaries, notably the Methodist William *Shaw, were more pro-settler and attacked him for his stance. By the late 1840s even the central state, on whom Philip had long relied, was turning against black rights. Philip died on 27 August 1851 in Hankey, South Africa, amongst the 'Cape folk' whose cause he had championed for so long.

Bibliography
A. Ross, *John Philip (1775–1851): Missions, Race and Politics in South Africa* (Aberdeen: Aberdeen University Press, 1986).

D. J. GOODHEW

■ **PICKERING, Henry** (1858–1941), Brethren publisher and writer, was born in Kenton, near Newcastle-upon-Tyne, on 31 January 1858. His father, John, was a stone quarryman, and the young Pickering was religiously inclined, singing in the village church choir. In 1874 he had an evangelical conversion at a mission held in a barn by the Open Brethren missionary J. Cecil Hoyle. Pickering had ambitions to become a teacher, but under Hoyle's influence he joined a Brethren congregation that met in a house at Dinnington Colliery, Northumberland, which led him to withdraw from his training at a Church of England school. Instead, he established the Crown Press in his father's house in about 1880 and soon added religious colportage to the business. Among his early ventures was printing Pickering's Penny Packets of assorted gospel tracts, and on Saturdays he engaged in evangelism through a stall at Consett market, Durham. On 21 July 1887 he married Mary Jane Johnstone, the daughter of a Newcastle gardener. Their four children all became active evangelical Christians, notably Ruth (later Mrs Charles Stokes), who became a missionary, and their only son Cecil, who became his father's partner in business.

In 1886 Pickering moved to Glasgow to manage the Bible Book Depot, which had been established ten years earlier by the itinerant Brethren evangelist Donald Ross. From 1893, when Pickering was joined in partnership by the printer William Inglis, the business was known as Pickering & Inglis. In addition to a vast quantity of gospel tracts, the firm issued twelve monthly magazines, principally for Christian workers, for use in evangelism and for devotional and didactic purposes. Pickering edited five of these, including from 1914 (when he succeeded J. R. Caldwell) until his death, *The Witness*, the principal Brethren magazine, which had reached a monthly circulation of some 30,000 by the 1940s. From 1916, in the 'Witness Watchtower' column, he commented on contemporary events from a fundamentalist, dispensationalist perspective. Most of the books Pickering & Inglis published were by Brethren writers, but in the inter-war period its influence was increasingly felt throughout conservative evangelicalism, and greater numbers of non-Brethren authors were published, including preachers associated with the Keswick Convention.

In Glasgow Pickering joined the Brethren congregations in the Marble Hall and, from 1897, Elim Hall, and he became one of the principal preachers among the Scottish Open Brethren. For a time he was affiliated with the stricter faction associated with the magazine *Needed Truth*, but he did not follow their secessionist tendencies; he became known as the leading exponent of less restrictive, more open interdenominational and social practices and was regarded with some suspicion by the more conservative elements. For example, during the First World War he refused to pronounce that conscientious objection to fighting was the only acceptable course. He proclaimed in 1929 that 'the Witness has ever stood for loyalty to King and Country'. Although he was critical of the term, in the 1920s he enthusiastically promoted the concerns of fundamentalism, claiming the Brethren were 'True fundamentalists, although they prefer to abide by the titles given by God'. His Brethren fundamentalism was given clearest expression in *The Believer's Blue Book* (1930). Pickering wrote another dozen books, many of them compilations of illustrative anecdotes for use by preachers, such as *1000 Acts and Facts* (n.d.), or outlines of sermons and children's talks, such as *How to Make and Show 100 Object Lessons* (1922). In the latter he advocated making models to illustrate texts or topics for children, a technique that he did much to popularize. His interest in Brethren history was expressed in the collection *Chief Men Among the Brethren* (1918; [2]1931), which consisted of short biographical sketches of individuals who were significant in the development of the movement.

Pickering & Inglis was strengthened by its acquisition in 1919 of the London publishers,

Alfred Holness. In 1922, to oversee his firm's expanding influence throughout Britain, Pickering moved to north London, where he became a member of Grove Green Hall. A coiner of pithy phrases, he seasoned his talks and sermons with humour and frequently used alliteration and acrostics. He was fond of children, with whom he could readily establish a rapport, and was much in demand as a children's speaker. In 1940, after a serious illness and to escape bombing, Pickering moved to Largs, Ayrshire, where he died on 20 January 1941.

Bibliography

J. A. H. Dempster, 'Aspects of Brethren Publishing Enterprise in Late Nineteenth Century Scotland', *Publishing History* 20 (1986), pp. 61–101; N. T. R. Dickson, *Brethren in Scotland 1838–2000: A Social Study of an Evangelical Movement* (Carlisle: Paternoster Press, 2002).

N. DICKSON

■ **PIERSON, Arthur Tappan** (1837–1911), pastor, speaker and author, played a significant role in the promotion of worldwide mission at the end of the nineteenth century, so contributing to the origins of the modern ecumenical movement. He also promoted in America the holiness teaching associated with the English Keswick Convention.

Descended from seventeenth-century Puritan immigrants from Yorkshire, Pierson was born on 6 March 1837 in New York, where his father, an accountant by profession, was an elder in the Thirteenth Street Presbyterian Church. After initial schooling in New York, he spent a year at boarding school in Tarrytown-on-the-Hudson, New York state. During this time Pierson was converted when thirteen years old through a series of revival meetings held in the local Methodist church, where he then attended a probationers' class-meeting. In 1852 Pierson joined his father's Presbyterian church in New York, and the following year entered Hamilton College in Clinton, New York state. His ultimate aim was to prepare for Christian ministry, but on the basis of evident aptitudes rather than any specific sense of 'call'. Revivals that were taking place in the vicinity of the college under Charles G. *Finney had an impact on college life, and Pierson himself was instrumental in a number of conversions as a Bible class leader at the village church. By the time revival occurred in the city of New York in 1857, Pierson had returned there to attend Union Theological Seminary, a conservative Presbyterian seminary, and this experience of revival and rapid church growth shaped his future ideals and convictions with regard to evangelism.

In September 1860 Pierson was called to First Congregational Church, Binghampton, New York state, the first of his five pastorates in the United States. He became known as a versatile and forceful preacher with a particular interest in overseas missionary activity. At Fort Street Presbyterian Church, Detroit, in the 1870s he became increasingly irked by what he came to regard as the formality and exclusiveness of church life and worship, believing that these were a hindrance to effective evangelistic outreach to the masses. In 1878 he met the Brethren preacher and philanthropist George *Müller of Bristol, whose influence on Pierson over the next two decades would be considerable. Impressed by the Brethren's dispensational approach to the interpretation of prophecy, which he claimed unlocked '[t]wo thirds of the Book which had been sealed to me ... ', Pierson abandoned his postmillennial position in favour of a premillennial expectation of Christ's imminent return. His ecclesiological ideals, including his views on baptism, were also shifting away from those of paedobaptist Presbyterianism. He was now looking for 'an undenominational sort of church, with a font for immersion of those who believe in that form of baptism'. It was this broader outlook, evident as Pierson became increasingly known across America as a writer and conference speaker, that led to the surprising invitation issued to him, a Presbyterian, to fill C. H. *Spurgeon's pulpit at the Metropolitan Tabernacle in London, perhaps the leading Baptist church in the world. Pierson supplied the Metropolitan Tabernacle pulpit during Spurgeon's final illness and after his death, from October 1891 to September 1892, and again in 1893. It was not, however, until 1896 that he himself was baptized as a believer by J. A. Spurgeon in an unusual private ceremony at West Croydon Baptist Church in Surrey, an act which provoked public criticism and resulted in

his removal from the Presbyterian ministry. Pierson remained outside all ecclesiastical bodies for the remainder of his life, although his relations with Presbyterianism were subsequently restored. Deterred from joining the Baptists by the practices of a closed table and closed membership, he spent a good deal of time with Brethren in Bristol from 1897 while writing the biography of George Müller and subsequently that of Müller's son-in-law and successor, James Wright, who died in 1905.

It was for his advocacy of world evangelization and as a promoter of the holiness tradition associated with the Keswick Convention that Pierson became most widely known. In the Missionary Review, a periodical that he edited for twenty-five years, Pierson published in 1885, 'A Plan to Evangelise the World', which concluded with a call for the establishment of an international council in order to 'hasten the coming of the Lord ... by speedily preaching the Gospel ...'. This initiative for world mission had already been enthusiastically endorsed by the evangelist D. L. *Moody when Pierson addressed the 1885 Northfield Conference in a similar vein. In his book The Crisis of Missions, published in 1886, he urged: 'The logic of the Scripture argument for worldwide evangelism is itself overwhelming'. It was in an address at a student conference in Mt Hermon the same year that Pierson called for 'the evangelization of the world in this generation', a phrase which, although not original, became the watchword that summed up the zeal and urgency that characterized missionary activity in the late nineteenth century. 'The Evangelization of the World in this Generation' was first adopted officially as a motto in America by the Student Volunteer Movement (SVM) in 1888, and subsequently by the Student Volunteer Missionary Union of Great Britain at the Liverpool Conference of 1896. The SVM, whose beginnings can be traced to the 1886 Mt Hermon conference, represented an attempt to move beyond scattered individual commitment to create a mass movement of students for global mission. In the Missionary Review Pierson broke new ground by an undenominational approach, reporting on the work of a wide range of missionary societies, and the SVM was very influential in bringing churches together.

Many of the early pioneers of the ecumenical movement of the twentieth century were drawn as young men into the student missionary movement by the appeal that Pierson had instigated.

At the Northfield Conference in 1895 Pierson was powerfully affected by the teaching of Andrew *Murray and H. W. Webb-Peploe. Both were associated with the Keswick Convention in England, the focal point of holiness teaching, which promoted the attainment of a higher level of spiritual life through faith rather than by effort. 'I entered that day into the consciousness of the rest of faith ...' wrote Pierson. At the Keswick Convention of 1897 Pierson made a public confession of the sins of impatience, pride and self-will, giving testimony to 'the new victories that had enriched his life and the new power that had marked his service'. Pierson became a regular Keswick speaker, and his address in 1905 was particularly noted, with a Church of England rector present recording colourfully: '... the Holy Spirit fell. The speaker was kept from completing his address by the sobs and cries of Christians who confessed their failures and sins.' Alongside established Keswick leaders, such as Charles Inwood and F. B. *Meyer, Pierson was instrumental in extending the influence of Keswick teaching to Northfield, Boston, and a number of other places in the United States, where Keswick-style conventions were inaugurated.

While Pierson could describe himself in later years as 'a renegade Presbyterio-Baptist-Brethren compound', his pan-denominational outlook with its particular focus on the goal of global evangelization caught the mood among evangelicals in the late nineteenth century and afforded him a role akin to that of a world statesman in the realm of transatlantic evangelicalism.

Bibliography

J. Kennedy Maclean, *Dr. Pierson and His Message* (London: Marshall, n.d.); D. Lotz, 'The Watchword for World Evangelization: "The Evangelization of the World in this Generation"', *Baptist Quarterly* 34.8 (October 1992), pp. 398–408; D. L. Pierson, *Arthur T. Pierson: A Biography By His Son* (London: James Nisbet, 1912).

R. N. SHUFF

■ **PINK, Arthur Walkington** (1886–1952), British Baptist minister and author, was active in the pastorate and also in an itinerant ministry in the United States and Australia from 1910 to 1934, when he withdrew from public ministry to return to Britain. Eventually he settled in the Outer Hebrides and devoted himself entirely to a writing ministry for the remainder of his life; the majority of his works were published only after his death.

Arthur W. Pink was born in Nottingham on 1 April 1886. His parents were Nonconformist Christians, who sought to raise him as such. Young Arthur's education was extensive, and he applied himself with discipline. However, he was not yet a believer.

By the age of twenty-two Pink was a successful businessman, but still not a Christian. He was a rising leader in the Theosophy Society and was being considered for leadership in the movement. He was scheduled to speak twice at a conference in his home town. When he came home after speaking the first time, his father quoted to him Proverbs 14:12, 'There is a way which seemeth right unto a man, but the end thereof are the ways of death.' This verse sent him into his room, and he emerged a converted man, who then went and preached the gospel to the Theosophy Society.

Following his conversion, he plunged himself into the study of Scripture. He rejected formal training, being convinced that the theological colleges were teaching errors. He did, finally, in 1910 travel to the United States to study at Moody Bible Institute in Chicago, but he left before completing his first summer semester. A strong individualistic spirit, along with a disciplined study habit, had convinced him that he could study on his own. In the years that followed he was an avid reader of the Puritans and other expositional writers. These authors became the foundation of his future writings.

From Chicago, Pink moved to Silverton, Colorado, to pastor a church. He went next to Garden Grove, California, and then to Kentucky, where he pastored two (probably Baptist) churches, one in Burkesville, and the other in Albany. While in Kentucky, Pink, at the age of thirty-one, married twenty-three year old Vera E. Russell on 16 November 1916.

From Kentucky the Pinks moved to

Spartanburg, South Carolina, in July of 1917, where he pastored the Northside Baptist Church. (No record of his own baptism exists, but he must have been baptized by immersion before this date.) Here he wrote his most influential book, *The Sovereignty of God*. This strong Calvinistic work caused problems in his church and with friends, publishers and readers. The first edition sold slowly. In the following years, Pink longed to leave Spartanburg, but no doors would open. He began to think that God might desire him devote himself entirely to his writing ministry. The pressure to leave, and having nowhere to go, led to deep depression, even a nervous breakdown. He resigned from the church in January 1920 with little desire ever to pastor again.

Pink moved to Swengel, Pennsylvania, to be close to his publisher. But he was soon in California, working in various cities. In the autumn of 1920 Brother Thompson, an evangelist who had seen many conversions in a tent mission in Oakland, enlisted Pink to teach the new converts. There followed one of the best periods of Pink's ministry, and he continued speaking to crowds of hundreds until April 1921, but the burden to write continued to trouble him.

Later in 1921 Pink began what would eventually become his entire ministry, a periodical entitled *Studies in the Scriptures*. The Pinks, through all their travels, together maintained this monthly journal of biblical exposition, which had a mailing list of around a thousand.

On 3 March 1925 the Pinks left for Australia where, after a period of successful ministry, he was censured by the Baptist Union for denying human free will. Turning to the Particular (Calvinistic) Baptists, he pastored a Particular church, until it censored him for believing in human free will. The reason for this second censure was his belief in the free offer of the gospel and in human responsibility to believe the gospel. After forming a new, independent church, he resigned from it on 25 March 1928, and left for England on 20 July. This pastorate was his last. Pink was still a staunch Calvinist, but he had rejected a premillennial dispensational view of Scripture in favour of covenant theology, including an amillennial view of eschatology.

The Pinks' return to England afforded no opportunities to preach. Therefore on 22 May 1929 they returned to America, hoping that old friends would welcome them. But when Pink was rejected in Kentucky and California, and in the light of what he perceived to be the serious compromises in the churches, an attitude of isolationism began to invade his mind. On 5 September 1934 the Pinks left for England, hoping that the response would be different there. But again the search for acceptance and ministry proved futile, both in England and in Scotland.

On 24 September 1940 the Pinks moved for the last time, from the Brighton-Hove area on the south coast of England to Stornoway in the Outer Hebrides. Their home had been strafed by a German aircraft passing over their town to bomb London.

From his new residence, Pink maintained his independent status, and continued to produce his monthly periodical, which he had never ceased to publish through all his travels and even during the war. He continued to issue warnings about what he regarded as false churches, and encouraged withdrawal if necessary. The Pinks did not attend any church, but Pink spent Sundays ministering by letters to his readers. For the next twelve years he lived in isolation, leaving his home only for a daily walk. When people came to meet him (and a visit demanded a long trip), he usually refused to receive them.

Pink died on 15 July 1952 at the age of sixty-seven. He was buried in an unmarked grave in a cemetery on the outskirts of Stornoway. Vera Pink kept the periodical in print until December 1953, using material Pink had prepared. Vera Pink died on 17 July 1962 at the age of sixty-nine.

It cannot be denied, even in the light of his unique characteristics, that Pink was committed to knowing and doing God's will. He believed himself called in his final years to use his pen, not his tongue, to minister to a few people. In later years his voluminous writings, which during his lifetime were known only to a few, were rediscovered; hundreds of thousands of books of his writings have been printed since his death. Through these Pink became a strong bridge between the Puritans of the past and the believers of the last half of the twentieth century. He was one of several writers whose work encouraged a revival of historic Calvinism in the last half of the twentieth century.

Bibliography
R. P. Belcher, *Arthur W. Pink – Born to Write* (Columbia: Richbarry Press, 1980); I. Murray, *The Life of Arthur W. Pink* (Edinburgh: Banner of Truth Trust, 1981).

R. P. BELCHER

■ **POPE, William Burt** (1822–1903), Wesleyan Methodist minister and theologian, was born in Horton, Nova Scotia, on 19 February 1822, the third of the six sons of John and Catherine Pope. All six entered the ministry; one, Thomas, later became an Oratorian. John Pope was a Cornishman, sent to Nova Scotia by the Wesleyan Methodist Missionary Society in 1820. He was transferred to St Vincent three years later, but ill health compelled him to return to England in 1827, and the family settled near Plymouth.

William Pope was educated in the village school at Hooe and then at Saltash. In 1837 he was sent to Bedeque, Prince Edward Island, to join his uncle Joseph's shipbuilding business. He used the sea voyage to improve his knowledge of German and astronomy. After a year, Pope returned to Plymouth, finding his elder brothers Thomas and George preparing to enter the Wesleyan ministry. Pope was already reading theology, particularly the works of William Paley and Richard *Watson, in addition to studying Latin, Greek, French and German. Although intended for a medical career, in 1840 he was accepted as a candidate for the ministry by the Cornwall Wesleyan Methodist Synod, approved by a connexional examination committee and enrolled in the Theological Institution at Hoxton under Dr John Hannah. Pope attended and appreciated Hannah's theology lectures, but he was largely left to study by himself, adding Hebrew and Arabic to his stock of languages. An early biographer, drawing on his Hoxton journal, noted that 'already can be traced the disposition to take too serious a view of his religious condition, which deepened towards the close of his life into unrelieved gloom'.

Pope left Hoxton in 1842 for a succession of circuit appointments, and in 1845 he married Ann Eliza Lethbridge, of Modbury, near Plymouth. Two of their nine children died in early life, leaving four daughters and three sons. Pope was not an outstanding success as a circuit minister. Naturally shy and introspective, his Wesleyan obituarist described him in 1903 as 'the quiet man who walked with God'. He was a conscientious, if absent-minded, pastor, able to pass acquaintances in the street without recognizing them. F. L. Wiseman recalled Pope's conviction that 'If I have a call, it is to preach the Gospel to the unsophisticated,' but a Kentish Methodist who knew him during his stay in the county in the late 1840s exclaimed in amazement when he became president of Conference (1877) that there was not a local preacher on the circuit plan who could not preach better. After appointments in Kingsbridge, Liskeard, Jersey, Sandwich, Dover and Halifax, Pope moved to larger circuits: London (City Road), Hull, Manchester (Oxford Road), Leeds (Brunswick) and Southport. During his time in Manchester he became secretary of the local committee responsible for the management of the Didsbury branch of the Wesleyan Theological Institution. When John Hannah, who had moved to Didsbury from Hoxton in 1842, announced his impending retirement, Pope was designated his successor, assisting with the teaching from 1866 and taking on the full responsibilities of theological tutor a year later.

Didsbury was 'an almost ideal appointment' for Pope, affording plenty of opportunity for study and writing. He observed the Wesleyan discipline of early rising, beginning work regularly at 4am. He maintained an astonishing range of intellectual interests, from mathematics and astronomy to languages and literature. The science lecturer at Didsbury recalled that Pope 'was *au fait* with everything'. He established an observatory at the college and bequeathed his telescope to Didsbury. It was reported that he was found during sessions of the Conference of which he was president sitting in a vestry reading a German treatise on mathematics. At a time when German theology was not widely read in England, Pope translated a number of works into English, notably Stier's *Words of the Lord Jesus* and commentaries on 1 John by Ebrard and Haupt. He was a co-founder of the *London Quarterly Review* in 1853, a regular contributor from 1858, and editor from 1860 until 1883, co-editing with J. H. Rigg from 1883 to 1886. His articles in the *LQR* included a stinging critique of *Essays and Reviews* ('an elaborate specimen of the latest theology of the Neologian section of the English Church') and surveys of German biblical and theological works, praising conservative scholars like Hengstenberg and Delitzsch and attacking the radicals as 'destructive critics' and 'rationalists'.

Pope continued to acknowledge an intellectual debt to John Hannah and published Hannah's *Introductory Lectures on the Study of Christian Theology*, with a memoir of the author, in 1872. Pope's own theological lectures formed the basis for his massive *Compendium of Christian Theology*, published in one volume in 1875 and expanded to three in 1879–1880. In the judgment of Pope's first posthumous biographer, the *Compendium* offered 'the best formulation of Methodist Arminianism into a coherent and well-proportioned system of thought'; a subsequent assessment described it as 'a monument of nineteenth-century conservative theology of the best type'. Based on detailed scriptural exegesis and a careful and catholic survey of historical theology, key themes were the rule of faith, the doctrine of God, the mediatorial work of Christ and the administration of redemption, including a discussion of the distinctive Wesleyan emphasis on entire sanctification. *The Person of Christ* was the subject of a separate publication, in which Pope expanded the text of his 1871 Fernley Lecture.

The general conservatism of Pope's theology was leavened by a deeply devotional spirit and a mystical bent. He recorded a great triumph in the revision of the Wesleyan catechism in 1881, when he persuaded the committee, in spite of the opposition of Dr George Osborn, to alter the first question from 'What is God? An infinite and eternal Spirit' to 'Who is God? Our Father', a development later taken further by J. S. Lidgett. On occasion, his mystical language could descend into obscurity; a course of midweek sermons on Philippians at Didsbury, open to the general public, delighted the students but had a 'rather disastrous' effect on the rest of the congregation. On reading a piece of his own work, Pope said: 'I

don't quite know what that means; but the more I think about it, the nearer I come to knowing what I must have meant at the time I wrote it.'

In wider Methodist circles Pope's watchword was 'the maximum of adaptation with the minimum of change'. He opposed the admission of lay representatives to the Wesleyan Conference in the 1870s, but presided over the Conference that gave formal sanction to the scheme of lay representation. From his presidential year (1877–1878) until 1885 he was chairman of the Manchester District. In 1877 he was awarded a DD by the University of Edinburgh to add to the DD granted by the Wesleyan University in the United States in 1865.

Pope's introspective nature left him vulnerable to periods of intense loneliness and spiritual depression. This weakness, combined with ill health, led to his retirement from Didsbury in 1886. He lived for a further seventeen years in seclusion in London, where he died on 5 July 1903.

Bibliography

W. B. Brash and C. J. Wright (eds.), *Didsbury College Centenary 1842–1942* (London: Epworth Press, 1942); R. W. Moss, *The Rev. W. B. Pope, D.D. Theologian and Saint* (London: Robert Culley, 1909).

M. WELLINGS

■ **PYE-SMITH, John** (1774–1851), Congregational educator and theologian, was in the view of one modern historian amongst the best known Nonconformist theologians of the first half of the nineteenth century. Another noted that not since Philip *Doddridge had any one man had such a pervasive influence on the world of Dissent. Born in Sheffield on 2 March 1774 to John Smith, bookseller, and his wife Martha, he received no formal education and was apprenticed to his father. On 21 November 1792 he was admitted to membership of the Congregational Church on profession of faith. In 1796 he served as the temporary editor of the radical Sheffield journal *The Iris* during the hymn-writer James Montgomery's brief imprisonment for libel.

Later that year Pye-Smith entered Rotherham Academy to train for the Congregational ministry under Edward *Williams, the noted exponent of 'modern' or 'new system' Calvinism. After a distinguished student career, he stayed on as classical tutor before being called to Homerton Academy in 1801. He remained at Homerton for the rest of his career, becoming theological tutor (i.e. principal) in 1806, and establishing himself as one of the outstanding theological teachers of the nineteenth century. Indeed 'Homerton' and 'Pye-Smith' became synonymous. One of his pupils, the historian Robert Halley (1796–1876), later principal of New College, London, thought him the 'ablest and best' of English Congregationalism's theological tutors. Another described him as a 'professor of all things in general ... almost a walking encyclopaedia'. Even in the age of the polymath, Pye-Smith's range of interests was notable. Equally at home in Dutch, Italian, German and French, as well as the ancient languages, his writing and thinking ranged over chemistry, geology, astronomy, philosophy, biblical studies and theology.

Pye-Smith is remembered particularly for his involvement in three central theological debates in the early nineteenth century: the defence of trinitarian orthodoxy in the face of Unitarianism, the relationship between the geological sciences and theology and the inspiration of Scripture. During his long career his theological method remained constant. He was a man of the Enlightenment. In his theology belief depended on evidence, and therefore (unusually for an evangelical) knowledge was of more significance in his apologetic method than experience. That theological foundation, added to his immense learning, made him a formidable defender of trinitarian orthodoxy against rationalism and deism. Yale awarded him an honorary DD for his *Letters to Thomas Belsham* (1807), the noted Unitarian theologian, and his *Scripture Testimony to the Messiah* (1818–1821) was a solid and powerful defence of the Trinity.

Pye-Smith was at the forefront of those who sought to integrate the physical sciences and theology. His most notable achievement was his 1839 Congregational lecture, 'The relation between the Holy Scriptures and some parts of geological science'. This was a measured response to Lyell's *Principles of Geology* (1830). Lyell showed that geology proved the earth to be much older than previously thought, and that uniformitarian-

ism was a more tenable hypothesis about the nature of creation than catastrophism. Pye-Smith attempted to bring together the findings of the new science of geology and the exegesis of Genesis. Uniformitarianism, he argued, was a more accurate reflection of biblical teaching than catastrophism. His lecture was courageous, for in it he showed himself prepared to abandon popular theories of creation and the flood, and to adopt a more subtle reading of Scripture than that of mere 'common sense', in the pursuit of truth. The works of creation and the Word of God in Scripture '... are streams from the same source, and, though they flow in different directions, they necessarily partake of the same qualities of truth, wisdom and goodness.' Therefore there must be harmony between them. It was for this work that the Royal Society elected him a fellow.

The third debate with which Pye-Smith was involved concerned the inspiration of Scripture. Like most early nineteenth-century evangelicals, he followed Philip Doddridge's view and distinguished between different modes of inspiration. According to this view, some passages of Scripture reveal more of the mind of God than others. In 1816 that position was seriously challenged from Geneva by the Scottish theologian Robert *Haldane in *The Evidence and Authority of Divine Revelation*. The whole of Scripture, Haldane argued, in all its mystery, should be received as divine teaching. Haldane's thesis would probably not have attracted much attention but for the Apocrypha controversy of the early 1820s. Haldane protested that the British and Foreign Bible Society's expedient policy of publishing the Apocrypha in Bibles distributed in Europe was a deliberate mingling of inspired and uninspired material and should be stopped. Pye-Smith entered the debate in 1826, defending the French theologian Dr Haffner's preface that was used by the Society in those Bibles. Pye-Smith lent support to Haffner's view of inspiration, and added a statement of his own (which was very similar to Haffner's preface). At Haldane's instigation Alexander Carson, an Ulster Baptist, inveighed against Pye-Smith in a pamphlet war in which Pye-Smith clearly had the upper hand. The debate raged on within evangelical circles. Pye-Smith retained his old-fashioned inductive approach, examining each book of

Scripture carefully before deciding whether it was inspired or not; he had serious doubts about the authority of the Song of Songs and the book of Esther. The Romantic deductive approach of Haldane, and later Louis Gaussen (*Theopnustia*, 1841), was completely alien to one as thoroughly schooled in Enlightenment method as Pye-Smith.

Pye-Smith was not simply a theological teacher; he was also a minister. His work at Homerton was complemented by a pastorate at the nearby Gravel Pits Lane Congregational Chapel, which he served faithfully for forty-seven years. He was a Dissenter to his core, espousing not just the predictable causes (the Anti-State Church Society, the Anti-Corn Law League etc), but also the less fashionable. He was a determined advocate of temperance as early as 1831, and was one of the early vice-presidents of the Peace Society long before pacifism became respectable. His independence of mind also showed itself liturgically. He eschewed the wearing of clerical dress, yet championed and introduced weekly communion at Homerton in the face of hostile opposition.

Undergirding all Pye-Smith's work, however, was a simple evangelical piety. 'He prayed', wrote one of his students, 'not as one *thinking* of God, but as one *seeing* him.' He died in Guildford on 5 February 1851, having lived just long enough to see his beloved Homerton unite with Hoxton Academy and Hackney Academy to form New College, London.

Bibliography

J. Medway, *Memoirs of the Life and Writings of John Pye-Smith, D.D., LL.D* (London: Jackson & Walford, 1853); G. F. Nuttall, *New College, London and its Library* (London: Dr Williams' Trust, 1977).

D. G. CORNICK

■ **RADER, Paul** (1879–1938), American evangelist and religious broadcasting pioneer, was born in Denver, Colorado, the son of a Methodist minister. A gifted American-football player and boxer, his athletic exploits and days spent as a cowboy coloured his later sermons and added to his popularity. Rader never earned an academic degree, but between 1898 and 1903 he was a student and football player at various colleges including the University of Colorado and Hamline University in St Paul, Minnesota. After his father accepted a pastorate in Tacoma, Washington, Rader moved west, spending the 1903–1904 academic year as an instructor at the University of Puget Sound. Rader married a member of his father's Tacoma congregation, Mary Caughran; the couple had three daughters. Intrigued by liberal theology and the Social Gospel, Rader was ordained as a Congregational minister in 1904 and pastored churches in Massachusetts and Oregon. Increasingly, however, he doubted the truthfulness of Christianity and in 1909 left the ministry, embarking on a series of business ventures.

While in New York City on business in 1912, Rader came into contact with the Christian and Missionary Alliance (C&MA). Moved by the dispensational, holiness-influenced theology of Alliance founder A. B. *Simpson, Rader underwent a dramatic reconversion experience. He subsequently became one of Simpson's protégés and by 1914 was a travelling Alliance evangelist. While conducting a revival in Chicago in December of that year, Rader was invited to lead a series of meetings at the non-denominational Moody Church. The revival was so successful that he became the church's new pastor. With Rader at the helm, Moody Church outgrew its premises, moving into a 5,000-seat wooden tabernacle at the corner of LaSalle and North Avenues to promote an aggressive, year-round programme of evangelism.

With his success at Moody Church, Rader became increasingly important on the national revival circuit. This, in turn, increased his visibility within the C&MA, leading to his election as a vice-president in 1919, and election as president upon Simpson's death later that year. Rather than moving to the Alliance headquarters in Nyack, New York, however, Rader decided to retain the Moody Church pastorate and to use Chicago as his base of operations. This decision quickly caused problems within both the church and the Alliance. A six-month tour of Alliance missions served as the final blow to his leadership at the church, and he resigned in 1921.

Following his resignation, Rader embarked on a series of fundraising trips for C&MA

missions, but in June 1922 he was invited back to Chicago for an evangelistic campaign. The meetings on the city's north side proved so successful that Rader again decided to make Chicago his base of operations. His new 4,000-seat Chicago Gospel Tabernacle quickly became a regional fundamentalist centre with nightly services, a rapidly changing rota of visiting speakers and musical groups and a diverse set of programmes targeting men, women, teenagers and children. Rader's decision, however, caused new conflicts with the C&MA. His divided loyalties and insistence that the Alliance follow his lead in a new 'Tabernacle strategy' further strained his relations with a number of leaders in the movement, and in 1924 Rader was forced to resign as president.

Free from his denominational duties, Rader devoted himself to the innovative ethos of the Chicago 'Tab'. One of his most important strategies was his enthusiastic embrace of radio at a time when many fundamentalists had grave doubts about the propriety of the new medium. Rader's first broadcast over Chicago's municipally owned station, WBU, on 17 June 1922 was a publicity gimmick for his meetings. The response of listeners, however, was so great that Rader became convinced that radio was a dramatic, God-given evangelistic tool. Between 1925 and 1930 Rader's Tabernacle became the largest religious presence on Chicago radio through all-day Sunday broadcasts over WHT and, later WBBM/WJBT ('Where Jesus Blesses Thousands'). Rader's efforts were the first major attempt to support an ongoing religious broadcast through the purchase of air-time funded mostly by listeners' contributions. In 1930 Rader's daily 'Breakfast Brigade' became the first independent fundamentalist programme to be broadcast over a national network when it went on air over the Columbia Broadcasting System.

The coming of the Depression, combined with Rader's broadcasting efforts and continual expansion of programmes, put a heavy financial strain on the Tabernacle. Rader's personal non-profit corporation eventually declared itself bankrupt, and in the spring of 1933 he left a greatly weakened Chicago Gospel Tabernacle. Having lost his high-profile venue, Rader endured a series of short-lived evangelistic enterprises over the next few years, including a period at the Fort Wayne Gospel Tabernacle. Plagued by debt and ill health, he moved his family to Hollywood, California in 1936. Rader died there of prostate cancer two years later.

The innovative spirit that characterized Paul Rader's years in Chicago had an enduring influence on the shape of the emerging evangelical movement in the 1940s and beyond. His direct influence was embodied in a number of converts and youthful protégés including, Charles E. *Fuller, leading radio evangelist and founder of Fuller Theological Seminary; Clarence W. Jones, founder of shortwave missionary station HCJB in Ecuador; Torrey Johnson, first president of Youth for Christ; Lance Latham, who began the AWANA children's programmes, and many others. Most influential, however, was Rader's example in harnessing the influence of popular culture and the power of mass media in the service of evangelism. His successful broadcasting was central to the development of evangelical radio work and laid the foundation for the eventual dominance of evangelical broadcasters within the 'Electronic Church'.

Bibliography

L. K. Eskridge, 'Only Believe: Paul Rader and the Chicago Gospel Tabernacle, 1922–1933' (MA thesis, University of Maryland, 1985); R. L. Niklaus, J. S. Sawin and S. J. Stoesz, *All For Jesus: God at Work in the Christian and Missionary Alliance Over One Hundred Years* (Camp Mill: Christian Publications, 1986); W. L. Tucker, *The Redemption of Paul Rader* (New York: The Book Stall, 1918).

L. ESKRIDGE

■ **RAIKES, Robert** (1736–1811), pioneer of the Sunday school movement, was born in September 1736 and baptized at St Mary de Crypt, Gloucester, on the twenty-fourth day of that month. His father, also called Robert, had founded the *Gloucester Journal* in 1722. His paternal grandfather, Richard, was vicar of Hessle near Hull, and his mother Mary's father was Richard Drew, vicar of Nailsworth in Gloucestershire. Raikes was attached to the Church of England throughout his life, serving as overseer of the poor for the parish of St Mary de Crypt and a member of its Vestry

Meeting. He was a deeply religious man of benevolent disposition rather than evangelical fervour.

Raikes' early education was in the same school at which George *Whitefield had been taught, St Mary de Crypt. At the age of fourteen he began to attend the College (Cathedral) School. He was apprenticed to his father's printing business from 1755 until his father's death in 1757. On 12 July he took over the running of the *Gloucester Journal*, which he managed until his retirement as proprietor and editor in 1802.

Raikes' brothers, William, Thomas and Charles, all went into business in London. Thomas became a director of the Bank of England and was a friend of William Pitt and William *Wilberforce. Robert Raikes married Anne, the only daughter of the squire Thomas Trigge, in December 1767 at St James's Church, Piccadilly, London. They had ten children, eight of whom survived to adulthood. The two youngest, Robert Napier and William Henley Raikes, entered the church and the army respectively. Most of their sisters were married to men serving in the armed forces.

Raikes remained in Gloucester all his life, reaching the apex of the business community, acquiring a substantial fortune but dispensing much to local charities. He served as vice-president of the Severn Humane Society and a joint trustee of the Gloucester Provident Society, displaying a benevolent spirit of humanitarian concern for the poor of the city and county of Gloucester.

Robert Raikes followed the example of his father in publicizing good causes and upholding the forces of law and order. He attempted to soften the harshness of penal policy whilst condemning unrepented acts of savagery against person and property. He visited Gloucester prison and published accounts of the appalling conditions he found. These came to the attention of John *Howard, the prison reformer, who commended Raikes' actions for the physical relief of inmates in his *State of the Prisons* (1776). Raikes was committed to the cause of humanitarian reform. He not only visited prisoners, but also taught them. He corresponded with men condemned to death or to deportation and raised money to pay the debts of men burdened with insolvency. He was also an advocate of the anti-slave trade movement. His teaching in prisons reflected his general interest in popular education as a means of enforcing the social mores of practical Christianity, which he had learned from his reading of *The Whole Duty of Man*, of which he published a new edition in 1780. Raikes saw the church as crucial to social stability.

It was as the 'founder of Sunday schools' that Raikes was best known. It is arguable whether this title is entirely justified, though in the popular imagination, fired by his enthusiastic biographers, it was his name that became most associated with the tremendous growth of Sunday schools in the period from 1780 to 1810. His was not an original contribution, other than as the main publicist of a movement that grew very rapidly in his lifetime. Laqueur's judgment is that Raikes was 'a symbol for one strand of [the Sunday Schools'] history' (*Religion and Respectability*, p. 21). He was a typical middle-class provincial philanthropist for whom popular education was a means of reducing threats to law and order in an age of anxiety as well as an evangelistic opportunity to introduce children to the Bible and the catechism for the betterment of the moral and spiritual values of the next generation.

Christians had made earlier contributions to elementary and popular education, such as those of the (Anglican) Ferrar sisters of Little Gidding and (the Dissenter) Joseph Alleine of Bristol in the seventeenth century. The work of the SPCK charity schools was particularly important in the early eighteenth century, and individuals affected by Methodism and the Evangelical Revival from the 1730s took up the opportunities afforded by Sunday schools. John Valton, the Methodist itinerant preacher, David Simpson, vicar of Christ Church Macclesfield, and Hannah Ball of High Wycombe, whose work was commended by John *Wesley, were among many who started such schools.

So Raikes was not the first to found a Sunday school when in 1780 he employed four women to teach the children of the poor of Gloucester on Sundays. The part played in this venture by Thomas Stock, headmaster of the Cathedral School, who as a curate of a Berkshire parish had started a Sunday school in Ashbury in 1777, has been disputed, as has the suggestion that Raikes knew of such work through Sophia Cooke (from the city) and William King (from the Calvinistic Methodist Tabernacle at Dursley). Stock certainly contributed to the cost of the Gloucester schools and superintended the work of the teachers, a role understated in subsequent accounts. The accidental nature of the establishment reflected a pattern of localized responses to the need to provide useful pursuits for young people on Sundays.

That this localized response grew into a huge movement is mainly due to social circumstances and Raikes' publishing contacts, particularly Colonel Townley of Rochdale, to whom he wrote in 1783 commending his Sunday schools. The letter subsequently found its way into many of the provincial newspapers of the northern industrial towns, and accounts of the enterprise appeared in the national *Gentleman's Magazine* and *Arminian Magazine*.

Subsequently, Raikes' enthusiastic advocacy of Sunday schools was taken up by the Anglican establishment, especially after the support of Bishops Beilby Porteous of Chester and Henry Ryder of Gloucester became public knowledge. The publicizing of the perceived effectiveness of the schools in changing the behaviour of the poor through the influence of their children was undoubtedly his main contribution to the movement. The Sunday School Society, established in 1785, resolved in 1787 to make Raikes an honorary member as 'the original founder, as well as a liberal promoter of Sunday Schools', a recognition that received royal approval when he was received at Windsor by the King and Queen. Raikes also publicized the efforts of Sarah Trimmer, author of the *Oeconomy of Charity* (1787), to create Schools of Industry as another tier of popular education for the poor.

Raikes welcomed the further extension of popular education through the British and National Day Schools, which augmented the work of evening and Sunday schools. He died on 5 April 1811, aged seventy-four, and was buried in the family vault at his local parish church of St Mary de Crypt, Gloucester.

Bibliography

F. Booth, *Robert Raikes of Gloucester* (Redhill: NCEC, 1980); J. H. Harris (ed.), *Robert Raikes: The Man and His Work* (London: Simpkin Marshall, 1899); T. W. Lacqueur,

Religion and Respectability: Sunday Schools and Working Class Culture 1780–1850 (New Haven: Yale University Press, 1975).

T. S. A. MACQUIBAN

■ **RAMABAI, Pandita** (1858–1922), Indian educator and reformer, was born the youngest child of a Brahmin couple, Anant Shastri Dongre and his second wife, Lakshmibai. Her scholarly father taught his wife to read Sanskrit and instructed her in Hindu sacred literature. She, in turn, taught her daughter. Ramabai spent her early childhood in the forest of Gangamul in Karnataka, where her father ran a school and worked rice fields. Frequent pilgrimages absorbed her older childhood years. The family walked through much of India, stopping at holy places and making an uncertain living by reciting sacred texts. They contributed any money they received (except what they needed in order to survive) to Brahmin holy men.

Ramabai's father defied tradition by resisting social pressure to contract a marriage in her childhood. Her parents treated her as her brother's equal and continued her education. Deeply religious, she knew considerable hardship and learned to rely on her conscience and her own inner self. Her parents died in 1874, victims of a severe famine in the Madras presidency. Her married sister died of cholera in 1875. Ramabai and her brother Srinivas Shastri continued walking through India, though they routinely experienced extreme poverty and hunger.

In 1878 they came to Calcutta, where university scholars examined Ramabai publicly and bestowed on her the titles Pandita and Sarasvati. Leaders in the Brahmo Samaj (a reform society with ties to prominent American Unitarians) welcomed her support for the cause of reform, and Ramabai began lecturing on the emancipation of women. She grounded her reasoning in Hindu sacred writings and won acclaim as an effective speaker and an advocate for women's rights.

Ramabai's brother died of cholera in 1880, and she broke caste to marry his Bengalese friend, Bipin Behari Das Medhavi. For two happy years the couple lived in Kochar, Assam. Then in 1882 cholera took Medhavi, and Ramabai was left a widow with an infant daughter, Manoramabai. She journeyed south and made her home in Pune, near her birthplace. There she continued her advocacy of reform and moved easily in the large Brahmin community. Disagreements soon arose, however, for even Brahmins who supported reforms envisaged that they would take place within a patriarchal framework focused on home and marriage. Ramabai, who knew the stigma of widowhood, took up the cause of high-caste widows and argued passionately for a woman's right to enter a profession. On 1 June 1882 she established the Arya Mahila Samaj, a women's association dedicated to mobilizing women in support of social reform. In September 1882 she addressed the acclaimed British Hunter Commission on Education, making a case for general education for women and training for female physicians. She then decided to study English in preparation for study in England, which seemed the obvious next step to an influential career in India.

Ramabai arrived in England in 1883. She stayed first with the Wantage Sisters in their Anglo-Catholic convent in Wantage. There she was converted to Christianity and was baptized. In 1884 she began studying and teaching at Cheltenham Ladies' College, where the influential female educator Dorothea Beale became her mentor. Forced by impaired hearing to relinquish her dreams of a medical career, Ramabai decided to learn all she could about female education. To this end, she accepted an invitation to the United States in 1886. In Philadelphia, Rachel Bodley, chemist and president of the Women's Medical College, became her ardent promoter. For the next two years, Ramabai travelled the United States and investigated its educational system. Churches and reform-minded Protestants of every kind rallied to her and embraced her dream of creating a non-sectarian home and school for high-caste Hindu widows. She raised support by publishing *The High Caste Hindu Woman* (1885), a book describing the social oppression she intended to address. In 1898 the Ramabai Association was founded, with Edward Everett Hale, Phillips Brooks and Frances *Willard among its founding officers. This Association promised Ramabai ten years of funding and enabled her to implement her plan. The Women's Christian Temperance Union pledged support both by giving Ramabai a leadership position in the Union's new international network and by creating Ramabai Circles in local WCTU chapters.

Ramabai began modestly in Bombay. Sensitive to potential difficulties, she appointed leading Hindu reformers to her board of directors and pledged to respect caste rules. Before long her Christian example led some of the girls to explore Christianity. This interest soon disrupted her school. Public outrage and the withdrawal of many students threatened its future, but the storm eventually subsided, and a reorganized local board of directors took charge. After several years, Ramabai moved the centre of her work to the Pune area, and that work grew dramatically during two prolonged periods of famine. A growing number of dependants prompted her to open a community at Kedgaon. By 1900 she was providing for some 2,000 female orphans and widows and for a few hundred neglected boys. Her community was a model of efficient organization, in which Indian dress was worn and Indian customs were maintained, but Christian teaching infused all aspects of life. Known as Mukti, the community ran a farm to provide much of its food, offered basic education and taught crafts and skills that set people on a path to self-sufficiency.

Throughout the 1890s, Ramabai's understanding of Christian faith grew. She first professed faith in an Anglo-Catholic context. In the United States she moved easily among all kinds of Protestants, from reform-minded Unitarians to holiness Methodists. In India she came under the influence of visiting Western evangelists such as the American Dwight Pentecost, who taught her about the new birth, and Keswick missioners from England who urged her to embrace the 'overcoming' life of 'holiness by faith in Jesus'. Deeply influenced by the writings of the eccentric English rector and evangelist William Haslam, Ramabai began attending revival conventions and camp meetings in India. When she returned to the United States in 1898 to report to the Ramabai Association, she had clearly embraced a more evangelical revivalist piety than the one she had professed a decade earlier. She enrolled her daughter and several of her young Indian widows in the holiness school near Rochester, New York, that became Roberts Wesleyan College. On her return trip to India, she addressed the annual Keswick Convention's missionary meeting, pleading for female missionaries for India.

In the twentieth century Manoramabai became her mother's able assistant and amanuensis. Circular letters from Manoramabai kept American, British and Australian Protestants aware of events at Mukti Mission. Various missionaries assisted Ramabai's efforts; some undertook short-term assignments at Mukti, while others joined Ramabai's regular staff. Among her most influential long-term associates was Minnie Abrams, a one-time Methodist Women's Missionary Society missionary, whose interest in village evangelism made her a valuable colleague. From her arrival in 1898 she began organizing evangelistic outreaches in the surrounding area and training Ramabai's young people for evangelism and Christian witness.

The Mukti Mission became the setting for two well-publicized revivals. In 1905, in the aftermath of the Welsh Revival, Mukti residents experienced a prolonged season of spiritual renewal. Another awakening in 1906 and 1907 assumed a more Pentecostal flavour; many reported that the young women were able miraculously to utter prayers, praise and prophecy in English. This fervour subsided rather quickly, but not before Pentecostals had identified the widely known Mukti Mission as a place touched by their movement. Minnie Abrams recounted this revival in a pamphlet, *The Baptism of the Holy Ghost and Fire*, which was very influential among Pentecostals. Ramabai never endorsed the Pentecostal movement, nor did she speak in tongues, but Minnie Abrams and other missionary associates did both and tirelessly promoted the Mukti Mission among the growing Pentecostal constituency. In 1908 Abrams left the Mukti Mission to return to the United States.

From 1900 Ramabai devoted herself almost exclusively to the preparation of a Marathi Bible. Designed with helps for lay evangelists, the Bible became her legacy to her people. She also prepared a Marathi concordance based on Greek and Hebrew etymology. Her many tracts and her 'Life of Christ' circulated widely.

In 1919 Ramabai received the Kaiser-I-Hind medal for outstanding contributions to Indian society. The untimely death in 1920

of her daughter and presumed successor Manoramabai shocked the extended Mukti family. In April 1922, after a brief illness, Ramabai died at Kedgaon. She left her work to the supervision of Indian and missionary Christians with the provision that a representative of the Christian and Missionary Alliance should chair the Mukti Mission Board.

In her own time, Ramabai enjoyed the esteem of the Protestant world. Western Christians in particular commended her integration of Christian faith and Indian life. In the late twentieth century, Indian feminist scholars began exploring and acknowledging her larger contributions to modern India.

Bibliography
U. Chakravarti, *Rewriting History: The Life and Times of Pandita Ramabai* (Kali for Women, 1998); M. Kosambi, *Pandita Ramabai Through Her Own Words* (New Delhi: Oxford University Press, 2000).

E. L. BLUMHOFER

■ **RAMM, Bernard** (1916–1992), Baptist theologian, was a leading theological voice within the coalition initially known as the 'new evangelicalism' or 'neo-evangelicalism', that, beginning in the 1940s, emerged from American fundamentalism. Although a Baptist for most of his life, Ramm typified the neo-evangelical ethos in the sense that his Christian identity and his understanding of the Christian faith were more clearly shaped by his participation in the fledgling evangelical movement than by his affiliation to his chosen denomination. Moreover, he epitomized the typically neo-evangelical goal of engaging in, rather than withdrawing from, the challenges posed by the theological discussions under way in the mainstream seminaries and the changes taking place in the wider culture. In so doing, Ramm became a model and inspiration for other evangelical scholars.

Ramm was born in 1916 in the mining city of Butte, Montana. From his early youth he was fascinated by science and assumed that he would grow up to become a scientist. Some time during the summer prior to his planned entrance to the University of Washington, however, Ramm underwent an instantaneous, radical and life-transforming conversion. His university training, which he completed in 1938, focused not on science but on speech and philosophy.

From 1938 to 1941 Ramm pursued the BD programme at Eastern Baptist Theological Seminary in Philadelphia, a school that had been founded to carry the conservative banner within the Northern Baptist Convention (now the American Baptist Churches). His final year at Eastern included graduate studies at the University of Pennsylvania and an interim pastorate in New York City. Although two short pastorates followed, in Seattle (1942–1943) and Glendale, California (1943–1944), Ramm was to make his contribution to evangelicalism through his lengthy and successful academic career, which was launched in 1943 when he was appointed Professor of Biblical Languages at the Los Angeles Baptist Theological Seminary. The next academic year he became head of the department of Philosophy and Apologetics at the Bible Institute of Los Angeles (Biola), where he taught until 1951.

While serving on the Biola faculty, Ramm enrolled in the University of Southern California, earning an MA in 1947 and a PhD in 1950. By focusing on philosophy of science, he was able to combine his long-standing interest in science with his training in philosophy. The result was a doctoral dissertation entitled, 'An Investigation of Some Recent Efforts to Justify Metaphysical Statements from Science with Special Reference to Physics'. Ramm's teaching career led him to Bethel College and Seminary (1951–1954), Baylor University (1954–1959) and finally the American Baptist Seminary of the West (formerly the California Baptist Theological Seminary). His long tenure of service at ABSW (1959–1974, 1978–1986) was briefly interrupted by a sojourn at his alma mater, Eastern Baptist Seminary (1974–1977).

Ramm's theological endeavours were motivated by the typically neo-evangelical concern to reaffirm the classical doctrines of the Christian faith within the context of a world shaped by the Enlightenment in a manner that avoided the 'obscurantism' of fundamentalism. To this end, Ramm focused on three major areas: apologetics, the interface of the Bible and science and biblical authority.

As its title indicates, Ramm's first book, *Problems in Christian Apologetics* (Portland:

Western Baptist Theological Seminary, 1949), was devoted to apologetics. In 1953 two further studies were published, *Types of Apologetic Systems* (Wheaton: Van Kampen, 1953) and *Protestant Christian Evidences* (Chicago: Moody, 1953). In these early works Ramm pursued an approach often called 'evidentialism', that is, the apologetic strategy that offers evidences for the truth of the Christian faith drawn from data (or 'facts', to use Ramm's designation) that can be observed or verified, at least in theory, by everyone. By 1958, however, Ramm was moving towards a change in his approach to apologetics, which finally led to a fourth book on the topic, *The God Who Makes a Difference* (Waco: Word, 1972). Convinced that no set of individual facts could prove the faith, he now argued for Christianity as a postulate or hypothesis. In addition, he introduced a distinction between 'certitude' and 'certainty', asserting that although a believer can gain full spiritual certitude about the great truths of personal salvation, only a high degree of probability can be attributed to the historical claims of the Christian faith. In Ramm's estimation, the error of the fundamentalists lay in their desire to claim rational certainty for the history narrated by the Bible.

Although apologetics consumed Ramm's earliest literary efforts, it was his attempt to bring the Bible and science into dialogue that catapulted him, as a young thinker, into the evangelical limelight. In a controversial book with a seemingly audacious title, *The Christian View of Science and Scripture* (Grand Rapids: Eerdmans, 1954), Ramm called evangelicals away from the fundamentalist approach that set Christianity scientific findings in opposition, and back to what he viewed as the 'noble tradition', in which God was seen as the author of both creation and redemption, and of which the operative assumption was the agreement between true science and the Bible. In issuing this call, Ramm not only sought to harmonize science with Scripture, but also boldly declared that the Bible contained culturally conditioned statements, and asserted that the biblical writers were simply not teachers of science in the modern sense. In 1950 Ramm had spelled out the hermeneutical basis for his case in his book, *Protestant Biblical Interpretation* (Boston: Wilde, 1950). In this work he argued for an intelligent biblicism, including the principle that revelation is accommodated and therefore has an 'anthropomorphic character' that the exegete must acknowledge. Ramm then applied this approach to one particular biblical book, Exodus, in the non-technical, lay-oriented book, *His Way Out* (Glendale: Regal, 1974).

As the 1950s gave way to the 1960s, Ramm published three books dealing with his third major area of interest, the question of Scripture, revelation and theological authority: *The Pattern of Religious Authority* (Grand Rapids: Eerdmans, 1958), *The Witness of the Spirit* (Grand Rapids: Eerdmans, 1959) and *Special Revelation and the Word of God* (Grand Rapids: Eerdmans, 1961). Like his concern for the interface of the Bible and science, this interest also served the apologetic goal of demonstrating the truth of the Christian faith. Ramm located ultimate authority in the divine revelation (which in the final analysis is Christ) and sought to bring together inspired Scripture and the illumined reader, and hence the outer and the inner, or the objective and the subjective, dimensions of biblical authority, in keeping with what he saw as the teaching of the Reformers.

Ramm's concern to set forth credible theology in the modern world eventually led him to embrace the approach of Karl Barth as the paradigm for modern evangelicalism. In his controversial book *After Fundamentalism* (San Francisco: Harper & Row, 1983), Ramm claimed, against the typical American evangelical reading of Barth, that Barth had been doing exactly what Ramm had himself set out to do, namely, to restate Reformed theology in a manner that took Enlightenment concerns seriously without capitulating to them. Ramm's momentous rediscovery of Barth appeared to free him finally to turn away from issues of theological foundation (apologetics, Bible and science, and theological authority) and to engage in constructive theology. The result was two books dealing with two core Christian doctrines, sin and Christ: *Offense to Reason* (San Francisco: Harper & Row, 1985) and *An Evangelical Christology* (Nashville: Thomas Nelson, 1985). Yet not even in these works did Ramm leave behind his interest in the apologetic task and in the dialogue with science that had occupied his attention throughout his career. On the contrary, he had come to see that constructive theology was in a sense apologetic by nature and consequently that it necessarily included a conversation with the reigning scientific paradigms of the day.

More important than the particular proposals he articulated in response to the central issues he tackled, Bernard Ramm's legacy lies in his call to evangelical theologians to move out of the intellectual ghetto fundamentalism had created, so as to engage the modern world with a credible presentation of the truth of the Christian faith. By turning his face towards modern thinking (specifically towards contemporary scientific advances and non-evangelical theologies) Ramm laid the foundation for evangelical thinkers to engage in positive dialogue with their context, not only to bear witness to the truth, but also to learn from other traditions and viewpoints.

Bibliography

S. J. Grenz (ed.), *Perspectives on Theology in the Contemporary World: Essays in Honor of Bernard Ramm* (Macon: Mercer University Press, 1990); S. J. Grenz and R. E. Olson, *Twentieth Century Theology: God and the World in a Transitional Age* (Downers Grove: IVP, 1992); B. Ramm, *The Evangelical Heritage* (Grand Rapids: Baker Book House, 2000).

S. J. GRENZ

■ **RAWLYK, George** (1935–1995), Canadian historian, was born in Thorold, Ontario, on 19 May 1935. His parents were from the Ukraine, and Ukrainian was the household language for Rawlyk and his two older sisters. Rawlyk's primary early influences outside the home were radical labour organizers and a mission conducted in his neighbourhood by a single woman, Mary Renton, for the Baptist Convention of Ontario and Quebec. When he was in the tenth grade he had what he later told his sisters was a 'spiritual experience' at a weekend sponsored by the Inter-School Christian Fellowship. Thereafter he worked for several years with Mary Renton in the mission and soon joined a Baptist church. He remained an active member of local Baptist churches for the rest of his life. He was also a lifelong democratic socialist and firm supporter of the New Democratic Party.

In 1957 Rawlyk received a bachelor's degree in history from McMaster University, where he was also a standout center on the football team. He was a Rhodes Scholar at Oxford from 1957 to 1959, and then returned to North America, where he pursued advanced study in Canadian history at the University of Rochester (MA 1962, PhD 1967). Rawlyk taught at Mount Allison University in New Brunswick and Dalhousie University in Nova Scotia before moving in 1963 to the history department of Queen's University in Ontario. From 1976 to 1985 he chaired the Queen's department during a tumultuous period of rapid expansion at Queen's and throughout Canadian academia.

Rawlyk first made his mark as a student of the eighteenth century, particularly of relations between New England and the Maritime colonies (e.g. *Nova Scotia's Massachusetts*, 1973). Much of his interest in Maritime history centred on the meteoric career of Henry *Alline (1743–1784), a revivalist whose powerful itinerant preaching promoted a 'New Light stir' in the 1770s and 1780s, but which was also influential in keeping the attention of Nova Scotians on local concerns and so making them unresponsive to New Englanders' invitation to join the American Revolution. Alline's populist style, intense preoccupation with spirituality and ardent commitment to Christian communities made up of ordinary men and women continued to fascinate Rawlyk.

It was not, however, until Rawlyk was at the mid-point of his career that he discovered academic resources that enabled him to write about Alline (and religion more generally) in terms that respected both the integrity of spiritual experience and the conventions of academic history. These resources included accounts of cultural hegemony from the Marxist theorist Antonio Gramsci and descriptions of the liminality of religious communities from the anthropologist Victor Turner. But they came primarily from the example of other North American historians who were beginning to publish academic works on evangelical groups. George Marsden's *Fundamentalism and American Culture* (1980) was of first importance among these works.

Much writing followed, especially on Canadian radical evangelicalism in the late eighteenth and early nineteenth centuries, most notably *Ravished by the Spirit: Revivals, Maritime Baptists and Henry Alline* (1984) and *The Canada Fire: Radical Evangelicalism in British North America, 1775–1812* (1994). Publications concerning the more general religious history of Canada included two pioneering edited collections, *The Canadian Protestant Experience, 1760–1990* (1990) and *Aspects of the Canadian Evangelical Experience* (1997). Finally, in cooperation with the public opinion researcher Angus Reid, Rawlyk began to write on religion in contemporary Canada, especially the signs of traditional evangelical commitment found among conservative Protestant groups, but also those found among mainstream Protestants and Roman Catholics (see especially *'Is Jesus Your Personal Saviour?' in Search of Canadian Evangelicalism in the 1990s*, 1996). Throughout the work published in his latter decades, Rawlyk insisted on the irreducible integrity of Christian experience. As he once wrote with characteristic forthrightness: 'Religious conversions have actually occurred; peoples' lives have apparently been profoundly and permanently changed. ... Conversions still take place and so do religious revivals' (*'Wrapped Up in God': A Study of Several Canadian Revivals and Revivalists*, 1988, p. ix).

During his tenure at Queen's, Rawlyk was feared but also revered as a demanding teacher. As a research mentor, he supervised more than 120 theses and dissertations on a wide range of topics in Canadian political, social and religious history. As teacher and mentor at Queen's, as the editor of an influential series in religious history from the McGill–Queen's University Press and through many acts of extraordinary personal kindness to students and friends, Rawlyk exerted a singular influence both on scholarship about evangelicals in Canada and as a Christian scholar himself. He died on 23 November 1995 from complications arising from a car accident two weeks earlier. Six weeks before his death he had been awarded the Doctor of Civil Law degree from Acadia University for his pivotal role in promoting the study of Maritime history and the importance of religion in Canada.

Bibliography

P. L. Coops and D. J. Hessler, 'George Alexander Rawlyk: A Bibliography, 1962–1996', *Acadiensis: Journal of the History of the Atlantic Region* 25.2 (1996), pp. 159–173 (in same issue, 'George Rawlyk Remembered', pp. 151–158); D. C. Goodwin (ed.), *Revivals, Baptists, and George Rawlyk* (Wolfville, Nova Scotia: Acadia Divinity College, 2000); M. Hutchinson, interview with Rawlyk, *Lucas: An Evangelical History Review* (Sydney, Australia) 14 (Dec. 1992), pp. 58–73; M. A. Noll, 'George Rawlyk's Contribution to Canadian History as a Contribution to United States History: A Preliminary Probe', *Fides et Historia* 23.1 (2000), pp. 1–17.

M. A. NOLL

■ **REES, Paul Stromberg** (1900–1991), holiness teacher, was born on 4 September 1900 in Providence, Rhode Island, to Seth Cook Rees, a noted evangelist, and his second wife, Frida Stromberg Rees. In 1908 the family moved to Pasadena, California, where the children of the second marriage received their education. In 1917 Seth Rees formed the Pilgrim Tabernacle Church, which in 1922 joined with others to create the Pilgrim Holiness Church.

Paul inherited his father's taste for oratory and his zeal for evangelism and holiness. He was seventeen when he preached his first sermon, at a rescue mission. In 1920 he formally joined his father as associate pastor of Pilgrim Tabernacle and was ordained the next year while a student at the University of Southern California, from which he graduated Phi Beta Kappa in 1923. Although he did not pursue formal graduate training, Rees retained an abiding love for books and learning all his life, and was awarded six honorary doctorates (1939–1982).

During the years from 1928 to 1932 Rees served as ministerial superintendent of Detroit Laymen's Holiness Tabernacle. From 1938 to 1958 he was pastor of First Covenant Church in Minneapolis, Minnesota, where he established a reputation as one of the leaders of the growing national and international evangelical movement. From 1942 to 1985 Rees was a member of the Board of Administration of the National Association of Evangelicals (NAE). In 1950 he became vice-president of the Evangelical Covenant Church of America (until 1955), and during the years 1952 to 1954 was president of the NAE. Beginning in 1954, he served as minister to ministers for four Billy *Graham Crusades in the US and abroad.

When Rees retired from First Covenant Church in 1958 he became vice-president at large of World Vision International, serving from 1964 as director of Pastors' Conferences for that organization as well. Rees retired from World Vision in 1975, but remained active in ministry around the world until late in his life. He preached his last sermon at the age of ninety, at Easter 1991, a few weeks before his death.

Rees was a strong advocate of the doctrine and experience of holiness, and devoted many years of active service to institutions that shared his commitment. From 1935 to 1965 he was a member of the Board of Trustees of Asbury College, and from 1967 to 1983 was on the Board of Asbury Theological Seminary, retiring as an honorary life member. He also served on the Board of Directors of William Penn College (Iowa) from 1950 to 1958.

In addition to his work in administration and public speaking, Rees spoke regularly on Christian radio programmes and was a prolific journalist. He served as editor and wrote for leading Christian journals, spending long periods in leadership positions for *The Herald, Christianity Today, The Covenant Companion, Eternity* and *World Vision*. He wrote a number of pamphlets and short pieces that were published separately and fourteen books. The first of these was a biography of his father (1934). Among those that followed were *The Adequate Man: Paul in Philippians* (1959) and *Men of Action in the Book of Acts* (1966). His last book was *Don't Sleep Through the Revolution* (1969). Rees' writing showed his love for reading, revealing without ostentation his broad knowledge of theological and devotional literature, and of fiction, history and current events as well.

Rees was an eloquent and persuasive preacher, who spoke often at Bible and other conferences and at camp meetings. One associate recalls that 'to hear him speak was to hear music'. Another wrote of the 'clarity', 'winsomeness' and 'artistry' of Rees' sermons. Although committed to the Wesleyan doctrine of holiness and to its practical application in worldwide Christian ministry, Rees was not narrowly doctrinaire, and exercised an important influence among Christians of all kinds. In a testament written towards the end of his career he warned that 'idolatry' (of traditions, forms and customs) was 'one of the most frequent undetected sins of Christians'. He was particularly effective at, and is still fondly remembered for, pastoral conferences of American missionaries serving overseas, particularly in East Asia.

Rees married Edith P. Brown in 1926. The couple had three children. He died on 20 May 1991 in Boca Raton, Florida.

Bibliography

G. D. Black (ed.), *An Empowered Witness: Sermons and Writings of Paul S. Rees* (Kansas City: Beacon Hill Press, 1997). The extensive Paul S. Rees papers are held in the library of Asbury Theological Seminary in Wilmore, Kentucky.

E. H. McKINLEY

■ **REVELL, Fleming Hewitt** (1849–1931), Christian publisher, businessman and philanthropist, was born in Chicago, Illinois, to Fleming H. and Emma Manning Revell. His parents had emigrated to America from England. Emma Revell came from a long line of English ancestors, and Fleming, Sr, was descended from the French Huguenots who escaped to Northern Ireland. Fleming, Sr, settled in London, where he worked as a shipbuilder. When the European side of the Atlantic dealt him financial adversity, he moved his family to America in 1849. He secured employment in Chicago, constructing boats for the Lake Michigan trade, but financial security still eluded the family. So young Fleming, at the age of only nine, left school and obtained employment in a chemist's shop to assist his father in supporting his mother and three sisters.

One of Revell's sisters, Emma, married the well-known American evangelist Dwight Lyman *Moody in the early 1860s. Revell's high regard for his dynamic brother-in-law (added to the fact that Moody was several years his senior) enabled Moody to influence

him profoundly. Late in 1868 Moody suggested that Revell abandon his post at the chemist's shop and dedicate himself to a career that would build the kingdom of Christ more directly. Though Revell was a practising Presbyterian, devoted to prayer and earnest about his commitment to Christ, he did not feel called to be a preacher. After some prayer and more persuasion from Moody, he embarked upon a non-denominational Christian publishing venture to provide literature for believers who wanted to be mature in Christ and equipped for ministry. This endeavour dominated the remainder of his life.

In January 1869, with the aid of Dwight and Emma Moody, Revell began to produce a modest religious monthly entitled *Everybody's Paper* and imprinted a book, *Grace and Truth* by William P. Mackay. His account ledgers report long days spent travelling the Midwest selling subscriptions for his periodical. He solicited a few subscriptions in every town and quickly built up a substantial base of support. Also in 1869, Revell met Josephine Barbour of Michigan while she was visiting the Moodys on a trip home from Tennessee. She also had been influenced by Moody and had recently completed three years as a missionary teacher to former slaves at his behest. Fleming and Josephine were drawn to one another instantly and, on 12 September 1872, were married in her home town of Romeo, Michigan. They began their married life in Chicago and eventually had two children: a son, Fleming Hewitt, Jr, and a daughter, Elisabeth. Fleming graduated from Yale and eventually joined his father's work and married Marion Cornell. Elisabeth married Max Shoop and moved to France.

The Chicago fire of 1871 completely destroyed Revell's new business while he was on holiday in England, but he would not be thwarted. He re-established his publishing company and *Everybody's Paper*, and went on to publish *Words of Life*, *Temperance Tales* and *The Sunday School Lesson Illustrator*, all of which achieved national circulation. Within a decade of starting his business he was well on his way to becoming the largest publisher of religious literature in North America. His association with Moody made success a virtual certainty. As the only authorized publisher of Moody's materials at that time, he produced Moody's tracts, sermons and writings in cloth and paper bindings. These products sold by the hundred thousands. Revell then added books for Moody's readers to his list of publications, including a sizeable amount of premillennialist literature, which challenged the then popular postmillennial view of the end times. By 1880 his list comprised around a hundred titles, besides booklets, hymnals and Sunday school periodicals. Over the next two decades, several of Revell's publications became best-sellers, and his company became the largest American publisher of Christian literature. At that time it published over 300 books a year. Revell published the works of several prominent evangelical preachers, evangelists and missionaries of his era, including Samuel Dickey Gordon, author of the 'Quiet Talks' series, Hannah Whitall *Smith and Adoniram Judson Gordon. In 1890 Revell's business was incorporated as the Fleming H. Revell Company. To supplement the Chicago operation, he opened a branch in New York. Later he opened branches in Toronto, London and Edinburgh. In producing a variety of printed material he enlarged the scope of conventional evangelical literature. His company boasted a young adult's department, sold standard Sunday school libraries of fifty volumes for $25.75 and distributed all the Sunday school resources of the period, offering picture cards and colourful floral mottoes to supplement them.

Revell was invited into the American Publishers' Association at its conception in 1900. He moved from Evanston, Illinois, to Riverdale-on-Hudson, New York, in 1906 and subsequently moved the company's headquarters to that city. At Revell Company's fiftieth anniversary, friends and colleagues surprised him with a dinner in New York. There his peers celebrated his accomplishments and affirmed his commitment to Christ. His success as a publisher was indisputable.

Revell was also generous with his time and his money, and dedicated both to causes beyond his company. He participated in the Niagra Conference. Through Moody he became acquainted with Northfield School in Massachusetts, and provided it with financial support. Later he became a trustee of Northfield Seminary. Further, he served as a trustee of Wheaton College during the presidency of his close friend Charles Blanchard. He was also a member of the board of home missions of the Presbyterian Church and a trustee of the Polytechnic Institute in Puerto Rico, which was managed by the Presbyterian Board of National Missions. He served as director of the New York YMCA and treasurer of the American Mission to Lepers. Revell was an astute businessman whose work as an investor and director in the New York Life Insurance Company furnished him with a substantial fortune. Known as a philanthropist, he invested wisely, and he charitably distributed his wealth to numerous Christian causes.

By the end of his career, Revell was a wise and experienced man. Sixty years of publishing gave him a keen awareness of the potential of religious books, and his annual vacations in Europe and the Near East equipped him with an understanding of world issues. His wife Josephine passed away in 1924, just a few months after their golden wedding anniversary. In 1929 Revell relinquished the presidency of his company and placed it in the hands of his son, Fleming Hewitt Revell, Jr. The elder Revell continued his involvement by serving as chairman of the board of directors. Late in 1931 he fell at home and fractured his pelvis. Eight days later, on 11 October 1931, he died in Yonkers, New York, from complications related to his injury. Philip E. Howard, a fellow publisher and the friend who wrote his obituary, remarked that 'his whole manner gave you a welcome' and named him 'one of the most noted of our American publishers'.

Bibliography

D. Malone, 'Revell, Fleming Hewitt', DAB, vol. VIII (New York: Charles Scribner's Sons, 1963), pp. 512–513; P. C. Wilt, 'Revell, Fleming Hewitt', Dictionary of Christianity in America (Downers Grove: IVP, 1990), p. 1009.

T. L. COOPER

■ **RICE, John R.** (1895–1980), fundamentalist evangelist, was born on 11 December 1895 near Gainesville, Texas. His family struggled financially during his childhood in west Texas, but as a young man he managed to earn enough money to attend college, graduating from Decatur Baptist College in 1918 and Baylor University in 1920 with an AB degree. The following year, hoping to earn a Master's degree and gain a college position, he enrolled in the education department at the University of Chicago, but dropped out within months to pursue a career in the ministry. In the autumn of 1921, Rice married his college sweetheart, Lloys McClure Cooke, and enrolled at Southwestern Baptist Theological Seminary in Fort Worth, Texas. He spent two years there working towards, but not completing, a Master's degree in theology. He received no further formal education, though he was later awarded honorary doctorates from four institutions, including Los Angeles Theological Seminary (1936) and Bob Jones College (1945).

Rice accepted his academic training and honours with gratitude but considered them ornamental next to the real business of his life, evangelism. Starting in 1926, he became a full-time itinerant preacher, travelling first throughout Texas and later throughout the whole country, delivering emotional and fiery sermons. He used Dallas as his home base from 1932 to 1940, then Wheaton, Illinois from 1940 to 1963 and finally Murfreesboro, Tennessee from 1963 to 1980. Rice laboured, with some success, to recreate the massive, city-wide campaigns of Dwight L. *Moody and Billy *Sunday, but ultimately found more influence through the pen than through the pulpit. In 1934 he founded *The Sword of the Lord*, a weekly newspaper dedicated to 'soul-winning', which he edited until his death. From humble beginnings, Rice built up the circulation to a peak of 300,000 in the mid-1970s. Meanwhile, he sponsored regular Sword of the Lord Conferences on Soul Winning and Revival, which provided training for aspiring evangelists, and he authored over one hundred books and nearly as many booklets and tracts. Many of his writings focused on evangelism, including his most famous, a tract written early in his career and entitled, 'What Must I Do To Be Saved?' Over forty-eight million copies had been printed by 1980.

As Rice won souls to Christ, he also made enemies. He personified the militant side of fundamentalism, berating modernism and demanding separation from 'infidels'. Rice often attacked liberal clergy, but he was more troubled by evangelicals who seemed to waver, especially Southern Baptists and neo-evangelicals. Born, raised and educated in the Southern Baptist Convention, he left in 1927 out of loyalty to his separatist mentor, J. Frank Norris. Rice also complained about the inclusion of evolution in the curriculum at Baylor University and the denomination's attempt to silence conservative critics. As a result, he spent the rest of his life as an independent Baptist and a vocal critic of the SBC.

Rice's break with neo-evangelicals was also a family matter. He watched the rebirth of evangelicalism from close range. In 1940 he moved from Dallas to Wheaton so that his children, six daughters, could attend Wheaton College. When in 1952 Rice formed the Sword Cooperating Board, he invited Bob Cook of Youth for Christ International and Billy *Graham to join. In 1957, however, when Graham included theological liberals on the committee for his New York City crusade, Rice cut ties with the young evangelist and with neo-evangelicalism more broadly. In 1963 Rice symbolized this division by relocating his headquarters from Wheaton to Murfreesboro, a move probably inspired by more than the financial reasons cited by his adoring biographer. From the 1950s to the 1970s, Rice continued to criticize evangelicals, opposing their acceptance of the Revised Standard Version of the Bible, objecting to the writings of E. J. *Carnell and even complaining about a liberal drift at Moody Bible Institute.

Rice embodied fundamentalism in other ways as well. He affirmed the core of its theology, summed up each week in the masthead of *The Sword of the Lord*: 'An Independent Christian Weekly, Standing for the Verbal Inspiration of the Bible, the Deity of Christ, His Blood Atonement, Salvation by Faith, New Testament Soul Winning and the Premillennial Return of Christ.' He spoke out against Pentecostalism and Catholicism. He railed against all manner of worldliness, including dancing, drinking, tobacco, petting and movies. His anti-feminist tirades and defence of patriarchy won him particular fame and infamy, especially with the publication, *Bobbed Hair, Bossy Wives, and Female Preachers* (1941).

Rice never shied away from controversial topics. His political comments, for example, were as strident as his theological ones. He defended the Second World War and the Vietnam War, attacked communism and socialism, opposed the Civil Rights Movement and endorsed conservative politicians such as Barry Goldwater and George Wallace. Rice offered harsh explanations for tragic assassinations, suggesting that John F. Kennedy had suffered divine wrath for the sins of his 'liquor-selling' father and that the rabble-rousing Martin Luther King, Jr had received his just deserts. Rice was equally frank about sensitive private matters, especially sex. Not only did his warnings about petting, suggestive clothing and dancing include plenty of details; so also did his celebration of the nuptial bed. In *The Home – Courtship, Marriage, and Children* (1945), for instance, Rice included a chapter on 'Normal Sex Life in Marriage' in which he endorsed frequent intercourse and encouraged extensive foreplay to aid both husband and wife in reaching a climax. Such candour often made Rice a target of criticism himself, but it probably boosted his popularity as well.

Rice's appeal also stemmed from his ability to employ tabloid-style journalism to proclaim fundamentalist doctrine. Dramatic, sometimes cartoon, drawings appeared on the cover of his publications, such as the flaming sword on his weekly paper. Rice opened one of his books *Is God a Bully?* (1958) by announcing that it contained 'seven sensational sermons', all of which were 'arousing, shocking, [and] pointed' (p. 5). In these, as in his other writings, he borrowed titillating news accounts of murders and sex crimes to illustrate biblical lessons. His language was equally colourful. In one 1935 diatribe he condemned dancing as the 'Child of the Brothel, Sister of Drunkenness, Lewdness, Divorce and Murder, The Mother of Lust – A Road to Hell!' (*What's Wrong With The Dance*, p. 3). Late in life Rice seemed to acknowledge his strange link to the tabloids. In 1980 he bought a full-page advertisement in the *National Enquirer* complete with a free phone number for ordering his books and a year's subscription to *The Sword of the Lord*.

Rice's success also resulted from his unrelenting drive. Into his seventies, he travelled widely, preaching and leading tours of the Holy Land. His wife described the 'life of an evangelist's wife' as the 'loneliest life on earth' and recalled that she saw more of Rice's secretary than of her husband (*Fundamentalist Journal* 1, p. 29). He wrote many of his books while on the road and dictated messages incessantly. Rice put nearly all of his income back into Sword ministries, saving only a modest amount for personal expenses, and he constantly pressured staff to increase circulation of the weekly paper. After more than half a century of public ministry, Rice slowed down in his eighties and died on 29 December 1980 in Murfreesboro. The old warrior had just turned eighty-five.

Bibliography
R. L. Sumner, *Man Sent From God: A Biography of Dr. John R. Rice* (Grand Rapids: Eerdmans, 1959); V. Walden, *John R. Rice: 'The Captain of Our Team'* (Murfreesboro: Sword of the Lord Publishers, 1990).

M. J. SIDER-ROSE

■ **RIDLEY, John Gotch** (1896–1976), evangelist, was the son of Thomas Ridley, a company director for Gordon and Gotch. John Gotch Ridley received his middle name from his mother, a member of the successful Gotch family. Fascinated by history and the story of Christian soldiers (such as Gordon of Khartoum and Henry Havelock), Ridley was glad to enlist with the First AIF in October 1915. He had already been converted, at William Lamb's strongly premillennialist Burton St Baptist Church in Sydney. His spirituality would continue to express the 'higher Christian life' perfectionism of Keswick and the millennial commitment to mission of the CIM. His assertiveness in evangelism reflected his military background, and in later years he would travel the imperial territories as a 'soldier for Christ'. The following story, from one of Ridley's few taped sermons, typifies his integration of narrative, personal experience of war and evangelism: 'Courage is essential in the Christian life ... I can never forget the courage of an officer in France at my first bayonet charge – a terrible thing a bayonet charge if you have ever been in it. With an awful artillery barrage in front of us and men falling left and right in our breastworks, and to see this calm young officer a couple of years older than myself looking along the breastworks and saying,

"I'll lead your line over, sergeant." And he picked up his trench coat and threw it over his shoulder, and he lit a cigarette, and with a wave of his arm said cheerily, "Come along boys!" and over the top he walked into a terrific fire. He fell riddled by bullets, but I never forgot the heroism of Lieutenant Briggs. And here the Lord takes this heroic virtue [of courage, in Mark 8:38] and presents it to us.'

Ridley served with the 53rd Battalion at Armentieres, Bellicourt, Egypt and Fromelles; he was shot in the face, and his vocal cords were severly damaged. He had been leading Bible studies enthusiastically in the trenches, but now he thought he would never speak properly again. In time, he recovered remarkably from the physical effects of the wound, though he had to fight the psychological effects (repeated nervous debilitation and collapse, headaches, loss of confidence) for the rest of his life, without assistance from psychology or drugs. In 1918 he was awarded the Military Cross for his bravery in repeatedly carrying the wounded, rations and ammunition under fire at the battle of Bellicourt.

Ridley returned home and became student pastor at Maroubra Baptist Church, the only church in which he ever held a permanent position (though he was later to be acting pastor at Katoomba Baptist and Auckland Tabernacle among others). His Military Cross opened a number of important pulpits to him. For instance, in 1961 he reminisced about standing in the pulpit of Stanmore Baptist Church still in uniform 'forty-two years before' (in 1919), telling stories of the war and relating them to the demands of Christ. His health deteriorated, however, ruling out the possibility of a missionary career with the CIM. Although he continued to regard missionaries such as David *Brainerd and Hudson *Taylor's great associate, William Burns, as his heroes, for a short while he worked on a sheep farm.

Convalescing in Blackheath in the Blue Mountains, Ridley met his wife Dorothy (née Chapman). Despite his disability he had a significant impact on the local Blackheath church; Dorothy, her sister and her whole family were soon drawn to evangelical Baptist Christianity. While in Blackheath he used to visit an old hermit, whose words ('You are the only man who ever cared for my soul')

encouraged Ridley to pursue his calling. His sense that God had spoken to him, saying 'Be strong and work, for I am with you', drove him to conquer his disability with rigorous military discipline through prayer and preparation. Thereafter he always emphasized the importance of the personal spiritual and devotional life; he prayed much himself and wrote extensively on prayer in booklets such as *The Deep, Sweet Well of Love*. His tracts were produced and distributed wherever Australian forces fought in the Second World War through the work of the Melbourne publisher S. John Bacon. Ridley published some thirteen books, four volumes of poems, more than twenty poems in leaflet form and over 100 booklets and tracts.

After their marriage in 1926, Ridley and Dorothy drove the horsedrawn carriage of the 'Australian Bush Crusade' (1926–1935) through the bush to isolated hamlets and small towns. As his health improved, Ridley's faith mission began local revival meetings, at first in association with local Baptist churches, and then increasingly in union tent missions in which a number of churches cooperated. Ridley was a committed Baptist, and he taught the great conservative doctrines of grace, repentance from sin and the return of Christ; his missions (with those of Wilfred Jarvis) resulted in the rapid growth of Baptist congregations in many parts of NSW, particular in the Armidale-Glen Innes areas and around the North Rivers (Grafton, Lismore, Casino etc.). After the outbreak of the Second World War, Ridley undertook chaplaincy and welfare work with Campaigners for Christ in army camps and on troop transports.

Although Ridley was an effective personal evangelist (many people would date their conversion from a conversation with him on a train or a bus during one of his long journeys), he was above all a preacher. It is one of the ironies of history that Ridley is remembered today largely for his preaching on Isaiah 57:15 at Burton Street Baptist in November 1932. His sermon, 'Where will you spend eternity?', was heard by Arthur Stace, a barely literate ex-alcoholic convert of R. B. S. Hammond. 'God really grabbed hold of Stace when Ridley said, Eternity, eternity! Oh that I could shout and sound eternity all over the streets of Sydney! You have to meet eternity. Where will you spend eternity?'

Stace was deeply affected; he took a piece of chalk out of his pocket and began to scrawl the word 'Eternity' on the pavement. His copperplate 'signature' was to become iconic in Sydney, even among non-Christians.

Ridley's preaching was so powerful (at a time when the influence of the pulpit was declining) partly because of his sense of inadequacy and partly because of his personality; his war experience and sense of weakness made him uncomfortable in informal settings, but his sermons could be carefully crafted and expansively illustrated (by bodily movement and from Christian history). Dorothy used to see him write out a sermon in full, pace his office memorizing the text and pray over it for hours before preaching seemingly without reference to the notes before him. Ridley was not good at committee work, and he avoided bureaucracy and attempts to 'organize' his work in the way that would enable later evangelists (such as Billy *Graham) to make a powerful impact. Consequently, his work was pre-eminently in local revivals scattered across Australia, New Zealand and later the USA and Britain (where he campaigned on behalf of Mildmay). After the birth of their daughter, Ruth, Dorothy could no longer travel so much, and Ridley worked increasingly with Baptist pastors and companions such as Alf Davey, John Owen and John Woodhouse. The bush missions declined, but Ridley's influence in the great pulpits of the Baptist church (Auburn, Ashfield, Burton Street and above all with C. J. Tinsley at Stanmore), and on the growing numbers of young men who passed through the Baptist Theological Union (later to be named after his great friend and principal of the college, G. H. *Morling), increased. He was known to the Young family (see *Young, Florence) through his own family and others, and he began to receive regular invitations to speak at the popular Katoomba and Upwey/Belgrave Heights conventions. Through the widespread influence of missions promoters such as Northcote Deck, he was also invited to speak abroad.

As Ridley's fame grew, he sought (with Alf Davey and others) to multiply the impact of his evangelism by cooperating in the founding of the Australian Institute for Evangelism on Mt Pleasant in the Illawarra region of NSW. This in turn grew into the international evangelistic agency Ambassadors for Christ, and the Illawarra Bible College. When Ambassadors lost the Stanwell Tops property, Ridley continued his other work rather than become involved in the recriminations. By then, he had already become entangled in the rising opposition among Baptists to the public presence of Pentecostalism in Australia. Some of his younger associates, such as John Woodham, received the distinctive Pentecostal experience known as 'baptism in the Holy Spirit' evidenced by speaking in tongues, through the ministry of the AOG minister Philip Duncan. Duncan's message was in many ways attractive to Ridley. Duncan too had been converted at Burton Street Baptist (through Ridley's influence, according to Dorothy) and shared William Lamb's premillennialism. (In later years, he would be a founder of the prophetic journal *Herald of Hope*.) Duncan and his father Fred, an elder in the church, were asked to leave in a confrontation arising from the ministry of Smith *Wigglesworth, but they stayed in touch with those members of their family who remained Baptists. Ridley shared their outlook and spirituality. In one of the few taped addresses, from 1961, he prays: 'May there be a willingness of heart to cease resisting the Holy Spirit who would fain [sic] draw souls to the Father through the sacrifice of the Son. And O, our God, we pray for the anointing of the Holy Ghost, the opening of the mouth, the loosening of the tongue, the liberty of the Spirit, to bring thy truth of grand redemption before the eyes of thy people tonight. And may there be a response of spirit, soul and mind to this great truth, that Christ died for us. Hear us then and grant that tonight there might be seals of thy power, and souls greatly blessed ...'

The news that Ridley had 'gone over' to the despised Pentecostals caused outrage at the Institute and in the Baptist Union. His name was dropped from preaching rotas, and his itinerant career declined rapidly. Worst of all was the unkindness his family suffered from Baptists afraid of the influence a man of Ridley's stature would have on the youth of the church. In the end, Ridley circulated a letter denying that he had separated from the church (though not, significantly, the validity of his experience). His career recovered, and now that the Baptist Union of NSW has been significantly influenced by the charismatic movement, he can be seen as a man ahead of his time rather than a renegade.

John Ridley, the soldier evangelist, was without equal in his influence on Australian itinerant evangelism in the pre-Billy Graham era. He was not always appreciated. To liberal Baptists, he represented an old revivalist technique irrelevant to the modern world. Respectable Baptists disliked his appeals, which some thought were laboured. Undeniably, Ridley's style was that of his own generation, but his powerful preaching and the continuous flow of his converts into church and ministry (particularly in places such as Glen Innes) gave the Baptist church an evangelical character that continues to be evident to this day. Above all, his was a life of great achievement made possible only through enormous self-discipline and courage.

Bibliography

H. E. Evans, *Soldier and Evangelist: the Story of Rev John G Ridley, MC* (BHSNSW: Eastwood, 1980); P. Rahme, *The Messenger & The Message Behind Mr. Eternity* (John G. Ridley MC, 'The Echoes of Eternity'); J. G. Ridley, *Milestones of Mercy* (Sydney: Christian Press, 1957); J. G. Ridley, 'My experiences in the charge of the 53rd Battalion, 19 July, 1916 at Armentieres', TSS, Australian War Memorial; 'Studio portrait of Lieutenant (Lt) John Gotch Ridley, of the 53rd Battalion, and his wife Dorothy (née Chapman)', P03254.001 Australian War Memorial; 'Courage', sermon, Stanmore Baptist Church, c. 1965, CSAC Archives.

M. HUTCHINSON

■ **RIDLEY, Nicholas** (c. 1503–1555), Bishop of London and martyr, was the closest ally of Thomas *Cranmer, Archbishop of Canterbury, in the establishment of the Protestant Reformation in England during the reign of Edward VI (1547–1553). His burning at the stake, along with fellow-Reformer Hugh *Latimer, in the reign of Mary Tudor (1553–1558) helped to confirm the convictions of the Reformers among the people of England.

Born sometime between 1502 and 1504 in South Tynedale, Northumberland, Ridley was the son of Christopher Ridley, of a prominent family in the somewhat primitive and violent borderland. With financial help from his uncle, Dr Robert Ridley, he entered Pembroke Hall, Cambridge in 1518, gaining his BA in 1521 and MA in 1525, by which time he had become a fellow of Pembroke Hall. After studies in Paris and Louvain, by the end of 1530 he had gained recognition as one of the most effective debaters in the University of Cambridge.

By 1534 Ridley was identified with the party of Protestant reform. He became one of Cranmer's chaplains in 1537, when he received the BD from Cambridge and was made vicar of Herne in Kent. In July 1540 he received his DD and in October was elected master of Pembroke Hall. About this time he was appointed a chaplain to Henry VIII, and in April 1541 he was installed as a prebendary of Canterbury Cathedral.

Ridley became convinced, probably in 1545, that the doctrine of transubstantiation in the mass was false. The writings of the ninth-century monk Ratramnus of Corbie persuaded him that the presence of Christ in the Lord's Supper was spiritual (though real) rather than corporeal, and Ridley in turn persuaded Cranmer around 1546.

With the accession of Edward VI in 1547 Ridley became an active leader in the Reformation of the English church. Consecrated Bishop of Rochester in September of that year, he supported Cranmer in the removal of images and in the reform of worship in the First Book of Common Prayer. Around the end of 1549 he replaced the altar in the cathedral of Rochester with a wooden table. Appointed Bishop of London in April 1550, he removed the altars from St Paul's and throughout the diocese of London.

Despite these strong reforming tendencies, Ridley opposed the scruples of John *Hooper concerning the use of vestments in his consecration as Bishop of Gloucester. In a dispute that ran from October 1550 until Hooper's eventual consecration with vestments in March 1551, Ridley argued that since vestments were a matter of indifference, it was within the authority of church and of state to prescribe them. Ridley's position prevailed after Hooper was imprisoned for a while for the sake of his conscience.

Early in 1552 Ridley preached before Edward VI on the importance of charity, and the king asked his advice as to how he might make provision for the poor. Ridley proposed a school for children of the poor, a hospital for the sick and a place of correction for vagabonds and harlots. By the end of Edward's life the first of these proposals had been implemented.

Upon the death of Edward VI on 6 July 1553, Ridley openly advocated the transfer of the crown to Lady Jane Grey rather than to the Catholic Mary Tudor. As a result he was soon imprisoned in the Tower of London. Because of overcrowding in the prison after the defeat of Wyatt's rebellion in January 1554, Ridley, Cranmer, Latimer and John Bradford were put in the same quarters and had several weeks to review the Scriptures together in preparation for trial concerning their views on the Lord's Supper. Along with Cranmer and Latimer, Ridley was transferred to Bocardo prison in Oxford, there to await his trial and execution.

During his time in prison he was active in writing to persuade Protestants to hold firm to their convictions. Through various agents he was able to transport both writings and funds to Bradford, now in the King's Bench prison in London, as the burning of Reformers began in February 1555. Before Hooper's martyrdom Ridley wrote him a letter of reconciliation. The trials of Ridley and Latimer took place in Oxford in the autumn, and they were taken to their execution together on 16 October 1555. Cranmer witnessed their burning from his prison window.

As they were chained to the stake, the older Latimer said, 'Be of good comfort, Master Ridley, and play the man. We shall this day light such a candle by God's grace, in England, as I trust shall never be put out.'

Bibliography

D. M. Loades, *The Oxford Martyrs* (New York: Stein & Day, 1970); D. MacCulloch, *Thomas Cranmer: A Life* (New Haven: Yale University Press, 1996); J. G. Ridley, *Nicholas Ridley: A Biography* (London: Longmans, Green & Co., 1957).

W. S. BARKER

■ **RILEY, William Bell** (1861–1947), fundamentalist leader and minister, was born in Green County, Indiana. His childhood was spent working on his family's tobacco farm in Kentucky. As a youth Riley felt called to become a minister. He attended Hanover College, graduating in 1885 as the top debater in his class. He went on to Southern Baptist Seminary in Louisville, graduating in 1888, and then accepted a pastorate in Lafayette, Indiana. While there he married Lillian Howard; they eventually had six children, and remained married until her death in 1931. (Two years later he married Marie Acomb, Dean of Women at Northwestern Bible School.)

After a brief period in Bloomington, Illinois, in 1893 Riley accepted the pastorate of Chicago's Calvary Baptist Church. Overwhelmed by the city's great size, in 1897 the ambitious young minister moved on to the First Baptist Church of Minneapolis. Seeking to make First Baptist a soulwinning centre, Riley eliminated pew rents, added altar calls to Sunday morning services and held revival services on Sunday evenings and during the week. Although some dismayed members sought Riley's removal, his supporters thwarted their efforts, and the critics eventually departed. Under Riley, First Baptist enjoyed remarkable growth, from 585 members in 1897 to 3,550 members at his retirement in 1942.

In his sermons Riley emphasized two doctrines that would become the theological core of fundamentalism: biblical inerrancy and dispensational premillennialism. For Riley, the belief that the Bible was literally accurate, without error, led naturally to the complex eschatological system developed by John Nelson *Darby. An aggressive proponent of dispensationalism, by the early 1900s Riley was a regular speaker at prophecy conferences, while at the same time devoting four months a year to revival services across America. Soon Riley had a national reputation in conservative evangelical circles.

Riley laid the groundwork for his fundamentalist crusade with two books: *The Finality of the Higher Criticism* (1909) and *The Menace of Modernism* (1917). In the former he concentrated on the infiltration of modernism into Protestant churches and seminaries; in the latter he detailed how America's schools denigrated Christianity while promoting Darwinism. *Menace* came out during the First

World War, when many Americans feared for the survival of Western civilization. As the war continued, evangelicals, convinced that modernist theology contributed to 'German barbarism', became increasingly receptive to Riley's suggestion, first advanced in *Finality*, that conservatives should join in an anti-modernist alliance.

To that end, in May 1919 Riley transformed a prophecy conference in Philadelphia into the first meeting of the World's Christian Fundamentals Association (WCFA). Riley envisaged his WCFA (he was founder, president and dominant force) as the headquarters of a 'fundamentalist' crusade to remove modernism from Protestant denominations. But while the Philadelphia conference was followed by a series of rallies throughout the nation, it was soon clear that the WCFA would not fulfil Riley's dream. Not only did other conservative leaders object to obeying Riley's commands, but the WCFA had little more than moral support to offer disenchanted conservatives in mainstream churches.

By 1921 Riley had shifted the organization's focus from removing modernism from denominations to removing evolution from state schools. Riley and his fellow fundamentalists were convinced not only that Darwinism contradicted Christian orthodoxy, but also that with its emphasis on 'survival of the fittest' it threatened to destroy America's moral foundations. Responding to this dire threat, Riley engaged in at least twenty-five 'debates' against evolutionists, using populist rhetoric, ridicule and humour to embarrass and confound his opponents in front of rowdy audiences often packed with fundamentalists. Riley's WCFA also orchestrated campaigns throughout the United States to ban the teaching of evolution; it succeeded in a number of southern states, including Tennessee, where Riley prevailed upon William Jennings *Bryan to defend the WCFA-supported anti-evolution statute in the Scopes Trial (1925). Riley also campaigned to make the teaching of evolution illegal in his home state of Minnesota; the result was a humiliating defeat in 1927, which was followed two years later by Riley's resignation as WCFA leader.

Riley's work as fundamentalist crusader, however, extended beyond the WCFA. In his own denomination, the Northern Baptist Convention (NBC), Riley was a leader in the campaign to eliminate modernism. In 1920 he helped to organize the Fundamentalist Fellowship, which demanded that the NBC scrutinize its schools for modernism; when this scrutiny resulted in a report commending Baptist schools for their orthodoxy, Riley called on the denomination to adopt the New Hampshire Confession as its official creed. Soundly defeated, an angry Riley led militant conservatives into the newly created Baptist Bible Union, which tried to push through anti-modernist measures at the 1924, 1925 and 1926 denominational conventions. These efforts failed badly, with many conservatives voting against the militants. Although Riley stayed in the denomination, many Baptist fundamentalists abandoned it.

Riley's fundamentalist crusade was moribund by the late 1920s. Then came the Great Depression and the New Deal. In response to these personal and national disasters (Riley despised the Roosevelt administration), the bitter fundamentalist patriarch focused his animus on an ancient scapegoat, the Jews. Throughout the 1930s Riley aggressively promoted the notion of an international Jewish conspiracy seeking world domination: having captured power in the Soviet Union, 'Jewish-Bolshevik' operatives were also succeeding in the United States, as evinced by the spread of Darwinism and the collectivist schemes of the New Deal. Riley lauded Adolf Hitler for 'heroically' resisting the Jewish conspiracy; he did not abandon this praise until faced with possible federal prosecution during the Second World War.

Riley did more in the 1930s and 1940s, however, than propagate anti-Semitism. Besides pastoring the largest Baptist church in Minnesota, he also presided over Northwestern Bible School of Minneapolis. Founded by Riley in 1902 with seven students and one First Baptist classroom, by 1946 Northwestern had expanded to include a theological seminary and a liberal arts college, with 700 full-time students, and another 1,000 students taking evening classes.

Like all his enterprises, Northwestern was dominated by Riley. His goal was an institution that would indoctrinate men (and some women) in fundamentalist theology while training them for positions in full-time religious work. The results were remarkable; by 1940 nearly 500 Northwestern graduates were serving as ministers and missionaries across the globe. Over 220 held pastorates in the upper Midwest, where Riley and his school served as the hub of a regional fundamentalist empire. The school provided churches with a variety of resources, including Sunday school materials, *The Northwestern Pilot*, a nationally circulated periodical edited by Riley, and visiting evangelists and Vacation Bible School workers. Most importantly, Northwestern provided ministers; Riley not only handpicked individuals for particular churches, but he would also regularly visit 'his boys', making sure that they were continuing to adhere to fundamentalist theology.

Riley's influence was greatest in Minnesota. By 1930 over one-third of Baptist ministers in Minnesota were Northwestern graduates. Prompted by Riley, in 1936 these fundamentalist ministers engineered a takeover of the Minnesota Baptist Convention. Riley immediately became the organization's dominant figure. President in the mid-1940s, he pushed member churches to withhold funds from the parent body, the Northern Baptist Convention, which Riley still viewed as dominated by modernists. In October 1947 Riley finally withdrew from the denomination. He died two months later; shortly thereafter the Minnesota Baptist Convention followed its hero and pulled out of the Northern Baptist Convention.

William Bell Riley was the first great leader of American fundamentalism. When his national crusade foundered, Riley turned to the Midwest, where he created the prototype of contemporary personality-based fundamentalist organizations.

Bibliography

M. A. Riley, *The Dynamic of a Dream: The Life Story of Dr. William B. Riley* (Grand Rapids: Eerdmans, 1938); C. A. Russell, 'William Bell Riley: Organizational Fundamentalist', in C. A. Russell (ed.), *Voices of American Fundamentalism: Seven Biographical Studies* (Philadelphia: Westminster Press, 1976); W. V. Trollinger, Jr, *God's Empire: William Bell Riley and Midwestern Fundamentalism* (Madison: University of Wisconsin Press, 1990).

W. V. TROLLINGER, JR

■ **RIPPON, John** (1751–1836), Baptist minister and hymnodist, was born on 29 April 1751 at Tiverton, Devon, the first of four children born to John Rippon, a serge maker and lay Baptist minister, and his wife Jane Hopkins. Born into a devout Baptist family, Rippon was converted and then baptized on 25 September 1767. Sensing a call to the Baptist ministry, Rippon entered the Bristol Baptist Academy in 1769. Here Hugh and Caleb Evans, tutors at the college, confirmed in Rippon the moderate evangelical form of Calvinism that shaped his life and ministry.

Despite his youth and theological views, after a trial period of more than a year, Rippon was called in 1773 to be pastor of the prestigious Carter Lane Baptist Church, Southwark, where his predecessor was the high Calvinist theologian John *Gill. Both Gill and Rippon remained pastors until they died, so that between them they served this church for 117 years. Rippon's enthusiastic advocacy of the moderate Calvinism that transformed the Particular Baptists during his lifetime helped him to become the leading Baptist minister in London and his church the largest and most influential of Baptist churches. Rippon was a colloquial, even eccentric, preacher in style, with 'a manly voice', and he made direct appeals to his hearers to receive the gospel. Over a thousand people joined his church during his pastorate.

Many wealthy Baptist lay leaders were members of this congregation: men such as the merchant William Burls, who was treasurer for many denominational funds, including that of the Baptist Missionary Society, and the miniature portrait painter Robert Bowyer. Members of Carter Lane were involved in numerous Dissenting and evangelical enterprises. No fewer than nineteen men from Carter Lane were recognized as Baptist preachers during Rippon's time, notably Joseph Swain and William Henry Angas. There were also many poor and needy people in the congregation, prompting Rippon to establish almshouses in 1803. In his old age the church declined in numbers and influence; the process was accelerated by the need to relocate the chapel to New Park Street in 1833 because of the building of the new London bridge, but more by Rippon's refusal to retire from the church, even when he was unable to officiate.

One key factor in Rippon's influence among Baptists was the *Baptist Annual Register*, which he edited from 1790 to 1802. The *Register* both reflected and stimulated the new evangelical life in Particular Baptist churches in both England and America, although Rippon's interest was wider than the Baptists. Rippon was a strong supporter of the Americans in the War of Independence and retained a lifelong fascination with the United States. He publicized the work of William *Carey and the Baptist Missionary Society, promoted itinerant village evangelism in which he was a regular participant, compiled lists of churches and statistics, preserved significant historical material and generally helped to give a sense of identity and mission to the Baptist churches of England. His extensive personal correspondence with Baptists in England, America and Europe, and with pioneer missionaries in India, was a mammoth task. He was rewarded with a DD from The Baptist College (now Brown University) in Providence, Rhode Island in 1792.

Rippon's influence was even more widely expressed through his hymnody. He published the first Baptist hymn-book to gain universal acceptance in England. His *Selection of Hymns* was first published in 1787 and was revised with twenty-seven editions in his lifetime; the forty-fourth edition, called the 'Comprehensive Rippon', appeared in 1844. For a generation Baptists in both Britain and America sang from Rippon's collection. Designed to complement the hymn collections of Isaac *Watts (an arrangement of whose hymns and songs he published in 1801), Rippon's collection drew widely on the outpouring of hymns that the revival movement stimulated. About 150 of the hymns had not been previously published, and new verses by contemporary Baptist writers such as Samuel Stennett (thirty-eight hymns) and Benjamin Beddome (forty-two) were included. About a third of the hymns in the first edition are known to have been by Baptists. Rippon drew heavily from other traditions. The most utilized author was Philip *Doddridge (105 hymns), and Rippon introduced twenty-four of Charles *Wesley's hymns to Baptists. His main concern was that the hymns selected were 'truly evangelical'. Rippon noted that in his collection 'Churchmen and Dissenters, Watts and Tate, Wesley

and Toplady, England and America, sing side by side'.

Rippon occasionally altered the theology of hymns, but generally his editing was designed to improve their literary worth. His arrangement of the collection reflected the homiletical bias of Dissenting worship. Rippon wrote several hymns himself, although he is best remembered for his extensive alterations to Edward Perronet's hymn, 'All hail the power of Jesu's name!'

The influence of Rippon's hymnody was profound, not only as an aid to the quality of Baptist worship, but also because, like any good hymn-book, his collection helped to shape the theology and devotional practice of a generation. Rippon also produced a companion *Tune Book* in 1791, which pioneered among Baptists the linking of hymns with particular tunes. This production codified the best tunes being used in Dissenting churches at the time and added a number of new ones.

Rippon styled himself 'the willing servant of all the churches'. This service was expressed in his leadership of numerous denominational committees and organizations, such as the Baptist Board (a London meeting of ministers), the Baptist Fund (which helped to finance smaller churches), mission societies and a range of Dissenting societies, such as the General Body of the Three Denominations (Presbyterians, Congregationalists and Baptists), which advocated full civil liberty for Dissenters. Rippon was a leading figure in the formation of the Baptist Union in England in 1812 and did more than any other person to promote a sense of denominational identity and unity among Particular Baptists.

Rippon had a deep interest in the history of Dissenters. He collected manuscripts from churches, and various supplements to the *Register* were published, including a history of Welsh Baptists by Joshua Thomas, an account of the origins of the Scotch Baptists, various local church histories from both Britain and America, and biographical details of evangelicals such as John *Wesley, George *Whitefield and Lady *Huntingdon.

Rippon personally wrote histories of Bristol Baptist Academy (1796) and the Society for Promoting Religious Knowledge among the Poor (1802), as well as memoirs for Andrew Gifford (1784), John Gill (c. 1809) and Abraham Booth (1806). He was fascinated with

Bunhill Fields, the important burial ground for many Puritans and Dissenters in London, collected details of all those buried between 1713 and 1790 (some 40,000), made copies of all the inscriptions and prepared a massive history of all the significant figures interred there. This was not published, although his manuscript volumes survive.

Rippon married Sarah Pyne on 7 December 1773 at St Olave's, Southwark, and they had four children. John Rippon died in London on 17 December 1836 and was buried in Bunhill Fields.

Bibliography
K. R. Manley, *'Redeeming Love Proclaim': John Rippon and the Baptists* (Carlisle: Paternoster, f.c.).

K. R. MANLEY

■ **ROBERTS, Evan** (1878–1951), Welsh revivalist, was born on 8 June 1878 in Island House, Loughor, Glamorgan, the son of Henry and Hannah Roberts. His parents were faithful members of the Moriah Calvinistic Methodist church, and Evan's upbringing was typical of Welsh Victorian Nonconformity; sincere piety was combined with an appreciation for poetry, song and the culture of the eisteddfod (a gathering for competitions in music, poetry, drama etc.). He began working as a coalminer at an early age, moving eastwards to Nantgarw and then to Mountain Ash in the Cynon Valley, before returning to Pontarddulais in west Wales in 1902 to begin an apprenticeship as a blacksmith. No sooner had he begun learning his new craft than he began preaching and was promptly drawn towards ministry in the Calvinistic Methodist Connexion. Having been commended by his presbytery, he began studies at the denomination's preparatory school at Newcastle Emlyn, Carmarthenshire, early in 1904. He was, however, afflicted by a dilemma: whether to proceed with his studies or simply to begin the work of saving souls to which he increasingly felt that he had been called.

Roberts had been pious even as a child, and following his reception into church membership at the age of thirteen he had thrown much of his energy into Sunday school work and other aspects of chapel life. His devotion deepened with the years, and while at Newcastle Emlyn he displayed a prayer life of unusual intensity. He regularly experienced feelings of rapture and claimed to have received over twenty ecstatic visions during the earlier part of 1904, which left him elated but strangely perplexed. These culminated in a momentous experience at Blaenannerch, Cardiganshire, on 29 September in which he believed himself to have broken by the Spirit in order to be used mightily by God in the salvation of souls throughout Wales.

There were already signs in other parts of the country that spirituality was being quickened and that a powerful revival had already begun. The local Calvinistic Methodists, first at New Quay and then at Blaenannerch, had experienced a dramatic renewal since the beginning of the year, and it was as part of this movement that Roberts felt the Spirit bidding him to forgo his training in order to begin a public ministry of evangelism and exhortation. A month later, in the course of a sermon by the Methodist patriarch Evan Phillips at Newcastle Emlyn, he was given an assurance of his call, and the next day, 31 October, he returned to his home church of Moriah, Loughor, to begin the work of renewal among the congregation's youth.

The four conditions of blessing that Roberts claimed the Spirit had revealed, namely, separation from all known sin, renunciation of all things that were morally dubious, immediate obedience to the promptings of the Holy Spirit and public confession of Christ, became the basis for his mission, and by the end of the week dramatic scenes of quite exceptional emotional power were drawing unprecedented congregations. According to the *Western Mail* 'Evan Roberts ... has been causing great surprise by his extraordinary orations at Moriah Chapel, that place of worship having been besieged by dense crowds of people unable to obtain admission. Such excitement has prevailed that the road in which the chapel is situated has been lined with people from end to end ...' (10 November 1904). It was the press's coverage of what was potentially an explosive story that turned Roberts from an obscure and inexperienced student preacher into the perceived leader of the rapidly developing 'Welsh' revival.

Invitations soon came for him to lead missions throughout Wales. His first mission journey, lasting from 13 November to

24 December, took him to the mining valleys of east Glamorgan. His verve, youthfulness, attractive personality and patent sincerity were effective means of popularizing the revival cause, while the contribution made by his brother Dan, his fellow student Sidney Evans, the soloist Sam Jenkins and more strikingly (and controversially) his band of female assistants, masked incipient theological problems. A second journey between 28 December 1904 and 3 February 1905 took him to the Swansea, Neath and Merthyr valleys, but by this time opposition to both his message and his methods was intensifying. It was voiced most pointedly by Peter Price, a Congregational minister at Dowlais, who stated that Roberts's emphasis on direct and unmediated divine inspiration denied the need for the objective preaching of the person and work of Christ and so created 'a sham revival', which was hindering 'the true revival' that had long preceded Roberts' work. The malicious and personal tone of Price's criticisms served only to garner Roberts even more popularity and support and undermined his critique. Yet there were those who, while not endorsing his invective, would later agree with the substance of his claim. A third journey between 8 and 21 February to the Ogwr, Llynfi and Afan valleys in mid-Glamorgan was cut short by the revivalist's decision while at Neath to spend a week in seclusion refusing any contact with the outside world. This 'silent week', which attracted huge popular speculation, added to the mystique that was now being attached to Evan Roberts, especially since he was seen to have been afflicted by paroxysms and extreme agonies of soul during his most recent public meetings and was tending more and more towards subjectivism in his public statements.

Following a short break, Roberts left for Liverpool on 28 March to lead his next mission, which had been organized by the city's Welsh churches. It was here that the near clairvoyant tendency that had already become such a marked feature of his ministry was given full rein. He would claim regularly during the next fortnight that he knew by divine intuition of particular individuals' specific sins and of their need to repent openly in order for his meetings to continue. These claims caused some consternation, though there was ample evidence of scores of people professing conversion or renewed consecration. The physical manifestations of Roberts' deepening agonies of spirit caused his hosts to become seriously worried about his psychological health, and following medical advice he took a month's rest at Capel Curig in the heart of Snowdonia in order to recuperate and plan ahead. A fifth journey, to Anglesey, Caernarfon and Bala in north Wales, began on 6 June and lasted until 3 July, during which time the revivalist, now fully recovered from his mental stress and much more balanced in his message and delivery, addressed over thirty meetings, which attracted some 20,000 listeners, of whom many were deeply impressed by his ministry. By the summer of 1905 Roberts had become more wary of overt emotionalism and no longer spoke of the four 'conditions' of revival; in fact his theological emphasis was moving from the subjective workings of the Holy Spirit to the objective content of the atoning work of Christ. Two further missionary tours at the end of the year, the first to the valleys of Glamorgan between 15 November and 2 December and the other in north Wales before Christmas, suggested that the extreme excitement of the earlier period was abating and that the renewal was moving into a more prosaic phase. Roberts' next missionary journey, in Caernarfonshire between 4 and 18 January 1906, would be his last; by this time the revival itself was coming to an end.

Apart from occasional appearances in religious gatherings, by 1909 Roberts had departed from the public sphere in order to undertake a ministry of intercession under the patronage of Mrs Jessie Penn-Lewis, a wealthy Christian laywoman from Leicester. Their joint volume *War on the Saints* (1912) is an indictment of the revival and indicates the extent of Roberts' disenchantment with many of the phenomena that had occurred at the time. After a decade and a half in Leicester, the former revivalist returned to Wales and lived in obscurity in a Cardiff suburb until his death, aged seventy-three, on 29 January 1951.

Bibliography

B. P. Jones, *An Instrument of Revival: The Complete Life of Evan Roberts 1878–1951* (New Jersey: Bridge Publications, 1995); D. M. Phillips, *Evan Roberts, the Great*

Welsh Revivalist and his Work (London: Marshall Bros., 1906).

D. D. MORGAN

■ **ROBERTS, Granville Oral** (1918–), healing evangelist and television preacher, was a central figure in an extraordinary Pentecostal/charismatic revival that reshaped the demography of Protestantism in the second half of the twentieth century. In 1947 he launched an independent healing ministry that made him a worldwide celebrity within a decade, and in the 1950s and 1960s he pioneered new techniques in the use of television that once again greatly expanded his influence. Both through his television programmes and through Oral Roberts University, which opened in 1965, Roberts facilitated the spread of the Pentecostal understanding of the gifts of the Holy Spirit and divine healing into mainstream Protestant churches and the Roman Catholic Church.

Roberts was born in a log house on a farm in Pontotoc County, Oklahoma, the son of Ellis Melvin Roberts and Claudius Irwin. After several years of scratching a marginal living from his Oklahoma farm, in 1916 Ellis Roberts began preaching in the small and scattered Oklahoma congregations of the Pentecostal Holiness Church. The Pentecostal movement, with its emphasis on speaking in tongues as the initial evidence of the baptism of the Holy Spirit, was little more than a decade old when Ellis became a minister, and at the time the Pentecostal Holiness Church claimed just over 5,000 members. Ellis Roberts spent the remainder of his life pastoring small churches in the South. His son Oral received the Pentecostal 'baptism of the Holy Spirit' at a camp meeting in 1936 and was ordained to the ministry by the Pentecostal Holiness Church. The next year he joined his father as an itinerant evangelist.

A defining spiritual crisis in Roberts' early life occurred in July 1935, when he experienced what he believed was a miraculous healing from tuberculosis and stuttering during a tent meeting in Ada, Oklahoma. In later years Roberts recited the story of his healing hundreds of times; it became a part of the hagiography of the healing revival that swept America in the 1950s and 1960s. Always given to listening for the voice of God in subjective and intuitive ways, as his parents had been, Roberts believed that after his healing God had called him to take healing to his generation.

In 1938 Roberts married Evelyn Lutman Fahnestock, a bright and sensible young schoolteacher whose common sense provided stability for the Roberts family and good advice for her husband throughout their lives. The two had a strong marriage and no hint of moral scandal ever surfaced in the Oral Roberts organization. The couple had four children; their youngest son, Richard Lee, joined the Oral Roberts organization in 1968. In 1993 he succeeded his father as president of Oral Roberts University.

By 1947 Oral Roberts was the local pastor of the Pentecostal Holiness church in Enid, Oklahoma, one of the larger congregations in his small denomination. About a year earlier an enigmatic evangelist named William Branham had begun holding extraordinary healing revivals throughout the country, attracting thousands of Pentecostals from scores of independent denominations to his meetings. They were hungry for an outbreak of the miraculous. News of the revivals swept through the Pentecostal subculture in America and triggered a vast pan-Pentecostal revival. Sensing that something exceptional was afoot, Roberts boldly resigned his secure position as a local church pastor, moved to Tulsa and launched an independent itinerant ministry.

In the early 1950s the Roberts ministry prospered; he conducted healing campaigns all over the United States and in more than fifty other countries. Huge audiences crowded into his tents, which steadily grew in size, reaching a capacity of more than 12,500. By Pentecostal standards, Roberts' meetings were models of decorum, featuring long, Scripture-filled sermons followed by an altar call; conspicuously absent were public manifestations of the gifts of the Spirit. Each service ended with Roberts praying for the sick. During his healing services Roberts felt a 'manifestation of God's presence' in his 'right hand' that, according to contemporaries, gave him a 'commanding power over demons, over disease and over sin'. All through the 1950s thousands of people paraded across the platform at the front of his tent seeking his prayers and healing touch. In the 1960s crowds began to dwindle slightly and increasingly Roberts' campaigns were held in auditoriums, but still thousands flocked to hear him preach and see him minister to the sick. By the time he stopped holding campaigns in 1968, an estimated one million people had passed through his healing line and millions more had witnessed one of his healing revivals, heard his sermons, answered his altar calls or become financial 'partners for deliverance'.

In contrast to many of the less sophisticated evangelists who participated in the American healing revival, Roberts was an excellent organizer and businessman. As his ministry mushroomed, he built an efficient staff team in Tulsa to handle the growing volume of mail that brought in floods of contributions and prayer requests from his partners. Within five years, Roberts had pieced together a radio network of more than 500 stations. In 1947 he began publishing a monthly magazine, *Healing Waters* (which went through a series of name changes before becoming *Abundant Life* in 1956), to keep his partners informed about his crusades and to present them with financial challenges. At the peak of his career Roberts' mailing list contained well over a million names.

Like Billy *Graham, Oral Roberts grasped the enormous potential of television in the early 1950s. His early efforts to produce a studio programme were not very successful but, with the development of cameras capable of recording the services in his dimly lit tent, in 1955 he launched weekly broadcasts of his crusades. The programmes shocked many Americans, but they thrilled the Pentecostal subculture that supported Roberts' healing campaigns. For the first time millions of Americans were exposed to the miraculous claims of the healing evangelists and heard their upbeat message of hope and health, which Roberts captured in cryptic slogans that proved to be ideal for television consumption.

At first, Roberts found it difficult to persuade television stations to broadcast his programme; his work was ridiculed by the press as 'fake healing'. Roberts' success triggered efforts to pass federal legislation banning the sale of time for religious programmes, but those efforts failed. By the late 1950s Roberts had put together a large network of stations that blanketed the country and made him one of the most recognizable religious leaders in the world. Television's biggest risk for Roberts and other evangelists was its enormous costs, but from the beginning his partners gave generously to support his programmes.

The healing revival of the 1950s that spawned the Roberts ministry and scores of smaller ones was supported largely by Pentecostals. In the early 1950s Pentecostal denominations began withdrawing support from independent healing ministers, whose financial appeals and healing claims grew more and more extreme. Oral Roberts, however, was widely respected as the most responsible and theologically orthodox of all of the healing ministers who appeared after the Second World War, and he maintained a working relationship with most of the Pentecostal denominational leaders into the 1960s. At the same time, Roberts was a catalyst in taking the Pentecostal message outside the borders of the old Pentecostal denominations. In 1951 he helped in the founding of the Full Gospel Business Men's Fellowship International, and his crusades and television programmes did much to lay the foundation for the charismatic movement, which expanded rapidly at the end of the 1960s.

In 1965 Oral Roberts University opened in Tulsa, and Roberts assumed the position of president of the university. ORU became the most prestigious Pentecostal private educational institution in America; its futuristic campus in Tulsa was a showpiece for the Oral Roberts organization. At the end of the twentieth century Oral Roberts University boasted a student population of more than 5,000 and was one of the fastest growing and most respected private institutions in the southwest.

By the early 1960s Oral Roberts was keenly aware that the Pentecostal message of divine healing and the gifts of the Spirit had begun to receive a sympathetic hearing by many people in mainstream Protestant churches and in the Roman Catholic Church. Sensing the changing climate, in 1968 Roberts made a series of high-risk decisions that shocked many of his closest advisors. First, he stopped holding crusades and discontinued his television programme. Then he resigned his ordination in the Pentecostal Holiness Church to become a Methodist minister and a member of the prestigious Boston Avenue Methodist

Church in Tulsa. Roberts insisted that he had changed none of his convictions, but he believed that there was a new openness in the Methodist Church to the charismatic message.

Then, in 1969, Roberts returned to television in peak viewing time with a series of hour-long specials. Slickly produced by Hollywood producer Dick Ross, the programmes featured the talented World Action singers from Oral Roberts University and a stream of well-known show business personalities. The shows were stunning financial and broadcasting successes, attracting viewing audiences as large as 64 million. Roberts proved that well-produced religious programmes could compete with secular ones, launching the modern entertainment-based electronic church. By the time Roberts stopped producing his hour-long specials in 1979, their impact had been immense. A 1980 Gallup Poll revealed that 84% of the American public recognized the name of Oral Roberts.

By the mid-1970s Oral Roberts had done much to improve his public image and had escaped most of the stigma of being a tent 'faith healer'. But Roberts entered a new period of controversy when he announced in 1975 that Oral Roberts University would open seven new graduate colleges, including a school of medicine. His grandiose plan for a medical school that would combine 'prayer and medicine' expanded in 1977 when he announced the construction of the City of Faith, a huge complex including a thirty-storey, 777 bed hospital, a sixty-storey clinic and diagnostic centre, and a twenty-storey medical research centre. The immense expense of constructing the City of Faith (around $250 million), combined with the expense of operating a medical college, placed unbearable financial strains on the organization. The City of Faith never attracted the number of patients that Roberts had anticipated, and it met fierce resistance from the medical establishment in Tulsa. It closed in 1990.

During the years in which the City of Faith was being constructed, Roberts resorted to some of the most high-pressure fund-raising techniques ever employed by television evangelists, once again raising thunderous objections from critics. Coincidentally, Roberts' extreme appeals for funding came at the same time as a media frenzy was focusing on sexual and financial scandals involving evangelists Jim Bakker and Jimmy *Swaggart. Although no hint of financial or moral wrongdoing ever surfaced in Roberts' life or ministry, in the public mind Roberts' appeals to build the City of Faith were seen as a part of a pattern of irresponsibility in independent organizations.

Although not a theologian, Oral Roberts thought seriously about the basic tenets of his belief in miracles, healing and the gifts of the Holy Spirit. Perhaps more than any other single person, Roberts was responsible for adding to Pentecostal theology the 'prosperity message', in which it was asserted that God approved of success and money. Roberts claimed to have discovered this message in 3 John 2, and regarded it as one of the more poignant insights of his career; the idea contributed much to the attractiveness of his preaching to upwardly mobile people in the United States and around the world. In the final analysis Roberts' most significant contribution to the Pentecostal/charismatic movement was his ability to popularize the content of the theology. Roberts summarized his message in phrases repeated thousands of times on television, and in his writings, which sold in millions: 'Something good is going to happen to you'; 'God is a good God'; 'Expect a miracle'; 'He that is in you is greater than he that is in the world'.

Oral Roberts was a consummate subjective personality who believed that, when he was spiritually open, his feelings were nothing less than the voice of God. When he felt strongly that God was leading him, his determination to obey was virtually unshakeable, even if what he took to be God's instructions were fraught with difficulties and dangers. During his long career he made many critical decisions that left his imprint on healing revivalism, religious television, Pentecostal theology, Christian education and the spread of the charismatic movement around the world.

Bibliography

D. E. Harrell, Jr, *All Things Are Possible: The Healing and Charismatic Revivals in Modern America* (Bloomington: Indiana University Press, 1975); D. E. Harrell, Jr, *Oral Roberts: An American Life* (Bloomington: Indiana University Press, 1985); E. Roberts, *His*

Darling Wife, Evelyn (New York: Dell Publishing Co., 1976); O. Roberts, *Expect a Miracle: My Life and Ministry* (Nashville: Thomas Nelson, 1995); W. A. Robinson, *Oral: The Warm, Intimate, Unauthorized Portrait of a Man of God* (Los Angeles: Acton House, 1976).

D. E. HARRELL, JR

■ **ROBERTSON, Pat** (1930–), minister, television personality and businessman, and political activist, was born Marion Gordon Robertson on 22 March 1930, in Lexington, Virginia, in the heart of the Blue Ridge Mountains, the son of Absalom Willis Robertson and Josephine Ragland Willis. Robertson's father was an attorney, who held political office in Virginia from 1915 to 1966, broken only by his service during the First World War. During those years he served in the Senate of Virginia, the US House of Representatives and, beginning in 1946, in the United States Senate. In the Senate he established a record as a rigid conservative in fiscal policy. He was narrowly defeated in 1966 at the age of seventy-nine.

As the child of a senator, young Pat Robertson grew up surrounded by symbols of patriotism and privilege, often visiting his father in Washington, DC. At the age of nineteen he graduated *summa cum laude* from Washington and Lee University, a prestigious institution in his home town of Lexington. He earned a Phi Beta Kappa key and was rewarded by his father with a summer in London, where he studied the Fine Arts at the University of London. Robertson graduated from Washington and Lee with a commission in the Marine Corps, and from 1950 to 1952 he served as an officer in Japan and Korea.

After his discharge in 1952, he entered Yale University Law School. In 1954, while still a student, he married Adelia Elmer, a nursing student at Yale. After his graduation in 1955, Robertson went through a disappointing series of job changes and a failed business venture and settled into a period of introspection and religious experimentation.

At the instigation of his deeply religious mother, Robertson came into contact with some of the leaders of the growing evangelical movement in America, decided to become a minister, and in 1956 enrolled in The Biblical Seminary in New York City. During his three years at the seminary, Robertson searched restlessly for deeper religious experiences. His contacts with Pentecostal students at the seminary led him into a number of life-changing encounters with evangelical/Pentecostal pioneers, most notably the publisher Robert Walker and the Lutheran charismatic pioneer Harald Bredesen. Shepherded by Bredesen, Robertson and other students from the seminary began visiting small Pentecostal churches in New York City. In 1957 Robertson received the 'baptism of the Holy Spirit', speaking in what he believed was an 'African dialect' while praying for a fellow student. He, Bredesen and some of the other students at the seminary were part of a growing number of Christians from mainstream denominational backgrounds who embraced the Pentecostal experience in the 1960s and became pioneers in the charismatic movement.

Much to the consternation of his father, who believed that his son had a brilliant future ahead in business, Pat Robertson ministered in the slums of New York City before purchasing a run-down UHF television station in Portsmouth, Virginia, to which he gave the grandiose name 'the Christian Broadcasting Network' (CBN) in 1960. During the months in which he was trying to launch the television station, Robertson was ordained in the Southern Baptist Church and began working as minister of education at the Freemason Baptist Church in inner-city Norfolk. CBN broadcast its first programme in October 1961. During the 1960s Robertson explored many financial avenues in the effort to sustain his unsteady venture, before initiating a highly successful series of telethons; the first in 1963 solicited 700 contributors, who became members of a 'club' giving $10 per month to support the station. 'The 700 Club' subsequently became the name of a chat-show programme that was begun in 1966, hosted by Robertson, and that continues to the present as a news/magazine programme promoting Robertson's views; it is one of the longest running television programmes in the history of the industry. Robertson and his programme remained unashamedly charismatic, and by the end of the 1960s he was one of the foremost celebrities in the rapidly expanding Pentecostal/charismatic movement.

The expansion of CBN was an unbroken success story. In 1979 a new headquarters building was dedicated that housed two state-of-the-art television studios and other recording facilities valued at more than $20 million. A year earlier Robertson had unveiled plans to build a graduate university; the opening of Regents University (originally called CBN University) symbolized a new period of influence and expansion in the Robertson organization. Envisaged as a graduate centre for training conservative religious leaders in many areas, including law and business, Regents also trained a generation of charismatic young people in the latest media skills. At the end of the century, Regents, with Robertson as its chancellor, was the most prestigious educational institution associated with the Pentecostal/charismatic movement.

In 1977 Robertson began a rapid expansion of his cable network, becoming one of the pioneers of satellite transmission. By the end of the 1970s CBN was financially self-sufficient, and in 1981 Robertson made a decision to abandon exclusively religious broadcasting in favour of programmes on a variety of subjects. In 1988 the network took the name 'The Family Channel' and became one of the nation's leading cable systems. In 1990, partly because the financial profitability of the Family Channel threatened the tax-exempt status of Robertson's organization, the network was separated and sold to International Family Entertainment Inc., a group of private investors. In 1997 IFE was sold to Fox Kids Worldwide, Inc. As a result of these financial deals, Regents University received more than $200 million in endowment.

Another affiliated organization, Operation Blessing International Relief and Development Corporation, was founded by Robertson in 1978 to distribute aid to underprivileged people in the United States and abroad.

Pat Robertson had always been interested in politics, and during the 1980s, as evangelicals became more and more involved politically, 'The 700 Club' increased its political comment. Robertson became a key figure in the emergence of the so-called 'religious right' before and after Ronald Reagan's election in 1980. Robertson possessed two advantages that separated him from other leaders of the 'religious right'. In the first place, his religious base was enormous because of his television exposure and because he was in touch with the millions of Americans who had embraced the Pentecostal/charismatic revival, not simply with a narrow denominational or fundamentalist constituency. In the second place, by background and by training Robertson brought to the political scene a depth of political knowledge and skill unprecedented among religious leaders.

In 1986 Robertson began exploring the possibility of running for the presidency, and in 1988 he entered the Republican primaries, surprising many by winning the Iowa caucuses. After losing in the South Carolina primary, Robertson withdrew from the race, but he has remained an important influence in the development of conservative politics in America. He serves as president of the Christian Coalition of America, which has done much to encourage conservative Christians to become politically active and to train them in the tactics of local politics. In 2000 the Christian Coalition claimed more than a million supporters in 1,500 local chapters in all fifty states. In 1990 Robertson created the American Center for Law and Justice as a conservative balance to the American Civil Liberties Union in the filing of lawsuits.

Robertson is the author of ten books, several of them bestsellers. He resigned his ordination in 1988 during his run for the presidency, but he was reordained in 2000 and recommitted himself to his religious objectives. Robertson's CBN empire is presently housed on a 700 acre complex in Virginia Beach. The elegant Williamsburg-style buildings symbolize the success and patriotism of Pat Robertson and his ministry. CBN is at present a diverse organization. Its Operation Blessing International is one of the largest private relief organizations in the country. 'The 700 Club' is viewed by millions of Americans regularly and in around fifty countries abroad. The organization's annual budget is estimated at more than $200 million, and CBN employs around 1,000 people.

Bibliography

D. E. Harrell, Jr, *Pat Robertson: A Personal, Political and Religious Portrait* (San Francisco: Harper & Row, 1987); Pat Robertson with Jamie Buckingham, *Shout It From the*

Housetops (Plainfield: Logos International, 1972).

D. E. HARRELL, JR

■ **ROBINSON, Harry S. D.** (1927–), Canadian Anglican minister, was born the son of John R. Robinson, a wealthy and prominent Toronto lawyer, and Elizabeth Marion (née Boultbee). His grandfather was 'Black Jack' Robinson, the editor of the *Toronto Telegram* for some thirty-five years. Robinson's mother was a devout Anglican; his Presbyterian father attended an Anglican church with his wife but never took communion, reflecting his Calvinist upbringing, which had convinced him that he was not among the elect.

After completing his secondary schooling at the University of Toronto School, Robinson became involved in the early camp ministry associated with the fledgling Inter-Varsity Christian Fellowship (IVCF) movement in Canada. At the age of twenty-two he began his university education, reading for a BA in English and history at the University of Toronto. While an undergraduate, he lived in Wycliffe College, an evangelical Anglican seminary affiliated to the University of Toronto, and was deeply involved with IVCF in the student work on campus.

Upon his graduation in 1952, he studied in England for a year at Oak Hill Theological College, an Anglican seminary north of London. His lecturers included Derek Kidner, the renowned Old Testament scholar, and Alan Stibbs; fellow students included Michael Baughen, later Bishop of Chester. During this time he met and befriended lifelong associates: John R. W. *Stott, then the remarkably young rector of All Souls', Langham Place, in London; James I. *Packer, then a budding Anglican theologian; and Dick Lucas, later rector for many years of St Helen's, Bishopsgate, in London. In this way, Robinson became part of a growing international fellowship of Anglican evangelical ministers who in the second half of the twentieth century did much to revive the fortunes of the evangelical grouping within the global Anglican communion.

In 1953 Robinson returned to Toronto and enrolled for his second year of theological studies at Wycliffe College, graduating in 1955. In the same year he married Frances Adams, a nurse, who later trained in and practised family counselling. Together they had three daughters and one son.

Robinson was ordained in 1955 and did a curacy in Kingston, Ontario before becoming rector of the Church of the Redeemer in north Kingston. Here he was mentored by Canon (later Bishop) Desmond Hunt, then the widely respected rector of St James, Kingston, a parish known for its student ministry. In 1963 Robinson moved to Toronto to become rector of 'Trinity East', better known as 'Little Trinity', a slum parish near inner-city Toronto with a long history of staunch 'low churchmanship' and proud of its 'hot Protestant' credentials. Under his leadership Little Trinity grew and developed a ministry to students, particularly those at the University of Toronto. Robinson also became well known as a conference speaker and university missioner, working closely with IVCF.

In 1978, in a surprising turn of events, Robinson was offered the rectorship of St John's Anglican Church in the Shaughnessy area of Vancouver. The church was located in one of Vancouver's wealthiest areas and had a history as a centre of high churchmanship in British Columbia. In spite of its reputation, St John's was in serious decline and financial difficulty, and its lay leaders were hopeful that Robinson could effect positive change. Aid for the task came in 1979 when his old friend James Packer arrived in Vancouver to become professor of theology at Regent College (an evangelical graduate school) as well as Robinson's honorary assistant at the church. When Robinson retired in 1992, St John's was arguably attracting the largest number of Sunday attenders of any Anglican church in Canada.

Robinson's success in parish ministry must undoubtedly be attributed to his genius as a preacher. While committed as a conservative evangelical to the consecutive exposition of Scripture as the best way to build people up in the Christian faith, his highly original approach to the task reflected an innate creativity and an ability to use insightful narrative to disarm his listeners. Widely read and deeply culturally aware, his preaching combined piercing irony with deep spiritual insight and genuine humility.

In 1995 he was awarded an honorary doctorate by Wycliffe College, Toronto. In his retirement he gave himself to an itinerant ministry, and from 1996 served as the first chaplain to the fledgling Anglican Studies Program at Regent College. Although neither recognized nor honoured by a largely hostile church bureaucracy, Robinson will undoubtedly be remembered as one of Canada's most influential Anglicans of the second half of the twentieth century. His younger brother, Tom, became a well-known evangelical Anglican minister in Atlantic Canada, founding Barnabas Anglican Ministries and playing a key role in the establishment of the Anglican Essentials movement in Canada in the early 1990s.

D. M. LEWIS

■ **ROBINSON, John** (?1576–1625), English Separatist, was a leader of the movement during the first quarter of the seventeenth century and a major intellectual and ecclesiastical influence upon the Pilgrim Fathers in America.

Obscurity surrounds Robinson's early life. He was born c. 1576 in the parish of Sturton-le-Steeple in Nottinghamshire, where it appears that his family were socially well placed and had close links to the local clergy. He matriculated at Corpus Christi College, Cambridge on 9 April 1592. He received a BA in 1596, became a fellow in 1597 on the grounds of his outstanding academic abilities and took his MA in 1599. During his time at Cambridge, Robinson came under the influence of the powerful preacher and Reformed theologian William *Perkins and was associated with a group of other young men in the Perkins circle who were to become significant Christian leaders, including William *Ames and John *Smyth. Issues such as conformity, the nature of the church and its government, and the adequacy or otherwise of the Prayer Book settlement were being hotly disputed at this time, and the debates must have had a profound effect upon Robinson.

In the early years of the seventeenth century, Robinson seems to have been a minister in Norfolk. Then, in 1607 he joined a gathered church at Scrooby Manor in Nottinghamshire. His decision to embrace separatism was the result of his links (from 1605) with non-conforming groups and of the increasingly evident unwillingness of James I to lend support to those desiring further reformation within the church. Robinson's separatism was tempered somewhat by pragmatism; he continued to preach in conforming churches for a year, partly in order to win over more converts to the separatist cause.

In 1608 the Archbishop of York instituted a campaign to crush separatism within his archdiocese and, in the resulting debacle, Robinson moved to Amsterdam, where he joined the separatist church led by Francis Johnson. The church, however, was passing through a series of controversies and so, on 2 February 1609, Robinson and a number of others were granted permission by the authorities at Leiden to move there, which they did at some point before May of the same year. Many of Robinson's congregation were clothweavers, and the cloth trade at Leiden offered opportunities for alleviating their abject poverty.

Although Robinson's soteriology remained firmly Reformed, his separatist ecclesiology served to divide him from the Puritan mainstream who remained within the Church of England, albeit often unhappily. Robinson engaged in controversy some time before 1612 with Ames, his old Cambridge companion, and now living in The Hague, over terms of communion. Then, at a later date, he clashed with John Smyth, another former Cambridge colleague, who had adopted the same separatist views as Robinson regarding the church but had combined these with a commitment to believer's baptism and an increasingly Arminian understanding of grace.

Robinson matriculated in theology at the University of Leiden in 1615, in order to continue his theological studies serving as pastor of his church. From 1617, however, he started to make preparations to move his congregation to America in order to provide them with a better environment. In 1620 financial backing for the journey was finally obtained, and Robinson committed himself to going if a majority of his church members agreed to the move. In the event, only a minority did and Robinson was reluctantly obliged to stay. It is, however, generally considered that his greatest moment as a Christian leader was that of his sermon on Ezra 8:21 that he is supposed to have delivered to the pilgrims on 21 July 1621, the day before they departed from Delft to

Southampton, whence they continued their journey on *The Mayflower*.

Although Robinson was never to join his congregation in America, he nevertheless remained a dominant force in the establishment of the pilgrims' church through the correspondence that he maintained with the leaders in the colony. He died of the plague on 1 March 1625 and was buried in Leiden.

Most of Robinson's works were controversial. His *magnum opus* was a collection of miscellaneous essays and aphorisms, *Observations Divine and Morall*, which was completed shortly before his death and published at Leiden in 1625. As a theologian, he was one of the first English Reformed Separatists and thus stands at the inception of a tradition which was to be continued by John *Cotton and was to bear fruit in the English Independents of the 1640s and 1650s, decisively shaping the nature of later English Puritanism and early English non-conformity.

Bibliography

W. H. Burgess, *John Robinson* (London: Williams & Norgate, 1920); O. S. Davis, *John Robinson, the Pilgrim Pastor* (Boston: The Pilgrim Press, 1903); T. George, *John Robinson and the English Separatist Tradition* (Macon: Mercer University Press, 1982).
C. R. TRUEMAN

■ **ROOKMAAKER, Henderik Roelof** (1922–1977), Dutch art historian, greatly influenced international evangelical thinking on the arts in the mid- and later twentieth century. Dr H. R. (Hans) Rookmaaker held academic posts at Leiden University and then the Free University of Amsterdam, where he was appointed Professor of Art History in 1964, but it was mainly through his lectures and writings outside Holland that he gained wide recognition as a Christian authority on the arts. At a strategic time in the mid-1960s, when evangelical opinion was still shaped by a legacy of suspicion about involvement in the arts, Rookmaaker began to lecture regularly in Britain and North America and became a guide, counsellor and friend to many art students, artists and scholars in evangelical circles. He offered a sharp critique of the secularizing impulse that had shaped modernist art, but at the same time he encouraged

evangelicals to participate in the contemporary art world and to value artistic work as important in its own right. Rookmaaker taught that art did not have to deal with overtly religious themes in order to justify its place in Christian life; art that was well crafted and that represented reality in truth and sincerity was already doing what God ordained for it. With the publication of his *Modern Art and the Death of a Culture* in 1970, the impact of Rookmaaker's thinking was extended well beyond those who heard him lecture. After numerous reprints and translations into various European and Asiatic languages, this pioneering book has become known to evangelicals worldwide.

Rookmaaker's ability to help evangelicals to shrug off their burden of doubt about the value of art was due in part to his coming as an outsider into evangelical life and not being formed by its traditions or daunted by its preconceptions. There was in fact little religion and no church affiliation in Rookmaaker's upbringing. He was born in The Hague in 1922 into a family of colonial administrators in the former Dutch East Indies (now the Republic of Indonesia) and spent his childhood alternately in the tropics and at school in The Hague. Since the colonial regime was clearly ending and would hold no future for him, he began training as an officer in the Dutch navy on the eve of the outbreak of war. In May 1940 the Netherlands capitulated to the Nazis, and as a member of the Dutch armed forces the young Rookmaaker spent much of the war interned in prison camps. In prison he was initially given little to read but the Bible, but this he studied thoroughly and as a result became convinced of its truth and accepted Christ as his Saviour. His first steps as a convert were guided by an older officer, Captain (later Professor) J. P. A. Mekkes, who also introduced him to the tradition of Dutch Reformed thought and in particular to the contemporary neo-Calvinist philosophical work of Herman *Dooyeweerd. The neo-Calvinist conviction that all aspects of life or reality have their own allotted place in creation and in the redeeming purpose of God became (and remained) the leitmotif of Rookmaaker's thinking. Rookmaaker found his own niche in neo-Calvinist philosophy by focusing on an aspect of life that other Dutch thinkers had scarcely studied: aesthetics and the arts. When the liberation of his country came in 1945, he resolved to pursue a new career as a Christian in the academic study of art.

Rookmaaker began studies in the history of art at the University of Amsterdam in 1946, taking a BA-equivalent examination in 1949, an MA-equivalent in 1953, and finally completing and publishing his doctoral thesis *Synthetist Art Theories* in 1959. Rookmaaker married Anky Huitker in 1949, and until he became a university lecturer at Leiden in 1957 they supported a young family on his earnings from part-time teaching and from art criticism that he wrote from 1949 to 1956 for the daily newspaper *Trouw*, which served a generally Dutch Reformed readership. His regular art reviews complemented his academic research and developed his capacity to write for a non-academic audience. Moreover, Rookmaaker, a jazz enthusiast since his teens, grew to be a recognized authority on African-American music; he published a Dutch book entitled *jazz blues spirituals* (1960) and edited and annotated the series of 'Classic Jazz Masters' reissues for Riverside Records. His knowledge of music as well as of art was much in evidence when he later came to lecture and write for an international evangelical audience.

Rookmaaker's links with the evangelical world were forged in 1948 when he began a close friendship with the American minister Francis *Schaeffer, who was to found the study centre L'Abri Fellowship in Switzerland. Rookmaaker stimulated Schaeffer's interest in art and in his turn was influenced by Schaeffer's evangelical approach to the life of faith. Though Rookmaaker remained a member of the Dutch (Free) Reformed Church and of the neo-Calvinist school of philosophy, his attitude to personal prayer, witness and outreach became more evangelical than Dutch Calvinist. Rookmaaker consciously sought to combine the strengths of these two Bible-believing traditions in his life and teaching. He encouraged Dutch Christians to be more outgoing in their faith, while on the international scene he pointed evangelicals to perspectives on art and culture that were Dutch Calvinist in origin. Rookmaaker's fusion of two traditions greatly benefited evangelical thought and practice in

the arts, though some evangelical scholars have criticized him for failing to develop a theology of the arts. On that point, however, Rookmaaker remained true to his neo-Calvinist tradition, in which a Christian understanding of fields such as art and art scholarship is formulated in philosophical rather than theological terms. None the less, Rookmaaker's writings were rich in direct references to the Bible. He tested the world-views of artists and cultural movements in the light of biblical norms and often drew on the prophets to challenge apostasy and warn against the dangers of a lukewarm church.

One channel through which Rookmaaker's teachings reached an international evangelical audience was L'Abri Fellowship, which in the 1960s and 1970s opened new study centres in countries such as the United States, Britain and (at Rookmaaker's instigation) the Netherlands. Another important channel was the work of the Inter-Varsity Fellowship (IVF, now UCCF) in Britain. By the mid-1960s, the IVF team of travelling secretaries appointed to guide Christian students included someone designated for work among students in the arts. Successive holders of this post learned to value Rookmaaker's warm friendship and guidance, and he quickly became established as the main visiting lecturer and conference speaker in this branch of IVF work. Fittingly, it was the Inter-Varsity Press that first published his influential book *Modern Art and the Death of a Culture* in 1970.

Many evangelicals who went on to make substantial careers in the arts in the later twentieth century owed much in their youth to the small, rotund, grey-suited and pipe-smoking Dutchman, who not only guided them authoritatively through the problems of modern art history but also belied his professorial appearance by analysing the popular music of their time and telling them to which obscure blues recordings the Rolling Stones had been listening. The shock was great when in 1977 Rookmaaker died suddenly, at home, of a heart attack; he had appeared to be well and was working on new projects. Appreciation of Rookmaaker's thought has scarcely diminished, however, and publication of a series of volumes in English covering his complete works began in 2002.

Bibliography
J. S. Begbie, *Voicing Creation's Praise: Towards a Theology of the Arts* (Edinburgh: T. & T. Clark, 1991); G. Birtwistle, 'H. R. Rookmaaker: The Shaping of his Thought', in *Art, Artists and Gauguin: The Complete Works of Hans R. Rookmaaker*, vol. 1 (Carlisle: Piquant, 2002), pp. xv–xxxiii.

G. BIRTWISTLE

■ **ROSEVEARE, Helen** (1925–), missionary to the Congo, was born in 1925 at Haileybury College, Hertfordshire, where her father was a mathematics teacher. As a teenager seeking for God, she initially turned to high Anglicanism. Later, while studying medicine at Newnham College, Cambridge, she encountered the Christian Union, and was converted at a house-party in the winter of 1945. As a new convert, she had a sense that God wanted her to go abroad, so after completing her medical studies she spent six months at the Worldwide Evangelization Crusade college at Crystal Palace. After being selected to go to the Congo, she spent a short period in Belgium learning French and studying tropical medicine, before leaving for Africa in February 1953, reaching the mission station of Iambi in mid-March.

Later Roseveare was to write that the following eleven years involved 'hard work and happiness, mingled with heart-breaks and disillusionments'. She quickly found that there was far more work at the station than she could easily handle, and within a few months she had started a nurses' training school, having become convinced that her main task was to train nurse-evangelists who could run dispensaries and clinics in different places.

In October 1955 she was asked to take over the abandoned maternity and leprosy centre seven miles away in Nebobongo. Much of the work had to be done from the beginning, and Roseveare and one other missionary, with their African helpers, had to learn the arts of brick-making and building. The centre became a 100-bed hospital with maternity services, a leprosy-care centre and children's home, forty-eight rural clinics and a training school for paramedics. Roseveare was working constantly, overseeing the whole mission, as well as carrying on with teaching and

medical work. Although she knew she was working too hard, she commented later how difficult it was, 'with no other medical help ... for 150 miles in any direction', to take time to rest. In 1958 she returned home for a year's much-needed furlough, also taking the opportunity to gain further medical experience before returning to Africa.

In 1960 the Congo gained its independence from Belgium. John Mangadima, a medical auxiliary and a good friend of Roseveare's, was then appointed director of the centre. In all her work Roseveare was eager to work with Africans as equals. A period of uncertainty followed independence, eventually leading in 1964 to civil war, which saw the destruction of all that she and her team had established. Ten Protestant missionaries, Roseveare among them, were seized by the rebels and endured five months' traumatic captivity. Initially this consisted of several weeks' house arrest, but after that time they were moved, imprisoned and ill-treated, suffering beatings and rape before eventually being rescued. Roseveare came to understand this experience as part of the privilege of sharing in the sufferings of Christ. In her first book, *Give Me This Mountain* (1966), she recounted some of the difficulties and joys of these years, explaining her view that the Christian life consists of times of joy and times of shadow, and how the latter can be a journey onwards towards the next mountain, rather than times of despair. Her second book, *He Gave Us a Valley* (1976), gives more detail about her captivity, and recounts her second period of missionary work.

This began with Roseveare's return to Africa in 1966, where after an initial period back at Nebobongo she spent most of the next seven years establishing a new medical centre in Nyankunde, northeastern Zaire. This became a 250-bed hospital with a maternity complex and leprosy-care centre, a training college for paramedics, regional centres and a 'flying doctor' service. Here, too, there was heartache and betrayal, as well as the accomplishment of much useful work.

After twenty years in the Congo, Roseveare finally returned home to the UK in 1973 for health reasons, settling in Northern Ireland. At the end of the twentieth century she was still travelling the world as a speaker, encouraging people to give their lives to mission, and inspiring them with the account of her own experience of the Christian life, both mountains and valleys.

Bibliography
A. Burgess, *Daylight Must Come: The Story of Dr Helen Roseveare* (London: Pan Books, 1977); H. Roseveare, *Give Me This Mountain* (London: IVP, 1966); H. Roseveare, *He Gave Us a Valley* (Leicester: IVP, 1976).

L. WILSON

■ **RUTHERFORD, Samuel** (c. 1600–1661), Scottish Reformed theologian, was born around 1600 in Nisbet, near Crailing in southeast Scotland. A key early influence upon him was the minister of Crailing, David Calderwood, a Presbyterian polemicist who was deprived of his charge in 1617 for protesting against royal ecclesiastical policies.

Rutherford entered the University of Edinburgh in 1617 and graduated in 1621. In 1623 he was appointed regent of humanity at the university, and he seems to have associated with the radical Presbyterian merchants John Mein and William Rigg, who led protests against the Five Articles of Perth and organized illegal conventicles. However, an entry in the burgh records of Edinburgh for 3 February 1626 declares that Rutherford had 'fallin in furnicatioun with Euphame Hamilton, and hes committit ane grit scandle in the college'. A child was born to Hamilton and Rutherford in April 1626, by which time they may well have married. But the scandal lost Rutherford his position as a regent. Chastened, he turned his thoughts towards parish ministry.

In 1627 he became the minister of Anwoth in Galloway. It was here that he gained a reputation as a tireless pastor and activist. 'He used ordinarily to rise by three a clock in the morning', wrote his fellow minister John Livingstone, and 'was the instrument of much good among a poor ignorant people, many of which he brought to the knowledge and practise of religion'. He established a network of connections with the gentry of southwest Scotland and orchestrated a Presbyterian campaign against royal ecclesiastical policy. He disseminated political information, intervened in burgh elections, wrote his own catechism, organized seasons of fasting and

prayer concerning the corruption of the church, wrote a Latin treatise against Arminianism and circulated manuscript treatises he had written to justify conventicles. His activities came to the attention of the authorities, and in 1636 he was deprived of his charge and placed under house arrest in the episcopalian stronghold of Aberdeen. Frustrated at his confinement, in 1636 and 1637 Rutherford released a torrent of letters to godly women, nobles, lairds, burgesses and ministers all over Scotland, many of which were copied and circulated among devout Presbyterians.

Following the signing of the National Covenant in February 1638, Rutherford returned to Anwoth and became a leading figure among the Covenanter clergy. In October 1639 he became professor of divinity at New College, St Andrews, where he set about overturning the episcopalian legacy. On the eve of the second Bishops' War in August 1640, he preached a series of crusading sermons to the Scottish army.

Between November 1643 and November 1647, Rutherford was in London as one of the Scottish commissioners to the Westminster Assembly. In these four years he participated fully in the Assembly's debates over church government and published a number of major works, including *Lex, Rex: or the Law and the Prince* (1644), an erudite and sometimes bitter defence of armed resistance to Charles I. Rutherford's main responsibility in London was to advance the Presbyterian cause. He began with great hopes of building 'the waste places of Zion in another kingdom', but was soon disillusioned by the state of English Puritanism and complained of 'Multitudes of Anabaptists, Antinomians, Familists, Separatists'. Within the Assembly, Erastians and Independents led a spirited campaign against the Scottish model of divine right Presbyterianism. Rutherford had already offered a critique of New England Congregationalism in *A Peaceable Plea for Paul's Presbytery* (1642), but he now followed this up with major works against Independency and Erastianism, *The Due Right of Presbyteries* (1644) and *The Divine Right of Church Government and Excommunication* (1646). His calls for the suppression of dissent earned him a place in *Milton's sonnet 'On the New Forcers of Conscience under the Long Parliament'. In

A Free Disputation against Pretended Liberty of Conscience (1649), Rutherford condemned radical Puritan tolerationists and reasserted the traditional Protestant doctrine of religious coercion. The book has been described by Owen Chadwick as 'the ablest defence of religious persecution written in the seventeenth century'.

By the time he prepared to return to Scotland in November 1647, Rutherford was deeply pessimistic about the English situation. Although he had witnessed the abolition of episcopacy and Parliament's adoption of a diluted system of Presbyterian church government, he was aware that the Independents were growing in strength. A month after his return to Scotland, the moderate Covenanters signed an Engagement with Charles I. Rutherford campaigned vigorously against this alliance. The defeat of the Engagers' army at Preston in August 1648 allowed the radical Presbyterians to establish a militant 'kirk party' regime. Rutherford was now at the height of his influence in Scotland. He was elected to professorships at Edinburgh University and at the new University of Harderwyck in the Netherlands, but chose to remain in St Andrews and assist the cause of reformation in Scotland.

After the execution of Charles I in January 1649, the Covenanters proclaimed Charles II king of Great Britain and Ireland. When Charles visited Scotland in July 1650, he was subjected to a lengthy speech from Rutherford 'running mutch upon what was the dewtie of kings'. As the Covenanters prepared to fight *Cromwell's army, Rutherford was convinced that victory for the cause was imminent. The defeat at Dunbar in September 1650 came as a shattering blow and split the Covenanters into two factions. The moderate Resolutioners wished to forge a new alliance with the Engagers, but Rutherford supported the hardline Remonstrants or Protestors, who insisted on further purging of church and state. Throughout the 1650s, the Remonstrant–Resolutioner dispute bitterly divided the Church of Scotland, and Rutherford became alienated from many former friends. He continued to preach and to publish major theological works such as *Disputatio Scholastica de Divina Providentia* (1649) and *The Covenant of Life Opened* (1655).

In September 1660, following the Restoration of Charles II, copies of *Lex, Rex* were publicly burned, and Rutherford was deprived of his position in the university and his charge in the church, and confined to his own house. He was cited to appear before Parliament on a charge of treason, and his friends feared that he might well face execution. However, early in 1661 Rutherford fell seriously ill. On 8 March he issued a last will and testimony, and near the end of the month, he died.

Rutherford's posthumous reputation rested on his *Letters*, which were first published in the Netherlands in 1664 and quickly became a classic of evangelical Protestant piety. They combined tough-minded reflection on affliction and divine judgment with mystical raptures extolling the ravishing beauty of Christ in the language of the Song of Songs. They were lavishly praised by Richard *Baxter and C. H. *Spurgeon, and have been republished no fewer than eighty times in various English editions, and at least fifteen times in Dutch. Their popularity serves as a reminder of how the affectionate and enthusiastic spirituality of the Puritans flowed into the new evangelicalism. Rutherford became known as 'the saint of the Covenant', and devout evangelicals even made pilgrimages to Anwoth. Collections of his sermons were also republished, including *The Trial and Triumph of Faith* (1645), *Communion Sermons* (1877) and *Quaint Sermons* (1885), but his controversial writings gathered dust and were largely forgotten. The exception was *Lex, Rex*, which was republished in the mid-nineteenth century and celebrated as a great defence of Whig liberties. In the early 1980s *Lex, Rex* was championed by Francis *Schaeffer in *A Christian Manifesto* (1981), which used Rutherford to legitimize civil disobedience over abortion, and claimed (inaccurately) that the book had been a major influence on the founding fathers of the American republic. *Lex, Rex* itself was republished by supporters of the Christian Right, and in 1982 Schaeffer's associate John Whitehead even established a major legal defence organization called The Rutherford Institute to defend religious liberties against the secular state. In 1983 a group of Scottish evangelicals founded Rutherford House to promote Reformed theology through conferences and publishing. As pietist, political theorist and theologian, Rutherford's writings continue to influence modern evangelicalism.

Bibliography
A. Bonar (ed.), *Letters of Samuel Rutherford* (Edinburgh: Banner of Truth, 1984); J. Coffey, *Politics, Religion and the British Revolutions: The Mind of Samuel Rutherford* (Cambridge: Cambridge University Press, 1997).

J. COFFEY

■ **RYDER, Henry** (1777–1836), Anglican bishop, was born on 21 July 1777, the youngest son of Nathaniel, first baron of Harrowby, and Elizabeth, daughter of Richard Terrick, Bishop of Peterborough and London. Educated initially at Harrow, Ryder graduated (MA) from St John's College, Cambridge, in 1798, and achieved his DD in 1813.

Ordained in 1800 by Bishop Cornwallis, Ryder first served in the curacy of Sandon, the residence of the Harrowby family. In 1801 he was presented to the living of Lutterworth, and in 1805 also took on the adjoining parish of Claybrooke. Ryder excelled in his role as parish priest, fulfilling the many aspects of his ministry energetically and still finding time to read, particularly the Early Fathers, and to study the Scriptures with a scholar's eye. His advantaged background did not prevent him mixing with ease among the diverse social classes with whom he came into contact. In 1808 Ryder became canon of Windsor, a role that he fulfilled with characteristic charm and energy. His sermons delighted George III, and he took particular pains over instructing the St George's Chapel choristers in religious matters. His influence even reached the troops stationed at Windsor's barracks.

In the early years of his ministry Ryder clearly distanced himself from the evangelical movement within the Church of England. So strong were his feelings against evangelical principles that when invited to preach at the Archdeacon's visitation in 1807, he took the opportunity to attack the movement on the grounds that it stood at odds with the principles of the main body of the church. However, his opposition lasted less than four years; by 1811 he had changed his allegiance to such an extent that he chaired a meeting of Leicester's Bible Society. Finally, he became an enthusiastic supporter of the move-ment after reading some of John *Newton's works.

Having become a staunch evangelical, Ryder was appointed to the deanery of Wells. This appointment was not well received by the representatives of the staid churchmanship that existed there. Changes instigated by Ryder, including the introduction of an evening service, the content of his sermons and his preaching in surrounding parishes, merely confirmed the suspicions of the older members of the chapter. Though much of his teaching and practice was regarded by his critics as overt Methodism, preaching in local parishes was, to Ryder, merely a way of repaying the contribution the parishes had made towards the endowment of the deanery at Wells. During his time there he came into contact with other noted evangelicals, Hannah *More and Thomas Gisborne.

Gisborne in particular was impressed by the work Ryder did at Wells, and in 1815 Ryder was offered the bishopric of Gloucester. The offer was not well received by everyone; Ryder's elder brother sat in the House of Lords, and many considered that this connection 'identified [him] with a party'. It was to the benefit of the people of Gloucester that Lord Dudley Ryder overcame the opposition, though a good deal of ill will remained among the clergy of the diocese. Henry Ryder's charming personality soon commended him to them, and they realized that he was an altogether better bishop than they had feared he might be.

Ryder was the first evangelical bishop in the Church of England, and one of the most prolific preachers of his time. He often preached three times on a Sunday, examined children in the Gloucester National School on Sunday afternoons and held weekly lectures in parish churches. In 1818 Hannah More testified in the *Christian Observer* that while visiting her during an illness he had 'confirmed thousands, consecrated one church and two churchyards, and preached nine sermons in ten days'. In addition to performing his more standard duties, in 1816 Ryder established the Gloucester Diocesan Association, which promoted education for the poor, and he had a good deal of influence in the setting up of the female penitentiary. Despite all the work that he did within the diocese of Gloucester, his evangelical practices still provoked unrest among some members of the clergy. Dr Thomas, Archdeacon of Bath, found it necessary to rebuke him publicly for chairing a meeting of the Church Missionary Society.

The energy with which Ryder carried out his diocesan duties in Gloucester did not go unnoticed. In 1824 he was translated to Lichfield, a large diocese that had been left without an effective leader during the later years of the episcopate of Bishop Cornwallis. The scope that Lichfield offered Ryder was virtually limitless; his having grown up there was an added bonus. In a time of country-wide diocesan regeneration, Ryder used both this and the parish system to the advantage of the population. Providing sufficient 'sittings' was a prime focus of his episcopate. In his first charge, Ryder identified the 'wants of [his] Diocese', of which the greatest was the need for new churches. The essence of his ministry was that the word of God was for everyone, and as a bishop he strove to make sure that everyone, regardless of social standing, could receive it. His visitation revealed that some twenty-seven parishes were in dire need of additional churches; they were currently able to offer 'sittings' to only 20% of the population. By the time of his second visitation 32,000 'sittings' had been, or were in the process of being, provided. Of the 150,000 'sittings' provided during his episcopate over 116,500 were made available free of charge, allowing the poorest people to hear the word.

Ryder was not just a builder of churches. Through his charges he impressed upon his clergy the importance of their position; he expected no less from them than he was prepared to give himself. No-one, he urged his clergy, in self-examination should be found wanting in his ministry: 'See that you never cease your labour, care and diligence, until you have done all that lieth in you, according to your bounden duty, to bring all such, as are or may be committed to your charge unto that agreement in faith and knowledge of God.'

Preaching with passion, he urged his clergy to 'warn every man, and teach every man'. However, he tempered his charge with realism by acknowledging that not everyone was a 'teachable hearer'. The increase in rent-free 'sittings' was designed to provide access to God for the 'teachable hearer'. National Schools and Sunday schools (in almost every parish) were useful for teaching the younger population, but in his visitation Ryder found that the provision for teaching morality and religion to children was woefully inadequate; the large numbers of children made effective teaching impossible. Ryder sought to provide a school, ideally attached to the new church building, for every district. In this way, he believed, the whole population could be transformed by instilling in them from an early age all that was right and good, preventing the ingress of badness and evil, reversing the growth in juvenile delinquency and creating 'profitable members of the community'.

Ryder's pouring out of his whole self into his ministry led to his early death. He died on 31 March 1836, aged 59. In addition to his indefatigable work for the church he married Sophia, the daughter of Thomas March Phillipps, and fathered ten sons and three daughters. Only his son Charles, who drowned at sea in 1825, did not survive him.

Bibliography

G. C. B. Davies, *The First Evangelical Bishop: Some Aspects of the Life of Henry Ryder* (Cambridge: Tyndale Church History Lecture, 1957); T. D. Ryder, *A Memoir of the Hon. and Rt. Rev. Henry Ryder* (1886).

P. J. CADLE

■ **RYERSON, Adolphus Egerton** (1803–1882), Canadian Methodist minister and educator, was born on 24 March in Charlotteville Township, Upper Canada, the fifth of six sons born to Colonel Joseph and Mehetable Ryerson, United Empire Loyalists. All but one son entered the Methodist ministry. Although his brothers John and William also provided leadership for the fledgling denomination, Egerton's career was the most distinguished. His brother George gained notoriety by his high-profile defection to the Irvingite Catholic Apostolic Church, but Egerton's contribution to the history of Canadian evangelicalism was more traditional, if not more staid. Egerton Ryerson's life spanned the era in which his native colony moved from Upper Canada's frontier conditions to the settled state of the 'modern' Canadian province of Ontario. Far from being a passive observer, Ryerson contributed significantly to shaping the emerging society, in which his beloved Methodism achieved a dominant position. At Ryerson's death, it was Ontario's largest denomination, attracting roughly one in three Protestants.

Converted at the age of twelve, during revivals after the war of 1812, Ryerson avoided arousing his 'Tory' Anglican father's wrath until he was eighteen. Forced to decide between formal membership of the Methodist church and continuing to live at home, he left. (He was later reconciled to his father.) For two years he helped his brother George in his work as a schoolteacher. On his twenty-second birthday, Ryerson began itinerant circuit preaching, replacing his seriously ill brother, William. In 1826 he became a missionary to the Mississauga Indians, west of York (now Toronto). Despite sharing common prejudices about the supposed inferiority of the natives, he respected them enough to gain limited fluency in their language. During his time with them, he formed what became a lifelong friendship with the native Methodist preacher Peter Jones. When appointed to regular circuits in subsequent years, he continued to visit nearby native congregations. He continued to travel extensively on horseback and preach almost daily for some years, but the course of his life began to change dramatically. He became one of Upper Canada's leading controversialists.

The colony's 1791 constitution had reserved one-seventh of all land for the support of a Protestant clergy. Church of England parsons enjoyed a monopoly on performing marriages until 1798, when the regulations were relaxed slightly (the pastors of most denominations were recognized in 1830); until 1828 other denominations were denied the corporate status required to hold in-trust chapels and burying grounds. When Archdeacon John Strachan's sermon at the funeral of Jacob Mountain, Canada's first Protestant bishop, was published in 1826, Ryerson countered its attack on 'Yankee Methodists' and other religious 'dissenters' with a lengthy article in the radical reform journal Colonial Advocate. Thus began a series of battles in print with Tory Anglicans and Roman Catholics on the one hand and, after Ryerson's exposure to atheistic radicals while in Great Britain in 1833, erstwhile reformer friends on the other. Although his secular political alignments changed, he remained true to his primary goal of promoting practical religious freedom.

In 1829 Ryerson was appointed founding editor of the Methodists' Christian Guardian and travelled to New York City to obtain a printing press. Circulation rose rapidly, as Ryerson attracted non-Methodist readers who shared his aim of full disestablishment of the colonial branch of the Church of England. With a few short breaks, he held the editorship until 1840. The 1829 conference also designated him 'book steward', a post in which he laid the foundations for what became the 'Ryerson Press'.

Occasionally, Ryerson turned his disputatious nature on other Methodists. His role in the 1833 union of British Methodist missions with existing Upper Canadian Episcopal Methodism was as acrimonious as it was important. His belligerent agitation for union provoked the most serious split in nineteenth-century Canadian Methodism, as a substantial minority withdrew from a continuing Episcopal Methodist Church. Ryerson also played a central part in the 1840 disruption of the Methodist union he had engineered and the 1847 reconciliation of British and central Canadian Methodists.

Ryerson's first significant foray into educational work came in 1842, when he assumed the principalship of the Methodists' Victoria College. Although he had had little formal preparation for this role, he had some knowledge of classical literature and languages. Victoria freed Canadian Methodists from dependence upon British-educated ministers, allowing them to develop skilled, indigenous leadership earlier than most denominations, a crucial factor in Methodism's massive numerical expansion. Although Ryerson's stay at Victoria was short, he left his mark upon its students, the next generation of leadership in the pulpit and the lecture hall. The expense of maintaining the school also led to a modification of the Methodists' voluntaryism. Refusing to condone the use of proceeds from the sale of Clergy Reserve lands for pastoral work, the Methodists none the less accepted grants for this costly educational work.

The work for which Ryerson is most famous began in 1844, when he became the colony's Chief Superintendent of Education. He travelled extensively in the United States and Europe to study educational systems.

Especially impressed by Prussian order and Irish textbooks, he adopted both for use in Ontario. His other innovations included standardized teacher training (begun in 1847; the first 'Normal School' building opened in 1852) and scholarly publishing on pedagogy (from 1848 to 1875 he edited the *Journal of Education for Upper Canada*). The value that leaders such as Ryerson placed on the study of history as a means of finding moral direction led them to collect artwork and artifacts for public display. The Royal Ontario Museum and the Ontario College of Art both trace their roots to Ryerson's first Normal School. His contributions to church and state were recognized during his lifetime in the form of two honorary doctorates: a DD from Wesleyan University, Connecticut (1842) and an LLD from Victoria College (1861).

For Ryerson, the purpose of education was not merely the inculcating of polite refinement. His educational philosophy, developed in an era before the withering impact of Darwinism and higher criticism upon general acceptance of the Bible's veracity, entailed presenting a generic (i.e. Protestant) Christianity to all students. They were to learn biblical basics, not denominational distinctives. At the root of his philosophy lay a postmillennial eschatology: the belief that regenerated individuals, working together through a variety of religious and secular institutions, could bring about the millennial kingdom of Christ through a non-revolutionary process. Christ would return to bring this process of moral improvement to its climax and lay claim to the perfected society. Universal state-funded education played an indispensable role in the process. Salvation was impossible by education alone, but Ryerson aimed to create an environment in which conversion was facilitated by the shaping of students' minds by a broad range of useful Christian knowledge. Political exigencies led to compromises in the 1850s, when separate Roman Catholic schools were given government funding (a continuing source of political strife into the late twentieth century).

Ryerson's polemics did not end with the 1854 settlement of the Clergy Reserves. In the same year he briefly withdrew from the Methodist Conference, objecting to ministers' being required to attend 'class' meetings. His secular political involvement continued; his friends included Canada's first prime minister, John A. Macdonald. In particular, he defended his educational reforms; he was keenly stung by charges (ironic in light of his lifelong struggle for liberty) that he had introduced 'Prussian despotism' into Ontario schools. He became increasingly defensive about his reputation, particularly after accusations of impropriety in his handling of public money (he was exonerated). Notwithstanding his leadership role in the 1874 reunion of Canadian Wesleyan and New Connexion Methodists, it may be argued that his earlier pugnacity made his death one of a handful necessary in order to achieve the full reunion of Canadian Methodism in 1884.

Ryerson's health began to fail in 1862. He continued, nevertheless, to develop Ontario's educational system, the 1871 School Act being the capstone of his career. The school system he left behind was one of the first modern public services in the province. He retired less than enthusiastically in 1876, and the government reorganized his department, making it directly responsible to a cabinet minister. In retirement he wrote several books, including one on Loyalists. Ryerson died on 19 February 1882 and is buried in Toronto. His name lives on: the Normal School's site now hosts Ryerson Polytechnical University, and many Ontario public schools are named in his honour.

Bibliography

J. G. Hodgins (ed.), '*The Story of My Life*' by the Late Rev. Egerton Ryerson, D.D., LLD. *(Being Reminiscences of Sixty Years' Public Service in Canada)* (Toronto: William Briggs, 1883); C. B. Sissons, *Egerton Ryerson, His Life and Letters*, 2 vols. (Toronto: Clarke, Irwin, 1937, 1947).

C. M. STEINACHER

■ **RYLAND, John** (1753–1825), Baptist pastor, educator and mission enthusiast, was one of a group of Northamptonshire pastors who, on the basis of their reading of Scripture and the works of Jonathan *Edwards (after whom Ryland named his son), sought to liberate Particular Baptist churches from hyper-Calvinism. They were successful in replacing an older inward-looking Calvinist theology by a new evangelical understanding of the tradition, which both revitalized the churches' work at home and gave birth to the modern missionary movement. A close friend of Andrew *Fuller, Ryland was equally opposed to both 'Pelagian pride' and 'Antinomian licentiousness'.

Born in Warwick on 29 January 1753, John Ryland was the son of John Collett Ryland, the Baptist pastor there, who has been described as a 'burly and explosive' Calvinist. A precocious child, who was able to read Psalm 23 in Hebrew at the age of five, Ryland taught himself the classics, and from the age of fifteen assisted his father in the school that he ran. Ryland subsequently became an able orientalist.

Converted as a teenager, Ryland began preaching in village churches and at College Street on week nights. In 1771 the Northampton church confirmed his call to ministry. Ten years later he became co-pastor to his father, and became sole pastor in 1785 when his father moved to Enfield, Middlesex, where poor money management caused him to become financially dependent on his generous son. Ryland was very active in the Northamptonshire Association, a model of a new-style association organized for mission. He twice served as moderator, in 1785 and 1792, but in 1794, after two years of deliberations and hesitations, he moved from Northampton to the pastorate of Broadmead, Bristol, which he combined with the presidency of Bristol Baptist College. He was well suited to his new work, since College Street had had both open membership and an open table, whilst at Broadmead he was pastor to a separate paedo-baptist congregation as well as to the Baptist one. At this time Brown University conferred an honorary doctorate on the largely self-taught Ryland.

It was Ryland's copy of Edwards' *Humble Attempt to Promote Explicit Agreement and Visible Union of God's People in Extraordinary Prayer* that was to provide the stimulus for the Northamptonshire pastors' famous Prayer Call of 1784, which was an essential prerequisite to the founding of the Baptist Missionary Society (BMS) eight years later. The three pastors involved were John Ryland of Northampton, John Sutcliff of Olney and Andrew Fuller of Kettering. Together they were successful in expounding a new missionary Calvinism that revolution-

ized the lives of English Particular Baptists. Of the three, only Sutcliff was college trained. Ryland was at the centre of the group that supported the youthful William *Carey, whom he had baptized in 1783; he encouraged Carey's increasing interest in the conversion of the heathen and in the formation of a society to pursue such aims. It was appropriate that Ryland should be one of those formally involved in commissioning Carey and his companion, Dr John Thomas, for missionary service in India.

Soon after the BMS was founded, Ryland, as a result of his move to Bristol, found himself in a strategic position to win west-country Baptist support for the new project. At the same time he increased the quality of the college's work, and under his leadership it moved into new purpose-built accommodation, which was finally completed in 1812.

Fuller's expectation that Christopher Anderson of Edinburgh would succeed him as secretary of the BMS was not generally shared when Fuller died in 1815. Ryland was asked to carry out the task, and did so for three years, initially with the assistance of James Hinton of Oxford, but it proved almost impossible for one who was already both pastor and college 'principal'. In 1818 John Dyer was appointed full-time co-secretary. Ryland remained nominal secretary until his death in Bristol on 25 May 1825, but Dyer was the principal director of the society's affairs from 1818, and particularly from 1819, when the office moved to London. Ryland had written that he 'trembled for the ark of the mission when it should be transported to London and fall into the hands of mere counting-house men'. Tension with Carey and his colleagues had been growing and would lead to the separation of the Serampore missionaries from the parent society for a decade from 1827. Ryland himself was particularly concerned with the developing work in the West Indies, and spent much time travelling to commend the cause in Britain. He also prepared petitions to Parliament on missionary matters.

Ryland enjoyed close friendships with Evangelical Anglicans, especially Toplady, *Scott and John Newton, with the last of whom he had a fascinating correspondence, which is extant among other Ryland letters in Bristol. His more than thirty published works include *Advice to Students of Divinity* (1770), *The Difficulties of the Christian Ministry and the Means of Surmounting Them* (1802), *Serious Remarks on the Different Representations of Evangelical Doctrine by the Professed Friends of the Gospel* (two parts, 1817, 1818) and *The Practical Influence of Evangelical Religion* (1819).

Bibliography
J. Culross, *The Three Rylands* (1897); G. Gordon, 'The Call of Dr John Ryland, Junior', *Baptist Quarterly* (1992), pp. 214ff.; J. E. Ryland, *Pastoral Memorials* (1826).

J. H. Y. BRIGGS

■ **RYLE, John Charles** (1816–1900), Anglican bishop, was born on 10 May 1816, the eldest son of John Ryle, a private banker and MP for Macclesfield (1833–1837), and Susanna, daughter of Charles Hunt of Wirksworth, Derbyshire. He was educated at Eton and then Oxford, being Fell Exhibitioner at Christ Church in 1834 and Craven scholar in 1836. He graduated in 1838, achieving his MA in 1871 and being created DD, by diploma, in 1880.

Ryle's family, since his great-grandmother's conversion by John *Wesley during a visit to Macclesfield, had been committed Wesleyan Methodists, who supported and funded several chapels in Macclesfield. In 1837 Ryle experienced his own conversion. First, Algernon Coote, a friend from Eton, urged him to 'think, repent and pray'; then he heard the epistle one Sunday afternoon in church: 'By grace are ye saved (pause) through faith (pause) and that not of yourselves (pause) it is the gift of God.' The succession of phrases brought full conviction to Ryle. 'Nothing,' he said, 'to this day appeared to me so clear and distinct as my own sinfulness, Christ's presence, the value of the Bible, the absolute necessity of coming out of the world, and the need of being born again, and the enormous folly of the whole doctrine of Baptismal Regeneration.' Having earlier studied the Thirty-Nine Articles at Eton (in a failed attempt to pass the Duke of Newcastle's scholarship), and the Thirty-Nine Articles, the Bible, the Prayer Book and church history for his finals at Christ Church, Ryle was ordained into the Church

of England by Charles Sumner on 12 December 1841, though he had been raised as a Methodist and had intended to pursue a career in politics.

Ryle became curate of Exbury, Hampshire (1841–1842). He was required to provide not only pastoral care, but also medical advice to his flock. Despite his less than complimentary opinion of his congregation of mostly agricultural workers, that they were 'a rich, dull, stupid set of people', he soon filled the chapel.

Ryle moved on to St Thomas, Winchester (1843–1844). He summed up the spiritual condition of Winchester thus: 'The whole place is in a very dead state ... worldliness reigned supreme in the close.' Ryle clearly regarded this lack of commitment as a challenge. He had soon filled the church, necessitating its rebuilding, instituted mid-week Bible lectures at the infant schools, and became superintendent of the district visitors' society. Such was his popularity that he was offered a £300 increase in stipend in an unsuccessful attempt to prevent his moving to Helmingham. There he came into contact with a number of prominent evangelicals, including Archbishop John Bird *Sumner, Admiral Harcourt and Admiral Hope.

Having formerly used other people's tracts, at Helmingham Ryle began to write his own, his first publication being 'I have somewhat to say unto thee', the first sermon he preached there. It was distributed free of charge throughout the parish. During his lifetime he published hundreds of tracts and over thirty books.

Ryle next moved to Stradbroke (1861–1880), where he successfully undertook a major restoration of the church. Part of the work included a new pulpit, which bore the inscription 'Woe is unto me if I preach not the Gospel'; Ryle personally supervised the carving and afterwards underscored the word 'not'. By the time he left the parish he was able to provide a seat in church for everyone and a place for every child in his school. In 1870 he became rural dean of Hoxne, and in 1872 honorary canon at Norwich.

In March 1880 Ryle accepted the offer of the deanery of Salisbury; he felt that by doing so he would be able to further the evangelical cause. However, before he could take up this post he was appointed to the new diocese of Liverpool in rather unusual circumstances.

The general election of 1880 saw the defeat of Disraeli by Gladstone. Liverpool's MP, Lord Sandon, informed Disraeli that his constituents wanted their bishop to be chosen by the Queen's current advisors rather than those appointed by Gladstone. According to Sandon, they had requested Ryle by name. His acceptance was required almost instantly as the old government would be replaced within a week. Apparently unwilling to accept no for an answer, Sandon secured Ryle's acceptance despite his age and relative poverty.

Liverpool had a multinational population of 1,100,000 and was a centre for commerce. Poverty and living conditions were appalling. Ryle's first Diocesan Charge urged his clergy to work effectively; they were the visible church, working among the people. Less formal, more effective contact with the churches was achieved through parish visits and the Annual Diocesan Conference, to which every ordained cleric, and two lay people from each parish, were invited.

Summing up the state of his diocese, Ryle said: 'you might as well send out of the Mersey a Cunard or a White Star steamer, with a crew of only twenty men all told, and expect her to cross the Atlantic and reach New York in safety'. He aimed to direct the 'restless activity' of the diocese by providing more 'living agents', an infrastructure in which they could operate, and the necessary oversight. Ryle promoted the office of Scripture Reader, paying lay men to complement the ordained ministry: 'the lay agent may do excellent service by sowing the seed and cutting down the corn. But if the crop is not to rot on the ground, the sheaves must be bound up and stored away in the barn, and this is the presbyter's work.' Fifty Readers took services in mission rooms, organized Sunday schools and visited the sick.

Between 1880 and 1890 twenty-seven churches and forty-eight mission halls were completed; the number of incumbents rose by twenty-two and that of curates by sixty-six; the number of confirmations rose from 4,500 in 1880 to 8,300 in 1890. Liverpool did not have a cathedral, and though Ryle accepted that there were good reasons for building one, he felt that money could be better invested at parish level.

In 1886 Ryle set up the Diocesan Clergy Pension Fund. He created institutions that supplemented the income of small livings, aided church building schemes, helped to meet church expenses in poor parishes, promoted and assisted education and assisted clergy widows and daughters. He also made sure that all the parishes that could assist others did so.

Preaching, whether from the pulpit or through tracts, was John Ryle's forte: 'You preach the Gospel of Jesus Christ so fully and clearly that everybody can understand it. If Christ crucified has not His rightful place in your sermons, and sin is not exposed as it should be, and your people are not plainly told what they ought to be and do, your preaching is no use.' Many of his tracts are still in print, in updated language; they still convey a powerful message, in a simple style.

Ryle married three times. His first wife was Matilda Charlotte Louisa, daughter of John Pemberton Plumptre of Fredville, Kent, whom he married in 1845; they had a daughter, Georgina Matilda. Matilda died in June 1847 having never recovered after Georgina's birth. In 1850 Ryle married Jessie Elizabeth, daughter of John Walker of Crawfordjohn, Lanarkshire, a long-standing friend and godmother to Georgina. Despite being sickly for all but the first six months of their marriage, she produced a daughter, Jessie Isabella, and three sons, Reginald John, Herbert Edward, and Arthur Johnston. She died of Bright's disease in May 1860. In 1861 Ryle married Henrietta, daughter of Lieutenant Colonel Legh Clowes. She assisted him by working in his Sunday school, playing the organ and bringing up his children. She died in 1889.

In failing health, Ryle retired on 1 March 1900; he died three months later.

Bibliography

J. C. Ryle, *Knots Untied being plain statements on disputed points in religion from the standpoint of an evangelical churchman* (London: 1898); P. Toon (ed.), *John Charles Ryle, an Autobiography* (Cambridge: 1975); P. Toon and M. Smout, *John Charles Ryle: Evangelical Bishop* (Cambridge: J. Clarke, 1976).

P. J. CADLE

■ **RYRIE, Charles C.** (1925–), dispensationalist theologian, teacher and author, was born on 2 March 1925 in St Louis, Missouri, and lived his early life in Alton, Illinois. He was converted at the age of five. After graduating from high school and spending a semester at Stony Brook School on Long Island, Ryrie attended Haverford College near Philadelphia. There he majored in mathematics, intending to become a banker. Other influences, however, led to a change in his plans. The strongest of these was Lewis Sperry *Chafer, the president of Dallas Theological Seminary and a family friend. Ryrie met privately with Chafer in Philadelphia in 1943 and dedicated his life to Christian ministry. Shortly thereafter he enrolled at Dallas Theological Seminary, from which he earned a ThM (1947) and a ThD (1949). He was ordained to the ministry by the First Baptist Church of Alton, Illinois.

After teaching at Westmont College in California from 1948 to 1951, Ryrie pursued a doctorate at the University of Edinburgh. He completed his PhD in 1954, meanwhile returning to Dallas Seminary in 1953 to teach systematic theology. In 1958 Ryrie became president of Philadelphia College of Bible (now Philadelphia Biblical University). He led this institution through a crucial period, during which it received state approval to grant degrees. Returning in 1962 to Dallas Seminary, he became Chair of the Department of Systematic Theology and Dean of Doctoral Studies. He remained at Dallas until he retired in 1983.

Since his retirement Ryrie has had an international ministry of lecturing, writing and teaching. He has taught regularly at Word of Life Bible Institute (New York) and since 1991 has been an adjunct professor at Philadelphia Biblical University. He received an honorary LittD from Liberty Baptist Theological Seminary in 1981. For many years he has been a member of the First Baptist Church of Dallas, Texas.

Ryrie has been a gifted communicator. His hallmarks are precision of interpretation, conciseness of statement and clarity of expression. He has made profound doctrines accessible even to the theologically untrained by focusing on the essence of issues, eliminating non-essentials and expressing ideas lucidly and simply. He has displayed unreserved devotion to Scripture and has expressed his convictions in a straightforward but irenic spirit.

Ryrie's simple communication was first manifested in collections of object lessons for children. But more substantial contributions soon followed, fuelled by his doctoral dissertations, class notes, chapel addresses and current theological debates. The result has been some thirty books and numerous articles and pamphlets, many now translated into other languages, on a broad range of biblical subjects.

Ryrie's first major work was *The Basis of the Premillennial Faith* (1953). A revision of his ThD dissertation, it argues that premillennialism rests not on one passage in Revelation 20 but on a hermeneutic that interprets the Bible literally and takes into account the grammar and contexts of many prophetic passages. Another early work was *Neo-orthodoxy* (1956), which briefly summarizes the theologies of several neo-orthodox scholars and examines their logical implications. This was followed by *The Role of Women in the Church* (1958), an adaptation of his PhD dissertation at Edinburgh.

In *Biblical Theology of the New Testament* (1959) Ryrie proposes a theological approach in which 'theology is a part of the very fabric of the Bible itself and not something that has been forced upon it or read into it'. It 'deals systematically with the historically conditioned progress of the self-revelation of God as deposited in the Bible'. Typical of Ryrie's simple yet penetrating writing style are *The Grace of God* (1963) and *The Holy Spirit* (1965). In the first he pursues the idea that grace brings liberty, but critiques both legalism and licence. In the second he develops a non-charismatic interpretation of the Holy Spirit's person and work.

Ryrie's commitment to dispensational theology receives full exposure in *Dispensationalism Today* (1965; republished 1995 as *Dispensationalism: Revised and Expanded*). In this work he seeks to correct perceived misconceptions about dispensationalism and to represent accurately how it is currently being taught. Defining a dispensation as 'a distinguishable economy in the outworking of God's purpose', he discovers in Scripture at least three dispensations: law (Old Testament Israel), grace (the church), and the millennial kingdom. In every economy, he declares, God's way of salvation remains the same.

Ryrie expounded his theology of Christian

living in *Balancing the Christian Life* (1969). Developing the thesis that 'genuine and wholesome spirituality is the goal of all Christian living', he deals with biblical concepts, personal responsibilities and practical problems related to the Christian life. One of these 'practical problems', the question of whether Christ must be Lord to be one's Saviour, became the occasion for another book, *So Great Salvation* (1989). Responding to John F. MacArthur's *The Gospel According to Jesus* (1988), which accused Ryrie and others of teaching an 'easy believism', Ryrie insists on the unconditional nature of divine grace and the uniquely gracious invitation of the gospel.

Meanwhile, Ryrie provided systematic theology for the lay student. His brief *Survey of Bible Doctrine* (1972), based on the assumption that God wants every believer to understand the Bible, was followed in 1986 by *Basic Theology*, a more comprehensive work for the non-professional reader. *Basic Theology* follows the usual categories of systematic theology and presupposes the inerrancy of Scripture and a 'normal', or 'plain', interpretation of it.

Ryrie also sought a biblical approach to social issues. *You Mean the Bible Teaches That ...* (1974; reissued 1991 as *Biblical Answers to Contemporary Issues*), seeks to apply biblical teaching to thirteen current issues. *What You Should Know About Social Responsibility* (1982) also deals with selected issues, but seeks a broader scriptural 'agenda' for social involvement. Such involvement, according to Ryrie, is not the gospel but a logical outworking of it.

The book for which Ryrie is most widely known is *The Ryrie Study Bible* (1976; expanded 1994–1995). Available in the King James, New King James, New American Standard and New International versions, it seeks to illuminate the biblical text through explanatory exegetical notes, graphics and other helps. While Ryrie's premillennial, dispensational views are often evident in his notes, his avoidance of dogmatism and presentation of alternative views have made his *Study Bible* acceptable to a broad spectrum of conservative Christians.

Ryrie's contributions understandably draw differing responses. His moderate dispensationalism and cautious openness to social involvement have appealed to many, although those of a covenant persuasion remain unconvinced. Charismatics disagree with his interpretation of spiritual gifts, and others see antinomianism lurking in his view of God's grace. Even his conciseness and simplicity, refreshing for many in their study of Scripture, is not appreciated by all. When does 'simple' become 'simplistic'? Are theological nuances that are clear to Ryrie himself always evident to his hearer or reader? Are relevant issues that cry out for discussion left untouched? The style that feeds some apparently leaves others craving more.

Ryrie's greatest legacy may well be making the Scriptures he reveres more understandable to lay people. Indeed, he would be pleased to be remembered for this. He has declared, '... the best thing I can do for people is to urge them to expose themselves to the Bible. All the books, tracts, arguments, sermons, and seminars ... don't hold a candle to the ability of the Word to lead people to faith and then to Christlikeness. Read the Word. Love the Word. And live the Word.'

Bibliography

W. Willis et al. (eds.), *Basic Theology: Applied* (Wheaton: Victor, 1995).

R. E. WENGER

■ **SANDERS, John Oswald** (1902–1992), missions director and author, was the son of a intensely studious Welsh-born clerk and bookseller, Alfred Sanders, and his Dunedin-born, able and musically talented though mentally unstable wife, Margaret Menzies Miller. He was born in the family home in Invercargill on 17 October 1902 and was educated at Southland Boys High School. At the age of sixteen he was employed as a clerk by the law firm of Frederick Hall-Jones and commenced extramural study for a law degree, which he completed in 1922. He learned administrative skills in his humble role in this firm.

The Sanders family belonged to the tradition of warm interdenominational evangelicalism that flourished in the Scottish settlements of Otago and Southland. They attended the Brethren assembly in Invercargill, were involved in the South Island committee of the China Inland Mission

(CIM), and attended the annual conference for spiritual awakening, modelled on the Keswick Convention, that was held at Pounawea in South Otago. Thus Sanders imbibed the tradition of CIM spirituality. He experienced a childhood conversion in 1911, but the turning-point of his life was his dedication of himself to missionary service at the Pounawea conference during the week after Christmas 1921. This commitment led him to decline a partnership in Hall-Jones' firm. He instead decided to attend the new Bible Training Institute (BTI) founded by Joseph *Kemp in Auckland, in order to prepare for missionary service in South America.

Sanders' studies ended abruptly when his father became ill and he was called home to support the family. They moved to Dunedin, where he was employed by John Wilkinson, a prominent lawyer and evangelical lay preacher. Sanders' evangelical faith owed much to this employer. Then in 1926 he was invited to serve as the field representative of the BTI and later that year he became secretary and treasurer of the Institute and moved with his dependents to Auckland. On 19 December 1931 he married Edith Mary Dobson, the daughter of a fruit farmer from Omihi in Canterbury. The couple had one son, John Wilbur Sanders, born on 21 September 1936.

Sanders was increasingly drawn into every aspect of the teaching and administration of the rapidly growing BTI, and he succeeded C. J. Rolls as superintendent in 1931. After the death of Kemp in 1933, he took effective charge of the Institute, where he put to use his considerable gifts of Christian administration. Sanders never spared himself in the task of developing the Institute. As secretary and then superintendent he was an all-purpose administrator. He promoted the Institute shrewdly and firmly controlled its youthful students. He was also a systematic teacher, issuing highly schematic summaries of Christian teaching in which he classified doctrines rather than evaluating them. He persuaded the BTI board to found a Christian bookshop, conducted weekly mission services and supported and spoke regularly at the annual Ngaruawahia Christian Convention. He encouraged a wide variety of missionary organizations and was instrumental in the formation of the United Maori Mission in

1936. His work was exhausting, and he nearly suffered burnout, but his faith and common sense sustained him.

Sanders was a passionate but unpretentious and compelling preacher, and his reputation soon spread to Australia. In March 1946 he accepted an invitation to become the Australian representative of the CIM, based in Melbourne. Firmness, decisiveness and an instinctive feel for the wisest policy made him a highly effective national director. Consequently, when in 1954 the CIM, the largest missionary organization in the world, faced a crisis after its expulsion from China and made the decision to appoint a general director, it chose Sanders for the role. Sanders oversaw the CIM's reorganization into the Overseas Missionary Fellowship (OMF) with masterly skill. Based in Singapore, he became well known in evangelical circles throughout the world for his efficiency, his skill in reasoning and planning and his ability to listen. He evaluated missionaries and strategies shrewdly. He was a missionary statesman whose work was firmly grounded in reality.

Sanders' reputation as an author increased in his years as OMF director. In the 1920s he had begun writing magazine articles for the BTI magazine, The Reaper, and he soon began to write books, mostly on the spiritual life and the qualities required for Christian leadership. Some thirty-two books on devotional and biblical topics flowed from his pen, and more than two million copies were printed in all, including translations into some twenty-three languages. All of them exhibited the same practical spirituality, forthright directness and sane faith.

After his retirement to Auckland in 1969, Sanders received numerous invitations to speak to institutions all over the world, and until the year of his death he was constantly travelling and inspiring audiences. His first wife died of cancer in Melbourne on 25 September 1966, and he later married Mary Miller, née Kemp, daughter of the founder of the BTI; she died on 12 December 1972. Sanders then acted for two years as principal of the Christian Leaders Training College in Banz, New Guinea. He was awarded the OBE in the Queen's Birthday Honours list in 1980 and an honorary doctorate was finally conferred on him at his old Institute (now called the Bible College of New Zealand) in 1992, just before his death in Auckland on 24 October of that year.

Called J. O. or Ossie by his friends, Sanders was a man of common sense and wisdom, not easily swayed by emotion, and a natural if austere leader. He was afflicted by shyness since childhood, which he overcame only after the death of his second wife. A tall man with sharp piercing eyes and a clear and well-ordered mind, he was a highly incisive preacher, organizer and counsellor. His understanding of American evangelicalism, which was better than that of many others in the ex-colonial world, helped him in his work for OMF. As a preacher his favourite subject was the life of Caleb, the Old Testament character who to the end of his life sought opportunities to conquer mountains. Sanders did much to preserve the link between devotional life and missionary commitment in evangelicalism, both in New Zealand and beyond.

Bibliography
R. and G. Roberts, *To Fight Better: A Biography of J. Oswald Sanders* (Crowborough: Highland Books/OMF, 1989); J. O. Sanders, *This I Remember* (Eastbourne: Kingsway Publications, 1982).

P. J. LINEHAM

■ **SANGSTER, William Edwin Robert** (1900–1960), British Methodist minister, became known for his preaching and writing ministry. The central focus of his theology was not only the need for all people to be saved, but also the typical Wesleyan notion that Christians needed to strive for holiness, or what John *Wesley described as Christian Perfection or Scriptural Holiness. He was convinced that if the church were to preach this message, societies would be completely transformed. He therefore strongly challenged the immorality and secularism that, in his judgment, were eroding post-war British society. He captivated large audiences with his uncompromising message and took it to the masses through the publication of his sermons in the national press.

William Sangster was born on 5 June 1900 near City Road, London. He was a natural scholar at school and a keen reader, and at the age of nine he was awarded a scholarship to Hoxton Central School. Sangster was introduced to the Christian faith when, from about 1909, he became associated through a friend with Radnor Street Mission, a Methodist Hall. It was here that he encountered the theology of John Wesley, particularly the doctrines of the assurance of salvation and Christian perfection. (It was here also that he met his future wife, Margaret Conway.) During a prayer meeting at the Mission in October 1913 he made a commitment to follow Jesus Christ. His main aim then became the sharing of his faith. He preached his first sermon at the Mission when he was sixteen years old. A year later he became a fully accredited local preacher. Family circumstances forced Sangster to leave school at fifteen, and he took up the position of office boy at a London accountancy firm. He first felt called to the Methodist ministry at the age of seventeen.

In June 1918 Sangster joined the army, and he served with the Queen's Royal West Surrey Regiment. He was considered for a commission, but was rejected because some of the officers did not want a 'holy Joe' in the mess. He missed the horrors of the Western Front and in 1919 was sent to Germany. While he was there a Methodist padre encouraged him to offer himself for ordination.

In 1920 Sangster began to attend Handsworth College, Birmingham, but he later moved to Richmond College. In April 1923 he was sent to deputize for the Revd William Tapper at the County Road Methodist Church in Liverpool, and in August of that year he was sent to Littlehampton in Sussex as a probationer minister in the Bognor circuit. He was ordained in Wesley Chapel, Priory Street, York on 27 July 1926, and was married soon after. His first appointment as an ordained minister was to Conwy in North Wales. A year into his ministry there, he completed his BA degree externally through London University.

In 1929 Sangster took over the Methodist church in Aintree, Liverpool. By this time he was recognized as a preacher, and was able to draw crowds of up to 700 people. In 1930 he began making final preparations to complete an MA degree. However, his health failed so that he could not complete the degree, and he entered a period of spiritual crisis. He became self-critical, blaming himself for being ambitious, and began to seek a special blessing, which he believed would come through prayer and striving after holiness. Drawing on his Wesleyan theology, he reached the conclusion that he needed God's grace in every aspect of his life and therefore to be entirely sanctified, and in 1931 his quest culminated in a deep experience. His first book, *Why Jesus Never Wrote a Book*, explains his new understanding of holiness.

In 1932 Sangster moved from Merseyside to the Queen Street Central Hall, Scarborough. He was moved in 1936 to the Brunswick Church in Leeds, known as a Methodist 'cathedral'. In 1937 he finally completed his MA and became an external examiner to Richmond College in ethics and philosophy. Following the death of the Revd Dr Dinsdale Young of Westminster Central Hall, London in January 1938, Sangster was appointed to replace him, and he moved there in 1939.

During the Second World War, Central Hall became a refuge for many through Sangster's work among those who had lost everything during the blitz. He also drew vast crowds to services. In 1942 he completed his doctorate (PhD, London University), which was later published under the title *The Path to Perfection*. By the end of the war, Sangster had become a national figure, being known particularly for his pronouncements on moral and social issues. He was also respected for his simple yet direct preaching.

Sangster was elected president of the Methodist Conference for 1950–1951. He was concerned about the decline in the number of local preachers, and put forward the idea of 'schools for preachers' for both ministers and laymen. At the ministerial session of Conference he pleaded with his colleagues to preach 'Scriptural Holiness', arguing that it was vital for there to be a distinct difference in behaviour between church members and society in general.

Sangster's mind was focused on the need for spiritual revival, and he eagerly participated in evangelistic crusades, sharing platforms with (for example) Billy *Graham and Alan Redpath. He was increasingly convinced that Methodism's task was to 'spread Christian holiness throughout the land'. He stated: 'Methodism's task will remain unfinished until all the ransomed church of God has seen this gleaming facet of truth.'

Sangster was forthright in denouncing what he regarded as the evils of post-war society. In 1953 he made headline news with the publication of his sermon entitled, 'What would a Revival of Religion do for Britain?' In it he claimed that Christ was the ultimate solution for the problems of society and that Christianity was the 'buttress of decency'.

In 1954 Sangster was elected secretary of the Home Mission Department. He held 'Schools of Evangelism', day conferences to train ordinary people to share their faith with others. He also established the 'Prayer Life Movement'. Prayer cells were formed, and within a year they had over 2,000 members. By the end of 1957 it was apparent that Sangster's health was failing, and by the Conference of 1958, it was clear that he was seriously ill. He was later diagnosed as suffering from progressive muscular atrophy. He died on 24 May (Wesley Day), 1960.

Sangster had a deep passion for souls. His preaching was characterized by the call for personal salvation, but his Wesleyan heritage led him also to focus on holiness. He claimed that *Luther's '... immense (and Scriptural) stress upon faith – and faith only – was left unbalanced by the lack of a complementary passion for holiness'. He affirmed the 'rich treasures of Catholic spirituality', adding that Methodism was indebted to both Protestantism and Catholicism. This position did not compromise his distinctive evangelical commitment: he affirmed only that part of Catholicism, namely holiness, that he believed to conform with the essence of biblical Christianity.

More than anything else, Sangster was therefore a 'herald of holiness'. He saw Entire Sanctification or Perfect Love as the greatest need of the Christian church. He maintained that 'God can do so much more with sin than just forgive it'. In his *Path to Perfection* he claimed that '... there is an experience of the Holy Spirit, available to all who will seek it ... which imparts spiritual power far above the level enjoyed by the average Christian...' He was convinced that it was possible for a Christian's heart to be made pure.

Sangster published very widely throughout his ministry. The major works that have had the most lasting impact are, *The Path to Perfection* (1943), *The Pure in Heart: A Study in Christian Sanctity* (1954) and the *Westminster*

Sermons (1960, 1961). He published numerous devotional works and also contributed to many newspapers, including the *Christian Herald*, the *Spectator* and the *Sunday Times*.

Bibliography

P. Sangster, *Doctor Sangster* (London: Epworth, 1962); S. R. Valentine, *William Edwin Sangster* (Peterborough: Foundery Press, 1998).

D. R. OWEN

■ **SANKEY, Ira David** (1840–1908), singer and hymn-writer, was born in Edinburg, a small town in Lawrence County, western Pennsylvania, on 28 August 1840. Sacred music played a central role in the Sankey family. David and Mary Sankey, devout Methodists, spent long winter evenings with their children around their fireplace singing hymns. In this way, Ira Sankey learned to read music and to harmonize. In 1857 the family moved to Newcastle, Pennsylvania. There Ira attended high school and began working in the bank of which his father was president. There, too, he joined the Methodist church, where he found a role as Sunday school superintendent and choir director. The congregation, who had not previously used musical instruments, soon acceded to Sankey's introduction of an organ to accompany congregational and choral singing. Sankey also developed an ability as a soloist.

Sankey honed his musical ability during the Civil War. Among the first from his town to volunteer in response to Lincoln's first call for troops, Sankey did not neglect his musical interests while soldiering. He organized a male choir, which assisted his company's chaplain. His term expired before the war ended, and he returned to work again with his father, now a collector of internal revenue. On 9 September 1863 Sankey married Fanny V. Edwards. They had two sons, Ira Allen and John.

For the next few years Sankey built a reputation as a singer at Sunday school conventions and political rallies in western Pennsylvania and eastern Ohio. Active in the YMCA, Sankey was appointed a delegate to the 1870 meeting of the International Convention of the YMCA in Indianapolis. There his introduction to D. L. *Moody abruptly changed his life.

Sankey had read of Moody, and his curiosity to see him in action led him to a 6am prayer meeting in a Baptist church at which Moody was scheduled to preside. Sankey arrived late and sat beside a friend who urged him to do something to improve the singing. At the first opportunity, Sankey began to sing William *Cowper's 'There Is a Fountain Filled With Blood'. Delighted with the effect, Moody after the service asked Sankey to move to Chicago and help in his work. Sankey, bewildered, demurred. The next day Moody summoned Sankey to meet him at a street corner and at once put him to work drawing a crowd with a song. Six months later, Sankey agreed to spend a week with Moody in Chicago. He then resigned his position with the Internal Revenue Service and moved early in 1871 to Chicago.

In June 1873 the Sankeys and the Moodys sailed for England. The Sankeys left their two young children at home. Sankey took with him only two books: his Bible and his musical scrapbook, a personal collection of songs he had found useful over the years. Moody and Sankey began their ministry in York. The modest initial turnout belied what would follow. Over the next two years, the two men became a sensation. Sankey accompanied himself on a portable reed organ, and his baritone voice dramatically reinforced Moody's message. In response to popular demand, Sankey issued a modest collection of his twenty-three most popular solos as *Sacred Songs and Solos Sung by Ira D. Sankey at the Meetings of Mr. Moody of Chicago*. The first edition sold out in less than a day, and successive expanded printings culminated in the 1200-song hymnal, *Gospel Hymns 1–6*. The book sold millions of copies, and Moody and Sankey donated the royalties to various causes.

Sankey had an unerring eye for appropriate musical texts to support Moody's sermons. Perhaps his best-known find was a poem he took from a newspaper, 'The Ninety-and-Nine'. During a service at which Moody preached on the New Testament parable of the lost sheep, Sankey spontaneously composed a tune, and the song became an enduring feature of Moody/Sankey meetings.

When Moody and Sankey returned to the United States late in 1875, their reputation preceded them. They conducted their first urban evangelistic campaign in Brooklyn, where the crowds that thronged every meeting made it evident that even the largest venues available were inadequate. For the next few years, they travelled throughout the United States, spending prolonged periods in major cities. Sankey continued to work on his expanding hymnal. As he endeared himself to audiences across the nation, sales followed apace. From 1881 to 1884, Moody and Sankey again toured England, making their first forays into British university culture. Meanwhile, in 1880, Moody had begun orchestrating annual series of summer conventions in his boyhood home town, Northfield, Massachusetts. The Sankeys purchased a summer home in this lovely setting in the Connecticut River valley, and the appreciative crowds of Christian workers, college students and women's groups eagerly embraced his musical leadership.

Sankey played an important role in reshaping the music of popular Christianity. He promoted the use of gospel hymns, with their emphases on personal testimony, religious experience, exhortation and invitation. He provided gospel hymn tunes and modelled the use of gospel music to achieve a desired effect. His best-selling hymnals popularized the texts and tunes of a new generation of hymn-writers, many of whom used the gospel hymn style. Upbeat singable music had what some called 'congregationality'. Tunes that borrowed heavily from folk and popular music helped to make the new hymnody accessible. The enormous following and detailed press coverage that Sankey's music gained enabled gospel hymnody soon to penetrate the churches. Many church musicians resisted the new music, which they regarded as undignified and populist, and attempted to confine it to social meetings, youth gatherings and revival meetings. At camp meetings, on street corners, at Christian Endeavor rallies, in YMCA halls and in modest urban missions, catchy gospel tunes and their simple texts became musical standards. Slowly some of the 'better' Sankey favourites found their way into denominational hymnals. In the meantime, Sankey's body of musical texts fuelled a growing industry of popular hymnal publishing.

Not surprisingly, Sankey participated directly in this endeavour. In the 1890s he was involved briefly on the operations side of Biglow and Main, formerly Bradbury Music Company, one of the country's premier publishers of gospel and Sunday school hymnals. Sankey's son, Ira A. Sankey, became part owner of the company and carried forward his father's commitment to presenting the evangelical message in song. Through the publishing house, an emerging group of gospel singers kept in touch with each other's work and cooperated with one another. Sankey knew personally everyone who mattered in the explosion of gospel hymn singing that swept the nation in the last quarter of the nineteenth century. And his influence crossed language boundaries into America's growing ethnic communities. During the 1890s, for example, Sankey worked with Walter Rauschenbusch to prepare a German edition of his *Gospel Hymns*. Missionaries also carried the music Sankey promoted around the world, where the songs in translation quickly became an important component of the burgeoning missionary movement. The Sankeys travelled beyond Europe in 1898, singing their songs and visiting the sights of the Holy Land and Egypt. When they returned, Sankey worked among the troops bound for Cuba in the Spanish American War. In the 1890s he accepted many invitations to provide the teaching programme he called 'Gospel Song and Story' in churches in the United States, Canada and Britain.

After Moody's death in 1899, Sankey spent most of his time in his spacious home in Brooklyn, New York. Over several years his eyesight failed until he was entirely blind. But he still sat at the organ in his music room, working over gospel songs. He died in Brooklyn on 13 August 1908 and is buried with many Brooklyn notables in Greenlawn Cemetery.

His association with Moody gave Sankey incalculable influence on the music of popular Protestantism. He helped to introduce instrumental accompaniment into settings in which there had long been objections to it and popularized a body of music that was accessible to the masses. Side by side with Moody, Sankey became a key figure in many of the evangelical endeavours of his day. The royalties from Sankey's hymnals built schools, churches and YMCA halls in Britain and America. Thanks to Sankey's success, evangelists since Moody have generally relied on the services of a singer.

Bibliography

J. Findlay, *Dwight L. Moody, American Evangelist, 1837–1899* (Chicago: University of Chicago Press, 1969); W. G. McLoughlin, *Modern Revivalism* (New York: Ronald Press, 1959); W. E. Moody, *The Life of D. L. Moody* (New York: Fleming H. Revell, 1900); I. D. Sankey, *My Life and the Story of the Gospel Hymns* (New York: Harper & Brothers, 1906).

E. L. BLUMHOFER

■ **SCHAEFFER, Francis August** (1912–1984), American Presbyterian pastor, missionary and apologist, became one of the foremost shapers of evangelicalism since the Second World War. He was little in stature, 'sad faced' (as *Time* dubbed him), and had a slightly high-pitched voice. In later life he cut a striking figure in knickerbockers and a goatee beard. John *Stott, writing after his death in 1984, called him 'a prophet for the sixties'. He was often caught up in controversy, being dogged, like so many evangelicals, by the issue of ecclesiastical and cultural separatism. His life is marked by three phases: his time as a fundamentalist pastor, embroiled in ecclesiastical separatism, which was changed for ever by his encounter with Europe in 1947 and 1948; the prelude to and development of the work of L'Abri Fellowship, first in Switzerland and later in the UK and elsewhere, with its open-home policy and increasing emphasis upon community as the ultimate apologetic for Christian faith; and finally his move into Christian political activism, which grew out of his endeavours to communicate through the central contemporary medium of film. Francis Schaeffer saw this activism as a natural extension of taking seriously the Lordship of Christ, which had gradually become the integration point of his theology, through all his struggles with separatism and the related issue of cultural transformation.

Francis Schaeffer's apologetic approach was shaped in a pastoral and mission context because he believed that personality is at the centre of reality. And if Christians really believe that, he felt, they are obliged to value the people they encounter. Most of his writings grew out of his conversations and discussions with people who came to L'Abri, his home high in the Swiss Alps. His distinctive lectures and discussion sessions also developed from these.

Francis Schaeffer was the child of working-class parents of German ancestry. He was born on 30 January 1912 in Germantown, Pennsylvania. As a child he helped his father in his duties as a caretaker, which included carpentry. By the age of seventeen, Schaeffer was working part-time on a fish wagon. He later admitted to having 'barely made it' in high school. But a dramatic change took place in his intellectual development while he was teaching English to a Russian count. The count was practising by reading a book in English on Greek philosophy. Schaeffer started to read the Bible alongside this classical reading. He was surprised to find answers to the deep philosophical questions he had begun to ask. His dawning excitement was never to leave him, even through times of radical re-examination of his beliefs.

After high school Schaeffer enrolled at the Drexel Institute as an engineering student. His parents wanted him to be a craftsman like his father, but he increasingly felt an unmistakable calling from God to be a pastor. The autumn of the next year found him at Hampden-Sydney College in southern Virginia. As he studied for the ministry, various indications of the unusual quality of his character became evident: the way in which he faced bullying, his participation in a Sunday school for black people in the vicinity and his service as president of the Student Christian Association.

The next year Schaeffer met Edith Seville at the First Presbyterian Church of Germantown. In her he discovered an attractive friend and ally against liberal attacks upon the integrity of Scripture. In 1935, after he graduated *magna cum laude*, the two cast their fortunes together in marriage. They both shaped the later work of L'Abri, and Edith Schaeffer's books significantly added to the overall impact of Schaeffer's writings. In the first ten years of their marriage three daughters were born.

In September 1935 Francis Schaeffer entered Westminster Theological Seminary, founded six years before, when Princeton

Seminary shifted decisively towards theological modernism. His lecturers in this period included Cornelius *Van Til (1895–1987), J. Gresham *Machen (1881–1937) and John *Murray (1898–1975). When Machen's growing controversy with the Presbyterian Church in the USA led to his being expelled from the ministry, Schaeffer and several others, including Carl *McIntire, felt compelled to separate from the denomination as well. A further division led to the founding of the fundamentalist Faith Theological Seminary. Schaeffer moved from Westminster to Faith to complete his studies (BD, 1938), and then became the first minister of the newly organized Bible Presbyterian Church (BPC), which had split in 1937 from the Presbyterian Church of America, later renamed the Orthodox Presbyterian Church (OPC), over issues such as dispensational premillennialism. He was based in Grove City, Pennsylvania. In 1941 he moved to a church in Chester, in the same state, where he identified with the many working-class members of his congregation, both city and country people. In 1943 the Schaeffer family moved to St Louis, where they began a local organization called Children for Christ. The movement eventually spread to other churches and then to other denominations. The Independent Board for Presbyterian Foreign Missions authorized Schaeffer to make a fact-finding tour of Europe in 1947. After this the board asked him to prepare for an international conference in Amsterdam in August 1948. Thus it happened that in February 1948 the Schaeffer family set sail for Europe.

In Amsterdam Francis Schaeffer met a serious and brilliant young Dutch student of art history named Hans *Rookmaaker. On discovering that Schaeffer was an American, Rookmaaker, whose main passion was music, approached him for a brief talk about black music. They walked the streets of Amsterdam until 4am in lively discussion. Rookmaaker recalled this as the first of 'many long talks about faith, philosophy, reality, art, the modern world and their mutual relations'. It was the start of a long and deeply significant association, one of Francis Schaeffer's few close friendships. Rookmaaker exposed Schaeffer to a rich Dutch intellectual tradition that owed an enormous debt to Abraham *Kuyper and others, reinforcing in the American seminal ideas he had received with delight from his old teacher, Van Til.

In the next few years the Schaeffers settled in Switzerland, their son Frank was born, and they worked industriously with children and warned evangelical churches about liberalism and what Schaeffer perceived as the more subtle threat of neo-orthodoxy, specifically as embodied in the theology of Karl Barth, whom Schaeffer visited at his Swiss home. To depict what he considered to be the dangers of neo-orthodoxy, Schaeffer focused on the historical context of religious existentialism, developing ideas that were later expressed more fully in Escape From Reason (1968), The God Who Is There (1968) and other books. At about the same time the husband-and-wife team created Sunday school material that was based on the gospel of Luke and later published as Everybody Can Know (1973).

In the Sunday School Times of 16 June and 23 June 1951, Schaeffer published an article on 'The Secret of Power and Enjoyment of the Lord: The Need for Both Purity and Love in the Christian Life'. His words reflected a deep spiritual struggle, associated with a lifelong wrestling with depression and the strong emotions that always moved him. Sometimes these emotions exploded in stormy outbursts (unseen by all except those close to him), but most often signified a profound and noticeable empathy for people.

Schaeffer's heartfelt words about power and enjoyment of the Lord recalled his experience of the previous winter, when he had paced up and down in his hayloft in the Swiss village of Champéry when the weather was wet, and walked the countryside when it was dry, re-examining the basis of his faith and commitment to the Lord. Without a present reality, he concluded, an orthodox theology does not lead to power and enjoyment of the Lord. Schaeffer always believed that without this deep struggle the work of L'Abri would never have started. There were several testing years, however, before it was inaugurated in 1955, and the Schaeffers finally broke their links with their mission board and with separatism. Eventually young people from all over the globe began streaming up to the Schaeffers' alpine home in an obscure part of Switzerland, a pilgrimage perhaps unique in the history of evangelicalism. By word of mouth, the news had spread to college and university students in a rapidly globalizing world that there was a place in the Alps where one could get honest answers to life's deepest questions. By 1968 over one thousand hours of audiotape of Schaeffer's lectures and discussions, covering such themes as true spirituality, the books of Romans and Revelation, the Westminster Confession and various cultural issues, had been recorded.

A turning-point in the development of L'Abri was the founding of a similar work in England in 1958, after Schaeffer had given lectures in Oxford and elsewhere in Britain. That work was eventually to be led by Ranald Macaulay, who married the Schaeffers' second daughter, Susan. The establishment of an English L'Abri was symbolic of the deep influence Schaeffer was to have on a generation of British evangelicals. In particular, he forged warm and significant links with the Inter-Varsity Fellowship (now called the Universities' and Colleges' Christian Fellowship). He also took a deep interest in what was happening both on the British theological scene and in British culture, especially when its rock music began to have a worldwide influence. Like the long-term community-based work of L'Abri in Switzerland, speaking tours of British and American universities and colleges gradually became an integral part of Schaeffer's ministry.

Schaeffer's first mainstream published book was *Escape from Reason*. In it he chronicled the roots of what we now recognize as postmodernism. *Escape from Reason* reveals the framework for much of his life's work as a pastor, apologist and latterly campaigner for human rights. Not surprisingly, his little book, which reads like an intellectual slideshow, has provoked criticisms, which also apply to some of his other publications. Some have disputed his thumbnail sketches of great historical figures, even though his central portrayals of Aquinas and Kierkegaard have a respectable scholarly pedigree.

Another essential book in Schaeffer's corpus was in preparation before and published in the UK soon after *Escape from Reason*. *The God Who Is There* picks up the thesis of the first book, tracing the origins of modern relativism in knowledge and morals to an abandonment of the perennial human search for a unified field of knowledge. All

that gives meaning to human beings and their society and culture is relegated to the realm of the mystical and non-rational. Because the modern person is typically 'below the line of despair', we have to rethink Christian apologetics and evangelism. We must now begin by recognizing that an evangelical proclamation of the gospel is radical in the modern world and how it differs from liberal and neo-orthodox theology. Schaeffer goes on to commend a person-centred apologetics that will be effective in our day.

Underlying both *Escape from Reason* and *The God Who Is There* is a concern for the issue of knowledge. Schaeffer had demonstrated that shifting approaches to knowledge in the recent and distant history of the West had had dramatic consequences for how we live (and die). He turned once again to this matter in *He Is There and He Is Not Silent* (1972), arguing that only the historic Christian faith gives adequate answers in the fundamental areas of metaphysics, morals and epistemology. Schaeffer was the author of over twenty books and booklets. The core books of the corpus, the first of which was not published until he was fifty-six, are the trilogy just mentioned. It is essential, however, to read *True Spirituality* (1971) to get to the heartbeat of his theology.

Schaeffer's unshakeable realism, his concern for the practice of truth in his generation, eventually led him to an activist stance in defence of the rights of the unborn child, the weak and the elderly. He was encouraged in this by his son Frank, a filmmaker and later a novelist, who in 1990 abandoned his father's evangelicalism in favour of Greek Orthodoxy. Frank's two comic novels are heavily fictionalized accounts of his childhood that nevertheless are hard not to read as a lampoon of L'Abri.

Schaeffer spoke at various seminars in the USA and UK where his first film series, *How Should We Then Live?* was shown. This pattern anticipated screening of the more controversial series *Whatever Happened to the Human Race?*, a project in which Everett Koop, later Surgeon General of the United States, collaborated. Their concern was the widespread increase in abortion on demand, and the concomitant peril of euthanasia. Schaeffer and Koop attributed this development to a monolithic acceptance of moral and epistemological relativism in the West. The tangible blessings that had accrued to society from Christian insights into human nature were rapidly being eroded by the new secular humanism. Such blessings were interpreted by the New Christian Right as being particularly embodied in traditional American social values. Schaeffer soon became the intellectual leader of the Moral Majority, deeply influencing Pat *Robertson, Tim *LaHaye, Jerry *Falwell and others, and came to the attention of President Ronald Reagan, whose administration was seen as an open door of opportunity for evangelical political impact.

While filming the second series, Schaeffer learned that he had cancer of the lymph system. Only immediate medical action saved his life, and thereafter frequent courses of chemotherapy were necessary. The shadow of death intensified his concern to do what he could to try to reverse the rise in abortion rates, a trend he found horrific. In aligning with the New Christian Right, Schaeffer was putting into practice his developing concept of cobelligerency. At the close of his life, Schaeffer was involved not only in the pro-life controversy, but also in the 'battle for the Bible'. He had helped to found the International Council on Biblical Inerrancy in 1977.

He died on 15 May 1984, shortly after a seminar tour associated with his final book, *The Great Evangelical Disaster* (1984), written with the help of his publisher Lane Dennis. L'Abri continues actively in several countries, including the United States, Britain, the Netherlands, Korea and Switzerland.

Bibliography

C. Catherwood, *Five Evangelical Leaders* (London: Hodder & Stoughton, 1984; Fearn, Ross-shire: Christian Focus, 1994); L. T. Dennis (ed.), *Francis Schaeffer: Portraits of the Man and His Work* (Westchester: Crossway, 1986); M. S. Hamilton, 'The Dissatisfaction of Francis Schaeffer', *Christianity Today*, 3 March 1997, pp. 22–30; R. W. Ruegsegger, *Reflections on Francis Schaeffer* (Grand Rapids: Zondervan, 1986); E. Schaeffer, *L'Abri* (Wheaton: Tyndale, 1969); E. Schaeffer, *The Tapestry* (Waco: Word, 1981).

C. DURIEZ

■ **SCHAFF, Philip** (1819–1893), church historian and ecumenist, was born in Chur, Switzerland on New Year's Day 1819. Raised in the Pietist atmosphere of Württemberg, he entered the boys' academy in Kornthal in 1834 and experienced a dramatic conversion while there. He moved on to the *Gymnasium* in Stuttgart, where he came to believe that his calling was to be a poet. He turned his attention to theological studies, however, and matriculated at the University of Tübingen in 1837. The greatest influences upon him while there were C. F. Schmid and J. A. Dorner, especially the latter, whose combination of scholarly erudition and warm Christian faith he found attractive. Schaff rejected the higher criticism of Tübingen's D. F. Strauss and F. C. Baur, later admitting his admiration for their intellectual brilliance but completely rejecting what he saw as their faithless destruction of the foundations of Christianity. Schaff's third year of theological study took him to Halle, where he worked as secretary and librarian for F. A. G. Tholuck, and Berlin, where he came under the influence of August Neander. Neander's 'mediating theology', with its combination of scholarship and piety, provided a model for Schaff, and his whole career would be shaped by the 'evangelical catholicism' characteristic of Neander and others at Berlin. Schaff completed his theological studies in 1841 and published his first book, *The Sin Against the Holy Ghost*, not knowing that the ideas expressed in it would cause opponents to bring heresy charges against him within a few years.

Schaff loved to travel and spent the next fourteen months on a tour of Italy and Sicily with a pupil and his family. In the autumn of 1842 he began his teaching career in Berlin as a *Privatdocent*. His prospects of a professorship at a German university were promising, but he left that possibility behind and turned to the New World by accepting an invitation to teach at the tiny German Reformed seminary in Mercersburg, Pennsylvania.

Schaff arrived in Mercersburg in August 1844 and immediately faced criticism because of his harsh words about America in his ordination sermon at Elberfeld the previous April. Responding to what he perceived to be his 'Macedonian call', Schaff expressed his concerns over the triple threats of heathenism, Romanism and sectarianism faced by the church in America. The German immigrants to America, he said, were in danger of sinking into 'an abyss of heathenism' in 'the land so free from restraint'.

An additional storm of protest arose after Schaff gave his inaugural address as professor at Mercersburg Seminary. Expanded and published in 1845 as *The Principle of Protestantism*, the address stressed the continuity within Christianity from the early to the contemporary church, including the church of the Middle Ages. Although the Protestant Reformation was a necessary development in Christian history, Schaff insisted that rather than being a revolutionary redirection of the faith, it was in basic continuity with the pattern of organic development in the church. He also expressed his desire for the development of an 'evangelical catholic' church in the future. The young professor had not reckoned with the strength of anti-Catholic feeling in his new homeland, however, and some of those who had invited him to the seminary now charged him with heresy. Almost a year later, the synod of the German Reformed Church exonerated Schaff, but his ideas would continue to be a source of controversy for years to come.

More happy was Schaff's discovery that his colleague on the faculty at Mercersburg, John Williamson *Nevin, was a theologian whose pilgrimage had led him to a position remarkably similar to Schaff's own. They would work together in various contexts for the next two decades, developing what came to be known as the Mercersburg Theology. Schaff and Nevin were convinced that the 'church question' was the most important theological issue of the day and that the historical development of the church towards an 'evangelical catholic' identity demanded a strong critique of the American churches' tendency towards individualism, rationalism and sectarianism.

In 1845 Schaff married Elizabeth Schley of Frederick City, Maryland. The couple had eight children, of whom three (two sons and a daughter) outlived their parents.

In his next two books, *What is Church History?* (1846) and *History of the Apostolic Church* (1851; ET, 1853), and in numerous articles in the journal *Der deutsche Kirchenfreund*, which he founded in 1848 and edited for the next six years, Schaff unfolded his understanding of the development of Christianity through time. Schaff and Nevin also worked together as editors and major contributors to the *Mercersburg Review*, which became the primary vehicle for the Mercersburg Theology.

A significant event in Schaff's theological development was his visit to Europe in 1853–1854. The first of fourteen such journeys, this visit allowed him to share his insights into the religious life of the United States with his former teachers and colleagues. His book of reflections, *Amerika* (1854; translated and expanded as *America: A Sketch of the Political, Social, and Religious Character of the United States of North America*, 1855), described in detail both the weaknesses and the admirable strengths of Christianity in his adopted homeland. Schaff lamented the sectarian divisions and relatively shallow intellectual and cultural life of the United States, but he also saw the dawning of a new day when the spirit of God would 'call forth from the chaos a beautiful creation'. In fact, Schaff argued that America was destined to play a distinctive role in the future of Christianity.

By the mid-1850s, Schaff had begun to feel increasingly isolated in Mercersburg. With the move of Marshall College from Mercersburg to Lancaster in 1853, the ongoing financial struggles of the seminary and the disruptions in southern Pennsylvania brought by the Civil War in 1862 and 1863, Schaff looked for opportunities elsewhere. In 1865, after a two-year leave of absence from Mercersburg Seminary, he accepted a post with the New York Sabbath Committee, which he held until 1870, when he joined the faculty of Union Theological Seminary in New York. Schaff taught at Union until just before his death, holding various chairs, including those of Encyclopedia and Christian Symbolics (1870–1873), Hebrew (1873–1874), Biblical Literature (1874–1887) and Church History (1887–1893). During his time in New York, Schaff founded in 1867 the American branch of the Evangelical Alliance and was the primary organizer and promoter of that group's international meeting in New York in 1873. One of Schaff's most arduous and remarkable contributions was as president from 1872 to 1884 of the American Committee for Bible Revision, which worked with the British Committee to revise the King James Version of the Bible. Amazingly, for a non-native English speaker and a scholar whose primary vocation was not biblical studies, Schaff worked tirelessly and effectively to engender cooperation and bring the translation project to completion.

Schaff worked on two major multi-volume works of enduring value during his years at Union: his three-volume *Creeds of Christendom*, which appeared in 1877, and his *History of the Christian Church*, for which Schaff wrote four volumes covering the early church up to Gregory VII and two volumes on the Protestant Reformation. The first volume had appeared in 1856, and the final one from his pen was published in 1892. Schaff's son David added two more volumes on the medieval church after his father's death. Schaff also edited a number of important works, including an American edition of Lange's German Bible commentary and an edition of the *Select Library of the Nicene and Post-Nicene Fathers of the Christian Church*.

Schaff was instrumental in the founding of the Society of Biblical Literature in 1880 and was the founder of the American Society of Church History in 1888, serving as that organization's president until his death. He intended both organizations to create opportunities for ecumenical and international cooperation among scholars.

Schaff's final and fitting address, 'The Reunion of Christendom', was delivered at the World's Parliament of Religions at Chicago in 1893. Revealing his amazingly broad conception of the Christian family, Schaff accorded a dazzling array of Christian groups a role in the evangelical catholic church that he believed was developing in America. Through scholarship, through ecumenical organizations and through appreciation for the Christian tradition in all its variety, Schaff advocated the reunion of Christendom. Not quite a month after his trip to Chicago, Schaff died at his home in New York City on 20 October 1893.

Bibliography

S. Graham, *Cosmos in the Chaos: Philip Schaff's Interpretation of Nineteenth-Century American Religion* (Grand Rapids: Eerdmans, 1995); K. Penzel (ed.), *Philip Schaff: Historian and Ambassador of the Universal Church,* *Selected Writings* (Macon: Mercer University Press, 1991); G. Shriver, *Philip Schaff: Christian Scholar and Ecumenical Prophet* (Macon: Mercer University Press, 1987).

S. R. GRAHAM

■ **SCHMUCKER, Samuel S.** (1799–1873), American Lutheran theologian, sought to recapture interest in Lutheranism among his contemporaries while recasting it in an American idiom. His work as a theological educator and author took part of nineteenth-century Lutheranism in one direction even as other major figures, such as C. F. W. *Walther in the Missouri Synod and Charles Porterfield Krauth in the General Council, took a different course.

Schmucker was born on 28 February 1799, in Hagerstown, Maryland. His grandfather Nikolaus had emigrated to Virginia from Michelstadt in Hesse-Darmstadt, Germany. His father, Johann Georg, had studied theology with Paul Henkel and was a Lutheran pastor in the Pennsylvania Ministerium. Schmucker himself attended an academy in York, Pennsylvania, the University of Pennsylvania and finally Princeton Theological Seminary. Ordained in 1821, he first served a Lutheran parish in New Market, Virginia. He was active in shaping the organization and theology of the General Synod, founded that same year.

When the General Synod set up its seminary and college in Gettysburg, Pennsylvania in 1826, Schmucker was called to lead the school. He was the only member of staff for the first four years and remained at Gettysburg seminary for nearly four decades; he taught some 400 students.

Schmucker felt obliged as a teacher in the church to write constantly; he produced books and periodicals expounding evangelical theology, especially at a popular level. His better-known works include *Elements of Popular Theology* (1834), *Psychology or Elements of a New System of Mental Philosophy* (1842), *The Lutheran Manual on Scriptural Principles* (1855) and *The Lutheran Symbols, or Vindication of American Lutheranism* (1856). He wrote many articles for *The Lutheran Observer* and *The Evangelical Review*. His interest in moving the church from an old-world Lutheran identity to a place in wider

American society was still to be seen in his final work, *The Unity of Christ's Church* (1870).

Schmucker faced a double challenge: American Protestantism had been greatly influenced by the Enlightenment, and its identity had become indistinct after the American Revolution as its ties to Europe grew weaker. Schmucker sought to strengthen Lutheran identity as he understood it, while also enlisting wider support for active evangelical church life. His concern over the issue of identity was seen first in his *Formula for the Government and Discipline of the Lutheran Church in America*, a kind of constitution for churches in Virginia and Maryland, which was adopted by the General Synod. Rationalism and deism from Germany and England had not penetrated Lutheran circles as deeply as they had affected other traditions, but their influence was beginning to be felt. Yet ironically, although Schmucker set out to stem the exodus from the Lutheran church, his efforts to enlist allies from other confessions would erode his own.

Lutheran identity in nineteenth-century America was complicated by the issue of language. German remained popular in many places. Many nineteenth-century immigrants had felt they could maintain their identity only by leaving Germany, and the continued use of their mother tongue in theological training, publications and public worship helped them to preserve it in their new home. However, Schmucker's own circle was making the transition to English, though they lacked both literature in English and English-speaking clergy. Schmucker's literary output, written in English, was designed to meet the need for publications, and his Gettysburg seminary provided pastors. But Schmucker sought further changes. In the face of the Enlightenment challenge and with time and distance weakening the church's links to Europe and its sense of identity, he believed it was necessary to forge a new identity for American Lutherans and to rally them around beliefs essential to their own time. The attempt to define that identity and those rallying points resulted in a major dispute over what it meant to be a Lutheran. Even the need for the name itself was called into question.

Unlike European countries, the United States had no territorial confession or national church. Denominationalism generated a plurality of churches, and their geographical overlap became increasingly complex. Schmucker believed that bold action was required to meet these challenges. Instead of disputing with evangelical members of other denominations, Lutherans should confront their real foes: 'fundamental errorists' in their own church and unbelievers outside it. It was important for American Lutherans to increase their vision: to look beyond themselves and be more accepting of other Protestants. To that end, Schmucker called on them to break free from tradition and move beyond historical positions that they maintained only by inertia. Everything must be open to review: 'the authority of the fathers, whether they be Nicene or Ante-Nicene, Roman or Protestant'. He first made his views public in 1838 with his *Fraternal Appeal to the American Churches with a Plan for Catholic Union on Apostolic Principles*.

Lutheran identity was defined primarily by the Augsburg Confession and *Luther's Small Catechism. The Confession had been put before Emperor Charles V in Augsburg in 1530, when those supporting Luther's movement stood in danger of condemnation and tried to use the document to demonstrate that they were truly within the Catholic Church. The Catechism was the means by which parents had handed on the core of Lutheran theology to their children in the home. But the needs of the sixteenth-century German church had now given way to new challenges. Schmucker sought to create a wider American evangelical alliance that would be better able than a single denomination to ensure its own survival and that could respond effectively to the circumstances of his day. To that end he drew up the Definite Platform and published it anonymously in 1855. It was an 'American recension' of the Augsburg Confession and purported to represent the position of the General Synod. It was never formally adopted, though many sympathized with it. Of the twenty-one primary articles in the Augsburg Confession, twelve were omitted or drastically rewritten. Additional articles (22–28) from the original document that dealt with abuses of the Reformation era were dropped completely. Schmucker sought to recast evangelical theology for his own age, moving beyond a Lutheran identity that had been developed long before and was now a stumbling-block, and a confession that, unless it was modified, was now largely obsolete.

Schmucker hoped to encourage non-Lutheran evangelicals to speak against what he saw as the external threat to Christianity: an increasingly powerful paganism promoted by atheists and rationalists. Instead he found himself opposed from within his own church. He was attacked by those intent on stopping him from undermining the confessional identity of 'old Lutheranism' in favour of a more general Protestantism. Schmucker was forced to defend himself against those he called 'intolerant symbolists, formalists, and orthodoxists' who, he believed, would condemn American evangelical Christianity to extinction in the long run. As a result of this dispute, Schmucker's interest in Philip *Melanchthon (he named his son Beal Melanchthon) led his opponents to regard Melanchthon too with suspicion. Melanchthon wrote the first version of the Augsburg Confession, but in his later Variata he changed some of its language, and so legitimated some crypto-Calvinist views. Some believed that Schmucker too was diluting orthodox theology.

Some Lutherans supported Schmucker, and a more open, tolerant Lutheranism emerged, which was willing to view its confessional documents more as an echo from the past than as a contemporary statement of faith. Other Lutherans warned against sacrificing the identity they had sought to transplant and preserve, though they too faced the challenge of engaging with an ever-changing culture. The debate generated by the Definite Platform over what it means to be 'confessional' and 'Lutheran' has continued beyond Schmucker's death (on 26 July 1873, at Gettysburg) and even to the present.

Bibliography

A. R. Wentz, *Pioneer in Christian Unity: Samuel Simon Schmucker* (Philadelphia: Fortress Press, 1967); P. P. Kuenning, *The Rise and Fall of American Lutheran Pietism: The Rejection of an Activist Heritage* (Macon: Mercer University Press, 1988); N. O. Forness (ed.), *The Papers of the Schmucker Bicentennial* (Gettysburg: Gettysburg College, 2000).

R. ROSIN

■ **SCOFIELD, Cyrus Ingerson** (1843–1921), dispensationalist author, was born in Lenawee County, Michigan, near the town of Clinton in 1843. His mother died from complications related to his birth. As a boy he and his devout Episcopalian family moved to Wilson County, Tennessee, near Lebanon; he lived in the slave South until the age of seventeen. Scofield intended to go to college, but his plans were changed by the Civil War. He enlisted and served throughout the war, receiving the Cross of Honor for bravery at the battle of Antietam. He never received the formal education that he had planned. After the war, Scofield moved to St Louis, Missouri and studied law while working as a clerk in a law practice. After moving to Atchison, Kansas, he was admitted to the Kansas Bar in 1869 and later served as an elected representative to the Kansas legislature and as an appointed US attorney.

Having married before moving to Kansas, Scofield was subsequently divorced and returned to St Louis, leaving behind his ex-wife and two young daughters. The circumstances of this phase of his life are somewhat unclear, but his troubles appear to have been related to alcohol abuse. Once back in St Louis, he experienced an evangelical conversion and soon afterwards assisted in a Dwight L. *Moody revival campaign. He was licensed to preach at the Hyde Park Congregational Church, where he worked from 1880 to 1882.

In 1882 Scofield moved to Dallas, Texas to become pastor of a Congregational mission church. He was ordained there and saw the church grow to over 500 members by the time he left in 1895. While in Dallas he was profoundly influenced by James H. Brooks, a Presbyterian minister who had read works by the dispensationalist John Nelson *Darby and other so-called Plymouth Brethren authors. Scofield began to offer a correspondence Bible course for which over 7,000 people were soon enrolled. The course marked the beginning of Scofield's career as a Bible expositor, which would make him one of the most significant evangelical fundamentalists of his era, perhaps of the entire twentieth century. His book *Rightly Dividing the Word of Truth* (1888) established him as a leading advocate of dispensational premillennialism. At this time he was also heavily involved in missions, serving as denominational missions superintendent for the south and southwest and founding the Central American Mission in 1890. At Moody's request Scofield left Dallas in 1895 to become pastor of a Congregational church in Northfield, Massachusetts, where he became deeply involved with the Northfield Bible Conference, eventually becoming president of the Northfield Bible Training School.

After returning to Dallas briefly in 1903, Scofield left his pastorate to devote himself full-time to the project for which he is famous, *The Scofield Reference Bible*, which was published by Oxford University Press in 1909. In 1908 Scofield transferred to the Presbyterian Church in the US. He eventually moved to New York City, where he ran a correspondence course and night school. In 1914 he and Lewis Sperry *Chafer founded the Philadelphia School of the Bible, and he spent the last seven years of his life updating and revising his reference Bible and participating in other projects initiated by the early fundamentalist movement.

Scofield believed that the Bible was a 'self-interpreting' book, but he laboured diligently to ensure that readers understood it in a dispensational context. Starting with a basic translation (the AV text), he and his seven consulting editors revised some passages to uncover what they believed to be the true meaning. They also defined important theological terms such as atonement and justification and inserted into the text outlines that included dispensational divisions. Scofield also made his own paragraph divisions, with headings and sub-headings. The reference Bible included footnotes in which important themes such as fulfilled and unfulfilled prophecy were discussed. A nine-member committee revised Scofield's Bible in 1967, retaining the dispensational system while updating the wording. In this edition Bishop Ussher's dating system, which Scofield had added in 1917, was dropped.

The Scofield Reference Bible is a prime example of the Baconian approach to the Bible that marked early twentieth-century fundamentalism. Scofield and others believed that they could come to an objective understanding of Scripture by employing the early modern scientific method. His lack of formal training was actually an advantage, he

believed, because it left his mind uncluttered and undiluted by human scholarship so that he could render the text plainly. For Scofield and other early fundamentalists, the Bible was a storehouse of theological facts that needed merely to be categorized and presented in an orderly fashion to be understood properly. Nowhere was this conviction more apparent than in the chain referencing method of biblical study that Scofield employed. Chain referencing starts with the first occurrence of a particular theme, then provides cross-references to all the passages in the Bible in which that theme is addressed. Scofield and reference Bible readers believed that by following this method one could learn everything that the Holy Spirit had revealed on any biblical theme. Further commentary was unnecessary. This approach resembled the Baconian approach to science, which emphasizes observation and categorization of the facts of nature. Fundamentalists eschewed all theories except dispensationalism, which they saw as the interpretive key to rightly dividing the Word.

Scofield's Bible played a major role in early fundamentalism's adoption of dispensational premillennialism. Brought to the US in the nineteenth century largely by Darby, by the 1920s this system had become popular among fundamentalists. By around 1960, after many fundamentalists had begun to think of themselves as neo-evangelicals, virtually all who retained the name 'fundamentalist' were dispensationalists. Dispensationalists divide history into distinct periods or dispensations, usually seven in number, and teach that God relates to humankind differently in each period. Each dispensation emphasizes a particular principle. Typically, the dispensations are innocence, conscience, human government, promise, law, grace and kingdom. God's redemptive work has a different meaning depending on the dispensation, and to understand passages of Scripture correctly, one must know to which dispensation a passage applies. For example, during the dispensation of law, there was, in Scofield's own words, an emphasis on 'legal obedience as the condition for salvation', but in the dispensation of grace this condition was changed to 'acceptance or rejection of Christ'. Scofield's dispensationalism was also pretribulation rapturist; like most fundamentalists, he taught that believers will be raptured to heaven before the onset of the great tribulation of the end times that will precede the kingdom dispensation.

It would be hard to overstate the significance of *The Scofield Reference Bible*. It has sold over two million copies, and it is the Bible that many fundamentalist churches present to new converts. Its notes, paragraph and dispensational divisions, headings and sub-headings can seem as much a part of Scripture as the text itself.

Bibliography

C. G. Trumbull, *The Life Story of C. I. Scofield* (New York: Oxford University Press, 1920); C. I. Scofield (ed.), *The Scofield Reference Bible* (New York: Oxford University Press, 1909, expanded 1917); C. I. Scofield, *Rightly Dividing the Word of Truth* (Westwood: Revell, 1896); G. M. Marsden, *Fundamentalism and American Culture* (New York: Oxford University Press, 1980).

B. HANKINS

■ **SCOTT, Thomas** (1747–1821), Anglican clergyman and commentator, was born in a small farmhouse at Braytoft in Lincolnshire. He began his schooling locally at Burgh, and then at eight years of age was sent to Bennington near Boston (Lincolnshire) for two years to continue his education in a school kept by a clergyman. From an early age he seemed to have a scholarly bent and a good aptitude for Latin. Although his father raised livestock, he wanted one of his sons to enter a learned profession, and so Scott was sent for further schooling at Scorton in Yorkshire in the hope that he would enter medicine. He continued at Scorton until 1762, when he was bound as an apprentice to a surgeon and apothecary at Alford, some eight miles from the family home. Within two months, however, Scott was dismissed for 'gross misconduct'. He returned home disgraced and was assigned the hardest tasks on the farm. He remained a farm labourer for nine years.

Scott now began to reflect more seriously on the state of his own soul, particularly in preparation for holy communion. He had a good deal of solitude on the farm and so spent much time in introspection. In a pattern common in evangelical biography, he would make moral resolutions, relapse into wrongdoing and then renew his resolutions when warning was given of the next sacrament. As he put it, 'The same ground was gone over again, and with the same issue.' Yet before his devotional anxiety could be resolved, he came across a Socinian commentary on the Scriptures and was immediately captivated. Scott tells the story of his theological development in his autobiography, *The Force of Truth* (1779).

Finding that he did not stand to inherit the farm but could well remain a day-labourer all his life, Scott resumed his private study of Greek and Latin with the intention of applying for holy orders. Then one day he walked away from the farm. Unexpectedly, he was supported by a local clergyman and by the Archdeacon of Lincoln, Gordon Scott. His plans were thrown into doubt, however, when the Bishop of Lincoln, John Green, required a testimonial letter and a letter from his father indicating his approval. In the end Scott's family rallied to his support, and his father gave his permission. In his autobiography, he sums up his ordination in one long periodic sentence: 'After having concealed my real sentiments under the mask of general expressions; after having subscribed Articles directly contrary to my then belief; and after having blasphemously declared, in the presence of God, and of the congregation, in the most solemn manner, sealing it with the Lord's supper, that I judged myself to be inwardly moved by the Holy Ghost to take that office upon me (not knowing or believing that there was a Holy Ghost), on September the 20th, 1772, I was ordained a Deacon.'

Scott was priested early the next year and moved to Buckinghamshire to take up a curacy at Stoke Goldington and Weston Underwood under Dr Dowbiggen, who had married the niece of the bishop. It was here that he met Jane Kell, whom he married in 1774. He remained a studious minister, teaching himself Hebrew and continuing his reading in the classics.

Two years earlier, about the time of his ordination, he had begun reading Bishop Burnet's *History of His Own Time* (1734), a book that concludes with a charge to the clergy of the established church to be more worthy pastors. Scott now began to be troubled about having entered into the ministry for unworthy motives and by his neglect of his parishioners. In January 1774 two of his parishioners lay at the point of death, and he did not visit. Yet he discovered that the neighbouring minister, John *Newton of Olney, had called on them several times. In 1775 he moved to a neighbouring curacy at Ravenstone, where he would remain for two years. Preoccupied with his own intellectual ability, he was eager to enter into theological debate with Newton and to demolish his Calvinistic beliefs. A converted slave-trader and a hymn-writer, Newton was well known as an evangelical. After some familiarity had been established, Scott sought to draw him into an epistolary controversy. The correspondence lasted from May to December, but much to Scott's vexation, Newton would not be drawn. He treated each of Scott's provocations as an earnest spiritual question, and acted the part of a spiritual director. At the same time, Scott was troubled in conscience about the Thirty-Nine Articles, all the more so because he had some hope of preferment, which would require his renewed subscription *ex animo*. Since the Feathers Tavern Petition in 1772, subscription had become a controversial issue in the established church, and the Unitarian Theophilus Lindsey had recently published his own *Apology* (1774) for leaving the Church of England altogether; he held views similar to Scott's. The stage was set for a crisis, but Scott's accession to evangelical views was not through a climactic evangelical conversion experience. On the contrary, his conscience led him to renewed study over the course of two years. Indeed, the central and longest section of *The Force of Truth* reads almost as a bibliographic essay, as Scott recounts some twenty-three books he read on his journey back to mainstream Christian belief. By 1777 he had reasoned his way into evangelical Calvinism.

In 1777 Scott moved to a larger house at Weston Underwood, where he preached and lectured several times a week. The vicar of his curacy at Ravenstone noticed a change in the earnestness of Scott's sermons. Moreover, Scott was preaching for an hour at a time, and always producing new sermons. The vicar claimed to know clergymen who preached for only ten minutes, and added that he himself had only fifty-four or fifty-five sermons and these had served him well enough for more than fifty years. Scott had clearly been revitalized by his change of views, and he was now often regarded as a 'Methodist'. Indeed, he now claimed that the beliefs of the Methodists were simply those held by the Reformers and expressed in the Articles of the Church of England.

In 1779 he published *The Force of Truth*, and two years later he became the curate of Olney, which had formerly been Newton's parish. The parishioners at Olney did not, however, flock to Scott's services as they had to Newton's. Some complained that they wanted more 'variety' and that Scott was too severe. For Scott's part, he found many of the people inclined to antinomianism. He therefore found the invitation to become chaplain at the Lock Hospital in London in 1785 a welcome one, and he soon added to this post a lectureship at St Mildred's, Bread Street and St Margaret's, Lothbury. However, the board of governors and the congregation attached to the hospital were aristocratic, and Scott's preaching was too direct and 'scolding' for them. When he emphasized Christian duties, they thought him Arminian; when he defended himself, they thought him more Calvinist than they. He had thoughts of leaving, but his wife persuaded him to stay. In London he joined in the discussions of the Eclectic Society with John Newton and other leading evangelicals, and out of these discussions came the plan to organize the Church Missionary Society. Scott served as the first secretary for the mission, preached its first anniversary sermon, and later tutored several of its candidate missionaries. In September 1790 his wife died, leaving him four young children, and he remarried that same year. He left London in 1803 to take up his last cure as rector of Aston Standford in Buckinghamshire, and he would remain there until his death in 1821.

Scott wrote a number of theological essays, but his greatest undertaking was his commentary on the whole Bible, begun in January 1788 and concluded in June 1792. Scott's method was to reprint the scriptural text and intersperse 'practical observations' applying the text to the reader, and then to offer further critical commentary on the original context in detailed footnotes. The commentary was originally published in 174 weekly parts. It was Scott's *magnum opus*, and he invested his own money to help the financially troubled publisher complete the project. But in the end the first publisher went bankrupt, and Scott was for years involved in crippling debts and lawsuits on account of the commentary. Notwithstanding these problems, the commentary was popular, and by his death 12,000 copies had been printed in England and more than 25,000 in America.

Scott was probably the most intellectually capable and theologically astute evangelical clergyman in the Church of England in his generation. Newton once introduced him to some Dissenters in the Midlands as the man he expected would prove to be 'the Jonathan *Edwards of Old England'. His collected *Theological Works* (1805–1808) were published in five volumes, but his most reprinted works were his *Force of Truth* and his commentary. The former was a distinctive work of intellectual autobiography and evangelical apologetics, and his *Commentary* was standard reading for Victorian evangelicals, so much so that he became known simply as 'the commentator'. His influence extended beyond the evangelical party. John Henry Newman possessed both of these works and others by Scott, claiming that it was he 'who made a deeper impression on my mind than any other, and to whom (humanly speaking) I almost owe my soul'.

Bibliography

J. Scott, *The Life of the Rev. Thomas Scott* (London: L. B. Seeley & Son, 1822).

D. B. HINDMARSH

■ **SCROGGIE, William Graham** (1877–1958), Baptist Bible teacher, was brought up in a strongly evangelical family. His mother was a native of Newburgh, and his father moved there in 1866 to undertake evangelistic work. James Scroggie later moved within Scotland and England a number of times. In 1875, when living in Annan, the family suffered a shattering blow; their three children, all under the age of five, died of scarlet fever. This story was later told by Graham Scroggie's mother in *The Story of a Life in the Love of God*. Graham Scroggie, who was born two years later, wrote a preface to this book, and clearly his parents' faith made a deep impression on him.

At an early age Scroggie felt an urge to become a preacher, and in his twentieth year he began training at the Pastors' College (later Spurgeon's College), London. He spoke of his two years at the Pastors' College as having had a 'creative and inspiring influence' on him, although he was critical of some omissions from his training, especially in the area of spirituality. In 1900 Scroggie married Florence Hudson; the couple had one son, Marcus. Scroggie's first period of service as a Baptist pastor was at Leytonstone in Essex. It was a ministry that came to a premature end after two years. Scroggie described this period as one of inner conflict, during which he felt spiritually bankrupt and almost a spiritual casualty. It led to a new experience in which, as he was to put it later, the Bible and Christ came alive to him.

Scroggie felt that he had to give up his first pastorate and start afresh. His next pastorate, in Halifax, was also short-lived. In this case it was his strong convictions about what was described as a 'questionable form of entertainment' in the church that led to his resignation. For the next two years Scroggie was without a pastorate.

After this rather uncertain start in pastoral ministry, Scroggie went on to significant ministries in Sunderland and in Edinburgh. In 1907 he accepted a call to the very active Bethesda Free Church in Sunderland, a church that claimed to have a hundred lay preachers, and in 1916 he moved to Charlotte Chapel, Edinburgh, Scotland's largest Baptist church. Scroggie's ministry at Charlotte Chapel attracted 1,000 people every Sunday, and hundreds also came to his midweek Bible school.

Scroggie resigned from Charlotte Chapel on account of ill health in 1933, spent six months in New Zealand at the Auckland Tabernacle and then almost five years in itinerant ministry in the USA, Canada, Australia and South Africa. From 1938 to 1944 he was minister of Spurgeon's Metropolitan Tabernacle in London. In 1943, when London Bible College was formed and a principal was required, an invitation was issued to Scroggie. Although he accepted, the post required too much administrative work and he relinquished it. Scroggie's first wife

Florence died, and in 1941 he married Joan Hooker, whose mother was the first principal of Ridgelands College, a missionary training college in Wimbledon. Scroggie died in 1958.

Scroggie exercised a significant influence in a number of areas. The first was that of evangelical spirituality in the first half of the twentieth century. In 1950 he was called 'indisputably the foremost living Keswick teacher', at a time when for most conservative evangelicals in Britain the teaching offered at the annual Keswick Convention, in the English Lake District, was of a quality not found on any other platform. At the heart of the spiritual life, for Scroggie, was a conscious decision to make Christ Lord of one's life. Scroggie argued that although Keswick spoke of the 'Spirit-filled' life, this idea was derived from that of Christ's Lordship, which in his view was Keswick's distinctive message. In 1951 Jean Rees, a popular evangelical writer, noted that at Keswick Scroggie had opposed the idea of 'Let go – and let God' and had said that victory came through 'fighting and striving to make true in experience what is true for us positionally'.

A second area of influence was that of preaching. Scroggie's vision was of a ministry, whether in local churches or at large conventions, that offered solid biblical exposition and spiritual application. His ability to deliver this kind of material effectively at Keswick is evidenced by his popularity as a speaker at Keswick's Bible Readings. Scroggie delivered this series of convention addresses on no fewer than twelve occasions, beginning in 1914, and was determined that they should exemplify the highest standards of exposition.

This stress on preaching affected Scroggie's view of the priorities of the local pastor. An important condition that he made before he accepted the call to Charlotte Chapel was that he should not have to do 'social pastoral visiting'. His pastoral work was directed to those who were sick, bereaved or in other special need. His perception was that his call was not to be an evangelist or a pastor but a Bible teacher. As a mark of his commitment to Bible teaching, Scroggie guided thousands of students through his own four-year correspondence course.

A further significant topic addressed by Scroggie was revivalist experiences. In 1912, when minister in Sunderland, which was a centre for the growing British Pentecostal movement, Scroggie wrote three articles in his church magazine on the baptism of the Holy Spirit and tongues. These were later published as a small book. Scroggie considered that errors over the baptism of the Spirit were especially due to the desire to associate the blessing of the Spirit with the gift of tongues. The careful Scot also believed that in many Pentecostal meetings there was a 'surrender of common sense'. When there was an outbreak of revivalist fervour at Keswick in 1922, Scroggie called for an intelligent, reasonable faith. Despite his caution, Scroggie did not deny the possibility of contemporary speaking in tongues.

Although he was outspoken and at times rather legalistic, Scroggie also attempted to transcend divisions between evangelicals. Speaking at one Keswick Convention on the subject of the Apostles' Creed, he argued that given the conflicts of the 1920s over theological modernism (with fundamentalists calling for evangelicals to leave the existing denominations), it was preferable to use the Apostles' Creed as a widely accepted basis of faith than for small groups to construct their own bases of belief and split from the wider church.

Graham Scroggie was awarded an honorary DD from Edinburgh University in 1927. The dean of the faculty of divinity of Edinburgh University, W. P. Paterson, spoke of Scroggie's 'unusual influence in the City as a preacher and missioner', his place as a 'prominent representative of the Keswick Movement, which has done so much to deepen the life and refine the ideals of Evangelicalism', and the work to which Scroggie had especially devoted himself, which was 'the study and teaching of the Bible in its twofold character of a Divine revelation and a great literature'.

Scroggie's books, which numbered over thirty, were widely read by evangelicals. No biography of Scroggie has been written, but his influence was profound. As a result of his thinking, spirituality came to be seen by many mid-century evangelicals in Britain and elsewhere as obedience to the Lordship of Christ in everyday life.

Bibliography

I. M. Randall, 'Graham Scroggie and Evangelical Spirituality', *The Scottish Bulletin of*

Evangelical Theology 18.1 (2000); J. J. Scroggie, edited by W. G. Scroggie, *The Story of a Life in the Love of God* (London: Pickering & Inglis, 1939).

I. M. RANDALL

■ **SEYMOUR, William Joseph** (1870–1922), founding pastor of the Azusa Street Mission, was born on 2 May 1870 in Centerville, Louisiana, the child of former black slaves, Simon and Phyllis Seymour, whose emancipation preceded William's birth by a mere four-and-a-half years. Although they were 'freedmen', the Seymour family struggled to survive in the face of mounting racial violence; William was raised amidst the disintegration of post-Civil War reconstruction. His opportunities were few; as he was working with his parents on the sugar plantations, formal education was out of reach. Nevertheless, Seymour revealed a robust intellect by teaching himself to read and write. He was particularly attracted to the Bible, which, coupled with the vibrant faith of the Negro-Spiritual tradition, caused him to develop a highly sensitive spirituality. From his youth his growing Christian faith, marked by a definite expectation of Christ's imminent return, was attended by dreams and visions. However, he did not join any particular church; he would leave the southern bayous before doing so.

In 1895 Seymour left his then known world, travelling north to settle in Indianapolis. Finding work as a waiter in an inner-city hotel, he then joined the Simpson Chapel Methodist Episcopal Church. Although the church was all black, the denomination was noted for its interracial vision, a characteristic that would later become a hallmark of Seymour's ecclesiology. After a five-year stay, Seymour moved east to Cincinnati, Ohio, where he met the influential holiness teacher, Martin Wells Knapp. Although by this time the Methodist Episcopal Church was drifting from its commitment to racial inclusiveness Knapp, a Methodist evangelist, encouraged racial integration in his public meetings. Knapp's inclusive vision, his belief in divine healing and his stress upon the return of Christ elicited an enthusiastic response from Seymour.

Seymour found a more perfect embodiment of Knapp's ideals in the Evening Light Saints. The Saints were restorationists, who believed that the present-day church was tragically compromised with the world, having lost the spiritual power of the church in apostolic times. Convinced that history was drawing to a close, they emphasized the preparation of the believer for the imminent return of Christ; an end-time outpouring of the Holy Spirit would bring a perfect cleansing of the heart, or sanctification, to those who looked for it. They were also interracial. Seymour readily imbibed all their teaching.

While with the Evening Light Saints, Seymour sensed a call to enter full-time ministry. He resisted it, however, and shortly thereafter was stricken with smallpox. The dangerous virus left Seymour weakened, but alive. With his complexion scarred and permanent loss of vision in his left eye, Seymour claimed that the disease was chastisement from God for his hesitation to obey the heavenly vision. Accordingly, he accepted ordination with the Saints and began a life of itinerant evangelism.

In 1903 Seymour left for Texas to search for family members who had been lost to slavery. He found them in Houston and settled there. For the next two years Seymour travelled widely, ministering in various holiness churches, and being acclaimed as a 'wonderful preacher'. In 1905 an evangelist called Charles F. *Parham came to Houston to hold meetings under the banner of the 'Apostolic Faith Movement'. Disillusioned with the claims of holiness teachers to possess apostolic power, Parham had been obsessed with discovering tangible evidence for a genuine baptism of the Holy Spirit. In 1901 people had begun to speak in tongues at his Kansas Bible College. Four years later in Texas, he forthrightly preached tongues as the 'Bible evidence' for the baptism of the Holy Spirit. Among those convinced by his message was Lucy Farrow, pastor of a black holiness church, who followed Parham to his home in Kansas. In her absence she left Seymour to lead her congregation. Seymour's preaching made a strong impression upon his hearers, most noticeably upon a visitor from Los Angeles, Mrs Neely Terry, who on her return to California described him as a notably godly pastor.

Two months after her departure, Lucy

Farrow returned to Houston with Parham and related her experience of speaking in tongues. They argued that this was the evidence of the return of apostolic power to the church. Interested, Seymour gained admission to Parham's Bible class in Houston. Though the law prevented him from joining a white class, Seymour sat in the hall beside a door that was deliberately left ajar. Parham's message persuaded Seymour that sanctification was not synonymous with Spirit-baptism, but rather a precondition of it. Glossolalia, or more precisely xenoglossy, was both the evidence of this baptism and the means of fulfilling the missionary mandate. Although he did not speak in tongues himself, in a few weeks Seymour had accepted the message he would preach for the rest of his life: saved, sanctified and filled with the Holy Spirit.

At this time a black holiness congregation in Los Angeles was in need of a pastor. On the recommendation of Neely Terry, Julia Hutchins, a leading member of the church, invited Seymour to fill the position. Believing this invitation to be a call from God, Seymour accepted at once. By January 1906, he was travelling west by train.

Los Angeles proved to be ground already prepared for the seed Seymour was bearing. The city was experiencing renewal as a fresh spiritual hunger swept through numerous congregations. Reports from the Welsh revival had led many leaders into protracted periods of fasting and prayer for a similar work of God in Los Angeles. Frank Bartleman, an itinerant evangelist, and Joseph Smale, the pastor of The New Testament Church, typified the current dissatisfaction with lifeless creeds and the longing for something new. Not everyone, however, was ready for the radical doctrine Seymour brought into this spiritual ferment.

Without hesitation, Seymour presented to his new congregation the teaching he had learned from Parham. This was a bold step to take; in effect, he was informing his holiness listeners that their experience of sanctification was not what the Bible called 'Holy Spirit baptism'. The result was a decisive split. Hutchins padlocked the doors of the church against Seymour, while some other members of the congregation followed their new pastor to the home of Mr and Mrs Edward Lee, where he was giving himself to prayer and fasting. Soon his piety attracted the attention of Richard and Ruth Asbery, who invited him to their home to conduct regular prayer meetings. This house, 214 North Bonnie Brae Street, became a new centre of spiritual revival. A small prayer group, including men and women, white and black, gathered around Seymour as they sought to receive the blessing he was describing. On 9 April 1906 Edward Lee requested Seymour to pray for him that he might receive the blessing that they were seeking; immediately Lee began to speak in tongues. This event was followed by numerous similar experiences over the next several days. On 12 April Seymour himself received the experience. Soon the house was full, with people overflowing into the surrounding yard. Divine healings were reported, people fell into trances, and many spoke in tongues. Men and women were stunned by an acute sense of God's presence. For Seymour, this was the fulfilment of scriptural prophecy; the end of the age was at hand, and the latter rain had begun.

Soon the congregation moved out of 214 North Bonnie Brae Street into a newly acquired property at 312 Azusa Street. The location, in an industrialized neighbourhood, was unattractive to visitors; yet many came to the barn-like, two-storey mission, which was bordered by livery stables and a shop that sold gravestones. It was, in Seymour's estimation, an ideal location, recalling the humble scene in Bethlehem. Moreover, the surroundings were attractive to those previously marginalized by more 'proper' church buildings.

Within a month of its opening, the mission hall was filled to capacity, holding services every day of the week, three times a day, often late into the night. A modest pulpit made of shoe crates was situated in the centre of the room, with pews made of rough planks and nail kegs laid in a circular formation around it. All races and classes mingled. Indeed, the movement's interracial character was one of its outstanding features; Bartleman says that 'The "color line" was washed away in the blood.' At a time when America was bitterly divided between white and black, the racial harmony achieved at these meetings was momentous.

The mission attracted the attention of the radical evangelical world at large. Men and women from as far away as China made the trip to Los Angeles to visit the famous Azusa Street. Much of this attention was made possible by the mission's newspaper, *The Apostolic Faith*, which was sent out worldwide to as many as 50,000 recipients from 1906 until 1908. The paper created a worldwide interest in the Los Angeles phenomenon and brought many people to the mission. Moreover, numerous missionaries were sent abroad. Almost from its inception, Azusa Street enjoyed worldwide influence, and it has since been hailed as the spiritual parent of Pentecostals around the globe.

Anti-sectarianism was consistently upheld as a chief tenet of the movement, but divisions soon arose. Invited to Los Angeles by Seymour in October 1906, Parham was sickened by what he saw. Though no doubt disturbed by what he deemed to be fanaticism, Parham, a self-declared racist, was evidently repelled by the interracial meetings. His consequent denunciations of Azusa Street split the movement; many of his sympathizers followed him to a rival mission. In the following years, Parham remained one of the mission's most strident critics.

The unity of the movement was further damaged by Seymour's marriage on 13 May 1908 to Jennie Evans Moore, one of the original workers at the mission, to the chagrin of her fellow worker Clara Lum. Accusing Seymour of being unmindful of Christ's imminent return, Lum, the mission secretary and chief coordinator of the mission's newspaper, left Azusa Street for another mission in Portland, Oregon. She took part of the mission's mailing list, and Seymour travelled to Portland in an attempt to recover it. He failed, and the end of 1909 marked the end of Azusa's 'glory years'.

As a preacher, Seymour was less flamboyant than might have been expected. He revealed no flair for polished oratory, though his preaching was very powerful. His discourse was measured and simple, not in the explosive style normally associated with revival preachers. He was noted for his humility, often putting his head inside a wooden shoe crate to hide himself from the limelight. William Durham, a contemporary of Seymour, called him the 'meekest man' he had ever met, whose power was in his weakness. In terms of his theology, Seymour defies simple classification

as a 'Pentecostal'; indeed, he was strikingly different from his theological descendants. Seymour was clearly reluctant to define speaking in tongues as the necessary initial evidence of being filled with the Spirit, remarking: 'Some people today cannot believe they have the Holy Ghost without some outward sign: that is Heathenism . . . It is all right to have the signs following, but not to pin our faith in outward manifestations.' For Seymour, the real evidence of receiving the Spirit was the fruit of the Spirit, namely love: 'If you get angry, or speak evil, or backbite, I care not how many tongues you may have, you have not the baptism with the Holy Spirit.'

Sadly, in spite of Seymour's emphasis on love and brotherly acceptance, harsh exclusivity tainted the Azusa Street Mission. Seymour equated all those who had not received the Spirit's fullness with the foolish virgins of Christ's parable, and warned that any who did not receive the baptism of the Spirit would be excluded from the rapture of the church. The mission's publication recounted graphic visions of non-compliant holiness believers falling into the mouth of hell to the glee of laughing demons beneath.

Seymour spent his final years in less than favourable conditions. After another schism in 1911, Azusa Street dwindled to small numbers, losing its distinctive interracial character. Azusa became a small black church of approximately twenty people, with a white person attending only occasionally. Seymour spent the following years in obscurity, though he travelled widely as a preacher. In 1915 he published his *Doctrines and Disciplines*, and rewrote the Azusa constitution, stipulating that the future leader of the mission must be 'a man of color'. In 1918 Seymour admitted, uncharacteristically, that he did not feel well, but he continued his preaching engagements around the USA. On 28 September 1922 William Seymour died, suffering a massive heart attack while dictating a letter. His burial was simple, the plain redwood casket mirroring the obscurity in which he died. His gravestone, which can be seen today, describes him as 'Our Pastor, Rev. William J. Seymour', reflecting the humility he exhibited as a leader.

Bibliography

F. Bartleman, *Azusa Street* (Plainfield: Logos

International, 1980); D. J. Nelson, 'For Such a Time as This: The Story of Bishop William J. Seymour and the Azusa Street Revival' (PhD dissertation, University of Birmingham, England, 1981); G. Wacker, *Heaven Below: Early Pentecostals and American Culture* (Cambridge, MA: Harvard University Press, 2001).

J. VICKERY

■ **SHAFTESBURY, (Seventh) Earl of** (1801–1885), Victorian philanthropist and social reformer, was born Anthony Ashley Cooper in London on 28 April 1801. From the age of ten to the age of fifty he was known as Lord Ashley; on his father's death in 1851 he inherited the title of Earl of Shaftesbury, membership in the House of Lords and the family estates. His father was a powerful figure in the House of Lords, but his parenting left much to be desired. His son later described him as a 'selfish and cold-hearted bully'. Yet, of his two parents his mother seems to have been the worse; his most charitable description of her was a 'fiend'. The daughter of the Duke of Marlborough, she was a socialite who was as popular with her peers as she was neglectful of her children.

The most important influence in Shaftesbury's childhoood was Maria Milles (pronounced Millis), a middle-aged evangelical servant who had been his mother's personal maid from the time she was a girl. Maria cared for and nurtured the boy's soul, leading him to a personal faith at the age of six. Her death four years later almost destroyed him. One biographer suggests he might well have suffered a 'total collapse', but instead the boy found courage to persevere in the faith Maria had imparted. He continued throughout his life the habits she had inculcated of daily prayer and Bible reading.

From the age of seven, Shaftesbury attended an unreformed public school; the hell on earth that he experienced there can hardly be imagined. As he recalled: 'The place was bad, wicked, filthy; and the treatment was starvation and cruelty.' The fact that home life was only a lesser purgatory probably only intensified his feelings. He became very protective of his younger siblings, and this concern to protect the weaker members of his family was, as an adult, extended to the wider society. Although Shaftesbury's compassionate humanitarianism probably owed a debt to his childhood experiences of neglect and oppression, his involvements were nurtured also by a strong sense of personal responsibility, which his Christian faith taught him and which his evangelicalism reinforced. His schooling situation improved when at the age of twelve he was sent to Harrow, the famous school for the sons of the British elite. From Harrow he went on to Oxford University, where he worked hard and took a degree (something not required of aristocrats in his day), achieving a first-class in classics.

For several years after Oxford, Shaftesbury accomplished little, wandering from one country home to the next because he was not welcome in his family's homes and a moderate allowance from his father necessitated his sponging off his wealthy friends. The only eventful occurrence in these years was his short-lived love affair with a young lady in Vienna who eventually married Prince Metternich. Shaftesbury's election as a Tory MP at the age of twenty-five was the start of a remarkable political career which was to span the next fifty-nine years: twenty-three years in the Commons, and thirty-four years in the Lords. He was first elected in Woodstock (1826), then for Dorchester in 1830 and 1831. In October 1831 he won a by-election in Dorset, where he remained Tory member until his resignation in 1845. He returned to the Commons as member for Bath in 1847, until he entered the Lords in 1851. His periods of political office were, however, very short; he was at the India Board of Control from 1828 to 1830 and the Admiralty from 1834 to 1835, but thereafter did not hold public office.

Shaftesbury's wedding to Lady Emily (Minny) Cowper in 1830 was the beginning of a remarkably happy marriage. Initially people thought it a most unlikely and worldly match for such a pious man; Minny's mother was Lady Cowper, well known as the mistress of Lord Palmerston, although she was married to Lord Cowper. Minny was almost certainly the illegitimate daughter of Lord Palmerston, who married Lady Cowper in 1839 following the death of her husband. Furthermore, Shaftesbury's family was clearly Tory and the Cowpers were leading Whigs;

Lord Melbourne, the Whig prime minister, was Emily's uncle, and Palmerston would eventually be Whig foreign minister and prime minister. Shaftesbury's father so deeply disapproved of the marriage that it led to a nine-year breach between father and son. The Cowper family was remarkably supportive and generous towards the couple. Lord Ashley and his wife apparently loved each other deeply and together had some ten children, four of whom predeceased him. Minny was both his greatest supporter and a key adviser; it was she who urged him in 1833 to take on the factory reform cause.

Although not from an evangelical family, from 1826 Shaftesbury began to be drawn in an evangelical direction through his reading of a Bible commentary by Thomas *Scott. By the early 1830s his evangelical commitments had become firmer; he became more explicitly concerned with declaring his faith to his friends and family and began to align himself with some evangelical political causes (notably sabbatarianism).

Any assessment of Shaftesbury's significance is difficult because his interests were so wide-ranging. He is best remembered for his involvement in securing a series of Factory Acts between 1833 and 1847 that prohibited the employment of children under the age of thirteen in factories and limited the working day of women and young people to ten and a half hours on weekdays and to seven and a half hours on Saturdays. In seeking such legislation he worked closely with a coalition of working-class labourers and used the press very effectively in mobilizing public opinion. His opponents were opposed on principle to any interference by the Government in the economy and deeply resented his lecturing them on their social responsibilities. In the early 1840s Shaftesbury secured the appointment of a Royal Commission to investigate the state of mines; its report in 1842 so shocked the nation that he was able to procure a Mines and Collieries Act that prohibited the employment of women and children under the age of ten in the mines.

There were other social causes in which Shaftesbury was a leading figure, many of which involved the exploitation of children: a series of Chimney Sweeps Acts brought to an end the use of small boys to hand-sweep the chimneys of English homes, which caused the disfigurement or early death of many; the Common Lodging-Houses Act of 1851 (which Charles Dickens called 'the finest piece of legislation enacted in England') provided for the registration and inspection of housing for the poor. Another cause that he took up was very unpopular in Victorian Britain, though Geoffrey Best has suggested that it was his most significant: the reform of the treatment of the insane. Shaftesbury was chair of the 'Lunacy Commission' for forty years, and whenever Parliament called another Royal Commission to investigate the issue, he was the leading expert witness.

Outside Parliament Shaftesbury was equally active in promoting voluntary philanthropic initiatives to address social ills. Introduced to the worst of London's slums by the lay evangelists employed by the evangelical London City Mission, he came to know first-hand the worst of urban destitution. He always insisted on personal investigation, whether it involved descending into the bowels of a coal mine, or meeting with gatherings of thieves and pickpockets in order to understand personally their predicament. He was an ardent advocate of 'ragged schools' for destitute and homeless children, which sought to provide them with basic literacy and job skills; he promoted emigration schemes to enable people to begin new lives in distant British colonies; he supported dozens of societies designed to help costermongers, flowergirls (who sold flowers on the streets), milliners and a host of others. He was a key figure in the Society for Improving the Condition of the Labouring Classes, begun in 1844, which focused on improving housing, and thereby public health. He was also a leading promoter of legislation to implement sanitation reform, serving as a member of the Board of Health (1848–1854) and working closely with Edwin Chadwick, the great proponent of utilitarianism. The range of his involvements astounded his contemporaries. After finishing Shaftesbury's biography Cardinal Henry Manning wrote: 'What a retrospect of work done. It makes me feel that my life has been wasted.'

In addition to his domestic social concerns, Shaftesbury spoke out forcefully on international issues. He was an advocate of political and religious liberty, and frequently pushed the British Government to use its influence to secure fair treatment for minority religious groups abroad. He was concerned with the just treatment of indigenous peoples in British colonies and worked with the Aboriginal Protection Society. In 1843 he denounced the British Government's provocation of the First Opium War with China.

Alongside Shaftesbury's multi-faceted social concerns one must set his many religious involvements. In the mid-1830s he became involved in Anglican home and foreign missionary societies. He played a key role in the formation of the Church Pastoral Aid Society in 1836 and remained its president for the rest of his life. He was especially concerned with efforts to convert the Jews and was an active supporter of the Jews' Society (the London Society for the Promotion of Christianity Amongst the Jews), serving as its president in 1848. He also believed fervently that the Jews were to be restored to Palestine and was the leading Gentile Zionist of the nineteenth century.

At home Shaftesbury backed the interdenominational London City Mission and the British and Foreign Bible Society. In the late 1850s he promoted a movement that sought to provide 'seeker-friendly' religious services for the working classes in theatres and public halls. He was deeply attached to the Bible and never ceased to denounce in the most colourful language those theologians whom he felt were undermining scriptural authority.

Shaftesbury was an unwavering supporter of the principle of an established church. He always sought to defend the privileges of the Church of England and protect its Protestant character, which he felt was at the core of British national identity. Part of his understanding of Britain's duties to God included 'keeping the Sabbath day holy'; this involved him in sabbatarian campaigns that were highly unpopular in some quarters, such as his effort in the late 1840s to stop Sunday postal services. Shaftesbury, however, was not a killjoy and did not oppose enjoyment and recreation on a Sunday, if it did not involve Sunday labour.

Although Shaftesbury was opposed to Roman Catholicism, he was most concerned with the growth of the Oxford Movement or what was termed 'Tractarianism', 'Anglo-Catholicism' or 'Puseyism'. He particularly detested this movement because he felt that it was an attempt to introduce Catholic teaching into the Church of England; ironically, the key figure in the movement, E. B. Pusey, was Shaftesbury's cousin. In the decade of Palmerston's prime ministership (between 1855 and 1865), Shaftesbury's advice on the appointment of bishops bore significant fruit in the raising of six well-known evangelicals to the episcopal bench.

From 1835 Shaftesbury became a close friend of Edward *Bickersteth, an evangelical Anglican minister and widely-respected author. Bickersteth had been the secretary of the Church Missionary Society, and his influence undoubtedly affected Shaftesbury's concern with evangelism at home and abroad. Bickersteth was a recent convert to premillennialism and an ardent advocate of Jewish missions; he was also an outspoken critic of many aspects of British imperialism. Shaftesbury likewise embraced premillennialism, ever looking forward to the Second Coming without ever attempting to set its date. For him, premillennialism was an incentive to social activism. After Bickersteth's death in 1850, the key influence on Shaftesbury was Alexander Haldane, a wealthy and influential lawyer who had a major role in the direction of *The Record* newspaper, a highly opinionated, abrasive and fiercely evangelical publication. Haldane's influence may account for the fact that in his later years Shaftesbury seemed to retreat into an isolated position, becoming highly critical of the Tractarians and even of fellow evangelicals whom he felt were not effectively resisting them.

Shaftesbury was always interested in the fostering and development of science, and in his late twenties he even considered leaving politics to become an astronomer. He always encouraged scientific experimentation, believing that eventually science would confirm the Bible. He did, however, strongly oppose experimentation on animals, and towards the end of his life was an early advocate of the anti-vivisection movement. Although he saw merits in the temperance movement, he was not a teetotaller. Nineteenth-century photographs of him give the impression that he was overly sombre and serious, but many of his contemporaries found him a fascinating, humorous and convivial personality.

Shaftesbury's own thinking was also influenced by Robert Southey, the British poet laureate and one of the leading Romantics. Southey urged the necessity of Government intervention in the economy to address social ills, a view which was contrary to the *laissez-faire* views popular amongst both Whigs and Tories at the time. Shaftesbury's social involvements were indebted to a combination of the Tory paternalism that Southey had encouraged, an evangelical social conscience radicalized by his belief in the need to give an account to Christ for his actions upon Christ's imminent return, and his sense of responsibility for the Christian stewardship of his aristocratic position. Related to all of this was his desire to reconcile the working classes to the existing social order. Above all, however, Shaftesbury believed that the Creator had made both body and soul, and that both had to be taken seriously and made fit for God's service.

The coming of the Reform Act of 1867 broadened the political franchise in Great Britain, and Shaftesbury became aware that the working classes could now take care of their own political interests. He also feared that state intervention was going too far, particularly in the field of education. In 1870 universal public education ended the need for his beloved ragged schools. Although he retained an interest in social questions, he became more negative, despondent and critical. Shaftesbury's happy family life was immensely important to him, and he was deeply devoted to both his wife and his children. The death of his sixteen-year-old son Francis in 1848 almost unnerved him; Francis had shared his parents' deep faith and they were both very attached to him. Minny's passing in 1872 was equally difficult to bear. Perhaps Shaftesbury's greatest disappointment in life was Anthony, his eldest son and heir. He lacked his father's intellect, faith and character, and although he succeeded him as earl in 1885, Anthony committed suicide the following year. Shaftesbury's personal health was long troubled by headaches and digestive problems that probably contributed to his hypersensitivity towards others and to his mood swings between elation and despair. In spite of such inner weaknesses, Shaftesbury became both Victorian Britain's best-known evangelical and its greatest social reformer.

Bibliography

G. Battiscombe, *Shaftesbury: A Biography of the Seventh Earl* (London: Constable, 1974); G. F. A. Best, *Shaftesbury* (London: Batsford, 1964); G. B. A. M. Finlayson, *The Seventh Earl of Shaftesbury, 1801–1885* (London: Eyre Methuen, 1981); J. L. Hammond and B. Hammond, *Lord Shaftesbury* (London: Constable, 1923); E. Hodder, *The Life and Work of the Seventh Earl of Shaftesbury, K. G.*, 3 vols. (London: Cassel & Co., 1887); J. Pollock, *Shaftesbury: The Poor Man's Earl* (London: Hodder & Stoughton, 1985).

D. M. LEWIS

■ **SHAKARIAN, Demos** (1913–1993), founder and leader of the Full Gospel Businessmen's Fellowship International (FGBMFI), was the architect of a parachurch organization specializing in the mobilization of businessmen for Christian fellowship and service. FGBMFI emerged from the healing revival movement of the 1940s and 50s in the United States, but grew most rapidly in partnership with the charismatic movement of the 1960s and 70s. Targeting businessmen in non-church settings, and endorsing 'pentecostal' experiences without apology, FGBMFI grew from humble beginnings in 1953 to become a monolithic international organization twenty-five years later, supporting 1,723 chapters in sixty-six countries.

Demos Shakarian was the son of Armenian immigrants who had settled in California in 1905. His family had strong Christian roots. In Kara Kala, Armenia, the Shakarians were Presbyterian, but the Molokans, an ecstatic Orthodox sect, influenced their church profoundly. Their decision to emigrate to the United States resulted from the vision of a young Russian boy, which predicted doom for the people of Kara Kala if they did not leave their homeland. Demos' grandfather's family settled in Los Angeles. Nine years later the Turks massacred the inhabitants of Kara Kala during the First World War.

Soon after Demos was born on 21 July 1913, his father moved the family to Downey, California to begin a dairy business. Shakarian entered the business and became a partner. He also devoted time to the youth work of the church. When he married Rose in 1932,

Shakarian was well established as a successful dairy farmer. By then, he and his father owned the largest dairy herd in California.

Business, however, was not wholly satisfying to Shakarian; he had a strong sense of spiritual destiny. He was not called to be a preacher, but he began utilizing his relational and business skills to promote evangelism. He organized rallies with well-known speakers and mobilized pastors from various denominations to provide ministry and follow-up. Shakarian gave time and money to these rallies, and they produced positive results.

Yet Shakarian's experience in ministry revealed a disturbing trend in the Christian world of his day. Many American men did not consider Christianity to be compatible with masculinity. Shakarian was grieved that most successful businessmen rarely attended Christian services, and he began to consider a new course of action. He would bring men together in places familiar to them, such as hotels and restaurants, and Christian laymen would explain how their lives had been changed by the power of Jesus. He would call his organization the 'Full Gospel Business Men's Fellowship International': 'Full Gospel', because speakers could talk freely about anything in the Bible, including healing, tongues and deliverance; 'Business Men's', because it would be run by laymen (full-time ministers would not be officers); 'Fellowship' because the organization would represent a coming together of equals outside a church setting; and 'International', because of the scope of its work.

When the healing evangelist Oral *Roberts was in Los Angeles for a crusade in 1951, Shakarian shared his idea with him. Roberts was supportive. He publicized Shakarian's first meeting and agreed to be the speaker. On the morning of Saturday 13 October, only twenty-one men attended the meeting, at Clifton's Cafeteria. Yet the group was encouraged as Roberts finished his address by prophesying that out of this small group, 1,000 chapters would emerge.

This strong beginning was followed by fourteen months of failure. The Los Angeles chapter continued to meet regularly, but attendance remained small. Shakarian took his vision to other cities, both nationally and internationally. He spent thousands of dollars of his own money, but was unable to start a single new chapter. One of the members told Shakarian that he would not give five cents for the entire organization.

Shakarian was ready to abandon his idea. He notified the chapter that the meeting on Saturday 26 December 1952 would be the last. On the night before, he refused to sleep. While praying, he had a vision, in which he was elevated above the nations of the earth. He saw millions of men, shoulder to shoulder, but they were in chains. Their faces were lifeless and miserable. He wept as he realized that they were dead. Then the vision changed. The men's faces suddenly came alive, and their chains were removed. Their faces radiated joy. Shakarian interpreted this vivid vision to mean that FGBMFI should not die.

The meeting the next morning was a breakthrough. The man who had declared the organization to be worthless made a large contribution. Another man had driven over 400 miles through the night to attend. A printer by trade, he offered his printing press and expertise; he became the editor of *Voice* magazine, the organization's periodical. Regular printings of *Voice* magazine would later exceed 500,000 copies.

In 1953 nine new chapters of FGBMFI were founded, and the first annual convention was held in Los Angeles, attended by 600 members. The organization's early growth resulted in part from the influence of the healing evangelists Oral Roberts and William Branham. The healing revival movement of the 1950s was both the product and the platform of the FGBMFI. The international growth of the organization resulted partly from the popularity of the evangelist Tommy Hicks. The first chapter outside the USA was founded in 1955, in Johannesburg, South Africa. In 1956 many new chapters were established in other countries. After ten years, known as the 'Decade of Destiny', FGBMFI supported some 300 chapters and 100,000 members.

Yet in the 1960s the organization grew even more rapidly. FGBMFI associated itself more closely with the rapidly expanding charismatic movement. Shakarian worked with a wide variety of Protestant denominations. He continued to emphasize the interdenominational nature of FGBMFI. He encouraged his members to stay in their churches, and to invest their gifts in their local churches, not in FGBMFI. As the charismatic movement developed links with Roman Catholicism, many Catholics became involved in FGBMFI.

The twenty-fifth anniversary of the organization in 1978 was a high point. In that year, 134 conventions were held. The 'Good News' television programme was being broadcast on over 300 stations, and 1,700 chapters were meeting in sixty-six nations. In 1980 FGBMFI celebrated the opening of new headquarters in Costa Mesa, California. Membership continued to increase through the 1980s, reaching 700,000. FGBMFI had become the most successful and far-reaching laymen's organization in Christian history.

Shakarian suffered a stroke in 1984. While he was incapacitated, the leadership of FGBMFI was reorganized. Shakarian recovered his health and was able to reassume control by 1989, but as a result of the leadership crisis membership had been cut in half. Before Shakarian died on 23 July 1993, he installed his son Richard as the second president. Richard had been closely involved in the work for many years. With effective leadership in place, FGBMFI has enjoyed new growth by attracting a new generation of Christian businessmen.

Today's FGBMFI will struggle to achieve the success of the organization under the leadership of Demos Shakarian. FGBMFI was well placed to benefit from the charismatic movement during its period of greatest influence and growth. At the same time, FGBMFI enabled the movement to develop more rapidly and broadly.

Bibliography

D. Shakarian, *The Happiest People on Earth* (Old Tappan: Fleming H. Revell, 1975); V. Fotherby, *The Awakening Giant* (London: Marshall Pickering, 2000); V. Synan, *Under His Banner* (Costa Mesa: Gift Publications, 1992).

D. W. DORRIES

■ **SHAW, William** (1798–1872), minister and missionary, was born on 8 December 1798 in Glasgow, Scotland. Shaw was Methodist minister to the white settler community of the Eastern Cape and a missionary amongst the Xhosa in the same region from 1820 to 1856. Then he returned to England, where he was prominent in Methodist circles until his death on 4 December 1872 in London. Much admired for his pastoral, evangelistic and diplomatic work, Shaw has more recently been criticized as an apologist for the settlers and for facilitating colonialism.

Shaw, the son of a sergeant in the North York militia, grew up in an army barracks and initially intended to enter his father's profession. Conversion to Methodism when aged fourteen made life in the services difficult, and he was demobilized in 1815. Shaw married Ann Maw in 1817, and following her death in 1854 he married a Mrs Ogle in 1857. After working as a school teacher and lay minister, he left for South Africa as Methodist chaplain to the Sephton party of settlers and as a missionary.

William and Ann Shaw reached the Eastern Cape of South Africa in 1820; he was one of only three clergy amongst the party. He helped to found the settlement of Salem and by his great energy and concern rapidly built up a network of ministers and societies. Shaw, like many in the party, combined lowly social origins with energy that had been thwarted in Britain. In the Eastern Cape the new community rapidly began to prosper. Shaw's approach was ecumenical. He used the Book of Common Prayer and the Love Feast and attracted many who were not themselves Methodists.

Shaw's ambitions extended well beyond the white community. Of the settlement at Salem he declared, 'This station will be the key to Kaffirland.' Initially the Government opposed Shaw's desire to work beyond the boundary of the colony with the Xhosa people, but relented in 1823. Shaw then founded a series of mission stations across what is now Transkei, extending as far as Natal. By 1834 there were six stations amongst the Xhosa, compared to the rival London Missionary Society's one.

Shaw was alive to the material as well as the spiritual needs of those he sought to convert. His popularity amongst the Gqunukhwebe was due in part to his ability to negotiate peace between them and the colony, win them grazing rights and start a trading store. The work was strenuous and frustrating. By the time Shaw left South Africa in 1856, he had seen the settlement at Butterworth burnt down three times in the ongoing conflicts between the Xhosa, the colonial state and the settlers.

From 1829, apart from a visit to England between 1833 and 1837, Shaw lived in the regional centre of Grahamstown. There he supervised an expanding number of ministers, lay preachers and missionaries. By 1860 there were twenty-two ministers and forty-four chapels for settlers. In 1837 Shaw was appointed General Superintendent of the Wesleyan Missions in South Eastern Africa. In this role he travelled a great deal, had much influence with the colonial Government and sought to mediate in the frequent frontier conflicts.

The combination of exhausting work and the death of Shaw's first wife in 1854 led to a breakdown in his health, and he returned to Britain in 1856. There he remained active in Methodism, being president of the Conference in 1865 and chairman of the Bristol and York districts. In 1860 his *The Story of My Mission in South Eastern Africa* appeared. In 1869 Shaw retired to London.

Shaw's work in South Africa was characterized by his twin concerns for the settlers and the indigenous population. In 1822, at the opening of the Grahamstown Chapel, Shaw spoke of his joy at the mixing of the races and their common testimonies of conversion. However, much of his work was less irenic. Unlike the LMS missionary John *Philip, Shaw retained close links with the settler community, and he clashed with Philip, who believed that the black peoples were being unjustly treated by the settlers. When Shaw returned to England he promoted the settler view, that they were innocent of any injustice, against the 'unfounded calumny' propagated by Philip. Shaw blamed the vacillating border policy of the British state for the conflicts, but saw the main problem as 'the moral state and habits of the Caffre tribes'. Like all nomadic tribes, he claimed, they had an inclination towards robbery, which could be checked by a combination of Christian faith and a settled way of life. Both Shaw and Philip lobbied the British Government to extend the frontier of the colony, although they differed on how the Xhosa should be treated. In 1838 and 1839 the two missionaries fiercely attacked one another in letters that Shaw later published. Although in the 1830s the state avoided further annexation, it soon extended its control over the Ciskei and Natal.

Shaw was far more suspicious of the central state in London than was Philip. The latter saw it as a restraint on settler depredations, whereas Shaw was more positive towards the settler community. Both advanced the cause of empire, but Shaw had less empathy for the black populations. His missions stations have been seen as 'Christian fortresses [that] would enable peaceable incursions to be made into surrounding heathenism'. Shaw worked closely with a succession of colonial governors. Thus when the Bhaca community was attacked by a Boer force in 1840, it appealed to Shaw, who secured for it the protection of British forces controlled by the governor, Napier. This incident contributed to the British decision of 1842 to occupy Natal.

The South African historian George Cory declared, 'Of the honoured names among the 1820 settlers, it is doubtful whether there is one which is worthy of being held in greater veneration than that of the Rev. William Shaw.' Largely for the reasons that led Cory to praise Shaw, the opinion of historians has swung against him in recent years. His enormous evangelistic energy and strategic vision have ensured that even today the area in which he worked remains a centre for Methodism, but his support of settler interests illustrates one of the pitfalls of missionary work in nineteenth-century Africa.

Bibliography

W. Hammond-Tooke (ed.), *The Journal of William Shaw* (Cape Town: A. A. Balkema, 1972); T. Keegan, *Colonial South Africa and the Origins of the Racial Order* (London: Leicester University Press, 1996); B. Stanley, *The Bible and the Flag: Protestant Missionaries and British Imperialism in the Nineteenth and Twentieth Centuries* (Leicester: Apollos, 1990).

D. J. GOODHEW

■ **SHEA, George Beverly, 'Bev'** (1909–), soloist, was born the fourth of eight children to Adam J. Shea and his wife Maude on 1 February 1909 in Winchester, Ontario. Both his parents were from Canada; his father was a Methodist pastor, and his mother had a talent for music that she passed on to her son, teaching him to play the piano and appreciate gospel music. Shea first sang publicly in the choir at Sunnyside Wesleyan Church in Ottawa, where his father served as pastor.

Shea went to Annesley College, a private, nondenominational institution, and joined a vocal quartet. There he met Erma Scharfe, whom he married in Ottawa on 16 June 1934. He sang his first public solo at the age of seventeen during a Christian camp meeting. In 1927 he made a public declaration of faith at another series of special services held in his father's church.

Shea moved to upstate New York in 1928, where he attended Houghton College. Leaving Houghton after one year for financial reasons, Shea moved to New York City and found work on Wall Street as an insurance clerk for Mutual of New York. At the same time he took lessons from some of the world's leading voice instructors and became a radio vocalist. When offered a lucrative radio contract that would have compromised his personal standards, Shea reached a point of decision. Learning of his dilemma, his mother placed a poem entitled 'I'd Rather Have Jesus' by Rhea F. Miller on the Bell piano in their home. Shea, finding the verses, composed music for them. The hymn became a source of inspiration and direction for him, as well as a gospel favourite. He has since chosen to spend his life singing gospel music, and declines opportunities to sing in secular arenas.

At the request of Dr Will Houghton, president of Moody Bible Institute, Shea moved to Chicago and began working as a staff announcer for Moody's radio station, WMBI. He soon became a popular radio personality as the host and featured vocalist on the station's 'Hymns from the Chapel'.

In 1943 the young evangelist Billy *Graham persuaded Shea to sing on his radio show, 'Songs in the Night'. Graham needed a well-known hymn-singer for his new Sunday night programme, and invited Shea to fill the role, making him the first person employed by Graham to assist in evangelism. Four years later, Shea began his full-time employment with the Billy Graham Evangelistic Association (BGEA) as the soloist for its crusades.

Shea resigned his position at WMBI when offered an opportunity to sing on WCFL's new programme, 'Club Time'. The show moved to network television in 1945.

At the BGEA crusades Shea's vocal selections always preceded Graham's preaching; twelve to fifteen of Graham's favourites comprised the bulk of Shea's repertoire. For over fifty years he was the premier vocalist at Graham's meetings, and on his weekly radio programme, 'Hour of Decision', Shea has performed before an estimated 200 million people in eighty countries. He has also produced over seventy albums with RCA during his years as a Christian musician. He produced the first recording of the familiar hymn 'How Great Thou Art'.

Early in his career Shea signed the 'Modesto Manifesto', an agreement with Graham, Cliff Barrows and Grady Wilson designed to preserve their ministerial integrity. They decided not to travel alone with any women besides their wives, avoid boasting about their accomplishments, de-emphasize offerings and forgo public criticism of churches and ministers.

Shea received an honorary Doctor of Fine Arts degree from Houghton College in 1956, and in 1972 he received a Doctorate of Sacred Music from Trinity College, Illinois. He was awarded a Grammy for his album 'Southland Favorites' in 1966, and was invited into the Gospel Music Association Hall of Fame in Nashville. He has published three autobiographical works: Then Sings My Soul (1968), Singing I Go (1971) and Songs That Lift the Heart (1972).

Shea's son Ronald was born in 1948 in Western Springs, Illinois, and also works for the BGEA. A daughter, Elaine, was born two years later. Erma and Shea were married until 1976, when she died of cancer. Shea later married Karlene Aceto, who worked as a receptionist at the BGEA. They spend their summers in Quebec at a cottage Shea owns, and live in the mountains of Montreat, North Carolina, a mile from the Grahams' home.

Bibliography
G. B. Shea, Then Sings My Soul (Old Tappan, New Jersey: Fleming H. Revell, 1968).

T. L. COOPER

■ SHEDD, William G. T. (1820–1894), Presbyterian theologian and educator, was born a sixth-generation descendent of Massachusetts Puritans. His father, Marshall, was the Congregational minister in Acton. He graduated from the University of Vermont (1839), where he was influenced in the study of European Romanticism by philosophy professor James Marsh, one of the leading defenders of Kant and Coleridge in America. While teaching in New York for a year, Shedd made a profession of faith and entered the Presbyterian Church.

Becoming convinced that he was called to the ministry, Shedd studied at Andover Theological Seminary (1840–1843) with Edwards A. Park, Leonard Woods, Moses Stuart and Edward Robinson. Here he became strongly attached to the Old School theology of Woods as more historical and less provincial than that of the New School. More impressed by Augustine and Anselm than by *Edwards or *Hopkins, he promoted a distinctive blend of orthodox Reformed theology and Romantic historicism throughout his life.

Ordained as a Congregational minister, Shedd pastored a church in Brandon, Vermont (1843–1845) before returning to the University of Vermont as professor of English literature (1845–1852). In 1852 he was called to the chair of sacred rhetoric in Auburn Theological Seminary and joined the New School Presbyterian Church. During his years at Auburn he prepared his *Homiletics and Pastoral Theology* (1867) and *Discourses and Essays* (1856), which explored various aspects of language and rhetoric and discussed disputed doctrines such as original sin. Shedd rejected Jonathan Edwards' understanding of the will as determined, insisting that the very heart of original sin was that 'man asserted his authority only by affronting God'.

In 1854 Shedd returned to the Congregational church as chair of church history at Andover Theological Seminary, even though his Old School convictions regarding original sin and the doctrine of the atonement were increasingly anomalous in New England. His *Lectures upon the Philosophy of History* (1856) further explored the importance of a historical approach to Christian doctrine in the defence of Reformed orthodoxy. Employing Augustine's image of the two cities, Shedd argued that secular history was fundamentally sinful, just as the natural person could not please God. Therefore, church history recorded the drama of redemption and the gradual transformation of the new humanity.

This understanding of sin and grace in history prevented Shedd from falling into what he called 'the idolatry of automatic progress'; in his view sin frequently led the church to reject the truth and fall into error and heresy.

Shedd served on the faculty of Andover until 1862, when he received a welcome call to assist Gardiner Spring at the Old School Presbyterian Brick Church in New York City. While at Brick Church he edited his church history lectures and produced his *History of Christian Doctrine* (1863), which was the 'first attempt in English literature to write an account of the gradual construction of all the doctrines of the Christian religion'. In this volume Shedd focused on the formulation of 'Nicene trinitarianism, Augustinian anthropology, and Anselmic soteriology', firmly planting his theological roots in patristic and medieval orthodoxy.

Union Theological Seminary in New York City called Shedd as professor of New Testament literature in 1863, and then transferred him to systematic theology in 1874 as the replacement for Henry Boynton Smith. Although the seminary was New School, Shedd remained Old School, working for the reunion of the two churches. While at Union, he published numerous works, including a *Commentary on the Epistle to the Romans* (1879; he considered the epistle 'an inspired system of theology'), *Calvinism, Pure and Mixed* (1893), *Orthodoxy and Heresy* (1893) and *Dogmatic Theology* (1889–1894), along with such pastoral writings as *Sermons to the Natural Man* (1871) and *Sermons to the Spiritual Man* (1884).

Unlike most Old School theologians who relied upon Scottish common-sense realism, Shedd utilized the philosophy of Romanticism to buttress orthodox Reformed theology, insisting upon the importance of the organic evolutionary development of doctrine. Convinced that the church continued to increase in its understanding of God, Shedd argued that although denominations may have deficient theology, they differ little in 'practical piety and devout feeling'.

Shedd utilized the idea of evolution to describe the processes of the history of doctrine more than a decade before Darwin applied it to biology, but Shedd forcefully argued against the idea of evolutionary biology. While admitting the possibility of a kind of progressive creation, he denied that the organic could evolve from the inorganic, or that humans could evolve from animals. Shedd favoured an inductive approach to science, and supposed that the reason why so many naturalists had become agnostics was in part due to the move towards deduction in scientific circles.

Shedd was not a churchman in the manner of Charles *Hodge and Robert L. *Dabney. He was a member of only one General Assembly (1868), at which he defended the orthodoxy of the New School, but he was convinced that the reunion of Old and New School would not be complete until the northern and southern churches were reunited. As Shedd put it, 'The theologizing of Breckinridge, *Thornwell and Dabney should be mingled with that of *Alexander, Richards, Smith, and Hodge.'

None the less, Shedd did contribute in writing to the debates of the late nineteenth-century Presbyterian Church. He vigorously opposed efforts to revise the Westminster Confession, claiming that any modification in the direction of Arminianism would weaken historic Calvinism, which he believed was derived from the Bible. Shedd also clearly rejected the higher criticism advocated by Charles Briggs, his colleague at Union Seminary, and denied that Presbyterian ministers should be allowed to teach views derived from it.

Bibliography

J. DeWitt, 'William Greenough Thayer Shedd', Presbyterian and Reformed Review 21.2 (1895), pp. 295–322; B. V. Munger, 'William Greenough Thayer Shedd: Reformed Traditionalist, 1820–1894' (PhD dissertation, Duke University, 1957); G. S. Smith, The Seeds of Secularization: Calvinism, Culture, and Pluralism in America, 1870–1915 (Grand Rapids: Christian University Press, 1985).

P. J. WALLACE

■ **SHERWOOD, Mary Martha** (1775–1851), writer, wrote over 350 pamphlets, tracts, essays, travel books and novels for both children and adults. She was best known for her children's story The Fairchild Family (1818), still regarded as a classic in the early years of the twentieth century but later execrated for its allegedly morbid 'Victorian' moralizing. She was born in 1775 to Dr George Butt, rector of Stanford, Worcestershire, and his wife Martha (née Sherwood) and grew up in a world of landed gentry with literary connections. Always an imaginative child, she began writing stories at the age of six. At the Abbey School, Reading, in addition to acquiring the usual young lady's education, she came under the influence of French emigrés such as Dr Valpy. Her first novels, The Traditions and Margarita, were written in 1794, and in 1801 she published Susan Grey, the first of many works with a moral and didactic purpose. In 1803 she married her cousin, Captain Henry Sherwood of the 53rd Regiment of Infantry, and in 1805 sailed for India with the regiment, leaving their year-old daughter Mary with her aunt Lucy to be brought up in the healthier climate of Kidderminster.

After a voyage which included a hostile encounter in the Indian Ocean with a French squadron under Admiral Linois, the Sherwoods arrived in Madras. The new environment at once shed a different light on Mary's conventional Christian faith. She was horrified to find that the East India Company's Presidency encouraged 'heathen practices', and was especially distressed by the evidence of cruelties to women. She moved with the regiment to Calcutta and then to Dinapore, where her son Henry was born on Christmas Day. She had passed the time of her pregnancy quietly (apart from the travelling), writing another didactic story, Lucy Clare (1805), keeping her copious journal and reading Law's Serious Call. Quietness was not usually characteristic of her; shortly after Henry's birth, while also caring for orphan children in her own household, she also set up a school, which soon had fifty European and Indian pupils. In 1806 she moved to Berhampore, where her daughter Lucy Martha was born in 1807. Here she met the chaplain Mr Parson, whom she identified as the first 'Simeonite' (after the evangelical Charles *Simeon) she had met. She gladly embraced evangelical teaching on original sin, finding release from her persistent sense of guilt at perceived moral failures. Clarity of doctrine was of great importance to her; she was later to be sharply critical of her evangelical mentors for their postmillenarian theology. During her time in India, however, she too was convinced that the whole world must be converted by human agency, prior to Christ's thousand-year reign on earth.

These convictions gave new impetus to Sherwood's teaching and writing, as well as leading her to give up dancing and public amusements. The death of her son Henry in 1807 was an additional factor in this time of spiritual ferment. In the same year, travelling between Berhampore, Dinapore and Cawnpore, she met Henry *Martyn. He proved a spiritual guide, an inspiration and a stimulus to her work. Through the death of Lucy Martha in 1808, the births of Lucy Elizabeth in 1809 and Emily in 1811 and constant travelling, she continued to teach and to write in support of Martyn's mission work. A visit to Calcutta gave her an opportunity to observe the work of the Baptist missionaries there. She learned Hindustani in order to translate *Bunyan's Pilgrim's Progress. When it proved impossible to render Bunyan's ideas in Indian thought-forms she wrote an inculturated version entitled The Indian Pilgrim (1810), as well as an Indian catechism. In 1811 Martyn left India for Persia, where he died in 1812. Sherwood continued her work in association with Mr Parson, beginning work in Meerut in 1812 on The Child's Manual, later published as The Fairchild Family. Her son Henry Martyn was born in 1813 and her daughter Sophia in 1815. In that year her children's story Little Henry and His Bearer was published in England and became an instant success. Arriving in Calcutta en route for England, she found herself famous.

On returning to England in 1816, Sherwood went to live with her mother in Worcester, becoming effectively head of the family on the latter's death in 1817. From 1821 to 1829 she and her sister kept a school for young ladies, offering French, astronomy, geography and history in addition to the basics, with the learned languages if required. She continued her routine of vigorous household supervision, charitable work and writing. The first part of The Fairchild Family was published in 1817. Later criticized as macabre, it imparted moral lessons by means of scenes which had become familiar to her in India, the most famous being that in which the children are taken to see an executed criminal.

From 1822 she presided over a charity set up to build a penitentiary in Worcester, but in 1827 she was removed from the committee after severe personal disagreements. Writing took priority once again; she published eighty items in eight years. These included Henry Milner, one of her most popular children's books, and then a series of novels for adults: The Lady of the Manor (1825), Roxobel (1831), The Nun, Victoria (1833) and The Monk of Cimiès (1839). The first of these was intended as a confirmation guide for young ladies; the others had a strongly anti-Roman Catholic tone. The second and third parts of The Fairchild Family were also written at this time. She replaced Jane Taylor as a writer for The Youth's Magazine, and worked for ten years on a Hebrew typological dictionary. Captain Sherwood, now retired from the Army, learned Hebrew so that he could act as her research assistant, and her daughters Sophia and Emily collaborated in some of her writing. She travelled extensively in France and northern Italy between 1830 and 1844, writing travel books as she went. Her doctrinal views continued to develop; in addition to adopting a premillennial eschatology, expecting the world's conversion to be brought about by direct divine intervention before the inauguration of Christ's rule, she became convinced of the universality of salvation. Conversations with Pastor Malan in Geneva and the death of her daughter Emily in 1833, led her to see salvation as entirely unconditional, dependent only on the work of Christ. This brought her into conflict with fellow evangelicals, and in 1835 she was banned from the asylum in Worcester where she had been teaching the inmates. She continued to write and to be published, in England and elsewhere. Her works were popular in America, and Little Henry and His Bearer was translated into French, German, Hindustani, Chinese and Sinhalese and had gone into thirty editions in English by 1840.

By the time of her death in 1851, Sherwood had become a household name because of her children's books. She was not the first to write for children, nor the first to use stories to impart moral teaching, but her powers of observation and description and her sheer prolixity and industry made her outstanding in her field. Like other women of her generation, she combined domestic responsibilities with professional activity. She was fortunate enough to survive childbirth in India; the new experiences of the subcontinent were thus able to inform her writing. Her encounter with evangelical piety helped to focus her already formidable energy and personal assurance. In the course of the twentieth century, the sentiments of her children's books went out of favour; recent criticism has accorded more sympathetic treatment to this gifted writer and ardent evangelical.

Bibliography
I. Gilchrist (ed.), *The Life of Mrs. Sherwood, by Mrs. Sophia Kelly* (London: Robert Sutton, 1854); F. J. H. Darton (ed.), *The Life and Times of Mrs. Sherwood (1775–1852) from the Diaries of Captain and Mrs. Sherwood* (London: Wells Gardner, Darton & Co., 1910); N. Royde-Smith, *The State of Mind of Mrs. Sherwood* (London: Macmillan, 1946); M. N. Cutt, *Mrs. Sherwood and Her Books for Children: A Study* (London: Juvenile Library, 1974).

M. JONES

■ **SHIELDS, Thomas Todhunter** (1873–1955), Baptist pastor and fundamentalist leader, was born on 1 November 1873 in Bristol, England, the son of a Primitive Methodist pastor, and remained proudly English. His father adopted Baptist principles and shortly thereafter, in 1888, emigrated to Canada, where he served as pastor of various small Ontario Baptist churches. He was an immensely influential figure in his son's life; the young Shields had no formal theological education and was mentored by his father. From early childhood, travelling with his father on his circuit, he had felt a call to ministry. So, after his conversion in 1891, he immediately began to prepare himself.

Shields served as pastor of various small Ontario Baptist churches, each one a little larger than the one before: Florence (from October 1894), Dutton (from 1895), where he was ordained in 1897, Delhi (from 1897), and finally Wentworth Street, Hamilton (from 1900). After spending 1903–1904 working as an evangelist, he moved to Adelaide Street in London, Ontario. Here he became prominent within the Baptist world. By 1906 a new building had been completed; it was expanded to seat 1,200 in 1908. The Baptist Convention of Ontario and Quebec (BCOQ) voted Shields onto its Home Missions Board. He shared the 1908 BCOQ assembly platform with E. Y. *Mullins, and began to receive invitations to preach from across North America. In 1910 he was faced with a choice between moving to New York or becoming pastor of Jarvis Street Baptist Church, Toronto. He chose to stay in Canada.

Although the BCOQ was troubled by controversy in 1910, Shields played only a minor role. In that year Elmore Harris, founder of Walmer Road Baptist Church and Toronto Bible College, charged I. G. Matthews of McMaster College with heresy. The dispute was resolved when Shields seconded the resolution of John MacNeill, pastor of Walmer Road, which affirmed a high Christology.

Shields' reputation grew during this period. He was awarded honorary DDs in 1917 by Temple University and in 1918 by McMaster. He was also able to fulfil a lifelong ambition by preaching at *Spurgeon's Metropolitan Tabernacle in London in both 1915 and 1918. Profoundly influenced by Spurgeon, Shields saw himself as a Calvinistic Baptist; his theology was also formed by the Puritans. Like most Ontario Baptists of the time, Shields began his ministry by emphasizing Christology, which shaped his preaching and theology. But after the First World War, he began to regard the inerrancy of the biblical text as the first theological principle. For his opponents in the ensuing controversies, soul liberty moved to the primary place. Both groups continued strongly to emphasize Christology, but it was now subordinated to other principles.

In 1919 Shields challenged an editorial in the *Canadian Baptist* entitled 'Inspiration and Authority of Scripture'. His response was widely welcomed, and the annual Assembly supported him. In 1920 Shields was appointed to McMaster's Board of Governors. But then his attempt to restrict the organist and choir of Jarvis Street provoked a dispute. This was exacerbated by a sermon on worldly amusements, and it left many of the wealthy members deeply alienated. In the autumn of 1921, 341 members left to form Central Baptist, later Park Road Baptist Church.

It was, however, McMaster that was permanently to shape Shields' reputation. In

1923 W. H. P. Faunce of Brown University was awarded an honorary LLD. Shields was furious; Faunce and Brown, he felt, did not represent the theological values of Canadian Baptists. Again he won support from the Assembly, but provoked the hostility of the Convention's leadership. Then, in 1925, L. H. Marshall was appointed to the McMaster faculty. Shields, who had been absent when the decision was taken, suspected Marshall of liberalism and called for an investigation. The Board, believing that the appointment process had been sufficiently rigorous, rejected his call. Shields' continuing opposition to the appointment led in 1926 to the loss of his right to serve as an Assembly delegate. Then, in an unprecedented action, the BCOQ applied to the Canadian Parliament for legislation and in 1927 expelled Jarvis Street Church from the Convention along with all churches sympathetic to the Regular Baptist Missionary and Education Society of Canada.

This society was the result of Shields' efforts in the 1920s to construct a denomination within a denomination. At Jarvis Street, Shields restructured the church, eliminating many committees and demanding continuous evangelism. Unlike most Baptists, he was not committed to a democratic form of church government. Monthly business meetings were eliminated. Although an annual meeting still formalized all key decisions, the running of the church was placed in the hands of the deacons. Shields justified the changes by reference to the church's rapid growth; by 1924 the Sunday school had more than 1,000 children and was one of the largest in Canada, while church members numbered more than 2,000. In 1922 Shields established *The Gospel Witness*. It would become a weekly newspaper and in its most successful period had over 30,000 subscribers in sixty different countries, over 3,000 of whom were ministers. From 1930 Shields' ideas were also popularized by a weekly two-hour radio programme. A movement to develop Christian education for church members, begun in 1924 and modelled on Spurgeon's College, grew into the Toronto Baptist Seminary, which was established in 1927. To protect the church against the problems he had encountered in the BCOQ, Shields placed all the activities of Jarvis Street under the direct control of the church's deacons. In 1927 he

established the Regular Baptist Missionary and Education Society of Canada.

In 1927 the thirty churches that had left the BCOQ formed the Union of Regular Baptist Churches of Ontario and Quebec, electing Shields as president. Many of these churches professed militant premillennial dispensationalism. When the amillennialist Shields tried to gain greater control over the group by bringing the independent women's and youth fellowships under the control of the Union, the premillennial churches ('Scofieldites') objected strongly. Shields expelled them from the Union, and in 1933 they formed the Fellowship of Independent Baptist Churches of Canada. Then in 1949, Shields expelled W. Gordon Brown, the dean of the seminary, and all the faculty left with Brown. As a result, the Union forced Shields to resign as president. Shields responded by taking Jarvis Street out of the Union. He became president of a tiny denomination, the Association of Regular Baptist Churches of Canada.

On the international scene Shields was very influential. He was involved in establishing, and served as president of, the Baptist Bible Union in 1923. His selection as president reflects the power of his personality: he differed with most of his American colleagues on eschatology, a major issue; most of them were premillennial dispensationalists. As president, Shields led the Union in one of its most controversial projects: its takeover of Des Moines University in Iowa in 1927. Shields was appointed president of the university. He tried tightly to control the theology and behaviour of both the faculty and the students, and in what must surely be one of the more unusual developments in American educational history, he required the students to stand while 'God Save The King' was sung. Following resignations from the faculty and student riots in 1929 the Board was held in the local prison for its own protection. The university closed at the end of the semester.

Shields was a staunch Baptist and his principles were non-negotiable, even when they were costly to him. For many years Jarvis Street assessed its own property and paid a voluntary tax to the city. Shields' principles limited his cooperation with his fundamentalist allies, but he was able to make common cause with them on a range of issues, including prohibition, opposition to the funding of

Catholic schools, Sabbath observance and restricting the role of women. Two of his major projects drew together more divergent partners. One of these was the Canadian Protestant League, which was formed as a result of Shields' discontent over French Catholic opposition to conscription in the First World War. It renewed its activites in 1941 in response to further opposition, expressed most publicly in a mass on Parliament Hill. Shields united and gave voice to a significant part of the Protestant community, but with the advent of peace the League began to decline. Shields resigned as president in 1950.

Shields then gave his full attention to the International Council of Churches. He and Carl *McIntire had formed this group in 1948 as an alternative to the World Council of Churches; Shields wrote its doctrinal statement. In 1949, at the age of seventy-five, he travelled the world with McIntire to promote the group.

When Shields died in Toronto on 4 April 1955, he was well loved and respected within his circle, but that circle had become much smaller during his career. He left hundreds of published sermons, scores of articles and numerous books, including *The Plot That Failed* (Toronto: The Gospel Witness, 1937); *The Doctrines of Grace* (Toronto: The Gospel Witness, 1955) and *Christ in the Old Testament* (Toronto: The Gospel Witness, 1972).

Bibliography

L. K. Tarr, *T. T. Shields (1873–1955)* (Grand Rapids: Baker Book House, 1967); A. Russell, 'Thomas Todhunter Shields, Canadian Fundamentalist', *Ontario History* 70.4 (1978), pp. 263–280.

D. A. GOERTZ

■ **SIMEON, Charles** (1759–1836), Anglican clergyman and evangelical leader, was born in Reading on 24 September 1759, the fourth son of Richard and Elizabeth Simeon, and was educated at Eton College. He had ugly features and was given the nickname 'Chin Simeon'. He was known for his sporting ability and his love of horses and clothes. As a young man he was something of a dandy, and before his conversion spent £50 a year on his clothes. At this stage religion meant little to him. He gained a scholarship to King's College, Cambridge, and soon after his arrival he was told that he was expected to attend the termly communion service. This challenged Simeon to examine himself. He joined the Society for Promoting Christian Knowledge (SPCK) and began to read Christian books. These included the anonymously written *The Whole Duty of Man*, and books on communion by the Nonjuror John Kettlewell and Bishop Thomas Wilson. Simeon's conversion was dramatic. He awoke early on Easter day, 4 April 1779, and cried out, 'Jesus Christ is risen today; Hallelujah! Hallelujah!' At that time there were few evangelicals at Cambridge, and he lacked Christian fellowship. Although the chapel services were badly conducted and lifeless, the services in the Book of Common Prayer sustained him and became 'as marrow and fatness' for his soul. He rose early and spent hours each day in personal Bible study and prayer.

In May 1782 Simeon was ordained deacon by James Yorke, the Bishop of Ely, to a college fellowship. Soon after this he met Henry *Venn, the rector of Yelling, near Cambridge, and John Berridge, the vicar of Everton, Bedfordshire. In matters of church order Simeon was more influenced by Henry Venn. After his ordination Simeon began to preach at St Edward's Church, Cambridge. During the absence of the vicar, Christopher Atkinson, he filled the building such that it was reportedly as crowded as a theatre on the first night of a new play. In the autumn the parish clerk welcomed back the incumbent with the words, 'O, sir, I am so glad you are come; now we shall have some room!' As Simeon made preparations to leave Cambridge, the living of Holy Trinity Church became vacant by the death of Henry Therond. Immediately Simeon encouraged his father to approach the patron, his friend, the Bishop of Ely, to appoint him. The matter was soon settled. The bishop offered Simeon the living, and though still only a deacon he began his incumbency in November 1782 on a stipend of £40 a year. In the following year he gained his BA (he received his MA in 1786) and was ordained priest in September by John Hinchcliffe, the Bishop of Peterborough and Master of Trinity College. In addition, Simeon remained a fellow of King's College and subsequently held a number of college posts.

For the next thirty years Simeon experienced hostility towards his evangelical ministry. When the churchwardens shut the main church doors and the pew-owners locked their pews, Simeon provided benches in the aisles, but they were removed. When he held an evening service in a rented room in a neighbouring parish, he was accused of being a 'Methodist'. At first he had only a small congregation, but soon undergraduates began to attend the church. Within two years, twenty-four students were attending, and eventually half of the congregation of over 1,100 people were undergraduates. Over the course of his fifty-four year ministry at Holy Trinity Church, Simeon influenced thirteen to fourteen generations of students. In 1790 Simeon began a fortnightly sermon class for those intending to be ordained, and when he moved to a larger set of college rooms in 1812, he commenced a weekly conversation party open to all undergraduates. By the late 1820s between fifteen and twenty men attended the sermon class and between sixty to eighty attended the conversation party. Simeon sat on a high stool near the fireplace in his drawing room. His attentive audience sat on chairs and benches and in the window recesses, and he invited them to ask him questions. As they listened two servants served tea. At a time when there was no formal ordination training, it is estimated that about 1,000 future clergy came under Simeon's influence, over twenty of whom became chaplains to the East India Company and three Church Missionary Society (CMS) missionaries. Those men who were influenced by Simeon, whether as clergy or members of other professions, became known as Simeonites or 'Sims' and were identified as a recognizable 'school of divinity'.

Simeon outlined his convictions in a series of hour-long university sermons, five on the 'excellence of the liturgy' and two on 'evangelical religion'. His threefold test for a sermon was: does it humble the sinner, exalt the Saviour and promote holiness? When he began his preaching ministry, Simeon had to develop his own style and presentation. In 1792 he read 'An Essay on the Composition of a Sermon' by the French Reformed minister Jean Claude. Simeon found that their prin-

ciples were identical and used the essay as the basis for his lectures on sermon composition. The fruit of Simeon's preaching is found in *Horae Homileticae*, his twenty volumes of sermon outlines (together with a volume of indexes and his abridgment of Claude's essay). 'My Horae', as Simeon called it, developed over a number of years. In 1796 100 sermon outlines were published, 500 in 1800, 2,000 in 1820 and finally 2,536 in 1833. The final version, which cost ten guineas, was dedicated to William Howley, the Archbishop of Canterbury. 'Throughout the whole I have laboured to maintain that spirit of moderation which so eminently distinguishes the established church, giving to every revealed truth ... its proper place, and that precise measure of consideration which it seemed to occupy in the inspired volume.' Alongside Simeon's *magnum opus* he published an improved edition of Benjamin Jenks' devotional manual *Prayers and Offices of Devotion for Family and for Particular Persons* (1822).

Simeon made clear his theological position. He was neither an Arminian nor a Calvinist but described himself as 'a moderate Calvinist' or 'a Bible Christian'. He opposed all human systems of divinity. His maxim was simple: 'Be Bible Christians, not system Christians.' He loved simplicity and insisted that the Bible should speak for itself. In disputed matters he maintained that the truth lay not in the middle but at both extremes. He regarded himself as a man swimming the Atlantic, 'I have no fear of striking one hand against Europe and the other against America.'

Simeon was known for his distinctive mode of preaching, and his appearance in the pulpit was captured in a series of six silhouettes by A. Edouart. They show him expounding, acquiring, entreating, imploring, imparting and concluding. He was an earnest, clear spoken preacher. He could be quite emotional, and his tears could flow in the pulpit. Yet moving as his sermons were, Simeon had his detractors. As he preached, drunken students would enter Holy Trinity: some simply scoffed; some sauntered up the aisle and stared at him; some threw stones and broke the windows; and others destroyed his composure by flinging open the doors and yelling 'Charlie'.

From 1783 Simeon preached in the villages around Cambridge, and at Holy Trinity he generally preached twice on Sundays. This pattern continued throughout most of his ministry, apart from when he was indisposed and lost his voice. When he was older, he preached only once on Sundays. From 1796 he was assisted by curates, who included Thomas Thomason and Henry *Martyn (both of whom served and died overseas), and his biographer and successor, William Carus. On two occasions Simeon's friends helped him to celebrate his jubilees. The first, in 1829, marked his seventieth birthday, and the second, in 1832, marked his fifty-year incumbency at Holy Trinity.

Simeon's spirituality was shaped by the Book of Common Prayer, which he considered to be 'a composition of unrivalled excellence'. He maintained that the finest sight short of heaven was of a congregation rightly using the liturgy. After the Bible, he regarded the Thirty-Nine Articles of Religion, the Book of Homilies and the liturgy to be 'the standard of divine truth'. He preached on the liturgy and taught his followers to value it; this example enabled them to remain loyal to the Church of England. However, his stance caused his critics to say that he was more of a churchman than a gospel man. Although Simeon appreciated the prayers of other denominations, he regarded the Prayer Book as far superior. In his view, 'The extemporaneous effusions that are used in other places bear no comparison with the formularies of our church.' When in Scotland, he worshipped with the Presbyterians, but he was always glad to return south of the border so that he could use the Book of Common Prayer.

Simeon cultivated friendships with those who were ordained and helped to find them suitable curacies. But at that time there were few openings for evangelical clergy and only limited evangelical patronage. From 1813 Simeon was one of the Thornton Trustees, but they had only twelve livings at their disposal. Three years later Simeon began to purchase the right to appoint ministers to livings, and by his death he had acquired the patronage of twenty-one churches. Some of the livings that he bought were spas such as Cheltenham, Bath and Bridlington, while others were in urban centres such as Derby and Bradford (in the twentieth century these two churches became cathedrals). At that time the trade in livings was a speculative venture, but Simeon could honestly say that whereas others 'purchase *income*, I purchase *spheres*, wherein the prosperity of the established church, and the kingdom of our blessed Lord, may be advanced'. The large sums of money required for these acquisitions came from a legacy from his brother and by substantial gifts from his friends.

Simeon was a country member of the Clapham Sect, and its members shared a number of concerns, including the abolition of the slave trade and the distribution of the Scriptures. In 1804 Simeon supported the formation of the British and Foreign Bible Society. Seven years later there was considerable opposition in Cambridge to the establishment of an auxiliary of the Bible Society. However, Simeon together with other evangelical leaders supported the undergraduate initiative.

Simeon was fully committed to the parochial system. His own parish had a population of between 1,000 and 1,500 residents. In it Simeon developed a visitation scheme and formed six societies or classes for the 120 members who made up the core of his non-student congregation. There were separate societies for men and women, and he met with them each month. At the same time, Simeon was also deeply committed to overseas mission. As early as 1787 he was invited to support the setting up of a mission in Bengal, and he subsequently encouraged individuals to become chaplains to the East India Company. In 1796 he posed a question to the London-based Eclectic Society: 'With what propriety, and in what mode, can a mission be attempted to the heathen from the established church?' But the Anglican members did not want to interfere with the work of the existing agencies, the SPCK and the Society for the Propagation of the Gospel, nor to join forces with the newly formed interdenominational London Missionary Society. Three years later, at another meeting of the Eclectic Society, Simeon asked three pertinent questions: 'What can we do? When shall we do it? How shall we do it?' The subsequent discussions led directly to the formation in April 1799 of 'The [Church Missionary] Society for missions to Africa and the East'. Simeon was a country member of the committee and preached the second anniversary sermon in 1802. Two years later the first collection for CMS at Cambridge took place at Holy Trinity Church. However, India was always Simeon's chief concern. Before a bishop was appointed he jokingly referred to the country as his diocese, but after 1814 he said, 'I modestly call it my province.' Like many of his contemporaries, Simeon became deeply committed to the evangelization of the Jews. He was so preoccupied with the cause that he was described as being 'Jew mad', and 'the chief friend of Israel in this country'. He was convinced that the 'Jews should be pressed with vital Christianity at once'. He fully supported the London Society for Promoting Christianity amongst the Jews (later known as the Church's Ministry among Jewish People) and became a trustee and committee member after it became exclusively Anglican in 1815. He frequently spoke at the meetings of the Society and preached annual sermons in 1811 and 1818. He contributed to the erection of the Episcopal Jews' Chapel in Palestine Place, Bethnal Green, London, and travelled hundreds of miles each year preaching and raising funds for the Society. In 1829 he also helped to establish the Operative Jewish Converts' Institution, which provided much needed employment for converted Jews.

Most years Simeon used his vacations to go on extensive preaching tours. Just months before his death he spent eight weeks visiting some of the midland parishes of which he was the patron. What he saw deeply moved him; his principles were being worked out in a variety of non-university settings. At Cheltenham his joy was immense; he experienced what he described as almost 'a heaven on earth'.

Simeon died unmarried, in Cambridge, on 13 November 1836 and was buried in the chapel of King's College.

Bibliography

A. W. Brown, *Recollections of the Conversation Parties of the Rev. Charles Simeon MA* (London: Hamilton, 1863); W. Carus, *Memoirs of the Life of the Rev. Charles Simeon MA* (London: Hatchard, 1847); H. E. Hopkins, *Charles Simeon of Cambridge* (Sevenoaks: Hodder & Stoughton, 1977); H. C. G. Moule, *Charles Simeon* (London: Methuen, 1892); A. Pollard and M. Hennell (eds.), *Charles Simeon 1759–1836* (London: SPCK, 1959); C. Smyth, *Simeon and Church Order* (Cambridge: CUP, 1940).

A. F. MUNDEN

■ **SIMPSON, Albert Benjamin** (1843–1919), founder of the Christian and Missionary Alliance, was born on 15 December 1843 in Bayview, Prince Edward Island, to pious Presbyterian parents who made their living in the island economy through the provisioning and building of ships. Albert shared in an heritage of faith and missions. Through his parents, his life was deeply touched by the ministry of John Geddie, pioneer missionary to the New Hebrides Islands. When Albert was four, an empire-wide depression forced the Simpsons to leave Prince Edward Island and seek their fortune in the then frontier farming area of Chatham, Ontario. It was there that the young Simpson was raised and experienced conversion.

Albert Simpson was a sensitive, frail and deeply impressionable youth and, as he recounts it, his religious upbringing made him deeply aware of the demands of a stern and distant God. At the age of fifteen he underwent a personal crisis characterized by months of mental and spiritual turmoil, culminating in the typical evangelical experience known as the new birth. He felt himself called to study for the ministry, and in 1861 entered Knox College, Toronto, to study for the ministry of the Canada Presbyterian Church.

Intellectually and spiritually, Knox College was an exciting place to be, and Simpson drank deeply of the spirit of faith and activism which permeated the institution. He proved to be not only an exceptional student but a gifted and much sought-after speaker as well. His rising profile within the Canada Presbyterian Church was confirmed when in 1865, at the age of twenty-two, he was called to the pastorate of Knox's Presbyterian Church, Hamilton, one of the leading churches of the denomination.

Over the next seven years, Simpson conducted a successful ministry in Hamilton. Yet, for all his apparent success as an urban pastor, he found himself growing increasingly dissatisfied with the traditional forms of ministry he practised. This restlessness was heightened when he came into contact with the innovative urban evangelism of Dwight L.

*Moody and the YMCA movement and the worldwide evangelical ecumenism of the Evangelical Alliance.

In 1874, sensing God's call to a broader ministry, Simpson left Hamilton to take up the pastorate of Chestnut Street Presbyterian Church, Louisville, Kentucky. Over the next five years Simpson's conception of ministry changed dramatically as he was influenced by one after another of the various new trends within late nineteenth-century evangelicalism. Feeling increasingly dissatisfied with his own spiritual life, Simpson was drawn to the teachings of the holiness movement. After reading William Boardman's *The Higher Christian Life*, he underwent a powerful experience, which he regarded as one of sanctification, and to which thereafter he attributed the tremendous power and success of his life's ministry. Soon after Simpson played a major role in a series of D. W. Whittle and P. P. Bliss revival meetings which shook Louisville in 1875. Simpson believed he saw in these meetings the limitless power of the Holy Spirit for witness and for changing lives.

Beyond urban evangelism, Simpson felt increasingly drawn to overseas missions; although he would never become a missionary himself, later he became one of the most successful missions administrators of his time. Simpson credited much of his rising passion for evangelism and missions to his adoption of premillennial and prophetic doctrines that emphasized the imminent return of the Lord and the extreme peril of those not ready to meet him.

In late 1879 Simpson moved to New York, where he spent a short, dissatisfying period as minister of New York's prestigious Thirteenth Street Presbyterian Church. Once in the teeming metropolis, however, he felt himself called irresistibly to begin a new ministry, one that would reach out to the 'unchurched masses', as he called them, in unconventional and innovative ways. He resigned from Presbyterian ministry and began an independent fellowship which, in a few short years, developed in many different ways. It was during this time of spiritual ferment that Simpson, never possessed of a sturdy constitution, experienced healing and soon became one of the leading exponents of the divine healing movement.

Between 1881 and 1887 Simpson's fellowship grew rapidly. In his pulpit ministry he was known as a spellbinding preacher with a deep knowledge of the Scriptures and a passionate love for God. He and his congregation provided social welfare to New York's 'untouchables', cared for orphans, educated lay people for ministry and missions, conducted high-profile evangelistic missions and healing campaigns, published a highly regarded missions periodical entitled *The Gospel in All Lands* and promoted foreign missions.

Among Simpson's concerns, missions quickly predominated. In 1887 he founded two fellowships which would eventually merge to become the Christian and Missionary Alliance, an ecumenical and evangelical fellowship dedicated to promoting the deeper Christian life and reaching the world for Christ. The Alliance spread rapidly to Canada, where a dominion auxiliary was established under John Salmon in 1889; it counted among its numbers such prominent figures as William Howland, the crusading mayor of Toronto, Dr Jenny Trout, the pioneering woman doctor, and William Christie, the biscuit maker. By 1897 Simpson's organization was one of the leading missionary organizations, supporting more than 300 missionaries overseas.

At the end of the nineteenth century and into the early twentieth, Simpson was on the cutting edge of the 'Forward Movements' of North American evangelicalism and played a crucial role in giving them shape and focus. The Alliance's motto 'Jesus Christ, Saviour, Sanctifier, Healer and Coming King' (known as the fourfold gospel) became the triumphant rallying cry for a new generation of evangelicals dissatisfied with traditional forms of piety and drawn to reach the world for Christ. Simpson's hymns, such as 'Jesus Only' and 'Himself', set their evangelistic passion to music.

With notoriety, however, came controversy as well. Simpson was criticized for his promotion of divine healing, a doctrine most of his evangelical counterparts did not share. His first missionary expedition to the Congo ended in disaster and brought him criticism from other missions organizations. And in the first decade of the twentieth century, Simpson found himself under attack from Pentecostals, who insisted, as Simpson could not, that speaking in tongues was a necessary evidence of the filling of the Holy Spirit. As a result, many prominent members of the Alliance broke with Simpson, going on to provide crucial early leadership for the newly emerging Pentecostal movement.

A. B. Simpson had a profound influence upon North American evangelical spirituality. He was a restless spiritual visionary who was passionately committed to what he believed to be the work of the Holy Spirit in the last days. He was a man of deep and profound spiritual passions, and many could identify with his teaching on struggle, failure and ultimate victory in Christ. And throughout his long and diverse ministry one theme predominated: 'Jesus Only'. When he died on 29 October 1919, the Christian and Missionary Alliance circled the globe.

Bibliography

L. Reynolds, *Footprints: The Beginnings of the Christian and Missionary Alliance in Canada* (Toronto: The Christian and Missionary Alliance in Canada, 1992); A. W. W. Tozer, *A. B. Simpson: A Study in Spiritual Altitude* (Harrisburg: Christian Publications, 1943); A. E. Thompson, *A. B. Simpson: His Life and Work* (Harrisburg: Christian Publications, 1920).

D. REID

■ **SMITH, Hannah Whitall** (1832–1911) and **Robert Pearsall** (1827–1898), Quaker holiness/deeper-life lay evangelists, authors and social activists, were married in Philadelphia, Pennsylvania in 1851. Both were born Philadelphia birthright Quakers. Robert's parents were John Jay and Rachel Pearsall Smith. Jay Smith, an editor and publisher, also ran the city's public library. Hannah's parents were John Mickle and Mary Tatum Whitall. John became the heir of the Whitall-Tatum glass company. Their families' extensive social and financial resources allowed the Smiths, throughout most their lives, to pursue their personal and family interests relatively free of financial concerns.

After their marriage, Robert encouraged Hannah to further her education, but the birth of her first child followed by five more children ended her aspirations. Only three of her

children lived into adulthood: Mary Logan Whitall, the wife first of Frank Costelloe, the Irish barrister and Member of Parliament, and then of the noted art historian Bernard Berenson; Logan Pearsall, the Oxford professor and creator of the literary genre trivia; and Alys Pearsall, the first wife of Bertrand Russell.

Robert and Hannah both professed personal spiritual conversion in the religious revival of 1857–1858. Schisms within traditional Quakerism and the growing exclusiveness with which it reacted to the new American revival movements led both Hannah and Robert to resign their membership of the Society of Friends soon after their conversions. Robert eventually became a Presbyterian. Hannah, during their deep involvement with the post-Civil War revival movements, found the teachings of the Methodists to be most compatible with her traditional Quakerism but never joined the denomination. She later re-joined the Society of Friends.

Methodist employees of the Millville, New Jersey Whitall-Tatum glass factory managed by Robert first introduced the Smiths to Methodist Wesleyan/holiness teaching during the Civil War. Soon after, both of them testified to experiencing the Methodist 'second blessing' of heart purity at the first national camp meetings sponsored by the newly organized National Camp Meeting Association for the Promotion of Holiness. The personal commitment of this non-Methodist lay couple to their newly found spiritual cause, as well as their established social prominence, quickly made Hannah and Robert much sought after speakers within a growing network of revival services and summer camp meetings in Pennsylvania and surrounding states. They also published books and articles promoting Christian holiness. Hannah's account of the untimely death of their son Frank and the holiness revival he had been fostering at Princeton (*Frank, The Record of a Happy Life* [Philadelphia, 1873]), along with Robert's *Holiness by Faith* (Boston, 1870) and his *Walking in the Light* (Boston, 1872), especially helped to prepare the way for the couple's Wesleyan/Holiness evangelism, which accompanied the general wave of spiritual renewal then spreading across England, Europe and around the world.

Hannah's idyllic childhood under the care of a doting father who had the personal resources to see to her every need had made it easy for her to see God as an infinitely loving father who, in his wisdom and love, could and would unfailingly supply his children's every need. Though she, like many Quakers of her day, had come to value the authority of the written word over her tradition's reliance on 'the Inner Light', she held firmly to a muted universalistic concept of God's ultimate restitution of all of fallen humankind. From time to time these suspect views threatened her ministry among the evangelicals of her time. However, her vigorous involvement in contemporary spiritual renewal and social reform causes, accompanied by her willingness to forgo any public promotion of her questionable opinions, generally negated doubts about her evangelical credentials.

In 1874 Hannah joined her husband in England, where Robert had became deeply involved in a series of seemingly spontaneous and progressively more dramatic ecumenical holiness renewal meetings. Clergy and lay people from the Church of England and the free churches gathered to hear the Smiths' message of Christian consecration, sanctification by faith and victorious living. Meetings at Oxford, Cambridge and Broadlands, the country estate of Lord and Lady Mount Temple in Hampshire and a centre of the movement, were followed by an evangelistic tour of Europe by Robert in the spring of 1875. In Europe he found support for his message not only among the free churches, but also among the established Evangelical Lutheran and Reformed churches.

The culmination of these meetings was the Brighton Convention for the Promotion of Christian Holiness in May 1875. More than 8,000 clergy and theologians from England and Europe met for ten days of teaching and worship. The most popular sessions of the Brighton Convention were those in which Hannah preached her practical secrets of the happy Christian life to audiences of 5,000 or more, mostly clergymen who were theologically opposed to the preaching ministry of women. She became known as 'the angel of the churches'.

Rumours of moral and doctrinal deviance on Robert's part began to spread immediately after the close of the Brighton Convention. They brought a swift and tragic end to the Smiths' ministry in England. Even though on their return to America they found that the rumours of failure had not diminished their opportunities for ministry there, in effect their revivalist ministry also ended at this time. In 1888 the family moved to England, where they lived for the rest of their lives as expatriates. Robert never recovered from the events of 1875. He gradually gave up all his Christian commitments and died alienated, but not separated, from his family. Plagued by a manic depressive nature for most of his life, he was now happiest when engaged in his Buddhist meditations in his spacious tree house at the family's home at Friday's Hill, south of London. He died in 1898.

In spite of its brevity, the Smiths' ministry had broad and lasting effects. The Keswick Convention was the result of their English and European evangelism. Their ministry also helped to shape the German Inner City Movement and brought powerful renewal to the Fellowship Movement within the Lutheran and Reformed churches in Germany and Switzerland. The Wesleyan/holiness theme of the revival popularized the central theological themes of the Methodist and evangelical churches of Europe. Many of the pioneers of early European Pentecostalism were also deeply rooted in these traditions.

After Robert's 'fall', Hannah redirected her unusual physical and spiritual energies into the concerns of her family, her writing and the many reform movements that she supported. She served as one of the first presidents of the Pennsylvania state chapter of the Women's Christian Temperance Union and later became the first national superintendent of its evangelistic arm. A lifelong friend and supporter of Frances *Willard, she was instrumental in her election to the presidency of the movement. Hannah and her daughter Alys were also instrumental in working with their mutual friends, Frances Willard and Lady Somerset, leader of the British temperance movement, in creating the International Women's Temperance Union. Hannah actively supported the temperance movement's broader campaign for women's suffrage. She maintained a full schedule, speaking on behalf of various causes, from women's rights to animal rights. During the same period she was a frequent speaker in

Quaker and other churches, continuing her lifelong practice of maintaining an active involvement in evangelical religion and broader political and social movements while retaining considerable influence in each.

Her book, *The Christian's Secret of a Happy Life* (Boston, 1875), quickly became one of the classics of evangelical devotional literature. In the first hundred years after its initial publication it went through more than thirty different English editions and numerous foreign language editions in every major and many lesser-known languages, selling over 2 million copies. Of her seventeen other books the most influential were *The Unselfishness of God* (1902), a spiritual autobiography, and *The God of All Comfort* (1906). She died at her son Logan's home at Iffley Place near Oxford in 1911.

Bibliography

M. E. Dieter, 'The Holiness Revival in Nineteenth Century Europe', *Westminster Theological Journal* 9 (spring 1974), pp. 15–27; H. Whitall Smith, *The Unselfishness of God and How I Discovered It* (New York, London: Fleming H. Revell, 1903); B. Strachey, *Remarkable Relations: the Story of the Pearsall Smith Family* (London: Victor Gollancz, 1980).

M. E. DIETER

■ **SMITH, John Taylor** (1860–1938), Anglican bishop, was the only person to hold the offices of honorary chaplain to the Queen, bishop and Chaplain-General. Taylor Smith was born on 20 April 1860 in Kendal in Westmorland (now Cumbria). His father, James Smith, was a coal agent. He was closer to his mother Jane and, due to his affection for her, preferred the surname Taylor Smith rather than his given surname, Taylor being his mother's maiden name.

Although Taylor Smith was famous for his finely crafted and well delivered sermons and talks, he was not academically gifted. He attended Kendal Grammar School but left early; because of lack of money and ability he did not attempt a degree at a university. Since his conversion at the age of eleven, Taylor Smith had been interested in the 'winning of souls', as he put it, and at the age of twenty-one he decided to become a priest. He attended St John's Hall, Highbury, more commonly known as the London College of Divinity, from 1882 to 1885, and received a third class in the preliminary examinations for holy orders. Given his well-known impish sense of humour, it is not surprising that Taylor Smith was amused by and proud of his honorary DDs from the universities of Durham (1897) and St Andrews (1911) and his CVO (1906), CB (1921) and KCB (1925).

Taylor Smith was, above all else, an 'uncompromising evangelical'; the evidence for this characterization is not hard to find. Taylor Smith decided to become a priest while attending a service at Carlisle Cathedral, during which he believed that God spoke to him. He accepted the offices of diocesan missioner in Sierra Leone (1890–1897), Bishop of Sierra Leone (1897–1901) and Chaplain-General (1901–1925) only after becoming certain that God was calling him to them, and he turned down others, such as the bishopric of Uganda, because he lacked this certainty. Furthermore, Taylor Smith believed that preaching was an essential task of a Christian minister; 'Woe to me if I do not preach the gospel' was one of his mottoes.

As his ministry in Sierra Leone shows, Taylor Smith mixed his very obvious evangelicalism with tolerance, generosity and a willingness to listen to people who disagreed with him. Earnest Ingham, the Bishop of Sierra Leone, wanted a canon-missioner 'to deepen the spiritual life of the church', and Taylor Smith undertook this task with typical gusto. Some of Taylor Smith's efforts were quite conventional: he organized and participated regularly in the Sunday and weeknight services; as dean of St George Cathedral in Freetown (1897–1901), he launched an appeal for funds to restore the cathedral; and he travelled all over the diocese on ten- to fourteen-day tours visiting churches in the hinterland. It was Taylor Smith's unconventional methods that endeared him to the diocese, however. At St George, for example, he inaugurated a regular service for children, a weekly Wednesday evening meeting for men and, unusual at that time, a cathedral chapter composed mainly of Sierra Leonians. After the British Government withdrew its financial subsidy of the diocese, thus disestablishing the church, Taylor Smith reorganized the finances so that all the native pastors were paid regularly, arguing that this arrangement would ensure their loyalty to the church. And, in a diocese that the historian Stephen Neill described as 'fractious', Taylor Smith promoted unity by bringing the disputants together, regaling them with his humorous interpretation of incidents in the Bible and encouraging them to rededicate their lives to God's service.

Taylor Smith was a traditional evangelical. He read the Bible every morning (during what he called his 'quiet time'), was a teetotaler and a non-smoker, exercised regularly and never attended the theatre. He also sought out opportunities to convert people, stated publicly and frequently the importance of moral purity and emphasized the need for a disciplined Christian life. A typical example of his approach to life is an encounter with an army officer who, thinking that Taylor Smith might condemn his lifestyle, pointed out that God had given humans physical cravings and desires. After convincing the officer that God had also given humans mental and spiritual cravings, Taylor Smith said, 'If you gratify your spiritual desires, and your mental desires, then you can gratify your physical desires.' When the officer met Taylor Smith two years later, he credited this conversation as the beginning of his conversion.

Taylor Smith was president or vice-president of a number of evangelical organizations. These included the World's Evangelical Alliance, an international movement to promote unity among evangelical churches, the Alliance of Honour, an interdenominational movement to promote moral purity, the Boys Brigade and the Scripture Union.

However, Taylor Smith was not an austere evangelical. He was a popular preacher; people from Queen Victoria to attendees at the Keswick Conventions liked his sermons. Taylor Smith's outlook on life was so youthful that friends and acquaintances called him 'everybody's bishop' and the 'man who never grew up'. Furthermore, he brought a sharp sense of humour to every occasion. Asked once why he had never married, he replied that he was married to the church and had never met any other woman worth his time.

Taylor Smith's published works are mainly sermons and addresses. His three major works are *Receiving the Abundance of Life* (1934), an address given at the Keswick Convention of 1934, *Abiding and Abounding* (1936), an address given at the Keswick Convention of 1936, and *From a Bishop's Basket* (1940), twelve sermons published posthumously.

Taylor Smith died on 28 March 1938 aboard the S. S. *Orion* as he was returning to England from Australia (where he was the main speaker at the Katoomba Convention, an Australian equivalent of the Keswick Conventions). After his death the governors of the London College of Divinity passed a special resolution calling Taylor Smith 'one of the most distinguished sons of the College' (he was the first student from the institution to become a bishop) and noting that his 'whole life was inspired and directed' by a clear vision of God, a 'conviction of the living truth of God's word written and unwavering assurance of personal salvation in Christ'.

Bibliography

E. L. Langston, *Bishop Taylor Smith, 1860–1938: Bishop and Chaplain-General* (London: Church Book Room Press, 1948); P. O. Ruoff, *Spiritual Secrets from Bishop Taylor Smith's Bible* (London: Marshall, Morgan & Scott, 1944); M. Whitlow, *J. Taylor Smith K.C.B., C.V.O., D.D.: Everybody's Bishop* (London: Lutterworth Press, 1938).

K. A. FRANCIS

■ **SMITH, Oswald Jeffrey** (1889–1986), Canadian pastor, was born on 8 November 1889 in Odessa, Ontario, the oldest of ten children, and was frequently ill as a child. The death of his younger sister when he was fifteen provoked a religious crisis that was resolved only with his conversion at the 1906 *Torrey-Alexander meetings in Toronto.

Between 1908 and 1909 Smith worked as a colporteur, first in Ontario and then among the logging camps and Native villages of coastal British Columbia. Feeling called back to Toronto to study in 1909, he enrolled instead in Manitoba College, Winnipeg. Although he met Jonathan *Goforth and discovered Charles *Finney (the single most influential figure in the shaping of his ministry) while there, he regarded the year as wasted.

In 1910, at Toronto Bible Training School, Smith's passion for mission increased. He held his first evangelistic crusade, worked as a pastor of a small church and travelled for the Pocket Testament League. After graduation in 1912, he enrolled in McCormick Seminary, Chicago, where again he combined his studies with evangelistic crusades and pastoral work. He was ordained in the Presbyterian church. Smith also spent a memorable summer among the mountain people of Kentucky.

Smith always felt a strong sense of call to Toronto. In 1915 he was called as associate pastor at Dale Presbyterian, the second largest Presbyterian church in Canada. His years there were tumultuous but stimulating. Smith took the senior role in 1916 but was forced to resign in 1918. Unable to find work, he went to Vancouver with the Shantyman's Christian Association, then realized his mistake and returned to Toronto.

Again Smith was unable to find work, so in 1920, solely by faith, he booked a 750-seat hall and founded the Gospel Tabernacle. Within months he had merged this with the nearby Parkdale Tabernacle of the Christian and Missionary Alliance. Starting with a congregation of twenty-four, he ordered a 1,500-seat tent and began evangelistic meetings. Dramatic growth followed; so in 1922 Smith built the Alliance Tabernacle. Here the main elements of his strategy were developed. Colourful services and a succession of famous preachers and musicians drew people to the church, while a wide range of evangelistic projects involved them in its work. The Tabernacle Publishers produced numerous tracts by Smith and magazines for a host of audiences. Smith was transformed by his first missionary tour, with William Felter of the Russian Missionary Society in 1924. He began to raise money for mission societies.

Smith's years at the Tabernacle were also controversial. He felt that the Alliance was less than sympathetic towards his transdenominational vision for mission, while they believed that he centred too much authority in himself. In 1926 Smith resigned to serve as district superintendent for Central and Eastern Canada and then to become pastor of the Alliance's Gospel Tabernacle of Los Angeles in 1927. Again, he realized that leaving Toronto was a mistake, but he felt duty bound to spend a year in Los Angeles. That year, while preaching in Tampa, he had the experience known as 'baptism in the Holy Spirit', which transformed his ministry and placed him firmly in the Keswick holiness tradition. Smith's time with the Alliance shaped its Canadian churches. He turned it from a movement focused mainly on holiness into an evangelistic organization with a strong emphasis on premillennial dispensationalism and separatist sympathies.

Back in Toronto Smith joined his old friend Paul *Rader (a former Alliance president) in The Worldwide Christian Couriers, and in 1928 they founded the Cosmopolitan Tabernacle (later renamed People's Church). Because of their Alliance background they drew many people away from the Alliance Tabernacle. They emphasized evangelism, the deeper life, foreign mission and the second coming. The church had no 'membership' or denominational ties. Structure was minimal; Smith appointed all the corporation officers.

In 1930 Smith rented the vacant St James Square Presbyterian Church. Believing that one should never bore the people, he gave a key role to music and guests. Smith also discovered the power of radio. Soon not only was his service being broadcast, but he was also hosting *The Back Home Hour*, a variety show following the evening service. Later, Smith would also use television, film and audio cassettes. His popularity was immense. Even after the church moved in 1934 to the larger former Central Methodist building, Smith frequently had to plead with radio listeners not to try to come to the services, in order to leave room for the non-Christians.

Smith was driven by a passion for mission, and raising the needed money was the task to which he dedicated his life. For this purpose he brought a succession of missionary speakers and evangelists to People's Church and supported them with pictures and colourful stories from his twenty missionary and evangelistic journeys to over seventy countries. Smith was also a master of the slogan. He encouraged giving by saying 'Why should anyone hear the gospel twice before everyone has heard it once?' and 'I must go or send a substitute'. He raised yet more money with the slogan 'Faith promise offerings'.

In 1959 Smith's son Paul fulfilled his father's dream by taking over People's Church. Paul moved the church to the northern part of the city in 1962.

Smith wrote thirty-five books, which were

translated into 128 languages; over six million copies had been sold by the time of his death. He also wrote poetry; over 1,200 of his poems have survived, and more than 200 have been set to music.

Smith's influence on evangelicalism was immense; many of its leaders were his friends. In recognition of this influence he received honorary degrees from numerous institutions, including a Doctorate of Divinity from Asbury College, a Doctorate of Literature from Bob Jones University, a Doctorate of Laws from Houghton College and a Doctorate of Humanities from the California School of Theology. He died in Toronto on 25 January 1986. Billy *Graham spoke at his funeral.

Bibliography
D. Hall. *Not Made For Defeat* (Grand Rapids: Zondervan, 1969); L. Neely, *Fire in His Bones* (Wheaton: Tyndale House, 1982).

D. A. GOERTZ

■ **SMYTH, John** (?1570–1612), Baptist leader, went to Christ's College in 1586, where he was tutored by Francis Johnson, who would later lead Henry *Ainsworth's separatist congregation in Amsterdam. He was ordained by the Bishop of Lincoln and then elected to a fellowship at his college in 1594. By 1597 he was becoming increasingly concerned about the true nature and right constitution of the church. By 1598 he had left his fellowship, and on 27 September 1600 he was appointed as lecturer to the Corporation of the City of Lincoln. At this stage he was a Puritan and faithful to the Church of England.

Smyth's moderate Puritan views did not last long. At a meeting of the Corporation of the City of Lincoln on 13 October 1602, he was released from his duties. It has been suggested that his dismissal was the result of tensions within the Lincoln Corporation, but he may already have been moving towards Separatist views. Certainly he was by this time questioning whether certain practices of the Church of England were based on Scripture. In 1603 he wrote *The Bright Morning Starre* and in 1605 *A Paterne of True Prayer*; in both these works he criticized the established church.

Eventually Smyth embraced the Separatist view, believing that the church, rightly constituted, was 'a company of faithful people separated from all uncleanness and joined together by a covenant of the Lord'. He argued in favour of congregational polity, believing that the church was made up of all those who were joined together in a promise to live in obedience to God's will, already made known to them or yet to be revealed.

By 1606 Smyth had joined with a group of Separatists in Gainsborough that included John *Robinson, William Brewster and William *Bradford, who would later settle in the New World. Due to persecution, in 1607 Smyth and another leader, Thomas Helwys, emigrated with a group of church members to Holland and settled in Amsterdam. For a time they met with the congregation associated with Francis Johnson and Henry Ainsworth, before some differences in doctrine became apparent, especially regarding their understanding of worship and the duties of ministers. In 1608 Smyth outlined these differences in a work entitled *The differences of the Churches of the separation (1608)*.

Smyth and Helwys shared with other Separatists a desire for a pure church. On the basis of their reading of Scripture, they insisted that the church was best organized as a gathered covenant community. Like many Separatists, Smyth began to feel uneasy about the baptism that he and others had received within the Church of England. By 1609 he had rejected infant baptism and was arguing in favour of baptism for believers only.

For Smyth the baptism that he and others had received was false in at least two ways. First, it was administered by a false church and secondly, it was performed on infants and not on professing believers. In order to reconstitute the church on what he believed to be a proper foundation, Smyth took the unusual step of baptizing himself, probably by affusion or pouring, and then he baptized Helwys and about forty others.

It was not long before Smyth came into contact with a group of Mennonites who practised believer's baptism and began to regret his decision to baptize himself and others. Smyth then renounced his baptism and called on members of the congregation to do the same. They refused to comply with his request and the congregation split. In

1611 Helwys and a small band of followers returned to England, where they established the first Baptist church on English soil.

Smyth drew up a confession of faith, which expressed his belief in general atonement and congregational church polity. But he died while waiting to be admitted to membership by the Mennonites. Although he did not remain a Baptist, Smyth is recognized along with Thomas Helwys as an early Baptist leader whose writings provided the theological foundation for Baptist doctrine and polity.

Bibliography

W. T. Whitley (ed.), *The Works of John Smyth*, 2 vols. (Cambridge: Cambridge University Press, 1915); B. R. White, *The English Separatist Tradition, from the Marian Martyrs to the Pilgrim Fathers* (Oxford: Oxford Theological Monographs, 1971).

K. E. SMITH

■ **SPENER, Philipp Jakob** (1635–1705), Lutheran pastor and early leader of the Lutheran Pietist movement, was born into an atmosphere of pervasive Arndtian piety and raised in the milieu of the lesser imperial aristocracy who later did much for the Pietist party. His father, Johann Philipp Spener, was a jurist and councillor to the lords of Rappoltstein at Rappoltsweiler in Upper Alsace, where Philipp Jakob was born on 13 January 1635. His early education was undertaken by his godmother, Countess Agatha von Rappoltstein. Her death when he was thirteen occasioned an intense desire for his own decease, a melancholy shaped by his reading in the English Puritans. From 1651 to 1659 Spener studied at the University of Strasburg, first philosophy, then theology. But he also received a basic historical training, which enabled him to perform a fundamental service to German heraldry and genealogy. This achievement might have led to a call to a chair in Tübingen and a turning from theology; in the event it helps to explain his success in mobilizing support from the 'pious counts' later in his career. In 1663, appointed a Free Preacher in Strasburg, he seemed to be heading for an academic career, identified with the Reform Orthodoxy of his tutor, Dannhauer. In 1664 he married

Susanna Ehrhardt, the daughter of a Strasburg patrician. These prospects were ended in 1666 by an unexpected call to be Senior of the Lutheran clergy at Frankfurt am Main. Spener was young for this appointment, but the vacancy had long been unfilled, and Strasburg made no attempt to keep him. Spener's twenty years' service in Frankfurt were a decisive period in his life. Prolonged study of *Luther and of the Apocalypse combined with practical experience laid the foundation of his mature views and of the *Pia Desideria* (1675), the programmatic writing, originally a preface to an edition of Arndt's lectionary sermons, that formed the substance of his policy for the renewal of the Lutheran churches.

Spener's first decade in Frankfurt taught him that an alternative to the reform hopes cherished in Lutheran Orthodoxy was now indispensable; it was vain to wait for state action, and clerical clamour for public repentance made little impact upon the habit and deference that sustained conventional Christian observance. Orthodoxy had relied too much on a combination of pressure from above, a highly articulated doctrinal system guaranteed against polemical attack, and the moral incentive of an impending last judgment to induce repentance before it was too late. Spener sought to introduce the leaven of the spiritual priesthood of all believers. There should be a Bible in every hand and class-meetings in which the faithful should exercise their calling by instructing, encouraging and warning each other. An altered moral imperative marked the real breach between Spener and Orthodoxy; he proclaimed 'the hope of better times', believing that this present age would not end until all the scriptural promises to the church, including the conversion of the Jews, were fulfilled. The need now was not repentance before it was too late, but work for the renewal of the church in the knowledge that it would bring the supreme blessing of Christ's return nearer. Instead of seeking to discipline the recalcitrant, Spener proposed to develop the spiritual talents of the willing. Preaching should be directed to the same end, the practical edification of the inner person.

Unlike the Reformed, the Lutherans had no tradition of gatherings outside the official liturgy, and Orthodox fears of schism, encouraged by the approaches of William Penn, the English Quaker, for settlers for his new colony in Pennsylvania, seemed justified when Johann Jakob Schütz, Spener's right-hand man in the Frankfurt class, seceded to join the Labadists. Spener circulated proof copies of the *Desideria* for comment, and in 1678 republished it in Latin in order to reach Lutheran theologians abroad. The response was moderate, but on the whole favourable. But irreparable damage was done by the secessions; the example of anti-Pietist legislation in Hesse-Darmstadt in 1678 was followed in other states; Spener's brother-in-law, Johann Heinrich Horb, was driven from his parish by the Strasburg Orthodox; Schütz was refused a public burial in Frankfurt. Spener's Pietism ceased to be an aspect of a broader devotional movement in Lutheranism and became a party defined by opposition to radical pietism (which Spener watched carefully) on one side, and on the other to an increasingly venomous Orthodox party. The original *collegium pietatis* or class-meeting changed character, being addressed only by Spener himself or by theological students; later in his career in Dresden and Berlin Spener experimented with it no further.

In 1686 Spener accepted a call to be Senior Court Chaplain in Dresden, a position that, since the Elector of Saxony was the head of the Corpus Evangelicorum (the Protestant party in the Imperial Diet), was the nearest to that of a Primate possessed by the German Lutheran churches. But his relations with the elector were always distant, and his private influence was exercised mainly through the ladies of the court. For public ministry he turned to catechizing, for which he had in 1677 published a system that depended less on memorizing than on meditation and Bible reading. In 1688 catechetical exercises were introduced throughout electoral Saxony, and they became well-known elsewhere in Germany. But in 1690 ferocious struggles began between the Orthodox and Pietists in Leipzig (occasioned by A. H. *Francke), Hamburg and elsewhere. Although Spener was not directly involved, he was closely connected with the Pietist leaders, and his own optimistic eschatology was violently attacked in print, the Wittenberg theological faculty detecting no fewer than 263 breaches of the Augsburg Confession. At the same time, the elector determined to get him out of Dresden,

and in 1691 he negotiated with the Elector of Brandenburg the offer of the Provostship of the Nikolaikirche in Berlin and a place on the consistorial council.

This much less prestigious opening Spener accepted without reluctance, and his fifteen years in Berlin proved to be the most fruitful of his life. Hohenzollern toleration protected him from the worst of religious polemic, and the creation of the new University of Halle/Saale enabled him to offer employment to the leaders of Leipzig Pietism. From this safe haven he was able to provide a future for the Pietist party in Prussian employment; he strengthened it in Württemberg and elsewhere. Spener was also enabled to complete his literary work. After he had produced a history of the Pietist movement (*Wahrhaftige Erzählung vom Pietismo*) in 1697, he withdrew from Pietist controversies and prepared his correspondence for publication in six huge volumes (two of which appeared posthumously). This correspondence, the largest in Protestant Germany during that period, embracing innumerable expert theological opinions on particular points and letters to men and women of every social rank and religious party, is the real monument to Spener's influence. He had, however, one great battle left, a controversy with the Unitarians, focused on Christology. This he completed just before his death on 5 February 1705.

Spener not only founded the Pietist movement; he also exercised a breadth of influence unrivalled by his colleagues and endeared himself to the later spokesmen of the German Enlightenment by his opposition to Aristotelianism and his sympathy for natural science and experimental methods. It is odd that it was the next generation of Pietists who consolidated both his work and his thought, who self-consciously looked beyond the Lutheran world and brought Spener's influence to bear at second-hand upon the Anglo-Saxon evangelical movements.

Bibliography

M. Brecht (ed.), in *Geschichte des Pietismus* (Göttingen: Vandenhoek & Ruprecht, 1993), vol. 1, pp. 281–389; P. Grünberg, *Philipp Jakob Spener*, 3 vols. (Göttingen: Vandenhoek & Ruprecht, 1893–1906); J. Wallmann, in M. Greschat (ed.), *Gestalten der Kirchengeschichte* (Stuttgart: Kohlhammer, 1982), vol. 7, pp. 205–224; J. Wallmann, *Philip Jakob Spener und die Anfänge des Pietismus* (Tübingen: J. C. B. Mohr [Paul Siebeck], ²1986).

W. R. WARD

■ **SPURGEON, Charles Haddon** (1834–1892), English Baptist minister and author, was the eldest son of John Spurgeon (1810–1902), an Independent (Congregational) minister in Tollesbury, near Colchester. His younger brother, James, became a minister and served as associate pastor to his famous brother. Charles was profoundly influenced by his grandfather, James Spurgeon (1776–1864), a highly regarded preacher and the minister of an Independent congregation in the tiny village of Stambourne, Essex, for fifty-four years. Because of family hardship, Spurgeon lived with his grandparents in Stambourne from near the end of his first year until the age of six. Here he experienced the rural life of pre-industrial England.

Spurgeon's formal education has been described as 'mediocre', but it prepared him for his life's work, preaching. During his early years, he often slipped into the attic and read the enormous folio works of martyrs, Puritans and especially John *Bunyan. He returned from Stambourne to live with his parents, first in Colchester and later in Maidstone, where his father pastored small congregations. After education in two local schools, he became a junior tutor at an Anglican school in Newmarket (1849), where he developed some measure of proficiency in Greek, Latin and philosophy. He then moved to an assistant master's post at a Cambridge school, which he held until 1851.

Later Spurgeon frequently referred to his profound spiritual convictions during these early years. Being raised in an environment where prayer, Bible study, catechizing, church attendance and the reading of devotional classics were regular practices, he knew the Christian faith. But this knowledge only compounded his sense of need. In an 1878 sermon he said, 'I distinctly recollect the time when I could not rest because of sin, and sought the Lord, while yet a child, with bitter anguish.' In another sermon he noted, 'I recollect when I used to say to myself when I was quite a lad, "If God does not punish me

for my sin, he ought to do so." That thought used to come to me again and again.'

Despite these deep impressions, it was not until 6 January 1850 that Spurgeon was converted. His story is quite straightforward. He rose early in the morning to pray and read his Bible. He set out for Colchester to attend a church that his mother had recommended. A snowstorm diverted him; thus he took a side street and entered the Artillery Street Primitive Methodist Chapel. An unknown substitute lay preacher preached from Isaiah 45:22 ('Look unto me ... ').

Spurgeon's *Autobiography* records what happened: 'He had not much to say, thank God, for that compelled him to keep on repeating his text, and there was nothing needed, by me at any rate, except his text. Then, stopping, he pointed to where I was sitting under the gallery, and he said, "That young man there looks very miserable" ... and he shouted, as I think only a Primitive Methodist can, "Look! Look, young man! Look now!" Then I had this vision ... not a vision to my eyes, but to my heart. I saw what a Saviour Christ was ... Now I can never tell you how it was, but I no sooner saw whom I was to believe than I also understood what it was to believe, and I did believe in one moment.'

During the next few weeks Spurgeon searched the Scriptures with great joy, and became convinced that he should be baptized. Securing his parents' permission, he walked eight miles to be immersed in the River Lark (at Isleham, Cambridgeshire) on 3 May 1850. He took his first communion at St Andrew's Baptist Church, Cambridge the following Sunday.

Within a few years Spurgeon became the best-known preacher in the world. He preached his first sermon, compelled by a friend and unprepared, at Taversham. He was only sixteen. By October 1851 he had become the pastor of Waterbeach Baptist Chapel near Cambridge. Within months the crowds had grown remarkably, albeit during a time of widescale evangelical revival. Spurgeon preached in the surrounding area of Cambridge, in chapels, cottages and the open air. His two-year ministry in the thatched-roof Waterbeach Chapel saw attendance grow from forty to 400. It was here that he began to publish his 'Waterbeach Tracts'. In

November 1853 a member of the historic New Park Street Chapel in London (where famous Baptist ministers such as Benjamin Keach, John *Gill, John *Rippon and Joseph Angus had served) heard Spurgeon and reported his impressions. On 18 December 1853 the nineteen-year-old minister preached his first sermon in London. He preached as a guest for the first three Sundays of January 1854, and was subsequently called as pastor.

New Park Street Chapel began to grow immediately under Spurgeon's preaching. To say he became an overnight sensation is not to overstate the fact. The building was almost immediately expanded to seat 1,500 (with standing room for 500 more), but still the crowds could not be contained. While plans were under way for a larger building Spurgeon preached at the famous Exeter Hall. In time this building, which seated over 4,000, also became inadequate. Sunday services were eventually held at the Surrey Music Hall, seating 10,000. By the age of twenty-two Spurgeon had become the most popular preacher of his day, yet he was despised by many in the press as 'the boy preacher'. *The Ipswich Express* said his sermons were 'redolent of bad taste, vulgar, and theatrical'. Spurgeon replied, 'I am perhaps vulgar, but it is not intentional, save that I must and will make the people listen. My firm conviction is that we have had quite enough polite preachers, and many require a change.'

At the first service at Surrey Hall, on the evening of 19 October 1856, a famous tragedy took place. With the building overflowing and thousands still outside wanting to get in, someone (probably with malicious intent) yelled, 'Fire!' In the mass confusion seven people were trampled to death. Spurgeon was devastated. He was literally carried from the pulpit to a friend's home and experienced profound depression for days. He later wrote, 'Perhaps never a soul went so near the burning furnace, and yet came away unharmed.' Two weeks later he returned to Surrey Hall, and morning services continued there from 1856 to 1859.

In 1861 Spurgeon preached to the largest indoor crowd ever recorded. He spoke, on a national day of fasting and prayer, to 23,654 at the famous Crystal Palace. In March 1861 the Metropolitan Tabernacle, with a seating capacity of nearly 6,000, was finally opened,

debt free. This would be the home of Spurgeon's congregation, and the centre of his distinguished pulpit ministry, until his death. For thirty-one years the average attendance for both morning and evening worship was said to approach 6,000. On Sunday evenings as many as 1,000 members were employed in various activities outside the Tabernacle. Once each quarter Spurgeon asked members not to attend the following Sunday evening so that the 'unsaved' might have seats. During his ministry a total of 14,692 members were added to the church, nearly 11,000 by baptism. At his death the membership of the church was 5,328, and there were 127 lay ministers serving in and around London in twenty-three mission stations.

In early 1856 Charles Spurgeon married Susanna Thompson. They had twin sons, Charles and Thomas, who both became Baptist ministers. In 1856 Spurgeon began to tutor one student. He took a second student the next year. When he formally organized this work into the Pastors' College, with the goal of training men with a limited formal education, the initial enrolment comprised eight students. The training consisted of a two-year course in mathematics, logic, homiletics, pastoral theology, English composition and biblical Greek and Hebrew. Spurgeon spoke to the students every Friday. His comments evolved into one of his best-known books, *Lectures to My Students*. The breadth of his understanding was demonstrated by his appointment of the first principal of the college, George Rogers of Camberwall, a Congregationalist. Speaking at the Tabernacle in 1884, D. L. *Moody referred to 'the 600 servants of God who have gone out from this college'. By Spurgeon's death the number was close to 1,000.

The publication of Spurgeon's sermons began in 1855. They were printed, published and mailed to subscribers, and were even published in newspapers around the world. Other initiatives followed. In 1867 the Stockwell orphanage for boys and girls opened. It would eventually include twelve houses and accommodate over 500 children. Almshouses for the poor were founded (1868). An association for the dissemination of gospel literature (Metropolitan Colportage Association, 1866) had scores of workers. Local mission work was done by students in the slums of

London; they established churches and Sunday schools. By 1865 Spurgeon had begun publication of *The Sword and Trowel*, a monthly magazine that contained both original material and news of his ministry. A prolific writer, Spurgeon authored some 135 books, was editor of twenty-eight others and produced a number of pamphlets and albums. In all, he produced over 200 titles. In 1875 Spurgeon's wife established a fund with the royalties in order to provide Christian books for needy pastors.

Spurgeon had a keenly developed social and political awareness and often found himself in the middle of national debates. He once wrote, 'Every God-fearing man should give his vote with as much devotion as he prays.' At the same time, he sought to avoid making the pulpit a place for partisanship. Like most Nonconformist ministers of the time he supported the Liberal Party. He was an outspoken advocate for the disestablishment of the Church of England. He supported measures to ensure Sabbath observance, favoured restrictions on alcohol and offered public prayer against bad housing in central London. He also openly denounced slavery in the United States in 1860, calling it 'a soul-destroying sin'.

Spurgeon was also a controversialist. In 1864 he preached one of his most famous sermons, 'Baptismal Regeneration'. His target was the influence of the Roman Catholic John Henry Newman and the rising Anglo-Catholic movement. (This sermon alone soon sold over 350,000 copies.) In the 1860s Spurgeon withdrew from the Evangelical Alliance (he rejoined later), and in the 1880s engaged in the much more serious 'down grade' controversy within the Baptist Union. Failing to persuade the Union to adopt a clear Statement of Faith he withdrew (1887) because of his suspicion that doctrinal laxity was growing. Even some conservative evangelical ministers thought that Spurgeon was sometimes unnecessarily divisive.

Spurgeon had great gifts, both natural and spiritual, and he knew great suffering. Not only did he suffer from chronic illness (rheumatic gout and frequent bouts of depression), but also his wife became an invalid in 1868. The effect of slander, opposition from several London pastors and public scorn in the press all took a heavy toll on him. Further, the labours of his huge ministry were a great burden, though one he relished. Spurgeon had a firm, clear conviction that God was sovereign. He was not, however, a fatalist. He noted, 'Fate is blind; providence has eyes.' He observed of his own trials, 'The way to stronger faith usually lies along the rough pathway of sorrow.' Later in life he would spend long periods of time at Mentone in France, to escape the cold, wet climate of London winters.

What was Spurgeon's theology? He was a Baptist by conviction. He also affirmed divine election and human responsibility with equal passion. His theology was biblical and spiritual, without being rational and systematic. There is no doubt that Spurgeon was an evangelical Calvinist. At the opening of the Metropolitan Tabernacle in 1861 he preached a series of sermons on the 'five points of Calvinism'. A reflective person by nature, he has been properly called 'The Heir of the Puritans'. One historian noted that Spurgeon found three things in the Puritans which he believed to be in short supply in the evangelicalism of his own day: 'rigorous theology, warm spirituality, and down-to-earth practicality'. He was premillennial, without embracing the more speculative views of the time. He also opposed holiness movements and strongly rejected higher criticism, defending the infallibility of the Scriptures.

Spurgeon was the best-known preacher of his time. Many still consider him the best preacher, if not the most popular one, in church history. The noted twentieth-century German pastor and theologian Helmut Thielicke, said: 'Sell all [the books] that you have ... and buy Spurgeon.' Today, over a hundred years after his death, there is more material by Spurgeon in print than by any other Christian author, living or deceased. His first published sermon was in a Paternoster series called the 'penny pulpit'. It met with incredible success. His sermons were collected and published as single volumes at the end of each year. In 1861 these volumes became *The Metropolitan Tabernacle Pulpit*. After Spurgeon died the series was continued using his stenographically recorded messages. The series ended in 1917 due to the hardship of wartime conditions. The complete set of sixty-three volumes is still in print and contains 3,544 sermons.

Spurgeon was clearly an entrepreneur, a remarkable 'speed reader', and a person with a 'photographic memory'. He was a natural orator who mastered the English Bible. He was also an artist who painted word-pictures with illustrations, wit, proverbs and extemporaneous, clear English. Nineteenth-century Britain included perhaps the greatest collection of pulpit orators of any century, including H. P. Liddon, Joseph *Parker, F. W. Farrar, Hugh Price *Hughes, F. W. *Meyer, Alexander *McLaren, R. W. *Dale and Alexander Whyte. All of them drew great crowds, but none like Spurgeon's, and he drew the crowds to the end of his life. Like many other great evangelical preachers, he believed that the key to his preaching was this: 'I take my text and make a bee-line to the cross.'

Spurgeon preached his last sermon at the Tabernacle on 7 June 1891. During the months that followed he experienced failing health. He died at the Hotel Beau Rivage in Mentone on 31 January 1892, at the age of fifty-seven. After a service in France, his body was taken to London, and four funeral services were held on Wednesday 10 February. One service was held for members of the Tabernacle, one for ministers and students, a third for 'Christian workers' and a fourth for the general public. A final service was held on 11 February, and Spurgeon's body was buried at West Norwood Cemetery, London, on 12 February. The grave is marked to this day with the words: 'Here lies the body of Charles Haddon Spurgeon Waiting for the Appearing of His Lord and Saviour Jesus Christ.'

Bibliography

E. Hayden, *Searchlight on Spurgeon* (Pasadena: Pilgrim Publications, 1973); E. Hayden, *Unforgettable Spurgeon* (Belfast: Ambassador Productions, 1997); P. Kruppa, *Charles Haddon Spurgeon: A Preacher's Progress* (New York: Garland, 1982); G. H. Pike, *The Life and Work of Charles Haddon Spurgeon*, 2 vols. (Edinburgh: Banner of Truth, repr. 1991); C. Ray, *The Life of Charles Haddon Spurgeon* (London: Passmore & Alabaster, 1903); C. H. Spurgeon, *The Autobiography of Charles H. Spurgeon*, 4 vols. (New York: Revell, 1898).

J. ARMSTRONG

■ **STEARNS, Shubal** (1706–1771), Separate Baptist revivalist, carried the fire and fervour of the Great Awakening in New England to the southern back country in the generation before the American Revolution.

Shubal Stearns was born in Boston, Massachusetts on 28 January 1706. In his youth his family moved to Tolland, Connecticut, where he joined the Congregational Church. During George *Whitefield's second tour of New England in 1745, he was converted. Whitefield's revival created a stir among the New England established churches. The churches marked by a great number of conversions came to be called 'New Light' churches. People were not admitted as members of these churches without a 'profession of vital religion'. This policy separated these revitalized churches from the established churches and around 1744 caused them to be labelled 'Separates'.

Following his conversion, Shubal Stearns laboured among the New Lights until 1751, when he became acquainted with some Baptists, who convinced him that believers' baptism was a duty. After a thorough study of the Scriptures, he became a Baptist and persuaded so many of his fellow church members to withdraw from Congregationalism that he was able to form a Baptist church in Tolland. In May the church ordained Stearns as pastor, and he served it for three years.

Then, with his strong faith in the immediate guidance of the Spirit, Stearns felt compelled to search for a special place to preach the gospel on the western frontier. Five couples, nearly all of them Stearns's relatives, decided to move with their pastor and his wife: Peter Stearns, Ebenezer Stearns, Shubal Stearns, Jr, Enos Stinson, Jonathan Polk and their wives. The little itinerating fellowship put all their possessions in carts, left New England and headed south for western Virginia.

They probably left Tolland in July 1754 and made their way to New York, then to Philadelphia. They continued to Baltimore, where they turned west by travelling up the Potomac Valley. Stopping first at Opeckon Creek in Berkeley County, Stearns found a Baptist church there under the pastoral care of John Garrard, who received him cordially. He also met his brother-in-law Daniel *Marshall, who had just returned from a mission among the Mohawk Indians. They joined their companies and decided to settle for a time on Cacapon Creek in Hampshire County, about thirty miles from Winchester.

When Stearns met little success in the area, however, he felt restless and began to think about moving on. Some of his friends had moved to North Carolina, and when he received their letters informing him about the spiritual hunger of people in the piedmont area, he decided to move south. The party left northwestern Virginia in the summer of 1755 and travelled down the Shenandoah Valley, crossed the Blue Ridge Mountains, and two hundred miles down the trail came to their resting place: Guilford (now Randolph) County, North Carolina.

The place Stearns chose to settle, called Sandy Creek, was a strategic location, a crossroads of frontier trails. Thousands of frontiersmen and their families passed through the area annually. Within three years the Sandy Creek Church, started by the New Englanders, had planted two sister churches, and in a few more years it had grown from the original sixteen members to 606 members. The key to this growth was Stearns' itinerant ministry. Although he lacked formal preparation for the ministry, he was a man of vision, action and unusual preaching skill. Baptist historian Morgan Edwards reports that his voice was 'musical and strong', and he could use it 'to make soft impressions on the heart' or 'to throw the animal system into tumults'. His hearers often broke into tears, trembling or screaming.

Stearns also had unusual organizational skills. He seemed to sense that an association would bring stability and uniformity to the multiplying churches. Thus he took the lead in the formation of the Sandy Creek Association, the first association of Baptist churches in North Carolina, and then sent out revivalists into the neighbouring colonies of Virginia, South Carolina and Georgia. Churches multiplied, but due to the difficulties of travel to the association meetings Stearns agreed in 1770 to the division of the association into three parts: North Carolina, South Carolina and Virginia.

Stearns died in 1771, having completed sixteen years of missionary labour in the South. The next year his associates identified forty-two churches that traced their origin to the Sandy Creek Church, and 125 ministers who had gone out from it.

Bibliography

W. L. Lumpkin, *Baptist Foundations in the South* (Nashville: Broadman Press, 1961); R. B. Semple, *History of the Baptists in Virginia* (Lafayette: Church Research and Archives, 1976).

B. SHELLEY

■ **STEPHEN, James** (1758–1832), slavery abolitionist, was born in Poole, Dorset, England on 30 June 1758. The second son of a Scottish-born solicitor of the same name, he attended several schools, including one at Kensington Green; he spent a term at the exclusive Winchester School but had to withdraw for financial reasons. With family help he attended Marischal College in Aberdeen, Scotland, finally settling in London in 1778 to work as a newspaper reporter. The death in 1781 of an uncle, a doctor and West Indian planter on St Christopher's, enriched James's elder brother William, who financed James's training as a barrister.

While studying at Kensington Green, Stephen fell in love with Anna (familiarly known as Nancy) Stent, sister of his close friend, Thomas Stent. They became secretly engaged at the age of fourteen and renewed their engagement after Stephen's return to London. However, while Tom Stent was abroad, Stephen also fell in love with Stent's beloved, a more exciting woman than Stent's sister; he fathered a son, William, by her in 1781. Stephen was in love with both women, but in 1783 he married Nancy Stent, who was given the care of her rival's illegitimate child. (Stephen used only the pseudonym 'Maria Rivers' to identify the woman.)

In 1783 Stephen went to St Christopher's to practise law; his wife soon followed, and they raised their family there. In Barbados he was horrified to witness a trial in which two blacks were convicted of rape by worthless evidence and then burnt alive. This event proved to be a turning-point in his life. Stephen came to despise slavery and began to correspond with William *Wilberforce, who was emerging as the parliamentary leader of those opposed to the slave trade. In 1788–1789 Stephen travelled to England and made personal contact with Wilberforce. From 1789 to 1794 he secretly became the chief West Indian source of information against the trade. During this period, Stephen worked principally for American shipowners seeking to recover cargoes that had been brought into St Christopher's as prizes.

Stephen returned to England in 1794 and practised in the prize appeal court of the Privy Council, being made a Master in Chancery in 1811. Once in England, Stephen became one of Wilberforce's closest friends. Before this time, Stephen had been at best a very nominal Christian; it was through Wilberforce that he underwent an evangelical conversion. In 1796 he moved to Clapham, where he became a key leader of the famous 'Clapham Sect', the zealous band of evangelicals eager to abolish the slave trade. Rough in his ways and heated in his language, Stephen was perhaps the least sophisticated of its members, but one of the most colourful, passionate and attractive.

A formidable debater and pamphleteer, with first-hand knowledge of the slave trade, Stephen was elected as a Tory MP for Tralee in 1808, serving for four years before becoming MP for East Grinstead (1812–1815). In Parliament Stephen became a close friend of Spencer *Perceval, a leading anti-slavery supporter and, from 1809, the British prime minister. (Perceval died in Stephen's arms in the lobby of the House of Commons in 1812, felled by an assassin's bullet.) Though unsophisticated, his brilliant legal mind and eloquent pen made him a formidable champion of abolition. Throughout his writings, from *The Crisis of the Sugar Colonies* (1802) to *The Slavery of the British West Indies Delineated* (1824–1830), runs the theme that God judges the actions of individuals and nations. Stephen interpreted the Napoleonic Wars and the revolutions and civil wars plaguing Europe as God's judgments 'on the nations of Europe, for their grievous and impious oppression of the African race'.

Another important work was Stephen's (originally) anonymous pamphlet published in 1805: *War in Disguise; Or the Frauds of the Neutral Flags*. In this Stephen drew on his West Indian experience to argue that Britain had never abandoned the right during a war to prevent neutrals carrying on a trade that had been prohibited to them in peacetime. (Prior to the war France had a strict monopoly on its colonial trade.) *War in Disguise* decried the practice of French ships carrying slave-produced goods from the French West

Indies and then heading for an American port where they began flying the American flag in order, as neutral ships, to make their way to France and Spain. Stephen probably drafted the famous Orders in Council of 1807, which sought to end the practice and thereby enraged the American government. In this way, he was, perhaps more than anyone else, responsible for the war of 1812. In 1815 he resigned from Parliament in protest over Lord Liverpool's refusal to adopt his scheme to establish a slave registry in the West Indies, believing that this alone could prevent the reintroduction of the slave trade. Perhaps Stephen's greatest literary work was his unfinished *Autobiography*, a providential interpretation of his life, written for his children. Although the work runs to over four hundred pages, it covers only his first twenty-five years.

Stephen's wife Nancy died in 1796, and in 1800 he married Wilberforce's widowed sister, Sarah Clarke. Stephen fathered six children, of whom the eldest, William, became a Buckinghamshire vicar, and the third, James, a distinguished civil servant. His second wife died in 1816, and in 1819 he moved to Great Missenden to be near his son William. In retirement he spent much time with his old friend Wilberforce. Stephen died at Bath, in Somerset, on 10 October 1832, a year before Wilberforce's death.

It is arguable that among the abolitionists Stephen was second only to Wilberforce. He was also the head of one of the most distinguished families in Victorian England. His son, Sir James Stephen, was a long-time colonial undersecretary. His grandsons included Sir James Fitzjames Stephen, judge of the High Court of Justice, and Sir Leslie Stephen, famous editor of the *Dictionary of National Biography*. The writer Virginia Woolf, was his great grand-daughter.

Bibliography

N. G. Annan, *Leslie Stephen: The Godless Victorian* (London: Weidenfeld & Nicolson, 1984); E. M. Howse, *Saints in Politics* (Toronto: University of Toronto, 1952); J. Pollock, *Shaftesbury: The Poor Man's Earl* (London: Hodder & Stoughton, 1985); G. Stephen, *Anti-Slavery Recollections* (London: Hatchards, 1854).

D. M. LEWIS

■ **STEWART**, **James Stuart** (1896–1990), preacher and scholar, was born on 21 July 1896 in Dundee. His father, William Stewart, was in business and later became secretary of the YMCA in Dundee, where he had an effective Bible-class ministry among young men for many years. His mother was Katharine Jane Duke, daughter of the Revd John Duke, also of Dundee. J. S., as he was known, thus grew up in an atmosphere of biblically based devotion, in which his preaching and teaching career was to be rooted. At Dundee High School he learned to love literature and football, and at the University of St Andrews he gained a first-class degree in classics in 1916. He served on the Western Front, and then in Manchester as a code-breaker. After the war he studied for the ministry of the United Free Church of Scotland at New College Edinburgh, and then for a year at the University of Bonn. His first academic task was to work with his Edinburgh teacher H. R. Mackintosh in translating Schleiermacher's *The Christian Faith* (published in 1928).

Stewart was minister at Auchterarder United Free Church from 1924 to 1928, and then at Beechgrove, Aberdeen from 1928 to 1935. In 1929 the United Free Church and the Church of Scotland reunited and Stewart became a minister of the established church. In 1935 he moved to North Morningside Church in Edinburgh, and he remained there until 1947, when he became Professor of New Testament Language, Literature and Theology in the University of Edinburgh and New College, as colleague to Professor W. Manson. He retired from this post in 1966, and spent the next 24 years in Edinburgh. He married Rosamund Barron in 1931 and they had two sons, Robin, who became a minister in the Church of Scotland, and Jack, who became a lecturer in English in Canada.

Stewart was a shy and reticent man who did not find small talk easy, yet he is remembered not only for his outstanding preaching, but also for his faithfulness in visiting his congregations and his assiduity in praying for them. In a rare personal insight in one of his sermons he says: 'for myself (if you will allow a personal word), I have been in the habit for some years now of using the Communion Roll as a manual of prayer – taking three families each day: so that there is not a soul of the 1560 on the Roll who is not prayed about personally by name at regular intervals.' His interest in and kindness to his students, both those who were studying for the ministry of the churches in Scotland, and those who came, mainly from the USA, to do research under his supervision, was proverbial. When a student was assigned to him for personal spiritual guidance, Stewart might be reticent in private conversation, but when he prayed with the student he was eloquent, and his prayers were remembered.

Stewart's love of literature embellished his thorough knowledge of the Scriptures, and his sermons, many of which are in print, show his powers of imagination and well-nourished insight. His copy of T. S. Eliot's *Murder in the Cathedral* was heavily annotated and underlined, like many other books that he loved and used. Although all his sermons are basically biblical, they are enriched with well-chosen quotations from classical nineteenth-century and contemporary writers and with insights from his own experience. Basically Stewart sought to expound and apply Scripture and to challenge and encourage his hearers. He was not afraid to use the same sermon many times, with due modifications, and to send them to a wider public in his books.

Stewart's books form a large part of his legacy. Like his sermons they were intended to serve God and reach as many readers as possible. For the Bible classes of the Church of Scotland he produced in 1932 a handbook, *The Life and Teaching of Jesus*, which was kept in print until recently and widely used. His most academic work of these years was delivered as the Cunningham Lectures in Edinburgh in 1934 and published under the title, *A Man in Christ: the Vital Elements of St Paul's Religion*. This book, showing a grasp of the latest British and continental scholarship, was produced in the context of a busy ministry, and is still valuable.

As befits a preacher, two of Stewart's best-loved books concern the art and craft of preaching. *Heralds of God* is the published form of the Warrack lectures delivered in Edinburgh and St Andrews. It was published in 1946 and much later republished as *Teach Yourself Preaching*. In it Stewart deals in memorable language with the preacher, the preacher's task and the preacher's method. His later book, *A Faith To Proclaim*, which appeared in 1953, is based on the Lyman *Beecher Lectures, delivered at Yale University in 1952, and concentrates on the teacher's message. The centrality of Christ is evident in all its chapters. Never in all his works and lectures did Stewart lose sight of the great theme of Christian belief and life, God's love in Christ. He travelled widely as a guest scholar, to Princeton and Berkeley, California as well as to Yale, and in 1959 he was for three months Turnbull Trust preacher in Melbourne, Australia.

After Stewart became Professor of New Testament Language, Literature and Theology at New College in 1947, he published little for the world of scholarship besides a number of articles in learned journals. His lectures were crowded, not only with students who were required to take his classes. All lectures began with prayer, as was the general custom in these days, and all are remembered as leading to devotion. Yet they were not sermons, but contained the best of contemporary scholarship. Many theses were completed under his supervision, often by postgraduates from far parts of the English-speaking world. Although Stewart was regarded as a self-effacing man, he valued certain honours. He was made a chaplain to the King in 1952, and soon thereafter to the new Queen. In 1962 he became moderator of the General Assembly of the Church of Scotland, and travelled widely in that post as an ambassador for his church.

Stewart retired in 1966 and continued to live in Edinburgh, occupying pulpits regularly in many churches. For many years during the summer months he occupied the pulpit in St George's West Church of Scotland, in Edinburgh's West End, often drawing large crowds. Several books of his sermons were published in his lifetime, most notably *The Gates of New Life* (1937), *The Strong Name* (1940) and *The Wind of the Spirit* (1968). After Stewart died, J. Gordon Grant edited a selection of unpublished sermons, *Walking With God* (1996), and his sermons continue to be read, and in some form, preached. He himself continued to preach, in a changing church scene, for many years. He outlived his wife and died on 1 July 1990 at the age of almost ninety-four.

Stewart was orthodox, but never obscurantist. He appreciated New Testament scholarship that illuminated his beloved Scriptures.

He loved to worship and to sing, and he loved classical music, especially Elgar. He was not afraid of unpopular opinions, and supported Mary Lusk, later Levison, in her wish to enter the ministry. At a time when Billy *Graham was regarded with suspicion, he befriended him. He met him on his first campaign in Scotland in 1956, and their friendship was to last until the end of his life. It would be quite wrong not to mention his enthusiasm for football, especially for the Heart of Midlothian, to which he was chaplain, and whose games he enjoyed attending.

Bibliography
R. Barbour, *J. S. Stewart in a Nutshell* (Edinburgh: The Handsel Press, 2000).
D. B. MURRAY

■ **STODDARD, Solomon** (1643–1729), Congregational theologian and minister, was born in late September 1643 and baptized in Boston, Massachusetts on 1 October 1643 when he was about four days old. Anthony Stoddard, his father, was a distinguished Boston merchant, and Mary Downing, his mother, a niece of John *Winthrop (1588–1649), the first governor of Massachusetts Bay. Educated at Harvard College, Stoddard graduated in 1662 and was subsequently appointed in 1666 as a tutor at his alma mater. After a short period as a chaplain in Barbados (1667–1669), Stoddard received a call in March 1670 to be pastor of the Congregational church in Northampton, Massachusetts. That same month he married Esther Mather (1640–1736), the widow of his predecessor at the church, Eleazar Mather (d. 1669). Among the twelve children that they raised (three of them Eleazar Mather's) was Esther Stoddard (1672–1770), the mother of the premier American theologian of the eighteenth century, Jonathan *Edwards (1703–1758).

Stoddard did not actually become a member of the Northampton congregation until April 1672. He was ordained that September. The two-year gap between his being called to preach to the church and his becoming a member and being ordained is probably related to the fact that until 1672 he had 'really no experimental acquaintance with the Gospel'. This statement may mean that he was not converted, or simply that he lacked assurance. At the Lord's Table, presumably at some point in 1672, he was given 'a full and glorious view of Christ and his great love for men as shown in his redemptive work'.

Reasoning in part from his own experience, Stoddard would eventually embrace the view that the Lord's Supper was *the* place where sinners were most likely to receive spiritual light and understanding. Around the time that Stoddard assumed the pastorate of the Northampton congregation, the Half-Way Covenant was adopted by the church. This measure, which had been promulgated by a 1662 synod in Boston, allowed the unregenerate children of believing parents to have their infants baptized provided that they embraced the Christian worldview and sought to lead a moral life. Participation in the Lord's Supper and voting remained the privilege of those who could profess conversion and thus were full members of the church.

By 1677 it appears that Stoddard was questioning the efficacy of the Half-Way Covenant, which was designed to encourage those who were 'half-way' members to go the whole distance and be converted. The influential Boston theologian Increase Mather (1639–1723), Stoddard's brother-in-law by marriage, noted in a sermon that he preached on 23 May 1677 that there were some in New England (and Stoddard is most likely in view) who were determined 'to bring all Persons to the Lords Supper, who have an Historical Faith, and are not scandalous in life, although they never had Experience of a work of Regeneration on their Souls' (*A Discourse Concerning the Danger of Apostasy* [Boston, 1679], p. 84). Stoddard was coming to the conviction that the Half-way Covenant actually hindered the progression of 'half-way' members towards conversion.

Two years later, at the Reforming Synod of 1679, Stoddard and Increase Mather debated the issue, though there is no clear evidence that Stoddard had yet reached the view Mather would later describe as Stoddard's 'strangest notion', namely that the Lord's Table is 'a converting ordinance'. There was also argument within his own church against Stoddard's deepening convictions. A sermon he preached in 1690 on Galatians 3:1 clearly indicates that he had come to the firm belief

that 'the Lord's Supper is appointed ... for the begetting of grace as well as for the strengthening of grace'.

Stoddard's innovation, known today as Stoddardeanism, was strongly attacked first by Edward Taylor (c. 1645–1729), a fellow pastor in nearby Westfield, who the twentieth century has discovered to be the most accomplished American poet of the era. Increase Mather was probably the fiercest opponent of Stoddardeanism. He and Stoddard carried on a debate in the press throughout the first decade of the eighteenth century. Stoddard's able defence of his views in such works as *The Doctrine of Instituted Churches* (London, 1700), *The Inexcusableness of Neglecting the Worship of God, under a Pretence of Being in an Unconverted Condition* (Boston, 1708) and *An Appeal to the Learned* (1709) won over to his views many pastors and churches in western Massachusetts. These works also defended Presbyterianism and thus further alienated men such as Mather who were firmly committed to a congregational model of church government.

At the heart of Stoddard's ministry was evangelism. 'Conversion,' he observed, 'is the greatest change men undergo in this world.' His church experienced five distinct seasons of revival (1679, 1683, 1690, 1712 and 1718) and probably more individuals were converted under his preaching than in any other church in New England. Three of his finest works delineate a theology of conversion in which he stressed that the sinner must and can prepare himself or herself for conversion: *The Safety of Appearing at the Day of Judgement* (Boston, 1687), *The Efficacy of the Fear of Hell* (Boston, 1713) and *A Treatise Concerning Conversion* (Boston, 1719).

Stoddard also believed that certain types of preaching hinder evangelism, especially preaching that is tied to written notes. On the other hand, 'when sermons are delivered without notes, the looks and gesture of the Minister, is a great means to command attention and stir up affection'. Moreover, good preaching is both doctrinal and designed to awaken sinners to their perishing state. 'We are not sent into the pulpit to shew our wit and eloquence, but to set the consciences of men on fire; not to nourish the vain humours of people, but to lance and wound the consciences of men.' Here Stoddard anticipated much of the preaching characteristic of the Great Awakening.

Stoddard's emphasis on the authority of the minister within the congregation (part of his Presbyterian platform and evident in *An Examination of the Power of the Fraternity* [1718]), his theological influence over the churches along the Connecticut River in Massachusetts and Connecticut and his vigorous preaching style earned him the sobriquet of 'Pope'. By the 1720s Pope Stoddard was beginning to feel his age. In 1725 a young minister was paid £13 to assist him, and in 1727 his grandson Jonathan Edwards came to be his permanent assistant. Edwards noted that his grandfather 'retained his powers, surprisingly to the last', but in his final years his eyesight was much diminished.

The power of Stoddard's distinct theological perspective is well seen in that twenty years after his death, when Jonathan Edwards, who succeeded him as pastor of the Northampton church, sought to restrict access to the Table once again to believers, he was met with fierce resistance. And due to his position on this key issue, one that was so much at odds with Stoddardeanism, Edwards was eventually dismissed as pastor in 1750.

Bibliography

T. M. and V. L. Davis (eds.), *Edward Taylor vs. Solomon Stoddard: The Nature of the Lord's Supper* (Boston: Twayne Publishers, 1981); K. J. Hardman, *The Spiritual Awakeners: American Revivlaists from Solomon Stoddard to D. L. Moody* (Chicago: Moody Press, 1983); P. Miller, 'Solomon Stoddard, 1643–1729', *Harvard Theological Review* 34 (1941), pp. 277–320; T. A. Schafer, 'Solomon Stoddard and the Theology of the Revival', in S. C. Henry (ed.), *A Miscellany of American Christianity* (Durham: Duke University Press, 1963), pp. 328–361.

M. A. G. HAYKIN

■ **STOKES, George Gabriel** (1819–1903), mathematical physicist, was the Lucasian Professor of Mathematics at Cambridge University from 1849 to 1903 and president of the Royal Society of London from 1885 to 1890.

Stokes was born on 13 August 1819 in Skreen, County Sligo, where his father was rector in the Church of Ireland. His mother, Elizabeth Haughton, was the daughter of a rector in the Church of Ireland. Stokes' earliest education came from his parents and the parish clerk. In 1832 he was sent to Dr R. H. Wall's school in Dublin, and in 1835 he entered Bristol College. He matriculated at Pembroke College, Cambridge in 1837 and graduated as senior wrangler and first Smith's prizeman in 1841. He began publishing a series of papers, on the viscosity within fluids and on the new wave theory of light, which quickly established his reputation. In 1852 he published a striking paper on 'fluorescence'; he coined the word himself. As secretary of the Royal Society from 1854 to 1885, he was instrumental in modernizing *The Philosophical Transactions of the Royal Society*. On 4 July 1857 he married Mary Susanna Robinson, daughter of the Irish astronomer Thomas Romney Robinson. He taught many future fellows of the Royal Society as Lucasian professor and in the 1890s published important papers on the new physics of radioactivity, electrons and X-rays. He died in Cambridge on 1 February 1903.

To the end of his life Stokes followed the evangelical views learned from his father, though he incorporated various unorthodox conclusions within that overall framework. As one centre of the evangelical wing of the Church of England, early Victorian Cambridge University was a congenial home for the young Stokes. He was required to study William Paley's *Evidences of Christianity* (1794), and he also embraced the design argument for God's existence as presented in Paley's *Natural Theology* (1802). However, the Bible rather than nature was always Stokes' primary source of religious truth. His twenty Gifford lectures, published in two volumes as *Natural Theology* (1891, 1893), were thus a difficult assignment, for the terms of the lectures restricted him to arguments based on natural theology rather than biblical revelation.

The doctrine of conditional immortality was his principal religious concern. He had found the idea of eternal damnation horrifying and repugnant even as a child. He re-examined the Bible and was influenced by the Congregational minister Edward White, whose *Life in Christ* (1846) espoused the view that immortality was not necessary but conditional on right belief. Instead of suffering perpetual torture, the unsaved were annihilated. Stokes regarded this as a welcome and fair doctrine, but also as one rooted in biblical evidence, John 3:16 being one of the verses he cited in its support. Moreover, he praised the value of the doctrine in missionary work and tried to persuade the Church Missionary Society to accept it. He published *Conditional Immortality: A Help to Sceptics* in 1897. According to Stokes, the erroneous concept of humanity's necessary immortality is part of Plato's pernicious influence on Christian theology, and that of the dualism of soul and body is another Platonic mistake. The Bible supports the doctrine of tripartite human nature; a human being consists of body, soul and spirit. Distinct from soul, spirit is a person's (potentially) immortal essence. Stokes also thought that spirit was unconscious in the period between death and the final judgment, arguing largely by analogy with his experience of not noticing the passage of time during a faint.

Stokes sought a proper balance between science and religion during a contentious age. The Bible, Stokes declared, was true even in matters of geology and biology, but not in a slavishly literal sense. Early Victorian theologians had mistakenly rejected modern geology because of such literalism. Extreme Darwinians, however, erred in overlooking discontinuities in the fossil record and in extending biological evolution into an antireligious materialism. Stokes thought that the biblically supported concept of God's continuing creative action over the course of geological time explained the fossil record sufficiently well. Even if the evidence ever actually supported Darwin, he argued, evolutionary theory would not undermine either the idea of God's continued involvement in natural processes or the truth of the Bible.

Bibliography

J. Larmor (ed.), *Memoir and Scientific Correspondence of the Late Sir George Gabriel Stokes*, 2 vols. (Cambridge: Cambridge University Press, 1907); D. B. Wilson, 'A Physicist's Alternative to Materialism: The Religious Thought of George Gabriel Stokes', *Victorian Studies* 28 (1984), pp. 69–96; D. B. Wilson, *Kelvin and Stokes: A Comparative Study in Victorian Physics* (Bristol: Adam Hilger, 1987); D. B. Wilson, 'Stokes and Kelvin, Cambridge and Glasgow, Light and Heat', in P. Harman and S. Mitton (eds.), *Cambridge Scientific Minds* (Cambridge: Cambridge University Press, 2002), pp. 104–122.

D. B. WILSON

■ **STONE, Barton W.** (1772–1844), founding leader in the Christian Church (Disciples of Christ) and evangelist, was born near Port Tobacco, Maryland on 24 December 1772, to Episcopalian farmer parents. Upon the death of his father, his mother moved the family to Pittsylvania County, Virginia. In 1790, so as to obtain a classical education, he began studies in Guilford, North Carolina, at an academy run by David Caldwell, a New Light Presbyterian. Though Stone anticipated a career in law, his thoughts turned to the ministry because of revivalistic stirrings generated by the renowned New Light evangelist, James *McGready.

McGready declared that humans were unable to know and enjoy God and as a result would suffer ultimate condemnation, except those elected by God through Christ. Though impressed by McGready's preaching, Stone was not converted until over a year later (1793) when he heard William Hodge, who proclaimed that sinners were greatly loved by God. After withdrawing to the woods, Stone had an experience that he identified with the love of God and was converted.

Stone, now twenty-one, considered taking up a ministry among the Presbyterians. It was necessary to read theology and undergo an examination in order to be ordained. Stone struggled through theological treatises and the Westminster Confession, studying the doctrines of the Trinity, the atonement, election and predestination, but had difficulty with the conventional Presbyterian positions. After a period in Georgia teaching Latin and Greek he returned to North Carolina.

Stone travelled to Tennessee, preaching in various places. In 1798 he was appointed minister at Cane Ridge and Concord in Bourbon County, Kentucky. Before his ordination, Stone declared that he was willing to affirm the Confession 'as far as it was consistent with the Word of God'. In the spring of 1801 Stone went to Logan County, Kentucky, west of

Bowling Green, to observe first-hand the fires of revival stirred by James McGready. Stone perceived the events there as 'passing strange'; nevertheless, he was amazed at the emboldened manner in which converts told others of their conversion. In July of 1801 Stone married Elizabeth Campbell, who bore five children, and died in 1810. In August 1801 Stone returned to Cain Ridge determined to reproduce what he had witnessed in Logan County. The outcome of his return proved to be a defining episode in American religious history, that is, the great Cain Ridge camp meeting. Perhaps as many as 20,000 came; the largest groups were the Presbyterians and Methodists, but numerous Baptists also attended. As a result of the Awakening, Stone and his Presbyterian associates, Richard McNemar, Robert Marshall, John Thompson, John Dunlavy and David Purviance, came into conflict with the three presbyteries of the region.

In 1803 the six ministers formed the independent Springfield Presbytery, so titled because of its connections with Springfield, Ohio. In June 1804, after persistent conflict with the other presbyteries and, convinced that the millennium might be on the horizon, they decided to abolish the presbytery in order, as they stated in the 'Last Will and Testament', to 'sink into union with the body of Christ at large'. The document was drafted by McNemar and discussed and signed by the other five. They decided to take the name 'Christian', encouraged by Rice Haggard, who had proposed it to the Virginia, James O'Kelly Christians. Some of the charges brought against them had to do with the atonement and Christology. Stone had published statements that were not consistent with the Nicean and Westminster Confessions. He held that Christ was begotten of God and, therefore, not equal with God. Within seven years McNemar and Dunlavy had left for the Shakers, and Marshall and Thompson had returned to the ministry of the Presbyterian Church. Stone emerged as the chief leader among the growing Christian Churches. When Elizabeth, Stone's first wife, died, he married her cousin, Celia Wilson Bowen, in 1812 at her home a few miles north of Nashville. They had six children. After a year in Kentucky they were persuaded to move to a farm near Nashville, then in 1815 to Lexington.

Stone first met Alexander *Campbell in 1824 when Campbell visited Kentucky to preach among the Baptist Churches. At that time Stone was teaching in his own private school, and in 1826 he began editing The Christian Messenger. He had occasional exchanges with Campbell in this journal and in Campbell's Christian Baptist; Campbell chided Stone for being too speculative in regard to the doctrine of the atonement, the Trinity and Christology. Stone proposed to Campbell as early as 1829 that their two groups should consider themselves one. By that time the Campbell reformers had in effect moved out from the Baptists and had perhaps 5,000 members, while those associated with Stone west of the Appalachians numbered more than 12,000. Stone continued to press for unity, but Campbell was reluctant; he underlined differences in regard to the necessity of baptism and the name 'Christian', preferring what he regarded as an older name, 'disciples of Christ'. Stone established a friendly relationship with John T. Johnson of the Campbell reformers and in 1831 announced that Johnson would join him in editing The Christian Messenger. After discussions at Georgetown in January 1832, the union of the two groups in that region of Kentucky was announced, and people were selected to travel throughout the surrounding states to encourage further mergers. Several of the Stone churches and their leaders did not support the merger, including David Purviance, who objected on the grounds that prayers for sinners and the anticipation of the Holy Spirit would decline among the churches.

Stone came rather early to the view that slavery was a pernicious evil. His wife had inherited slaves, and it seems that one reason for their move to Jacksonville, Illinois in 1834 was that since by law the Stones could not free the slaves, as they were attached to the estate, they could relinquish their ownership only by moving away. Stone favoured the sending of all slaves to Liberia, where (he believed) they could found colonies and evangelize the rest of Africa. He worked in the American Colonization Society, the purpose of which was to raise private funds to assist the repatriation; he thought it was only a matter of time until Congress appropriated federal funds for it. Stone viewed the unifying of the churches and the abolition of slavery as signs that the millennium was near. Beginning in 1842, he recommended that Christians not participate in civil government because of the party system and the authorities' failure to abolish slavery. He came to believe that the government and laws of Jesus were sufficient to rule the world and by July 1844 was arguing argued for non-resistance. Stone died on a trip to Missouri in the home of his daughter in Hannibal on 9 November 1844.

Bibliography
B. W. Stone and J. Rogers, *The Biography of Rev. Barton Warren Stone* (Cincinnati: J. A. & U. P. James, 1847); R. Thompson (ed.), *Voices from Cane Ridge* (St Louis: Bethany Press, 1954); C. C. Ware, *Barton Warren Stone, Pathfinder of Christian Union* (St Louis: Bethany Press, 1932); D. N. Williams, *Barton Stone: A Spiritual Biography* (St Louis: Chalice Press, 2000). For many of the published writings of Stone, see: *http://www.mun.ca/rels/restmov/texts/bstone/stone.html*

T. H. OLBRICHT

■ **STORR, Vernon Faithfull** (1869–1940), Anglican minister and author, was the best-known advocate of liberal evangelicalism in the Church of England in the early twentieth century. Storr was born on 4 December 1869 in Muddenpilly, near Madras, India; although he was an English national, his father Edward worked for the Madras Civil Service at that time. He married his cousin Katherine Cecilia Storr on 4 February 1902, and they had four children: Mary, born in July 1903; Noel, born in December 1905; Rachel, born in November 1910; and Tony, born in May 1920.

Storr won a scholarship to Queen's College, Oxford in 1888 (although he did not receive the full value of the scholarship until his second term because Queen's gave money only to students born in the United Kingdom until he persuaded the college authorities to change this policy) and received his BA in 1892, a First Class in the Humanities. In 1894 University College, Oxford offered him a fellowship, and he received an MA in 1895; he lectured in philosophy and tutored students reading logic, the philosopher-theologian B. H. Streeter being one of his students.

In 1893 and 1894 Queen's made Storr the Aubrey Moore Theological Student, and this award suggested that he would immediately embark on a clerical career; in fact, he did not accept a curacy until 1900, partly because of his uncertainty about the priesthood as a career, and partly because he was unsure whether he should ally himself to the catholic or the evangelical wing of the church. In 1900, having been ordained a deacon, he became the assistant curate of Haslemere in the diocese of Winchester, and he retained a connection with the diocese until 1921. In 1901 Queen's offered Storr the living of Bramshott in Hampshire; he was ordained a priest and became the rector there.

The close connection between Storr's clerical and academic careers continued for the rest of his life. In 1906 he became the rector of Headbourne-Worthy, a benefice held by University College, because it was a smaller parish and so would allow him more opportunities to write, and thus to fulfil the obligation of the fellowship he had accepted in 1905. As a result of his work as examining chaplain for the Bishop of Winchester (1902–1903) and Archbishop of Canterbury (1903–1936), Storr was invited by Bishop Ryle to become a residentiary canon of Winchester (1907–1916). His writing on the philosophy of religion and his preaching (he was the Select Preacher at Oxford in 1908 and 1909 and at Cambridge in 1909 and 1922) led Prime Minister Lloyd George to ask him to become a canon of Westminster in 1920, Archbishops Davidson and Lang to appoint him a member of the Archbishops' Commission on Christian Doctrine in 1922 (he served until 1937) and the lawyers at Lincoln's Inn to invite him to become the Warburton Lecturer in 1923 (he served until 1937).

Although Storr was a committed evangelical, he was tolerant, with a concern for the ethical implications of his theological position, and able, according to Archbishop William Temple, to 'appreciate the views of others'; nevertheless, he was firm in his own views. In 1916 he took the positions of rector of Bentley in Hampshire and honorary canon of Winchester because he did not like the 'Catholicism' of the bishop, Edward Talbot. George Harris, Storr's biographer, describes his major academic book *The Development of*

English Theology in the Nineteenth Century as 'severe in [its] judgment of the Tractarian Movement as a whole', and in a lecture given at Oxford University in 1922 entitled 'A Crisis in the Church' Storr described evangelicalism and Anglo-Catholicism as 'two radically opposed systems of thought contending for the soul of the Church of England'.

In 1923 Storr began work with the Anglican Evangelical Group Movement (AEGM), an enterprise that solidified his reputation as one of the foremost apologists for evangelicalism. The group, whose membership was initially confined to clergy, claimed in its objectives to be committed to 'spiritual religion', a 'belief in freedom' and a 'reliance on the Gospel rather than on tradition'. Storr, along with his future biographer George Harris, became the joint editor of fifty-three pamphlets issued by the AEGM, honorary organizing secretary in 1930 and president in 1930, 1935 and 1940. Storr also wrote six pamphlets for the AEGM, including its first, on the subject of God, and one on the relationship between Jesus Christ and the Old Testament (both published in 1923). Storr's pamphlets emphasized his view that traditional evangelical positions (e.g., belief in God) were tenable in the light of current thinking and knowledge.

Storr's concern with contemporary thought was an important facet of his liberal approach to evangelicalism. The AEGM's claim that 'Christianity has nothing to fear from criticism or new discovery' could serve as Storr's philosophy of life. From the time of his attendance at lectures on biology during his extra year at Queen's, Storr had sought to rationalize his Christianity and contemporary thought. In one of his lectures on philosophy to students at Cambridge he stated simply that 'there can be little or no doubt that the theory of evolution must be accepted as the best hypothesis which science has been able to frame to cover the known results reached by the investigations of the morphologist, embryologist and paleontologist.' Not surprisingly, given his inclinations, Storr became a reviewer for *The Guardian* of books on evolution and science for nearly twenty years and became involved in the Cromer Convention, an annual meeting of evangelicals in the 1920s that explored the relationship between evangelicalism and contemporary thought.

Although Storr would have wished it otherwise, his work as an apologist and philosopher dwarfed his historical and academic writing. One reason was his health, which seemed to break down whenever he worked too hard on academic projects, and another was his church responsibilities. After 1921 he was both canon and treasurer of Westminster Abbey (1926–1931), governor of Westminster School (1931–1936) and Abbey Chronicler (1931–1937). Storr turned down the offices of Regius Professor of Divinity at Oxford, Dean of Canterbury (three times), Bishop of Peterborough and Bishop of Worcester because he believed they would curtail further his opportunities to pursue the projects in which he was interested.

Storr was a prolific author, particularly of pamphlets explaining important aspects of evangelicalism. He wrote more than forty pamphlets and books, as well as articles on religion for *The Times* throughout the 1930s. His major academic work is *The Development of English Theology in the Nineteenth Century, 1800–1860* (1913), an attempt to show how the 'ideas and tendencies' of the late eighteenth century left 'a complex problem of theological reconstruction' as a legacy to the nineteenth century; he intended to cover the period from 1860 to 1900 in a second book but never completed it. Storr's other important publications are: *Development and Divine Purpose* (1906), *The Inspiration of the Bible* (1908), *What it Means to be a Christian* (1918), *Christianity and Immortality* (1918), *My Duty towards Foreign Missions* (1919), *The Moral Argument for Theism* (1921), *Reservation* (1923), *The Missionary Genius of the Bible* (1924), *My Faith* (1927), *From Abraham to Christ: Studies in the Development of the Theism of the Old Testament, Warburton Lectures, 1923–1927* (1928), *The Bible in the Modern Mind* (1928), *The Oxford Movement: A Liberal Evangelical View* (1933), *Spiritual Liberty: A Study of Liberal Evangelicalism* (1934), *Freedom and Tradition: A Study of Liberal Evangelicalism* (1940).

Storr died in Tunbridge Wells, Kent on 25 October 1940, and as an obituary in *The Times* noted, 'What is remarkable about him is his fruitful application to the study of the philosophy of religion.'

Bibliography

G. H. Harris, *Vernon Faithfull Storr: A Memoir* (London: SPCK, 1943).

K. A. FRANCIS

■ **STOTT, John Robert Walmsley** (1921–), Anglican clergyman and author, was born in London to Dr Arnold Stott and Lily Stott. His father was a distinguished physician (who was eventually appointed a physician to the Royal Household) with a busy practice based in the family home on Harley Street. Although his father was a secularist, his mother, who had a Lutheran heritage, taught John and his sisters as children to read the Bible and 'say their prayers', and took them to Sunday school at All Souls', Langham Place near their home. The family had musical interests, and John learned the cello. From his father John acquired an early interest in the natural world, making frequent visits to parks and the nearby London Zoo. He began with a butterfly collection but turned quickly to birdwatching, which developed into a major interest. At the age of eight he was sent to boarding school at Oakley Hall in Gloucestershire, arriving as the youngest boy at the school and leaving as head boy.

Stott earned a scholarship in 1935 to the prestigious Rugby School, which his father also had attended. John continued to play his cello in the school orchestra and was a soloist in the chapel choir. His parents, hoping that he would pursue a career in the diplomatic or foreign service, sent him to spend summers in Germany and France to develop his natural aptitude for languages. Although Stott was confirmed in the Anglican Church in 1936 and participated in the formal religious routines of the school, as an early adolescent his interest in Christianity was minimal. As an adult, John recalled that as a teenager he became aware of 'a great fixed gulf' between his high ideals and 'the kind of person he was'. This perception prepared him to 'open the door to Christ', in an unemotional but clear conversion experience in February 1938, through the ministry of Eric *Nash (widely known as 'Bash'). Stott eventually wrote that 'what brought me to Christ was a sense of defeat and of estrangement, and the astonishing news that the historic Christ offered to meet the very needs of which I

was conscious.' Nash was deeply influential in Stott's formative years as a new convert, during which his boyhood habits of Bible reading and prayer came alive: 'when I was born again and the Holy Spirit came to dwell within me, the Bible immediately began to be a new book for me.' He accompanied Nash in his evangelistic ministry, in which he began to hone his public speaking skills. Meanwhile, he excelled academically at Rugby, played the title role in Shakepeare's *Richard II*, and became head boy. By the age of seventeen, Stott was convinced that he was called to ordained ministry in the Church of England; his father strongly opposed his decision.

At Trinity College, Cambridge between 1940 and 1944, Stott studied modern and medieval languages (especially French and German), then theology, earning a double first-class degree, and was elected a Senior Scholar. He received the BA in 1943 (MA 1947). Stott later recalled that he arrived in wartime Cambridge as 'a very wobbly and vulnerable Christian'. His faith was strengthened through involvement with the Cambridge Inter-Collegiate Christian Union (CICCU), a prominent evangelical and multi-denominational student ministry which provided him with 'friendships, teaching, books and opportunities for service'. Eventually his busy involvement in Christian work led him to abandon the cello. Stott began to exercise leadership using his pastoral, evangelistic and teaching gifts among his peers at Cambridge and serving for several years as Nash's valuable 'right-hand man' in the running of summer camps ('Bash camps') and school-boys' vacation house parties. In 1944–1945 he trained for ordination at Ridley Hall, Cambridge, where he studied under such scholars as C. H. Dodd, C. F. D. Moule and John Burnaby. In this period, however, Stott encountered a predominantly liberal theological environment, which he later described as 'a spiritual wilderness' that drove him to more thorough biblical study.

When Stott was ordained in December 1945, he returned to London as assistant curate at All Souls', Langham Place, where the rector, Harold Earnshaw-Smith, provided a positive role model of evangelical preaching and pastoral care. In 1950 Stott became rector and moved into 12 Weymouth Street; his drawing-room was the very room in which he had attended Sunday school as a child. As rector he established five priorities for the congregation: prayer, expository preaching, regular evangelism, careful discipling of new believers and systematic training of lay leaders. The church's reputation for parochial evangelism grew through the fruitfulness of regular 'guest services' and lay outreach. Through his parish work and growing preaching ministry throughout Britain, Stott became recognized as a leader of a younger generation of rising evangelical clergy. From the early 1950s to the late 1970s, Stott conducted many evangelistic missions at major universities in Britain (including Cambridge and Oxford, several times), North America (including Harvard and Yale), Australia and South Africa. Addresses given at his early missions formed the basis for his book *Basic Christianity* (1958), which one commentator called 'the definitive evangelistic paperback for at least a generation'. This book has been translated into over twenty-five languages and has sold around two million copies. Stott's short evangelistic booklet, *Becoming a Christian* (1950), reprinted over 100 times, has been used globally. It was supplemented with a companion booklet, *Being a Christian* (1957). As a key figure in the Evangelical Alliance, Stott was instrumental in orchestrating Billy *Graham's Harringay (1954) and Wembley (1955) crusades, through which he forged a warm and lasting friendship with Graham. In 1959 he was appointed a Chaplain to the Queen, and he became an Extra Chaplain in 1991.

Stott's ministry always extended beyond Anglican circles and included a widening range of students and pastors. For instance, three times during the 1960s (and three more times in the 1970s) he gave the Bible readings at the annual Keswick Convention, a major gathering of British evangelicals. He held office as president of a number of major evangelical societies, including the British Evangelical Alliance, Scripture Union and TEAR Fund (The Evangelical Alliance Relief Fund), and served for four terms as president of the Inter-Varsity Fellowship (later the Universities and Colleges Christian Fellowship). His prominence within North American evangelicalism was reflected in his role as Bible expositor on six occasions in the 1960s and 70s at the triennial Urbana Missionary

Convention organized by the Inter-Varsity Christian Fellowship. His stature internationally was evident in his pivotal role in the 1974 International Congress on World Evangelization held at Lausanne, Switzerland. Organized by the Billy Graham Evangelistic Association, the Congress was a defining moment in twentieth-century evangelicalism. Stott handled two crucial assignments that testified to his position as what one observer called 'the theological leader of worldwide evangelicalism'. First, he gave an opening address on the nature of biblical evangelism, which included biblical definitions of five key words: mission, evangelism, dialogue, salvation and conversion. Secondly, he chaired the drafting committee of the Lausanne Covenant, a concise theological statement of Christian belief and commitment that became very influential in evangelical circles. The Covenant was noteworthy particularly for its balanced stance on the relation between evangelism and social action. As a major contributor in the subsequent 'Lausanne Movement', Stott served on the executive committee of the continuation committee, and he chaired its sub-group on theology and education until 1981. A second international congress was held in Manila in 1989, where Stott chaired the drafting committee of the 'Manila Manifesto', which called 'the whole church to take the whole gospel to the whole world'. Stott's work as an evangelist and mission strategist provided the background for a widely read book, *Christian Mission in the Modern World* (1975).

With a growing international vision and desire for networking among leaders committed to a revitalized evangelical witness within Anglicanism, Stott spearheaded the establishment of the Evangelical Fellowship in the Anglican Communion (EFAC) in 1961 and chaired its British branch, the Church of England Evangelical Council, from 1967 to 1984. Stott was the chief architect and official chairman of a landmark gathering that he later called 'our evangelical coming of age', the National Evangelical Anglican Congress (NEAC) at Keele in 1967, at which he and Michael Green were the final editors of the official statement. Stott also chaired the second NEAC in 1977 held in Nottingham. Alister McGrath has suggested that the growth of post-war English evangelicalism was attributable more to Stott to than any other person; he 'became a role model for a younger generation of evangelical ordinands in England'.

As Stott's worldwide ministry grew, in 1970 Michael Baughen assumed primary pastoral responsibility for All Souls' as vicar, while Stott remained as rector with reduced everyday duties that allowed him to travel extensively overseas. In 1975 Baughen became rector, and Stott took the honorary role of rector emeritus. His travel throughout Africa, Asia, the Middle East and South America for over thirty years was dedicated mainly to evangelistic missions, preaching tours and clergy conferences (and almost always included a little birdwatching). His pastoral warmth, capacity for friendship, biblical commitment and theological acumen encouraged and influenced many pastors and leaders, who commonly refer to him affectionately as 'Uncle John'. At the same time, continued fellowship with Christians in the developing world heightened Stott's sensitivity to issues of poverty and injustice, helping him to develop his increasingly holistic understanding of the gospel. A strategic concern to equip Christian leaders in the developing world, especially teachers at theological colleges and future writers, led Stott to found the Langham Trust (now Langham Partnership International), which provided scholarships for 'Langham Scholars' to pursue advanced theological degrees (usually in Europe or North America) and distributed evangelical literature to pastors and theological libraries. In his later years, Stott gave priority to this work. After his eightieth birthday, he handed over the direction of the Langham Partnership to Christopher Wright, a respected biblical scholar and educator.

A hallmark of Stott's vision has been the necessity and urgency of relating the gospel to the needs and concerns of the contemporary world. This led him to establish the London Institute for Contemporary Christianity in 1982; he served as its first director, then as president from 1986. It was designed as 'neither a theological college nor a missionary training college, but a lay institute' and was modelled to a certain degree on Regent College, Vancouver, where Stott had lectured on several occasions. Stott wrote that its purpose was 'to help students become more complete

Christians in their personal and home life, and more effective Christians in their professional and public life' so that 'integrated Christians' would 'penetrate the secular world with a more integrated gospel'. Likewise, a commitment to biblical faithfulness in contemporary life prompted him to initiate a series of Bible expositions aptly called 'The Bible Speaks Today', to which he contributed volumes on Galatians, 1 Timothy, 2 Timothy and Titus, Ephesians, Acts, Thessalonians, Romans and the Sermon on the Mount. Stott's own approach to preaching was articulated in his book *I Believe in Preaching* (1982; North American title *Between Two Worlds*). Stott advocated the practice of expository preaching rooted in a 'double listening' to the text of Scripture and to current needs, in order to 'build bridges' between the ancient and contemporary worlds. One of Stott's distinctive themes was the challenge of 'drawing out' the meaning of Scripture rather than imposing one's own mind upon the Bible, so that the Scriptures themselves speak authoritatively. His concern for the application of biblical principles to every area of society and a range of moral issues was expressed in *Issues Facing Christians Today* (1984), published in North American as *Involvement*. In *The Cross of Christ* (1986), which some theologians consider his *magnum opus*, he argues that 'the cross transforms everything. It gives a new, worshipping relationship to God, a new and balanced understanding of ourselves, a new incentive to give ourselves in mission, a new love of our enemies, and a new courage to face the perplexities of suffering.' He offers a 'personal plea' and 'spiritual legacy' in *Evangelical Truth* (1999), and his consistent focus on the gospel is encapsulated in *The Incomparable Christ* (2001). Also among his later writings is the fruit of his lifelong fascination with birdwatching, *The Birds Our Teachers* (1999), which includes meditations on various types of birds as well as over 150 photographs by the author. In recognition of his 'services to the Church as Theologian and Author', Stott was awarded the Lambeth Doctor of Divinity degree by the Archbishop of Canterbury, Robert Runcie, in 1983.

Respected for his careful preparation, continuous study and precise articulation of complicated topics, Stott undertook extensive reading and writing at a scenic cottage in Wales called 'The Hookses', where he also offered hospitality to a wide variety of conferences, groups and visitors. His biographer has noted that Stott's pattern has been to write 'what he first taught' (in lectures, expository addresses or sermons). His vast literary output, comprising over forty books, was enhanced by ongoing involvement with a wide range of study groups, the administrative support of a hardworking secretary, Frances Whitehead, and a series of capable study assistants (usually young theological graduates). Stott, who never married, acknowledged that with the responsibilities of a family he could never have travelled or written as he had.

Stott's influence upon global evangelicalism was rooted in several convergent factors. His personal life was marked by self-discipline, prayerfulness and humility, traits constantly admired by all those whom he influenced. His preaching and teaching were strongly biblical and well-organized and consistently probed the Bible's relevance and implications at both personal and social levels. His writings were exegetically grounded and unusually fair-minded, exhibiting notable simplicity and clarity of expression, qualities that were valued highly by pastors as well as educated laypeople. Stott's theology expressed a cross-centred, deeply trinitarian form of classical evangelical faith and constantly exemplified a perspective he liked to call 'balanced, biblical Christianity' ('BBC'), bringing together in harmony concerns that too often are opposed: personal and corporate, inward and outward, prayer and action, evangelism and social concern, word and Spirit, boldness and compassion. His natural constitution included a first-rate mind and the physical stamina needed for an itinerant ministry; his temperament included a gracious tenacity and 'teutonic thoroughness' (as Dudley-Smith called it), which enabled him to write prolifically and contribute significantly to a host of organizations and movements throughout over fifty years of ministry.

Stott declined the opportunity to become a bishop (several times), archbishop (of Sydney, Australia), theological college lecturer (at several institutions) and principal (of Wycliffe Hall, Oxford) and organizational executive (President of the World Evangelical Fellowship). Like his chief historical mentor, Charles *Simeon of Cambridge, he continued to be based at a single church throughout his entire career. He devoted his energies to supporting existing movements and organizations from All Souls', while using his strategic vision to establish new ones. As a scholarly pastor rather than academic scholar, whose teaching and writing were grounded in an ongoing engagement in the church's biblical exposition and evangelism, Stott became, according to the historian Adrian Hastings, 'one of the most influential figures in the Christian world' who was 'the recognized senior theologian and thinker of world evangelicalism'.

Bibliography

T. Dudley-Smith, *John Stott, The Making of A Leader: The Early Years* (Leicester: Inter-Varsity Press, 1999); T. Dudley-Smith, *John Stott, A Global Ministry: The Later Years* (Leicester: Inter-Varsity Press, 2001); D. Wells, 'Guardian of God's Word', *Christianity Today* (16 September 1996).

J. P. GREENMAN

■ **STOWE, Harriet Beecher** (1811–1896), novelist and writer, was born on 14 June 1811 in Litchfield, Connecticut. Her father was Lyman *Beecher, one of the foremost American Presbyterian evangelicals of the nineteenth century. Beecher, sometimes known as Brimstone Beecher, was an ardent evangelical preacher in the pulpit and also an outspoken leader of social causes, including opposition to slavery. His legacy included six sons who became ministers, one of whom, Henry Ward Beecher, was perhaps the most well-known popular preacher of the Gilded Age era. Lyman Beecher also had seven daughters, the eldest of whom, Catharine, was a leader in the promotion of both the higher education of women and the domestic qualities of motherhood, home and hearth. Harriet, the second daughter, was thus part of one of the most wide-ranging and influential New England families of the century; moreover, her father's brand of orthodoxy would continue to influence her through the major period of her artistic achievement, even though much of her writing ostensibly critiqued the harshness and the cold logic of what she came to regard as New England's dominant religion.

Harriet made a decision to serve Jesus Christ at the age of thirteen, as a result of one of her father's sermons. Lyman Beecher was a very persuasive and powerful preacher, who regularly put pressure on his children to make an evangelical profession of faith in order to experience the 'second birth'. Harriet did so, probably in May or June 1825, when she reported to her father that Christ had taken her for his own.

Harriet's faith would face many tests throughout her childhood and adult life. Her mother died when Harriet was only four years old; her husband struggled with financial difficulties throughout the early years of their marriage; and Harriet herself endured the grief of losing four of her own children in tragic circumstances. Meanwhile, the United States was undergoing major social and cultural changes that would issue finally in the many tragic events culminating in the Civil War. As a result, Harriet's personal faith underwent severe challenges that caused the reflective and highly intelligent young woman to question and examine the fundamental beliefs of her Christian worldview. These challenges became central themes of many of her novels and stories. Moreover, she was the author of scores of essays, poems, editorials and theological reflections in which she openly discussed her religious and social views on numerous topics. Most of these appeared in newspapers or magazines and are difficult to locate today.

After her mother died, Harriet became closer to her sister Catharine. She attended and later taught in Catharine's school, the Hartford Female Academy, and wrote books with her at a fairly young age. When her father Lyman was called in 1832 to become president of Lane Theological Seminary, a new Presbyterian school in Cincinnati, Ohio, she moved west with him and Catharine. There she met Calvin Stowe, a professor and clergyman who was strongly opposed to slavery. He was nine years her senior, and his deceased wife, Eliza Tyler, had been a dear friend of hers. Their subsequent marriage in 1836 was born of their common grief. The Stowes moved to Maine in 1850 when Calvin accepted a position at Bowdoin College.

Within two years of the wedding, Harriet had had three children, increasing her household responsibilities and financial worries as Calvin's salary from the college diminished. Harriet continued her work as a loving and caring homemaker while writing for local magazines and newspapers. Her ardent letters to her surviving children revealed a strongly evangelical spirit, encouraging them to seek Christ and conform their hearts and lives to him.

However, Stowe's years as a mother were also marked by tragedy. She was traumatized by the deaths of four of her seven children. The first, and the one with the most significant effects, was the loss in the summer of 1849 of Samuel Charles (nicknamed 'Charley'), who died at the age of eighteen months from cholera. Years later she would lose an older son, Henry, who drowned while a student at Dartmouth College, her son Frederick, who became an alcoholic and never recovered from the wounds he sustained at Gettysburg in the Civil War, and her daughter Georgiana, who died in her forties, having lost her health and mind as a result of morphine addiction. Stowe was survived by her twin daughters, Eliza and Isabella, and a son, Charles Edward.

As a mother who had herself mourned deeply for a lost child, Stowe felt a bond with the many slave mothers who lost their own children to the auction block. The work of the Underground Railroad had deeply touched both Calvin and Harriet, and they participated directly by housing and becoming friends with fugitive slaves in their home. By the late 1840s, however, the anti-slavery movement had greatly expanded, energized by newspaper editors, lecturers, authors and clergymen. Then the Fugitive Slave Act was passed in 1850, controversially granting Southerners the right to pursue fugitive slaves into the free states. It also implicitly forced the North to keep watch for runaway slaves and to return them when they were found. This law, working in conjunction with the profound grief still haunting Stowe from the death of her beloved Charley the year before, aroused her anger.

At this time Stowe received a letter from her sister-in-law, Mrs Edward Beecher, exhorting her: 'If I could use a pen as you can, I would write something that will make this whole nation feel what an accursed thing slavery is.' Having read this challenging letter,

Stowe rose to her feet, crumpled the letter and vowed, 'I will write something ... I will if I live.' Then in February 1851, while taking communion at a church meeting, Stowe had a vision of a saintly African American slave who, while being mercilessly beaten to death, was heard to be praying for his tormentors in Christ-like fashion. In this momentary vision was the seed that became her greatest literary triumph. Significantly from a religious viewpoint, after Stowe became an acclaimed author, she asserted that she did not write *Uncle Tom's Cabin*; God wrote it, she said, and she served merely as his instrument.

Uncle Tom's Cabin; or, Life Among the Lowly, is one of the most politically charged and controversial works of fiction in American history. It is a testimony to the novel's great impact that, when Abraham Lincoln met Stowe at the White House in 1862, he reportedly greeted her with the words, 'So you're the little woman who wrote the book that started this great war!' (Whether the statement was actually made by Lincoln, or is legendary, is a matter of dispute.) First published in 1851 as a serial in *The National Era*, an abolitionist newspaper, *Uncle Tom's Cabin* was printed as a book in 1852 and became one of the most phenomenal bestsellers of the century. In a wide-ranging and epic-like novel, Stowe created dozens of memorable characters who portrayed the inhumanity of slavery, the humanity of the slaves, and the insidious, corrupting influence this 'peculiar institution' had upon the whole nation. The climax of the story was derived explicitly from the vision of the communion service: the Christ-like Uncle Tom being martyred at the hands of the demonic Simon Legree. The death of the angelic Little Eva and the escape of Eliza over the frozen Ohio River, each of which constituted an aspect of 'passing over', became two of the most famous literary scenes of the century. Other important characters, including George Shelby, George Harris, Cassy, Chloe, Topsy and Augustine St Clare, brought the rich story to life while simultaneously galvanizing antislavery sentiment throughout the land. Although for many decades *Uncle Tom's Cabin* fell out of favour among literary critics, in recent decades it has regained its stature as a major American novel of exceptional importance. Its value as a record of the cultural and religious worldviews of its time has been particularly noted. The novel also exhibits an almost encyclopedic knowledge of the rhetorical preoccupations of the antebellum era. In addition, its status as a major American novel written by a woman has issued in its use by various feminist critics investigating the domestic and sentimental ideologies of the period.

After 1852 Harriet Beecher Stowe's fortune was established, and hers was a name known by all educated Americans. She continued to publish books, at the rate of about one a year, for the rest of her life, but none achieved the extraordinary success of her great masterpiece. Among her most notable works were *A Key to Uncle Tom's Cabin* (1853), which presented an abundance of evidence supporting her version of slavery in the South; the novel *Dred: A Tale of the Great Dismal Swamp* (1856), which depicts a runaway slave community and more radically violent slave resistance; *The Minister's Wooing* (1859), which dramatizes a variety of religious issues current among theologians in New England; and *The Pearl of Orr's Island* (1862), *Oldtown Folks* (1869) and *Poganuc People* (1878), all of which demonstrate Stowe's mastery of the form of literature called 'local colour', the close and nuanced study of the habits and lifestyles of small interknit communities. These last three novels were highly prized by the growing local colour movement of the post-Civil War era, and would influence important writers such as Sarah Orne Jewett and Mary Wilkins Freeman. Stowe also continued to publish numerous essays and other writings in a variety of journals such as the *Atlantic*, the *Independent* and the *Christian Union*. Having moved to Hartford in 1864, she spent the last decades of her life there in the famous 'Nook Farm' community that included Mark Twain, Charles Dudley Warner and other notable writers and ministers. As her health and mental acuity rather deteriorated with age, she lived a quiet life there until her death on 1 July 1896.

Bibliography

J. Hedrick, *Harriet Beecher Stowe: A Life* (New York: Oxford University Press, 1994); F. Wilson, *Crusader in Crinoline: The Life of*

Harriet Beecher Stowe (Philadelphia: J. P. Lippincott, 1941).

H. K. BUSH, JR

■ **STRONG, Augustus Hopkins** (1836–1921), American Baptist theologian, seminary president and church leader, was born on 3 August 1836, in Rochester, New York to Alvah and Catherine Hopkins Strong, descendants of an old-stock family that traced its roots to the Puritan Great Migration of 1630. The Strongs ranked among Rochester's leading citizens: Alvah published the *Rochester Democrat*; Henry Strong, Augustus's brother, became president of Eastman Kodak.

After preparatory training at Rochester Collegiate Institute, Strong attended Yale College (AB 1857), where he was converted through the ministry of Charles *Finney. Returning home, he enrolled at Rochester Theological Seminary, from which he graduated in 1859. As was customary for young men of his class and era, Strong then embarked on a year of travel and study abroad, primarily at the University of Berlin.

Strong returned to a nation on the brink of civil war. After a year in his father's newspaper office he accepted the pastorate of First Baptist Church, Haverhill, Massachusetts, where he remained throughout the war (1861–1865). Haverhill served as a springboard to First Baptist Church, Cleveland, Ohio, one of America's pre-eminent congregations, to whom Strong preached for the next seven years. The Cleveland pulpit raised him to the pinnacle of Baptist society. He oversaw a congregation of enviable size, wealth and prestige, and counted John D. Rockefeller among his parishioners. Strong and Rockefeller would remain lifelong friends, and their relationship became familial when Rockefeller's daughter, Bessie, married Strong's eldest son, Charles.

Strong was now a man of refinement and erudition with ties to great wealth and esteemed for his well-wrought sermons, and his name came naturally to the lips of the trustees of leading Baptist educational institutions. He refused the presidency of Brown University, but accepted the presidency and chair of systematic theology at Rochester Theological Seminary. Only thirty-six years of age, Strong left Cleveland for his home town and alma mater, where he would preside for the next forty years (1872–1912).

At Rochester Strong became a towering figure in Baptist circles. Widely regarded as one of the great Baptist theologians of the day, his work as an administrator, fundraiser and church leader, and his role as a friend and father figure to the Baptist elite, had a quieter but equally enduring effect on Northern Baptists and their educational culture. He welcomed associates as theologically disparate as William Bell *Riley and William Rainey Harper and as ideologically disparate as Walter Rauschenbusch and Rockefeller. Despite the acrimony that engulfed American Protestantism in the final decades of his life, he remained one of the few authorities quoted and admired by liberals and conservatives alike.

Strong's *Systematic Theology*, first published in 1886, was his *magnum opus* in the truest sense. By 1909 it had passed through eight editions and grown to three volumes. Constantly revised and amended, it was a record of his evolving thought and, to a great extent, the evolving thought of his generation. In the end, Strong was content to let this intensely personal work stand as his 'monument'. In its original form it had been a learned summary of the best of Baptist orthodoxy, firmly rooted in the Reformed tradition as defined by historic formulae such as the New Hampshire Confession and the Saybrook Platform. In its final form it was a monument, not only to Strong, but, according to Grant Wacker, to the entire tradition of Baptist systematics and its encounter with 'the dilemma of historical consciousness'.

By the late 1890s Strong had come to believe that history and human consciousness had a role in the apprehension of religious truth (perhaps under the influence of his son Charles, a protégé of William James and close friend of George Santayana) and to respect 'higher criticism', which subjected holy writ to painstaking literary and historical analysis. The seventh edition of his *Systematic Theology* (1902) showed the effect of these developments. Among the new departures were a strong emphasis on divine immanence and the adoption of theistic evolution as an ontological model. Most distressing to his conservative friends, however, was Strong's revised understanding of biblical revelation. In 1886, he saw the Bible as 'an infallible and sufficient rule of faith and practice'. In 1902 he described it as a 'record of progressive divine revelation, sufficient ... to lead every honest inquirer to Christ and salvation'. A doctrine of biblical inerrancy, in short, had become a doctrine of biblical efficacy.

Strong had not jettisoned the tenets of Reformed orthodoxy. Rather, he had attempted to renovate the epistemic underpinnings of those tenets. 'Ethical monism', the ontological system elaborated in *Christ in Creation and Ethical Monism* (1899), was the linchpin of his revised project. It began with the scholastic truism that God is the sole Ground of Being (the 'monism' in 'ethical monism'), making all existence ultimately a manifestation, albeit 'finite, partial, graded', of the one substance, God. The 'ethical' in 'ethical monism' referred to Strong's paradoxical assertion that within the one supreme substance, a moral or 'psychological dualism' existed whereby 'the soul is personally distinct from matter on the one hand and from God on the other'. Finally, Strong's system was radically Christocentric; the Father represented Being in pure potentiality, the Son the actualization or 'depotentiation' of that Being. History was but 'the exfoliation of Christ's life in time' (Wacker, p. 108).

In the charged atmosphere of *fin-de-siècle* American Protestantism, Strong satisfied noone. Conservatives spied incipient pantheism and creeping modernism; liberals saw token modernization ornamenting an obsolete system. Critics on all sides, however, agreed that Strong had positioned a vast, essentially orthodox edifice on historicist scaffolding utterly incapable of supporting it. Interpreters since that time have largely agreed. However, placed in its professional and political context and in the light of more recent intellectual revolutions, Strong's 'struggle to hold together ancient faith and modern epistemology' (Wacker, p. 1) merits a more positive appraisal.

Strong's theology cannot be separated from his role as a diplomat and administrator of the first order. In addition to his work at Rochester, he presided in turn over the General Convention of Baptists of North America, the American Baptist Foreign Mission Society and the American Baptist Education Society, and served on the boards of the New York Baptist Union for Ministerial Education and Vassar College. His genteel upbringing, the demands of Baptist statecraft and his awareness of his leadership role left him temperamentally and vocationally predisposed to mediate and reconcile, to hold constituencies together (much like fellow seminary president, E. Y. *Mullins). Not surprisingly, he proceeded to unite new theology and orthodox rationalism, the immanent and the transcendent, even opposing eschatologies (Christ's return would be 'pre-millennial spiritually, but post-millennial physically'). Each pole represented a valued constituency, a cluster of respected friends, or a coterie of esteemed colleagues.

In the last decade of his life Strong seems to have veered sharply to the right, though less so than has been suggested. As a guardian of the Baptist community and its traditions, he was alarmed by the 'practical Unitarianism' of liberal scholars and its enervating effect on the ministry and on Baptist mission societies in particular, as he noted in *A Tour of the Missions* (1918). Nevertheless, while decrying the abandonment of orthodoxy, he never retracted his own theological revisions, including his views on inerrancy, higher criticism and theistic evolution. Nor did he allow that historicism inevitably led to naturalism (a logical absurdity within the framework of ethical monism). Fittingly, his final word, published posthumously, took both fundamentalists and liberals to task. Neither, he argued in *What Shall I Believe?* (1922), fully appreciated the significance of the incarnation. Fundamentalists ignored its historical implications, liberals its doctrinal implications.

Finally, it should be noted that in the bitter competition between fundamentalists and modernists for the hearts, minds and institutions of American Christians, each camp was dedicated as a matter of principle to the premise that their respective theologies and epistemologies were mutually exclusive. To admit otherwise was to invite disaster. A century later, however, in a postmodern age in which the construction of logic has itself been historicized, assessments are different. Strong's synthesis, as a particular historical-cultural option, may seem as tenable a foundation for theology as any, and it has in its favour its grounding in Baptist communal tradition.

Strong should be remembered not only as a theologian and churchman, but also as a patron of the Social Gospel and an advocate of social justice, including a woman's right to suffrage, ordination and postgraduate education. He was a staunch defender of academic freedom, which he encouraged at Rochester and practised through the appointment of scholars such as Rauschenbusch and Albert Henry Newman. The idea of a Baptist postgraduate research university on the European model was also his, although friendly rivals outmanoeuvred him in the end, persuading Rockefeller to found it in Chicago rather than New York City, as Strong had hoped.

Strong was married to Harriet Savage (1861–1914) and after her death to Marguerite Jones (1915–1921). He had six children: Charles, Mary, John, Cora, Kate and Laura. He died in the city of his birth on 29 November 1921. His publications, in addition to those noted above, include *Lectures on Theology* (1876), *Philosophy and Religion* (1888, 1912), *The Great Poets and Their Theology* (1897) and *Union with Christ: A Chapter of Systematic Theology* (1913).

Bibliography
G. Wacker, *Augustus H. Strong and the Dilemma of Historical Consciousness* (Macon: Mercer University Press, 1985); T. George and D. Dockery, *Baptist Theologians* (Nashville: Broadman Press, 1990); D. Crerar (ed.), *Autobiography of Augustus Hopkins Strong* (Valley Forge: Judson Press, 1981).
R. G. ROBINS

■ **STRONG, Josiah** (1847–1916), Congregational clergyman and Progressive reformer, was one of America's most prominent Protestant Christians during its Gilded Age and Progressive Era. Serving successively as Congregational pastor, General Secretary of the Congregationalist Home Missionary Society, President of the Evangelical Alliance and founder/President of the American Institute for Social Service, Strong was an outspoken advocate of reform, the Social Gospel and international interdenominationalism. Throughout his career he called upon American Protestants to fulfil what he saw as their primary calling, namely bringing Christianity and Anglo-Saxon civilization to a world crying out for liberty. Because of his best-selling 1885 book, *Our Country: Its Possible Future and Its Present Crisis*, many scholars have labelled Strong an 'imperial expansionist' and 'jingoistic' advocate of America's 'manifest destiny'. This well-established yet uncharitable and somewhat misinformed historical evaluation has led generations of Americans to misunderstand Strong and his call for social reform. Although he believed in the superiority of American civilization and advocated the Anglo-Saxon racism characteristic of his day, he opposed political expansionism and the extension of abusive American corporate hegemony. He argued that the United States had a worldwide mission to promote international understanding, economic advancement, peace, justice and Christian morality. Sometimes controversial and often misunderstood, Strong occupied the centre ground of American Protestantism at the turn of the twentieth century. To know him is to know the pulse of Christendom, American style.

Josiah Strong was born on 19 January 1847 in Naperville, Illinois, the son of Josiah Strong and Elizabeth Webster. At five years of age he moved with his family to Hudson, Ohio. After graduating from Western Reserve College in 1869 and Lane Theological Seminary in 1871, the newly married (to Alice Bisbee at Chardon, Ohio in August 1871) Strong was ordained to the Congregational ministry on 8 September 1871 and installed as pastor of a home missionary church in Cheyenne, Wyoming. After two years of service in Wyoming, Strong served as chaplain and instructor in theology at Western Reserve College from 1873 to 1876, and from 1876 to 1881 he served as pastor of First Congregational Church in Sandusky, Ohio. In 1881 Strong became General Secretary of the Congregationalist Home Missionary Society, responsible for overseeing the denomination's work in Ohio, Kentucky, West Virginia and western Pennsylvania. From 1884 to 1886 he served as minister of the Central Congregational Church in Cincinnati, Ohio.

While pastor of Central Congregational Church, Strong published his most famous work, *Our Country: Its Possible Future and Its Present Crisis* (1885). By the time of

Strong's death, the book had sold over 176,000 copies, and individual chapters had been reprinted in hundreds of newspapers, magazines, pamphlets and other occasional publications. His ideas were popular and largely representative of American Protestantism at the turn of the century. *Our Country* called for evangelism and social reform in Strong's 'Christian' America by affirming morality in politics, Anglo-Saxon racism, American cultural superiority and the nation's manifest destiny to spread democracy and Christianity around the globe. According to Strong, the United States was the world's best example of 'civil liberty' and 'spiritual Christianity', and therefore it was divinely commissioned to be its brothers' cultural guardian. The future of Western civilization was in the hands of American Christians, who had the power to 'hasten or retard the coming of Christ's kingdom in the world by hundreds, and perhaps thousands, of years'. Affirming the leadership and responsibility of the United States in the context of his postmillennial vision of global Christian democracy, Strong wrote, 'We of this generation and nation occupy the Gibraltar of the ages which commands the world's future.'

In *Our Country* Strong identified eight perils to be overcome in the United States and the world: immigration, Romanism, Catholic and secular challenges to the state schools, Mormonism, drunkenness, socialism, materialism and problems associated with growing cities. Each of these was a threat to the moral fabric and Protestant Christian identity of the United States. Strong's ideal America was Anglo-Saxon, Protestant, democratic and spiritually pure. He strongly believed that Anglo-Saxons were God's chosen people, destined to bring redemption and democracy to the world. The nation's admixture of alien immigrants (many of them Catholic) was dangerous: 'Glory is departing from many a New England village, because men alien in blood, in religion, and in civilization, are taking possession.' Yet at the same time, it provided a unique opportunity, because the ideals of civil liberty and spiritual Christianity had equipped Americans to be missionaries, first to immigrant newcomers and then to the world. Immigrants were thus a blessing in disguise, as they provided the pathway to internationalism through the assimilation of inferior races. Anglo-Saxons were a tool in the hands of God to redeem the world, break down national identities and hasten the return of Jesus Christ.

Our Country raised Strong to a position of national leadership. The year after its publication he was elected general secretary of the Evangelical Alliance, an interdenominational organization that affirmed spiritual revival, social reform, the superiority of Western civilization, and middle-class Victorian values. In this post he promoted social reform and practical Protestant cooperation in addressing social ills. During his years as head of the Evangelical Alliance, Strong came to express the core programme of the growing Social Gospel, a movement of which he was 'the apogee … the dynamo, the revivalist, the organizer, and … the most irrepressible spirit' (Ahlstrom, *A Religious History of the American People*, pp. 798–799). By the turn of the century Strong had turned his attention away from individual salvation and was promoting social reform in the nation's cities.

In order to address issues of urban decay, Strong began to utilize the new social scientific methods being used in the nation's universities. Frustrated with the conservatism of the Evangelical Alliance, Strong left in 1898 to create the League for Social Service (called the American Institute for Social Service after 1902). Through this organization he sought to conduct social research, educate the public about social issues and promote social reforms. The Institute produced hundreds of publications aimed at inspiring American congregations to join forces in the fight against poverty, drunkenness, political corruption and other social ills. Strong also founded the Safety First movement, to improve working conditions in US factories, and the American Museum of Safety. In 1908 Strong assisted in the creation of the Federal Council of Churches, which did much to promote social reform throughout the century. By promoting the Institute's programme of social reform, Strong sought to bring about the kingdom of God on earth. His leadership of the Institute and his affirmation of Progressive values illustrate the important role Protestant Christianity and its leaders played in the Progressive movement, a role which is often undervalued and underestimated.

Strong published many other books in addition to *Our Country*. While secretary of the Evangelical Alliance he published his second most important book, *The New Era* (1893), in which he attempted to explain why the closing years of the nineteenth century were a focal point of history. The book discussed the historical contributions of the Anglo-Saxons, in whom (Strong claimed) were united the best qualities of the Hebrews, Greeks and Romans, America's rural and urban problems and new methods for addressing them, namely denominational co-operation and social scientific research. *The Twentieth Century City* (1898) and *The Challenge of the City* (1907) analysed the growth and problems of the city and proposed remedies: a new patriotism based on commitment to the public good, the application of the social teachings of the gospel, the ministry of institutional churches and legislative reforms achieved through the power of the press and enlightened public opinion. Strong also wrote *Religious Movements for Social Betterment* (1900), *Expansion Under New World Conditions* (1900) and *The Next Great Awakening* (1902), which evaluated social reform crusades in the light of the kingdom of God and Christ's social teachings and sought to motivate Christians to support them. *Social Progress: A Yearbook* (1904–1906) presented a wide array of global economic, industrial, social and religious statistics. *Our World: The New World Life* (1913) contended that industry, peace and ideals had become global issues, and *Our World: The New World Religion* (1915) argued that Jesus established 'world principles' that were the basis for solving great world problems and for realizing the new world ideal. Strong also wrote two books of devotional/practical theology: *The Times and Young Men* (1916) and *My Religion in Every-Day Life* (1910). Finally, he edited a monthly periodical entitled *The Gospel of the Kingdom* (founded 1908) and published many articles, sermons, addresses etc. He died in New York City on 28 April 1916.

Bibliography

D. R. Muller, 'Josiah Strong and the Challenge of the City' (PhD dissertation, New York University, 1955); D. R. Muller, 'The Social Philosophy of Josiah Strong: Social Christianity and American Progressivism', *Church History* (June 1959), pp. 183–201; D. R. Muller, 'Josiah Strong and American Nationalism: A Reevaluation', *Journal of American History* (December 1966), pp. 487–503; E. T. Root, 'Josiah Strong: A Modern Prophet of the Social Gospel', *New Church Review* (June 1922), pp. 47–54; J. Strong, *Our Country: Its Possible Future and Its Present Crisis*, ed. J. Herbst (Cambridge, MA: Harvard University Press, 1963).

K. W. PETERSON

■ **STUDD, C. (Charles) T. (Thomas)** (1860–1931), founder of Worldwide Evangelization Crusade (WEC), was the youngest of three sons born to Edward Studd, a wealthy retired jute and indigo planter living in Wiltshire, England. A talented athlete by the age of sixteen, he was captain of his cricket team at Eton College. At Trinity College, Cambridge, where he continued his education, he became nationally recognized as England's most talented cricketer. He experienced profound spiritual renewal under the ministry of D. L. *Moody and Ira *Sankey, and became an influential member of that remarkable group of Cambridge students known as the 'Cambridge Seven', young graduates of wealth and privilege who renounced their promising careers to serve as missionaries to China. As one of England's best known and most popular athletes, Studd's decision to devote his life to missionary service caused a sensation in the public press and launched the Student Volunteer Movement (SVM). Studd sailed for China in 1885 under the auspices of the China Inland Mission (CIM), arousing both sharp criticism and deep admiration for his seemingly reckless endorsement and practice of that mission society's radical incarnational principles; he would provoke this mixed reaction for the rest of his life. After his twenty-fifth birthday, he gave away nine-tenths of his inheritance to a variety of Christian societies. His motto would be, 'If Christ be God and died for me, then no sacrifice can be too great for me to make for him.' In China he married Priscilla Livingston Stewart (1864–1929), a young Irish woman from Ulster whose temperament and dedication corresponded to his own. His wedding gift to her was a tithe of his inheritance, which she promptly gave away completely. They had four daughters.

Returning to England in 1894, broken in health, the couple gave what remained of their property to CIM. For the next six years Studd itinerated throughout the United States and Britain on behalf of the SVM, before moving to India in 1900 to serve as minister of the English-speaking church at Ootacamund. Once again compelled by poor health to return to England in 1906, he resumed his speaking ministry. In 1910, still sickly and against the wishes of his ailing wife, he embarked for Africa, returning one year later to establish the Heart of Africa Mission, later to become WEC. In 1913, accompanied by his future son-in-law Alfred Buxton (1891–1940), Studd began what many would regard as a quixotic eighteen-year missionary career in the Belgian Congo (People's Democratic Republic of Congo). Inspiring from afar as an example, as a field leader and colleague he proved to be an obstinate and incompetent administrator, provoking bitter and sustained conflicts with family, fellow missionaries and Africans until his death. Except for a single visit in 1928, his wife remained in England throughout Studd's sojourn in Africa. She died in 1929, a virtual widow. After Studd's death at Ibambi in July 1931, his strife-riven organization began to flourish under the capable leadership of another famous son-in-law, Norman P. Grubb (1895–1993). Today WEC, still evincing the radical spirit of its founder, is an international community of some 1,682 missionaries serving in more than seventy countries.

Bibliography

J. T. Erskine, *Millionaire for God: The Story of C. T. Studd* (London: Lutterworth Press, 1968); N. P. Grubb, *C. T. Studd: Cricketer and Pioneer* (London: Religious Tract Society, 1933); J. C. Pollock, *The Cambridge Seven: A Fire in China – C. T. Studd and His Friends* (Leicester: Inter-Varsity Press, 1996).

J. J. BONK

■ **SUMNER, John Bird** (1780–1862), Archbishop of Canterbury, was born on 25 February 1780, the eldest son of the Revd Robert Sumner and Hannah Bird. His younger brother was Charles Richard Sumner (Bishop of Winchester). Educated initially at Eton, he proceeded to King's College, Cambridge, being elected scholar in November 1798 and fellow in November 1801. He held the King's Betham scholarship until 1803, won the Browne medal for best Latin ode in 1800 and was Hulsean prizeman in 1802. He received a BA in 1803, an MA in 1807 and a DD in 1828.

In 1802 Sumner became an assistant master at Eton and was ordained by Bishop Douglas (Salisbury) in 1803. On 31 March 1803, he married Marianne, daughter of George Robertson, a naval captain. In accordance with common practice, he was required to give up his King's fellowship, though he was later elected fellow at Eton (1817). In 1818 he was nominated to the parish of Mapledurham, Oxfordshire. With Mapledurham bringing him £1,000 a year and his Eton fellowship a further £800, Sumner became unusually wealthy. In 1820, promoted by Shute Barrington, Bishop of Oxford, he was appointed to the ninth prebendal stall at Durham, moving to the fifth stall in 1826 and to the second stall in 1827, each being better endowed than the last. Having declined the offer of the diocese of Sodor and Man in 1827, he accepted Chester in 1828. In 1848 he became Archbishop of Canterbury, following Howley's death.

Sumner was a moderate evangelical closely linked with the Clapham Sect. Living out his theory that societies 'show an anxious zeal against ungodliness and formal religion', he became closely involved with many societies, including the Church Missionary Society, British and Foreign Bible Society, Church Pastoral Aid Society, Lord's Day Observance Society, Society for the Propagation of the Gospel and Society for Promoting Christian Knowledge, becoming vice-president of the British and Foreign Bible Society in 1848. His belief in the sanctity of the Sabbath led him to demand that Palmerston close the National Gallery and British Museum on Sundays, though his major achievement in this area was the banning of Sunday afternoon military band concerts in all London parks.

In summarizing Sumner's character A. C. Benson wrote: 'he was a man of extraordinary self-restraint and method, regulating the employment of his time, his money, his hours of sleeping, eating and exercise by the strictest rules'. His self-discipline and methodical nature were evident in his approach to educational standards, the New Poor Law and church building; he always took a reasoned and practical line, though he was not known as an independent thinker.

Honest poverty, he felt, was a natural state created by God. However, he had little sympathy for those whose poverty was created by their own imprudent and foolish behaviour. Personal responsibility stood high on Sumner's list of priorities; all should be encouraged to do their utmost to fulfil their many obligations. Sumner would not countenance complacency either in himself or in others. For this reason he requested an amendment to the Pluralities Bill on the basis that it was reasonable for a clergyman to hold two neighbouring parishes (no more than three miles apart by the nearest road and providing one had a value of less than £100). At a time when many clergy families lived in genteel poverty this provision encouraged them to maximize their efforts to alleviate their situation.

In the Lords Sumner voted for the Catholic Emancipation Bill, because he felt that the number of Catholics was about to decline. He admitted that he might have voted differently had he envisaged its stability or growth.

Education for the masses was one of Sumner's major concerns. In the diocese of Chester both schools and churches were inadequate. Manchester, then one parish, had only one church for 200,000 people, but Sumner understood that building alone would not solve the problem: 'We have not multiplied the shepherds, as the flocks became more numerous: we have not added fresh folds, when our enclosures had become too full and overcrowded.' Similarly, he recognized that the lack of good schoolteachers inhibited the moral and spiritual growth of children. Sumner helped Henry Raikes to establish the first teacher training college, believing that parents would be prepared to pay a little for their children to gain a better education.

Sumner wanted the masses to be able to understand Scripture, and to that end he wrote a number of commentaries. In his preaching Sumner revealed himself to be a crucicentric evangelical; almost every sermon or address referred to the crucifixion in some way. Only by really understanding what had taken place on the cross, he believed, could people truly become warm, living and breathing Christians instead of cold-hearted, pharisaical Christians lacking any real, living faith.

In his Charge of 1829, Sumner spoke to his clergy about their purpose, that humankind be 'brought to God'. However, whilst others spoke of teaching people right from wrong, Sumner told his clergy that this was not necessary: '[M]en do not so much require to be instructed in moral truths as in religious obligation. They are no strangers to the broad distinction between right and wrong, holiness and ungodliness. They commonly acknowledge them in words, whilst they practically confound them. They need to be convinced, not what sin is, but of the sinfulness of sin: to be taught that the "wages of sin is death", eternal death. And the atonement made by the Son of God, the sacrifice of the cross, is the great instrument of working this conviction.'

In a move to maximize the efficacy of the church, Sumner urged his clergy to appoint lay people as district visitors, who would bring the word of God to greater numbers by 'visiting and examining schools, by reading and praying with the infirm and aged, by consoling the fatherless and widows and pursuing the many ways by which it is the power of one Christian to benefit and receive another.' Drawing on his own experiences of working with the poor, as he had done in Cambridge and Eton, Sumner was able to provide practical guidance and encouragement.

Sumner was a staunch opponent of the Oxford Movement, referring to it as 'a revival of the worst evils of the "Romish System" '. However, in dealing with matters of ritual he was always careful to reply in a tempered fashion, providing reasoned answers derived from careful reading, or even refusing to take sides. Samuel Wilberforce believed that Sumner was indecisive and incapable of fulfilling the duties of his office, referring to 'the fearful weakness caused by the character of the Primate'. However, this comment should be evaluated in the light of the fact that Samuel Wilberforce was a candidate for the primacy after the death of Archbishop Howley. But though Sumner undoubtedly applied himself to the practical issues facing the church and achieved much, Randall Davidson too felt that he was not the right person for the primacy at that time; according to Davidson an energetic High Churchman would have been more effective.

Sumner and his wife Marianne had ten children. Marianne died in 1829, but her death was not permitted to interrupt Sumner's work. Exhibiting his great self-restraint, he promised to 'forget my own loss and the destitution of my family', saying that 'a clergyman who has his heart in his profession is the happiest of men; in the business of his life at least, if not in actual temperament.' He died on 6 September 1862, his health having declined under pressure of work.

Bibliography

N. Scotland, *John Bird Sumner, Evangelical Bishop* (Leominster: Gracewing, 1995).

P. J. CADLE

■ **SUNDAY, William Ashley, Jr** (1862–1935), evangelist and professional baseball player, was born in Story County, Iowa, USA, the son of William Ashley Sunday, Sr, a farmer and American Civil War (Union) soldier, and Mary Jane Corey.

Sunday was born in a two-room cabin on a small rented farm. His father, a Union Army private, died of influenza a few weeks after William was born. His mother made valiant efforts to farm the land, but poverty overcame the family. Therefore, in 1872 Billy and his twelve-year-old brother Edward had to be sent to the Civil War Soldiers' Orphan Home in Glenwood, Iowa. In 1874 the boys were moved to the Davenport, Iowa Orphan Home. They lived there until 1876 and received some education. Then both boys chose to leave the orphanage and hire themselves out as farm hands in Story County.

In 1877 Billy Sunday moved to Nevada, Iowa, where he sporadically attended high school, lived with a Civil War veteran and his wife, and hired himself out as a janitor, stable keeper and hotel clerk. During his three years in Nevada he played for a local baseball team, demonstrating superb athletic prowess marked by unusual agility and speed. Because of Sunday's running speed the fire brigade at Marshalltown, Iowa recruited him to be a member of their volunteer department. In return they secured him a job in a furniture shop and guaranteed him a place in the Marshalltown baseball team.

Although Sunday never finished high school, he did help the Marshalltown baseball team to earn a statewide reputation. By 1881, in part because of his base-stealing and fielding ability, the Marshalltown nine was one of the best in Iowa. In 1882 Sunday was the star of the team, and he led them to the state championship. Because of his exploits as a baserunner and left fielder, Sunday came to the attention of Adrian 'Cap' Anson, captain and manager of the National League's Chicago White Stockings, who are today the Chicago Cubs. In the spring of 1883 Sunday took the train to Chicago, where he passed a trial for the twelve-member squad. Sunday played for five years for the White Stockings (1883–1887). In 1887 he batted .291 and stole thirty-four bases.

The Pittsburgh Pirates bought Sunday from Chicago in 1888, and for the next two and a half seasons (1888–1890) he led the team in stolen bases. In mid-season 1890, by now a nationally recognized baserunner, he was sold to Philadelphia. That year he batted .257 and stole eighty-four bases.

By 1890 Sunday was at the peak of his baseball career. At the age of twenty-seven he was earning $400 per month at a time when the average industrial worker earned $380 per year. He had a national reputation, his health was excellent, and more than one major league baseball club wanted him in their squad. Nevertheless, several events in the previous four years led to his resignation from professional sports in the winter of 1890.

During the 1886 baseball season Sunday professed faith in Jesus Christ for the first time. After being confronted by a street evangelist, he later went to the Pacific Garden Mission, a Chicago street mission, where he heard sermons urging the listeners to repent of their sins and follow Jesus Christ. One night in the summer of 1886 Sunday responded to an altar call. In the wake of this event he began studying the Bible, attending prayer meetings and changing his worldly lifestyle. Sunday also became active in the Chicago Young Men's Christian Association, where he became one of their preaching evangelists during the close season.

In 1886 Sunday did more than convert to the Christian faith and become a lay preacher;

he also became a member of Chicago's prestigious Jefferson Park Presbyterian Church. There he met Helen Amelia Thompson, the daughter of a wealthy Chicago businessman. Their relationship flourished, and they were married on 5 September 1888. Their marriage produced four children: Helen (1890), George Marquis (1892), William Ashley, Jr (1901) and Paul Thompson (1907).

Sunday's new religion gradually rivalled and then surpassed his love for baseball. Indeed, by the winter of 1890 he and his wife had agreed that he should resign from professional baseball and devote his life to preaching the gospel. Commitment to Christ, not money, was the impetus behind the career change. Sunday was offered a $3,500 baseball contract for seven months' work in 1891. He turned down the offer, choosing instead to take a salary of under $1,000 for eleven and a half months as a Bible teacher and evangelist with the Chicago YMCA. Sunday worked for the YMCA until 1893, when he joined a well-known evangelist J. Wilbur Chapman as a travelling associate evangelist. Britain's F. B. *Meyer and America's D. L. *Moody had nurtured Chapman in the faith. For the next two and a half years Chapman became a mentor to Sunday. The older, well-established preacher taught the former farmer and baseball player how to dress appropriately and relate to church leaders; he also helped Sunday to improve his preaching skills.

In 1896, much to the dismay of the Sunday family, J. Wilbur Chapman accepted a call to become pastor of a Philadelphia church. Without forewarning, the young evangelist found himself with no mentor, no salary and no invitations for ministry. Billy and Helen Sunday fell on their knees together, beseeching God for guidance. Six days later a telegram arrived asking Sunday to preach a series of evangelistic messages at Garner, Iowa. With shouts of joy the unemployed preacher accepted. From that day until his death nearly four decades later he never lacked invitations to preach.

The newly independent evangelist began his first crusade on 7 January 1896 in Garner, Iowa. Sunday was to conduct over 250 crusades in all sizes of towns and cities in the United States. Although he was invited to hold evangelistic meetings in other countries on several continents, he prayerfully concluded that he was to restrict his ministry to the United States. Most of his crusades were held nightly over two or three weeks, with morning and afternoon meetings during the days for special interest groups such as women, businessmen, young people and Sunday school teachers. From 1896 until his death in 1935, the zealous evangelist maintained a hectic schedule of travel and preaching.

Sunday ultimately preached to over 100 million people. Approximately one million people responded to his altar calls, in which they were asked to walk his famous 'sawdust trails' and commit their lives to Jesus Christ. These 'sawdust trails' were Sunday's trademark, taking their name from his early campaigns in the Pacific northwest, in which the floors of meeting halls and hastily constructed tabernacles were covered with sawdust. This material was free or inexpensive, and the mud, melted snow and dust could be easily swept away after each meeting.

By the 1920s Christians and non-Christians alike recognized the famous 'Baseball Evangelist' as an American phenomenon who had preached the gospel to more people in more cities than anyone in world history. When he led extensive crusades of several weeks' duration in such places as San Francisco, Chicago, Cleveland, Boston, New York and Philadelphia, his meetings were daily front-page news for weeks at a time. Statistics of attendance and altar-call respondents were considered newsworthy. In addition, many newspapers reprinted his sermons verbatim, causing millions more to feel the impact of his messages.

Billy Sunday became a household name in early twentieth-century America because he gave hope to so many people. His message of salvation for all sinners who cried out for mercy gave hope to guilt-laden sinners. Furthermore, he gave hope to the millions of poor rural and small town dwellers who migrated to the cities looking for an escape from the poverty and drudgery of unmechanized rural life. Sunday's biography is a rags to riches story. Not only did he emerge from an orphanage and rural poverty to achieve fame in major league baseball, he also became still more famous as a gifted orator and preacher. A theatrical man, he could make audiences laugh as well as weep. He was already famous by the time of the First World War and dined with presidents, socialized with leaders in the sports and entertainment world, enjoyed his standing as one of America's most admired men and befriended the nation's economic power elite. A human dynamo famous for his energy and enthusiasm, Sunday earned over a million dollars, sought the Republican nomination for President of the United States and ran for Vice-President with the Prohibition Party. He also sold a syndicated column to numerous newspapers and published books of his sermons, which sold thousands of copies.

Although Sunday never attended college or seminary, the Presbyterian Church ordained him in 1903. Despite his desire to be recognized as an independent evangelist, he remained a Presbyterian all his life. Until the First World War the mainstream denomination enjoyed its association with America's most famous preacher; however, by 1917 some Presbyterian leaders were embarrassed that Sunday carried ordination papers from their church. By that time his earnings brought shame to the Presbyterian Church and nearly caused them to set a limit on their preachers' earnings. Sunday was accountable to no-one for his financial income and expenses. He received no salary but paid his expenses from the offerings. Usually he gave away the nightly offerings, after paying his rent and workers, to a local charity. He kept only the final night's 'love offering' for himself, but that might raise over $100,000 in a major city. Many criticized him for this policy.

During his career, Sunday was untouched by scandal, although he was criticized for his affluence. Much of his income went to charities, but many observers felt suspicious of a preacher who taught of the poor Nazarene yet earned such large sums of money. In fairness to Sunday, it should be noted that he gave much of his money away, and most of the criticism directed against him resulted from his ever-increasing identification with conservative causes. He openly endorsed Republican candidates for political office, and ardently campaigned for the prohibition of the sale of alcoholic beverages during the 1910s. Indeed, many of his contemporaries credited the passage of the Eighteenth Amendment to the US Constitution to his enthusiasm for the Prohibitionist cause.

Sunday's popularity waned after 1920

because he was older, his causes were less celebrated and some of his Republican political friends (e.g. Herbert Hoover) were unpopular after 1929. Nevertheless, he always had a large following. Crowds thronged to hear him preach. When he died an estimated 15–20,000 people passed his open coffin at Chicago's Moody Church. His followers came from every ethnic group and from all walks of life. He spoke a language people understood and called them back to traditional values during a time of great change. He became the leader of those who wanted to keep biblical, conservative Christianity alive in an increasingly secular society.

Although countless people testified to making first-time decisions for Christ under Sunday's preaching, and numerous others recommitted their lives and found encouragement from the famous preacher, his life was marred by family difficulties. The Sunday children became a source of much pain for their parents. Only Helen seems to have been a strong Christian. She married Mark Haines; they had a son, Paul, and she died at the age of forty-two from complications resulting from a disease similar to multiple sclerosis. The three sons, on the other hand, were overly indulged by their parents, who felt guilty about leaving them alone for weeks with their sister or a housekeeper. Unruly and seldom disciplined, all three boys suffered from drinking problems, pursued promiscuous lifestyles and died young and out of fellowship with the Christian community.

During his lifetime Billy Sunday was criticized for failing to raise his boys well, and he was ridiculed by the press and some church leaders for his excessive income, but these attacks were minor compared to those of some Christian leaders on his altar calls at the end of each service. Sunday believed that people could and must make a decision to repent and follow Christ, so he invited and encouraged them to do so. But many predestinarians believed this invitational style of evangelism, which became much more popular as other evangelists and ministers copied Sunday, to be theologically errant. Sunday was attacked as an 'Arminian' by many Calvinists. Some even called him a heretic. Yet it must be recognized that regardless of his methods, countless thousands of lives were changed and drinking establishments, gambling dens and houses of ill repute went out of business in communities where he preached for two or more weeks.

Bibliography

R. A. Bruns, *Preacher: Billy Sunday and Big-Time American Evangelism* (New York: W. W. Norton, 1992); L. W. Dorsett, *Billy Sunday and the Redemption of Urban America* (Grand Rapids: Eerdmans, 1991); W. G. McLaughlin, Jr, *Billy Sunday Was His Real Name* (Chicago: University of Chicago Press, 1955).

L. W. DORSETT

■ **SWAGGART, Jimmy Lee** (1935–), television preacher and gospel musician, was born on 15 March 1935 near Ferriday, Louisiana. His parents, Willie Leon Swaggart and Minnie Bell Herron, who married when they were teenagers, raised their family in the depths of Depression poverty. Swaggart's father was a marginal labourer and ne'er-do-well until 1942, when he became a member of the Assemblies of God and changed his lifestyle. In the late 1940s he became an itinerant preacher, planting churches in Louisiana. Although young Jimmy Swaggart chafed under the strict moral standards imposed on all Pentecostals during those years, he was converted and had the experience known as 'baptism in the Holy Spirit' at the age of eight. At the age of seventeen he married Frances Anderson, who was a member of the Assemblies of God church in Wisner, Louisiana. A forceful and talented woman, Frances became Swaggart's most important and trusted advisor. They had one son, Donnie, who has become an evangelist himself and an important member of the Swaggart ministry team.

After marrying, Swaggart eked out a living while working at odd jobs, at the same time conducting street meetings in nearby towns. Swaggart was fascinated by the healing revivalists who were holding crusades around the country in the early 1950s, particularly William Branham, and in 1958, at the age of twenty-two, he began working as a full-time evangelist. His evangelistic career was initially built on the success of his cousin Jerry Lee Lewis, who had become a national rock 'n' roll recording celebrity in 1958. Swaggart frequently made references to his famous cousin in his sermons.

Swaggart and two of his cousins, Jerry Lee Lewis and country music star Mickey Gilley, drew from the same creative musical sources in the South, where gospel, country and black musical styles were being fused in creative new ways. All three credited a local black friend, 'old Sam', with a critical role in the formation of their musical styles. From the beginning of Swaggart's evangelistic career, his rhythmic piano playing and stylistic singing were his trademark and, many believed, the primary reason for his success.

Swaggart's musical style troubled some Assemblies of God ministers, and in 1959 the Louisiana District of the Assemblies of God declined to ordain him, though he was ordained the next year. In 1959 Swaggart began recording gospel albums; the sales of his recordings rapidly escalated after Jerry Lee Lewis persuaded Sun Records in Memphis, one of the largest producers of rock 'n' roll hits in the 1960s, to record a Swaggart album. By the end of the 1960s, Swaggart was the most popular evangelist in the Assemblies of God; in 1969 he launched an immensely popular radio programme that featured both his preaching and his music. 'The Campmeeting Hour' expanded rapidly, feeding and being fed by the growing popularity of Swaggart's records. Swaggart put the receipts from his recordings back into the ministry, and by 1977 his radio network included around 600 stations.

In 1972 Swaggart began holding weekend crusades in auditoriums throughout the nation because the crowds who came to hear him would no longer fit into local churches. The Swaggart meetings filled a void because the most popular Pentecostal evangelists who had launched revival ministries after the Second World War had stopped holding campaigns, most notably Oral *Roberts in 1968. Swaggart's well-organized campaigns, strongly backed by the Assemblies of God nationally and locally, once again expanded his base of supporters. The campaigns included Swaggart's animated and doctrine-filled sermons and a musical programme that featured probably the most talented ensemble of singers and musicians ever to be part of an evangelistic organization.

In 1973 Swaggart began producing a weekly half-hour television programme, which became an hour-long programme in 1977. By that time the programme was being broadcast on more than 100 stations. By 1983 Swaggart's programme had become the most popular syndicated religious programme in America according to the Arbitron ratings. An estimated 15 million Americans watched his weekly broadcast; he built a network of more than 3,000 stations in 145 countries, which carried his programme to an estimated worldwide audience of 300 million. Once again building on Swaggart's musical talents, the programme rapidly became more popular, at a time when viewing figures for religious television were growing at a remarkable rate.

During the decade from 1977 to 1987 the Jimmy Swaggart Evangelistic Association, based in Baton Rouge, Louisiana, became a huge financial empire with budgets surpassing $150,000,000 annually. On a 300-acre site Swaggart built a $30 million headquarters that included a state-of-the-art television production centre. The organization also constructed a 7,500 seat Family Worship Center, which was attended regularly by more than 10,000 people, and opened a college (Jimmy Swaggart Bible College). During these years, Swaggart conducted huge campaigns outside the United States. In addition, at its peak in the mid-1980s, the Swaggart organization supported more than 600 indigenous missionaries in 115 countries and more than 100 Bible colleges.

Jimmy Swaggart's most important lasting legacy is probably the impact of his message and techniques in Latin America and elsewhere in the developing world. In addition to his campaigns, his television programmes were broadcast in much of the world; his organization dubbed tapes of his crusades into twenty-five languages in studios in Baton Rouge. By the middle of the 1980s Jimmy Swaggart may well have been the most widely known and emulated Protestant in the world. One poll in the 1980s reported that Swaggart's programme was watched by more than 75% of Central American churchgoers and that nearly 70% of Latin Americans felt that Swaggart's teachings were more 'useful' than those taught in institutional churches.

More than most independent revivalists who preceded him, Swaggart in his preaching adhered closely to orthodox Pentecostal theology, and although his campaigns attracted a wide variety of people, Pentecostals provided his support base. In addition to the money that he put into denominational causes, his orthodoxy made him the favourite son of the Assemblies of God. Their relationship with him contributed much to Swaggart's success, but it also proved to be extremely beneficial to the Assemblies of God around the world.

In a stunning series of revelations in 1988, broadcast nationally and around the world, Swaggart was accused of being involved in voyeuristic activities with a prostitute in New Orleans. In a dramatic broadcast on 21 February Swaggart delivered what may well have been the most watched sermon in history. He confessed that he had 'wronged' his wife, his family, his denomination, his church and the 'hundreds of millions that I have stood before in over a hundred countries of the world' and offered a tearful apology: 'I have sinned against you, and I beg your forgiveness.' Swaggart refused the rehabilitative discipline prescribed by the Assemblies of God, who demanded that he cease all public activities for a year, believing that it would kill his ministry, and in April 1988 his ordination was removed.

The scandal had a devastating effect on the Swaggart organization, causing an almost total collapse of support from Pentecostal denominations and a greatly diminished income. None the less, Swaggart persevered in the 1990s, and by the end of the century he was broadcasting on television throughout the country and in thirty foreign countries. The organization also operated a World Evangelism Bible College and Seminary in Baton Rouge and a local church that met in his Family Worship Center. Though his record sales have diminished through the years, he is still a popular recording artist. Swaggart is one of the best-selling gospel music artists of all time, having sold more than fifteen million copies of his recordings.

Bibliography

M. J. Giuliano, *Thrice Born: The Rhetorical Comeback of Jimmy Swaggart* (Macon: Mercer University Press, 1999); A. Rowe Seaman, *Swaggart: An Unauthorized Biography of an American Evangelist* (New York: Continuum, 1999); J. L. Swaggart, *To*

Cross A River (Baton Rouge: Jimmy Swaggart Ministries, 1984).

D. E. HARRELL, JR

■ **SWEETING, George** (1924–), minister and president of Moody Bible Institute (MBI), was born in Haledon, New Jersey, just a year after his parents emigrated to the USA from Scotland. Sweeting's parents placed a high value on religious instruction, and so young George, with his three sisters and two brothers, grew up attending local evangelical churches. In 1938 his parents joined Hawthorne Gospel Church, and it was there that Sweeting met his future wife, Margaret Hilda Schnell, whom he married in 1947.

Even in his late teens, Sweeting already possessed the zeal for evangelism that would characterize his life. After dedicating his life to Jesus Christ and Christian ministry during the summer before his junior year in high school, he immediately began to share his faith with his classroom peers, leading forty-one to Christ during his senior year. After high school Sweeting followed his older brother to study at 'Mr *Moody's School' in Chicago, where he sharpened his preaching and evangelistic abilities through MBI's compulsory practical work. He became locally famous for his use of chalk drawing and a portable easel for evangelism ('illustrated sermons'), travelling in the midwest on most weekends. (In the 1950s he published two books on chalk-drawing technique for preachers.) Sweeting received his diploma in 1945, and in 1946 commenced a two-year BA at Gordon College in Wenham, Massachusetts. While a student, Sweeting continued to feel a strong call to direct involvement in evangelism and preaching and at one time turned down an offer to lead the department of missions at Gordon. At this time Herrmann Braunlin, pastor of Sweeting's home church, Hawthorne Gospel, asked him to be his assistant pastor. Sweeting accepted this call for eighteen months, then took the senior pastorate at Grace Church in Passaic.

Sweeting's intense desire to preach drove him in the 1950s to resign from his position as pastor and to take his message to the road. He returned to what he knew best, the itinerant life of a chalk artist and evangelist. Sweeting preached almost every day to hundreds of people, crossing state and national boundaries in pursuit of ministry opportunities. His travelling 'crusades' (with an entourage that included a large tent transported from city to city by a tractor-trailer with 'Christ is the Answer' painted on the sides) lasted until the oldest of his four sons became a teenager in 1961. Sweeting then took the pastorate of another New Jersey church, Madison Avenue Baptist in Paterson. Madison Avenue was a prestigious evangelical church struggling with low attendance and a lack of enthusiasm when Sweeting arrived. But their new pastor provided a vision for growth and maturity that revitalized the church in just a few years. Moody Memorial Church in Chicago had similar problems, and parishioners there soon began imploring Sweeting to fill their three-year vacancy for a pastor. After much deliberation, Sweeting accepted the call and moved his family west.

George Sweeting ministered at Moody Church for five years before he succeeded William Culbertson as president of MBI. During his time as president (1971–1987), Sweeting promoted the growth of the institution while keeping evangelism central to his vision. He worked to expand Moody's ministry through radio, books and magazines; he founded Moody's annual Pastors' Conference; and he initiated the Advanced Studies Program that eventually led to the formation of the Moody Graduate School. Sweeting also believed that Moody should continue its historic mission to the city of Chicago and thus resisted proposals to move the institute to the suburbs. Sweeting encouraged MBI to remain true to D. L. Moody's vision of inclusive and apolitical evangelism. In these and other ways, Sweeting led the institute more by providing a compelling vision than by managerial prowess. In 1987, after guiding the MBI through a major centennial celebration, Sweeting decided to resign from the presidency and became the institute's chancellor until his retirement in 1999. He is presently chancellor-emeritus of MBI and continues to write and speak widely on Christian topics.

Sweeting's biographer attributes to him a 'generous impulse'. He has avoided controversy by disposition and hence has encouraged MBI to move away from an embattled fundamentalism. He once described himself as a 'fundamentalist in doctrine and an evangelical in spirit'. His passion for evangelism and his preaching of, in his words, an 'inclusive gospel' have stressed the positive, transformative aspects of his and Moody's fundamentalist inheritance over against the negative tendency to draw rigid battle lines. Sweeting has written over thirty books, including *How to Begin the Christian Life* (Chicago: Moody Press, 1975) which has sold nearly a million copies in ten languages, and *The No-Guilt Guide to Witnessing* (Wheaton: Victor Books, 1991).

Bibliography
J. B. Jenkins, *A Generous Impulse: The Story of George Sweeting* (Chicago: Moody Press, 1987).

R. B. BADEMAN

■ **TAYLOR, James Hudson** (1832–1905), medical missionary and founder of the interdenominational China Island Mission, of which he was general director for nearly forty years, was born in Barnsley, Yorkshire on 21 May 1832 to James Taylor, apothecary and proprietor of a chemist's shop, and Amelia (née Hudson). His was a devout Methodist home and upbringing. His great-grandfather, a stonemason, had helped to build the chapel that the family attended and had entertained John *Wesley in 1786. His father was a Methodist lay preacher with a special interest in the evangelization of China. Hudson Taylor experienced conversion in 1849 after a period of questioning. In his *Retrospect* he saw himself indebted to the prayers of his mother and his sister Amelia, a close confidant who was to marry Benjamin Broomhall, home director and leading figure in the CIM; four of their children served as missionaries of the society in China. After local schooling and experience of work in his father's shop and a local bank, Taylor became medical assistant to Robert Hardey, a doctor in Hull, a practising Methodist and member of his mother's extended family. In Hull he joined a Brethren assembly under the ministry of Andrew Jukes, previously an ordained Anglican. Here he was baptized as a believer. He remained convinced of the rightness of believer's baptism for the rest of his life, though never exclusively, cooperating fully with paedo-baptists later in the CIM. His interest in China, awakened by his father, was stimulated by reports of Karl Gutzlaff's work in *The Gleaner in the Missionary Field*. Taylor corresponded with the Chinese Association in London about his call to missionary service; its leaders encouraged him towards medical training by offering to meet his fees. In Hull he heard of the work of George *Müller of Bristol and his ministry to orphans, conducted financially on principles of faith without direct appeals for funds, an approach Taylor adopted in his personal life and later in the work of CIM.

In 1852 Taylor began his medical studies at the London Hospital. Political developments in China after 1842, occasioned by Western political and economic pressure (which included the import of opium from British India), had by then extended the foothold for missionary work secured by pioneers such as Robert *Morrison and William Milne in Canton to five 'treaty ports'. More significantly for Taylor's immediate future, the outbreak of the Taiping rebellion, which initially appeared to be a Christian uprising, caused him and the leaders of the China Evangelization Society to decide to cut short his medical course so that he could sail to China in 1853. He sailed in the *Dumfries*, narrowly escaping shipwreck in the Irish Sea, and arrived in Shanghai on 1 March 1854. Here he was welcomed by the missionary community, mostly comprised of members of the London Missionary Society and the Church Missionary Society, with whom he was to conduct his early evangelistic tours into the interior, first with Joseph Edkins (LMS) in 1854, and then with the Revd John Burdon (CMS) in 1855 down the Yangtze river. In all he helped to distribute some 3,000 New Testaments in Chinese supplied by the Bible Society.

Shanghai itself was under war conditions, with rebels and Imperial troops disputing control. Taylor himself narrowly escaped death from both a bullet and a cannonball. He was joined by Dr William Parker, a Scots Presbyterian minister of the China Evangelization Society in 1854, but both had reasons to be dissatisfied with the CES: Taylor's initial salary was set at $80 per annum at a time when CMS gave their missionaries $700, and Parker experienced much incompetence. In 1857 Taylor resigned from the CES. By then he had become convinced of the need to identify with the Chinese people by adopting Chinese dress and the 'queue' (pigtail), at least partly on the advice of the veteran LMS missionary Dr W. H. Medhurst, who had himself adopted it when on visits to the interior. His lack of formal membership of any society and European criticism, both within and beyond the missionary compound, of his policy of Chinese identification, may account for his struggle with certain CMS figures (Miss Aldersey and W. A. Russell) over his marriage to Maria Dyer on 20 January 1858. Maria was the daughter of a missionary clergyman and a firm leader in her own right, who supported him in the crucial early days of the CIM; her early death was a great loss to him and to the mission. His friend and long-serving American missionary W. A. P. Martin described the early Taylor as 'a mystic, absorbed in religious dreams, waiting to have his work revealed ... not idle but aimless' (Pollock, pp, 67–68).

In 1860 the Taylors returned to England, and Hudson resumed his medical studies. He also worked long hours on a translation of the New Testament into the Ningpo dialect with the CMS missionary and scholar F. F. Gough. Taylor qualified as a Member of the Royal College of Surgeons in 1862. In China the treaty of Tientsin had opened ten extra ports in 1858 and made travel up the Yangtze legal for foreigners. General Gordon finally defeated the Taipings in 1864. The opportunities of the interior, allied to his sense of responsibility for millions of Chinese dying without the gospel, brought Taylor to a personal crisis point on a visit to Brighton in 1865. He wrote: 'unable to bear the sight of a congregation of a thousand or more Christian people rejoicing in their own security, while millions were perishing for lack of knowledge, I wandered out on the sands alone in great spiritual agony; and there the Lord conquered my unbelief [that is, Taylor's doubts about his own adequacy as a Christian missionary leader] and I surrendered myself to God for this service. I told him all the responsibility as to issues or consequences must rest with him ...'.

Taylor prayed for twenty-four fellow workers, two each for the eleven provinces and two for Manchuria. CIM was named and born in 1865; William Berger, a long-standing friend and experienced businessman of Saint Hill, East Grinstead, agreed to act as home director. Missionaries were to go out with no assured salary, and there were to be no direct appeals for money; CIM was the first of the 'faith missions'. By this time Hudson Taylor had become personally acquainted with George Müller, whose example he had admired in Hull days, and he had also warmed to the spirituality of the Mildmay Conference, begun by William *Pennefather and precursor of the Keswick Convention, where Taylor himself later shared the platform with such leading evangelicals as the Anglican Handley *Moule and the Baptist F. B. *Meyer. C. H. *Spurgeon became a friend and supporter after a meeting with Taylor in 1864. Taylor published *China: its spiritual needs and claims* in 1865, which showed his gifts as a highly effective popular communicator. There were seven editions by 1887, and 10,000 copies were sold. Taylor proved an equally effective platform advocate for China and was invited by the evangelist Grattan *Guinness to meetings in Dublin in 1866. Guinness was to assist CIM with the selection and training of candidates from his missionary training institute in East London, and his daughter Geraldine married Taylor's second son, Howard, and was co-author of a widely read biography of Taylor.

In 1866 a party of sixteen missionaries sailed in the *Lammermuir*. Two typhoons in September brought them very close to total loss by shipwreck. At Anjer Taylor agreed to baptize as believers some members of the party. Of this episode J. C. Pollock wrote: 'Hudson Taylor committed the worst misjudgement of his life. He had founded an unsectarian mission, announcing unequivocally that in matters of denominational conscience each missionary should be free ... To allow his personal convictions to interfere with members of another church ... flatly contradicted his interdenominational principle' (Pollock, p. 135). Certainly the episode occasioned criticism, not least from the respected CMS missionary (later bishop) G. E. Moule.

Certain fundamental principles of CIM should be noted, as they distinguished the mission from the start. First, Taylor tried to insist on Chinese dress, the value of which as a means of identification, especially in the interior, he had proved himself. Secondly, the mission was directed from the field, rather than (as for LMS, CMS and BMS) from offices in London. Taylor himself was director, and all CIM missionaries accepted his authority on becoming members. This principle led Taylor's friend W. A. P. Martin to refer to him as 'the Loyola of Protestant missions in China' (Broomhall, VII, p. 511). CIM workers, like Ignatius Loyola's Jesuits, were to accept the director's rulings and policies in their arduous lives, although in practice his authority was exercised with great understanding, and dissenters (such as Lewis Nicol on the dress issue) were treated with a greater degree of leniency than William Berger felt to be good for the mission. Thirdly, Taylor willingly accepted as missionaries those with lower educational attainments than other societies required, working men (Nicol was a blacksmith) who could prove themselves in the field by their character and spirituality. Fourthly, Taylor was a pioneer in the use of young unmarried women as missionaries to the interior, a policy that attracted much criticism but proved its value in practice. Fifthly, the mission was genuinely interdenominational, including Methodists, Anglicans, Presbyterians and others. Taylor was a self-confessed Baptist in later life but regarded himself as 'head of a pan-denominational mission' (Broomhall, VII, p. 156). Sixthly, considerable emphasis was placed on itinerancy for the purpose of preaching the gospel where Christ had not been named, and journeys of thousands of miles were made by CIM pioneers to the borders of Tibet, Burma and Manchuria. Nevertheless, Bishop Frank Houghton, general director of CIM from 1940, correctly pointed out that Taylor had always believed in church planting as the goal of the mission, the establishing of indigenous churches which, in the phrase used by Henry *Venn of CMS, were 'self-governing, self-supporting and self-extending'. Seventhly, in the severe trials which came upon the mission, supremely in the Boxer violence but also in other events, Taylor refused indemnities, believing that the proper Christian response was to forgive insults, destruction of premises and even martyrdom.

In 1865 the great city of Hangzhou became CIM's base. G. E. Moule of CMS had gone there in 1864. He gave a friendly welcome to the missionaries, but under the influence of Lewis Nicol and others he became a critic of mission policy on dress and unmarried women, so that Berger had to defend the mission in London. In 1869 it was attacked in the House of Lords by the Duke of Somerset and others for creating disturbances in the interior embarrassing to the government, though it was defended in the debate by Bishop Magee (9 March 1869). Taylor regarded 1870 as his hardest year; the massacre of French missionaries at Tianjin in June was followed by Maria's death soon after that of her baby son in July and the death of his son Samuel. Illness forced him to return to England in 1871, where he was prostrated by spinal problems, married Jennie Faulding, his CIM colleague, accepted William Berger's resignation, replacing him ultimately with Benjamin Broomhall, and (in 1875) launched *China's millions*, a successful journal and a further example of his effectiveness as a communicator.

In 1877, after initial misgivings, Taylor showed that he and the mission could maintain their position in the company of other missions and their leaders in the Shanghai Missionary Conference. CIM provided aid in the great famine of that year, when Timothy Richard of BMS enhanced his reputation for able humanitarianism. He and Taylor were to differ radically on theology, however, when Richard became a critic of the scriptural conservatism of CIM and won over some of their missionaries to his viewpoint. In 1885 CIM's public profile was hugely boosted by the enlisting of the 'Cambridge Seven', a group that comprised two sporting heroes, the Cambridge and England cricketer C. T. *Studd and the Cambridge rowing 'blue' S. P. Smith, the well-born Montagu Beauchamp, W. W. Cassels, later an Anglican bishop, Arthur and Cecil Polhill-Turner and Dixon Hoste, Taylor's successor as general director. Their impact was such that 50,000 copies of *China's millions* proved too few to report their doings to the public, and a farewell meeting at Exeter Hall in London drew 3,500 people. By the end of 1885, CIM numbered 200 missionaries compared to the sixteen on the *Lammermuir* in 1865.

Between 1885 and 1905 Taylor, at first reluctantly, made CIM an international organization. Branches were formed in Canada and the USA, with Henry Frost as a leader and D. L. *Moody as a supporter; Moody's Northfield Conferences led many to offer themselves for missionary service. A council formed on the same basis as that in London, on which Benjamin Broomhall served, represented North America. Hesitations in London were allayed by Taylor's personal tact and persuasion. Scandinavian associates and full members were added to CIM, not least through the efforts of Frederik Franson, the Swedish revival leader. Taylor visited Australia and Tasmania, from where more missionaries were recruited in 1890. Prayer for 100 missionaries in 1887 became prayer for 1,000 in 1890. By 1897 the number of Chinese Christians in churches planted by CIM reached 80,000. A time of terrible sifting followed in the Boxer rising of 1898-1900, when violence against foreigners was actively encouraged by the reigning empress. Taylor had gone from Australia to the New York Ecumenical Conference of 1900, attended by some 200,000 people, at which he spoke memorably on China's needs. Speaking in Boston with A. T. *Pierson, he suffered a breakdown and was recovering in Davos, Switzerland when the worst news of the Boxers emerged. CIM lost fifty-eight missionaries and twenty-one children out of a total of one hundred and thirty Protestant martyrs, but once more Taylor refused indemnities. He realized the need for a director in the field and appointed Dixon Hoste as acting general director. Hoste was confirmed in 1902 as full director, a post he occupied for thirty years (1902-1932). After the loss of his second wife in Switzerland, Taylor decided to visit China in 1905. He died, appropriately, in the capital city of the province that had proved hardest for CIM to enter, Changsha in Hunan, on 3 June 1905. His mottoes, printed on the outside cover of *China's millions* in Chinese script, had been 'Ebenezer' and 'Jehovah Jireh', translated as 'Hitherto the Lord has helped us' and 'The Lord will provide'. K. S. Latourette called him, 'one of the four or five most influential foreigners who came to China in the nineteenth century for any purpose, religious or secular'. At his death CIM consisted of 825 missionaries in some 300 stations across China.

Bibliography

A. J. Broomhall, *Hudson Taylor and China's Open Century*, 7 vols. (London: Hodder & Stoughton, 1981-1989); Dr and Mrs Howard Taylor, *Hudson Taylor in Early Years: the Growth of a Soul* (London: CIM, 1911); Dr and Mrs Howard Taylor, *Hudson Taylor and the China Inland Mission: the Growth of a Work of God* (London: CIM, 1918); J. Hudson Taylor, *A Retrospect* (London: Morgan & Scott, 1875); J. C. Pollock, *Hudson Taylor and Maria* (London: Hodder & Stoughton, 1962); R. Steer, *J. Hudson Taylor: a Man in Christ* (London: OMF, 1993).

T. E. YATES

■ **TAYLOR, Nathaniel William** (1786-1858), Congregational minister and theologian, was born on 23 June 1786 in New Milford, Connecticut to Nathaniel Taylor, a wealthy farmer and apothecary, and Ann Northrup Taylor, another prominent citizen of New Milford. He was the grandson of the Revd Nathanael Taylor, the first of the Taylor clan to live in New Milford, the town's Congregational pastor for half a century and a member of the Yale Corporation from 1774 to 1800.

After some time in the preparatory school of the Edwardsian minister, Azel Backus, who had succeeded Joseph *Bellamy in the Congregational pulpit of Bethlehem, Connecticut, Taylor matriculated at Yale College in the autumn of 1800. He quickly fell under the influence of Yale's president, Timothy *Dwight, a grandson of Jonathan *Edwards and a champion of New England's Congregational standing order. Suffering from visual impairment and what he called 'rheumatism', Taylor had to withdraw to his home in New Milford for an extended period of recovery. But he returned to Yale to graduate with the class of 1807, experiencing conversion under Dwight's ministry at the end of his junior year (1806). As one of Taylor's own students recounted the event, 'There was a classmate and particular friend of his, who at the same time, by the working of the Divine Spirit, was concerned for his eternal interests. The two friends communicated their feelings to each other. And one day, while walking together, they raised the question whether they should call on President Dwight, who had invited all persons thoughtful upon religion to call and converse with him. At length, while still talking and doubting on that question, they came to Dr. Dwight's gate. There they stopped and hesitated. Soon, Taylor said, "Well, I shall go in." "Well," rejoined his companion, "I think I will not, to-day." Taylor did go in. And the result of his conversation with that eminent Christian guide, was that he gave himself to Christ, in a covenant never to be broken.'

After graduation, Taylor stayed on in New Haven to serve as Dwight's amanuensis, drafting numerous letters and sermons for his functionally blind mentor. He lived in the Dwight family home from 1808 to 1809, and also read theology with Dwight in 1810. During this time, Taylor and Dwight became intimate soul mates, Taylor's thought and approach to ministry being shaped profoundly by the ageing president. As Taylor's friend Leonard Bacon would put it later, 'to say that [Taylor] was a favorite pupil of President Dwight, does not adequately express the intimacy of the relation between them'.

Taylor married his childhood sweetheart and second cousin, Rebecca Marie Hine, on 15 October 1810. Rebecca was the only daughter of Major Beebe Hine and Lois Northrop Hine; her family kept an inn on New Milford's green, where the wedding was held. After staying a few days in New Milford so that Taylor could preach to his home congregation, the newlyweds then moved back to New Haven to establish a home of their own. In 1812 they moved into the house in which they would live for the rest of their lives, raise a family and entertain a host of friends and visiting dignitaries. A clapboard colonial house, it was situated on the southwest corner of New Haven's Temple and Wall Streets, just north of the town green.

Taylor had received his licence to preach from the New Haven West Association on 21 August 1810. After supply preaching in various churches, he received a permanent call to one of the most prominent Congregational churches in all of New England, New Haven's Center Church, on 16 July 1811. The call was less than unanimous, and the youthful Taylor was reluctant to accept it. But with some encouragement from Dwight and a second call from the church, Taylor finally accepted,

and was ordained and installed on 8 April 1812. He was to become an enormously successful pastor. Overseeing revivals at the church in 1815, 1816 and 1820–1821, he added 400 members to its roll in only a decade.

In 1822 Taylor was recruited to serve as the inaugural Dwight Professor of Didactic Theology at Yale's fledgling school of theology. He resigned his position at the Center Church and by the end of the 1820s had become the most controversial theologian in America. Along with his colleagues Chauncey A. Goodrich and Eleazar T. Fitch, Taylor propounded a modification of Edwards' evangelical Calvinism remembered ever since as 'New Haven theology'. His *Concio ad Clerum*, delivered in 1828 at the annual meeting of Connecticut's Congregational clergy, marked the beginning of the notorious 'Taylorite' controversy.

Taylor's New Haven theology included five major hallmarks. First, he redefined the doctrine of original sin so as to exclude the notion that the entire human race is held guilty for Adam's sin. Taylor granted that all human beings are born with sinful natures, or natures that will lead to sin 'in all the appropriate circumstances of our being'. He denied, however, that we are born with natures to which God has attached a positive sinful charge, a denial intended to keep unrepentant sinners from blaming God for their moral problems.

Secondly, Taylor redefined the traditional Edwardsian understanding of the freedom of the will. Whereas Edwards had distinguished between the unregenerate sinner's 'natural ability' to repent and his or her 'moral inability' to do the same, Taylor abandoned the language of inability altogether. While granting that sin is 'certain' prior to regeneration, he insisted that it is not 'necessary'. Again, this claim was intended to prevent the unrepentant from using Calvinist necessitarianism as a crutch.

Thirdly, Taylor employed the theme of God's moral government, which had been developed by earlier Edwardsians, as a superstructure for his theology. Practically speaking, this meant that the Taylorites consistently described God's efficacious grace in what they called 'moral' rather than 'physical' terms. Granting that God's grace always effects what God wants it to effect, they suggested that it does so morally, by winning over the will, rather than physically or coercively.

Fourthly, the Taylorites propounded an ardently infralapsarian theodicy, denying that sin is a necessary part of God's plan of salvation. According to Taylor, God knew from eternity that to create an optimal system of moral government he would have to allow humans the freedom to rebel through sin. He did not actively will this sin, however. He only permitted it to take place, as an evil necessary for the greater good of the moral universe.

Fifthly, Taylor repudiated the doctrine of the sinfulness of 'unregenerate doings', which had been advocated by some of his Edwardsian predecessors. He agreed with them that prior to regeneration all that one does, including one's use of the means of grace, is sinful. But he insisted that during one's regeneration there is a moment when one's mind is convinced of the reliabilty of the Bible by the power of the Holy Spirit and thus assents to the truthfulness of the gospel without sin.

These teachings led to a schism among Connecticut Congregationalists in the early 1830s and the ultimate dissolution of New England's Edwardsian tradition. Taylor's arch-rivals, the Revds Bennet Tyler and Asahel Nettleton, succeeded by 1833 in forming an alternative 'Pastoral Union' for Connecticut's Congregational clergy. In 1834 this Pastoral Union founded a seminary that would vie for students with Taylor and Yale for years to come. Naming it the Theological Institute of Connecticut (later Hartford Theological Seminary), they built it in tiny East Windsor, Connecticut, literally (and symbolically) right down the street from Edwards' birth place.

Though the so-called 'Taylorite–Tylerite' controversy subsided in the 1840s and 1850s, its fragmentation of the region's churches severely weakened New England Calvinism. By the time of Taylor's death in New Haven on 22 March 1858, the religious culture of Edwardsian New England was dying too.

Taylor's most significant work was published in New Haven's *Quarterly Christian Spectator* in the 1820s and 1830s. But an extensive series of his lectures and sermons was published posthumously in four volumes: namely, his *Practical Sermons* (1858), *Essays, Lectures, Etc., upon Select Topics in Revealed Theology* (1859) and *Lectures on the Moral Government of God*, 2 vols. (1859).

Bibliography

S. E. Mead, *Nathaniel William Taylor, 1786–1858: A Connecticut Liberal* (Chicago: University of Chicago Press, 1942); D. A. Sweeney, *Nathaniel Taylor, New Haven Theology and the Legacy of Jonathan Edwards* (New York: Oxford University Press, 2002).

D. A. SWEENEY

■ **TAYLOR, William George** (1845–1934), Australian Methodist evangelist, was born on 18 January 1845 in Knayton, Yorkshire, the son of John and Mary Taylor, devout Wesleyans. Educated at Stokesly Grammar School, he was apprenticed to 'iron kings' Gilkes, Wilson and Pease as an accountant in 1859. After his conversion in March 1857 in an intense class-meeting, Taylor began preaching in 1861, and in 1862 it was his joy to land his 'first fish', as he described the first person converted through his ministry. His life-time commitment to vigorous evangelism was unwavering.

Taylor began training for the Wesleyan ministry at Richmond College in 1868, where an influential fellow-student was Hugh Price *Hughes, but he volunteered to serve the Australian Conference in 1870, reaching Sydney in January 1871. Ordained in 1874, Taylor's remarkable Australian ministry began as an associate minister at Albert Street, Brisbane and continued at Warwick, where he married Ann Robey in 1874, Toowoomba and the Manning River circuit. In 1882 he went to the Glebe circuit in inner Sydney. In each place revival was evidenced by numerous converts, all carefully recorded in Taylor's diary, which was the basis of his later, powerful autobiography *The Life-story of an Australian Evangelist* (London: Epworth Press, 1920). Gifted musically, a careful organizer and passionately evangelical in his preaching, Taylor became one of Australia's outstanding evangelists.

Taylor's major work was at Sydney's 'Old York Street', as the mother church of Wesleyan Methodism was affectionately known, where he reluctantly accepted an appointment in 1884. The previously large church was in decline, largely due to what Taylor described as 'the seductive call of the suburbs'. Some had advocated selling the property, and Taylor's appointment was thought to afford a last chance of developing a strong Methodist centre in the heart of the city.

Taylor's unorthodox approach was soon successful. He named the church 'the Central Methodist Mission' and used as his motto 'A Living Christ for a Dying World'. Apart from a year as a 'supernumary' and special assignments at William Street in the city and in the provincial town of Bathurst, Taylor remained at the Mission until his retirement in 1913.

Open-air meetings using brass bands and striking advertising to attract seamen from the nearby docks, as well as a strong emphasis on prayer, led to initial growth in the Mission's congregation. The traditional class-meetings were maintained, and a large number of volunteers were drawn into the leadership of the programmes. Taylor gradually developed the Mission into one of the great mission-style churches similar to those established in England by his friends Charles Garrett, 'my ideal and my copy', and Hugh Price Hughes. Various 'service organizations' were begun, such as a Seamen's Mission (1886); an evangelists' training institute and a 'Sisters of the People' movement (formed in 1890) engaged in practical care and evangelism in the slums of the inner city. Other organizations included a home for destitute children, a 'Medical Institute for Treatment of Inebriates', a women's shelter, a workmen's home and a 'male immigration depot'. General philanthropic work, providing food and clothing to 'the deserving poor', was another feature of the church's ministry.

Through all these activities Taylor maintained a primary focus on evangelism, and his social outreach was seen as an expression of that primary responsibility. Each Saturday night Taylor led a 'consecration service' for all Mission workers. Wealthy laymen, especially the Hon. Ebenezer Vickery, gave generously to Taylor's projects, most notably during the move from the York Street site to the Lyceum Theatre in Pitt Street in 1905. Under Taylor the Central Methodist Mission became one of Australia's leading churches. He also served as president of the Wesleyan Conference in 1896.

Taylor continued in active support of evangelical causes until his death at Lindfield, NSW, in 1934. His special contribution was as a bridge between the older traditional Wesleyan emphases on holiness (he had helped to found the Association for the Promotion of Holiness in 1885) and evangelism, which he upheld, and the newer, more socially oriented ministry needed in a large city mission.

Bibliography
D. Wright, *Mantle of Christ: A History of the Sydney Central Methodist Mission* (St Lucia: University of Queensland Press, 1984); D. Wright and E. Clancy, *The Methodists: A History of Methodism in NSW* (St Leonards: Allen & Unwin, 1993).

K. R. MANLEY

■ **TEN BOOM, Corrie** (1892–1983), writer and speaker, is best known for writing *The Hiding Place* (1971), an account of her activities and imprisonment during the Second World War. She grew up in Haarlem, Holland, where her father was a watchmaker. After her sister Nollie and brother Willem had married, and her mother had died, she continued to live with her father Casper and sister Betsie in the family house they called the Beje. Betsie ran the house and Corrie trained as a watchmaker, becoming the first woman in Holland to qualify. She was also involved in charitable ventures, such as a church for the mentally handicapped. Her father was loved and respected locally and had a special love for the Jews.

In Holland Corrie's extended family and friends watched developments in 1930s Germany with concern, but were mostly taken by surprise when the Nazis invaded. Once it became apparent that Jews were being victimized, it was natural to Corrie that she should help them to escape. Her brother Willem was already involved in the underground, and with his help she started to run an operation helping Jews to leave the city. When that became problematic, she began hiding them in their ramshackle house. In total over 700 Jews passed through the house, and Corrie organized a network of around eighty helpers. A secret room (the hiding place) was built behind her bedroom, and an alarm system was installed.

In February 1944 the family was betrayed by an informer. Six people managed to hide in the secret room, but the Ten Booms were arrested. Corrie's father Casper, aged eighty-four and not in good health, died in the Scheveningen prison only ten days later. Her brother Willem was released after a few weeks, but died in December 1946. Corrie and Betsie were transferred first to Vught, and then to Ravensbruck concentration camp. In all these situations the sisters were sustained by their faith. In Ravensbruck they changed the atmosphere in their hut by showing love to the other prisoners and organizing daily gatherings for Scripture reading and prayer. These gatherings gradually grew in numbers, but because the room was infested with fleas, the guards never came in to stop them. Betsie became gradually weaker, finally dying in December 1944. In her last days she talked to her sister about a place for people to recuperate after the war, describing a large house with tall windows, a broad staircase, statues set in the wall, and beautiful gardens, and also a concentration camp without the wire, painted green with many flowers around it. Corrie was released not long after her sister's death, possibly due to an administrative error.

After the war, Corrie fulfilled Betsie's vision and became involved in the care and rehabilitation of prisoners-of-war. She acquired a house in Bloemendaal, which matched almost exactly Betsie's description of the place with tall windows, where disabled people and ex-prisoners found a home, and she then raised money for the purchase of Darmstadt concentration camp, the subject of Betsie's second vision, where ex-prisoners and others affected by the war could live. Corrie also started speaking about her experiences and became well known in evangelical circles, visiting many countries all over the world. She learnt first-hand about forgiveness when she met an ex-guard who had since been converted. About 1965 the first of a series of companions began to live and travel with her. Corrie moved to California in 1977, but a year later a serious stroke almost completely incapacitated her, although with the help of her assistants she was still able to answer some correspondence. She died at her home on her ninety-first birthday, 15 April 1983.

Corrie's account of her war-time experiences, *The Hiding Place*, was published in 1971 and became very popular in evangelical circles, selling four and a half million copies by the end of the last century. It was made into a film in 1975 and received some good reviews. Although she is known primarily for this story, she wrote many other works as well, in Dutch and English.

Bibliography

C. Ten Boom, *The Hiding Place* (London: Hodder & Stoughton, 1972).

L. WILSON

■ **TENNENT, Gilbert** (1703–1764), New Side Presbyterian pastor and revivalist, was born in County Armagh, Ireland, the eldest son of William Tennent. The family emigrated to Pennsylvania in 1718, and Gilbert received his MA from Yale College (1725). Ordained by the presbytery of Philadelphia in 1726, he was called to pastor in New Brunswick, New Jersey, where he met the fiery Dutch Reformed minister Theodore Frelinghuysen, whose emphasis on conversion and pietist theology encouraged him to focus on those aspects of Ulster Scots piety. By 1734 revivals had begun, and by the time George *Whitefield visited Tennent in 1739, they were thriving. Whitefield encouraged Tennent to engage in a preaching tour of New England in the winter of 1740–1741; it proved highly successful.

By 1735 Tennent had been joined in his revival efforts in the Raritan Valley by several young pastors who came to finish their pastoral training under his supervision after studying with his father at the Log College. In 1734 Gilbert Tennent encouraged the synod of Philadelphia to examine candidates and even current ministers for 'the evidences of the grace of God'. The synod instead required all presbyteries to 'diligently examine all the candidates for the ministry in their experiences of a work of sanctifying grace in their hearts'. Rather than focusing on conversion, the synod's directive emphasized sanctification.

By 1737 Tennent and his supporters had begun to itinerate throughout several presbyteries, and wherever they went, division and disorder seemed to follow. In 1738 the synod decided that in order to keep the peace, the revivalists should be given their own presbytery, and presbytery boundaries were redrawn to include the majority of the revivalists in the new presbytery of New Brunswick. The Intrusion Act of 1739 allowed a presbytery to forbid a minister from preaching within its bounds if it judged that his preaching was divisive.

At Nottingham, Pennsylvania, Tennent replied with his most famous sermon, 'The Danger of an Unconverted Ministry' (1740), in which he claimed that many of the ministers in the synod of Philadelphia were unconverted 'Pharisee-Teachers'. Calling upon his hearers to support the work of the revivalists with prayer and money, he advocated preaching the terrors of the law in order to bring about conviction of sin and true repentance. Within a year of the sermon's publication, more than a dozen congregations had split in order to avoid the ministrations of 'unregenerate' pastors.

At the synod of 1740 Tennent claimed that anyone who was opposed to the revivals was opposed to the work of God, and therefore devoid of the Spirit of God, and he accused such people of being hypocrites who did not care for Christ's flock, but he refused to name names. In 1741 there was a split in the synod, and in 1745 the revivalists formed the synod of New York.

In 1743 Tennent accepted a call to pastor the nondenominational tabernacle that Whitefield's followers had opened in Philadelphia. Once settled in the city, Tennent began moving away from his earlier extemporaneous preaching style and rustic dress, provoking from one disillusioned follower the caustic accusation that he was 'turning back to Old Presbyterianism, and a State of dead Forms'.

This change was largely caused by Tennent's encounter with Nicholas von *Zinzendorf and the Moravians, who accused Tennent and the Great Awakening of not going far enough. The radical pietism and emotionalism of the Moravians convinced Tennent that his condemnation of other Presbyterian ministers had been too strong. Tennent realized that his objections to the Moravians were virtually identical to the anti-revivalists' objections to him. Further, George Whitefield's opposition to Tennent's

pastorate in the 'New Building' led to heightened tensions between them, and resulted in Tennent's declaration that although he remained supportive of Whitefield, he believed his Anglican colleague was insufficiently committed to orthodox Calvinism.

Tennent admitted in his *Irenicum Ecclesiasticum* (1749) that he could not 'find that the Christians of the three first Centuries after CHRIST made gracious experiences, or the Church's Judgment about them Terms of Communion'. So rather than judging the spiritual state of others, Tennent now advocated reunion with the Old Side because they were orthodox in doctrine and regular in life. Although this return to Scottish piety aroused the ire of some of his revivalist colleagues and did not immediately allay the suspicions of the Old Side ministers, it did provide the initial groundwork for reunion nine years later, and in 1758 Tennent was elected moderator of the reunited synod of New York and Philadelphia.

Bibliography

M. J. Coalter, Jr, *Gilbert Tennent, Son of Thunder* (New York and London: Greenwood Press, 1986); M. Westerkamp, *The Triumph of the Laity: Scots-Irish Piety and the Great Awakening, 1625–1760* (New York: Oxford, 1988).

P. J. WALLACE

■ **THOMAS, W. H. Griffith** (1861–1924), Anglican theologian, writer and international conference speaker, served the evangelical world in Britain, Canada and the United States amidst the crises of the early twentieth century. William Henry Griffith Thomas was born in Oswestry, Shropshire, England. As his father died before Thomas's own birth (2 January 1861), and the death of his grandfather (who was his guardian) was attended by litigation, Thomas was obliged to leave school at fourteen years old. Already an involved layman in his Anglican parish, he had a definitive evangelical conversion in 1878, an experience he never forgot. About eighteen months later he had an experience of sanctification that quickly brought him into contact with Keswick holiness teaching. His spiritual passion continued to grow after he went up to London to work in the office of a relative. He proved to be a bright student, keen to study biblical Greek into the night. Thomas soon came to the attention of the local vicar, who offered him a lay curacy in his parish, a paid position. This allowed him to leave his job, to assist the vicar and to enrol in the three-year divinity programme at King's College, where he excelled and gained the patronage of the principal, Henry *Wace.

Thomas was ordained deacon in 1885 but declined any new appointment until 1889. As a senior curate now, under A. M. W. Christopher at the evangelical parish of St Aldate's, Oxford, Thomas's academic abilities became obvious to the wider ecclesiastical world. He began theological studies at Christ Church and earned his BD at the age of thirty-four. In 1896 Thomas accepted an invitation to serve the proprietary chapel at Portman Square, London and started advanced theological study. The next few years were happy. Thomas was married (1898) and soon became a father; the chapel succeeded and was regularized as the parish of St Paul (1902); he completed most of the work on his doctoral dissertation; and he came to national and international attention through his preaching and lecturing. He also completed his popular evangelical exposition of theology and the Christian life, *The Catholic Faith: A Manual of Instruction for Members of the Church of England*, the first of many well-known books.

Thomas's academic career commenced with his appointment as principal of the evangelical Anglican Wycliffe Hall, Oxford (1905), and the DD granted to him by Oxford for his dissertation on the Holy Spirit, published immediately as *A Sacrament of our Redemption*. At Wycliffe Hall he did much of the lecturing and formation of students for ordination. His writing, his interdenominational speaking in North America and the growing testimony of evangelical Anglicans in England to his abilities led to several career opportunities.

In 1910, weary from his administrative load and eager to take up more lecturing and writing opportunities, Thomas accepted the offer of Wycliffe College, Toronto, another evangelical Anglican seminary, of a post as professor of theology. His nine years there made him widely known in North America. In 1913 he delivered the Stone Lectures at Princeton, published as *The Holy Spirit of God*.

But his professional relationship with the administration and council of Wycliffe College grew increasingly tense, and led to one of the most surprising dismissals in evangelical history. A ten-point 'Special Report' prepared by the executive committee charged Thomas with not making the interests of the college his priority. In his response of early 1919 Thomas gave voice to his sense of hurt and betrayal. He argued that he had done everything to which he had agreed and more, though his original salary and housing arrangements had not been honoured. Nor had he for some years after he arrived been allowed to teach theology courses reserved for H. J. Cody (rector of St Paul's, Bloor Street, since 1907 and defeated candidate in the diocese of Toronto episcopal elections of 1909). Thomas felt he had tried but failed to prove himself enough of a Canadian Anglican to satisfy his critics. So, he argued, he accepted invitations to speak or lecture on theology (regardless of denomination or nation), rather than the invitations of major donors in the Wycliffe circle, who expected him to engage in Anglican politics. Thomas was unwilling to be enlisted in the battles between evangelicals and Anglo-Catholics during the revision of the Canadian Prayer Book. After a last attempt at compromise by both sides, Thomas's resignation was demanded, offered and received before the end of the spring 1919 term.

Thomas's reputation was not damaged, in spite of stories about his departure in Canada's largest dailies. A nervous *ad hoc* publicity committee consisting of H. J. Cody, Dyson *Hague and others prepared Wycliffe for a possible public backlash, though decorum in the end prevailed. Thomas remained popular in Canada, where he had travelled widely as a Wycliffe professor, and Wycliffe luminaries continued to praise his Anglican publications. But Thomas quickly moved to Philadelphia to take up a variety of writing and speaking responsibilities, including the editing of *The Sunday School Times* and leadership of the American, sanctification-oriented Victorious Life conferences, both of which he had long supported. It was there that he helped to plan with Lewis Sperry *Chafer and others the projected Evangelical Theological College, later Dallas Theological Seminary. In the midst of many engagements that took him from China and Japan in 1920 to King's College, Halifax, in the spring of 1924, his body failed. He died suddenly in Philadelphia on 2 June 1924. His posthumous *The Principles of Theology: An Introduction to the Thirty-Nine Articles* (London: Church Book Room Press, 1930) proved highly popular and remained in print for decades.

Thomas can be best described as a moderate Anglican evangelical who consciously held to the Reformation tradition. He was a responsible and widely read scholar who chose to give his life less to original research than to theology in the service of the international church. Yet he was never Calvinist enough for Benjamin *Warfield or Pentecostal enough for zealots within the Victorious Life movement or dispensationalist enough for Charles *Scofield and others with whom he agreed to cooperate. Not polemical but surprisingly irenic by nature, he saved his harder words for the extremes of Anglo-Catholic theology, and in later life for aggressive modernism. Even then he generally avoided politics, and as the fundamentalist–modernist controversy broke out in America he consistently refused to utter the shibboleths (which he blamed on 'puritanism') about historical criticism or biblical inerrancy or matters of science that were essentials for many with whom he worked. Nor did he agree to stop quoting James *Orr or P. T. *Forsyth, moderate conservatives with whom he had a deep sympathy but who did not fit the agenda of many around him. Christ as revealed in the Bible was supremely authoritative for him. But Christianity was above all 'spiritual'. He quarrelled with tight intellectual systems (for which he blamed 'rationalism'), as they elevated the fatal limitations of human logic above the limitless power of the Holy Spirit to lead Christians into the spiritual experience of divine truth.

Bibliography
M. Guthrie Clarke, *William Henry Griffith Thomas, 1861–1924: Minister, Scholar, Teacher, Great Churchman* (London: Church Book Room Press, 1949); R. Lum, 'W. H. Griffith Thomas and Emergent American Fundamentalism' (PhD thesis, Dallas Theological Seminary, 1994); W. Katerburg, 'W. H. Griffith Thomas: Anglicanism, Fundamentalism, and Modernity', in W. Katerburg,

Modernity and the Dilemma of North American Anglican Identities, 1880–1950 (Montreal, London, Ithaca: McGill–Queen's University Press, 2001); Council Minutes, Archives, Wycliffe College, Toronto.

P. H. FRIESEN

■ **THORNTON, Henry** (1760–1815), philanthropist, economist, banker and Member of Parliament, was born on 10 March 1760, the son of John Thornton, who was known as an evangelical philanthropist and one of Europe's wealthiest merchants. Surprisingly, however, Henry received a very poor private education. He began working in a counting house at the age of eighteen, joining his father's when aged twenty, and became a partner at the age of twenty-three. The following year he joined the bank of Downe, Free and Thornton. In the 1780s, however, Thornton secretly despised his evangelical father, and did not share his religious convictions. His attitude changed largely through the influence of his cousin, William *Wilberforce, whose conversion in 1785 affected his whole family.

In 1782 Thorton considered an invitation to stand for Parliament in a by-election for one of Hull's two seats (the other was held by Wilberforce) but declined when he became aware that he was expected to buy votes. Later in the same year he stood for Southwark, where he again refused the customary payment expected by voters; none the less he was elected and held the seat for the next thirty-three years.

A reputation for political independence and moral integrity earned Thornton the respect of many. He was no orator and rarely spoke in Parliament, but his sincerity, cool-headedness and shrewd financial advice on economic matters carried great weight in parliamentary committees. In 1802 he published *An Enquiry into the Nature and Effects of the Paper Credit of Great Britain*, which was praised by John Stuart Mill and established his reputation as an economist. In it he opposed Adam Smith's view that paper currency in circulation could never exceed the supply of gold and silver. Some twentieth-century economists judged Thornton to be the peer of David Ricardo, if not his master. The same year he published a pamphlet on *The Probable Effects of the Peace upon the Commercial Interests of Great Britain*. Thornton became a director and governor of the Bank of England. (His older brother, Samuel, was also an evangelical MP and governor of the Bank of England.)

Thornton projected a cold and hard exterior, but this was a cover for a warm and generous heart that led him to become the leading philanthropist of his day. His cousin and closest friend, William Wilberforce, quipped of him that 'Sweetest fruit hath the sourest rind'. Thornton was ever concerned with the systematic relief of the poor and efforts to provide them with inoculations, employment and education. A special interest of his was the education of the deaf.

Thornton was far more than a wealthy and generous philanthropist; he also provided the organizational skill that held the Clapham Sect together. (The Clapham Sect was an informal group of wealthy and powerful evangelicals best remembered for its leadership of the movement to abolish the British slave trade.) It was Thornton's estate, Battersea Rise, in the village of Clapham that was the centre of the group; it was the home of Wilberforce for five years before his marriage in 1797. Wilberforce provided the personal conviviality which inexorably drew people into his orbit; Thornton was the administrative expert, the wise counsellor and incredibly hard-working leader who laboured alongside Wilberforce to ensure that discussion led to action.

One of Thornton's earliest initiatives was his role in the founding of the Sierra Leone colony, designed to be a home for freed slaves. It was intended to be the base from which Christianity would be introduced into west Africa, the slave trade suppressed and Africa 'civilized' and educated. The intelligence behind much of the organization was Thornton's; much of the capital came from Thornton and Wilberforce. In 1791 Thornton introduced a parliamentary Bill that created the Sierra Leone Company; he then secured the financing, set out the constitution, identified a governor and arranged the provision of settlers. Throughout its existence he was the company's chairman. Eventually in 1808 he convinced the British government to take over Sierra Leone and make it a Crown, instead of a company, colony. Although the project cost him a considerable amount of money,

Thornton was convinced that the investment was a wise one. Thornton consistently supported Wilberforce's anti-slave trade measures and in 1791 suggested the formation of an African Institution, which was eventually established in 1807.

Thornton's other great causes, along with abolition, were British India and Christian missions abroad. The key influence on him regarding India was his good friend Charles Grant, who argued that the expansion of the East India Company's holdings in India was both morally wrong and politically inexpedient. However, once the conquests had been made and there was no likelihood of them being given up, Grant insisted that Britain was under a moral obligation to provide India with good government based on Christian principles. In his view, Britain was morally and politically obliged to stay in India. These views Thornton fully endorsed. He helped to design and implement the strategy for the Claphamites' campaign in 1813 to insert clauses in the charter of the East India Company that would allow Christian missionaries into India. Thornton was the first treasurer of both the Church Missionary Society (1799) and the British and Foreign Bible Society (1804). His business prospered, and until his marriage to Marianne Sykes in 1796 he gave away six-sevenths of his income; following his marriage this giving was reduced to one-third. He supported schools for the poor and especially the work of his friend, Hannah *More.

Thornton also collaborated with Hannah More in writing many of the famous *Cheap Repository Tracts*, and edited several which More wrote herself. These, along with a commentary on the Old Testament and many family prayers were published or re-published posthumously and achieved a wide readership. He deliberately left his children only modest fortunes, arguing that his example of personal frugality combined with extravagant generosity was a richer legacy.

Thornton died on 16 January 1815 at Wilberforce's house after a year of ill health; his wife died later the same year, leaving their nine children orphans. Their guardian was the family's young friend, Robert H. Inglis (later Sir Robert, MP). That at Thornton's death the term 'philanthropist' was widely regarded as synonymous with 'evangelical' was in some measure due to his example.

Bibliography

S. Meacham, *Henry Thornton of Clapham* (Cambridge, MA: Harvard University Press, 1964); R. G. Thorne, *House of Commons 1790–1834* (London: Secker and Warburg, 1986); R. I. and S. Wilberforce, *The Life of William Wilberforce*, 5 vols. (London: J. Murray, 1838); J. Pollock, *Wilberforce* (London: Constable, 1977).

D. M. LEWIS

■ **THORNWELL, James Henley** (1812–1862), southern Old School Presbyterian theologian and educator, was born to an English plantation overseer and a Calvinist Baptist mother in South Carolina. His father's death in 1825 left his family impoverished, and Thornwell's education was overseen and financed by neighbouring gentry, who were impressed with the boy's intellectual abilities. He was apprenticed to his patron William Robbins, a lawyer, but at the age of sixteen determined to study theology.

Thornwell entered South Carolina College in 1830, where he studied with the famous scientist and free-thinker, Thomas Cooper, graduating in 1831 at the top of his class. While teaching in Sumterville, he joined the Concord Presbyterian Church after becoming convinced of the truth of Presbyterian doctrine by reading the *Westminster Confession of Faith*. After becoming principal of the Cheraw Academy in 1832, he applied to the Harmony presbytery in 1833 as a ministerial candidate. While his testimony as to his personal religious experience was unsatisfactory, the presbytery believed they saw potential in him and so accepted him. In 1834 he received an offer to study at Andover Seminary, where he encountered New School theology and New England manners, both of which were distasteful to him. Harvard Divinity School, though no more to his theological taste, at least offered courses in German and Hebrew, so he took courses there before returning to South Carolina in October 1834. Upon his return he was licensed by Harmony presbytery, and the following spring was ordained by Bethel presbytery as pastor at Lancasterville.

Thornwell's preaching and pastoral labours in his three congregations were quite successful, but he was not satisfied that he himself felt the message of the gospel as well as he understood it. Late in 1835 Thornwell married Nancy Witherspoon (great-niece of John Witherspoon). They had nine children, four of whom died in childhood.

In 1837 Thornwell became professor of *belles-lettres* and logic at South Carolina College, but after three semesters he resigned to return to the pastorate, this time that of the prestigious First Presbyterian Church of Columbia. Within a year, however, he was back at the college, this time as chaplain and professor of sacred literature and the evidences of Christianity. Here he would remain from 1840 to 1851, and here he established his reputation within the Presbyterian church.

Virulently opposed to 'papism', Thornwell engaged in ongoing polemics with the Roman Catholic press, as in his *Arguments of Romanists from the Infallibility of the Church and the Testimony of the Fathers in Behalf of the Apocrypha Discussed and Refuted* (1845), and his dynamic two-hour speech against the validity of Roman Catholic baptism effectively convinced the 1845 Old School Presbyterian General Assembly to declare that such baptism was invalid. In 1847 he was elected moderator of the General Assembly at the age of thirty-four. A vigorous churchman, he regularly contributed to religious periodicals, helping to found *The Southern Presbyterian Review* in 1847.

After Thornwell accepted a call to Charleston's Glebe Street Presbyterian Church in 1851, South Carolina College offered him its presidency, which he took only after his congregation reluctantly released him. As president of the state college, Thornwell had considerable influence not only in the church but in the state as well.

Thornwell's influence at South Carolina College developed in the wake of the removal of the deist Thomas Cooper from the college presidency in 1834. Although a state school, the college became so identified with Thornwell and the Presbyterians in the public mind that whereas South Carolina Methodists, Baptists and Lutherans established their own colleges in the antebellum era, Presbyterians did not. Three of the four college presidents who followed Cooper were Presbyterians, and the one non-Presbyterian president said of Thornwell (after he had been called by a Presbyterian church in Baltimore in 1845) that he was 'the representative of the Presbyterian church, which embraces the bone and sinew of the State, without whose support the institution cannot exist'.

The triumph of Thornwell and the Presbyterians came through the growth of the churches and the success of the evangelical appropriation of Scottish common-sense realism and Baconian induction in arguing that science demonstrated the existence of God through the evidence of creation in nature. Perennially concerned to utilize reason in the defence of Christianity, Thornwell was influential in his attempt to maintain the harmony of science and religion, arguing that the 'days' of Genesis 1 could be interpreted as long epochs. In 1859 he encouraged the establishment of the Perkins professorship of natural science in connection with revelation at Columbia Seminary.

In 1855 Thornwell's desire to serve in the church led him to leave South Carolina College once again and become professor of didactic and polemic theology at Columbia Theological Seminary. While at Columbia, Thornwell briefly edited the declining *Southern Quarterly Review* from 1856 to 1857.

Sometimes known as the 'Calhoun of the church', Thornwell increasingly identified himself with the famous statesman and his genteel conservatism. The social chaos of revolutionary Europe and industrial America gradually convinced Thornwell and his peers that southern society and its 'institutions' needed to be defended from such anarchy.

Although he had been a unionist in the crises of 1830 and 1850, Thornwell argued for the secession of the whole south in 1860, and was asked by the new southern Presbyterian church to write an 'Address of the Presbyterian Church in the Confederate States of America to All the Churches of Jesus Christ Throughout the Earth' (1862), defending the formation of the PCCSA in the light of the 'Spring Resolutions' made by the 1861 Old School General Assembly, which required all Presbyterians to render obedience to the federal government. He died four months before his fiftieth birthday in August 1862, hoping for 'the victory of his new nation and the values which, for him as for many others, it cherished and symbolized to the world'. His lectures and essays found in *The Collected Writings of James Henley Thornwell* (4 vols., 1871–1873) were edited and published posthumously by his friends John B. Adger and John L. Girardeau.

Generally considered the most brilliant debater in the Presbyterian church, many of Thornwell's distinctive views became the orthodoxy of the southern Presbyterian church, such as his view that baptized infants were not subjects of church discipline until they personally professed faith. Thornwell was convinced that both the theology and the polity of the church must be drawn from Scripture alone. Therefore, he believed that lay elders had essentially the same office as ministers, and so could participate in the ordination of ministers; thus he elevated the ruling elder in Presbyterian polity. Likewise, he argued that the church could not surrender its divine missionary calling to autonomous boards or voluntary societies, and that therefore all missions must be conducted by the church. He also insisted that the church should not speak on purely social or political questions, but should enforce only scriptural duties, and since Scripture never condemns slavery, neither could the church. Scripture did, however, regulate how masters and slaves should relate to one another, so Thornwell did address that subject in such publications as *The Rights and Duties of Masters: A Sermon Preached at the Dedication of a Church Erected in Charleston, South Carolina, for the Benefit and Instruction of the Coloured Population* (1850).

Bibliography

J. O. Farmer, Jr, *The Metaphysical Confederacy: James Henley Thornwell and the Synthesis of Southern Values* (Macon: Mercer University Press, 1986); E. B. Holifield, *The Gentlemen Theologians: American Theology in Southern Culture, 1795–1860* (Durham: Duke University Press, 1978); B. M. Palmer, *The Life and Letters of James Henley Thornwell* (Richmond: Whittet & Shepperson, 1875).

P. J. WALLACE

■ **TINDLEY, Charles Albert** (185?–1933), gospel song writer and pastor, was a prominent figure in American black music history. Probably because Tindley was a legend in his time, it seems not unlikely that some of the stories of his life are apocryphal, such as the assertion that, desperate as a boy for literacy, he walked fourteen miles one night to attend a reading class. Since 1970 his life and work have received renewed attention owing to a revival of interest in the history of gospel music, but for the most part scholars must rely on the accounts of Tindley's admiring followers.

Almost certainly Tindley was born in the 1850s to slave parents, Charles and Ester Tindley, in the town of Berlin on the eastern shore of Maryland. His mother died when he was a small boy, and his father hired him out to various families in the area. His childhood was undoubtedly hard and full of labour, and he was deprived of the benefit of education, including Sunday school. Apparently, he taught himself reading and writing; as he grew into young manhood and the Civil War made it more permissible for African Americans to seek an education, it seems he was able to obtain assistance from adults. For instance, a friendly rabbi is said to have helped him to acquire some Greek and Latin (ordinary elements of secondary school and college education of the time, especially of ministerial training).

Some time in the early 1870s Tindley moved to Philadelphia, joining the early stream of migration of rural and small-town blacks to the nation's cities. In fact, he was able to join a small group of Berlin African American migrants on their way to Philadelphia. Also in the early 1870s he married Daisy Henry; they were to have eight children. His first work in Philadelphia was menial; he carried bricks and also acted as a sexton, maintaining the buildings of the John Wesley Methodist Episcopal Church. All the while his ambition for an education remained intense, and it is said that he took a correspondence course from Boston Theological Seminary. Finally, he took an examination for the Methodist ministry and is said to have achieved the second highest score. (The number of entrants is unknown.) Another possibly apocryphal story has the other ministerial candidates, somewhat envious of his impressive performance, asking him what he had to prepare himself for a career as a minister. Tindley replied, 'Nothing but a broom.'

According to the usual Methodist practice of the time, Tindley was assigned to a succession of pastorates in the New Jersey, Maryland and Delaware area. His last charge before returning to Philadelphia was at the Ezion Methodist Episcopal Church, where in 1822 Peter Spencer had published the second hymn book intended for a black congregation. (The first such book was Richard *Allen's, in 1801.) By 1900 Tindley had advanced to the office of presiding elder for the Wilmington district.

Early in the new century, probably in 1902, Tindley was called as minister to the very church that he had once served as a sexton; the call must have been especially gratifying. By all accounts he enjoyed a highly successful ministry. He began with a congregation of 130 and buildings valued at $10,000; at the end of his ministry the church had 10,000 members, and its property was valued at half a million dollars. Tindley's was an 'institutional' church, one of a number of urban churches, both white and black, that engaged not only in worship and prayer, but also in community work. It distributed food and clothing for the indigent; if it followed the example of other institutional churches, it may also have taught basic literacy. Undoubtedly it provided both instruction in the sight reading of music and the opportunity to sing or play in musical groups; members of the church wrote several notable choruses.

Tindley was particularly interested in music, though he does not appear to have received any formal education in this area. He composed his songs and carried them in his head until he found someone trained in music to write them down for him. It is not difficult to imagine the source of Tindley's interest. Black church culture was in part a musical culture, especially in Philadelphia, where sacred music concerts under church auspices had been staged since the antebellum period. Tindley formed a series of publishing companies and produced a first book of religious songs, including some of his own composition, in 1905 (*Song Echoes*) and another in 1916 (*New Songs of Paradise*). His growing reputation as a composer of gospel songs was confirmed by the 1921 publication of the widely used African American sacred song collection *Gospel Pearls*, which included six of his songs.

Because of their interest in Tindley as a composer of gospel songs, scholars have tended to underestimate his role as a minister. But apparently he was a gripping preacher, who sometimes sang his own compositions during or at the conclusion of his sermons. Standing straight and tall at 6 ft 2 in., he had an imposing presence. Whites as well as blacks flocked to his sermons, and it was said that if one did not arrive by 9.30 for the 11am service, one would not get a seat. His congregations were so big that eventually he hired sports stadiums to accommodate Easter and Christmas services. Probably the apotheosis of Tindley's ministerial career was in 1924, when a new building was erected specifically to accommodate more of those who wanted to hear him preach. The 'Tindley Temple', as the structure was called, seated 3,200.

Like most church projects, black and white, the Tindley Temple was badly affected by the economic crash in 1929. A large debt was still outstanding, and Tindley was growing old. His wife had died in 1924. There are hints that dissension began to diminish the success of the Temple. Tindley died in 1933 of blood poisoning.

Tindley has been lionized as the inventor of the gospel song: the 'grandfather of gospel' to Thomas A. *Dorsey's 'father of gospel'. Dorsey asserted in 1942 that Tindley 'originated this style of music [i.e. gospel songs], and what I wanted to do was further what Tindley started'. It may be more correct, though, to see Tindley as one of a number of composers, white and black, who used popular secular melody, narratives about becoming a Christian and staying the course, and sometimes spritely rhythm to encourage Americans in the singing of religious music and thereby fill revival halls. One could say that Tindley, like *Moody's musical collaborator Ira *Sankey, democratized church music. Where before the aspiration in many city (and certainly middle-class black) churches had been for high-toned sacred works from the pens of Bach, Handel, Mozart and a few classically trained black composers, Tindley and others (e.g. Lucie Campbell and William Henry Sherwood, who included his own songs in his publications Soothing Songs Hymnal [1891] and Harp of Zion and BYPU Hymnal [1893]) encouraged a demand for simple, singable words and tunes. Tindley also made these songs part of the black musical idiom, or perhaps it is more accurate to say that his

compositions left room for that idiom. Samuel Floyd notes in his history of black music that Tindley 'created space in his songs to accommodate the call-and-response figures and improvisations that, along with flatted thirds and sevenths ['blue notes'] and other core-culture performance practices, would come to make the style'.

Some of the best known of Tindley's forty-six published pieces are 'Stand By Me', 'We'll Understand It Better By and By' and 'What Are They Doing in Heaven Today?' He also is responsible for a version of 'We Shall Overcome', revived in the 1960s during the civil rights struggles.

Bibliography

H. C. Boyer, 'Charles Albert Tindley: Progenitor of Black-American Gospel Music', *Black Perspective in Music*, 11 (Fall 1983), pp. 103–132.

V. L. BRERETON

■ **TORRANCE, Thomas F.** (1913–), Reformed theologian, was born on 30 August 1913 in Chengdu, in the Sichuan province of western China. He was the eldest son of Thomas Torrance, a member of the Church of Scotland, and his wife Annie Elizabeth, an Anglican. His parents directed the work of the Sichuan Agency of the American Bible Society mission in Shanghai, and they lived the Christian life in an uncommonly gracious and natural way. Torrance read and memorized Scripture daily and took an active part in family prayer and worship. His parents showed him constantly that belief in the gospel ought to lead to mission and care for others.

In 1925 attacks upon foreigners and missionaries in China increased markedly, in response to the Shanghai incident of 30 May (in which British troops opened fire upon unarmed students), and by July 1926 no more than 500 out of 8,000 Protestant missionaries were left in the interior of China. The Torrance family were forced to return to Scotland in 1927. Torrance's father eventually returned to China for six years (1928–1934), leaving Annie and their six children to settle in Edinburgh so that the younger Thomas could begin studies in classics and philosophy.

Torrance's life as a student began in earnest at the University of Edinburgh (1931–1934), where he encountered A. E. Taylor (a Plato scholar) and Norman Kemp Smith (an authority on Kant and Hume). Taylor's Gifford lectures of 1930, with their emphasis upon 'the given', left a distinct and lasting impression upon the whole of Torrance's later work on critical realism in theology and science, evident in his belief that both theology and science function *a posteriori*. Taylor and Smith's enthusiasm for philosophy of science led Torrance to give serious attention to the natural world. He has one of the foremost *theological* minds in the philosophy of science; not only has he published significant works in the field; he also became a member of the Académie Internationale de Philosophie des Sciences (in 1976) and received the Templeton Prize for Progress in Religion (1978).

As an undergraduate, Torrance became increasingly dissatisfied with the account of revelation and Scripture offered to him by evangelical Christians, with whom he felt an otherwise close affinity. He was ill at ease with what he later called 'the rather rationalistic and fundamentalistic way of interpreting the Bible being advocated in Inter-Varsity Fellowship circles'. But just as Torrance was perplexed by the 'deterministic Calvinism which was then mistakenly being imported into the thinking of the Christian Union', he was also disturbed by the rationalistic liberalism of many of his university professors. He did not resolve this dilemma until he began theological studies at New College, Edinburgh.

After completing his MA in classical languages and philosophy (1934), Torrance began formal training in theology at New College. Under the supervision of H. R. Mackintosh, the leading Scottish evangelical systematic theologian of the period, Torrance encountered intellectually serious dogmatics, genuine evangelical faith and passion for Christian mission. Mackintosh's influence may be seen most clearly in Torrance's emphasis on the Nicene definition of the unity of Christ as the fully divine and incarnate Son of God, notably in his mature treatment of *homoousios*. Torrance also maintains that what is encountered in revelation is neither information about God, nor 'propositional truth', but God's being in act.

After completing the BD degree at Edinburgh, Torrance was awarded the Aitken Fellowship, which provided him with sufficient funding to conduct research at an institution of his choice. He chose to study with Karl Barth at the University of Basle in 1937–1938. His choice was wise: not only did he obtain the DTh degree at Basle (1946) and eventually publish his dissertation, *The Doctrine of Grace in the Apostolic Fathers* (1948); he also began a lifelong engagement with Karl Barth. With Geoffrey Bromiley, Torrance directed for twenty-five years the editorial and translation work of the English edition of Barth's *Kirchliche Dogmatik* (*Church Dogmatics*). Barth demonstrated the esteem in which he held Torrance by choosing him as his successor in the Chair of Dogmatics at the University of Basle. Torrance, however, regretfully turned down the post, deciding to remain as Professor of Christian Dogmatics at Edinburgh.

For two years (1950–1952), Torrance occupied the Chair of Church History at Edinburgh. On the retirement of G. T. Thompson in 1952, Torrance moved to the Chair in Christian Dogmatics (1952–1979). In the course of his teaching career and scholarly life, Torrance has published over thirty-five monographs and over 500 articles, pamphlets, ecumenical reports and edited books. His work has received numerous awards; in 1969 he was the first ever British recipient of the Collins Award, for Theological Science. His works on the philosophy of science, epistemology and the scientific nature of the dogmatic enterprise include *Space, Time and Incarnation* (1969), *God and Rationality* (1971), *Transformation and Convergence in the Frame of Knowledge* (1984) and his most advanced book in this area, *Reality and Scientific Theology* (1985). Torrance's expertise in Reformation and *Calvin studies is evident in his extensive editorial work on *Tracts and Treatises on the Reformation by John Calvin* (1958) and the twelve volumes of *Calvin's New Testament Commentaries* (1959–1973). Perhaps even more important are his *Calvin's Doctrine of Man* (1949) and *The Hermeneutics of John Calvin* (1988). His great affection for and expertise in patristic studies is ably demonstrated in *Divine Meaning: Studies in Patristic Hermeneutics* (1995). His long-standing participation in ecumenical dialogue is faithfully represented in the two-volume work *Conflict and Agreement in the Church* (1959, 1960). His most constructive dogmatic work is found in *The Mediation of Christ* (1984, 1992), *The Trinitarian Faith* (1988), *Karl Barth: Biblical and Evangelical Theologian* (1990) and *The Christian Doctrine of God* (1996).

Torrance's theological work demonstrates clearly the benefits of listening closely to the witness of Athanasius, Calvin and Barth. His long-standing commitment to a theology that is both scientific (critical) and trinitarian in form ought not to obscure the truly evangelical nature of his work. For Torrance the objectivity of God's gracious and effectual self-revelation in the divine Word, Jesus Christ, remains the hope of the world.

Bibliography

A. E. McGrath, *T. F. Torrance: An Intellectual Biography* (Edinburgh: T. & T. Clark, 1999); E. M. Colyer, *How to Read T. F. Torrance: Understanding His Trinitarian & Scientific Theology* (Downers Grove: Inter-Varsity Press, 2001).

M. HUSBANDS

■ **TORREY, Reuben Archer** (1856–1928), fundamentalist educator and evangelist, was born in Hoboken, New Jersey. His father was a prosperous manufacturer, and R. A. Torrey enjoyed a comfortable childhood, first in Brooklyn, and then on a large estate in Geneva, New York. He attended Yale University (BA, 1875) and then Yale Divinity School (BD, 1878).

After graduating from divinity school, Torrey served as minister of the Congregational Church of Garrettsville, Ohio. While there, in 1879, Torrey married Clara Belle Smith; he and Clara eventually had four children. In 1882 Torrey resigned his post; he spent the next year in theological studies at the German universities of Leipzig and Erlangen. When he returned to the United States, Torrey accepted the pastorate of the tiny Open Door Congregational Church in Minneapolis. In 1886 he organized the People's Church in downtown Minneapolis while at the same time serving as superintendent of a struggling urban mission.

In choosing Minneapolis, Torrey rejected a job offer from an established church in his home town of Brooklyn. Despite his upperclass upbringing, educational pedigree and personal struggle with religious scepticism, Torrey was committed to preaching a conservative theology to common people. An encounter with Dwight *Moody while in divinity school helped to spur him in this direction. In 1889 the famous evangelist, having heard of Torrey's successes in Minneapolis, invited him to come to Chicago to serve as the superintendent of his new Bible Institute. Not surprisingly, Torrey accepted the offer. Five years later he also assumed the pastorate of Moody's Chicago Avenue Church, an appointment which further confirmed the perception that he was the great man's heir apparent.

Torrey managed financial and curricular affairs at the Bible Institute. In keeping with Moody's vision, he wanted to provide the students with a practical education that prepared them for Christian service. In his own course on Bible doctrine, which was the centrepiece of the curriculum, Torrey taught a conservative theology while relentlessly emphasizing that students were to make use of their knowledge. As Torrey's successor, James M. *Gray, later said: 'To [Torrey], almost more than to D. L. Moody, does the Institute still owe its reputation for turning out men and women stimulated and equipped to deal face to face and heart to heart with human souls about salvation.' Torrey's influence as educator spread beyond the confines of the school he administered, as other Bible institutes deliberately strove to emulate the Chicago institution.

Given his success as superintendent, it was not surprising that, after Moody's death in 1899, Torrey was made president of the renamed Moody Bible Institute (MBI). But like his mentor, Torrey was possessed by evangelistic fervour. In 1901 he embarked on a four-year worldwide tour, in which (assisted by singer Charles M. Alexander, with whom he would later quarrel over Alexander's efforts to make money from his hymnbooks) he preached to over fifteen million people in Australia, New Zealand, Japan, China, India and finally, Great Britain, where the crusade culminated in a five-month rally in London. Then Torrey returned to North

America, where he spent much of the next six years holding revival meetings in Cleveland, San Francisco, Atlanta, Philadelphia, Toronto, Ottawa and a host of other large and medium-sized cities.

As a revivalist Torrey's style could not have been further from that of his evangelistic contemporary Billy *Sunday. Torrey was as formal as Sunday was informal; the historian William McLoughlin has observed that on the street Torrey 'usually wore a high hat, and he always talked as though he had one on'. In the pulpit, wearing a white bow-tie and starched collar, Torrey deliberately eschewed emotionalism, approaching his sermon like an attorney coolly presenting the evidence before a jury. He was also deliberately interdenominational, repeatedly and proudly telling his audiences that he was an 'Episcopresbygationalaptist!'

Torrey's evangelistic schedule kept him away from the Chicago Avenue Church and MBI for long periods of time. In 1906 he resigned his pastorate. Two years later, because the school was continuing to expand, and because of some administrative conflicts, Torrey resigned as MBI president. For the next few years he concentrated on evangelism, even returning to the British Isles in 1911. He also continued to write popular religious books, eventually publishing more than forty. But in 1912 Torrey agreed to serve as dean of the recently founded Bible Institute of Los Angeles (BIOLA). At BIOLA Torrey handled administrative duties while also teaching the Bible doctrine course, just as he had at Moody. Further duplicating his Chicago experience, in 1915 he accepted the pastorate of the Church of the Open Door, an interdenominational church connected with the school.

In his preaching and writing Torrey repeatedly emphasized what he regarded as the evils of drinking, dancing and card-playing, the importance of personal conversion and piety, the work of the Holy Spirit and, as an ardent dispensational premillennialist, the second coming of Christ. But as the twentieth century progressed, Torrey became increasingly concerned over what he saw as the rapid spread of theological modernism and evolutionism in America. For Torrey, not only were such ideas unChristian and unscientific (as he proclaimed in a 1906 revival message, 'there

is not one single instance of scientifically observed and recorded transmutation of species'), but the acceptance of such foolish notions threatened the very future of the nation. He proclaimed in his 1918 publication, *What the War Teaches*, that it was the German acceptance of these ideas that had caused the Great War, 'with its cruelty, its lust, its murder, its rape, its agony, its death, and its almost universal dissolution and hell'. If the United States was not to follow Germany's example, evolutionism and modernism had to be rooted out of American schools, seminaries and churches.

Of course, many other conservative evangelicals shared Torrey's concerns. Out of these anxieties came the fundamentalist movement. Torrey was, in effect, present at its creation. He served as editor of the final two volumes of *The Fundamentals*, the twelve-volume proclamation of conservative doctrine published between 1910 and 1915. Furthermore, in 1918 he hosted a gathering of leading Protestant conservatives at his summer home in Montrose, Pennsylvania, out of which came the World's Christian Fundamentals Association; Torrey enthusiastically supported its anti-modernist campaigns. By 1923 Torrey, in 'The Battle Within the Churches', was arguing for a radical restructuring of American Protestantism, with biblical literalism as the point of division: 'The old denominational differences have lost their significance. The [new] alignment should be along the line of whether people accept the Bible as the inerrant Word of God or not.'

But although Torrey was one of the founders of the fundamentalist movement, by the 1920s his best years were behind him, and he left primary leadership of the anti-evolutionist and anti-modernist crusades to William Bell *Riley and others. In 1924 Torrey, disturbed by BIOLA's fiscal laxity and moves towards a liberal arts curriculum, resigned his positions at the school and at the Church of the Open Door. He devoted the last years of his life to evangelistic campaigns and the Montrose Bible Conference in Pennsylvania, which he had founded in 1908. Torrey died in 1928 at his home in Asheville, North Carolina.

Reuben Torrey was one of the most important evangelicals of his generation. Author, educator, evangelist and minister, Torrey may have been most significant in his role as a transitional figure between nineteenth-century revivalism and millennarianism and twentieth-century fundamentalism.

Bibliography
G. M. Marsden, *Fundamentalism and American Culture: The Shaping of Twentieth-Century Evangelicalism, 1870–1925* (New York: Oxford University Press, 1980); R. Martin, *R. A. Torrey: Apostle of Certainty* (Murfreesboro: Sword of the Lord Publishers, 1976); W. G. McLoughlin, Jr, *Modern Revivalism: Charles Grandison Finney to Billy Graham* (New York: Ronald Press, 1959).

W. V. TROLLINGER, JR

■ **TOZER, A. W.** (1897–1963), Christian Missionary Alliance minister and author, was born on 21 April 1897 in what is now the town of Newburg in rural western Pennsylvania. The third of six children, he spent his first fifteen years in the town of his birth helping on the family farm and attending the local one-room grammar school. The family seldom attended church. What little spiritual nurture Tozer received during this period came from his paternal grandmother and his own reading. When he was ten years old, the family home was destroyed by fire, and soon afterwards his father experienced the first of several nervous breakdowns. For the next five years the young Tozer assumed most of the responsibility for the farm. Then, in 1912, the family moved to Akron, Ohio. Hoping to take advantage of his new and enlarged surroundings, Tozer, now fifteen, enrolled in the nearby high school. After just one day, however, he concluded that he could make better progress than the school curriculum allowed by following a path of independent reading and study. He set himself a course of learning, and for the next few years earned his living cutting rubber.

During this time an encounter with a Christian neighbour challenged Tozer to begin seriously thinking about the state of his soul. A year later, in 1915, the message of an old street preacher brought him to a point of spiritual decision. According to his own account, he immediately returned home, took refuge in an attic room and there called upon God's 'saving mercies in Christ'. Following his conversion, he joined Grace Methodist Episcopal Church, where he met Ada Cecelia Pfautz, whom he married on 26 April 1918. Together they raised seven children. A year before their wedding, in the home of his soon to be mother-in-law, Tozer underwent what he considered the defining moment of his Christian life, what he called 'the filling of the Holy Spirit'. '[I]n faith', he recalled, 'I took a leap away from everything that was unimportant to that which was most important: to be possessed by the Holy Spirit of the living God ... Any tiny work that God has ever done through me and through my ministry for Him dates back to that hour when I was filled with the Spirit' (*In Pursuit of God*, p. 44).

Preaching was Tozer's choice of ministry from the beginning, and he first engaged in it on the streets of Akron. But his church discouraged him because of his lack of formal college and seminary education. He soon found acceptance, however, with a group of street evangelists from the nearby Christian and Missionary Alliance church, whose pastor not only encouraged his preaching, but also opened his library to him and his own pulpit on occasion. Tozer's preaching caught the attention of the area superintendent of CMA churches, and in 1919 he recommended Tozer to an Alliance church in West Virginia. Tozer accepted the charge and was ordained by the CMA the following year. After serving two churches in West Virginia, he took a pastorate in Toledo, Ohio, where he ministered until 1924. In December of that year he received a call from an influential Alliance church in Indianapolis, Indiana.

The move to Indianapolis proved a turning-point in Tozer's ministry. Until this time, his congregations had been small and his preaching had been primarily evangelistic. The congregation at Indianapolis, however, was different in several important ways. It was significantly larger and more educated than Tozer's previous churches, and the congregation expected pastoral rather than evangelistic preaching. The shift in emphasis in his preaching necessitated a new and intense focus in his reading and study. It was not unusual to see the young minister carrying an armload of books to and from the public library on a weekly basis.

After four years of successful ministry in Indianapolis, Tozer accepted an invitation to become the pastor of Chicago's Southside Gospel Tabernacle (later named the Southside Alliance Church), on the condition that he would not be required to do visitation, but could spend every day in study, prayer and meditation in preparation of his sermons. During the four years at Indianapolis he had become convinced that God had specifically called him to the ministry of preaching and to teaching. Although unusual, Tozer's conditions were accepted, and he remained in Chicago for the next thirty-one years. From 1946 to 1950 he also served as vice-president of the Christian and Missionary Alliance, and in 1950 he became the editor of the *Alliance Magazine*, a position he maintained, apart from two years, until his death. He also hosted a popular morning radio programme entitled 'Talks from a Pastor's Study' and broadcast by WMBI, the radio station of Moody Bible Institute. In 1959 he moved to Toronto to become the preaching minister of the Avenue Road Alliance Church, where he remained until his death in 1963.

Today, Tozer is best known for his books. He published nine during his lifetime (seven during his years in Chicago and three while in Toronto), and nearly thirty additional books, drawn from various editorials and tape recordings of sermons, have been published since his death. Most prominent among them are his seasoned spiritual discourse, *The Pursuit of God* (1948), and his study on the attributes of God, *The Knowledge of the Holy* (1961). But successful and influential as his published work has been, Tozer was by calling and conviction primarily a preacher and teacher. The majority of his books consist of revised sermons, and the greater part of his days and nights, and his prayers, readings and meditations, were given to sermon preparation. The themes of the person and work of the Holy Spirit, purity of heart, the indwelling Christ and the importance of worship dominated his preaching. Tozer believed that the expository preaching of God's word was an imperative for the church, but he also believed that expository preaching alone did not guarantee that what was preached would be spiritually nourishing. '[I]t is not mere words that nourish the soul', he states in the preface to *The Pursuit of God*, 'but God Himself, and unless and until the hearers find God in personal experience they are not the

better for having heard the truth.' He never tired of warning against what he perceived to be a prevailing emphasis within evanglicalism on fundamentals and rightness of doctrine to the neglect of the power of the Holy Spirit. This prophetic and somewhat mystical streak put him out of step with many mainstream evangelical groups. He had, for example, little sympathy for the National Association of Evangelicals and succeeded in dissuading the Alliance from joining the Association during his lifetime.

Tozer's Christian life was characterized by intense discipline and deep devotion and was indelibly marked by the mystics Fénelon, Bernard of Clairvaux and Julian of Norwich among others. His last book was a collection of poetry entitled *The Christian Book of Mystical Verse* (1963). Near the end of his life, Tozer stated, 'I have found God cordial and generous and in every way easy to live with' (*Twentieth Century Prophet*, p. 15). Tozer died on Sunday 12 May 1963 at the age of sixty-six. The epitaph inscribed on his gravestone reads, 'A Man of God'.

Bibliography

D. J. Fant, *A. W. Tozer: A Twentieth Century Prophet* (Harrisburg: Christian Publications, 1964); J. L. Snyder, *In the Pursuit of God: The Life of A. W. Tozer* (Camp Hill: Christian Publications, 1991).

C. W. MITCHELL

■ **TYNDALE, William** (c. 1494–1536), Bible translator, was born in the early 1490s, somewhere around the town of Dursley near the river Severn. The Tyndales (who also called themselves Hutchins) were an important family in the west of Gloucestershire. William, together with at least two brothers, came from a lesser branch of the family. He went as a student to Magdalen Hall, Oxford, which was later incorporated into Hertford College. There he gained his Bachelor of Arts (1512) and his Master of Arts (1515). Exactly where Tyndale spent the second half of that decade is not certain, but the tradition points to further studies at Oxford and some time spent at Cambridge University. Cambridge was rife with Lutheran ideas around the early 1520s, and it is possible that Tyndale acquired his Protestant convictions while studying there. At a later date he expressed his dissatisfaction with the teaching of theology at the universities: 'In the universities they have ordained that no man shall look on the Scripture until he be noselled in heathen learning eight or nine years, and armed with false principles with which he is clean shut out of the understanding of the Scripture.'

In 1521 Tyndale left the university world to join the household of Sir John Walsh at Little Sodbury Manor, north of Bath. It is not certain what role Tyndale played in the household, but he may have been the chaplain (he was ordained at some point) or a tutor to the children or a secretary to Sir John. While at the house, he made an English translation of Erasmus's *Enchiridion*. Many of the local clergy came to dine at the manor. Their visits gave Tyndale the opportunity both to be shocked by their ignorance of the Bible and to become embroiled in controversy with them. One such cleric declared that 'We were better to be without God's laws than the pope's', to which Tyndale responded: 'If God spare my life, ere many years pass, I will cause a boy that driveth the plough shall know more of the Scriptures than thou dost.' Here Tyndale was echoing Erasmus's famous wish in the preface to his Greek New Testament: 'I would to God that the ploughman would sing a text of the Scripture at his plough and that the weaver would hum them to the tune of his shuttle.' Tyndale had 'perceived by experience how that it was impossible to establish the lay people in any truth, except the scripture were plainly laid before their eyes in their mother tongue, that they might see the process, order, and meaning of the text'.

Tyndale had felt the call to translate the Bible into English. At this time the only English translation available was the Wyclif Bible, which was distributed clandestinely by the Lollards, the followers of John *Wyclif. But this had never been printed. Furthermore, it was inaccurate in many ways, having been translated from the Latin Vulgate edition rather than the original Greek and Hebrew. Because of the Lollard threat, the church had in 1408 banned the unauthorized translation of the Bible into English. So Tyndale left Little Sodbury Manor in search of ecclesiastical approval for his projected translation. In 1523 he went to London and obtained an interview with the bishop of London, Cuthbert Tunstall. This was a shrewd choice as Tunstall was a scholarly man and a friend of Erasmus. But Tunstall was more concerned to prevent the growth of Lutheranism than to promote the English Bible, and Tyndale received no encouragement from him.

Tyndale stayed on in London for a year, where he received financial support from a wealthy cloth merchant by the name of Humphrey Monmouth. He preached there a number of times at St Dunstan's in the West, one of the City churches. By the end of the year he 'understood at the last not only that there was no room in my lord of London's palace to translate the new testament, but also that there was no place to do it in all England'. With the backing of Monmouth and other merchants, Tyndale resolved to leave the country in order to engage in the work of translation. So in 1524 he sailed for Germany, never to return. It appears that he first went to Wittenberg to study. Contemporaries such as Thomas More refer to his time there. There is also an entry in the matriculation register for 27 May 1524 reading 'Guillelmus Daltici Ex Anglia'. If the final 'ci' is a copyist's error for 'n' we have an anagram of 'Tindal' with the two syllables reversed.

In Germany Tyndale worked on the New Testament translation, which was complete by 1525. It was entrusted to the printer Peter Quentell at Cologne, and the pages began to roll off the press. But one of the print workers spoke too freely over his wine, and news of the project came to the ears of Johann Dobneck, alias Cochlaeus, a leading opponent of the Reformation. He arranged a raid on the press, but Tyndale had been warned and had fled with the pages so far printed. Only one incomplete copy of this edition survives, extending as far as Matthew 22, though according to Cochlaeus the printers had reached as far as Mark. This printing reveals Tyndale's considerable dependence upon *Luther. The order of the books as seen by the contents page, the woodcuts used, the prologue and the marginal notes are all heavily influenced by Luther's 1522 New Testament to the extent of substantial borrowing of material in some places.

Tyndale moved with his assistant, the ex-friar William Roye, to Worms, a more sympathetic environment, where the first complete New Testament was printed in 1526 by Peter Schoeffer. This edition contained no prologues or notes, either to hasten production or to avoid possible obstacles to its favourable reception in England. Of the three or six thousand copies printed, only two have survived. There is a simple reason why so few copies of Tyndale's early editions survive. They were smuggled into England and the bishops did all they could to eradicate them. In 1526 none other than Cuthbert Tunstall preached against the translation, claiming to have discovered 2,000 errors in it, and had copies ceremoniously burnt at St Paul's. The following year the archbishop of Canterbury was buying up copies in order to have them burnt. An amusing story is told of how a little later Tunstall was in Antwerp and an English merchant called Augustine Packington offered to buy up for him the stock of New Testaments so that they could be burnt. The bishop gave Packington the money, which he passed on to Tyndale to finance the next revised edition. 'And so forward went the bargain, the bishop had the books, Packington had the thanks, and Tyndale had the money.' The result was a renewed flood of imported Testaments, and Tunstall realized that he had been outwitted.

At some stage after the 1526 printing of the New Testament Tyndale moved to Antwerp, one of the main European centres of printing, where there was a sizeable community of English merchants, who paid him a regular stipend. From 1528 all of his works were published there. It was there in 1530 that his translation of the Pentateuch, made with the help of Miles Coverdale, was printed. The following year saw the publication of his translation of Jonah. No more of the Old Testament was published by Tyndale, but there is strong evidence that the translation of the historical books (Joshua to 2 Chronicles) in the 1537 *Matthew's Bible* was Tyndale's, the rest of the Old Testament being Coverdale's translation. There were also a number of further editions of the New Testament. Tyndale continually revised the translation, in the light of suggestions received and of his own further thoughts. Some, but not all, of the editions contained marginal notes. The purpose of these was mainly to explain the meaning of the text, but at times Tyndale could not resist the temptation to apply the text against the papacy.

Tyndale translated directly from the Greek and Hebrew, with occasional reference to the Latin Vulgate and Luther's German translation. His style is homely and intended for the ordinary person, in keeping with his original aim to make the Bible widely known. In the following extract from the 1526 edition (Romans 12:1–2) the original spelling has been retained:

'I beseeche you therfore brethren by the mercifulness of God, that ye make youre bodyes a quicke sacrifise, holy and acceptable unto God which is youre resonable servynge off God. And fassion note youre selves lyke unto this worlde. But be ye chaunged [in youre shape] by the renuynge of youre wittes that ye may fele what thynge that good, that acceptable and perfaicte will of god is.'

Tyndale also wrote prologues to each book of the Bible, some based on Luther's. These were important for introducing the theology of the Reformation to their readers.

Tyndale planned to complete the translation of the Old Testament, but this was not to be. In 1535 he was living with Thomas Poyntz, a relative of Lady Walsh of Little Sodbury, and his wife. His influential hosts afforded him a certain measure of protection, but this proved to be inadequate. In May of that year he was betrayed by a fellow Englishman, Henry Phillips, who induced Tyndale to venture onto the streets of Antwerp, where he was ambushed and seized while walking down a narrow passage. He was taken to the state prison in the castle of Vilvorde, near Brussels. After more than a year of confinement, Tyndale was put on trial in August 1536 and condemned as a heretic; then he was formally defrocked and excommunicated. His execution was deferred for another two months. Early in October (traditionally on the 6th), having refused to recant, he was strangled and then burnt at the stake in Brussels. His last words were reported to be 'Lord, open the king of England's eyes.'

Tyndale's translation was banned in England and destroyed when it was found. But its influence was considerable, even in the reign of Henry VIII, which remained a difficult time for Protestants. In 1535 Miles Coverdale produced the first ever complete printed edition of the Bible in English. For diplomatic reasons, Tyndale was not named, but the translation was heavily dependent upon his. By this time there was an archbishop of Canterbury (Thomas *Cranmer) and a vicar-general (Thomas Cromwell) who were both committed to the Protestant cause. They persuaded Henry to approve the publication of the Coverdale translation. By 1539 every parish church in England was required to make a copy of the English Bible available to all of its parishioners. All of the available translations were substantially based upon Tyndale's. Thus, although Tyndale had not been personally rehabilitated, his cause had triumphed, as had the substance of his translation. Tyndale can justly be called 'the father of the English Bible'. It would not be much of an exaggeration to say that almost every English New Testament until recently was merely a revision of Tyndale's. Some 90% of his words passed into the King James Version and about 75% into the Revised Standard Version.

Tyndale is famous as a Bible translator, but translation was not his only work. He wrote a number of books, including expositions of 1 John (1531) and the sermon on the mount (1533). He also published a number of other works. The Parable of Wicked Mammon (1528) is on the theme of justification by faith alone, though with an Augustinian emphasis on faith bringing about a moral renewal leading to good works. It was heavily dependent upon Luther's Sermon von dem unrechten Mammon, and in places Tyndale simply translated Luther. In this work Tyndale identifies the papacy with the Antichrist. The Obedience of a Christian Man (1528) is Tyndale's most influential treatise, in which he argues for obedience to civil authority, except where loyalty to God is concerned. It is reported that Henry VIII read parts of this work and was delighted with it, especially its subordination of the church to royal authority. Henry was less delighted with Tyndale's strong rejection of divorce in his The Practice of Prelates (1530), the original subtitle of which was Whether the Kynges grace maye be separated from hys quene, because she was his brothers wyfe. Here he chronicles the relations between the crown and the papacy and presents an unfavourable portrait of the king. This book served to turn Henry against Tyndale. In 1530 Tyndale published an expanded version of the preface to his first, incomplete New Testament, entitled A Pathway into the Holy Scripture.

After Tyndale's death A Brief Declaration of the Sacraments was found amongst his papers; it was published in about 1548. In this he argues for a Reformed rather than Lutheran view of Christ's presence in the Lord's Supper.

Tyndale is also famous for his literary battle with Thomas More. In 1529 More attacked 'the captain of English heretics' in his Dialogue Concerning Heresies. Two years later Tyndale replied with an Answer to Sir Thomas More's Dialogue. More responded with a lengthy and tedious Confutation in two volumes (1532, 1533). The two men were unable to agree, because of their different starting points. For More, the true church is the historic Catholic Church, in communion with Rome, which is infallible. Whoever opposes the teaching of this church is a heretic. It was because of this belief that More had many 'heretics' burnt at the stake, and it was because of this belief that More was himself prepared to go to the scaffold. For Tyndale, on the other hand, the true faith is to be found in Scripture and any church that denies it is under the control of the Antichrist.

What were the influences upon Tyndale? Undoubtedly, he was influenced by Renaissance humanism. The very concern to translate the Bible from the original languages revealed this influence, as did his use of the latest tools of scholarship to aid him in the task. Tyndale based his translation of the New Testament primarily on Erasmus's Greek edition with its new Latin translation (1516). Clearly Tyndale was also influenced by the Reformers in general and by Luther in particular. In his first (incomplete) edition of the New Testament and in some of his other writings this influence extends to wholesale copying of material from Luther. But Tyndale was an independent thinker, not just a disciple of Luther. He differed from Luther at a number of key points, such as his view of covenant, his view that the Law imposes a permanent obligation on the Christian and his rejection of Luther's doctrine of the 'real presence'. Hardest of all to measure is the influence upon Tyndale of Wyclif and the Lollards. Both laid a heavy stress on reading the Bible in English and both arrived at a negative assessment of the Church of Rome in the light of those Scriptures.

Bibliography

D. Daniell, *William Tyndale: A Biography* (New Haven & London: Yale University Press, 1994); J. F. Mozley, *William Tyndale* (London: SPCK; New York: Macmillan, 1937); C. H. Williams, *William Tyndale* (London: Nelson, 1969).

A. N. S. LANE

■ **VAN DER KEMP, Johannes** (1747–1811), missionary and physician, was born on 7 May 1747 in Rotterdam, Holland. He was most famous for his work as a missionary for the Congregationalist London Missionary Society (LMS) in South Africa, but was a man of many gifts. Van der Kemp's work in South Africa brought him into conflict with the white population, and he remained a subject of controversy after his death, being seen variously as an early liberal, a misguided sentimentalist or a tool of imperialism.

Johannes Van der Kemp was educated at Dordrecht and then the University of Leyden, where he studied medicine, philosophy and theology but left without gaining a degree. He joined the Dragoon Guards and was rapidly promoted to the rank of captain. During this time Van der Kemp formally joined the Dutch Reformed Church, but it meant little to him, and his life was characterized by a series of affairs. In 1773 his then mistress bore him a daughter.

Van der Kemp was already characterized by a 'proud humility', which was evident throughout his life. In 1780 he defied convention by marrying Christina Helena Frank, who was considered to be beneath him, and the resulting opposition from his fellow officers led him to resign his commission. He then moved to Edinburgh, where he completed his medical training, qualifying as MD in 1782. By this stage, his thinking had taken him towards deism, although he did not publicly disavow Christianity.

In the same year, Van der Kemp returned to Holland to work as a doctor. In 1791 came the turning-point of his life, the death of his wife and daughter in a boating accident. In his grief, Van der Kemp came to accept the deity of Christ and the Reformed faith. He was involved as a medical officer in defending Holland in its war with revolutionary France. In 1795 he felt strongly called to missionary work after hearing of the formation of the LMS.

In 1797 Van der Kemp was ordained by the Scottish Presbyterian Church in London, although the Presbyterian character of his ministry had no particular significance. He founded a missionary society (the Nederlandshe Zendinggenootschap) and set out for the Cape, reaching it on 31 March 1799. One of the first LMS missionaries in South Africa, he founded 'The South African Society for Promoting the Spread of Christ's Kingdom' whilst at the Cape and then set out for the eastern frontier of the colony. This was in a highly confused state; there was much fighting. His initial companions proved unable to face the strain, but in 1801 he was joined by A. A. Vaderlingen and James Read. In 1801 Van der Kemp founded a settlement for the Khoisan population, first at Graaf Reinet, then from 1802 at Botha's Place, where it acted as a refuge from settler violence. Due to widespread violence in 1803 he again moved the settlement, to Bethelsdorp, an area with poor land, but well situated for military protection from the government. There he again offered refuge to labourers from settler demands and refused to let the residents become serfs. His shifting mission station was the first LMS institution in South Africa.

In 1805 the Batavian government tried to restrict Van der Kemp's work by banning him from teaching Khoisan to write and then forced him to come to Cape Town. The new British government allowed him to return to Bethelsdorp in 1806, when he remarried, to a black woman named Sara whom he had redeemed from slavery and with whom he had four children, scandalizing the white community. Thereafter Van der Kemp found himself in frequent conflict with both government and colonists. He attempted to sway opinion in London in order to prevent the worst abuses, but failed to prevent the passage of new laws in 1809 to restrict Khoisan freedoms. After Van der Kemp's death the government agreed to a 'Black Circuit' (1812) to examine his charges, but this sided mostly with the settlers. In 1811 he returned to Cape Town, hoping to start a mission in Madagascar. This did not materialize, but during this time he was made superintendent of LMS missions in South Africa. He suffered deep depression shortly before his death in Cape Town on 15 December 1811.

In a number of respects Van der Kemp was deeply influenced by Enlightenment Europe. His conversion involved acceptance of the Reformed faith, but it also made him wary of reason and gave him a preference for feeling and a strongly egalitarian disposition. In the Cape this disposition was expressed in his opposition to slavery and readiness to adapt to black culture. In particular, Van der Kemp was an excellent linguist, who began the process of translation of Christian literature into Xhosa and Khoi. His 'Specimen of ye Kaffra Language' in *Transactions of the Missionary Society* (London, 1803) is one of the earliest studies of Bantu languages. The regime at Bethelsdorp was a quasi-Benedictine mix of work and prayer. Communion was central to the life of the settlement. Van der Kemp shared Khoisan lifestyle to a degree unthinkable to many later missionaries and readily encouraged black preachers and evangelists. His beliefs seeped into the mentality of the region. Thus his emphasis on the second coming may have informed the later Kat River Rebellion of 1851 and Xhosa cattle killing of 1857.

To Van der Kemp the nominal Christian was more evil than a non-Christian. Fortified by belief in the imminence of the second coming, he spoke of how he 'loathed civilised society'. Van der Kemp's views led him to a form of early liberation theology. When protesting against the Batavian governor Janssens over the treatment of the Khoisan, he argued that if the government 'should acquiesce in the misdeeds against the guiltless, then should the cry to heaven of the oppressed bring their deliverance and therewith the frustration of the governor's plans'.

Van der Kemp's work in South Africa was intertwined with the expansion of European colonialism. His work with black people has been seen as a palliative for colonialism, and Bethelsdorp undoubtedly helped Khoisan to adapt to the new economic order. But colonist violence existed before his arrival, and by his actions he questioned and partially checked it. In his concern for the humanity and culture of those he sought to evangelize he was ahead of many who followed him. By his bridging of black and colonial cultures he offered colonized peoples a new way of life as the former ways disappeared.

Van der Kemp represented an early generation of missionaries: strident in theology, socially ambiguous in status, egalitarian in sympathies and semi-detached from their sending societies. They worked in turbulent times, mixing evangelistic zeal with social action more easily than did missionaries of the mid- and late-nineteenth century. Van der Kemp was a champion of the rights of black people, but promoted some aspects of colonialism at the same time.

Bibliography

E. Elbourne, 'Concerning Missionaries: the Case of Van der Kemp', *Journal of Southern African Studies*, 17, 1 (1991); I. H. Enklaar, *Life and Work of Dr J. Th. Van der Kemp, 1747–1811: Missionary Pioneer and Protagonist of Racial Equality in South Africa* (Cape Town and Rotterdam: A. A. Balkema, 1988).

D. J. GOODHEW

■ **VAN TIL, Cornelius** (1895–1987), Reformed theologian and apologist, was born in Grootegast, Holland. At the age of ten, he moved with his family to Highland, Indiana. The Van Tils were members of the Christian Reformed Church, and Cornelius attended institutions associated with that denomination: the Calvin Preparatory School, Calvin College and (for one year) Calvin Theological Seminary, all in Grand Rapids, Michigan. He transferred to Princeton Theological Seminary to complete his theological education and earned his ThM there in 1925. Simultaneously, he studied philosophy at Princeton University and completed his PhD in 1927. His dissertation, supervised by Archibald Allan Bowman, entitled 'God and the Absolute', compared Reformed theology's view of God with the absolute of philosophical idealism. In September 1925 Van Til married Rena Klooster. The Van Tils had one son, Earl. Rena died in 1978.

Van Til pastored a Christian Reformed church in Spring Lake, Michigan, taking a leave of absence to teach apologetics at Princeton Seminary during the academic year 1928–1929. The seminary offered him the chair of apologetics at the end of that period, but he turned down the offer and returned to Spring Lake. He was strongly inclined to remain in the pastorate, and he did not want to cooperate in the reorganization of the seminary authorized that spring by the General Assembly of the Presbyterian Church, USA. He believed that reorganization would purge the seminary of its historic stand for orthodox Calvinism and make it more representative of liberal theological viewpoints in the church. Those viewpoints included that of the Auburn Affirmation of 1924, in which 1,300 ministers declared that such doctrines as biblical infallibility, the virgin birth of Christ, his substitutionary atonement, his bodily resurrection and his literal second coming were humanly formulated 'theories' and not to be required of ministerial candidates.

Other members of the Princeton faculty also opposed the reorganization. Chief among these was J. Gresham *Machen, author of *Christianity and Liberalism* (Grand Rapids: Eerdmans, 1923), who left Princeton Seminary with others to found, in 1929, Westminster Theological Seminary in Philadelphia, an institution devoted to Presbyterian doctrine, but independent of denominational control. Van Til reluctantly left his pastorate to join the new seminary. He taught apologetics and systematic theology at Westminster until his retirement in 1972, and continued to teach occasionally until 1979.

In 1936 Machen was suspended from the ministry of the Presbyterian Church, USA for his founding and support of a nondenominational, theologically conservative mission agency. He then founded, with others, a new denomination, originally called the Presbyterian Church of America, later the Orthodox Presbyterian Church. In sympathy with Machen, Van Til transferred his ministerial membership from the Christian Reformed Church to the new denomination, where he remained for the rest of his life.

Major influences on Van Til's thought were the Dutch Reformed theologians, particularly Abraham *Kuyper (who emphasized that Christ is Lord of all areas of human life) and the dogmatician Herman *Bavinck. Kuyper and Bavinck disparaged apologetics because they believed that it tended to put human reason above Scripture. Van Til's teachers

at Princeton, however, emphasized that Christianity has nothing to fear from rational scrutiny and is fully capable of rational defence. Van Til sought to do justice to both these insights, by developing an approach to apologetics that was rational, but based on a biblical concept of rationality.

Van Til's studies of philosophical idealism, first under Henry Jellema at Calvin and later under A. A. Bowman, and his interaction with writings of the British apologist James *Orr convinced him that all human thought is governed by *presuppositions*. (Hence Van Til is sometimes called a 'presuppositionalist', though he was not enthusiastic about that label.) Presuppositions, he believed, cannot be proved by usual methods, since they serve as the basis of all proof. But they can be proved 'transcendentally', by showing that they are necessary for all rational thought and must be true if there is to be any meaning or order in the world. Van Til sought to reconstruct Christian apologetics so that it would establish the Christian God as the presupposition of thought, rather than one rational conclusion among many.

Van Til disparaged the 'traditional method' of establishing the truth of Christianity by theistic proofs and historical evidences, because he believed that this tradition began with data considered intelligible apart from God and then proved God's existence from them. On the contrary, he argued, if we concede that anything is intelligible apart from the God of Scripture, we have lost the battle at the outset. So we should, rather, use a transcendental method, showing that the various forms of non-Christian thought ('would-be autonomous reasoning', as he put it) reduce to meaninglessness, that they can account for precisely nothing, and that the Christian world and life view can make sense of everything.

It is the doctrine of the Trinity, Van Til argued, that provides the ultimate answer to the 'problem of the one and the many', the problem of how we can distinguish one thing from another, though we can identify them only by general properties. It is the doctrine of God's sovereign, eternal plan that guarantees that the world is an intelligible whole. It is the doctrine of revelation that guarantees we can have true knowledge of God and his creation. There are mysteries in the Christian faith, but these are to be expected once we renounce the self-sufficiency of human reason and trust God on the basis of his Word. The creator–creature distinction, Van Til argued, is the key to metaphysics, epistemology and ethics.

Van Til was thought by some critics to have left no room for the use of evidence in apologetics, but he rejected this criticism: evidence is useful when used within a transcendental argument based on biblical presuppositions. But is this not, critics persisted, a circular argument, to prove Christianity on the basis of Christian presuppositions? Yes, said Van Til, it is circular in a sense. But, he argues, every system of thought is circular when arguing for its most fundamental presuppositions (e.g. a rationalist can defend the authority of reason only by using reason), and the Christian circle is the only one that renders reality intelligible on its own terms.

Non-Christian thought, Van Til argues, collapses into meaninglessness, because of the noetic effects of sin. The unbeliever knows God (Romans 1:18–21) but suppresses the truth (1:18, 21–32). Therefore, there is an 'antithesis' between Christian and unbelieving thought, between the wisdom of God and the wisdom of the world. Although unbelievers know and state truth on occasion, they do so only by being inconsistent with respect to their presuppositions and by relying (contrary to their intention) on the Christian world-view. The unbeliever knows truth as 'borrowed capital'.

Van Til's publications exceeded 300, including nearly forty books. Among the most important are *Christian Apologetics* (1975), *The Defense of Christianity and My Credo* (1971) and *The Defense of the Faith* (1955, ²1963). Most of Van Til's writings, plus many audio lectures and sermons, can be found on the CD-ROM, *The Works of Cornelius Van Til* (published by Labels Army Co., available from P & R Publishers). On that CD, and also available separately, is the most complete bibliography of Van Til's works, *A Guide to the Writings of Cornelius Van Til, 1895–1987*, by Eric D. Bristley.

Bibliography

G. L. Bahnsen, *Van Til's Apologetic: Readings and Analysis* (Phillipsburg: Presbyterian & Reformed Publishing Co., 1998); J. M. Frame, *Cornelius Van Til: An Analysis of His Thought* (Phillipsburg: Presbyterian & Reformed Publishing Co., 1995); W. White, *Van Til – Defender of the Faith* (Nashville and New York: Thomas Nelson, 1979).

J. M. FRAME

■ **VARLEY, Henry** (1835–1912), evangelist, was born in Tattershall, Lincolnshire, his father a brewer and his mother an evangelical schoolmistress. In 1846 he moved to London and found work as an apprentice butcher. Not long after arriving in London he attended a Bible class at Baptist *Noel's Chapel in John Street, Bedford Row. He was converted in 1851 under Noel's preaching, joined the church, and was baptized by Noel the following year. In 1854 he sailed for the gold rush colony of Victoria, Australia, to seek his fortune. He was not successful on the goldfields but prospered as a butcher in Geelong. In 1857 he returned to London to marry his childhood sweetheart, Sarah Pickworth, and set up in business as a butcher. He prospered and won a reputation for integrity. However, it was not long before he was involved in full-time ministry. He tentatively began with a mission to pig feeders at Notting Hill. Only twelve adults and a few children attended the first service he led. It was a small beginning in a not very encouraging environment, but the work flourished to the extent that a church, the Free Tabernacle, was founded and Varley became its minister.

A natural restlessness led Varley increasingly to devote his time to itinerant evangelism throughout Britain. His reputation grew, and in the 1870s he enjoyed successful campaigns in the United States and Canada. In 1877 he was invited to Melbourne by the evangelical leadership there, and he spent two years doing evangelistic work in the city and colony, and the neighbouring colonies, before returning to England, where his wife was providing the leadership at the Free Tabernacle.

In 1888 he returned again to Melbourne, where most of his children were to settle. Melbourne was to be his base as he continued his itinerancy in the Australian colonies, though four of the years in which he called Melbourne 'home' were spent overseas, including visits to the west coast of the United States and England. In 1896 he returned to England, and remained busy in his last years, which included a brief final visit to Melbourne in 1904–1905. He died of asthma, a lifelong disability, in 1912 in Brighton, England. His friend F. B. *Meyer named him as one of the great evangelists of the Victorian era.

Varley's theology and spirituality were standard fare for most evangelists of his time: individualistic and subjective, populist and rather narrow, dismissive of scholarship, shaped by the Deeper Life movement and with an emphasis on prayer.

According to Meyer, 'He had a fine presence, a melodious and powerful voice, a copious vocabulary, and at times a terrific intensity into which he flung the full strength of his manhood.' He was sometimes called 'the second *Spurgeon'; and like his friend Spurgeon he was most successful among the lower middle and artisan classes. His style was appropriate to his background and revivalist aims; he was outspoken (a 'fearless denouncer of evil'), uncompromising, powerful and clear. In his preaching he focused on the need for individual conversion and expressed himself forcefully on the social evils of the day, though without addressing the problem of systemic evil or the need for social righteousness. A ready pen supplemented his preaching; he wrote a large number of pamphlets and booklets, some of them quite lengthy. The content of his preaching and writing style was significantly influenced by a polemical streak, which drew pungent criticism from the secular press.

Though usually regarded as one of the Brethren, he eschewed church affiliation, his independence masking a barely concealed separatism, like Spurgeon's but unlike that of his American friend and peer, the warmhearted, irenic D. L. *Moody. This separatism limited his lasting impact on Melbourne. For all his ability and energy he never managed to establish a hold on the imagination of the Melbourne evangelical leadership. His failure was due partly to his itinerancy, but mostly to the confidence of the local evangelicals in their own identity, their own ability and their denominational loyalties; the populist Varley could never dominate them. With his militantly conservative theology and ecclesiology Varley, again like Spurgeon, may be thought of as a proto-fundamentalist, displaying those features that characterized post-1920s fundamentalism.

In his time Varley was well known, but his influence and contribution were ephemeral; he did not leave anything tangible to perpetuate his contribution and memory. He did not found a denomination as did *Wesley, nor a church and college as did Spurgeon and Moody, nor an organization as did *Booth. In England his son Henry became a prominent Baptist minister; in Melbourne his son Frank was a well-known evangelist in the forthright and uncompromising mould of his father, and his other sons were an important part of the evangelical network.

Bibliography

D. Paproth, 'Henry Varley and the Melbourne Evangelicals', *Journal of Religious History* (June 2001); 'Henry Varley Down Under', parts 1 and 2, *Lucas: An Evangelical History Review*, 2001 and 2002; H. Varley Jr, *Henry Varley's Life Story* (London: Alfred Holness, n.d.).

D. PAPROTH

■ **VENN, Henry** (1796–1873), Anglican clergyman and missionary statesman, was born at Clapham, near London, on 10 February 1796, the son of John Venn, the rector of Clapham. He was educated at Queens' College, Cambridge, where he matriculated in 1814 and graduated BA in 1819, MA in 1821 and BD in 1828. He was ordained deacon in 1819 by the bishop of Ely and priest in 1820 by the bishop of Norwich. Venn served a curacy at St Dunstan's in the West in London between 1821 and 1824 and then returned to Queens', where he had been elected to a fellowship in 1819. He also served a term as a university proctor in 1825. In 1827 Venn was appointed by his father's friend William *Wilberforce to the curacy of Drypool on the outskirts of Hull. In 1829 he married Martha, the daughter of Nicholas Sykes of Hull, whose large marriage settlement provided the couple with lifetime financial security. He remained at Drypool for a further five years and took all the measures that might have been expected of an active evangelical parish priest. He appears to have given particular emphasis to a ministry among young adults, and already by 1829 he had 160 individuals in his confirmation class. In 1834 Venn was appointed by Daniel

*Wilson, the vicar of Islington, to the curacy of St John's Holloway, where he remained for a further twelve years. He was appointed to an honorary prebend of St Paul's Cathedral in 1846.

In 1840 Martha Venn died, and the following year Henry accepted a temporary part-time position as honorary clerical secretary of the Church Missionary Society (CMS). In 1846 Venn decided to devote himself full-time to the CMS, and he remained as its secretary for a further twenty-six years until 1872.

As secretary, Venn had considerable advantages. He was not only the son of one of the founders and original committee members of CMS, but he also possessed great skills in committee work, supported by a commitment to meticulous preparation and a formidable command of detail. Consequently, although he was never constitutionally at the head of the society, he rapidly became its effective leader. In the middle years of the nineteenth century, CMS faced three major groups of issues: the question of finance, the relationship between the society and the structures of the Church of England and the future shape of missions and their relations with local Christian communities.

Venn's assumption of the position of secretary coincided with a period of financial crisis for CMS. The society found itself, for the first time, with an income insufficient to maintain the expanding work in its main mission fields, accumulating debts and little capital. A subcommittee of influential bankers was established to make recommendations, and Venn consequently presided in his first few years over a programme of moderate retrenchment and a major expansion of the home organization with a view to achieving a substantial increase in the income of the society. This process was successful, and by the mid-1840s the society had achieved a position of relative prosperity, which it retained until the 1870s. Particularly important was the development of a system of local associations and association secretaries covering the whole of England and acting as conduits of information about the activities of the society to its supporters and of resources for the central organization.

The issue of the relationship between the society and the structures of the church arose

both at home, where the CMS had received little support from an episcopate that was suspicious of its evangelicalism, and abroad, where it came into conflict with colonial bishops over the issue of the control of its agents. Venn made a crucial contribution to the amelioration of these difficulties as a member of the CMS committee in the 1830s by advocating a formal recognition of the rights of bishops to license missionaries while at the same time continuing to assert the right of the CMS, as a voluntary society, to control the operations of its own agents. This approach paved the way for an accommodation with the establishment, a process assisted by the appointment of more sympathetic bishops both at home and in the colonies; the consecration of Daniel Wilson as bishop of Calcutta in 1834 was particularly important.

It was, however, the third set of issues, those relating to mission strategy, with which Venn became most strongly associated. He seems to have begun his work with the assumption that European superintendence of work in the mission field was essential. However, by the 1850s, because of concern about the detrimental effects of paternalism, he had begun to advocate (along with Rufus Anderson, the secretary of the American Board of Commissioners for Foreign Missions) the 'three selves' principle: that is, that the object of mission was to establish indigenous churches that were self-governing, self-supporting and self-propagating. On this view, missions were strictly temporary, a form of scaffolding, which should be removed as the native church matured and the missionaries worked themselves out of a job. This process has been called 'the euthanasia of a mission'. Moreover, Venn believed, native bishops should be appointed as soon as possible to head the new churches and prevent their subordination to missionaries or white colonial bishops. By the 1860s, Venn was beginning to put these principles into practice. In 1860, for example, the native pastorate organization in Sierra Leone took over the running of the majority of parishes, although European influence in the church remained strong. In 1864 Venn's policy on the episcopate came to fruition with the consecration of Samuel Ajayi *Crowther as a bishop for West Africa. Venn's mission strategy also included a concern for the economic development of western Africa, both as a check to the slave trade and as a means of facilitating the creation of a self-supporting indigenous church. Although criticism of his policy with regard to indigenous churches strengthened in the last quarter of the nineteenth century, resulting in, *inter alia*, Bishop Crowther's resignation in 1892, Venn's enduring reputation as one of the most creative and influential missionary thinkers of the century seems amply warranted.

Despite a prolonged period of ill health in the 1860s, which led him to attempt to retire in 1862, Venn's central position in CMS combined with his various skills propelled him into the position of spokesman for the evangelical tradition within the Church of England. He became a confidant of J. B. *Sumner as archbishop of Canterbury, was involved in a number of other evangelical societies and was temporarily editor of *The Christian Observer* in 1869. He was appointed as a representative evangelical to the parliamentary commissions on clerical subscription and ritual. Venn finally resigned as CMS clerical secretary in November 1872 and, after suffering a stroke, died on 13 January 1873. Venn's commitments left him with relatively little time for writing, and his only substantial works were biographical in nature: *The life and a selection from the letters of the Rev. H. Venn, Author of 'The Complete Duty of Man'* (London: J. Hatchard, 1834), an edition of the letters of his grandfather together with a short 'life' written by his father, and *The Missionary Life and Labours of Francis Xavier taken from his own correspondence: with a sketch of the general results of Roman Catholic Missions among the Heathen* (London: Longman, 1862).

Bibliography

W. R. Shenk, *Henry Venn – Missionary Statesman* (Maryknoll: Orbis Books, 1983); T. E. Yates, *Venn and Victorian Bishops Abroad* (London: SPCK, 1978).

M. A. SMITH

■ **VINE, William Edwy** (1873–1949), Brethren lay theologian and missionary administrator, was born in Blandford, Dorset, where his father kept a boarding school. In 1875 it moved to Exeter, where it was known as Mount Radford School. Vine's parents were Open Brethren, and Vine was converted in early childhood and, at the age of fourteen and after baptism, became a member of the Gospel Hall, Fore Street, Exeter. He was to remain a lifelong adherent of the Brethren movement. At the age of seventeen Vine became a teacher in his father's school and began studying part time at the University College of Wales, Aberystwyth, to prepare for a University of London degree. He graduated from London in 1905 with an MA in classics. In 1899 Vine married Pheobe Baxendale, a former pupil of his father. They had five children, one of whom, Christine, later the wife of Gordon Fountain, became a medical missionary in India, and a further two, Edwin and Winifred, worked overseas as a surgeon and nurse respectively. When the children were young, Vine frequently played games with them, had a tennis court constructed for their benefit and, being an accomplished violin player, held occasional musical evenings.

In 1904, on the death of his father, Vine and his brother Theodore became joint headmasters of the school. About this time, in association with the Brethren itinerant preacher C. F. Hogg, Vine conducted a correspondence course in Bible study; his notes were later published as commentaries on Thessalonians and Galatians (1914 and 1922). Vine also ran a course in Greek grammar and eventually published *New Testament Greek Grammar: A Course in Self Help* (1931). In 1909 he was asked by W. H. Bennet and W. E. Sparks to assist them as an editor of *Echoes of Service*, the Brethren missionary magazine, which had its offices in Bath, Somerset. The Brethren had no central administrative institutions but a substantial number of overseas missionaries: 600 in 1909 and 1,120 by 1949. It was the editors of the magazine who maintained communications with them, provided informal pastoral advice and acted as a clearing house for financial support. From 1910 Vine worked part-time as an editor and in the school, but in 1911 he became a full-time editor and moved to Bath. There he joined the Manvers Hall congregation, eventually becoming its leading elder; upon the deaths of his co-editors Vine became, in addition, the senior figure at *Echoes of Service*. He gave Bible study lectures at the training home for female missionary candidates that was established in Bath about 1921 and handled some sixty to seventy letters daily from missionaries. He also answered the many questions on Scripture which Brethren members addressed to the editors.

Vine published some nineteen books and a number of pamphlets in his lifetime and co-authored a further four books with C. F. Hogg. A number of these works were commentaries, but he also wrote more widely in theology. Vine taught the inerrancy and plenary inspiration of the Scriptures, views expressed in *The Divine Inspiration of the Bible* (1923). The two later works that he jointly wrote with Hogg were on eschatology, and they approached this subject from a premillennialist viewpoint, although they modified traditional Brethren dispensationalism on several points. *The Church and the Churches* (c. 1929) expounded Open Brethren ecclesiology, and *The Divine Plan of Missions* (1927) laid great stress on gathering converts into local congregations. However, Vine's principal work was *An Expository Dictionary of New Testament Words* (four volumes, 1939–1941). The work, designed for the non-specialist reader, listed all the significant occurrences in the New Testament of many Greek words, expounding their meanings and listing the English words by which they were translated. It benefited greatly from Vine's knowledge of classical Greek, Hellenistic vernacular literature and the Septuagint. He paid tribute to the comments on the manuscript made by the then classics lecturer F. F. *Bruce; Bruce in return later described Vine's scholarship as 'wide, accurate and up-to-date, and withal unobtrusive' (foreword to the one-volume edition, 1952).

Small of stature, Vine was an Edwardian gentleman in appearance. The writer Anne Arnott, who as a child attended Manvers Hall, described him as being 'a loving and impetuous man, inclined to pour his feelings into words' (*The Brethren* [1969], p. 24). From 1927 he suffered from incurable heart disease and was subject to fainting spells; nevertheless, he maintained his rigorous work schedule. He died on 2 November 1949. Earlier that day he had written his last editorial for *Echoes of Service* on 'to me to live is Christ' (Philippians 1:21).

Bibliography
P. O. Ruoff, W. E. *Vine: His Life and Ministry* (London: Oliphants, 1951); F. R. Coad, *A History of the Brethren Movement* (Exeter: Paternoster, ²1976).

N. DICKSON

■ **WACE, Henry** (1836–1924), Anglican clergyman and scholar, was born in London on 10 December 1836, son of the Revd Richard H. Wace. His father was forced through illness to resign his parish work and spent the rest of his life teaching pupils at Goring in Oxfordshire and Wadhurst in Sussex. Wace was educated at Marlborough College, Rugby School and King's College, London before going up in 1856 to Oxford University. He matriculated at Trinity College but soon moved with a scholarship to Brasenose College. In 1911 he was to be elected an honorary fellow of Brasenose, where his son, the Revd Henry C. Wace, was also a fellow.

After graduation Wace was ordained by Bishop Tait to a curacy at St Luke's, Berwick Street, London. Two years later, in 1863, he became curate of St James's, Piccadilly serving under J. E. Kempe; he left in 1870 for the lectureship of Grosvenor Chapel. He worked at Lincoln's Inn as chaplain (1872–1880) and preacher (1880–1896). In 1875 Wace was appointed Professor of Ecclesiastical History at King's College, London, and he became principal in 1884 when Alfred Barry was elected as Archbishop of Sydney. During this period, he was involved in some major scholarly initiatives. For instance, he edited the section of the *Speaker's Commentary* on the Bible that dealt with the Apocrypha (2 vols., 1888) and collaborated with William Smith in editing *A Dictionary of Christian Biography, Literature, Sects and Doctrines during the First Eight Centuries* (4 vols., 1877–1887) and with Philip *Schaff and others in editing *A Select Library of Nicene and Post-Nicene Fathers of the Christian Church* (14 vols., 1890–1900). During Wace's principalship, King's College suffered a severe financial crisis and was threatened with closure. As a denominational institution, it did not receive a government grant, and public subscriptions were not enough to address the emergency. Furthermore, a joint petition by King's

College and University College for a charter to establish a new 'Albert University of London' was rejected after lengthy negotiations and two Royal Commissions. Meanwhile, the college attracted unwelcome controversy in 1891 when it sacked Alfred Momerie, Professor of Logic and Metaphysics, for denying the atonement and the Trinity. Wace left King's in 1896 and resigned from the college council six years later in protest at its decision to abolish religious tests.

While at King's Wace gained several ecclesiastical honours. He was awarded a prebendal stall at St Paul's Cathedral, London in 1881 on the nomination of Bishop Jackson and a Doctorate of Divinity at Oxford University in 1883, and he became an examining chaplain to the Archbishop of Canterbury and a chaplain to the Queen. In 1896 he was appointed rector of St Michael's, Cornhill, London by the Drapers' Company, in succession to Bishop Alfred Earle. Nevertheless, to the surprise of his contemporaries, Wace remained without important preferment until he was chosen as Dean of Canterbury after the death of Frederic Farrar in 1903. He worked to raise more than £30,000 for the repair of the cathedral's fabric and was rewarded on his eighty-fifth birthday with the freedom of the city. An able administrator, he gave his support to numerous evangelical organizations. For instance, he was president of the councils of the London College of Divinity and St John's Hall, Durham, and chairman of the governors of Weymouth College and Trent College. Likewise he worked on behalf of King's College Hospital and the Clergy Mutual Insurance Society. Wace died at Canterbury on 9 January 1924.

Wace was a staunch Protestant and thought the title 'evangelical' was 'one of the most glorious designations which Christian men, and especially Christian ministers, can bear'. He became an expert in theological controversy and a determined advocate of the Reformation Settlement of the Church of England, being described as 'a champion by voice and pen for the vital truths of Bible Christianity' (*Journal of the Transactions of the Victoria Institute* 56 [1924], p. 1). He sought to encourage better understanding of the Reformers' teaching, editing *Luther's Primary Works* (1896) with C. A. Buchheim,

and his collected essays on this topic were published as *Principles of the Reformation* (1910). Wace firmly resisted the spread of ritualism in the Church of England, believing it to be a revival of the errors of medieval Roman Catholicism, and headed the National Church League. He opposed plans to revise the Book of Common Prayer lest its Protestant character be destroyed, and warned that the legalization of mass vestments and reservation of the sacrament were foolish concessions to 'Anglo-Catholics' motivated by the bishops' desire to avoid discontent. Nevertheless, in an attempt to secure peace in the church, Wace proposed in 1903 that, subject to Scripture, variations in ritual and doctrine should be admissible if they were in general usage in the first six centuries. This suggestion, which followed Bishop Jewell's appeal to antiquity in his arguments against Roman Catholics, won favour from people of very different theological views, but it never proved practicable. As a result of Wace's ability to win the favour of non-evangelicals he was chosen as chairman for the Fulham Conferences of 1900 and 1901, small 'round table' discussions called by the bishop of London to debate eucharistic doctrine and auricular confession.

Wace resisted not only ritualism, but also the spread of rationalism, both inside and outside the church. He challenged the methods of the 'higher' biblical critics and rejected their radical conclusions, arguing instead for the traditional understanding of the age, authorship and accuracy of the Bible. The Bible Churchmen's Missionary Society, which separated from the Church Missionary Society in 1922 because of disagreement about the doctrine of Scripture, chose him as its vice-president. Wace was actively engaged in debates about 'science' and 'faith', and was president of the Victoria Institute, which aimed to explore questions of philosophy and science, and to reconcile any apparent discrepancies between them and 'the great truths revealed in Holy Scripture'. At the Church Congress of 1888 he claimed that 'agnostics', if honest, would accept the name 'infidels'; this statement led to a heated exchange with Thomas Huxley in the pages of the *Nineteenth Century*, later published as *Christianity and Agnosticism* (1895). Elsewhere Wace attacked the teaching of other opponents of biblical Christianity, such as

Matthew Arnold, Charles Darwin, Cotter Morison, Ernest Renan, Herbert Spencer and Mrs Humphry Ward.

Wace was a prolific author and a prominent preacher. As a young curate he came to the attention of John Delane, editor of the *Times*, through a letter to the newspaper about the Colenso crisis, and he was invited to become a leader writer. This task he undertook regularly for over twenty years, and he remained an occasional correspondent to the end of his life. He also contributed frequently to journals such as the *Quarterly Review* and *Churchman*, and was often a speaker at the Islington Clerical Conference and the Church Congress. His papers in the *Clergyman's Magazine* were published as *Some Central Points of Our Lord's Ministry* (1890), and those in the *Record* newspaper as *Some Questions of the Day* (2 vols., 1912–1914). Wace delivered the Boyle Lectures for 1874–1875 at the Chapel Royal, Whitehall, published as *Christianity and Morality*, the Bampton Lectures for 1879 at Oxford University, published as *The Foundations of Faith*, and the Warburton Lectures for 1894–1898 at Lincoln's Inn, published as *Prophecy Jewish and Christian*. Other collections of his addresses appeared in print as *The Gospel and its Witnesses* (1883), *The Sacrifice of Christ* (1898), *The War and the Gospel* (1917), *The Story of the Passion* (1922) and *The Story of the Resurrection* (1923).

A. ATHERSTONE

■ **WAGNER, Charles Peter** (1930–), church growth specialist and author, was born in New York City to Charles Graham and Mary Wagner. He married Doris Mueller in 1950 and they have had three children. He came to be regarded as one of the most prominent evangelical church growth experts in the world today.

Wagner is a leader in several organizations. He is Chancellor of the Wagner Leadership Institute (1998–present) and President of Global Harvest Ministries (1992–present). He also serves as International Apostle for the Strategic Prayer Network (1990–present) and as Apostle for the Apostolic Council of Educational Accountability (1998–present), the Apostolic Council of Prophetic Elders (1999–present) and the Apostolic Roundtable

of Deliverance Ministries (2000–present). He is Presiding Apostle for the International Coalition of Apostles (1999–present). Wagner was educated at Rutgers University (BS, 1952), Fuller Theological Seminary (MDiv, 1955), Princeton Theological Seminary (ThM, 1962), Fuller Theological Seminary School of World Missions (MA in Missiology, 1968) and the University of California (PhD in Social Ethics 1977). He was ordained in 1955 by the Conservative Christian Congregational Conference and in the 1990s by Glory of Zion International. He served as a missionary in Bolivia with the Andes Evangelical Mission (now SIM International) and the South American Mission from 1956 to 1971. During those years he also served as a professor at George Allen Theological Seminary in Cochabamba and as associate general director of the Andes Evangelical Mission (1964–1971).

Wagner joined the faculty of Fuller Theological Seminary School of World Mission in 1971 as assistant to the church-growth specialist Donald McGavran. He soon became a significant scholar and leader in the field of missions and church growth. His professional work at Fuller included serving as professor from 1971 to 1998 and as vice-president of the Charles E. Fuller Institute for Evangelism and Church Growth (1971–1991). In 1984 he was appointed to a teaching chair as the first Donald A. McGavran Professor of Church Growth. While serving for nearly three decades on the faculty of Fuller Theological Seminary, Wagner conducted research, taught extensively on church growth and other areas of practical theology and cross-cultural missions, published numerous academic and professional works and travelled widely as a speaker and consultant.

Wagner took a major role in the Lausanne Committee on World Evangelization from 1974 to 1989. His international stature as an evangelical and church growth expert increased as he served as a founding member and on the executive committee. He was the first chairperson of the Lausanne Strategy Working Group that focused on unreached people groups. On the basis of this work he initiated and co-edited with Edward R. Dayton the *Unreached Peoples* annuals, which were regarded as a major contribution to contemporary missiology.

Wagner's other organizational roles have included: founding president of The North American Society for Church Growth (1985), founding president of Global Harvest Ministries (1992) and the leadership of several organizations related to his work with apostolic and prophetic charismatic ministry. During the 1990s he began to speak and publish on the subject of apostolic leadership and apostolic churches, and he founded and co-founded several 'apostolic' organizations for the promotion of education, prophetic ministry and prayer.

Although Wagner has been influential in the wider evangelical world, his extensive research into and writing on the Pentecostal and charismatic movements have given him particular expertise in these areas. Through his longtime association with the charismatic leader John *Wimber, leader of the Vineyard Movement, and their joint teaching of a controversial course on charismatic ministry at Fuller Theological Seminary entitled, 'MC 510 Signs and Wonders' (1984), he became identified with the charismatic movement. He is credited with originating the term 'third wave', to designate the increased openness among other evangelicals to the miraculous power of the Holy Spirit and joint ministry with Pentecostals and charismatics.

In 1992 Wagner further strengthened his affiliation with charismatic leaders and joined Pastor Ted Haggard and George Otis, Jr, in establishing the World Prayer Center in Colorado Springs. Wagner moved his own operation to Colorado Springs and began developing organizations to promote apostolic and prophetic ministry and spiritual warfare. He became involved with other charismatic leaders such as Cindy Jacobs, Billy Joe Daugherty and Bill Hammond. During this period he ended his formal association with Fuller Theological Seminary and established his own non-traditional school, called 'Wagner Leadership Institute'.

Wagner's scholarly career can be broken down into three distinct periods. The first was the 1970s and early 1980s, when Wagner was under the influence of Donald McGavran, whom he credited with teaching him that the best way to learn about church growth is to study growing churches. During this period he focused on the technical principles of church growth, and his research led him to

the conclusion that the most significant factor that made churches grow rapidly was an emphasis on the present day supernatural work of the Holy Spirit. His next period of research extended from the late 1980s to the mid 1990s, when he experienced a paradigm shift to what he would later call 'spiritual principles' of church growth. This transition was related to his involvement with John Wimber and the Vineyard Church movement and led him to emphasize supernatural signs and wonders, prayer and spiritual warfare as methods of evangelism and church growth. The third period, which began in the mid 1990s, involved a change in focus to what Wagner calls 'the apostolic reformation of the church', an ecclesiastical movement of churches that embody what he regards as the best technical and spiritual principles of church growth. He identifies various churches as models of this new movement; they range from independent charismatic and evangelical community churches to mainstream denominational churches. They include the Willow Creek Community Church in Chicago (led by Bill Hybels), Victory Christian Center in Tulsa (led by Billy Joe Daugherty), Hope Chapel in Kaneohe (led by Ralph Moore), Christian International Ministries Network in Santa Rosa Beach (led by Bill Hammond) and Faith Community Baptist Church in Singapore (led by Pastor Lawrence Khong).

Wagner became prominent in the church during the last quarter of the twentieth century because of his broad experience and extensive knowledge as a missionary, church growth expert and researcher of the charismatic movement. He published his observations and theories and established a broad readership among church leaders and educators of various traditions. A prolific writer, Wagner has written or edited over fifty books, including significant works on missiology, church growth, social ethics, ecclesiology, Pentecostalism and spirituality. He has also published hundreds of articles in periodicals and professional journals. His better known books include: *Latin America Theology: Radical or Evangelical?* (1970), *The Protestant Movement in Bolivia* (1970), *Frontiers in Missionary Strategy* (1972), *Church/Missions Tensions Today* (ed. 1972), *Look Out! The Pentecostals are Coming* (1973), *Your Church*

Can Grow: Seven Vital Signs of a Healthy Church (1976), *Your Spiritual Gifts Can Make Your Church Grow* (1979, 1994), *Your Church Can Be Healthy* (1979), *Our Kind of People: The Ethical Dimensions of Church Growth in America* (1979), *Church Growth and the Whole Gospel* (1981), *On The Crest of the Wave: Becoming a World Christian* (1983), *Leading Your Church to Growth* (1984), *Strategies for Church Growth: Tools for Planning Evangelism and Missions* (1987), *Signs and Wonders Today* (ed., rev. ed. 1987), *Strategies for Church Growth* (1989), *How to Have a Healing Ministry* (1988), *Church Planting for a Greater Harvest* (1990), *Engaging the Enemy* (1991), *Warfare Prayer* (1992), *Prayer Shield* (1992), *Breaking Strongholds in Your City* (1993), *Churches that Pray* (1993), *Confronting the Powers* (1996), *The Healthy Church* (1996), *The Rising Revival* (ed. 1998), *Confronting the Queen of Heaven* (1998), *Radical Holiness for Radical Living* (1998), *The Every Church Guide to Growth* (co-author, 1998), *The New Apostolic Churches* (ed. 1998), *Church Quake* (1999), *Apostles and Prophets The Foundation of the Church* (2000), *Acts of the Holy Spirit* (2000), *Seven Power Principles that I didn't Learn in Seminary* (2000) and *Apostles of the City* (2000).

Bibliography

C. P. Wagner (ed.), *The New Apostolic Churches* (Ventura: Regal Books, 1998).

D. HEDGES

■ **WALLIS, Arthur** (1922–1988), British author and elder statesman of 'restorationism', was born in Dublin, the son of Captain Reginald and Mrs Mary Wallis. He was converted in his childhood and educated at Christian schools in England: Winterdyne Preparatory School, Southport, and Monkton Combe School, Bath. After a short period of clerical work, he entered full-time Christian service, trusting God for his finances.

Deciding against further institutional education, Wallis pursued a rigorous course of personal biblical studies alongside a correspondence course in New Testament Greek. In 1942 he was baptized by Alan Redpath at Duke Street Baptist Church, Richmond. In the same year he enlisted in the army and,

after training at Sandhurst, saw action with the Royal Tank Regiment in North Africa and Italy, where he was wounded. After the war he changed his views on military service and became a conscientious objector. He married Eileen Hemingway in 1949, and they had one son, Jonathan.

During Wallis's teenage years his father, a popular and gifted preacher, had asked Leith Samuel to 'see that my boys get my message'. Samuel thus became a mentor to Arthur, and their relationship flowered into a lasting friendship.

Wallis's early church affiliation was with the Open Brethren. The veteran and unconventional Brethren teacher, G. H. Lang, led him to believe in the Pentecostal experience known as 'baptism in the Holy Spirit', and in the present availability of the gifts of the Spirit. This belief, his personal studies and his reading of R. A. *Torrey and Andrew *Murray, led him to a powerful experience, which he ascribed to the Holy Spirit, in March 1951. His links with the Brethren thereafter became inevitably weaker. However, he rejected the Pentecostal teaching on tongues as the initial evidence of baptism in the Spirit and did not speak in tongues himself until 1962.

Early in his life Wallis developed an interest in revival, through a visit at the age of fifteen to Loughor, Wales, where the Welsh Revival of 1904 had begun. Conversations with an elderly convert from that revival created a desire to see revival for himself. Hearing of the Lewis Awakening, a localized revival in the Hebrides (1949–1951), he visited the area and spent time with the instrument of that revival, Duncan Campbell.

In 1952 Wallis met David Lillie, another Lang devotee and the leader of a Brethren assembly in Exeter. Lillie's passion for the restoration of the church to New Testament ideals complemented Wallis's passion for revival, and these two elements quickly became inseparable in Wallis's thinking. From 1958 the two men convened a series of conferences to share their vision with other leaders.

Saddened by the fading of the Lewis Awakening, Wallis became even more convinced that only churches established on sound New Testament lines could prevent revival power from dissipating. Such churches, he held, would be 'self-governing, self-supporting, self-edifying, self-propagating'. They would be made up of committed believers only, joined on the basis of organic relationship rather than denominational structure. They would also experience the power and gifts of the Holy Spirit and would be open to all the 'Ephesians 4 ministries', including present-day apostles and prophets.

Meanwhile, Wallis was leading an independent church in his home village of Talaton, Devon, as well as pursuing an itinerant teaching ministry, conducting evangelistic missions and running Supplyline, a missionary support organization. His first book, destined to become a classic on revival, was *In the Day of Thy Power – The Scriptural Principles of Revival* (1956). Leith Samuel and G. H. Lang vetted the manuscript and Duncan Campbell wrote the foreword.

A twenty-month period in New Zealand in 1963–1964 put Wallis in the midst of a growing controversy over 'the things of the Spirit' that was dividing the large Brethren movement in that country. A passionate advocate of Christian unity, he found the division distressing. He was supported during this time by Campbell McAlpine, in whom he found a kindred spirit. Later, back in Britain, Wallis, McAlpine and the South African Denis Clark became close friends and together addressed many conferences on revival, the Spirit-filled life and the restoration of the church. From 1965 Wallis also spoke at conferences organized by the Fountain Trust and in due course joined the Trust's advisory council. This commitment identified him as a bridge-builder: his own conviction was that denominationalism was alien to the will of God, yet the Fountain Trust chiefly represented leaders committed to bringing renewal to the historic denominations.

Wallis was a man of prayer. Slow to reach decisions, he would pray, and often fast, until he was certain that he had heard from God. His next three major books reflected these emphases: *God's Chosen Fast – A Spiritual and Practical Guide to Fasting* (1968), *Pray in the Spirit – The Work of the Holy Spirit in the Ministry of Prayer* (1970) and a manual on spiritual warfare, *Into Battle* (1973).

Keen to deepen his understanding of biblical prophecy, in 1972 Wallis convened a series of meetings to explore the subject with a group of six other itinerant preachers. Out of these meetings came a conviction that God was calling them to covenant relationship of the 'David and Jonathan' kind. The circle was later widened, with Wallis, as the oldest man and convenor, acting as chairman. But there was division here too, over how 'grace', as distinct from 'law', should determine one's approach to issues such as drinking alcohol, Sunday observance and personal devotions. Wallis, who took a conservative line on these issues, worked hard to mend the breaches.

An abridged and updated edition of Wallis's first book was issued in 1979 as *Rain From Heaven – Revival in Scripture and History*. It acknowledged the 'charismatic movement' as a move of God but denied that it was revival. Wallis in fact believed the movement to be weakening; he attributed the decline to compromise, chiefly on the part of its leaders. He addressed this concern, among others, in *The Radical Christian* (1981), where he described the evangelicalism of his day as 'leavened with unreality, hypocrisy and compromise'. This book, in spite of its challenging tone, led to many invitations to preach overseas.

In 1979 Wallis moved to Bradford, in the north of England, to be closer to Bryn Jones's 'Harvestime' team and to serve as editor of *Restoration* magazine, to which he also contributed many articles. Three years later he moved south again to help Tony Morton, leader of The Community Church, Southampton, and of the Cornerstone team. Wallis cultivated these 'team' links in spite of his misgivings about the scriptural basis for 'apostolic teams' as fixed groupings.

Wallis's discipling materials, tested in the Southampton church, were published as *Living God's Way* (1984), which was followed in 1987 by a further series, *On To Maturity*. Trips to China in 1984 and 1985 to visit the growing underground church led to the writing of *China Miracle – A Voice to the Church in the West* (1985). Shortly after this Wallis developed health problems, and he died suddenly during a prayer retreat in Sheffield in September 1988.

Wallis's influence was far greater than that of his writings. Many of the next generation of 'new church' leaders saw him as a wise confidant and father-figure, while those in more traditional circles accepted him as a gracious and persuasive ambassador for the restoration movement.

Bibliography
J. R. Wallis, *Arthur Wallis: Radical Christian* (Eastbourne: Kingsway, 1991).

D. MATTHEW

■ **WALTHER, Carl F. W.** (1811–1887), Lutheran clergyman, theologian and seminary president, was one of North American Lutheranism's most influential and effective leaders. He served as founding president of the Lutheran Church, Missouri Synod and was president of Concordia Theological Seminary in St Louis for over thirty years. Heavily influenced by Lutheran confessionalism and continental Pietism, Walther opposed rationalistic liberalism and remained a fierce advocate of orthodox Lutheranism throughout his long career, during which he helped to define the theological and cultural parameters of Lutheranism in the New World. An immigrant from Saxony, Walther assisted in the construction of lasting ecclesiastical and educational institutions, becoming one of the key German-American leaders of the nineteenth century.

Walther was born in Langenchursdorf, Saxony (25 October 1811), the son of Gottlob Henrich Wilhelm Walther, a Lutheran pastor, and Johanna Wilhelmina Zschenderlein. Walther's father was a third-generation Lutheran pastor, who occupied the same pastoral charge in Langenchursdorf that had been held by Walther's grandfather. Carl was the eighth of twelve children, only six of whom lived to adulthood. He was called 'Ferdinand' by his family. Educated at first by his father, he began attending school at the age of eight in Hohenstein. After two years, he entered the Latin School in Schneeberg. He began theological studies at the University of Leipzig in October 1829.

During his first year of studies Walther experienced intense anxiety over his personal salvation. He sought counsel from Martin Stephan, a pastor at St John's Lutheran Church in Dresden. Stephan was an orthodox Lutheran and theological conservative, who adamantly opposed the rationalism taking hold of Europe's universities and the state church of Saxony. Stephan's written reply to Walther assured him of his salvation and assuaged his spiritual crisis. Stephan would remain an important figure in Walther's life, eventually encouraging him to emigrate to North America with a group of Lutheran pilgrims who hoped to preserve the orthodox faith.

During his university years in Leipzig, Walther contracted a near-fatal lung disease. Setting aside his formal studies for six months, he read *Luther's works intensely while he convalesced. This period would become significant for his future, because in reading Luther closely he became convinced of the biblical basis of Luther's theology and became unshakeably committed to a firm confessionalism. In 1833 he passed his first series of examinations, which authorized him to serve as tutor for the Friedmann Loeber family in Cahla. On 15 January 1837 he was ordained in Bräunsdorf, Saxony and became sole pastor of the church *Zum Guten Hirten* where he also taught religion classes at a local school.

While in Bräunsdorf he continued his association with Martin Stephan. In the late 1830s Stephan began to fear that rationalism was threatening to extinguish true Christianity in the state church of Saxony. An advocate of pure Lutheranism, he also protested against the Prussian Union, which had forced a union between Lutheran and Reformed churches. As a result, Stephan began to organize his disciples into a spiritual organization (*Gesellschaft*) for emigration to the United States. In November 1838 Stephan and approximately 700 supporters, among them Walther and his older brother Otto, left Germany from Bremen in five ships. Stephan claimed absolute authority over the emigrant band and named himself 'bishop'. They landed in New Orleans in 1839 (Walther himself arrived on the ship *Johann Georg* on 5 January 1839) and quickly settled in St Louis and Perry County, Missouri. These immigrants were part of the pre-Gilded-Age emigration which brought over 2.5 million Germans to North America. Stephan's heavy-handed leadership and domineering intransigence nearly brought the group to ruin both spiritually and economically. In late May 1839 Walther and other key leaders in the community banished Stephan from the *Gesellschaft* for financial and sexual misconduct. This experience would profoundly affect Walther's theology and polity. Recalling the abuses committed by the Saxon state church and Martin Stephan, throughout his career Walther sought to preclude further cases of clerical tyranny by investing the governing authority of the church in congregations rather than the clergy.

The events of 1839 led to a crisis of theological and ecclesiastical identity for the fledgling Lutheran group. Who or what were they exactly? They were not a 'pure' church, for they had no ordained bishop; they were no longer affiliated with the state church of Saxony, and they found themselves in a land of ethnic pluralism and religious voluntarism. Could they properly be considered a 'church' at all? At the 'Altenburg Disputation', two public debates held in Altenburg, Missouri in April 1841, Walther laid the foundation for the unique polity of the Lutheran Church Missouri Synod. Seeking theological and political solutions to the questions of the troubled Gesellschaft, Walther studied Luther's ecclesiology carefully and determined that the band of immigrants could properly call themselves a true 'church', even though they were far from perfect and plagued with controversy. In Altenburg he also developed a Free Church ecclesiology within a Lutheran confessional context by defending congregational polity. He would spend his career defending his views against those such as the Lutheran theologian J. K. Wilhelm *Löhe and the immigrant pastor A. A. Grabau, who advocated a more hierarchical polity.

At the Altenburg Disputation, Walther resolved the Gesellschaft's theological crisis and provided a theological foundation for Lutheranism in North America and the beginnings of the Lutheran Church Missouri Synod. Following the meetings, he became pastor of the immigrant congregation in St Louis named Trinity Lutheran Church, a congregation whose previous pastor was his recently deceased older brother. In September 1841 he married Emilie Buenger, a fellow member of the original Gesellschaft; and they subsequently had six children. From his position as pastor of Trinity Lutheran, Walther launched a career as a church organizer, theological educator and religious publisher. In September 1844 he published the first issue of De Lutheraner, a religious newspaper

designed 'to call together those who are correct in the faith' and which bore the slogan 'God's Word and Luther's doctrine pure shall now and evermore endure'.

In 1847 Walther helped to organize an inter-congregational body of Saxon immigrants, which eventually became the Lutheran Church Missouri Synod. Originally entitled the 'German Evangelical Lutheran Synod of Missouri, Ohio and Other States', the Synod dropped the word 'German' from its title during the First World War under pressure from '100% Americanism' policies and took its present name in 1947. Walther served as president of that body from its founding to 1850, and again from 1864 to 1878. In October 1849 he was elected Professor of Theology at the Missouri Synod's Concordia Seminary. He served as president of Concordia from 1854 to 1887. In 1853 he founded a theological journal entitled Lehre und Wehre. Later he edited the dogmatic compendium of the Lutheran orthodox theologian Johann Wilhelm Baier and promoted the St Louis edition of Luther's works. As a tireless proponent of unity among American Lutherans he assisted in sponsoring a series of conferences and colloquies from 1856 to 1867. Walther later helped to found the Lutheran Synodical Conference (1872), a federation of American Lutheran synods that grew out of the colloquies. A brilliant theologian and respected leader, Walther used his platforms as professor, denominational president and seminary president to promote orthodox Lutheranism in North America.

Throughout the nineteenth century the Lutheran Church Missouri Synod remained a German ethnic denomination; as a result, it related to American evangelicalism only at its margins. The Synod was in its early stages of development and ethnically circumscribed when large-scale German immigration commenced, from which it received regular cultural replenishing that slowed the Americanization process. German Lutherans during the late nineteenth century were almost untouched by the millenarian movement, the precursor of American fundamentalism; so most scholars do not refer to them as 'evangelical'. Even though they resembled fundamentalists in many ways, the two groups were never co-terminous, as their methods, motivations and cultural circumstances always remained distinct.

In the last decade of his life Walther became embroiled in a bitter controversy with other Lutherans over the theological issue of predestination. Accused of crypto-Calvinism by his detractors, he believed that God predestines to salvation whoever he chooses to save by an eternal election that is based solely upon the merits of Christ. He further declared that God's election in no way derives from the subsequent faith or conduct of the saved, but instead becomes the cause of their faith and good works. Claiming to hold unswervingly to the orthodox Lutheran position, Walther had little tolerance for his opponents. He died in St Louis on 7 May 1887.

Bibliography
W. O. Forster, *Zion on the Mississippi: The Settlement of the Saxon Lutherans in Missouri, 1839–1841* (St Louis: Concordia, 1953); C. S. Meyer (trans. and ed.), *Letters of C. F. W. Walther: A Selection* (Philadelphia: Fortress Press, 1969); L. W. Spitz, Sr, *The Life of Dr. C. F. W. Walther* (St Louis: Concordia, 1961); M. L. Rudnick, *Fundamentalism and the Missouri Synod: A Historical Study of their Interaction and Mutual Influence* (St Louis: Concordia, 1966); A. R. Suelflow, *Servant of the Word: The Life and Ministry of C. F. W. Walther* (St Louis: Concordia, 2001); R. A. Suelflow (trans.), *Selected Writings of C. F. W. Walther: Selected Letters* (St Louis: R. A. Suelflow, 1981).

K. W. PETERSON

■ **WALVOORD, John Flipse** (1910–2002), dispensationalist and Dallas Seminary president, was born 1 May 1910 in Sheboygan, Wisconsin, the youngest of the three children of John Garrett Walvoord (a teacher and principal) and Mary Flipse Walvoord. Mary's difficult pregnancy with John threatened her life, but the couple refused their doctor's recommendation of an abortion, and she lived to be nearly 102. In 1925 they moved to Racine, Wisconsin, where John completed his high school education.

Despite his devout family and several years of daily Scripture reading, Walvoord came to faith in Christ only when, at the age of fifteen and through the ministry of William McCarrell, he recognized he was attempting to earn his salvation. Walvoord graduated from Wheaton College in three and a half years (BA, 1931), with a Greek major and Latin minor, having also participated in football, track and field events and state and national debating competitions. Choosing the Evangelical Theological College (later Dallas Theological Seminary) in preference to Princeton Theological Seminary, he graduated in three years (ThB and ThM, 1934).

For most of his time at college and seminary, Walvoord planned to be a missionary in China, but by his graduation he believed that God was leading him in another direction. Called in 1934 to be pastor of Rosen Heights Presbyterian Church in Fort Worth, Texas, he stayed for sixteen years, with an additional year as interim pastor while the church sought a successor. Despite mounting controversy in the denomination over dispensationalism, he served for ten years as stated clerk of the Fort Worth presbytery and twice as head of presbytery. During his first years at Fort Worth he earned his ThD (Evangelical Theological College, 1936), and later he gained an MA in philosophy (Texas Christian University, 1945).

Walvoord married Geraldine Lundgren in her home in Geneva, Illinois on 28 June 1939 after a romance of about seven years. They had four children, John Edward, James Randall, Timothy and Paul.

The founding president of Dallas Theological Seminary, Lewis Sperry *Chafer, asked Walvoord to serve as acting registrar (1935) and then as registrar (1936–1945) and Associate Professor of Systematic Theology (beginning in 1936). From 1940 to 1945 Walvoord added the role of secretary of the faculty to his responsibilities, relinquishing it in 1945 to become assistant to the president, though he actually assumed many of the daily presidential responsibilities since Chafer's health was declining. Despite his rigorous schedule, during this period Walvoord also published *The Doctrine of the Holy Spirit* (1943, rev. 1954, 1958).

When Walvoord became assistant to the president, the school was seriously in debt and technically bankrupt. Chafer's resolute refusal to solicit directly for funds, a form of George *Müller's 'faith principle', largely accounted for the seminary's financial predicament. Without violating that policy, Walvoord 'persuaded Dr. Chafer to send out a newsletter, a President's letter every six weeks or two months, simply stating what was going on, and enclosing an envelope'. Within three months, the school began to pay its current expenses. 'From 1945 to 1952, when Dr. Chafer died, we didn't retire the debt, but we paid the bills in full, and paid the faculty in full for the first time since the school began' (Mink, p. 71).

After Chafer died in August 1952, the seminary board opened a sealed letter he had left for them, in which he named Walvoord as his successor, to the surprise of all. Walvoord was inaugurated in February 1953, at the dedication of Chafer Chapel.

Walvoord left the Fort Worth church in 1951 because of his increasing seminary responsibilities, but the Dallas presbytery refused to accept the transfer into their jurisdiction, despite the Fort Worth presbytery's letter certifying that he had 'left in good standing'.

Walvoord joined Reinhardt Bible Church (Dallas) and also the Independent Fundamental Churches of America (IFCA), founded in 1930 by his former pastor McCarrell. Walvoord and Dallas Seminary were prominently associated with the separatist IFCA, especially during the 1950s and 1960s.

Walvoord assumed Chafer's role as editor of *Bibliotheca Sacra* (1952–1985). He served as president of the Evangelical Theological Society (1954) and edited a volume of papers from its annual meeting (published 1957). Despite his administrative and teaching responsibilities, he published many books, including *The Return of the Lord* (1955), *The Rapture Question* (1957, rev. 1979), *The Millennial Kingdom* (1959), *The Revelation of Jesus Christ* (1966), *Jesus Christ Our Lord* (1969), *Daniel, the Key to Prophetic Revelation* (1971) and *The Blessed Hope and the Tribulation* (1976). He also served on the editorial board that revised the *Scofield Reference Bible* (1967). *Israel in Prophecy* (1962), *The Church in Prophecy* (1964) and *The Nations in Prophecy* (1967) were republished in one volume as *Israel, the Nations, and the Church in Prophecy* (1988). He revised Chafer's *Major Bible Themes* (1974) and abridged Chafer's eight-volume *Systematic Theology* in two volumes (1988).

Chafer had divided the seminary's governing board into two groups because its members had different abilities. One group was responsible for education and the other for business; the business manager was charged with care of the school's finances and real estate. This arrangement removed educational matters from the control of businessmen, but Walvoord soon learned that it also removed non-academic matters from presidential control. Walvoord's attention to detail throughout the school frustrated him considerably because he was required to obtain approval for expenditure from the business manager, C. Fred Lincoln, who had held the post since 1926. When Lincoln retired in 1967, presidential authority was extended to include business affairs.

Under Walvoord's leadership, the school flourished, and it received regional accreditation in 1969. The seminary added new departments in Christian education and world missions, an extensive summer school programme and a winter session, and and began to offer a two-year MA (1974) and the Doctor of Ministry degree (1980). Despite opposition and the loss of some funding, African-Americans were enrolled (1968) and then added to the administrative staff (1975) and the faculty (1979). Women were enrolled, first in the MA course (1974) and later in the four-year ThM course (1986). Three major buildings were constructed – a library (1960) and two classroom buildings (1974) – and others purchased. Under Walvoord's leadership members of the faculty were encouraged to pursue graduate work at major universities in the US and Britain, and many of them earned second doctorates in addition to Dallas's ThD. Walvoord retired in 1986, becoming Chancellor and, in 2001, Chancellor Emeritus; the latter appointment marked his seventy years at the seminary. Walvoord died in Texas on 20 December 2002.

Walvoord's writings focused on dispensational eschatology, rather than more general exposition of dispensationalism as a system. Writing both to instruct sympathetic Bible students and to answer critics of dispensationalism, he expounded a dispensational approach to prophecy, emphasizing the pretribulational rapture of the church and the premillennial return of Christ. Just as Chafer had developed C. I. *Scofield's teachings into a systematic theology, so Walvoord developed and revised Chafer's theology.

Walvoord's greatest contribution was Dallas Theological Seminary, which grew from 251 students in the autumn of 1952 to 1,647 in the spring of 1986. He stabilized the school's precarious finances, established effective administrative structures, gathered a distinguished faculty and raised academic standards. An efficient administrator and strong, visionary leader, he concentrated decision-making in his own hands, though this strategy had both advantages and disadvantages. Walvoord's enduring legacy for dispensationalism is the seminary and its thousands of graduates serving around the world.

Bibliography

T. G. Mink, 'John F. Walvoord at Dallas Theological Seminary' (PhD dissertation, North Texas State University, 1987); R. A. Renfer, 'History of Dallas Theological Seminary' (PhD dissertation, University of Texas, 1959).

S. R. SPENCER

■ WARFIELD, Benjamin Breckinridge (1851–1921), American Presbyterian theologian, was Professor of Didactic and Polemical Theology at Princeton Theological Seminary from 1887 to his death. A prodigious scholar, writer, reviewer and editor, he continued the tradition of Charles *Hodge and A. A. *Hodge, appraising and addressing contemporary intellectual currents from the standpoint of Calvinism. Warfield shaped two generations of national leaders in American Presbyterianism, including many major figures in the fundamentalist and moderate camps of the Presbyterian Church (USA). Evangelicals and fundamentalists to this day look to Warfield's writings on biblical inerrancy, apologetics, evolution, theological method and miracles with a mixture of reverence and disapproval.

Warfield was born on 5 November 1851 outside Lexington, Kentucky, to William Warfield, a gentleman farmer and authority on the breeding of short-horned cattle, and Mary Cabell Breckinridge, daughter of the vociferous Presbyterian theologian, editor and politician, Robert Jefferson Breckinridge. The Civil War, waged during Warfield's adolescence, split his mother's family into Union and Secession factions, his parents' town house serving as headquarters for the Union side of the family. His sister's death of typhoid fever, the killing of an uncle and the schism of the Presbyterian church into Northern and Southern denominations followed in 1866. Warfield himself contracted typhoid and according to family lore lost his recollection of the past, but gained a nearly photographic memory of everything he would read thereafter.

Warfield entered Princeton College as a sophomore in 1868, when the Scottish philosopher James *McCosh arrived to assume the presidency. Warfield warmed to McCosh's belief in the harmony of science and religion, and after graduating as valedictorian in 1871, he planned to pursue a scientific career. While touring Europe with college friends he decided instead to prepare for the ministry. He returned to Lexington, worked as an editor for the *Farmer's Home Journal* and in 1873 entered Princeton Seminary. There he studied under the venerable Charles Hodge, whose combination of firm orthodoxy and a tender spirit persuaded Warfield (nicknamed 'the pugilist' in college) to adopt a more temperate and scholarly approach to polemics than his grandfather's. But it was Hodge's son, New Testament professor Caspar Wistar Hodge (Warfield called him 'my divinity on earth'), who fired his imagination for his future career. Warfield graduated in 1876, married Annie Pearce Kinkead of Lexington, and went with her to Leipzig to study New Testament theology and biblical criticism. He attended the lectures of Luthardt, Harnack and Delitzsch from November until February; then throat trouble drove him to Italy to recuperate. The couple returned home in the summer. This short period provided Warfield with his only personal contact with the theological work of German universities, a stunning fact in view of his mastery of their literature and method in ensuing years.

After brief service as a preacher in Baltimore and Dayton, Warfield was called in 1878 to teach New Testament at Western Theological Seminary near Pittsburgh. His mastery of German methods in the service of conservative understandings of scriptural authority, exemplified in 'Inspiration' (1881) and *An Introduction to the Textual Criticism of the New Testament* (1886), soon led to job offers from other seminaries. Princeton called him to the chair of the Hodges and a career change from biblical studies to systematics. There he directed his energies to specific polemical issues, editing and writing for Princeton's theological quarterlies, two of which he founded himself: the *Presbyterian and Reformed Review* (1890–1902) and the *Princeton Theological Review* (1903–1929). He also worked with William M. McPheeters in editing *The Bible Student* (1900–1903).

In the 1890s Warfield assembled a promising young faculty that enjoyed great influence in the Presbyterian Church. The denomination adopted a strong statement of biblical inerrancy, resisted a move to soften the Calvinism of the Westminster standard, and ousted Charles Briggs for holding higher critical views of biblical authorship. Warfield actively supported all these moves. In those same years, unfortunately, Annie Warfield became a permanent invalid. Warfield had served on the Committee of Missions for Freedmen and had attended the General Assembly at Saratoga and the Pan-Presbyterian Conference in Belfast, but now he forsook denominational activity to stay by her side. His confinement to Princeton enabled him to produce the impressive journals and scholarship that comprise his chief legacy. In addition to a vast array of articles and reviews, collected in a ten-volume series of *Works* (1927–1932), he contributed poems to various newspapers and published several volumes of sermons. He died after teaching his classes on 16 February 1921.

The theme of Warfield's life's work is the hearty embrace of modern scholarship to support Calvinist doctrine, explicate the supernatural character of Christianity and defend the authority of the Bible. He became a premier exponent of biblical inerrancy, evidentialist apologetics, cessationism and theistic evolution, all the while resisting theological developments hostile to Calvinism at home and abroad. Warfield wrote in response to the intellectual currents and challenges of his day, hence the disparate collection of topics he covered; yet a logic and coherence pervades the whole. Later writers tend to sympathize with some of Warfield's positions while faulting him for others, overlooking key principles that unite his work. First, Warfield sought to expound biblical and Calvinistic doctrine and worldview in the language and with the methodology of modern investigation. Secondly, he employed the concept of God's concursive operation with his creatures (natural laws, human agency), according to which God directs and superintends all that comes to pass. Thirdly, recognition of concursus entails attention to process over time. Warfield believed that modern thought underlined the importance of these venerable Calvinistic notions, and they pervade his multifarious combination of conservatism and modernity and his use of modernity against modernism.

Warfield embraced his age's fascination with system-building, devoting much effort to 'theological encyclopedia', the proper structure of theology. Theology is the science of God (not of religious experience), and as such it requires proper grounding in fact. Apologetics thus lies at the beginning of the whole enterprise, not at its end. One establishes the reasonableness of belief in a personal God, then his verbal revelation of himself in the Scriptures, and from there builds up a solid system of divinity. This 'evidentialism' followed the British empirical tradition of Paley (natural theology) and Butler (Christian evidences) so common in American collegiate education and typified at McCosh's and Hodge's Princeton. The Princetonian use of Scottish common-sense realism has been frequently noted, especially in contrast to the 'presuppositionalism' of Dutch theologians Abraham *Kuyper and Herman *Bavinck. Warfield worked hard to have Kuyper's works translated and published in America, and brought both men to Princeton for special series of lectures (1899 and 1909). But he disputed their claim that regeneration set Christians apart from all other thinkers, for it effectively eliminated the common ground of natural theology that Warfield made fundamental to his system. As he famously put it in 1903, Christianity is 'the Apologetical religion ... clothed with the mission to reason its way to dominion'.

Warfield's evidentialism went hand-in-hand with a conviction that Christianity in modern nations required well-educated ministers capable of holding their own as theologians among the panoply of professional scientists. He insisted on intellectual rigour at Princeton, prompting a student protest and dividing the faculty over curricular issues in the practically-minded, activist 1910s. Charges of rationalism greeted his efforts, as they would those of his successors throughout the century.

But Warfield marshalled evidences and worked out a structured, scientific theology in order to defend the supernaturalism of Christianity. He analyzed the principles behind the recast doctrine soon to be called 'liberal' and 'modernist'. In the theology of Albrecht Ritschl, for example, sin is ignorance, curable through the attainment of Christlike consciousness and ethical life in Christian community. This view is deism in modern dress, Warfield declared: it implies that God is far away and silent, working always and only through natural causes. Christianity, in contrast, hinges on the unmediated working of Christ's power in regenerating the sinful heart. 'When will the Church at large awaken to the fact that the problem which "the newer religious thinking" is putting before her is simply the old eighteenth-century problem in a fresh form?' he asked in 1895. 'Is Christianity a natural religion, the crown and capstone it may be of natural religion, but only natural religion for all that? Or is Christianity a supernatural religion – supernatural in origin, in sanctions, in power and in issue?' Every Christian heart is, properly speaking, a miracle, and Calvinism is the most supernaturalistic of confessions on this point.

Warfield's defence of supernatural Christianity centred on the issue of special revelation, the authority of the Scriptures. In response to A. C. McGiffert's inaugural address in 1895, Warfield declared, 'The Church did not grow up by natural law; it was founded. And the authoritative teachers sent forth by Christ to found His Church carried with them … a body of divine Scriptures, which they imposed on the Church that they founded as its code of law.' This infallible foundation differs from natural revelation in several respects. It proclaims God's specific, saving work in historical particulars unimagined by natural religion. Apart from Scripture we know God only as creator and judge, leaving us in despair over our sinfulness. Secondly, the Bible is an authority external to the individual, calling us to faith in a person known with some objectivity, not just inwardly. For Warfield the defining aspect of faith is its resting on external authority; this sets it apart from both the rationalism and the mysticism of natural religion. Finally, Scripture is infallible: God, who cannot lie, provided his word through plenary (full), verbal inspiration (down to the very words), so that the Bible is errorless in all God intended it to affirm, including matters scientific and historical.

Warfield articulated this doctrine of inerrancy most famously in an article entitled 'Inspiration', co-authored with A. A. Hodge for the *Presbyterian Review* of 1881. They argued that the Scriptures 'not only contain, but are, the word of God', without error in the original manuscripts. They carefully guarded their thesis against confusion with the dictation theory, exploring the varieties of concursive operation involved in the production of the Bible. Elsewhere Warfield answered many of the criticisms of the doctrine of inerrancy. To those who faulted his recourse to a set of vanished originals, he responded that textual criticism has very largely replicated them in our hands. To those who said that the doctrine makes faith in the Bible precarious, subject to destruction at the discovery of even one error in scientific or historical fact, Warfield countered that there is a 'sentimental presumption' in favour of Scripture's veracity, deriving from its evident power in experience and its dearness to the church. Moreover, it is not necessary to prove the Scripture errorless; the burden of proof lay rather on its challengers, who must show absolutely that the error resides in the text rather than its interpretation, and in the original rather than the copy. Most important for Warfield is the pervasive claim of the Scriptures themselves to be the very word of God.

Warfield's belief in supernaturalism and concursus, together with his great confidence in science, yielded interesting results. Among them were his espousal of evolutionism, his opposition to the 'perfectionism' of holiness and higher-life movements, and his belief that miracles ceased after the generation of the apostles.

From his college days onwards Warfield suspected that species originated, as Darwin suggested, by descent with modification. But with Charles Hodge he rejected the Darwinian doctrine that evolution happened by chance. Natural selection seemed quite plausible to a scion of cattle-breeders, and he even found in *Calvin's reading of the six days of creation a doctrine of providence that amounted to 'pure evolutionism'. Natural selection, like any law of nature, is an instance of divine activity concursive with secondary causes. Warfield required directly supernatural activity only at the creation *ex nihilo* of the original matter of the universe, the creation of the first human soul (though this was probably implanted in a body that had evolved from beasts), the biblical miracles and the regeneration of individual hearts. Yet he refused to elevate evolution to the status of assured fact or to make it the self-sufficient explanation of all reality. He bemoaned the tendency of scientists to pervert evolution into a vehicle for materialistic monism.

Evolution for Warfield is no substitute for creation; rather, it is the method of divine providence once life has been created, a particularly grand instance of the general principle that God works chiefly by process. The idea of supernatural process lies at the heart of Protestantism, for the distinction between creation and providence/evolution was just the distinction between justification and sanctification. We are justified by God's unilateral action from outside, creating a new heart in us; thereafter we are sanctified by the ongoing work of the Holy Spirit working concursively with efforts that spring from our regenerated heart. This principle of supernatural process animated Warfield's extensive polemics against perfectionists, among whom he included such diverse figures as the liberal Albrecht Ritschl, the revivalist Charles *Finney and the Victorious Life apostle Hannah Whitall *Smith. They shared the belief that 'complete salvation is ... coincident with justification', so that 'all sense of continued sinfulness is a clear disproof of present salvation'. Ritschl's perfectionism, according to Warfield, flowed from his insufficiently supernaturalist understanding of providence; Victorious Life perfectionism, for all its belief in the nearness

of God, shared the same source. 'Men are unwilling that either the world or themselves should be saved by God's secular methods', Warfield wrote. 'They ask to be made glorified saints in the twinkling of an eye ... They look every day for the cataclysm in which alone they can recognize God's salvation'. For Warfield, God works with us in sanctifying us; Calvinistic activism springs from a robust doctrine of supernatural concursive process.

In 1918 Warfield published *Counterfeit Miracles*, denying the possibility of miracles after the apostles on the grounds that the purpose of miracle is to authenticate a revelation. His argument displays some of the anti-Catholicism of his maternal grandfather and highlights the degree to which Warfield shared the scientific worldview of his generation, but it also shows how completely a vocal defender of supernaturalism could locate the supernatural, apart from creation, the biblical miracles and regeneration, in 'God's secular methods'.

Warfield championed Westminster Calvinism as 'the ripest fruit of Reformed creed-making', the mature development of potentialities inherent in that 'perfect seed' of doctrine, the Bible. This growth analogy allowed him to affirm both a fixed body of truth and its progressive unfolding in history. On this model only, argued Warfield, was true theological progress possible, for progress required building on the past, and building towards a goal. With this principle in mind he produced sizeable studies of Tertullian, Augustine and Calvin, seeking in them the trunk of the tree whose crown, in his view, was Westminster Calvinism: pure religion, pure evangelicalism and pure theism. It is not insignificant that Warfield worked tirelessly to oppose the revision of the Confession. He won in 1893 and lost in 1904, but in one of his last surviving letters he wrote, 'I am a flaming optimist. That's because I am a Calvinist.'

Bibliography

J. E. Meeter and R. Nicole, *A Bibliography of Benjamin Breckinridge Warfield, 1851–1921* (Nutley: Presbyterian & Reformed Publishing Co., 1974); D. F. Wells (ed.), *The Princeton Theology* (Grand Rapids: Baker, 1989).

B. J. GUNDLACH

■ **WARREN, Max Alexander Cunningham** (1904–1977), Anglican evangelical missionary statesman and writer, was born on 13 August 1904 in Dun Laoghaire, Ireland, to parents who were missionaries in North India. His father was ordained in the Church of Ireland. After a childhood in India, Warren was educated in England at Marlborough and Jesus College, Cambridge (1923–1926), where he was awarded a history scholarship. He obtained first-classes in both history and theology and was Lightfoot Scholar in ecclesiastical history. The study of history remained an abiding interest, and he read widely, not least in nineteenth-century British imperial and colonial studies. His wife, Mary (née Collett), was also a Cambridge history graduate (Girton College, 1922–1925).

After ordination training at Ridley Hall, Warren offered himself as a lay missionary to northern Nigeria as a member of the 'Hausa band' formed in 1924, and arrived in Nigeria in December 1927. He joined there Dr W. R. Miller, a long-serving Church Missionary Society (CMS) medical missionary in Muslim Nigeria, based in Zaria and Kano. Warren's health broke down after serving in Zaria for less than a year, during which time he had both admired Miller and disagreed with his missionary policy. During his long convalescence from tuberculosis, and through the intervention of a Christian counsellor, Warren had a profound spiritual experience, recorded in his autobiography, *Crowded Canvas* (1974), pp. 65–68, as a discovery of the personal love of God in his own weakness and despair at the time. After three years as an invalid, he married Mary and was ordained in Winchester Cathedral in the same month, May 1932. The couple were to have two children, Rosemary (b. 1934) and Pat (b. 1936), who married the CMS missionary Roger Hooker and served with him in India.

Warren became curate of St John's, Boscombe, a flourishing evangelical church, and also youth organizer for the diocese (1932–1936). His zeal for evangelism was expressed through a large-scale evangelical mission in Bournemouth, in which over a hundred students from Oxford and Cambridge took part, led by Warren's boyhood friend, Bryan Green, then chaplain to the Oxford Pastorate; Green wrote of it as 'brilliantly planned'. This student mission was a fitting preparation for

Warren's next appointment as vicar of Holy Trinity, Cambridge (1936–1942), the church Charles *Simeon had served. Warren acted as secretary of the Cambridge Pastorate, which, like its Oxford equivalent, sought to extend Christian work among members of the university. Warren faced the challenges of the Second World War by turning to the Old Testament prophets, not least Habakkuk, as interpreters of history who trusted God in the face of cataclysmic events. In 1942 he initiated the Evangelical Fellowship of Theological Literature, which aimed to renew theological scholarship among evangelicals and bring together in one body conservative and liberal under the single label 'evangelical' after the divisions of 1922 (for example, that between the more conservative Bible Churchman's Missionary Society and the CMS).

In the same year Warren became General Secretary of CMS (1942–1963), a position of great influence that he was to find supremely satisfying. Beyond the society and its leadership, his influence was exercised by his authorship of the CMS newsletters. These monthly reflections on Christian mission and the world order, economic, political and religious, acquired a readership of some 14,000. His penetrating analysis of the context and practice of mission were read by politicians and diplomats as well as by missionaries and clergy.

For CMS, Warren's secretariat coincided with the adjustment to post-colonialism, the movement to independence not only of India in 1947 but also of nations in West, Central and East Africa where CMS had worked, and the growth of national churches in Ghana, Nigeria, Uganda, Kenya and Tanzania. Skill was needed in adjusting to the new realities and this Warren displayed as a missionary statesman *par excellence*.

A leading issue addressed in the newsletters was the Christian relationship to the resurgent world religions. Warren had himself been deeply impressed by Kenneth (A. K.) Cragg's *The Call of the Minaret* (1956), in which the case for sensitive dialogue with Islam was advanced with great erudition and sympathy, without loss of emphasis on Christian distinctiveness. As well as urging his readers to study this book, Warren launched a series of works by writers with personal experience of alternative religious traditions, the 'Christian Presence' series. In his general introduction as editor he explained that the aim was 'in approaching another people, another culture, another religion ... to take off one's shoes, for the place we are approaching is holy. Else we may find we are treading on men's dreams ... we have to sit where they sit, to enter sympathetically into the pains, griefs and joys of their history ... we have, in a word, to be "present" with them' (J. V. Taylor, *The Primal Vision* [1961], pp. 10–11). Cragg supplied *Sandals at the Mosque* (1959) to this series, which included studies by J. V. Taylor (African religion) and George Appleton (Buddhism).

In this period Warren also attended International Missionary Council (IMC) meetings at Whitby, Ontario (1947), where he acted as chaplain, Willingen (1952), Evanston, Illinois (1954) and Ghana (1957/8). He argued vigorously against the merger proposed between the World Council of Churches (WCC) and the IMC, believing that the latter retained the confidence of many missionary bodies, and that this would be lost if its distinctive life was absorbed into the larger body. Despite his pleas, the merger took place at the New Delhi meeting of the WCC in 1961.

In 1963 Warren retired from CMS and was appointed canon and sub-dean of Westminster Abbey (1963–1973). He was invited to give two sets of lectures in the Cambridge divinity faculty. The first series was published as *The Missionary Movement from Britain in Modern History* (1965) and the second as *Social History and Christian Mission* (1967). In his spare moments at CMS and after, he had studied and catalogued the voluminous papers and correspondence of his great predecessor, Henry *Venn, CMS secretary from 1841 to 1872. This work bore fruit in *To Apply the Gospel* (1971), an introduction to Venn's writings and missiology.

Warren continued to address theological and missiological issues after his retirement from Westminster Abbey. His essay on religious pluralism and the theology of religions of John Hick, an extended critique entitled 'The Uniqueness of Christ' (*Modern Churchman*, vol. 18 [1974], pp. 55–66), was judged by F. W. Dillistone, his biographer, to be the best article he ever wrote. Of his many other writings, some of the most significant were *The Christian Mission* (1951), a study on

church and state, *Caesar the Beloved Enemy* (1955), *Revival – An Enquiry* (1954) and *I Believe in the Great Commission* (1976). He died on 22 August 1977 and received an extended obituary in *The Times* of 25 August.

If there is a single interpretative key to Warren's life, it is the emphasis on freedom and flexibility in mission. It led him to espouse the voluntary principle for the missionary society and was at the root of his opposition to the merger of IMC and WCC. Warren expressed it in a pamphlet review of a volume on modern Anglican expansion, *Iona and Rome* (1946), in which he advocated Celtic approaches to mission in preference to an emphasis on hierarchy and diocesanization. He remained a lifelong opponent of the static, the bureaucratic and 'tidiness' as the enemy of initiative and spiritual dynamism.

Bibliography

F. W. Dillistone, *Into All the World: A Biography of Max Warren* (London: Hodder & Stoughton, 1980); M. Warren, *Crowded Canvas: Some Experiences of a Life-time* (London: Hodder & Stoughton, 1974); T. E. Yates, 'Evangelicalism Without Hyphens: Max Warren, the Tradition and Theology of Mission', *Anvil*, 2.3 (1985), pp. 231–245; G. Kings, *Christianity Connected: Hindus, Muslims and the World in the Letters of Max Warren and Roger Hooker* (Zoetermeer: Boekencentrum, 2002).

T. E. YATES

■ **WATSON, David Christopher Knight** (1933–1984), Anglican clergyman and evangelist, was born on 7 March 1933 at Catterick, Yorkshire, the son of Godfrey and Peggy Watson. His father was deeply committed to Christian Science, but after his death the family became Anglicans. Watson was educated at Bedford School and Wellington College, Berkshire. Though he excelled at school, he took no interest in Christianity, and after national service described he himself as a humanist and atheist. However, while at St John's College, Cambridge, Watson made a simple commitment to Christ and became involved with the Cambridge Inter-Collegiate Christian Union. He graduated BA in 1957 (MA in 1961). As a student he became involved with the 'Bash camps' at Iwerne

Minster, Dorset, led by E. J. H. *Nash. Their simple and direct presentation of the gospel to public-school boys helped to develop Watson's ability as a communicator, which, together with his organizational gifts, later made him an influential church leader.

After training at Ridley Hall, Cambridge, Watson was ordained deacon in 1959 and priest in 1960. His first two curacies were in contrasting settings. The first was at St Mark's, Gillingham, which began to experience charismatic renewal during his time there. The second, from 1962, was at Holy Sepulchre (the Round Church), Cambridge, where his gifts began to be more widely recognized. In 1964 he married Elizabeth Anne MacEwan Smith and they had two children.

In 1965 Watson became the curate-in-charge of St Cuthbert's, Pearsholm Green, York. His aim was simple: to preach the gospel and to develop a charismatic understanding of the work of the Holy Spirit. The result of much hard work, expository preaching and prayer was the creation of a lively and dynamic congregation. It eventually outgrew the building, and in 1973 it transferred to St Michael-le-Belfrey, situated immediately opposite York Minster. Two thirds of the congregation came from other churches in the city and county, and a third were new Christians. The church, including Watson and his family, experimented with a number of household communities. Within the church a pattern of shared leadership developed, which included curates, drama and dance specialists and talented musicians, all of whom complemented Watson's unique gifts. Between 1978 and 1983 Watson conducted fifty-eight missions in five continents. Venues included universities, public schools and prisons, and some missions were city-wide 'Festivals of Praise'. Watson wrote a number of books, including I Believe in Evangelism (1977) and I Believe in the Church (1978). A report on the church concluded that 'St Michael-le-Belfrey is not an ordinary Anglican parish. It represents the coming together of a particular person with his own gifts; a particular family with their own faith and vision; a particular moment in the life of the churches in a city and deanery, and in the processes of English society in the [19]70s.'

Much of the success of the church was due to David Watson. He was a gracious, charming, open person, and his upper-middle-class, public-school background was evident in his speech. At the same time, he willingly exposed his own weakness and vulnerability. From the mid 1960s he suffered from asthma and debilitating bouts of depression. His emphases were evangelism, renewal and reconciliation; he promoted the last of these particularly in Ireland and South Africa and between charismatics and non-charismatics. He was not a controversialist: he was prepared to work with Roman Catholics and caused some concern among evangelicals when he described the Reformation as one of the greatest tragedies in the history of the church, which had brought division into the body of Christ.

Watson moved to London in 1982 with the intention of fulfilling an even wider ministry. Soon afterwards he published his autobiography, You are My God (1983), and was diagnosed with cancer. In April 1983 he gave a moving BBC radio interview, 'A case for healing', and in the same year wrote the posthumously published Fear no Evil (1984). Watson died in London on 18 February 1984. A number of memorial services were held, the largest at York Minister and St Paul's Cathedral, London. Writing at the time, the then Archbishop of Canterbury, Robert Runcie, said, 'No sensitive observer of the Church of England over the past twenty years could fail to notice the impact of David Watson. So many people came to faith or were renewed in faith through his ministry that God's blessing upon his life and work seemed self-evident.'

Bibliography
E. England (ed.), David Watson: a Portrait by his Friends (Crowborough: Highland, 1985); T. Saunders and H. Sansom, David Watson: a Biography (Sevenoaks: Hodder & Stoughton, 1992).

A. F. MUNDEN

■ **WATSON, Richard** (1781–1833), Wesleyan Methodist minister and theologian, was born on 22 February 1781 at Barton-upon-Humber, Lincolnshire, the seventh of the eighteen children of Thomas and Ann Watson. Thomas Watson was a saddler with Dissenting sympathies, whose enthusiastic support for the building of a chapel in Barton cost him customers and led to the family's move to Lincoln in 1789. Ann Watson, a Londoner, was 'a woman of superior mind'.

Richard Watson's education began at the age of six, when he was sent to the school of Matthew Barnett, curate of St Peter's, Barton. Barnett introduced Watson to Latin. At an early age Watson was already an avid reader. After two years at a private school in Lincoln, Watson attended Lincoln Grammar School until he was fourteen, when he became an apprentice carpenter and joiner. Although by this time his parents had become Wesleyan Methodists, Watson turned against Christianity for a while, and also allowed most of his studies to lapse. A desire to gather material to use in argument with a staunchly Calvinist acquaintance led him to attend the Wesleyan chapel, and this attendance resulted in his conversion. He preached his first sermon at the age of fifteen, and his reputation grew to the point where he was invited to take over the duties of the Wesleyan minister at Newark, who was unwell. The Conference of 1796 received Watson as a preacher on trial, and he served circuits in Ashby-de-la-Zouch, Castle Donington, Leicester and Derby, before being received into full connexion in 1800. The guidance of Jonathan Edmondson, his superintendent in Leicester, was important in directing Watson's reading, as he developed his understanding of the biblical languages and of theology. An interest in doctrinal controversy, however, and a willingness intellectually to explore opinions other than his own, led to misgivings concerning his orthodoxy during his appointment in the Hinckley circuit (1800–1801). Although formal charges were never brought, Watson was wounded by the unfounded suspicions, resigned from the ministry and later left the connexion. Shortly afterwards he joined the recently formed Methodist New Connexion. His wife, Mary Henshaw, whom he married in 1801, was the daughter of a New Connexion local preacher; they had a son and a daughter.

Watson soon became a New Connexion preacher, serving in Manchester and then in Liverpool. He was elected secretary of the Conference several times, was invited to write the Conference's pastoral address to the societies, published a pamphlet defending the continuation of the war with Napoleonic France and became a regular leader-writer for *The Liverpool Courier*. Dissatisfaction with the discipline of the New Connexion led to his resignation in 1811, and in 1812, with the support of Joseph Entwisle and Jabez *Bunting, he was reinstated as a Wesleyan minister.

The next twenty years of Watson's life were spent at the heart of the Wesleyan connexion. After circuit appointments in Wakefield and Hull, he moved to London in 1816 as one of the secretaries of the newly founded Wesleyan Methodist Missionary Society (WMMS), becoming Resident Secretary (without circuit responsibilities) in 1821. Apart from two years in Manchester (1827–1829), he spent the rest of his ministry in London, organizing the rapidly expanding work of the WMMS, corresponding with missionaries, writing the annual reports of the Society and defending Wesleyan missions, especially those in the West Indies, against press and parliamentary criticism of their alleged incitement of unrest on the plantations. The latter responsibility increasingly involved Watson in the campaign against slavery; he followed Bunting's lead in supporting the Anti-Slavery Society, addressed the Society's Exeter Hall meeting in April 1831 and drafted resolutions on slavery for the Wesleyan Conferences of 1830 and 1832. Watson served on a variety of other connexional committees, was first secretary of the General Chapel Fund (1817) and was elected President of Conference in 1826. A firm supporter of connexional polity and discipline, he responded to the agitation of the Protestant Methodists provoked by the Leeds organ controversy of 1827 by publishing a critique of their congregationalist ecclesiology in *An Affectionate Address* (1828).

Watson's gifts as a polemicist were employed in responding to comments denying the eternal sonship of Christ in Adam *Clarke's *Commentary*. Watson's *Remarks on the Eternal Sonship and the Use of Reason in Matters of Revelation* (1818) not only defended orthodox Christology but also included a discussion of theological method, suggesting that Clarke's rationalist principles of biblical interpretation were susceptible to Arian and Socinian development in the hands of less reliable exegetes. Two years later,

Watson was asked by the connexion to reply to Southey's *Life of Wesley* (1820), which he did so robustly in his *Observations on Southey's Life of Wesley: Being a Defence of the Character, Labours, and Opinions of the Founder of Methodism against the Misrepresentations of that Publication* that George IV reputedly expressed sympathy for the Poet Laureate, and Watson's early twentieth-century biographer gently chided him for failing to appreciate the real merits and insights of Southey's work.

Among Watson's constructive works were a *Biblical and Theological Dictionary* (1831), a biography of *Wesley (1831), a catechism on Christian evidences (1824) and a volume of *Conversations with the Young* (1830). He was also given responsibility for selecting hymns for the 1831 Wesleyan supplement to Wesley's 1780 hymnbook. His major work, however, was his *Theological Institutes: Or, A View of the Evidences, Doctrines, Morals, and Institutions of Christianity*, which he began writing in 1821, and which appeared in six parts between 1823 and 1829. The *Institutes* represented the first effective systematization of Wesleyan theology, perhaps stimulated by anxieties provoked during the controversy over eternal sonship, that the doctrinal standards provided by the writings of Wesley and *Fletcher were inadequate to deal with contemporary questions. Watson's presentation marked a change of focus from Wesley's 'distinctive mode of practical theology' to a more deductive, systematic and propositional approach underpinned by an emphasis on the authority of Scripture. In the words of Watson's first biographer, Thomas Jackson, 'As a theologian, the distinguishing peculiarity of his mind was an absolute submission to the authority of holy Scripture.' Much of the first part of the *Institutes* was devoted to an exposition of this authority. Significantly, Watson was working on an exposition of the whole of the New Testament at the time of his death, in London, on 8 January 1833.

Despite many years of ill health, Watson was an imposing figure, standing six feet two inches tall and with a square and lofty brow: 'the biggest brow I ever saw', according to Benjamin Gregory. As a preacher, he made too many demands on the intellect of his hearers to be truly popular, but he was reputed none the less to be a clear and lucid speaker; a politician who attended a sermon at City Road with Joseph Butterworth, the Methodist publisher and MP, remarked on the sheer intellectual ability of a preacher who could sustain an extemporary address for two hours. Ecclesiastically, Watson's sympathies lay with the Church of England rather than with Dissent, and he admired the Anglican liturgy, commending its use among the Methodists. His influence on the organization of nineteenth-century Wesleyan Methodism was substantial and on its theology, unrivalled.

Bibliography

E. J. Brailsford, *Richard Watson. Theologian and Missionary Advocate* (London: C. H. Kelly, 1906); T. Jackson, *Memoirs of the Life and Writings of the Revd Richard Watson* (London: John Mason, 1834); W. Willan, *Sermons and Outlines by the Revd Richard Watson* (London: Hamilton, Adams & Co., 1865).

M. WELLINGS

■ **WATTS, Isaac** (1674–1748), hymnwriter, was born on 17 July 1674 in Southampton and died at Stoke Newington, London on 25 November 1748. His father, an active Dissenter, was twice imprisoned. Thus from early childhood, Watts knew personally the privations and restrictions facing Dissenters. He received a classical education at Southampton Grammar School, having been introduced to Latin and Greek by his father, who kept a boarding school in the town. This classical education was to be very important to his works, in which there are obvious references to both the style and the content of classical literature. Watts was offered the chance of a university education, but he was required as a condition to become a member of the Church of England; determined to remain a Dissenter, he was barred from university, but he spent four years at Stoke Newington Academy (1690–1694), studying classics, logic, Hebrew and divinity. After spending two years at home, from 1696 Watts was for five years the resident tutor to the son of Sir John Hartopp; during this time he devoted himself to Hebrew and divinity. From 1698 to 1701, despite bouts of illness, he preached frequently. In 1701, having travelled to Bath and Tonbridge Wells to alleviate his fever and weakness, he returned to London, and in 1702 became the pastor of a popular Independent meeting place in Mark Lane. In 1703 an additional pastor was appointed to oversee the growing congregation. Preaching commitments, combined with constant study, left Watts in poor health, vulnerable to fever and headaches. Because of this, in 1712, unable to continue working as a minister, he took up residence in the household of Sir Thomas and Lady Abney, where he stayed for the rest of his life.

The intellectual history of Watts' times brings his work into sharper focus. In 1645 the Royal Society was founded. John Wilkins, a founder member, was to have a personal influence on Watts, as Watts acknowledged in 1715 in 'A Guide to Prayer' (G. Burder [ed.], *The Works of the Reverend and Learned Isaac Watts, D.D. in Six Volumes* [London, 1810]). Isaac Newton was the president of the Society from 1703 to 1727, a period in which much of Watts' work was written; references to Newton in that work point to his influence upon it. In 1690 John Locke published his two works *Of Government*, which were very influential in shaping liberal and democratic ideas. Watts thus grew up in an age of question and analysis, in which established beliefs were criticized and the importance of reason, which was for Watts 'the glory of human nature', was emphasized. Deism, a rational movement that criticized the Bible and rejected certain traditional Christian doctrines, flourished at this time; Watts' writing on deist philosophy becomes more significant when its background is understood. He saw a sincere deist as one 'who will sooner or later become a Christian'. However, Watts stressed that reason was subordinate to God's revelation in the life and work of Jesus Christ.

Although Watts is remembered as a hymn-writer, his literary output was wide-ranging. The long list of his publications includes *Horae Lyricae* (1706, 1709), *Hymns & Spiritual Songs* (1707), *Divine Songs for Children* (1715), *Psalms of David* (1719), *Logic* (1725; used as a text at Oxford), *Knowledge of Heavens & Earth* (1726), *Philosophical Essays* (1733) and *Relinquiae Juveniles* (1734). Watts' exposition of and dissertations on the *Christian Doctrine of the Trinity*

(1722) are a timely reminder of his century's questioning of Christian doctrine. Watts argued that Independent ministers who could not sign a Trinitarian statement of faith should not be excluded from fellowship. His own treatises on the doctrine of the Trinity, particularly his essay 'The Glory of Christ', provoked suspicions of Unitarianism; these were reinforced by the later destruction of some of his work by his executors. Watts possessed an open, enquiring mind, sought persistently after truth and refused to accept the dictates of mere custom. His writings on the Trinity demonstrate his preoccupation with reasoned explanation: 'I want to have this wonderful doctrine of the all-sufficience of thy Son and thy Spirit made a little plainer' (*Works iv*, p. 160). Widely recognized in his lifetime as a scholar with considerable theological and philosophical acumen, Watts received an honorary degree in 1728 from Edinburgh University.

In 1706 Watts published the first edition of *Horae Lyricae* (*Works iv*, pp. 423–499) in two volumes. In 1709 it was expanded to three volumes, including a much longer preface but omitting some of the psalms. The language used in this work is poetic and devotional, with metaphysical conceits; it links Watts with Donne and Herbert and earned him the respect of Samuel Johnson and a place in *Lives of the Poets*. *Horae Lyricae* contains sonnets, Latin poems, Pindaric odes, blank verse, experiments with verse form, rhythm and metre, as in 'Divine Judgements' (*Works iv*, p. 451), which is a daring, technical experiment in English Sapphics. This alarmingly vivid and graphic poem, written in hendecasyllabic metre with a short fourth line, displays a vision of Hell akin to that of medieval doom painting:

> Hopeless mortals! how they scream and
> shiver,
> While devils push them to the pit wide-
> yawning,
> Hideous and gloomy, to receive them
> headlong
> Down to the centre!

Some of Watts' early poetry reveals Miltonic influence, but the significance of *Horae Lyricae* lies partly in its affinity to the poetry of John Donne. Watts, in writing of divine love in the poem 'Mutual love stronger than Death' (*Works iv*, p. 451), uses sensuous, physical images: 'he seiz'd me in his arms'; 'with force divinely sweet'. These are as forceful and shocking as Donne's poetry.

Horae Lyricae is divided into three books, entitled 'Sacred to Devotion and Piety', 'To Vertue, Honour and Friendship' and 'To the Memory of the Dead'. Although the first book contains some hymns, for example 'God is a name my soul adores', in much of the poetry Watts is trying to express something of the Godhead, to define the indefinable. 'Happy Frailty' (*Works iv*, p. 445) uses imagery more often associated with Blake; Watts marvels at the 'clod of Earth design'd / T'enclose a heavenly star'. The contrasting images of the clod and the star are very vivid, and the word 'design'd' suggests the purposeful work of the creator. 'True Monarchy, 1701' (*Works iv*, p. 465) reveals the importance that Watts placed on self-discipline, with its reference to 'the Man / That chains his rebel will to Reason's throne'.

In discussing the importance of the cadence, the rise and fall of a phrase, Watts refers to the poetry of Milton, Dryden and Pope, and their influence is evident in his *Hymns and Spiritual Songs* (3 vols., 1707; *Works iv*, pp. 257–368). The hymns are mostly in four metres and set to common tunes; Watts aims to create a smooth sound with restrained metaphors. He harnesses his poetical skill to produce a controlled, simple construction, using clarity and unerring choice of language to achieve his object: 'to make the sense plain and obvious'. Although the subject matter is biblical, the thoughts and feelings expressed in many of the hymns are personal, as in 'Come, Holy Spirit, heavenly dove' (1707; *Works iv*, p. 307). An invocation, much of its effect and strength lies in its contrasts. The hymn starts and finishes with the quickening (life-giving) power of the Holy Spirit; the two intervening verses include phrases such as 'in vain', 'languishing hosannas', 'dying devotion' and 'faint and cold love', which contrast with the fire, 'the flame of sacred love', that the Holy Spirit will bring. The description of human failure ('in vain we tune; in vain we strive') emphasizes the 'quickening powers' of the Holy Spirit. A common theme in Watts' hymnody is the duty laid upon humans to praise God for his creation, but Watts also stresses human

inadequacy and inability to comprehend the marvel of that creation and the mystery that surrounds the Godhead. In verse 4 of 'I give immortal praise' (*Works iv*, p. 356) Watts praises the mystery of the Trinity whilst asserting the fallibility of reason. In his later work *Strength and Weakness of Human Reason* (1731; *Works ii*, p. 319) Watts tried to lead his readers to see that reason must be subjugated to divine revelation, as in the last line of 'I give immortal praise':

> Where reason fails with all her powers,
> There faith prevails, and love adores.

This hymn and 'The Lord Jehovah reigns' (*Works iv*, p. 345) have a six-line verse. Watts uses this structure because it allows him to use the last two lines of each verse as a summary of the preceding four lines. The last verse of 'The Lord Jehovah reigns' comprises four lines of rhetorical questions and Watts' answer: 'I love his name, I love his word, / Join all my powers to praise the Lord.' This desire to praise God for his creation and redemption is perhaps best exemplified in the hymn which Erik Routley described as 'the greatest of all hymns on the Atonement written since the Reformation' (*Hymns Today & Tomorrow*, 1966, p. 68). In the hymn 'Nature with open volume stands' (*Works iv*, p. 350) the poetic imagination is expressed clearly in the devotional content.

> Here his whole name appears complete:
> Nor wit can guess, nor reason prove
> Which of the letters best is writ –
> The Power, the Wisdom, or the Love.

In this third verse Watts develops the image of the 'open volume' in verse 1: the whole name of God is a product of its various letters (his attributes), which man's wit and reason, so important in the eighteenth century, cannot comprehend. In this verse and verse 4 lines 2 and 3 are run on; in other verses lines 3 and 4 emphasize the thought expressed in lines 1 and 2. The structure is noteworthy because the word 'here' that opens these two central verses refers to the cross. Christ's redemption on the cross is thus the climax of the 'volume'.

The mystical element in Watts' poetry is evident in the hymn 'Give me the wings of faith to rise' (*Works iv*, p. 337). The 'clouds of witnesses' in the last verse complete the image of 'the veil' in verse 1. The wings of faith transcend earthly reason, allowing a glimpse of immortality and a temporary union with those beyond death.

'I'm not ashamed to own my Lord' (*Works iv*, p. 282), which is based on 2 Timothy 1:12, exemplifies Watts' faith and assurance of salvation and his evangelistic zeal. The expressions 'I know', 'his promise stands' and 'appointing my soul a place' in verses 2 to 4 follow Watts' opening defence of his Lord, in which he asserts the glory of the cross. This whole hymn almost implies the existence of a covenant between Watts and God. Perhaps the best-known hymn in *Hymns and Spiritual Songs* is a communion hymn, 'When I survey the wondrous cross' (*Works iv*, p. 349). It presents the futility and worthlessness of all that humans have to offer when it is placed alongside the greatness of God's love for them, portrayed in the death of Christ. Watts uses contrasts to heighten awareness of this incomprehensible sacrifice:

When I survey the wondrous cross
On which the Prince of glory died,
My richest gain I count but loss,
And pour contempt on all my pride.

Watts' description of the pain of crucifixion, 'his dying crimson like a robe / Spreads o'er his body on the tree', is transformed by its own imagery into something like a medieval icon. The last verse moves from marvel and vivid description to complete personal commitment:

Love so amazing, so divine
Demands my soul, my life, my all.

In this hymn Watts begins as the controlled objective hymn-writer but ends as the personal evangelist. Because of its cruci-centrism, it was to become a favourite of the later evangelical movement.

Divine Songs attempted in easy language for the use of Children (1715; *Works iv*, p. 389) must have become widely known, because 'How doth the little busy bee' (*Works iv*, p. 399) was parodied in Lewis Carroll's *Alice in Wonderland* in 1865, and in 1868 Louisa May Alcott used 'Birds in their little nests agree' in *Little Women*. The content of some of these songs conveys dread rather than guidance, but they influenced William Blake's *Songs of Innocence* (see D. Barratt, R. Pooley and L. Ryken [eds.], *The Discerning Reader* [Leicester: IVP, 1995], pp. 195–217). One hymn from *Divine Songs* has found a place in recent hymnals; 'I sing the almighty power of God' appears in *Hymns & Psalms* (1983) and *Rejoice and Sing* (1991).

The Royal Society was also interested in the reform of psalmody, and Watts makes a great contribution to this: *The Psalms of David imitated in the language of the New Testament* (1719; *Works iv*, pp. 241–368). In the preface Watts explains to the reader how he has omitted some material from the Psalms, paraphrased the text and included references to Messianic fulfilment in order to update the content, 'to accommodate the book of Psalms to Christian worship'. Somewhat limited by the dearth of suitable tunes at the time and by the practice of giving out of a psalm line by line, Watts' psalms may appear restricted in metre, but in the preface he states that he has used the three most useful metres. He defends his language thus: 'I have coupled all my lines by rhymes much more than either Mr. Tate or Dr. Patrick have done; which is certainly most musical and agreeable to the ear where rhyme is used at all. I have always avoided the language of the poets where it did not suit the language of the gospel.' The psalms, expressed in concise, structured, controlled language, combine the themes of human wonder at God's creation with God's redeeming grace, fulfilled in Christ. Psalm 8, in common metre, exemplifies this combination: 'wondrous', 'exalted' and 'glories' in verse 1 emphasize God's greatness, while 'moon', 'stars' and 'moving worlds' in verse 2 underline God's creative power; 'dwells . . . so far below' stresses man's insignificance; and verse 8, by the use of contrasts such as 'crown'd' and 'bow'd to death', recalls Christ's triumph over death. The psalms are based on the original text, but most include an additional line or verse that presents the gospel message of the risen Christ. However, there is a notable exception: 'O God our help in ages past' (*Works iv*, p. 191). Often used at remembrance and funeral services, and originally entitled 'Man frail, and God eternal', this hymn from the *Psalms of David* is well known and is sung by millions of people, from various Christian traditions every year. In it Watts expresses the security resulting from God's protection in words such as 'shelter', 'home', 'secure', 'sufficient' and 'guard'. 'Our help', 'our hope', 'our home', 'past' and 'years to come' are phrases that convey assurance in an uncertain world. The permanence of God's protection is contrasted (in almost nihilistic terms) with the transitory world where 'Time ... bears all its sons away'. Based on the first five verses of Psalm 90, this hymn is close to its original and does not explicitly express a Messianic hope. Rather it is a splendid statement of God's omnipotence and permanence in contrast to human transience.

Watts is the first great hymnographer. He adheres strictly to metrical pattern and controlled verse form, but his religious fervour and simple, evangelical use of the Scriptures, coupled with his poetic imagination, combine with his technical skill to produce what J. R. Watson calls 'a recognizable and impressive art form' (*Companion to Hymn & Psalms*, 1988, p. 21).

Bibliography

L. F. Benson, *The English Hymn* (London: Hodder & Stoughton, 1915); H. Escott, *Isaac Watts, Hymnographer* (London: Independent Press, 1962); J. R. Watson, *The English Hymn* (Oxford: Oxford University Press, 1997).

M. HARRIS

■ **WESLEY, Charles** (1707–1788), co-founder of Methodism and hymn-writer, was born on 18 December 1707 in Epworth, England, where his father, Samuel, was the Anglican rector. He was the eighteenth child born to Samuel and Susanna Wesley and was five years younger than his more famous brother, John *Wesley. After receiving his elementary education from his mother, Charles entered Westminster School in April 1716, where his eldest brother, Samuel Wesley, was Master. In 1726 Charles entered Christ Church College, Oxford, as a King's Scholar, where he earned the BA and MA.

During his first year at Oxford Charles's seriousness about religion diminished significantly, but in his second year he gave himself, with a few other students, to diligent study and religious practice, which earned them the name 'Methodists'. John Wesley left his curacy at Epworth and brought his leadership and organizational skills to their assistance. Soon these young men had formed the so-called 'Oxford Holy Club', with rules, resolutions and patterns of piety drawn from the Scriptures and the practices of the early church. Charles's buoyant personality contributed much to the Holy Club.

Charles believed that he was best suited for an academic life, but his brother John had other plans for him. As Charles explained to Dr Chandler: 'I took my Masters Degree, and only thought of spending all my days at Oxford. But my brother, who always had the ascendent over me, persuaded me to accompany him and Mr. Oglethorpe to Georgia. I exceedingly dreaded entering into holy orders; but he overruled me here also, and I was ordained Deacon by the Bishop of Oxford, Dr. Potter, and the next Sunday, Priest, by the Bishop of London, Dr. Gibson' (Tyson, *Reader*, p. 59). The Wesley brothers, with two friends from the Oxford Holy Club, went to Georgia as missionaries, under the auspices of the Anglican Society for the Propagation of the Christian Gospel (SPCG). John was to serve as pastor of the citizens of Savannah; Charles's duties were divided between being secretary to General Oglethorpe, secretary for Indian Affairs, and pastor to the settlers of Frederica. They arrived in St Simons Island, Georgia, on 9 March 1736, and soon began their respective tasks.

It quickly became apparent that Charles Wesley was ill suited for the rough, rural life he met in Frederica. He also seemed to be unsuitable for his congregation, as his High Church rubrics and concerns were not appreciated by the straightforward colonials. He became too deeply involved in local gossip and parish intrigue; within three weeks of his arriving in the country, Charles's parishioners were refusing to greet him when they passed on the only street in town. As Charles reported to Chandler: 'The hardship of lying on the ground, &c., soon threw me into a Fever and Dysentery, which in half a year forced me to return to England.'

Disappointment over the apparent failure of his Georgia mission, his recurrent illness and the patient witness of the Moravian mechanic John Bray, prepared Charles for his conversion. On Pentecost Sunday, 21 May 1738, after professing resolute faith in Christ, Charles wrote: 'I felt a violent opposition and reluctance to believe; yet still the Spirit of God strove with my own and the evil spirit, till by degrees he chased away the darkness of my unbelief. I found myself convinced, I know not how, nor when; and immediately fell into intercession ... I now found myself at peace with God, and rejoiced in hope of loving Christ. My temper for the rest of the day was, mistrust of my own great, but before unknown, weakness. I saw that by faith I stood; by the continual support of faith, which kept me from falling, though of my self I am ever sinking into sin. I went to bed still sensible of my own weakness ... yet content of Christ's protection' (Tyson, *Reader*, p. 99).

Two days later, on 23 May 1738, Charles Wesley began composing the lyrics to 'An hymn upon my conversion'. The next evening his brother John visited him on his way home from a meeting in Aldersgate Street. John had good news: 'I believe!' He and Charles sang the 'conversion hymn' in celebration of their shared experiences. Exactly which 'conversion hymn' the Wesleys sang that night is a matter of some debate. A case can be made from the brothers' journals for any one of three: 'Christ the Friend of Sinners' ('Where shall my wondering soul begin?'), 'Free Grace' ('And can it be, that I should gain'), and 'A Hymn for Whitsunday' ('Granted is the Saviour's prayer'). Charles's 'Congratulations to a Friend Upon Believing in Christ' ('What morn on thee with sweeter ray') was probably written after the event, in celebration of his brother's conversion. The hymn which became (arguably) his most famous, 'O for a thousand tongues to sing', was written (as its original title implies) 'For the Anniversary Day of One's Conversion'.

Charles Wesley is best known as an evangelical hymn-writer. He wrote over 9,000 hymns and sacred poems in a busy half-century of ministry. As many as 400 of his compositions are found in modern hymn-books; the most famous of these include 'And can it be?', 'Christ the Lord has risen today', 'Hark! the herald-angels sing', 'Love divine, all loves excelling' and 'O for a thousand tongues to sing'. Although Charles

Wesley was a capable keyboard musician, he confined himself to composing lyrics. These were written in a vast array of metres, many of which could easily be adapted to fit popular tunes.

As a hymn-writer, however, Charles Wesley was primarily a Methodist evangelist. Many of his hymns reflect the biblical texts used in his sermons, or celebrate the evangelical experiences chronicled in his journal. Charles's hymns were constructed to vivify, illustrate and inculcate Methodist doctrines, and were profoundly shaped by the Authorized Version of the Bible. As J. E. Rattenbury wryly wrote: 'a skillful man, if the Bible were lost, might extract it from Wesley's hymns. They contain the Bible in solution' (*Evangelical Doctrines*, p. 48). Charles's hymns were invariably Christocentric, and virtually every hymn included Methodist doctrinal distinctives such as 'universal redemption' (unlimited atonement and general election) and 'full salvation' (justification and sanctification). That John Wesley understood his brother's hymns as theological compositions is amply demonstrated by his use of them to illustrate and supplement his *Standard Sermons*; eighteen of the fifty-three sermons employ Charles's hymns.

Charles Wesley was an effective evangelist, partly because of his poet's way with words. When his sermon 'Awake, Thou that Sleepest' was published as a pamphlet it became one of the Wesleys' best selling publications. In the first decade of their cooperative ministry Charles joined his brother John in his innovative outdoor preaching and itinerant ministry. His journal for these years chronicles his incessant travel and numerous sermons.

Charles and John Wesley's mostly harmonious partnership in ministry was only occasionally strained. John rightly described himself as 'the head' and Charles as 'the heart' of their work. Charles annotated more than one of John's epistolary directives with the words: 'Trying to bring ME under HIS yoke.' But Charles was capable of independent and impetuous action, as in the 'Grace Murray affair', in which he intervened in John's courtship, marrying Grace to another suitor. Charles was even more a son of the Anglican Church than John was, and he resented the growing power of the Methodist lay preachers. On Christian perfection, John usually preached the 'instantaneous blessing', whereas Charles regarded sanctification as a process that was not normally completed until the life to come.

After marrying Sarah (Sally) Gwynne in 1749, however, Charles lived a more settled life, though he continued to minister, first in Bristol and then in London (1771–1788). He died in London on 29 March 1788 and was buried in the graveyard of his Anglican parish church in Marylebone.

Bibliography
F. Baker, *Charles Wesley as Revealed by His Letters* (London: Epworth Press, 1948); F. Baker, *The Representative Verse of Charles Wesley* (London: Epworth Press, 1962); S. T. Kimbrough (ed.), *Charles Wesley Poet and Theologian* (Nashville: Abingdon Press, 1992); J. E. Rattenbury, *Evangelical Doctrines of Charles Wesley's Hymns* (London: Epworth Press, 1948); J. R. Tyson (ed.), *Charles Wesley: A Reader* (New York and Oxford: Oxford University Press, 1989); J. R. Tyson, *Charles Wesley on Sanctification: A Biographical and Theological Study* (Grand Rapids: Zondervan, 1986).

J. R. TYSON

■ **WESLEY, John** (1703–1791), founder of the Methodist movement, was the second surviving son of Samuel Wesley, the rector of Epworth, and Susanna Annesley, the daughter of a Dissenting minister. His parents provided early training that was a combination of High Church religion, Puritan discipline and academic rigour. After six years at Charterhouse School, London (1713–1720), Wesley matriculated at Christ Church, Oxford. After receiving his BA degree in 1724, he pursued an academic career and in the following four years was ordained deacon, accepted a fellowship at Lincoln College, received his MA and was ordained priest.

Wesley's ordination studies led him to embrace holy living in the tradition of Jeremy Taylor, William Law and Thomas à Kempis. He began a life of meditative piety that focused on the virtues in an attempt to imitate the life of Christ. He began to measure his spirituality through disciplined self-examination and diary-keeping, not un-

like Ignatius Loyola. In 1729 his brother *Charles and two other friends joined him in this venture. By the early 1730s, at the suggestion of a friend, William Morgan, they had begun to add to their agenda of study and piety a more public programme of social work, such as educating orphans and visiting prisoners. At this point Wesley's Arminian theology was seen as a 'new method' by many Calvinists, and he lived strictly by method and rule (he had a method for everything from reading to visiting), so his followers became known as 'Methodists'. By 1734 they numbered about fifty (including Benjamin Ingham and George *Whitefield), in a network of small groups throughout several colleges of Oxford University. Wesley later referred to this Oxford period as 'the first rise of Methodism'.

In 1732 Wesley, like his father earlier, became a corresponding member of the Society for Promoting Christian Knowledge. When his father died in 1735, John answered the Society's invitation to become a volunteer missionary to the new colony of Georgia, recently founded by his father's friend Colonel James Oglethorpe. Subsequently appointed by the Society for the Propagation of the Gospel as parish priest of Savannah, where he served with some limited success, Wesley became enamoured of Sophey Hopkey, niece of the chief magistrate, Thomas Causton. His High Church inclinations and failed courtship of Sophey sharpened his criticism of Causton and Oglethorpe, whom he believed to be guilty of mismanagement. At the magistrate's instigation a grand jury indicted Wesley on a variety of trumped-up charges, which led to his hasty departure from Georgia in 1737. Nevertheless, he had helped the congregation at Savannah to grow, partly perhaps because of his personal notoriety and affinity to anti-establishment rebels. Because of his institution of small society meetings outside church services, first at Frederica and then at Savannah, he called this period 'the second rise of Methodism'.

Back in England, Wesley continued his activities within the religious society movement and pursued his spiritual search for assurance of salvation, which had been encouraged by his contact with some German pietists in Georgia, especially Augustt Hermann Spangenberg. His quest was furthered by his association in London with the Moravian Peter *Böhler, with whom he formed a society in Fetter Lane, London, in May 1738, which he later called the 'third rise of Methodism'. On Pentecost Sunday of that year, his brother Charles had an experience of assurance that the Moravians had been presenting as a prerequisite to salvation or calling oneself a Christian. Three days later, on 24 May, John Wesley had a similar experience in a society meeting in Aldersgate Street. He said that his 'heart was strangely warmed' and that he felt 'an assurance that Christ had died for me'. He then adopted the Moravian practice of claiming that he was now a Christian, 'justified by faith alone', whereas previously he had been trusting in his own righteousness. Although he had been preaching 'salvation by faith' since March 1738 at Peter Böhler's suggestion, he declared that a 'new era' in his life began in April of the following year when he started preaching this theology of 'faith alone' and 'free grace' in the open air in Bristol to thousands of people at a time.

For the next decade Wesley questioned and rejected many of the Moravian assumptions that had led him to see faith as the sole means of salvation. His maturing theology affirmed the necessity of both faith and ('in some sense') works, though it was grounded and dominated by the theme of grace. His emphasis on free grace, along with his espousal of the Arminian emphasis on free will, led him also to challenge directly the doctrine of the 'eternal decrees' (predestination) espoused by George Whitefield and other Calvinists.

The Wesleyan revival was part of a larger worldwide 'evangelical revival'; in America this was often called the Great Awakening. Not all Wesley's friends joined him or stayed with him; George Whitefield's Calvinist leanings drew him into a separate, parallel, Calvinistic Methodist revival. Until the mid-1740s Whitefield was the main target of most anti-Methodist literature, his notoriety arising from his exuberant preaching style. The spread of the Wesleyan revival and the increasing organization of the movement during this period involved not only extensive travel for the Wesley brothers, but also the coordination of local revivals, many of them initiated and led by lay preachers who wanted to associate with the Wesleyans. John asserted that God had raised up the Methodist preachers 'to reform the nation, especially the Church, and to spread Scriptural holiness across the land'.

Although Wesley's preaching could not match the oratorical mastery of Whitefield, his preaching in the open air often attracted thousands of listeners. His style was apparently devoid of the bombast usually expected from an evangelist; one eyewitness even observed that Wesley might be mistaken for a talking marble statue if he had not moved one hand to turn the pages of his sermon. But like that of Jonathan *Edwards, whose writings influenced Wesley, the content of his message moved his listeners far more than the manner of its delivery.

Wesley believed that the proper development of the United Societies of the People Called Methodists depended upon uniformity of doctrine and disciplined Christian living. To these ends, he called his preachers together for annual conferences to promote doctrinal integrity and uniform practices. The published minutes of these meetings began to provide a handbook of Methodist thought and organization. Although the only requirement for joining a Methodist society was the desire 'to flee from the wrath to come and be saved from sin', Wesley's 'General Rules' outlined the specific ways in which the members should demonstrate their desire for salvation: by doing all the good they could, avoiding evil of every kind (the main kinds were listed) and attending to the means of grace. These rules were enforced by quarterly examinations of members and the award of 'class tickets' to those who passed. Largely because of this strict discipline, the Methodist movement in England never grew very fast during the eighteenth century. It was a noticeable but small minority; the 72,000 British members at the time of Wesley's death represented less than 1% of the population.

Unlike Whitefield, Wesley spent as much time organizing his followers into societies as he did preaching to the masses, to ensure that his people enjoyed spiritual fellowship and nurture and did not become 'a rope of sand'. The laity provided much of the leadership for the societies: preachers, class leaders, band leaders, stewards, trustees, visitors of the sick. For these leaders, Wesley not only developed rules and 'methods' for their groups, but also provided educational and devotional publications for their edification. Wesley published over four hundred books and pamphlets for his people, including a fifty-volume *Christian Library* with extracts from what he thought to be the most important works of divinity in the history of Christian thought. His eight volumes of published 'sermons' (1787–1788) were composed largely of written treatises on Christian theology, nurture and edification rather than transcripts of his more anecdotal preaching; Sir Walter Scott remembered Wesley's preaching because of his stories. His collected works (1772–1774) comprised thirty-two volumes. He also published textbooks of history, science, logic, languages, classics and other subjects that he thought a good mind should master. The college he founded at Kingswood, near Bristol, provided a curriculum for children and a course of 'academical learning' that in his view surpassed in quality an Oxford or Cambridge batchelor's degree.

Although most elements of Wesley's movement were intended to renew the Church of England, they gave the Methodists a sense of identity that eventually led to their separation from the church after Wesley's death. During his lifetime, he constantly reiterated his intention 'not to separate', but by the 1780s many people, including his brother Charles, were reading his actions as implying *de facto* separation. Since the middle of the century, the movement had spread into Scotland, Ireland and the American colonies. Following the revolt of the colonies and the return to England of the Anglican clergy, Wesley ordained his own leaders to provide sacramental services and episcopal leadership for the American Methodists, who were organized into a separate church, the Methodist Episcopal Church. He refused to ordain Methodist preachers in countries where the Anglican church retained a presence.

The Methodist 'connexion', organized around those preachers 'in connexion with' John Wesley, was an identifiable phenomenon on the religious scene in the early 1740s. Their detractors included not only those, such as Calvinists and Moravians, who disagreed with aspects of their theology, but also satirical writers, whose portrayals of Wesley's ideas and actions were encouraged by the popular distrust of religious enthusiasm and fanaticism. The shortcomings of Wesley's private life largely escaped public notice, however, especially his aborted engagement in 1749 to Grace Murray (whom his brother Charles married to one of John's preachers while John was out of the country), and the failure of his marriage (in 1752) to a wealthy London widow, Mary Vazeille (who left him after a few years because of her jealousy, spite and perhaps loneliness). His attention was always directed to the work of renewing the church, to which he believed God was directing him.

Wesley's theology was forged in the midst of controversy and tempered by his understanding and experience of 'the Scripture way of salvation'. Although his theological pilgrimage was influenced by Pietism, Puritanism, mysticism and the early church, his basic theological framework continued to reflect his Church of England heritage. His attempt to hold divergent positions in tension produced a 'mediating' theology, although his occasional forays into controversy led him at times to stress one or another side of an argument. His mature theology seen as a whole includes both sacramentalism and evangelism, free will and free grace, faith and good works, without any inconsistency. Although he was probably less unchanging through his lifetime than he sometimes claimed, there is more continuity between the young and the old Wesley than has usually been acknowledged.

Wesley's preaching centred upon what he termed 'the three grand scriptural doctrines – original sin, justification by faith, and holiness consequent thereon'. He occasionally varied his terminology; in one place he refers to the main doctrines of Methodism as (1) repentance, which he called the 'porch of religion', (2) justification by grace through faith, the 'door of religion', and (3) sanctification or holiness, 'religion itself'. The possibility of experiencing entire sanctification, or Christian perfection, in this lifetime was an essential Wesleyan doctrine, which discouraged most clergy of the established church from joining his revival. Wesley insisted that he was not teaching 'perfectionism', merely that it was possible, by God's grace, fully to love God and one's neighbour in this life, but his terminology obscured his explanations. His conviction that one could experience assurance of salvation (both forgiveness or justification, and holiness or sanctification) created further tension, even though it was a lifelong emphasis that shaped his own spiritual pilgrimage. Perversion of his doctrines by his own preachers, such as the perfectionists Thomas Maxfield and John Bell, did not help his cause.

Wesley required his lay preachers, many of whom were uneducated, to preach 'no other doctrines' than those contained in his collection of published sermons and his commentary on the New Testament. These doctrines, distinctively evangelical but in accord with the Church of England standards, were also impressed upon his people through hundreds of popular hymns written and published by the Wesley brothers.

Wesley devised a variety of means to assist his people, including schools for both girls and boys, medical clinics for the indigent, loan funds for small business ventures, subsidized housing for widows and children and pension funds for 'tired and worn out preachers, their widows and children'. For the poor of his societies, he collected clothes, food and money. His published *Journal* is a monument to Methodism rather than to himself, an unabashed piece of propaganda for his movement, filled with accounts of pious lives and holy deaths, earthly enemies and divine retribution. His bibliography reflects his wide range of interests, from theology to poetry, science to philosophy, travel to novels, classics to bestsellers. He became a model of Christian activity, or as one contemporary Swedish observer, Professor J. H. Liden, noted, he was 'the personification of piety'.

Nevertheless, Wesley was the target of persistent attack, especially during the first generation of the Methodist revival. He did, however, outlive most of his early detractors and became a respected example of human and spiritual energy in his old age. For over half a century, he travelled the country, covering an estimated quarter of a million miles, preaching over 40,000 times and publishing over 400 works. He was not afraid to challenge the government's view of the causes of poverty; he was not slow to attack English support of the slave trade. One of his last letters was to the young William *Wilberforce, MP, asking him to persuade Parliament to abolish that 'vile abomination', slavery in America.

Wesley became, as one obituary noted, the most famous private person in England. More than one observer during his lifetime noted a 'venerableness' in his manner, which increased in his later years. From the age of forty he was a subject for many portrait painters, including several Fellows of the Royal Academy, such as Sir Joshua Reynolds, Nathaniel Hone and William Hamilton. Pottery busts were created by the Staffordshire craftsmen Enoch Wood and Josiah Wedgewood. One contemporary, Thomas Haweis, described Wesley as 'of the inferior size, his visage marked with intelligence, singularly neat and plain in his dress; a little cast in his eye, observable on particular occasions; upright, graceful, and remarkably active'. From an early age, he saw himself as a 'brand plucked from the fire', but always disclaimed any sense of special destiny. He has often been viewed as an autocratic leader, but his friends recognized his ability to listen. One colleague noted that Wesley possessed a fund of historical knowledge and anecdote that 'rendered his company as entertaining as instructive'. As a preacher he was outshone by George Whitefield; as a hymn-writer he was surpassed by his brother Charles. As a theologian he was more synthetic than original; as an organizer he shaped a movement that never included even 1% of the population of his homeland. Nevertheless, the energy that he exhibited well into his eighties, as well as the total impact of his person and message upon Great Britain, has generated a reputation that belies his diminutive physique; his influence is often portrayed in nearly epic proportions.

Wesley died in his eighty-eighth year. To avoid a public commotion, his body was buried privately at 5am on the morning of his public funeral service. His obituary in the *Gentleman's Magazine* (1791) noted that he was 'one of the few characters who outlived enmity and prejudice, and received, in his latter years, every mark of respect from every denomination', and that 'he must be considered as one of the most extraordinary characters this or any age ever produced'.

Bibliography

R. P. Heitzenrater, *The Elusive Mr. Wesley* (Nashville: Abingdon Press, 1984); R. P.

Heitzenrater, *Wesley and the People called Methodists* (Nashville: Abingdon Press, 1995); H. D. Rack, *Reasonable Enthusiast* (Philadelphia: Trinity Press International, 1989); L. Tyerman, *The Life and Times of the Rev. John Wesley* (London: Hodder & Stoughton, 1871).

R. P. HEITZENRATER

■ **WHITEFIELD, George** (1714–1770), evangelist, was born in Gloucester on 16 December 1714 to an innkeeper and wine merchant, who died when his son was just two years old. Frequently in his ministry Whitefield confessed that as a boy working in his father's public house he mimicked the kinds of behaviour he observed there: lying, swearing and even stealing. But at an early age he also showed signs of the great oratorical gifts that would make him a spellbinding preacher. As a student at St Mary de Crypt, George first displayed his remarkable gifts of elocution and his passion for acting, but deteriorating family circumstances interrupted his schooling. Desiring to prepare George for a life in business, his mother apprenticed him to his older brother James, a Bristol merchant engaged in the American trade. But George would later claim that God's providence led him away from a life in business. First, he and his brother's wife could not relate well, and he had to leave Bristol. And secondly, a family friend came forward with sufficient funds to enable him to enter Pembroke College at Oxford University.

While at Oxford, George experienced a profound 'new birth', the evangelical designation for a spiritual conversion. He had joined a small band of zealous students, who were often ridiculed by scoffing classmates as the 'Holy Club', and the group's leader John *Wesley suggested that he read Henry Scougal's *The Life of God Within the Soul of Man* (1677). In perusing the book, Whitefield realized that what the author called 'falsely placed religion' described his own experience: 'going to church, doing hurt to no one, being constant in the duties of the closet [prayer], and now and then reaching out ... to give alms to ... poor neighbours.' He came to believe that 'true religion was [nothing less than] union of the soul with God, and Christ formed within'. He testified that as he read

those words, 'a ray of Divine light ... instantaneously darted upon my soul, and from that moment, but not till then, did I know that I must be a new creature.' George's conversion gave him a message and a mission: he vowed to preach the necessity of the new birth to men and women near and far.

Whitefield indeed took the Great Commission seriously throughout his thirty-three years of preaching (1737–1770), making seven trips to America and four to Scotland as well as travelling extensively in England and Wales. His appeal was particularly powerful in America and Scotland, where, before his arrival, local awakenings had already begun under the leadership of local pastors. In both places, he fanned the flames of revival far beyond each locality with his dynamic preaching and his widespread appeal. As an itinerant, he ignored parish boundaries and preached the gospel to people everywhere, and as an ecumenist, he paid little attention to sectarian distinctions. Although a lifelong member of the Church of England, he was one of its severest critics because the church, in his opinion, neglected such fundamental Protestant doctrines as justification and sanctification. Yet he resisted appeals by Scottish Presbyterians who urged him to leave the Anglican Church and join them, arguing that he preached, not for any particular church, but for the kingdom of God.

During his first American journey in 1739, Whitefield launched the charity that would be his sole institutional legacy, the orphan house in Georgia. Seeing that the many orphans in Georgia lacked both physical and spiritual nourishment, he established an orphanage and school outside Savannah, calling it 'Bethesda', the House of Mercy. At its peak, Bethesda was home to more than one hundred boys and girls, and through the course of Whitefield's ministry, it became known to his followers in Britain and America. He organized preaching tours partly in order to raise funds for Bethesda, collecting about £15,000 in total. His supporters viewed the Georgia orphan house as a symbol of the evangelist's sacrifice; his critics saw it as a fund-raising scam. For Whitefield, Bethesda was a financial burden, but a labour of love on behalf of children who, like himself, lacked parents who could take care of them.

In 1741 Whitefield married the thirty-six-year-old Elizabeth James, a widow from Abergavenny, Wales, who had recently experienced the new birth. Whitefield had been looking for a 'helpmeet' who would travel with him on his preaching journeys and assist him at the orphan house. George and Elizabeth had one child, a son born in 1743, who died just one year later, ironically at the Bell Inn in Gloucester where George had been born. Elizabeth was his faithful companion for twenty-eight years until her death in London in 1769, just before he departed for America, where he would die a year later.

Though committed to a simple, unchanging message of the necessity of the new birth, Whitefield was an innovator in the means of delivering that message. He was a pioneer in the advertising of preaching services in daily newspapers; going far beyond the customary announcement of when and where a service was to be held, he reported the number of people who attended, an estimate of how many experienced conversion, and a comment on how his preaching affected the audience. When London churches closed their pulpits to him because he criticized the clergy for not preaching the 'one thing needful', Whitefield became an itinerant, preaching outdoors wherever he found a crowd of people: at racecourses, in marketplaces, outside the Kingswood coal mines and in London's great public parks. His 'print and preach' strategy proved effective in attracting ever larger crowds. In 1739 crowds estimated at twenty, thirty, forty and even fifty thousand people came to hear him preach. Reading about these throngs from a distance, Benjamin Franklin was sceptical, unconvinced that an unamplified voice could be heard by such a large audience out of doors. When Whitefield reached Philadelphia later that year, Franklin conducted an experiment. Starting from the dais where Whitefield was preaching, Franklin walked to a point where traffic noise began to drown out the preacher's voice, reckoned that distance to be the radius of a semi-circle, allotted a certain number of square feet for each person facing Whitefield and calculated that he could be easily heard by crowds of more than thirty thousand people. The large American crowds testify, in part, to the effectiveness of the months of newspaper publicity that preceded his arrival in the colonies.

Although advance publicity helped to promote Whitefield's services, his performance in the pulpit inspired people to attend service after service. Whitefield's dramatic performances inspired comparisons between the preacher and London's premier actor, David Garrick. Whitefield's preaching did more than convey meaning through words; it transported his listeners through the experiences of sin and salvation. In his popular sermon, 'The Eternity of Hell-Torments', he did more than describe the horrors of hell, placing sinners in hell itself and giving them voice: 'O wretched Man that I am, who shall deliver me from the Body of Death! Are all the Grand Deceiver's inviting Promises come to this? O Damned Apostate! Oh that I had never hearkened to his beguiling Insinuations! Oh that I had rejected his very first Suggestions with the utmost Detestation and Abhorrence! Oh that I had taken up my cross and followed Christ! But alas! These reflections come now too late. But must I live for ever tormented in these Flames? Oh, Eternity! That thought fills me with Despair. I cannot, will not, yet I must be miserable for ever.'

Dramatizations such as this transfixed his audiences. Sarah Edwards, wife of Jonathan *Edwards, one of the staunchest supporters of the Great Awakening, testified to the effects of Whitefield's oratory: 'It is wonderful to see what a spell he casts over an audience by proclaiming the simplest truths of the Bible. I have seen upwards of a thousand people hang on his words with breathless silence, broken only by an occasional half-suppressed sob ... A prejudiced person, I know, might say that this is all theatrical artifice and display; but not so will anyone think who has seen and known him.'

Whitefield's preaching even moved the sceptic Benjamin Franklin, who counted the evangelist as a friend even though he rejected his message. Franklin described Whitefield's performance and observed that his itinerancy gave him an advantage: 'By hearing him often I came to distinguish easily between sermons newly compos'd, & those which he had often preach'd in the Course of his Travels. His Delivery of the latter was so improv'd by frequent Repetitions, that every Accent, every Emphasis, every Modulation of Voice, was so perfectly well turn'd and well plac'd, that without being interested in the Subject, a Pleasure of much the same kind with that receiv'd from an excellent Piece of Music. This is an Advantage itinerant Preachers have over those who are stationary: as the latter cannot well improve their Delivery of a Sermon by so many Rehearsals.'

On one occasion, knowing that Whitefield would finish his sermon with a collection to support his newly founded orphan house in Georgia, Franklin vowed not to contribute to the fund because Whitefield had ignored his plea to establish the charity in Pennsylvania. But as Whitefield proceeded to make his case, Franklin said that he began to soften and dropped his copper coins in the collection plate. Then with another 'Stroke of his Oratory', Franklin added his silver dollars. Finally, Franklin reported, Whitefield 'finish'd so admirably, that I empty'd my Pocket wholly into the Collector's Dish, Gold and all'.

In addition to being a 'Divine Dramatist', George Whitefield was also a 'Pedlar in Divinity'. Opponents of the Great Awakening used this epithet pejoratively, to denote a self-promoting preacher travelling about the countryside 'selling' his brand of religion in the hope of realizing private gain. An anonymous writer to *The Boston Weekly News-Letter* suggested that existing laws designed to regulate 'Pedlars in Trade' be extended 'for the discouragement of Pedlars in Divinity also'. Part of the writer's concern was the enormous success that the innovative preacher was enjoying. Although they were critical of Whitefield's commercial methods, one group of Boston laymen conceded that these were successful. They noted that his advance publicity had prepared Bostonians for his visit in 1740. Because of newspaper advertisements and reports, his 'Name and Character were very great among us before his Arrival,' and 'he had made such a Noise and Bustle in Europe and America that the Expectations of the People and their Curiosity were very much rais'd both to see him, and hear him preach.'

Whitefield had been reluctant to exploit the press to promote his revival services. In agreeing to allow his travelling companion and soon-to-be publicist, William Seward, to place advertisements in London dailies, Whitefield departed from the course followed by his mentor John Wesley. When Seward approached Wesley with the idea of advertising his itinerancy, Wesley rejected the notion as a tasteless 'sounding of the trumpet'. Whitefield himself was embarrassed and angry when, without his knowledge or approval, Seward first placed an advertisement, in the 19 September 1737 edition of the London *Daily Advertiser*. The short piece depicted the evangelist as a selfless young man who was forgoing lucrative appointments in England to undertake a dangerous missionary journey to Georgia. But the results convinced him that newspaper publicity was a means of making the gospel known to large numbers of people who might not otherwise have known of his preaching. One observer reported that, shortly after the first advertisement, 'everybody ran after him' because his name 'was everywhere made known'. From that time, Whitefield followed the 'print and preach' strategy, and he became the best-known evangelist in the North Atlantic world.

Both John Wesley and George Whitefield took seriously the Great Commission to preach the gospel throughout the world. On separate and numerous occasions, each expressed his view of the whole world as his parish, but they assumed very different roles in the service of that global parish. Wesley emphasized organization and discipline, starting with small cells of pious evangelicals who committed themselves to a deeper faith and binding them together into larger bodies of believers who eventually became the Methodist Church. Whitefield had neither the time for nor interest in such painstaking, methodical work. He saw himself as a preacher, as one who sowed gospel seeds, recognizing that others, like Wesley, needed to follow him and water those seeds.

In addition to assuming different roles in the propagation of the gospel, Whitefield and John Wesley engaged in a much publicized theological dispute. While in America on his first preaching tour in 1740, Whitefield read Wesley's sermon on free grace, and charged his friend and mentor with embracing Arminianism. Whitefield clung to the Calvinist perspective in which God is viewed as the sole agent in salvation, holding that human beings were incapable of doing anything towards their own redemption. Disturbed that Wesley had denied what Whitefield regarded as a central doctrine, the latter published an open letter to Wesley arguing that free grace was a dangerous teaching similar to the (supposed) Catholic emphasis on good works at the expense of God's grace. Though the two men remained friends, their differences led to a split in the Methodist movement, with Wesley organizing the Arminian wing, while Whitefield identified with the Calvinist wing.

The towering figure among Calvinistic Methodists was the Countess of *Huntingdon, a person of great significance in Whitefield's ministry. After experiencing the new birth in the late 1730s, she became Whitefield's greatest benefactor. In addition to providing much-needed funds for his preaching tours and his orphanage, she introduced him to members of the aristocracy, including Lord Bolingbroke and the Earl of Chesterfield. Whitefield became chaplain to the Countess and, while in London preaching to huge crowds in the public parks, he would also hold private services in her home. In the late 1740s the Countess funded an evangelical seminary at Trevecca, Wales and helped to organize the Calvinistic Methodist Church. Although Whitefield lent his support to the group, he did not join, wishing instead to maintain his ecumenical stance. However, he maintained a close friendship with the Countess and arranged that upon his death his beloved Georgia orphan house would be placed in her trust.

Wherever he went, Whitefield both united and divided Christians. In America, denominations split over the revival he led. Congregationalists divided into New Lights, who supported the awakening, and Old Lights, who opposed it. Similarly, Presbyterians in the middle colonies separated into Old Sides and New Sides. His supporters heralded Whitefield as a fearless servant of God who was a powerful instrument of a special dispensation of God's grace. They believed that throughout history, whenever faith grew dark, God anointed an extraordinary figure who pointed to a new light of grace, and that Whitefield was such a person. His opponents disagreed. First, they were sceptical of claims that the revival was a 'work of God', arguing instead that the so-called revival was more of a human invention than a divine outpouring.

They charged Whitefield with shameless self-promotion and thought that his reported crowd figures were grossly exaggerated, a charge to which Whitefield himself gave some credibility in 1756 when he revised his *Journals* and lowered some of the estimates. His critics dismissed many of the testimonies regarding conversions as enthusiastic responses to emotional preaching. To them, the real test of the new birth was changed behaviour, and the critics saw little evidence of a more moral society as a result of the revival.

When George Whitefield died at Newburyport, Massachusetts on 30 September 1770, he left no denomination or sect. However, his legacy is powerful and enduring, and he is remembered by many as the father of modern evangelical revivalism. From Charles Grandison *Finney in the early nineteenth century to Billy *Graham in the late twentieth, evangelists have mentioned Whitefield as an inspiring forerunner. Though he lacked the means available to people such as Graham to reach a worldwide audience, Whitefield recognized the powerful link between the printed and the preached word and between advance publicity and preparation and the success of revival services. Like his successors, he took the Great Commission seriously, and used all means available to preach the necessity of the new birth to strangers at a distance.

Bibliography

George Whitefield's Journals (London: Banner of Truth Trust, 1960); J. Gillies (ed.), *The Works of the Reverend George Whitefield*, 6 vols. (London: 1771–1772); F. Lambert, *'Pedlar in Divinity': George Whitefield and the Transatlantic Revivals, 1737–1770* (Princeton: Princeton University Press, 1994); H. S. Stout, *The Divine Dramatist: George Whitefield and the Rise of Modern Evangelicalism* (Grand Rapids: Eerdmans, 1991).

F. LAMBERT

■ **WIGGLESWORTH, Smith** (1859–1947), British Pentecostal healing evangelist, was a plumber from Bradford, Yorkshire, who did not learn to read easily until adult life and was unknown outside his home town until his late forties.

Since his death, Wigglesworth has become a legend amongst Pentecostals and charismatics; an internet search in late 2000 yielded well over 1,000 sites about him or containing his sermons. Much of this reputation results from his work as a healing evangelist, and perhaps from his simple biblicism and uneducated background, which epitomize the Pentecostal-charismatic ideal of Spirit-empowerment overriding natural and social limitations.

Wigglesworth's education was neglected because from the age of six he had to help support his family. First he went to work 'pulling and cleaning turnips ... from morning until night'; then from the age of seven he laboured at the woollen mill with his father and brother for twelve hours a day.

Wigglesworth was converted at the age of eight in his grandmother's Wesleyan Methodist chapel. Neither of his parents was a Christian at that time, but he was involved shortly afterwards in the conversion of his mother. Wigglesworth joined the Salvation Army at the age of sixteen, but the following year he was won over to believers' baptism and dispensationalism by a Plymouth Brethren man at the mill. With this background, he was a good candidate for recruitment by the Pentecostal movement when it emerged in the first decade of the twentieth century.

In 1882 he married Mary Jane (known to all as 'Polly') Featherstone, who also had experience as a Salvation Army officer and evangelist. She was the better preacher of the two, and Wigglesworth, during the early years of his marriage, directed more and more of his energies into his plumbing business, using skills he had acquired from his Brethren friend at the mill. Although his business prospered, it had the effect of cooling his Christian zeal and causing him to become irritated at his wife's continuing evangelistic activities and her consequent late arrivals home. For a couple of years, indeed, he abandoned his Christian life entirely, and was eventually brought back to it only through his wife's faithful and spirited witness.

From the late 1880s the couple included healing meetings in the activities of the Bowland Street Mission Hall, which they ran. A number of notable healings were attested, the most dramatic being that of the local Baptist minister's wife, who was supposed by her friends to be on her deathbed but immediately recovered after prayer and went on to outlive her husband by several years. Wigglesworth himself claimed to have been healed, once of a chronic ailment and once of acute appendicitis.

When he heard of the outbreak of speaking in tongues at Sunderland in 1907, Wigglesworth travelled north to investigate. Thomas Ball Barratt, an Englishman pastoring a Methodist church in Norway, had received the 'baptism in the Spirit' with tongues on a visit to the United States and had consequently been implored by the minister of All Saints, Sunderland, Alexander *Boddy, to visit and share his experiences. This he did in September 1907, and thus Pentecostalism made its first entry into Britain. After a few days' stay, Wigglesworth received what he now called 'the real Baptism in the Holy Spirit' as the Pentecostals were defining it, that is, with the sign of speaking in tongues. (His previous definition of this baptism, as principally involving sanctification, had been conditioned by his background in the holiness movement. This earlier understanding he now, by implication, dismissed: 'I might have received anointings previously'.)

The following Sunday Wigglesworth preached in his own Mission Hall back in Bradford. His previous efforts had been so miserable that they were infrequent; most of the preaching had been provided by his doughty wife. But she had questioned his Sunderland experience and challenged him to give evidence of it in the pulpit. She gave her judgment by crying out during the sermon, 'That's not my Smith, Lord, that's not my Smith!' Amid emotional scenes, the congregation embraced Wigglesworth's Pentecostal experience for themselves. During the years that followed, the Wigglesworths were involved in spreading the Pentecostal movement around the country, with Smith now taking the lead in preaching.

Wigglesworth received severe personal blows some years later. Polly died suddenly in 1913 as she was coming out of the Mission Hall, where she had been preaching. Two years later his younger son George died. Smith's faith remained unshaken. When he was asked why, when he prayed for healing for others, his daughter Alice remained deaf (as she had been from birth), he replied that it was because of 'her lack of faith', and few were sure whether or not he was joking.

In the years after the First World War Wigglesworth's reputation and career as a preacher became international. He had visited North America for several months after the outbreak of war, but with the coming of peace he had the opportunity to visit Norway, Sweden, Denmark, France and Switzerland. Preaching tours in India and Ceylon (Sri Lanka), Australia and New Zealand followed. In all of them Wigglesworth conducted evangelistic and healing campaigns. He later claimed that he had seen three dead people raised to life, as well as the restoring of sight to the blind.

Wigglesworth's blunt manner and simplistic biblicism seemed harsh to many. He often treated roughly those who came forward for healing in his meetings, demanding that crippled people run up and down after he had prayed for them and even, on occasion, striking the afflicted part of a person's body as he prayed. He sometimes claimed, perhaps with some exaggeration, to have read nothing but the Bible. Although several editions of his sermons were printed, he denied having actually written them, and insisted that they were the work of people who had taken notes from his preaching. Such claims have done nothing since to detract from the popularity of these sermons.

Wigglesworth was accompanied on many of his travels by his daughter Alice, and sometimes also by her husband, James Salter. The couple had gone as missionaries to Africa, but James agreed to work alone on the mission-field for much of the time so that his wife could accompany her father.

One of the most famous incidents in Wigglesworth's life occurred late in his career, and by its nature almost guaranteed his continuing significance for church life through the rest of the century. On a trip to South Africa in 1936, he met the young David *du Plessis, then general secretary of the Apostolic Faith Mission in that country. Wigglesworth gave him a dramatic prophecy, subsequently fulfilled, of the rise of the charismatic movement among the historic denominations. Du Plessis was bewildered, and queried it with Wigglesworth, not at the time but when the two men met again in England after the Second World War. Wigglesworth reaffirmed the content of the prophecy, whilst emphasizing that he himself would see no part of its fulfilment, but that du Plessis would play a significant role.

Wigglesworth died on 12 March 1947, whilst attending the funeral of a friend. He was accompanied to the end by his faithful son-in-law, James Salter.

Bibliography
S. H. Frodsham, *Smith Wigglesworth, Apostle of Faith* (Nottingham: Assemblies of God Publishing House, 1949); J. Hywel-Davies, *Baptised by Fire: the Story of Smith Wigglesworth* (Sevenoaks: Hodder & Stoughton, 1987).

M. PEARSE

■ **WILBERFORCE, William** (1759–1833), abolitionist and philanthropist, was born in Hull on 24 August 1759, the only son of Robert Wilberforce and Elizabeth (née Bird). His family were merchants who had made a considerable fortune trading with the Baltic states. Wilberforce was first educated at Hull Grammar School under Joseph Milner, an evangelical Anglican minister. His father died when Wilberforce was nine, and his mother sent him to stay near London with his wealthy uncle and aunt, William and Hannah Wilberforce. Through their influence, and to the great horror of his mother, he underwent an evangelical conversion at the age of twelve. His letters home and his behaviour during periodic visits to Hull so alarmed her that she withdrew him from the care of his uncle and aunt and sent him as a boarder at Pocklington School near Hull (1771–1776). Under his mother's close supervision the effects of this early conversion seem to have disappeared.

A year before Wilberforce entered St John's College, Cambridge in 1776 (BA, 1781; MA, 1788), his grandfather died, and he came into a considerable inheritance. When he went up to Cambridge, his evangelicalism was well behind him, and he was as worldly as any of his peers, and vastly popular. Witty, charming, erudite, eloquent and hospitable, not to mention exceedingly wealthy, Wilberforce as an undergraduate displayed the characteristics which combined to give him a 'power of gravitation' over his peers; he was a natural leader who drew friends and followers into his orbit. He did not take his studies very seriously.

In the winter of 1779–1780 Wilberforce moved to London, where he befriended William Pitt, who was then studying for the bar. Both determined to enter Parliament. To this end Wilberforce spent a sizeable fortune (between £8,000 and £9,000) being elected MP for Hull in September 1780, only a few weeks after attaining the age of majority. The young bachelor MP took London high society by storm, demonstrating, in one biographer's words, that 'his grace, polish, charm and wit could overcome any lingering prejudices against him as the son of a tradesman. London society would tolerate almost anyone who was amusing, civilized and rich.' Later in life his friends remarked how even Wilberforce's most implacable foes could be won over by his charm in a matter of a few hours. As Lord Milton observed, Wilberforce displayed a 'close union between the most rigid principles and the most gay and playful disposition'. Wilberforce became Pitt's closest friend at the very time that Pitt's star was rising above the political firmament; Pitt was soon to be Chancellor of the Exchequer and, by the age of twenty-four, Britain's Prime Minister. In the early 1780s Wilberforce and Pitt were inseparable, frequenting London's exclusive gentlemen's clubs, where they talked, drank and gambled with the rich and famous.

In 1785 Wilberforce was re-elected to Parliament as the MP for Yorkshire rather than Hull. Yorkshire was one of the most prestigious and powerful seats in Parliament; with his eloquent, conversational style, Wilberforce was soon known as one of Parliament's leading debaters. His friendship with Pitt strengthened, although it did not result in a cabinet post. Wilberforce generally supported Pitt politically, but emerged as an independent-minded politician.

In 1784 Wilberforce decided on a European tour and invited an Irish friend to accompany him. When the friend declined, Wilberforce asked Isaac Milner, the brother of Joseph Milner (his former schoolmaster) to join him. Isaac, an Anglican clergyman, was known as a brilliant Cambridge scientist and mathematician. Unaware of Milner's evangelical convictions, Wilberforce was surprised to find that someone whom he could respect intellectually could also embrace religious views, which he did not view as *de rigueur*. Together they read and discussed Philip *Doddridge's *The Rise and Progress of Religion in the Soul* and the Greek New Testament. The trip was interrupted by political events in England in late 1784 but resumed soon after.

At the start of the first tour Wilberforce was a conventional Anglican with Unitarian sympathies; at the end of it he was convinced of the truth of key Christian doctrines. At the conclusion of the second tour he began to undergo the classical Christian experience of 'conviction of sin', which has so often accompanied the conversions of great Christians. He sought further counsel from John *Newton, the leading Anglican evangelical in London. By October 1785 the 'great change', as he termed it, had occurred. His conversion may in fact have been a 're-conversion', but to many of his friends it was as unwelcome as it was unexpected. For a time Wilberforce toyed with becoming an Anglican clergyman; both Newton and Pitt dissuaded him, convinced that the nation needed his public service.

After a long period of self-questioning and prayer Wilberforce reached his famous conclusion that 'God has set before me two great objects: the suppression of the slave trade and the reformation of manners [i.e. morality]'. Wilberforce's embracing of the anti-slavery cause appears to be a distinct effect of his embracing of evangelical Christianity. In the early 1780s he had shown no particular interest in the matter, and a popular myth that he had written against slavery as a youth cannot be substantiated. Clearly Newton, a former slave trader himself, encouraged him to take up the cause, but another key influence was the evangelical MP Sir Charles Middleton (later Lord Barham, first Lord of the Admiralty at the time of Trafalgar). Middleton urged Wilberforce to bring the matter forward in Parliament in late 1786 and introduced him to James Ramsay, an Anglican minister who had long experience in the West Indies. In his 1784 *Inquiry into the Effects of Putting a Stop to the African Slave Trade, and of Granting Liberty to the Slaves in the British Sugar Colonies* he argued that Britain owed compensation to Africa because of the 'horrid barbarities' that the British had precipitated.

In May 1787 Wilberforce told friends of his decision to take on the slave trade. His ultimate aim was the abolition of slavery itself, but he knew that the slave trade had to be stopped before abolition could be effected. Even with Pitt's personal support, the road to abolition was far more difficult than he originally anticipated. John *Wesley, who had attacked slavery in his Thoughts on Slavery (1774), wrote to encourage Wilberforce and to caution him about the enormous difficulties he would encounter. The wealthy West Indian slave-owners were skilful opponents and brilliant obstructionists. Wilberforce's health handicapped him as well; in 1788 his doctors despaired of his life, and he suffered for the rest of his days from what appears to have been ulcerative colitis, caused by stress. Only a daily intake of opium (the aspirin of the day) enabled him to continue.

Wilberforce's opening speech launching the campaign on 11 May 1789 was, in Edmund Burke's view, one of the greatest speeches in Parliament's history, but the planters persuaded Parliament to delay action by gathering its own evidence. Wilberforce's attempt to introduce a bill abolishing the slave trade was defeated in the Commons on 20 April 1791 (by 163 votes to 88). The following year his motion was amended to include the word 'gradual' and passed with a target date of 1 January 1796. However, the motion was nullified by the House of Lords, which called for more evidence. Similarly, a bill to prohibit the carrying of slaves in British ships to foreign ports failed in 1793 and 1794.

By 1795 Britain was distracted by its war with France, and Wilberforce became somewhat estranged from Pitt because he did not feel the government was trying hard enough to achieve peace. Despite repeated defeats in the Commons (1796, 1797, 1798, 1799), Wilberforce persisted. In May 1804 the Commons passed an abolition bill by a surprisingly wide margin (124 to 49), but the Cabinet told Wilberforce that the bill would have to wait a year. Pitt's death in January 1806 led to the formation of a coalition government more favourable to abolition. Following general elections late in 1806, a bill was introduced in the Lords by Lord Grenville, the prime minister, in February 1807 and then by Wilberforce in the Commons. The motion passed easily in both houses and was given royal assent on 25 March 1807. Slave emancipation would not follow until 1833, and in the early 1820s Wilberforce passed the leadership of the campaign on to a younger set of leaders, chief among them the young evangelical MP, Thomas Fowell *Buxton.

Wilberforce's effort to reform British 'manners' or morality was perhaps a more daunting task than that of slave trade abolition. As early as 1787 he determined to establish a society to aid him in his task, and he enlisted the great and powerful in the plan. First he persuaded George III to issue a formal 'Royal Proclamation against Vice and Immorality', as was customary on the accession of a new monarch. Wilberforce's society sought to enforce the proclamation through legal prosecution of offenders and by offering support to magistrates. Originally known as the 'Proclamation Society', it was renamed 'The Society for the Suppression of Vice' in 1802. A close ally in this effort was Hannah *More.

In 1797 Wilberforce published A Practical View of the Prevailing Religious System of Professed Christians in the Higher and Middle Classes in this Country, Contrasted with Real Christianity. At the time, no-one thought of Wilberforce as an author, and when he first proposed the idea of a religious book written by a politician, his publisher doubted that there would be any interest in the work. The book, however, turned out to be a bestseller and probably did more than any other single publication to promote the revival of evangelical Christianity in early nineteenth-century Britain. It played a key role in the conversions of many people, including Thomas *Chalmers and Leigh Richmond.

A central theme of A Practical View was the message that 'serious religion', Wilberforce's code words for evangelicalism, is the best cement of civil society because it effectively reinforces the social obligations of both the poor and the rich. In Wilberforce's reading of history, the French Revolution and the debacle that followed was due to a wholesale capitulation to secular Enlightenment thought; all of Europe was now paying the price of France's abandonment of its Christian heritage. The message that A Practical View articulated included an emphasis on the social utility of the Christian faith, which many English came to regard as a compelling response to the threat posed by the French Revolution. In social terms, one of the most important themes developed by Wilberforce is the concept of duty that came to be so prominent in the Victorian mind.

While his pen was important, it was Wilberforce's remarkable ability with people that enabled him to create one of the most influential networks in British history. Wilberforce was a 'networker'; he naturally drew people to himself, and when he needed assistance, talent and fortune were at his command. One of his nineteenth-century biographers likened him to a prime minister surrounded by his cabinet of Clapham philanthropists. In this cabinet his friends had specific portfolios: James *Stephen and Zachary *Macaulay, the slave trade; Lord Teignmouth, the Bible Society; Henry *Thornton (MP and leading economist), finance; Charles Grant, British India; Zachary Macaulay and Hannah More, public relations; the minister without portfolio was Thomas Babington, who offered general advice where needed. For spiritual counsel Wilberforce relied on John Venn, rector of Clapham, Isaac Milner (by then president of Queen's College, Cambridge) and Charles *Simeon of Cambridge. The Claphamites were committed to a 'practical Christianity', which expressed itself in the areas of private philanthropy, education and moral and social reform, much of it through voluntary societies.

In 1797 at the age of thirty-seven, Wilberforce married Barbara Ann Spooner, thus beginning 'thirty-five years of undiluted happiness'. By this time Wilberforce was already a national celebrity and a very busy politician; over the next ten years his family life became even busier with the birth of four sons and two daughters. Wilberforce viewed his own role as father as more important than his role as politician. The primary consideration behind his resignation in 1812 of his Commons seat for Yorkshire (the most coveted seat in Parliament) was his concern for the moral and religious education of his six children.

Wilberforce and his wealthy cousin Henry Thornton set an example of generous philanthropy. Wilberforce's leadership in establishing voluntary societies to bring public attention to their philanthropic causes was crucial. One historian has calculated that Wilberforce was a member of the committee of some sixty-nine voluntary societies.

Three other concerns lay close to Wilberforce's heart: the Christianization of British India, the evangelization of Africa and the growth of the evangelical party within the Church of England. Next to the slave trade no other matter occupied him more than Indian missions. Wilberforce hoped to gain permission for Christian missionaries to enter India, but knew he first had to overcome the opposition of the East India Company, which ruled British India. In 1793, when the Company's charter came up for its twenty-year renewal, Wilberforce almost succeeded in having a clause inserted requiring the Company to admit British schoolteachers and missionaries. Beginning in 1812, Wilberforce mounted a massive and successful lobbying effort to persuade Parliament to insert 'missionary clauses' in the charter upon its renewal in 1813. In the interim, the Claphamites sought to work within the East India Company by having evangelical clergymen sent out as Company chaplains to prepare the way for future missionaries.

Another important concern was the debt that Wilberforce felt Britain owed to Africa because of its involvement in the slave trade. In 1787 Granville Sharp had been approached by Africans living in London, who asked him to assist them in re-settling in West Africa. With help from the Treasury a self-sustaining community was founded in Sierra Leone. In 1791 the Sierra Leone Company was chartered by Parliament as a company colony; Wilberforce and his cousin Henry Thornton invested heavily in the expensive and ill-fated venture. The Claphamites had great hopes that Sierra Leone would be a 'province of freedom' for freed slaves and the launching pad for the Christianization of West Africa, but the realization of this dream took much longer than was initially expected.

Wilberforce's other great concern was the evangelical grouping within the Church of England. Much of the remarkable growth of Anglican evangelicalism in the period between 1790 and 1830 was due to the work of Wilberforce and his Clapham friends, and to the influence of Charles Simeon of Cambridge, with whom Wilberforce collaborated closely. The Claphamites sought to avoid public association with Protestant Nonconformity and to affirm their loyalty to both church and state. A key part of their strategy was the creation of *The Christian Observer*, a monthly periodical founded in 1802 and edited by Zachary Macaulay. By this means the Claphamites could address key political and social issues from an evangelical Anglican perspective. However, by the late 1820s it was clear that the majority of evangelical clergy and perhaps an even larger percentage of laity were dissatisfied with Wilberforce's leadership. Many were especially unhappy with his support of Catholic Emancipation (1829), which removed many civil disabilities from Roman Catholics and allowed them to sit in Parliament.

Wilberforce's theology and spirituality were deeply influenced by Puritan writers: his favourite authors were seventeenth-century English Puritans and men profoundly influenced by them. Wilberforce was influenced by contemporary Calvinists as well, such as John Newton, John Witherspoon, and Thomas *Scott, but he declined to be known as a Calvinist himself. The writer who affected him most was Philip Doddridge, whose influence was exerted principally through his *Rise and Progress of Religion in the Soul*, which played a role in Wilberforce's conversion.

Wilberforce was famous for what he termed his 'launchers'; he would devise ways in which he could launch into a discussion of 'serious' religion in talks with less-than-serious friends. Reginald Coupland recounts a story, which Wilberforce often told against himself, of how he was once visiting an old friend, a member of the House of Lords, at his sick bed and wondering how he might gently introduce the topic of religion. The visit was interrupted by the arrival of another visitor who asked the ailing man how he was doing. He responded, 'As well as I can be with Wilberforce sitting here and telling me I am going to hell.' But as Coupland comments, 'When the little man came in late to a dinner-party, bristling, maybe, with "launchers", every face, says a contemporary, "lighted up with pleasure at his entry".'

From 1812 Wilberforce stood for the less arduous constituency of Bramber and continued his involvement in many of the societies which he had helped to create. Over the next thirteen years in Parliament (he resigned in February 1825) his political actions proved controversial and damaged his reputation in the minds of many. As early as 1799 he had introduced a bill that eventually became the hated Combination Act, which prevented workers from uniting to form unions, reasoning that he was saving the poor from opportunistic political agitators. For reasons of national security he supported the Corn Laws (1815), which were unpopular with the poor because they raised the price of bread for the masses. Along with the majority of educated Englishmen he supported the suspension of Habeas Corpus in the period following the ending of the Napoleonic Wars (1815–1817), because he believed this was necessary to defend the British constitution. He also played a controversial role in settling the claims of Queen Caroline (1820).

Wilberforce resigned from Parliament in 1825, but his health had been in serious decline for a decade. In 1830 financial disaster struck the family when his eldest son and namesake was involved in a disastrous business venture that depleted the family's resources. Wilberforce turned down offers from friends to pay off his son's debts, which ran to some £50,000; the Wilberforces gave up their London home and went to live with one of their clerical sons. The death of their eldest daughter in 1820 had deeply affected Wilberforce; their second daughter died in 1832. After convalescing from a bout of influenza in Bath in 1833, Wilberforce returned to London, where he died on 29 July 1833. Just before his death, he heard of the second reading (approval in principle) of the bill to abolish slavery. Parliament honoured him in death with a suspension of business on the day of his funeral, and the family acquiesced in Parliament's request that he be buried in Westminster Abbey.

Bibliography

R. Coupland, *Wilberforce* (London: Collins, 1923); R. Furneaux, *William Wilberforce* (London: H. Hamilton, 1974); J. Pollock, *Wilberforce* (London: Constable, 1977); M. A. Pura, *Vital Christianity: The Life and Spirituality of William Wilberforce* (Toronto: Clement Publishing, 2002); R. I. and S. Wilberforce, *The Life of William Wilberforce*, 5 vols. (London: J. Murray, 1838).

D. M. LEWIS

■ **WILEY, Henry Orton** (1877–1961), Nazarene theologian and college president, was born in Marquette, Nebraska on 15 November 1877. He moved to Medford, Oregon and attended Oregon State Normal School, graduating in 1898. He became a registered pharmacist and served for several years as a minister in the United Brethren Church. Wiley married Alice May House on 8 November 1902. The couple had four children: Alma Pearl, Lester Vernon, Henry Ward and Alice Ruth. Wiley completed his BA at the University of the Pacific in 1910 and received the BD (1910), STM (1916) and STD (1929) degrees from the Pacific School of Religion. During his studies at the University of California, Berkeley (1900–1902), he served as pastor of small Church of the Brethren congregations nearby. After an experience of 'sanctification' Wiley joined the Church of the Nazarene; he became associate pastor of the congregation in Berkeley (1905–1909), and in 1909 founding pastor of the San José church. In 1910 he began his first term (1910–1916) as president of Pasadena College (now, Point Loma Nazarene University). He resigned in March 1916, frustrated by the interference of the Board of Trustees and the quarrelling of the faculty and local clergy.

Wiley then became president of Northwest Nazarene College, Nampa, Idaho (1916–1926). While there, he began his long term as General Secretary of the Board of Education of the Church of the Nazarene, which lasted from 1915 to the early 1940s. From 1926 to 1928 he again served as president of Pasadena College. Wiley then moved to Kansas City to serve (1928–1936) as editor of *The Herald of Holiness*, the official publication of the denomination. However, Pasadena College, again in debt, called Wiley back for a third term as president (1933–1948). In his roles as president and denominational executive, he was instrumental in transforming the Church of the Nazarene Bible schools into liberal arts colleges.

Wiley's greatest contribution to the Holiness movement was as an author. His massive three-volume *Christian Theology* (Kansas City: Nazarene Publishing House, 1940–1943) remains the tradition's standard scholarly theological synthesis. More than any other thinker, he enabled Holiness theologians to interact with the other main currents of theological reflection in American religious culture while remaining true to their own tradition. An abbreviated version of the work, *Introduction to Christian Theology* (Kansas City: Beacon Hill Press, 1959), was published in cooperation with Paul T. Culbertson. Wiley also wrote a commentary, *The Epistle to the Hebrews* (Kansas City: Beacon Hill Press, 1959). With Nazarene educator E. P. Elleysen, he co-authored two volumes on pedagogy: *The Principles of Teaching* (Kansas City: Nazarene Publishing House, 1925) and *A Study of the Pupil* (Kansas City: Nazarene Publishing House, 1926). Three volumes of his sermons were published: *God Has the Answer* (Kansas City: Beacon Hill Press, 1956), *The Pentecostal Promise* (Kansas City: Beacon Hill Press, 1963) and *The Harps of God* (Kansas City: Beacon Hill Press, 1971).

Wiley died in Pasadena on 22 August 1961. Extensive archives are kept at Point Loma Nazarene University, San Diego, Northwest Nazarene University, Nampa and the Church of the Nazarene Archives, Kansas City.

Bibliography
P. M. Bassett, 'A Study in the Theology of the Early Holiness Movement', *Methodist History*, 13 (April 1975), pp. 61–84; R. E. Kirkemo, *For Zion's Sake: A History of Pasadena/Point Loma College* (San Diego: Point Loma Press, 1992); J. M. Price, 'An Educational Biography of H. Orton Wiley, 1877–1961' (PhD dissertation, University of Kansas, 2001); T. L. Smith, *Called Unto Holiness: The Story of the Nazarenes: The Formative Years* (Kansas City: Nazarene Publishing House, 1962).

D. BUNDY

■ **WILKERSON, David Ray** (1931–), Pentecostal evangelist, founder of Teen Challenge and Times Square Church, was born in Hammond, Indiana on 19 May 1931 to Kenneth and Ann Wilkerson, both ministers of the General Council of the Assemblies of God (AG). The younger Wilkerson attended the denomination's Central Bible Institute (now College) in Springfield, Missouri for one year (1950–1951). He married Gwen Carosso in 1953, and the couple had four children. Licensed to preach in the same year, he was ordained in 1955.

Wilkerson pastored two small Assemblies of God churches in Scottsdale and Philipsburg, Pennsylvania, before coming to national attention in 1958. In February 1958 he read an article in *Life* magazine that told the story of seven teenage boys who were on trial in New York City for murder. After studying the artist's depiction of the young men in the courtroom, he wept and wondered if they had ever heard the good news of Jesus Christ. Sharing the *Life* article with his congregation at a Wednesday evening service, Wilkerson explained that he felt divinely led to visit the defendants in prison but lacked the funds to do so. In response church members contributed $75 to cover his expenses.

Arriving in New York City, Wilkerson learned that he needed the permission of the trial judge to visit the prison. Since the judge's life had been threatened and his telephone disconnected, the only way to secure permission was to attend the trial and afterwards request to speak to the judge in his chambers. When Wilkerson stepped out into the aisle to address him, the judge, fearing assassination, hid behind the bench and police officers ejected the young preacher from the building. While Wilkerson was being held by two officers, newspaper reporters photographed him. The picture appeared the next day, 1 March 1958, on the front page of *The New York Daily News*. Although Wilkerson never gained access to the young men, the story opened his way to the gangs of the city, who called him 'the guy the cops don't like'.

Wilkerson's ministry drastically changed as he dedicated his life to the evangelization and rehabilitation of inner-city young people. Without any certain financial support, he resigned his pastorate and with his family moved to New York City and became a street preacher. In July he also began to hold religious services in the St Nicholas Arena, and he later opened an office on Staten Island. Local Assemblies of God pastors sympathized with his activities and held a meeting at Glad Tidings Tabernacle (AG) in Manhattan in December 1958 to plan for the future. The twenty in attendance pledged five dollars a week to underwrite his ministry. Nine of the pastors present formed a central committee that became the board of directors of Teen Age Evangelism, as Teen Challenge was originally known. A year later the fledgling organization opened its first in-patient centre for addicts in Brooklyn. From this inauspicious beginning emerged Teen Challenge, an agency devoted to evangelism and the rehabilitation of adolescents with chemical dependencies and debilitating lifestyles. In the decade that followed, Wilkerson and his helpers encouraged Christian young people to become involved in evangelizing the gangs of New York City and directed converts to local churches to be grounded in their new-found faith.

As Wilkerson travelled across the country preaching in churches and promoting the work of Teen Challenge, he took with him former addicts and prostitutes, who shared their testimonies of conversion and deliverance. Through their startling stories, many congregations in the largely rural and suburban constituency of the AG learned for the first time about the problems of inner-city young people and the plight of those living in urban areas.

With the expansion of Teen Challenge to other cities, additional programmes were required for the care of former addicts. More adept as an evangelist than as an administrator, Wilkerson relied on others to further develop the enterprise, such as his brother, Don Wilkerson, who directed the centre in Brooklyn, and Frank M. Reynolds, who founded the Teen Challenge Training Center in Rehrersburg, Pennsylvania. Although Teen Challenge came under the general oversight of AG Home Missions in 1963, it gained favour and financial backing from a broad range of Christian organizations, ranging from the Kathryn *Kuhlman Foundation of Pittsburgh, Pennsylvania to the Roman Catholic Archdiocese of Cincinnati, Ohio. Eventually Teen Challenge became international in scope with over 150 centres in the United States and 250 overseas. Through the years the biblically based organization has received praise for the high rate of permanent recovery among those enrolled in the programme.

Because of the expanding scope of his ministry, in 1971 Wilkerson left New York City and moved to Lindale, Texas, where he founded World Challenge, Inc. to serve as an umbrella organization for his evangelistic campaigns, publishing, video production, drug and rehabilitation centres, feeding programmes and other activities. In 1987 he returned to New York City to open the non-denominational Times Square Church in the historic Mark Hellinger Theater at 51st Street and Broadway in Manhattan. In the same year he relinquished his AG ministerial credentials. While remaining faithful to the denomination's doctrinal beliefs, Wilkerson informed church leaders that he wanted Times Square Church to have the freedom to ordain its own candidates for ministry, a practice not possible for a local church in the more restrictive AG. With a current congregation of over 7,000, representing over 100 nationalities, the church focuses on evangelism and aid to the poor, the hungry, the destitute and the addicted. The church produces an audiotape series of Wilkerson's sermons entitled *Times Square Church Pulpit Series*.

In the early years of Teen Challenge, Nicky Cruz, leader of the powerful Mau Mau gang, became a Christian as a result of Wilkerson's street preaching. This inspired Wilkerson to write (with John and Elizabeth Sherrill) his best-known book, *The Cross and the Switchblade* (1963), a publication that also contributed to the beginning of the Catholic charismatic renewal in 1967. In 1969 the book became the basis for a film of the same name (1969) starring Pat Boone as Wilkerson and Erik Estrada as Cruz. Wilkerson's other books include *A Positive Cure for Drug Addiction* (1963), *Twelve Angels from Hell* (1965) with Leonard Ravenhill, *Little People* (1966) with Phyllis Murphy, *I'm Not Mad at God* (1967), *Hey, Preach – You're Coming Through!* (1968), *Parents on Trial: Why Kids Go Wrong – or Right* (1968) with Claire Cox, *Purple Violet Squish* (1969), *Rebel's Bible* (1970), *David Wilkerson Speaks Out* (1973), *Beyond the Cross and the Switchblade* (1974), *The Vision* (1974), *Judgment on America* (1975), *Christian Maturity Manual* (1977), *Sipping Saints* (1978), *Racing Toward Judgment* (1982), *Set the Trumpet to Thy Mouth: Hosea 8:1* (1985) and *America's Last Call* (1998).

The ministry of David Wilkerson reflects the rugged individualism characteristic of Pentecostalism, which brought many of the AG's programmes into existence. Originally viewed with suspicion by some Pentecostals for the social aspect of its work, Teen Challenge represented one of the earliest and most successful efforts in the Pentecostal movement at combining gospel proclamation with humanitarian assistance. On a broader scale than was possible within the AG, Wilkerson has continued with his fiercely prophetic (and sometimes speculative) voice, holistic mission and pragmatic approach to urban ministry.

Bibliography

E. L. Blumhofer, *The Assemblies of God: A Chapter in the Story of American Pentecostalism*, 2 vols. (Springfield: Gospel Publishing House, 1989); D. Wilkerson, *The Cross Is Still Mightier Than the Switchblade* (Shippensburg: Treasure House, 1996).

G. B. McGee

■ **WILLARD, Frances E.** (1839–1898), temperance leader and social reformer, was called 'Frank' by her friends and family, but was known as 'St Frances' to hundreds of thousands of temperance supporters around the world. One of the most widely recognized women of her day, she was a tireless organizer and advocate for the cause of what she called 'Home Protection', travelling thousands of miles on its behalf, and regularly speaking to crowds numbered in the thousands.

Frances Willard was born into a family with a strong Puritan heritage. Her parents, Josiah Flint Willard and Mary Hill Willard, came from families that had been in New England for more than two hundred years. On her father's side Frances was a descendant of Simon Willard, a Puritan who arrived in the Massachusetts Colony in 1634. A year and a half later he became one of the founders of Concord. Ironically, Simon Willard received from the Massachusetts General Court a monopoly to sell alcohol in the town. He was also a supporter of the founding of Harvard College.

Simon Willard's fourth son, Samuel, was a graduate of Harvard and served as pastor of Boston's Old South Church. He protested against the witchcraft hysteria in Salem. One of those hanged as a witch was John Willard, who was probably a cousin. Frances Willard took great pride in the fact that an ancestor of hers had actively defended the so-called witches of Salem.

Raised on adjoining farms in western New York, Josiah Willard and Mary Hill were the same age and knew each other well. Their families were active in the community and in their church. The couple were mature adults when they married at the age of twenty-six. Their firstborn child died in infancy. Their second child was Frances's older brother, Oliver. The third child, a daughter named Caroline Elizabeth, died at the age of fourteen months, about a year before Frances Elizabeth Caroline was born on 28 September 1839. Willard had one other sibling, a sister named Mary, born in 1843.

In 1841 Josiah Willard moved his family further west to Oberlin, Ohio. There he entered the preparatory school of Oberlin College so that he could fulfil a childhood dream of becoming a Christian minister. While in Oberlin, Mary Hill Willard took advantage of the coeducational system there and enrolled for classes herself. By all accounts, the family was quite happy and content at Oberlin. The contentment was shattered by Josiah Willard's sudden illness, an 'attack of hemorrhage of the lungs'. His doctor recommended that he leave Oberlin for work in the open air. The family thus left Ohio in 1846 for the open prairies of Wisconsin.

The Willards moved to a farm in Janesville, Wisconsin. The farm would later grow to a thousand acres. After Wisconsin attained statehood in 1848, Josiah Willard served one term in the state's House of Representatives. In Wisconsin the family began attending the Methodist church because there was no other church available. They had been members of the Congregational church in Oberlin. Willard remained a Methodist for the rest of her life and drew much strength and support from her Methodist connections.

Willard's education began at home, where her mother was her first teacher. Oliver had been walking the four miles into Janesville to attend the state school there, but Josiah Willard felt that his daughters were too young to make the trip. He also believed that girls belonged in the home. Willard's education was informal until the family moved in 1857 to Evanston, Illinois, where she enrolled in the North Western Female College. She graduated in 1859 with a 'Laureate of Science'.

Following her graduation, Willard started out on her career as an educator, taking a teaching position at a one-room school in Harlem (now River Forest), Illinois. She left the school after one term to take a position at the Kankakee Academy in Kankakee, Illinois, a school owned by a family friend. Again leaving after a single term, Willard returned to the school at Harlem. In both places Willard felt the pain of separation from her family, and although she had begun her work hopefully, it proved unsatisfactory to her. She returned briefly to North Western Female College, but then suffered a bout of depression over the death of her sister Mary. Believing that a change of scene would help her out of her depression, Willard accepted a position at the Pittsburgh Female College. In 1866 she became preceptress at Genesee Wesleyan Seminary in Lima, New York, not far from Churchville. Although this work was her most satisfying experience as a teacher, Willard spent only one year at Genesee. It was there that she met Kate Jackson, whose father sent the two young women on an extended European tour.

Frances Willard and Kate Jackson travelled for over two years, exploring much of the British Isles, Europe, imperial Russia and the area around the Mediterranean. Willard helped to support herself on the tour by writing articles for newspapers. It was also during her European tour that she began to develop her commitment to progress for women, a cause that would be her main motivation in her work as both an educator and as a social reformer.

On her return to Evanston, Willard began her career as an educator of women by accepting the presidency of the Evanston Ladies College, which had been created in 1869 as a more rigorous institution than the North Western Female College. By 1871, the Ladies College had become the women's division of Northwestern University. Under Willard's guidance and leadership the college developed innovative and effective educational policies and practices. Willard also faced serious conflict with the president of Northwestern University, a former fiancé, Charles Fowler, who brought his personal and acrimonious feelings into their professional relationship. After a few years of struggles with Fowler and with the Board of Trustees of the university, Willard finally decided that her future in the institution was limited and would probably never be satisfying for her. This decision led to her resignation and an unfulfilling conclusion to her career as an educator of women.

In June 1874 at the age of thirty-five Willard was jobless, had no savings and faced an unsure future. Fortunately at the same time that she was resigning from Northwestern an unplanned and widespread women's movement started to emerge. All across the United States women began gathering for prayer and social action. These 'praying bands' focused on the perceived threat to the American home posed by alcohol use and abuse. The praying women marched on bars, poured alcoholic beverages into city gutters and on the ground, and generally made known their dissatisfaction with a society that condoned and even licensed the sale and use of alcohol. For these women, many of whom were evangelicals, primarily Methodists, Baptists and Presbyterians, such practices ought not to exist in what they believed was a 'Christian nation', and they resolved to achieve reforms. Willard saw in this nascent movement the opportunity to do for the cause of women in American society what she had been unable to accomplish in the field of education.

Willard was perhaps not an obvious choice to lead women in their fight for temperance. During her European tour she had drunk wine and beer without any apparent qualms, so she may have had no moral objection to alcohol or may have developed one since the tour. In any case, when she received an invitation from a group of temperance women in Chicago to lead their efforts, she accepted it and began her second career, that of a social reformer and activist.

Out of the praying bands grew a strong impulse towards organization, and the women created the Woman's Christian Temperance Union (WCTU). Willard's prominent position as the president of the Chicago organization enabled her to take a leading role in the early days of the national movement. But her leadership at all levels of the Union, although it was recognized immediately, did not take her to the presidency until 1879. For five years Willard fought with the Union's leaders, especially with the president, Mrs Annie Wittenmyer, over the issue of votes for women.

For Willard, who as a young woman had watched enviously as her older brother Oliver went to cast his vote in an election, suffrage was an important way in which women would be able to exercise their power in the world outside the home. But observing the constant controversy surrounding the women's suffrage movement, Willard was careful to couch her own views in terms of what she called 'home protection'. She believed that the only way that women could protect their homes from the dangers of alcohol was by exercising the franchise and electing leaders and supporting laws and ordinances that would make temperance the norm for society.

Once she had accepted leadership in the temperance movement, Willard turned aside from it only once. For several months in 1877 she worked as an associate of evangelist Dwight L. *Moody. Moody was impressed by Willard's organizational abilities and by her appeal to women. For her part, Willard saw the work as a great opportunity to spread her temperance gospel. But the association was short-lived. Moody objected to Willard appearing on the same stage with her good friend and fellow temperance activist, Mary Livermore, who was a Unitarian.

Even after assuming the office of president of the Union Willard faced some opposition. She believed that the WCTU should be concerned about more than just temperance and so developed a threefold emphasis for the Union's work: temperance, labour, and 'woman'. These three broad themes allowed Willard to create a wide-ranging reform movement that touched on matters of education, the legal age of sexual consent for women, home economics and politics. These all fitted into her 'Do-Everything Policy'. Eventually the Union would develop thirty-nine departments to realize the expansive and all-encompassing vision of its president.

The Do-Everything Policy eventually led Willard into the male-dominated arena of politics. She was instrumental in the development of a national prohibition party to compete with the two major parties. This political activity was more than a little distasteful to many within the WCTU, but even when the opposition was strongest Willard was able to maintain her position of authority. She was even able to assist in the establishment of a World WCTU in 1891 and to serve as its first president. She held the presidencies of both unions from that year until her death.

During her years as national president of the WCTU Willard travelled widely, averaging an estimated 15,000 to 20,000 miles per year on the road and fewer than three weeks a year at home. She made numerous trips throughout the South and to Europe. Wherever she went she dealt with an astounding volume of correspondence, and she never lost control of the WCTU.

In her journals Willard expressed a desire to be famous and widely loved and admitted to having a driving ambition for success. She was a politically shrewd women in an age when women had no voice in the political life of the United States. She was a tireless organizer and a visionary for the burgeoning women's movement. Her death was a hard blow to the WCTU and its members.

At the time of her death on 17 February 1898 Willard was in New York City preparing for a voyage to England. Her health had been precarious for some time and took a drastic turn for the worse. News of her death spread rapidly, being reported in newspapers across the country and around the world. Thousands attended memorial services in New York City, Chicago and Evanston, Illinois to pay their respects to 'St Frances', while hundreds more were turned away in each place. Willard was buried at Rose Hill Cemetery in Chicago.

After Willard's death the opposition to her far-reaching work in the WCTU took control and began dismantling much of what she had laboured to create. The campaign for temperance, always a part of Willard's work, was brought to the fore to the detriment of other concerns. The Union dissociated itself from politics almost entirely, and the suffrage movement was given a low priority. Other parts of Willard's programme were eliminated altogether.

But Frances Willard's fame did not end with her death. The leadership of the Union, those who had so vigorously opposed her in her life, began to use her memory to create a myth about her in order to sustain the more tightly focused programme of the WCTU.

One of the lasting tributes to Willard was paid about a year after her death, when the Illinois state legislature passed a bill providing funds for a statue to be made and placed in Statuary Hall in the US Capitol building in Washington, DC as one of the state's two allotted submissions. Willard's companion and personal secretary for the final twenty-one years of her life and her first biographer, Anna Gordon, had urged the Illinois legislature to pay this tribute and oversaw the creation of the statue. Congress accepted it on the eighth anniversary of Willard's death, 17 February 1905. The memorial was the first honouring a woman to be placed in the Statuary Hall collection.

Bibliography
F. E. Willard, *Glimpses of Fifty Years: The Autobiography of an American Woman* (Chicago: Woman's Temperance Publishing Association, 1892); R. Bordin, *Frances Willard: A Biography* (Chapel Hill: The University of North Carolina Press, 1986); M. Earhart, *Frances Willard: From Prayer to Politics* (Chicago: University of Chicago Press, 1944).

T. L. FARIS

■ **WILLIAMS, Edward** (1750–1813), Independent (Congregational) theologian and educator, was born on 14 November 1750 at Glan-clwyd, North Wales, the son of Thomas and Anne Williams. The family was Anglican and of fairly substantial yeoman stock, and Edward was provided with a better education than were most of his neighbours. He was taught Latin at a grammar school in nearby St Asaph with a view to a career in the established church, but finding that prospect uncongenial he prevailed upon his parents to allow him to train as a lawyer. As a result Williams transferred to a preparatory school at Caerwys, Flintshire and was tutored by John Lloyd, the parish curate. It was there that he came to know a fellow pupil, Thomas Jones of Caerwys, who was destined, as Thomas Jones of Denbigh, to become a leader among the Welsh Calvinistic Methodists and the finest theologian in his connexion.

Though gifted and able, Williams was a sensitive and as yet spiritually unstable youth. Realizing that he had no vocation for a career in the law, he returned home after a year to assist his father on the farm. His reading included Thomas à Kempis and books on practical holiness, but he was as yet unsure about the concept of salvation by Christ alone on the basis of his finished sacrifice on the cross. Much troubled by his doubts, he sought the company of the local Methodists and especially the help of Robert Llwyd, the so-called 'father' of Methodism in the Vale of Clwyd, who was a tenant at the nearby farm of Plasashpool. He accompanied Llwyd to a service at Tŷ Modlen, Llandyrnog, to listen to the preaching of the Methodist clergyman Daniel Rowland who, along with Howel *Harris, was the foremost leader of the Welsh Calvinistic Methodists, and began to be drawn to the Methodist way. Yet his conversion, he claimed, occurred not there but 'in a despicable barn' at Cefn-y-gwrdu, Llangwyfan, under the ministrations of an unnamed lay exhorter. He was about eighteen years old at the time.

Williams' father was far from happy with his son's Methodist proclivities. He tried persuading him to forsake them and renew his earlier intention to become a clergyman in the Church of England. To entice him in that direction he promised to sponsor him at Oxford, and in preparation for university Williams enrolled for further study under the scholarly David Ellis, curate of Drewen, Merionethshire. The plan to proceed to Oxford was thwarted by his unfortunate experience of observing the drunken high spirits of some candidates for orders on their way to an ordination service at St Asaph Cathedral. His suspicion of the established church deepened and he decided that were he to be ordained, it would not be as a clergyman of the Church of England.

The Welsh Calvinistic Methodists at this time were still nominally attached to the established church. Despite its less than satisfactory spiritual state, they had no desire to secede and were very wary of Dissent. Williams, though, had now come into contact with Daniel Lloyd, the Independent minister at the Lôn Swan church in Denbigh, where he soon sought membership. Although indebted to the Methodists, he found their overt emotionalism increasingly distasteful, while the decorum and intellectual rigour of orthodox Dissent attracted him more and more. Lloyd, who was only five years older than Williams and an alumnus of the Abergavenny academy, was a thoughtful preacher and a staunch

Calvinist, and soon became the younger man's mentor and guide. Williams began preaching among the Independents and in 1771 enrolled at the Abergavenny academy. His parents, by now more or less reconciled with their son's Dissent (and happier with it than with his earlier Methodism), acquiesced in his choice and afforded him (somewhat fitful) support.

Williams remained at Abergavenny for four years. The curriculum there included divinity, classical and patristic literature in Latin and Greek, Hebrew, French, philosophy, logic, geometry, astronomy, algebra, rhetoric, sermon composition and church history. The discipline was bracing, and the academic standards were high. The principal, Benjamin Davies, later head of the Homerton academy, regarded Williams as a very able and perhaps over-conscientious student possessed of 'an eminent degree of serious piety; in that he excelled, in my judgement, all the young men placed under my direction'. The theological tone at Abergavenny was much influenced by the Protestant scholasticism of Francis Turretin, *Calvin's successor in Geneva, though Williams was also impressed by the natural theology of the Cambridge Platonists, Ralph Cudworth in particular. According to his biography his general doctrinal position even then was 'moderately Calvinistic' while his preaching, which was noted for its exceptional clarity, combined the dynamic evangelicalism of his Methodist days with the studied didacticism of the Older Dissent.

Edward Williams was ordained to serve the pastorate of Ross-on-Wye, Herefordshire in June 1775, and moved to the Independent church at Oswestry, Shropshire, two years later. He also ran a school. In 1781, responding to a request by the evangelical philanthropist Willelma Campbell, Viscountess Glenorchy, he began training young men for the Dissenting ministry. No sooner had he begun this work than an invitation arrived from Abergavenny for him to succeed Benjamin Davies as the academy's principal. Although he felt that he could not accept this invitation, the Congregational Fund Board was sufficiently eager for him to undertake the work that it allowed the transfer of his institution to Oswestry, where Williams could combine his work for Lady Glenorchy with that of the academy. This transfer was completed by mid-1782.

As well as teaching and writing (while at Oswestry he published editions of works by Matthias Maurice and John *Owen along with a substantial apologia for infant baptism which prompted the University of Edinburgh to confer on him an honorary DD), Williams established Sunday schools and was active in evangelism, not least into neighbouring North Wales. The pressure of work was such that he felt that he had to resign his principalship, and in October 1791 he accepted a call to the less onerous work of pastor at Carrs Lane church in Birmingham. While in Birmingham he took much interest in the then new field of overseas missions and became one of the first directors of the London Missionary Society. Although Williams was by now a much revered leader among the Independents, there were those who felt that his academic talents and obvious skill in the training of Dissenting ministers were not being put to the best use, and in 1795 he was invited to head the academy at Rotherham, Yorkshire, and to undertake ministerial duties at the Masborogh Independent church. His work at Rotherham was unsparing: seminary teaching, preaching both at his home church and further afield, evangelism and church extension in surrounding areas, and on a national level leadership in denominational affairs and involvement in the missionary society. His publications included fourteen volumes on different aspects of doctrinal and practical theology, editions of the works of Isaac *Watts, Philip *Doddridge and Jonathan *Edwards, and a volume of 600 hymns, as well as a variety of essays in *The Evangelical Magazine*. Following an exceptionally productive career he died, aged sixty-three, on 9 March 1813.

Although Williams was a key figure in all aspects of Congregational life, it was as a theologian that he made his most significant contribution. Two works especially, *An Essay on the Equity of Divine Government and the Sovereignty of Divine Grace* (1809) and *A Defence of Modern Calvinism* (1812), signalled a new phase in the development of Dissenting theology in England and Wales. Dissatisfied with a Calvinism which emphasized the divine decrees at the expense of a free human response to the gospel call, Williams rejected the concept of limited atonement and God's active reprobation of the impenitent. God's gracious election in Christ corresponded with the ability of men and women to use the means of grace in order to believe the gospel and so be saved. God's will was the salvation of all; it was the duty of all to turn to God, who would grant them grace to respond to his call in obedience and faith. Positioned between high Calvinism on the one hand and Arminianism on the other, the moderate or 'modern' Calvinism espoused by Williams became accepted as Dissenting orthodoxy for much of the nineteenth century.

Bibliography

J. Gilbert, *Memoir of the Life and Writings of the late Rev. Edward Williams DD* (London: F. Wesley, 1825); W. T. Owen, *Edward Williams DD: His Life, Thought and Influence* (Cardiff: University of Wales Press, 1963).

D. D. MORGAN

■ **WILLIAMS, Sir George** (1821–1905), philanthropist and founder of the Young Men's Christian Association (YMCA), was born on 11 October 1821 at Ashway Farm, Dulverton, Somerset and baptized at Dulverton parish church on 10 December 1821. He was the youngest son of Amos Williams and Ann Betty Vickery. Williamses had farmed at Exford since at least the early seventeenth century; Amos had leased Ashway since 1809, his 381 acres making him Lord Caernarvon's chief tenant on the Pixton estate. Four of his sons became farmers and George should have been the fifth to do so; after an education appropriate to his station (a dame school in Dulverton, and Gloyns's, a private school in Tiverton), he went at the age of thirteen to work at Ashway. In 1836, however, he was apprenticed to Bridgwater's leading draper, Henry William Holmes.

That move determined Williams' religious and vocational future. Most Williamses were Anglicans; Holmes was a Congregationalist. Williams began to attend Zion Congregational Church, Bridgwater. He was converted in 1837, joined the church on 4 February 1838 and became a teetotaler in 1839. By 1842, after a short period with a draper brother in North Petherton, Williams was in London, working at Hitchcock & Rogers, 72 St Paul's Churchyard, a drapery business employing 150 assistants of both sexes, most of them living on the premises. His salary was £40.

St Paul's Churchyard was a centre of the drapery trade and Hitchcock's, which had twelve departments by 1837, was one of its leading houses. It was dominated by George Hitchcock, a fellow westcountryman. Williams made rapid progress. By 1844 he was buyer and manager of the drapery department. In December 1842 he transferred his church membership to the King's Weigh House, one of London's oldest Congregational churches; under the ministry of Thomas Binney, it was one of its most influential.

Williams had an infectious gift for friendship. He was also a good judge of character. Drapery throve on discerning relationships carefully maintained, and Williams kept his friendships, like his family relationships, in good order. In Bridgwater he had been active in Bible class, Sunday school and prayer meeting. He had also been influenced by C. G. *Finney's Lectures to Professing Christians and Lectures on Revivals of Religion. In London these concerns intensified. Williams worked in the City for the Weigh House's Domestic Misssion and Sunday School, in the West End for Craven Chapel's open-air preaching and tract distribution, and in Southwark for Surrey Chapel's Ragged School. On Sundays he sermon-tasted, sampling the leading Nonconformist and evangelical Anglican preachers, and on weekdays he worked steadily to improve the tone at Hitchcock's. An intensely religious spirit developed there, and a dozen young men, Anglicans, Baptists, Congregationalists and Methodists, mostly Hitchcock's employees, met on 6 June 1844 to form what was minuted as 'a society which should have for its object the arousing of converted men in the different drapery Establishments in the Metropolis to a sense of their obligation and responsibility as Christians in diffusing knowledge to those around them either through the medium of prayer meetings or any other meetings they think proper' (Binfield, p. 120). This developed into the London YMCA (the name was suggested by another Hitchcock's man, C. W. Smith).

Williams' life thereafter revolved around the firm and the YMCA, his success in the former underpinning his influence in the latter. Hitchcock's had a good reputation. Its hours were long (7am to 9pm), but George Hitchcock supported the Early Closing Association, introduced winter closing at 7pm in 1843 and a Saturday half-holiday a decade later. On 9 June 1853 Williams married Hitchcock's daughter Helen at St James's Paddington, and the firm became George Hitchcock, Williams & Co. Williams became sole proprietor in 1863. Although the retail side was maintained, Williams concentrated on the wholesale side. In the 1860s the firm exhibited in London, Paris and Amsterdam. Although it refused to leave the City for the West End, it opened showrooms in the English provinces, developed a profitable French connection and exploited opportunities in Australasia, North America and South Africa. The City premises expanded greatly. In 1871 the firm employed 209 people; by 1901 its employees numbered nearly 1,000.

If George Williams determined the firm's direction, its success was consolidated by his sons Frederick and Howard and his nephew John Williams, and it was underlined by the family's marriages with the families of Thomas *Cook, the tour operator, and Matthew Hodder, the publisher. Three of John Williams' sons brought to the publishing house Hodder and Stoughton (almost next door to Hitchcock, Williams) in the twentieth century the flair which had characterized Hitchcock's in the nineteenth century. One of them, Sir J. E. Hodder-Williams (1876–1927), was George Williams' authorized biographer.

It was, however, the YMCA that brought George Williams into the public eye. At Hitchcock's there developed the auxiliary and mutual improvement societies that began to flower in Nonconformist chapels and were easily replicated in the YMCAs planted by Williams and his friends on their business travels. Similar associations already existed in Britain and the Continent, but Williams' organizing abilities, his many business contacts and his increasing family contacts (he had missionary and settler relatives in most continents) helped to fuse them into a loosely yet closely federated international movement, of which he became the representative figure.

Williams' sense of place was judicious but clear. He succeeded George Hitchcock as treasurer of London YMCA in 1863 and Lord

*Shaftesbury as president in 1886. When the English National Council of YMCAs was founded, he became its first president (1881), and he was the driving force in adapting Exeter Hall as the headquarters for both the London YMCA and the National Council. His most characteristic representative role, however, was with the World's Alliance of YMCAs. This had been initiated in 1855, when a conference held in Paris under the wing of the Evangelical Alliance adopted the 'Paris Basis' as the foundation for an international association of young men; Williams was one of the oldest young men present. Until 1878 the Alliance was effectively run from London. Tensions grew as the world movement grew, and in 1878–1879 Williams played a vital role in establishing the Alliance in Geneva (it claims to have been Geneva's first such international organization) under the secretaryship of a young banker, Charles Fermaud.

Williams' shrewdness, his financial generosity and his availability made him indispensable. He was almost invariably at the YMCA's frequent international conferences. He knew the continental and North American movements intimately, was trusted by their leaders, eased the tensions between them and ensured the steady working of the International Committee that evolved when the Alliance moved to Geneva.

By 1894 Williams was the movement's Grand Old Man. The jubilee of the London YMCA was marked by an international conference; in that year there were 150,000 members in Britain, 120,000 in Germany and 450,000 in the United States. In July Williams was knighted. In April 1905 the YMCA's International Jubilee was celebrated in Paris. Williams was present, sharing the honorary world presidency with the Swedish Prince Oscar Bernadotte. There were by then 7,773 associations worldwide.

Until his marriage Williams was an assiduous member of the Weigh House. After his marriage he returned to Anglicanism, worshipping first at Trinity Church, Little Queen Street, and then at the Portman Chapel, whose incumbent, J. W. Reeve, had performed his marriage ceremony and where Lord Shaftesbury worshipped. Williams became a churchwarden.

Williams' move to Portman Chapel was significant. He continued to grace Congregational events, such as the laying of foundation stones and the opening of new churches, especially where family connections were involved, but Portman Chapel was relatively convenient for his successive homes at 30 Woburn Square and 13 Russell Square, and it was in tune with his evangelicalism. Samuel Garratt of Little Queen Street was a premillennialist, like many of the preachers Williams had heard in the 1840s, and was active in the Prophecy Investigation Society. Like them, Williams was a supporter of the British Society for Propagation of the Gospel among the Jews, chairing its annual meeting in 1884 and 1892. This was turning into the world of the Keswick Convention, the Mildmay Conferences and the World Student Christian Federation, and all found ready support in YMCA circles.

Williams' attitudes were predictable. He disliked drink, tobacco, the theatre and unpunctuality, but he combined his dislikes with a discerning pragmatism. He was politically conservative, and his family was increasingly politically Conservative. On the platform he was compellingly incoherent, but behind the scenes he was a wise and effective mediator, credible by virtue of his broad spectrum of business and religious associates. He was more than a benignly shrewd operator; he was a statesmanlike philanthropist who fully merited a great funeral at St Paul's Cathedral and burial in its crypt on 14 November 1905. He left £248,450 gross.

Bibliography

The archives of YMCA England (Birmingham University Library); C. Binfield, *George Williams and the YMCA. A Study in Victorian Social Attitudes* (London: Heinemann 1973); Sir J. E. Hodder-Williams, *The Life of Sir George Williams* (London: Hodder & Stoughton, 1906); C. P. Shedd (ed.), *History of the World's Alliance of Young Men's Christian Associations* (London: SPCK, 1955).

C. BINFIELD

■ **WILLIAMS, Henry** (1792–1867), pioneer missionary in New Zealand, was born on 11 February 1792 in Gosport, Hampshire, the fifth of eight children of a prosperous lace manufacturer and his wife, Mary Marsh. In 1796 the family moved to Nottingham, where Williams' father became prominent in civic affairs. In 1806 Williams joined the Royal Navy as a midshipman, following a family tradition. Sailing on ships that cruised in the Bay of Biscay and the Indian Ocean, he was promoted to lieutenant before the end of the Napoleonic War, when he was discharged on half-pay at the age of twenty-three. Back on land he lived with his brother-in-law, Edward Garrard Marsh (an evangelical clergyman), and became interested in the work of the Church Missionary Society (CMS).

On 20 January 1818 at Nuneaton Courtenay, Oxfordshire, Williams married Marianne Coldham, the daughter of another Nottingham lacemaker, also prominent in community affairs. The couple shared an enthusiasm for mission, and in 1819 Williams volunteered his services as a captain to the CMS mission in New Zealand, which had been pioneered in 1814 by three laymen. The couple were initially accepted as lay missionaries, but CMS felt that Williams would be more useful if he was ordained, and Marsh prepared him for his ordination as deacon on 2 June 1822 and his priesting on 16 June 1822. Three children were born before the Williams' departure to New Zealand; eleven more were born in New Zealand.

CMS were hesitant about sending an able man to a mission embroiled in troubles; they had just discovered that one of the first missionaries, Thomas Kendall, had taken a young Maori woman as a mistress, and other missionaries were supplying guns to the indigenous Maori people. The couple left following plentiful exhortations from the CMS committee to obedience, exemplary family life and the placing of spiritual responsibilities ahead of secular business.

The family arrived in Sydney on 27 February 1823, and they reached New Zealand on 3 August 1823. At that time there were two CMS mission stations in the country, both of them in the Bay of Islands in the far north. Williams established a third base in the same bay at Paihia and helped the chaplain of New South Wales and supervisor of the New Zealand mission, Samuel *Marsden, to dismiss Kendall because of his mistress and (a few months later) the other ordained

missionary, John Butler, for drunkenness. A number of lay missionaries remained.

Williams quickly established a firm sense of direction. He developed relationships with local Maori chiefs, being always tactful yet insistent on Christian values. He organized classes for the missionaries to learn the Maori language. Soon he had built a chapel and founded schools. He made a breakthrough with the conversion of the chief Rangi and the launching of a ship, the *Herald*, in 1826, which fulfilled his original aspiration and made the mission independent of Bay of Islands tribes. The arrival of Williams' brother William that same year enabled the translation of the Bible to proceed; William had a university education and was a natural linguist.

Henry Williams was then given independent responsibility by CMS and was thus able to abandon Marsden's policy of evangelizing the Maori only after 'civilizing' them. But Williams was concerned about the violence in Maori society and increasingly played a role as a peacemaker between warring tribes. The mission was gradually extended, despite a crisis in 1827 when the Wesleyan mission, which had good relations with CMS, was expelled by Maori from Whangaroa, further north. In the 1830s the scale and impact of the mission increased greatly, but Williams insisted that baptisms be restricted to those who could give a clear profession of faith. By the mid 1830s the chapels were crowded, and new chiefs were asking for missionaries to be resident. Williams, however, was acutely conscious of the threat from the growing number of European traders, who had very different moral standards from those of the missionaries, and he also learned that a French Catholic bishop was to be sent to New Zealand and that settlements of English people were being planned.

Williams urged the London committee of CMS to seek British intervention to protect New Zealand for the Maori people and the mission. His plea was successful, but in unexpected ways. The British government authorized the annexation of New Zealand, not to exclude settlers but rather to regulate them. They did so by sending Captain William Hobson, himself a supporter of CMS, to New Zealand, and the treaty he offered to Maori people to induce them to accept colonial status was translated by Henry Williams and strongly endorsed by him when it was signed in Waitangi on 6 February 1840.

In many ways this treaty marked a turning-point for the mission. Although the British administration was sympathetic to CMS, secular authority displaced missionary influence and placed Williams in a compromised and uncomfortable position between Maori and government as a friend of both, who was vulnerable as tensions increased. Williams' response was to become even more emphatic and insistent on what he saw as right. But this authoritarian style was inappropriate, because the mission had gained a new and unsympathetic master in Bishop George A. Selwyn, a Crown appointee. Selwyn was of High Church disposition, and he did not approve of Williams' emphatic evangelicalism. When Williams challenged Governor George Grey's methods of securing Maori land for European settlers, the governor responded by attacking Williams' own land purchases, which he had made in the 1830s in order to provide for his large family. Williams' integrity was called into question, and when he refused to withdraw, CMS dismissed him on the advice of Bishop Selwyn.

Williams retreated to the family home at Pakaraka. Although he was reinstated in 1854 at the joint request of Grey and Selwyn, the mission was never the same again, and CMS began to make plans for handing it over to the Anglican Church in New Zealand. The mission had lost its considerable reputation with Maori, as secular authorities and other missions strongly challenged its dominance. Williams lost much of his enthusiasm and sense of purpose in the face of these events, and as the colony descended into racial warfare in the 1860s, he and Bishop Selwyn were attacked by both sides, and Maori deserted the European-led church. Henry Williams died on 16 July 1867, grieved at the course of events. His wife Marianne, who had worked hard with him, died on 16 December 1879.

Henry Williams was a fine model of the first-generation evangelical missionary. He was quite clear about the need for Maori conversion, and he insisted upon a clear profession of faith from converts. Rejecting Marsden's view that Maori should be 'civilized' before evangelization could take place,

he reshaped his mission on more definitely evangelical principles. He also recognized that an evangelical mission had to put the Bible in the hands of local people, and he placed the task of translation in the hands of his brother and Robert Maunsell, who both had university training. The Anglican character of his evangelicalism was evident in his defence of his church's privileges and in his relationships with Maori chiefs, to whom he gave clear and emphatic guidance. He was also anxious to secure the cooperation of the British authorities and worked with CMS leaders in England to facilitate British intervention in the affairs of New Zealand. His evangelicalism was conservative and cautious; his churchmanship was deliberately low, and consequently he was highly suspicious of the High Church symbolism introduced by Selwyn. Williams is often seen in New Zealand in primarily political terms, but these cannot explain his remarkable combination of virtues and values.

Bibliography

N. Benfell, 'The Shape of the New Society: Selwyn, CMS and the New Zealand Company in Fierce Debate – Martyr to the Cause? Henry Williams and His Tribulations', in R. Glen (ed.), *Mission and Moko: Aspects of the Work of the Church Missionary Society in New Zealand 1814–1882* (Christchurch: Latimer Fellowship of New Zealand, 1992), pp. 73–109; H. F. Carleton, *The Life of Henry Williams* (Auckland: Upton & Co., 1874–1877); L. M. Rogers (ed.), *The Early Journals of Henry Williams 1826–40* (Christchurch: Pegasus, 1961); L. M. Rogers, *Te Wiremu: A Biography of Henry Williams* (Christchurch: Pegasus, 1973).

P. J. LINEHAM

■ **WILLIAMS, John** (1796–1839), South Pacific missionary, so captured the public imagination by his explorations and later martyrdom that he is said to have become modern Britain's first missionary hero.

Williams was born in Tottenham. At the age of fourteen he was made apprentice to Enoch Tonkin, one of his mother's Christian friends, with whom he remained for seven years, showing a flair for metal-work. On 3 January 1814 he was converted while listening to Timothy East preach on Mark 8:36–37, in the Old Whitfield Chapel near the City Road. Williams' mother had attended Tottenham and Edmonton Congregational Chapels and had come under the influence of William Romaine in her youth. Williams attended the London Tabernacle during the ministry of Matthew Wilks, a Calvinistic Methodist evangelical. By July 1816 Williams had applied to the directors of the London Missionary Society, amongst whom Wilks was a moving force. They decided to send him without further training to the South Pacific. Williams married Mary Chauner on 29 October 1816. He reached Moorea, in the Society Islands, on 17 November 1817. Shortly after his arrival, Williams was sent to Huahine to assist with a new mission, and eventually to the island of Raiatea, on 11 September 1818.

Christianity had before his arrival become the national religion of Raiatea, but there was said to be a lack of moral transformation among the Raiateans. Since Williams saw a close link between industry, civilization and conversion, he urged them to build a respectable European settlement. Williams himself built a house, replete with French sashes and Venetian blinds, tables and chairs, a yard for English poultry and a plot with English vegetables. One historian has argued that this concern with lifestyle was a product of his bourgeois aspirations, a result of his middle-class ancestry. But another has rightly claimed that it was shared by virtually all English missionaries of that era; they all 'dressed and slept English and wanted to eat and drink English'.

Williams was never content at his station and always longed to do greater things for the gospel. He wrote to the directors asking to be moved to a more populous station. Before his letter was answered, the chief of the island of Rurutu visited Raiatea. The chief was so impressed with the change in Raiatea that he asked Williams to provide him with teachers. Soon the idols of Rurutu were sent to Raiatea as a sign of the nation's conversion. From this moment the true potential of his station dawned on Williams; Raiatea could be the centre of an expanding sphere of influence. Williams later wrote, in perhaps his most famous sentence: 'For my own part, I cannot content myself within the narrow limits of a single reef.' For the rest of his life he never thought of himself as restricted to one station, as did other missionaries. He cast himself more as a roving evangelist.

Williams and his wife were first plagued by elephantiasis in their early years on Raiatea. While recovering in Sydney, Williams decided to purchase a vessel called The Endeavour, which was to be the means of increasing the islands' 'intercourse with civilised countries'. After returning to Raiatea on The Endeavour, via New Zealand, he set off again on 4 July 1823 for Aitutaki. Happy at the island's transformation and pleased with the work of the teachers he had left there, he was intrigued by accounts of an island called Rarotonga, which was not on the map. The story of his voyage in search for that island later became part of many early twentieth-century Sunday school books. His claim to be the discoverer of Rarotonga was later contested.

On Williams' return to Raiatea, the censures of the directors awaited him; they disapproved of his purchase of The Endeavour, claiming that missionaries should not concern themselves with commercial matters. Williams was forced to sell the vessel and remained in Raiatea for three years. In April 1827 he accompanied the Pitmans, new missionaries, to Rarotonga. On their arrival, he was pleased to see that the inhabitants had heeded the teaching of the Raiatean missionaries. Williams encouraged the Rarotongans to build a new chapel, mastered the language, translated John's Gospel and the Epistle to the Galatians into Rarotongan and helped the chiefs and king to establish new laws.

Whilst on Rarotonga, waiting for a vessel to take him back to Raiatea, Williams again saw the necessity of a ship for the progress of his mission work. As none was expected, Williams set himself the task of building a vessel, which he called the Messenger of Peace. In a feat that aroused much admiration, he made the cordage, the sails, the substitutes for nails, oakum, pitch and paint, the anchors and the pintles of the rudder, using simple tools: a pick-axe, an adze and a hoe. On 24 May 1830 he left on his next major voyage, pioneering the way into the Samoan Islands. After being received well, he left some teachers on these islands and returned to Rarotonga, where there was much work to keep him busy.

A violent storm had destroyed much of Rarotonga, which he helped to rebuild; he translated more of the Bible into the island's language and attempted to stem the tide of alcoholism on Raiatea. He was finally able to get away to visit Samoa again on 11 October 1832. He was greeted warmly. At Sapapalli, the ladies performed a 'heavenly dance' for Williams. They sang, 'Now our land is saved, and evil practices have ceased. How we feel for the lotu! Come! let us sleep and dream of Viriamu.'

Viriamu, as Williams was called in Samoan, was no doubt ecstatic, but such incidents aroused the suspicions of his colleagues and the directors, who believed that Williams was making a name for himself rather than the gospel.

In order for Mary Williams to recover from illness, and also to accelerate the publication of the Bible in Rarotongan, Williams returned to England shortly after this Samoan voyage, arriving in London on 12 June 1834. He captivated audiences around the country with descriptions of the spread of the gospel in the Pacific. His *A Narrative of Missionary Enterprises* was designed to be acceptable to the nobility, the gentry, men of science and explorers, so that evangelicals could then secure their support. No missionary work had secured for itself so wide a circulation. (The book's sales increased sharply following Williams' martyrdom, when a 'People's Edition' was published.) With the help of his increased following, Williams was able to purchase *The Camden* as a permanent missionary ship for the islands.

A farewell ceremony was held for Williams on 4 April 1838. On returning to the islands, Williams made his new home at Fastetootai, in the Samoan islands, amongst a tribe that was seen as the most despised in the region. Having travelled from there to the Hervey and Society Islands, Williams again set out for new territory in the New Hebrides. Calling at Apia in the Samoan Islands, Williams moved on to Rotuma, and then to Tanna, where he was received well, though he was unable to communicate the purpose of his visit. On 18 November 1839 he wrote the last entry in his diary, perhaps in reference to his reception at Tanna: 'This is a memorable day, a day which will be transmitted to posterity, and the record of events which have this day transpired

will [be] exist after those who have taken an active part in them have retired into the shades of oblivion and the results of this day will be...'

Two days later, when Williams landed on Erromanga, he was martyred with his friend Harris. The circumstances surrounding their deaths are far from clear. It is possible that Williams landed on Erromanga on the day of a local feast. According to a later source, a previous visitor had also landed on the day of a feast and had stolen women and food, and the Erromangans could have been seeking revenge. Charles *Spurgeon identifies the previous visitor as the son of a missionary, whilst other sources say he was a sandalwood trader. More mysterious still is the claim that Williams knew that he would die. His last diary entry above, and his inability to sleep the night before the landing on Erromanga, were used to support this theory. Harris' body, it is said, was consumed on the shore. Some accounts suggest that Williams' body was also consumed, whilst others claim that it was carried away to be exchanged for pigs that were eaten at the feast. Some remains are said to have been retrieved later.

In one of many books written in his honour, it was said: 'John Williams will be venerated as one of the most illustrious Fathers of the New Era – as one of the royal line of Stephen and Antipas, and other martyrs of our God.' Though now largely forgotten, he remained a household name amongst evangelicals till a few decades ago. Seven ships were named in his honour, to take missionaries and supplies between the islands of the South Seas. The money for these ships was raised by Sunday school children around Britain and in the colonies. The last ship, *John Williams VII*, was launched in 1962 and left the mission service in 1972.

Bibliography

E. Prout, *Memoirs of the Life of the Rev. John Williams* (London: John Snow, 1843); J. Williams, *A Narrative of Missionary Enterprises in the South Sea Islands* (London: John Snow, 1837); miscellaneous papers and images in the Archives of the School of Oriental and African Studies, University of London.

S. SIVASUNDARAM

■ **WILLIAMS, John Rodman** (1918–), educator and Presbyterian charismatic theologian, was born on 21 August 1918 in Clyde, North Carolina to John Rodman and Odessa Lee (née Medford) Williams and was raised in a Presbyterian manse. He earned an AB from Davidson College in 1939, a BD (1943) and ThM (1944) from Union Theological Seminary and a PhD from Columbia University and Union Theological Seminary in 1954. Towards the end of his doctoral studies and while preaching at an Easter service, he fully embraced Christ as his risen Lord. In 1943 he married Johanna Servaas; the couple had three children.

Ordained to the ministry in the (Southern) Presbyterian Church in the US in 1943, Williams served as a chaplain in the Marine Corps (1944–1946), associate professor of philosophy and religion at Beloit College in Wisconsin (1949–1952), pastor of First Presbyterian Church, Rockford, Illinois (1952–1959) and professor of systematic theology and philosophy of religion at Austin Presbyterian Theological Seminary in Texas (1959–1972). As a leading theologian in his denomination, his work extended far beyond the classroom to the Task Force on Evangelism (1965–1967) and chairmanship of the Permanent Theological Committee (1970–1971) of the Presbyterian Church in the US. He also served as a member of the Faith and Order Commission of the World Council of Churches (1964–1973), the North American Theological Committee of the World Alliance of Reformed Churches (1967–1975), the Writing Committee and Council of Theologians of the Consultation on Evangelical Affirmations at Trinity Evangelical Divinity School (1989) and the North American Church Council (1993–1994).

It was in 1965 that Williams' academic work took a dramatically new direction after he testified to receiving 'baptism in the Holy Spirit' and speaking in tongues. From that time, he became a prominent voice among Presbyterian charismatics and, with his already established reputation as a theologian, added considerable theological depth to the charismatic movement. He subsequently served as president of the International Presbyterian Charismatic Communion (1972–1973) and played a notable role on the study commission of the Presbyterian Church in the

US that produced the document, 'The Person and Work of the Holy Spirit, with Special Reference to "The Baptism in the Holy Spirit"', submitted to the 111th General Assembly in 1971. This contributed to the acceptance of the charismatic renewal within his own denomination and the broader Reformed tradition.

Williams' leadership role among charismatics and classical Pentecostals grew with his service as president and professor of theology at the short-lived Melodyland School of Theology (1972–1982), sponsored by Melodyland Christian Center in Anaheim, California. He also participated in the first quinquennium of the international Roman Catholic and Classical Pentecostal Dialogue (1972–1976). In 1982 he joined the faculty of Regent University School of Divinity in Virginia Beach, Virginia. He served as president of the Society for Pentecostal Studies in 1985. Academic lectureships took him to Yale Divinity School, Guilford College, the University of Melbourne, Gordon-Conwell Theological Seminary and Princeton Theological Seminary.

A prolific author, Williams has written popular articles for many Christian publications, academic studies for various theological journals and several books. The latter include *The Era of the Spirit* (1971), *The Pentecostal Reality* (1972) and *The Gift of the Holy Spirit Today* (1980). His *magnum opus*, *Renewal Theology*, appeared in its completed form in 1992. Williams also worked as a contributing editor for the *Layman's Commentary on the Holy Spirit* (1972) and as an advisory consultant for the *Logos International Bible Commentary: Matthew, Mark, Luke* (1981). In recognition of his theological contributions, students and colleagues presented a Festschrift to him, entitled *Spirit and Renewal: Essays in Honor of J. Rodman Williams* (ed. M. W. Wilson), on the occasion of his seventh-fifth birthday and the fiftieth anniversary of his ordination.

Over the years, the evolution of Williams' understanding of Spirit baptism moved him away from other charismatic theologians who identified the gift of the Holy Spirit with salvation. Rather than viewing it simply as an actualization of what lies dormant in the faith of a believer, he concluded that the charismatic ministry of the Spirit stems from a distinct action of God subsequent to conversion. The gift, therefore, brings spiritual empowerment for Christian witness and a greater openness to the working of the charismatic gifts in the life and mission of the church. This approach, more closely related in some ways to classical Pentecostal teachings, has extended his theological influence to Pentecostals worldwide.

Bibliography

W. A. Elwell, *Handbook of Evangelical Theologians* (Grand Rapids: Baker Book House, 1993).

G. B. McGEE

■ **WILLIAMS, Roger** (1603?–1683), minister and founder of the Rhode Island colony, is recognized as one of the earliest proponents of 'liberty of conscience', or the right of individuals to practise the form of Christianity that their convictions dictate without government interference. Williams believed strongly in liberty of conscience because his piety was so important to him; he felt constrained to do what he saw as God's will and could not bear any government forcing him to act against it.

Williams was born around 1603 to a middle-class London family, and under the patronage of Sir Edward Coke entered Pembroke College, Cambridge, in 1624. Williams received his BA at Pembroke in 1627 and accepted employment as a Church of England chaplain for Sir William Masham in the county of Essex in 1629. Although Williams' relationship in these years to the increasingly troubled Puritan movement remains unclear, it is likely that he became acquainted with John *Winthrop in 1629, and eight months after Winthrop and his company set sail for Massachusetts, Williams and his wife did likewise, arriving in the New World in early 1631.

Williams soon accepted a pastorate at Salem, but only after offending some of Boston's leaders by turning down an appointment there. Salem soon withdrew its offer at the urging of the Boston authorities, and the Williamses moved to the Plymouth colony in southeastern New England. Williams hoped that he would have more affinity with the Separatists in Plymouth: religious dissenters who, unlike the Puritans, had broken completely with the Church of England. While in Plymouth, Williams wrote his first book, *A Key into the Language of America* (1643), which was both an anthropological survey and a defence of the rights of native Americans against what he saw as forced, illegitimate conversion by the English settlers.

By the end of 1633 Williams had grown dissatisfied with Plymouth and decided to return to Salem. The General Court of Massachusetts was suspicious of his activities, especially after he was appointed Teaching Elder of Salem's church in 1635. By late 1635 Massachusetts had had enough of Williams' controversial opinions on the treatment of the Indians and his increasingly public criticism of state authority, and so in October the magistrates banished him and his family from Massachusetts. Before leaving in January 1636, Williams engaged in a celebrated debate with John *Cotton over the rights of the natives and the nature of the church.

Williams, his family and a few followers spent the winter among the Pokanoket Indians of Narragansett Bay in southeastern New England, and then in the spring of 1636 they established a new, permanent settlement on the west bank of the Seekonk River, calling it 'Providence' as a testimony to God's deliverance. Williams became the political leader of the new colony and built a surprisingly good relationship with the Narragansetts despite the war between the Massachusetts Bay colony and the Pequot Indians from 1636 to 1638. Williams displayed a greater respect for native American culture than most of his contemporaries did and believed that peaceful coexistence was a better policy than fighting over settlement and land use. Williams' relations with Massachusetts remained uneasy because of his respect for the Indians and Rhode Island's developing reputation as a refuge for religious radicals and dissenters from the New England way. Providence quickly put into law Williams' convictions concerning liberty of conscience, and in 1639 he decided to become a Baptist and helped to found the first Baptist church in America. Characteristically, however, he soon grew disenchanted even with the Baptists and eventually left organized religion altogether. Williams' inability to maintain fellowship with any denomination or movement certainly limited his impact among contemporaries, if not upon posterity.

In 1643 Williams decided to return to his native London in order to secure a charter for Rhode Island and also to publish his *Key to the Language of America* and perhaps his best-known work, *The Bloudy Tenent of Persecution* (1644), a harsh attack on Massachusetts' repression of religious dissidents. In the turmoil of the English Civil War, and with the help of friends in Parliament, Williams was able to win the charter and publish his books, and in 1644 he sailed back to New England. He hoped that the patent for Rhode Island would define the previously uncertain political status of the growing English settlements within the colony, and for three years he governed Rhode Island with some success. But in 1651 a political rival, William Coddington, arrived from England with yet another parliamentary commission, which made him the governor of the young colony for life. Reluctantly, Williams sailed yet again to London in 1651 in order to stabilize the colony's government and confirm the 1644 patent. This time he was not quite so successful, but he did manage to nullify Coddington's commission and also to publish another contribution to the pamphlet war he had started with John Cotton and others, *The Bloudy Tenent Yet More Bloudy* (1652). Williams also made friends with his fellow religious radicals Oliver *Cromwell and John *Milton during this second visit. He returned again to Rhode Island in 1654.

Williams was again elected leader of Rhode Island on his return, but his election did not end the political turmoil in the colony. In 1655 Williams wrote a letter to the citizens of Providence that critics have seen as the beginning of a retreat from his democratic positions. The letter made a modest appeal to government authority in the protection of common interests and appealed to the citizenry to work together to make their experiment in democracy and liberty work. Williams' troubles continued unabated, however, until 1663, when the restored King Charles II granted Rhode Island and Providence Plantations a royal charter that specifically guaranteed its inhabitants liberty of conscience.

As time passed and controversy continued, Williams began to withdraw from political leadership in the colony, but he did not withdraw from theological controversy. Increasingly he engaged with the Quakers who were settling in the free environment of Rhode Island in ever greater numbers; the colony even elected a Quaker governor in 1672. In the same year Williams publicly debated with Quaker leaders in Newport and Providence, somewhat ironically trying to disprove their theology of 'Inner Light', or the revelation to individuals of divine truth. He published an account of his challenge to the Quakers in *George Fox Digg'd Out of His Burrowes* (1676). When the brutal King Philip's War broke out between the English colonists and southeastern New England's Indians in 1675, Williams' appeals for restraint were largely unheeded, and in 1676 a band of Indians attacked Providence and even burned his home. After the war Williams helped to capture Indian combatants, who were then sold into slavery. He spent his final years trying to resolve Rhode Island's continuing political disputes and writing theology, and in early 1683 he died in Providence.

Some early historians, such as the Baptist leader Isaac *Backus, admired Williams' defence of religious liberty and fervent piety, but later ones, particularly those from the twentieth century, have seen him as America's earliest proponent of freedom of expression and practice, sometimes downplaying his earnest advocacy of correct Christian belief.

Bibliography
E. S. Gaustad, *Liberty of Conscience: Roger Williams in America* (Grand Rapids: Eerdmans, 1991); J. D. Knowles, *Memoir of Roger Williams: the Founder of the State of Rhode Island* (Boston: Lincoln, Edmands, 1834); R. Williams, *The Complete Writings of Roger Williams*, 7 vols. (New York: Russell & Russell, 1963).

T. S. KIDD

■ **WILLIAMS, William** (1717–1791), hymn-writer, poet, author and pioneer of Welsh Calvinistic Methodism, was born in 1717 at Cefn-coed in the parish of Llanfair-ar-y-bryn, three miles from Llandovery in Carmarthenshire. He was the fourth child of John and Dorothy Williams, and as his father was a ruling elder at the Congregational church at Cefnarthen, he was given a Nonconformist upbringing. Thomas *Charles of Bala said it was intended that Williams should become a doctor, but around 1737, while attending the Dissenting academy at either Chancefield or Llwyn-llwyd near Hay-on-Wye, he heard Howell *Harris preaching outside Talgarth church and was converted. Turning his back on Dissent, he was ordained deacon on 3 August 1740 by Nicholas Claggett, the bishop of St David's, and thereafter served as a curate at Llanwrtyd, Llanfihangel Abergwesyn and Llanddewi Abergwesyn. Accused in June 1743 before the bishop's court of neglecting his duties, presumably because of his Methodist activities, he was later refused ordination as a priest, but even before the official charges had been brought against him it had been decided by the Welsh Calvinistic Methodist Association during its meeting in April that he should leave his curacies and become an assistant to Daniel Rowland. This he did after being found guilty by the court on 26 January 1744, and he spent the remainder of his life as an itinerant Methodist preacher, a role that allowed him not only to exercise his ministry over a wide area but also to concentrate on his literary work. Together with Daniel Rowland and Howell Davies, he was recognized as one of the leaders of the Welsh Methodist movement. Following his marriage to Mary Francis of Llansawel sometime around 1748, he moved to live at Pantycelyn, the farm on which his mother had been raised. From then on, his own name and that of the farm became synonymous. Williams died on 11 January 1791 and was buried at Llanfair-ar-y-bryn.

Though an effective preacher and a popular exhorter, Williams' main contribution to the Methodist Revival was literary. His hymns, because of their popularity, contributed greatly to the development of the Revival, and they appeared regularly in various collections published between 1744 (Aleluia) and 1787 (Rhai Hymnau Newyddion). Williams also produced two English language collections: Hosannah to the Son of David (1759) and Gloria in Excelsis (1772). The most famous of his English hymns, 'Guide me, O thou great Jehovah', appeared in the second of these.

He also composed, in Welsh, two epic poems of over 1,000 stanzas each; Golwg ar Deyrnas Crist (A View of Christ's Kingdom, 1756) described Christ's Lordship in creation, providence and grace, while Bywyd a Marwolaeth Theomemphus (The Life and Death of Theomemphus, 1764) portrayed the spiritual pilgrimage from reprobation to salvation. Williams also wrote many other poems, including nearly thirty elegies in memory of various notable people who had either been influenced by the Revival or had contributed to it.

Williams' numerous prose works were intended for the edification of converts; these included his Pantheologia or History of the World's Religions (1762 and 1779), mostly comprising translations of works by others. His own original works are much more significant and include Llythyr Martha Philopur (Martha Philopur's Letter, 1762), Atteb Philo-Evangelius (Philo-Evangelius' Answer, 1763), Crocodil Afon yr Aifft (The Crocodile of the Egyptian River, 1767), Hanes Tri Wŷr o Sodom a'r Aifft (The Story of Three Men from Sodom and Egypt, 1768), Aurora Borealis (1774), Ductor Nuptiarum neu Gyfarwyddwr Priodas (A Guide to Marriage, 1777) and Drws y Society Profiad (The Door to the Society Meeting, 1777).

Williams published nearly ninety books, pamphlets and tracts during his lifetime and is today regarded as one of the giants of Welsh literature. Not only did his works provide solace and encouragement to many Methodists and provide them with a means of expressing their deepest convictions and feelings; they also safeguarded for posterity some of the spirit and warmth of the Revival, and it is for that reason that they are still read and sung today.

Bibliography

E. Evans, Pursued by God (Bridgend: Evangelical Press of Wales, 1996); G. T. Hughes, Williams Pantycelyn (Cardiff: University of Wales Press, 1983); D. Ll. Morgan, The Great Awakening in Wales (London: Epworth Press, 1988); G. M. Roberts, Y Pêr Ganiedydd, 2 vols. (Aberystwyth: Gwasg Aberystwyth, 1949, 1958); M. Stephens (ed.), The New Companion to the Literature of Wales (Cardiff: University of Wales Press, 1998).

G. TUDUR

■ **WILSON, Daniel** (1778–1858), Anglican evangelical and fifth bishop of Calcutta in India, was born on 2 July 1778 into a prosperous family in London, his father, Stephen, being a wealthy manufacturer of silk. It had been expected that he would follow his father into the family business, but in October 1797 he felt called to the ministry of the Church of England. He was educated at St Edmund Hall, Oxford, and graduated with a BA in 1802 and an MA in 1804. He married his cousin, Ann Wilson, on 23 January 1803. The progress of the eight-month courtship was recorded in his Latin journal; the account ended with the words 'Our wedding was solemnized, (amidst) happiest omens.'

After his graduation and ordination, Wilson served briefly as a curate at Chobham and Bisley in Surrey. He then returned to St Edmund Hall as a tutor and vice-principal, and also served in the parish of Worton in Oxfordshire. By 1808 he was the assistant curate of St John's Chapel, Bloomsbury, where he preached to many influential Anglicans of his day, including the *Wilberforce family. When he became vicar of St John's in 1812 he resigned his Oxford position to devote himself full time to the work of the ministry. In 1824 he was appointed to the parish of St Mary's Islington, which was in the patronage of his family.

In 1827 Wilson preached a series of sermons on the 'The Divine Authority and Perpetual Obligation of the Lord's Day'. Published in 1831, these sermons reflect Wilson's evangelical piety and commitment to a careful exegesis of Scripture. They also provided 'the spark which lit the first flame' of the Lord's Day Observance Society, which is still in existence.

In 1832 Wilson was nominated for the office of Bishop of Calcutta in India. The position had been offered to several other candidates, who had all rejected it. Wilson was consecrated to the office on 29 April and set sail for India on 19 June. On his arrival in Calcutta on 5 November, he found the diocese in a state of some disarray. Four of his predecessors had all died in office after very short episcopates, and so the authority of the office and its administrative structures had been weakened. He lost little time in beginning work and was able to bring about administrative reform and re-impose the authority of the bishop's office. During his tenure as bishop he undertook seven visitations of his diocese and was instrumental in the building of a new cathedral in Calcutta, involving himself in the design and construction and contributing generously from his own income.

Wilson's episcopate was particularly influential because of his approach to mission. He changed the way in which the church related to the Hindu caste system, which classified people socially on the basis of their birth. When he arrived in India he discovered that most missionaries, both Catholic and Protestant, were prepared to tolerate the caste system. He, however, was convinced that its retention was a disgrace to the Christian church and encouraged and allowed many to return to the Hindu faith. On 5 July 1833 he issued a letter to Anglican missionaries in which he wrote: 'the distinctions of castes must be abandoned, decidedly, immediately, finally; and those who profess to belong to Christ must give this proof of their having really put off, concerning the former conversation, the old and having really put on the new man, in Jesus Christ. The Gospel recognizes no distinctions such as those of castes, imposed by a heathen usage, bearing in some respect a supposed religious obligation, condemning those in the lower ranks to perpetual abasement, placing an immovable barrier against all general advance and fellowship on the one hand, and preventing those of Christian love on the other.'

Wilson's letter was met with loud protests, particularly in southern India, but he pursued his plan to abolish church recognition of the caste system. He issued a second letter on 17 January 1834 in which he outlined a five point plan: 'The Converts of all sit together in church. They come without distinction to the Lord's Table. The country priest or catechist receives into his house anyone that comes to him ... whatever the caste. Godfathers and godmothers are taken indiscriminately from what-ever caste. In the church-yard no separate place is allotted for the interment of those of higher castes as they are called.'

This policy, which became known as 'the Wilson line', initially resulted in a loss of members from many churches and missions, but by the 1860s this trend had been reversed. The church in India began to see rapid growth through the conversion of some of the poorest people to Christianity. What had initially appeared to be a disastrous policy began to reap rewards as people saw that the church was prepared to reach out with the gospel to all people regardless of their social or economic class and to proclaim the message that Christianity was open to all, even the most marginalized.

As his work in India demonstrated, Wilson was not afraid of controversy. He became involved in the debate in the Church of England regarding the Oxford Movement and what he perceived as the abandonment of Protestant beliefs in favour of those held by Roman Catholics. This theme would recur in his preaching and writing.

Wilson's strong views on the caste system and the Oxford Movement caused one biographer to say that he was characterized by 'spiritual egotism' and had 'a technical view of religion ... typical of evangelicals'. A more sympathetic observer has written that in his life and work Wilson sought to maintain and defend 'the core of the gospel of Jesus'.

During his career Wilson wrote several books. These included: *Sermons on Various Subjects of Christian Doctrine and Practice* (1818); *The Evidences of Christianity* (1830); *The Divine Authority and Perpetual Obligation of the Lord's Day* (1831); *Sermons in India during a Primary Visitation* (1838); *Sufficiency of Scripture as a Rule of Faith* (1841); *Expository Lectures on St. Paul's Epistle to the Colossians* (1845) and *The Bishop of Calcutta's farewell to India: five sermons* (1846).

Bibliography

J. Bateman, *Life of the Right Rev. Daniel Wilson, D.D., late Lord Bishop of Calcutta and Metropolitan of India* (London: J. Murray, 1859); H. Cnattingus, *Bishops and Societies: A Study of Anglican Colonial Missionary Expansion 1698–1850* (London: SPCK, 1952); C. R. A. Hoole, 'A Nineteenth Century Church Growth Debate: India', *Evangelical Review of Theology*, 19 (October, 1995), pp. 381–386.

S. FINLAYSON

■ **WIMBER, John** (1934–1997), founder of the Association of Vineyard Churches, was a leading proponent of 'signs and wonders' within the charismatic movement. In 1962 he organized and played with the Righteous Brothers rock 'n' roll group. After a conversion experience in 1963, he pursued biblical studies at Azusa Pacific University in California. Wimber was recorded (ordained) in 1970 by the California Yearly meeting of Friends (Quakers) and served as co-pastor of the Yorba Linda Friends Church for five years.

In 1974 Wimber joined the missiologist C. Peter *Wagner in pioneering the Charles E. Fuller Institute. As a church consultant, he travelled widely, analysing local churches and offering advice on how to foster growth. He read reports by Wagner of healing and deliverance from evil spirits in South America, which resulted in large numbers of conversions and church growth. Through his study of Scripture Wimber concluded that Jesus always combined the proclamation of the kingdom of God with its demonstration by casting out demons, healing the sick or raising the dead. Such signs and wonders authenticated the gospel and broke down people's resistance to it.

Wimber found a theological framework for his views in the writings of George Eldon *Ladd, such as *A Theology of the New Testament*. For Ladd, Jesus came to wrest the kingdom of the world away from Satan and to free it from bondage to sin, sickness, demons and death. In his healing and exorcisms, the kingly reign of God was near. Jesus' followers have been enlisted to share in Christ's ministry and do battle with Satan, by performing the same works that Jesus did and proclaiming the presence of the kingdom of God.

By 1977 a Sunday evening fellowship meeting of the Yorba Linda church had become increasingly charismatic, and its leaders, including Wimber, were asked to leave. About sixty of them followed him into a new church affiliated with the neighbouring Calvary Chapel of Costa Mesa, and its pastor, Chuck Smith.

In church services Wimber began to emphasize 'power evangelism', in which the proclamation of the gospel is accompanied by a demonstration of God's power and presence through 'signs and wonders'. Soon there were many reports of dramatic healing, and hundreds of conversions. During one three-and-a-half-month period, Wimber estimated some 1,700 people were converted to Christ. Meanwhile, the Calvary Chapel leadership, including Smith, became concerned over the emphasis on supernatural manifestations in church meetings. In 1982 Wimber and his church joined the fledgling Vineyard Churches movement, which had separated from Calvary Chapels over similar issues. That same year Wimber became the leader of Vineyard Churches.

Wimber's church grew to number 5,000 members, while he spearheaded an aggressive church-planting programme that eventually resulted in the Association of Vineyard Churches. During his years of ministry with the Quakers he had hoped to renew his and other denominations. His subsequent experiences with the Friends and then with Calvary Chapel led him to the conclusion that the Vineyard movement must become a denomination. The initially loose affiliation of churches is today a well-defined denomination, with a statement of faith affirming traditional orthodoxy in the context of the kingly reign of God manifested in signs and wonders and the proclamation of the gospel. In the USA churches are members of the national denomination, while in the UK recognized Senior Pastors are members and their churches are 'affiliated'. In both countries the national church body exercises discipline over its pastors in matters of doctrine and conduct, which includes the possible revocation of ordination papers. Within those parameters, local churches are self-governing. In all Vineyard churches ordination is conferred by a local senior pastor in cooperation with regional and national church authorities.

From 1982 to 1985 Wimber taught a course in Fuller Seminary's School of World Mission, 'The Miraculous and Church Growth'. Hundreds came to hear his lectures and then to experience a workshop in which many were reportedly 'slain in the Spirit', while others were healed or had demons exorcised. In response to the ensuing controversy, the seminary concluded that 'signs and wonders' are miracles intended to signal the advent of Christ rather than the normal concomitant of ministry today. The course was restructured and the workshops cancelled.

Wimber meanwhile commissioned teams who conducted seminars on Vineyard principles around the world. The teams would contact pastors and congregations in an area and offer to hold a 'Signs and Wonders' seminar. If local support was forthcoming, many people would attend. After a follow-up seminar, Vineyard fellowships would be planted, incorporating many of the people who attended the seminar. Sometimes existing congregations would petition to be 'adopted'. Wimber himself decided which congregations and which ministers were accepted for Vineyard status. He had final authority, although he also consulted his leaders.

In 1988 Wimber became enamoured of the ministry team of the Kansas City Fellowship, who became known as the 'Kansas City Prophets'. He called on Vineyard pastors to receive their ministry. A great interest in prophecy developed, and self-styled prophets began giving messages to their pastors regarding staff changes and presented 'revelations' directing individuals to begin ministry in specific locations. Some of Wimber's associates grew concerned over the movement's preoccupation with the predictive prophecy of supposedly select, authoritative prophets, since it contradicted the Vineyard emphasis on the exercise of spiritual gifts by all members of the body of Christ. Several Vineyard pastors and their churches left the fellowship. In 1992 Wimber rescinded his approval of the Kansas City Fellowship model of prophecy. Although he continued to have final authority, he began to work more closely with a team of regional pastoral coordinators.

A phenomenon known as 'holy laughter' later swept through many Vineyard churches; spontaneous laughter and animal noises such as barking and roaring reportedly erupted from congregations, sometimes during sermons. The phenomenon was seen as a fresh outpouring from the Holy Spirit. Imported from South Africa through Rodney Howard-Browne, it erupted in 1994 at the Toronto Airport Vineyard in Toronto, where John Arnott was the pastor. Initially, Wimber adopted a wait-and-see attitude, saying that while he could find no scriptural support for the phenomenon, he felt it was 'just people responding to God'. In December 1995 he moved to disenfranchise the Toronto Airport Vineyard, saying that it was 'going over the edge' by encouraging such behaviour and making it the focus of services.

At a Vineyard pastors' conference in 1992, Wimber listed ten characteristics of the church as he understood it: (1) accurate biblical teaching; (2) contemporary worship in the freedom of the Holy Spirit; (3) the gifts of the Holy Spirit in operation; (4) small-group ministry; (5) ministry to the poor, widows, orphans and those who are broken; (6) physical healing with an emphasis on signs and wonders; (7) missions; (8) unity within the whole body of Christ; (9) evangelistic outreach; and (10) equipping of the saints for ministry. The Association of Vineyard Churches in the USA considers these its 'genetic code'. In 2002 there were more than 850 Vineyard churches located in seventy countries and organized into autonomous Associations of Vineyard Churches. Wimber died in Santa Ana, California in 1997 from a massive brain haemorrhage.

Bibliography

T. Smail, A. Walker and N. Wright, *Charismatic Renewal* (London: SPCK, 1995; Minneapolis: Bethany House Publishers, 1994 [US title *The Love of Power or the Power of Love*]); C. Wimber, *John Wimber: The Way It Was* (London: Hodder & Stoughton, 1999); J. Wimber and K. Springer, *Power Evangelism* (San Francisco: Harper & Row, 1986); J. Wimber and K. Springer, *Power Points* (San Francisco: Harper & Row, 1991).

D. P. THIMELL

■ **WINTHROP, John** (1588–1649), first governor of Massachusetts Bay Colony, believed that English Puritans had a great opportunity to establish a 'New England' in the New World. Winthrop wrote his famous sermon, 'A Modell of Christian Charity', and delivered it to settlers on board the *Arbella* during their Atlantic crossing in 1630. In the sermon he outlined his plans for a colony founded on the bonds of love and righteousness among Christians. He exhorted the colonists to create a community that honoured God; 'wee shall be as a Citty upon a Hill' (Rutman, p. 4). This memorable phrase lived on in the American consciousness; the nation's sense of identity is partly based on the idea of its mission.

John Winthrop was born in Suffolk, England to the prosperous family of Adam and Anne Winthrop. He entered Trinity College, Cambridge in 1603, at the age of fifteen. Two years later he left without a degree to help his father to manage the family estate. He followed his father into the legal profession and became Suffolk's justice of the peace in 1617. Soon he had a thriving law practice in London and was appointed an attorney to the court of wards and liveries, where he drafted petitions for parliament. By 1619 he had acquired the position of lord of Groton manor from his ageing father.

Winthrop married Margaret Tyndal in April 1618, after suffering the loss of his first two wives. The Winthrops were committed adherents of the Puritan wing of the Church of England. Winthrop combined a disciplined and moral life with warm devotion. In a letter to a friend he described his relationship with God in terms echoing the Song of Solomon: 'Drawe us with the sweetnesse of thine odours, that we may runne after thee, allure us, and speak kindly to thy servantes, that thou maist possess us as thine owne' (Morgan, p. 12).

As a Puritan, John Winthrop believed that a nation existed in holy covenant with God. God showered his blessings or judgments upon a people according to their willingness to follow the divine law. Convinced that English society was corrupt, the Puritans feared for the future of the nation. Puritan leaders, through prophetic preaching and writing, sought to awaken England from what they believed was its spiritual and moral stupor. Consequently, under the reign of King Charles I, Puritans found themselves in disfavour with the monarch. They finally lost all hope that England might be reformed when the crown sought to establish high Anglicanism as the uniform style of worship.

In response to the social and religious changes in England, some Puritan merchants decided to explore the idea of a settlement in America. In March 1629 they received a royal charter granting them legal rights to land in New England. They approached John Winthrop to lead the colony as its governor. Winthrop was attracted by the opportunities for financial gain and political leadership afforded by the new enterprise. What he found most appealing, however, was the unprecedented opportunity to create a community free from the religious entanglements of the Old World and based solely upon the laws of God. Accordingly, he accepted the one-year offer as governor on 20 October 1629. The popular Winthrop held the office of governor of Massachusetts Bay for several terms: 1630–1634, 1637–1640, 1642–1644 and 1646–1649.

Four hundred men, women and children arrived in New England on 12 June 1630. Eventually, in what became known as the Great Migration, another 15,000 to 20,000 people would make the journey across the Atlantic to Massachusetts Bay. The colonists suffered most severely during the first winter, losing two hundred people in the harsh conditions. Winthrop, however, found the colonial life invigorating and thrived in the demanding conditions. In a letter home to Margaret he wrote, 'I like so well to be heer, as I doe not repent my comminge: and if I were to come againe, I would not have altered my course, though I had foreseene all these Afflictions: I never fared better in my life, never slept better, never had more content of minde' (Morgan, p. 62). Margaret and the rest of his family joined him in the autumn of 1631.

Governor Winthrop's vision of a 'Citty upon a Hill' helped to sustain the settlers during the difficult early years of the colony. His firm grip on power also contributed to stability and order. Winthrop's governmental authority extended beyond the administration of laws pertaining to drunkenness, stealing and murder to include the enforcement of religious conformity. As a result, there was little room for religious dissent within the Massachusetts Bay colony.

Roger *Williams, a Puritan minister, arrived during the settlers' first winter in Massachusetts Bay. He refused an invitation to become pastor of the Boston church. Williams was a Separatist who could countenance no compromise with the Church of England. The Massachusetts Bay colony still had formal ties with the Anglican Church. Therefore, in the opinion of Williams, the colonial churches were spiritually compromised.

Williams' charismatic personality made his views attractive to others. In 1633 he was persuaded to accept a ministerial position at the Salem church. Soon his separatist teachings provoked the opposition of the civil authorities. The Massachusetts authorities, including Winthrop, quickly became involved; they perceived in Williams a direct threat to the unity and stability of the colony. Williams argued that the government had no right to interfere in religious affairs. After a short trial in 1635, the magistrates expelled Williams from the settlement.

Winthrop did not abandon Williams after his expulsion from the colony. Over the next five years they continued to exchange letters. Winthrop urged Williams to reconsider his separatist beliefs. As a result of these discussions, Williams did change his mind regarding separatism. He made the free practice of religion the defining characteristic of Rhode Island.

The influence of Anne *Hutchinson also threatened the fulfilment of John Winthrop's dream of a 'Citty upon a Hill'. Hutchinson came to Boston in 1633 as a follower of the popular pastor John *Cotton. Weekly small-group meetings were held in her home to discuss Cotton's sermons. She came to the attention of Winthrop and the civil magistrates when it was reported that she and her followers claimed to be able to discern who lived 'under the covenant of grace' (the saved) and who lived 'under the covenant of works' (the unsaved). The controversy intensified when they asserted that with the exception of John Cotton and Anne Hutchinson's brother-in-law, John Wheelwright, all the pastors in the Massachusetts Bay colony were living 'under the covenant of works'. Winthrop brought Hutchinson to trial in 1638 on a charge of antinomianism. Hutchinson defended herself well until she was asked how she knew the things she claimed to know. She declared that God spoke directly to her without the aid of the Bible, 'by a voice of his own spirit to my soul' (Morgan, p. 152). The magisterial authorities immediately found her guilty of antinomianism and expelled her from Massachusetts Bay.

John Winthrop was an inveterate recorder of daily life. During his long career he kept meticulous notes about the events that shaped the Puritan settlement. Published as the *History of New England from 1630 to 1649* (1959), these are the most valuable primary source for the history of Massachusetts Bay colony in its earliest years.

Bibliography
E. S. Morgan, *The Puritan Dilemma: The Story of John Winthrop* (Little, Brown & Co., 1958); D. B. Rutman, *Winthrop's Boston: Portrait of a Puritan Town, 1630–1649* (W. W. Norton & Co., 1965).

J. L. THOMAS

■ **WOODS, Charles Wilfrid Stacey** (1909–1983), student missionary, evangelist and founder of the International Fellowship of Evangelical Students (IFES), was the son of a Brethren evangelist, Frederick Woods, and the Stilwells, a prominent Bendigo legal family. The family was originally Anglican, but Fred was converted under the influence of his Brethren mother, and emphasized conversion throughout his life. Woods thus inherited a tradition of itineracy, conversionism and the dynamic interaction between Anglican openness and Brethren sectarianism that was to sustain much Anglican world mission. It was shared by his chief associates throughout his life: Howard *Guinness, Vincent Craven and the Lutheran pietist Charles Troutman. His sister Rosemary was to marry Wilfred Hutchison, who was born into a Brethren family but went on to become secretary to the Anglican diocese of Sydney and secretary of the Church of England in Australia's General Synod. Woods 'could never pinpoint the date of his conversion. He feared and loved the Lord from earliest childhood', and it was perhaps this experience that enabled him to understand and commit himself to youth evangelism.

In 1920 Woods moved with his family to Sydney, where he attended a Boys' School, and later he studied for the University of Sydney BA (English and history) at night while working in a steel foundry during the day. Though his 'moment of belief' was not a crisis experience, he certainly had such a moment at a camp at Broken Bay (1924) run by the CSSM missioner Edmund Clarke, when it became clear to him and his friend Vincent Craven that evangelism was their calling. Through participation in beach missions and orphanage work, in the Brethren world and in university evangelical Anglicanism, Woods became involved in the global division between Protestant fundamentalism and liberalism.

While on a camp in Austimer with Trevor Morris in 1929, Woods received the brochure that was to change his life. Dallas Theological Seminary had been established for only five years (under the name of 'Evangelical Theological College'), but its position in American fundamentalist circles (secured for it by W. H. Griffith *Thomas and Lewis Sperry *Chafer) was at the time rivalled only by J. O. Buswell's Wheaton College near Chicago. Woods' father had been in New York, where he had met Dr George Gill, who prompted him to send Woods to Dallas. It was to be another year before Woods could move to the United States, however, and in 1930 Howard Guinness came to Australia and worked with him and Craven at Broken Bay. Guinness' vision for global student evangelism and charismatic leadership were attractive to the two only slightly younger men. Clearly Woods and Craven also made an impact on Guinness, who would remember and refer to them in later years.

The strong relationships on which this early work was grounded would typify Woods' whole career. In September 1930, he boarded the *Aorangi* for North America alone, but typically he became friends with other Christians on board: Paul Guinness, Howard's uncle, and (although they were in first-class accommodation and Woods was in steerage) the parents of his future friend and associate in the Canadian Inter-Varsity Fellowship, Arthur Hill. Arriving in Vancouver just before his twenty-first birthday, Woods made contact with local evangelical students and then travelled to Dallas by train and car. On the way he encountered another leading American evangelical, Robert Hall Glover, the Canadian born Home Director for North America of the China Inland Mission (CIM). Glover invited Woods to spend time at the CIM mission at Victoria Beach, Manitoba; he was to do so several times in the following years, and the experienced proved to be his real introduction to Canada. His immediate goal, however, was Dallas, which he reached in the middle of the Great Depression. A bank crash wiped out the savings he had put aside for his course, and he only narrowly escaped being 'sent down'. At the same time, however, he clearly had the ability to attract support. Between 1930 and 1935, he visited Hawaii three times, while in 1931 and 1933 he followed up Glover's invitation to Canada with a visit to the CSSM camp at Victoria Beach, via Toronto. In 1933, he transferred to Wheaton College in order to finish his BA, so that he could in turn take his BTh from Dallas; he graduated from both institutions in 1934. While in Wheaton, he became a member of the Anglican Church, and also became friends with a number of people who would have an important impact on his ministry, including Charles Troutman, whom he would later invite to work in Canada, and who would become his representative in the United States in the early years of the IVCF. At the end of his studies, Woods then had to choose between Howard Guinness' offer of work in India on his way home to ordination in Australia and Arthur Hill's invitation to act as general secretary of the IVCF in Canada. Guinness' cancellation of the visit to India changed Woods' life. Toronto became his base of operations for the next eighteen years, as he began energetically to encourage the growth of student work across the country.

By 1936 the political situation in Europe was deteriorating and the League of Nations was becoming weak. In that year Woods visited student conventions in Finland and Switzerland, which, with his previous international experience, gave him a vision for a worldwide student movement. Toronto was a good place from which to realize such a vision. It was a centre of worldwide Protestant missions and within the British Commonwealth, but it was also close to the emerging great power, the USA. In 1936 Woods and Troutman went as observers to the Convention of the League of Evangelical Students in Chicago. Two years later, the IVCF-USA was to be born out of this network on the campus of the University of Michigan. In 1938, Woods married Yvonne Ritchie; in 1939 his father died in Toronto while visiting the new couple; and in 1940 their first child, Stephen, was born. In 1941 Woods moved to Wheaton to lead the American student work, which was incorporated in January 1942; at the same time he continued to coordinate the Canadian work through various visits. The British Inter-Varsity model had to be modified for the American context. When the Delaware delegate Barbara Boyer visited Campus in the Woods in 1946, many students

asked her in what state Delaware was. Woods, neither Canadian nor American, was well qualified to bridge the cultural divide at a critical time.

Ironically, while Woods, an Australian, moved into the USA, the entry of the USA into the Second World War took many of his evangelical contemporaries into the army and over to Australia. As a result, during the 1950s, while an Australian ran the IVCF in North America, and Vincent Craven (in Canada with the RAF) became interested in camp work, two Americans (Troutman and Warner Hutchinson) ran InterVarsity in Australia and New Zealand. Woods also sought to extend InterVarsity into Latin America, through the good offices of the Latin American Mission, in which many American InterVarsity graduates were to serve. In 1937 he and Troutman had visited Mexico as part of a long tour of the whole continent. In 1944 Woods spent a month there, including in his itinerary Mexico City, Pueblo, Orizaba, Bogota, Medellin, Cartagena and Barranquilla, and exercising, with people such as Edward Pentecost, his now well-honed 'holy opportunism' and ability to connect with people of prominence. When his flying boat was forced into Jamaica for repairs, for instance, he took advantage of the delay to contact people who had studied at McGill University in Montreal. 'This unplanned, unscheduled layover was in God's plan and foresight,' he says. 'I was able to visit schools, learn of the preparation for the opening of the University, and meet with church leaders and Christians in education. They urged that we help them.' Through *HIS* magazine and Woods' ability to organize, IVCF gained a presence throughout the continent that prepared it for the boom in university enrolments around the world after the Second World War. By 1950 thirty-five staff were serving students in 499 InterVarsity chapters across the country.

When the end of the war was announced, Woods was at Campus in the Woods. With a keen eye for strategy, he was aware that the increase in student numbers in America and Canada would be reflected around the world, and he chose this moment to create an international body. IVCF held its first missionary convention in Toronto (because of its CIM and SIM heritage) in 1946, with 500 delegates and some of the leading neo-evangelical leaders of the day, including Harold *Ockenga, J. G. Holdcroft, Bakht Singh, Robert McQuilkin and L. E. *Maxwell. In 1948 the convention moved to Urbana, outside Chicago, and within a decade had grown to more than 2,000 delegates. By 1964 numbers had reached 6,000, and by 1993 over 17,000. The convention became a major contributor to global Protestant missions. The process that led to the founding of IFES began in 1946, when Woods met Martyn *Lloyd-Jones and other leaders at Oxford in England. The organizing committee came together again at Phillips Brooks House, Harvard, in August 1947 to create networks to 'awaken and deepen personal faith in the Lord Jesus Christ and to further evangelistic work among students throughout the world'. From its original ten member movements, by 1996 IFES had expanded to comprise over 130, including a number of huge movements that have been the means for sustained revival in places such as Nigeria. Much of this expansion took place under Woods' leadership; he was the first elected general secretary, working from Lausanne for some twenty-eight years. He developed a fearsome reputation for work (he could, for instance, dictate up to seventy letters in a day) and for organization. Most of the European movements, for instance, existed before the advent of IFES, but it was Woods who encouraged the formalizing of offices and functions and who pressed for the holding of regular events and the acquisition of such centres as La Salsicaia in Grosseto and Schloss Mittersill in Austria. More often than not, he achieved his goals because of his ability to share his vision with people who had the resources to realize it.

Not everyone appreciated the changes in IVCF after the war. Some, such as the pietist Troutman, saw its growth as a particularly American form of corporatism, which had little place in the heart religion of the gospel. For Woods, however, rational means and theology (a Brethren hallmark) were simply tools for the extension of the kingdom. The gospel was something one did; as he noted in his 1954 Urbana address, 'A Single Eye', his focus was single, his energy channelled, his mission clear: 'If a Christian has a single eye, if God is his goal, if he really is living for eternity and not for himself and for earthly prosperity

and success, then his whole body will be full of light. He will know God's will. God can speak to him revealing His truth, His will, His way. Such a man will hear God's call. The man with a single eye is a man of unclouded vision. He is not in darkness because of habitual sin. The things of this life do not becloud his vision of the eternal city.'

He did not count success by numbers, though numbers at Urbana were large by the time he preached on the text 'Whatsover he saith unto you, do it' at the 1957 Convention: 'I almost tremble, when we realize the large number of people who are here, lest we put our confidence in numbers, lest we measure success in terms of the accounting of this world. The very fact that we are so many constitutes a danger. We may feel we haven't got to look to God. And in reality, the very fact that we are so many means that we must look to God as never before.'

The movement had 'moved forward on its knees. From the beginning great emphasis was given to the morning watch, the quiet time, personal devotions ... The Christian life is vital fellowship with the Father, Son and Holy Spirit.' Woods' career was a particularly Australian mix of pragmatic, selfless commitment put at the service of what he believed was the highest cause possible. Charles Stacey Woods died in Lausanne on 10 April 1983, leaving a family still very active in European and student mission, and a worldwide legacy.

Bibliography
C. S. Woods, *The Growth of a Work of God* (Downers Grove: IVP, 1978); C. S. Woods, *Some Ways of God* (Downers Grove: IVP, 1975); interviews, W. V. Craven, Charles Troutman et al., CSAC Archives; personal correspondence, Y. K. Woods and S. Woods; personal correspondence, Bruce Kaye, General Secretary, Anglican Church in Australia.
M. HUTCHINSON

■ **WRIGHT, James Elwin** (1890–1973), leader of American nondenominational agencies, was born in Corinth, Vermont, to Joel Adams and Mary Melissa (née Goodwin) Wright. He grew up in a family dedicated to ministry. His father, who supported his ministry by property development, founded the nondenominational First Fruit Harvesters. In 1898 the elder Wright established a Christian community on land he had purchased in Rumney, New Hampshire and set out to evangelize New England. In 1908, after a 'latter rain' experience including widespread speaking in tongues, the organization began planting Pentecostal churches throughout the region.

At the age of fifteen, Wright joined his father's property business, which he later expanded, opening offices in Boston and Florida. The work took him throughout the state and brought to his attention its many abused and neglected children. In 1911 Wright and his new wife Florence Dunkling opened Bethesda Home on land the Harvesters had purchased near their Rumney grounds. For eight years the Wrights directed life at Bethesda. During this time Wright became involved in child welfare legislation and served as chairman of the legislative committee for the New Hampshire State Conference of Social Work. He contributed to the passing of numerous laws designed to protect children, including one of the country's first Mother's Aid Bills (1915). Before resigning to pursue theological education at the Christian and Missionary Alliance's Missionary Training Institute in Nyack, New York, he organized the New Hampshire Welfare Association (1918).

In 1924 the Harvesters' board asked Wright to assume the leadership. He refused, believing that the organization had departed from its original charter to evangelize and promote unity among all Christians. Instead, it was functioning like a denomination, planting Pentecostal churches. Wright, though sympathetic to many aspects of the Pentecostal movement, argued in *The Baptism of the Holy Ghost and its Relation to Speaking in Tongues* (1922) that 'speaking in tongues is a sign and not the evidence of the baptism of the Holy Ghost'. He agreed to assume the leadership only when the Harvesters' board yielded to his demand that the organization return to its original purpose.

Almost immediately, Wright ended the Harvesters' church-planting activities and channelled the group's energies towards evangelism, encouraging believers and fostering cooperation between existing churches. Summer camp meetings and annual confer-

ences for ministers and Christian workers attracted participants from a wide variety of denominations, including Baptists, Episcopalians, Methodists, Pentecostals and Presbyterians. At Wright's insistence the organization's new charter declared, 'We believe very deeply in the unity of the body of Christ, the church ... composed of all believers everywhere ... [and] we recognize all believers in the fundamentals expressed in the Apostles' Creed, as Church members' (1927).

Wright expanded his programmes and organized travelling Bible conferences throughout New England. The response was overwhelming. In 1931, at the third annual Pastors' Conference, the Harvesters changed its name to the New England Fellowship (NEF). By 1935 over 1,000 churches were participating in the NEF, which every year held dozens of evangelistic rallies, organized hundreds of Bible conferences, ran summer camps at Rumney, distributed Christian literature and promoted Christian radio broadcasts. Wright invited leading clergy to his conferences, including Harold J. *Ockenga from Boston's Park Street Congregational Church, William Bell *Riley, founder of Northwestern Bible College and Seminary, Moody Memorial Church's Henry *Ironside and Wheaton College president J. Oliver Buswell. At a time when many conservative Christians were caught up in the fundamentalist-modernist battles within their churches, the NEF grew rapidly. In the *New England Fellowship Monthly*, Wright urged Christians to remain in their churches. 'We have never encouraged or fostered a split in any church,' he wrote in 1940. 'On the contrary we [are] always ... counseling patience in the hope of an ultimate clearing up of the difficulties.'

Conservative Christians took note of the success of the NEF, and by 1937 Wright found himself involved in conversations about the creation of a national organization. In 1941 a group of interested ministers met at Moody Bible Institute to discuss the idea, and the following summer a national conference was held in St Louis, Missouri. Wright played a critical role in planning and organizing the new group, which was soon named the National Association of Evangelicals (NAE). Although his heart was in New England, Wright with great reluctance accepted the position of executive secretary and remained with the organization until 1957. During these years he wrote several books including *The Old Fashioned Revival Hour* (1940), *Evangelical Action* (1942) and *Manna in the Morning* (1943). Wright spent his last years in Rumney, New Hampshire.

Bibliography

E. Evans, *The Wright Vision* (Lanham: University Press of America, 1991).

K. BERENDS

■ **WYCLIF, John** (c. 1330–1384), reforming theologian, was born into a wealthy Yorkshire family, probably from the neighbourhood of Richmond. His life may be divided into three phases. He studied at Oxford University and by 1360 had become the master of Balliol College. At that time this was not the prestigious post that it is today; Wyclif was still studying for his MA. On gaining this the following year, he was ordained and resigned the mastership, becoming instead the absentee rector of a Lincolnshire church, a better source of income. This enabled him to continue his academic career at Oxford, and by 1370 he had become its leading philosopher and theologian. Between 1365 and 1372 he wrote a comprehensive series of philosophical treatises (*Summa de Ente*), some of which still await publication. The most important one, his *Universals*, was not published till 1985! He had also begun to develop radical ideas on lordship, which he expounded in his *Civil Dominion*. There he argued that it is only the godly who can rightfully exercise lordship and that ungodly rulers have no legitimate authority. Since the monastic orders were committed to poverty, all their considerable wealth was unjustly held and did not legitimately belong to them. The clergy of the time were notoriously corrupt, and Wyclif argued that their dishonesty gave the secular authorities the right to confiscate church property.

With views like these it is not surprising that Wyclif in the early 1370s entered the service of the Crown, thus beginning the second phase of his life. His teachings on the church's wealth were very convenient for the secular government. At that time the church was immensely wealthy, owning about a third of all land in England, and yet it claimed exemption from taxation. Wyclif's doctrines could be used to threaten the clergy, in order to extort taxes from them to finance an expensive war with France. They could also be used in negotiations with the papacy over the pope's alleged right to tax the English clergy, to finance his own wars. Wyclif joined a delegation sent to Bruges in 1374 to negotiate with the papacy. During the 1370s he enjoyed the support and protection of John of Gaunt, the Duke of Lancaster. In 1377 Pope Gregory XI condemned eighteen of Wyclif's statements, and the English bishops tried to put him on trial at St Paul's Cathedral, but John of Gaunt intervened on his behalf.

All was soon to change, however. In 1377 King Edward III died, and the power of the duke was reduced. The following year saw the election of a rival pope and the beginning of the forty-year Great Schism, in which two or more popes confronted one another. Rome now had far more pressing concerns than John Wyclif, but the English government no longer needed his doctrines in order to manipulate the church.

In 1378 Wyclif entered the final phase of his life. He was no longer needed in public life and so was able to return to his studies at Oxford. His ideas also became more radical. Wyclif was not alone in attacking the corruption and abuses in the church, but he was the one major figure at that time to go behind the practices to attack the doctrines of contemporary Catholicism. This attack led to his losing the government's favour, but his former patrons continued to exert enough pressure on his behalf to protect him from the attacks of the English clergy. Another trial, at Lambeth in 1378, was thwarted by the queen mother's support for Wyclif.

Wyclif broke with Catholic tradition in making Scripture the final authority. In 1378 he wrote *The Truth of Holy Scripture*, in which he portrayed the Bible as the ultimate norm, by which the church, tradition, councils and even the pope must be tested. Scripture contains all that is necessary for salvation; there is no need for additional traditions. Furthermore, all Christians, not just the clergy, ought to read it for themselves. For this reason, Wyclif encouraged the translation of the Bible into the everyday language of the time. This translation is now known as the Wyclif Bible, although the extent of his involvement is uncertain. He also sent out 'Poor Preachers' as evangelists to distribute and preach from the Bible. These itinerant lay preachers were not a complete novelty and in many ways resembled the early friars, except in their opposition to the church authorities.

In exalting the Bible, Wyclif also challenged the authority of the papacy. In his 1379 *The Power of the Pope*, he argued that the papacy is an office instituted by humans, not by God. Like William of Ockham before him, he argued that the pope's power does not extend to secular government. Furthermore, the pope's authority is not derived directly from his office but depends on his having the moral character of Peter. A pope who does not follow Jesus Christ is the Antichrist. Later Wyclif went further and rejected the papacy completely, seeing all popes (not just bad popes) as Antichrist. He was critical not just of the papacy but also of the behaviour of the other clergy and the religious orders, attacking them in his works *Simony*, *Apostasy* and *Blasphemy*.

In 1379 in his *Apostasy* and in the following year more fully in his *The Eucharist*, Wyclif opposed the Roman doctrine of transubstantiation: the belief that the substance of the eucharistic bread is changed into the substance of Christ's body, while the 'accidents' of bread (its physical characteristics) remain. He denounced it on several grounds: it was a recent innovation (defined at the Fourth Lateran Council in 1215); it was philosophically incoherent; it was contrary to Scripture. Wyclif did not deny that in some sense Christ's body and blood are present in the Eucharist, but insisted that the bread and wine remain. Here he believed himself to be following older Catholic tradition, as found in Fathers such as Ambrose and Augustine. Wyclif noted in a sermon that honest citizens do not let friars into their wine cellars for fear that they might bless the wine and turn every barrel into mere accidents!

The bishops put increasing pressure on the university authorities to act against Wyclif, but were resisted. In 1381, however, there was a Peasants' Revolt, and John Ball, one of its leaders, was alleged to be a disciple of Wyclif. Although Wyclif disowned the revolt, he found himself banished from Oxford and withdrew to Lutterworth, near Rugby, whose absentee rector he had been since 1374. There he devoted his remaining years to further writing, protected from the wrath of the church by his noble patrons. In 1382 he suffered a stroke, which was followed by another in December 1384. He died on New Year's Eve.

Wyclif's disciples in England became known as Lollards. They included a number of gentry until an abortive rebellion in 1414, after which they became an underground lower-class movement. The Lollards helped to prepare the ground for the English Reformation, by distributing the English Bible and by fomenting discontent with the Roman Church. Wyclif's influence also spread beyond England. At Oxford he had pupils from Bohemia who took copies of his writings home with them, where they influenced the reformer Jan *Hus. Hus was burnt at the stake in 1415 at the Council of Konstanz (1414–1418), and the council also took the opportunity to condemn forty-five 'errors' of Wyclif. Wyclif's bones were dug up and burnt in 1428. A later chronicler commented: 'They burnt his bones to ashes and cast them into the Swift, a neighbouring brook running hard by. Thus the brook conveyed his ashes into the Avon, the Avon into the Severn, the Severn into the narrow seas and they into the main ocean. And so the ashes of Wyclif are symbolic of his doctrine, which is now spread throughout the world.'

Bibliography

H. B. Workman, *John Wyclif: A Study of the English Medieval Church*, 2 vols. (Oxford: Oxford University Press, 1926); K. B. McFarlane, *Wycliffe and English Non-Conformity* (Harmondsworth: Penguin, [1952] repr. 1972); A. Kenny, *Wyclif* (Oxford: Oxford University Press, 1985).

A. N. S. LANE

■ **YODER, John Howard** (1927–1997), Mennonite theologian, was born on 29 December 1927, just outside Smithville in northern Ohio, the son of Howard C. and Ethel (née Good) Yoder. He was raised in the Oak Grove Mennonite Church and from the age of seven lived in the nearby town of Wooster. Yoder was descended from several generations of influential leaders within the Mennonite Church on both sides of his family. It was also obvious from an early age that he had extraordinary gifts, especially intellectual gifts.

Yoder moved to Goshen College, a Mennonite college in Indiana, in 1945. He graduated with a BA two years later. Two of his teachers were especially important in his spiritual and intellectual development. Only a year earlier Guy Hershberger had published his significant book *War, Peace, and Nonresistance* and, more importantly, Harold Bender had published his American Society of Church History presidential address, 'The Anabaptist Vision'. For centuries the sixteenth-century Anabaptist movement had been defined negatively. Bender's essay, an exciting reinterpretation of the movement, inspired commitment to discipleship, Christian community, non-violence and service among a generation of Mennonites. For the academically inclined, it also served as a call for further research by Mennonites into the Anabaptist origins of their denomination. Conveniently, Bender had founded in 1927 *The Mennonite Quarterly Review*, an academic journal that provided a forum for serious research on sixteenth-century Anabaptism and Mennonite life.

John Yoder was among those who were inspired to serve their church and through it the world. In April 1949 Yoder began an assignment with the Mennonite Central Committee in France, initially comprising youth work and a peace testimony. Soon Yoder was overseeing a small network of childrens' homes that provided food and shelter for children made orphans by the war. Additionally, Yoder was asked to work for the healing of divisions within French Mennonite churches. A history of the French Mennonites says that 'few men will have exercised such a profound influence in [the churches'] transformation in this post-war period'. Yoder was also, almost from the time he arrived in Europe, involved in ecumenical discussions about peace.

In the autumn of 1950 Yoder became a part-time student at the University of Basel, and he became full-time in 1954. He studied with many of the luminaries there, including Walter Eichrodt and Walter Baumgartner in Old Testament, Oscar Cullmann in New Testament, Karl Jaspers in philosophy and Karl Barth in dogmatics. He took five structured courses and five colloquiums with Barth, although Barth was not his doctoral supervisor. Yoder wrote his doctoral thesis (and a subsequent volume), under the supervision of Ernst Staehelin, on the disputations between the magisterial Reformers and the Anabaptists in early sixteenth-century Switzerland. (After his thesis was published, in 1962, he received his DTh *insigne cum laude*.)

The lectures and essays Yoder wrote in Europe prefigured much of his life's work. He wrote about Reinhold Niebuhr, Karl Barth, the Christian witness to the state, ecumenical relations and 'the politics of the Messiah'. On 12 July 1952 Yoder married the French Mennonite Anne Marie Guth. Between 1953 and 1969 they had seven children, six of whom survived infancy. In 1957 Yoder and his family moved to the US. During their first year in the States Yoder worked in one of the Yoder greenhouses. During the 1958–1959 academic year he taught at Goshen College during a tutor's sabbatical. Then beginning in the autumn of 1959, Yoder worked full-time as an administrative assistant for overseas missions at the Mennonite Board of Missions (MBM) in Elkhart, Indiana. From the beginning of his time at the mission board he initiated contacts with evangelical leaders, the National Association of Evangelicals and the National Council of Churches. For more than twenty years, beginning in 1961, he worked in various roles for the World Council of Churches. From 1965 to 1970 Yoder was an associate consultant with MBM.

From 1960 to 1965 Yoder was a part-time instructor at the Associated Mennonite Biblical Seminaries in Elkhart. In 1965 he became a full-time professor at the seminaries, remaining there until 1977. From 1970 to 1973 he was also president of Goshen Biblical Seminary (one of the two 'associated' Mennonite seminaries), and he was acting dean of the same school during the academic year 1972–1973. From 1967 Yoder taught an occasional course at the University of Notre Dame. In the autumn of 1977 Yoder became a full-time professor at the University of Notre Dame; Goshen Biblical Seminary bought a quarter of his time until the spring of 1984. From the autumn of 1984 until his death in late 1997 Yoder taught only at Notre Dame. During the 1970s he taught for a year in Argentina (1970–1971), France (1974–1975) and Jerusalem (1975–1976). Yoder also undertook lecture tours in more than twenty countries and taught intensive, short courses at three institutions in as many countries. His fluency in French, German and Spanish helped him in his work.

Yoder wrote hundreds of articles in five languages as well as seventeen books; a few more will be published posthumously. The heart of Yoder's thought is expressed in six of his books: For the Nations, The Royal Priesthood, The Priestly Kingdom, Nevertheless, The Christian Witness to the State and The Politics of Jesus. The Politics of Jesus has been translated into nine languages, sold more than 90,000 copies and influenced many Christians, both academic and otherwise. Jim Wallis, editor of Sojourners magazine, says that 'John Yoder inspired a whole generation of Christians to follow the way of Jesus into social action and peacemaking'. J. Philip Wogaman, in his book, Christian Ethics: A Historical Introduction, names Yoder as one of a handful of the 'formative Christian moral thinkers' of the twentieth century.

Following allegations of sexual misconduct, Yoder was placed under the discipline of the Mennonite Church in June 1992. In the summer of 1996 the disciplinary process was successfully concluded; the Church Life Commission and the Indiana-Michigan Mennonite Conference encouraged 'Yoder and the church to use his gifts of writing and teaching'. Yoder died on 30 December 1997.

Over the last three decades at least seven master's theses and sixteen doctoral theses have been written in which Yoder's thought is a major component. In the 1980s, when the liberal American Christian magazine The Christian Century published an article entitled 'The Years of the Evangelicals', Yoder was pictured on the cover with Billy *Graham, Carl F. H. *Henry, Francis *Schaeffer and George Marsden. In 1993 Stanley Hauerwas said that 'when Christians look back on this century of theology in America The Politics of Jesus will be seen as a new beginning'. In April 2000 Christianity Today, an American evangelical magazine, named The Politics of Jesus one of the ten best books of the twentieth century. Without question, John Howard Yoder has had and continues to have a significant influence among evangelicals.

Bibliography
C. A. Carter, The Politics of the Cross: The Theology and Social Ethics of John Howard Yoder (Grand Rapids: Brazos Press, 2001); S. Hauerwas, 'The Nonresistant Church: The Theological Ethics of John Howard Yoder', in Vision and Virtue (Notre Dame: University of Notre Dame Press, 1981); S. Hauerwas, C. K. Huebner, H. J. Huebner and M. T. Nation (eds.), The Wisdom of the Cross: Essays in Honor of John Howard Yoder (Grand Rapids: Eerdmans, 1999); M. T. Nation, 'A Comprehensive Bibliography of the Writings of John Howard Yoder', The Mennonite Quarterly Review, LXXI (January 1997), pp. 93–145; M. T. Nation, The Ecumenical Patience & Vocation of John Howard Yoder (Grand Rapids: Eerdmans, 2002).

M. T. NATION

■ YOUNG, Florence Selina Harriett (1856–1940), missionary leader, was born on 10 October 1856 in the family home at Motueka, near Hamilton, New Zealand, the second youngest of three sisters and three brothers. Her father, Henry, was a well connected and wealthy member of the Brethren. Having joined the East India Company in his youth, he quickly became the youngest judge in India, with a promising future. However, he resigned and returned to England, where as one of the early Brethren he engaged in preaching, 'depending on God' for his needs. His ability, restlessness, independence and religious fervour were shared by his daughter. In 1838 he married Catherine Eccles, and they emigrated to New Zealand and began farming in the South Island.

Florence's formal education was limited to three years at boarding school in England from 1871 to 1874. On her return to New Zealand she underwent a classic evangelical conversion at a prayer meeting in Dunedin. In 1878 she emigrated with her brothers and widowed father to Australia. The brothers spent eighteen months investigating business opportunities in Fiji, New South Wales and Queensland before buying a sugar plantation at Fairymead near Bundaberg, Queensland, in

1880. Before Florence settled there she visited England, Scotland, France and Italy with her father and one of her brothers. While in London she attended the Mildmay Conference in 1880 and 1881.

Young returned to Fairymead in 1882, and her attention was drawn to the Kanakas, labourers from Melanesia imported to work on the sugar plantations from 1870; some 15,000 came to Australia before the Queensland government banned further immigration. Young's perception of the Kanakas' religious plight was heightened by the apathy of the local churches, the refusal of the Melanesian Mission and the London Missionary Society to work among them, and the evangelical missionary challenge she had heard at Mildmay.

In working among the Kanakas, Young concentrated on evangelism and teaching them to read the Bible. Her success and desire to extend the work to other plantations led to the founding of the Queensland Kanaka Mission in 1886. Like many other nineteenth-century voluntary missions, the QKM was evangelical, unsectarian, based on 'faith principles' (Young had been influenced by her father and by hearing George *Müller when he visited Sydney) and focused on 'soul winning'.

In 1888–1889 Young visited England and India, where she was impressed by the work of the Church of England Zenana Mission. In the following year she met Hudson *Taylor in Brisbane. He was interested in the QKM, and she was interested in his pioneering policy of allowing single women a role in mission work. In 1891 a ban on the importing of labour into Queensland, with a consequent limitation of the work of QKM, seemed imminent, and Young decided on a career with CIM.

During Young's first missionary term in China (1891–1894) the Queensland government re-introduced Kanaka labour, and there was dissension in QKM. Taylor advised her to return home, especially as she had suffered a breakdown; her autobiography does not mention whether it was mental or physical. Back in Queensland she resolved the troubles, but she returned to China from 1897 until the Boxer Rebellion forced her to leave in 1900. Her health precluded further work in China, and in any case the QKM had grown and needed more superintendence.

In 1901 the newly formed federal government passed the Immigration Control Act, which prevented further importation of coloured labour and forced the repatriation of those already in Queensland. But the work of QKM did not come to an end; the mission received appeals for help from Malaita in the Solomon Islands. The Roman Catholics and the Church of England's Melanesian Mission were operating in the Solomons, but they were not acceptable to those Malaitans who had been influenced by the strictly evangelical QKM. At first Young sought help from the evangelical Church Missionary Association, but it said that QKM itself should begin work in the islands. So in January 1904 the Solomon Islands branch of QKM was formed; this was to be Young's work for the rest of her life. In April Young, with three male missionaries and a female chaperone, toured the islands to assess the prospects. Some changes were made in the constitution of QKM to make the council an advisory one, the yacht Evangel was purchased, and missionary work in the Solomons began. In 1907 QKM changed its name to the South Seas Evangelical Mission.

Young moved to Sydney, from where she superintended the growing work. Her influence was pervasive; she ran the office and mission home, visited the field, oversaw candidates, accounts, teaching materials and correspondence and spoke on behalf of the mission. After she suffered a slight stroke in 1927, William Mallis, an experienced missionary in India, was invited to become general director. Although his contribution was valued, his term of office lasted only four years. Young was always in the background, reluctant to relinquish control, and she remained honorary secretary, handing over the job only a month before she died on 28 May 1940 in Sydney. At her death the members of SSEM congregations numbered 9,000 out of 40,000 Malaitans, and the South Seas Evangelical Church may be regarded as her legacy. She and the Young family were generous benefactors to the mission, investing much of their money, time and energy in it.

Young's achievements were considerable. She founded and served with two missions and worked overseas with another. Her personal fiefdom, SSEM, was an antipodean example of the non- or inter-denominational missions that were founded in the late nine-teenth century. Young was one of those single, emancipated Victorian women who found opportunities in mission work and channelled their energy and drive into it. She was a woman of prayer and had a motherly concern for her missionaries. But she did not always work well with others, because of her forceful personality and need to control, and her individualistic Keswick spirituality, narrow theology, independent approach and overriding conviction that she knew the will of God restricted her impact.

Bibliography

D. Hilliard, 'The South Seas Evangelical Mission in the Solomon Islands. The Foundation Years', *Journal of Pacific History*, 4 (1969), pp. 41–64; F. S. H. Young, *Pearls from the Pacific* (London: Marshall, Morgan & Scott, 1925).

D. PAPROTH

■ **ZIMMERMAN, Thomas Fletcher** (1912–1991), denominational executive and international Pentecostal leader, was born in Indianapolis on 26 March 1912 to Thomas Fletcher and Carrie (née Kenagy) Zimmerman, who were both of Pennsylvania Dutch descent. Lay leaders in a local Methodist Protestant congregation, their religious views changed radically as a result of Carrie's healing from tuberculosis in 1917 following prayer by Pentecostals who visited their home.

Controversy over the Zimmermans' new-found belief in faith healing and other Pentecostal teachings prompted their pastor to suggest that they join a Pentecostal church. Consequently they became members of the Apostolic Church led by John Price, where the younger Zimmerman later became active in ministry under his tutelage. Following graduation from high school, he received a scholarship to Indiana University at Bloomington, where he studied for two years. After the unexpected death of his father, he returned home to assist his mother in the family bakery business. In 1933 he married Price's daughter Elizabeth, and the couple eventually had three children.

Two years later, Zimmerman left Indianapolis to lead a small congregation in Harrodsburg. In 1936 he was ordained by the central district of the General Council of the Assemblies of God (AG). Zimmerman gradually came to prominence in the denomination as he served several large congregations in Illinois, Missouri and Ohio. In 1945, while pastor of Central Assembly of God in Springfield, where the denomination's headquarters was based, he helped to organize the AG radio department. In 1953 he was elected to serve as one of the four assistant general superintendents. Within a few years, he had worked in every part of the headquarters and also contributed to the founding of Evangel University in Springfield. He became the general superintendent in 1959 and held the post until 1985. For extensive community service, he received the 'Springfieldian of the Year Award' in 1974 from the Springfield Area Chamber of Commerce.

Following his election as general superintendent, Zimmerman seized the opportunity to prepare the AG for new initiatives in evangelism and church growth. He led the denomination into a major study of itself in order to clarify its mission in the world. This fostered new programmes that welded professional and lay ministries together, and culminated in the Council on Evangelism in 1968 in St Louis and organizational restructuring at the 1971 General Council meeting in Kansas City. These years proved to be among the most productive of Zimmerman's long period of office. The new initiatives contributed to unprecedented growth, but also accelerated the enlarging of the denomination's bureaucracy.

Zimmerman's stature among evangelical leaders grew after his attendance at the organizational meeting of the National Association of Evangelicals (NAE) in 1942 and his work in establishing National Religious Broadcasters two years later. In 1960 he became the first Pentecostal to be elected as president of the NAE, and in the following years he became the best-known spokesperson of organized classical Pentecostalism. His engaging personality and organizational skills served the AG well, and also the wider Pentecostal movement, in part through his leadership on the Advisory Board of the Pentecostal World Conference.

Long-standing friendships with conservative evangelical leaders led to Zimmerman's participation in the promotion of the

American evangelical agenda abroad under the leadership of Billy *Graham. As a result, Zimmerman played key roles in the World Congress on Evangelism in 1966 and on the executive committee of the Lausanne Committee for World Evangelization. He also presided over the planning committees for the American Festival of Evangelism in Kansas City in 1981, served as chairman of the executive committee of 'Key '73', an evangelistic campaign in North America, and was a member of the board of managers of the American Bible Society.

The benefits of identification with the wider evangelical community, however, were gained at a price as the distinctive Pentecostal spirituality of the AG began to wither at the grassroots. Zimmerman and other church executives were also persuaded, in view of the AG's affiliation with the NAE and its eschatological speculations, to keep the denomination isolated from the wider church world; it distanced itself from the World Council of Churches and the charismatic movement in the mainstream Protestant and Roman Catholic churches, and did not join in formal dialogue with the Roman Catholic Church.

Thomas F. Zimmerman died on 2 January 1991. His papers are held at the Billy Graham Center, Wheaton and the Flower Pentecostal Heritage Center, Springfield.

Bibliography
E. L. Blumhofer, *Restoring the Faith: The Assemblies of God, Pentecostalism, and American Culture* (Urbana: University of Illinois Press, 1993); C. M. Robeck, Jr, 'The Assemblies of God and Ecumenical Cooperation: 1920–1965', in W. M. and R. P. Menzies (eds.), *Pentecostalism in Context* (Sheffield: Sheffield Academic Press, 1997), pp. 107–150.

G. B. McGee

■ **ZINZENDORF, Nikolaus Ludwig von** (1700–1760), German Pietist and Moravian leader, represents the third generation of Pietist renewal following those of Philipp Jakob *Spener and August Hermann *Francke. He was the founder of the *Herrnhut Brüdergemeine*, the Moravian Church (the first free church to emerge from the Pietist movement). Although Zinzendorf was by training a lawyer rather than a theologian, his teaching profoundly influenced the piety of the *Herrnhut Brüdergemeine*. This was very different from that of the Pietist movement at Halle, with its strong emphasis on sin and correspondingly rigorous understanding of the conversion experience. For the mature Zinzendorf, the Christian life consists of a 'living faith' and continuous 'participation' with the crucified Saviour. He understood this experience as a gift, as the 'merit' of Christ's death on the cross, which manifested themselves in a cheerfulness and joy in redemption that were typical of the Moravian Church and were reflected even in the lighthearted Baroque style and layout of their enclosed, self-contained settlements. So Zinzendorf did not understand Christ's Lordship and presence in terms of his having laid down his humanity, such that he no longer bore the wounds of his crucifixion. Rather, he continued to bear his humanity and the wounds of his sacrifice as signs of his infinite love for us. The Moravian Brethren's daily sense of a significant and intimate fellowship with the electing Christ was most clearly expressed in the agreement of the synod held in London in September 1741, in which Jesus Christ alone was recognized as the chief elder of the church. This agreement reflected the Brethren's belief that Christ actively guides his church through the Word, by daily 'watchwords' (quotations from the Bible and hymns) and through his presence in prayer.

Born in Dresden, Zinzendorf was the son of George Ludwig von Zinzendorf (a high-ranking Saxon official who died in 1700). Following the early death of his father, he was raised as her protégé by his educated maternal grandmother, Henriette Katharina von Gersdorf, on her estate in Großhennersdorf near Zittau. In 1710 Zinzendorf entered August Hermann Francke's Pädagogium at Halle, where he was inspired by Francke's missionary work. Between 1716 and 1719 he studied law at Wittenberg but cherished his personal contact with theologians. Undertaking a gentleman's 'Grand Tour' through the Netherlands and on to Paris, he developed a close friendship with the cardinal Louis Antoine de Noailles. After his travels, he acquired a civil service position in the court at Dresden. On 7 September 1722, he was married to Countess Erdmuthe Dorothea von Reuß-Ebersdorf and acquired an estate at Berthelsdorf near Zittau, where he eventually established a religious community.

In 1722 German-speaking Moravian refugees, members of the *Unitas Fratrum* fleeing from the region of Fulneck because of their religious convictions, were permitted by Zinzendorf to settle on his land. He organized them into a settlement called 'Herrnhut'.

In 1727, as a result of serious tensions within this community, which even the Berthelsdorf pastor Johann Andreas Rothe was unable to resolve, Zinzendorf issued statutes that organized the external and internal life of the settlement. Its spiritual life was considerably improved by Zinzendorf's astute organization and leadership. Not only did he organize the community into small spiritual cell groups of approximately four to eight people (called 'bands'); he also revitalized its public worship with new liturgical forms, including a 'love feast', 'Easter litany' and times of prayer (*Stundengebet*) and singing (*Singstunde*). This experience of renewal reached its high point after the celebration of the Lord's Supper on 13 August 1727, when the Berthelsdorf community experienced a profound sense of the nearness of Christ. Moravian Brethren were subsequently sent from the Herrnhut community, on the pattern of the mission of the early church, to make contact with Christians of all denominations. This mission was undertaken, through visits, correspondence and prayer, for the purpose of creating a greater sense of Christian community. The first missionaries were sent in 1732 to Greenland and to St Thomas in the Caribbean.

Even as the Herrnhut community was taking shape, in 1729 Zinzendorf began to distance himself from Halle and consciously to oppose the developing Enlightenment. He read the Bible in the original languages. Through his dispute with the free-thinker Johann Konrad Dippel (in whose rationalist view of the love of God there was no place for the biblical notion of the 'wrath of God'), the death of Christ, as a ransom and the basis of reconciliation with God, became very important to Zinzendorf. His new insight was reflected in his affirmation that Christ's death was to be understood as an atonement *for us*, stating that 'Since 1734, the reconciling

sacrifice of Jesus has openly become our material basis against all evil in life and practice'. From this point Christ the 'man of sorrows' was for Zinzendorf the foundation of all true theology, ethics and knowledge of sin. In 1738, after attracting the favourable attention of the Prussian King Friedrich Wilhelm I, Zinzendorf delivered revivalist sermons in Berlin. The transcripts of these 'Berlin Sermons' were later published in multiple editions and translated into other languages.

Not wishing to leave his brothers and sisters alone on the mission field, Zinzendorf left for St Thomas at the end of 1738. In 1741 he travelled from London to North America in order to consolidate the Brethren settlements in Pennsylvania (at Bethlehem and Nazareth). Although he had initially sought to organize the various religious sects into ecumenical synods in the hope of fostering church unity, he learned the value of existing Christian denominations. Zinzendorf negotiated an agreement with the Bohemian Brethren in Poland to allow the Moravians to baptize and hold communion services on the mission field. In 1735 the court chaplain, Daniel Ernst Jablonsky, consecrated David Nitschmann as a bishop, and in 1737 he also consecrated Zinzendorf. Zinzendorf's expulsion from Saxony in 1736 had already prepared the way for independence, and his consecration effected a final break with the Lutheran national church.

A new centre developed in Wetteravia (northeast of Frankfurt) in Herrnhaag and Marienborn, in the territory of the religiously tolerant and open-minded Count Ernst Casmir I von Ysenburg-Büdingen. Herrnhaag was intended as the supreme model of a cheerful and childlike community; its expressive and lyrical idiom was given voice most poignantly in the appendixes to the Herrnhuter hymnal. The community claimed that Christ was present in their midst, attributed their exuberance to the Spirit and set aside their previous structures of leadership; as a result, they soon provoked strong opposition. In 1749 Zinzendorf criticized Herrnhaag, describing the period between 1743 and 1749 as the time of 'Satan's sifting' (a reference to Luke 22:31). After Ysenberg-Büdingen's death in 1749, the government insisted that Zinzendorf's community be disbanded. As a result, its members left to join other Brethren communities in Neuwied (Germany) and North America.

From 1749 to 1755 Zinzendorf stayed mostly in London and developed Lindsey House into a new centre. Following an Act of Parliament of 24 June 1749, in which the *Unitas Fratrum* was officially recognized as an 'Ancient Protestant Episcopal Church', Zinzendorf sought to move the *Brüder-gemeine*'s effective centre of operations to London, from where he could oversee its foreign mission. Through the encouragement of the publisher James Hutton, who became a member of the Brethren community, Zinzendorf published the first English Brethren hymnbook and a summary of his thoughts, *Maxims, Theological Ideas and Sentences*, compiled by John Gambold (London, 1751). A number of polemical tracts against the Brethren were also published at this time. The work of John Cennick and others led to an increase in the number of communities in central England, Wales and Ireland. In 1755 Zinzendorf returned to Saxony, where he resumed the nurture of the Brethren communities. In 1760 mission stations existed among Native Americans and in Greenland, Surinam, the West Indies, Jamaica, Antigua and Berbice. The Brethren communities in Europe, comprising those in Germany, the Netherlands and Switzerland, had grown to 5,747 members, and those in Great Britain to 3,422 members, by 1760.

Zinzendorf's Moravians were instrumental in John *Wesley's spiritual development, and their ethos and distinctives influenced early Methodism more generally. Zinzendorf's most important personal achievement was not his theological writings and sermons, but the organization and spiritual care that he gave to his worldwide, ecumenical free church. This church, which emerged from Lutheranism, came to define itself with reference to the Augsburg Confession as an ecumenical statement of faith. Combining the traditions of the Moravian church with the legacy of the Reformation, and setting these upon the foundation of Pietism, this church represents an early example of what would today be called an ecumenical church.

Bibliography

E. Beyreuther, *Zinzendorf-Biographie*, 3 vols.

(Marburg: 1957–1961); E. Geiger, *Nikolaus Ludwig von Zinzendorf: Seine Lebensgeschichte* (Holzgerlingen: 1999); C. Podmore, *The Moravian Church in England, 1728–1760* (Oxford: 1998); J. R. Weinlick, *Count Zinzendorf: The Story of his Life and Leadership in the Renewed Moravian Church* (Nashville: 1956); *Zinzendorf und die Herrnhuter Brüder: Quellen zur Geschichte der Brüder-Unität von 1722–1760*, hg. v. Hans-Christoph Hahn und Hellmut Reichel, Hamburg 1977; *Graf ohne Grenzen: Leben und Werk von Nikolaus Ludwig Graf von Zinzendorf*. Ausstellungskatalog, Herrnhut 2000.

D. MEYER
tr. M. HUSBANDS

■ **ZWINGLI, Ulrich** (or Huldrych) (1484–1531), Swiss Reformer, was the founder of Reformed Protestantism. He was born on New Year's Day 1484, a mere fifty-two days after *Luther, at Wildhaus, some forty miles from Zurich. He matriculated at the University of Vienna in 1498 but for some reason left. In 1502 he matriculated at the University of Basel, where he was taught by the reform-minded Thomas Wyttenbach, becoming Bachelor of Arts in 1504 and Master of Arts in 1506. That year he was appointed parish priest of the town of Glarus and so was ordained in September, a few months short of the canonical age of twenty-three.

Swiss soldiers were in great demand as mercenaries; such service was a lucrative source of income. Zwingli served for a time as an army chaplain, but his attitude changed after he witnessed the disastrous Battle of Marignano in 1515, in which over 6,000 Swiss soldiers were killed, and he came to regard the mercenary trade as immoral. His preaching against it was not well received at Glarus, so in 1516 Zwingli moved to become parish priest at Einsiedeln, then as now a popular centre of Marian devotion. While at Glarus and Einsiedeln Zwingli read widely, and it was during this time that the foundations of his Reformed beliefs were laid. In particular, he came to believe in the supreme and final role of Scripture. In 1518 Zwingli became parish priest at the Grossmünster (Great Cathedral) at Zurich. There, on his thirty-fifth birthday, he began to preach systematically through whole books of the Bible, starting with Matthew. This practice was common in the early church, but in Zwingli's time it was a radical innovation. Soon after his arrival at Zurich there was a severe outbreak of the plague, which killed nearly a third of the population. Zwingli stayed to minister to the sick and himself caught the plague, nearly dying. In 1522 he secretly married Anna Reinhart, having failed to get permission to marry from the bishop of Konstanz. Two years later their marriage was made public. They had four children.

Zwingli reached Protestant convictions at about the same time as Luther, largely independently of him. Their backgrounds were different. Luther was taught the 'modern way' by the disciples of Gabriel Biel, while Zwingli was trained in the 'old way' of Thomas Aquinas. Zwingli was also strongly influenced by the humanism of Erasmus, more so than Luther. As a result of these educational differences, Luther and Zwingli approached theology differently. In particular, Zwingli felt that no doctrine should be contrary to reason, while Luther allowed considerably less role for reason in theology. This difference was seen especially in their respective attitudes towards the presence of Jesus Christ in the Lord's Supper.

At Zurich Zwingli gradually introduced reform, at first with the approval of the Roman Catholic authorities. As late as 1523 he received a warm letter from the pope! In 1522 he produced the first of his many Reformation writings, which helped to spread his ideas widely in Switzerland. In 1523 there were two public disputations at Zurich; as a result the city council gave its support to the evangelical cause. At the first of these disputations Zwingli put forward sixty-seven theses, on which he also wrote a *Commentary*. The following year all statues and pictures were removed from the churches, as were organs. The Reformation in Zurich was largely complete by 1525, when the mass was abolished, being replaced by a simple communion service. That year Zwingli composed a *Commentary on True and False Religion*, dedicated to King Francis I of France, in which he contrasts his understanding of biblical truth with the alleged errors of the Roman church. Other Swiss cantons also decided for the reform, and Zwingli's goal of a united evangelical Switzerland looked to be attainable. To this end he formed an alliance of evangelical cantons, but the Roman Catholic cantons felt threatened and formed a rival alliance. The outcome was war in 1529. After a lull, fighting broke out again in 1531, and Zwingli was killed on the battlefield on 11 October at Kappel.

One of Zwingli's first writings was his *The Clarity and Certainty of God's Word*, published in 1522, in which he affirmed the final authority of Scripture. God's word is certain and also clear, though it can be misunderstood. But when God speaks to his children his word brings its own clarity with it, and it can be understood without human instruction because the Holy Spirit illuminates us and enables us to see God's word in its own light. The word of God must not be subjected to an infallible human interpreter such as the pope or a council. Certainty comes not from human learning, nor from church authority, but from humbly listening to God himself.

Zwingli discovered in practice that sincerely seeking to hear God's word did not necessarily end all disagreement. He found himself engaged in controversy with two other reform groups over the nature of the sacraments. First, there were those at Zurich, led by Conrad Grebel and Felix Mantz, who wanted a more radical reform. They were not satisfied with a Reformed state church but wanted a voluntary church of committed Christians, to be entered by adult baptism. At first Zwingli and these radicals had much in common, but by 1525 they were quarrelling. There was a public disputation, and the city council decided against the radicals, who then rebaptized those of their number who had been baptized as babies. The city council exiled them, but Mantz returned and was executed by drowning in 1527. In 1525 Zwingli wrote his *Baptism, Rebaptism and the Baptism of Infants*, in which he defended infant baptism, arguing that baptism is the sign of the covenant and the covenant embraces the whole family and not just the individual. But while he maintained the practice of infant baptism, Zwingli (unlike Luther) abandoned the Catholic belief that baptism bestows (even on infants) new birth and the forgiveness of sins. He came to see baptism as primarily an outward sign of faith.

The second controversy was with Luther, over the presence of Jesus Christ in the Lord's Supper. Luther rejected the Roman doctrine of transubstantiation, but continued to believe in the real presence of Christ's body and blood 'in, with and under' the bread and the wine. Zwingli was persuaded to abandon this belief in 1524 by the Dutchman Cornelius Hoen. From then on he rejected the doctrine of real presence and maintained that the bread and the wine are merely symbols of Christ's body and blood. The Lord's Supper is a thanksgiving memorial in which we look back to the work of Jesus Christ on the cross. It is also a fellowship meal in which the body of Christ is present in the form of the congregation. These views Zwingli set out in his *Clear Exposition of Christ's Last Supper* (1526). Luther and Zwingli met together with others at the Marburg Colloquy in October 1529 in an attempt to resolve their differences, but without success. Zwingli maintained his views to the end, reaffirming them in his last writing, a brief *Exposition of the Faith* written in the (vain) hope of winning Francis I for the Reformed faith.

Zwingli met an early death on the battlefield. There was no time for his thought to mature or for him to write a systematic exposition of Reformed theology. This task was left to *Calvin, with the result that Reformed Protestantism is known as Calvinism, not Zwinglianism. But if the building was left to others and if Zwingli was to a large extent forgotten, the fact remains that it was he who laid the foundations of Swiss Protestantism and Reformed theology.

Bibliography

U. Gäbler, *Huldrych Zwingli: His Life and Work* (Edinburgh: T. & T. Clark, 1987); G. R. Potter, *Zwingli* (Cambridge: Cambridge University Press, 1976).

A. N. S. LANE

INDEX OF NAMES

INDEX OF SUBJECTS

INDEX OF ARTICLES